MICROECONOMICS

MICROECONOMICS

Theory and Applications

Fourth Edition

DOMINICK SALVATORE

Fordham University

New York   Oxford
OXFORD UNIVERSITY PRESS
2003

Oxford University Press

Oxford   New York
Auckland Bangkok Buenos Aires Cape Town Chennai
Dar es Salaam Delhi Hong Kong Istanbul Karachi Kolkata
Kuala Lumpur Madrid Melbourne Mexico City Mumbai
Nairobi São Paulo Shanghai Singapore Taipei Tokyo Toronto

Copyright © 2003 by Oxford University Press, Inc.

Published by Oxford University Press, Inc.
198 Madison Avenue, New York, New York, 10016
http://www.oup-usa.org

Oxford is a registered trademark of Oxford University Press

Library of Congress Cataloging-in-Publication Data

Salvatore, Dominick.
   Microeconomics: theory and applications / Dominick Salvatore.—4th ed.
     p. cm.
   Includes indexes.
   ISBN 0-19-513995-X
   1. Microeconomics. I. Title.

   HB172 .S139 2002
   338.5—dc21   2002068402

Printing number: 9 8 7 6 5 4 3 2 1

Printed in the United States of America
on acid-free paper

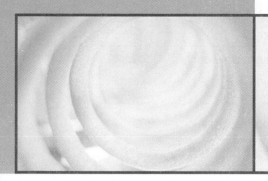

BRIEF CONTENTS

* Core Chapter

v

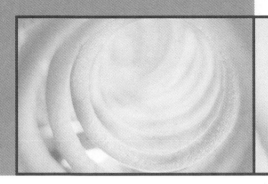

CONTENTS

PART TWO   Theory of Consumer Behavior and Demand   55

LIST OF EXAMPLES AND AT THE FRONTIER

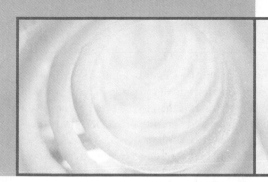

PREFACE

T his is the fourth edition of a text that has enjoyed enviable market success in an increasingly crowded field and has been adopted at hundreds of colleges throughout the United States and the English-speaking world. The text has also been translated into several languages.

I had three principal aims in writing this text: to present a judicial blend of the standard topics of traditional microeconomic theory and the many exciting recent developments in the field; to bring important but neglected international aspects into the course; and to devise a number of fresh, realistic, and truly useful examples that could vividly demonstrate modern microeconomic theory at work.

This is a text for modern undergraduate courses in intermediate microeconomics in economics and business programs. A prior course in principles of economics is required, and only simple geometry is used. There is an optional mathematical appendix at the end of the text for students who have had calculus.

THE MODERN APPROACH TO MICROECONOMICS

A unique feature of this text is that it presents a judicial blend of all the standard topics of traditional microeconomic theory as well as the many exciting recent developments in the field. *Some of the exciting new theoretical developments covered in this text are:* learning curves, new pricing practices, contestable markets, experimental economics, new advances in game theory, financial microeconomics, the theory of public choice, industrial policies and firm competitiveness, and the economics of information.

Each chapter has a section called "At the Frontier," which presents recent and exciting applications or more advanced theoretical developments in microeconomics today. Some of these are Nonclearing Market Theory; The Marketing Revolution with Micromarketing; The New Computer-Aided Production Revolution and the International Competitiveness of U.S. Firms; Minimizing Costs Internationally—The New Economies of Scale; Auctioning Airwaves; Windows 95—A Near Software Monopoly—Lands Microsoft in the Courts; The Art of Devising Air Fares; The Virtual Corporation; Derivatives: Useful but Dangerous; and The Internet and the Information Revolution.

INTERNATIONAL DIMENSION OF MICROECONOMICS

Another unique feature of this text is the introduction of an international dimension into microeconomics to reflect the globalization of production and distribution in today's world. Other microeconomics texts approach microeconomics as if the international economy did not exist. However, many of the commodities we consume are imported, and firms today purchase many inputs abroad and sell an increasing share of their outputs overseas. Even more importantly, domestic firms face more and more competition from foreign producers. None of these issues are reflected in current microeconomic texts, and I feel it is time to rectify such deficiencies by incorporating international ramifications throughout the intermediate course.

Modern microeconomics should deal with the effect of imports on domestic prices, the international convergence of tastes, technological progress and international competitiveness, minimizing costs internationally, the new economies of scale, dumping, immigration and domestic wages, domestic production and strategic trade policies, and other such topics.

PUTTING THE THEORY TO WORK

To introduce more realism than most other microeconomics texts offer, this text includes five to eight demarked examples in each chapter—not the usual tired examples but truly relevant and modern ones. These examples (138 in all—more than in any other text) show how theory can be used to analyze and yield possible solutions to important present-day economic problems. My intention is to demonstrate that only by "putting theory to work" does theory truly come alive. Examples deepen understanding of the theory and enhance motivation by displaying the usefulness of theory in specific modern contexts.

Some of the exciting new examples are: Fighting the Drug War by Reducing Demand and Supply; Gillette Introduces the Sensor and Mach3 Razors—Two Truly Global Products; What Is an "American" Car?; America's Gambling Craze; General Motors Decides Smaller Is Better; How Do Firms Get New Technology?; The Market-Sharing Ivy Cartel; Wal-Mart's Preemptive Marketing Strategy; Deregulation and the New Merger Boom; From Welfare to Work—The Success of Welfare Reform in the United States; The Market for Dumping Rights; and Do Golden Parachutes Reward Failure?

OTHER INNOVATIVE FEATURES OF THIS BOOK

I have tried to balance traditional topics with contemporary concerns in these ways:

A new chapter has been included on *Choice Under Uncertainty* (Chapter 6) to reflect the fact that most consumer choices made in the real world are made under conditions of uncertainty rather than certainty. The chapter includes a discussion of how risk and uncertainty affect demand choices, how to measure risk, utility theory and risk aversion, and insurance and gambling.

A chapter on *Game Theory* (Chapter 12) presents a clear introduction to advances that have been made in this field, and it provides significant insights into modern business behavior in oligopolistic markets. There is a discussion of the prisoners' dilemma, price and nonprice competition, threats, commitments, credibility, entry deterrence, repeated games, and strategic moves.

A chapter on *Market Structure, Efficiency, and Regulation* (Chapter 13) examines the efficiency implications of monopoly, monopolistic competition, and oligopoly. It also evaluates the case for deregulation of economic activities.

A complete chapter concentrates on *Financial Microeconomics* (Chapter 16). Financial microeconomics, in general, and the cost of capital, in particular, is of growing importance in today's world, but they are not covered in most other microeconomics texts.

The Economics of Information (Chapter 19)—another important, modern topic—is covered by a full-length chapter. The chapter deals with the economics of search, asymmetric information and adverse selection, moral hazard, market signaling, the principal-agent problem, the efficiency wage theory, and other topics.

Other important topics covered are: the concept of the margin as the key unifying theme in all of microeconomics, the characteristics approach to consumer demand theory, learning curves, the new economies of scale, two-part tariff, tying, bundling, limit pricing, cost-plus pricing, contestable markets, experimental economics, the theory of public choice, and effluent fees for optimal pollution control.

More advanced optional topics are covered (in chapter appendices): theory of revealed preference, the characteristics approach to consumer demand theory, index numbers and changes in consumer welfare, demand estimation and forecasting, Cobb–Douglas production function, extensions and uses of production and cost analysis, the Cournot and Stackelberg models, and others.

The *At the Frontier* section in each chapter presents very recent applications or more advanced theoretical developments in microeconomics.

New or Expanded Treatment in the Fourth Edition

- The number of examples has been increased to 138 in this edition; previous examples were either replaced with more recent ones or updated.
- Nonclearing market theories are examined in Chapter 2.
- The theory of revealed preference is presented in Chapter 3.
- The characteristics approach to consumer demand theory is introduced in Chapter 4.
- The new Chapter 6, on choice under uncertainty, has been added.
- The new production revolution is examined in Chapter 7.
- The new international economies of scale are discussed in Chapter 8.
- The functioning of markets and experimental economics is examined in Chapter 13.
- The economics of discrimination is discussed in Chapter 15.
- Measures of income inequalities and rising income inequalities in the United States are examined in Chapter 17.
- Efficiency versus equity in U.S. tax reform is discussed in Chapter 18.
- Internet Site Addresses for the most important topics are discussed in each chapter.

ORGANIZATION OF THE TEXT

The text is organized into six parts:

- *Part One* (Chapters 1 and 2) introduces microeconomic theory and reviews some principles of economics. This part shows clearly the importance and relevance of the international dimension in microeconomic theory and how it will be integrated into this text.
- *Part Two* (Chapters 3–6) presents the theory of consumer behavior and demand. It examines how consumers maximize utility and how an individual's and the market's demand curves are derived. It shows the measurement and usefulness of the various demand elasticities, and it examines choice under uncertainty.
- *Part Three* (Chapters 7–9) examines the theory of production, cost, and pricing in competitive markets. The international aspects of domestic production are shown throughout.
- *Part Four* (Chapters 10–13) focuses on the theory of the firm in imperfectly competitive markets. It brings together the theory of consumer behavior and demand (from Part Two) and the theory of production and costs (from Part Three) to analyze how price and output are determined under various types of imperfectly competitive markets.
- *Part Five* (Chapters 14–16) examines the theory of input pricing and employment (i.e., how input prices and the level of their employment are determined in the market). As in previous parts of the text, the presentation of the theory is reinforced with many real-world examples and important modern applications.
- *Part Six* (Chapters 17–19) presents the theory of general equilibrium and welfare economics, examines the role of the government in the economy, and deals with the economics of information. This part interrelates with material covered in all the previous parts of the text.

The nine core chapters are 1, 3–5, 7–10, and 14. Additional chapters and topics may be emphasized at the discretion of the instructor.

PEDAGOGICAL FEATURES

This text has been carefully planned to facilitate student learning using the following pedagogical features:

- The main sections of each chapter are numbered for easy reference, and longer sections are broken into two or more subsections.
- All of the graphs and diagrams are carefully explained in the text and then summarized briefly in the captions.
- Diagrams are generally drawn on numerical scales to allow the reading of answers in actual numbers rather than simply as distances. Consistent, judicious use of color and shading in the illustrations aid student understanding.
- No calculus is used in the text, but an extensive (and optional) Mathematical Appendix is given at the end of the book.
- A glossary of important terms is given at the end of the text.

Each chapter also contains the following teaching aids:

- Key terms are boldfaced when they are first introduced and are listed at the end of each chapter; definitions, arranged alphabetically, are provided in the Glossary at the end of the text.
- A *Summary* reviews the main points covered in the chapter.
- Twelve *Review Questions* help the student remember the material covered in the chapter.
- Twelve *Problems* ask students to actually apply and put to use what they learned from the chapter. Answers to selected problems, marked by an asterisk (*), are provided at the end of the book for the type of quick feedback that is so essential to effective learning.

ACCOMPANYING SUPPLEMENTS

The following ancillaries are available for use with this book:

1. A substantial *Instructor's Manual,* written by the text author, is available. It includes chapter objectives, lecture suggestions, detailed answers to all end-of-chapter questions and problems, a set of 25 multiple-choice questions and answers for each chapter that I personally feel cover the most important ideas in each chapter. The *Manual* also includes *additional examples and problems* (with answers) for class discussions and/or examinations. Finally, there is an annotated list of *Supplementary Readings* with references on the various topics covered in each chapter. The *Manual* was prepared with as much care as the text itself.

2. A separate *Test Bank,* prepared by Professor Mary Lesser of Iona College, contains nearly 1,000 multiple-choice questions with answers and is available to adopters of the text. This comprehensive *Test Bank,* more extensive than that of any competing text, is also available in computerized form for custom test-making on IBM PCs, Macintosh, and compatibles.

3. PowerPoint presentations of all figures and tables in the text are available to adopters of the text.

4. A *Study Guide,* prepared by Professor Mary Lesser of Iona College, is available from Oxford University Press to assist students in text content review and practice. It provides, for each text chapter, a review of concepts from previous chapters, an annotated chapter outline, fill-in the blanks, and a wealth of multiple-choice questions with answers.

5. A *Website* for the text that includes at least one other example for each chapter and includes updates of other material.

ACKNOWLEDGMENTS

This text grew out of the undergraduate and graduate courses in microeconomics that I have been teaching at Fordham University during the past 20 years. I was very fortunate to have had many excellent students who, with their questions and comments, have contributed much to the clarity of exposition of this text.

I owe a great intellectual debt to my brilliant former teachers: William Baumol (New York and Princeton Universities), Victor Fuchs (Stanford University and National Bureau of Economic Research), Jack Johnston (University of California), and Lawrence Klein (University of Pennsylvania and Wharton School of Business). It is incredible how many of the insights that one gains as a superb economist's student live on for the rest of one's life.

Many of my colleagues in the Department of Economics at Fordham University made numerous comments that significantly improved the final product. Professors Joseph Cammarosano and Derrick Reagle in particular read through the entire manuscript and made invaluable notes for improvements. Many valuable suggestions were also made by Janis Barry, Cristopher Cornell, Clive Daniel, Eugene Diulio, Edward Dowling, George von Furstenberg, Duncan James, James Lothian, Henry Schwalbenberg, and Greg Winczewski.

The following professors reviewed the fourth edition of this text and made many valuable suggestions for improvements: John Cochran, Metropolitan State College of Denver; Mehidi Haririan, Bloomsburg University of Pennsylvania; Michael Magura, University of Toledo; Michael Szenberg, Pace University; Robert Whaples, Wake Forest University.

The following professors reviewed the previous editions of this book, and their numerous and excellent comments resulted in a much improved text: Mary Acker, Iona College; Richard Ballman, Augustana College; Taeho Bark, Georgetown University; Joseph Barr, Framingham State College; William Beaty, Tarelton State University; Gordon Bennett, University of Southern Florida; Charles Berry, University of Cincinnati; Joseph Brada, Arizona State University; Charles Breeden, Marquette University; Robert Brooker, Gannon University; William Buchanan, University of Texas—Permian Basin; John Cochran, Metropolitan State College; Elizabeth Erikson, University of Akron; G. R. Ghorashi, Stockton State College; James Giordano, Villanova University; Paulette Graziano, University of Illinois; Ralph Gunderson, University of Wisconsin—Oshkosh; Simon Hakim, Temple University; John D. Harford, Cleveland State University; Mehdi Haririan, Bloomsburgh University of Pennsylvania; Andy Harvey, St. Mary's University; Paul M. Hayashi, The University of Texas—Arlington; Roy Hensley, University of Miami; Thomas R. Ireland, University of Missouri—St. Louis; Joseph Jadlow, Oklahoma State University; H. A. Jafri, Tarleton State University; Joseph Kiernin, Fairleigh Dickinson University; Janet Koscianski, Shippensburg University; Vani Kotcherlakota, University of Nebraska—Kerney; W. E. Kuhn, University of Alabama; Louis Lopilato, Mercy College; Mike Magura, University of Toledo; Jessica McGraw, University of Texas at Arlington; Larry Mielnicki, New York University; Stephen Miller, University of Connecticut; Thomas Mitchell., Southern Illinois University—Carbodale; Peter Murrell, University of Maryland; Kathryn Nantz, Fairfield University; Felix Ndukwe, Lafayette College; Patricia Nichol, Texas Tech University; Lee Norman, Idaho State University; Edward O'Relley, North Dakota State University; Patrick O'Sullivan, State University of New York—Old Westbury; Paul Okello, University of Texas—Arlington; Donal Owen, Texas Tech University; Ray

Pepin, Stonehill College; Martin Richardson, Georgetown University; Howard Ross, Baruch College; Timothy P. Roth, University of Texas—El Paso; Siamack Shojai, Manhattan College; Philip Sorensen, Florida State University; Charles Stuart, University of California—Santa Barbara; Michael Szenberg, Pace University; Allen Wilkins, University of Wisconsin—Madison; Anne E. Winkler, University of Missouri—St. Louis; H. A. Zavareei, West Virginia Institute of Technology.

Finally, I would like to express my gratitude to Linda Harris for her outstanding development effort and to the entire staff of Oxford University Press, especially Paul Donnelly and Stephen McGroarty, for their truly expert assistance throughout this project. My thanks also go to Angela Bates and Rae Fortunato (the department secretaries at Fordham University) for their efficiency and cheerful dispositions.

Dominick Salvatore

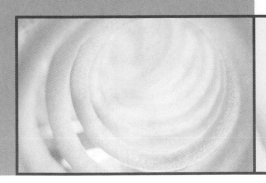

ABOUT THE AUTHOR

Dominick Salvatore is Distinguished Professor of Economics at Fordham University. He was President of the International Trade and Finance Association; Chairman of the Economics Section of the New York Academy of Sciences; Chairman of the Society for Policy Modeling; and consultant to the Economics Policy Institute in Washington, the United Nations, and the World Bank.

Professor Salvatore is the author of 38 books including *Managerial Economics in a Global Economy,* 5th edition (2003) and *International Economics,* 8th edition (2003). He has also written the *Schaum's Outline of Microeconomic Theory,* 3rd edition (1992), which was translated in ten languages and sold more than one-half million copies.

Professor Salvatore is the editor of the *Handbook Series in Economics* for the Greenwood Press. He is coeditor of the *Journal of Policy Modeling* and *Open Economies Review* and is Associate Editor of the *American Economist* (the Journal of the International Honor Society in Economics). His research has been published in more than 100 articles in leading scholarly journals and presented at numerous national and international conferences.

MICROECONOMICS

PART ONE

Introduction to Microeconomics

Part One (Chapters 1 and 2) presents an introduction to microeconomic theory and a review of some basic tools of economics. Chapter 1 deals with scarcity as the fundamental economic fact facing every society and examines the function and purpose of microeconomic theory and its methodology. Chapter 1 also discusses the concept of the margin as the central unifying theme in microeconomics and examines the importance of introducing an international dimension in microeconomic analysis. The "At the Frontier" section discusses agreement and disagreement among economists on the most important economic questions of the day. Chapter 2 is a brief review of the concepts of demand, supply, and equilibrium. In addition, the chapter examines the benefits and costs resulting from the growing interdependence of the United States in the world economy, while the "At the Frontier" section discusses nonclearing market theories.

CHAPTER 1

Introduction

Microeconomic theory is perhaps the most important course in all economics and business programs. Microeconomic theory can help us answer such questions as why there is a trade-off between spending on health care and spending on other goods and services; why the price of housing has risen sharply in recent years; why the price of beef is higher than the price of chicken; why the price of gasoline rose sharply during the 1970s and declined in the 1980s; why textiles are produced with much machinery and few workers in the United States but with many workers and a small amount of machinery in India; why there are only a handful of automakers but many wheat farmers in the United States; why the courts ordered the breakup of AT&T in 1982; why physicians earn more than cab drivers and college professors; why raising the minimum wage leads to increased youth unemployment; why environmental pollution arises and how it can be regulated; and why the government provides some goods and services such as national defense. Microeconomic theory provides the tools for understanding how the U.S. economy and most other economies operate.

Microeconomic theory is also the basis for most "applied" fields of economics such as industrial economics, labor economics, natural resources and environmental economics, agricultural economics, regional economics, public finance, development economics, and international economics.

In this introductory chapter, we define the subject matter and the methodology of microeconomics. We begin by examining the meaning of scarcity as the fundamental economic fact facing every society. We then discuss the basic functions that all economic systems must somehow perform and the way they are performed in a free-enterprise economic system, such as that of the United States. We also examine why the concept of the margin is the central unifying theme in microeconomics and the importance of introducing an international dimension into microeconomic analysis. Subsequently, we examine the role of theory or models in microeconomics, discuss the basic methodology of economics, and distinguish between positive and normative analysis. The "At the Frontier" section discusses agreement and disagreement among economists on the most important economic issues of the day.

3

1.1	WANTS AND SCARCITY

Economics deals with the allocation of scarce resources among alternative uses to satisfy human wants. The essence of this definition rests on the meaning of human wants and resources, and on the scarcity of economic resources in relation to insatiable human wants.

Can Human Wants Ever Be Fully Satisfied?

Human wants refer to all the goods, services, and conditions of life that individuals desire. These wants vary among different people, over different periods of time, and in different locations. However, human wants always seem to be greater than the goods and services available to satisfy them. Although we may be able to get all the hamburgers, beer, pencils, and magazines we desire, there are always more and better things that we are unable to obtain. In short, the sum total of all human wants can never be fully satisfied.

Economic resources are the inputs, the factors, or the means of producing the goods and services we want. They can be classified broadly into *land* (or natural resources), *labor* (or human resources), and *capital*. These are the resources that firms must pay to hire. Land refers to the fertility of the soil, the climate, the forests, and the mineral deposits present in the soil. Labor refers to all human effort, both physical and mental, that can be directed toward producing desired goods and services. It includes entrepreneurial talent that combines other labor, capital, and natural resources to produce new, better, or cheaper products. Finally, capital refers to the machinery, factories, equipment, tools, inventories, irrigation, and transportation and communications networks. All of these "produced" resources facilitate the production of other goods and services. In the economist's sense, money is not capital because it does not produce anything. Money simply facilitates the exchange of goods and services.

Scarcity: The Pervasive Economic Problem

Resources have alternative uses. For example, a particular piece of land could be used for a factory, housing, roads, or a park. A laborer could provide cleaning services, be a porter, construct bridges, or provide other manual services. A student could be trained to become an accountant, a lawyer, or an economist. A tractor could be used to construct a road or a dam. Steel could be used to build a car or a bridge. Because economic resources are limited, they command a price. While air may be unlimited and free for the purpose of operating an internal-combustion engine, *clean* air to breathe is not free if it requires the installation and operation of antipollution equipment.

Because resources are generally limited, the amount of goods and services that any society can produce is also limited. Thus, the society must choose which commodities to produce and which to sacrifice. In short, society can only satisfy some of its wants. If human wants were limited or resources unlimited, there would be no scarcity and there would be no need to study economics.

Over time, the size and skills of the labor force rise, new resources are discovered and new uses are found for available land and natural resources, the nation's stock of capital is increased, and technology improves. Through these advances, the nation's ability to produce goods and services increases. But human wants always seem to move well ahead of society's ability to satisfy them. Thus, scarcity remains. Scarcity is the fundamental economic fact of every society (see Example 1–1).

EXAMPLE 1–1
More Health Care Means Less of Other Goods and Services

One of the most serious concerns of individuals, businesses, and governments in the United States and in most other countries today is the explosion of health-care costs. More than 13% of national income was spent for health care in 2000 in the United States, up from 4% in 1940 and 7% in 1970. Health-care costs have thus risen much faster than income and now exceed $4,600 per person living in the United States. There is, of course, nothing wrong with spending more on health care if that is what society wants. But a higher proportion of income spent on health care means that proportionately less is available for all other goods and services. Resources are scarce and incomes are limited, and so we cannot have more of everything.

Despite spending more on health care than any other country, both in absolute amount and as a proportion of national income, nearly 43 million people or 16% of Americans have no medical insurance, infant mortality is higher in the United States than in many other advanced nations, and life expectancy is lower. What is even more serious is that large cost increases are built in the U.S. health-care system because of an aging population, the development of new and more expensive medical technologies and medicines, and the move to third party (private and government-sponsored health insurance plans), which reduced the incentive to contain medical expenses.

In the attempt to contain costs, the United States rapidly moved to a system of managed care or HMOs (health-maintenance organizations, the term commonly used for managed-care providers) during the past decade, and these now cover over 160 million people. HMOs try to contain health-care costs by providing a flat fee per person to health care providers (physicians, hospitals, etc.) and limiting patients' access to specialists. This made physicians angry at their loss of income and made patients furious at the restrictions on the treatment that they can receive, and it prompted Congress to introduce a "Patients Bill of Rights" in order to overcome some of these restrictions. The upshot of all of this is that exploding health-care costs are likely to remain one of the most serious economic problems facing Americans (and people in other nations).

Sources: M. Feldstein, "The Economics of Health Care: What Have We Learned? What Have I Learned?," American Economic Review, May 1995, pp. 28–49; "Health Care in America—Your Money or Your Life," The Economist, March 1998, pp. 23–25; U. E. Reinhardt, "Health Care for the Aging Baby Boom: Lessons from Abroad," Journal of Economic Perspectives, Spring 2000, pp. 71–84; and "Organizational Innovations to Contain Health Costs," Economic Report of the President, 2001, pp. 225–229; and "Propelled by Drugs and Hospital Costs, Health Spending Surged in 2000," New York Times, January 8, 2002, p. 14.

1.2 | FUNCTIONS OF AN ECONOMIC SYSTEM

Faced with the pervasiveness of scarcity, all societies, from the most primitive to the most advanced, must somehow determine (1) what to produce, (2) how to produce, (3) for whom to produce, (4) how to provide for the growth of the system, and (5) how to ration a given quantity of a commodity over time. Let us see how the **price system** performs each of these functions under a free-enterprise system (such as our own). In a **free-enterprise system** individuals own property and individuals and firms make private economic decisions.

What to produce refers to which goods and services a society chooses to produce and in what quantities to produce them. No society can produce all the goods and services it wants, so it must choose which to produce and which to forgo. Over time, only those goods and services for which consumers are willing and able to pay a price sufficiently high to cover at least the costs of production will generally be produced. Automobile manufacturers will not produce cars costing $1 million if no one is there to purchase them. Consumers can generally induce firms to produce more of a commodity by paying a higher price for it. On the other hand, a reduction in the price that consumers are willing to pay for a commodity will usually result in a decline in the output of the commodity. For example, an increase in the price of milk and a reduction in the price of eggs are signals to farmers to raise more cows and fewer chickens.

How to produce refers to the way in which resources or inputs are organized to produce the goods and services that consumers want. Should textiles be produced with a great deal of labor and little capital or with little labor and a great deal of capital? Since the prices of resources reflect their relative scarcity, firms will combine them in such a way as to minimize costs of production. By doing so, they will use resources in the most efficient and productive way to produce those commodities that society wants and values the most. When the price of a resource rises, firms will attempt to economize on the use of that resource and substitute cheaper resources so as to minimize their production costs. For example, a rise in the minimum wage leads firms to substitute machinery for some unskilled labor.

For whom to produce deals with the way that the output is distributed among the members of society. Those individuals who possess the most valued skills or own a greater amount of other resources will receive higher incomes and will be able to pay and coax firms to produce more of the commodities they want. Their greater monetary "votes" enable them to satisfy more of their wants. For example, society produces more goods and services for the average physician than for the average clerk because the former has a much greater income than the latter.

In all but the most primitive societies there is still another function that the economic system must perform: It must provide for the growth of the nation. Although governments can affect the rate of **economic growth** with tax incentives and with incentives for research, education, and training, the price system is also important. For example, interest payments provide the savers an incentive to postpone present consumption, thereby releasing resources to increase society's stock of capital goods. Capital accumulation and technological improvements are stimulated by the expectations of profits. Similarly, the incentive of higher wages (the price of labor services) induces people to acquire more training and education, which increases their productivity. Through capital accumulation, technological improvements, and increases in the quantity and quality (productivity) of labor, a nation grows over time.

Finally, an economic system must allocate a given quantity of a commodity over time. **Rationing over time** is also accomplished by the price system. For example, the price of wheat is not so low immediately after harvest that all the wheat is consumed very quickly, thus leaving no wheat for the rest of the year. Instead, some people (speculators) will buy some wheat soon after harvest (when the price is low) and sell it later (before the next harvest) when the price is higher; the available wheat is thus rationed throughout the year.

1.3   MICROECONOMIC THEORY AND THE PRICE SYSTEM

In this section, we define the subject matter of microeconomic theory, briefly examine the determination and function of prices in a system of free enterprise, and show how governments affect the operation of the economic system. We will see that prices play such an important role that microeconomic theory is often referred to as "price theory."

The Circular Flow of Economic Activity

Microeconomic theory studies the economic behavior of *individual* decision-making units such as individual consumers, resource owners, and business firms, and the operation of individual markets in a free-enterprise economy. This is to be contrasted with **macroeconomic theory,** which studies (a) the total or *aggregate* level of output and national income and (b) the level of national employment, consumption, investment, and prices for the economy *viewed as a whole.* Both microeconomics and macroeconomics provide very useful tools of analysis and both are important. While macroeconomics often makes the headlines, microeconomics attempts to explain some of the most important economic and social problems of the day. These range from the high cost of energy, to welfare programs, environmental pollution, rent control, minimum wages, safety regulations, rising medical costs, monopoly, discrimination, labor unions, wages and leisure, crime and punishment, taxation and subsidies, and so on.

Microeconomics focuses attention on two broad categories of economic units: households and business firms, and it examines the operation of two types of markets: the market for goods and services, and the market for economic resources. The interaction of households and business firms in the markets for goods and services and in the markets for economic resources represents the core of the free-enterprise economic system. Specifically, households own the labor, the capital, the land, and the natural resources that business firms require to produce the goods and services households want. Business firms pay to households wages, salaries, interest, rents, and so on, for the services and resources that households provide. Households then use the income that they receive from business firms to purchase the goods and services produced by business firms. The income of households are the production costs of business firms. The expenditures of households are the receipts of business firms. The so-called **circular flow of economic activity** is complete.

The circular flow of economic activity can be visualized in Figure 1.1. The inner loop shows the flow of economic resources from households to business firms and the flow of goods and services from business firms to households. The outer loop shows the flow of money incomes from business firms to households and the flow of consumption expenditures from households to business firms. Thus, the inner loop represents production flows while the outer loop represents financial flows.

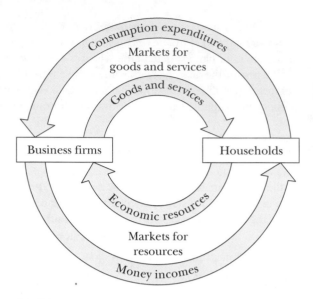

FIGURE 1.1   The Circular Flow of Economic Activity
The inner loop shows the flow of resources from households to
business firms and shows the flow of goods and services from
business firms to households. The outer loop shows the flow of
money incomes from business firms to households and shows
the flow of consumption expenditures from households to
business firms. The prices of goods and services are
determined in the top half of the figure, and the prices of
resources are determined in the bottom half of the figure.

Looking at it from a different perspective, we see that the top part of Figure 1.1 shows
the flow of goods and services from business firms to households and the opposite flow of
consumption expenditures from households to business firms. Here are the markets where
goods and services are bought and sold. The bottom part of Figure 1.1 shows the flow of resources from households to business firms and the opposite flow of money incomes to
households. Here are the markets where resources or their services are bought and sold.

Specifically, the top loop shows consumers' purchases of foods, clothing, housing,
health care, education, transportation, recreation, vacations, and so on, and the expenditures that consumers incur to pay for them. The bottom loop shows the labor time, the capital, the land, and the entrepreneurship that individuals provide to firms in return for wages,
interest, rent, and profits, which represent the incomes with which consumers purchase the
goods and services they want.

Determination and Function of Prices

The prices of goods and services are determined in the markets for goods and services (the
top half of Figure 1.1), while the prices of resources and their services are determined in the
markets for resources (the bottom half of Figure 1.1). If households want to purchase more

of a commodity than is placed on the market by business firms, the price of the commodity will be bid up until the *shortage* of the commodity is eliminated. This occurs because at a higher price, households will want to *purchase less* of the commodity while business firms will want to *produce more* of the commodity. For example, if automobile prices rise, consumers will want to purchase fewer automobiles while automakers will want to produce more automobiles. Automakers can produce more automobiles at higher prices because they are able to bid resources (labor, capital, and land) away from other uses.

On the other hand, if households want to purchase less of a commodity than business firms place on the market, the price of the commodity will fall until the *surplus* of the commodity disappears. This occurs because at a lower price, households will want to *purchase more* of the commodity while business firms will want to *produce less* of the commodity. For example, if consumers want to purchase less beef than farmers send to market, the price of beef falls until the quantity demanded of beef matches the quantity supplied. In the process, farmers will hire fewer resources so that some resources will be freed to produce more of other commodities that consumers value more highly. Thus, it is the system of commodity prices that determines which commodities are produced and in what quantities (the "what to produce" question of the previous section) and how resources are used.

Turning to factor markets, if households provide less of a resource or service than business firms want to hire at a given price, the price of the resource will be bid up until the shortage of the resource is eliminated. This occurs because at higher resource prices, households will usually provide more of the resource or service while business firms will economize on the use of the resource (so as to minimize production costs). For example, if hospitals want to hire more nurses than are available, nurses' salaries rise. This results in more people entering nursing schools and in hospitals economizing on the use of nurses (for example, by employing more orderlies at lower salaries to perform some of the tasks previously performed by nurses). The process continues until the adjustment (i.e., the shortage of nurses) is eliminated.[1]

On the other hand, if too much of a resource is made available at a given price, the price falls until the surplus is eliminated. This occurs because at lower resource prices, households will usually provide less of the resource or service while business firms will substitute in production the cheaper resource for the more expensive one (so as to minimize production costs). Thus, in a free-enterprise economy it is the system of resource prices that determines how production is organized and how the income of resource owners is established (the "how to produce" and the "for whom to produce" questions of the previous section).

It is because of the crucial function of prices in determining what goods are produced and in what quantities, how production is organized, and how output or income is distributed that microeconomic theory is often referred to as **price theory.**[2] Example 1–2 shows how the weather affects the supply and, hence, the price of agricultural commodities in the United States and abroad.

---

[1] The shortage of nurses may last many years if the demand for hospital care and for nurses outstrips the increasing number of nurses being trained or if market imperfections and government involvement prevents wages from rising to the equilibrium level. This is what seems to have happened in fact in many areas of the United States.

[2] In imperfectly competitive markets (monopoly, monopolistic competition, and oligopoly) the price system does not function as smoothly as indicated above and the determination of commodity and resource prices and quantities is more complex.

EXAMPLE 1-2

Drought in Kansas Sends Wheat Prices Soaring

During 1988 and 1989, Kansas suffered the worst drought since the "dust bowl" days of the early 1930s. Kansas normally produces more than one-third of the nation's crop of hard red winter wheat (the wheat used for making bread), and with about 40% of this crop destroyed by the drought, wheat prices shot up from about $2.50 per bushel in 1987 to over $4.25 in spring 1989. American wheat stocks were heavily depleted, and American wheat exports fell sharply. The drought in the United States also encouraged Canada, Argentina, and Australia to plant more wheat and replace U.S. wheat exports to other nations such as Russia. The wheat market is actually one big global market.

Consumer prices in the United States did not increase very much, however, because a $1 loaf of bread contains only 4 cents' worth of wheat (the rest reflects manufacturing and marketing costs) and because food prices represent only one-sixth of the consumer price index. Most wheat farmers' income also increased because wheat prices rose proportionately more than the reduction in crops and because the U.S. government provided a subsidy ranging from $3.17 to $3.80 for each bushel of wheat lost to drought. The rains came back in 1990, however, and wheat output increased and wheat prices declined. The cycle of drought, reduced output, and rising prices followed by good weather, large outputs, and lower prices (and higher government subsidies) was repeated a number of times during the 1990s.

The weather affected not only the output of wheat but also the output of corn, soybeans, and cotton, and not only in the United States but also in other large producing countries, such as Brazil and Argentina—thus, influencing world prices, trade, and the consumption of these commodities around the world. This example vividly portrays the workings of the price system, the effect of government intervention, and the large interdependence that exists in the world economy today.

Sources: T. Tregarthen, "Drought Sends Farm Prices Soaring," *The Margin,* January/February 1989, pp. 22–23; "Farmers Are Back in the Green," *Business Week,* June 11, 1990, pp. 18–19; and "Strong Harvests Set to Restrain Wheat Price Rise," *Financial Times,* January 27, 2000, p. 34.

What Role for the Government?

So far our discussion has deliberately excluded government. Bringing government into the picture will modify somewhat the operation of the system, but it will not, in a free-enterprise system such as that of the United States, replace the operation of markets. Governments affect the circular flow of economic activity by purchasing goods and services for public consumption (education, defense, police, and so on) that compete with privately consumed goods and services. Governments may themselves produce some goods and services, thereby leaving fewer resources for business firms to use. Most importantly, governments, through taxes and subsidies, usually redistribute income from the rich to the poor. By doing so, they can greatly affect the circular flow of economic activity. Governments also use taxes to discourage the consumption of certain commodities such as alcohol and tobacco and provide incentives for the consumption of others such as housing and education. Thus, the United States operates under a **mixed economy** comprising private enterprise and government actions and policies.

Although government policies certainly affect the circular flow of economic activity in a free-enterprise system, they do not replace the price system.[3] This can be contrasted with a centrally planned economy such as that of the former Soviet Union, where most economic decisions were made almost exclusively by government officials or planning committees. In this type of economy, the government rather than the market sets prices. The result is usually persistent shortages of certain commodities and excess production of others. Thus, central planning is usually less efficient than a free-enterprise system (see Example 1–3).

In the United States and other free-enterprise or mixed economies, the price system operates so smoothly that people are not even aware of it. Only on rare occasions (usually as a result of government interference) do we become aware that something is wrong. The long lines at most gas stations during the petroleum crisis in 1979 were the result of the U.S. government's attempt to keep gasoline prices below the market or equilibrium level. When price controls were eliminated and the price of gasoline was allowed to rise to the market level, gasoline lines disappeared. When bad weather sharply reduced the output of Florida oranges in 1977 and 1981 and that of fresh fruits and vegetables in 1984, no waiting lines were seen outside food stores in the United States. The prices of oranges and vegetables simply rose, and this rationed available supplies to match the amounts that consumers wanted to purchase at the higher prices.

EXAMPLE 1–3
Economic Inefficiencies Cause Collapse of Communist Regimes

In 1957, Communist Party Chair Nikita Khrushchev proudly asserted that the Soviet Union would "bury" the United States—not with atomic warheads but with superior productive power. Instead, in 1989 the Soviet Union and former Eastern European communist regimes collapsed as a result of massive economic failures. Consumer goods were shabby, assortment was very limited, and shortages of even basic foodstuffs were common. Automobiles, refrigerators, TV sets, and other durable goods were primitive by world standards. In computers and machine tools, the former Soviet Union was a decade behind the United States and its standard of living was less than one-third that of the United States. These massive economic failures were the direct result of the command economy that operated throughout the communist world. Economic decisions were centralized, capital goods or the means of production were owned by the state, and incentives were lacking or grossly distorted.

---

[3] Government sometimes does replace the price system in some markets by imposing price controls such as rent ceilings and minimum wages. In general, however, in a free-enterprise economy such as that of the United States, government works through the market (with taxes, subsidies, and state-owned enterprises) rather than supplanting it. See "How We Got Here," *Wall Street Journal*, September 27, 1999, pp. R6 and R8; and Mehdi Haririan, *State Owned Enterprises in a Mixed Economy* (Boulder: Westview Press, 1989).

The collapse of communism brought severe economic dislocations in the form of sharply reduced outputs, rising unemployment, rapid inflation, huge budget deficits, unsustainable international debts, and disrupted trade relations. Poland, Hungary, the Czech Republic, and the other countries in central and eastern Europe, as well as Russia and the other republics of the former Soviet Union have been struggling for the past decade to set up working market economies. This is a monumental task after decades of central planning and gross inefficiencies.

The establishment of a market economy requires (1) freeing prices and wages from government control (so that goods and resources can be efficiently allocated by markets); (2) transferring productive resources from the state to private ownership (i.e., privatizing the economy); (3) opening the economy to competition and liberalizing international trade (i.e., replacing state trading with trade based on market principles); and (4) establishing the legal and institutional framework necessary for the functioning of a market economy (such as property rights, a Western-style banking system, a capital market, cost accounting, business law, etc.). The problems of transition to a market economy are enormous and are likely to take the rest of this decade or longer to accomplish.

Sources: W. Easterly and Stanley Fischer, "What We Can Learn from the Soviet Collapse," *Finance and Development,* December 1994, pp. 2–5; "Assessing the Reform Record in the Transition Economies," *International Monetary Fund Survey,* January 9, 1995, pp. 1–6; and D. Salvatore, "The Problems of Transition, EU Enlargement, and Globalization," *Empirica,* July 2001, pp. 1–21.

1.4   THE MARGIN: THE KEY UNIFYING CONCEPT IN MICROECONOMICS

In this section, we provide an overview of the crucial importance of the margin as the central unifying theme in all of microeconomics and examine some clarifications on its use.

The Crucial Importance of the Concept of the Margin

Because of scarcity, all economic activities give rise to some benefits but also involve some costs. The aim of economic decisions is to maximize net benefits. Net benefits increase as long as the marginal or extra benefit from an action exceeds the marginal or extra cost resulting from the action. Net benefits are maximized when the **marginal benefit** is equal to the **marginal cost** (see Example 1–4). This concept applies to all economic decisions and market transactions. It applies to consumers in spending their income, to firms in organizing production, to workers in choosing how many hours to work, to students in deciding how much to study each subject and how many hours to work after classes, and to individuals in determining how much to save out of their income. It also applies in deciding how much pollution society should allow, in choosing the optimal amount of information to gather, in choosing the optimal amount of government regulation of the economy, and so on. Indeed, the **concept of the margin** and **marginal analysis** represent the key unifying concepts in all of microeconomics.

Specifically, the aim of consumers is to maximize the satisfaction or net benefit that they receive from spending their limited income. The net benefit or satisfaction of a consumer increases as long as the marginal or extra benefit that he or she receives from consuming one additional unit of a commodity exceeds the marginal or opportunity cost of forgoing or giving up the consumption of another commodity. A consumer maximizes satisfaction when the marginal benefit that he or she receives per dollar spent on every commodity is equal. More concretely, if the satisfaction or benefit that an individual gets from consuming one extra hamburger with a price of $2 is more than twice as large as the satisfaction of consuming a hot dog with a price of $1, then the individual would increase net benefits or satisfaction by consuming more hamburgers and fewer hot dogs. As the individual does this, the marginal benefit of consuming each additional hamburger declines, while the marginal loss in giving up each additional hot dog increases. The individual maximizes net benefits when the marginal benefit per dollar spent on each becomes equal. This central unifying theme of the margin in consumer behavior and demand is examined in Part Two (Chapters 3–6) of the text.

EXAMPLE 1–4

Marginal Analysis in TV Advertising

Table 1.1 shows a firm's total and marginal benefits and costs of increasing the number of TV spots per week. With each additional TV spot, the firm's total benefits (sales or revenues) increase, but the extra or marginal benefit declines. The reason is that each additional TV spot reaches fewer and fewer additional people and becomes less effective in inducing more consumers to buy the product. At the same time, the extra or marginal cost of each TV spot remains at $4,000. The last column of the table shows that the net benefit (total benefits or revenues minus total costs) is maximized at $30,000 when the firm airs four TV spots per week, at which the marginal benefit equals the marginal cost. Note that in cases like this where we deal with whole units (i.e., where we cannot buy a fraction of a TV spot), the net benefit of $30,000 also results when the firm airs three TV spots per week, but only with four TV spots is the marginal benefit equal to the marginal cost, and this is the general rule that we follow to maximize net benefits (see point E in Figure 1.2).

TABLE 1.1   Benefits and Costs of TV Spots

Number of TV Spots	Total Benefits	Marginal Benefits	Total Costs	Marginal Cost	Net Benefit
1	$20,000	—	$4,000	—	$16,000
2	34,000	$14,000	8,000	$4,000	26,000
3	42,000	8,000	12,000	4,000	30,000
4	**46,000**	**4,000**	**16,000**	**4,000**	**30,000**
5	48,000	2,000	20,000	4,000	28,000
6	49,000	1,000	24,000	4,000	25,000

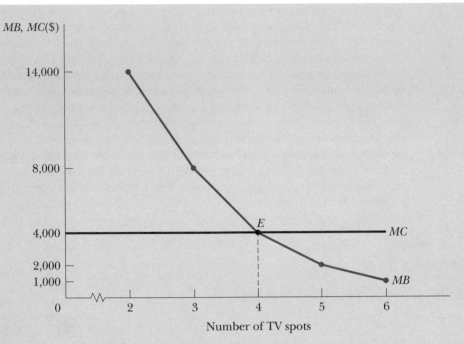

FIGURE 1.2   Marginal Benefit and Marginal Cost of TV Advertising   The marginal benefit (*MB*) of each additional TV spot declines while the marginal cost (*MC*) is constant at $4,000. The net benefit is maximized at point *E* at which *MB = MC*.

To be noted is that the very high cost TV advertising today is a far cry from the first TV ad (a 20-second spot for a Bulova clock that was broadcast on July 1, 1941) that cost $9. As the cost of reaching mass audiences rises and direct marketing to individuals becomes more effective (see "At the Frontier" for Chapter 5), advertisers are shifting some of their advertising expenditures to these other channels (the ability to measure the effectiveness of advertising on sales remains, however, elusive).

Sources: "Ad Industry Benefits of a Recovery," *Wall Street Journal,* February 8, 1993, p. B1; "Target Micromarkets Is Way to Success," *Wall Street Journal,* May 31, 1995; p. A1; "Commercial Breakdown," *Financial Times,* August 1999, p. 11; and "New Economy," *New York Times,* August 27, 2001, p. C4.

Similarly, it pays for a firm to expand output as long as the marginal or extra revenue that it receives from selling each additional unit of the commodity exceeds the marginal or extra cost of producing it. But as the firm produces and sells more units of the commodity, the marginal revenue may decline while its marginal cost rises. The firm maximizes total profits when the marginal revenue is equal to the marginal cost. The application of the marginal concept in firms' production decisions is examined in detail in Part Three (Chapters 7–9) of the text. The same general concept applies to an individual's decision on how many hours to work. The individual will maximize welfare when the marginal benefit he or she receives from the wages of an extra hour of work just matches the marginal cost in terms of the leisure or earnings and consumption foregone by not working the extra hour. The optimal amount of savings by an individual is the amount at which the marginal benefit from the interest earned from saving an extra dollar just matches the marginal cost of postponing spending the dollar on present consumption. These applications of marginal analysis are examined in Part Five (Chapters 14–16).

Similarly, the optimal amount of government regulation of the economic system is the amount at which the marginal benefit of such intervention just matches its marginal cost. The same concept applies to the gathering of information. Gathering information provides some benefits but involves some costs. Thus, the optimal amount of information gathering is the amount at which the marginal benefit equals the marginal cost. These uses of the marginal concept are examined in Part Six (Chapters 17–19) of the text.

Some Clarifications on the Use of the Margin

Several clarifications are in order on the application of the concept of the margin and marginal analysis in microeconomics. First, the maximization of net benefits by marginal analysis does not imply that individuals are entirely selfish and does not preclude a certain degree of altruistic behavior. A more selfish person will maximize satisfaction in terms of material goods and services that the individual himself or herself consumes. A less selfish person will maximize satisfaction by using part of his or her income or resources in helping others. Similarly, a firm may contribute part of its profits to some "worthy causes" or choose to maximize sales rather than profits. Second, individuals, firms, and governments seldom have all the information required to maximize net benefits at the margin precisely. The concept of optimization at the margin is nevertheless an invaluable tool of analysis because it provides the motivation or driving force for most economic actions. Even when individuals and firms are not explicitly trying to maximize net benefits, they often behave as if they are. In fact, the assumption has very good predictive power. Third, marginal analysis leads to the maximization of individual benefits but not to the maximization of the welfare of society as a whole when private benefits and costs differ from social benefits and costs. One situation that leads to this arises in the presence of imperfect competition and justifies government intervention in the economic system to overcome the problem, or at least to minimize its harmful impact. Indeed, whenever some individuals in society can be made better off without making someone else worse off, there is a case for government intervention at the margin to improve society's welfare. When production and consumption can no longer be reorganized so as to improve the welfare of some without at the same time reducing the welfare of others, society is said to be at **Pareto optimum.** These applications of marginal analysis are examined in Part Four (Chapters 10–13) and Part Six (Chapters 17–19) of the text.

Despite these clarifications and qualifications, we can clearly see that the concept of the margin and marginal analysis provide the central unifying theme in all of micro-economics.

SPECIALIZATION, EXCHANGE, AND THE INTERNATIONAL FRAMEWORK OF MICROECONOMICS

In this section we discuss specialization and exchange and the need to provide an international framework for the study of microeconomics.

Specialization and Exchange

Two important characteristics that greatly increase the efficiency of market economies are specialization in production and exchange. **Specialization** refers to the use of labor and other resources in performing those tasks in which each resource is most efficient. Efficiency and output are then maximized. For example, by concentrating in the production of food, farmers produce a much greater output than if they tried to be self-sufficient and make their own clothing and manufacture all the utensils and equipment they need. By avoiding being "the jack of all trades" and specializing instead in the production of food, where they are most efficient, the farmers' output becomes much greater. Farmers can then exchange some of their excess food for the clothes, utensils, and equipment that they need and, as a result, be able to consume more of every good.

But there is an even more important aspect of specialization that increases the efficiency of labor still more. This is division of labor. **Division of labor** refers to the breaking up of a task into a number of smaller, more *specialized* tasks and assigning each of these tasks to different workers. Such a division of labor is likely to greatly increase workers' efficiency by allowing each of them to become more proficient at performing one task, developing shortcuts in the performance of the task, and avoiding the time lost from shifting from one task to another.

Specialization and division of labor, however, create the need for **exchange.** When individuals perform only one task in the production of a single commodity, there is a need for them to exchange part of their output for all the other things that they want. This exchange is greatly facilitated by the use of money. That is, in a monetized economy, individuals are paid in money for their work and can use this income to purchase in the market desired goods and services.

Specialization in production occurs not only at the individual level but also at the regional and national levels. A region or nation can specialize in the production of those goods and services in which it has a **comparative advantage** or is relatively more efficient, and then exchange part of its output for the output of other regions or nations. By doing so, each region or nation will end up consuming more than it could if it tried to be self-sufficient. Trade or exchange makes possible specialization in production and provides benefits to all parties to the exchange. This is discussed in detail in Part Three (Chapters 7–9) of the text.

The International Framework of Microeconomics

As consumers, we purchase Japanese Toyotas and German Mercedes, Italian handbags and French perfumes, Hong Kong clothes and Taiwanese calculators, Scotch whiskey and Swiss chocolates, Canadian fish and Mexican tomatoes, Costa Rican bananas and Brazilian coffee. Often, we are not even aware that the products we consume, or parts of them, are made abroad. For example, imported cloth is used in American-made suits, many American brand-name shoes are entirely manufactured abroad, and a great deal of the orange juice that we drink is imported. American multinational corporations produce and import many parts and components from abroad and export an increasing share of their output. Most of the parts and components of the IBM PC are in fact manufactured abroad (see Example 1–5), and more than one-third of IBM revenues and profits are generated abroad. General Motors and Ford face stiff competition from Toyota, Nissan, and Honda, and many U.S. steel companies are today near bankruptcy as a result of foreign competition and rising steel imports.

EXAMPLE 1–5

Even the IBM PC and the Boeing 777 Are Not All American!

Table 1.2 shows that of the total manufacturing cost of $860 for the IBM PC in 1985, $625 was for parts and components made abroad (of which, $230 was from U.S.-owned plants). Even though all the parts made overseas could be manufactured domestically, they would have cost more and would have led to higher PC prices in the United States (and reduced competitiveness of IBM PCs in international markets). Today, even a larger proportion of parts and components going into the IBM PC are made abroad. Similarly, only 13 of the 33 major components of the new Boeing 777 jetliner are made in the United States, 7 are made in Japan, and another 13 in other countries (Australia, Canada, England, France, Italy, and South Korea).

TABLE 1.2	Distribution of Manufacturing Costs for the IBM PC in the United States and Abroad			
Total manufacturing cost:				$860
Portion made abroad:			$625	
in U.S.-owned plants		$230		
in foreign-owned plants		$395		
Distribution of manufacturing costs:				
Monochrome monitor	(Korea)	$ 85		
Semiconductors	(Japan)	105		
Semiconductors	(U.S.)	105		
Power supply	(Japan)	60		
Graphic printer	(Japan)	160		
Floppy disk drives	(Singapore)	165		
Assembly of disk drives	(U.S.)	25		
Keyboard	(Japan)	50		
Case and final assembly	(U.S.)	105		
		$860		

Sources: "America's High Tech Crisis," Business Week, March 11, 1985, pp. 56–67; and Boeing news release 1998.

In view of the **internationalization of economic activity** and the international repercussions of domestic competitiveness policies, we cannot study microeconomics in an international vacuum. The large and growing degree of interdependence of the United States in the world economy today makes a closed-economy approach to the study of microeconomics unrealistic. This text will explicitly introduce and integrate the international dimension into the body of traditional microeconomics to reflect the globalization of most economic activities in the world today.[4]

1.6   MODELS, METHODOLOGY, AND VALUE JUDGMENTS

We will now discuss the meaning and function of theory or models, examine the methodology of economics and distinguish between positive and normative analysis.

Models and Methodology

In microeconomic theory, we seek to predict and explain the economic behavior of individual consumers, resource owners, and business firms and the operation of individual markets. For this purpose we use models. A **model** abstracts from the many details surrounding an event and identifies a few of the most important determinants of the event. For example, the amount of a commodity that an individual demands over a given period of time depends on the price of the commodity, the individual's income, and the price of related commodities (i.e., substitute and complementary commodities). It also depends on the individual's age, gender, education, background, whether the individual is single or married, whether he or she owns a house or rents, the amount of money he or she has in the bank, the stocks the individual owns, the individual's expectations of future income and prices, geographic location, climate, and many other considerations.

However, given the consumer's tastes and preferences, demand theory identifies the price of the commodity, the individual's income, and the price of related commodities as the most important determinants of the amount of a commodity demanded by an individual. Although it may be *unrealistic* to focus only on these three considerations, demand theory postulates that these are generally capable of predicting accurately and explaining consumer behavior and demand. One could, of course, include additional considerations or variables to gain a fuller or more complete explanation of consumer demand, but that would defeat the main purpose of the theory or model, which is to simplify and generalize.

A theory or model usually results from casual observation of the real world. For example, we may observe that consumers generally purchase less of a commodity when its price rises. Before such a theory of demand can be accepted, however, we must go back to the real world to test it. We must make sure that individuals in different places and over different periods of time do indeed, as a group, purchase less of a commodity when its price rises. Only after many such successful tests and the absence of contradictory results can we accept the theory and make use of it in subsequent analysis to predict and explain consumer

---

[4] See D. Salvatore, "Globalization and International Competitiveness," in S. Shojai, ed., *Globalization: Virtue or Vice?* (New York: Praeger, 2001), pp. 7–21.

behavior. If, on the other hand, test results contradict the model, then the model must be discarded and a new one formulated.

To summarize, a theory or model is usually developed by casual observation of the real world, but we must then go back to the real world to determine whether the implications or predictions of the theory are indeed correct. Only then can we accept the theory or model. According to the Nobel Laureate economist Milton Friedman, a model is not tested by the realism or lack of realism of its assumptions, but rather by its ability to predict accurately and explain. The assumptions of the model are usually unrealistic in that they must necessarily represent a simplification and generalization of reality. However, if the model predicts accurately and explains the event, it is tentatively accepted. For example, demand theory, as originally developed, was based on the assumption that utility (i.e., the satisfaction that a consumer receives from the consumption of a commodity) is cardinally measurable (i.e., we can attach specific numerical values to it). This assumption is clearly unrealistic. Nevertheless, we accept the theory of demand because it leads to the correct prediction that a consumer will purchase less of a commodity when its price rises (other things, such as the consumer's income and the price of related commodities, remaining equal).

While most assumptions represent simplifications of reality, and to that extent are unrealistic, most economists take a broader position. According to these economists, the appropriate **methodology of economics** (and science in general) is to test a theory not only by its ability to predict accurately, but also by whether the predictions follow logically from the assumptions and by the internal consistency of those assumptions. For example, the theory of perfect competition postulates that the economy operates most efficiently when consumers and producers are too small individually to affect prices and output. But this theory cannot be tested for the economy as a whole. It can only be tested by tracing the loss of welfare of individual consumers when the atomistic assumptions of the theory do not hold. Thus, an adequate test of the theory requires not only confirming that the predictions are accurate but also showing how the outcome follows logically or results directly from the assumptions.

Throughout this text we will look at many economic theories or models that seek to predict and explain the economic behavior of consumers, resource owners, and business firms as they interact in the markets for goods, services, and resources. The models presented are generally those that have already been successfully tested. In a microeconomic theory course, we are not concerned with the actual testing of these theories or models, but rather with their presentation, usefulness, and applications.

Positive and Normative Analysis

In discussing the methodology of economic analysis, an important distinction is also made between positive and normative analysis. **Positive analysis** studies what *is*. It is concerned with how the economic system performs the basic functions of what to produce, how to produce, for whom to produce, how it provides for growth, and how it rations the available supply of a good over time. In other words, how is the price of a commodity, service, or resource actually determined in the market? How do producers combine resources to minimize costs of production? How does the number of firms in a market and the type of product they produce affect the determination of the price and quantity sold of the commodity? How do the number and type of owners and users of a resource affect the price and quantity of the resource placed on the market? How do specific taxes and subsidies affect the production and consumption of various commodities and the use of various resources? What are the effects of minimum wages on employment and incomes? The level of real wages on work and leisure? Rent control on the availability of housing? Deregulation of gas on gas prices and consumption? How does the economic system provide for the growth of the nation? How does it ration the available supply of a commodity over time? All of these and many more topics fall within the realm of positive analysis. For the most part, positive analysis is factual or hypothetically testable and objective in nature, and it is devoid of ethical or value judgments.

Normative analysis, on the other hand, studies what *ought* to be. It is concerned with how the basic economic functions *should* be performed. Normative analysis is thus based on value judgments and, as such, is subjective and controversial. Whereas positive analysis is independent of normative analysis, normative analysis is based on positive analysis and the value judgments of society. Controversies in positive analysis can be (and are) usually resolved by the collection of more or better market data. On the other hand, controversies in normative analysis usually are not, and cannot, be resolved. Take, for example, the case of providing national health insurance for everybody. Many people favor it, but others are opposed, and no amount of economic analysis can resolve the controversy. Economists can provide an analysis of the *economic* costs and benefits of national health insurance. Such an analysis can be useful in clarifying the economic issues involved, but it is not likely to lead to general agreement on the proposition that national health insurance should or should not be provided for everybody. The economists' tools of analysis and logic can be applied to determine the economic benefits and costs of normative questions, but it is society as a whole (through elected representatives) that must make normative decisions.

It is extremely important in economics to specify exactly when we are leaving the real world of positive analysis and entering that of normative analysis—that is, when disagreements can be resolved by the collection of more or better data (facts) and when ethical or value judgments are involved. This book is primarily concerned with positive analysis. A statement such as "universal national health insurance should be established" is a proposition of normative analysis because it is based on value judgments. Normative analysis will be discussed in detail in Chapters 17 and 18.

AT THE FRONTIER
Do Economists Ever Agree on Anything?

Y ou have probably heard some of the many jokes about economists disagreeing on almost everything. "How many opinions on the same subject do you expect to find in a room with three economists?" Answer: "four." In response to an economist's answer framed as "on the one hand . . . and on the other . . . ," President Truman is supposed to have snapped: "Give me a one-handed economist." Such jokes do not seem justified according to the results of a recent study.

Table 1.3 reports the responses to 10 of 40 propositions form 464 respondents to a questionnaire sent to a random sample of 1,350 economists in 1992. Table 1.3 shows that the vast majority of economists agreed on the first three propositions (that a ceiling on rents reduces the quantity and quality of housing, that tariffs and

TABLE 1.3　Responses of Economists of Various Propositions

Proposition	Percentage of Respondents Who	
	Agreed	Disagreed*
1. A ceiling on rents reduces the quantity and quality of housing available.	92.9	6.5
2. Tariffs and import quotas usually reduce general economic welfare.	92.6	6.5
3. Fiscal policy (e.g., tax cuts and/or expenditure increase) has a significant stimulative impact on a less than fully employed economy.	89.9	9.1
4. Cash payments increase the welfare of recipients to a greater degree than do transfers-in-kind of equal cash value.	83.9	15.1
5. A large federal budget deficit has an adverse effect on the economy.	82.7	15.7
6. The redistribution of income distribution within the U.S. is a legitimate role for government.	81.9	16.8
7. A minimum wage increases unemployment among young and unskilled workers.	78.9	20.5
8. Antitrust laws should be enforced vigorously to reduce monopoly power from its current level.	71.8	27.6
9. Reducing the regulatory power of the Environmental Protection Agency (EPA) would improve the efficiency of the U.S. economy.	36.0	62.3
10. The U.S. government should retaliate against (foreign) dumping and subsidies in international trade.	50.2	47.6

*The sum of the percentages of those who agree and disagree does not add to 100 because of nonrespondents to the particular question.

import quotas usually reduce general economic welfare, and that fiscal policy has a significant stimulative effect on a less than fully employed economy), but strongly disagreed on the last two propositions. In general, there was much more agreement on questions of microeconomics (which are overrepresented in the propositions reported in Table 1.3) than on questions of macroeconomics.

But even on the questions that elicit widespread agreement among economists, the gap between the public's (especially non-college graduates) and economists' views are very wide. There is, however, a great deal of agreement on what are the major issues that society faces today (i.e., the state of the economy, education, health care, taxes, crime, and international conditions).

Sources: R. M. Alston, J. R. Kearl, and M. B. Vaughan, "Is There a Consensus Among Economists in the 1990's?," *American Economic Review,* May 1992, pp. 203–209; R. J. Blendon et al., "Bridging the Gap Between the Public's and Economists' Views of the Economy," *Journal of Economic Perspectives,* summer 1997, pp. 105–118; and "The Politics of Prosperity," *Business Week,* August 7, 2000, pp. 104–108.

SUMMARY

1. Economics deals with the allocation of scarce resources among alternative uses to satisfy human wants. Scarcity of resources and commodities is the fundamental economic fact of every society.

2. All societies must decide what to produce, how to produce, for whom to produce, how to provide for the growth of the system, and how to ration a given amount of a commodity over time. Under a free-enterprise or mixed economic system such as that in the United States, it is the price system that performs these functions, for the most part.

3. Microeconomic theory studies the economic behavior of individual decision-making units such as individual consumers, resource owners, and business firms and the operation of individual markets in a free-enterprise economy. This is contrasted with macroeconomic theory, which studies the economy viewed as a whole. Microeconomic theory focuses attention on households and business firms as they interact in the markets for goods and services and resources.

4. Because of scarcity, all economic activities give rise to some benefits but also involve some costs. The aim of economic decisions is to maximize net benefits. Net benefits increase as long as the marginal or extra benefit from an action exceeds the marginal or extra cost resulting from the action. Net benefits are maximized when the marginal benefit is equal to the marginal cost. This concept applies to all economic decisions and market transactions. It applies as much to the consumption decisions of individuals as to the production decisions of firms, the supply choices of input owners, and government decisions. Indeed, the concepts of the margin and marginal analysis represent the key unifying concepts in all of microeconomics.

5. Specialization and exchange are two important characteristics that greatly increase the efficiency of individuals and firms in market economies. Many of the commodities we consume today are imported, and American firms purchase many inputs abroad, sell an increasing share of their products to other nations, and face increasing competition from foreign firms in the U.S. market and around the world. The international flow of capital, technology, and skilled labor has also reached unprecedented dimensions. In view of such internationalization of economic activity in the world today, it is essential to introduce an international dimension into the body of traditional microeconomics.

6. Theories make use of models. A model abstracts from the details surrounding an event and seeks to identify a few of the most important determinants of an event. A model is tested by its predictive ability, the consistency of its assumptions, and the logic with which the predictions follow from the assumptions. There is more agreement among economists than is commonly believed.

KEY TERMS

Economics
Human wants
Economic resources
Price system
Free-enterprise system
What to produce
How to produce
For whom to produce
Economic growth
Rationing over time

Microeconomic theory
Macroeconomic theory
Circular flow of economic activity
Price theory
Mixed economy
Marginal benefit
Marginal cost
Concept of the margin
Marginal analysis
Pareto optimum

Specialization
Division of labor
Exchange
Comparative advantage
Internationalization of economic activity
Model
Methodology of economics
Positive analysis
Normative analysis

REVIEW QUESTIONS

1. Will the problem of scarcity disappear over time as standards of living increase?

2. Distinguish between the real and the financial flows that link product and factor markets.

3. Explain in terms of the circular flow of economic activity why some individuals are richer while others are poorer.

4. Explain why some football players earn more than others. Why would a team sign a superstar for millions of dollars when it could sign a good player for much less?

5. Does a firm maximize its total revenue when it maximizes its total profits?

6. It has been proven that a speed limit of 55 MPH, rather than 65 MPH, on the nation's highways saves lives and fuel. Is there any cost in keeping the speed limit at 55 MPH?

7. Why is it that imports and exports as a percentage of gross national product (GNP) are much smaller in the United States than in Switzerland?

8. What is the relationship between import prices and domestic prices?

9. What happens to the dollar price of Japanese exports to the United States and to the yen price of U.S. exports to Japan if the Japanese yen increases in value with respect to the U.S. dollar?

10. Two models predict equally well, but one is based on a larger number of assumptions and the logic with which the predictions follow from the assumptions is more intricate than for another model. Why is the second model better?

11. A model using three variables explains 85% of an event (say, a price increase), while another model, using ten variables, explains 95% of the event. Which of the two models is better? Why?

12. The government should pass more stringent pollution control laws. Do you agree? What can economists contribute to the discussion?

PROBLEMS

*1. Why do we study microeconomics?

2. Explain why an increasing proportion of income spent on health care does not necessarily involve a reduction in the quantity of all other goods and services that can be purchased overtime. In what way is exploding health care costs related to the problem of scarcity?

3. Briefly explain how the sharp increase in petroleum prices since the fall of 1973 affected driving habits and the production of cars in the United States since then.

4. Explain why India produces textiles with much more labor relative to capital than does the United States.

5. Explain how the introduction of government affects the circular flow of economic activity.

*6. Explain the effect of government setting the price of a commodity
   a. below equilibrium with a price ceiling;
   b. above equilibrium with a price floor.

7. How does the concept of the margin provide a key unifying concept in microeconomics?

8. Using some data obtained from a publication such as *The Survey of Current Business, The U.S. Statistical Abstract,* or *International Financial Statistics* available in your library, show that the interdependence of the U.S. economy with the rest of the world has increased sharply during the past three decades.

9. a. If two models predict equally well but one is more complicated than the other, indicate which one you would use and why.
   b. Indicate how you would determine which of the two models is more complex.

10. a. Explain how you would go about constructing a model to predict total sales of American-made cars in the United States next year.
   b. Indicate how you would test your model.

* = Answer provided at end of book.

11. Economists often disagree on economic matters, so economics is not a science. True or false? Explain.

*12. Briefly indicate which aspects of the redistribution of income from higher- to lower-income people involve

    a. positive analysis;

    b. normative analysis.

INTERNET SITE ADDRESSES

For the state of the U.S. economy, see the *Economic Report of the President* at:

    http://www.access.gpo.gov.eop

General directories and indexes of economic information are:

    YAHOO—Economics:
    http://www.yahoo.com/Social_Science/Economics/

    Infoseek—Economics:
    http://www.infoseek.com/Business/Economics

For U.S. economic data, indicators and statistics, see:

    Bureau of Economic Analysis:
    http://www.bea.doc.gov/

    Bureau of Labor Statistics: http://stats.bls.gov/

    Census Bureau: http://www.census.gov/

    Department of Commerce: http://www.doc.gov/

    Department of the Treasury:
    http://www.ustreas.gov/

Economic Indicators Monthly:
http://www.gpo.ucop.edu/catalog/econind.html

Economic History Services:
http://www.eh.net/hmit

National Bureau of Economic Analysis:
http://www.nber.org

The gateway to all the major federal statistical sites: http://www.fedstats.gov

For international economic data, indicators and statistics, see:

    International Monetary Fund: http://IMF.org

    Organization for Economic Cooperation and Development: http://oecd.org

    World Bank: http://worldbank.org

    World Trade Organization: http://www.wto.org

CHAPTER 2

Basic Demand and Supply Analysis

ave you ever stopped to think about how the price of a commodity (say, the price of your favorite music compact disc) is determined and why it often changes over time? In this chapter we seek to answer these questions by providing an overview of how markets function. We begin by defining the concept of a market. Next we discuss the meaning of demand and a change in demand. After reviewing supply, we examine how the interaction of the forces of market demand and supply determine the equilibrium price and quantity of a commodity. Then we examine how the equilibrium price and quantity of a commodity are affected by changes in demand and supply and by imports. Finally, we examine the effect of modifications and interferences in the operation of markets. So widespread is the applicability of the market model, that one could safely start answering any question of microeconomics by saying that it depends on demand and supply. Note, however, the "At the Frontier" discussion of nonclearing market theories.

2.1   MARKET ANALYSIS

Most of microeconomic analysis is devoted to the study of how individual markets operate. A **market** is an institutional arrangement under which buyers and sellers can exchange some quantity of a good or service at a mutually agreeable price. Markets provide the framework for the analysis of the forces of demand and supply that, together, determine commodity and resource prices. As explained in Chapter 1, prices play the central role in microeconomic analysis.

A market can, but need not, be a specific place or location where buyers and sellers actually come face to face for the purpose of transacting their business. For example, the New York Stock Exchange is located in a building at 11 Wall Street in New York City. On the other hand, the market for college professors has no specific location; rather, it refers to all the formal and informal information networks on teaching opportunities throughout the nation. There is a market for each good, service, or resource bought and sold in the economy. Some of these markets are local, some are regional, and others are national or international in character.

Throughout this chapter, we assume that markets are perfectly competitive. A **perfectly competitive market** is one in which there are so many buyers and sellers of a product that each of them cannot affect the price of the product, all units of the product are homogeneous or identical, resources are mobile, and knowledge of the market is perfect. For the purpose of the present chapter, this definition of a perfectly competitive market suffices. A more detailed definition and analysis of this and other types of markets is given in Chapter 9 and in Part Three of the text.

2.2 | MARKET DEMAND

The concept of demand is one of the most crucial in microeconomic theory and in all of economics. In this section, we review the concepts of the market demand schedule and the market demand curve, and examine the meaning of a change in demand.

Demand Schedule and Demand Curve

A **market demand schedule** is a table showing the quantity of a commodity that consumers are willing and able to purchase over a given period of time at each price of the commodity, while holding constant all other relevant economic variables on which demand depends (the *ceteris paribus* assumption). Among the variables held constant are consumers' incomes, their tastes, the prices of related commodities (substitutes and complements), and the number of consumers in the market.

For example, Table 2.1 provides a hypothetical daily demand schedule for hamburgers in a large market (say, New York City, Chicago, or Los Angeles). At the price of $2.00 per hamburger, the quantity demanded is 2 million hamburgers per day. At the lower price of $1.50, the quantity demanded is 4 million hamburgers per day. At the price of $1.00, the quantity demanded is 6 million hamburgers, and at the prices of $0.75 and $0.50, the quantity demanded is 7 and 8 million hamburgers, respectively.

At lower prices, greater quantities of hamburgers are demanded. Each additional hamburger consumed per day provides declining marginal or extra benefit, and so consumers

TABLE 2.1	Market Demand Schedule for Hamburgers	
Price Per Hamburger	Quantity Demanded Per Day (Million Hamburgers)	
$2.00	2	
1.50	4	
1.00	6	
0.75	7	
0.50	8	

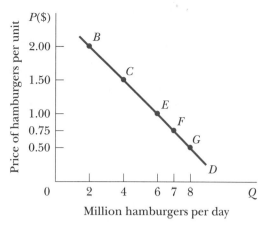

FIGURE 2.1 Market Demand Curve for Hamburgers Market demand curve *D* shows that at lower hamburger prices, greater quantities are demanded. This is reflected in the negative slope of the demand curve and is referred to as the "law of demand."

would only purchase greater quantities at lower prices. This is true for most commodities. Lower commodity prices will also bring more consumers into the market. The inverse price-quantity relationship (indicating that a greater quantity of the commodity is demanded at lower prices and a smaller quantity at higher prices) is called the **law of demand.**

By plotting on a graph the various price-quantity combinations given by the market demand schedule, we obtain the **market demand curve** for the commodity. The price per unit of the commodity is usually measured along the vertical axis, while the quantity demanded of the commodity per unit of time is measured along the horizontal axis. For example, Figure 2.1 shows the market demand curve for hamburgers corresponding to the market demand schedule of Table 2.1. The demand curve has a *negative slope;* that is, it slopes downward to the right. This negative slope is a reflection of the law of demand or inverse price-quantity relationship.

The various points on the demand curve represent *alternative* price-quantity combinations. For example, at the price of $2.00 per hamburger, the quantity demanded is 2 million hamburgers (point *B* in Figure 2.1). If the price is $1.50, the quantity demanded is 4 million hamburgers (point *C*), and so on. A demand curve also shows the maximum price consumers are willing to pay to purchase each quantity of a commodity per unit of time. For example, the demand curve of Figure 2.1 shows that the *demand price* (i.e., the maximum price that consumers are willing to pay) for 2 million hamburgers is $2.00 per hamburger (point *B*); for 4 million hamburgers, the demand price is $1.50, and so on. Finally, a particular demand curve refers to a specific period of time. The demand curve of Figure 2.1 is for one day. The demand curve for hamburgers for a month is correspondingly higher.[1]

---

[1] The demand curve can, but need not, be a straight line.

Changes in Demand

A demand curve can shift so that more or less of the commodity would be demanded at any commodity price. The entire demand curve for a commodity would shift with a change in (1) consumers' incomes, (2) consumers' tastes, (3) the price of related commodities, (4) the number of consumers in the market, or in any other variable held constant in drawing a market demand curve. For example, with a rise in consumer income the demand curve for most commodities (normal goods) shifts to the right, because consumers can then afford to purchase more of each commodity at each price. The same is true if consumers' tastes change (or if the quality of the product improves) so that they demand more of the commodity at each price, or if the number of consumers in the market increases.

A demand curve also shifts to the right if the price of a substitute commodity rises or if the price of a complementary commodity falls. For example, if the price of hot dogs (a substitute for hamburgers) *rises*, people will switch some of their purchases away from hot dogs and demand more hamburgers at each and every price of hamburgers (a rightward shift in the demand for hamburgers). Similarly, if the price of the bun (a complement of hamburgers) *falls,* the demand for hamburgers also shifts to the right (since the price of a hamburger with the bun is then lower).

On the other hand, the demand curve for a commodity usually shifts to the left (so that less of it is demanded at each price) with a decline in consumer income, a decrease in the price of substitute commodities, or a decrease in the number of consumers in the market. The demand curve also shifts to the left if the price of complementary commodities rises or if consumer tastes change so that they demand less of the commodity at each price.

Figure 2.2 shows D, the original demand curve for hamburgers (from Figure 2.1) and D', a higher demand curve for hamburgers. With D', consumers demand more hamburgers

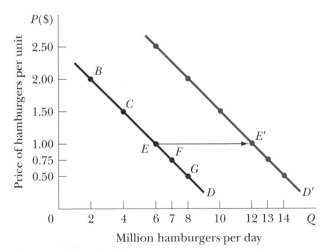

FIGURE 2.2   Change in Demand for Hamburgers
Consumers demand more hamburgers at each price when the demand curve shifts to the right from D to D'. Thus, at $P = \$1.00$, consumers purchase 12 million hamburgers with D' instead of only 6 million with D.

at each price. For example, at the price of $1.00, consumers demand 12 million hamburgers per day (point E') as compared with 6 million demanded (point E) on curve D. The shift from D to D' leads consumers to demand 6 million *additional* hamburgers per day at each price.

A shift in demand is referred to as a *change in demand* and must be clearly distinguished from a *change in the quantity demanded,* which refers instead to a movement along a given demand curve as a result of a change in the commodity price. Thus, the shift in demand from D to D' is an increase in demand, while the movement along D, say, from point E to point F, is a change in the quantity demanded. The change in demand is caused by the change in the economic variables that are held constant in drawing a given demand curve (the *ceteris paribus* assumption), whereas a change in the quantity demanded is a movement along a given demand curve as a result of a change in the price of the commodity (with all the other economic variables on which demand depends remaining constant).

2.3   MARKET SUPPLY

We have examined the market demand, now it is time to turn to the supply side.

Supply Schedule and Supply Curve

A **market supply schedule** is a table showing the quantity supplied of a commodity at each price for a given period of time. It assumes that technology, resource prices, and, for agricultural commodities, weather conditions are held constant (the *ceteris paribus* assumption). Table 2.2 gives a hypothetical daily supply schedule for hamburgers. Starting at the bottom, the table shows that at the price of $0.50 per hamburger, the quantity supplied is 2 million hamburgers per day. At the higher price of $0.75 per hamburger, the quantity supplied is 4 million hamburgers per day. At the price of $1.00, the quantity supplied is 6 million hamburgers per day, and so on. Higher hamburger prices allow producers to bid resources away from other uses and supply greater quantities of hamburgers.

The various price-quantity combinations of a supply schedule can be plotted on a graph to obtain the **market supply curve** for the commodity. For example, Figure 2.3 shows the market supply curve for hamburgers corresponding to the market supply schedule of

TABLE 2.2 Market Supply Schedule for Hamburgers	
Price Per Hamburger	Quantity Supplied Per Day (Million Hamburgers)
$2.00	14
1.50	10
1.00	6
0.75	4
0.50	2

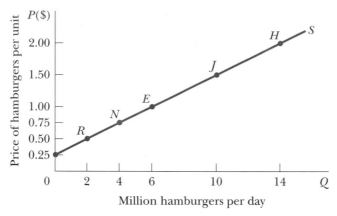

FIGURE 2.3   Market Supply Curve for Hamburgers   Market supply curve *S* shows that higher hamburger prices induce producers to supply greater quantities.

Table 2.2. The *positive slope* of the supply curve (i.e., its upward-to-the-right inclination) reflects the fact that higher prices must be paid to producers to cover rising marginal, or extra, costs and thus induce them to supply greater quantities of the commodity.

As with the demand curve, the various points on the supply curve represent *alternative* price–quantity combinations. For example, at the price of $0.50 per hamburger, the quantity supplied is 2 million hamburgers per day (point *R* in Figure 2.3). If instead the price is $0.75, the quantity supplied is 4 million hamburgers (point *N*), and so on. A supply curve also shows the *minimum* price that producers must receive to cover their rising marginal costs and supply each quantity of the commodity. For example, the supply curve of Figure 2.3 shows that the *supply price* (i.e., the minimum price that suppliers must receive) in order to supply 2 million hamburgers per day is $0.50 (point *R*); for 4 million hamburgers, the supply price is $0.75 (point *N*), and so on. A particular supply curve is drawn for a specific period of time. The supply curve of Figure 2.3 is for one day. The supply curve of hamburgers for a month is correspondingly larger or farther out.[2]

Changes in Supply

An improvement in technology, a reduction in the price of resources used in the production of the commodity, and, for agricultural commodities, more favorable weather conditions (i.e., a change in the *ceteris paribus* assumption) would cause the entire supply curve of the commodity to shift to the right. Producers would then supply more of the commodity at each price. For example, Figure 2.4 shows that at the price of $1.00, producers supply 12 million hamburgers per day (point *E′*) with *S′* as opposed to only 6 million hamburgers with *S*.

The shift to the right from *S* to *S′* is referred to as *an increase in supply.* This must be clearly distinguished from *an increase in the quantity supplied,* which is instead a movement

---

[2] As in the case of demand, the supply curve can, but need not, be a straight line.

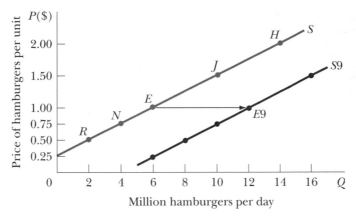

FIGURE 2.4   Change in the Supply of Hamburgers   When the
supply curve shifts to the right from S to S', producers supply more
hamburgers at each price. Thus, at P = $1.00, producers supply
12 million hamburgers with S' instead of only 6 million with S.

on a given supply curve in the upward direction (as, for example, from point *E* to point *J*, in
Figure 2.4) resulting from an increase in the commodity price (from $1.00 to $1.50). On the
other hand, a decrease in supply refers to a leftward shift in the supply curve and must be
clearly distinguished from a decrease in the quantity supplied of the commodity (which is a
movement down a supply curve and results from a decline in the commodity price).

2.4   WHEN IS A MARKET IN EQUILIBRIUM?[3]

We now examine how the interaction of the forces of demand and supply determines the
equilibrium price and quantity of a commodity in a perfectly competitive market. A market
is in equilibrium when no buyer or seller has any incentive to change the quantity of the
commodity that he or she buys or sells at the given price. The **equilibrium price** of a commodity is the price at which the quantity demanded of the commodity equals the quantity
supplied and the market clears. The process by which equilibrium is reached in the marketplace can be shown with a table and illustrated graphically.

Table 2.3 brings together the market demand and supply schedules for hamburgers
from Tables 2.1 and 2.2. From Table 2.3, we see that only at $P = \$1.00$ is the quantity sup-
plied of hamburgers equal to the quantity demanded and the market clears. Thus, $P = \$1.00$ is the equilibrium price and $Q = 6$ million hamburgers per day is the equilibrium
quantity.

At prices above the equilibrium price, the quantity supplied exceeds the quantity
demanded and there is a **surplus** of the commodity, which drives the price down. For
example, at $P = \$2.00$, the quantity supplied (QS) is 14 million hamburgers, the quantity

---

[3] An algebraic analysis of how equilibrium is determined for this case is given in the appendix to this chapter.
A more general analysis is provided in section A1.11 of the Mathematical Appendix at the end of the book.

TABLE 2.3	Market Supply Schedule, Market Demand Schedule, and Equilibrium			
Price Per Hamburger	Quantity Supplied Per Day (Million Hamburgers)	Quantity Demanded Per Day (Million Hamburgers)	Surplus (+) or Shortage (−)	Pressure on Price
$2.00	14	2	12	Downward
1.50	10	4	6	Downward
1.00	6	6	0	Equilibrium
0.75	4	7	−3	Upward
0.50	2	8	−6	Upward

demanded (QD) is 2 million hamburgers, so there is a surplus of 12 million hamburgers per day (see the first line of Table 2.3). Sellers must reduce prices to get rid of their unwanted inventory accumulations of hamburgers. At lower prices, producers supply smaller quantities and consumers demand larger quantities until the equilibrium price of $1.00 is reached, at which the quantity supplied of 6 million hamburgers per day equals the quantity demanded and the market clears.

On the other hand, at prices below the equilibrium price, the quantity supplied falls short of the quantity demanded and there is a **shortage** of the commodity, which drives the price up. For example, at $P = \$0.50$, $QS = 2$ million hamburgers while $QD = 8$ million hamburgers, so that there is a shortage of 6 million hamburgers per day (see the last line of Table 2.3). The price of hamburgers is then bid up by consumers who want more hamburgers than are available at the low price of $0.50. As the price of hamburgers is bid up, producers supply greater quantities while consumers demand smaller quantities until the equilibrium price of $P = \$1.00$ is reached, at which $QS = QD = 6$ million hamburgers per day and the market clears. Thus, bidding drives price and quantity to their equilibrium level.

The determination of the equilibrium price can also be shown graphically by bringing together on the same graph the market demand curve of Figure 2.1 and the market supply curve of Figure 2.3. In Figure 2.5 the intersection of the market demand curve and the market supply curve of hamburgers at point E defines the equilibrium price of $1.00 per hamburger and the equilibrium quantity of 6 million hamburgers per day.

At higher prices, there is an excess supply or surplus of the commodity (the top shaded area in Figure 2.5). Suppliers then lower prices to sell their excess supplies. The surplus is eliminated only when suppliers have lowered their price to the equilibrium level. On the other hand, at below equilibrium prices, the excess demand or shortage (the bottom shaded area in the figure) drives the price up to the equilibrium level. This occurs because consumers are unable to purchase all of the commodity they want at below-equilibrium prices and they bid up the price. The shortage is eliminated only when consumers have bid up the price to the equilibrium level, that is, only at $P = \$1.00$, $QS = QD = 6$ million hamburgers per day, and the market is in equilibrium (clears). So, both demand and supply play a role in determining price.

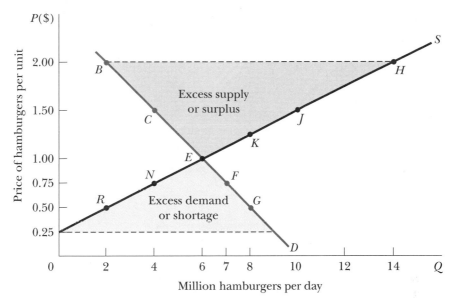

FIGURE 2.5   Demand, Supply, and Equilibrium   The intersection of *D* and *S* at point *E* defines the equilibrium price of $1.00 per hamburger and the equilibrium quantity of 6 million hamburgers per day. At *P* larger than $1.00, the resulting surplus will drive *P* down toward equilibrium. At *P* smaller than $1.00, the resulting shortage will drive *P* up toward equilibrium.

Equilibrium is the condition which, once achieved, tends to persist in time. That is, as long as buyers and sellers do not change their behavior and *D* and *S* do not change, the equilibrium point remains the same.

At a particular point in time, the observed price may or may not be the equilibrium price. However, we know that market forces generally push the market price toward equilibrium. This may occur very rapidly or very slowly. Before the market price reaches a particular equilibrium price, demand and supply may change (shift), defining a new equilibrium price. For now we will assume that, in the absence of price controls, the market price *is* the equilibrium price.

2.5   ADJUSTMENT TO CHANGES IN DEMAND AND SUPPLY: COMPARATIVE STATIC ANALYSIS

What is the effect of a change in the behavior of buyers and sellers, and hence in demand and supply, on the equilibrium price and quantity of a commodity? Because the behavior of buyers and sellers often does change, causing demand and supply curves to shift over time, it is important to analyze how these shifts affect equilibrium. This analysis is called **comparative static analysis.**

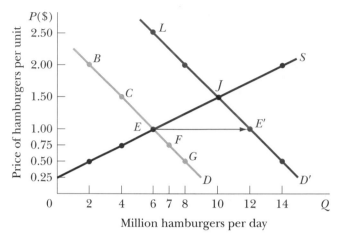

FIGURE 2.6   Adjustment to an Increase in Demand   *D* and *S* are the original demand and supply curves (as in Figure 2.5). The shift from *D* to *D'* results in a temporary shortage of hamburgers, which drives the price up to *P* = $1.50 at which *QS* = *QD* = 10 million hamburgers.

Adjustment to Changes in Demand

We have seen that the market demand curve for a commodity shifts as a result of a change in consumers' income, their tastes, the price of substitutes and complements, and the number of consumers in the market (i.e., a change in the *ceteris paribus* assumption). Given the market supply curve of a commodity, an increase in demand (a rightward shift of the entire demand curve) results both in a higher equilibrium price and a higher equilibrium quantity. A reduction in demand has the opposite effect.

Figure 2.6 shows a shift from *D* to *D'* resulting, for example, from an increase in consumers' income. The shift results in a temporary shortage of 6 million hamburgers (*EE'* in the figure) at the original equilibrium price of *P* = $1.00 (point *E*). As a result, the price of hamburgers is bid up to *P* = $1.50 at which *QS* = *QD* = 10 million hamburgers. As the price of hamburgers rises to *P* = $1.50, the quantity demanded declines (from point *E'* to point *J* along *D'*) while the quantity supplied increases (from point *E* to point *J* along *S*) until the new equilibrium point *J* is reached. At the new equilibrium point *J*, both *P* and *Q* are higher than at the old equilibrium point *E* and the market, once again, clears.

Adjustment to Changes in Supply

The market supply curve of a commodity can shift as a result of a change in technology, resource prices, or weather conditions (for agricultural commodities). Given the market demand curve for the commodity, an increase in supply (a rightward shift of the entire supply curve) results in a lower equilibrium price but a larger equilibrium quantity. A reduction in supply has the opposite effect.

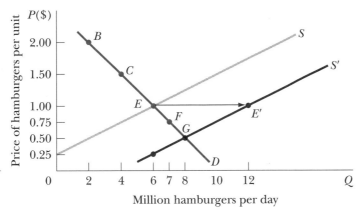

FIGURE 2.7   Adjustment to an Increase in Supply D and S are the original demand and supply curves. The shift from S to S' results in a temporary surplus of hamburgers, which drives the price down to $P = \$0.50$ at which $QS = QD = 8$ million hamburgers.

Figure 2.7 shows a shift from S to S' resulting, for example, from a reduction in the price of beef. The shift results in a temporary surplus of 6 million hamburgers (EE' in the figure) at the original equilibrium price of $P = \$1.00$ (point E). To get rid of their surplus, sellers reduce their price to $P = \$0.50$, at which $QS = QD = 8$ million hamburgers. As the price of hamburgers falls to $P = \$0.50$, the quantity demanded increases (from point E to point G along D) while the quantity supplied decreases (from point E' to point G along S') until the new equilibrium point G is reached. At new equilibrium point G, P is lower and Q is higher than at old equilibrium point E and the market, once again, clears.

Starting from Figure 2.5, you should be able to show what happens to the equilibrium price and quantity if both the demand and supply of hamburgers increase, if both decrease, or if one increases and the other decreases. We can similarly examine the effect of changes in demand and supply on the equilibrium price and quantity of any other commodity or service (see Example 2–1).

EXAMPLE 2–1

Changes in Demand and Supply and Coffee Prices

Changes in the demand and the supply of coffee explain why world wholesale coffee prices have fallen by nearly a half from 1999 to 2001 and why they are now at their lowest level in three decades. The sharp decline in coffee price threw millions of small coffee farmers and their families in developing countries into extreme poverty, while multinational food companies (such as Nestlé) and coffee shops (such as Starbucks) posted very high profits from coffee sales.

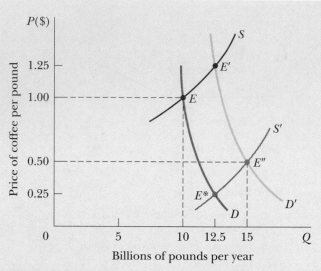

FIGURE 2.8   Demand, Supply and Coffee Prices   Curves *D* and *S* refer, respectively, to the world's demand and supply curve for coffee. Curves *D* and *S* intersect at point *E*, giving the equilibrium price of coffee of $1.00 and the equilibrium quantity of 10 billion pounds per year. If *D* and *S* shifted, respectively, to *D'* to *S'*, the new equilibrium point would be *E''*, giving the price of $0.50 and the quantity of 15 million pounds per year.

The problem in the coffee market arose from the fact that the supply of coffee increased faster than its demand, causing coffee prices to fall. Since coffee prices fell faster than quantities increased, the earnings of coffee farmers also declined. This can be shown with Figure 2.8, where *D* represents the world's demand curve for coffee and *S* represents the world's supply curve. Curves *D* and *S* intersect at the equilibrium world price of coffee of $1 per pound and the equilibrium quantity of 10 billion pounds per year (point *E* in the figure), giving coffee farmers a total revenue (income) of $10 billion per year. If, over time, *D* shifts to *D'* and *S* shifts to *S'*, the world price of coffee falls to $0.50 per pound and the quantity rises to 15 billion pounds per year (shown by new equilibrium point *E''* in the figure). This, however, produces a total revenue (income) for coffee farmers of only $7.5 billion per year. If only *D* shifted to *D'*, the price of coffee would be $1.25 (point *E'* in the figure); while if only *S* shifted to *S'*, the price of coffee would be $0.25 (point *E**).

During the past few years, the supply of coffee has been increasing at twice the rate of the increase in demand as a result of new countries (such as Vietnam) starting to produce and export coffee on a large scale and others (such as Indonesia and Brazil) sharply increasing exports. This caused the price of coffee that growers received to fall from $1.40 per pound in 1998 to as low as $0.48 in June 2002, which is lower than the production costs of many poor small farmers. As more efficient larger farmers increased their production to make up for the reduction in price, the market supply curve for coffee shifted to the right, causing coffee prices to fall even lower.

A plan drawn up in May 2000 by the 28-member Association of Coffee Producing Countries (ACPC) sponsored by Brazil and Colombia (respectively, the world's largest and third largest coffee exporter) failed to reduce coffee exports and stabilize prices. Prospects for price increases in the next few years do not seem bright, unless bad weather sharply cuts coffee production around the world.

Sources: "Coffee Producers Expecting More Tough Years in Saturated Market," *Financial Times,* December 29, 2000, p. 18; "Drowning in Cheap Coffee," *The Economist,* September 29, 2001, pp. 43–44; "For Coffee Traders, Disaster Comes in Pairs," *New York Times,* October 28, 2001, p. 4; and "Crisis Call to Coffee Growers," *Financial Times,* April 16, 2002, p. 23.

2.6 | DOMESTIC DEMAND AND SUPPLY, IMPORTS, AND PRICES

When the domestic price of a commodity is higher than the commodity price abroad, the nation will import the commodity until domestic and foreign prices are equalized, in the absence of trade restrictions and assuming no transportation costs. This is shown in Figure 2.9. Curves D_T and S_T in Panels A and C refer to the demand and supply curves for textiles in the United States and in the rest of the world per year, respectively. Panel A shows that in the absence of trade, the United States would produce and consume 200 million yards of textiles at the price of $3 per yard (point F). Panel C shows that the rest of

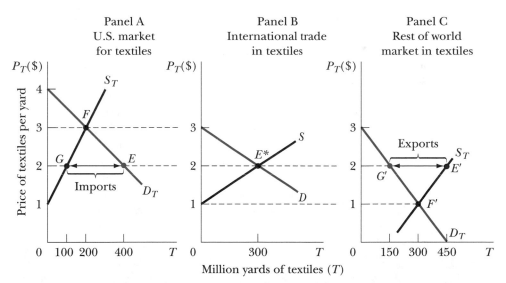

FIGURE 2.9   Equilibrium Commodity Price with Trade   The U.S. demand for textile imports (*D*) in Panel B is derived from the excess demand at below–equilibrium prices in the absence of trade in Panel A. On the other hand, the foreign supply of textile exports to the United States (*S*) in Panel B is derived from the foreign excess supply at above–equilibrium prices in the absence of trade in Panel C. The *D* and *S* curves intersect at point *E** in Panel B, establishing the equilibrium price of $2 per yard and the equilibrium quantity of textiles traded of 300 million yards.

the world produces and consumes 300 million yards at the price of $1 per yard (point F'). With free trade in textiles, and assuming (for simplicity) zero transportation costs, the price of textiles will be $2 per yard both in the United States and abroad. The United States will import 300 million yards of textiles (EG in Panel A), which is equal to the textile exports of the rest of the world ($E'G'$ in Panel C). This result, which is easily visualized by examining Panels A and C only, is formally derived in Panel B.

Panel B shows the U.S. demand for textile imports (D) and the foreign supply curve of textile exports (S). The U.S. demand for textile imports in Panel B is derived from the U.S. **excess demand** for textiles at each price below the U.S. equilibrium price in Panel A. Specifically, at the equilibrium price of $3 per yard, the United States produces and consumes 200 million yards of textiles (point F in Panel A). This corresponds to the vertical intercept of the U.S. demand curve for textile imports (D) in Panel B. At $P_T = \$2$, the United States produces 100 million yards domestically (point G in Panel A), consumes 400 million yards (point E in Panel A), and thus imports 300 million yards (EG in Panel A). This corresponds to point E^* on the U.S. demand curve for textile imports (D) in Panel B.

The foreign supply curve of textile exports to the United States (S in Panel B) is derived from the **excess supply** of textiles in the rest of the world at prices above the equilibrium price in Panel C. Specifically, at the equilibrium price of $1 per yard, the rest of the world produces and consumes 300 million yards of textiles (point F' in Panel C). This corresponds to the vertical intercept of the supply curve of textile exports of the rest of the world (S) in Panel B. At $P_T = \$2$, the rest of the world produces 450 million yards (point E' in Panel C), consumes 150 million yards (point G' in Panel C), and exports 300 million yards ($E'G'$ in Panel C). This corresponds to point E^* on the supply curve of textile exports of the rest of the world (S) in Panel B.

The U.S. demand curve for textile imports (D in Panel B) intersects the foreign supply curve of textile exports from the rest of the world (S in Panel B) at point E^*, resulting in the equilibrium quantity of textiles traded of 300 million yards at the equilibrium price of $2 per yard. Just as for any other commodity, the equilibrium price and quantity of textiles traded is given at the intersection of the demand and supply curves. Note that in the absence of any obstruction to trade in textiles and assuming no transportation costs, the price of textiles is equal in the United States and abroad. Thus, the price of textiles with trade is lower in the United States and higher in the rest of the world than in the absence of trade. With transportation costs, the price of textiles in the United States would exceed the price of textiles in the rest of the world by the cost of transportation.

This analysis clearly shows that in today's interdependent world, the tendency for the domestic price of a commodity to rise is moderated by the inflow of imports of the commodity. This is certainly the case for automobiles in the United States (see Example 2–2).

EXAMPLE 2–2

The Large U.S. Automotive Trade Deficit Keeps U.S. Auto Prices Down

Table 2.4 shows that even though automobiles were by far the largest U.S. imports and exports, the United States had an automotive trade deficit of nearly $116 billion in 2000. This represented more than one quarter of the total U.S. trade deficit for that year. Without

TABLE 2.4	The Major Goods Exports and Imports of the United States in 2000 (billions of dollars)		
Imports	**Value**	**Exports**	**Value**
Automobiles	$195.9	Automobiles	$80.2
Petroleum	120.2	Semiconductors	60.1
Computers	89.8	Computers	55.5
Textiles	63.3	Chemicals	52.3
Household appliances	56.4	Aircraft	48.1
Semiconductors	48.4	Food and beverages	43.3
Electrical generating machinery	39.7	Electrical generating machinery	35.8
Chemicals	34.4	Telecommunication equipment	31.3
Food and beverages	32.8	Scientific and medical equipment	19.4
Telecommunications equipment	31.9	Household appliances	18.5

such automobile imports, automobile prices in the United States would have been more than $1,000 higher than they were. Table 2.4 also shows that the other major imports of the United States in 2000 were petroleum, computers, and textiles, while the other main exports were semiconductors, computers and chemicals. Since the price of all traded goods are affected (sometimes a lot) by imports and exports, it would not make much sense to study microeconomic theory, in general, and the process whereby equilibrium prices are determined, in particular, without considering imports and exports in our highly globalized and interdependent world.

Source: U.S. Department of Commerce, *Survey of Current Business* (Washington, D.C.: U.S. Government Printing Office, July 2001), pp. 60–63.

2.7 | INTERFERING WITH VERSUS WORKING THROUGH THE MARKET

In the analysis presented so far in this chapter, we have implicitly assumed that the market is allowed to operate without government or other interferences. In that case, demand and supply determine the equilibrium price and quantity for each commodity or service. If, on the other hand, the government interfered with the operation of the market by imposing effective price controls (say, in the form of rent control or an agricultural price-support program), the market would not be allowed to operate and a persistent shortage or surplus of the commodity or service would result. Contrast this situation with *working through or within the market* (as, for example, with the imposition of an excise tax or the federal antidrug program). Working through the market would result in a shift in demand or supply, but the equilibrium price and quantity of the commodity or service would still be determined by demand and supply, and no persistent shortage or surplus would arise.

Current, real-world examples can illustrate the differences. Example 2–3 shows the detrimental effect of rent control in New York City. Example 2–4 shows the waste that results from U.S. agricultural price-support programs and why many people want to do away with them. On the other hand, Example 2–5 examines the economic effects of working through the market with the imposition of an excise tax, while Example 2–6 shows how the federal antidrug program seeks to reduce drug use in the United States by reducing the demand and supply of illegal drugs.

By interfering with the working of markets, rent control, price ceilings on gasoline, and agricultural price-support programs create huge waste and inefficiencies in the economy. These arise because markets communicate crucial information to consumers about the relative availability of goods and services, and to suppliers about the relative value that consumers place on various goods and services. Without the free flow of information transmitted through market prices, persistent shortages and surpluses—and waste—arise. Working through the market (see Examples 2–5 and 2–6) leads to different (and better) results.

EXAMPLE 2–3

Rent Control Harms the Housing Market

"There is probably nothing that distorts a city worse than rent regulation. It accelerates the abandonment of marginal buildings, deters the improvement of good ones, and creates wondrous windfalls for the middle class—all the while harming those it was meant to help, the poor."[4] More than 90% of economists would agree (see Table 1.3). Rent control was adopted in New York City as an emergency measure during World War II, but it has been kept ever since. Although rent control is most stringent in New York City, today more than 200 cities (including Boston, Los Angeles, and San Francisco) have some form of rent control. More than 10% of rental housing in the United States is under rent control.

Rent controls are **price ceilings** or maximum rents set below equilibrium rents. Although designed to keep housing affordable, the effect has been just the opposite—a shortage of apartments. For example, Figure 2.10 might refer to the market for apartment rentals in New York City. Without rent control (and assuming, for simplicity, that all apartments are identical), the equilibrium rent is $1,000 and the equilibrium number of apartments rented is 1.6 million. At the controlled rent of $600 per month, 2 million apartments could be rented. Only 1.2 million apartments are available at that rent, so there is a shortage of 800,000 apartments. Indeed, apartment seekers would be willing to pay a rent of $1,400 per month rather than go without an apartment when only 1.2 million apartments are available.[5]

Rent control introduces many predictable distortions into the housing market. First, as we have seen, rent control results in a shortage of apartments for rent. This is evidenced by the great difficulty and time required to find a vacant, rent-controlled apartment to rent. Second, owners of rent-controlled apartments usually cut maintenance and

---

[4] "End Rent Control," *New York Times,* May 12, 1987, p. 30.

[5] A Price ceiling at or above the equilibrium price has no effect. For example, rent is $1,000 and the number of apartments rented is equal to 1.6 million in Figure 2.10 regardless of whether a rent ceiling of $1,000 or higher is imposed. Only if rent control or the maximum rent allowed by law is below the equilibrium rent of $1,000 does a shortage of apartments for rent result.

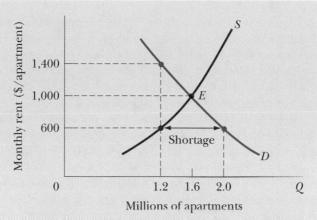

FIGURE 2.10   Rent Control   At the controlled rent of $600 per month, 2.0 million apartments could be rented. Only 1.2 million apartments are available at that rent, so there is a shortage of 800,000 million apartments. Apartment seekers would be willing to pay a rent of $1,400 per month when only 1.2 million apartments are available.

repairs to reduce costs, and so the quality of housing deteriorates. Because of the shortages to which rent control gives rise, apartments vacated as a result of inadequate maintenance can be filled easily and quickly. Third, rent control reduces the return on investment in rental housing, and so fewer rental apartments will be constructed.[6] Fourth, rent control encourages conversion into cooperatives (since their *price* is not controlled), which further reduces the supply of rent-controlled apartments.[7] Finally, with rent control, there must be a substitute for market price allocation; that is, nonprice rationing is likely to take place as landlords favor families with few or no children or pets and families with higher incomes.

In summary, we can predict that rent control leads to (1) a shortage of rental housing, (2) lower maintenance, (3) inadequate allocation of resources to the construction of new rental housing, (4) reduction in the stock of rental housing through conversion into cooperatives and condominiums, and (5) nonprice rationing of apartments for rent. One study revealed that the vacancy rate of rent-controlled apartments in New York City was less than 1%, expenditures on repairs were only about half as much as on non-controlled apartments, and the shortage of new rental housing construction amounted to over $3 billion. One way to eliminate the housing shortage and other distortions introduced by rent control, and at the same time protect tenants in residence from sudden sharp rent increases, is to decontrol apartments only as they become vacant. Indeed, New York City passed a law in 1997 that permitted landlords to increase the rent by as much as 20% when a rent-controlled apartment became vacant and eliminated all regulations when, upon vacancy, the rent rose beyond $2,000.

---

[6] To overcome this, rent control laws usually exempt new apartments.
[7] Many localities have passed laws restricting this practice.

Similar distortions result from the imposition of price ceilings on other commodities and services. For example, it was estimated that the price ceiling on gasoline in the United States in the summer of 1979 (at the height of the petroleum crisis) resulted in $200 million in lost time and 100 million gallons of gas wasted per month from waiting in long lines to obtain gasoline. Black markets also sprung up as some consumers were willing to pay a higher price for gasoline rather than stand in lines, and some suppliers were willing to accommodate them at higher prices. When price control was abolished, gasoline prices rose to the equilibrium level and long lines at the pumps and other market distortions soon disappeared. Similarly, the cap placed on doctor reimbursements by third parties (see Example 1–1) led to a shortage of doctor services, which is reflected in delays that patients experience when trying to see a doctor. Another example is given by the wait that users experience before the requested information appears on their computer screens when "surfing the Net." This results from the government's resistance to levying charges based on Internet usage.

Sources: "End Rent Control," *New York Times,* May 12, 1987, p. 30; "A Model for Destroying a City," *Wall Street Journal,* March 12, 1993, p. A8; "Rent Deregulation Has Risen Sharply Under 1997 Law," *New York Times,* August 8, 1997, p. B1.

EXAMPLE 2–4

The Economics of U.S. Farm Support Programs

For more than 70 years, American agriculture has been the nation's largest recipient of political intervention and economic aid. Demand and supply analysis can again enlighten us on how the U.S. farm-support program worked and on the gross inefficiencies to which it led.

The federal government has used the following three basic methods to prop up farm incomes: (1) From the 1930s until 1973, the federal government operated a price-support program (i.e., it established a **price floor** or a minimum price above the equilibrium price) for several agricultural commodities to increase farm incomes. This resulted in a surplus of agricultural commodities, which was then purchased by the government. The government used part of the surplus to assist low-income people, to subsidize school lunch programs, and for foreign aid. But a great deal of the surplus had to be stored and some spoiled. (2) From the early 1930s, the government also provided incentives for farmers to keep part of their land idle to avoid ever-increasing surpluses. (3) Starting in 1973, the government also gave farmers a direct subsidy if the market price of certain commodities fell below a target price.

We can analyze the effect of these three farm-support programs with the aid of Figure 2.11 which refers to the wheat market. In the absence of any support program, wheat farmers produce the equilibrium quantity of 2 billion bushels per year, sell it at the equilibrium price of $3 per bushel, and realize a total income of $6 billion. If the government establishes a price floor of $4 per bushel for wheat, farmers supply 2.2 billion bushels

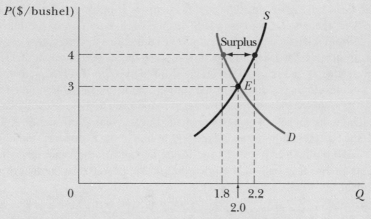

Billions of bushels of wheat per year

FIGURE 2.11   Agricultural Support Programs   At the price floor of $4 per bushel, farmers supply 2.2 billion bushels, consumers purchase 1.8 billion bushels, and the government purchases the surplus of 0.4 billion bushels at a total cost of $1.6 billion.

per year, consumers purchase only 1.8 billion bushels, and the government must purchase the surplus of 0.4 billion bushels at the support price of $4 per bushel, for a total cost of $1.6 billion. This does not include the cost of storing the surplus. The price floor has no effect if the market price rises above it.

If, through acreage restriction, output falls from 2.2 to 2.1 billion bushels at the supported price of $4 per bushel, the surplus declines to 0.3 billion bushels, and the cost of the price-support program falls to $1.2 billion. With direct subsidies, farmers sell the equilibrium quantity of 2 billion bushels at the equilibrium price of $3 per bushel, and the government then provides farmers a direct subsidy of $1 per bushel at a total cost of $2 billion (if the government sets the target price for wheat at $4 per bushel). With a direct subsidy, however, there is no storage problem, and consumers obtain wheat at the lower market price of $3 per bushel.

The Fair Act of 1996 (more often called the "Freedom to Farm Act") freed U.S. farmers from government production controls but was supposed to gradually phase out farm subsidies. When commodity prices plummeted in 1998, however, U.S. farmers lobbied Congress and received nearly $3 billion in emergency assistance payments on top of the huge payments they were still receiving under the other farm programs (that were supposed to be phased out). Emergency assistance payments increased to $7.5 billion in 1999, $9 billion in 2000, and $20 billion in 2001. Furthermore, most of the assistance went to very large growers rather than to small family farms. Thus, instead of liberalizing agriculture, as agreed at the World Trade Organization (the Geneva-based international institution that regulates international trade), the U.S. farming sector was as protected in 2001 as it was in 1996.

The farm bill signed into law by President Bush in May 2002 that will run from 2003 to 2008 increased subsidies to U.S. farmers even more. This represented a reversal of course from what the President had proposed in 2001 (i.e., to shift U.S. farm policy away from subsidies and toward freer markets and more open international trade in agricultural products) and is likely to create even more trade friction with the European Union and developing countries in the future. The European Union and Japan are, of course, just as guilty. Indeed, they provide even more aid to their farmers than the United States. The total amount of farm aid provided in the year 2000 was $49 billion in the United States, $60 billion in Japan, and $90 billion in the European Union. This comes to over $350 dollars per person living in the United States, Japan, and the European Union, and more than half of the price that farmers receive for some crops represent government subsidies.

Sources: "Farmers Harvest a Bumper Crop of Subsidies," *Wall Street Journal,* August 10, 1999, p. A24; "Far From Being Dead, Federal Subsidies Are Fueling Many Big Farms," *New York Times,* May 14, 2001; "Treaties May Curb Farmers' Subsidies," *New York Times,* August 31, 2001, p. 1; OECD, *Agricultural Policies in OECD Countries* (Paris: OECD, 2001); "Administration Seeks to Shift Farm Policy from Subsidies," *New York Times,* September 20, 2001, p. 12; "Reversing Course, Bush Signs Bill Raising Farm Subsidies," *New York Times,* May 14, 2002, p. 16; "U.S. Farm Bill Poses Threat to Trade Talks, Says Australia," *Financial Times,* May 14, 2002, p. 4.

EXAMPLE 2-5

Working through the Market with an Excise Tax

An **excise tax** is a tax on each unit of a commodity.[8] If collected from sellers, the tax causes the supply curve to shift upward by the amount of the tax, because sellers require that much more per unit to supply each amount of the commodity. The result is that consumers purchase a smaller quantity at a higher price, while sellers receive a smaller *net* price after payment of the tax. Thus, consumers and producers share the burden or **incidence of a tax.**

We can analyze the effect of an excise tax collected from sellers through the use of Figure 2.12. In the figure, D and S are the demand and supply curves of hamburgers with the equilibrium defined at point E (at which $P = \$1.00$ and $Q = 6$ million hamburgers, as in Figure 2.5). If a tax of $0.75 per hamburger is collected from sellers, S shifts up by the amount of the tax to S'', since sellers now require a price $0.75 higher than before to realize the same net after-tax price. Now D and S'' define equilibrium point C with $Q = 4$ million hamburgers and $P = \$1.50$, or $0.50 higher than before the imposition of the tax. Thus, at the new equilibrium point, consumers purchase a smaller quantity and pay a higher price. Sellers also receive the smaller net price of $0.75 (the price of $1.50 paid by consumers minus the $0.75 collected by the government on each hamburger sold).

---

[8] An excise tax can be of a given dollar amount *per unit* of the commodity or of a given percentage of the price of the commodity (ad valorem). If all units of the commodity are of equal quality and price (as we assume here), the per-unit and the ad valorem excise tax are equal and the distinction is unnecessary.

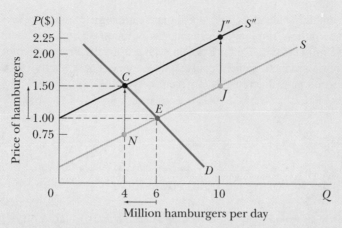

FIGURE 2.12   Effect of an Excise Tax With *D* and *S*, *P* = $1.00 and *Q* = 6 million hamburgers (point *E*), as in Figure 2.5. If the tax of $0.75 per hamburger is collected from sellers, *S* shifts up by $0.75 to *S*". With *D* and *S*", *Q* = 4 million hamburgers and *P* = $1.50 for consumers (point *C*), but sellers receive a net price of only $0.75 after paying the $0.75 tax per unit.

In the case shown in Figure 2.12, two-thirds of the burden of the tax falls on consumers and one-third on sellers. That is, consumers pay $0.50 more and sellers receive a net price that is $0.25 less than before the imposition of the excise tax. Thus, even though the tax is collected from sellers, the forces of demand and supply are such that sellers are able to pass on or shift part of the burden of the tax to consumers in the form of a higher price for hamburgers. Given the supply of a commodity, the less sensitive the quantity demanded is to price (i.e., the steeper the demand curve), the greater is the share of the tax paid by consumers in the form of higher prices. On the other hand, given the demand for a commodity, the less sensitive the quantity supplied is to price (i.e., the steeper the supply curve), the smaller is the share of the tax paid by consumers and the larger is the share left to be paid by sellers (see Problem 12 at the end of the chapter).

If the government collected the tax of $0.75 per hamburger from buyers or consumers rather than from sellers, *D* would shift down by $0.75 to *D*" (pencil *D*" in Figure 2.12 through point *N*, parallel to *D*). With *D*" and *S*, *Q* = 4 million hamburgers, *P* = $0.75 (that buyers pay to sellers) and then buyers have to pay the tax of $0.75 per hamburger to the government. Again, consumers pay $1.50, which is $0.50 more than the previous equilibrium price, and sellers receive $0.25 less. Therefore, the net result is the same whether the tax is collected from sellers or from buyers.

Sometimes governments use excise taxes not only to raise money but also to discourage the use of a product, such as cigarettes, which is harmful to health. An excise tax on cigarettes increases their price and discourages their use. An alternative would be

for the government to conduct an educational campaign explaining, especially to teenagers, the harm from smoking. In general, governments do both. Another type of excise tax is the **import tariff.** This is a tax on each unit of the imported commodity. As such, it has both a production and a consumption effects; these, as well as the welfare effects of a per-unit tax and an import tariff, are analyzed in Section 9.8.

EXAMPLE 2-6

Fighting the Drug War by Reducing Demand and Supply

The battle against illegal drug use in the United States is being fought by trying to reduce their demand and supply. The federal government is trying to shift the demand curve for illegal drugs down and to the left through an educational campaign to explain the destructive effect of illegal drugs. By itself, this campaign would reduce sales and the price for illegal drugs (compare equilibrium point E in Figure 2.13) before the government

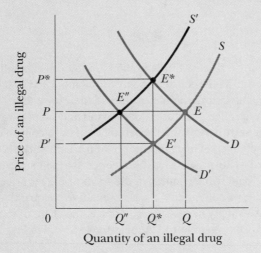

Figure 2.13   Reducing the Demand and Supply for Illegal Drugs D and S refer to the demand and supply curves for illegal drugs before the government campaign to reduce demand and supply. With D and S, the equilibrium price of drugs is P and the equilibrium quantity is Q. With a reduction in demand from D to D', the equilibrium price of drugs falls to P' and the sales to Q^*. With a reduction (leftward shift) in supply from S to S', the price rises to P^* and sales fall to Q^*. With D' and S', the price is P and sales Q''.

campaign with equilibrium point E' after a successful government campaign to reduce demand. The government is also trying to reduce the supply of illegal drugs by providing payments (subsidies) to Bolivian, Colombian, and Peruvian farmers (who raise most of the coca crop from which a majority of the cocaine entering the United States is extracted) to shift to other crops and by increasing border surveillance and interdiction (seizures) of illegal drugs entering the United States. By itself, this would shift the supply curve for illegal drugs upward and to the left and lead to reduced sales and higher drug prices (compare equilibrium point E with E^* in Figure 2.13).

Thus, both a reduced demand and a reduced supply would lower sales of illegal drugs, but the former would also reduce the price of illegal drugs while the latter would increase drug prices. If both the demand and the supply of drugs were reduced, drug sales would fall, but drug prices would remain unchanged (compare equilibrium point E'' to E), increase, or decrease, respectively, depending on whether the downward shift in the demand curve is equal, smaller, or greater than the upward or leftward shift in the supply curve.

Therefore, we cannot determine by looking only at drug prices whether the government campaign is successful. Specifically, if the reduction in drug prices is due to a reduction in demand, the campaign can be said to be successful because it is accompanied by reduced sales. But the reduction in drug prices could also result from an increased drug supply. In that case, the campaign against illegal drugs would not be successful. It all depends on whether the price reduction is accompanied by a reduction or an increase in drug sales. On the other hand, if at the same time that the demand for illegal drugs declines their supply increases, drug prices will definitely fall, but sales can remain the same, decrease, or increase depending, respectively, on whether the leftward shift in the demand curve is equal, greater, or smaller than the rightward shift in the supply curve (you can clearly see this by penciling in these changes in Figure 2.13). Despite some recent dramatic successes in apprehending and jailing some powerful Colombian drug lords, the flow of cocaine to American cities seems to be increasing and prices falling. It seems that the drug war is being lost!

AT THE FRONTIER
Nonclearing Markets Theory

In this chapter we have seen how an excess demand for a commodity is automatically eliminated by a price rise and an excess supply is eliminated by a price decline. Markets clear by quantity responses to price changes resulting from a disequilibrium. Some real-world markets, however, do not clear and do not seem to move toward clearing. For example, financial markets (especially credit markets) often do not clear. That is, we often observe excessive demand or excessive supply of credit that persists over time. Sometimes nonclearing markets also arise in labor, commodity, and other markets. To explain these situations, economists have developed **nonclearing markets theory.**

Continued. . .

The new theory of nonclearing markets postulates that sometimes markets do not clear, because economic agents react to both price signals (as in traditional theory) and to quantity signals. In particular, economic agents sometimes deliberately create a disequilibrium situation because of the advantages that they can extract from the persistence of a surplus or a shortage of the commodity or service that they sell or buy. One of the main insights of nonclearing markets theory is that a disequilibrium in one market can actually create desirable *spillover effects* in a related market.

For example, ticket prices for concerts by a superstar, such as Billy Joel or Madonna, are often deliberately set below the equilibrium price so as to create a shortage (i.e., excess demand) for tickets. Long lines form in front of ticket booths long before tickets go on sale and all available tickets are quickly sold out as soon as they do go on sale. The news media report on the long lines to get tickets and interview some of the people camped outside ticket booths days before the tickets go on sale, fans talk about the hot concert coming up, and an aura of anticipation and success is created. Promoters play this price game in the expectation that all the "hype" about the concert and the free publicity that it gets will lead to much greater sales of the star's recordings, and that these spillovers will more than make up for the loss of revenue by pricing concert tickets below the equilibrium level. The same occurs in pricing admission tickets to Disneyland or meals at a chic restaurant. Lines in front of the new restaurant and word of mouth are the best and cheapest forms of advertising that the restaurant could have. Most people believe that if it is difficult to get into the restaurant, it must be great.

These and other examples of nonclearing markets do not mean that the traditional theory of clearing markets examined in this chapter is wrong, but only that the traditional theory is not applicable in some cases where shortages or surpluses are deliberately created and tend to persist over time. The theory of nonclearing markets acknowledges this fact and tries to explain it. In the ticket example above, it is clear that excess demand for tickets is fully and voluntarily planned by the price-maker or promoter as a way to increase overall or combined revenues from the concert and the sales of the star's recordings.

Sources: "Nonclearing Markets: Microeconomic Concepts and Macroeconomic Applications," *Journal of Economic Literature,* June 1993, pp. 732–761 and "So Long, Supply and Demand," *Wall Street Journal,* January 1, 2000, p. R31.

SUMMARY

1. Most of microeconomic analysis is devoted to the study of how individual markets operate. A market is in equilibrium when no buyer or seller has any incentive to change the quantity of the good, service, or resource that he or she buys or sells at the given price. Markets provide the framework for the analysis of the forces of demand and supply that determine commodity and resource prices. A market can, but need not, be a specific place or location. A perfectly competitive market is a market in which no buyer or seller can affect the price of the product,

all units of the products are homogeneous, resources are mobile, and knowledge of the market is perfect.

2. A market demand schedule is a table showing the quantity demanded of a commodity at each price over a given time period while holding constant all other relevant economic variables on which demand depends. The market demand curve is the graphic representation of the demand schedule. It is negatively sloped, which reflects the inverse price-quantity relationship or the law of demand. A change in consumers' incomes, tastes for the commodity, the number of consumers in the market, or the price of substitutes or complements shifts the demand curve.

3. A market supply schedule is a table showing the quantity supplied of a commodity at each price over a given time period. The market supply curve is the graphic representation of the supply schedule. Because of rising marginal costs, the supply curve is usually positively sloped, which indicates that producers supply more of the commodity at higher prices. A change in technology, resource prices, and, for agricultural commodities, weather conditions, shifts the supply curve.

4. The equilibrium price and quantity of a commodity are defined at the intersection of the market demand and supply curves of the commodity. At higher than equilibrium prices, there is a surplus of the commodity, which leads sellers to lower their prices to the equilibrium level. At lower than equilibrium prices, there is a shortage of the commodity, which leads consumers to bid prices up to the equilibrium level. Equilibrium is the condition that, once achieved, tends to persist.

5. An increase in demand (a rightward shift in the demand curve) results in an increase in both the equilibrium price and quantity of the commodity. A decrease in demand has the opposite effect. On the other hand, an increase in supply (a rightward shift in the supply curve) results in a lower equilibrium price but a higher equilibrium quantity. A decrease in supply has the opposite effect.

6. A nation's demand for imports is derived from the nation's excess demand for the importable commodity at below-equilibrium prices in the absence of trade. On the other hand, the foreign supply of exports of the commodity is derived from the foreign excess supply of the commodity at above-equilibrium prices in the absence of trade. The equilibrium price and quantity of the traded commodity are given at the intersection of the demand and supply curves of imports of the commodity. In today's interdependent world, the tendency for the domestic price of a commodity to rise is moderated by the inflow of imports of the commodity.

7. A price ceiling below the equilibrium price (such as rent control) leads to a shortage of the commodity and possibly black markets. A price floor above the equilibrium price (as for some agricultural commodities) leads to a surplus of the commodity. Given the supply of a commodity, the steeper the demand for the commodity, the greater the burden or incidence of a per-unit tax on consumers. The federal antidrug program relies on reducing the demand and supply of illegal drugs. Some real-world markets do not clear, and this fact gave rise to a new nonclearing market theory.

KEY TERMS

Market	Equilibrium price	Price ceiling
Perfectly competitive market	Surplus	Price floor
Market demand schedule	Shortage	Excise tax
Law of demand	Equilibrium	Incidence of a tax
Market demand curve	Comparative static analysis	Import tariff
Market supply schedule	Excess demand	Nonclearing markets theory
Market supply curve	Excess supply	

REVIEW QUESTIONS

1. Which of the following cause demand to increase? An increase in consumers' income, an increase in the price of substitutes, an increase in the price of complements, an increase in the number of consumers in the market.

2. Will the supply curve shift to the right or to the left if (a) technology improves or (b) input prices increase? (c) What happens if both (a) and (b) occur?

3. Explain why $Q = 4$ is not the equilibrium quantity in Figure 2.5 and how equilibrium is reached.

4. Explain why $Q = 8$ is not the equilibrium quantity in Figure 2.5 and how equilibrium is reached.

5. Using comparative static analysis, explain how a wheat shortage was avoided in the United States after the drought in Kansas in 1988 and 1989 (described in Example 1–2).

6. Was the increase in the demand for large automobiles in the United States since the collapse of petroleum prices in 1986 rational? Do you foresee any difficulty for the United States if this trend continues?

7. Why is the textile price of $1.50 in Figure 2.9 not the equilibrium price?

8. What would be the difference in textile prices between the United States and the rest of the world if textiles were freely traded but the cost of transporting each yard of textiles between the United States and the rest of the world was $1? What would be the quantity of textiles traded?

9. a. When is the price ceiling or price floor ineffective?

   b. What is an example of an effective price ceiling? What is its effect?

   c. What is an example of an effective price floor? What is its effect?

10. Does it make any difference whether an excise tax is collected from sellers or from buyers? Why?

11. Determine the minimum size of a prohibitive tariff in Figure 2.9 in the absence of transportation costs.

12. How does nonclearing markets theory explain why markets sometimes do not clear?

PROBLEMS

1. Given the following demand schedule of a commodity

P($)	6	5	4	3	2	1	0
QD	0	10	20	30	40	50	60

show that by substituting the prices given in the table into the following demand equation or function, you obtain the corresponding quantities demanded given in the table:

$$QD = 60 - 10P$$

*2. a. Derive the demand schedule from the following demand function:

$$QD' = 80 - 10P$$

   b. On the same graph, plot the demand schedule of Problem 1 and label it D and

the demand curve of part (a) of this problem and label it D'.

   c. Does D' represent an increase in demand or an increase in the quantity demanded? Why?

3. a. Derive the supply schedule from the following supply function:

$$QS = 10P$$

   b. Derive the supply schedule from the following supply function:

$$QS' = 20 + 10P$$

   c. On the same graph, plot the supply schedule of part (a) and label it S and the supply curve of part (b) and label it S'.

   d. What may have caused S to shift to S'?

*4. a. Construct a table similar to Table 2.3 giving the supply schedule of Problem 3(a), and the

---

* = Answer provided at end of book.

demand schedule of Problem 1. In the same table identify the equilibrium price and quantity of the commodity, the surplus or shortage at prices other than the equilibrium price, and the pressure on price with a surplus or a shortage.

b. Show your results of part (a) graphically.

5. Using the demand function of Problem 1 and the supply function of Problem 3(a), determine the equilibrium price and quantity algebraically.

6. a. Repeat the procedure in Problem 4(a) for the supply schedule of Problem 3(b) and the demand schedule of Problem 2(a).

b. Show your results of part (a) graphically.

c. On the same graph, draw D and S from Problem 4(b) and D' and S' from Problem 6(b). What general conclusion can you reach as to the effect of an increase in the demand and supply of a commodity on the equilibrium price and quantity of the commodity?

7. On separate sets of axes, show that

a. a decrease in demand reduces the equilibrium price and quantity of the commodity.

b. a decrease in supply increases price but reduces quantity.

c. a decrease in both demand and supply will reduce quantity but may increase, reduce, or leave price unchanged.

8. On separate sets of axes, show that

a. an increase in both demand and supply will increase quantity and may increase, reduce, or leave price unchanged.

b. a decrease in demand and an increase in supply will reduce price but may increase, decrease, or leave quantity unchanged.

c. an increase in demand and a decrease in supply will increase price but may increase, decrease, or leave quantity unchanged.

*9. Indicate what happens in the market for hamburgers if

a. the price of hot dogs increases.

b. a disease develops that kills a large proportion of cattle.

c. a new breed of cattle is developed with much faster growth.

d. medical research proves that this new breed results in hamburgers with less cholesterol.

e. a direct subsidy on each head of cattle is given to farmers raising cattle.

10. Using Panels A and C of Figure 2.9, show the price of textiles in the United States and in the rest of the world. Also show the quantity of textiles traded if the cost of transportation for each yard of cloth is $1 and if this cost falls equally on the United States and the rest of the world.

11. With reference to your answer to Problem 4(a), indicate the effect of the government imposing on the commodity a

a. price ceiling of $P = \$2$.

b. price ceiling of $P = \$3$.

c. price ceiling higher than $P = \$3$.

d. price floor of $P = \$5$.

e. price floor of $P = \$4$.

f. price floor equal to or smaller than $P = \$3$.

*12. Draw a figure showing that

a. given the supply of a commodity, the less sensitive the quantity demanded is to price (i.e., the steeper the demand curve), the greater is the share of the tax paid by consumers in the form of higher prices.

b. given the demand for a commodity, the less sensitive the quantity supplied is to price (i.e., the steeper the supply curve), the smaller is the share of the tax paid by consumers and the larger is the share paid by sellers.

APPENDIX   THE ALGEBRA OF DEMAND, SUPPLY, AND EQUILIBRIUM

In this appendix, we show the algebraic analysis corresponding to the graphical analysis of equilibrium, surplus and shortages, shifts in the demand and supply functions, and the effect of an excise tax shown in this chapter.

Market Equilibrium Algebraically

To show the algebraic determination of equilibrium, we begin by expressing the market demand curve of Figure 2.1 and the supply curve of Figure 2.3 algebraically, as follows:

$$QD = 10 - 4P \qquad\qquad [1]$$

$$QS = -2 + 8P \qquad\qquad [2]$$

From equation [1], we see that if $P = \$2$, $QD = 2$; if $P = \$1$, $QD = 6$, and if $P = \$0.50$, $QD = 8$, as shown by demand curve D in Figure 2.1. Similarly, from equation [2], we see that if $P = \$0.50$, $QS = 2$; if $P = \$1$, $QS = 6$, and if $P = \$2$, $QS = 14$, as shown by supply curve S in Figure 2.3.

To find the equilibrium price ($\overline{P}$) we set

$$QD = QS \qquad\qquad [3]$$

and get

$$10 - 4P = -2 + 8P$$

$$12 = 12P$$

Thus,

$$\overline{P} = \$1 \qquad\qquad [4]$$

Substituting the equilibrium price of $\overline{P} = \$1$ either into demand equation [1] or supply equation [2], we get the equilibrium quantity ($\overline{Q}$) of

$$QD = 10 - 4(\$1) = 6 = \overline{Q} \qquad\qquad [1A]$$

or

$$QS = -2 + 8(\$1) = 6 = \overline{Q} \qquad\qquad [2A]$$

as shown by point E in Figure 2.5.

At the nonequilibrium price of $P = \$1.50$,

$$QD = 10 - 4(\$1.50) = 4$$

while

$$QS = -2 + 8(\$1.50) = 10$$

Thus, we would have a surplus of 6 units, as shown in Figure 2.5.

On the other hand, at $P = \$0.50$,

$$QD = 10 - 4(\$0.50) = 8$$

while

$$QS = -2 + 8(\$0.50) = 2$$

Thus, we would have a shortage of 6 units, as shown in Figure 2.5.

Shifts in Demand and Supply, and Equilibrium

The shift in the demand curve from D to D' in Figure 2.2 can be represented algebraically by

$$QD' = 16 - 4P \qquad [5]$$

The new equilibrium price is determined by setting QD' equal to QS. That is,

$$16 - 4P = -2 + 8P \qquad [6]$$
$$18 = 12P$$

Thus,

$$\overline{P} = \$1.50 \qquad [7]$$

and

$$QD' = 16 - 4(\$1.50) = 10 = \overline{Q} \qquad [5A]$$

or

$$QS = -2 + 8(\$1.50) = 10 = \overline{Q} \qquad [2B]$$

as shown by equilibrium point J in Figure 2.6.

On the other hand, the shift in the supply curve from S to S' in Figure 2.4 can be represented algebraically by

$$QS' = 4 + 8P \qquad [8]$$

The new equilibrium price is determined by setting QD equal to QS'. That is,

$$10 - 4P = 4 + 8P \qquad [9]$$
$$10 - 4P = 4 + 8P$$
$$6 = 12P$$

Thus,

$$\overline{P} = \$0.50 \qquad [10]$$

and

$$QD = 10 - 4(\$0.50) = 8 = \overline{Q} \qquad [1B]$$

or

$$QS' = 4 + 8(\$0.50) = 8 = \overline{Q} \qquad [8A]$$

as shown by equilibrium point G in Figure 2.6.

The Effect of an Excise Tax

The effect of the excise tax shown by the shift of S to S' in Figure 2.12 can be represented algebraically by

$$QS'' = -8 + 8P \qquad [11]$$

Setting QD equal to QS'', we get the equilibrium price of

$$10 - 4P = -8 + 8P \qquad [12]$$
$$18 = 12P$$

Thus,

$$\overline{P} = \$1.50 \qquad [13]$$

and

$$QD = 10 - 4(\$1.50) = 4 = \overline{Q} \qquad [1C]$$

or

$$QS'' = -8 + 8(\$1.50) = 4 = \overline{Q} \qquad [11A]$$

as shown by equilibrium point C in Figure 2.12.

At $Q = 4$, sellers get a net price of

$$QS = -2 + 8P$$
$$4 = -2 + 8P \qquad [2C]$$
$$6 = 8P$$
$$P = \$0.75 \qquad [12]$$

as shown by point N in Figure 2.12.

For a more general and advanced algebraic analysis of demand, supply, and equilibrium, see section A.11 of the Mathematical Appendix at the end of the book.

INTERNET SITE ADDRESSES

An excellent presentation of demand, supply and equilibrium is:

http://price.bus.okstate.edu/archive/Econ3113_963/Shows/Chapter2/chap_02.htm

Market conditions and prices for coffee are found in:

http://www.ico.org/markinf.htm

http://www.oxfam.org.uk/whatnew/press.coffee.htm

For agricultural policies in OECD countries, see:

http://www.oecd.org/publications/e-book/51011.pdf

Information on tax rates in the various States of the United States is found in:

http://www.taxadmin.org/fta/rate/sales.html

http://www.taxadmin.org/fta/rate/tax_stru.html

Data on the International transactions of the United States are found in the Bureau of Economic Analysis web site:

http://bea.doc.gov and clicking "international data."

General directories and indexes of economic information are:

YAHOO—Economics:
http://www.yahoo.com/Social_Science/Economics/

PART TWO

Theory of Consumer Behavior and Demand

P art Two (Chapters 3–6) presents the theory of consumer behavior and demand. Chapter 3 examines the tastes of the consumer and how the consumer maximizes utility or satisfaction in spending his or her income. These concepts are used and extended in Chapter 4 to derive the consumer's demand curve for a commodity. Chapter 5 shows how, by aggregating or summing up individual consumers' demand curves, we get the market demand curve for the commodity. Chapter 5 also examines in detail the measurement and usefulness of various demand elasticities. Chapter 6 discusses consumer choices in the face of uncertainty. Each chapter in Part Two includes an "At the Frontier" section with some new theories or applications of consumer behavior and demand, and Chapters 4 and 5 also have an optional appendix presenting some more advanced topics in consumer demand theory.

CHAPTER 3

Consumer Preferences and Choice

I n this chapter, we begin the formal study of microeconomics by examining the economic behavior of the consumer. A consumer is an individual or a household composed of one or more individuals. The consumer is the basic economic unit that determines which commodities are purchased and in what quantities. Millions of such decisions are made each day on the more than $10 trillion worth of goods and services produced by the American economy each year.

What guides these individual consumer decisions? Why do consumers purchase some commodities and not others? How do they decide how much to purchase of each commodity? What is the aim of a rational consumer in spending income? These are some of the important questions to which we seek answers in this chapter. The theory of consumer behavior and choice is the first step in the derivation of the market demand curve, the importance of which was clearly demonstrated in Chapter 2.

We begin the study of the economic behavior of the consumer by examining tastes. Consumers' tastes can be related to utility concepts or indifference curves. These are discussed in the first two sections of the chapter. In Section 3.3, we examine the convergence of tastes internationally. We then introduce the budget line, which gives the constraints or limitations consumer's face in purchasing goods and services. Constraints arise because the commodities that the consumer wants command a price in the marketplace (i.e., they are not free) and the consumer has limited income. Thus, the budget line reflects the familiar and pervasive economic fact of scarcity as it pertains to the individual consumer.

Because the consumer's wants are unlimited or, in any event, exceed his or her ability to satisfy them all, it is important that the consumer spend income so as to maximize satisfaction. Thus, a model is provided to illustrate and predict how a rational consumer maximizes satisfaction, given his or her tastes (indifference curves) and the constraints that the consumer faces (the budget line). The "At the Frontier" section presents a different way to examine consumer tastes and derive a consumer's indifference curves.

The several real-world examples and important applications presented in the chapter demonstrate the relevance and usefulness of the theory of consumer behavior and choice.

TABLE 3.1 Total and Marginal Utility		
Q_X	TU_X	MU_X
0	0	. . .
1	10	10
2	16	6
3	20	4
4	22	2
5	22	0
6	20	−2

3.1   UTILITY ANALYSIS

In this section, we discuss the meaning of utility, distinguish between total utility and marginal utility, and examine the important difference between cardinal and ordinal utility. The concept of utility is used here to introduce the consumer's tastes. The analysis of consumer tastes is a crucial step in determining how a consumer maximizes satisfaction in spending income.

Total and Marginal Utility

Goods are desired because of their ability to satisfy human wants. The property of a good that enables it to satisfy human wants is called **utility.** As individuals consume more of a good per time period, their **total utility** (*TU*) or satisfaction increases, but their marginal utility diminishes. **Marginal utility** (*MU*) is the extra utility received from consuming one additional unit of the good per unit of time while holding constant the quantity consumed of all other commodities.

For example, Table 3.1 indicates that one hamburger per day (or, more generally, one unit of good *X* per period of time) gives the consumer a total utility (*TU*) of 10 utils, where a **util** is an arbitrary unit of utility. Total utility increases with each additional hamburger consumed until the fifth one, which leaves total utility unchanged. This is the *saturation point.* Consuming the sixth hamburger then leads to a decline in total utility because of storage or disposal problems.[1] The third column of Table 3.1 gives the extra or marginal utility resulting from the consumption of each *additional* hamburger. Marginal utility is positive but declines until the fifth hamburger, for which it is zero, and becomes negative for the sixth hamburger.

Plotting the values given in Table 3.1, we obtain Figure 3.1, with the top panel showing total utility and the bottom panel showing marginal utility. The total and marginal utility curves are obtained by joining the midpoints of the bars measuring *TU* and *MU* at each level of consumption. Note that the *TU* rises by smaller and smaller amounts (the shaded areas)

---

[1] That is, some effort (disutility), no matter how small, is required to get rid of the sixth hamburger. Assuming that the individual cannot sell the sixth hamburger, he or she would not want it even for free.

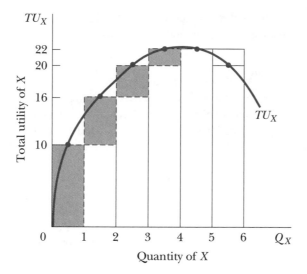

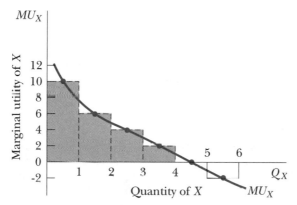

FIGURE 3.1   Total and Marginal Utility   In the top panel, total utility (*TU*) increases by smaller and smaller amounts (the shaded areas) and so the marginal utility (*MU*) in the bottom panel declines. *TU* remains unchanged with the consumption of the fifth hamburger, and so *MU* is zero. After the fifth hamburger per day, *TU* declines and *MU* is negative.

and so the *MU* declines. The consumer reaches saturation after consuming the fourth hamburger. Thus, *TU* remains unchanged with the consumption of the fifth hamburger and *MU* is zero. After the fifth hamburger, *TU* declines and so *MU* is negative. The negative slope or downward-to-the-right inclination of the *MU* curve reflects the **law of diminishing marginal utility.**

Utility schedules reflect tastes of a particular individual; that is, they are unique to the individual and reflect his or her own particular subjective preferences and perceptions.

Different individuals may have different tastes and different utility schedules. Utility schedules remain unchanged so long as the individual's tastes remain the same.

Cardinal or Ordinal Utility?

The concept of utility discussed in the previous section was introduced at about the same time, in the early 1870s, by William Stanley Jevons of Great Britain, Carl Menger of Austria, and Léon Walras of France. They believed that the utility an individual receives from consuming each quantity of a good or basket of goods could be measured cardinally just like weight, height, or temperature.[2]

Cardinal utility means that an individual can attach specific values or numbers of utils from consuming each quantity of a good or basket of goods. In Table 3.1 we saw that the individual received 10 utils from consuming one hamburger. He received 16 utils, or 6 additional utils, from consuming two hamburgers. The consumption of the third hamburger gave this individual 4 extra utils, or two-thirds as many extra utils, as the second hamburger. Thus, Table 3.1 and Figure 3.1 reflect cardinal utility. They actually provide an index of satisfaction for the individual.

In contrast, **ordinal utility** only *ranks* the utility received from consuming various amounts of a good or baskets of goods. Ordinal utility specifies that consuming two hamburgers gives the individual more utility than when consuming one hamburger, but it does not specify exactly how much additional utility the second hamburger provides. Similarly, ordinal utility would say only that three hamburgers give this individual more utility than two hamburgers, but *not* how many more utils.[3]

Ordinal utility is a much weaker notion than cardinal utility because it only requires that the consumer be able to rank baskets of goods in the order of his or her preference. That is, when presented with a choice between any two baskets of goods, ordinal utility requires only that the individual indicate if he or she prefers the first basket, the second basket, or is indifferent between the two. It does not require that the individual specify how many more utils he or she receives from the preferred basket. *In short, ordinal utility only ranks various consumption bundles, whereas cardinal utility provides an actual index or measure of satisfaction.*

The distinction between cardinal and ordinal utility is important because a theory of consumer behavior can be developed on the weaker assumption of ordinal utility without the need for a cardinal measure. And a theory that reaches the same conclusion as another on weaker assumptions is a superior theory.[4] Utility theory provides a convenient introduction to the analysis of consumer tastes and to the more rigorous indifference

---

[2] A market basket of goods can be defined as containing specific quantities of various goods and services. For example, one basket may contain one hamburger, one soft drink, and a ticket to a ball game, while another basket may contain two soft drinks and two movie tickets.

[3] To be sure, numerical values could be attached to the utility received by the individual from consuming various hamburgers, even with ordinal utility. However, with ordinal utility, higher utility values only indicate higher rankings of utility, and no importance can be attached to actual numerical differences in utility. For example, 20 utils can only be interpreted as giving more utility than 10 utils, but not twice as much. Thus, to indicate rising utility rankings, numbers such as 5, 10, 20; 8, 15, 17; or I (lowest), II, and III are equivalent.

[4] This is like producing a given output with fewer or cheaper inputs, or achieving the same medical result (such as control of high blood pressure) with less or weaker medication.

curve approach. It is also useful for the analysis of consumer choices in the face of uncertainty, which is presented in Chapter 6. Example 3–1 examines the relationship between money income and happiness.

EXAMPLE 3–1

Does Money Buy Happiness?

Does money buy happiness? Philosophers have long pondered this question. Economists have now gotten involved with their analysis in trying to answer this age-old question. Table 3.2 shows that there is a significant positive relationship between income and happiness in the United States. The table shows that the "mean happiness rating" (based on a score of "very happy" = 4, "pretty happy" = 2, and "not too happy" = 0) was generally higher for higher incomes. The mean happiness rating is only 1.8 for households with income of less than $10,000 but 2.8 for households with income in excess of $75,000. Yes, money does seem to buy happiness. The only exception seems to be the slight decline in the mean happiness rating for households in the $40,000–$49,999 income range as compared with households in the $30,000–$39,999 income range. Otherwise, higher incomes seem to bring greater happiness. The same general result was obtained in every country in which this type of survey was conducted.

In addition, the percentage of Americans interviewed who regarded themselves as "very happy" varied over time and for different groups of people. It was 34% in the early 1970s but only 30% in the late 1990s. It seems that as income rose, expectations rose even faster and reduced the level of happiness. The happiness of American men has grown during the past three decades, while that of women (despite the gains in the job market and the reduction in gender discrimination) declined sharply. Blacks were less happy than whites, but the black–white gap diminished over time. The results are similar in the United Kingdom. The results also indicate that it would take about $100,000 extra per year to reimburse the average American for the suffering associated with divorce or death

TABLE 3.2	Percent Distribution of Population by Happiness at Various Levels of Income, United States, 1994
Total Household Income	**Mean Happiness Rating**
All income groups	2.4
$75,000 and over	2.8
50,000–74,999	2.6
40,000–49,999	2.4
30,000–39,999	2.5
20,000–29,999	2.3
10,000–19,999	2.1
Less than 10,000	1.8

Source: Easterlin (2000, p. 468).

of the spouse (the biggest depressants on reported happiness) and $60,000 extra per year to reimburse him or her for the pain of unemployment (the second largest depressant).

Sources: R. A. Easterlin, "Income and Happiness," *Economic Journal,* July 2000; D. Blanchflower and A. Oswald, "Well-Being over Time in Britain and the USA," *NBER Working Paper 7487,* January 2000; "Does Money Buy Happiness," *Wall Street Journal,* January 4, 2002, p. A7; and B. S. Frey and A. Stutzer, "What Can Economists Learn from Happiness Research," *Journal of Economic Literature,* June 2002.

3.2   CONSUMER'S TASTES: INDIFFERENCE CURVES

In this section, we define indifference curves and examine their characteristics. Indifference curves were first introduced by the English economist F. Y. Edgeworth in the 1880s. The concept was refined and used extensively by the Italian economist Vilfredo Pareto in the early 1900s. Indifference curves were popularized and greatly extended in application in the 1930s by two other English economists: R. G. D. Allen and John R. Hicks. Indifference curves are a crucial tool of analysis because they are used to represent an ordinal measure of the tastes and preferences of the consumer and to show how the consumer maximizes utility in spending income.

Indifference Curves—What Do They Show?[5]

Consumers' tastes can be examined with ordinal utility. An ordinal measure of utility is based on three assumptions. First, we assume that when faced with any two baskets of goods, the consumer can determine whether he or she prefers basket *A* to basket *B*, *B* to *A*, or whether he or she is indifferent between the two. Second, we assume that the tastes of the consumer are *consistent* or *transitive.* That is, if the consumer states that he or she prefers basket *A* to basket *B* and also that he or she prefers basket *B* to basket *C*, then that consumer will prefer *A* to *C*. Third, we assume that more of a commodity is preferred to less; that is, we assume that the commodity is a **good** rather than a **bad,** and the consumer is never satiated with the commodity.[6] The three assumptions can be used to represent an individual's tastes with indifference curves. In order to conduct the analysis by plane geometry, we will assume throughout that there are only two goods, *X* and *Y.*

An **indifference curve** shows the various combinations of two goods that give the consumer equal utility or satisfaction. A higher indifference curve refers to a higher level of satisfaction, and a lower indifference curve refers to less satisfaction. However, we have no indication as to how much additional satisfaction or utility a higher indifference curve indicates. That is, different indifference curves simply provide an ordering or ranking of the individual's preference.

For example, Table 3.3 gives an indifference schedule showing the various combinations of hamburgers (good *X*) and soft drinks (good *Y*) that give the consumer equal satisfaction. This information is plotted as indifference curve U_1 in the left panel of Figure 3.2.

---

[5] For a mathematical presentation of indifference curves and their characteristics using rudimentary calculus, see Section A.1 of the Mathematical Appendix at the end of the book.

[6] Examples of bads are pollution, garbage, and disease, of which less is preferred to more.

TABLE 3.3	Indifference Schedule	
Hamburgers (X)	Soft Drinks (Y)	Combinations
1	10	A
2	6	B
4	3	C
7	1	F

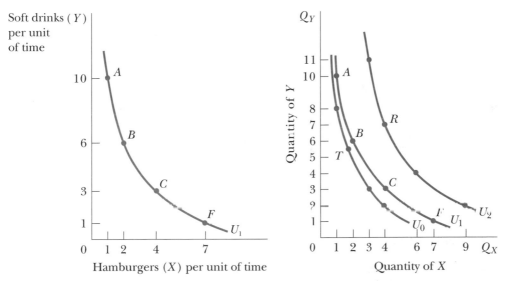

FIGURE 3.2   Indifference Curves   The individual is indifferent among combinations A, B, C, and F since they all lie on indifference curve U_1. U_1 refers to a higher level of satisfaction than U_0, but to a lower level than U_2.

The right panel repeats indifference curve U_1 along with a higher indifference curve (U_2) and a lower one (U_0).

Indifference curve U_1 shows that one hamburger and ten soft drinks per unit of time (combination A) give the consumer the same level of satisfaction as two hamburgers and six soft drinks (combination B), four hamburgers and three soft drinks (combination C), or seven hamburgers and one soft drink (combination F). On the other hand, combination R (four hamburgers and seven soft drinks) has both more hamburgers and more soft drinks than combination B (see the right panel of Figure 3.2), and so it refers to a higher level of satisfaction. Thus, combination R and all the other combinations that give the same level of satisfaction as combination R define higher indifference curve U_2. Finally, all combinations on U_0 give the same satisfaction as combination T, and combination T refers to both fewer hamburgers and fewer soft drinks than (and therefore is inferior to) combination B on U_1.

Although in Figure 3.2 we have drawn only three indifference curves, there is an indifference curve going through each point in the XY plane (i.e., referring to each possible combination of good X and good Y). That is, between any two indifference curves,

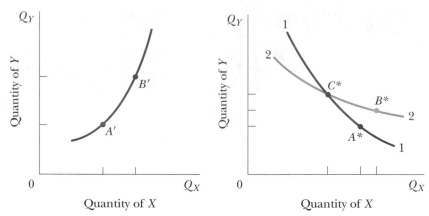

FIGURE 3.3   Indifference Curves Cannot Be Positively Sloped or Intersect
In the left panel, the positively sloped curve cannot be an indifference curve because it shows that combination B'', which contains more of X and Y than combination A', gives equal satisfaction to the consumer as A'. In the right panel, since C^* is on curves 1 and 2, it should give the same satisfaction as A^* and B^*, but this is impossible because B^* has more of X and Y than A^*. Thus, indifference curves cannot intersect.

an additional curve can always be drawn. The entire set of indifference curves is called an **indifference map** and reflects the entire set of tastes and preferences of the consumer.

Characteristics of Indifference Curves

Indifference curves are usually negatively sloped, cannot intersect, and are convex to the origin (see Figure 3.2). Indifference curves are negatively sloped because if one basket of goods X and Y contains more of X, it will have to contain less of Y than another basket in order for the two baskets to give the same level of satisfaction and be on the same indifference curve. For example, since basket B on indifference curve U_1 in Figure 3.2 contains more hamburgers (good X) than basket A, basket B must contain fewer soft drinks (good Y) for the consumer to be on indifference curve U_1.

A positively sloped curve would indicate that one basket containing more of both commodities gives the same utility or satisfaction to the consumer as another basket containing less of both commodities (and no other commodity). Because we are dealing with goods rather than bads, such a curve could not possibly be an indifference curve. For example, in the left panel of Figure 3.3, combination B' contains more of X and more of Y than combination A', and so the positively sloped curve on which B' and A' lie cannot be an indifference curve. That is, B' must be on a higher indifference curve than A' if X and Y are both goods.[7]

Indifference curves also cannot intersect. Intersecting curves are inconsistent with the definition of indifference curves. For example, if curve 1 and curve 2 in the right panel of Figure 3.3 were indifference curves, they would indicate that basket A^* is equivalent to basket C^* since both A^* and C^* are on curve 1, and also that basket B^* is equivalent to

---

[7] Only if either X or Y were a bad would the indifference curve be positively sloped as in the left panel of Figure 3.3.

basket C^* since both B^* and C^* are on curve 2. By transitivity, B^* should then be equivalent to A^*. However, this is impossible because basket B^* contains more of both good X and good Y than basket A^*. Thus, indifference curves cannot intersect.

Indifference curves are usually convex to the origin; that is, they lie above any tangent to the curve. Convexity results from or is a reflection of a decreasing marginal rate of substitution, which is discussed next.

The Marginal Rate of Substitution

The **marginal rate of substitution (MRS)** refers to the amount of one good that an individual is willing to give up for an additional unit of another good while maintaining the same level of satisfaction or remaining on the same indifference curve. For example, the marginal rate of substitution of good X for good Y (MRS_{XY}) refers to the amount of Y that the individual is willing to exchange per unit of X and maintain the same level of satisfaction. Note that MRS_{XY} measures the downward vertical distance (the amount of Y that the individual is willing to give up) per unit of horizontal distance (i.e., per additional unit of X required) to remain on the same indifference curve. That is, $MRS_{XY} = -\Delta Y/\Delta X$. Because of the reduction in Y, MRS_{XY} is negative. However, we multiply by -1 and express MRS_{XY} as a positive value.

For example, starting at point A on U_1 in Figure 3.4, the individual is willing to give up four units of Y for one additional unit of X and reach point B on U_1. Thus, $MRS_{XY} = -(-4/1) = 4$. This is the absolute (or positive value of the) slope of the chord from point A to point B on U_1. Between point B and point C on U_1, $MRS_{XY} = 3/2 = 1.5$ (the absolute slope of chord BC). Between points C and F, $MRS_{XY} = 2/3 = 0.67$. At a particular point on the indifference curve, MRS_{XY} is given by the absolute slope of the tangent to the indifference curve at that point. Different individuals usually have different indifference curves and different MRS_{XY} (at points where their indifference curves have different slopes).

We can relate indifference curves to the preceding utility analysis by pointing out that all combinations of goods X and Y on a given indifference curve refer to the same level of total utility for the individual. Thus, for a movement down a given indifference curve, the gain in utility in consuming more of good X must be equal to the loss in utility in consuming less of good Y. Specifically, the increase in consumption of good X (ΔX) times the marginal utility that the individual receives from consuming each additional unit of X (MU_X) must be equal to the reduction in Y ($-\Delta Y$) times the marginal utility of Y (MU_Y). That is,

$$(\Delta X)(MU_X) = -(\Delta Y)(MU_Y) \qquad [3.1]$$

so that

$$MU_X/MU_Y = -\Delta Y/\Delta X = MRS_{XY} \qquad [3.2]$$

Thus, MRS_{XY} is equal to the absolute slope of the indifference curve and to the ratio of the marginal utilities.

Note that MRS_{XY} (i.e., the absolute slope of the indifference curve) declines as we move down the indifference curve. This follows from, or is a reflection of, the convexity of the indifference curve. That is, as the individual moves down an indifference curve and is left with less and less Y (say, soft drinks) and more and more X (say, hamburgers), each remaining unit of Y becomes more valuable to the individual and each additional unit of X becomes less valuable. Thus, the individual is willing to give up less and less of Y to obtain each additional unit of X. It is this property that makes MRS_{XY} diminish and indifference

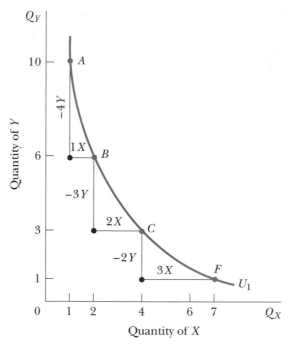

FIGURE 3.4   Marginal Rate of Substitution (MRS)
Starting at point A, the individual is willing to give up 4
units of Y for one additional unit of X and reach point B on
U_1. Thus, $MRS_{XY} = 4$ (the absolute slope of chord AB).
Between points B and C, $MRS_{XY} = 3/2$. Between C and F,
$MRS_{XY} = 2/3$. MRS_{XY} declines as the individual moves
down the indifference curve.

curves convex to the origin. We will see in Section 3.5 the crucial role that convexity plays
in consumer utility maximization.[8]

Some Special Types of Indifference Curves

Although indifference curves are usually negatively sloped and convex to the origin, they
may sometimes assume other shapes, as shown in Figure 3.5. Horizontal indifference
curves, as in the top left panel of Figure 3.5, would indicate that commodity X is a **neuter;**
that is, the consumer is indifferent between having more or less of the commodity. Vertical
indifference curves, as in the top right panel of Figure 3.5, would indicate instead that
commodity Y is a neuter.

The bottom left panel of figure 3.5 shows indifference curves that are negatively
sloped straight lines. Here, MRS_{XY} or the absolute slope of the indifference curves is constant. This means that an individual is always willing to give up the same amount of good Y

---

[8] A movement along an indifference curve in the upward direction measures MRS_{YX}, which also diminishes.

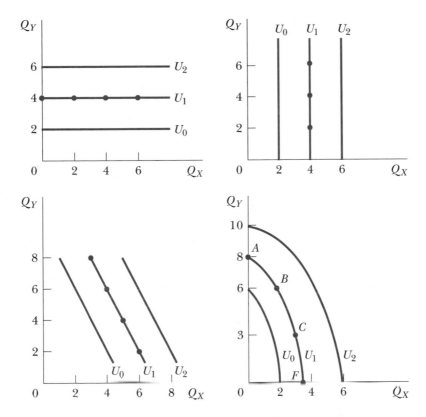

FIGURE 3.5   Some Unusual Indifference Curves   Horizontal indifference curves, as in the top left panel, indicate that X is a neuter; that is, the consumer is indifferent between having more or less of it. Vertical indifference curves, as in the top right panel, would indicate instead that commodity Y is a neuter. Indifference curves that are negatively sloped straight lines, as in the bottom left panel, indicate that MRS_{XY} is constant, and so X and Y are perfect substitutes for the individual. The bottom right panel shows indifference curves that are concave to the origin (i.e., MRS_{XY} increases).

(say, two cups of tea) for each additional unit of good X (one cup of coffee). Therefore, good X and two units of good Y are *perfect substitutes* for this individual.

Finally, the bottom right panel shows indifference curves that are concave rather than convex to the origin. This means that the individual is willing to give up more and more units of good Y for each additional unit of X (i.e., MRS_{XY} increases). For example, between points A and B on U_1, $MRS_{XY} = 2/2 = 1$; between B and C, $MRS_{XY} = 3/1 = 3$; and between C and F, $MRS_{XY} = 3/0.5 = 6$. In Section 3.5, we will see that in this unusual case, the individual would end up consuming only good X or only good Y.

Even though indifference curves can assume any of the shapes shown in Figure 3.5, they are usually negatively sloped, nonintersecting, and convex to the origin. These characteristics have been confirmed experimentally.[9] Because it is difficult to derive indifference

---

[9] See, for example, K. R. MacCrimmon and M. Toda, "The Experimental Determination of Indifference Curves," *Review of Economic Studies*, October 1969.

curves experimentally, however, firms try to determine consumers' preferences by marketing studies, as explained in Example 3–2.

EXAMPLE 3–2

How Ford Decided on the Characteristics of Its Taurus

Firms can learn about consumers' preferences by conducting or commissioning marketing studies to identify the most important characteristics of a product, say, styling and performance for automobiles, and to determine how much more consumers would be willing to pay to have more of each attribute, or how they would trade off more of one attribute for less of another. This approach to consumer demand theory, which focuses on the characteristics or attributes of goods and on their worth or *hedonic prices* rather than on the goods themselves, was pioneered by Kelvin Lancaster (see "At the Frontier" in Chapter 4). This is in fact how the Ford Motor Company decided on the characteristics of its 1986 Taurus.

Specifically, Ford determined by marketing research that the two most important characteristics of an automobile for the majority of consumers were styling (i.e., design and interior features) and performance (i.e., acceleration and handling) and then produced its Taurus in 1986 that incorporated those characteristics. The rest is history (the Taurus regained in 1992 its status of the best-selling car in America—a position that it had lost to the Honda Accord in 1989). Ford also used this approach to decide on the characteristics of the all-new 1996 Taurus, the first major overhaul since its 1986 launch, at a cost of $2.8 billion, as well as in deciding the characteristics of its world cars, Focus, launched in 1998 and Mondeo introduced in 2000. Other automakers, such as General Motors, followed similar procedures in determining the characteristics of their automobiles. During the past few years, U.S. automakers have shifted somewhat toward producing "sports wagons," which are a cross between sedans and sport-utility vehicles (SUVs) to reflect recent changes in consumer tastes.

Market studies can also be used to determine how consumers' tastes have changed over time. In terms of indifference curves, a reduction in the consumer's taste for commodity X (hamburgers) in relation to commodity Y (soft drinks) would be reflected in a flattening of the indifference curve of Figure 3.4, indicating that the consumer would now be willing to give up less of Y for each additional unit of X. The different tastes of different consumers are also reflected in the shapes of their indifference curves. The consumer who prefers soft drinks to hamburgers will have a flatter indifferences curve than a consumer who does not.

Sources: "Ford Puts Its Future on the Line," *New York Times Magazine,* December 4, 1985, pp. 94–110; V. Bajic, "Automobiles and Implicit Markets: An Estimate of a Structural Demand Model for Automobile Characteristics," *Applied Economics,* April 1993, pp. 541–551; "The Shape of a New Machine," *Business Week,* July 24, 1995, pp. 60–66; "Ford Hopes Its New Focus Will Be a Global Best Seller," *Wall Street Journal,* October 8, 1998, p. B10; S. Berry, J. Levinsohn, and A. Pakes, "Differentiated Products Demand Systems from a Combination of Macro and Micro Data: The New Car Market," National Bureau of Economic Research, *Working Paper 6481,* March 1998; and "Ford's Taurus Loses Favor to New-Age 'Sport Wagon,'" *New York Times,* February 7, 2002, p. B1.

3.3   INTERNATIONAL CONVERGENCE OF TASTES

A rapid convergence of tastes is taking place in the world today. Tastes in the United States affect tastes around the world and tastes abroad strongly influence tastes in the United States. Coca-Cola and jeans are only two of the most obvious U.S. products that have become household items around the world. One can see Adidas sneakers and Walkman personal stereos on joggers from Central Park in New York City to Tivoli Gardens in Copenhagen. You can eat Big Macs in Piazza di Spagna in Rome or Pushkin Square in Moscow. We find Japanese cars and VCRs in New York and in New Delhi, French perfumes in Paris and in Cairo, and Perrier in practically every major (and not so major) city around the world. Texas Instruments and Canon calculators, Dell and Hitachi portable PCs, and Xerox and Minolta copiers are found in offices and homes more or less everywhere. With more rapid communications and more frequent travel, the worldwide convergence of tastes has even accelerated. This has greatly expanded our range of consumer choices and forced producers to think in terms of global production and marketing to remain competitive in today's rapidly shrinking world.

In his 1983 article "The Globalization of Markets" in the *Harvard Business Review,* Theodore Levitt asserted that consumers from New York to Frankfurt to Tokyo want similar products and that success for producers in the future would require more and more standardized products and pricing around the world. In fact, in country after country, we are seeing the emergence of a middle-class consumer lifestyle based on a taste for comfort, convenience, and speed. In the food business, this means packaged, fast-to-prepare, and ready-to-eat products. Market researchers have discovered that similarities in living styles among middle-class people all over the world are much greater than we once thought and are growing with rising incomes and education levels. Of course, some differences in tastes will always remain among people of different nations, but with the tremendous improvement in telecommunications, transportation, and travel, the cross-fertilization of cultures and convergence of tastes can only be expected to accelerate. This trend has important implications for consumers, producers, and sellers of an increasing number and types of products and services.

EXAMPLE 3–3
Gillette Introduces the Sensor and Mach3 Razors—Two Truly Global Products

As tastes become global, firms are responding more and more with truly global products. These are introduced more or less simultaneously in most countries of the world with little or no local variation. This is leading to what has been aptly called the "global supermarket." For example, in 1990, Gillette introduced its new Sensor Razor at the same time in most nations of the world and advertised it with virtually the same TV spots (ad campaign) in 19 countries in Europe and North America. In 1994, Gillette introduced an upgrade of the Sensor Razor called SensorExcell with a high-tech edge. By

1998, Gillette had sold over 400 million of Sensor and SensorExcell razors and more than 8 billion twin-blade cartridges, and it had captured an incredible 71% of the global blade market. Then in April 1998, Gillette unveiled the Mach3, the company's most important new product since the Sensor. It has three blades with a new revolutionary edge produced with chipmaking technology that took five years to develop. Gillette developed its new razor in stealth secrecy at the astounding cost of over $750 million, and spent another $300 million to advertise it. Since it went on sale in July 1998, the Mach3 has proved to be an even bigger success than the Sensor Razor, and in April 2002 Gillette introduced its Mach3 Turbo razor (an evolution of its Mach3) worldwide. Despite its great marketing success in razors, however, Gillette's stumbled in some of its other products and its overall profits fell in the late 1990s and early 2000s.

The trend toward the global supermarket is rapidly spreading in Europe as borders fade and as Europe's single currency (the euro) brings prices closer across the continent. A growing number of companies are creating "Euro-brands"—a single product for most countries of Europe—and advertising them with "Euro-ads," which are identical or nearly identical across countries, except for language. Many national differences in taste will, of course, remain; for example, Nestlé markets more than 200 blends of Nescafé to cater to differences in tastes in different markets. But the converging trend in tastes around the world is unmistakable and is likely to lead to more and more global products. This is true not only in foods and inexpensive consumer products but also in automobiles, tires, portable computers, phones, and many other durable products.

Sources: "Building the Global Supermarket," *New York Times,* November 18, 1988, p. D1; "Gillette's World View: One Blade Fits All," *Wall Street Journal,* January 3, 1994, p. C3; "Gillette Finally Reveals Its Vision of the Future, and it Has 3 Blades," *Wall Street Journal,* April 4, 1998, p. A1; "Gillette, Defying Economy, Introduces a $9 Razor Set," *New York Times,* October 31, 2001, p. C4; "Selling in Europe: Borders Fade," *New York Times,* May 31, 1990, p. D1; "Converging Prices Mean Trouble for European Retailers," *Financial Times,* June 18, 1999, p. 27; "Can Nestlé Be the Very Best?," *Fortune,* November 13, 2001, pp. 353–360.

3.4 | THE CONSUMER'S INCOME AND PRICE CONSTRAINTS: THE BUDGET LINE

In this section, we introduce the constraints or limitations faced by a consumer in satisfying his or her wants. In order to conduct the analysis by plane geometry, we assume that the consumer spends all of his or her income on only two goods, X and Y. We will see that the constraints of the consumer can then be represented by a line called the budget line. The position of the budget line and changes in it can best be understood by looking at its endpoints.

Definition of the Budget Line

In Section 3.2, we saw that we can represent a consumer's tastes with an indifference map. We now introduce the constraints or limitations that a consumer faces in attempting to

satisfy his or her wants. The amount of goods that a consumer can purchase over a given period of time is limited by the consumer's income and by the prices of the goods that he or
she must pay. In what follows we assume (realistically) that the consumer cannot affect the
price of the goods he or she purchases. In economics jargon, we say that the consumer faces
a **budget constraint** due to his or her limited income and the given prices of goods.

By assuming that a consumer spends all of his or her income on good X (hamburgers)
and on good Y (soft drinks), we can express the budget constraint as

$$P_X Q_X + P_Y Q_Y = I \tag{3.3}$$

where P_X is the price of good X, Q_X is the quantity of good X, P_Y is the price of good Y, Q_Y
is the quantity of good Y, and I is the consumer's money income. Equation [3.3] postulates
that the price of X times the quantity of X plus the price of Y times the quantity of Y equals
the consumer's money income. That is, the amount of money spent on X plus the amount
spent on Y equals the consumer's income.[10]

Suppose that $P_X = \$2$, $P_Y = \$1$, and $I = \$10$ per unit of time. This could, for example,
be the situation of a student who has $10 per day to spend on snacks of hamburgers (good X)
priced at $2 each and on soft drinks (good Y) priced at $1 each. By spending all income on
Y, the consumer could purchase $10Y$ and $0X$. This defines endpoint J on the vertical axis of
Figure 3.6. Alternatively, by spending all income on X, the consumer could purchase $5X$ and
$0Y$. This defines endpoint K on the horizontal axis. By joining endpoints J and K with a
straight line we get the consumer's **budget line.** This line shows the various combinations
of X and Y that the consumer can purchase by spending all income at the given prices of the
two goods. For example, starting at endpoint J, the consumer could give up two units of Y
and use the $2 not spent on Y to purchase the first unit of X and reach point L. By giving up
another $2Y$, he or she could purchase the second unit of X. The slope of -2 of budget line JK
shows that for each $2Y$ the consumer gives up, he or she can purchase $1X$ more.

By rearranging equation [3.3], we can express the consumer's budget constraint in a
different and more useful form, as follows. By subtracting the term $P_X Q_X$ from both sides
of equation [3.3] we get

$$P_Y Q_Y = I - P_X Q_X \tag{3.3A}$$

By then dividing both sides of equation [3.3A] by P_Y, we isolate Q_Y on the left-hand side
and define equation [3.4]:

$$Q_Y = I/P_Y - (P_X/P_Y)Q_X \tag{3.4}$$

The first term on the right-hand side of equation [3.4] is the vertical or Y-intercept of the budget line and $-P_X/P_Y$ is the slope of the budget line. For example, continuing to use $P_X = \$2$,
$P_Y = \$1$, and $I = \$10$, we get $I/P_Y = 10$ for the Y-intercept (endpoint J in Figure 3.6) and
$-P_X/P_Y = -2$ for the slope of the budget line. The slope of the budget line refers to the rate
at which the two goods can be exchanged for one another in the market (i.e., $2Y$ for $1X$).

The consumer can purchase any combination of X and Y on the budget line or in the
shaded area below the budget line (called *budget space*). For example, at point B the individual would spend $4 to purchase $2X$ and the remaining $6 to purchase $6Y$. At point M, he

---

[10] Equation [3.3] could be generalized to deal with any number of goods. However, as pointed out, we deal with
only two goods for purposes of diagrammatic analysis.

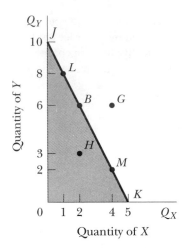

FIGURE 3.6   The Budget Line
With an income of $I = \$10$, and
$P_Y = \$1$ and $P_X = \$2$, we get
budget line JK. This shows that the
consumer can purchase $10Y$ and $0X$
(endpoint J), $8Y$ and $1X$ (point L),
$6Y$ and $2X$ (point B), or ... $0Y$ and
$5X$ (endpoint K). $I/P_Y = \$10/\$1 =$
10 is the vertical or Y-intercept of
the budget line and $-P_X/P_Y =$
$-\$2/\$1 = -2$ is the slope.

or she would spend $8 to purchase $4X$ and the remaining $2 to purchase $2Y$. On the other hand, at a point such as H in the shaded area below the budget line (i.e., in the budget space), the individual would spend $4 to purchase $2X$ and $3 to purchase $3Y$ and be left with $3 of unspent income. In what follows, we assume that the consumer *does* spend all of his or her income and is on the budget line. Because of the income and price constraints, the consumer cannot reach combinations of X and Y above the budget line. For example, the individual cannot purchase combination G ($4X$, $6Y$) because it requires an expenditure of $14 ($8 to purchase $4X$ plus $6 to purchase $6Y$).

Changes in Income and Prices and the Budget Line

A particular budget line refers to a specific level of the consumer's income and specific prices of the two goods. If the consumer's income and/or the price of good X or good Y change, the budget line will also change. When only the consumer's income changes, the budget line will shift up if income (I) rises and down if I falls, but the slope of the budget line remains unchanged. For example, the left panel of Figure 3.7 shows budget line JK (the same as in Figure 3.6 with $I = \$10$), higher budget line $J'K'$ with $I = \$15$, and still higher budget line $J''K''$ with $I = \$20$ per day. P_X and P_Y do not change, so the three budget lines

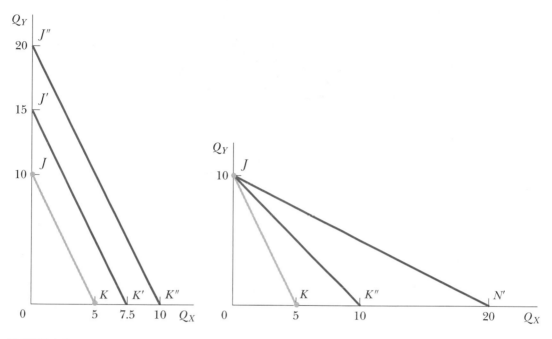

FIGURE 3.7   Changes in the Budget Line   The left panel shows budget line *JK* (the same as in Figure 3.6 with *I* = $10), higher budget line *J'K'* with *I* = $15, and still higher budget line *J"K"* with *I* = $20 per day. P_X and P_Y do not change, so the three budget lines are parallel and their slopes are equal. The right panel shows budget line *JK* with P_X = $2, budget line *JK"* with P_X = $1, and budget line *JN"* with P_X = $0.50. The vertical or *Y*-intercept (endpoint *J*) remains the same because income and P_Y do not change. The slope of budget line *JK"* is $-P_X/P_Y = -\$1/\$1 = -1$, while the slope of budget line *JN'* is $-1/2$.

are parallel and their slopes are equal. If the consumer's income falls, the budget line shifts down but remains parallel.

If only the price of good *X* changes, the vertical or *Y*-intercept remains unchanged, and the budget line rotates upward or counterclockwise if P_X falls and downward or clockwise if P_X rises. For example, the right panel of Figure 3.7 shows budget line *JK* (the same as in Figure 3.6 at P_X = $2), budget line *JK"* with P_X = $1, and budget line *JN'* with P_X = $0.50. The vertical intercept (endpoint *J*) remains the same because *I* and P_Y do not change. The slope of budget line *JK"* is $-P_X/P_Y = -\$1/\$1 = -1$. The slope of budget line *JN'* is $-1/2$. With an increase in P_X, the budget line rotates clockwise and becomes steeper.

On the other hand, if only the price of *Y* changes, the horizontal or *X*-intercept will be the same, but the budget line will rotate upward if P_Y falls and downward if P_Y rises. For example, with *I* = $10, P_X = $2, and P_Y = $0.50 (rather than P_Y = $1), the new vertical or *Y*-intercept is Q_Y = 20 and the slope of the new budget line is $-P_X/P_Y = -4$. With P_Y = $2, the new *Y*-intercept is Q_Y = 5 and $-P_X/P_Y = -1$ (you should be able to sketch these lines). Finally, with a proportionate reduction in P_X and P_Y and constant *I*, there will be a parallel upward shift in the budget line; with a proportionate increase in P_X and P_Y and constant *I*, there will be a parallel downward shift in the budget line.

EXAMPLE 3-4

Time as a Constraint

In the discussion of the budget line above, we have assumed only two constraints: the consumers's income and the given prices of the two goods. In the real world, consumers are also likely to face a time constraint. That is, since the consumption of goods requires time, which is also limited, time often represents another constraint faced by consumers. This explains the increasing popularity of precooked or ready-to-eat foods, restaurant meals delivered at home, and the use of many other time-saving goods and services. But the cost of saving time can be very expensive—thus proving the truth of the old saying that "time is money."

For example, the food industry is introducing more and more foods that are easy and quick to prepare, but these foods carry with them a much higher price. A meal that could be prepared from scratch for a few dollars might cost instead more than $10 in its ready-to-serve variety which requires only a few minutes to heat up. More and more people are also eating out and incurring much higher costs in order to save the time it takes to prepare home meals. McDonald's, Burger King, Taco Bell, and other fast-food companies are not just selling food, but fast food, and for that customers are willing to pay more than for the same kind of food at traditional food outlets, which require more waiting time. Better still, many suburbanites are increasingly reaching for the phone, not the frying pan, at dinner time to arrange for the home delivery of restaurant meals, adding even more to the price or cost of a meal.

Time is also a factor in considering transportation costs. One could fly roundtrip from New York to Paris or London in 15 hours with a regular airline ticket for $1,000 or on the supersonic Concorde in half the time for about $7,200. Since the real or true cost of the trip includes not only the price of the airline ticket but also travel time, we can expect most of the passengers on the Concorde to be high-level executives for whom the travel time saved is very valuable.

Sources: "Suburban Life in the Hectic 1990s: Dinner Delivered," *New York Times,* November 20, 1992, p. B1; "How Much Will People Pay to Save a Few Minutes of Cooking? Plenty," *Wall Street Journal,* July 25, 1985, p. B1; and "The Concorde Destination," *New York Times,* September 28, 1979, p. 26.

3.5   CONSUMER'S CHOICE

We will now bring together the tastes and preferences of the consumer (given by his or her indifference map) and the income and price constraints faced by the consumer (given by his or her budget line) to examine how the consumer determines which goods to purchase and in what quantities to maximize utility or satisfaction. As we will see in the next chapter, utility maximization is essential for the derivation of the consumer's demand curve for a commodity (which is a major objective of this part of the text).

Utility Maximization

Given the tastes of the consumer (reflected in his or her indifference map), the **rational consumer** seeks to maximize the utility or satisfaction received in spending his or her income. A rational consumer maximizes utility by trying to attain the highest indifference curve possible, given his or her budget line. This occurs where an indifference curve is tangent to the budget line so that the slope of the indifference curve (the MRS_{XY}) is equal to the slope of the budget line (P_X/P_Y). Thus, the condition for **constrained utility maximization, consumer optimization,** or **consumer equilibrium** occurs where the consumer spends all income (i.e., he or she is on the budget line) and

$$MRS_{XY} = P_X/P_Y \qquad\qquad [3.5]$$

Figure 3.8 brings together on the same set of axes the consumer indifference curves of Figure 3.2 and the budget line of Figure 3.6 to determine the point of utility maximization. Figure 3.8 shows that the consumer maximizes utility at point B where indifference curve U_1 is tangent to budget line JK. At point B, the consumer is on the budget line and $MRS_{XY} = P_X/P_Y = 2$. Indifference curve U_1 is the highest that the consumer can reach with his or her budget line. Thus, to maximize utility the consumer should spend \$4 to purchase $2X$ and the remaining \$6 to purchase $6Y$. Any other combination of goods X and Y that the consumer could purchase (those on or below the budget line) provides less utility. For example, the consumer could spend all income to purchase combination L, but this would be on lower indifference curve U_0.

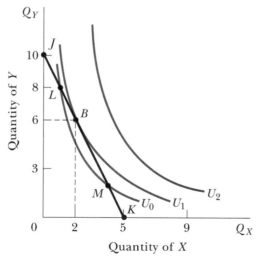

FIGURE 3.8   Constrained Utility Maximization
The consumer maximizes utility at point B, where indifference curve U_1 is tangent to budget line JK. At point B, $MRS_{XY} = P_X/P_Y = 2$. Indifference curve U_1 is the highest that the consumer can reach with his or her budget line. Thus, the consumer should purchase $2X$ and $6Y$.

At point L the consumer is willing to give up more of Y than he or she has to in the market to obtain one additional unit of X. That is, MRS_{XY} (the absolute slope of indifference curve U_0 at point L) exceeds the value of P_X/P_Y (the absolute slope of budget line JK). Thus, starting from point L, the consumer can increase his or her satisfaction by purchasing less of Y and more of X until he or she reaches point B on U_1, where the slopes of U_1 and the budget line are equal (i.e., $MRS_{XY} = P_X/P_Y = 2$). On the other hand, starting from point M, where $MRS_{XY} < P_X/P_Y$, the consumer can increase his or her satisfaction by purchasing less of X and more of Y until he or she reaches point B on U_1, where $MRS_{XY} = P_X/P_Y$. One tangency point such as B is assured by the fact that there is an indifference curve going through each point in the XY commodity space. The consumer cannot reach indifference curve U_2 with the present income and the given prices of goods X and Y.[11]

Utility maximization is more prevalent (as a general aim of individuals) than it may at first seem. It is observed not only in consumers as they attempt to maximize utility in spending income but also in many other individuals—including criminals. For example, a study found that the rate of robberies and burglaries was positively related to the gains and inversely related to the costs of (i.e., punishment for) criminal activity.[12] Utility maximization can also be used to analyze the effect of government warnings on consumption, as Example 3–5 shows.

EXAMPLE 3–5

Utility Maximization and Government Warnings on Junk Food

Suppose that in Figure 3.9, good X refers to milk and good Y refers to soda, $P_X = \$1$, $P_Y = \$1$, and the consumer spends his or her entire weekly allowance of \$10 on milk and sodas. Suppose also that the consumer maximizes utility by spending \$3 to purchase three containers of milk and \$7 to purchase seven sodas (point B on indifference curve U_1) before any government warning on the danger of dental cavities and obesity from sodas. After the warning, the consumer's tastes may change away from sodas and toward milk. It may be argued that government warnings change the information available to consumers rather than tastes; that is, the warning affects consumers' perception as to the ability of various goods to satisfy their wants—see M. Shodell, "Risky Business," *Science,* October 1985.

The effect of the government warning can be shown with dashed indifference curves U_0' and U_1'. Note that U_0' is steeper than U_1 at than original optimization point B, indicating that after the warning the individual is willing to give up more sodas for an additional

[11] For a mathematical presentation of utility maximization using rudimentary calculus, see Section A.2 of the Mathematical Appendix.

[12] See I. Ehrlich, "Participation in Illegitimate Activities: A Theoretical and Empirical Investigation," *Journal of Political Economy,* May/June 1973; W. T. Dickens, "Crime and Punishment Again: The Economic Approach with a Psychological Twist," National Bureau of Economic Research, *Working Paper No. 1884,* April 1986; and A. Gaviria, "Increasing Returns and the Evolution of Violent Crimes: The Case of Colombia," *Journal of Development Economics,* February 2000.

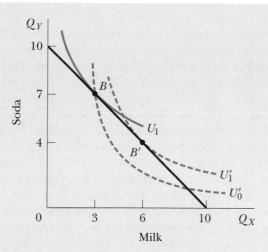

FIGURE 3.9   Effect of Government Warnings
The consumer maximizes utility by purchasing 3 containers of milk and 7 sodas (point B on indifference curve U_1) before the government warning on the consumption of sodas. After the warning, the consumer's tastes change and are shown by dashed indifference curves U'_0 and U'_1. The consumer now maximizes utility by purchasing 6 containers of milk and only 4 sodas (point B', where U'_1 is tangent to the budget line).

container of milk (i.e., MRS_{XY} is higher for U'_0 than for U_1 at point B). Now U'_0 can intersect U_1 because of the change in tastes. Note also that U'_0 involves less utility than U_1 at point B because the seven sodas (and the three containers of milk) provide less utility after the warning. After the warning, the consumer maximizes utility by consuming six containers of milk and only four sodas (point B', where U'_1 is tangent to the budget line).

The above analysis clearly shows how indifference curve analysis can be used to examine the effect of any government warning on consumption patterns, such the 1965 law requiring manufacturers to print on each pack of cigarettes sold in the United States the warning that cigarette smoking is dangerous to health. Indeed, the World Health Organization is now stepping up efforts to promote a global treaty to curb cigarette smoking. We can analyze the effect on consumption of any new information by examining the effect it has on the consumer's indifference map. Similarly, indifference curve analysis can be used to analyze the effect on consumer purchases of any regulation such as the one requiring drivers in many states to wear seat belts.

Sources: "Some States Fight Junk Food Sales in School," *New York Times,* September 9, 2001, p. 1 and "The World Health Organization Takes on Big Tobacco," *Fortune,* September 17, 2001, pp. 117–124.

Corner Solutions

If indifference curves are everywhere either flatter or steeper than the budget line, or if they are concave rather than convex to the origin, then the consumer maximizes utility by spending all income on either good Y or good X. These are called **corner solutions.**

In the left panel of Figure 3.10, indifference curves U_0, U_1, and U_2 are everywhere flatter than budget line JK, and U_1 is the highest indifference curve that the consumer can reach by purchasing $10Y$ and $0X$ (endpoint J). Point J is closest to the tangency point, which cannot be achieved. The individual could purchase $2X$ and $6Y$ and reach point B, but point B is on lower indifference curve U_0. Since point J is on the Y-axis (and involves the consumer spending all his or her income on good Y), it is called a corner solution.

The middle panel shows indifference curves that are everywhere steeper than the budget line, and U_1 is the highest indifference curve that the consumer can reach by spending all income to purchase $5X$ and $0Y$ (endpoint K). The individual could purchase $1X$ and $8Y$ at point L, but this is on lower indifference curve U_0. Point K is on the horizontal axis and involves the consumer spending all his or her income on good X, so point K is also a corner solution.

In the right panel, *concave* indifference curve U_1 is tangent to the budget line at point B, but this is not optimum because the consumer can reach higher indifference curve U_2 by spending all income to purchase $10Y$ and $0X$ (endpoint J). This is also a corner solution. Thus, the condition that an indifference curve must be tangent to the budget line for

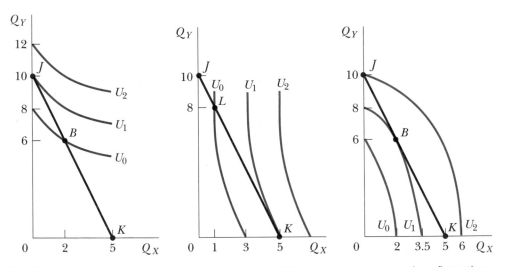

FIGURE 3.10   Corner Solutions   In the left panel, indifference curves are everywhere flatter than the budget line, and U_1 is the highest indifference curve that the consumer can reach by purchasing $10Y$ only (point J). The middle panel shows indifference curves everywhere steeper than the budget line, and U_1 is the highest indifference curve that the consumer can reach by spending all income to purchase $5X$ (point K). In the right panel, concave indifference curve U_1 is tangent to the budget line at point B, but this is not the optimum point because the consumer can reach higher indifference curve U_2 by consuming only good Y (point J).

optimization is true only when indifference curves assume their usual convex shape and are neither everywhere flatter nor steeper than the budget line.

Finally, although a consumer in the real world does not spend all of his or her income on one or a few goods, there are many more goods that he or she does not purchase because they are too expensive for the utility they provide. For example, few people purchase a $2,000 watch because the utility that most people get from the watch does not justify its $2,000 price. The nonconsumption of many goods in the real world can be explained by indifference curves which, though convex to the origin, are everywhere either flatter or steeper than the budget line, yielding corner rather than interior solutions. Corner solutions can also arise with rationing, as Example 3–6 shows.

EXAMPLE 3–6

Water Rationing in the West

Because goods are scarce, some method of allocating them among individuals is required. In a free-enterprise economy such as our own, the price system accomplishes this for the most part. Sometimes, however, the government rations goods, such as water in the West of the United States (as a result of recurrent droughts) and gasoline in 1974 and 1979 (at the height of the petroleum crisis). If the maximum amount of the good that the government allows is less than the individual would have purchased or used, the **rationing** will reduce the individual's level of satisfaction.

The effect of rationing on utility maximization and consumption can be examined with Figure 3.11. In the absence of rationing, the individual maximizes satisfaction at point B, where indifference curve U_1 is tangent to budget line JK, by consuming $2X$ and $6Y$ (as in Figure 3.8). Good X could refer to hours per week of lawn watering (in absence of an automatic water sprinkler system), while good Y could refer to hours per week of TV viewing. If the government did not allow the individual to use more than $1X$ per week, the budget line becomes JLK', with a kink at point L. Thus, rationing changes the constraints under which utility maximization occurs. The highest indifference curve that the individual can reach with budget line JLK' is now U_0 at point L, by consuming $1X$ and $8Y$. In our water rationing case, this refers to one hour of lawn watering and eight hours of TV viewing per week. With water rationing, the incentive arises to illegally water lawns at night under the cover of darkness. On the other hand, gasoline rationing during 1974 and 1979 led to long lines at the gas pump and to black markets where gasoline could be purchased illegally at a higher price without waiting. Thus, rationing leads to price distortions and inefficiencies.

If rations were $2X$ or more per week, the rationing system would not affect this consumer since he or she maximizes utility by purchasing $2X$ and $6Y$ (point B in the figure). Rationing is more likely to be binding or restrictive on high-income people than on low-income people (who may not have sufficient income to purchase even the allowed quantity of the rationed commodity). Thus, our model predicts that high-income people are more likely to make black-market purchases than low-income people. Effective rationing leads not only to black markets but also to "spillover" of consumer purchases on

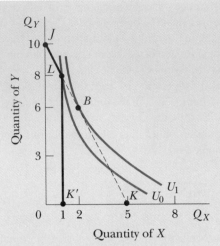

FIGURE 3.11   Rationing   In the absence of rationing, the individual maximizes satisfaction at point *B*, where indifference curve U_1 is tangent to budget line *JK*, and consumes 2*X* and 6*Y* (as in Figure 3.8). If the government did not allow the individual to purchase more than 1*X* per week, the budget line becomes *JLK′*, with a kink at point *L*. The highest indifference curve that the individual can reach with budget line *JLK′*, is now U_0 at point *L*, by consuming 1*X* and 8*Y*.

other goods not subject to rationing (or into savings). Both occurred in the United States during the 1974 and 1979 gasoline rationing periods. As pointed out in Section 2.7, allowing the market to operate (i.e., letting the price of the commodity reach its equilibrium level) eliminates the inefficiency of price controls and leads to much better results.

Sources: "Trickle-Down Economics," *Wall Street Journal,* August 23, 1999, p. A14; "Water Rights May Become More Liquid," *Wall Street Journal,* February 15, 1996, p. A2; and "W. C. Lee, "The Welfare Cost of Rationing-by-Queuing Across Markets," *Quarterly Journal of Economics,* July 1987.

Marginal Utility Approach to Utility Maximization

Until now we have examined constrained utility maximization with ordinal utility (i.e., with indifference curves). If utility were cardinally measurable, the condition for constrained utility maximization would be for the consumer to spend all income on *X* and *Y* in such a way that

$$\frac{MU_X}{P_X} = \frac{MU_Y}{P_Y} \qquad\qquad [3.6]$$

TABLE 3.4	Marginal Utility of X and Y		
Q_X	MU_X	Q_Y	MU_Y
1	10	4	5
2	6	5	4
3	4	6	3
4	2	7	2
5	0	8	1

Equation [3.6] reads, the marginal utility of good X divided by the price of good X equals the marginal utility of good Y divided by the price of good Y. MU_X/P_X is the extra or marginal utility per dollar spent on X. Likewise, MU_Y/P_Y is the marginal utility per dollar spent on Y. Thus, for constrained utility maximization or optimization, the marginal utility of the last dollar spent on X and Y should be the same.[13]

For example, Table 3.4 shows a portion of the declining marginal utility schedule for good X and good Y (from Table 3.1), on the assumption that MU_X is independent of MU_Y (i.e., that MU_X is not affected by how much Y the individual consumes, and MU_Y is not affected by the amount of X consumed). If the consumer's income is $I = \$10$, $P_X = \$2$, and $P_Y = \$1$, the consumer should spend $4 to purchase $2X$ and the remaining $6 to purchase $6Y$ so that equation [3.6] is satisfied. That is,

$$\frac{6 \text{ utils}}{\$2} = \frac{3 \text{ utils}}{\$1} \qquad [3.6A]$$

If the consumer spent only $2 to purchase $1X$ and the remaining $8 to purchase $8Y$, $MU_X/P_X = 10/2 = 5$ and $MU_Y/P_Y = 1/1 = 1$. The last (second) dollar spent on X thus gives the consumer five times as much utility as the last (eighth) dollar spent on Y and the consumer would not be maximizing utility. To be at an optimum, the consumer should purchase more of X (MU_X falls) and less of Y (MU_Y rises) until he or she purchases $2X$ and $6Y$, where equation [3.6] is satisfied.[14] This is the same result obtained with the indifference curve approach in Section 3.5. Note that even when the consumer purchases $1X$ and $4Y$ equation [3.6] is satisfied ($MU_X/P_X = 10/2 = MU_Y/P_Y = 5/1$), but the consumer would not be at an optimum because he or she would be spending only $6 of the $10 income.

The fact that the marginal utility approach gives the same result as the indifference curve approach (i.e., $2X$ and $6Y$) should not be surprising. In fact, we can easily show why this is so. By cross multiplication in equation [3.6], we get

$$\frac{MU_X}{MU_Y} = \frac{P_X}{P_Y} \qquad [3.7]$$

---

[13] We will see in footnote 14 that equation [3.6] also holds for the indifference curve approach.

[14] By giving up the eighth and the seventh units of Y, the individual loses 3 utils. By using the $2 not spent on Y to purchase the second unit of X, the individual receives 6 utils, for a net gain of 3 utils. Once the individual consumes $6Y$ and $2X$, equation [3.6] holds and he or she maximizes utility.

But we have shown in Section 3.2 that $MRS_{XY} = MU_X/MU_Y$ (see equation [3.2]) and in Section 3.5 that $MRS_{XY} = P_X/P_Y$ when the consumer maximizes utility (see equation [3.5]). Therefore, combining equations [3.2], [3.5], and [3.7], we can express the condition for consumer utility maximization as

$$MRS_{XY} = \frac{MU_X}{MU_Y} = \frac{P_X}{P_Y} \qquad [3.8]$$

Thus, the condition for consumer utility maximization with the marginal utility approach (i.e., equation [3.6]) is equivalent to that with the indifference curve approach (equation [3.5]), except for corner solutions. With both approaches, the value of equation [3.8] is 2.

AT THE FRONTIER
The Theory of Revealed Preference

Until now we have assumed that indifference curves are derived by asking the consumer to choose between various market baskets or combinations of commodities. Not only is this difficult and time consuming to do, but we also cannot be sure that consumers can or will provide trustworthy answers to direct questions about their preferences. According to the **theory of revealed preference** (developed by Paul Samuelson and John Hicks), a consumer's indifference curves can be derived from observing the actual market behavior of the consumer and without any need to inquire directly about preferences. For example, if a consumer purchases basket A rather than basket B, even though A is not cheaper than B, we can infer that the consumer prefers A to B.

The theory of revealed preference rests on the following assumptions:

1. The tastes of the consumer do not change over the period of the analysis.
2. The consumer's tastes are *consistent,* so that if the consumer purchases basket A rather than basket B, the consumer will never prefer B to A.
3. The consumer's tastes are *transitive,* so that if the consumer prefers A to B and B to C, the consumer will prefer A to C.
4. The consumer can be induced to purchase any basket of commodities if its price is lowered sufficiently.

Figure 3.12 shows how a consumer's indifference curve can be derived by revealed preference. Suppose that the consumer is observed to be at point *A* on budget line *NN* in the left panel. In this case, the consumer prefers *A* to any point on or below *NN*. On the other hand, points above and to the right of *A* are superior to *A* since they involve more of commodity *X* and commodity *Y*. Thus, the consumer's indifference curve must be tangent to budget line *NN* at point *A* and be above *NN* everywhere else. The indifference curve must also be to the left and below shaded area *LAM*. Such an indifference curve would be of the usual shape (i.e., negatively sloped and convex to the origin).

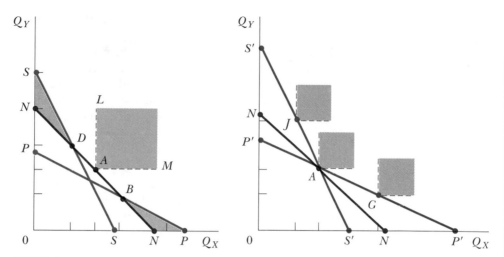

FIGURE 3.12   Derivation of an Indifference Curve by Revealed Preference   In the left panel, the consumer is originally at optimum at point *A* on *NN*. Thus, the indifference curve must be tangent to *NN* at point *A* and above *NN* everywhere else. It must also be to the left and below shaded area *LAM*. If the consumer is induced to purchase combination *B* (which is inferior to *A*) with budget line *PP*, we can eliminate shaded area *BPN*. Similarly, with combination *D* on budget line *SS*, shaded area *DSN* can be eliminated. Thus, the indifference curve must be above *SDBP*. In the right panel, the consumer prefers *G* to *A* with budget line *P'P'* and prefers *J* to *A* with budget line *S'S'*. Thus, the indifference curve must be below points *G* and *J*.

To locate more precisely the indifference curve in the *zone of ignorance* (i.e., in the area between *LAM* and *NN*), consider point *B* on *NN*. Point *B* is inferior to *A* since the consumer preferred *A* to *B*. However, the consumer could be induced to purchase *B* with budget line *PP* (i.e., with P_X/P_Y sufficiently lower than with *NN*). Since *A* is preferred to *B* and *B* is preferred to any point on *BP*, the indifference curve must be above *BP*. We have thus eliminated shaded area *BPN* from the zone of ignorance. Similarly, by choosing another point, such as *D*, we can, by following the same reasoning as for *B*, eliminate shaded area *DSN*. Thus, the indifference curve must lie above *SDBP* and be tangent to *NN* at point *A*.

The right panel of Figure 3.12 shows that we can chip away from the zone of ignorance immediately to the left of *LA* and below *AM*. Suppose that with budget line *P'P'* (which goes through point *A* and thus refers to the same real income as at *A*), the consumer chooses combination *G* (with more of *X* and less of *Y* than at *A*) because P_X/P_Y is lower than on *NN*. Points in the shaded area above and to the right of *G* are preferred to *G*, which is preferred to *A*. Thus, we have eliminated some of the upper zone of ignorance. Similarly, choosing another budget

Continued. . .

line, such as $S'S'$, we can eliminate the area above and to the right of a point such as J, which the consumer prefers to A at the higher P_X/P_Y given by $S'S'$. It follows that the indifference curve on which A falls must lie below points G and J. The process can be repeated any number of times to further reduce the upper and lower zones of ignorance, thereby locating the indifference curve more precisely. Note that the indifference curve derived is the one we need to show consumer equilibrium because it is the indifference curve that is tangent to the consumer's budget line.

Although somewhat impractical as a method for actually deriving indifference curves, the theory of revealed preference (particularly the idea that a consumer's tastes can be inferred or revealed by observing actual choices in the market place) has been very useful in many applied fields of economics such as public finance and international economics. The appendix to Chapter 4 applies the theory of revealed preference to measure changes in standards of living and consumer welfare during inflationary periods.

SUMMARY

1. The want-satisfying quality of a good is called utility. More units of a good increase total utility (TU) but the extra or marginal utility (MU) declines. The saturation point is reached when TU is maximum and MU is zero. Afterwards, TU declines and MU is negative. The decline in MU is known as the law of diminishing marginal utility. Cardinal utility actually provides an index of satisfaction for a consumer, whereas ordinal utility only ranks various consumption bundles.

2. The tastes of a consumer can be represented by indifference curves. These are based on the assumptions that the consumer can rank baskets of goods according to individual preferences, tastes are consistent and transitive, and the consumer prefers more of a good to less. An indifference curve shows the various combinations of two goods that give the consumer equal satisfaction. Higher indifference curves refer to more satisfaction and lower indifference curves to less. Indifference curves are negatively sloped, cannot intersect, and are convex to the origin. The marginal rate of substitution (MRS) measures how much of a good the consumer is willing to give up for one additional unit of the other good and remain on the same indifference curve. Indifference curves also generally exhibit diminishing MRS.

3. A rapid convergence of tastes is taking place in the world today. Tastes in the United States affect tastes around the world, and tastes abroad strongly influence tastes in the United States. With the tremendous improvement in telecommunications, transportation, and travel, the convergence of tastes can only be expected to accelerate—with important implications for us as consumers, for firms as producers, and for the study of microeconomics.

4. The budget line shows the various combinations of two goods (say, X and Y) that a consumer can purchase by spending all income (I) on the two goods at the given prices (P_X and P_Y). The vertical or Y-intercept of the budget line is given by I/P_Y and $-P_X/P_Y$ is the slope. The budget line shifts up if I increases and down if I decreases, but the slope remains unchanged. The budget line rotates upward if P_X falls and downward if P_X rises.

5. A rational consumer maximizes utility when reaching the highest indifference curve possible with the budget line. This occurs where an indifference curve is tangent to the budget line so that their slopes are equal (i.e., $MRS_{XY} = P_X/P_Y$). Government warnings or new information may change the shape and location of a consumer's indifference curves and the consumption pattern. If indifference curves are everywhere either flatter or steeper than the budget line or if they are concave, utility maximization requires the consumer to spend all income on either good Y or good X. These are called corner solutions. Corner solutions can also arise with rationing. The marginal utility approach postulates that the consumer maximizes utility when he or she spends all income and the marginal utility of the last dollar spent on X and Y are the same. Since $MRS_{XY} = MU_X/MU_Y = P_X/P_Y$, the marginal utility and the indifference curve approaches are equivalent. Indifference curves can also be derived by the theory of revealed preference.

KEY TERMS

Utility	Good	Budget line
Total Utility (*TU*)	Bad	Rational consumer
Marginal Utility (*MU*)	Indifference curve	Constrained utility maximization
Util	Indifference map	Consumer optimization
Law of diminishing marginal utility	Marginal rate of substitution (*MRS*)	Consumer equilibrium
Cardinal utility	Neuter	Corner solution
Ordinal utility	Budget constraint	Rationing
		Theory of revealed preference

REVIEW QUESTIONS

1. The utility approach to consumer demand theory is based on the assumption of cardinal utility, while the indifference curve approach is based on ordinal utility. Which approach is better? Why?

2. If Alan is indifferent between Coke and Pepsi, what would Alan's indifference curves look like?

3. The indifference curve between a good and garbage is positively sloped. True or false? Explain.

4. What is the relationship between two goods if the marginal rate of substitution between them is zero or infinite? Explain.

5. What is the marginal rate of substitution between two complementary goods?

6. Are indifference curves useless because it is difficult to derive them experimentally?

7. Why is there a convergence of tastes internationally?

8. If Jennifer's budget line has intercepts $20X$ and $30Y$ and $P_Y = \$10$, what is Jennifer's income? What is P_X? What is the slope of the budget line?

9. Must a consumer purchase some quantity of each commodity to be in equilibrium?

10. Janice spends her entire weekly food allowance of $42 on hamburgers and soft drinks. The price of a hamburger is $2, and the price of a soft drink is $1. Janice purchases 12 hamburgers and 18 soft drinks, and her marginal rate of substitution between hamburgers and soft drinks is 1. Is Janice in equilibrium? Explain.

11. Why is a consumer likely to be worse off when a product that he or she consumes is rationed?

12. In what way is the theory of revealed preference related to traditional consumer theory? What is its usefulness?

PROBLEMS

1. From the following total utility schedule

Q_X	0	1	2	3	4	5	6	7
TU_X	0	4	14	20	24	26	26	24

   a. derive the marginal utility schedule.

   b. plot the total and the marginal utility schedules.

   c. determine where the law of diminishing marginal utility begins to operate.

   d. find the saturation point.

4. Draw an indifference curve for an individual showing that

   a. good X and good Y are perfect complements.

   b. item X becomes a bad after 4 units.

   c. item Y becomes a bad after 3 units.

   d. MRS is increasing for both X and Y.

5. Suppose an individual has an income of $15 per time period, the price of good X is $1 and the price of good Y is also $1. That is, $I = \$15$, $P_X = \$1$, and $P_Y = \$1$.

Combination	U_1		U_2		U_3		U_4	
	Q_X	Q_Y	Q_X	Q_Y	Q_X	Q_Y	Q_X	Q_Y
A	3	12	6	12	8	15	10	13
B	4	7	7	9	9	12	12	10
C	6	4	9	6	11	9	14	8
F	9	2	12	4	15	6	18	6.4
G	14	1	15	3	19	5	20	6

2. The following table gives four indifference schedules of an individual.

   a. Using graph paper, plot the four indifference curves on the same set of axes.

   b. Calculate the marginal rate of substitution of X for Y between the various points on U_1.

   c. What is MRS_{XY} at point C on U_1?

   d. Can we tell how much better off the individual is on U_2 than on U_1?

*3. a. Starting with a given *equal* endowment of good X and good Y by individual A and individual B, draw A's and B's indifference curves on the same set of axes, showing that individual A has a preference for good X over good Y with respect to individual B.

   b. Explain why you drew individual A's and individual B's indifference curves as you did in Problem 3(a).

   a. Write the equation of the budget line of this individual in the form that indicates that the amount spent on good X plus the amount spent on good Y equals the individual's income.

   b. Write the equation of the budget line in the form that you can read off directly the vertical intercept and the slope of the line.

   c. Plot the budget line.

6. This problem involves drawing three graphs, one for each part of the problem. On the same set of axes, draw the budget line of Problem 5 (label it 2) and two other budget lines:

   a. One with $I = \$10$ (call it 1), and another with $I = \$20$ (label it 3), and with prices unchanged at $P_X = P_Y = \$1$.

   b. One with $P_X = \$0.50$, $P_Y = \$1$, and $I = \$15$ (label it 2A), and another with $P_X = \$2$ and the same P_Y and I (label it 2B).

_____

* = Answer provided at end of book.

c. One with $P_Y = \$2$, $P_X = \$1$, and $I = \$15$ (label it 2C), and another with $P_X = P_Y = \$2$ and $I = \$15$ (label it 2F).

*7. a. On the same set of axes, draw the indifference curves of Problem 2 and the budget line of Problem 5(c).

b. Where is the individual maximizing utility? How much of X and Y should he or she purchase to be at optimum? What is the general condition for constrained utility maximization?

c. Why is the individual not maximizing utility at point A? At point G?

d. Why can't the individual reach U_3 or U_4?

8. On the same set of axes (on graph paper), draw the indifference curves of problem 2 and budget lines

a. 1, 2, and 3 from Problem 6(a); label the points at which the individual maximizes utility with the various alternative budget lines.

b. 2 and 2A from Problem 6(b); label the points at which the individual maximizes utility on the various alternative budget lines: E and L.

*9. Given the following marginal utility schedule for good X and good Y for the individual, and given that the price of X and the price of Y are both $1, and that the individual spends all income of $7 on X and Y,

Q	1	2	3	4	5	6	7
MU_X	15	11	9	6	4	3	1
MU_Y	12	9	6	5	3	2	1

a. indicate how much of X and Y the individual should purchase to maximize utility.

b. show that the condition for constrained utility maximization is satisfied when the individual is at his or her optimum.

c. determine how much total utility the individual receives when he or she maximizes utility? How much utility would the individual get if he or she spent all income on X or Y?

10. Show on the same figure the effect of (1) an increase in cigarette prices, (2) an increase in consumers' incomes, and (3) a government warning that cigarette smoking is dangerous to health, all in such a way that the net effect of all three forces together leads to a net decline in cigarette smoking.

11. a. Draw a figure showing indifference curve U_2 tangent to the budget line at point B (8X), and a lower indifference curve (U_1) intersecting the budget line at point A (4X) and at point G (12X).

b. What happens if the government rations good X and allows the individual to purchase no more than 4X? No more than 8X? No more than 12X?

c. What would happen if the government instead mandated (as in the case of requiring auto insurance, seat belts, and so on) that the individual purchase at least 4X? 8X? 12X?

*12. Show by indifference curve analysis the choice of one couple not to have children and of another couple, with the same income and facing the same costs of having and raising children, to have one child.

INTERNET SITE ADDRESSES

CHAPTER 4

Consumer Behavior and Individual Demand

In Chapter 3 we saw how a consumer maximized utility by reaching the highest possible indifference curve with the given budget line. In this chapter, we examine how the consumer responds to changes in income and prices while holding tastes constant. Incomes and prices change frequently in the real world, so it is important to examine their individual effects on consumer behavior.

We begin by examining how the consumer responds to changes in his or her income when prices and tastes remain constant. This will allow us to derive a so-called Engel curve and to distinguish between normal and inferior goods. Then we examine the consumer's response to a change in the price of the good and derive the individual's demand curve for the good. This is the basic building block for the market demand curve of the good (to be derived in Chapter 5), the importance of which was outlined in Chapter 2.

After deriving an individual's demand curve, we discuss how to separate the substitution from the income effect of a price change for normal and inferior goods. The ability to separate graphically the income from the substitution effect of a price change is one of the most powerful tools of analysis of microeconomic theory, with many important applications. Subsequently, we examine the degree by which domestic and foreign goods and services are substitutable and the great relevance of this substitution in the study of microeconomics. We then consider some important applications of the theory presented in this chapter. These applications, together with the real-world examples included in the theory sections, highlight the importance of the theory of consumer behavior and demand. Finally, the "At the Frontier" section presents the characteristics approach to consumer theory, which provides some additional insights and uses of consumer theory. The optional appendix to this chapter deals with index numbers and how they are used to measure changes in consumer welfare.

CHANGES IN INCOME AND THE ENGEL CURVE

A change in the consumer's income shifts his or her budget line, and this shift affects consumer purchases. In this section we examine how a consumer reaches a new optimum position when income changes but prices and tastes do not.

Income–Consumption Curve and Engel Curve

By changing the consumer's money income while holding prices and tastes constant, we can derive the consumer's income–consumption curve. The **income–consumption curve** is the locus of (i.e., joins) consumer optimum points resulting when only the consumer's income varies. From the income–consumption curve we can then derive the consumer's Engel curve (discussed below).

For example, the top panel of Figure 4.1 shows that with budget line JK the consumer maximizes utility or is at an optimum at point B, where indifference curve U_1 is tangent to budget line JK and the consumer purchases $2X$ and $6Y$ (the same as in Figure 3.8). That is (continuing with the example from Chapter 3), the best way for the student to spend a daily income allowance of \$10 on snacks of hamburgers (good X) and soft drinks (good Y) is to purchase two hamburgers and six soft drinks per day. If the prices of hamburgers and soft drinks remain unchanged at $P_X = \$2$ and $P_Y = \$1$ but the daily income allowance rises from \$10 to \$15 and then to \$20, budget line JK shifts up to $J'K'$ and then to $J''K''$ (the same as in the left panel of Figure 3.7). The three budget lines are parallel because the prices of X and Y do not change.

With an income of \$15 and budget line $J'K'$, the consumer maximizes utility at point R, where indifference curve U_2 is tangent to budget line $J'K'$ and the consumer purchases $4X$ and $7Y$ (see the top panel of Figure 4.1). Indifference curve U_2 is the same as in the right panel of Figure 3.2 because tastes have not changed. Finally, with an income of \$20 and budget line $J''K''$, the consumer maximizes utility or is at an optimum at point S on U_3 by purchasing $5X$ and $10Y$ per unit of time (per day). By joining optimum points B, R, and S we get (a portion of) the income–consumption curve for this consumer (student). Thus, the income–consumption curve is the locus of consumer optimum points resulting when only the consumer's income varies.[1]

From the income–consumption curve in the top panel of Figure 4.1, we can derive the Engel curve in the bottom panel. The **Engel curve** shows the amount of a good that the consumer would purchase per unit of time at various income levels. To derive the Engel curve we keep the same horizontal scale as in the top panel but measure money income on the vertical axis.

The derivation of the Engel curve proceeds as follows. With a daily income allowance of \$10, the student maximizes utility by purchasing two hamburgers per day (point B) in

---

[1] At each point along the income–consumption curve the value of the MRS_{XY} is the same. This is because $-P_X/P_Y$ is the same for each of the budget lines (i.e., parallel lines have identical slopes).

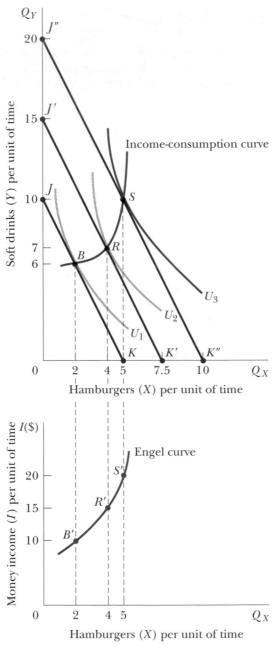

FIGURE 4.1   Income–Consumption Curve and Engel Curve   With budget lines *JK, J′K′, J″K″* and indifference curves U_1, U_2, and U_3 in the top panel, the individual maximizes utility at points *B, R,* and *S,* respectively. By joining optimum points *B, R,* and *S* we get the income–consumption curve (top panel). By then plotting income on the vertical axis and the various optimum quantities purchased of good *X* along the horizontal axis, we can derive the corresponding Engel curve *B′R′S′* in the bottom panel.

the top panel. This gives point B' (directly below point B) in the bottom panel. With an income allowance of $15, the student is at an optimum by purchasing four hamburgers (point R) in the top panel. This gives point R' in the bottom panel. Finally, with a daily income allowance of $20, the student maximizes utility by purchasing five hamburgers (point S in the top panel and S' in the bottom panel). By joining points B', R', and S' we get (a portion of) the Engel curve in the bottom panel. Thus, the Engel curve is derived from the income–consumption curve and shows the quantity of hamburgers per day (Q_X) that the student would purchase at various income levels (i.e., with various income allowances). Since the Engel curve is derived from points of consumer (student) utility maximization, $MRS_{XY} = P_X/P_Y$ at every point on the curve.

Engel curves are named after Ernst Engel, the German statistician of the second half of the nineteenth century who pioneered studies of family budgets and expenditure patterns. Sometimes Engel curves show the relationship between income and *expenditures* on various goods rather than the *quantity* purchased of various goods. However, because prices are held constant, we get the same result (i.e., the same Engel curve).

For some goods, the Engel curve may rise only gently. This indicates that a given increase in income leads to a proportionately larger increase in the quantity purchased of the good. These goods are sometimes referred to as "luxuries." Examples of luxuries may be education, recreation, and steaks and lobsters (for some people). On the other hand, the Engel curve for other goods may rise rather rapidly, indicating that a given increase in income leads to a proportionately smaller increase in the quantity purchased of these goods. These goods are called "necessities." Basic foodstuffs are usually regarded as necessities. A more precise definition of luxuries and necessities is given in Chapter 5.

EXAMPLE 4–1

Engel's Law After a Century

Table 4.1 gives the percentages of total consumption expenditures on various items for U.S. families in selected income classes in 1999. The table shows that higher-income families consistently spend a smaller percentage of their income than lower-income families on food but spend a larger percentage on personal insurance and pensions. Less regularity is found in the proportion of expenditures on other goods and services.

The decline in the proportion of total expenditures on food as income rises has been found to be true not only for the United States in the period of the survey, but also at other times and in other nations. Thus, food in general is a necessity rather than a luxury. This regularity is sometimes referred to as "Engel's law." Indeed, the higher the proportion of income spent on food in a nation, the poorer the nation is taken to be. For example, in India almost 50% of income is spent on food on the average.

TABLE 4.1	Percentage of Total Consumption by Income Class for U.S. Families in 1999						
	Annual Income						
Consumption Item	0– $9,999	$10,000– $19,999	$20,000– $29,999	$30,000– $39,999	$40,000– 49,000	$50,000– $69,000	$70,000 and over
Food	16.5%	15.3%	14.9%	14.4%	14.3%	13.2%	11.4
Housing	36.9%	35.0	32.6	31.0	31.0	30.0	30.0
Apparel and services	5.1	5.1	5.4	5.4	4.1	4.3	4.7
Transportation	16.3	18.8	19.0	19.9	20.5	19.9	17.4
Health care	6.4	8.1	7.0	5.6	5.0	4.8	3.7
Entertainment	4.7	4.5	4.6	4.8	4.6	5.6	5.4
Education	3.7	1.2	1.1	1.0	1.0	1.2	1.9
Insurance and pensions	2.1	3.6	6.4	8.8	11.1	12.9	15.9
Other	8.3	8.4	9.0	9.2	8.4	8.1	9.6
Total	100.0	100.0	100.0	100.0	100.0	100.0	100.0

Source: U.S. Department of Labor, Bureau of Labor Statistics, *Consumer Expenditures in 1999,* Report 949 (Washington, D.C.: May 2001), Table 2.

Normal and Inferior Goods

A **normal good** is one of which the consumer purchases more with an increase in income. An **inferior good** is one of which the consumer purchases less with an increase in income. Good X in Figure 4.1 is a normal good because the consumer purchases more of it with an increase in income. For example, an increase in the student's income allowance from $10 to $15 leads to an increase in the purchase of hamburgers from two to four per day. Thus, for a normal good, the income–consumption curve and the Engel curve are both positively sloped, as in Figure 4.1.

Figure 4.2 shows the income–consumption curve and the Engel curve for an inferior good. This results from supposing that the student, instead of spending the daily income allowance on soft drinks (good Y) and hamburgers (good X), spends it on soft drinks and candy bars (good Z), and supposing the student views candy bars as an inferior good.[2] With the price of soft drinks at $1 and the price of candy bars also at $1, the budget line of the student is JK' with a daily income allowance of $10 and $J'N$ with an income of $15 (see the top panel of Figure 4.2).

If indifference curves between soft drinks and candy bars are U_1' and U_2' the student maximizes satisfaction at point V, where indifference curve U_1' is tangent to budget line JK' with a

---

[2] Other commodities that are, perhaps, even more readily recognized as inferior goods in the United States today might be bologna and cheaper cuts of meats.

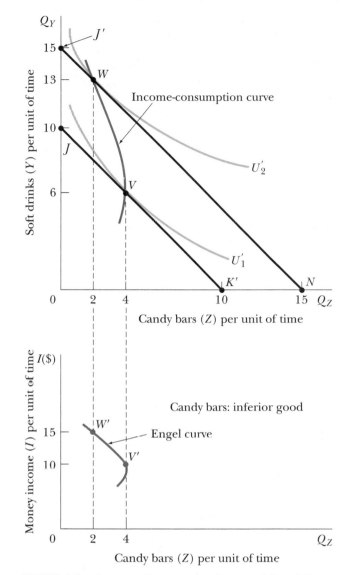

FIGURE 4.2   Income–Consumption Curve and Engel Curve for an Inferior Good   With budget lines *JK'* and *J'N* and indifference curves U_1' and U_2' in the top panel, the individual maximizes utility at points *V* and *W*, respectively. By joining points *V* and *W* we get the income–consumption curve (top panel). By then plotting income on the vertical axis and the optimum quantities purchased of good *Z* along the horizontal axis, we derive corresponding Engel curve *V'W'* in the bottom panel. Since the income–consumption curve and Engel curve are negatively sloped, good *Z* is an inferior good.

daily income allowance of $10. The student maximizes utility at point W, where indifference curve U_2' is tangent to budget line $J'N$ with an income of $15 (see the top panel of Figure 4.2). Thus, the consumer purchases four candy bars with an income of $10 and only two candy bars with an income of $15. Candy bars are, therefore, inferior goods for this student. The income–consumption curve for candy bars (VW in the top panel of Figure 4.2) and the corresponding Engel curve ($V'W'$ in the bottom panel) are both negatively sloped, indicating that the student purchases fewer candy bars as his or her income allowance increases.

The classification of a good as normal or inferior depends only on how a specific consumer views the particular good. Thus, the same candy bar can be regarded as a normal good by another student. Furthermore, a good can be regarded as a normal good by a consumer at a particular level of income and as an inferior good by the same consumer at a higher level of income. For example, with an allowance of $40 dollars per day, the student in the previous section may begin to regard hamburgers as an inferior good, because he or she now can afford steaks and lobsters. Also note that an inferior good is not a "bad" because more is preferred to less, and indifference curves remain negatively sloped (refer back to Section 3.2).

In the real world, most broadly defined goods such as food, clothing, housing, health care, education, and recreation are normal goods. Inferior goods are usually narrowly defined cheap goods, such as bologna, for which good substitutes are available. As pointed out earlier, a normal good can be further classified as a luxury or a necessity, depending on whether the quantity purchased increases proportionately more or less than the increase in income.

EXAMPLE 4–2

Many People Are Blowing Their Pension Money Long Before Retirement

There is a retirement crisis brewing in America today, not because people are not putting enough money into their retirement plans, but because they are taking billions of dollars out long before old age. Today, workers have many chances to take out their retirement money in the form of a lump sum before the usual retirement age. They can do so when they change jobs, when they work for a company that is sold and are thus ejected from their retirement plan, or by taking early retirement. But instead of putting their money into sound investments on which to live when they retire, many workers are blowing their lump-sum retirement-plan payouts on new cars, appliances, furniture, and boats, as well as in casinos.

A 1993 Labor Department study of how 60,000 households handled a retirement-plan lump sum showed that only 21% of the recipients rolled their money into Individual Retirement Accounts (IRAs), as recommended by financial planners. Almost 30% spent their lump sums on consumer products or used them to pay medical or educational expenses for themselves and their children, and another 23% put the money into a business or house or repaid debts. Younger people were more likely to spend rather than invest their retirement money into IRAs, but so did more than one-fifth of those in the 55–64 age group. Experts predict that by the end of the decade about half of the pension money in traditional firm-sponsored and firm-administered pension plans will have been distributed to the contributors. Employers prefer distributing pension money in a lump sum to employees because it saves them the cost of administering a string of retirement checks and other expenses. The problem is that many people treat their lump-sum pension money as a win at the lottery and go on spending spree, leaving little on which to live in their retirement years. Humans, it seems (and contrary to the usual assumption of rationality made by traditional economic theory), often behave quite irrationally! (Choices under uncertainty will be examined in detail in Chapter 6.)

Sources: "Offered a Lump Sum, Many Retirees Blow It and Risk Their Future," *Wall Street Journal,* July 31, 1995, p. A1; and "Borrowing on a 401k? Better Think Twice," *Wall Street Journal,* October 12, 2001, p. C1.

4.2   CHANGES IN PRICE AND THE INDIVIDUAL DEMAND CURVE

Commodity prices frequently change in the real world, and it is important to examine their effect on consumer behavior. A change in commodity prices changes the consumer budget line, and this affects consumer purchases. In this section we examine how the consumer reaches a new optimum position when the price of a good changes but the price of the other good, income, and tastes remain unchanged.

By changing the price of good X while holding constant the price of good Y, income, and tastes, we can derive the consumer's price–consumption curve for good X. The **price–consumption curve** for good X is the locus of (i.e., joins) consumer optimum points resulting when only the price of good X varies. From the price–consumption curve we can then derive the consumer's demand curve for good X.

For example, the top panel of Figure 4.3 shows once again that with budget line JK, the consumer maximizes utility or is at an optimum at point B, where indifference curve U_1 is tangent to budget line JK and the consumer purchases $2X$ and $6Y$ (the same as in Figure 3.8). Suppose that the consumer's income (i.e., the student allowance) remains unchanged at $I = \$10$ per day and the price of good Y (soft drinks) also remains constant at $P_Y = \$1$. A reduction in the price of good X (hamburgers) from $P_X = \$2$ to $P_X = \$1$ and then to $P_X = \$0.50$ would cause the consumer's budget line to become flatter or to rotate counterclockwise from JK to JK'' and then to JN' (the same as in the right panel of Figure 3.7).[3]

With $P_X = \$1$ and budget line JK'', the consumer maximizes utility at point E, where indifference curve U_2 is tangent to budget line JK'' and the consumer purchases $6X$ and $4Y$ (see the top panel of Figure 4.3). Indifference curve U_2 is the same as in the right panel of Figure 3.2 because tastes have not changed. Finally, with $P_X = \$0.50$ and budget line JN', the consumer maximizes utility or is at an optimum at point G on U_4 by purchasing $10X$

---

[3] Remember that the X-intercepts of the budget lines are obtained by I/P_X. Thus, with $I = \$10$ and $P_X = \$2$, we get endpoint K and budget line JK. With $P_X = \$1$, we get endpoint K'' and budget line JK'', and with $P_X = \$0.50$, we get endpoint N' and budget line JN'.

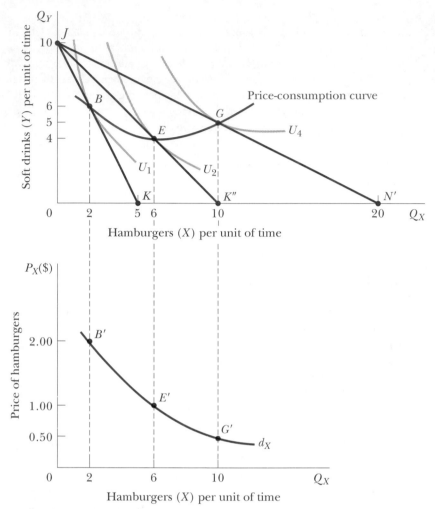

FIGURE 4.3   Price–Consumption Curve and the Individual's Demand Curve
The top panel shows that with $I = \$10$ and $P_Y = \$1$, the consumer is at an optimum at point B by purchasing $2X$ with $P_X = \$2$, at point E by purchasing $6X$ with $P_X = \$1$, and at point G by purchasing $10X$ with $P_X = \$0.50$. By joining points BEG, we get the price–consumption curve for good X. In the bottom panel, by plotting the optimum quantities of good X on the horizontal axis and the corresponding prices of good X on the vertical axis, we derive the individual's negatively sloped demand curve for good X, d_X.

and $5Y$ per unit of time (per day). By joining optimum points B, E, and G we get (a portion of) the price–consumption curve for this consumer (student). Thus, the price–consumption curve for good X is the locus of consumer optimum points resulting when only the price of X changes.[4]

---

[4] At each point along the price–consumption curve, $MRS_{XY} = P_X/P_Y$. However, unlike the case of the income–consumption curve, these ratios will vary because the budget lines are no longer parallel.

From the price–consumption curve in the top panel of Figure 4.3, we can derive the individual consumer's (student's) demand curve for good X in the bottom panel. The **individual's demand curve** for good X shows the amount of good X that the consumer would purchase per unit of time at various alternative prices of good X while holding everything else constant. It is derived by keeping the same horizontal scale as in the top panel but measuring the price of good X on the vertical axis.

The derivation of the individual's demand curve proceeds as follows. With $I = \$10$, $P_Y = \$1$, and $P_X = \$2$, the student maximizes utility by purchasing $2X$ (two hamburgers) per day (point B) in the top panel. This gives point B' (directly below point B) in the bottom panel. With $P_X = \$1$, the consumer is at optimum by purchasing $6X$ (point E) in the top panel. This gives point E' in the bottom panel. Finally, with $P_X = \$0.50$, the consumer maximizes utility by purchasing $10X$ (point G in the top panel and G' in the bottom panel). Other points could be similarly obtained. By joining points B', E', and G' we get the individual consumer's demand curve for good X, d_X, in the bottom panel. Thus, the demand curve is derived from the price–consumption curve and shows the quantity of the good that the consumer would purchase per unit of time at various alternative prices of the good while holding everything else constant (the *ceteris paribus* assumption).

We will see in Chapter 5 that the market demand curve for a good (our ultimate aim in Part Two of the text) is obtained from the addition or the horizontal summation of all individual consumers' demand curves for the good. Note that the individual consumer's demand curve for a good (d_x in the bottom panel of Figure 4.3) is negatively sloped. This reflects the *law of demand,* which postulates that the quantity purchased of a good per unit of time is inversely related to its price. Thus, the individual purchases more hamburgers per unit of time when their price falls and less of them when their price rises. Also note that an individual consumer's demand curve for a good is derived by holding constant the individual's tastes, his or her income, and the prices of other goods. If any of these change, the entire demand curve will shift. This is referred to as a change in demand as opposed to a change in the quantity demanded, which is a movement along a given demand curve as a result of a change in the price of the good while holding everything else constant (refer back to Section 2.2).

EXAMPLE 4–3

Higher Alcohol Prices Would Sharply Reduce Youth Alcohol Use and Traffic Deaths

Road accidents are the single largest cause of deaths among young people in America, and about half of the road fatalities are caused by young people driving while intoxicated. Efforts to reduce alcohol use by youths have centered on increasing the minimum legal age for purchasing and drinking alcohol, which is now 21 in all 50 states. The hope is that this will shift the demand curve for alcohol use by young people to the left (despite the fact that some forge identity cards to get around the rule). Surprisingly, little use has been made in the United States of an even more powerful deterrent to youth alcohol use—higher alcohol prices through higher federal alcohol taxes. In fact, the real price (i.e., the nominal price divided by the price index to adjust for inflation) of alcoholic beverages has declined by about 40% for beer and wine and 70% for hard liquor in the United States since 1951. Taxes are currently only about $2 per quart for beer and $3.60 for hard liquor in the United States, compared with $18.20 and $34.50 in England.

Using simulations for a sample of high school students, Douglas Coate and Michael Grossman found that by indexing the tax on beer to the rate of inflation (so as to keep the real price of beer constant at the 1951 level) would have cut the number of frequent young beer drinkers by about 20% and that this would have saved 1,660 lives from traffic accidents per year (twice as many as resulting from increasing the minimum legal drinking age from 18 to 21). Of course, raising taxes even higher so as to increase the real price of alcoholic beverages would have reduced drinking and road fatalities even more. This is not surprising, since most teenagers have much less disposable income than adults. Thus, increasing the price of alcoholic beverages would have a more powerful deterring effect on them than on older drinkers. What is surprising is that despite the predictions of economic theory and the confirmation of empirical studies, the government has chosen thus far not to use price as a powerful deterrent to youth alcohol use.

Sources: "Efforts to Reduce Teen Drinking May Provide Lessons," *Wall Street Journal,* August 10, 1995, p. B1; "Beer, Taxes and Death," *The Economist,* September 18, 1993, p. 33; Douglas Coate and Michael Grossman, "Effects of Alcoholic Beverage Prices and Legal Drinking Ages on Youth Alcohol Use," *Journal of Law and Economics,* April 1988, pp. 145–172; and "Traffic Death Rose in 2001, But Rates for Miles Fell," *The New York Times,* August 8, 2002, p. 21.

4.3   SUBSTITUTION AND INCOME EFFECTS

In this section, we separate the substitution effect from the income effect of a price change for both normal and inferior goods. This separation will give us an important analytical tool with wide applicability and will also allow us to examine the exception to the law of downward sloping demand.

How Are the Substitution and Income Effects Separated?[5]

We have seen in the previous section that when the price of a good falls the consumer buys more of it. This is the combined result of two separate forces at work called the substitution effect and the income effect. We now want to separate the total effect of a price change into these two components. We begin by first reviewing how the total effect of a price change (discussed in section 4.2) operates.

---

[5] The separation of the substitution effect from the income effect of a price change using rudimentary calculus is shown in section A.4 of the Mathematical Appendix at the end of the book.

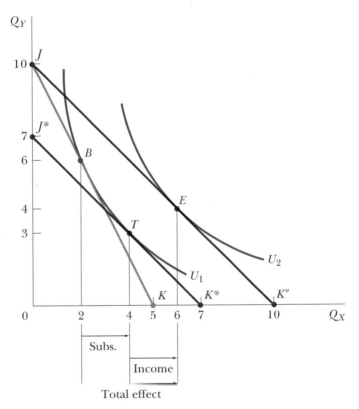

FIGURE 4.4   Income and Substitution Effects for a Normal Good   Starting from optimum point *B* (as in the top panel of Figure 4.3), we can isolate the substitution effect by drawing imaginary budget line *J*K** tangent to U_1 at *T*. The movement along U_1 from point *B* to point *T* is the substitution effect and results from the relative reduction in P_X only (with real income constant). The shift from point *T* on U_1 to point *E* on U_2 is then the income effect. The total effect ($BE = 4X$) equals the substitution effect ($BT = 2X$) plus the income effect ($TE = 2X$).

In Figure 4.4, $I = \$10$ and $P_Y = \$1$, and these remain constant. With $P_X = \$2$, we have budget line *JK* and the consumer maximizes utility at point *B* on indifference curve U_1 by purchasing $2X$. When the price of good X falls to $P_X = \$1$, the budget line becomes *JK″* and the consumer maximizes utility at point *E* on indifference curve U_2 by purchasing $6X$ (so far this is the same as in Figure 4.3). The increase in the quantity purchased from $2X$ to $6X$ is the total effect or the sum of the substitution and income effects. We are now ready to separate this total effect into its two components: the substitution effect and the income effect. *The substitution effect measures the increase in the quantity demanded of a good when its price falls resulting only from the relative price decline and independent of the change in real income.* On the other hand, *the income effect measures the increase in the quantity purchased of a good resulting only from the increase in real income that accompanies a price decline.*

First, consider the **substitution effect.** In Figure 4.4, we see that when the price of X falls from $P_X = \$2$ to $P_X = \$1$, the individual moves from point B on U_1 to point E on U_2 so that his or her level of satisfaction increases. Suppose that as P_X falls we could reduce the individual's money income sufficiently to keep him or her on original indifference curve U_1. We can show this by drawing hypothetical or imaginary budget line J^*K^* in Figure 4.4. Imaginary budget line J^*K^* is parallel to budget line JK'' so as to reflect the *new* set of relative prices (i.e., $P_X/P_Y = \$1/\$1 = 1$) and is below budget line JK'' in order to keep the individual at the original level of satisfaction (i.e., on indifference curve U_1).[6] The individual would then maximize satisfaction at point T, where indifference curve U_1 is tangent to imaginary budget line J^*K^* (so that $MRS_{XY} = P_X/P_Y = \$1/\$1 = 1$).

The movement along indifference curve U_1 from original point B to imaginary point T measures the substitution effect only (since the individual remains on the same indifference curve or level of satisfaction). From Figure 4.4, we see that the substitution effect, by itself, leads the individual to increase the quantity purchased of good X from two to four units when P_X falls from \$2 to \$1. That is, the individual substitutes hamburgers for, say, hot dogs and purchases two additional hamburgers and fewer hot dogs per unit of time. The substitution effect results exclusively from the reduction in the **relative price** of X (from $P_X/P_Y = \$2/\$1 = 2$ to $P_X/P_Y = \$1/\$1 = 1$) with the level of satisfaction held constant. Because indifference curves are convex, the substitution effect always involves an increase in the quantity demanded of a good when its price falls.

Next, consider the **income effect.** The shift from the imaginary point T on U_1 to the actual new point E on U_2 can be taken as a measure of the income effect. The shift from point T to point E does not involve any price change. That is, since the imaginary budget line J^*K^* and the actual new budget line JK'' are parallel, relative prices are the same (i.e., $P_X/P_Y = 1$ in both). The shift from indifference curve U_1 to U_2 can thus be taken as a measure of the increase in the individual's real income or purchasing power.[7] Because good X is a normal good, an increase in the consumer's purchasing power or real income leads him or her to purchase more of X (and other normal goods). In Figure 4.4, the income effect, by itself, leads the consumer to purchase two additional hamburgers (i.e., to go from $4X$ to $6X$).[8]

Thus, the total effect of the reduction in P_X ($BE = 4X$) equals the substitution effect ($BT = 2X$) plus the income effect ($TE = 2X$). The substitution effect reflects the increase in Q_X resulting only from the reduction in P_X and is independent of any change in the consumer's level of satisfaction or real income. On the other hand, the income effect reflects the increase in Q_X resulting only from the increase in satisfaction or real income. Only the total effect of the price change is actually observable in the real world, but we have been able, at least conceptually or experimentally, to separate this total effect into a substitution effect and an income effect.

---

[6] Budget line J^*K^* is imaginary in the sense that we do not actually observe it, unless the reduction in P_X is in fact accompanied by a lump-sum tax that removes \$3 ($JJ^* = K''K^*$) from the money income of the individual.

[7] The shift from point T to point E could be observed by giving back to the consumer the hypothetical lump-sum tax of \$3 collected earlier. Only with such an increase in real income or purchasing power can the consumer move from point T on U_1 to point E on U_2.

[8] It also leads the individual to purchase one additional soft drink (i.e., to go from $3Y$ to $4Y$). See Figure 4.4.

In Figure 4.4, the substitution effect and the income effect are of equal size. In the real world, the substitution effect is likely to be much larger than the income effect. The reason is that most goods have suitable substitutes, and when the price of a good falls, the quantity of the good purchased is likely to increase very much as consumers substitute the now-cheaper good for others. On the other hand, with the consumer purchasing many goods and spending only a small fraction of his or her income on any one good, the income effect of a price decline of any one good is likely to be small. There are, however, exceptional cases in which the income effect exceeds the substitution effect. Also note that although the substitution effect of a price reduction is always positive (i.e., it always leads to an increase in the quantity demanded of a good), the income effect can be positive if the good is normal or negative if the good is inferior.[9]

EXAMPLE 4-4

The Substitution and Income Effects of a Gasoline Tax

One of the biggest political battles being fought in Congress centers on energy policy in general and the size of the federal gasoline tax in particular. This is not a new battle. It is a battle that has been fought periodically every five years or so during the past three decades, every time the price of petroleum and American dependence on imported petroleum increased. It is surely a battle that will be fought again before the end of this decade because of the need for an energy policy in the United States.

Overall, gasoline taxes are now about 41 cents per gallon in the United States, as compared with more than $2 per gallon in Europe and Japan. Ever since the first petroleum crisis in 1973–1974, many in Congress have sought a gasoline tax of 50 cents per gallon. The tax would increase gasoline prices for American motorists and lead to a reduction in gasoline consumption and American dependence on foreign oil (which now stands at more than 50%, up from 35% in 1973). To avoid the deflationary impact (i.e., the reduction in purchasing power) of the tax on the economy, it has been proposed to either (a) return to consumers the amount of the tax collected on gasoline in the form of a *general* tax rebate unrelated to gasoline consumption or (b) reduce other taxes.

The gasoline tax, coupled with a general tax rebate to avoid the deflationary impact of a gasoline tax, relies on the distinction between the substitution effect and the income effect of an increase in gasoline prices. The substitution effect would result as people switch to cheaper means of transportation (trains, buses, subways), car pools, and more fuel-efficient cars and economize on the use of automobiles in general. The general income subsidy would then neutralize the reduction in real income associated with the increase in the price of gasoline. Thus, while the reduction in purchasing power would

---

[9] We could derive a demand curve along which real, rather than nominal, income is kept constant (i.e., showing or reflecting only the substitution effect). Such a demand curve would be steeper than the usual demand curve (which shows both the substitution and the income effects) if the good is normal (because in that case the income effect reinforces the substitution) and flatter than the usual demand curve if the good is inferior (because in that case part of the substitution effect would be neutralized by the opposite income effect).

be neutralized by the general income subsidy, the increase in the gasoline price would reduce its consumption. Despite strong opposition to a large increase in the gasoline tax from road builders, tourist interests, farm groups, the oil industry, and truckers, a large increase in the gasoline tax seems likely. Americans strongly prefer (and have relied on) tougher fuel-efficiency rules on automakers to reduce the growth of gasoline consumption. But with the spread in the popularity of the less fuel-efficient SUVs (sport-utility vehicles) in recent years, the effort to save on energy is not succeeding, and so the battle for a higher gasoline tax is likely to rage on.

Sources: A. A. Taheri, "Oil Shocks and the Dynamics of Substitution Adjustments in Industrial Fuels in the U.S.," *Applied Economics,* August 1994, pp. 751–756; "Oil Prices Generate Political Heat," *Wall Street Journal,* August 30, 2000, p. A18; "Looking for Ways to Save Gasoline," *Wall Street Journal,* July 12, 2001, p. A1; and "Want to Cut Gasoline Use? Raise Taxes," *Business Week,* May 27, 2002, p. 26.

Substitution and Income Effects for Inferior Goods

For a normal good, the substitution and the income effects of a price decline are both positive and reinforce each other in leading to a greater quantity purchased of the good. On the other hand, when the good is inferior, the income effect moves in the opposite direction from the substitution effect. That is, when the price of an inferior good falls, the substitution effect continues to operate as before to *increase* the quantity purchased of the good. This results from the convex shape of indifference curves. However, the increase in purchasing power or real income resulting from the price decline leads the consumer to purchase *less* of an inferior good. But, because the substitution effect is usually larger than the income effect, the quantity demanded of the inferior good increases when its price falls and the demand curve is still negatively sloped.

We can separate the substitution effect from the income effect of a price decline for an inferior good by returning to the candy bar (inferior good Z) example of the previous section. In the top panel of Figure 4.5, the consumer is originally at optimum at point V, where indifference curve U_1' is tangent to budget line JK' and the consumer purchases four candy bars (as in the top panel of Figure 4.2). If the price of candy bars declines from $P_Z = \$1$ to $P_Z = \$0.50$, the consumer moves to optimum point S, where indifference curve U_2' is tangent to budget line JN' and the consumer purchases $6Z$. The movement from point V to point S ($+2Z$) is the sum or net effect of the substitution and income effects.

To separate the substitution effect from the income effect, we now draw the imaginary budget line J^*N^*, which is lower than, but parallel to, budget line JN' and tangent to U_1' at point T. The movement along U_1' from the original point V to imaginary point T is the *substitution effect*. It results exclusively from the reduction in P_Z relative to P_Y and is independent of any increase in real income. Thus, the substitution effect, by itself, leads the individual to purchase four additional units of good Z per unit of time (from $4Z$ to $8Z$).

On the other hand, the movement from imaginary point T on U_1' to the new point S on U_2' can be taken as a measure of the *income effect*. It results exclusively from the increase in the level of satisfaction of the consumer with relative prices constant ($P_Z/P_Y = \$0.50/\$1 = 1/2$ for imaginary budget line J^*N^* and for new budget line JN'). The income effect, by itself, leads the consumer to purchase two *fewer* units of good Z per unit of time (from $8Z$ to $6Z$) because good Z is an inferior good.

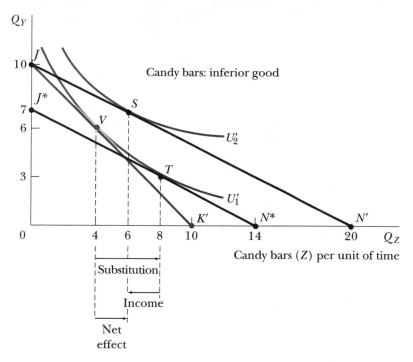

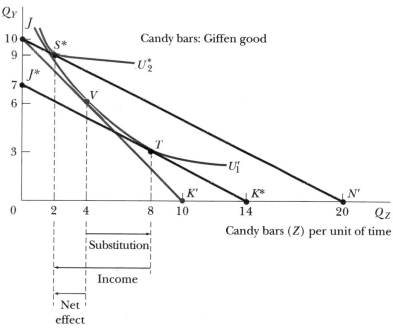

FIGURE 4.5   Income and Substitution Effects for Inferior Goods   Starting from optimum point *V* in the top panel, we can isolate the substitution effect by drawing J^*N^* parallel to *JN'* and tangent to U_1' at point *T*. The movement along U_1' from point *V* to point *T* is the substitution effect. The movement from point *T* on U_1' to point *S* on U_2' is the income effect. Since the income effect is negative, good *Z* is inferior. However, since the positive substitution effect exceeds the negative income effect, Q_Z increases when P_Z falls. In the bottom panel, the positive substitution effect ($VT = 4Z$) is smaller than the negative income effect ($TS^* = -6Z$), so that Q_Z declines by $2Z$ when P_Z falls. Good *Z* is then a Giffen good.

Thus, the total effect ($VS = 2Z$ given by the movement from point V on U_1' to point S on U_2') equals the positive substitution effect ($VT = 4Z$ given by the movement from point V to T on U_1') plus the negative income effect ($TS = -2Z$ given by the movement from point T on U_1' to point S on U_2'). However, since the positive substitution effect exceeds the negative income effect, the consumer purchases two additional units of good Z when its price declines. Thus, the demand curve for good Z is negatively sloped, even though good Z is an inferior good. That is, the consumer purchases $4Z$ at $P_Z = \$1$ and $6Z$ at $P_Z = \$0.50$.

On the other hand, if the positive substitution effect is smaller than the negative income effect when the price of an inferior good falls, then the demand curve for the inferior good is positively sloped. This very rarely, if ever, occurs in the real world, and is referred to as the **Giffen good,** after the nineteenth-century British economist, Robert Giffen, who supposedly first discussed it. Note that a Giffen good is an inferior good, but not all inferior goods are Giffen goods. If it existed, a Giffen good would lead to a positively sloped demand curve for the individual and would represent an exception to the law of negatively sloped demand.[10]

The bottom panel of Figure 4.5 is drawn on the assumption that good Z is now a Giffen good. In this panel, the consumer is originally at optimum point V and hypothetically moves to point T because of the substitution effect (as in the top panel). However, with *alternative* indifference curve U_2^* in the bottom panel (as opposed to U_2' in the top panel), the income effect is given by the movement from point T to point S^*. Point S^* is to the left of point T because good Z is an inferior good, so that an increase in real income leads to less of it being purchased. The total effect is now $VS^*(-2Z)$ and is equal to substitution effect VT ($4Z$) plus income effect $TS^*(-6Z)$. Because the positive substitution effect is smaller than the negative income effect, the quantity demanded of good Z *declines* when its price falls, and d_Z would be positively sloped over this range. That is, the individual would purchase $4Z$ at $P_Z = \$1$ but only $2Z$ at $P_Z = \$0.50$.

Although theoretically interesting, the Giffen paradox rarely, if ever, occurs in the real world. The reason is that inferior goods are usually narrowly defined goods for which suitable substitutes are available (so that the substitution effect usually exceeds the opposite income effect). Giffen thought that potatoes in nineteenth-century Ireland provided an example of the paradox, but subsequent research did not support his belief.[11]

The separation of the substitution effect from the income effect (and all of the analysis in this chapter) could easily be shown for a price increase rather than for a price decline. These alternatives are assigned as end-of-chapter problems.

4.4   SUBSTITUTION BETWEEN DOMESTIC AND FOREIGN GOODS

The substitution between domestic and foreign goods and services has reached an all-time high in the world today and is expected to continue to increase sharply in the future. This increase has been the result of (1) transportation costs having fallen to very low levels for

---

[10] If we kept real rather than nominal income constant in deriving the demand curve (i.e., if the demand curve showed or reflected only the substitution effect), there would be no Giffen exception to the law of negatively sloped demand.

[11] See S. Rosen, "Potatoes Paradoxes," *Journal of Political Economy,* December 1999.

most products, (2) increased knowledge of foreign products due to an international information revolution, (3) global advertising campaigns by multinational corporations, (4) the explosion of international travel, and (5) the rapid convergence of tastes internationally. For homogeneous products such as a particular grade of wheat or steel, and for many industrial products with precise specifications such as computer chips, fiber optics, and specialized machinery, substitutability between domestic and foreign products is almost perfect. Here, a small price difference can lead quickly to large shifts in sales from domestic to foreign sources and vice versa. Indeed, so fluid is the market for such products that governments often step in to protect these industries from foreign competition.

Even for differentiated products, such as automobiles and motorcycles, computers and copiers, watches and cameras, TV films and TV programs, soft drinks and cigarettes, soaps and detergents, commercial and military aircraft, and most other products that are similar but not identical, substitutability between domestic and foreign products is very high and continues to rise. Despite the quality problems of the past, U.S.-made automobiles today are highly substitutable for Japanese and European automobiles, and so are most other products. Indeed, intraindustry trade in such differentiated products now represents over 60% of total U.S. trade and an even larger percentage of the trade of most other industrial countries.[12] With many parts and components imported from many nations, and with production facilities and sales around the world often exceeding sales at home, even the distinction between domestic and foreign products is fast becoming obsolete.

EXAMPLE 4–5

What Is an "American" Car?

Strange as it may seem, the question of what is an American car may be difficult to answer. Should a Honda Accord produced in Ohio be considered American? What about a Chrysler minivan produced in Canada (especially now that Chrysler has been acquired by Germany's Mercedes-Benz)? Is a Kentucky Toyota or Mazda that uses nearly 50% of imported Japanese parts American? It is clearly becoming more and more difficult to define what is American, and opinions differ widely.

For some, any vehicle assembled in North America (the United States, Canada, and Mexico) should be considered American because these vehicles use U.S.-made parts. But the United Auto Workers union views cars built in Canada and Mexico as taking away U.S. jobs. Some regard automobiles produced by Japanese-owned plants in the United States as American because they provide jobs for Americans. Others regard production by these Japanese "transplants" as foreign, because the jobs they create were taken from the U.S. automakers, because they use nearly 40% of imported Japanese parts, and because they remit profits to Japan. What if Japanese transplants increased their use of American parts to 75% or 90%? Is the Ford Probe, built for Ford by Mazda in Mazda's Flat Rock Michigan plant, American?

---

[12] D. Salvatore, *International Economics,* 8th ed. (New York: John Wiley & Sons, 2003), Section 6.4.

It is difficult to decide exactly what is an American car—even after the American Automobile Labeling Act of 1992, which requires all automobiles sold in the United States to indicate what percentage of the car's parts are domestic or foreign. One could even ask if this question is relevant at all in a world growing more and more interdependent and globalized. In fact, rapid consolidation in the industry has left only five truly global automakers—General Motors, Ford, Toyota, DaimlerChrysler, and Volkswagen—and each has developed or is developing a truly world car (essentially the same basic type of automobile sold everywhere) and using parts from all over the world.

Sources: "Honda's Nationality Proves Troublesome for Free-Trade Pact," *The New York Times,* October 9, 1992, p. 1; "Want a U.S. Car? Read the Label," *The New York Times,* September 18, 1994, Section 3, p. 6; "Made in America? Not Exactly: Transplants Use Japanese Car Parts," *Wall Street Journal,* September 1, 1995, p. A3B; "Ford Hopes Its New Focus Will Be a Global Bestseller," *Wall Street Journal,* October 8, 1998, p. B10; "And Then There Were Five," *US News & World Report,* March 4, 2000, p. 46.

4.5   SOME APPLICATIONS OF INDIFFERENCE CURVE ANALYSIS

We now can apply the tools developed in this chapter to analyze the economics of the food stamp program, consumer surplus, and exchange. These applications deal only with the demand for goods and services, but the tools developed in this chapter have many other applications (examined in other parts of the text). For example, the distinction between the substitution and income effects is useful in analyzing the effect of overtime pay on the number of hours worked and on leisure time. Because this topic deals with the supply of labor, however, it is appropriately postponed until Chapter 14, which deals with input price and employment. Indifference curve analysis is also useful in analyzing the choice between borrowing or lending from present income (examined in Chapter 16), in general equilibrium and welfare economics (examined in Chapter 17), and in the analysis of time as an economic good (discussed more extensively in Chapter 19).

Is a Cash Subsidy Better Than Food Stamps?

Under the federal **food stamp program,** low-income families receive free food stamps, which they can use only to purchase food. At its peak in 1988, more than 4.8 million eligible low-income families received free food stamps at a cost of $12.4 billion to the federal government. The important question is whether it would have been better (i.e., provided more satisfaction) to have given an equal amount of subsidy in cash to these families.

We can examine this question using Figure 4.6. Suppose that, initially, a typical poor family has a weekly income of $100. If the poor family spent its entire weekly income on nonfood items, it could purchase $100 worth of nonfood items per week (point *A* on the vertical axis). On the other hand, if the poor family spent the entire $100 on food, it could purchase 100 units of food per week if the unit price of food were $1 (point *C* on the horizontal axis). The initial budget line of the family would be *AC.*

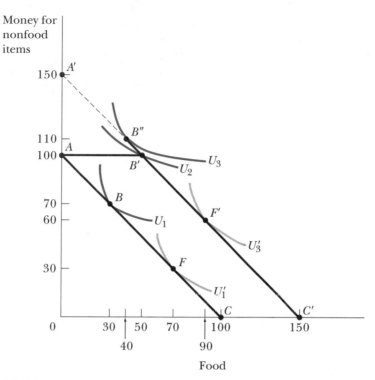

FIGURE 4.6   Food Stamps versus Cash Aid   A poor family's budget line, *AC*, becomes *AB'C'* with $50 worth of free food stamps per week, and *A'C'* with a $50 cash subsidy instead. The family maximizes utility at point *B* on U_1 without any aid, at point *B'* on U_2 with food stamps, and at point *B''* on U_3 with the cash subsidy. However, another family with the same original income and budget line *AC* but with a stronger preference for food may go instead from point *F* on U_1' to point *F'* on U_3' either with the cash subsidy or with food stamps.

With free food stamps that allow the family to purchase $50 worth of food per week, the budget line of the family becomes *AB'C'*, where *AB'* = *CC'* = 50. Combinations on dashed segment *A'B'* are not available with the food stamp program because the family would have to spend more than its $100 money income on nonfood items and less than the $50 of food stamps on food (and this is not possible if it cannot sell its food stamps). Were the government to provide $50 in cash rather than in food stamps, the budget line would then be *A'C'*. Thus, we have three alternative budget lines for the family: budget line *AC* without any aid, budget line *AB'C'* with $50 in food stamps, and budget line *A'C'* with $50 cash aid instead.

If the family's indifference curves are U_1, U_2, and U_3, the family maximizes utility at point *B* where U_1 is tangent to *AC* before receiving any aid, at point *B'* on U_2 with food stamps, and at point *B''* (preferred to *B'*) on U_3 with the cash subsidy. In this case, the cash subsidy allows the family to reach a higher indifference curve than do food stamps.[13] However, *another family* with the same initial income of $100 (and budget line *AC*) but stronger preference for food and facing indifference curves U_1' and U_3' will move instead from point *F* on U_1' to point *F'* on U_3', either with the cash subsidy or with food stamps. Thus, depending on the family's tastes, *a cash subsidy will not be worse than food stamps and may be better* (i.e., provide more satisfaction). Why then does the federal government continue to use food stamps? One reason is to improve nutrition.[14]

Consumer Surplus Measures Unpaid Benefits

Consumer surplus is the difference between what a consumer is willing to pay for a good and what he or she actually pays. It results because the consumer pays for *each* unit of the good only as much as he or she is willing to pay for the *last* unit of the good (which gives less utility than earlier units). We can see how consumer surplus arises and how it can be measured with the aid of Figure 4.7.

The figure shows that $5 is the maximum amount that the consumer is willing to pay for the first unit of good *X* (say, hamburgers) rather than go without it. Thus, the area of the first rectangle (with height of $5 and width of 1) measures the marginal value or benefit that the consumer gets from the first hamburger. After all, by being willing to purchase the first hamburger for $5, the consumer indicates that he or she prefers paying $5 for the first hamburger rather than keeping the $5 in cash or spending the $5 on other goods. The second unit of good *X* (hamburger) gives the consumer less utility than the first, and the consumer would be willing to pay $4 for it rather than go without it. Thus, $4 (the area of the second rectangle) can be taken as a measure of the marginal value or benefit of the second hamburger to the consumer. The third hamburger gives the consumer less utility than either the first or the second and so the consumer is willing to pay only $3 for it. Thus, the marginal value or benefit of the third hamburger is $3 and is given by the area of the third rectangle. For the fourth hamburger, the consumer would be willing to pay $2 (the area of the fourth rectangle), and this is a measure of the marginal value or benefit of the fourth hamburger, and so on.

To summarize, the consumer would be willing to pay $5 for the first hamburger, $4 for the second, $3 for the third, and $2 for the fourth, for a total of $14 for all four hamburgers. Thus, $14 is the total benefit that the consumer receives from purchasing four hamburgers. However, if the market price is $2 per hamburger, the consumer can purchase all four hamburgers at a total cost of (i.e., by actually spending) only $8. Because the consumer would be willing to pay $14 for the first four hamburgers rather than go entirely without them, but actually pays only $8, he or she enjoys a net benefit or *consumer surplus* equal to the difference ($6).

To put it another way, the consumer is willing to pay $5 for the first hamburger, but since he or she can purchase it for only $2, he or she receives a surplus of $3 for the first hamburger. Since the consumer is willing to pay $4 for the second hamburger but pays only $2, there is a surplus of $2 on the second hamburger. For the third hamburger, the consumer

---

[13] Both cost the government $50.

[14] Note that the indifference curves of the two *different* families shown in Figure 4.6 would cross if extended. It is only the individual indifference curves of each family that cannot cross.

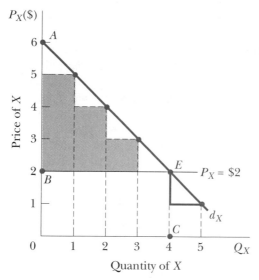

FIGURE 4.7   Consumer Surplus   The difference between what the consumer is willing to pay for $4X$ ($5 + $4 + $3 + $2 = $14) and what he or she actually pays ($8) is the consumer surplus (the shaded area that equals $6). If good X could be purchased in infinitesimally small units, the consumer surplus would equal the area under d_X and above $P_X = $2 (area $AEB = $8).

is willing to pay $3, but since he or she pays only $2, the surplus is $1. For the fourth hamburger, the consumer is willing to pay $2, and since he or she has to pay $2 for it, there is no surplus on the fourth hamburger. The consumer would not purchase the fifth hamburger because he or she is not willing to pay the $2 market price for it.

By adding the consumer surplus of $3 on the first hamburger, $2 on the second, $1 on the third, and $0 on the fourth, we get the consumer surplus of $6 obtained earlier. This is given by the sum of the shaded areas in the figure. The same result would have been obtained if the consumer had been asked for the maximum amount of money that he or she would have been willing to pay for four hamburgers rather than do entirely without them—*all or nothing.*

If hamburgers could have been purchased in smaller and smaller fractions of a whole hamburger, then the consumer surplus would have been given by the entire area under demand curve d_X above the market price of $2. That is, the consumer surplus would have been the area of triangle AEB, which is $(1/2)(4)(4) = $8. This exceeds the consumer surplus of $6 that we found by adding only the shaded areas in the figure. Specifically, the consumer would have been willing to pay $16 (the area of $OAEC$) for four hamburgers. Note that $OAEC$ is composed of triangle AEB plus rectangle $OBEC$. Since the consumer only pays $8 ($OBEC$), the consumer surplus is $8 ($AEB$). If P_X fell to $1, the consumer would purchase five hamburgers and the consumer's surplus would be $12.50 (the area under d_X and above

$P_X = \$1$ in the figure) if hamburgers could be purchased by infinitely small fractions of a whole hamburger.[15]

The concept of consumer surplus was first used by Jules Dupuit in 1844 and was subsequently refined and popularized by Alfred Marshall. The concept helped resolve the so-called **water-diamond paradox,** which plagued classical economists until 1870. Why is water, which is essential for life, so cheap, while diamonds, which are not essential, so expensive? The explanation is that because water is so plentiful (relatively cheap) and we use so much of it, the utility of the last unit is very little (washing the car), and we pay as little for all units of water as we are willing to pay for the last *nonessential* unit of it. On the other hand, diamonds are scarce in relation to demand, and because we use very little of them, the utility and price of the *last unit* are very great. The *total* utility and the consumer surplus from all the water used are far greater than the total utility and the consumer surplus from all the diamonds purchased. However, demand depends on marginal utility, not on total utility. In a desert, the first glass of water would be worth much more than any glassful of diamonds.

The above analysis referred to an individual's demand curve, but a similar analysis would also apply to a market demand curve. In subsequent chapters we will use the concept of consumer surplus to measure the benefits and costs of excise taxes, import tariffs, pollution control, government projects, and other microeconomic policies, as well as to measure the benefits and costs of alternative market structures.

Benefits from Exchange

Suppose that two individuals, A and B, have a given amount of good X and good Y and decide to trade some of these goods with each other. If the exchange is voluntary, the strong presumption is that both individuals gain from the exchange (otherwise, the individual who loses would simply refuse to trade). We can examine the process of voluntary exchange by indifference curve analysis.

Suppose that individual A's tastes and preferences for good X and good Y are shown by indifference curves U_1, U_2, and U_3 in the top left panel of Figure 4.8. Individual B's tastes and preferences are given by indifference curves U_1', U_2', and U_3' (with origin $0'$) in the top right panel. Initially, individual A has an allocation of $3X$ and $6Y$ (point C in the top left panel) and individual B has $7X$ and $2Y$ (point C' in the top right panel).

We now rotate individual B's indifference diagram by 180 degrees (so that origin $0'$ appears in the top right corner) and superimpose it on individual A's indifference diagram in such a way that the axes of the two diagrams form the so-called **Edgeworth box diagram,** shown in the bottom panel of Figure 4.8. The length of the box ($10X$) measures the combined amount of X initially owned by individual A ($3X$) and individual B ($7X$). The height of the box ($8Y$) measures the amount of Y initially owned by individual A ($6Y$) and individual B ($2Y$). A's indifference curves are convex to origin 0 (as usual), while B's indifference curves are convex to origin $0'$.

---

[15] Measuring consumer surplus by the area under the demand curve and above the prevailing market price is only an approximation (it is based on the assumption that a consumer's indifference curves are parallel), but for most purposes it is sufficiently accurate to be a useful tool of analysis. See, R. D. Willig, "Consumer Surplus without Apology," *American Economic Review,* September 1976. See, however, K. S. Lyon and Ming Yan, "Compensating Variation Consumer's Surplus Via Successive Approximations," *Applied Economics,* June 1995, pp. 547–554.

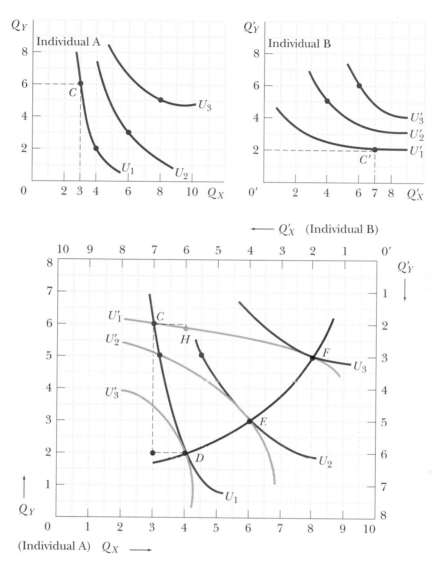

FIGURE 4.8   Edgeworth Box Diagram   The top left panel shows individual A's indifference curves, and the top right panel shows B's indifference curves. The box in the bottom panel is obtained by rotating B's indifference map diagram 180 degrees and superimposing it on A's diagram in such a way that the dimensions of the box equal the initial combined amounts of goods X and Y owned by A and B. Any point in the box refers to a particular distribution of X and Y between A and B. At point C, MRS_{XY} for the two individuals differs (U_1 and U_1' cross) and there is a basis for mutually beneficial exchange until a point between D and F on curve DEF is reached (where MRS_{XY} for A and B are equal).

Any point inside the box indicates how the total amount of X and Y may be distributed between the two individuals. For example, the initial distribution of X and Y given by point C indicates that individual A has $3X$ and $6Y$ (viewed from origin 0) and individual B has the remainder of $7X$ and $2Y$ (when viewed from origin $0'$) for a total of $10X$ and $8Y$

(the dimensions of the box). Individual A is on indifference curve U_1 and individual B is on indifference curve U_1'.

Since at point C (where U_1 and U_1' intersect) the marginal rate of substitution of good X for good Y (MRS_{XY}) for individual A exceeds MRS_{XY} for individual B, there is a basis for mutually beneficial exchange between the two individuals. Starting at point C, individual A would be willing to give up $4Y$ to get one additional unit of X (and move to point D on U_1). On the other hand, individual B would be willing to give up $1X$ for about 0.2 additional units of Y (and move to point H on U_1'). Because A is willing to give up more of Y than necessary to induce B to give up $1X$, there is a basis for trade in which individual A gives up some of Y in exchange for some of X from individual B.

Whenever the MRS_{XY} for the two individuals differs at the initial distribution of X and Y, either or both may gain from exchange. For example, starting from point C, if individual A exchanges $4Y$ for $1X$ with individual B, A would move from point C to point D along indifference curve U_1, while B would move from point C on U_1' to point D on U_3'. By moving from indifference curve U_1' to indifference curve U_3', individual B receives all of the gains from the exchange while individual A gains or loses nothing (since A remains on U_1). At point D, U_1 and U_3' are tangent, and so their slopes (MRS_{XY}) are equal. Thus, there is no basis for further exchange (at point D, the amount of Y that A is willing to give up for $1X$ is exactly equal to what B requires to give up $1X$). Any further exchange would make either one or both individuals worse off than they are at point D.

Alternatively, if individual A exchanged $1Y$ for $5X$ with individual B, individual A would move from point C on U_1 to point F on U_3, while individual B would move from point C to point F along U_1'. In this case, A would reap all the benefits from exchange while B would neither gain nor lose. At point F, MRS_{XY} for A equals MRS_{XY} for B and there is no further basis for exchange. Finally, starting again from point C on U_1 and U_1', if A exchanges $3Y$ for $3X$ with B and gets to point E, both individuals gain from the exchange since point E is on U_2 and U_2'.

Starting from any point within $CDEF$ but not on curve DEF, both individuals can gain from exchange by moving to a point on curve DEF between points D and F. The closer individual A gets to point F (i.e., the more shrewd A is as a bargainer), the greater is the proportion of the total gain from the exchange accruing to A and the less is left for B. The Edgeworth box is named after the English economist F. Y. Edgeworth, who in 1881 first outlined its construction. (We will return to exchange in greater detail in Chapter 17.)

AT THE FRONTIER
The Characteristics Approach to Consumer Theory

The **characteristics approach to consumer theory,** pioneered by Kelvin Lancaster, postulates that consumers demand a good because of the characteristics, properties, and attributes of the good, and it is these characteristics that give rise to utility.[16] For example, a consumer does not demand beef, as such, but rather the characteristics of protein and calories, which are the direct source of utility. But protein and calories are also provided (though in different proportions) by pork and chicken. Thus, a good usually possesses more than one characteristic, and any given characteristic is present in more than one good.

The characteristics approach to consumer theory can be shown graphically. In the top panel of Figure 4.9, the horizontal axis measures the characteristic of protein and the vertical axis measures calories. Suppose that the consumer's income is $10 and that $10 worth of pork provides the combination of protein and calories given by point A, while $10 worth of beef gives the combination at point B.[17] The budget line is then AB. Area $0AB$ is called the *feasible region* and budget line AB is the *efficiency frontier*. That is, the consumer can purchase any combination of protein and calories in area $A0B$, but he or she will maximize utility or satisfaction by choosing combinations on line AB.

If U_1 is a consumer's indifference curve in characteristics space (i.e., with characteristics protein and calories measured along the axes), the consumer maximizes utility at point C, where indifference curve U_1 is tangent to budget line AB. The consumer reaches point C by obtaining $0F$ characteristics from spending $5 on beef and FC characteristics from spending the remaining $5 on pork. $0F = 1/2 \, 0B$ and $0G = 1/2 \, 0A$. Note that FC equals $0G$, both in length and direction.[18]

In the bottom panel, a new good is introduced, chicken, which has half as many calories per unit of protein as beef. If $10 worth of chicken provides the combination of protein and calories given by point H, the budget line or efficiency frontier becomes AH. The consumer now maximizes utility at point J, where indifference curve U_2 is tangent to budget line AH. The consumer reaches point J by obtaining $0K$ characteristics from spending $5 on chicken and KJ (equals $0G$) characteristics from spending the remaining $5 on pork. No beef is now purchased.

The reduction in the price of a good can be shown by a proportionate outward movement along the characteristics ray of the good, while an increase in income can be shown by a proportionate outward shift of the entire budget line. These shifts will allow the consumer to reach a higher indifference curve as in traditional consumer theory.

The characteristics approach to consumer theory has several important advantages over traditional demand theory. First, substitution among goods can be easily explained in terms of some common characteristics of the goods. For example, according to this theory coffee and tea are substitutes because they both have the characteristic of being stimulants.

Continued. . .

---

[16] Kelvin Lancaster, *Consumer Demand: A New Approach* (New York: Columbia University Press, 1971).
[17] Note that the characteristics ray for pork has a slope four times larger than the characteristics ray for beef. Thus, pork provides four times as many calories per unit of protein as beef.
[18] FC and $0G$ are called vectors. Thus, the above is an example of vector analysis, whereby vector $0C$ (not shown in the top panel of Figure 4.9) is equal to the sum of vectors $0F$ and $0G$.

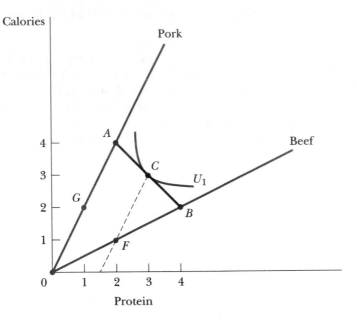

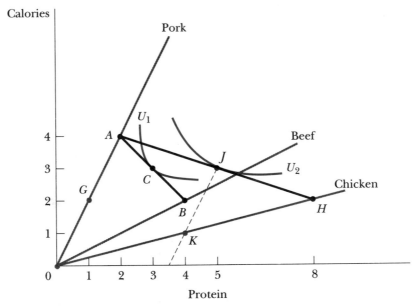

FIGURE 4.9   The Characteristics Approach to Consumer Demand Theory
In the top panel, $10 worth of pork gives the combination of protein and calories indicated by point *A* and $10 worth of beef gives the combination at point *B*. Thus, *AB* is the budget line. The consumer maximizes utility at point *C*, where U_1 is tangent to *AB*, by spending $5 on pork and $5 on beef, and receiving *OF* characteristics from beef and *FC* (equals *OG*) from pork. In the bottom panel, $10 worth of chicken gives point *H*, so that the budget line is *AH*. The consumer maximizes utility at point *J* on U_2 by spending $5 on pork and $5 on chicken, and obtaining *OK* characteristics from chicken and *KJ* (equals *OG*) characteristics from pork, with no beef purchased.

Second, the introduction of a new good can easily be taken care of by drawing a new ray from the origin reflecting the combination of the two characteristics of the new good. This was shown by the introduction of chicken in the bottom panel of Figure 4.9. However, the new good will only be purchased if its price is sufficiently low (e.g., chicken in the bottom panel of Figure 4.9). Had $10 worth of chicken provided only the combination of protein and calories given by point K on the characteristics ray for chicken, the budget line would become ABK and the consumer would maximize utility by remaining at point C and purchasing no chicken.

Third, a quality change can be shown by rotating the characteristics ray for the good. For example, the introduction of a new breed of leaner hogs resulting in pork with less calories per unit of protein can be shown by a clockwise rotation of the characteristics ray for pork. Finally, by comparing the price of two goods that are identical except for a particular characteristic, this approach permits the estimation of the implicit or *hedonic* price of the characteristic. For example, by comparing the price of houses that are otherwise identical except for some other characteristic, such as lower noise pollution, proximity to good schools, parks, and a good transportation network, we can estimate the implicit or hedonic price of each of these characteristics. Thus, if the price of a house that is near a park is $10,000 more than the price of another identical house that is not near a park, the characteristic of being closer to a park is worth $10,000.

One disadvantage of the theory is that some characteristics, such as taste and style, are subjective and cannot be measured explicitly. The problem is even more serious in dealing with the characteristics of services. Nevertheless, the hedonic approach is very useful because it allows at least an *implicit* measure of the various characteristics of each good.

SUMMARY

1. The income–consumption curve joins consumer optimum points resulting when only the consumer's income is varied. The Engel curve is derived from the income–consumption curve and shows the amount of a good that the consumer would purchase per unit of time at various income levels. A normal good is one of which the consumer purchases more with an increase in income. An inferior good is one of which the consumer purchases less with an increase in income. The income–consumption curve and the Engel curve are positively sloped for normal goods and negatively sloped for inferior goods.

2. The price–consumption curve for a good joins consumer optimum points resulting when only the price of the good varies. This curve shows the amount of the good that the consumer would purchase per unit of time at various prices of the good while holding everything else constant. The individual consumer's demand curve for a good is negatively sloped, reflecting the law of demand.

3. When the price of a good falls, consumers substitute this good for other goods and their real income rises. If the good is normal, the income effect reinforces the substitution effect in increasing the quantity purchased of the good. If the good is inferior, the substitution effect tends to increase while the income effect tends to reduce the quantity demanded of the good. Because the former usually exceeds the latter, the quantity demanded of the good increases

and the demand curve is negatively sloped. Only if the income effect overwhelms the opposite substitution effect for an inferior good will the quantity demanded of the good decrease when its price falls, and the demand curve will slope upward. This is called a Giffen good, but it has never really been observed in the real world.

4. With the substitutability between domestic and foreign goods and services having reached an all-time high in the world today, and with the expectation that it will rise even more in the future, the need to introduce an important international dimension in the study of microeconomics becomes even clearer.

5. A cash subsidy leads to an equal or greater increase in utility than a subsidy in kind (such as the food stamp program) that costs the same. The consumer surplus is given by the difference between what the consumer is willing to pay for a good and what the consumer actually pays for it. Its value can be approximated by the area under the demand curve and above the market price of the good. An Edgeworth box diagram is constructed by rotating an individual's indifference map diagram by 180 degrees and superimposing it on another's, so that the dimensions of the box equal the combined initial distribution of the two goods between the two individuals. The Edgeworth box diagram can be used to analyze voluntary exchange. The characteristics approach to consumer theory can be used to measure the implicit or hedonic price of a particular characteristic of a good or service.

KEY TERMS

Income–consumption curve
Engel curve
Normal good
Inferior good
Price-consumption curve
Individual's demand curve
Substitution effect

Relative price
Income effect
Giffen good
Food stamp program
Consumer surplus
Water-diamond paradox
Edgeworth box diagram

Characteristics approach to
   consumer theory
Income or expenditure
   index (E)
Laspeyres price index (L)
Paasche price index (P)

REVIEW QUESTIONS

1. A consumer buys an Oldsmobile for $20,000 instead of a Toyota for $22,000. Does this mean that the consumer prefers the Oldsmobile to a Toyota?

2. How would indifference curves between money and automobiles differ between two individuals with the same money income but with one having a stronger preference for automobiles than the other?

3. Why would the use of gasoline decline if its price rose as a result of a gasoline tax but the effect of the price rise was compensated by a tax rebate?

4. The income effect of a 20% increase in housing rents is larger than the effect of a 20% increase in the price of salt. True or false? Explain.

5. A demand curve showing only the substitution effect can never be positively sloped, not even theoretically. True or false? Explain.

6. Is a demand curve showing both the substitution and income effects flatter or steeper than the demand curve showing only the substitution effect? Explain.

7. Will a consumer purchase more or less of an inferior good when its price declines? Explain.

8. Can all goods purchased by a consumer be inferior?

9. In 2003, the Men's Hair Company increased the price of its shampoo and subsequently sold more shampoo than in 2002. Is the demand curve for this company's shampoo positively sloped? Explain.

10. Why is the gift of any good likely to provide less satisfaction to the recipient than an equal cash gift?

11. When would the gift of a good provide the recipient as much satisfaction as an equal cash gift?

12. How can a black market in food stamps be explained?

13. What are the advantages and disadvantages of the characteristics approach to consumer theory?

PROBLEMS

1. a. Derive the income-consumption curve and Engel curve from the indifference curves of Problem 2 in Chapter 3 and the budget lines from Problem 6(a) in Chapter 3. Is good X a normal or an inferior good? Why?

   b. Derive the Engel curve for good Y. Is good Y a normal or an inferior good? Why?

2. a. For the budget lines of Problem 6(a) in Chapter 3, draw indifference curves that show that good X is inferior; derive the income-consumption curve and the Engel curve for good X.

   b. Draw the Engel curve for good Y. Must good Y be normal?

*3. a. Derive the price-consumption curve and demand curve for good X from the indifference curves of Problem 2 in Chapter 3 and the budget lines from Problem 6(b) in Chapter 3 when the price of X falls from $P_X = \$2$ to $P_X = \$1$ and then to $P_X = \$0.50$.

   b. Use the figure for your answer to 3(a) to explain how you would derive the price-consumption curve and demand curve for good X when the price of X rises from $P_X = \$0.50$ to $P_X = \$1$ and then to $P_X = \$2$.

4. Using the indifference curves of Problem 2 in Chapter 3 and the budget lines of problem 6(b) in Chapter 3, separate the substitution effect from the income effect when the price of X falls from $P_X = \$2$ to $P_X = \$1$ and then from $P_X = \$1$ to $P_X = \$0.50$.

*5. Separate the substitution effect from the income effect for an *increase* in the price of an inferior good.

6. Separate the substitution effect from the income effect for an increase in price of a Giffen good.

*7. It is sometimes asserted that rice in very poor Asian countries might be an inferior good. Even though there is no evidence that this is indeed the case, explain the reasoning behind this assertion.

8. The average number of children per family has declined in the face of rapidly rising family incomes, so children must be an inferior good. True or false? Explain.

*9. Use indifference curve analysis to show that a poor family can be made to reach a given higher indifference curve with a smaller cash subsidy than with a subsidy in kind (such as, for example, by the government paying half of the market price of food for the family). Why might the government still prefer a subsidy in kind?

10. With reference to Figure 4.7 in the text, indicate the size of the consumer surplus when $P_X = \$3$ if

    a. good X can only be purchased in whole units.

    b. good X can be purchased in infinitesimally small fractional units.

11. With reference to Figure 4.8 in the text, indicate how exchange could take place starting from the initial distribution of good X and good Y between individual B given by the intersection of U_1 and U_2'.

12. Starting with the top panel of Figure 4.9, show

    a. a 50% reduction in the price of pork and its effect on consumer utility maximization.

    b. a 50% increase in the consumer's income and its effect on consumer utility maximization.

---

* = Answer provided at end of book.

APPENDIX   INDEX NUMBERS AND CHANGES IN CONSUMER WELFARE

In this appendix, we discuss index numbers and their use in measuring changes in standards of living or welfare, especially during inflationary periods. For example, workers and their unions are keen to know if money wages are keeping up with rising prices. Cost-of-living indices are often used for inflation adjustment in wage contracts, for pensions and welfare payments and, since 1984, even for tax payments. In this appendix, we will define three indices and, by comparing the values of these indices in two different time periods, determine if the standard of living has increased, decreased, or remained unchanged. For simplicity, we will assume that the consumer spends all income on only two commodities, X and Y.

Expenditure, Laspeyres, and Paasche Indices

To measure changes in the standard of living or welfare from one time period to another, we begin by defining three indices: the income or expenditure index, the Laspeyres price index, and the Paasche price index.

The **income or expenditure index** (E) is the ratio of period 1 to base period money income or expenditures. That is,

$$E = \frac{x_1 P_{x1} + y_1 P_{y1}}{x_0 P_{x0} + y_0 P_{y0}}$$ [4.1]

where x and y refer to the quantities of commodities X and Y purchased, respectively; P refers to price, and the subscripts "1" and "0" refer to period 1 and the base period, respectively.

Thus, the income and expenditure index is the sum of the product of period 1 quantities and their respective period 1 prices divided by the sum of the product of base period quantities and their respective base period prices. In short, E measures the ratio of the consumer's period 1 expenditures or income to the base period expenditures or income. If E is greater than 1, the individual's *money* income or expenditures have increased from the base period to period 1. However, since prices usually also rise, we cannot determine simply from the value of E whether the individual's *real* income or standard of living has also increased. To do that, we need to define the Laspeyres and the Paasche price indices and compare their values with that of the income or expenditure index.

The **Laspeyres price index** (L) is the ratio of the cost of *base period quantities* at period 1 prices relative to base period prices. That is,

$$L = \frac{x_0 P_{x1} + y_0 P_{y1}}{x_0 P_{x0} + y_0 P_{y0}}$$ [4.2]

In the Laspeyres price index, we use the base period quantities as the weights and measure the cost of purchasing these base period quantities at period 1 prices relative to base period prices.

The **Paasche price index** (P) is the ratio of the cost of *period 1 quantities* at period 1 prices relative to base period prices. That is,

$$P = \frac{x_1 P_{x1} + y_1 P_{y1}}{x_1 P_{x0} + y_1 P_{y0}}$$ [4.3]

TABLE 4.2 Hypothetical Quantity Price Data in a Base Period and in Period 1				
Period	x	Px	y	Py
0 (base)	4	$1	3	$2
1	3	2	6	1

In the Paasche price index, we use period 1 quantities as the weights and measure the cost of purchasing period 1 quantities at period 1 prices relative to base period prices. Thus, the difference between the Laspeyres and the Paasche price indices is that the former uses the base period quantities as the weights while the latter uses the period 1 quantities.

For example, using the hypothetical data in Table 4.2, we can calculate

$$E = \frac{x_1 P_{x1} + y_1 P_{y1}}{x_0 P_{x0} + y_0 P_{y0}} = \frac{(3)(\$2) + (6)(\$1)}{(4)(\$1) + (3)(\$2)} = \frac{\$12}{\$10} = 1.2 \text{ or } 120\%$$

$$L = \frac{x_0 P_{x1} + y_0 P_{y1}}{x_0 P_{x0} + y_0 P_{y0}} = \frac{(4)(\$2) + (3)(\$1)}{\$10} = \frac{\$11}{\$10} = 1.1 \text{ or } 110\%$$

$$P = \frac{x_1 P_{x1} + y_1 P_{y1}}{x_1 P_{x0} + y_1 P_{y0}} = \frac{\$12}{(3)(\$1) + (6)(\$2)} = \frac{\$12}{\$15} = 0.8 \text{ or } 80\%$$

How Are Changes in Consumer Welfare Measured?

Because some quantities and prices rise over time and others fall, it is often impossible to determine by simple inspection of the quantity-price data whether an individual's standard of living or welfare has increased, decreased, or remained unchanged from one time period to the next. To measure changes in the standard of living, we compare the value of the income or expenditure index to the values of the Laspeyres and the Paasche price indices.

An individual's standard of living is higher in period 1 than in the base period if E is greater than L. That is, the individual is better off in period 1 than in the base period if the increase in his or her money income (E) exceeds the increase in the cost of living using base-period quantities as weights (L). For example, since we calculated from Table 4.2 that $E = 1.2$ or 120% while $L = 1.1$ or 110%, the individual's standard of living increased from the base period to period 1 because his or her income has risen more than his or her costs or prices.

On the other hand, *the individual's standard of living is higher in the base period than in period 1 if E is smaller than P.* That is, the individual is better off in the base period than in period 1 if the increase in his or her money income (E) is smaller than the increase in the cost of living using period 1 quantities as the weights (P). If E is not smaller than P, the individual's standard of living is not higher in the base period. For example, since $E = 120\%$ and $P = 80\%$ from Table 4.2, the individual is not better off in the base period than in period 1. Thus, with E greater than L and E not smaller than P, the individual of the above numerical example is definitely better off in period 1 than in the base period.

Figure 4.10 presents a graphic interpretation of the numerical example of Table 4.2. In the figure, $I_0 I_0$ is the individual's budget line in the base period. That is, with $X = 4$, $P_X = \$1$, $Y = 3$, and $P_y = \$2$, the individual's total income (I) and expenditure in the base period is $10 (obtained from $4X$ times $1 plus $3Y$ times $2). If the individual had spent the entire base-period income of $10 on commodity X, he or she could have purchased $10X$. If instead the individual had spent his or her entire base-period income of $10 on commodity Y, he or she could have purchased $5Y$. This defines $I_0 I_0$ as the individual's budget line in the base period. The individual's purchase of $4X$ and $3Y$ in the base period (see the first row of Table 4.2) is indicated by point B_0 on budget line $I_0 I_0$. We can similarly determine from the second row of Table 4.2 that in period 1 the individual's income is $12 (obtained from $3X$ times $2 plus $6Y$ times $1), so that his or her budget line is $I_1 I_1$. The individual's purchase of $3X$ and $6Y$ in period 1 is indicated by point B_1 on budget line $I_1 I_1$.

From Figure 4.10 we can conclude that since point B_0 is below budget line $I_1 I_1$, the individual must be better off in period 1 than in the base period. That is, since B_0 was available to the individual in period 1 but was not chosen, the individual must be better off in period 1. Specifically, in period 1 the individual could have purchased the base period bundle (B_0) at period 1 prices by spending only $11 ($4X$ times $2 plus $3Y$ times $1) of his or her

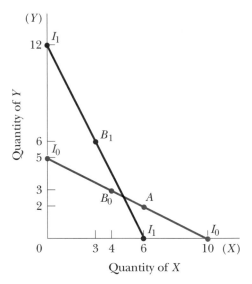

FIGURE 4.10   Changes in Consumer Welfare   An individual is better off at B_1 in period 1 than at B_0 in the base period because B_0 was available in period 1 (i.e., B_0 is below period 1 budget line $I_1 I_1$) but was not chosen. Had the individual been at point A in the base period, we would need the individual's indifference curves to determine if B_1 is superior, inferior, or equal to A.

period 1 income of $12. On the other hand, in the base period the individual could not have purchased period 1 quantities at base period prices since that would have required an expenditure of $15 (3X times $1 plus 6Y times $2), which would have exceeded his or her base period income of $10. Thus, the individual must be better off with B_1 in period 1 than with B_0 in the base period.

Had the individual been at a point such as A rather than at point B_0 on budget line I_0I_0 in the base period (see Figure 4.10), we could no longer determine without the individual's indifference curves whether the individual was better off in period 1, in the base period, or was equally well off in period 1 as in the base period. This would depend on whether point B_1 was on a higher, lower, or the same indifference curve as point A, respectively. You should be able to calculate from comparing point A on I_0I_0 in the base period to point B_1 on I_1I_1 in period 1 that $E = 120\%$, $L = 140\%$, and $P = 80\%$. Since E is not larger than L (so that the individual is not necessarily better off in period 1) but E is not smaller than P (so that the individual is not necessarily better off in the base period), we have conflicting results and we cannot tell whether the standard of living is higher, lower, or equal in period 1 as compared with the base period. This confirms the inconclusive results of the graphic analysis (in the absence of the individual's indifference curves) in Figure 4.10.

Because the Laspeyres price index (L) uses base period quantities as the weights, L becomes available sooner than the Paasche price index (P).[19] The most common of the price indices is the Consumer Price Index (CPI), which has been published monthly by the Bureau of Labor Statistics for more than sixty years. The CPI is a Laspeyres index for a "typical" urban family of four. It is the weighted average of the price of 400 goods and services purchased by consumers in the United States. The weights of the various commodities in the basket are periodically changed to reflect variations in consumption patterns. Other important (Laspeyres) price indices are the wholesale price index (WPI) and the GNP deflator. The latter is used to calculate GNP in real terms.

EXAMPLE 4–6
The Consumer Price Index, Inflation, and Changes in the Standard of Living

One application of index numbers is in measuring changes in real earnings and standards of living over time. According to the Bureau of Labor Statistics, total private non-agricultural weekly money earnings in the United States was $345.35 in 1990 and $472.73 in 2000. The CPI rose from 100 in 1990 to 131.8 in 2000. Dividing the weekly money earnings by the corresponding CPI, we find that weekly *real* earnings increased only slightly from $345.35 in 1990 to $358.67 in 2000. Since the CPI is known to have an upward bias, however, the true increase in real earnings may in fact have been somewhat greater.

---

[19] The Laspeyres price index also uses period 1 prices. However, period 1 prices become available much sooner than period 1 quantities.

According to the CPI Commission (set up by the Senate Finance Committee in 1995 and reporting in 1996), the consumer price index or CPI overstates the rate of inflation by about 1.1 percentage points, making the true rate of inflation in the United States in recent years closer to 2% rather than the reported 3%. According to the Commission's final report, of the 1.1 percentage point overstatement in the CPI, 0.6 percentage points were due to the failure of the CPI to take into account new products and quality changes, 0.4 percentage points were due to the failure to consider the substitution of goods in consumption as a result of changes in relative prices, and the remaining 0.1 percentage points resulted from not taking into consideration the availability of new outlets (stores) with cheaper prices. Some of these revisions in the calculation of the CPI have already been made and the others are in the process of being implemented.

These revisions in the CPI will save the U.S. government billions of dollars in lower cost-of-living adjustments to social security recipients; they will also lead to higher income tax collection (because of the slower increases in standard deductions); they will result in about $95 billion higher national savings (and lower national debt) per year, and they eliminate the underestimation in the growth of the real GDP of the nation. The CPI revisions will also affect the three million private-sector workers with union contracts tied to the CPI (and are likely to influence how much other employers pay as well).

Sources: M. J. Boskin et al., *Toward a More Accurate Measure of the Cost of Living* (Washington, D.C.: Senate Finance Committee, 1996); M. J. Boskin et al., "The CPI Commission: Findings and Recommendations," *American Economic Review,* May 1997; M. J. Boskin and D. W. Jorgenson, "Implications of Overstating Inflation for Indexing Government Programs and Understating Economic Progress," *American Economic Review,* May 1997; D. L. Costa, "Estimating Real Income in the U.S. from 1888 to 1994: Correcting CPI Bias Using Engle Curves," *Journal of Political Economy,* December 2001; B. W. Hamilton, "Using Engel's Law to Estimate CPI Bias," American Economic Review, June 2001; and M. F. Bryan and J. Gokhale, "The Consumer Price Index and National Savings," *Economic Commentary,* October 15, 1995.

EXAMPLE 4–7

Comparing the Standard of Living in Different Countries

One of the most commonly used measures of the standard of living or well-being of a nation is its per capita income. Using per capita income to compare standard of livings around the world presents some difficulties, however. First, some services provided by individuals for personal use (such as mowing the lawn) affect well-being but are not included in the measure of per capita income because the service is not purchased through the market. Only if the person hires a lawn service will the cost of the service be included in the GDP measure. Per capita incomes that do not include the imputed (estimated) value of these nonmarket services underestimate the standard of living in the nation. The underestimation is larger in poor than in rich countries because in poor countries more goods and services are produced for personal use rather than being sold in the market.

A second difficulty in making international comparisons arises because the per capita GDP of other nations must be converted into dollars. Conversion is troublesome because the exchange rate between the dollar and other currencies may not correctly reflect the purchasing power of the dollar in different nations. For example, if the real exchange rate between the dollar and the Philippines' pesos (P) is $1 = P2 when measured in dollars of equivalent purchasing power, a per capita GDP of P6,000 in the Philippines refers to a per capita income of $3,000. But if the actual exchange rate is $1 = P3, the same per capita income of P6,000 gives a per capita income of only $2,000. Thus, it is necessary to use dollars of equivalent purchasing power to convert the GDP per capita in dollars of different countries for purposes of international comparison.

Table 4.3 presents data on the per capita income of the United States and the six other leading industrial nations in the world (Japan, Germany, France, the United Kingdom, Italy, and Canada) and five large developing countries (South Korea, Mexico, Brazil, China, and India) for the year 2000. The second column of Table 4.3 gives the per capita income for each of the 12 nations in terms of U.S. dollars adjusted to include nonmarket goods and services and the true purchasing power of the dollar in different nations. Although not perfect, the adjusted GDP per capita is a more acceptable measure of the standard of living of a nation because it measures the true ability of the people of a nation to purchase goods and services in the market place.

According to this measure, the United States has the highest standard of living in the world, exceeding Canada's standard of living (the second richest nation shown in the table) by about 20%, and exceeding the standard of living of Japan (the nations with the third highest standard of living) by about 22% and that of other countries by still higher

TABLE 4.3 Measures of Standard of Living in the United States and Abroad in 2000

Country	Adjusted Per Capita Income	Unadjusted Per Capita Income
1. United States	$34,260	$34,260
2. Canada	27,330	21,050
3. Japan	26,460	34,210
4. Germany	25,010	25,050
5. France	24,470	23,670
6. United Kingdom	23,550	24,500
7. Italy	23,370	20,010
8. S. Korea	17,340	8,910
9. Mexico	8,810	5,080
10. Brazil	7,320	3,570
11. China	3,940	840
12. India	2,390	460

Source: World Bank, *World Development Report* (Washington, D.C.: World Bank, 2002, pp.232–233).

percentages. The third column of Table 4.3 gives the GDP per capita using the actual or unadjusted rather than adjusted exchange rates. With unadjusted per capita incomes, the ranking and the differences among the various countries are much greater, especially between developed and developing countries. While media sources often present these data, comparisons using the actual or unadjusted exchange data are obviously not appropriate.

Even the adjusted per capita income figures leave a great deal to be desired as measures of a nation's standard of living because the standard of living depends not only on the quantity of goods and services that individuals consume but also on many other considerations, such as the level of education, health, leisure, crime, and so on, of the population. The United Nations is trying to address this problem by devising a measure of the standard of living that includes some of these other considerations with its "human development index."

Sources: The World Bank, *World Development Report* (Washington, D.C.: World Bank, 2002) and United Nations Development Program, *Human Development Report* (New York: United Nations, 2001).

INTERNET SITE ADDRESSES

For an excellent presentation of the analysis of consumer behavior, see:

> http://price.bus.okstate.edu/archive/Econ3113_963/Shows/Chapter3/chap_03.htm
>
> http://price.bus.okstate.edu/archive/Econ3113_963/Shows/Chapter4/chap_04.htm

For data on total consumption by income classes for U.S. families to demonstrate Engel's Law and derive Engel's curves, see:

> http://stats.bls.gov/csxhome.htm

On teenage drinking and driving, and on what to do about it, see:

> http://www.firsteagle.com/tdd.htm
>
> http://www.niaaa.nih.gov/publications/iss20-4.htm
>
> http://www.healthdistrict.org/Survey98/factsheets/drinkdrive.htm

The level of and the debate on gasoline tax is examined at:

> http://www.cnn.com/2000/US/06/gas.prices.02/

> http://www.siteofthesentient.com/inframe/gasoline.html
>
> http://www.eia.doe.gov/pub/oil_gas/petroleum/analysis_publications/primer_on_gasoline_prices/html/petro.html
>
> http://www.bts.gov/transtu/indicators/Security/html/ US_Dependence_on_Oil_Imports.html

For a discussion of the sources of bias in measuring the consumer price index (CPI), as well as the use of the CPI to measure changes in the standard of living see:

> http://www.stat-usa.gov/BEN/boskin.pdf
>
> http://stats.bls.gov/cpihome.htm
>
> http://stats.bls.gov/blshome.html
>
> http://stats.bls.gov/mlr/

For the UN Human Development Report, see:

> http://www.undp.org/hdro

CHAPTER 5

Market Demand and Elasticities

I n this chapter, we begin by examining how the *market* demand curve for a commodity is obtained by summing up individual's demand curves for the commodity. As shown in Chapter 2, the market demand curve for a commodity, together with the market supply curve, determine the equilibrium price of the commodity. After deriving the market demand curve for a commodity, we discuss the various elasticities of demand, including price and income elasticities in international trade. Finally, since consumers' expenditures on a commodity represent the revenues of the producers or sellers of the commodity, we consider the producer's side of the market. This is done by examining total and marginal revenues from the sale of the commodity and their relationship to the price elasticity of demand.

An important dose of realism is introduced into the discussion by actual real-world estimates of the various elasticities for many commodities and the way they are used in the analysis of many current economic issues. The "At the Frontier" section then examines some new revolutionary marketing research approaches to demand estimation, while the optional appendix shows how demand is estimated and forecasted by regression analysis.

5.1 THE MARKET DEMAND FOR A COMMODITY

In this section, we examine how the market demand curve for a commodity is derived from the individuals' demand curves. The **market demand curve** for a commodity is simply the horizontal summation of the demand curves of all the consumers in the market. Thus, the market quantity demanded at each price is the sum of the individual quantities demanded at that price. For example, in the top of Figure 5.1, the market demand curve for hamburgers (commodity X) is obtained by the horizontal summation of the demand curve of individual 1 (d_1) and individual 2 (d_2), on the assumption that they are the only two consumers in the market. Thus, at the price of $1, the market quantity demanded of 10 hamburgers is the sum of the 6 hamburgers demanded by individual 1 and the 4 hamburgers demanded by individual 2.

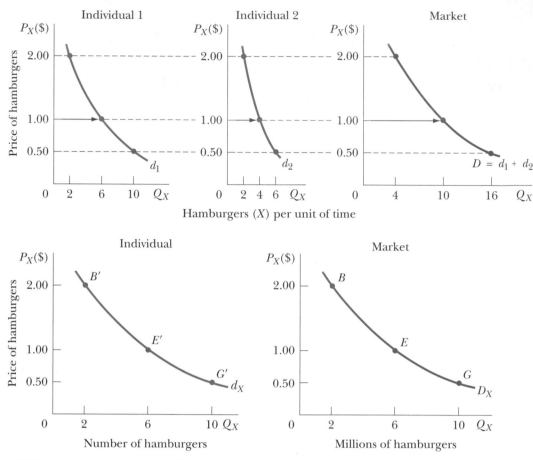

FIGURE 5.1   From Individual to Market Demand   The top part of the figure shows that the market demand curve for hamburgers, D, is obtained from the horizontal summation of the demand curve for hamburgers of individual 1 (d_1) and individual 2 (d_2). The bottom part of the figure shows an individual's demand curve, d_X, and the market demand curve, D_X, on the assumption that there are 1 million individuals in the market with demand curves for hamburgers identical to d_X.

If instead there were 1 million individuals in the market, each with demand curve d_X the market demand curve for hamburgers would be D_X (see the bottom part of Figure 5.1). Both D_X and d_X have the same shape, but the horizontal scale for D_X refers to millions of hamburgers. Note that d_X is the individual's demand curve for hamburgers derived in Chapter 4 (see Figure 4.3).

The market demand curve for a commodity shows the various quantities of the commodity demanded in the market per unit of time at various alternative prices of the commodity while holding everything else constant. The market demand curve for a commodity is negatively sloped (just as an individual's demand curve), indicating that price and quantity are inversely related. That is, the quantity demanded of the commodity increases when its price falls and decreases when its price rises. The variables held constant in drawing the market demand curve for a commodity are incomes, the prices of substitute and complementary commodities, tastes, and the number of consumers in the market. A change in any of these will cause the market demand curve for the commodity to shift (see Section 2.2).[1]

Finally, it must be pointed out that a market demand curve is simply the horizontal summation of the individual demand curves *only if* the consumption decisions of individual consumers are independent (i.e., in the absence of so-called *network externalities*). This is not always the case. For example, people sometimes demand a commodity because others are purchasing it, either to be "fashionable" and to "keep up with the Joneses" or because it makes the commodity more useful (as in the case of e-mail, which becomes more useful as more people use it). The result is a **bandwagon effect** or *positive network externality* and this makes the market demand curve for the commodity flatter or more elastic than otherwise.

At other times, the opposite or **snob effect** (a *negative network externality*) occurs as many consumers seek to be different and exclusive by demanding less of a commodity, as more people consume it. That is, as the price of a commodity falls and more people purchase the commodity, some people will stop buying it in order to stand out and be different. This tends to make the market demand curve steeper or less elastic than otherwise. There are then some individuals who, to impress other people, demand more of certain commodities (such as diamonds, mink coats, Rolls Royces, etc.) the more expensive these goods are. This form of "conspicuous consumption" is called the **Veblen effect** (after Thorstein Veblen, who introduced it). For example, some high-income people may be less willing to purchase a \$4,000 mink coat than a \$10,000 one when the latter clearly looks much more expensive. This also results in a steeper or less elastic market demand curve for the commodity than otherwise.[2]

In what follows, we assume that the bandwagon, snob, and Veblen effects are not significant, so that the market demand curve for the commodity can be obtained simply by the horizontal summation of the individual demand curves. Example 5–1 examines the market demand for Big Macs, Example 5–6 presents the various elasticities of the demand for alcoholic beverages, while Example 5–7 in the appendix to this chapter discusses the actual estimation and forecast of the demand for electricity in the United States.

EXAMPLE 5–1

The Demand for Big Macs

The market demand curve for hamburgers faced by McDonald's is the sum of the individuals' demand curves for hamburgers. What follows shows how the market demand curve for hamburgers changed over time as a result of competitive pressures and changes in consumers' tastes, and how McDonald's responded to these changes.

---

[1] A change in expectations about the future price of the commodity will also affect its demand curve. For example, the expectation that the price of the commodity will be lower in the future will shift the market demand curve to the left (so that less is demanded at each price in the current period) as consumers postpone some of their purchases of the commodity in anticipation of a lower price in the future.

[2] Conceivably, in some cases, the snob and Veblen effects could even make the market demand curve for the commodity positively sloped, though no such cases have yet been found in the real world.

With 28,700 restaurants in 121 countries and serving 45 million people around the world every day in 2001, McDonald's dwarfed the competition in the fast-food burger market. In the United States, McDonalds has 12,800 outlets compared with Burger King's 8,400 (its closest competitor in the U.S. market). After nearly three decades of double-digit gains, however, domestic sales at McDonald's have been growing slowly since the mid-1980s as a result of higher prices, changing tastes, demographic changes, increased competition from other fast-food chains and other forms of delivering fast foods and, more recently, because of the mad-cow disease in Europe.

Price increases at McDonald's exceeded inflation in each year since 1986. The average check at McDonald's now exceeds $4—a far cry from the 15-cent hamburger on which McDonald's got rich—and this sent customers streaming to lower-pricing competitors. Concern over cholesterol and calories has also reduced growth. In addition, the proportion of the 15- to 29-year-olds (the primary fast-food customers) in the total population has shrunk from 27.5% to 22.5% during the past decade. Increased competition from other fast-food chains (especially Burger King and Wendy's), other fast-food options (pizza, chicken, tacos, and so on), frozen fast foods, mobile units, and the vending machines have also slowed down the growth of demand for Big Macs. Finally, the breakout of the mad-cow disease in Europe during the past few years has also dampened the growth of hamburger sales there.

McDonald's did not sit idle but tried to meet its challenges head on by introducing new items on its menu and cutting prices. For example, in 1990 McDonald's introduced a value menu with small hamburgers selling for as little as 59 cents (down from 89 cents) and a combination of burger, french fries, and soft drink for as much as half off. In response to increased public concern about cholesterol and calories, McDonald's began publicizing the nutritional content of its menu offerings, substituted vegetable oils for beef tallow in frying its french fries, replaced ice cream with lowfat yogurt, introduced bran muffins and cereals to its breakfast menu, and, in 1991, introduced the McLean Deluxe—a new reduced-fat, quarter-pound hamburger on which McDonald's spent from $50 to $70 million to develop and promote. Then, in 1995, McDonald's introduced McPizza, in 1996 it introduced the Arch Deluxe, in 1997 it cut the price of a Big Mac from $1.90 to 55 cents with the purchase of French fries and a drink, and in 1999 it introduced the "Made For You" freshly cooked meals. To meet the increased competition from frozen fast foods, mobile units, and vending machines, an increasing number of McDonald's franchises set up drive-through and to combat the sales decline of hamburgers in Europe, it introduced more nonbeef items on its menu.

All of these efforts, however, failed to stimulate growth and McDonald's abandoned most of them. McDonald's just seems to have lost its golden touch at home, and that is why it is now rapidly expanding abroad, where it faces much less competition and where there is much more room for growth. In fact, by 2001 there were more McDonald's restaurants abroad (15,900) than in the United States (12,800). In recent years, McDonald's has been opening restaurants abroad at a rate four to five times as fast as in the United States, and it is now earning more than 60% of its profits in other countries. McDonald's now predicts that it will have more than 50,000 restaurants around the world (two-thirds of them outside the United States) by the end of this decade.

Sources: "An American Icon Wrestles with a Troubled Future," *New York Times,* May 12, 1991, Section 3, p. 1; "Too Skinny a Burger Is a Mighty Hard Sell, McDonald's Learns," *Wall Street Journal,* April 15, 1994, p. A1; "McDonald's: Can It Regain Its Golden Touch?" *Business Week,* March 9, 1988, pp. 70–77; "Getting Off Their McButts," *Business Week,* February 1999, pp. 84–88; "McDonald's Expects Earnings to Be Flat," *Wall Street Journal,* January 20, 2001, p. B10; "Missteps," *Forbes,* December 10, 2001, pp. 77–78; and "Fallen Arches," *Fortune,* April 29, 2002, pp. 74–76.

5.2 PRICE ELASTICITY OF MARKET DEMAND

In this section, we show how to measure the price elasticity of demand, both algebraically and graphically. We also examine the important relationship between the price elasticity of demand and the total expenditures of consumers on the commodity. That is, when the price of a commodity changes, will consumers' expenditures on the commodity increase, decrease, or remain unchanged? Finally, we examine the determinants or the factors that affect the value of the price elasticity of demand.

Measuring the Price Elasticity of Demand[3]

The price elasticity of demand measures the responsiveness in the quantity demanded of a commodity to a change in its price. This could be measured by the inverse of the slope of the demand curve (i.e., by $\Delta Q / \Delta P$).[4] The disadvantage is that the inverse of the slope is expressed in terms of the units of measurement. A change of 100,000 units in the quantity demanded of a commodity is very large if the commodity is new housing units, but it is not very large if the commodity is hamburgers. Similarly, a price change of one dollar is insignificant for houses, but very large for hamburgers. Thus, measuring the responsiveness in the quantity demanded of a commodity to a change in price by the inverse of the slope of the demand curve is not very useful. Furthermore, comparison of changes in quantity to changes in price across commodities is meaningless. These problems can be resolved by using percentage rather than absolute changes in quantity and prices.

In order to have a measure of the responsiveness in the quantity demanded of a commodity to a change in its price that is independent of the units of measurement, Alfred Marshall, the great English economist of the turn of the century, refined and popularized the concept of the price elasticity of demand. This measure is defined in terms of *relative* or *percentage* changes in quantity demanded and price. As such, price elasticity of demand is a pure number (i.e., it has no units attached to it), and its value is not affected by changes

---

[3] For a discussion of the price elasticity of demand using calculus, see Section A.5 of the Mathematical Appendix at the end of the book.

[4] Since the turn of the century, the convention in economics (started by Alfred Marshall) is to plot price on the vertical axis and quantity on the horizontal axis. Therefore, the quantity response to a change in price could be measured by $\Delta Q / \Delta P$, which is the inverse of the slope of the demand curve.

in the units of measurement. This also allows meaningful comparisons in the price elasticity of demand of different commodities.

The **price elasticity of demand** is given by the percentage change in the quantity demanded of a commodity divided by the percentage change in its price. Letting η (the Greek letter eta) stand for the coefficient of price elasticity of demand, ΔQ for the change in quantity demanded, and ΔP for the change in price, we have the formula for the price elasticity of demand:

$$\eta = \frac{\Delta Q/Q}{\Delta P/P} = \frac{\Delta Q}{\Delta P} \cdot \frac{P}{Q} \qquad [5.1]$$

Since quantity and price move in opposite directions, the value of η is negative. To compare price elasticities, however, we use their absolute value (i.e., their value without the negative sign). Thus, we say that a demand curve with a price elasticity of -2 is more elastic than a demand curve with a price elasticity of -1 (even though -2 is algebraically smaller than -1). Note that the inverse of the slope of the demand curve (i.e., $\Delta Q/\Delta P$) is a component, but only a component, of the price elasticity formula.

Formula [5.1] measures **point elasticity of demand** or the elasticity at a particular point on the demand curve. More frequently, we are interested in the price elasticity between two points on the demand curve. We then calculate the **arc elasticity of demand.** If we used formula [5.1] to measure arc elasticity, however, we would get different results depending on whether the price rises or falls.[5] To avoid this, we use the *average* of the two prices and the *average* of the two quantities in the calculations. Letting P_1 refer to the higher of the two prices (with Q_1 the quantity at P_1) and P_2 refer to the lower of the two prices (with Q_2 the corresponding quantity), we have the formula for arc elasticity of demand[6]:

$$\eta = \frac{\Delta Q}{\Delta P} \cdot \frac{(P_1 + P_2)/2}{(Q_1 + Q_2)/2} = \frac{\Delta Q}{\Delta P} \cdot \frac{(P_1 + P_2)}{(Q_1 + Q_2)} \qquad [5.2]$$

Using formula [5.1] to measure the elasticity for a *price decline* from point B ($Q = 2$, $P = \$2.00$) to point G ($Q = 10, P = \$0.50$) on the market demand curve in Figure 5.1, we get

$$\eta = \frac{8}{(-1.50)} \frac{2}{(2)} = -\frac{16}{3} = -5.33$$

On the other hand, measuring elasticity for a *price increase* from point G to point B on the same demand curve, we get

$$\eta = -\frac{8}{(1.50)} \frac{0.50}{(10)} = -\frac{4}{15} = -0.27$$

Using formula [5.2] for arc elasticity, we get

$$\eta = -\frac{8}{(1.50)} \frac{2.50}{(12)} = -\frac{20}{18} = -1.11$$

---

[5] As we will see below, this results because a different base is used in calculating percentage changes for a price increase than for a price decrease.
[6] For the second ratio in the formula, we could use $\overline{P}/\overline{Q}$, where the bar on P and Q refers to their average value.

The price elasticity of demand is usually different at and between different points on the demand curve, and it can range anywhere from zero to very large or infinite. Demand is said to be *elastic* if the absolute value of η is larger than 1, *unitary elastic* if the absolute value of η equals 1, and *inelastic* if the absolute value of η is smaller than 1.

Price Elasticity Graphically

We can also measure graphically the price elasticity at any point on a linear or nonlinear demand curve. To measure the price elasticity at point E on D_X in the left panel of Figure 5.2 (the same as in the right bottom panel in Figure 5.1), we proceed as follows. We draw tangent AEH to point E on D_X and drop perpendicular EJ to the quantity axis. The slope of tangent line AEH is negative and constant throughout and can be measured by

$$\frac{\Delta P}{\Delta Q} = -\frac{JE}{JH}$$

The first component of the price elasticity formula is the inverse of the slope of the demand curve or

$$\frac{\Delta Q}{\Delta P} = -\frac{JH}{JE}$$

The second component of the price elasticity formula is

$$\frac{P}{Q} = \frac{JE}{0J}$$

Reassembling the two components of the elasticity formula, we have

$$\eta = \frac{\Delta Q}{\Delta P} \cdot \frac{P}{Q} = -\frac{JH}{JE} \cdot \frac{JE}{0J} = -\frac{JH}{0J} = -\frac{6}{6} = -1$$

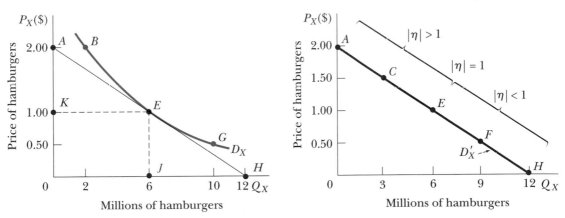

FIGURE 5.2   Measurement of Price Elasticity of Demand Graphically   In the left panel, the price elasticity at point E on D_X is measured by drawing tangent AEH to point E on D_X and dropping perpendicular EJ to the horizontal axis. At point E, $\eta = -JH/0J = -6/6 = -1$. In the right panel, the absolute value of $\eta = 1$ at point E (the midpoint of D_X'), $\eta > 1$ above the midpoint, and $\eta < 1$ below the midpoint.

That is, the price elasticity of D_X at point E in the left panel of Figure 5.2 is equal to 1. Since EJH, AKE, and AOH are similar triangles (see the left panel of Figure 5.2), the price elasticity of D_X at point E can be measured by any of the following ratios of distances:

$$\eta = -\frac{JH}{0J} = -\frac{K0}{AK} = -\frac{EH}{AE} \qquad [5.3]$$

The price elasticity of demand at any other point on D_X can be found in a similar way by drawing a tangent to D_X at that point and then proceeding as indicated above (see Problem 2). This provides a convenient and easy way to measure the price elasticity of demand at any point on a nonlinear demand curve.

The same procedure can be used to measure the price elasticity at any point on a straight-line demand curve. For example, by inspecting the right panel of Figure 5.2, we can find that $\eta = -9/3 = -3$ at point C on D'_X, $\eta = -3/9 = -1/3$ at point F, and $\eta = -6/6 = -1$ at point E (the midpoint of D'_X). Furthermore, $\eta \to \infty$ at point A and $\eta = 0$ at point H (see Problem 3). Thus, while the slope of a straight-line demand curve is constant throughout, its price elasticity varies between each point on (and its absolute value declines as we move down) the demand curve. As a general rule, a straight-line demand curve is unitary elastic at its geometric midpoint, price elastic above its midpoint, and inelastic below its midpoint (see the right panel of Figure 5.2).

Two other simple rules are useful in considering the price elasticity of demand. The first is that of two parallel demand curves (linear or nonlinear), the one further to the right has a smaller price elasticity at each price (see Problem 4(a), with answer at the end of the text). Second, when two demand curves intersect, the flatter of the two is more price elastic at the point of intersection (see Problem 4(b), with the answer also provided at the end of the text).

Price Elasticity and Total Expenditures

An important relationship exists between the price elasticity of demand and the total expenditures of consumers on the commodity. This relationship is often used in economics. It postulates that a decline in the commodity price results in an increase in total expenditures if demand is elastic, leaves total expenditures unchanged if demand is unitary elastic, and results in a decline in total expenditures if demand is inelastic.

Specifically, when the price of a commodity falls, total expenditures (price times quantity) increase if demand is elastic because the percentage increase in quantity (which by itself tends to increase total expenditures) exceeds the percentage decline in price (which by itself tends to reduce total expenditures). Total expenditures are maximum when $|\eta| = 1$ and decline thereafter. That is, when $|\eta| < 1$, a reduction in the commodity price leads to a percentage increase in the quantity demanded of the commodity that is smaller than the percentage reduction in price, and so total expenditures on the commodity decline. This is shown in Table 5.1, which refers to D'_X in Figure 5.2.

From Table 5.1 we see that between points A and E, $|\eta| > 1$ and total expenditures on the commodity increase as the commodity price declines. The opposite is true between points E and F over which $|\eta| < 1$. Total expenditures are maximum at point E

TABLE 5.1 Total Expenditures and Price Elasticity of Demand

Point	P_X ($)	Q_X (Million Units)	Total Expenditures (Million $)	Absolute Value of η
A	2.00	0	0	∞
C	1.50	3	4.5	3
E	1.00	6	6.0	1
F	0.50	9	4.5	1/3
H	0	12	0	0

(the geometric midpoint of D_X' in Figure 5.2). The general rule summarizing the relationship among total expenditures, price, and the price elasticity of demand is that *total expenditures and price move in opposite directions if demand is elastic and in the same direction if demand is inelastic* (see Table 5.1).

Figure 5.3 shows a demand curve that is unitary elastic throughout. Thus, $\eta = -JH/J0 = -6/6 = -1$ at point E on D^*, $\eta = -LJ/0L = -3/3 = -1$ at point B', and $\eta = -HN/0H = -12/12 = -1$ at point G'. Note that total expenditures (price times quantity) are constant ($6 million) at every point on D^*. This type of demand curve is a rectangular hyperbola. Its general equation is

$$Q = \frac{C}{P} \tag{5.4}$$

where Q is the quantity demanded, P is its price, and C is a constant (total expenditures). Thus, $P \cdot Q = C$. For example, at point B', $(P)(Q) = (\$2)(3) = \$6$. At point E, $(\$1)(6) = \$6$, and at point G', $(\$0.50)(12) = \$6$ also.

What Determines Price Elasticity?

Because the price elasticity of demand is so useful (i.e., it tells us, among other things, what happens to the level of total expenditures on the commodity when its price changes), it is important to identify the forces that determine its value. The size of the price elasticity of demand depends primarily on two factors. First and foremost, *the price elasticity of demand for a commodity is larger the closer and the greater are the number of available substitutes*. For example, the demand for coffee is more elastic than the demand for salt because coffee has better and more substitutes (tea and cocoa) than salt. Thus, the same percentage increase in the price of coffee and salt elicits a larger percentage reduction in the quantity demanded of coffee than of salt.

In general, a commodity has closer substitutes and thus a higher price elasticity of demand the more narrowly the commodity is defined. For example, the price elasticity for Marlboro cigarettes is much larger than for cigarettes in general, and still larger than for all tobacco products. If a commodity is defined so that it has perfect substitutes, its price

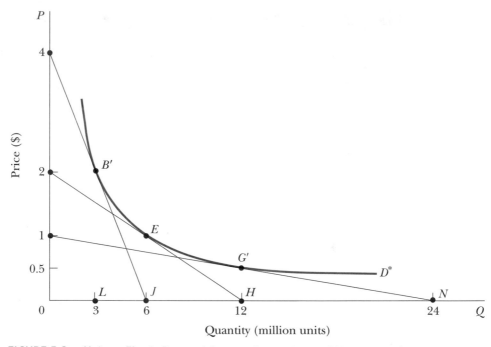

FIGURE 5.3   Unitary Elastic Demand Curve   Demand curve D^* has unitary elasticity throughout. Thus, $\eta = -JH/OJ = -6/6 = -1$ at point E, $\eta = -LJ/OL = -3/3 = -1$ at point B', and $\eta = -HN/OH = -12/12 = -1$ at point G'. Total expenditures $(P \cdot Q)$ are the same ($6 million) at every point on D^*. This demand curve is a rectangular hyperbola.

elasticity of demand is infinite. For example, if a wheat farmer attempted to increase his or her price above the market price, the farmer would lose all sales as buyers would switch all their wheat purchases to other farmers (who produce identical wheat).

Second, *price elasticity is larger, the longer is the period of time allowed for consumers to adjust to a change in the commodity price.* The reason for this is that it usually takes time for consumers to learn of a price change and to fully respond or adjust their purchases. For example, consumers may not be able to reduce much the quantity demanded of electricity soon after learning of an increase in the price of electricity. Over a period of several years, however, households can replace electric heaters with gas heaters, purchase appliances that consume less electricity, and so on. Thus, for a given price change, the quantity response *per unit of time* is usually much greater in the long run than in the short run, and so the absolute value of η is larger in the former than in the latter time period. This is clearly shown in Example 5–2.[7]

---

[7] Sometimes it is stated that the price elasticity of demand is larger the greater is the number of uses of the commodity. However, no satisfactory reason has been advanced as to why this should be so. It is also sometimes said that price elasticity is lower the smaller is the importance of the commodity in consumers' budgets (i.e., the smaller is the proportion of the consumers' incomes spent on the commodity). However, empirical estimates often contradict this.

EXAMPLE 5–2

The Price Elasticity for Clothing Increases with Time

The first row of Table 5.2 shows that the price elasticity of demand for clothing in the United States is −0.90 in the short run but rises to −2.90 in the long run. This means that a 1% increase in price leads to a reduction in the quantity demanded of clothing of only 0.90% in the short run but 2.90% in the long run. Although the price elasticity of demand for gasoline (the last row of Table 5.2) is three times higher in the long run than in the short run, both elasticities are very small. It seems that people cannot find suitable substitutes for gasoline even in the long run. The table also shows the short-run and long-run price elasticities of demand for a selected list of other commodities. The estimated price elasticity of demand for any commodity is likely to vary (sometimes widely) depending on the nation under consideration, the time period examined, and the estimation technique used. Thus, estimated price elasticity values should be used with caution.

Many economic policies (such as reducing American dependence on imported petroleum) rely crucially on price elasticities. For example, with the price of gasoline of about $1.50 per gallon and a short-run price elasticity of 0.2 (see Table 5.2), a $0.50 tax per gallon would increase the price of gasoline from about $1.50 to $2.00 per gallon, or by about 33%, and reduce the quantity demanded of gasoline by 6.6% $[(\eta)(\%\Delta P) = (-0.2)(0.33) = -6.6\% = \%\Delta Q]$ in the short run. With the price elasticity equal to 0.6 in the long run, the reduction in the quantity demanded of gasoline in the long run would still be about only 20%.

TABLE 5.2 Selected Price Elasticities of Demand

Commodity	Short Run	Long Run
Clothing*	−0.90	−2.90
Household natural gas[†]	−1.40	−2.10
Tobacco products[#]	−0.46	−1.89
Electricity (household)[#]	−0.13	−1.89
Foreign travel[#]	−0.14	−1.77
Wine[@]	−0.88	−1.17
Jewelry and watches[#]	−0.41	−0.67
Gasoline[&]	−0.20	−0.60

Sources:
*M. R. Baye, D. W. Jansen, and T. W. Lee, "Advertising in Complete Demand Systems," *Applied Economics,* Vol. 24, 1992.
[†]G. R. Lakshmanan and W. Anderson, "Residential Energy Demand in the United States," *Regional Science and Urban Economics,* August 1980.
[#]H. S. Houthakker and L. S. Taylor, *Consumer Demand in the United States: Analyses and Projections* (Cambridge, MA.: Harvard University Press, 1970).
[@]J. L. Sweeny, "The Response of Energy Demand to Higher Prices? What Have We Learned?" *American Economic Review,* May 1984.
[&]J. A. Johnson, E. H. Oksanen, M. R. Veall, and D. Fretz, "Short-run and Long-run Elasticities for Canadian Consumption of Alchoholic Beverages," *Review of Economics and Statistics,* February 1992.

5.3   INCOME ELASTICITY OF DEMAND[8]

In Section 4.1 we defined the **Engel curve** as showing the amount of a commodity that a consumer would purchase per unit of time at various income levels, while holding prices and tastes constant. We can measure the responsiveness or sensitivity in the quantity demanded of a commodity at any point on the Engel curve by the **income elasticity of demand.** This is defined as

$$\eta = \frac{\Delta Q/Q}{\Delta I/I} = \frac{\Delta Q}{\Delta I} \cdot \frac{I}{Q} \qquad [5.5]$$

where ΔQ is the change in the quantity purchased, ΔI is the change in income, Q is the original quantity, and I is the original money income of the consumer.

A commodity is normal if η_I is positive and inferior if η_I is negative. A normal good can be further classified as a **necessity** if η_I is less than 1 and as a **luxury** if η_I is greater than 1. In the real world, most broadly defined commodities such as food, clothing, housing, health care, education, and recreation are normal goods. Inferior goods are usually narrowly defined inexpensive goods, such as bologna, for which good substitutes are available. Among normal goods, food and clothing are necessities while education and recreation are luxuries.

This classification of goods into inferior and normal, and necessity and luxury, cannot be taken too seriously, however, because the same commodity can be regarded as a luxury by some individuals or at some income levels, and as a necessity or even as an inferior good by other individuals or at other income levels.[9] A simple geometric method can determine if a commodity is a luxury, a necessity, or an inferior good at each income level. If the tangent to the Engel curve is positively sloped and crosses the income axis, η_I exceeds 1 and the good is a luxury at that income level. If the tangent crosses the origin, $\eta_I = 1$. If the tangent crosses the horizontal axis, η_I is less than 1 and the commodity is a necessity at that income level. Finally, if the tangent to the Engel curve is negatively sloped, the commodity is an inferior good.

For example, Table 5.3 and Figure 5.4 show that the student in Chapters 3 and 4 would regard hamburgers as a luxury at income levels (allowances) of up to $15 per day. Hamburgers would become a necessity for daily allowances of between $15 and $30 and would be regarded as an inferior good at higher incomes (where the student could afford steaks and lobsters).

The concept and measurement of the income elasticity of demand and Engel curve can refer to a single customer or to the entire market. When referring to the entire market, Q and ΔQ are the total or the market quantity purchased and its change, while I and ΔI are the total or aggregate money income of all consumers in the market and its change.[10]

As pointed out in Section 4.1, the proportion of total expenditures on food declines as family incomes rise. This is referred to as **Engel's law.** Indeed, the higher the proportion of income spent on food, the poorer a family or nation is taken to be. For example, in the

---

[8] For a discussion of the income elasticity of demand using calculus, see Section A.5 of the Mathematical Appendix at the end of the book.

[9] Indeed, some economists feel that the necessity-luxury classification of goods is entirely spurious and meaningless.

[10] Remember, however, that the income elasticity of market demand is not well defined unless it is also specified on which commodities income increments are spent.

TABLE 5.3	Income Elasticity and Classification of Hamburgers (X) at Various Daily Income Allowances				
I	Q_x	%ΔQ_x	%ΔI	η_I	Classification
10	2	. . .	. . .	. . .	. . .
15	4	100	50	2.00	Luxury
20	5	25	33	0.76	Necessity
30	6	20	50	0.40	Necessity
40	4	−33	33	−1.00	Inferior

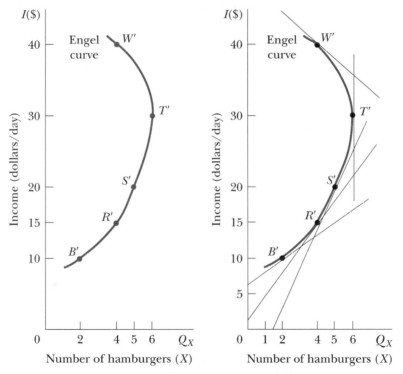

FIGURE 5.4   Engel Curve and Income Elasticity   Because the tangent to the Engel curve is positively sloped and crosses the income axis up to the daily income allowance of $15, hamburgers are a luxury for this individual. The tangent goes through the origin at *I* = $15 and η_I = 1 at that income level. Since the tangent is positively sloped and crosses the quantity axis from *I* = $15 to $30, hamburgers are a necessity between these income levels. For *I* higher than $30, the Engel curve is negatively sloped and hamburgers become an inferior good for this individual.

United States less than 20% of total family incomes is spent on food as compared with over 50% for India (a much poorer nation). As Example 5–3 shows, the income elasticity of demand can be very different for different products.

EXAMPLE 5–3

Transatlantic Air Travel Is a Luxury, Flour Is an Inferior Good

The third and last rows of Table 5.4 show, respectively, that the income elasticity of demand is 1.91 for transatlantic air travel and −0.36 for flour. This means that a 1% increase in consumers' income leads to a 1.91% increase in expenditures on foreign travel but to a 0.36% *reduction* in expenditures on flour. Thus, foreign travel is a (strong) luxury, while flour is a (weak) inferior good. The table shows that wine is also a luxury, while cigarettes, beer, nonbeverage sugar, and pork are necessities. Beef is on the border line.

Note that the income elasticities given in Table 5.4 are measured as the percentage change in expenditures on the various commodities (rather than the percentage change in the *quantity* purchased of the various commodities). To the extent that prices are held constant, however, we get the same results as if the percentage change in quantities were used. As pointed out, the interpretation of these income elasticity values is not as clear-cut and precise as for the price elasticity of demand discussed earlier.

TABLE 5.4   Selected Income Elasticities of Demand

Commodity	Income Elasticity
Wine*	2.59
Electricity (household)[†]	1.94
Transatlantic air travel[#]	1.91
Beef[@]	1.06
Cigarettes[&]	0.50
Beer*	0.46
Chicken[@]	0.28
Non-beverage sugar**	0.23
Pork[@]	0.14
Flour[†]	−0.36

Sources:
*J. A. Johnson, E. H. Oksanen, M. R. Veall, and D. Fretz, *op. cit.*
[†]H. S. Houthakker and L. S. Taylor, *op. cit.*
[#]J. M. Cigliano, "Price and Income Elasticities for Airline Travel: The North Atlantic Market," *Business Economics,* September 1980.
[@]D. B. Suits, "Agriculture," in W. Adams, ed., *Structure of American Industry* (New York: Macmillan, 1990).
[&]F. Calemaker, "Rational Addictive Behavior and Cigarette Smoking," *Journal of Political Economy,* August 1991.
**N. D. Uri, "A Note on the Estimation of the Demand for Sugar in the USA in the Presence of Measurement Error in the Data," *Applied Economics,* January 1995.

<table>
<tr><td>**5.4**</td><td>## CROSS ELASTICITY OF DEMAND[11]</td></tr>
</table>

We have seen in Section 2.2 that one of the things held constant in drawing the market demand curve for a commodity is the price of substitute and complementary commodities. Commodities X and Y are **substitutes** if more of X is purchased when the price of Y goes up. For example, consumers usually purchase more coffee when the price of tea rises. Thus, coffee and tea are substitutes. Other examples of substitutes include butter and margarine, hamburgers and hot dogs, Coca-Cola and Pepsi, electricity and gas, and so on.

On the other hand, commodities X and Y are **complements** if less of X is purchased when the price of Y goes up. For example, consumers usually purchase fewer lemons when the price of tea goes up. Thus, lemons and tea are complements. Other examples of commodities that are complements are coffee and cream, hamburgers and buns, hot dogs and mustard, cars and gasoline, and so on.

An increase in the price of a commodity leads to a reduction in the quantity demanded of the commodity (a movement along the demand curve for the commodity) but causes the demand curve for a substitute to shift to the right and the demand curve for a complement to shift to the left. For example, an increase in the price of tea will cause the demand for coffee (a substitute of tea) to shift to the right (so that more coffee is demanded at each coffee price) and the demand for lemons (a complement of tea) to shift to the left (so that fewer lemons are demanded at each lemon price).

We can measure the responsiveness or sensitivity in the quantity purchased of commodity X as a result of a change in the price of commodity Y by the **cross elasticity of demand** (η_{XY}). This is given by:

$$\eta_{XY} = \frac{\Delta Q_X / Q_X}{\Delta P_Y / P_Y} = \frac{\Delta Q_X}{\Delta P_Y} \cdot \frac{P_Y}{Q_X} \qquad [5.6]$$

where ΔQ_X is the change in the quantity purchased of X, ΔP_Y is the change in the price of Y, P_Y is the original price of Y, and Q_X is the original quantity of X. Note that in measuring η_{XY}, we hold constant P_X, consumers' incomes, their tastes, and the number of consumers in the market.

If η_{XY} is greater than zero, X and Y are substitutes because an increase in P_Y leads to an increase in Q_X as X is substituted for Y in consumption. On the other hand, if η_{XY} is less than zero, X and Y are complements because an increase in P_Y leads to a reduction in (Q_Y and) Q_X. The absolute value (i.e., the value without the sign) of the cross elasticity of demand measures the degree of substitution or complementarity. For example, if η_{XY} between coffee and tea is found to be larger than that between coffee and hot chocolate, this means that coffee and tea are better substitutes than coffee and hot chocolate. If η_{XY} is close to zero, X and Y are independent commodities. This may be the case with cars and pencils, telephones and chewing gum, pocket calculators and beer, and so on.

Several additional things must be kept in mind with respect to the cross elasticity of demand. First, the value of η_{XY} need not equal the value of η_{YX} because the responsiveness of Q_X to a change in P_Y need not equal the responsiveness of Q_Y to a change in P_X.

---

[11] For a discussion of the cross elasticity of demand using calculus, see Section A.5 of the Mathematical Appendix at the end of the book.

For example, a change in the price of coffee is likely to have a greater effect on the quantity of sugar (a complement of coffee) demanded than the other way around, since coffee is the more important of the two in terms of total expenditures.

Second, a high positive cross elasticity of demand is often used to define an industry since it indicates that the various commodities are very similar. For example, the cross elasticity of demand between Chevrolets and Oldsmobiles is very high, and so they belong to the same (auto) industry. This can lead to some difficulty, however. For example, how high must the positive cross elasticity between two commodities be for them to be in the same industry? Also, if the cross elasticity between cars and station wagons and between station wagons and trucks is "high," but the cross elasticity of demand between cars and trucks is "low," are cars and trucks in the same industry? In these cases the definition of the industry usually depends on the problem to be studied.

Third, the above definition of substitutes and complements is sometimes referred to as a "gross" definition; as such, it refers to the entire market response and reflects both the income and the substitution effects. For an individual consumer, there is a more rigorous definition (in terms of the substitution effect only) discussed in more advanced treaties.[12] Example 5–4 gives the estimated gross elasticity of demand between a number of products and shows its usefulness in the analysis of important economic issues.

EXAMPLE 5–4
Margarine and Butter Are Substitutes, Cereals and Fresh Fish Are Complements

The first row of Table 5.5 shows that the cross elasticity of demand of margarine with respect to the price of butter is 1.53. This means that a 1% increase in the price of butter leads to a 1.53% increase in the demand for margarine. Thus, margarine and butter are substitutes in the United States. On the other hand, the last row of Table 5.5 shows that the cross elasticity of demand of cereals with respect to fresh fish is −0.87. This means that a 1% increase in the price of cereals leads to a reduction in the demand for fresh fish by 0.87%. Thus, cereals (for example, bread) and fresh fish are complements. The table also shows the cross elasticity of demand of other selected commodities in the United States.

Cross price elasticities of demand have important economic applications—even in the courtroom, as the celebrated Cellophane Case shows (see, *U.S. Reports*, Vol. 351, Washington, D.C.: U.S. Government Printing Office, 1956, p. 400). In that case, the court decided that DuPont had not monopolized the market for cellophane even though it had 75% of the market. The reason? The cross price elasticity of demand between cellophane and other flexible packaging materials (waxed paper, aluminum foil, and others) was sufficiently high to indicate that the relevant market was not cellophane as such, but flexible packaging materials, and DuPont, with only a 20% market share, had not monopolized that market.

[12] See J. R. Hicks, *Value and Capital* (New York: Oxford University Press, 1946), p. 44.

TABLE 5.5 Selected Cross Elasticities of Demand	
Commodity	Cross-Pirce Elasticity
Margarine with respect to the price of butter	1.53*
Natural gas with respect to the price of electricity	0.80[†]
Pork with respect to the price of beef	0.40*
Chicken with respect to the price of pork	0.29*
Clothing with respect to the price of food	−0.18[#]
Entertainment with respect to the price of food	−0.72[@]
Cereals with respect to the price of fresh fish	−0.87[&]

Sources:
*D. M. Heien, "The Structure of Food Demand: Interrelatedness and Duality," *American Journal of Agricultural Economics,* May 1982.
[†]G. R. Lakshmanan and W. Anderson, *op. cit.*
[#]M. R. Baye, D. W. Jansen, and T. W. Lee, *op. cit.*
[@]E. T. Fujii et al., "An Almost Ideal Demand System for Visitor Expenditures," *Journal of Transport Economics and Policy,* May 1985.
[&]A. Deaton, "Estimation of Own- and Cross-Price Elasticities from Household Survey Data," *Journal of Econometrics,* September–October 1937.

5.5   PRICE AND INCOME ELASTICITIES OF IMPORTS AND EXPORTS

We have seen that when the price of a commodity falls, consumers purchase more of the commodity. The increase in the quantity purchased of the commodity resulting from a decline in its price (while holding everything else constant) is measured by the price elasticity of demand. The same is true for U.S. imports and exports. When import prices fall, domestic consumers import more from abroad. When the price of U.S. exports fall, foreigners purchase more American goods and U.S. exports rise. The increase in the quantity of U.S. imports and exports resulting from a price decline is measured, respectively, by the **price elasticity of demand for imports** and the **price elasticity of demand for exports.**

One complication arises, however, when we deal with imports and exports. The price of imports to U.S. consumers depends not only on prices in exporting nations (expressed in foreign currencies) but also on the rate of exchange between the dollar and foreign currencies. The rate of exchange between the dollar and a foreign currency is called the **exchange rate.** For example, the exchange rate (R) between the U.S. dollar and the euro (€), the currency of the 12-nation European Monetary Union (Austria, Belgium, Finland, France, Germany, Greece, Ireland, Italy, Luxembourg, Netherlands, Portugal, and Spain), is about 1. This means that U.S. consumers must pay $1 to get €1. Thus, the price of a music record that costs €1 in the European Monetary Union (EMU) is $1 to U.S. consumers. If the price of the record falls to €0.50 in the EMU, U.S. consumers will have to pay only $0.50 for the record. The price of an EMU record to U.S. consumers can also fall to $0.50, even if the price remains at €1 in the EMU, if the exchange rate between the dollar and the euro falls from $1 to €1 to $0.50 to €1.[13]

Exchange rates change very frequently in the real world. How exchange rates are determined and the reasons that they change are not important at this point (they are explained in the appendix to Chapter 9). What is important is that the *dollar* price of U.S. imports can change because of a change in foreign-currency prices abroad or because of a change in exchange rates. Regardless of the reason for the change in the price of U.S. imports, we can measure the increase in quantity of U.S. imports resulting from a fall in their *dollar* price by the price elasticity of demand for imports. Similarly, regardless of the reason for the change in the price of U.S. exports, we can measure the increase in quantity of U.S. exports resulting from a fall in their *dollar* price by the price elasticity of demand for U.S. exports. On the other hand, an increase in U.S. income leads to an increase in U.S. imports, while an increase in income in foreign countries leads to an increase in U.S. exports. These can be measured, respectively, by the **income elasticity of demand of imports** and the **income elasticity of demand for exports.**

EXAMPLE 5–5

Price and Income Elasticities for Imports and Exports in the Real World

The price elasticity of demand for U.S. manufactured imports has been estimated to be about 1.06 both in the short run and in the long run. That is, a 1% decline in the dollar price of U.S. imports of manufactured goods can be expected to lead to a 1.06% increase in the quantity demanded and thus leave their dollar value practically unchanged in the short run as well as in the long run.

On the other hand, the price elasticity of demand for U.S. exports of manufactured goods was estimated to be 0.48 in the short run and 1.67 in the long run. This means that a 1% decline in the price of U.S. exports can be expected to lead to an increase in the quantity of U.S. manufactured goods exports of 0.48% within a year or two of the price change and 1.67% in the long run (i.e., in a period of five years or so). Thus, a decline in U.S. export prices leads to U.S. earnings from manufactured exports to fall in the short run and to a rise in the long run.

Finally, the income elasticity of demand for imports was estimated to be 1.94 in the United States. This means that a 1% increase in U.S. income or GNP can be expected to lead to an increase of about 1.94% in U.S. imports. Thus, U.S. imports are normal goods and can be regarded as luxuries. The income elasticity of imports for the other six largest industrial countries (Japan, Germany, France, the United Kingdom, Italy, and Canada) range from 0.35 for Japan to 2.51 for the United Kingdom. On the other hand, the income elasticity of exports range from 0.80 for the United States and 1.60 for Italy.

---

[13] This is only the immediate outcome. Over time, the dollar price of U.S. imports is likely to fall by less than the indicated above because of other forces at work (that need not be examined here).

The price and income elasticities of imports and exports are important to individual consumers and producers in the United States and abroad, and they affect the level of economic activity in all the nations engaging in international trade.

Source: D. Salvatore, *International Economics,* 8th ed. (New York: John Wiley & Sons, 2003), Chapters 16 and 17.

| MARGINAL REVENUE AND ELASTICITY[14]

Up to this point, we have examined demand from the consumers' side only. However, consumers' expenditures on a commodity are the receipts or the total revenues of the sellers of the commodity. In this section, we look at the sellers' side of the market. We begin by defining marginal revenue and showing how the marginal revenue curve can be derived geometrically from the demand curve. Then we examine the relationship between marginal revenue, price, and the price elasticity of demand. Thus, the material in this section represents the link or bridge between the theory of demand (Part Two of the text) and the theory of the firm (Chapters 9–13).

Demand, Total Revenue, and Marginal Revenue

The total amount earned by sellers of a commodity is called **total revenue (*TR*)**; it is equal to the price per unit of the commodity times the quantity of the commodity sold. **Marginal revenue (*MR*)** is then the change in total revenue per unit change in the quantity sold; *MR* is calculated by dividing the change in total revenue (ΔTR) by the change in the quantity sold (ΔQ):

$$MR = \frac{\Delta TR}{\Delta Q} \qquad [5.7]$$

We can also show that the sum of the marginal revenues on all units of the commodity sold equals total revenue.

In Table 5.6, price (column 1) and quantity (column 2) give the demand schedule of the commodity. Price times quantity gives total revenue (column 3). The change in total revenue resulting from each additional unit of the commodity sold gives the marginal revenue (column 4). As a check on the calculations, we see that the sum of the marginal revenues equals total revenues (column 5). Note that TR/Q equals **average revenue** (*AR*), and $AR = P$ (the height of the demand curve).

The information given in Table 5.6 is plotted in Figure 5.5. The top panel gives the total revenue curve. The bottom panel gives the corresponding demand (*D*) and marginal revenue curves. Since *MR* is defined as the change in *TR* per unit change in *Q*, the *MR* values are plotted at the midpoint of each quantity interval in the bottom panel of Figure 5.5.

---

[14] For the definition of marginal revenue in terms of calculus, see Section A.7 of the Mathematical Appendix at the end of the book.

TABLE 5.6 Demand, Total Revenue, and Marginal Revenue

P (1)	Q (2)	TR (3)	MR (4)	Sum of MR's (5)
$11	0	$ 0	. . .	. . .
10	1	10	$10	$10
9	2	18	8	18
8	3	24	6	24
7	4	28	4	28
6	5	30	2	30
5	6	30	0	30
4	7	28	−2	28
3	8	24	−4	24

On the other hand, points on the TR and D curves are plotted *at* each level of output. For example, at $P = \$11$, $Q = 0$, and so TR (which equals P times Q) is zero and is plotted at the origin in the top panel of Figure 5.5. At $P = \$10$, $Q = 1$, and so $TR = \$10$ and MR ($\Delta TR/\Delta Q$) is also $\$10$. This TR value is plotted at $Q = 1$ in the top panel, while the corresponding MR is plotted between $Q = 0$ and $Q = 1$ (i.e., at $Q = 0.5$) in the bottom panel.

The MR curve starts at the same point on the vertical axis as the D curve and is everywhere else below the D curve. This is because to sell one more unit of the commodity, price must be lowered not only for the additional unit sold but also on all previous units. For example, we see in Table 5.6 that to sell the second unit of the commodity, price must be lowered from $\$10$ to $\$9$ on both units. Therefore, the MR on the second unit is given by $P = \$9$ (a point on D) minus the $\$1$ reduction on the price of the first unit. That is, $MR = \$8$, which is lower than P, so the MR curve is below the D curve (see the bottom panel of Figure 5.5). When D is elastic, MR is positive because an increase in Q increases TR. When D is unitary elastic, $MR = 0$ because an increase in Q leaves TR unchanged (at its maximum level). When D is inelastic, MR is negative because an increase in Q reduces TR (see the bottom panel of Figure 5.5). We will make a great deal of use of the relationship between the demand curve and the marginal revenue curve in Chapters 9–13, where we deal with the theory of the firm and market structure.

Geometry of Marginal Revenue Determination

The marginal revenue curve for a straight-line and for a nonlinear demand curve can easily be found geometrically. This is shown in Figure 5.6. In the left panel, we can find the marginal revenue corresponding to point C on D_X' by dropping perpendicular CJ to the vertical axis and CW to the horizontal axis, and then subtracting distance AJ from CW. This identifies point C'. Thus, at $Q = 3$, $P = WC = \$1.50$, and $MR = WC' = \$1.00$. Similarly, by dropping perpendiculars EK and EE' from point E on D_X' and subtracting distance AK from EE', we get point E'. Thus, at $Q = 6$, $P = E'E = \$1$, and $MR = 0$. By joining points C' and E' we derive the MR_X' curve shown in the left panel of Figure 5.6. Note that the MR_X' curve starts at point A (as the D_X' curve) and every point on it bisects (i.e., cuts in half) the distance from the D_X' curve to the vertical or price axis. (Indeed, this provides an alternative but equivalent method of deriving the MR curve geometrically for

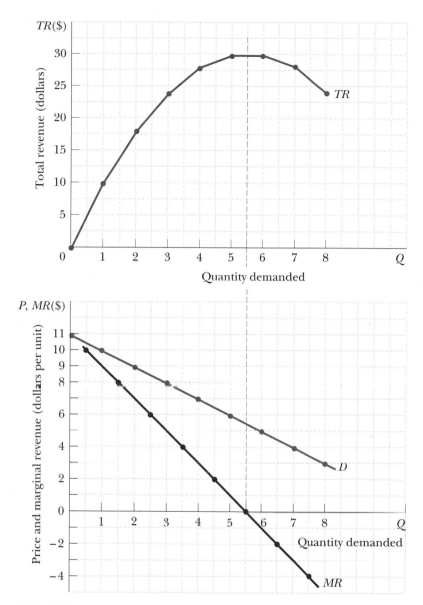

FIGURE 5.5   Total Revenue, Demand, and Marginal Revenue   Total revenue rises up to 5 units of the commodity sold, remains constant between 5 and 6 units, and declines thereafter. When *D* is elastic, *MR* is positive because *TR* increases. When *D* is unitary elastic, *MR* = 0 because *TR* is constant (at its maximum). When *D* is inelastic, *MR* is negative because *TR* declines (as *Q* increases).

a straight-line demand curve.) Thus, $JV = 1/2JC$, $KC' = 1/2KE$, and $0E' = 1/20H$ (see the figure).

To find the marginal revenue curve corresponding to any point on a nonlinear demand curve, we draw a tangent to the demand curve at that point and then proceed as described above. Thus, to find the marginal revenue corresponding to point B on D_X in the right panel

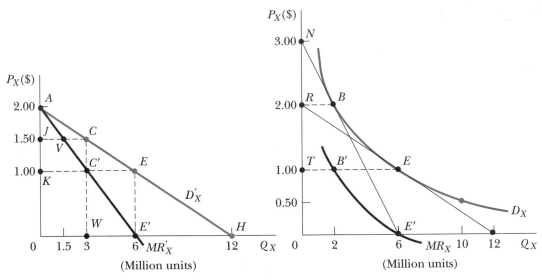

FIGURE 5.6   Marginal Revenue Determination   In the left panel, for point C on the D'_X curve, $MR = C'W$ and is obtained by subtracting distance AJ from price CW. For point E, $MR = 0$ and was obtained by subtracting distance $AK = EE'$ from P_X. In the right panel, to find the MR at point B we draw a tangent to the D_X curve at point B, and then we move down distance NR from point B. This identifies point B' on the MR_X curve. By moving down distance RT from point E on the D_X curve, we define point E' ($MR = 0$) on the MR_X curve.

of Figure 5.6, we draw the tangent to demand curve D_X at point B and move distance NR downward from point B. This identifies point B' on the MR_X curve. Another point on the MR_X curve is obtained by moving distance RT down from point E. This identifies point E'. Other points on the MR_X curve can be similarly obtained. By joining these points we get the MR_X curve for the D_X curve (see the right panel of Figure 5.6). Note that when the demand curve is nonlinear, the marginal revenue curve is also nonlinear.

Marginal Revenue, Price, and Elasticity[15]

There is an important and often-used relationship among marginal revenue, price, and the price elasticity of demand given by

$$MR = P(1 + 1/\eta) \qquad [5.8]$$

For example, at point C on D'_X in the left panel of Figure 5.6, $\eta = -WH/0W = -9/3 = -3$, and

$$MR = \$1.50(1 - 1/3) = \$1.00$$

---

[15] For a more straightforward derivation of expression [5.8] using simple calculus, see Section A.7 of the Mathematical Appendix at the end of the book.

(the same as WC' found earlier geometrically). At point E, $\eta = -E'H/0E' = -6/6 = -1$ and $MR = \$1.00(1 - 1/1) = \$1.00(0) = 0$. At point A, $\eta = -0H/0 = -12/0 = -\infty$, and $MR = \$2.00(1 - 1/\infty) = \$2.00(1 - 0) = \$2.00$.

Formula [5.8] also applies to nonlinear demand curves. For example, at point B on D_X in the right panel of Figure 5.6, $\eta = -4/2 = -2$ and

$$MR = \$2(1 - 1/2) = \$1.00$$

(the same as found earlier geometrically). Similarly, at point E, $\eta = -6/6 = -1$ and $MR = \$1.00(1 - 1/1) = 0$.

Formula [5.8] can be derived with reference to the straight-line demand curve in the left panel of Figure 5.6. Take, for example, point C on D'_X. At point C,

$$\eta = -\frac{WH}{0W} = -\frac{CH}{AC} = -\frac{J0}{AJ}$$

But $J0 = CW$ and, by congruent triangles, $AJ = CC'$. Hence,

$$\eta = -\frac{J0}{AJ} = -\frac{CW}{CC'} = -CW/(CW - C'W) = -\frac{P}{(P - C'W)} = -\frac{P}{(P - MR)}$$

With this result, we manipulate the equation algebraically, to isolate MR on the left-hand side:

$$\eta(P - MR) = -P$$

$$P - MR = -\frac{P}{\eta}$$

$$-MR = -\frac{P}{\eta} - P$$

$$MR = P + \frac{P}{\eta}$$

$$MR = P(1 + 1/\eta) \text{ (expression (5.8))}$$

So far, we have discussed the market demand curve for a commodity (D'_X or D_X in Figure 5.6). If there is only one producer or seller in the market (a monopolist), the firm faces the market demand curve for the commodity. When there is more than one producer or seller of the commodity, each firm will face a demand curve that is more elastic than the market demand curve because of the possible substitution among the products of the different firms. With a very large number of sellers of a homogeneous or identical product, the demand curve for the output of each firm might be horizontal or infinitely elastic (perfect competition). In this case the change in total revenue in selling one additional unit of the commodity (i.e., the marginal revenue) equals price. This is confirmed by using formula [5.8]; that is,

$$MR = P(1 - 1/\infty) = P$$

For example, in Figure 5.7, if the firm sells $5X$, its $TR = \$5$. If it sells $6X$, $TR = \$6$. Thus, $MR = P = \$1$, and the demand curve and the marginal revenue curves coincide. (The perfectly competitive model will be examined in Chapter 9.)

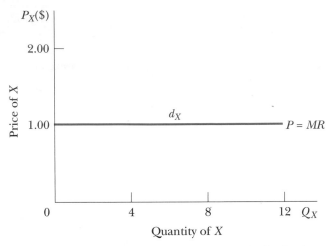

FIGURE 5.7   Demand Curve for the Output of a Perfectly Competitive Firm   The demand curve for the output of a perfectly competitive firm is horizontal or infinitely elastic. Thus, $P = MR$ and the demand curve and the marginal revenue curve coincide.

Example 5–6 gives the price, cross, and income elasticities of demand for beer, wine, and spirits in the United States and examines the relationship among the various elasticities as well as between price elasticities and total revenue. The "At the Frontier" section then examines some new revolutionizing approaches to consumer demand estimation and marketing.

EXAMPLE 5–6

The U.S. Consumer Demand for Alcoholic Beverages

Table 5.7 gives the price, cross, and income (expenditures) elasticities of the U.S. demand for alcoholic beverages (beer, wine, and spirits) estimated from U.S. Department of Agriculture individual and household food-consumption survey data for 1987–1988.

From Table 5.7, we see that the price elasticity of demand for beer (η_{XX}) is −0.23. This means that a 10% *increase* in the price of beer results in a 2.3% *reduction* in the quantity of beer demanded by U.S. consumers and thus to an *increase* in consumer expenditures on beer. The price elasticity of wine (η_{YY}) is −0.40 and that of spirits (η_{ZZ}) is −0.25, so that an increase in their price also leads consumers to demand a smaller quantity of wine and spirits, but also to spend more on these alcoholic beverages. Table 5.7 also shows that the cross price elasticity of demand for beer with respect to wine (η_{XY}) is 0.31 and with respect to spirits (η_{XZ}) is 0.15. This means that wine and spirits are substitutes for beer, with wine being a better substitute. Thus, a 10%

TABLE 5.7	Price, Cross, and Income Elasticities of Demand for Beer, Wine, and Spirits in the United States		
Beer		**Wine**	**Spirits**
$\eta_{XX} = -0.23$		$\eta_{YY} = -0.40$	$\eta_{ZZ} = -0.25$
$\eta_{XY} = 0.31$		$\eta_{YX} = 0.16$	$\eta_{ZX} = 0.07$
$\eta_{XZ} = 0.15$		$\eta_{YZ} = 0.10$	$\eta_{ZY} = 0.09$
$\eta_{XI} = -0.09$		$\eta_{YI} = 5.03$	$\eta_{ZI} = 1.21$

Legend: X = beer, Y = wine, Z = spirits, I = Income

increase in the price of wine will lead to a 3.1% increase in the demand for beer, while a 10% increase in the price of spirits leads to a 1.5% increase in the demand for beer. Note that the cross price elasticity of wine and spirits with respect to beer (i.e., η_{YX} and η_{ZX} in columns two and three of the table) are somewhat different from the cross price elasticity of demand for beer with respect to wine and spirits (η_{XY} and η_{XZ} in column one).

Finally, Table 5.7 shows that with $\eta_{XI} = -0.09$, $\eta_{YI} = 5.03$, and $\eta_{ZI} = 1.21$, a 10% increase in consumer income (expenditure) leads to a 0.9% *reduction* in the demand for beer, but to a 50.3% *increase* in the demand for wine, and a 12.1% *increase* in the demand for spirits. Thus, beer can be considered an inferior good, while wine and spirits can be regarded as luxuries (with wine being a much stronger luxury than spirits).

Sources: X. M. Gao, E. J. Wiles, and G. L. Kramer, "A Microeconometric Model of the U.S. Consumer Demand for Alcoholic Beverages," *Applied Economics,* January 1995, pp. 59–69.

AT THE FRONTIER
The Marketing Revolution with Micromarketing

While regression analysis (discussed in the appendix to this chapter) is by far the most useful and used method of estimating demand, **marketing research approaches to demand estimation** are being revolutionized and becoming increasingly important as a result of new technological developments that permit micromarketing.

There are several traditional marketing approaches to estimate market demand curves and elasticities. One involves *consumer surveys* using interviews or questionnaires in which consumers are asked how much of a commodity they would purchase at various prices. It is, however, generally agreed that this procedure

Continued. . .

yields very biased results, because consumers either cannot or will not give trust-worthy answers. Another traditional marketing approach to demand estimation is *consumer clinics,* in which consumers are given a sum of money and asked to spend it in a simulated store to see how they react to price changes. However, the sample of consumers must necessarily be small because this procedure is expensive. Also, the results are questionable because consumers are aware that they are in an artificial situation. Still another traditional marketing approach to demand estimation is a *market experiment,* whereby the seller increases the price of the commodity in one market or store and lowers it in another and then records the different quantities purchased in the two markets or stores. This procedure is questionable because a small sample is involved, the seller can permanently lose customers in the high-priced market or store, and only the immediate or short-run response to the price change is obtained.

Recent technological developments in telecommunications, however, have greatly changed and completely revitalized marketing research approaches to consumer demand estimation to the point where they have become crucial marketing tools and are bound to become even more important in the future. One such tool is micromarketing.

Today, more and more consumer-product companies are narrowing their marketing strategy from the region and city to the individual neighborhood and single store. The aim of such a detailed point-of-sale information, or **micromarketing,** is to identify on a store-by-store basis the types of products with the greatest potential appeal for the specific customers in the area. Using census data and checkout scanners, Market Metrics, a marketing research firm, now collects consumer information at more than 30,000 supermarkets around the country. For example, for a particular grocery store in Georgia, Pennsylvania, Market Metrics found that potential customers were predominantly white, blue collars, owned two cars, lived in households of three or four people, and had an average income of $54,421, and 26% of the people were below the age of 15. Based on these demographic and economic characteristics, Market Metrics determined that the strongest sellers in this market would be baby foods and grooming items, baking mixes, desserts, dry dinner mixes, cigarettes, laundry supplies, first aid products, and milk. Less strong would be sales of artificial sweeteners, tea, books, film, prepared food, yogurt, wine, and liquor. Such store-specific micromarketing is likely to become more and more common and necessary for successful retailing in the future.

As marketers refine their tools, they are increasingly taking aim at the ultimate narrow target: the individual consumer. Indeed, many companies, led by banks, are assembling customer profiles and employing sophisticated technology called *neural networks* in order to set up *one-to-one marketing* (also called relationship marketing or customer–relationship management). This seeks to reach the individual consumer and establish a learning relationship with each customer, starting from the most valuable ones. This is exactly what Amazon.com (the internet book seller) does when it reminds a customer that a book that might interest her has just come in. One-to-one marketing requires identifying the company's customers, differentiating among them, interacting with them, and customizing the product or service to fit each individual customer's needs.

For example, the Quaker Oats Company tracks how your household redeems coupons and uses the information to refine the coupons it will offer you in the future, and Merrill Lynch & Co. provides detailed financial information about its customers to its brokers in order to help them promote the company's financial products. Depositing a $10,000 check may thus eliminate the customer as a likely candidate for a car loan, but not for a home mortgage loan. It may even determine whether your telephone call gets answered first (if your profile, which comes up immediately on the bank's computer screen, identifies you as a valued customer) or last. Although it is not easy to set up one-to-one marketing and most companies may not yet be capable or ready for it, it is almost certain that marketing will be getting more and more personalized in the future.

Sources: "Know Your Customer," *The Wall Street Journal,* June 21, 1999, p. R18, and "Is Your Company Ready fo One-to-One Marketing?" *Harvard Business Review,* January–February 1999, pp. 151–160.

SUMMARY

1. The market demand curve for a commodity is obtained from the horizontal summation of the demand curves of all the individual consumers in the market and shows the total quantity demanded at various prices. It is negatively sloped; and, in drawing it, we must hold constant the consumers' incomes, the price of substitutes and complementary commodities, tastes, and the number of consumers in the market. The market demand curve is flatter or more elastic than otherwise with a bandwagon effect (a positive network externality), and steeper and less elastic when a snob effect (a negative network externality) is present, or with conspicuous expenditures or Veblen effect.

2. The price elasticity of demand is measured by the percentage change in the quantity demanded of a commodity divided by the percentage change in its price. By drawing a tangent to a point on a nonlinear demand curve and dropping a perpendicular to either axis, we can measure price elasticity at that point by the ratio of two distances. A straight-line demand curve is unitary elastic at its midpoint, elastic above the midpoint, and inelastic below the midpoint. Total expenditures and price move in opposite directions if demand is elastic and in the same direction if demand is inelastic. A rectangular hyperbola demand curve has unitary elasticity and constant total expenditures throughout. A demand curve is more elastic (a) the closer and the better are the available substitutes, and (b) the longer the adjustment period to the price change.

3. The income elasticity of demand (η_I) measures the percentage change in the quantity purchased of a commodity divided by the percentage change in consumers' incomes. A commodity is usually considered to be a necessity if η_I is between 0 and 1 and a luxury if η_I exceeds 1. η_I exceeds 1 if the tangent to the Engel curve is positively sloped and crosses the income axis. η_I is between 0 and 1 if the tangent to the Engel curve is positively sloped and crosses the quantity axis. If η_I is negative, the commodity is an inferior good and the Engel

curve is negatively sloped. According to Engel's law, the proportion of total expenditures on food declines as family incomes rise.

4. Commodities X and Y are substitutes if more of X is purchased when the price of Y goes up, and complements if less of X is purchased when the price of Y goes up. The cross elasticity of demand between commodities X and Y (η_{XY}) measures the percentage change in the quantity purchased of X divided by the percentage change in the price of Y. If η_{XY} is positive, X and Y are substitutes. If η_{XY} is negative, X and Y are complements, and if $\eta_{XY} = 0$, X and Y are independent commodities.

5. We can measure the increase in U.S. imports and exports as a result of a decline in their prices by their respective price elasticities of demand. The only complication is that the price of U.S. imports and exports is also affected by changes in the exchange rate. The exchange rate gives the number of units of the domestic currency required to purchase one unit of the foreign currency. We can also measure the income elasticity of demand for U.S. imports and for the imports of other nations.

6. The total revenue (TR) of sellers equals price times quantity. Marginal revenue (MR) is the change in TR per unit change in the quantity of the commodity sold. MR is positive when demand (D) is elastic because a reduction in price increases TR. When D is unitary elastic, $MR = 0$ because TR is constant (at its maximum). When D is inelastic, MR is negative because a reduction in price reduces TR. The MR curve for a straight-line D curve bisects the quantity axis. The MR at a point on a nonlinear D curve is found geometrically by drawing a tangent to the demand curve at that point. Marginal revenue, price, and price elasticity of demand are related by $MR = P(1 + 1/\eta)$. The demand curve facing a perfectly competitive firm is horizontal and $P = MR$ because η is infinite. Today, marketing research approaches to demand estimation are being revolutionized by new technological developments that permit micromarketing.

KEY TERMS

Market demand curve
Bandwagon effect
Snob effect
Veblen effect
Price elasticity of demand (η)
Point elasticity of demand
Arc elasticity of demand
Engel curve
Income elasticity of demand (η_I)
Necessity
Luxury

Engel's law
Substitutes
Complements
Cross elasticity of demand (η_{XY})
Price elasticity of demand for imports
Price elasticity of demand for exports
Exchange rate
Income elasticity of demand for imports

Income elasticity of demand for exports
Total Revenue (TR)
Marginal Revenue (MR)
Average Revenue (AR)
Marketing research approaches to consumer demand
Micromarketing
Identification problem
Multiple regression

REVIEW QUESTIONS

1. Which is more elastic, an individual's demand curve for a commodity or the market demand curve for a commodity? Why? Is this always true? Explain.

2. Will a decrease in a commodity price increase expenditures on that commodity? Why?

3. If the price of household natural gas increases by 10%, by how much can we expect the quantity

demanded of household natural gas and total expenditures on household natural gas to change in the short run and in the long run according to the elasticity values in Table 5.2?

4. Is the price elasticity of demand for Marlboro cigarettes more or less elastic than the demand for all tobacco products? Why? By how much would the quantity demanded of Marlboro cigarettes change in the long run if the price rose by 5% and the long-run price elasticity of demand is 3.56? If the price of all tobacco products also increased by 5%, would the quantity demanded of Marlboro cigarettes change by more or less as compared to the case when only the price of Marlboro cigarettes changed?

5. Suppose that a study has found that the price elasticity of demand for subway rides is 0.7 in Washington, D.C., and the mayor wants to cut the operating deficit of the subway system. Should the mayor contemplate increasing or decreasing the price of a subway ride? Why?

6. Can you say with reference to Table 5.4 whether producers and sellers of beef or pork, products would be affected more adversely from a recession?

7. Which of the following are more likely to have a positive cross elasticity of demand: pencils and paper, an IBM PC and a Dell PC, or automobiles and gasoline?

8. What other demand elasticities, besides those examined in this chapter, are likely to be important for beachwear? How would you measure such elasticities?

9. If the price of books in England falls by 10%, but at the same time the dollar appreciates (i.e., increases in value with respect to the British pound) by 10%, how is the U.S. demand for imported books from the United Kingdom likely to be affected?

10. If prices and exchange rates remain unchanged, but income rises by 4% in the United States and 3% in the rest of the world during a given year, by how much would U.S. imports from and exports to the rest of the world change if the income elasticity of demand for U.S. imports is 1.94 while the income elasticity of demand for U.S. exports is 0.80? How would the U.S. trade balance (exports minus imports) change over the year if it was balanced at the beginning of the year?

11. If the price of a product is $10 and the marginal revenue is $5, what is the price elasticity of demand for the product at that point?

12. If the demand curve faced by a firm is $d_X = P_X = 10, what is the price elasticity of demand at $Q_X = 10$? Between $Q_X = 10$ and $Q_X = 12$?

13. What are the marketing research approaches to demand estimation? What is meant by micromarketing?

PROBLEMS

1. Measure the price elasticity of the market demand curve in the left panel of Figure 5.2
   a. from point B to point E.
   b. from point E to point B.
   c. as an average over arc BE.

2. Measure graphically the price elasticity of demand curve D_X in the left panel of Figure 5.2
   a. at point B.
   b. at point G.

3. Using the general formula for the price elasticity of demand (i.e., equation [5.1]),

prove that
   a. $\eta = \infty$ at point A on D'_X in the right panel of Figure 5.2.
   b. $\eta = 0$ at point H in the same diagram.

*4. Explain the following.
   a. Of two parallel demand curves, the one further to the right has a smaller price elasticity at each price.
   b. When two demand curves intersect, the flatter of the two is more elastic at the point of intersection.

---

* = Answer provided at end of book.

5. Using only the total expenditures criterion, determine if the demand schedules given in the following table are elastic, inelastic, or unitary elastic.

$P(\$)$	5	4	3	2	1
Q_X	100	130	180	275	560
Q_Y	100	120	150	220	430
Q_Z	100	125	167	250	500

6. If the price elasticity of demand for Marlboro cigarettes is −6 and its price rose by 10%
   a. by how much would the quantity demanded decrease?
   b. would the consumers' total expenditures on Marlboro cigarettes increase, decrease or remain unchanged?
   c. If the price of all other brands of cigarettes also increased by 10%, what would happen to the quantity demanded of Marlboro? To consumers' expenditures on Marlboro?

7. From the following table

Q_X	100	250	350	400	300
I	\$10,000	15,000	20,000	25,000	30,000

   a. calculate the income elasticity of demand for commodity X between various income levels and determine what type of good is commodity X;
   b. plot the Engel curve; how can you tell from the shape of the Engel curve what type of good is commodity X?

*8. a. Explain why in a two-commodity world both commodities cannot be luxuries.
   b. What would be the effect on the quantity of cars purchased if consumers' incomes rose by 10% and the income elasticity of demand is 2.5?

9. Which of the following sets of commodities are likely to have positive cross elasticity of demand?
   a. aluminum and plastics
   b. wheat and corn
   c. pencils and paper
   d. private and public education
   e. gin and tonic
   f. ham and cheese
   g. men's and women's shoes

*10. Using the values for the price and income elasticity of demand for electricity and for the cross elasticity of demand between electricity and natural gas given in Tables 5.2, 5.4, and 5.5, answer the following questions:
   a. Is the demand for electricity elastic or inelastic in the short run? In the long run? How much would the quantity demanded of electricity change as a result of a 10% increase in its price in the short run? In the long run?
   b. Is electricity a necessity or a luxury? How much would electricity consumption change with a 10% increase in consumers' incomes?
   c. Is natural gas a substitute or complement of electricity? By how much would electricity consumption change with a 10% increase in the price of natural gas?

11. Given the following demand schedule

$P(\$)$	8	7	6	5	4	3	2	1	0
Q_X	0	1	2	3	4	5	6	7	8

   a. find the total revenue and the marginal revenue.
   b. plot the total revenue curve, the demand curve, and the marginal revenue curve.
   c. Using the formula relating marginal revenue, price, and elasticity, confirm the values of the marginal revenue found geometrically for $P = \$8$, for $P = \$4$, and for $P = \$2$.

12. Explain why a firm should never operate in the inelastic range of its demand curve.

*13. The following proposition (proved in Section A.6 of the Mathematical Appendix at the end of the text) is given:

$$K_X \eta_{XI} + K_Y \eta_{YI} = 1$$

where K_X is the proportion of the consumer's income I spent on commodity X (i.e., $K_X = P_X Q_X / I$, η_{XI} is the income elasticity of demand for commodity X, K_Y is the proportion of income spent on Y (i.e., $K_Y = P_Y Q_Y / I$), and η_{YI} is the income elasticity of demand for Y. Also, suppose that a consumer spends 75% of his or her income on commodity X and the income elasticity of demand for commodity X is 0.9. Assume that the individual consumes only commodities X and Y.

a. Find the income elasticity of demand for commodity Y.

b. What kind of commodity is Y? X? How high would the income elasticity of demand for X have to be before commodity Y becomes inferior?

APPENDIX   EMPIRICAL ESTIMATION OF DEMAND BY REGRESSION ANALYSIS

The most useful and used method of estimating market demand curves today is regression analysis. This method uses actual market data of the quantities purchased of the commodity at various prices over time (i.e., time series data) or for various consuming units or areas at one point in time (i.e., cross-section data). Indeed, all of the actual demand elasticities presented in the examples in this chapter were estimated by regression analysis. However, only if the scatter of quantity-price observations (points) fall as in the left panel of Figure 5.8 can we estimate a demand curve from the data. If the points fall as in the right panel, we face an **identification problem** and may be able to estimate neither a reliable demand curve nor a supply curve for the commodity from the data.[16]

When quantity price observations (points) fall as in the left panel of Figure 5.8, we can estimate the average demand curve for the good by correcting for the forces that cause the demand curve to shift (i.e., by correcting for the changes or differences in incomes and in the prices of related commodities). This is accomplished by the **multiple regression** statistical technique.[17] Regression analysis allows the economist to disentangle the independent effect of the various determinants of demand so as to identify from the data the average market demand curve for the commodity (such as dashed line D in the left panel).

To conduct the regression analysis, the researcher collects data on the quantity purchased of the good in question, its price, the income of consumers, and the price of one or more related commodities (substitutes and complements). Regression analysis allows the researcher to correct for the effect of changes or differences in consumers' incomes and in the prices of related commodities and permits the estimation of the average demand function that best fits the data (as, for example, D in the left panel of Figure 5.8). The values of all the collected variables are usually first transformed into logarithms because by

---

[16] Each quantity-price observation (point) is usually given by the intersection of a different (and unknown) demand and supply curve for the commodity. The reason for this is that demand and supply curves usually shift over time and are usually different for different consumers and in different places. When the points fall as in the left panel, we can correct for the forces that cause the demand curve to shift and derive an average demand curve from the data. When the points fall as in the right panel and the shifts in demand and supply are not independent, we are unable to do so.

[17] Regression analysis is explained in a course in statistics. For an introduction to regression analysis, see D. Salvatore and D. Reagle, *Statistics and Econometrics,* 2nd ed. (New York: McGraw-Hill, 2002, Chapters 6 and 7).

FIGURE 5.8   Scatter Diagram of Quantity–Price Observations When the scatter points of quantity–price observations fall as in the left panel, we can estimate an average demand curve from the data using regression analysis, such as dashed line *D*. However, when the points fall as in the right panel, we may be unable to estimate or identify either a reliable demand or supply curve.

doing so the estimated coefficients of the demand function are the various elasticities of demand.[18]

By regression analysis we estimate a demand function of the following form:

$$Q_X = a + bP_X + cI + eP_Y \qquad [5.9]$$

where Q_X, P_X, I, and P_Y usually refer to the logarithm of the quantity purchased of commodity X per unit of time, its price, the consumers' income, and the price of related commodity Y, respectively. $Q_X = a$ (the constant) when P_X, I, and P_Y are all zero. The estimated coefficient of P_X, b, is the price elasticity of demand (when the regression is performed on the data transformed into logarithms). On the other hand, c is the estimated income elasticity of demand, while e is the estimated cross elasticity of demand of good X for good Y.

For the demand curve of good X to obey the law of demand, the estimated b coefficient (η_X) must be negative (so that quantity demanded and price are inversely related). Good X is a necessity if the estimated c coefficient (η_I) is positive but smaller than 1. On the other hand, good X is a luxury if $c > 1$ and an inferior good if $c < 0$. If the estimated e coefficient (η_{XY}) is positive, good Y is a substitute for good X. If $e < 0$, good Y is a complement of good X. Regression analysis is also used to forecast future demand, as Example 5–7 illustrates.

---

[18] In order for the estimated coefficients to be elasticities, the value of each variable collected must first be transformed into the natural logarithm. Natural logs are those to the base 2.718 (as opposed to common logs, which are to the base 10). For example, the natural log of 100, written ln 100, is 4.61 (i.e., ln 100 = 4.61). This is obtained by looking up the number 100 in a table of natural logs or more simply using a pocket calculator. The time series or the cross-section data of each variable transformed into natural logs are then used to run the regression and obtain the various coefficients of the demand function. These estimated coefficients are the elasticities. Why this is so is explained in a course of mathematics for economists.

EXAMPLE 5-7

Estimating and Forecasting the U.S. Demand for Electricity

Estimating and forecasting the demand for electricity is very important because it takes many years to build new capacity to meet future needs. One such an estimate was provided by Halvorsen, who used multiple regression analysis to estimate the market demand equation for electricity with cross-sectional data transformed into natural logarithms for the 48 contiguous states in the United States for the year 1969.

Table 5.8 reports the estimated elasticity of demand for electricity for residential use in the United States with respect to the price of electricity, per capita income, the price of gas, and the number of customers in the market. Although the results of various studies differ somewhat, the results reported below indicate that the amount of electricity for residential use consumed in the United States would fall by 9.74% as a result of a 10% increase in the price of electricity, would increase by 7.14% with a 10% increase in per capita income, would increase by 1.59% with a 10% increase in the price of gas, and is proportional to the number of customers in the market. Thus, the market demand curve for electricity is negatively sloped, electricity is a normal good and a necessity, and gas is a substitute for electricity.

Using the above estimated demand elasticities and projecting the growth in per capita income, in the price of gas, in the number of customers in the market, and in the price of electricity, public utilities could forecast the growth in the demand for electricity in the United States so as to adequately plan new capacities to meet future needs. For example, if we assume that per capita income grows at 3% per year, the price of gas at 20% per year, the number of customers at 1% per year, and the price of electricity at 4% per year, we can forecast that the demand for electricity for residential use in the United States will expand at a rate of 2.43% per year. This rate is obtained by adding the products of the value of each elasticity to the projected growth of the corresponding variable, as indicated in the following equation:

$$Q = (0.714)(3\%) + (0.159)(20\%) + (1.000)(1\%) - (0.974)(4\%)$$
$$= 2.142 + 3.180 + 1.000 - 3.896$$
$$= 6.322 - 3.896$$
$$= 2.426$$

With different projections of the yearly growth in per capita income, the price of gas, the number of customers in the market, and the price of electricity, we will get correspondingly different results.

The above results are shown in Figure 5.9, where P_0 and Q_0 are the original price and quantity of electricity demanded in the United States on hypothetical demand curve D_0 in the base period (say, the current year). Demand curve D' results from the projected increase in per capita income, D'' results from the increase in the price of gas also, and D_1 results from the increase in the number of customers in the market as well. Thus, D_1 takes into account or reflects the cumulative effect of all the growth factors considered.

| TABLE 5.8 | Elasticities of Demand for Electricity for Residential Use in the United States |

Variable	Value
Price	−0.974
Per capita income	0.714
Price of gas	0.159
Number of customers	1.000

Sources: R. Halvorsen, "Demand for Electric Energy in the United States," *Southern Economic Journal,* April 1976.

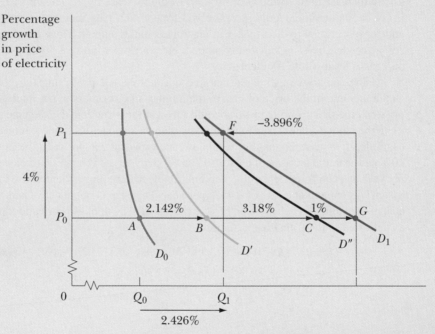

FIGURE 5.9   **Forecast of Electricity in the United States** P_0 and Q_0 are the original price and quantity of electricity demanded in the United States on hypothetical demand curve D_0. Demand curve D' results from projecting a 3% increase in per capita incomes, D'' by also projecting a 20% increase in the price of gas, and D_1 from a 1% increase in the number of customers in the market as well. If the price elasticity is also assumed to increase by 4% (from P_0 to P_1), the demand for electricity increases from 2.426% per year (the movement from point A on D_0 to point F on D_1).

Were the price of electricity to remain constant, the demand for electricity would rise by 6.322% per year (given by the movement from point A on D_0 to point G on D_1 in the figure). The projected increase in the price of electricity by 4% per year (from P_0 to P_1), by itself, will result in a decline in the quantity demanded of electricity by 3.896% (the movement from point G to point F on D_1). The net result of all forces at work gives rise to a net increase in Q of 2.426% per year (the movement from point A on D_0 to point F on D_1).

Until the mid-1990s when the deregulation of the electricity market started in the United States, the nation's regulatory commissions set low electricity rates and this discouraged the building of new power plants. Electrical power companies simply preferred charging higher electricity rates at times of peak demand rather than building the new plants. All this began to change during the past decade as the electricity market started to be deregulated. Botched-up deregulation, however, led to widespread electricity shortages, blackouts or brownouts, and sharply higher electricity prices in California and other western states during 2000 and 2001, and this slowed down, put on hold, or even reversed the deregulation process. The United States does need to build from 1,300 to 1,900 new power plants to meet future demand, which is expected to grow by 45% by the year 2020. Since it takes from 6 to 12 years to build a new plant, electrical power companies have no time to waste.

Sources: "R. Halvorsen, "Demand for Electric Energy in the United States," *Southern Economic Journal,* April 1976; "Value Networks—The Future of the U.S. Electric Utility Industry," Sloan Management Review, Summer 1997, pp. 21–34; "Plant-Building Gets a Boost from the U.S.," *Financial Times,* June 4, 2001, p. 1; and "The Lessons Learned," *Wall Street Journal,* September 17, 2001, p. R4.

INTERNET SITE ADDRESSES

An excellent presentation of the analysis of demand and elasticities is found in:

> http://price.bus.okstate.edu/archive/Econ3113_963/Shows/Chapter3/chap_03.htm
>
> http://price.bus.okstate.edu/archive/Econ3113_963/Shows/Chapter4/chap_04.htm

Information about McDonalds can be found at:

> http://www.mcdonalds.com

For the elasticity of demand for alcoholic beverages, see:

> http://tigger.uic.edu

> http://www.prevent.org/Winword/pb_PDFalcohol_tax_briefing1.pdf

The demand for electricity, deregulation, and shortages are examined in:

> http://www.eia.doe.gov/cneaf/electricity/dsm/dsm_sum.html
>
> http://www.msnbc.com/news/297115.asp?cp1=1
>
> http://www.opensecrets.org/news/electricity.htm
>
> http://www.rppi.org/ps280central.html

## CHAPTER 6

Choice Under Uncertainty

Traditional demand theory—as examined until now—implicitly assumed a riskless world. It assumed that consumers face complete certainty as to the results of the choices they make. Clearly, this is not the case in most instances. For example, when we purchase an automobile we cannot be certain as to how good it will turn out to be and how long it will last. Similarly, when we choose an occupation, we cannot be certain as to how rewarding it will be in relation to alternative occupations. Thus, the applicability of traditional economic theory is limited by the fact that it is based on the assumption of a riskless world, while most economic decisions are made in the face of risk or uncertainty.

In this chapter we extend traditional demand theory to deal with choices subject to risk or uncertainty. We begin the chapter by distinguishing between risk and uncertainty and introducing some of the concepts essential for risk analysis. Then we examine methods for measuring risk and for analyzing an individual's attitude toward risk. Subsequently, we discuss gambling and insurance, risk–return indifference curves, and their use in analyzing choices subject to risk. Finally, we summarize ways by which an individual or other economic agent can reduce risk. A large dosage of realism is introduced into the analysis by the many real-world examples included in the chapter. The "At the Frontier" section deals with foreign exchange risk and hedging.

6.1 RISK AND UNCERTAINTY IN DEMAND CHOICES

Consumer choices are made under conditions of certainty, risk, or uncertainty. **Certainty** refers to the situation where there is only one possible outcome to a decision, and this outcome is known precisely. For example, investing in Treasury bills leads to only one outcome (the amount of the yield), and this is known with certainty. The reason is that there is virtually no chance that the federal government will fail to redeem these securities at maturity or that it will default on interest payments. On the other hand, when there is more than one possible outcome to a decision, risk or uncertainty is present.

Risk refers to a situation where there is more than one possible outcome to a decision and the probability of each specific outcome is known or can be estimated. Thus, risk requires that the decision maker know all the possible outcomes of the decision and have some idea of the probability of each outcome's occurrence. For example, in tossing a coin, we can get either a head or a tail, and each has an equal (i.e., a 50–50) chance of occurring (if the coin is balanced). Similarly, investing in a stock can lead to a set of possible outcomes, and the probability of each possible outcome can be estimated from past experience. In general, the greater the variability (i.e., the greater the number and range) of possible outcomes, the greater the risk associated with the decision or action.

Uncertainty is the case when there is more than one possible outcome to a decision and where the probability of each specific outcome occurring is not known or even meaningful. This may be due to insufficient past information or instability in the structure of the variables. In extreme forms of uncertainty, not even the outcomes themselves are known. For example, drilling for oil in an unproven field carries with it uncertainty if the investor does not know either the possible oil outputs or their probability of occurrence.[1]

In the analysis of choices involving risk or uncertainty, we will utilize such concepts as strategy, states of nature, and payoff matrix. A *strategy* refers to one of several alternative courses of action that a decision maker can take to achieve a goal. For example, an individual may have to decide on how much of its savings to put in stocks (which can offer high returns but are subject to high volatility and risk) and how much in governments bonds (which offer lower returns but are also subject to low volatility and risk). *States of nature* refer to conditions in the future that will have a significant effect on the degree of success or failure of any strategy, but over which the decision maker has little or no control. For example, the economy may be booming, normal, or in a recession in the future. The decision maker has no control over the states of nature that will prevail in the future, but the future states of nature can affect the outcome of any strategy that he or she may adopt. The particular decision made will depend, therefore, on the decision-maker's knowledge or estimation of how the particular future state of nature will affect the outcome or result of each particular strategy (such as the return on stocks and bonds). Finally, a *payoff matrix* is a table that shows the possible outcomes or results of each strategy under each state of nature. For example, a payoff matrix may show the return that the individual would obtain from an investment if the economy will be booming, normal, or in a recession in the future.

EXAMPLE 6–1

The Risk Faced by Coca-Cola in Changing Its Secret Formula

On April 23, 1985, the Coca-Cola Company announced that it was changing its 99-year-old recipe for Coke. Coke is the leading soft drink in the world, and the company took an unusual risk in tampering with its highly successful product. The Coca-Cola Company felt that changing its recipe was a necessary strategy to ward off the challenge from

---

[1] Although the distinction between risk and uncertainty is theoretically important, in this chapter we follow the usual convention (when introducing this topic) of using these two terms interchangeably.

Pepsi-Cola, which had been chipping away at Coke's market lead over the years. The new Coke, with its sweeter and less fizzy taste, was clearly aimed at reversing Pepsi's market gains. Coca-Cola spent over $4 million to develop its new Coke and conducted taste tests on more than 190,000 consumers over a three-year period. These tests seemed to indicate that consumers preferred the new Coke over the old Coke by 61% to 39%. Coca-Cola then spent over $10 million on advertising its new product.

When the new Coke was finally introduced in May 1985, there was nothing short of a consumers' revolt against the new Coke, and in what is certainly one of the most stunning multimillion dollar about-faces in the history of marketing, the company felt compelled to bring back the old Coke under the brand name Coca-Cola Classic. The irony is that with the Classic and new Cokes sold side by side, Coca-Cola regained some of the market share that it had lost to Pepsi. While some people believed that Coca-Cola intended all along to reintroduce the old Coke and that the whole thing was part of a shrewd marketing strategy, most marketing experts are convinced that Coca-Cola had underestimated consumers' loyalty to the old Coke. This did not come up in the extensive taste tests conducted by Coca-Cola because the consumers tested were never informed that the company intended to *replace* the old Coke with the new Coke rather than sell them side by side. This example clearly shows that even a well-conceived strategy is risky and can lead to results estimated to have a small probability of occurrence. While Coca-Cola recuperated from the fiasco, most companies are not so lucky! In the meantime, the perennial cola battle for market supremacy between Coke and Pepsi rages on.

Sources: "Coca-Cola Changes Its Secret Formula in Use for 99 Years," *New York Times,* April 24, 1985, p. 1; " 'Old' Coke Coming Back After Outcry by Faithful," *New York Times,* July 11, 1985, p. 13; "Flops," *Business Week,* August 16, 1993, pp. 76–82; and "Facing Slow Sales, Coke and Pepsi Gear Up for New Battle," *Wall Street Journal,* April 16, 2001, p. B4.

6.2 | MEASURING RISK

In the previous section we defined risk as the situation where there is more than one possible outcome to a decision and the probability of each possible outcome is known or can be estimated. In this section we examine the meaning and characteristics of probability distributions, and then we use these concepts to develop a precise measure of risk.

Probability Distributions

The **probability** of an event is the chance or odds that the event will occur. For example, if we say that the probability of booming conditions in the economy next year is 0.25, or 25%, this means that there is 1 chance in 4 for this condition to occur. By listing all the possible outcomes of an event and the probability attached to each, we get a **probability distribution.** For example, if only three states of the economy are possible (boom, normal, or recession) and the probability of each occurring is specified, we have a probability

TABLE 6.1 Probability Distribution of States of the Economy	
State of the Economy	Probability of Occurrence
Boom	0.25
Normal	0.50
Recession	0.25
Total	1.00

distribution such as the one shown in Table 6.1. Note that the sum of the probabilities is 1, or 100%, since one of the three possible states of the economy must occur with certainty.

The concept of probability distribution is essential in evaluating and comparing different outcomes or investments. In general, the outcome or payoff from an investment (e.g., from the purchase of a stock) is generally highest when the economy is booming and smallest when the economy is in a recession (when the value of the stock is likely to fall). If we multiply each possible outcome or payoff of an investment by its probability of occurrence and add these products, we get the expected value of the investment. For example, if there are two possible outcomes for investment or event X with payoffs X_1 and X_2 and probabilities Pr_1 and Pr_2, then the expected value of X or $E(X)$ is

$$\text{Expected value of } X = E(X) = Pr_1\, X_1 + Pr_1\, X_1 \qquad [6.1]$$

If there are n possible outcomes, the expected value becomes

$$E(X) = Pr_1 X_1 + Pr_2 X_2 + \cdots + Pr_n X_n \qquad [6.2]$$

Thus, the **expected value** of an investment is the weighted average of all possible payoffs that can result from the investment under the various states of the economy, with the probability of those payoffs used as weights. The expected value of an investment is a very important consideration in deciding whether or not to make an investment and which of two or more investments is preferable.

For example, Table 6.2 presents the payoff matrix of investment A and investment B and shows how the expected value or mean of each investment is determined. In this case the expected value of each of the two investments is $500, but the range of outcomes or payoffs for investment A (from $400 in recession to $600 in boom) is much smaller than for investment B (from $200 in recession to $800 in boom).

The expected profit and the variability in the outcomes of investment A and investment B are shown in Figure 6.1, where the height of each bar measures the probability that a particular outcome (measured along the horizontal axis) will occur. Note that the relationship between the state of the economy and profits is much tighter (i.e., less dispersed) for investment A than for investment B. Thus, investment A is less risky than investment B. Since both investments have the same expected profit, investment A is preferable to investment B if the individual is risk averse (the usual case). Had the expected value of investment A been lower than for investment B, the individual would have to decide whether the lower risk from investment A compensates him or her for its lower expected value. In Section 6.3

TABLE 6.2	Calculation of the Expected Profits of the Two Investments			
Investment	(1) State of Economy	(2) Probability of Occurrence	(3) Outcome of Investment	(4) Expected Value (2) × (3)
A	Boom	0.25	$600	$150
	Normal	0.50	500	250
	Recession	0.25	400	100
			Expected earnings from investment A	$500
B	Boom	0.25	$800	$200
	Normal	0.50	500	250
	Recession	0.25	200	50
			Expected earnings from investment B	$500

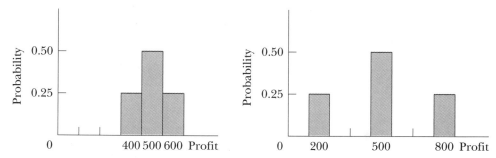

FIGURE 6.1   Probability Distribution of Profits from Investment A and Investment B   The expected profit is $500 for both projects A and B, but the range of profits (and therefore the risk) is much smaller for project A than for project B. For project A the range of profits is from $400 in a recession to $600 in a boom. For project B, the range of profits is from $200 in a recession to $800 in a boom.

we will show how an individual makes such decisions. Before doing that, however, we want to show how to measure risk more precisely.

The Standard Deviation

We have seen above that the tighter or the less dispersed a probability distribution, the smaller the risk of a particular strategy or decision. The reason is that there is a smaller probability that the actual outcome will deviate significantly from the expected value. We can measure the tightness or the degree of dispersion of a probability distribution by the standard deviation. Thus, the **standard deviation (sd)** measures the dispersion of possible outcomes from the expected value. The smaller the value of *sd*, the tighter or less dispersed the distribution—and the lower the risk attached to it.

| TABLE 6.3 | Calculation of the Standard Deviation of Profits for Investments A and B | | |

Deviation from Expected Value	Deviation Squared	Probability	Deviation Squares Times Probability
	Project A		
$600 − $500 = $100	$10,000	0.25	$2,500
500 − 500 = 0	0	0.50	0
400 − 500 = −100	10,000	0.25	2,500

Sum of deviations squared = Variance = $5,000
Standard deviation = Square root of variance = $70.71

	Project B		
$800 − $500 = $300	$90,000	0.25	$22,500
500 − 500 = 0	0	0.50	0
200 − 500 = −300	90,000	0.25	22,500

Sum of deviations squared = Variance = $45,000
Standard deviation = Square root of variance = $212.13

To find the value of the standard deviation (sd) of a particular probability distribution, we follow the three steps outlined below.

1. Subtract the expected value or the mean of the distribution from each possible outcome or payoff to obtain a set of deviations from the expected value.
2. Square each deviation, multiply the squared deviation by the probability of its expected outcome, and then sum these products. This weighted average of squared deviations from the mean is the *variance* of the distribution.
3. Take the square root of the variance to find the standard deviation (sd).[2]

Table 6.3 shows how to calculate the standard deviation of the probability distribution of payoffs or profits for investment A and investment B given in Table 6.2. The expected value was found earlier to be $500 for each investment. From Table 6.3, we see that the standard deviation of the probability distribution of payoffs for investment A is $70.71, while that for investment B is $212.13. These values provide a numerical measure of the absolute dispersion of payoffs from the expected value of each investment and confirm the greater dispersion of payoffs and risk for investment B than for investment A, shown earlier graphically in Figure 6.1. Note that risk analysis is useful not only in analyzing investments but also in examining any activity involving risk, as Example 6–2 demonstrates.

---

[2] The actual formula for the standard deviation (sd) is

$$sd = \sqrt{\sum_{i=1}^{n}(X_i - \overline{X})^2 \cdot \Pr_i}$$

where $\sum$ is the "sum of," X_i is payoff or outcome i (of n payoffs or outcomes), $\overline{X}$ is the mean or expected value of the distribution of X [i.e., $E(X)$], and $\Pr_i$ is the probability of occurrence of payoff or outcome i.

EXAMPLE 6–2

Risk and Crime Deterrence

Risk analysis can be used to analyze crime deterrence. A 1973 study found that criminals often respond to incentives in much the same way as people engaged in legitimate economic activities. For example, the rate of robberies and burglaries was found to be positively related to the gains and inversely related to the costs of (i.e., punishment for) criminal activity. It was found that for each 1% increase in the probability of being caught and sent to jail, the rate of robberies declined by 0.85% and for each 1% increase in the duration of imprisonment, the rate of burglaries declined by 0.9%. Thus, it seems that increasing the efficiency of the police in apprehending criminals and the imposition of stiffer sentences discourages crime.

Other studies, however, did not confirm this relationship but found that reducing the opportunity to commit crimes is a more effective way to reduce criminal activity. For example, a survey conducted by the *New York Times* in September 2000 found homicide rates to be higher in states with the death penalty than in states without it. Furthermore, homicide rates showed similar up-and-down trends over the years, thus offering little support to the contention that capital punishment is a deterrent. Some economists do not accept the results of these studies, however. They pointed out that if variations in other factors, such as the rate of unemployment, income inequality, and the likelihood of apprehension, as well as the existence of the death penalty, had been considered in the analysis, then the death penalty would have showed to be a significant deterrent.

Obviously, more empirical studies are needed to resolve this controversy, but risk analysis will necessarily have to be part of any such study. Indeed, risk analysis has already shown its usefulness in the analysis of crime. For example, it has been shown that the greater the probability of apprehension for a crime (and hence the lower the cost of law enforcement), the lighter the sentence. Thus, lovers' quarrels and brawls involving alcohol have the highest probability of being caught and also the lightest sentences. On the other hand, the crime of arson has an exceptionally low probability of apprehension and consequently the highest average sentence. Furthermore, risk analysis indicates that by increasing the penalty, law enforcement agencies can reduce the cost of enforcement. For example, imposing a fine of, say, $100 for a small crime and catching one violator in ten leads to an expected cost of apprehension for the violator of $10 ($100 times 0.1). But this has the same deterring effect as imposing a fine of $1,000 for the same crime and catching only one in 100 violators (which is much cheaper to do) since the expected cost of apprehension for the criminal is the same (i.e., $1,000 times 0.01 = $10).

Sources: I. Ehrlich, "Participation in Illegitimate Activities: A Theoretical and Empirical Investigation," *Journal of Political Economy,*" May/June 1973; W. T. Dickens, "Crime and Punishment Again: The Economic Approach with a Psychological Twist," National Bureau of Economic Research, *Working Paper No. 1884,* April 1986; E. Glaeser and B. Sacerdote, "The Determinants of Punishment: Deterrence, Incapacitation and Vengeance," National Bureau of Economic Research, *Working Paper No. 1884,* August 2000; and "States with no Death Penalty Share Lower Homicide Rates," *New York Times,* September 22, 2001, p. 1.

| 6.3 | ## UTILITY THEORY AND RISK AVERSION |

In this section we first examine the different views or preferences toward risk of different individuals and then use this information to examine consumers' choices in the face of risk. We will see that in making choices under risk or certainty the consumer maximizes utility or satisfaction. When risk or uncertainty is present, the consumer maximizes *expected* utility.

Different Preferences Toward Risk

Most individuals, faced with two alternative investments of equal expected value or profit, but different standard deviation or risk, will generally prefer the less risky investment (i.e., the one with the smaller standard deviation). That is, most individuals seek to minimize risks or are **risk averters.** Some individuals, however, may very well choose the more risky investment (i.e., are **risk seekers or lovers**), while still others may be indifferent to risk (i.e., are **risk neutral**). The reason is that different individuals have different preferences toward risk. Most individuals are **risk averters** because they face **diminishing marginal utility of money.** The meaning of diminishing, constant, and increasing marginal utility of money can be explained with the aid of Figure 6.2.

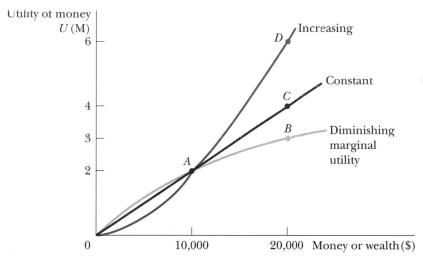

FIGURE 6.2   Diminishing, Constant, and Increasing Marginal Utility of Money
A $10,000 money income or wealth provides 2 utils of utility to a particular individual (point *A*), while $20,000 provides 3 utils (point *B*) if the total utility of money curve of the individual is concave or faces down (so that the marginal utility of money declines), 4 utils (point *C*) if the total utility curve is a straight line (so that the marginal utility is constant), and 6 utils (point *D*) if the total utility curve is convex or faces up (so that marginal utility increases). The individual would then be, respectively, a risk averter, risk neutral, or a risk seeker.

In Figure 6.2, money income or wealth is measured along the horizontal axis while the utility or satisfaction of money (measured in **utils**) is plotted along the vertical axis.[3] From the figure, we can see that $10,000 in money or wealth provides 2 utils of utility to a particular individual (point *A*), while $20,000 provides 3 utils (point *B*), 4 utils (point *C*), or 6 utils (point *D*), respectively, depending on the *total* utility of money curve for this individual being concave or facing down, a straight line, or convex (facing up).

If the *total* utility curve is concave or faces down, doubling the individual's income or wealth from $10,000 to $20,000 only increases his or her utility from 2 to 3 utils, so that the *marginal* utility of money (the slope of the total utility curve) diminishes for this individual. If the total utility of money curve is a straight line, doubling income also doubles utility, so that the marginal utility of money is constant. Finally, if the total utility of money curve is convex or faces up, doubling income more than doubles utility, so that the marginal utility of money income increases.

Most individuals are risk averters and face diminishing marginal utility of money (i.e., their total utility curve is concave or faces down—see Figure 6.2). To see why this is so, consider an offer to engage in a bet to win $10,000 if "head" turns up in the tossing of a coin or to lose $10,000 if "tail" comes up. Since the probability of a head or a tail is 0.5 or 50% and the amount of the win or loss is $10,000, the expected value of the money won or lost from the gamble is

$$0.5(\$10,000) + 0.5(-\$10,000) = 0 \qquad [6.3]$$

Even though the expected value of such a *fair game* is zero, a risk averter (an individual facing diminishing marginal utility of money) would gain less utility by winning $10,000 than he or she would lose by losing $10,000. Starting from point *A* in Figure 6.2, we see that by losing $10,000, the risk-averting individual loses 2 utils of utility if he or she loses $10,000 but gains only 1 util of utility if he or she wins $10,000. Even though the bet is fair (i.e., there is a 50–50 chance of winning or losing $10,000), the **expected utility** of the bet is negative. That is,

$$\text{Expected utility} = E(U) = 0.5(1 \text{ util}) + 0.5(-2 \text{ utils}) = -0.5 \qquad [6.4]$$

In such a case, the individual will refuse a fair bet.[4] From this, we can conclude that a risk-averting individual will not necessarily accept an investment with positive expected monetary value. To determine whether or not the individual would undertake the investment, we need to know his or her utility function of money or income.

Maximizing Expected Utility

To determine whether or not an individual should undertake an investment, he or she needs to determine the expected utility of the investment. For example, suppose that an investment

---

[3] As pointed out in Section 3.1, a *util* is a fictitious unit of utility. Here, we assume that the utility or satisfaction that a particular individual receives from various amounts of money income or wealth can be measured in terms of utils.

[4] With constant utility, $E(U) = 0.5(2 \text{ utils}) + 0.5(-2 \text{ utils}) = 0$ and the individual is risk neutral and indifferent to the bet. With increasing marginal utility, $E(U) = 0.5(4 \text{ utils}) + 0.5(-2 \text{ utils}) = 1$ and the individual is a risk seeker and would accept the bet.

has a 40% probability of providing profit of $20,000 and a 60% probability of resulting in a loss of $10,000. Since the *expected monetary return* of such a project is positive (see Table 6.4), a risk-neutral or a risk-seeking individual would undertake the project. However, if the individual is risk averse (the usual case) and his or her utility function is as indicated in Figure 6.3, the individual would not make the investment because the *expected utility* from the investment is negative (see Table 6.5).

Thus, even if the expected *monetary* return is positive, a risk-averse manager will not make the investment if the expected *utility* of the investment is negative. The general rule is that the individual seeks to maximize utility in a world of no risk or uncertainty, but

TABLE 6.4 Expected Return from the Investment

States of Nature	(1) Probability	(2) Monetary Outcome	(3) Expected Return (1) × (2)
Success	0.40	$20,000	$8,000
Failure	0.60	−$10,000	−6,000
			Expected return = $2,000

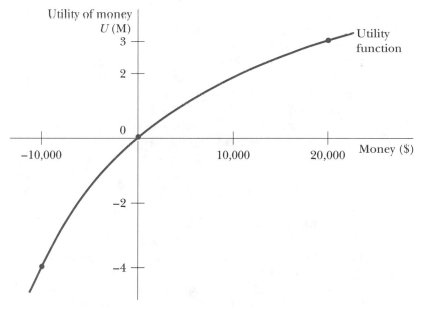

FIGURE 6.3   The Utility Function of a Risk-Averse Individual   An investment with a 40% probability of providing a return of $20,000 (3 utils of utility) and a 60% probability of resulting in a loss of $10,000 (−4 utils of utility) has an expected utility of (0.4)(3 utils) + (0.6)(−4 utils) = −1.2 utils, and it would not be made by the individual.

TABLE 6.5   Expected Utility from the Investment

States of Nature	(1) Probability	(2) Monetary Outcome	(3) Associated Utility	(4) Expected Return (1) × (3)
Success	0.40	$20,000	3	1.2
Failure	0.60	−$10,000	−4	−2.4
			Expected utility =	−1.2

maximizes *expected* utility in the face of risk.[5] Needless to say, even different risk-averse individuals have different utility functions and face different marginal utilities of money, and so even they can reach different conclusions with regard to the same investment. Being risk averse, it would seem irrational for most individuals to engage in gambling. Yet, America seems to be in the grip of a gambling craze (see Example 6–3).

EXAMPLE 6–3

America's Gambling Craze

There was a time, not too many years ago, when gambling was considered morally wrong and was illegal in most parts of the United States. The lust to get something for nothing, which gambling represents, was considered a weakness of character, and bookies and number racketeers were regarded not much better than drug dealers. All of that has changed and gambling has become America's favorite pastime. Today, gambling casinos can brag more than 100 million visitors per year—more than Major League Ballparks. Americans now spend more than $700 billion per year on all sorts of gambling from casinos to state lotteries, race track and off-track betting, sports betting, bingo, and so on—more than on movie theaters, books, amusement attractions, and recorded music *combined*. Gambling expenditures have been rising at more than 10% per year; there are now more than 42 state lotteries, and casinos, operating in 27 states. In fact, gambling flourishes in every state but Utah and Hawaii. Many go on vacation only where there is a casino, gambling is rampant in the nation's colleges, and electronics is even bringing gambling into homes, restaurants, and planes. In short, we have become a nation of gamblers, and gambling has become America's craze.

Why the change in America's tastes in favor of gambling? The boom in legal gambling can be largely attributed to state and local governments' desire to raise more money without increasing taxes. If many people would gamble anyway, why not legalize gambling and tax gambling profits to finance education and other social programs? But in doing so, state and local governments have encouraged gambling and increased

[5] Only for a risk-neutral individual does maximizing the expected monetary value or return correspond to maximizing expected utility.

its social costs. Many poor people spend a great deal of their meager incomes on gambling in the hope of a big win that would lift them out of their poverty. But for the vast majority of them, there is no big win and gambling represents a very regressive tax. With gambling legalized and even encouraged, more and more people can be expected to become compulsive or problem gamblers. As a cash business, gambling also lures criminals and organized crime and it corrupts public officials.

Gambling is also not as much as a net stimulus to the economy as it is often made out to be because it takes away from other forms of entertainment and other expenditures in general. For example, more than a quarter of a century ago, Atlantic City in New Jersey allowed casino gambling in order to revitalize the city. At the time, Atlantic City's unemployment rate was twice the state's unemployment rate. Today, more than 25 years and many casinos later, Atlantic City's unemployment rate is still twice the state's unemployment rate and many other of the city's ills remain. Why does America have such a craze for gambling if gambling seems irrational for risk averters? Because of the exaggerated hope of winning that many people have, because of the entertainment that gambling provides, and because many individuals may be risk averters for small gambles but risk lovers for big gambles.

Source: "Electronics Is Bringing Gambling into Homes, Restaurants and Planes," *Wall Street Journal,* August 16, 1995, p. A1; "America's Gambling Fever," *U.S. News & World Report,* January 15, 1996, pp. 53–51; "Gambling on the Future," *The Economist,* June 26, 1999, pp. 27–28; "The Economics of Casino Gambling," *The Journal of Economic Perspectives,* Summer 1999, pp. 173–192; National Gambling Impact Study Commission, *Final Report* (Washington, D.C.: U.S. Government Printing Office, August 3, 1999; and "Perfectas by Personal Computer," *Wall Street Journal,* August 27, 2001, p. B1.

6.4   INSURANCE AND GAMBLING

In this section we take a closer look at insurance and gambling. Specifically, we examine why some individuals insure themselves while others gamble, and, what seems entirely contradictory, why the same individual sometimes does both, buy insurance and gamble.

Why Do Some Individuals Buy Insurance?

We have seen in the previous section that a risk averter faces a total utility function of money that is concave or faces down, so that the marginal utility of money for the individual declines. This means that the individual prefers a given sum of money with certainty to any risky asset of equal expected value. It also means that an individual is willing to pay a small amount of money to avoid the small risk of incurring a large loss (i.e., to buy insurance).

For example, suppose that, as shown in Figure 6.4, an individual owns a small business that generates a daily income of $200 (point *A*) without a fire and $20 after a fire (point *B*), and the probability of no fire is $p = 0.899$ (i.e., 89.9%), so that the probability of a fire is $1 - p = 0.111$ (11.1%). Then the expected income from the business is

Expected income $= (0.889)(\$200) + (0.111)(\$20) = \$2.22 + \$178.8 = \$180.02$

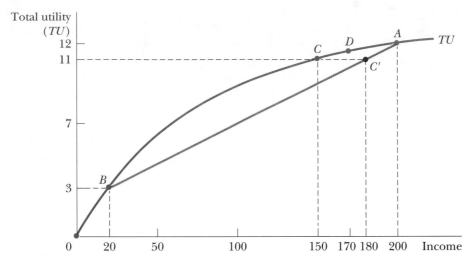

FIGURE 6.4   The Utility Function for an Insurer   The expected value of the business that provides a daily income of $200 (point A) with no fire and $20 with a fire (point B), and with the probability of 0.989 of no fire and 0.111 of a fire, is: (0.889)($200) + (0.111)($20) = $180 (point C'). The certain daily income of $150 (point C) gives the same utility to the individual as owning the business. Insuring against the loss resulting from a fire at a daily cost $30 leaves the individual with a higher level of utility (point D) than would owning the business without insurance (point C'). Thus, the individual will buy the insurance.

The income of $180.02 or $180 (rounded to the nearest dollar) is not actually available to the individual. That is, the individual faces only two alternatives: (1) an income of $200 with probability of 89.90% or (2) an income of $20 with probability of 11.1%. The expected income of $180 is a weighted average of these two alternatives using the probabilities as weights. However, the individual would never actually have the income of $180. Different probabilities of occurrence attached to the incomes of $200 and $20 would result in a different expected daily income. For example, with $p = 0.8$, the expected income from the business would be

$$\text{Expected income} = (0.8)(\$200) + (0.2)(\$20) = \$164$$

The utility of the expected income is given by the height of straight-line line (chord) BA at the point directly above the level of the expected income in Figure 6.4. For example, the utility of expected income of $180 is 11 utils (point C' on chord AB). This convenient geometric property results directly from the definition of the expected income (i.e., as the weighted average of the two alternative incomes using objective probabilities as the weights). The utility of the expected income does not fall on the total utility curve because the expected income is not an income that the individual can actually achieve (such as the income shown by point A or B).

From Figure 6.4 we can see that an income of $150 with certainty (point C on the individual's utility function) provides the individual with the same 11 utils of utility as a business that provides an expected (risky) income of $180 (point C' on chord AB). The distance

$CC' = \$30$ is called the **risk premium.** This is the maximum amount that the individual would be willing to pay to avoid the risk. Specifically, since a daily income of $150 with certainty provides the same utility to the individual as a risky business with an expected daily income of $180, the individual would be willing to pay up to $30 per day to insure himself or herself against a large loss from a fire.

Since, in our case, the individual already owns the business (rather than having to decide whether or not to enter it) and after a fire the business would still generate an income of $20 per day, he or she would actually be willing to pay up to $50 per day ($AC$ in Figure 6.4) to insure against the loss of the entire business. If the owner of the business could insure the business for $30 per day, he or she would definitely do so since that would put him or her at point D on the utility curve, and point D provides more utility (11.5 utils) than owning the business without insurance, which provides 11 utils of utility (point C'). Point D is on the utility curve because it is a daily income that the individual can actually achieve with insurance.[6]

Why Do Some Individuals Gamble?

Next we turn to the analysis of gambling. To do so, suppose that the individual of Figure 6.4, after having purchased the fire insurance for $30 (thus ending up with the certain daily income of $170 shown by point D in Figure 6.4), faces a total utility function that is convex or faces up (so that the marginal utility of money increases) *for higher incomes—* as shown in Figure 6.5. The individual now contemplates purchasing a lottery ticket costing $20 with a 20% probability of winning and receiving an extra daily income of $250.[7] After purchasing the ticket for $20, the individual's daily income would then either be $150 (shown by point C in Figure 6.5) if the individual does not win or $400 (the $150 from the business and the $250 from the win, as shown by point G in Figure 6.5) if he or she wins. Since the probability of winning is 0.2 or 20%, the expected value of the individual's income by purchasing the ticket is

$$\text{Expected value} = (\$150)(0.8) + (\$400)(0.2) = \$120 + \$80 = \$200$$

From Figure 6.5 we see that the individual's utility with purchasing the ticket that provides an expected income of $200 (point F' on chord CG) exceeds the individual's utility of the certain income of $170 without purchasing the ticket (point D on the total utility function of the individual). In fact, the utility that the individual receives by buying the lottery ticket (and continuing to hold on to his or her business) is equal to the certain daily income of $240 dollars (point F on the total utility function). Another way of looking at it is to realize that the individual prefers to purchase the lottery ticket and hold on to his or her business with an expected value of $200 (point F' on chord CG) than having $200 of certain income (point A on the total utility curve in Figure 6.5). This makes the individual a risk seeker or risk lover for increases in income.

---

[6] In Section 6.6 we will see why an insurance company would be willing to sell an insurance policy to the individual for a premium payment of $30 per day.

[7] Although lotteries usually provide one or two large prizes, people usually convert a lump-sum win into an annuity that provides a certain flow income over time in order to pay a lower tax rate.

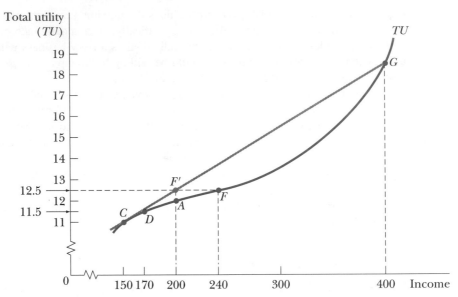

FIGURE 6.5   The Utility Function for a Gambler   With the purchase of a lottery ticket that costs $20, the individual's income is either $150 with 80% probability of not winning or $400 with a 20% probability of winning, resulting in the expected income of ($150)(0.2) + $400(0.2) = $200 (point F' on chord CG). This provides a higher utility for the individual than the certain sum of $200 (point A on the total utility curve). Indeed, buying the ticket gives the individual the same utility as the certain income of $240 (point F). Thus, the individual is a gambler for increases in income.

EXAMPLE 6–4

Gambling and Insuring by the Same Individual—A Seeming Contradiction

In the real world, we often observe individuals purchasing insurance and also gambling. For example, many people insure their homes against fire and also purchase lottery tickets. This behavior may seem contradictory. Why should the same individual act as a risk avoider (purchase insurance) and at the same time as a risk seeker (gamble)? One possible explanation for this seemingly contradictory behavior is provided by Milton Friedman and Leonard Savage, who postulate that the total utility of money curve may look like that in Figure 6.6. This total utility curve is concave or faces down (so that the marginal utility of money diminishes) at low levels of money income, and it is convex or faces up (so that the marginal utility of money increases) at higher levels of income. An individual with an income at or near the point of inflection on the total utility curve (point A) will find it advantageous both to spend a small amount of money to insure himself or herself against the small chance of a large loss (say, through a fire that destroys his or her home) and to purchase a lottery ticket providing a small chance of a large win. Starting with an income level at or near A, the individual would act as a risk avoider for

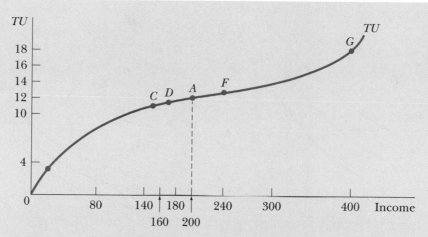

FIGURE 6.6   The Utility Function of an Individual Who Buys Insurance and Gambles   An individual whose income is $200 (point *A*), which is at or near the point of inflection of the total utility curve, will act as a risk averter and will spend a small amount of money to purchase insurance against the small chance of a large loss of income and at the same time will act as a risk seeker and gamble a small amount of money (say, to purchase a lottery ticket) that gives a small chance of a large win.

declines in income and as a risk seeker for increases in income. Indeed, Figure 6.6 was obtained by bringing together Figure 6.4 and Figure 6.5.

One shortcoming of the above analysis is that it rationalizes more than explains economic behavior in the face of risk. In fact, Kenneth Arrow has found that many people do not take out flood insurance even at favorable government-subsidized rates, whereas flight insurance and lotteries offer examples of people accepting extremely unfavorable odds. A recent study by Garrett and Sobel, however, did find that the utility curve of people who buy lottery ticket have the shape predicted by Friedman and Savage. Furthermore, financial planners and brokers do make a great deal of use of the concepts discussed above in trying to assess their clients' tolerance for risk in providing financial advice.

Sources: M. Friedman and L. J. Savage, "The Utility Analysis of Choices Involving Risk," *Journal of Political Economy,* August 1948; K. Arrow, "Risk Perception in Psychology and Economics," *Economic Inquiry,* January, 1982. T. A. Garrett and R. S. Sobel, "Gamblers Favor Skewness, Not Risks: Further Evidence from U.S. Lottery Games," *Economic Letters,* April 1999; and "Dealing with Risk," *Business Week,* January 17, 2000, pp. 102–112.

6.5   Risk Aversion and Indifference Curves

The extent of an individual's risk aversion can also be shown by indifference curves that relate expected income (measured along the vertical axis) to the variability of expected income (measured by the standard deviation along the horizontal axis). Each indifference

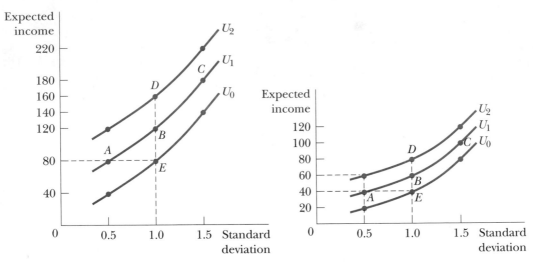

FIGURE 6.7   Indifference Curves for Risk-Averse Individuals   An increase in the standard deviation from 0.5 to 1.0 requires an increase in the expected income of $40 to keep the highly risk-averse individual shown in the left panel on indifference U_1 (compare point B with point A), while it requires an increase in the expected income of only $20 for the less risk-averse individual in the right panel.

curve shows all the combinations of standard deviation and expected income that give the individual the same level of utility or satisfaction. Since a higher variability of income (risk) must be compensated by a higher expected income, these indifference curves are positively sloped. Figure 6.7 shows two sets of such indifference curves. The indifference curves in the left panel are steep and refer to an individual who has a strong aversion to risk, while those in the right panel are flatter for a less risk-averse individual.

Specifically, indifference curve U_1 in the left panel shows that the individual is indifferent among the standard deviation of 0.5 and the expected income of $80 (point A), the standard deviation of 1.0 and the expected income of $120 (point B), and the standard deviation of 1.5 and the expected income of $180 (point C). Thus, indifference curve U_1 shows that, starting at point A, the individual requires an additional $40 in expected income to just compensate him or her for an increase in the standard deviation from 0.5 to 1.0 (and reach point B) and the individual requires an additional $60 in expected income to compensate him or her for an increase in the standard deviation from 1.0 to 1.5 (and reach point C). On the other hand, starting at point B on U_1, and the standard deviation of 1.0, the higher expected income of $160 puts the individual at point D on higher indifference curve U_2, while the lower expected income of $80 puts the individual at point E on lower indifference curve U_0. Finally, an increase in the standard deviation from 0.5 to 1.0 at the expected income of $80 shifts the individual from point A on U_1 to point E on lower indifference curve U_0.

The right panel of Figure 6.7 shows the indifference curves for an individual who is less risk averse than the individual in the left panel. For example, indifference curve U_1 in the right panel shows that the individual is indifferent among the expected income of $40 and standard deviation of 0.5 (point A), the expected income of $60 and standard deviation of 1.0 (point B), and the expected income of $100 and standard deviation of 1.5 (point C). On the other hand, for the standard deviation of 1.0, the higher expected income of $80 puts the individual at point D on higher indifference curve U_2 (from point B on U_1), while the lower expected income of $40 puts the individual at point E on a lower indifference curve U_0. Finally, an increase in the standard deviation from 0.5 to 1.0 at the expected income of $40 shifts the individual from point A on U_1 to point E on lower indifference curve U_0. The return-risk indifference curves discussed above can be used to determine the choice of the best investment portfolio for an individual (see Example 6–5).

EXAMPLE 6–5

Spreading Risks in the Choice of a Portfolio

Since investors are risk averse, on the average, they will hold a more risky portfolio of stocks and bonds only if it provides a higher return. The way by which an individual chooses an optimum investment portfolio can be shown by Figure 6.8.

In the figure, curve $ABCD$ is the individual's risk-return trade-off function or indifference curve. It shows that the individual is indifferent among a 10% rate of return on the investment with zero standard deviation (point A), a 14% rate of return with standard deviation of 0.5 (point B), a 20% rate of return with a standard deviation of 1.0 (point C), and a rate of return of 32% with a standard deviation of 1.5 (point D).

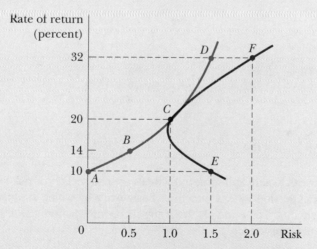

FIGURE 6.8   Choosing an Investment Portfolio   The risk-return trade-off function or indifference curve $ABCD$ shows the various risk-return trade-off combinations among which the investor is indifferent. On the other hand, frontier ECF represents the combinations of risk and return that are obtainable with mixed portfolios of asset E and asset F, with independent risk. The optimum portfolio for the investor is represented by point C, where the risk-return trade-off function or indifference curve $ABCD$ is tangent to frontier ECF.

Suppose also that there exist only two assets, with risk and return given by points E and F in Figure 6.8. If the risk of assets E and F are independent of each other, the investor can choose any mixed portfolio of assets E and F shown on the frontier or curve ECF. To understand the shape of frontier ECF, note that the return on a mixed portfolio will be between the return on asset E and on asset F alone, depending on the particular combination of the two assets in the portfolio. As far as risk is concerned, there are portfolios (such as that indicated by point C) on frontier ECF that have lower risks than those composed exclusively of either asset E or asset F. The reason for this can be gathered by assuming that the probability of a low return is $1/2$ on asset E and $1/4$ on asset F and that, for the moment, we take the probability of a low return as a measure of risk. If these probabilities are independent of each other, the probability of a low return on both assets E and F at the same time is $(1/2)(1/4) = 1/8$, which is smaller than for either asset E or F separately.

Given the risk–return trade-off function or indifference curve $ABCD$ shown in Figure 6.8, we can see that the optimum portfolio for this investor is the mixed portfolio indicated by point C, where risk–return indifference curve $ABCD$ is tangent to frontier ECF. Indeed, market evidence shows that a well-diversified portfolio containing various mixes of stocks, bonds, Treasury bills, real estate, and foreign securities can even-out a lot of the ups and downs of investing without sacrificing much in the way of returns. Of course, the type of portfolio that an investor actually chooses depends on his/her tolerance for risk, as shown by his or her risk–return trade-off functions or indifference curves.

Sources: H. M. Markowitz, "Portfolio Selection," *Journal of Finance,* March 1952, pp. 77–91; "For Volatile Times, the Psychology of Risk," *New York Times,* November 23, 1997, p. 3; "What's Your Risk Tolerance?," *Wall Street Journal,* January 23, 1998, p. C1W; "Dealing with Risk," *Business Week,* January 17, 2000, pp. 102–112; "Gauging Investors' Appetite for Risk," *Wall Street Journal,* September 18, 2001, p. C14; and "Just How Risky is Your Portfolio? *Fortune,* November 26, 2001, pp. 219–224.

6.6   REDUCING RISK AND UNCERTAINTY

We have seen above that, although some individuals are risk seekers or risk lovers, most are risk averters. In this section we examine three basic ways by which an individual can reduce risk or uncertainty. These are (1) gathering more information, (2) diversification or risk spreading, and (3) insurance.

Gathering More Information

Individuals and decision makers can often make better predictions and sharply reduce the risk or uncertainty surrounding a particular strategy or event by collecting more information. For example, by consulting *Consumer Reports,* consumers can determine how frequently a particular type of automobile or brand of refrigerators are likely to require repairs and take this information into consideration in their purchases. Similarly, investors can obtain information about the riskiness of a bond by checking Moody's, Standard & Poor, or other rating agencies' reports. Gathering information is costly, however, and the individual or manager should treat it as any other investment. That is, he or she should continue to gather information until the marginal benefit (return) from it is equal to the marginal cost. The *value of complete information* is the difference between the expected income or value of a choice with complete information and the expected value without complete information. The economics of information is examined in detail in Chapter 19.

Diversification

Another very important method of reducing risk or uncertainty is **diversification** or spreading the risks. Diversification involves investing a given amount of resources in a number of independent projects instead of investing them in a single one. This is an example of the old saying "Don't put all of your eggs in one basket." As long as the projects are not closely related, investing in a number of them can reduce the risk. If there is a *perfect negative correlation* between two activities (so that when one occurs, the other definitely will not), the risk can be entirely eliminated by engaging in both activities at the same time. Only if there is a perfect positive correlation between two events will engaging in both not reduce the risk at all. Under any other circumstance (i.e., when events are imperfectly correlated or entirely unrelated), diversification can reduce risks.

For example, a person can reduce risk by investing his or her money in a number of stocks instead of investing it in a single stock because the stocks of different companies do not exhibit perfect positive correlation. This can be accomplished more simply by buying shares of mutual funds. These are shares of companies that buy a large number of different stocks. Even doing so, however, does not eliminate all risks because in case of a recession the stocks of all companies tend more or less to fall. That is, while diversification can go a long way toward reducing risk, it cannot eliminate all of them. Systemic risks are nondiversifiable and remain.

Insurance

We have seen in Section 6.4 that risk averters can avoid risk by purchasing insurance. This involves paying a small sum to avoid the small risk of a big loss. The maximum price that an individual is willing to pay for insurance is equal to the risk premium. This is the difference between the expected value of a loss and a certain sum that provides the individual with the same utility.

For example, suppose that an individual owns a house worth $100,000 and faces a probability of 1 in 100, or 1%, that the house will burn down during any given year. The expected value of the loss from a fire during any year is then $(0.01)(\$100,000) = \$1,000$. If a fire insurance policy were offered to home owner for $1,000, a risk-averse home owner will definitely buy it. Such an insurance would be *fairly priced* or be *actuarially fair* because it is equal to the expected loss that it covers. In fact, a risk-averse home owner would be willing to pay much more for it, depending on his or her degree of risk aversion (as measured by the risk premium).

Would an insurance company be willing to sell such an insurance policy to home owners? To answer this question, suppose that the insurance company can sell the fire insurance to 100 homeowners. By insuring 100 homeowners, each paying an insurance premium of $1,000, and with the risk of 1% that one of the 100 insured homes will burn down during a year, the insurance company collects $100,000 in insurance premiums during the year and expects to pay out $100,000 for the one house that it expects to actually burn down during the year. Since the insurance company must also cover its operating expenses (i.e., the costs of administering the policy), however, it will actually have to charge a premium in excess of $1,000 for the insurance policy. With competition among insurance companies, the *insurance premium* will tend to exceed $1,000 only by the operating expenses of the insurance company. This will usually be much smaller than the *risk premium* that an individual home owner is willing to pay to avoid the risk of a fire, thus making the insurance policy still very advantageous to the average home owner.

EXAMPLE 6-6

Some Disasters as Nondiversifiable Risks

Some risks, such as those arising from a war, affect everyone. Such risks are nondiversifiable, and so insurance companies do not offer insurance against them because they cannot spread their risks. In recent years, some insurance companies have started viewing major natural disasters (hurricanes, flooding, earthquakes) as nondiversifiable risks. In the wake of the terrorist attack against the World Trade Center (WTC) in New York City on September 11, 2001, insurance companies would probably add losses from future terrorist attacks to the list on nondiversifiable (and hence noninsurable) risks in the absence of government help. Most insurance companies are reluctant to offer coverage for terrorist acts because they cannot calculate the risk and thus cannot set appropriate premiums.

It has been estimated that the insurance claims from the terrorist attack on the WTC will exceed $50 billion dollars to cover everything from the cost of rebuilding the WTC to reimbursing businesses for lost sales and paying workers' compensation claims. Losses to just 13 insurance companies that provided coverage at the WTC were estimated to exceed $7 billion. The terrorist attack against the WTC is surely the worst insurance disaster in history. It would result in some insurance companies actually going bankrupt and others refusing to sell insurance against acts of terrorism in the future or sharply increasing the cost of coverage without help from Washington. Lawmakers in Washington are now working on a proposal under which insurers would cover initial terrorism claims but their losses would be limited, with the government picking up the remainder.

Even before the attack on the WTC, however, many insurance companies refused to offer hurricane and earthquake insurance in many parts of the country that face a relatively high probability of occurrence of these catastrophic events in order to limit payment claims made on them. For example, insurers paid $12.5 billion for losses resulting from the 1994 Los Angeles Earthquake and $15.5 billion for the 1992 Hurricane Andrew. As an alternative, state-run insurance policies have been offered to households against these disasters in Florida and California, but they provide less protection and charge rates about three times higher than previously available commercial rates.

Sources: "For Insurers, Some Failures and Rate Jumps," *New York Times,* September 15, 2001, p. C1; "Under U.S. Plan, Taxpayers Would Cover Terror Claims," *New York Times,* October 7, 2001, p. B1; and "Can the Risk of Terrorism Be Calculated by Insurers?" *Wall Street Journal,* April 8, 2002, p. C1.

AT THE FRONTIER
Foreign Exchange Risks and Hedging

Portfolios with domestic and foreign securities usually enjoy lower overall volatility and higher dollar returns than portfolios with U.S. securities only. Many experts have traditionally recommended as much as 40% of a portfolio to be in foreign securities. Investing in foreign securities, however, gives rise to a foreign-exchange risk because the foreign currency can depreciate or decrease in value during the time of the investment.

For example, suppose that the return on European Monetary Union (EMU) securities is 15%, compared with 10% at home. As a U.S. investor, you might then want to invest part of your portfolio in the EMU. To do so, however, you must first exchange dollars for euros (€), the currency of the EMU, in order to make the investment. If the **foreign-exchange rate** is $1 to the euro (that is, $1/€1), you can, for example, purchase €10,000 of EMU securities for $10,000. In a year, however, the exchange rate might be $0.90/€1, indicating a 10% depreciation of the euro (i.e., each euro now buys 10% fewer dollars). In that case, you will earn 15% on your investment in terms of euros, but lose 10% on the foreign-exchange transaction, for a net *dollar* gain of only 5% (as compared with 10% on U.S. securities). Of course, the exchange rate at the end of the year might be $1.10/€1, which means that the euro appreciated by 10%, or that you would get 10% more dollars per euro. In that case, you would earn 15% on the euro investment *plus* another 10% on the foreign-exchange transaction. As an investor (rather than a speculator), however, you will probably want to avoid the risk of a large foreign-exchange loss and would not invest in the EMU unless you can hedge or cover the foreign-exchange risk.

Hedging refers to the covering of a foreign-exchange risk. Hedging is usually accomplished with a **forward contract.** This is an agreement to purchase or sell a specific amount of a foreign currency at a rate specified today for delivery at a specific future date. For example, suppose that an American exporter expects to receive €1 million in 3 months. At today's exchange rate of $1/€1, the exporter expects to receive $1 million in three months. To avoid the risk of a large euro depreciation by the time the exporter is to receive payment (and thus receive much fewer dollars than anticipated), the exporter hedges his foreign-exchange risk. He does so by selling €1 million forward at today's forward rate for delivery in three months, so as to coincide with the receipt of the €1 million from his exports. Even if today's forward rate is $0.99/€1, the exporter willingly "pays" 1 cent per euro to avoid the foreign-exchange risk. In 3 months, when the U.S. exporter receives the €1 million, he will be able to immediately exchange it for $990,000 by fulfilling the forward contract (and thus avoid a possible large foreign-exchange loss). An importer avoids the foreign-exchange risk by doing the opposite (see Problem 12).

Continued. . .

Hedging can also be accomplished with a **futures contract.** This is a standardized forward contract for *predetermined quantities* of the currency and *selected calendar dates* (for example, for €25,000 for March 15 delivery). As such, futures contracts are more liquid than forward contracts. There is a forward market in many currencies and a futures market in the world's most important currencies (the U.S. dollar, the euro, Japanese yen, British pound, Swiss franc, and Canadian dollar). Futures markets exist not only in currencies but also in many other financial instruments or derivatives (a broad class of transactions whose value is based on, or derived from, a financial market such as stocks, interest rates, or currencies) and commodities (corn, oats, soybeans, wheat, cotton; cocoa, coffee, orange juice; cattle, hogs, pork bellies; copper, gold, silver, platinum). Hedging in forward or futures markets reduces transaction costs and risks and increases the volume of domestic and foreign trade in the commodity, currency, or other financial instrument. Of course, forward and futures contracts can also be used for speculation, where they can lead to very large wins or huge losses.

Source: D. Salvatore, *International Economics,* 8th ed. (New York: John Wiley & Sons, 2003), Chapter 14.

SUMMARY

1. Most consumer choices are made in the face of risk or uncertainty. Risk refers to the situation where there is more than one possible outcome to a decision and the probability of each specific outcome is known or can be estimated. Under uncertainty, on the other hand, the probability of each specific outcome is not known or even meaningful. Choices involving risk utilize the concepts of strategy, states of nature, and payoff matrix.

2. The probability of an event is the chance or odds that the event will occur. A probability distribution lists all the possible outcomes of a decision and the probability attached to each. The expected value of an event is obtained by multiplying each possible outcome of the event by its probability of occurrence and then adding these products. The standard deviation (sd) measures the dispersion of possible outcomes from the expected value and is used as a measure of risk.

3. While some individuals are risk neutral or risk seekers, most are risk averters. Risk aversion is based on the principle of diminishing marginal utility of money, which is reflected in a total utility of money curve that is concave or faces down. A risk averter would not accept a fair bet, a risk-neutral individual would be indifferent to it, and a risk seeker would accept even some unfair bets. In investment decisions subject to risk, a risk-averse individual seeks to maximize expected utility rather than monetary returns. The expected utility of a decision or strategy is the sum of the product of the utility of each possible outcome and the probability of its occurrence.

4. A total utility curve that is concave or faces down (so that the marginal utility of money diminishes) for decreases in income and is convex or faces up (so that the marginal utility of money increases) for increases in income can be used to rationalize the seeming contradicting behavior of an individual buying insurance and gambling at the same time. The risk premium is the maximum amount that a risk-averse individual would be willing to pay to avoid a risk.

5. The extent of an individual's risk aversion can be shown by indifference curves. Each indifference curve shows all the combinations of standard deviation and expected income that give the individual the same level of utility or satisfaction. Since a higher variability of income (risk) must be compensated by a higher expected income, these indifference curves are positively sloped. The stronger the risk aversion of an individual, the steeper are his or her indifference curves. Risk–return indifference curves can be used to determine the choice of the best portfolio.

6. Individuals and decision makers can often make better predictions and sharply reduce the risk or uncertainty surrounding a particular strategy or event by collecting more information. They can also do so by diversification or risk spreading. Individuals can also reduce risks by buying insurance. Insurance premiums are usually higher than those actuarially fair to allow insurance companies to cover their operating expenses. But they are usually still much lower than the risk premium that risk-averting individuals are willing to pay. Some risks, such as those arising from wars, are nondiversifiable and insurance companies refuse to ensure them. The same is true for major natural disasters and terrorist attacks.

7. Including foreign securities in an investment portfolio can reduce risk (through diversification) and increase the rate of return, but also gives rise to a foreign-exchange risk because the foreign currency can depreciate during the time of the investment. Such foreign-exchange risk can be covered by hedging. This is usually accomplished with a forward or a futures contract. A forward contract is an agreement to purchase or sell a specific amount of a foreign currency at a rate specified today for delivery at a specific future date. A futures contract is a standardized forward contract for predetermined quantities of the currency and selected calendar dates.

KEY TERMS

Certainty	Risk seeker or lover	Risk premium
Risk	Risk neutral	Gambler
Uncertainty	Risk averter	Diversification
Probability	Diminishing marginal utility of	Foreign exchange rate
Probability distribution	money	Hedging
Expected value	Expected utility	Forward contract
Standard deviation (sd)	Insurer	Futures contract

REVIEW QUESTIONS

1. What is the meaning of risk, uncertainty? Why are these concepts important in the theory of consumer choice or demand?

2. What is meant by probability distribution, expected value, variance, standard deviation?

3. What is the value of the standard deviation if all the outcomes of a probability distribution are identical? Why is this so? What does this mean?

4. How does the process of consumer utility maximization differ in the case of certainty and risk?

5. What is the meaning of diminishing, constant, and increasing marginal utility of money?

6. Why is maximization of the expected value not a valid criterion in decision making subject to risk? Under what conditions would that criterion be valid?

7. What is the meaning of risk aversion, risk seeking or loving and risk neutrality?

8. Who is an insurer? A gambler? How can we measure the degree risk aversion or risk loving?

9. What is a risk premium? How is it measured?

10. What does a risk–return indifference curve show? What is its use?

11. How are risks and returns balanced in choosing a portfolio?

12. Why is decision making under uncertainty necessarily subjective?

13. What can an individual do to reduce risk?

14. Why does investing abroad involve a foreign exchange risk? How can such a risk be covered?

PROBLEMS

1. An individual has two investment opportunities, each involving an outlay of $10,000. The possible earnings from each investment and their respective probabilities are given in the following table.

	Investment I		Investment II		
Earnings	$4,000	$6,000	$3,000	$5,000	$7,000
Probability	0.6	0.4	0.4	0.3	0.3

  a. Calculate the expected earnings of each investment.
  b. Calculate the standard deviation of each investment.
  c. Determine which of the two investments the individual should choose.

2. An individual has to choose between investment A and investment B. The individual estimates that the income and probability of the income from each investment are given in the following table.

Investment A		Investment B	
Income	Probability	Income	Probability
$4,000	0.2	$4,000	0.3
5,000	0.3	6,000	0.4
6,000	0.3	8,000	0.3
7,000	0.2		

  a. Calculate the standard deviation of the distribution of each investment.
  b. Which of the two investments is more risky?
  c. Which investment should the individual choose?

3. An individual is considering two investment projects. Project A will return a loss of $45 if conditions are poor, a profit of $35 if conditions

are good, and a profit of $155 if conditions are excellent. Project B will return a loss of $100 if conditions are poor, a profit of $60 if conditions are good, and a profit of $300 if conditions are excellent. The probability distribution of conditions are as follows:

Conditions:	Poor	Good	Excellent
Probability:	40%	50%	10%

  a. Calculate the expected value of each project and identify the preferred project according to this criterion.
  b. Calculate the standard deviation of the expected value of each project and identify the project with the highest risk.

*4. An individual is considering two investment projects. Project A will return a loss of $5 if conditions are poor, a profit of $35 if conditions are good, and a profit of $95 if conditions are excellent. Project B will return a loss of $15 if conditions are poor, a profit of $45 if conditions are good, and a profit of $135 if conditions are excellent. The probability distribution of conditions are as follows:

Conditions:	Poor	Good	Excellent
Probability:	40%	50%	10%

  a. Calculate the expected value of each project and identify the preferred project according to this criterion.
  b. Calculate the standard deviation of the expected value of each project and identify the project with the highest risk.
  c. Which of the two projects should a risk-averse individual prefer?

5. a. What is the expected utility of an investment with a 40% probability of gaining 3 utils and

* = Answer provided at end of book.

a 60% probability of losing 1 util? Should a risk-averse individual undertake this project? (b) What if the payoff of the project were the same as above, except that the utility lost with a loss was 3 utils?

6. a. An investment has a 40% probability of providing a profit of $20,000, which would give an individual 4 utils of utility, and a 60% probability of losing $10,000, which would result in a loss of 3 utils for the individual. (a) What is the expected value of the investment? (b) What is the expected utility of the investment? (c) Should a risk-averse individual undertake this investment? Why?

*7. An individual is considering two investment projects. Project A will return a zero profit if conditions are poor, a profit of $16 if conditions are good, and a profit of $49 if conditions are excellent. Project B will return a profit of $4 if conditions are poor, a profit of $9 if conditions are good, and a profit of $49 if conditions are excellent. The probability distribution of conditions are as follows:

Conditions:	Poor	Good	Excellent
Probability:	40%	50%	10%

   a. Calculate the expected value of each project and identify the preferred project according to this criterion.

   b. The individual's utility function for profit is equal to the square root of the profit. Calculate the expected utility of each project and identify the preferred project according to this criterion.

   c. Is this individual risk averse, risk neutral, or risk seeking? Why?

8. An individual is considering two investment projects. Project A will return a zero profit if conditions are poor, a profit of $4 if conditions are good, and a profit of $8 if conditions are excellent. Project B will return a profit of $2 if conditions are poor, a profit of $3 if conditions are good, and a profit of $4 if conditions are excellent. The probability distribution of conditions are as follows:

Conditions:	Poor	Good	Excellent
Probability:	40%	50%	10%

   a. Calculate the expected value of each project and identify the preferred project according to this criterion.

   b. Assume that the individual's utility function for profit is $U(X) = X - 0.05X^2$. Calculate the expected utility of each project and identify the preferred project according to this criterion.

   c. Is this individual risk averse, risk neutral, or risk seeking? Why?

9. Suppose that a risk averse individual's income is $80 per day in Figure 6.6. Explain why this individual would not buy a lottery ticket that would increase his or her income to $200 per day with a win.

10. Suppose that a risk–return indifference curve of individual A starts on the vertical axis at a rate of return of 10% and is positively sloped, while an indifference curve of individual B starts on the vertical axis at a rate of return of 6% and is also positively sloped but less steep than the indifference curve of individual A. Finally, assume that an indifference curve of individual C starts on the vertical axis at a rate of 5% and is horizontal. (a) Which individual is risk neutral? And who is risk averse? Why? (b) Of the two risk-averse individuals, which is the least risk averse? Why? (c) What does the fact that individual A's indifference curve starts on the vertical axis at the rate of return of 10% mean?

11. An individual owns a house worth $100,000 with a probability of 1% that it will burn down in any year, which would result in a total loss. The individual's risk premium is $1,200, and he can purchase fire insurance on the house for $100 above fair or actuarial value of the loss. (a) Would the individual purchase the insurance? Why? (b) Why would an insurance company be willing to provide such insurance?

*12. A U.S. firm imports $200,000 worth of EMU goods and agrees to pay in three months. The exchange rate is $1.00/€1 today and the three-month forward rate is $1.01/€1. Explain how the importer can hedge his foreign-exchange risk.

INTERNET SITE ADDRESSES

For a discussion of risk analysis, see the Decision Analysis Society, a subdivision of the Institute of Operations Research and the Management Sciences, at:

http://www.fuqua.duke.edu/faculty/daweb

For the risk associated with air travel, see:

http://www.imsa.edu/team/spi/SADVI/sadvi97/riskexample.html

An analysis of what Coca-Cola is doing to meet its competition, see:

http://www.coke.com

The Final Report of the National Gambling Impact Commission examing gabling in America is found at:

http://www.Ngisc.gov/reports/finrpt.html

For the method of measuring risk used by J. P. Morgan and financial-markets portfolio theory, see:

http://www.jpmorgan.com

http://www.contingencyanalysis.com/glossarymodernportfoliotheory.html

For futures trading and hedging, see the Commodity Futures Trading Commission and the Chicago Mercantile Exchange Web sites at:

http://www.cftc.gov

http://www.cme.com/market/currency/index.html

PART THREE

Production, Costs, and Competitive Markets

P art Three (Chapters 7–9) presents the theory of production, cost, and pricing in competitive markets. Chapter 7 examines production theory, or how firms combine resources or inputs to produce final commodities. These concepts are then utilized and extended in Chapter 8 to examine costs of production and to derive the short-run and the long-run cost curves of the firm. Finally, Chapter 9 brings together the theory of consumer behavior and demand (from Part Two) with the theory of production and costs (from Chapters 7 and 8) to analyze how price and output are determined under perfect competition. The chapter appendices present more advanced topics in the theory of production, cost, and pricing. The presentation of the theory is reinforced throughout with many real-world examples, while the "At the Frontier" sections present some new and important developments in production and cost theory and in the operation of perfectly competitive markets.

## CHAPTER 7

Production Theory

In Part Two, we examined the theory of consumer behavior and demand. Our focus of attention was the consumer. In Part Three, we examine the theory of production, cost, and pricing in competitive markets. Here the focus is on the firm. This chapter examines the theory of production or how firms organize production; that is, we examine how firms combine resources or inputs to produce final commodities. Chapter 8 builds on the discussion and analyzes the costs of production of the firm. Then Chapter 9 brings together the theory of consumer behavior and demand with the theory of production and costs to analyze how price and output are determined under perfect competition.

This chapter begins with a discussion of the organization of production. We define the meaning of production, examine why firms exist, consider their aims, classify resources or inputs into various categories, and define the meaning of short-run and long-run production. From this, we go on to the theory of production when only one input is variable. This is accomplished by defining the total, the average, and the marginal product curve of the variable input. Production theory is subsequently extended to deal with two variable inputs by the introduction of isoquants.

From the theory of production where only one or two inputs are variable, we proceed to examine cases in which all inputs are variable. Here, we define the meaning of constant, increasing, and decreasing returns to scale, the conditions under which they arise, and their importance. Finally, we examine technological progress and international competitiveness.

The real-world examples included in this chapter highlight the importance and relevance of the theory of production, while the "At the Frontier" section discusses the new computer-aided revolution that is now sweeping America. The optional appendix examines the most used production function (the Cobb–Douglas) and its empirical estimation.

7.1 | RELATING OUTPUTS TO INPUTS

In this section, we examine the organization of production and classify inputs into various categories. We begin by focusing on the meaning and organization of production, why firms exist, and the aim of firms. Then we classify inputs into various broad categories. This section serves as a general background for the theory of production presented in subsequent sections.

Organization of Production

Production refers to the transformation of resources into outputs of goods and services. For example, General Motors hires workers who use machinery in factories to transform steel, plastic, glass, rubber, and so on into automobiles. The output of a firm can either be a final commodity such as automobiles or an intermediate product such as steel (which is used in the production of automobiles and other goods). The output can also be a service rather than a good. Examples of services are education, medicine, banking, legal counsel, accounting work, communications, transportation, storage, wholesaling, and retailing. Production is a flow concept or has a time dimension. In other words, production refers to the rate of output over a given period of time. This is to be distinguished from the stock of a commodity or input, which refers to the quantity of the commodity (such as the number of automobiles) or input (such as the tons of steel) at hand or available at a particular point in time.

More than 80% of all goods and services consumed in the United States are produced by firms. The remainder is produced by the government and such nonprofit organizations as the Red Cross, private colleges, foundations, and so on. A **firm** is an organization that combines and organizes resources for the purpose of producing goods and services for sale at a profit. There are millions of firms in the United States. These include proprietorships (firms owned by one individual), partnerships (owned by two or more individuals), and corporations (owned by stockholders). The way the firm is organized is not of primary concern in the study of microeconomic theory; what the firm does is. Firms arise because it would be inefficient and costly for workers and for the owners of capital and land to enter into and enforce contracts with one another to pool their resources for the purpose of producing goods and services.

Just as consumers seek to maximize utility or satisfaction, firms generally seek to maximize profits. Both consumers and firms can be regarded as maximizing entities. Profits refer to the revenue of the firm from the sale of the output after all costs have been deducted. Included in costs are not only the actual wages paid to hired workers and payments for purchasing other inputs, but also the income that the owner of the firm would earn by working for someone else and the return that he or she would receive from investing his or her capital in the best *alternative* use. For example, the owner of a delicatessen must include in his or her costs not only payments for the rental of the store, hired help, and for the purchase of the hams, cheeses, beers, milk, crackers, and so on in the store. He or she must also include as part of costs the foregone earnings of the money invested in the store as well as the earnings that he or she would receive by working for someone else in a similar capacity (e.g., as the manager of another delicatessen). The owner earns (economic) profits only if total revenue exceeds total costs (which include actual expenses and the alternatives foregone).

The profit-maximizing assumption provides the framework for analyzing the behavior of the firm in microeconomic theory. It is from this assumption that the behavior of the firm can be studied most fruitfully. This assumption has recently been challenged by the so-called "managerial theories of the firm," which postulate multiple goals for the firm. That is, after attaining "satisfactory" rather than maximum profits, the large modern corporation is said to seek to maintain or increase its market share, maximize sales or growth, maintain a large staff of executives and lavish offices, minimize uncertainty, create and maintain a good public image as a desirable member of the community and a good employer, and so on. However, because many of these goals can be regarded as indirect ways to earn and increase profits in the long run, we will retain the profit-maximizing assumption.

Classification of Inputs

Firms transform inputs into outputs. **Inputs,** resources, or factors of production are the means of producing the goods and services demanded by society. Inputs can be classified broadly into **labor or human resources** (including entrepreneurial talent), **capital or investment goods,** and **land or natural resources.** This threefold classification of inputs is only a convenient way to organize the discussion, however, and it does not convey the enormous variety of specific resources in each category. For example, labor includes clerks and assembly-line workers as well as accountants, teachers, engineers, doctors, and scientists. And we must consider the specific types of labor and other inputs required for the analysis of production of a particular firm or industry.[1]

Particularly important among inputs is **entrepreneurship,** which refers to the ability of some individuals to see opportunities to combine resources in new and more efficient ways to produce a particular commodity or to produce entirely new commodities. The motivation is the great profit possibilities that an entrepreneur may believe to exist. The entrepreneur either uses his or her resources to exploit these profit opportunities or, more likely, attempts to convince other people with large sums of money to put some of that money at his or her disposal to introduce new production techniques or new products and share in the potential profits. There are many examples of entrepreneurship during the late 1970s and early 1980s in the field of microcomputers. This was a time when some young engineers and computer experts sought to combine new and more powerful chips (the basic memory component of computers) to produce cheaper or better microcomputers. Some of these entrepreneurs were successful and became rich overnight (e.g., the developers of the Apple Computers). Most, however, had to abandon their dreams after huge losses. In any event, entrepreneurs play a crucial role in modern economies. They are responsible for the introduction of new technology and new products, and for most of the growth of the economy as a whole.

---

[1] The reason is that different skills require varying training costs and wages to be supplied. Thus, to analyze the production process of a particular firm or industry, we must consider the *specific* types of labor and other inputs that are required. Yet, for general theoretical work, it is often convenient to deal with the broad input categories of labor, capital, and land.

Inputs can be further classified into fixed and variable. **Fixed inputs** are those that cannot be varied or can be varied only with excessive cost during the time period under consideration. Examples of fixed inputs are the firm's plant and specialized equipment. For example, it takes many years for General Motors to build a new automobile plant and introduce robots to perform many repetitive assembly-line tasks. **Variable inputs,** on the other hand, are those that can be varied easily and on short notice during the time period under consideration. Examples of these are raw materials and many types of workers, particularly those with low levels of skills. Thus, whether an input is fixed or variable depends on the time horizon being considered. The time period during which at least one input is fixed is called the **short run,** and the time period during which all inputs are variable is called the **long run.** Obviously, the length of time it takes to vary all inputs (i.e., to be in the long run), varies for firms in different industries. For a street vendor of apples, the long run may be a day. For an apple farmer, it is at least five years (this is how long it takes for newly planted trees to begin bearing fruit).

7.2   PRODUCTION WITH ONE VARIABLE INPUT

In this section, we present the theory of production when only one input is variable. Thus, we are dealing with the short run. We begin by defining the total, the average, and the marginal product of the variable input and examining their relationship graphically, and then we discuss the important law of diminishing returns. Production theory with more than one variable input is taken up in subsequent sections.

Total, Average, and Marginal Product

A production function is a unique relationship between inputs and outputs. It can be represented by a table, a graph, or an equation and shows the maximum output of a commodity that can be produced per period of time with each set of inputs. Both output and inputs are measured in physical rather than monetary units. Technology is assumed to remain constant. A simple short-run production function is obtained by applying various amounts of labor to farm one acre of land and recording the resulting output or **total product (*TP*)** per period of time. This is illustrated by the first two columns of Table 7.1.

The first two columns of Table 7.1 provide a hypothetical production function for a farm using various quantities of labor (i.e., number of workers per year) to cultivate wheat on one acre of land (and using no other input). When no labor is used, total output or product is zero. With one unit of labor (1*L*), total product (*TP*) is 3 bushels of wheat per year. With 2*L*, *TP* = 8 bushels. With 3*L*, *TP* = 12 bushels, and so on.[2]

From the output or total product schedule we can derive the (per-unit) average and marginal product schedules for the input. Specifically, the total (physical) output or total product (*TP*) divided by the quantity of labor employed (*L*) equals the **average product** of

---

[2] The reason for the decline in *TP* when six units of labor are used will be discussed shortly.

TABLE 7.1	Total, Average, and Marginal Product of Labor in the Cultivation of Wheat on One Acre of Land (Bushels Per Year)		
Labor (Workers per Year) (1)	Output or Total Product (2)	Average Product of Labor (3)	Marginal Product of Labor (4)
0	0	. . .	. . .
1	3	3	3
2	8	4	5
3	12	4	4
4	14	3.5	2
5	14	2.8	0
6	12	2	−2

labor (AP_L). On the other hand, the change in output or total product per-unit change in the quantity of labor employed is equal to the **marginal product** of labor (MP_L).[3]

$$AP_L = \frac{TP}{L} \qquad [7.1]$$

and

$$MP_L = \frac{\Delta TP}{\Delta L} \qquad [7.2]$$

Column 3 in Table 7.1 gives the average product of labor (AP_L). This equals TP (column 2) divided by the quantity of labor used (column 1). Thus, with one unit of labor (1L), the AP_L equals 3/1 or 3 bushels. With 2L, AP_L is 8/2 or 4 bushels, and so on. Finally, column 4 reports the marginal product of labor (MP_L). This measures the change in total product per-unit change in labor. Since labor increases by one unit at a time in column 1, the MP_L in column 4 is obtained by subtracting successive quantities of the TP in column 2. For example, TP increases from 0 to 3 bushels when we add the first unit of labor. Thus, the MP_L is 3 bushels. For an increase in labor from 1L to 2L, TP increases from 3 to 8 bushels. Thus, the MP_L is 5 bushels. For an increase in labor from 2L to 3L, the MP_L is 4 bushels (12 − 8), and so on.

Plotting the total, average, and marginal product quantities of Table 7.1 gives the corresponding product curves shown in Figure 7.1. Note that TP grows to 14 bushels with 4L. It stays at 14 bushels with 5L and then declines to 12 bushels with 6L (see the top panel of Figure 7.1). The reason for this is that laborers get into each other's way and actually trample the wheat when the sixth worker is employed. In the bottom panel, we see that the AP_L curve rises to 4 bushels and then declines. Since the marginal product of labor refers to the

---

[3] In subsequent chapters, when the possibility arises of confusing the AP and the MP with their monetary values, they will be referred to as the average *physical* product and the marginal *physical* product.

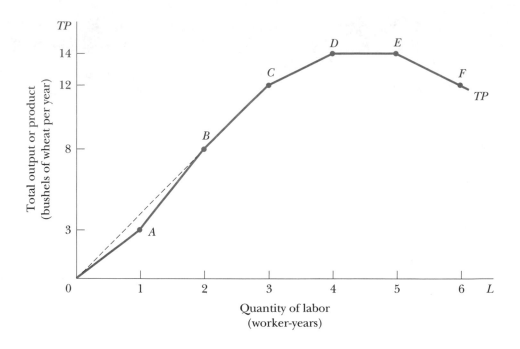

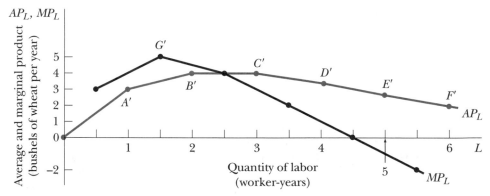

FIGURE 7.1   Total, Average, and Marginal Product Curves   The top panel shows the total output or total product (TP) curve. The AP_L at point A on the TP curve is 3 bushels (the slope of OA) and is plotted as A' in the bottom panel. The AP_L curve is the highest between $2L$ and $3L$. The MP_L between A and B on the TP curve is 5 bushels (the slope of AB) and is plotted between 1 and 2 in the bottom panel. The MP_L is highest at $1.5L$, $MP_L = AP_L$ at $2.5L$, $MP_L = 0$ at $4.5L$, and it is negative thereafter.

change in total product per-unit change in labor used, each value of the MP_L is plotted halfway between the quantities of labor used. Thus, the MP_L of 3 bushels, which results from increasing labor from $0L$ to $1L$, is plotted at $0.5L$; the MP_L of 5 bushels, which results from increasing labor from $1L$ to $2L$, is plotted at $1.5L$, and so on. The MP_L curve rises to 5 bushels at $1.5L$ and then declines. Past $4.5L$, the MP_L becomes negative.

The Geometry of Average and Marginal Product Curves

The shape of the average and marginal product of labor curves is determined by the shape of the corresponding total product curve. The AP_L at any point on the TP curve is equal to the slope of the straight line drawn from the origin to that point on the TP curve. Thus, the AP_L at point A on the TP curve in the top panel of Figure 7.1 is equal to the slope of $0A$. This equals 3/1 or 3 bushels and is plotted directly below A, as point A', in the bottom panel of Figure 7.1. Similarly, the AP_L at point B on the TP curve is equal to the slope of dashed line $0B$. This equals 8/2 or 4 bushels and is plotted as point B' in the bottom panel. At point C, the AP_L is again equal to 4. This is the highest AP_L. Past point C, the AP_L declines but remains positive as long as the TP is positive.

The MP_L between any two points on the TP curve is equal to the slope of the TP between the two points. Thus, the MP_L between the origin and point A on the TP curve in the top panel of Figure 7.1 is equal to the slope of $0A$. This is equal to 3 bushels and is plotted halfway between $0L$ and $1L$ (i.e., at $0.5L$) in the bottom panel of Figure 7.1. Similarly, the MP_L between points A and B on the TP curve is equal to the slope of AB. This is equal to 5 (the highest MP_L) and is plotted as point G' at $1.5L$ in the bottom panel. The MP_L between B and C on the TP curve is equal to the slope of BC. This equals 4 and is the same as the highest AP_L (the slope of $0B$ and $0C$). Between points D and E, TP remains unchanged and the $MP_L = 0$. Past point E, TP falls and MP_L becomes negative.

We have drawn the curves in Figure 7.1 under the assumption that labor is used in whole units. If this were not the case and labor time were infinitesimally divisible, we would have the smooth TP, AP_L, and MP_L curves shown in Figure 7.2. In this figure, the AP_L (given, as before, by the slope of a ray from the origin to the TP curve) rises up to point H on the TP curve in the top panel and then declines. Thus, the AP_L curve in the bottom panel rises up to point H' and declines thereafter (but remains positive as long as TP is positive). On the other hand, the MP_L at any point on the TP curve is equal to the slope of the tangent to the TP curve at that point. The slope of the TP curve rises up to point G (the point of inflection) and then declines. Thus, the MP_L curve in the bottom panel rises up to point G' and declines thereafter. The MP_L is zero at point I' directly below point I, where the TP is highest or has zero slope, and it becomes negative when TP begins to decline.[4]

Note that the MP_L curve reaches its maximum point before the AP_L curve. Furthermore, as long as the AP_L curve is rising, the MP_L curve is above it. When the AP_L curve is falling, the MP_L curve is below it, and when the AP_L curve is highest, the MP_L intersects the AP_L curve. The reason for this is that for the AP_L to rise, the MP_L must be greater than the average to pull the average up. For the AP_L to fall, the MP_L must be lower than the average to pull the average down. For the average product to be at a maximum (i.e., neither rising nor falling), the marginal product must be equal to the average (the slope of line $0H$). For example, for a student to increase his or her cumulative average test score, he or she must receive a grade on the next (marginal) test that exceeds his or her average. With a lower grade on the next test, the student's cumulative average will fall. If the grade on the next test equals the previous average, the cumulative average will remain unchanged.

---

[4] Note that the TP curve in Figure 7.2 has an initial portion over which it faces up (so that the MP_L increases). That is, up to point G, labor is used so sparsely on one acre of land that the MP_L increases as more labor is employed. This is usual but not always true. That is, in some cases, the TP curve faces down from the origin (so that MP_L falls from the very start). An example of this is discussed in the appendix to this chapter.

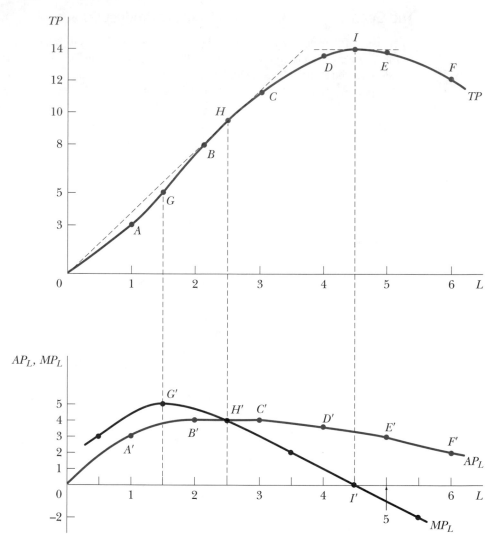

FIGURE 7.2 Geometry of Total, Average, and Marginal Product Curves With labor time infinitesimally divisible, we have smooth TP, AP_L, and MP_L curves. The AP_L (given by the slope of the line from the origin to a point on the TP curve) rises up to point H' and declines thereafter (but remains positive as long as TP is positive). The MP_L (given by the slope of the tangent to the TP curve) rises up to point G', becomes zero at I', and is negative thereafter. When the AP_L curve rises, the MP_L is above it; when the AP_L falls, the MP_L is below it; and when AP_L is highest, $MP_L = AP_L$.

The Law of Diminishing Returns

The decline in the MP_L curve in Figures 7.1 and 7.2 is a reflection of the **law of diminishing returns.** This is an empirical generalization or a physical law, not a proposition of economics. It postulates that as more units of a variable input are used with a fixed amount of other inputs, after a point, a smaller and smaller return will accrue to each additional unit of the variable input. In other words, the marginal (physical) product of the variable input eventually declines. This occurs because each additional unit of the variable input has less and less of the fixed inputs with which to work.

In Figure 7.2, the law of diminishing returns for labor begins to operate past point G' (i.e., when more than $1.5L$ is applied to one acre of land). Further additions of labor will eventually lead to zero and then to negative MP_L. Note that to observe the law of diminishing returns, at least one input (here, land) must be held constant. Technology is also assumed to remain unchanged. It should also be noted that when less than $1.5L$ is employed, labor is used too sparsely in the cultivation of one acre of land and the MP_L rises. Had land been kept constant at two acres instead of one, the TP, AP_L, and MP_L curves would retain their general shape but would all be higher, since each unit of labor would have more land to work with (see Section 7.3). Example 7–1 discusses the most famous historical application of the law of diminishing returns.

EXAMPLE 7–1
Economics—The Dismal Science Because of Diminishing Returns

In the early nineteenth century, Thomas Malthus (in his *Essay on the Principles of Population,* 1798) and other classical economists predicted that population growth in the face of fixed stocks of land and other nonhuman resources could doom humanity to a subsistence standard of living. That is, rapid population growth could reduce the average and the marginal product of labor sufficiently to keep people always near starvation. This gloomy prediction earned for economics the label of the "dismal science."

These predictions have not proved correct, especially for the United States and other industrial nations of the world where standards of living are much higher than they were a century or two ago. The reasons for the sharply increased standard of living are as follows: (1) The quantities of capital, land, and minerals used in production have vastly increased since the beginning of the nineteenth century; (2) population growth has slowed down considerably in the industrial nations; and (3) most importantly, very significant improvements in technology have greatly increased productivity.

Contrary to Mathus's dismal predictions, standards of living have in fact increased over the past century throughout most of the world. Malthus inappropriately applied a short-run law (the law of diminishing returns) to the long run (when technology can improve dramatically) and came up with a spectacularly wrong prediction! As Table 7.2 shows, food production per capita has increased during the 1980s and 1990s in all major developing-country groups (with the exception of sub-Saharan Africa) as a result of new high-yielding and disease-resistant grains, better fertilizer, more irrigation, and so on. The reduction in food production per capita in sub-Saharan Africa was due to internal strife, wars, and droughts.

TABLE 7.2	Index of Food Production per Capita in Major Developing-Country Groups in 1990 and in 2000 (1978–1981 = 100)	
Developing-Country Groups	Index in 1990	Index in 2000
East Asia and the Pacific (China)	127(133)	160(215)
South Asia (India)	116(119)	146(124)
Latin America (Brazil)	106(115)	118(149)
Middle East and North Africa (Egypt)	101(118)	107(151)
Sub-Saharan Africa (Ethiopia)	94(84)	94(74)

Source: World Bank and Food and Agriculture Organization, 2002.

7.3   PRODUCTION WITH TWO VARIABLE INPUTS

In this section we examine production theory with two variable inputs by introducing isoquants. We also show how to derive total product curves from an isoquant map, thereby highlighting the relationship between production with one and two variable inputs. We then examine the shape of isoquants in Section 7.4.

What Do Isoquants Show?

An **isoquant** shows the various combinations of two inputs (say, labor and capital) that can be used to produce a specific level of output. A higher isoquant refers to a larger output, whereas a lower isoquant refers to a smaller output. If the two variable inputs (labor and capital) are the only inputs used in production, we are in the long run. If the two variable inputs are used with other fixed inputs (say, land), we would still be in the short run.

Figure 7.3 gives a hypothetical production function, which shows the outputs (the $Q's$) that can be produced with various combinations of labor (L) and capital (K) per time period. For example, the left panel of the figure shows that 12 units of output (i.e., $12Q$) can be produced with 1 unit of labor (i.e., $1L$) and 5 units of capital (i.e., $5K$) or with $1L$ and $4K$.[5] The left panel also shows that $12Q$ can also be produced with $3L$ and $1K$ or with $6L$ and $1K$ per time period. On the other hand, the figure indicates that 26 units of output ($26Q$) could be produced with $2L$ and $5K$, $2L$ and $4K$, $3L$ and $2K$, and $6L$ and $2K$. From the figure, we can also determine the various combinations of L and K to produce $34Q$ and $38Q$. Note that to produce a greater output per time period, more labor, more capital, or both more labor and more capital are required. For visual aid, equal levels of output are joined together by a curve in the body of the left panel of Figure 7.3

Plotting the various combinations of labor and capital that can be used to produce 12, 26, 34, and 38 units of output per time period gives the isoquant for each of these levels of

---

[5] Of course, since inputs are not free, a firm would prefer to produce $12Q$ with $1L$ and $4K$ rather than with $1L$ and $5K$.

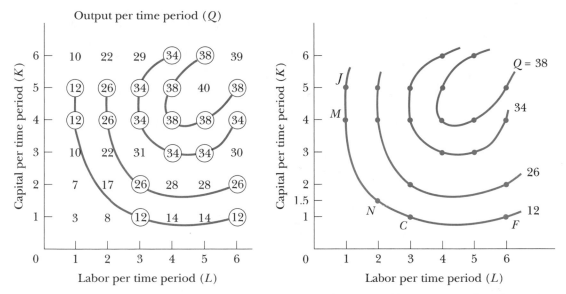

FIGURE 7.3   Production Function with Two Variable Inputs: Isoquants   The isoquants in the right panel are obtained from the data in the left panel. The lowest isoquant shows that 12 units of output can be produced with 1L and 5K (point J), 1L and 4K (point M), 2L and 1.5K (point N), 3L and 1K (point C), or 6L and 1K (point F). Higher isoquants refer to higher levels of output.

output shown in the right panel of Figure 7.3. The figure shows that 12 units of output (the lowest isoquant shown) can be produced with 1 unit of labor (1L) and 5 units of capital (5K). This defines point J. Twelve units of output can also be produced with 1L and 4K (point M), 3L and 1K (point C), and 6L and 1K (point F). Joining these points with a smooth curve, we obtain the isoquant for 12 units of output. Similarly, by plotting the various combinations of labor and capital that can be used to produce 26 units of output (2L and 5K, 2L and 4K, 3L and 2K, and 6L and 2K) and joining the resulting points by a smooth curve we get the isoquant for 26Q in the right panel of Figure 7.3. The isoquants for 34Q and 38Q in the figure can be similarly derived from the data in Figure 7.3.

Derivation of Total Product Curves from the Isoquant Map

By drawing a horizontal line across an isoquant map at the level at which the input measured along the vertical axis is fixed, we can generate the total product curve for the variable input measured along the horizontal axis. For example, by starting with the isoquant map in the right panel of Figure 7.3 and keeping capital constant at $K = 4$, we can derive the total product curve of labor for $K = 4$. This corresponds to the higher of the two TP curves in the bottom panel of Figure 7.4. Thus, from point M (1L and 4K) on the isoquant for 12Q in the top panel, we obtain point M' on the TP curve for $K = 4$ in the bottom panel. From point V (2L and 4K) on the isoquant for 26Q in the top panel, we derive point V' on the TP curve for $K = 4$ in the bottom panel, and so on. This is equivalent to reading across the row for $K = 4$ in the left panel of Figure 7.3.

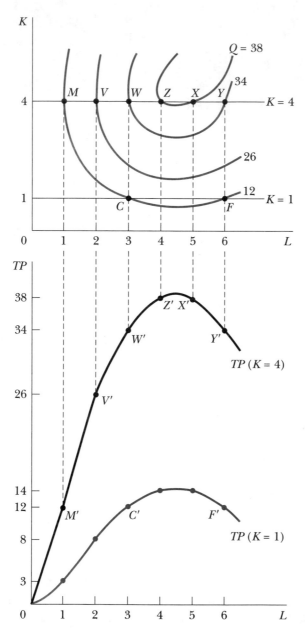

FIGURE 7.4   Derivation of Total Product Curves from the Isoquant Map   By keeping capital constant at $K = 4$ in the top panel, we can derive the higher of the two total product curves in the bottom panel. Thus, from point M ($1L$ and $4K$) on the isoquant for $12Q$ in the top panel, we obtain point M' on the TP curve for $K = 4$ in the bottom panel. From point V ($2L$ and $4K$) in the top panel we derive point V' in the bottom panel, and so on. With capital constant at $K = 1$ (i.e., reading across the row for $K = 1$ in the left panel of Figure 7.3), we get the lower total product curve in the bottom panel.

With capital held constant at the lower level of $K = 1$, we generate the lower total product curve in the bottom panel of Figure 7.4. This is equivalent to reading across the row for $K = 1$ in the left panel of Figure 7.3. Note that when capital is held constant at a smaller level, the *TP* curve for labor is lower because each unit of labor has less capital with which to work.

If, instead, we held the quantity of labor constant and changed the quantity of capital used, we would derive the *TP* curve for capital. This can be obtained by drawing a vertical line on the isoquant map at the level at which labor is held constant. This is equivalent to reading up to the appropriate column in the left panel of Figure 7.3. The higher the level at which labor is held constant, the higher is the total product curve of capital. From a given total product curve, we could then derive the corresponding average and marginal product curves, as shown in the bottom panel of Figure 7.2. Thus, Figure 7.3 could provide information about the long run as well as the short run, depending on whether labor and capital are the only two inputs and both are variable (the long run), or whether labor and capital are used with other fixed inputs (such as land), or either labor or capital is fixed (the short run).

<table>
<tr><td>**7.4**</td><td></td></tr>
</table>

THE SHAPE OF ISOQUANTS

In this section we examine the characteristics of isoquants, define the economic region of production, and consider the special cases where commodities can only be produced with fixed input combinations. We will see that the shape of isoquants plays as important a role in production theory as the shape of indifference curves plays in consumption theory.

Characteristics of Isoquants[6]

The characteristics of isoquants are crucial for understanding production theory with two variable inputs. Isoquants are similar to indifference curves. However, whereas an indifference curve shows the various combinations of two commodities that provide the consumer equal satisfaction (measured ordinally), an isoquant shows the various combinations of two inputs that give the same level of output (measured cardinally, or in actual units of the commodity).[7]

Isoquants have the same general characteristics of indifference curves. That is, they are negatively sloped in the economically relevant range, are convex to the origin, and do not intersect. These properties are shown in Figure 7.5.[8] The nonintersecting property of isoquants can easily be explained. Intersecting isoquants would mean that two different levels of output of the same commodity could be produced with the identical input combination (i.e., at the point where the isoquants intersect). This is impossible under our assumption that the most efficient production techniques are always used.

Isoquants are negatively sloped in the economically relevant range. This means that if the firm wants to reduce the quantity of capital used in production, it must increase the

---

[6] Compare Figure 7.5 with Figure 3.2.

[7] The positively sloped portions of the isoquants have been omitted in Figure 7.5 because they are irrelevant. The reason for this is discussed in the next subsection.

[8] The reasoning is exactly the opposite as for the decline in MP_L.

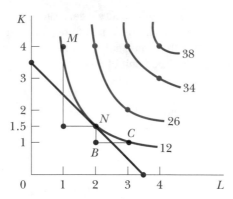

FIGURE 7.5   Marginal Rate of Technical Substitution (MRTS)   Between point M and point N on the isoquant for 12 units of output (12Q), the marginal rate of technical substitution of labor for capital ($MRTS_{LK}$) equals 2.5. Between point N and point C, $MRTS_{LK} = 1/2$. At point N, $MRTS_{LK} = 1$ (the absolute slope of the tangent to the isoquant at point N).

quantity of labor in order to continue to produce the same level of output (i.e., remain on the same isoquant). For example, starting at point M (1L and 4K) on the isoquant for 12 units of output (12Q), the firm could reduce the quantity of capital by 2.5K by adding 1L in production and reach point N on the same isoquant (see Figure 7.5). Thus, the average slope of the isoquant between points M and N is $-2.5K/1L$. The average slope between N and C is $-1/2$.

The absolute value of the slope of the isoquant is called the **marginal rate of technical substitution (MRTS)**. This is analogous to the marginal rate of substitution of one good for another in consumption, which is given by the absolute value of the slope of an indifference curve. For a downward movement along an isoquant, the marginal rate of technical substitution of labor for capital ($MRTS_{LK}$) is given by $-\Delta K/\Delta L$. It measures the amount of capital that the firm can give up by using one additional unit of labor and still remain on the same isoquant. Because of the reduction in K, $MRTS_{LK}$ is negative. However, we multiply by -1 and express $MRTS_{LK}$ as a positive value. Thus, the average $MRTS_{LK}$ between points M and N on the isoquant for 12Q is 2.5. Similarly, the average $MRTS_{LK}$ between points N and C is $1/2$. The $MRTS_{LK}$ at any point on an isoquant is given by the absolute value of the slope of the isoquant at that point. Thus, the $MRTS_{LK}$ at point N is 1 (the absolute value of the slope of the tangent to the isoquant at point N; see Figure 7.5).

The $MRTS_{LK}$ is also equal to MP_L/MP_K. To prove this, we begin by remembering that all points on an isoquant refer to the same level of output. Thus, for a movement down a given isoquant, the gain in output from using more labor must be equal to the loss in output from using less capital. Specifically, the increase in the quantity of labor used (ΔL) times the marginal product of labor (MP_L) must equal the reduction in the amount of capital used (ΔK) times the marginal product of capital (MP_K). That is,

$$(\Delta L)(MP_L) = -(\Delta K)(MP_K) \qquad [7.3]$$

so that

$$\frac{MP_L}{MP_K} = -\frac{\Delta K}{\Delta L} = MRTS_{LK} \qquad [7.4]$$

Thus, $MRTS_{LK}$ is equal to the absolute value of the slope of the isoquant and to the ratio of the marginal productivities.

Although we know that the absolute value of the slope of the isoquant or $MRTS_{LK}$ equals the ratio of MP_L to MP_K, we cannot infer from that the actual value of MP_L and MP_K. For example, at point N on the isoquant for $12Q$ in Figure 7.5, we know that $MRTS_{LK} = -\Delta K/\Delta L = MP_L/MP_K = 1$ (so that $MP_L = MP_K$), but we do not know what the individual values of MP_L and MP_K are. Similarly, we know that between points N and C on the isoquant for $12Q$, $MRTS_{LK} = -\Delta K/\Delta L = MP_L/MP_K = 1/2$ (so that $MP_L = 1/2MP_K$), but we do not know what the actual value of either marginal product is. These values can, however, be calculated from Figure 7.5.

For example, we can find the value, of MP_L and MP_K between points N and C on the isoquant for $12Q$ in Figure 7.5 by comparing point N ($2L$, $1.5K$) and point C ($3L$, $1K$) referring to $12Q$, to point B ($2L$, $1K$) referring to $8Q$ (see the left panel of Figure 7.3). The rightward movement from point B to point C keeps capital constant at $1K$ and increases labor by $1L$, and it results in an increase in output of $4Q$ (from $8Q$ to $12Q$). Thus, $MP_L = 4$. On the other hand, the upward movement from point B to point N keeps labor constant at $2L$ and increases capital by $1/2K$, and it also results in an increase in output of $4Q$. Thus, the $MP_K = 8$. With $MP_L = 4$ and $MP_K = 8$, $MP_L/MP_K = 4/8 = 1/2 = MRTS_{LK}$, as found earlier.

Within the economically relevant range, isoquants are not only negatively sloped but also convex to the origin. That is, as we move down along an isoquant, the absolute value of its slope or $MRTS_{LK}$ declines and the isoquant is convex (see Figure 7.5). The reason for this can best be explained by separating the movement down along an isoquant (say, from point N to point C along the isoquant for $12Q$ in Figure 7.5) into its two components: the movement to the right (from point B to point C) and the movement downward (from point N to point B). The increase in L with constant K (the movement from point B to point C) will lead to a decline in the MP_L because of diminishing returns. In addition, the reduction in K (the movement from point N to point B), by itself, will cause the entire MP_L curve to shift down. Thus, MP_L declines for both reasons. On the other hand, by using less K and more L, the MP_K rises.[9] With the MP_L declining and the MP_K rising as we move down along an isoquant, the $MRTS_{LK} = MP_L/MP_K$ will fall and the isoquant is convex to the origin.

Economic Region of Production

The firm would not operate on the positively sloped portion of an isoquant because it could produce the same level of output with less capital and less labor. For example, the firm would not produce $34Q$ at point P in Figure 7.6 because it could produce $34Q$ by using the

---

[9] For a mathematical presentation of isoquants and their characteristics, see Section A.8 of the Mathematical Appendix at the end of the book.

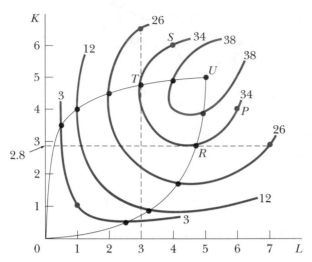

FIGURE 7.6   Economic Region of Production
Isoquants are positively sloped to the right of ridge line *ORU*
and to the left of or above ridge line *OTU*. The firm would
never produce at a point such as *P* or *S* in the positively
sloped portion of the isoquant because it could produce the
same output with less of both inputs.

smaller quantity of labor and capital indicated by point *R*. Similarly, the firm would not produce 34*Q* at point *S* because it could produce 34*Q* at point *T* with less *L* and *K*. Since inputs are not free, the firm would not want to produce in the positively sloped range of isoquants.

Ridge lines separate the relevant (i.e., the negatively sloped) from the irrelevant (or the positively sloped) portions of the isoquants. In Figure 7.6, ridge line *ORU* joins points on the various isoquants where the isoquants have zero slope (and thus zero $MRTS_{LK}$). The isoquants are negatively sloped to the left of this ridge line and positively sloped to the right. This means that starting, for example, at point *R* on the isoquant for 34*Q*, if the firm used more labor it would also have to use more capital to remain on the same isoquant (compare point *P* to point *R* on the isoquant for 34*Q*). Starting from point *R*, if the firm used more labor with the same amount of capital, the level of output would fall (i.e., the firm would fall back to a lower isoquant; see the dashed horizontal line at $K = 2.8$ in Figure 7.6). The same is true at all other points on ridge line *ORU*. Therefore, the MP_L must be negative to the right of this ridge line. Note that points on ridge line *ORU* specify the minimum quantity of capital required to produce the levels of output indicated by the various isoquants. Note also that at all points on this ridge line, $MRTS_{LK} = MP_L/MP_K = 0/MP_K = 0$.

On the other hand, ridge line *OTU* joins points where the isoquants have infinite slope (and thus infinite $MRTS_{LK}$). The isoquants are negatively sloped to the right of this ridge line and positively sloped to the left. This means that starting, for example, at point *T* on the isoquant for 34*Q*, if the firm used more capital it would also have to use more labor to remain on the same isoquant (compare point S to point T on the isoquant for $34Q$). Starting at point T, if the firm used more capital with the same quantity of labor, the level of output would fall (i.e., the firm would fall back to a lower isoquant; see the dashed vertical line at $L = 3$ in Figure 7.6). The same is true at all other points on ridge line $0TU$. Therefore, the MP_K must be negative to the left of or above this ridge line. Note that points on ridge line $0TU$ indicate the minimum quantity of labor required to produce the levels of output indicated by the various isoquants. Note also that at all points on this ridge line, $MRTS_{LK} = MP_L/MP_K = MP_L/0 =$ infinity.

Thus, we conclude that the negatively sloped portion of the isoquants within the ridge lines represents the economic region of production, where the MP_L and the MP_K are both positive but declining. Producers will never want to operate outside this region. As a result, from this point on, whenever we will draw isoquants, we will usually show only their negatively sloped portion. Indeed, some special types of production functions have isoquants without positively sloped portions.

Fixed-Proportions Production Functions

So far, we have drawn isoquants as smooth curves, indicating that there are many different (really, an infinite number of) input combinations that can be used to produce any output level. There are cases, however, where inputs can only be combined in fixed proportions in production. In such cases, there would be no possibility of input substitution in production and the isoquants would be at a right angle, or L-shaped.

For example, Figure 7.7 shows that 10 units of output ($10Q$) can only be produced at point A with $2L$ and $1K$. Employing more labor will not change output since $MP_L = 0$

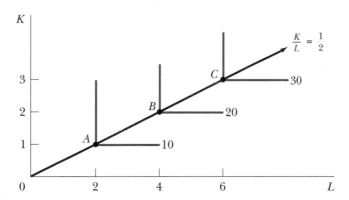

FIGURE 7.7   Fixed-Proportions Production Function   When isoquants are at right angles, or L-shaped, inputs must be used in fixed proportions in production. Thus, 10 units of output ($10Q$) can only be produced at point A with $2L$ and $1K$. Using more labor or capital would not change output; $20Q$ can only be produced with $4L$ and $2K$ (point B), and $30Q$ only with $6L$ and $3K$ (point C). Thus, output can only be produced at the constant or fixed capital-labor ratio or proportion of $K/L = 1/2$.

(the horizontal portion of the isoquant). Similarly, using more capital will not change output since $MP_K = 0$ (the vertical portion of the isoquant). Here, there is no possibility of substituting L for K in production and the $MRTS_{LK} = 0$. Production would only take place at the constant capital-labor ratio of $K/L = 1/2$. A larger output can only be produced by increasing both labor and capital in the same proportion. For example, $20Q$ can be produced at point B by using $4L$ and $2K$ at the constant K/L ratio of $1/2$. Similarly, $30Q$ can only be produced at point C with $6L$ and $3K$ and $K/L = 1/2$.

In the real world, some substitution of inputs in production is usually possible. The degree to which this is possible can be gathered from the curvature of the isoquants. In general, the smaller the curvature of the isoquants, the more easily inputs can be substituted for each other in production. On the other hand, the greater the curvature (i.e., the closer are isoquants to right angles, or L-shape), the more difficult is substitution. Being able to easily substitute inputs in production is extremely important in the real world. For example, if petroleum had good substitutes, users could easily have switched to alternative energy sources when petroleum prices rose sharply in the fall of 1973. Their energy bill would then not have risen very much. As it was, good substitutes were not readily available (certainly not in the short run), and so most energy users faced sharply higher energy costs. As Example 7–2 shows, gasoline and driving time can also be substituted for each other, and this can be shown by isoquants.

EXAMPLE 7–2

Trading Traveling Time for Gasoline Consumption on the Nation's Highways

Higher automobile speed reduces the driving time needed to cover a given distance but reduces gas mileage and thus increases gasoline consumption. It has been estimated that reducing the speed limit on the nation's highways from 65 to 55 mph reduced gasoline consumption by about 3%. The trade-off between traveling time and gasoline consumption for a 600-mile trip can be represented by the isoquant shown in Figure 7.8. In the figure, the vertical axis measures hours of traveling time, while the horizontal axis measures gallons of gasoline consumed. Gasoline and travel time are thus the inputs into the production of automobile transportation.

The isoquant in Figure 7.8 shows that at 50 mph, the 600 miles can be covered in 12 hours and with 16 gallons of gasoline, at 37.5 miles per gallon (point A). At 60 mph, the 600 miles can be covered in 10 hours and with 20 gallons of gasoline, at 30 miles per gallon (point B). Driving at 60 mph saves 2 hours of travel time (one scarce resource) but increases gasoline consumption by 4 gallons (another scarce resource). Thus, the trade-off or marginal rate of technical substitution ($MRTS$) of gasoline for travel time between point A and point B on the isoquant in Figure 7.8 is $1/2$. At 66.7 mph (assuming that the speed limit is above it), the 600 miles can be covered in 9 hours with 30 gallons of gasoline, at 20 miles per gallon (point C). Thus, the $MRTS$ of gasoline for travel time between points B and C is $1/10$.

In order to determine the most economical (i.e., the least cost) combination of gasoline and travel time to cover the 600 miles, we need to know the price of gasoline and

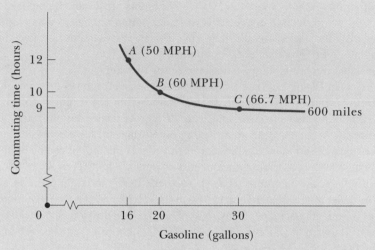

FIGURE 7.8   Speed Limit and Gasoline Consumption   Isoquant *ABC*
shows the trade-off between traveling time and gasoline consumption. At
50 MPH, 600 miles can be covered in 12 hours and with 16 gallons of
gasoline (point *A*). At 60 MPH, the 600 miles can be covered in 10 hours
and with 20 gallons of gasoline (point *B*). At 66.7 MPH, 600 miles can be
covered in 9 hours with 30 gallons (point *C*).

the value of time to the individual. This is addressed in the next chapter, where we take
up costs of production. If the price of gasoline were to increase, the individual would
want to substitute traveling time for gasoline (i.e., drive at a lower speed so as to increase gas mileage and save gasoline) to minimize the cost of traveling the 600 miles
(see Example 8–3). Note that there is also a trade-off between travel speed and safety
(i.e., lower speeds increase travel time but save lives).

Sources: C. A. Lave, "Speeding, Coordination, and the 55-mph Limit," *American Economic Review,*
December 1985, pp. 1159–1164; "U.S. Progress in Energy Efficiency Is Halting," *New York Times,*
February 27, 1989, p. 1; "Death Rate on U.S. Roads Reported at a Record Low," *New York Times,* October 27,
1998, p. 16; "Looking for Ways to Save Gasoline," *Wall Street Journal,* July 12, 2001, p. A1; and "CAFE
Leaves a Bitter Taste," *The Economist,* August 4, 2001, p. 54.

7.5   CONSTANT, INCREASING, AND DECREASING RETURNS TO SCALE

The word "scale" refers to the long-run situation where all inputs are changed in the same
proportion. The result might be constant, increasing, or decreasing returns. **Constant
returns to scale** refers to the situation where output changes by the *same* proportion as inputs. For example, if all inputs are increased by 10%, output also rises by 10%. If all inputs
are doubled, output also doubles. **Increasing returns to scale** refers to the case where output changes by a *larger* proportion than inputs. For example, if all inputs are increased by

10%, output increases by more than 10%. If all inputs are doubled, output more than doubles. Finally, with **decreasing returns to scale,** output changes by a *smaller* proportion than inputs. Thus, increasing all inputs by 10% increases output by less than 10%, and doubling all inputs, less than doubles output.

Constant, increasing, and decreasing returns to scale can be shown by the spacing of the isoquants in Figure 7.9. The left panel shows constant returns to scale. Here, doubling inputs from 3L and 3K to 6L and 6K doubles output from 100 (point A along ray 0D) to 200 (point B). Tripling inputs from 3L and 3K to 9L and 9K triples output from 100 (point A) to 300 (point C). Thus, 0$A = AB = BC$ along ray 0D and we have constant returns to scale. The middle panel shows increasing returns to scale. Here, output can be doubled or tripled by less than doubling or tripling the quantity of inputs. Thus, 0$A > AB > BC$ along ray 0D and the isoquants are compressed closer together. Finally, the right panel shows decreasing returns to scale. In this case, in order to double and triple output we must more than double and triple the quantity of inputs. Thus, 0$A < AB < BC$ and the isoquants move farther and farther apart. Note that in all three panels, the capital–labor ratio remains constant at $K/L = 1$ along ray 0D.

Constant returns to scale make sense. We would expect two similar workers using identical machines to produce twice as much output as one worker using one machine. Similarly, we would expect the output of two identical plants employing an equal number of workers of equal skill to produce double the output of a single plant. Nevertheless, increasing and decreasing returns to scale are also possible.

Increasing returns to scale arise because, as the scale of operation increases, a greater division of labor and specialization can take place and more specialized and productive machinery can be used. With a large scale of operation, each worker can be assigned to perform only one repetitive task rather than numerous ones. Workers become more proficient in the performance of the single task and avoid the time lost in moving from one machine to another. The result is higher productivity and increasing returns to scale. At higher scales of operation, more specialized and productive machinery can also be used. For example, using a conveyor belt to unload a small truck may not be justified, but it greatly increases efficiency in unloading a whole train or ship. In addition, some physical properties of equipment and machinery also lead to increasing returns to scale. Thus, doubling the diameter of a pipeline more than doubles the flow, doubling the weight of a ship more than doubles its capacity to transport cargo, and so on. Firms also need fewer supervisors, fewer spare parts, and smaller inventories per unit of output as the scale of operation increases.

Decreasing returns to scale arise primarily because, as the scale of operation increases, it becomes ever more difficult to manage the firm effectively and coordinate the various operations and divisions of the firm. The channels of communication become more complex, and the number of meetings, the paper work, and telephone bills increase more than proportionately to the increase in the scale of operation. All of this makes it increasingly difficult to ensure that the managers' directives and guidelines are properly carried out. Thus, efficiency decreases (this is sometimes referred to as "managerial diseconomies"). Decreasing returns to scale must be clearly distinguished from diminishing returns. *Decreasing returns to scale* refers to the long-run situation when all inputs are variable. On the other hand, *diminishing returns* refers to the short-run situation where at least one input is fixed. Diminishing returns in the short run is consistent with constant, increasing, or decreasing returns to scale in the long run.

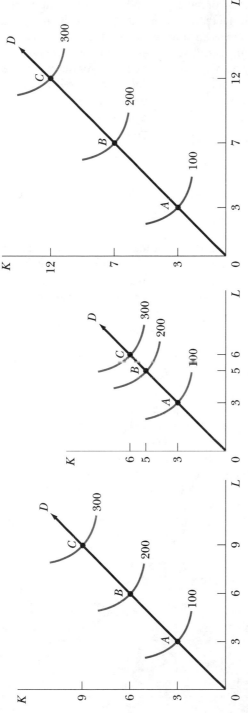

FIGURE 7.9 Constant, Increasing, and Decreasing Returns to Scale The left panel shows constant returns to scale. Here, doubling inputs from 3L and 3K to 6L and 6K doubles output from 100 (point A along ray OD) to 200 (point B). Tripling inputs to 9L and 9K triples output to 300 (point C). Thus, OA = AB = BC along ray OD. The middle panel shows increasing returns to scale. Here, output can be doubled or tripled by less than doubling or tripling the quantity of inputs. Thus, OA > AB > BC and the soquants become closer together. The right panel shows decreasing returns to scale. Here, output changes proportionately less than labor and capita and OA < AB < BC.

209

In the real world, the forces for increasing and decreasing returns to scale often operate side by side. The forces for increasing returns to scale usually prevail at small scales of operation. The tendency for increasing returns to scale may be balanced by the tendency for decreasing returns to scale at intermediate scales of operation. Eventually, the forces for increasing returns to scale may be overcome by the forces for decreasing returns to scale at very large scales of operation. Whether this is true for a particular firm can only be determined empirically. In the real world, most firms seem to exhibit near constant returns to scale (see Table 7.7 in the appendix to this chapter). As Example 7–3 shows, however, General Motors believes that it faces decreasing returns to scale and wants to shrink.

EXAMPLE 7–3

General Motors Decides Smaller Is Better

General Motors (GM), the third biggest corporation and the largest car maker in the world, had a turbulent decade in the 1990s. It started by incurring huge losses of $2 billion in 1990 and $4.5 billion in 1991 as the result of a bloated work force and management, low-capacity utilization, too many divisions and models, and high-cost suppliers. For a corporation that had been extolled as the epitome of a successful company in 1946, this was a dramatic decline indeed! As the data on sales per employee in Table 7.3 seem to indicate, GM was too large and faced strong decreasing returns to scale. Chrysler, on the other hand, could still have expanded to take advantage of increasing returns to scale (in fact, Chrysler merged with Germany's Daimler, the maker of Mercedes-Benz, in 1998). Ford, with the largest sales per employee, seemed to be just about the right size. It was clear that GM required a major restructuring—and this GM did throughout the 1990s.

As part of its reorganization plan announced in December 1991, GM closed 21 plants and shed 74,000 (50,000 blue-collar and 24,000 white-collar) workers from 1992 to 1994. The closing of plants eliminated GM's excess capacity of 2 million cars and trucks per year and left GM with a 5 to 5.5 million capacity in its North American operation and 33% of the U.S. car market, down from 46% in 1978 and 35% in 1991. Just closing plants and reducing GM's size, however, was not sufficient, and GM went through more restructuring during the mid-1990s. Although these increased efficiency,

TABLE 7.3	Total Sales, Employees and Sales per Employee at GM, Ford and Chrysler in 1991		
	Sales (in billion dollars)	Employees (in thousands)	Sales per Employee (in thousand dollars)
General Motors	123.1	756	162.7
Ford	88.3	333	265.4
Chrysler	29.4	123	238.8

Source: The Economist, May 2, 1992, p. 78.

its competitors did not stand still, and GM productivity still lagged in relation to that of its domestic competitors. For example, in 1998, GM required 34 worker-days to produce its average car, as compared with Chrysler's 32 and Ford's 30, and GM's share of the North American Car market declined further to 29%.

To close this productivity gap, GM consolidated its North American and international operations; reduced further the number of models it produced; cut average manufacturing time per vehicle; centralized its sales, service, and marketing system; and spinned off its auto-components group (Delphi Automotive Systems) and outsourced more of the assembly task. As GM was improving, Ford was facing setbacks resulting from the controversy over deadly rollovers of Ford Explorers equipped with Firestone tires, boardroom tensions (which led to the removal of its chief executive in fall 2001), and from competitors increasing their efficiency faster than Ford's. By 2002, GM has surpassed Ford on vehicle productivity, quality ratings, and profitability.

Sources: "Automobiles: GM Decides Smaller Is Better," *The Margin,* November/December 1988, p. 29; "GM Posts Record '91 Loss of $4.45 Billion, Sends Tough Message to UAW on Closings," *The New York Times,* February 25, 1992, p. 3; "The Decline and Fall of General Motors," *The Economist,* October 10, 1998, pp. 60–61; "Reviving GM," *Business Week,* February 1, 1999, pp. 114–122; "GM Narrows Productivity Gap with Ford" *The Wall Street Journal,* August 11, 2001, p. A3; "Ford Lost $5.4 Billion in 2001 After Charge for Revamping," *The Wall Street,* January 18, 2002, p. C2; "GM Pulls Well Ahead of Ford," *Financial Times,* April 22, 2002, p. 17; and "GM Outstrips Ford on Vehicle Productivity, Study Shows," *Financial Times,* June 14, 2002, p. 18.

7.6   TECHNOLOGICAL PROGRESS AND INTERNATIONAL COMPETITIVENESS

In this section, we examine the meaning and importance of technological progress and innovations in general and the crucial role they play in the international competitiveness of firms.

Meaning and Importance of Innovations

In our analyses so far, we have assumed a given technology. Over time, however, technological progress takes place. **Technological progress** refers to the development of new and better production techniques to make a given, improved, or an entirely new product. The introduction of innovations is the single most important determinant of a firm's long-term competitiveness at home and abroad. Innovations are basically of two types: **product innovation,** which refers to the introduction of new or improved products, and **process innovation,** the introduction of new or improved production processes. Contrary to popular belief, most innovations are incremental; that is, they involve more or less continuous small improvements in products or processes rather than a single, major technological breakthrough. Furthermore, most innovations involve the commercial utilization of ideas that may have been around for years. For example, it took a quarter of a century before firms (primarily Japanese ones) were able to perfect the flat video screen (invented in the mid-1960s by George Heilmeier of RCA) and introduce the screens commercially in portable personal computers (PCs).

Innovations can be examined with isoquants. A new or improved product requires an entirely new isoquant map showing the various combinations of inputs to produce each level of output of the new or improved product. On the other hand, a process innovation can be shown by a shift toward the origin of the firm's given product isoquants, showing that each level of output can be produced with fewer inputs after the innovation than before. Unless a firm aggressively and continuously improves its product or production process, it will inevitably be overtaken by other more innovative firms. To be successful in today's world, firms must adopt a global competitive strategy, which means that they must continuously scout the world for new product ideas and processes. It is also crucial for firms to have a presence, first through exports and then by local production, in the world's major markets. Larger sales mean increasing returns to scale in production and distribution, and they allow the firm to spend more on research and development and thus stay ahead of the competition.

The introduction of innovations is stimulated by strong domestic rivalry and geographic concentration—the former because it forces firms to constantly innovate or else lose market share (and even risk being driven entirely out of the market), the latter because it leads to the rapid spread of new ideas and the development of specialized machinery and other inputs for the industry. Sharp domestic rivalry and great geographic concentration make Japanese firms in many high-tech industries fierce competitors in the world economy today.[10]

The risk in introducing innovations is usually high. For example, eight of ten new products fail within a short time of their introduction. Even the most carefully introduced innovations can fail, as evidenced by the failure of RJR Nabisco's "smokeless cigarette" and Coca-Cola's change in 1985 of its 99-year-old recipe. Product innovations can also die because of poor planning and unexpected production problems. This happened, for example, to Weyerhauser. Encouraged by market testing that showed its diaper product was better than competitors' products and could be produced more cheaply, Weyerhauser introduced its UltraSoft diapers in 1990, but the product failed within a year because of unexpected production problems.[11]

EXAMPLE 7–4

How Do Firms Get New Technology?

Table 7.4 provides the results of a survey of 650 executives in 130 industries on the methods that U.S. firms use to acquire new technology. From the table, we see that the most important method of acquiring product and process innovations is by independent research and development (R&D) by the firm. The other methods of acquiring process innovations, arranged in order of decreasing importance, are: licensing

---

[10] See M. Porter, *The Competitive Advantage of Nations* (New York: The Free Press, 1990).
[11] See "Diaper's Failure Shows How Poor Plans, Unexpected Woes Can Kill New Products," *Wall Street Journal,* October 9, 1990, p. B1.

TABLE 7.4	Methods of Acquiring New Technology by American Firms	

Method of Acquisition	Rank	
	Process Innovation	Product Innovation
Independent R&D	1	1
Licensing	2	3
Publications or technical meetings	3	5
Reverse engineering	4	2
Hiring employees of innovating firms	5	4
Patent disclosures	6	6
Conversations with employees of innovating firms	7	7

Sources: R. E. Levin, "Appropriability, R&D Spending, and Technological Performance," *American Economic Review,* May 1988, pp. 424–428; "Spy vs. Spy: Are Your Company Secrets Safe?" *Fortune,* February 17, 1997, p. 136; "Drug Spies," *Fortune,* September 6, 1999, pp. 230–242; and "P&G Admits Spying on Unilever," *Financial Times,* August 31, 2001, p. 17.

technology by the firms that originally developed the technology, publications or technical meetings, reverse engineering (i.e., taking the competitive product apart and devising a method of producing a similar product), hiring employees of innovating firms, patent disclosures (i.e., from the detailed information available from the patent office which can be used to develop a similar technology or product in such a way as not to infringe on the patent), and information from conversations with employees of innovating firms (who may inadvertently provide secret information in the course of general conversations). For product innovations, reverse engineering becomes more important than licensing, and hiring employees from innovating firms is more important than publications or technical meetings. Last but not least (and something that firms would hardly admit—except when caught), firms try to obtain new technology by industrial espionage.

Innovations and the International Competitiveness of U.S. Firms

There has hardly been a technological breakthrough during the past four decades, from TVs to robots, from copiers to fax machines, from semiconductors to flat video screens, that was not made by an American firm or laboratory. According to the **product cycle model,** however, firms that first introduce an innovation eventually lose their export market and even their domestic market to foreign imitators who pay lower wages and generally face lower costs. In the meantime, however, technologically leading firms introduce even more advanced products and technologies.

The problem is that the period during which firms can exploit the benefits of successful innovations is becoming shorter and shorter before foreign imitators take the market away. In fact, in many cases American discoveries such as the fax machine and the flat video screen were first introduced and exploited commercially by foreign (Japanese) firms. Although many American firms remain world leaders in their industries (e.g., Boeing in commercial aircraft, IBM in mainframe computers, Hewlett-Packard in laser printers, Gillette in razors, Coca-Cola in soft drinks, and McDonald's in fast food—to mention only a few), firms in many other industries such as steel, automobiles, consumer electronics, and semiconductors lost international competitiveness to foreign competitors, especially the Japanese, during the 1970s and 1980s. One important reason for this was that American firms generally stressed product innovation, whereas Japanese firms stressed process innovations. Thus, even when American firms were the first to introduce a new product, Japanese firms were soon able to produce it better and more cheaply and in a few years were able to outsell American competitors both at home and abroad.[12]

Example 7–5 shows, however, how Xerox, through hard work and perseverance, was able to regain by the early 1990s the international competitiveness that it had lost to the Japanese during the late 1970s and early 1980s. Example 7–6 then provides an overall score card on the international competitiveness of American Industry in the early 1990s. Finally, the "At the Frontier" section shows how U.S. industry regained the ground lost to the Japanese during the 1970s and 1980s in a wide range of high-tech products as a result of the new revolution in computer-aided production that swept America. In any event, most of the trade now taking place among industrial nations is now **intraindustry trade** in differentiated manufactured products.

EXAMPLE 7–5

How Xerox Lost and Regained, but Is Now Struggling to Remain Internationally Competitive

The Xerox Corporation was the first to introduce the copying machine in 1959, based on its patented xerographic technology. Until 1970, Xerox had no competition and thus had little incentive to reduce manufacturing costs, improve quality, and increase customers' satisfaction. Even when Japanese firms entered the low end of the market with better and cheaper copiers in 1970 and began to take over this segment of the market, Xerox did not respond, concentrating instead on the mid and high ends of the market where profit margins were much higher. Xerox also used the profits from its copier business to expand into computers and office systems during the 1970s. It was not until 1979 that Xerox finally awakened to the seriousness of the Japanese threat. From so-called

---

[12] "In the Realm of Technology, Japan Seizes a Greater Role," *New York Times,* May 28, 1991, p. C1.

competitive benchmarking missions to Japan to compare relative production efficiency and product quality, Xerox was startled to find that Japanese competitors were producing copiers of higher quality at far lower costs and were positioning themselves to move up into the more profitable mid- and high-end segments of the market.

Faced with this life-threatening situation, Xerox, with the help of its Japanese subsidiary (Fuji Xerox), mounted a strong response that involved reorganization and integration of development and production, as well as ambitious companywide quality-control efforts. Employee involvement was greatly increased, suppliers were brought into the early stages of product design, and inventories and the number of suppliers were greatly reduced. Constant benchmarking was then used to test progress in the companywide quality-control program and customer satisfaction. By taking these drastic actions, Xerox was able to reverse the trend toward loss of market share to Japanese competitors, even at the low segment of the market.

History seemed to repeat itself, however, at the beginning of the new decade when Xerox once again found itself battling Japan's Cannon for supremacy in the new digital world of office information technology. This, despite the fact that during the second half of the 1990s Xerox had recast itself as a digital document and solutions company that combines hardware, software, and services into a service and consulting package, industry-by-industry.

Sources: The MIT Commission on Industrial Productivity, *Made in America* (Cambridge, MA: The MIT Press, 1989), pp. 270–277; "Japan Is Tough, But Xerox Prevails," *New York Times,* September 3, 1992, p. D1; "Xerox Recasts Itself as a Formidable Force in Digital Revolution," *Wall Street Journal,* February 2, 1999, p. A1; and "Downfall of Xerox," *Business Week,* March 5, 2001, pp. 82–92.

EXAMPLE 7–6

Score Card on American Industry

Table 7.5 presents a competitiveness scorecard on 13 key American industries in the early 1990s. An A implies a secure dominant position in the world; B suggests solid leadership with some other country (usually Japan and Germany); C implies weakness and continued decline; D refers to industries in which the United States is essentially out of the world competition. What is troubling from the data in Table 7.5 is not that the U.S. competitive scorecard was so bad—after all it did contain two A's and six B's—but that a decade earlier aerospace, computers, and telecommunications would also have received an A rating (instead of B+, C+, and B−, respectively) and cars and industrial equipment would have received a B rate.

In pharmaceuticals the United States is the world center for research and in forest products the United States is what Saudi Arabia is to oil. In aerospace the United States is the world leader but Europe's Airbus Industrie, formed in 1969 by German, French, British and Spanish aerospace companies, now has captured nearly half of the world market in commercial jets. In chemicals, food, and petroleum refining the United States

TABLE 7.5   Score Card on 13 Key American Industries

A	Pharmaceuticals
A	Forest Products
B+	Aerospace
B	Chemicals
B	Food
B	Scientific and Photographic Equipment
B	Petroleum refining
B−	Telecommunications Equipment
C+	Computers
C	Industrial and Farm Equipment
C	Motor Vehicles
C−	Metals
D	Electronics

Sources: "How American Industry Stacks Up," *Fortune,* March 9, 1992, pp. 30–46; "How American Industry Stacks Up Now," *Fortune,* April 18, 1994, pp. 52–64; "The United States as the Most Competitive Economy in the World," in D. Salvatore, *International Economics,* 8th ed. (New York: Wiley & Sons, 2003), Section 6.5B.

shares world leadership with the Europeans, and in scientific equipment and telecommunications with the Japanese and the Europeans. In computers, the United States faces stiff competiton from Japan but retains world leadership in software (the programs that run the computers). In industrial equipment and motor vehicles, Japan has proved a very formidable competitor. In metals, Japan and Europe are the world leaders, and in electronics, the United States has all but abandoned the field to Japan. As the "At the Frontier" section that follows shows, however, the decline in the international competitiveness of American industry came to an end and even reversed itself since the second half of the 1990s.

AT THE FRONTIER
The New Computer-Aided Production Revolution and the International Competitiveness of U.S. Firms

S ince the early 1990s, a veritable revolution in production has been taking place in the United States, based on computer-aided design and computer-aided manufacturing, which has greatly increased the productivity and international competitiveness of U.S. firms. **Computer-aided design (CAD)** allows research and development engineers to design a new product or component on a computer screen, quickly experiment with different alternative designs, and test the strength and reliability of different materials—all on the screen! Then, **computer-aided manufacturing (CAM)** issues instructions to a network of integrated machine tools to produce a prototype of the new or changed product. These developments allow firms to avoid many possible production problems, greatly speed up the time required to develop and introduce new or improved products, and reduce the optimal lot size or the production runs to achieve maximum production efficiency. This revolution has been taking place mostly in the United States, based primarily on its world leadership and superiority in computer software and computer networks.

These new developments have led to a new digital factory—an information-age marvel that is responsible for a quantum leap in the speed, flexibility, and productivity of U.S. firms resulting from the ingenious marriage of computer software and computer networks in industries as diverse as construction equipment, automobiles, PCs, and electronic pagers. This new digital factory has unheard agility that allows it to customize products down to one unit while achieving mass-production speed and efficiency. For example, as a Dell salesperson specifies an order for a PC for a particular consumer, the digitized data flow to the assembly line where production begins immediately and is completed in a very short time, so that the customer can have his or her customized PC in a day or two. This is sometimes called software-controlled continuous flow manufacturing—a process that is basically merging manufacturing and retailing. This much faster time-to-market and customizing capability is beginning to provide American firms with tremendous advantage over foreign competitors. As a result, after losing the competitive war during the 1980s and early 1990s, the United States regained all of its lost ground, and then some, since the mid-1990s.

Computer-aided design (CAD) is dramatically increasing the pace of innovations. For example, a designer can call up on the screen a car door she may working on, test opening and closing the door, run the window up and down. experiment with lighter materials, and direct machinery to make a prototype door. Such CAD allowed Chrysler to design and build its highly successful NEON subcompact car in 33 months instead of the usual 45 months. Even more exotically, scientists at Caterpillar, the largest earth-moving equipment builder in the world, test drive huge machinery that they are developing in virtual reality long before they are built. The Boeing 777 jetliner was developed entirely in this way. CAD is even used to design and simulate entire assembly lines, and it can be used to send production orders to suppliers' machinery so that, in a sense, they become an extension of the firm's plant. In short, we are likely to be at the dawn of the biggest revolution in manufacturing since the perfection of the industrial lathe in the year 1800. And with the U.S. undisputed superiority in software, it is unlikely that foreign competitors can easily copy and match the new American manufacturing genius anytime soon.

Source: "The Digital Factory," *Fortune,* November 14, 1994, pp. 92–110; and "The Totally Digital Factory May Not Be So Far Away," *Financial Times,* November 1, 2000, p. XII.

SUMMARY

1. Production refers to the transformation of resources or inputs into outputs of goods and services. A firm is an organization that combines and organizes resources for the purpose of producing goods and services for sale at a profit. In general, the aim of firms is to maximize profits. Profits refer to the revenue of the firm from the sale of the output after all costs have been deducted. Inputs can be broadly classified into labor, capital, and land, and into fixed and variable. Entrepreneurship refers to the introduction of new technologies and products to exploit perceived profit opportunities. The time period during which at least one input is fixed is called the short run. In the long run, all inputs are variable.

2. The production function is a unique relationship between inputs and output. It can be represented by a table, graph, or equation showing the maximum output or total product (TP) of a commodity that can be produced per time period with each set of inputs. Average product (AP) is total product divided by the quantity of the variable input used. Marginal product (MP) is the change in total output per-unit change in the variable input. The MP is above the AP when AP is rising, MP is below AP when AP is falling, and $MP = AP$ when AP is at a maximum. The declining portion of the MP curve reflects the law of diminishing returns.

3. An isoquant shows the various combinations of two inputs that can be used to produce a specific level of output. From the isoquant map, we can generate the total product curve of each input by holding the quantity of the other input constant.

4. Isoquants are negatively sloped in the economically relevant range, convex to the origin, and do not intersect. The absolute value of the slope of the isoquant is called the marginal rate of technical substitution ($MRTS$). This equals the ratio of the marginal product of the two inputs. As we move down along an isoquant the absolute value of its slope, or $MRTS$, declines and the isoquant is convex. Ridge lines separate the relevant (i.e., the negatively sloped) from the irrelevant (or positively sloped) portions of the isoquants. With right-angled, or L-shaped, isoquants, inputs can only be combined in fixed proportions in production.

5. Constant, increasing, and decreasing returns to scale refer to the situation where output changes, respectively, by the same, by a larger, and by a smaller proportion than do inputs. Returns to scale can be shown by the spacing of isoquants. Increasing returns to scale arise because of specialization and division of labor and from using specialized machinery. Decreasing returns to scale arise primarily because as the scale of operation increases, it becomes more and more difficult to manage the firm and coordinate its operations and divisions effectively. In the real world, most industries seem to exhibit near-constant returns to scale.

6. The introduction of innovations is the single most important determinant of a firm's long-term competitiveness. Product innovations refer to the introduction of new or improved products, while process innovations refer to the introduction of new or improved production processes. Many innovations are not successful because of poor planning and unexpected production problems. Since the early 1990s, a veritable revolution in production has been taking place in the United States based on computer-aided design and computer-aided manufacturing, which has greatly increased productivity and international competitiveness of U.S. firms.

KEY TERMS

Production	Capital or investment goods	Variable inputs
Firm	Land or natural resources	Short run
Inputs	Entrepreneurship	Long run
Labor or human resources	Fixed inputs	Production function

Total product (*TP*)
Average product (*AP*)
Marginal product (*MP*)
Law of diminishing returns
Isoquant
Marginal rate of technical
   substitution (*MRTS*)
Ridge lines

Constant returns to scale
Increasing returns to scale
Decreasing returns to
   scale
Technological progress
Product innovation
Process innovation
Product cycle model

Intraindustry trade
Computer-aided design
Computer-aided manufacturing
Cobb–Douglas production
   function
Output elasticity of labor
Output elasticity of capital
Homogeneous of degree 1

REVIEW QUESTIONS

1. Where on the total product and on the marginal product of labor curves of Figure 7.2 does the law of diminishing returns begin to operate? What gives rise to the law of diminishing returns?

2. What does the total product curve look like if diminishing returns set in after the first unit of labor is employed?

3. Would a rational producer be concerned with the average or the marginal product of an input in deciding whether or not to hire the input?

4. Which of the following points (5*L* and 7*K*, 3*L* and 9*K*, 4*L* and 5*K*, and 6*L* and 6*K*) cannot be on the same isoquant? Why?

5. If the marginal product of labor is 6 and the marginal rate of technical substitution between labor and capital is 1.5, what is the marginal product of capital?

6. Is the firm facing increasing, constant, or decreasing returns to scale if it expands

the quantity of labor and capital used in production from 10*L* and 10*K* to 13*L* and 13*K*, and output increases from 256 units to 300 units? Why?

7. Can a firm have a production function that exhibits increasing, constant, and decreasing returns to scale at different levels of output? Explain.

8. Is technical efficiency sufficient to determine at what point on an isoquant a firm operates? Why?

9. Is diminishing returns to a single factor of production consistent with constant or nonconstant returns to scale?

10. What is meant by an innovation? What are the different types of innovations?

11. What is the difference between technological progress and increasing returns to scale?

12. What is meant by the "digital factory"?

PROBLEMS

1. From the following production function, showing the bushels of corn raised on one acre of land by varying the amount of labor employed (in worker-years),

Labor	1	2	3	4	5	6
Output	8	20	30	34	34	30

   a. derive the average and the marginal product of labor.

b. plot the total, the average, and the marginal product curves.

2. Plot again the total product curve of Problem 1 on the assumption that labor time is infinitesimally divisible, and derive graphically the corresponding average and marginal product curves.

3. From the production function given in Table 7.6.

   a. derive the isoquants for 8 units of output, 8*Q*, 20*Q*, 25*Q*, 30*Q*, and 34*Q*.

TABLE 7.6 Production Function with Two Variable Inputs

Capital	(K)	6	6	18	25	30	30	25	
		5	8	20	30	34	34	30	
		4	8	20	30	34	34	30	Q
		3	6	18	25	30	30	25	
		2	4	13	20	25	25	20	
	↑	1	1	5	7	8	8	7	
	K								
		0	1	2	3	4	5	6	
		L	→			Labor		(L)	

b what is the relationship between Table 7.6 and the table in Problem 1?

4. From the isoquant map of Problem 3(a), derive

a. the total product curve for labor when the quantity of capital is held fixed at $K = 4$.

b. the average and the marginal product curves for labor from the total product curve of 4(a) above.

5. a. From Problem 3, redraw the isoquant for 20 units of output (20Q) and show how to measure the marginal rate of technical substitution of labor for capital (i.e., $MRTS_{LK}$) between the point where 2 units of labor and 4 units of capital (i.e., 2L and 4K) are used (call this point M) and the point where (3L, 2K) are used (call this point N). What is the $MRTS_{LK}$ at point N? At point C (4L, 1.5K)?

b. Find the value of the MP_L and MP_K for a movement from point N on the isoquant for 20Q and point N' (4L, 2K) and N'' (3L, 3K) on the isoquant for 25Q, and show that $MRTS_{LK} = MP_L/MP_K$.

c. Explain why the $MRTS_{LK}$ falls as we move down along the isoquant.

6. a. On the isoquant map of Problem 3, draw the ridge lines.

b. Explain why a firm would never produce below the lower ridge line or above the top ridge line.

*7. On the same set of axes draw two isoquants, one indicating that the two inputs must be combined in fixed proportions in production, and the other showing that inputs are perfect substitutes for each other.

*8. If the price of gasoline is $1.50 per gallon and travel time is worth $6.00 per hour to the individual, determine at which speed the cost of traveling the 600 miles is minimum in Figure 7.8.

9. Does the production function of Problem 3 exhibit constant, increasing, or decreasing returns to scale? Explain.

*10. Suppose that the production function for a commodity is given by

$$Q = 10\sqrt{LK}$$

where Q is the quantity of output, L is the quantity of labor, and K is the quantity of capital:

a. Indicate whether this production function exhibits constant, increasing, or decreasing returns to scale.

b. Does the production function exhibit diminishing returns? If so, when does the law of diminishing returns begin to operate? Could we ever get negative returns?

*11. Indicate whether each of the following statements is true or false and give the reason.

a. A student preparing for an examination should not study after reaching diminishing returns.

b. If large and small firms operate in the same industry, we must have constant returns to scale.

12. Explain the importance of the new production revolution for the international competitiveness of American firms.

___
* = Answer provided at end of book.

APPENDIX   THE COBB–DOUGLAS PRODUCTION FUNCTION

In this appendix, we present the Cobb–Douglas production function. This is the simplest and most widely used production function in empirical work today. We begin with the formula, which is followed by a simple illustration. Next we consider the methods available to empirically estimate the Cobb–Douglas production function and some of the difficulties involved. We conclude with some empirical results.

The Formula

The formula for the **Cobb–Douglas production function** is

$$Q = AL^{\alpha}K^{\beta} \qquad [7.5]$$

where Q = output in physical units, L = quantity of labor, K = quantity of capital, and A, α (alpha), and β (beta) are positive parameters estimated in each case from the data. The parameter A refers to technology. The more advanced the technology, the greater the value of A. The parameter α refers to the percentage increase in Q for a 1% increase in L, while holding K constant. Thus, α is the **output elasticity of labor.** For example, if $\alpha = 0.7$, this means that a 1% increase in the quantity of labor used (while holding the quantity of capital constant) leads to a 0.7% increase in output. Thus, the output elasticity of labor (α) is 0.7. Similarly, the parameter β refers to the percentage increase in Q for a 1% increase in K, while holding L constant. Thus, β is the **output elasticity of capital.** For example, if $\beta = 0.3$, this means that a 1% increase in K, while holding L constant, leads to a 0.3% increase in Q. Thus, the output elasticity of K (β) is 0.3.

In the above example, $\alpha + \beta = 0.7 + 0.3 = 1$. Thus, we have constant returns to scale. That is, a 1% increase in both L and K leads to a 1% increase in Q. Specifically, a 1% increase in L, by itself, leads to a 0.7% increase in Q; a 1% increase in K, by itself, leads to a 0.3% increase in Q. Thus, with an increase of both L and K by 1%, Q increases by a total of 1% also and we have constant returns to scale. Another name for constant returns to scale is **homogeneous of degree 1.**

On the other hand, if $\alpha + \beta > 1$, we have increasing returns to scale. That is, a 1% increase in L and K leads to a greater than 1% increase in Q. For example, if $\alpha = 0.8$ and $\beta = 0.3$, a 1% increase in L and K leads to a $0.8 + 0.3 = 1.1\%$ increase in Q. Finally, if $\alpha + \beta < 1$, we have decreasing returns to scale (i.e., an increase in L and K by 1% leads to an increase in Q of less than 1%).

Illustration

Suppose $A = 10$, $\alpha = \beta = 1/2$, and $\overline{K} = 4$ and is held constant (so that we are dealing with the short run). By substituting these values into equation [7.5], we get

$$Q = 10L^{1/2}4^{1/2} = 10\sqrt{4}\sqrt{L} \qquad [7.5A]$$

By then substituting alternative quantities of L used in production into equation [7.5A], we derive the total product (TP) schedule, and from it, the average product of labor (AP_L) and the marginal product of labor (MP_L) schedules. The results are given in Table 7.7.

Plotting the TP, the AP_L, and the MP_L schedules of Table 7.7 as Figure 7.10, we see that the Cobb–Douglas production function exhibits diminishing AP_L and MP_L from the

TABLE 7.7	Total, Average, and Marginal Product of Labor		
L	TP	AP_L	MP_L
0	0	. . .	. . .
1	20.00	20.00	20.00
2	28.28	14.14	8.28
3	34.64	11.55	6.36
4	40.00	10.00	5.36
5	44.72	8.94	4.72

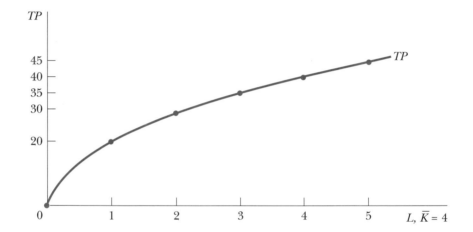

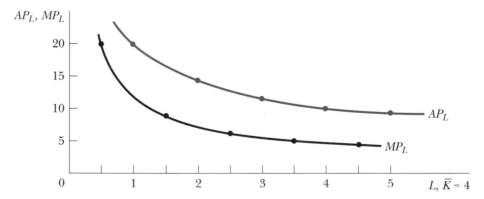

Figure 7.10   Total, Average, and Marginal Product of Labor for the Cobb-Douglas Production Function   This figure shows the TP, the AP_L, and the MP_L schedules given in Table 7.7. From the figure, we see that the AP_L and the MP_L decline from the very start and the MP_L never becomes negative for the Cobb-Douglas production function. Note that the MP_L is plotted between the various quantities of labor used and capital is held constant at $\overline{K} = 4$.

TABLE 7.8 Production in the Long Run

L	K	$10\sqrt{(L)(M)}$	Q
0	0	$10\sqrt{(0)(0)}$	0
1	1	$10\sqrt{(1)(1)}$	10
2	2	$10\sqrt{(2)(2)}$	20
3	3	$10\sqrt{(3)(3)}$	30
4	4	$10\sqrt{(4)(4)}$	40
5	5	$10\sqrt{(5)(5)}$	50

very start or with the first unit of L used, and that the MP_L never becomes negative. Note that the MP_L is plotted between the various quantities of labor used. The AP_L and the MP_L are functions of or depend only on the K/L ratio. That is, they remain the same regardless of how much L and K are used in production as long as the K/L ratio remains the same (as along any given ray from the origin).[13]

In the long run, both L and K are variable. Thus,

$$Q = 10L^{1/2}K^{1/2} = 10\sqrt{L}\sqrt{K} = 10\sqrt{LK} \qquad [7.5B]$$

Since $\alpha + \beta = 0.5 + 0.5 = 1$ in this case, we have constant returns to scale. This is shown in Table 7.8. Here, output grows at the same rate as the rate of increase in both inputs. For example, doubling the quantity of labor and capital used, from 1 to 2 units, doubles output from 10 to 20 units. Increasing L and K by 50%, from 2 to 3 units, increases Q by 50% from 20 to 30 units, and so on.

We can also define the isoquants for this Cobb–Douglas production function. For example, the isoquant for $50Q$ can be defined by substituting 50 for Q in equation [7.5B]. By then substituting various quantities of labor into the resulting equation, we get the corresponding quantities of capital required to produce the $50Q$:

$$50 = 10\sqrt{LK} \qquad [7.5C]$$
$$5 = \sqrt{LK}$$
$$25 = LK$$
$$\frac{25}{L} = K$$

Thus, if $L = 10$, $K = 2.5$; if $L = 5$, $K = 5$; if $L = 2.5$, $K = 10$, and so on. Other isoquants can be similarly derived. Isoquants are parallel along any ray from the origin and are equally spaced to reflect constant returns to scale (as in the left panel of Figure 7.9).

Empirical Estimation

One method of estimating the parameters of the Cobb–Douglas production function (i.e., A, α, and β) is to apply statistical (i.e., regression) analysis to time series data on the inputs

---

[13] This is proved in more advanced texts.

used and the output produced.[14] For example, the researcher may collect data on the number of automobiles produced by an automaker in each year from 1951 to 1997 and on the quantity of labor and capital used in each year to produce the automobiles. The data are usually transformed into natural logarithms (indicated by the symbol ln) and the regression analysis is conducted on the transformed data. The form of the estimated Cobb–Douglas production function is then

$$\ln Q = \ln A + \alpha \ln L + \beta \ln K \qquad [7.5D]$$

The researcher thus obtains an estimate of the value of $\ln A$, α, and β.[15] Of primary interest to the researcher is the value of α and β.[16]

Another method of estimating the value of A, α, and β is by regression analysis using cross-section data. In this case, the researcher collects data for a given year (or other time unit) for each of many producers or firms in a particular industry on the quantity of labor and capital used and the output produced. That is, instead of collecting data for one firm over many years (time series), the researcher now collects data for a given year for many firms in the same industry (cross section). As in the previous case, the researcher usually first transforms the data into natural logarithms and then estimates equation [7.5D] by regression analysis to obtain the values of parameters A, α, and β. Once again the researcher is primarily interested in the values of α and β. Table 7.9 in Example 7–7 presents the values of α and β estimated for various U.S. manufacturing industries.[17]

Input–output relationships can also be obtained from engineering studies. All of these methods (i.e., regression analysis using time series or cross-section data and engineering studies) face difficulties. One of these is that we must assume that the best production techniques are used by all firms at all times. Due to a lack of information or erroneous decisions, this may not be the case. Another difficulty arises in the measurement of the capital input, since machinery and equipment are of different types, ages (vintage), and productivities. A further shortcoming characteristic of engineering studies is that they typically cover only some production activities of the firm. Despite these and other problems, numerous studies have been conducted over the years using these different approaches. They have provided very useful information on production for the entire economy and for various industries.

EXAMPLE 7–7

Output Elasticity of Labor and Capital and Returns to Scale in U.S. and Canadian Manufacturing

Table 7.9 reports the estimated output elasticities of labor (α) and capital (β) for various U.S. manufacturing industries in 1957. The value of $\alpha = 0.90$ for furniture means that a 1% increase in the quantity of labor used (holding K constant) results in a 0.90% increase

---

[14] For a general discussion of regression analysis, see the appendix to Chapter 5.

[15] The value of parameter A can then be obtained by finding the antilog of $\ln A$.

[16] In Cobb–Douglas time series estimates, technological progress must also be accounted for. This is usually accomplished by including time (t) as an additional explanatory variable in equation [7.5D].

[17] Data for many firms in each of the various U.S. manufacturing industries for the year 1957 were used to estimate the values of α and β for each industry. Thus, these are cross-section estimates.

| TABLE 7.9 | Estimated Output Elasticity of Labor (α) and Capital (β) in U.S. Manufacturing |

Industry	α	β	$\alpha + \beta$
Furniture	0.90	0.21	1.11
Chemicals	0.89	0.20	1.09
Printing	0.62	0.46	1.08
Food, beverages	0.51	0.56	1.07
Rubber, plastics	0.58	0.48	1.06
Instruments	0.84	0.20	1.04
Lumber	0.65	0.39	1.04
Apparel	0.91	0.13	1.04
Leather	0.96	0.08	1.04
Electrical machinery	0.66	0.37	1.03
Nonelectrical machinery	0.62	0.40	1.02
Transport equipment	0.79	0.23	1.02
Textiles	0.88	0.12	1.00
Paper pulp	0.56	0.42	0.98
Primary metals	0.59	0.37	0.96
Petroleum	0.64	0.31	0.95

Sources: J. Moroney, "Cobb–Douglas Production Functions and Returns to Scale in U.S. Manufacturing Industry," *Western Economic Journal,* December 1967; and J. R. Baldwin and P. K. Goreki, *The Role of Scale in Canada/U.S. Productivity Differences in the Manufacturing Sector, 1970–1979* (Toronto: Toronto University Press, 1986).

in the quantity produced of furniture. The value of $\beta = 0.21$ means that a 1% increase in K (holding L constant) increases Q by 0.21%. Increasing both L and K by 1% increases Q by $0.90 + 0.21 = 1.11\%$. This means that the production of furniture is subject to increasing returns to scale.

The values of α and β reported in Table 7.9 were estimated by regression analysis using cross-section data for many firms in each industry for the year 1957. The value of α ranges from 0.51 for food and beverages to 0.96 for leather. This is the output elasticity of production and nonproduction workers combined. The value of β ranges from 0.08 for leather to 0.56 for food and beverages. Note that most industries exhibit close-to-constant returns to scale (i.e., the value of $\alpha + \beta$ is close to 1).

A similar study for 107 Canadian industries found that in 1979 the value of α ranged from 0.04 for watches and clocks to 1.26 for distilleries, the value of β ranged from 0.02 for flour and breakfast cereal products to 1.36 for glass manufacturers, while the values of $\alpha + \beta$ ranged from 2.20 (very strong economies of scale) for the feed industry to 0.82 (relatively strong diseconomies of scale) for tread mill. Thus, Canadian manufacturing industries seemed to exhibit a wider range of output elasticities of labor and capital as well as a wider range of economies and diseconomies of scale than U.S. firms.

INTERNET SITE ADDRESSES

An excellent presentation of production theory is found in:

> http://price.bus.okstate.edu/archive/Econ3113_963/Shows/Chapter6/index.htm

For gasoline consumption and substitution, see:

> http://www.techstandards.co.uk/system/index.html
>
> http://sciway.net/statistics/scsa98/en/en17.html

For production information on General Motors, Ford, Chrysler, and Toyota, see:

> General Motors: http://www.gm.com
>
> Ford: http://www.ford.com

Chrysler: http://www.chrysler.com

Toyota: http://www.Toyota.com

For competition between Xerox and Canon, see:

> Canon: http://www.usa.canon.com
>
> Xerox: http://www.xerox.com

For the virtual corporation and computer-aided design (CAD) and computer-aided manufacturing (CAM), see:

> Microsoft: http://www.microsoft.com
>
> Motorola: http://www.mot.com
>
> Dell: http://www.dell.com
>
> Caterpillar: http://www.caterpillar.com

CHAPTER 8

Costs of Production

I n this chapter, we consider the costs of production of the firm and their relationship to production theory (presented in Chapter 7). After examining the nature of costs, we derive short-run and long-run cost curves for the firm. These curves will be used to determine the profit-maximizing level of output for a perfectly competitive firm in Chapter 9 and for imperfectly competitive firms in Chapters 10–11. This chapter also introduces economies of scope and learning curves. The many real-world examples highlight the importance and relevance of the analysis, while the "At the Frontier" section examines the growing importance of international economies of scale. In the optional appendix, we examine in a more technical way the relationship between production and costs and the effect of input-price changes on production and costs.

8.1 THE NATURE OF PRODUCTION COSTS

From the firm's production function (showing the input combinations that the firm can use to produce various levels of output) and the price of inputs, we can derive the firm's cost functions. These functions show the minimum costs that the firm would incur in producing various levels of output. For simplicity, we assume that the firm is too small to affect the prices of the inputs it uses. Thus, the prices of inputs remain constant regardless of the quantity demanded by the firm. (The determination of input prices when the firm does and does not affect input prices is discussed in Part Five, Chapters 14–16.)

In economics, costs include explicit and implicit costs. **Explicit costs** are the actual out-of-pocket expenditures of the firm to purchase or hire the inputs it requires in production. These expenditures include the wages to hire labor, interest on borrowed capital, rent on land and buildings, and the expenditures on raw and semifinished materials. **Implicit costs** refer to the value of the inputs owned and used by the firm in its own production processes. The value of these owned inputs must be imputed or estimated from what these inputs could earn in their best alternative use.

227

Implicit costs include the maximum wages that the entrepreneur could earn in working for someone else in a similar capacity (say, as the manager of another firm), and the highest return that the firm could obtain from investing its capital elsewhere and renting out its land and other inputs to others. The inputs owned and used by the firm in its own production processes are not free to the firm, even though the firm can use them without any actual or explicit expenditures. Accountants traditionally include only actual expenditures in costs, whereas economists always include both explicit and implicit costs, or opportunity costs.[1]

The **opportunity cost** to a firm in using any input is what the input could earn in its best alternative use (outside the firm). This is true for inputs purchased or hired by the firm as well as for inputs owned and used by the firm in its own production. For example, a firm must pay wages of $20,000 per year to one of its employees if that is the amount the worker would earn in his or her best alternative occupation in another firm. If this firm attempted to pay less, the worker would simply seek employment in the other firm. Similarly, if the entrepreneur could earn more in managing another firm than in directing his or her own firm, it would not make much economic sense to continue to be self-employed.[2] Thus, for a firm to retain any input for its own use, it must include as a cost the opportunity cost that the input could earn in its best alternative use or employment. This is the **alternative** or **opportunity cost doctrine.** Similarly, the opportunity cost of attending college includes not only the explicit cost of tuition, books, and so on, but also the foregone earnings of not working (see Example 8–1).

Costs are also classified into private and social. **Private costs** are the opportunity costs incurred by *individuals and firms* in the process of producing goods and services. **Social costs** are the costs incurred by *society* as a whole. Social costs are higher than private costs when firms are able to escape some of the economic costs of production. For example, a firm dumping untreated waste into the air imposes a cost on society (in the form of higher cleaning bills, more breathing ailments, and so on) that is not reflected in the costs of the firm. Private costs can be made equal to social costs by public regulation requiring the firm to install antipollution equipment. In this and subsequent chapters, we will be primarily concerned with private costs. Social costs will be examined in detail in Chapter 18.

EXAMPLE 8–1
The Cost of Attending College

Table 8.1 reports the annual explicit and implicit or opportunity costs of attending a private college during the 2000–2001 academic year. Explicit costs include tuition, books, and supplies. Colleges also charge for room and board (meal plans), but the student would incur these expenses or the equivalent whether or not he or she attends college.

[1] For tax purposes, the accountant's definition of costs, which includes only explicit costs, is usually used. However, in economics, we must always consider both explicit and implicit, or opportunity costs.
[2] This is true unless the individual valued the freedom associated with being self-employed more than the extra income in managing a similar firm for someone else.

TABLE 8.1   Annual Cost of Attending a Private College

Explicit costs		
Tuition	$22,000	
Books and supplies	1,000	
Subtotal		$23,000
Implicit costs		
Foregone earnings	$15,000	
Foregone interest	345	
Subtotal		$15,345
Total opportunity costs		$38,345

Source: Admission Office, Fordham University.

Implicit costs include the student's foregone earnings by attending college rather than entering the labor force. It also includes the foregone interest on explicit costs (since these funds could have been lent at the going interest rate). Using the current low interest rate of 2% and assuming that half of the explicit costs are incurred at the beginning of each semester, we get the foregone interest of ($11,500)(0.02) = $230 for one year plus ($11,500)(0.02)/2 = $115 for six months, for a total of $345.

Note that the annual implicit costs of attending college are about two-thirds of the explicit costs. Attending a public four-year college is cheaper only to the extent that tuition for state residents in many states is about $4,000 (so that the total opportunity cost of attending a public college is about $19,000). For out-of-state residents, the annual cost of attending a public college may be close to $23,000. Most independent colleges and universities also provide financial aid to a large minority of students from low-income families, but this usually amounts to less than half of the tuition. The annual opportunity cost of attending an Ivy League college is more than $35,000, since tuition alone exceed $26,000 per year.

Sources: "As Endowments Slip at Colleges, Big Tuition Increases Fill the Void," *New York Times,* February 22, 2002, p. 1; "You're in. Now Pay up," *U.S. News & World Report,"* April 29, 2002, pp. 38–39; "Greater Share of Income Is Committed to College," *New York Times,* May 5, 2002, p. 18; and "State Schools Plan Big Tuition Jumps," *Wall Street Journal,* June 20, 2002, p. A1.

8.2   COST IN THE SHORT RUN

In this section, we examine the theory of cost in the short run. We first define fixed, variable, and total costs and draw these total cost curves. We then define average fixed cost, average variable cost, average total cost, and marginal cost and draw these per-unit cost curves. Finally, we show how per-unit cost curves can be derived graphically from the corresponding total cost curves.

Total Costs

In the short run, some inputs are fixed and some are variable; this leads to fixed and variable costs. **Total fixed costs (TFC)** are the total obligations of the firm per time period for all fixed inputs. These fixed or sunk costs include payments for renting the plant and equipment (or the depreciation on plant and equipment if the firm owns them), most kinds of insurance, property taxes, and some salaries (such as those of top management, which are fixed by contract and must be paid over the life of the contract whether the firm produces or not). Fixed costs are sometimes referred to as *sunk costs* by economists and *overhead costs* by business people. **Total variable costs (TVC)** are the total obligations of the firm per time period for all the variable inputs of the firm. These include payments for raw materials, fuels, most types of labor, excise taxes, and so on. **Total costs (TC)** equal TFC plus TVC.

Within the limits imposed by the given plant, the firm can vary its output in the short run by varying the quantity of the variable inputs used per period of time. This gives rise to TFC, TVC, and TC schedules and curves. These show, respectively, the *minimum* fixed, variable, and total costs of producing the various levels of output in the short run. In defining these cost schedules and curves, all inputs are valued at their opportunity cost, which includes both explicit and implicit costs.

Table 8.2 presents hypothetical TFC, TVC, and TC schedules. These schedules are then plotted in Figure 8.1. From Table 8.2, we see that TFC are $30 regardless of the level of output. This is reflected in Figure 8.1 in the horizontal TFC curve at the level of $30. TVC are zero when output is zero and rise as output rises. The shape of the TVC curve follows directly from the law of diminishing returns. Up to point W' (the point of inflection), the firm uses so little of the variable inputs with the fixed inputs that the law of diminishing returns is not yet operating. As a result, the TVC curve faces downward or rises at a decreasing rate. Past point W' (i.e., for output levels greater than 1.5), the law of diminishing returns operates and the TVC curve faces upward or rises at an increasing rate. Since $TC = TFC + TVC$, the TC curve has the same shape as the TVC curve but is $30 (the TFC) above it at each output level.

Per-Unit Costs

From total costs we can derive per-unit costs. These are even more important in the short-run analysis of the firm. **Average fixed cost (AFC)** equals total fixed costs divided by output. **Average variable cost (AVC)** equals total variable costs divided by output. **Average**

TABLE 8.2 Fixed, Variable, and Total Costs

Quantity of Output	Total Fixed Costs	Total Variable Costs	Total Costs
0	$30	$ 0	$ 30
1	30	20	50
2	30	30	60
3	30	45	75
4	30	80	110
5	30	145	175

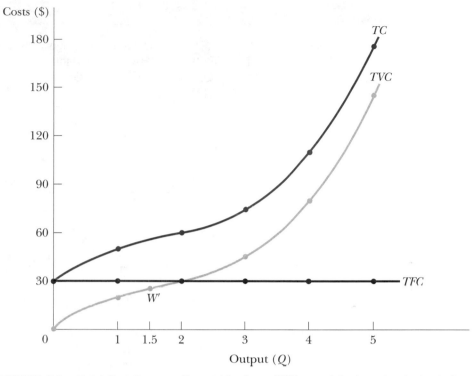

FIGURE 8.1   Total Cost Curves   The total fixed cost (*TFC*) curve is horizontal at the level of $30, regardless of the level of output. The total variable costs (*TVC*) are zero when output is zero and rise as output rises. Past point *W'*, the law of diminishing returns operates and the *TVC* curve faces upward or rises at an increasing rate. Total costs (*TC*) equal *TFC* plus *TVC*. Thus, the *TC* curve has the same shape as the *TVC* curve but is $30 above it at each output level.

total cost (*ATC*) equals total costs divided by output. *ATC* also equals *AFC* plus *AVC*. **Marginal cost (*MC*)** equals the change in *TC* or in *TVC* per unit change in output.

Table 8.3 presents the per-unit cost schedules derived from the corresponding total cost schedules of Table 8.2. The *AFC* values given in column 5 are obtained by dividing the *TFC* values in column 2 by the quantity of output in column 1. *AVC* (column 6) equals *TVC* (column 3) divided by output (column 1). *ATC* (column 7) equals *TC* (column 4) divided by output (column 1). *ATC* also equals *AFC* plus *AVC*. *MC* (column 8) is given by the change in *TVC* (column 3) or in *TC* (column 4) per unit change in output (column 1). Thus, *MC* does not depend on *TFC*.

The per-unit cost schedules given in Table 8.3 are plotted in Figure 8.2. Note that *MC* is plotted *between* the various levels of output. From Table 8.3 and Figure 8.2, we see that the *AFC* curve falls continuously, while the *AVC*, *ATC*, and *MC* curves first fall and then rise (i.e., they are U-shaped). Since the vertical distance between the *ATC* and the *AVC* curve equals *AFC*, a separate *AFC* curve is superfluous and can be omitted from the figure.

The reason the *AVC* curve is U-shaped can be explained as follows. With labor as the only variable input in the short run, *TVC* for any output level (*Q*) equals the given wage rate

TABLE 8.3 Total and Per-Unit Costs

Quantity of Output (1)	Total Fixed Costs (2)	Total Variable Costs (3)	Total Costs (4)	Average Fixed Cost (5)	Average Variable Cost (6)	Average Total Cost (7)	Marginal Cost (8)
1	$30	$ 20	$ 50	$30	$20	$50	$20
2	30	30	60	15	15	30	10
3	30	45	75	10	15	25	15
4	30	80	110	7.50	20	27.50	35
5	30	145	175	6	29	35	65

$(\overline{w})$ times the quantity of labor (L) used. Then,

$$AVC = \frac{TVC}{Q} = \frac{\overline{w}L}{Q} = \frac{\overline{w}}{Q/L} = \frac{\overline{w}}{AP_L} = \overline{w}\left(\frac{1}{AP_L}\right) \qquad [8.1]$$

With $\overline{w}$ constant and from our knowledge (from Section 7.2) that the average physical product of labor (AP_L or Q/L) usually rises first, reaches a maximum, and then falls, it follows that the AVC curve first falls, reaches a minimum, and then rises. Thus, the AVC curve is the monetized mirror image, reciprocal, or "dual" of the AP_L curve. Since the AVC curve is U-shaped, the ATC curve is also U-shaped. The ATC curve continues to fall after the AVC curve begins to rise because, for a while, the decline in AFC exceeds the rise in AVC (see Figure 8.2).

The U-shape of the MC curve can similarly be explained as follows:

$$MC = \frac{\Delta TVC}{\Delta Q} = \frac{\Delta(\overline{w}L)}{\Delta Q} = \frac{\overline{w}(\Delta L)}{\Delta Q} = \frac{\overline{w}}{\Delta Q/\Delta L} = \frac{\overline{w}}{MP_L} = \overline{w}\left(\frac{1}{MP_L}\right) \qquad [8.2]$$

Since the marginal product of labor (MP_L or $\Delta Q/\Delta L$) first rises, reaches a maximum, and then falls, it follows that the MC curve first falls, reaches a minimum, and then rises. Thus, the rising portion of the MC curve reflects the operation of the law of diminishing returns.[3]

The MC curve reaches its minimum point at a smaller level of output than the AVC and the ATC curves, and it intersects from below the AVC and the ATC curves at their lowest points (see Figure 8.2). The reason is that for average costs to fall, the marginal cost must be lower. For average costs to rise, the marginal cost must be higher. Also, for average costs neither to fall nor rise (i.e., to be at their lowest point), the marginal cost must be equal to them. Although the AVC, ATC, and MC curves are U-shaped, they sometimes have a fairly flat bottom (see Example 8–2).

Geometry of Per-Unit Cost Curves

The shapes of the per-unit cost curves are determined by the shapes of the corresponding total cost curves. The AVC and ATC are given, respectively, by the slope of a line (ray) from the origin to the TVC and TC curves, while the MC is given by the slope of the TC and the

[3] If factor prices increased, the MC and the other cost curves would shift up, as shown in the appendix to this chapter.

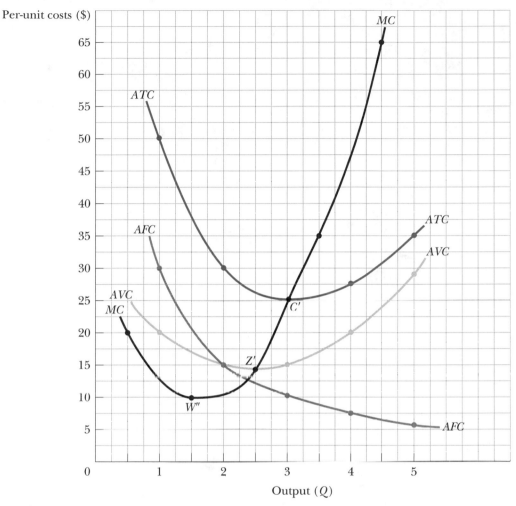

FIGURE 8.2   Per-Unit Cost Curves   The average fixed cost (*AFC*) curve falls continuously, while the average variable cost (*AVC*), average total cost (*ATC*), and marginal cost (*MC*) curves are U–shaped. The *MC* is plotted between the various output levels. The *ATC* curve falls as long as the decline in *AFC* exceeds the rise in *AVC*. The rising portion of the *MC* curve intersects from below the *AVC* and the *ATC* curves at their lowest point.

TVC curves. This is similar to the derivation of the average and marginal product curves from the total product curve in Section 7.2.

Figure 8.3 shows that the *AVC* at 1 and 4 units of output (*Q*) is given by the slope of ray 0*Y*, which is $20. Note that the slope of a ray from the origin to the *TVC* curve in the top panel falls up to point *Z* (where the ray from the origin is tangent to the *TVC* curve) and then rises. Thus, the *AVC* curve in the bottom panel falls up to point *Z'* (i.e., up to *Q* = 2.5) and rises thereafter. The bottom panel of Figure 8.3 also shows that the *ATC* at *Q* = 3 is $25 (the slope of ray 0*C* in the top panel). Note that the slope of a ray from the origin to the *TC* curve falls up to point *C* (where the ray from the origin is tangent to the *TC* curve) and then rises. Thus, the *ATC* curve falls up to point *C'* (i.e., up to *Q* = 3) and rises thereafter.

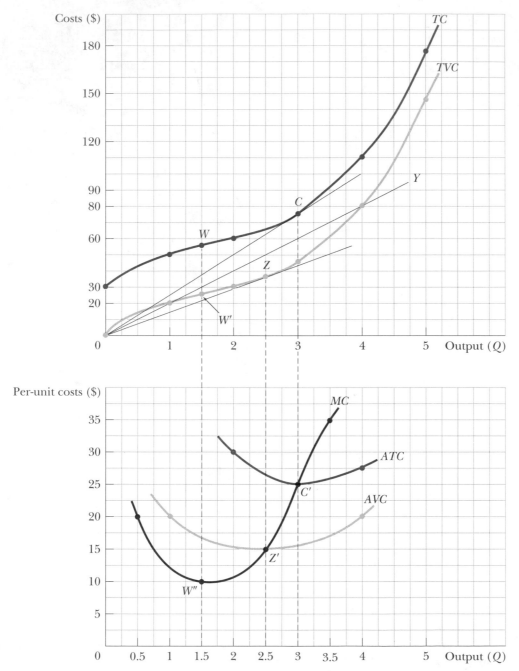

FIGURE 8.3   Graphic Derivation of Per-Unit Cost Curves   The *AVC* and *ATC* are given, respectively, by the slope of a line from the origin to the *TVC* and *TC* curves, while the *MC* curve is given by the slope of the *TC* or *TVC* curves. The slope of a ray from the origin to the *TVC* curve (the *AVC*) falls up to point *Z* and rises thereafter. The slope of a ray from the origin to the *TC* curve (the *ATC*) falls up to point *C* and rises thereafter. The slope of the *TC* and *TVC* curves (the *MC*) falls up to point *W* and *W'*, respectively, and then rises and intersects from below the *AVC* and the *ATC* curves at their lowest points.

The top panel of Figure 8.3 also shows that the slope of the *TC* and *TVC* curves falls up to point *W* and *W'* (the points of inflection) on the *TC* and *TVC* curves, respectively, and then rises. Thus, the *MC* curve in the bottom panel falls up to *W"* and rises thereafter. At point *Z*, the *MC* and *AVC* are both equal to the slope of ray 0Z. This is $35/2.5, or $14, and equals the lowest *AVC*. At point *C*, the *MC* and *ATC* are both equal to the slope of ray 0C. This is $75/3, or $25, and equals the lowest *ATC*. Note that the *AVC*, *ATC*, and *MC* curves derived geometrically in Figure 8.3 are identical to those in Figure 8.2 and correspond to the values in Table 8.3.

Not shown in Figure 8.3 (in order not to complicate the figure unnecessarily) is the geometrical derivation of the *AFC* curve. This, however, is very simple. For example, turning back for a moment to Figure 8.1, we can see that the *AFC* for one unit of output is equal to the slope of the ray from the origin to $Q = 1$ on the $TFC = \$30$ curve. This is $30/1, or $30. At $Q = 2, AFC = \$30/2 = \$15$. At $Q = 3, AFC = \$30/3 = \$10$, and so on. Note that because *TFC* are constant, *AFC* falls continuously as output rises. Thus, the *AFC* curve is a rectangular hyperbola (see Figure 8.2). As pointed out earlier, *AFC* is equal to the vertical distance between the *ATC* curve and the *AVC* curve, and so a separate *AFC* curve is not really necessary.

EXAMPLE 8–2
Per-Unit Cost Curves in Corn Production

Figure 8.4 shows the actual estimated *AVC*, *ATC*, and *MC* per bushel of corn raised on central Iowa farms. The per-unit cost curves in the figure have the same general shape as

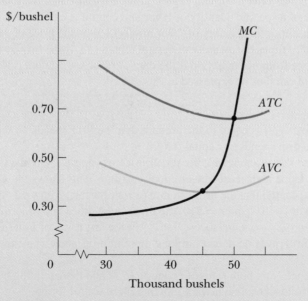

FIGURE 8.4   Average and Marginal Cost Curves in Corn Production   This figure shows the actual *AVC*, *ATC*, and *MC* curves per bushel of corn raised on Iowa farms. These curves have flat bottoms, and the *MC* curve rises steeply.

the typical curves examined earlier, but with flatter bottoms. Once *MC* starts rising, it does so very rapidly. This is true not only in raising corn but also in many other cases. For example, traveling costs (in terms of travel time) rise very steeply during peak hours on highways. Similarly, landing costs (in terms of landing time) at airports also rise rapidly during peak hours (3–5 P.M.).

Sources: D. Suits, "Agriculture," in W. Adams and J. Brock, *The Structure of the American Economy* (Englewood Cliffs, NJ: Prentice-Hall, 1995), p. 12; Samuel, "Traffic Congestion: A Solvable Problem," *Issues in Technology,* Spring 1999; "Road Pricing: The Solution to Highway Congestion," *The Margin,* Spring 1993; and Carlin and R. Park, "Marginal Cost Pricing of Airport Runway Capacity," *American Economic Review,* June 1970.

8.3   COST IN THE LONG RUN

In the long run, all inputs and costs are variable; that is, there are no fixed inputs and no fixed costs. In this section, we define isocost lines and examine how a firm chooses the combination of inputs to minimize the cost of producing a given level of output when all factors are variable.

Isocost Lines

Suppose that a firm uses only labor and capital in production. Then the total cost (*TC*) of the firm for the use of a specific quantity of labor and capital is equal to the price of labor (*w* or the wage rate) times the quantity of labor hired (*L*), plus the price of capital (*r* or the rental price of capital) times the quantity of capital rented (*K*). If the firm owns the capital, *r* is the rent foregone from not renting out the capital (such as machinery) to others. The total cost of the firm can thus be expressed as

$$TC = wL + rK \qquad [8.3]$$

That is, the total cost (*TC*) is equal to the amount that the firm spends on labor (*wL*) plus the amount that the firm spends on capital (*rK*).

Given the wage rate of labor (*w*), the rental price of capital (*r*), and a particular total cost (*TC*), we can define an **isocost line** or equal-cost line. This shows the various combinations of labor and capital that the firm can hire or rent for the given total cost. For example, for $TC_1 = \$80$, $w = \$10$, and $r = \$10$, the firm could either hire $8L$ or rent $8K$, or any combination of *L* and *K* shown on isocost line *RS* in the left panel of Figure 8.5. For each unit of capital the firm gives up, it can hire one more unit of labor. Thus, the slope of isocost line *RS* is -1.

By subtracting *wL* from both sides of equation [8.3] and then dividing by *r*, we get the general equation of an isocost line in the following more useful form:

$$K = TC/r - (w/r)L \qquad [8.4]$$

The first term on the right-hand side of equation [8.4] is the vertical or *Y*-intercept of the isocost line, and $-w/r$ is the slope. Thus, for $TC_1 = \$80$ and $w = r = \$10$, the vertical or

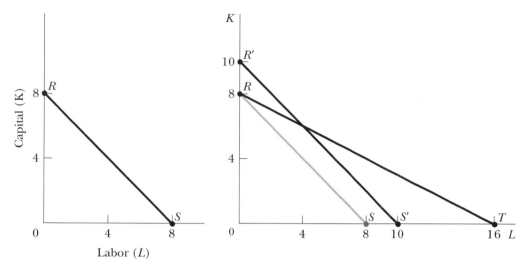

FIGURE 8.5   Isocost Lines   With capital measured along the vertical axis, for $TC_1 = \$80$ and $w = r = \$10$, the Y-intercept of the isocost line is $TC_1/r = \$80/\$10 = 8K$ and the slope is $-w/r = -\$10/\$10 = -1$. This gives budget line RS in the left and right panels. With $TC_2 = \$100$ and unchanged $w = r = \$10$, we have isocost line $R'S'$, with Y-intercept of $TC_2/r = \$100/\$10 = 10K$ and slope of $-w/r = -\$10/\$10 = -1$ in the right panel. With $TC_1 = \$80$ and $r = \$10$ but $w = \$5$, we have isocost line RT with slope of $-1/2$.

Y-intercept is $TC_1/r = \$80/\$10 = 8K$, and the slope is $-w/r = -\$10/\$10 = -1$ (see isocost line RS in the left panel of Figure 8.5).

A different total cost will define a different but parallel isocost line, while a different relative price of an input will define an isocost line with a different slope. For example, an increase in total expenditures to $TC_2 = \$100$ with unchanged $w = r = \$10$ will generate isocost line $R'S'$ in the right panel of Figure 8.5. The vertical or Y-intercept of isocost line $R'S'$ is equal to $TC_2/r = \$100/\$10 = 10K$ and its slope is $-w/r = -\$10/\$10 = -1$. With $TC_1 = \$80$ and $r = \$10$ but $w = \$5$, we have isocost line RT with slope of $-1/2$.

Note the symmetry between the isocost line and the budget line. In Section 3.4 we defined the *budget line* as showing the various combinations of two commodities that a consumer could purchase with a given money income. The *isocost line* shows the various combinations of two inputs that a firm can hire at a given total cost. However, whereas an individual's income is usually given and fixed over a specific period of time (so that we usually deal with only one budget line), a firm's total costs of production vary with output (so that we have a whole family of isocost lines).[4]

---

[4] A consumer's budget line can also change over a given period of time because consumers can save or borrow as well as vary the hours worked and type of job. However, these possibilities are usually not considered in order to keep the analysis simple.

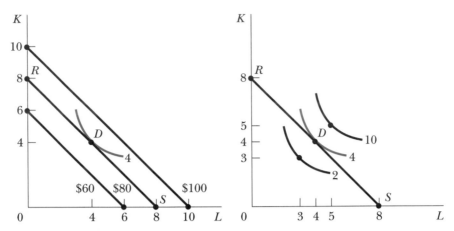

FIGURE 8.6   Optimal Input Combination   The left panel shows that *RS* is the lowest isocost with which the firm can reach isoquant 4*Q*. The firm minimized the cost of producing 4 units of output at point *D* by using 4*L* and 4*K* at a total cost of $80. The right panel shows that isoquant 4*Q* is the highest isoquant the firm can reach with isocost line *RS*. Thus, the firm maximizes output with a total cost of $80 by producing at point *D* and using 4*L* and 4*K*.

Least-Cost Input Combination[5]

To minimize the cost of producing a given level of output, the firm must produce at the point where an isocost line is tangent to the isoquant. For example, the left panel of Figure 8.6 shows that the minimum cost of producing four units of output (4*Q*) is $80 (isocost line *RS*). This is the lowest isocost line that will allow the firm to reach the isoquant for 4*Q*. The firm must produce at point *D* and use 4*L* (at the cost of $wL = \$40$) and 4*K* (at the cost of $rK = \$40$). This is the least-cost input combination. Any other input combination results in higher total costs for the firm to produce four units of output (i.e., to reach isoquant 4*Q*).

Minimizing the cost of producing a given level of output is equivalent to maximizing the output for a given cost outlay. The right panel of Figure 8.6 shows that the maximum output or highest isoquant that the firm could reach at the total cost of $80 (i.e., with isocost line *RS*) is the isoquant for 4*Q*. Thus, the condition for cost minimization is equivalent to the condition for output maximization. For both, the firm must produce where an isoquant and an isocost are tangent (point *D* in both panels of Figure 8.6). The concept of output maximization for a given cost outlay for a producer is completely analogous to the concept of consumer utility maximization for a given budget constraint, which was discussed in Section 3.5.

At the point of tangency, the absolute value of the slope of the isoquant or marginal rate of technical substitution of labor for capital is equal to the absolute value of the slope of the isocost line. That is,

$$MRTS_{LK} = w/r \qquad [8.5]$$

---

[5] For a mathematical presentation of cost minimization using rudimentary calculus, see Section A.9 of the Mathematical Appendix at the end of the book.

Since the $MRTS_{LK} = MP_L/MP_K$, we can rewrite the **least-cost input combination** as

$$MP_L/MP_K = w/r \qquad [8.6]$$

Cross multiplying, we get

$$MP_L/w = MP_K/r \qquad [8.6B]$$

Equation [8.6B] indicates that to minimize production costs (or maximize output for a given total cost), the extra output or marginal product per dollar spent on labor must be equal to the marginal product per dollar spent on capital. If $MP_L = 5$, $MP_K = 4$, and $w = r$, the firm would not be maximizing output or minimizing costs since it is getting more extra output for a dollar spent on labor than on capital. To maximize output or minimize costs, the firm would have to hire more labor and rent less capital. As the firm does this, the MP_L declines and the MP_K increases (because of diminishing returns). The process would have to continue until condition [8.6B] held. If w were higher than r, the MP_L would have to be proportionately higher than the MP_K for condition [8.6B] to hold.

The same general condition would have to hold to minimize production costs, no matter how many inputs the firm uses. That is, the MP per dollar spent on each input would have to be the same for all inputs. Another way of stating this is that, for costs to be minimized, an additional or marginal unit of output should cost the same whether it is produced with more labor or more capital.

Cost Minimization in the Long Run and in the Short Run

We have seen in the left panel of Figure 8.6 that the minimum cost of producing four units of output (4Q) is $80 when the firm uses four units of labor (4L) at $10 per unit and four units of capital (4K) at $10 per unit (point D, where the isoquant for 4Q is tangent to the isocost for $80). This is repeated in Figure 8.7. Figure 8.7 also shows that in the long run (when both L and K can be varied), the firm can produce 10Q with 5L and 5K at the *minimum* total cost of $100 (point H, where the isoquant for 10Q is tangent to the isocost for $100). Points D and H can also be interpreted as the points of maximum output for cost outlays of $80 and $100, respectively. Note that this production function exhibits strong economies of scale (i.e., 4L and 4K produce 4Q, while 5L and 5K produce 10Q).

If capital were fixed at 4K (in the short run), the *minimum cost* of producing 10Q would be higher, or $110, because the firm would have to use 7L and 4K (point V, where the isoquant for 10Q *crosses* the isocost for $110). Thus, the minimum cost of producing a given level of output is lower in the long run when both L and K are variable than in the short run when only L is variable. Note that at point V, the $MRTS_{LK} < w/r$. This means that the rate at which L can be substituted for K *in production* is smaller than the rate at which L can be substituted for K *in the market*. Thus, total costs can be reduced in the long run by using less labor and more capital in production. But this is impossible in the short run. As Example 8–3 shows, total costs would also be higher if government regulation prevented the attainment of the long-run cost minimization point.

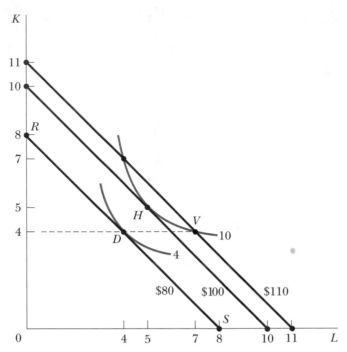

FIGURE 8.7   Long-Run and Short-Run Cost Minimization
Starting from point D, the firm minimizes the long-run cost of
producing 10Q at point H, where isoquant 10Q is tangent to the isocost
line for $100 and the firm uses 5L and 5K. If capital is fixed at 4K, the
firm minimizes the short-run cost of producing 10Q by using 7L and 4K
(point V, where the isoquant for 10Q crosses the isocost line for $110).

EXAMPLE 8–3

The Least-Cost Combination of Gasoline and Driving Time

Figure 8.8 repeats the isoquant of Figure 7.8, showing the various combinations of gasoline consumption and driving time required to cover 600 miles. If the price of gasoline
is $1.50 per gallon and the opportunity cost of driving time is $6.00 per hour, the minimum total cost for the trip would be $90. This is given by point B, where the isocost line
(with absolute slope of $1.50/$6.00 = 1/4) is tangent to the isoquant. Thus, to minimize
traveling cost, the individual would have to drive 10 hours at 60 mph and use 20 gallons
of gasoline. The individual would spend $30 on gasoline (20 gallons at $1.50 per gallon)
and incur an opportunity cost of $60 for travel time (10 hours of driving at $6.00 per
hour), for a total cost of $90 for the trip.

　　If the government set the speed limit at 50 mph, the trip would require 16 gallons of
gasoline and 12 hours of driving time (point A). The total cost of the trip would then be

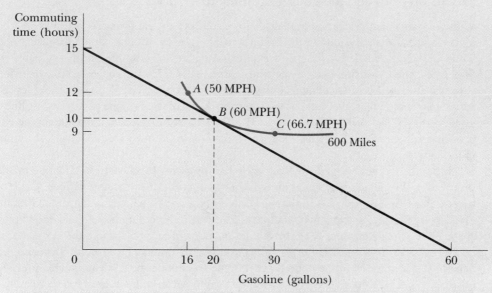

FIGURE 8.8   The Minimum Cost of a Trip   The minimum cost for the trip is $90 and is given at point *B*, where the isoquant is tangent to the isocost. The individual spends $30 on gasoline (20 gallons at $1.50 per gallon) and $60 in driving time (10 hours at $6.00 per hour).

$24 for gasoline (16 gallons at $1.50 per gallon) plus $72 for the driving time (12 hours at $6.00 per hour), or $96. Thus, enforcing a 50 mph speed limit saves gasoline but increases driving time and the total cost of the trip.

Thus, the final repeal of the 55-mile-an-hour law in 1995 (which had been imposed in 1974 at the start of the petroleum crisis to save gasoline) seems a rational response to the decline in gasoline prices (in relation to other prices) and the increase in real wages that has taken place since 1981. Opposition to the repeal of the 55-mile-an-hour law came primarily from those who believe that lower speed limits save lives. The reduction in gasoline price did, however, bring to a halt progress in energy efficiency.

Sources: C. A. Lave, "Speeding, Coordination, and the 55-mph Limit," *American Economic Review,* December 1985, pp. 1159–1164; "U.S., Progress in Energy Efficiency Is Halting," *New York Times,* February 27, 1989, p. 1; "Death Rate on U.S. Roads Reported at a Record Low," *New York Times,* October 27, 1998, p. 16; "Looking for Ways to Save Gasoline," *Wall Street Journal,* July 12, 2001, p. A1; "Senate Kills Effort to Raise Cars' Fuel Efficiency," *Wall Street Journal,* March 14, 2002, p. A2.

8.4   EXPANSION PATH AND LONG-RUN COST CURVES

In this section, we first define the firm's expansion path and, from it, derive the firm's long-run total cost curve. From the firm's long-run total cost curve, we then derive the firm's long-run average and marginal cost curves. Finally, we show the relationship between the firm's short-run and long-run average cost curves.

Expansion Path and the Long-Run Total Cost Curve

With constant input prices and higher total cost outlays by the firm, isocost lines will be higher and parallel. By joining the origin with the points of tangency of isoquants and the isocost lines, we derive the firm's **expansion path.** For example, in the top panel of Figure 8.9, the expansion path of the firm is line $0BDFHJN$. In this case, the expansion path is a straight line, indicating a constant capital-labor ratio (K/L) for all output levels. At the tangency points, the slope of the isoquants is equal to the slope of the isocost lines. That is, $MRTS_{LK} = MP_L/MP_K = w/r$, and $MP_L/w = MP_K/r$. Thus, points along the expansion path show the least-cost input combinations to produce various levels of output in the long run.

From the expansion path, we can derive the **long-run total cost (LTC)** curve of the firm. This curve shows the minimum long-run total costs of producing various levels of output. For example, point B in the top panel of Figure 8.9 indicates that the minimum total cost of producing two units of output ($2Q$) is $60 ($30 to purchase $3L$ and $30 to purchase $3K$). This gives point B' in the bottom panel of Figure 8.9, where the vertical axis measures total costs and the horizontal axis measures output. From point D in the top panel, we get point D' in the bottom panel. Other points on the LTC curve are similarly obtained. Note that the LTC curve starts at the origin because in the long run there are no fixed costs.

Derivation of the Long-Run Average and Marginal Cost Curves

The **long-run average cost (LAC)** curve is derived from the LTC curve in the same way as the short-run average total cost ($SATC$) curve is derived from the short-run total cost (STC) curve. For example, in Figure 8.10, the $LAC = $30 for two units of output ($2Q$) is obtained by dividing the LTC of $60 (point B' on the LTC curve in the top panel) by 2. This is the slope of the ray from the origin to point B' on the LTC curve and is plotted as point B in the bottom panel. Other points on the LAC curve are similarly obtained. Note that the slope of a line from the origin to the LTC curve falls up to point H' (in the top panel of Figure 8.10) and then rises. Thus, the LAC curve in the bottom panel falls up to point H ($10Q$) and rises thereafter. However, whereas the U-shape of the $SATC$ curve is explained by the law of diminishing returns, the U-shape of the LAC curve depends on the operation of increasing, constant, and decreasing returns to scale, respectively, as explained in Section 7.5.

The relationship between the *long-run* total and per-unit cost curves is generally the same as between the *short-run* total and per-unit cost curves and is also shown in Figure 8.10. The **long-run marginal cost (LMC)** curve is given by the slope of the LTC curve. From the top panel of Figure 8.10, we see that the slope of the LTC curve (the LMC) falls up to $Q = 7$ (the point of inflection) and rises thereafter. Also, the slope of the LTC curve (the LMC) is smaller than the slope of a ray from the origin to the LTC curve (the LAC) up to point H' and larger thereafter. At point H, $LMC = LAC$. Note that the LMC curve intersects from below the LAC curve at the lowest point of the latter. The LMC is $30 at $Q = 1$ because LTC increases from 0 to $60 when output rises from zero (the origin) to two units.

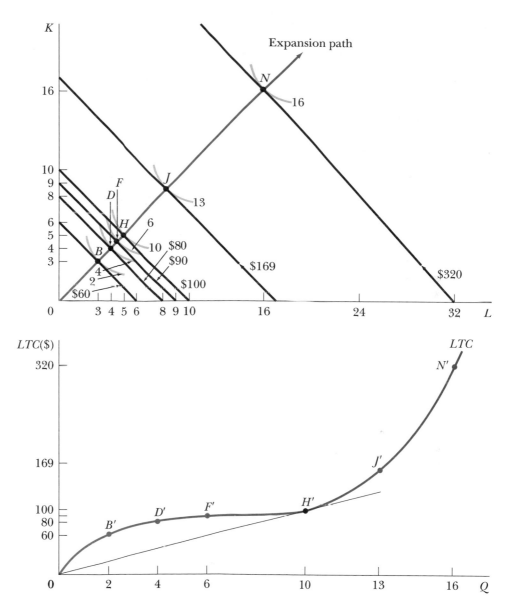

FIGURE 8.9   Derivation of the Expansion Path and the Long-Run Total Cost Curve   The expansion path of the firm is line *OBDFHJN* in the top panel. It is obtained by joining the origin with the points of tangency of isoquants with the isocost lines holding input prices constant. Points along the expansion path show the least-cost input combinations to produce various output levels in the long run. The long-run total cost curve in the bottom panel is derived from the expansion path. For example, point *B'* on the *LTC* curve is derived from point *B* on the expansion path. The *LTC* curve shows the minimum long-run total costs of producing various levels of output when the firm can build any desired scale of plant.

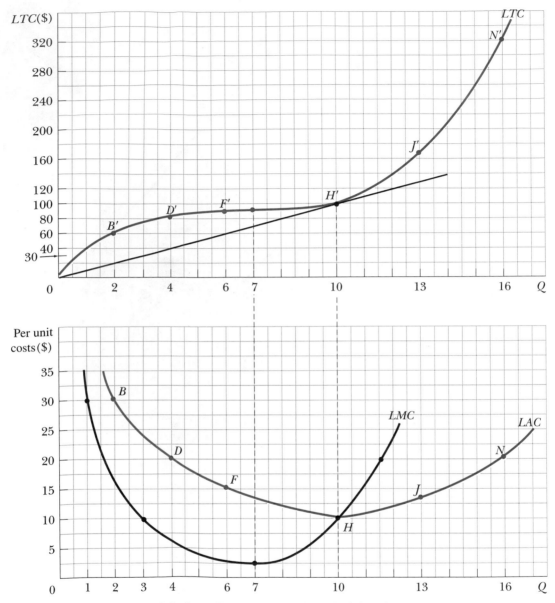

FIGURE 8.10   Derivation of the Long-Run Average and Marginal Cost Curves   The slope of a ray from the origin to the *LTC* curve in the top panel falls up to point *H'* and rises thereafter. Thus, the *LAC* curve in the bottom panel falls up to point *H* and rises thereafter. On the other hand, the slope of the *LTC* in the top panel (the *LMC* in the bottom panel) falls up to the point of inflection (at $Q = 7$) and then rises.

Thus, the change in *LTC* per unit change in output (the *LMC*) is $60/2 = \$30$. The *LMC* is $10 at $Q = 3$ because *LTC* increases from $60 to $80 for a two-unit increase in output (from $Q = 2$ to $Q = 4$). The other *LMC* values shown in Figure 8.10 are obtained in the same way.

The Relationship between Short- and Long-Run Average Cost Curves

There is an important relationship between the firm's *SATC* and *LAC* curves. Figure 8.11 shows that the *LAC* curve is tangent to various *SATC* curves. Each *SATC* curve represents the plant to be used to produce a particular level of output at minimum cost. The *LAC* curve is then the tangent to these *SATC* curves and shows the minimum cost of producing each level of output. For example, the lowest *LAC* (of $30) to produce two units of output results when the firm operates plant 1 at point *B* on its *SATC*₁ curve. The lowest *LAC* (of $20) to produce four units of output results when the firm operates plant 2 at point *D* on its *SATC*₂ curve. Four units of output could also be produced by the firm operating plant 1 at point *D** on its *SATC*₁ curve (see the figure). However, this would not represent the lowest cost of producing 4*Q* in the long run. Other points on the *LAC* curve are similarly obtained. Thus, the *LAC* curve shows the minimum per-unit cost of producing any level of output *when the firm can build any desired scale of plant*. Note that the *LAC* to produce 3*Q* is the same for plant 1 and plant 2 (point *C*).

With only six plant sizes, the *LAC* curve would be *ABCDE''FGHIJMNR* (the solid portion of the *SATC* curves). With the infinite or very large number of plant sizes that the firm could build in the long run, the *LAC* curve would be the smooth curve passing through points *BDFHJN* (that is, the "kink" at points *C*, *E''*, *G*, *I*, and *M* would be eliminated by having many plant sizes). Mathematically, the *LAC* curve is the "envelope" to the *SATC* curves.

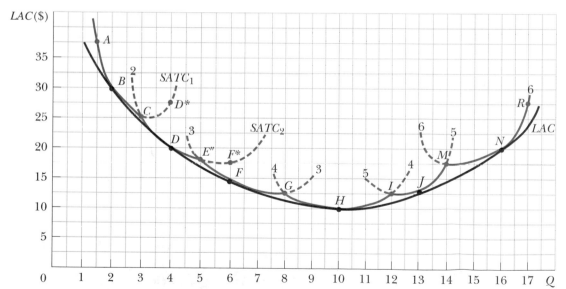

Figure 8.11   Relationship between Short- and Long-Run Average Cost Curves   The *LAC* curve is tangent to the *SATC* curves, each representing the plant size to produce a particular level of output at minimum cost. With only six plants, the *LAC* curve would be *ABCDE''FGHIJMNR* (the solid portion of the *SATC* curves). With the infinite or very large number of plant sizes that the firm could build in the long run, the *LAC* curve would be the smooth curve passing through points *BDFHJN*.

The long run is often referred to as the **planning horizon.** In the long run, the firm has the time to build the plant that minimizes the cost of producing any anticipated level of output. Once the plant has been built, the firm operates in the short run. Thus, the firm plans in the long run and operates in the short run. Example 8–4 shows the long run average cost curve in the generation of electricity.

EXAMPLE 8–4

Long-Run Average Cost Curve in Electricity Generation

Figure 8.12 shows the actual estimated *LAC* curve for a sample of 114 firms generating electricity in the United States in 1970. The figure shows that the *LAC* is lowest at the output level of about 32 billion kilowatt-hours. The *LAC*, however, is nearly L-shaped, indicating that *LAC* do not increase much for outputs greater than 32 billion kilowatt-hours. Electrical companies were able to avoid the increasing costs that they would have incurred in producing more power themselves to satisfy increasing consumer demand by buying more and more power from independent power producers. But all of this is changing very rapidly in the face of deregulation and the end of monopoly power by electrical companies (see Chapters 9 and 12). Furthermore, recent technological advances have greatly reduced the average cost of producing electricity with micro-turbine

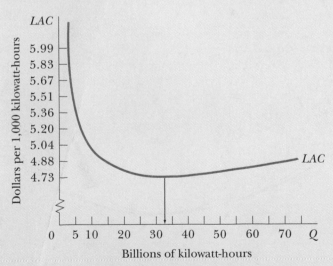

FIGURE 8.12   Long-Run Average Cost Curve in Electricity Generation   This figure shows the actual estimated *LAC* curve for a sample of 114 firms generating electricity in the United States in 1970. The lowest point on the *LAC* curve is at the output level of about 32 billion kilowatt-hours. However, the *LAC* curve is nearly L-shaped.

generators, and this may soon provide even small businesses with the choice of generating their own electricity efficiently.

Sources: L. Christensen and W. Green, "Economies of Scale in U.S. Electric Power Generation," *Journal of Political Economy,* August 1976, p. 674; Michael Weiner et al., "Value Networks—The Future of the U.S. Electric Utility Industry," *Sloan Management Review,* Summer 1997; "Energy: Power Unbound," *Wall Street Journal,* September 14, 1998, pp. R4 and R10; "Future Generations," *Wall Street Journal,* September 13, 1999, p. R8; and "End of the Power Price Surge Shocks U.S. Markets," Financial Times, September 11, 2001, p. 22.

8.5   SHAPE OF THE LONG-RUN AVERAGE COST CURVE

In Figures 8.10 and 8.11, the *LAC* curve has been drawn as U-shaped, just like the *SATC* curve. The reason for this similarity, however, is entirely different. The *SATC* curve turns upward when the rise in *AVC* (resulting from the operation of the law of diminishing returns) exceeds the decline in *AFC* (see Figure 8.2 and the discussion relating to it). However, in the long run, all inputs are variable (i.e., there are no fixed inputs) and so the law of diminishing returns is not applicable. The U-shape of the *LAC* curve depends instead on increasing and decreasing returns to scale. That is, as output expands from very low levels, increasing returns to scale prevail and cause the *LAC* curve to fall. As output continues to expand, the forces for decreasing returns to scale eventually begin to overtake the forces for increasing returns to scale and the *LAC* curve begins to rise.

As seen in Section 7.5, increasing returns to scale means that output rises proportionately more than inputs, and so the cost per unit of output falls if input prices remain constant. On the other hand, decreasing returns to scale means that output rises proportionately less than inputs, and so the cost per unit of output rises if input prices remain constant. Therefore, decreasing *LAC* and increasing returns to scale are two sides of the same coin.[6] Similarly, increasing *LAC* and decreasing returns to scale are equivalent. When the forces for increasing returns to scale are just balanced by the forces for decreasing returns to scale, we have constant returns to scale and the *LAC* curve is horizontal.

Empirical studies seem to indicate that in many industries the *LAC* curve has a very shallow bottom or is nearly L-shaped, as in Figure 8.12. This means that economies of scale are rather quickly exhausted, and constant or near-constant returns to scale prevail over a considerable range of output. This permits relatively small and large firms to coexist in the same industry (see Example 8–5). The smallest quantity at which the *LAC* curve reaches its minimum is called the **minimum efficient scale (MES).** The smaller the MES, the smaller the prevalence of economies of scale and the larger the number of firms that can operate efficiently in the industry (see Example 8–6).

Were increasing returns to scale to prevail over a very large range of output, large (and more efficient) firms would drive smaller firms out of business. In an extreme case, only

---

[6] Increasing returns to scale and decreasing costs and economies of scale are synonymous only if the firm keeps the capital-labor ratio unchanged as it expands its scale of operation.

one firm could most efficiently satisfy the entire market demand for the commodity. This is usually referred to as a "natural monopoly." In such cases, the government allows only one firm to operate in the market, but the firm is subject to regulation. Examples are provided by public utilities (such local electrical water and gas companies). Natural monopolies are discussed in detail in Chapter 13. On the other hand, the reason we do not often observe steeply rising *LAC* in the real world is that firms may generally know when their *LAC* would begin to rise rapidly and avoid expanding output in that range.

EXAMPLE 8–5
The Shape of the Long-Run Average Cost Curves in Various Industries

Table 8.4 gives the long-run average cost for small firms as a percentage of the long-run average cost of large firms in seven U.S. industries or sectors. The table shows that the *LAC* of small hospitals is 29% higher than for large hospitals. This implies that small hospitals operate in the declining portion of the *LAC* curve. For Ph.D.-granting institutions, the *LAC* for small universities is about 19% higher than for large ones. For most other industries, the *LAC* of small firms is not much different from the *LAC* for large firms in the same industry. These results are consistent with the widespread near-constant returns to scale reported in Table 7.9 and with L-shaped or at least flat-bottomed *LAC* curves. Only in trucking does the *LAC* curve seem mildly U-shaped (since small firms have lower *LAC* costs than large ones).

These above results are also consistent with those of a more extensive study conducted in India and in Canada. Of the 29 industries examined in India, 18 were found to have L- or nearly L-shaped *LAC* curves, 6 were found to have horizontal *LAC* curves or nearly so, and only 5 were found to be U-shaped. Of 94 manufacturing industries studied in Canada, 31 had a *LAC* curve that was L-shaped, 23 had a *LAC* that was horizontal,

TABLE 8.4	Long-Run Average Cost (LAC) of Small Firms as a Percentage of LAC of Large Firms
Industry	**Percentage**
Hospitals	129
Higher education	119
Commercial Banking	
Demand deposits	116
Installment loans	102
Electric power	112
Airline (local service)	100
Railroads	100
Trucking	95

18 had a *LAC* curve falling throughout, 14 had rising *LAC*, and only for 8 was the *LAC* curve U-shaped.

Sources: H. E. Frech and L. R. Mobley, "Resolving the Impasse on Hospital Scale Economies: A New Approach," *Applied Economics,* March 1995; H. Cohen, "Hospital Cost Curves with Emphasis on Measuring Patient Care Output," in H. Klarman (ed.), *Empirical Studies in Health Economics* (Baltimore: Johns Hopkins Press, 1979); R. K. Koshal and M. Koshal, "Quality and Economies of Scale in Higher Education," *Applied Economics,* Vol. 27, 1995; F. Bell and N. Murphy, *Costs in Commercial Banking* (Boston: Federal Reserve Bank of Boston, Research Report No. 41, 1968); L. Christensen and W. Greene, "Economies of Scale in U.S. Electric Power Generation," *Journal of Political Economy,* August 1976; G. Eads, M. Nerlove, and W. Raduchel, "A Long-Run Cost Function for the Local Service Airline Industry," *The Review of Economics and Statistics,* August 1969; Z. Griliches, "Cost Allocation in Railroad Regulation," *The Bell Journal of Economics and Management Science,* Spring 1972; R. Koenker, "Optimal Scale and the Size Distribution of American Trucking Firms," *Journal of Transport Economics and Policy,* January 1977; V. K. Gupta, "Cost Functions, Concentration, and Barriers to Entry in Twenty-Nine Manufacturing Industries in India," *Journal of Industrial Economics,* November 1968; B. Robidoux and J. Lester, "Econometric Estimates of Scale Economies in Canadian Manufacturing," *Applied Economics,* January 1992.

EXAMPLE 8–6

The Minimum Efficient Scale in Various U.S. Food Industries

Table 8.5 shows the minimum efficient scale (MES) as a percentage of output in various U.S. food industries in 1986. The table shows that the MES was 12.01% of the total cane sugar industry output. Thus, economies of scale seem to be very important in this industry. One way to interpret this is to say that if all firms in the industry were identical in size and were just large enough to produce at the smallest output at which their *LAC* curve was minimum, only eight firms could exist in this industry. This is to be contrasted with the mineral water industry, where the MES was 0.08% of the total industry output, so that economies of scale seem to be very small indeed and a very large number of firms could exist in the industry. For all the other industries studied, the MES is between these two extremes.

TABLE 8.5	Minimum Efficient Scale (MES) as a Percentage of Output in Various U.S. Food Industries		
Industry	MES as Percentage of Output	Industry	MES as Percentage of Output
Cane sugar	12.01	Beer	1.37
Breakfast cereals	9.47	Frozen food	0.92
Roasted coffee	5.82	Processed meat	0.26
Canned soup	2.59	Canned vegetables	0.17
Biscuits	2.04	Bread	0.12
Margarine	1.75	Mineral water	0.08

Source: J. Sutton, *Sunk Costs and Market Structure* (Cambridge, MA: MIT Press, 1991), pp. 106–105.

8.6	MULTIPRODUCT FIRMS AND DYNAMIC CHANGES IN COSTS

Until now, we have assumed that a firm produced a single product. In this section, we examine how a firm producing more than one product may face lower costs for each product than if it produced only one or fewer products. We also examine the reduction in costs that often occur as a firm gains experience or "learns" in the production of a given product.

Economies of Scope

In the real world, we often observe firms producing more than one product rather than a single product. For example, automobile companies produce cars and trucks, computer firms produce desktops and portables, universities produce teaching and research, and chicken farms produce poultry and eggs. **Economies of scope** are present if it is cheaper for a single firm to produce various products jointly than for separate firms to produce the same products independently.[7] For example, economies of scope exist if the total cost (TC) of jointly producing cars (C) and trucks (T) is smaller than if cars and trucks were produced independently by different firms. That is, economies of scope exist if

$$TC(C,T) < [TC(C,0) + TC(0,T)] \qquad [8.7]$$

In other words, economies of scope are present if it is more expensive to produce cars and trucks independently rather than jointly. If the opposite is the case (i.e., it is less expensive to produce cars and trucks independently than jointly), so that the direction of the above inequality sign is reversed, we would have **diseconomies of scope.**

Economies of scope may arise when products can be produced with common production facilities or other inputs, thus lowering costs. For example, automobiles and trucks can be produced with the same metal sheet and engine assembly facilities, and their joint production leads to a better utilization of those production facilities and lower costs than when automobiles and trucks are produced independently by different firms. Similarly, a small commuter airline may face lower costs if it also provides cargo services than if it provided only commuter service. Economies of scope also arise when a firm produces a second product in order to utilize the by-products (which before, the firm had to dispose at a cost) arising from the production of the first product. In addition, economies of scope can result from better marketing strategies and the better utilization of a common administration. Firms must constantly be alert to the possibility of profitably extending their product lines to exploit such economies of scope. Indeed, one reason for the existence of multiproduct conglomerates is the synergy or the increase in efficiency and lower costs arising from economies of scope.

Economies of scope must be clearly distinguished from economies of scale. There is simply no direct relationship between the two. For example, full-service banking arose because of the economies of scope in providing savings and checking deposits, loans,

---

[7] See J. C. Panzar and R. D. Willig, "Economies of Scope," *American Economic Review,* May 1981; and E. E. Bailey and A. F. Friedlaender, "Market Structure and Multiproduct Industries: A Review Article," *Journal of Economic Literature,* September 1982.

currency exchange, and data processing to customers by the same bank, and not because of economies of scale (which have been found to be fully exhausted for banks as small as with $25 million in deposits).[8] Sometimes, however, expected synergies and economies of scope fail to materialize and the conglomerate either fails or deliberately splits into separate entities. This is exactly what happened to ITT in 1995 when it decided to split into three different companies: an insurance company, an industrial product manufacturing business, and a casino, hotel, and sports company.[9] In 2000, AT&T announced its intention of splitting itself into four separate companies (business services, consumer products, wireless, and broadband).[10]

The Learning Curve

As a firm gains experience in the production of a commodity or service, its average cost of production usually declines. In other words, *for a given level of output per time period,* the increasing *cumulative total output* over many time periods often provides the manufacturing experience that enables the firm to significantly lower its average cost of production. The **learning curve** shows the decline in the average input cost of production with rising cumulative total outputs of the firm over time. For example, it might take 1,000 hours for an aircraft manufacturer to assemble the 100th aircraft, but only 700 hours to assemble the 200th aircraft because as managers and workers gain production experience they usually become more efficient, especially when the production process is relatively new. Contrast this with economies of scale, which refers to declining long-run average cost as the firm's output *per time period* increases.

The left panel of Figure 8.13 shows a learning curve that indicates that the average cost declines from $10 for producing the 10th unit of the product (point *H*), to $7 for producing the 20th unit (point *T*), and to $5 for producing the 40th unit of the product (point *W*). Average cost declines at a decreasing rate so that the learning curve is convex to the origin. This is the usual shape of learning curves; that is, firms usually achieve the largest decline in average input costs when the production process is relatively new and smaller declines as the firm matures.

The difference between the reduction in average costs due to learning and to increasing returns to scale is clarified by examining the right panel of Figure 8.13. In the figure, the reduction in long-run average cost (*LAC*) due to increasing returns to scale is shown by a movement, say from point *D* to point *F*, along the *LAC* curve (the same as in Figure 8.11) as output *per time period* increases. The reduction in *LAC* due to learning is instead shown by the downward shift in the *LAC* curve, say from point *D* to point *D**, for a given level of output per time period, but as the firm learns from a larger total cumulative output over many periods.

Learning curves have been documented in many manufacturing and service sectors including manufacturing of airplanes, appliances, ships, computer chips, refined petroleum

---

[8] T. G. Gilligan, M. Smirlock, and W. Marshall, "Scale and Scope Economies in the Multiproduct Banking Firm," *Journal of Monetary Economics,* October 1984.

[9] "ITT, The Quintessential Conglomerate, Plans to Split Up," *New York Times,* June 14, 1995, p. D1.

[10] "AT&T Gives Details of Pending Breakup," *New York Times,* May 12, 2001, p. C3.

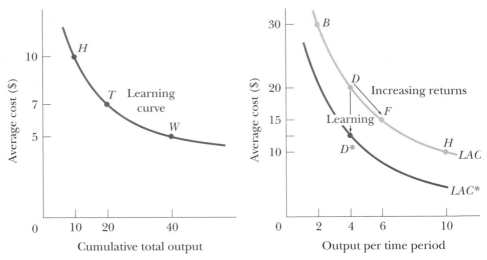

FIGURE 8.13   Learning and Increasing Returns Compared   The left panel shows that as the total cumulative output of the firm doubles from 10 to 20 units over time, the average cost declines from $10 to $7 (the movement from point *H* to point *T* on the learning curve). The right panel shows that *LAC* declines from $20 to $15 as output increases from 4 to 6 units per time period (the movement from point *D* to point *F* along the *LAC* curve) due to increasing returns to scale. But *LAC* falls from $20 to $12.50 to produce 4 units of output per time period as the firm learns from larger cumulative total outputs (the downward shift of the *LAC* curve from point *D* to point *D**).

products, and the operation of power plants. Learning curves have also been used to forecast the need for personnel, machinery, and raw materials and for scheduling production, determining the price at which to sell output, and even to evaluate suppliers' price quotations. For example, in its early days as a producer of computer chips, Texas Instruments adopted an aggressive price strategy based on the learning curve. Believing that the learning curve in chip production was steep, the firm kept unit prices very low to increase its total cumulative output rapidly, thereby learning by doing. The strategy was successful and the rest is history (Texas Instruments became one of the world's major players in this market).

How rapidly the learning curve (i.e., average input cost) declines can differ widely among firms and is greater the smaller the rate of employee turnover, the fewer production interruptions (which would lead to "forgetting"), and the greater the ability of the firm to transfer knowledge from the production of other similar products. The average cost typically declines by 20% to 30% for each doubling of cumulative output for many firms (see Example 8–7).[11]

---

[11] The classic paper on learning curves is K. Arrow, "The Economic Implication of Learning by Doing," *Review of Economic Studies,* June 1962. See also L. Argote and D. Epple, "Learning Curves in Manufacturing," *Science,* February 23, 1990, and D. A. Irwin and P. J. Klenow, "Learning-by-Doing Spillovers in the Semiconductor Industry," *Journal of Political Economy,* December 1994.

EXAMPLE 8–7

The Learning Curve for the Lockheed L-1011 Aircraft and for Semiconductors

Figure 8.14 shows the learning curve for the L-1011 aircraft that Lockheed produced between 1970 and 1984 in the United States. The figure shows that the number of worker-hours (in thousands) that Lockheed used was 900 to produce the 10th aircraft, 550 for the 20th, 400 for the 40th, 350 for the 50th, 300 for the 100th, and slightly lower than 300 to produce the 150th aircraft. This implies a learning rate of about 20%. Thus, a 10% increase in cumulative production would lead to a 2% reduction in cost. Learning essentially came to an end with the production of the 100th aircraft. After producing 150 of the L-1011, the rate of production slowed down considerably and the worker-hours required to produce each aircraft went back up to about 500,000 (not shown in the figure). This implies organizational forgetting when the rate of production slows

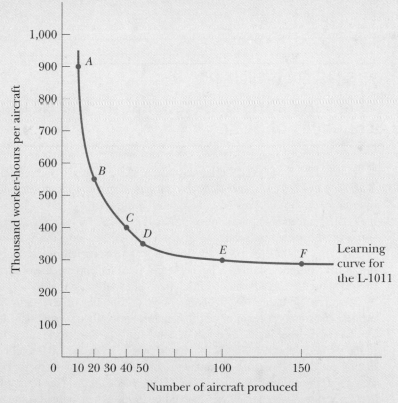

FIGURE 8.14   Learning Curve for the Lockheed 1011 Aircraft   The figure shows that the number of worker-hours (in thousands) that Lockheed used to produce its L-1011 aircraft declined at a about the rate of 20% and essentially came to an end when cumulative production reached about 100 aircraft.

down significantly (Lockheed stopped producing the L-1011 in 1984 after producing 250 aircraft).

Learning has also been important in the production of semiconductors (the memory chips that are used in personal computers, cellular telephones, electronic games, etc.). The semiconductor industry introduced seven generations of dynamic random access memory chips (DRAM) between 1974 and 1992. A study found that the learning rate in the production of each generation of DRAMs also averaged about 20%, so that a doubling of cumulative output reduced the average cost of production by about 20%. The study also found that there was no discernible difference in the speed of learning of U.S. and Japanese firms, but that intergenerational learning was low. That is, having a lower cost in the production of one generation of DRAMs was no guarantee of continued success in the production of the next generation.

Sources: C. L. Benkard, "Learning and Forgetting: The Dynamics of Aircraft Production," *American Economic Review,* September 2000; and D. A. Irwin and P. J. Klenow, "Learning-by-Doing Spillovers in the Semiconductor Industry," *Journal of Political Economy,* December 1994.

AT THE FRONTIER
Minimizing Costs Internationally—The New Economies of Scale

D uring the past decade, there has been a sharp increase in international trade in parts and components. Today, more and more products manufactured by international corporations have parts and components made in many different nations. The reason is to minimize production costs. For example, the motors of some Ford Fiestas are produced in the United Kingdom, the transmissions in France, the clutches in Spain, and the parts are assembled in Germany for sales throughout Europe. Similarly, Japanese and German cameras are often assembled in Singapore to take advantage of the much cheaper labor there.

Foreign "sourcing" of inputs is often not a matter of choice to earn higher profits, but simply a requirement to remain competitive. Firms that do not look abroad for cheaper inputs face loss of competitiveness in world markets and even in the domestic market. This is the reason that $625 of the $860 total cost of producing an IBM PC was outsourced from abroad and most of the major components going into the production of a Boeing 777 are made abroad (see Example 1–5). Of 26 major American companies surveyed in 1996, 22 outsourced some activity, up from 15 in 1992. U.S. firms now spend more than $100 billion on outsourcing and by doing so they cut costs by 10–15%. Outsourcing now accounts for more than one-third of total manufacturing costs by Japanese firms and this saves them more than 20% of production costs. Such low-cost offshore purchase of inputs is likely to continue to expand rapidly in the future and is being fostered by joint ventures, licensing arrangements, and other nonequity collaborative arrangements. Indeed, this represents one of the most dynamic aspects of the global business environment of today.

Not only are more and more inputs imported, but more and more firms are opening production facilities in more and more nations. For example, Nestlé, the largest Swiss company and the world's second largest food company, has production facilities in 59 countries, America's Gillette has facilities in 22 countries. In 1987, Ford had component factories and assembly plants in 26 different industrial sites in the United Kingdom, Germany, Belgium, France, Spain, and Portugal and employed more people abroad than in the United States (201,000 people abroad as compared with 181,000 in the United States). Bertelsman AG, the $7 billion German media empire, owns printing plants around the world and the Literary Guild Book Club, and it also prints books at competitors' plants and sells them through Time-owned Book-of-the-Month Club.

So widespread and growing is international trade in inputs and the opening of production facilities abroad that we are rapidly moving toward truly multinational firms with roots in many nations rather than in only one country, as in the past. This change affects not only the multinational companies. Indeed, more and more firms that, until a few years ago, operated exclusively in the domestic market are now purchasing increasing quantities of inputs and components and shifting some of their production to foreign nations. For example, Malachi Mixon, the American medical equipment company, now buys parts and components in half a dozen countries, from China to Colombia, when ten years ago it did all of its shopping at home. The popular Mazda Miata automobile, which is manufactured in Japan, was conceived in Mazda's California design lab by an American engineer at the same time that Mazda opened production facilities for other models in the United States.

Firms must constantly explore sources of cheaper inputs and overseas production to remain competitive in our rapidly shrinking world. Indeed, this process can be regarded as manufacturing's new (international) economies of scale in today's global economy. Just as companies were forced to rationalize operations within each country in the 1980s, they now face the challenge of integrating their operations for their entire system of manufacturing around the world to take advantage of the new **international economies of scale.** What is important is for the firm to focus on those components that are indispensable to the company's competitive position over subsequent product generations and "outsource" other components for which outside suppliers have a distinctive production advantage.

The new international economies of scale can be achieved in five basic areas: product development, purchasing, production, demand management, and order fulfillment. In product development, the firm can design a core product for the entire world economy by building into the product the possibility of variations and derivatives to meet the needs of local markets. Firms can achieve new economies of scale by purchasing raw materials, parts, and components on a global rather than on a local basis—no matter where their operations are located. Firms can

Continued. . .

also coordinate production in low-cost manufacturing centers with final assembly in high-cost locations near markets. They can forecast the demand for their products and undertake demand management on a world rather than on a national basis. Firms can achieve important economies of scale by shipping products from the plants closest to customers more quickly and with smaller inventory on a global basis. International economies of scale are likely to become even more important in the future as we move closer and closer to a truly global economy.

Sources: "Manufacturing's New Economies of Scale," *Harvard Business Review,* May–June 1992; "Strategic Outsourcing," *Harvard Business Review,* November–December 1992; "Strategic Outsourcing," *Sloan Management Review,* Summer 1994; "The New Dynamics of Global Manufacturing Site Location," *Sloan Management Review,* Summer 1994; and "A Sharp Sense of the Limits of Outsourcing," *Financial Times,* July 31, 2001, p. 10.

SUMMARY

1. In economics, costs include explicit and implicit costs. Explicit costs are the actual expenditures of the firm to purchase or hire inputs. Implicit costs refer to the value (imputed from their best alternative use) of the inputs owned and used by the firm in its own production process. The opportunity cost to a firm in using any input (whether owned or hired) is what the input could earn in its best alternative use. Costs are also classified into private and social. Private costs are those incurred by individuals and firms, while social costs are those incurred by society as a whole.

2. In the short run we have fixed, variable, and total costs. Total fixed costs (TFC) plus total variable costs (TVC) equal total costs (TC). The shape of the TVC curve follows directly from the law of diminishing returns. Average fixed cost (AFC) equals TFC/Q, where Q is output. Average variable cost (AVC) equals TVC/Q. Average total cost (ATC) equals TC/Q. $ATC = AFC$ plus AVC also. Marginal cost (MC) equals the change in TC or in TVC per-unit change in output. The AVC, ATC, and MC curves first fall and then rise (i.e., they are U-shaped). AVC and MC move inversely to the AP_L and the MP_L, respectively. The AVC and the ATC are given, respectively, by the slope of a line from the origin to the TVC and to the TC curves, while the MC is given by the slope of the TC and the TVC curves.

3. Given the wage rate of labor (w), the rental price of capital (r), and a particular total cost (TC), we can define the isocost line. This line shows the various combinations of L and K that the firm can hire in the long run. With K plotted along the vertical axis, the Y-intercept of the isocost line is TC/r and its slope is $-w/r$. To minimize production costs or maximize output, the firm must produce where an isoquant is tangent to an isocost line. At this point, $MRTS_{LK} = w/r$, and $MP_L/w = MP_K/r$. This means the MP per dollar spent on L must be equal to the MP per dollar spent on K. The minimum cost of producing a given level of output is usually lower in the long run than in the short run.

4. The expansion path joins the origin with the points of tangency of isoquants and isocost lines with input prices held constant. It shows the least-cost input combination to produce various output levels. From the expansion path, we can derive the long-run total cost (LTC) curve. This shows the minimum long-run total costs of producing various levels of output when the firm can build any desired plant. From the long-run total cost curve, we can then derive the long-run average and marginal cost curves. The long-run average cost (LAC) equals LTC/Q, while the long-run marginal cost (LMC) equals $\Delta LTC/\Delta Q$. The LAC curve is tangent to the short-run average total cost curves. The firm plans in the long run and operates in the short run.

5. The U-shape of the long-run average cost curve of the firm results from the operation of increasing, constant, and decreasing returns to scale, respectively. Empirical studies seem to indicate that in many industries the *LAC* curve has a very shallow bottom or is nearly L-shaped. This means that economies of scale are quickly exhausted, and constant or near-constant returns to scale prevail over a considerable range of output. This permits relatively small and large firms to coexist in the same industry. The smallest quantity at which the *LAC* curve reaches its minimum is called the minimum efficient scale (MES).

6. Economies of scope are present if it is cheaper for a firm to produce various products jointly than for separate firms to produce the same products independently. The opposite situation refers to diseconomies of scope. The learning curve shows the decline in the average cost of production with rising cumulative total outputs over time by the firm. During the past decade, there has been a sharp increase in international trade in parts and components, and more and more firms have opened production facilities abroad to keep production costs as low as possible and thus be able to meet the growing international competition. This process can be regarded as manufacturing's new (international) economies of scale in today's global economy.

KEY TERMS

Explicit costs
Implicit costs
Opportunity cost
Alternative or opportunity cost
  doctrine
Private costs
Social costs
Total Fixed Costs (*TFC*)
Total Variable Costs (*TVC*)

Total Costs (*TC*)
Averaged Fixed Cost (*AFC*)
Average Variable Cost (*AVC*)
Average Total Cost (*ATC*)
Marginal Cost (*MC*)
Isocost line
Least-cost input combination
Expansion path
Long-Run Total Cost (*LTC*)

Long-Run Average Cost (*LAC*)
Long-Run Marginal Cost (*LMC*)
Planning horizon
Minimum efficient scale (MES)
Economies of scope
Diseconomies of scope
Learning curve
International economies
  of scale

REVIEW QUESTIONS

1. An individual quits his job as a manager of a small photocopying business in which he was earning $30,000 per year and opens his own shop by renting a store for $5,000 per year, using $10,000 of his own money to rent the photocopying machines, and hiring a helper for $10,000 per year. What are the individual's accounting costs? What are his economic costs?

2. State colleges are more efficient than independent colleges in providing college education because they charge lower tuition. True or false? Explain.

3. Is the annual retainer paid by a firm to a lawyer a fixed or a variable cost?

4. How should a firm utilize each of two plants to minimize production costs for the firm as a whole?

5. If the marginal cost of a firm is rising, does this mean that its average cost is also rising?

6. Is it always better to hire a more qualified and productive worker than a less qualified and productive worker? Explain.

7. Is a firm minimizing costs if the marginal product of labor is six, the marginal product of capital is five, the wage rate is $2, and the interest on capital is $1? If not, what must the firm do to minimize costs?

8. Must a firm's long-run average cost curve be U-shaped if its long-run marginal cost curve is U-shaped?

9. What does the long-run marginal cost curve of a firm look like if its long-run average cost curve is L-shaped?

10. What is the difference between economies of scale, economies of scope, and the reduction in average costs as a result of learning?

11. Should a firm purchase abroad some parts and components needed to produce its product, even if that creates employment opportunities abroad instead of at home?

12. What is meant by "international economies of scale"?

PROBLEMS

*1. A woman working in a large duplicating (photocopying) establishment for $15,000 per year decides to open a small duplicating business of her own. She runs the operation by herself without hired help and invests no money of her own. She rents the premises for $10,000 per year and the machines for $30,000 per year. She spends $15,000 per year on supplies (paper, ink, envelopes), electricity, telephone, and so on. During the year her gross earnings are $65,000.

   a. How much are the explicit costs of this business?

   b. How much are the implicit costs?

   c. Should this woman remain in business after the year if she is indifferent between working for herself or for others in a similar capacity?

2. a. Plot the total fixed costs (TFC) curve, the total variable costs (TVC) curve, and the total costs (TC) curve given in the following table.

Quantity of Output	Total Variable Costs	Total Costs
0	$ 0	$ 30
1	20	50
2	30	60
3	48	78
4	90	120
5	170	200

   b. Explain the reason for the shape of the cost curves in 2(a) above.

3. a. Derive the average fixed costs (AFC), the average variable costs (AVC), the average total costs (ATC), and the marginal costs (MC) from the total cost schedules given in the table of Problem 2.

   b. Plot the AVC, ATC, and MC curves of 3(a) on a graph and explain the reason for their shape. How are AFC reflected in the figure?

   c. How can the AFC, AVC, ATC, and MC curves be derived geometrically?

*4. Electrical utility companies usually operate their most modern and efficient equipment around the clock and use their older and less efficient equipment only to meet periods of peak electricity demand.

   a. What does this imply for the short-run marginal cost of these firms?

   b. Why do these firms not replace all of their older equipment with newer equipment in the long run?

5. Suppose that the marginal product of the last worker employed by a firm is 30 units of output per day and the daily wage that the firm must pay is $20, while the marginal product of the last machine rented by the firm is 80 units of output per day and the daily rental price of the machine is $40.

   a. Why is this firm not maximizing output or minimizing costs in the long run?

   b. How can the firm maximize output or minimize costs?

6. With reference to Figure 8.7, answer the following questions.

   a. If capital were fixed at 5 units, what would be the minimum cost of producing 10 units of output in the short run?

   b. If capital were variable but labor fixed at 4 units, what would be the minimum cost of producing 10 units of output?

7. a. Suppose that $w = \$10$ and $r = \$10$ and the least-cost input combination is $3L$ and $3K$ to produce 2 units of output ($2Q$), $4L$ and $4K$ to produce $4Q$, $4.5L$ and $4.5K$ to produce $6Q$, $5L$ and $5K$ to produce $8Q$, $7.5L$ and $7.5K$ for $10Q$, and

* = Answer provided at end of book.

12L and 12K for 12Q. Draw the isocost lines, the isoquants, and the expansion path of the firm.

b. From the expansion path of 7(a), derive the long-run total cost curve of the firm.

c. Redraw your figure of 7(b) and on it draw the STC curve from the data given for Problem 2(a), the STC curve tangent to the LTC curve at Q = 8, and the STC curve tangent to the LTC curve at Q = 12.

8. a. From the LTC curve of the firm of Problem 7(b), derive the LAC and the LMC curves of the firm.

b. Redraw the figure of 8(a), and on the same figure draw the ATC and the MC curves of Problem 3(b). Also draw the ATC curve that forms the lowest point of the LAC curve at Q = 8 and the corresponding SMC curve. On the same figure, draw the ATC curve that is tangent to the LAC curve at Q = 12 and the corresponding SMC curve.

*9. a. Under what condition would the LTC curve be a positively sloped straight line through the origin?

b. What would then be the shape of the LAC and the LMC curves?

c. Would this be consistent with U-shaped STC curves?

d. Draw a figure showing your answer to 9(a), 9(b), and 9(c).

10. Suppose that in Figure 8.8 the opportunity cost of driving time remained at $6.00 per hour but the price of gasoline increased to $4.50 per gallon.

a. Approximately how much gasoline and driving time would the individual use for the trip of 600 miles?

b. What would be the minimum total cost of the trip?

11. a. Draw a figure showing that the best plant for a range of outputs may not be the best plant to produce a given level of output.

b. Why might the firm build the first rather than the second type of plant?

*12. Given the following learning curve equation,

$$AC - 1{,}000\,Q^{-0.3}$$

where AC refers to the average cost of production and Q to the total cumulative output of the firm over time, find the AC of the firm for producing the

a. 100th unit of the product.

b. 200th unit of the product.

c. 400th unit of the product.

d. Draw the learning curve from the results obtained from parts (a) to (c).

APPENDIX **EXTENSIONS AND USES OF PRODUCTION AND COST ANALYSIS**

This appendix shows how the total variable cost curve can be derived from the total product curve, examines input substitution in production to minimize costs, and shows the effect of an increase in input prices on the firm's cost curves.

Derivation of the Total Variable Cost Curve from the Total Product Curve

The top panel of Figure 8.15 reproduces the total product (TP) curve of Figure 7.2. With labor (L) as the only variable input and with the constant wage rate of $10, the total variable cost (TVC) of producing various quantities of output is given by TVC = $10L (the lower horizontal scale in the top panel). If we now transpose the axes and plot TVC on the vertical axis and output on the horizontal axis, we obtain the TVC curve shown in the bottom panel of Figure 8.15. Thus, the shape of the TVC curve is determined by the shape of the TP curve.

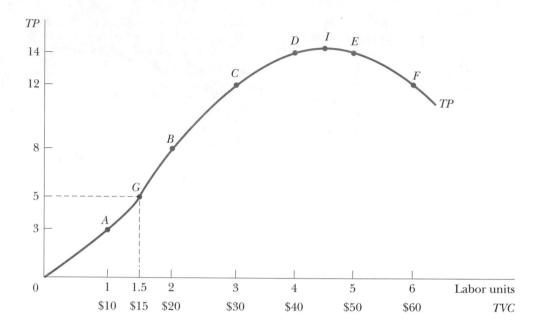

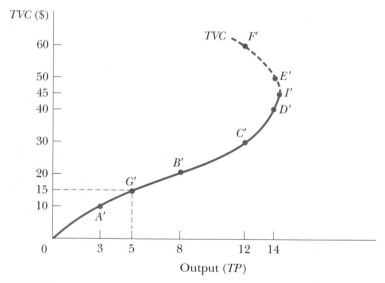

FIGURE 8.15   Derivation of the *TVC* Curve from the *TP* Curve   The top panel reproduces the *TP* curve of Figure 6.2. With labor (*L*) as the only variable input and with the constant wage rate of $10, *TVC* = $10*L* (the lower horizontal scale in the top panel). If we now transpose the axes and plot *TVC* on the vertical axis and output on the horizontal axis, we obtain the *TVC* curve shown in the bottom panel. At points *G* and *G'*, the law of diminishing returns begins to operate.

Note that the slope of the *TP* curve (or *MP_L*) rises up to point *G* (the point of inflection) in the top panel and then declines. On the other hand, the slope of the *TVC* curve (the *MC*) falls up to point *G'* (the point of inflection) in the bottom panel and then rises. At points *G* and *G'*, the law of diminishing returns begins to operate. The *MC* is the monetized mirror image or dual of the MP_L. That is, MC falls when MP_L rises, MC is minimum when MP_L is highest, and MC rises when MP_L falls. The same inverse relationship exists between the AVC and the AP_L. Note also that the TVC curve is dashed above point I' in the bottom panel because no firm would want to incur higher TVC to produce smaller outputs.

Input Substitution in Production to Minimize Costs

We now examine how a firm minimizes the cost of producing any given level of output by substituting a cheaper for a more expensive input in production. Figure 8.16 shows that with $TC = \$140$ and $w = r = \$10$, the firm minimizes the cost of producing $10Q$ by using $7K$ and $7L$ (point A, where isocost line FG is tangent to isoquant $10Q$). At point A, $K/L = 1$.

If r remains at $\$10$ but w falls to $\$5$, the isocost line becomes FH and the firm can reach an isoquant higher than $10Q$ with $TC = \$140$. The firm can now reach isoquant $10Q$ with $TC = \$100$. This is given by isocost $F'H'$, which is parallel to FH (i.e., $w/r = 1/2$ for both) and is tangent to isoquant $10Q$ at point B. At point B, $K/L = 1/2$. Thus, with a reduction in w (and constant r), a lower TC is required to produce a given level of output. To minimize production costs, the firm will have to substitute L for K in production, so that K/L declines.

The ease with which the firm can substitute L for K in production depends on the shape of the isoquant and can be measured by the elasticity of substitution (see Example 8–7). The flatter the isoquant, the easier it is to substitute L for K in production. On the other hand, if the isoquant is at a right angle, or L-shaped (as in Figure 7.7), no input substitution is possible (i.e., $MRTS_{LK} = 0$). In such a case, K/L will then always be constant regardless of input prices.

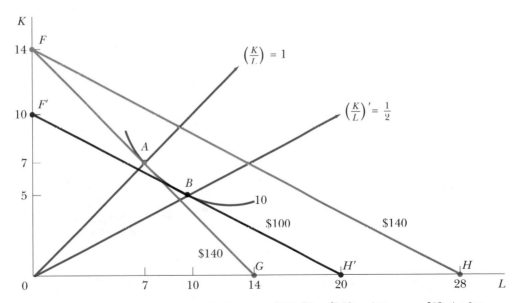

FIGURE 8.16   Input Substitution in Production   With $TC = \$140$ and $w = r = \$10$, the firm minimizes the cost of producing $10Q$ by using $7K$ and $7L$ (point A, where isocost FG is tangent to isoquant $10Q$). At point A, $K/L = 1$. If r remains at $\$10$ but w falls to $\$5$, the firm can reach isoquant $10Q$ with $TC = \$100$. The least-cost combination of L and K is then given by point B, where isocost $F'H'$ is tangent to isoquant $10Q$. At point B, $K/L = 1/2$.

EXAMPLE 8-8

The Elasticity of Substitution in Japanese Manufacturing Industries

A more precise method of measuring the ease with which a firm can substitute one input for another in production than looking at the curvature of the isoquant is with the *elasticity of substitution*. This is given by the percentage change in K/L with respect to the percentage change in P_L/P_K. The larger the value of this elasticity, the easier it is for the firm to substitute L for K in production. Table 8.6 gives the value of the elasticity of substitution of nonskilled labor for capital (σ_{NK}), skilled labor for capital (σ_{SK}), and nonskilled labor for skilled labor (σ_{NS}), in a number of Japanese manufacturing industries from 1970 to 1988.

TABLE 8.6 Elasticity of Substitution in Japanese Manufacturing Industries			
Industry	σ_{NK}	σ_{SK}	σ_{NS}
Food	0.14	0.62	0.38
Pulp and paper	0.76	0.75	1.32
Metal products	0.99	0.86	1.72
Non-electrical machinery	0.31	0.56	1.44
Electrical machinery	0.52	0.60	0.96
Precision instruments	0.67	0.62	1.15

The table shows that for the food industry, a 1% reduction in the wages of unskilled labor relative to the price of capital would lead to a 0.14% reduction in the capital-to-unskilled-labor ratio (while holding the wages of skilled labor constant), as firms substitute nonskilled labor for capital in production. This means that the isoquant between nonskilled labor and capital is almost L-shaped, offering little possibility of factor substitution in production. On the other hand, the elasticity of substitution between nonskilled and skilled workers of 1.72 for metal products implies a fairly flat isoquant and a strong possibility of substituting nonskilled for skilled workers. The table also shows that, except for the food industry, it is easier to substitute nonskilled for skilled labor than to substitute nonskilled or skilled labor for capital.

Source: K. Hashimoto and J.A. Heath, "Estimating Elasticities of Substitution by the CDE Production Function: An Application to Japanese Manufacturing Industries," Applied Economic, February 1995, p. 170.

INPUT PRICES AND THE FIRM'S COST CURVES

In deriving the firm's cost curves, input prices are kept constant. Per-unit costs differ at different levels of output because the physical productivity of inputs varies as output varies. If input prices do change, the AC and the MC curves of the firm will shift—up if input prices rise and down if input prices fall. These shifts are called external diseconomies and economies, respectively, and are examined in detail in Chapter 9.

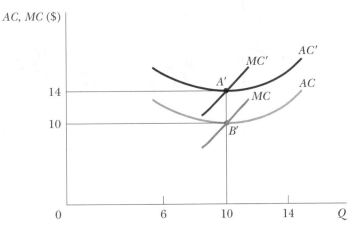

FIGURE 8.17   Input Prices and the *AC* and *MC* Curves   Point *B'*
on curve *AC* shows that with $w = \$5$, $AC = \$10$ for $Q = 10$ (from
point *B* in Figure 8.16). Point *A'* on curve *AC'* shows that with $w = \$10$,
$AC = \$14$ for $Q = 10$ (from point *A* in Figure 8.16). Thus, an increase in
w from $5 to $10 shifts *AC* and *MC* up to *AC'* and *MC'*.

For example, point *B* in Figure 8.16 shows that $10Q$ is produced at $TC = \$100$ when
$w = \$5$, so that $AC = \$10$. With $w = \$10$, the production of $10Q$ requires $TC = \$140$ (point A
in Figure 8.16), so that $AC' = \$14$. This is shown in Figure 8.17 by point *B'* and *A'* on
average cost curves *AC* and *AC'*, respectively. Note that the marginal cost curve will also
shift up from *MC* to *MC'* when *w* rises.

For simplicity, we assumed in Figure 8.17 that the firm produces at the lowest point on
its average cost curve before and after the increase in *w*. Be that as it may, the minimum cost
of producing a given level of output is always achieved by substituting the cheaper input (in
this case, capital) for the input that has become more expensive (labor) until the tangency
of the given isoquant with the new (steeper) isocost is reached (point *A* in Figure 8.16, at
which, once again, $MRTS_{LK} = w/r$).

INTERNET SITE ADDRESSES

For an excellent presentation of the theory of cost of
    production, see:
    http://price.bus.okstate.edu/archive/Econ3113_963/
    Shows/Chapter7/index.htm

For estimates of scale economies in electricity
generation, see:
    http://www.sel.com/
    http://www.treasury.nsw.gov.au/etf/etf95_5.htm

For economies or diseconomies of scale at General
Motors, Ford, and Chrysler, see:
    http://www.gm.com
    http://www.ford.com
    http://www.chrysler.com

For how far afield companies go to reduce costs, see:
    Southwest Airlines: http://www.southwest.com
    Domino's Pizza: http://www.dominos.com
    Federal Express: http://www.fedex.com
    GE Information Services: http://www.geis.com

For Learning curves, see:
    National Bureau of Economic Research:
    http://www.nber.org/papers/w7127

For competition in industry for commercial aircraft, see:
    Lockheed: http://www.lockheedmartin.com
    Boeing: http://www.boeing.com
    Airbus: http://www.airbus.com

CHAPTER 9

Price and Output Under Perfect Competition

In this chapter, we bring together the theory of consumer behavior and demand (from Part Two) and the theory of production and costs (from Chapters 7 and 8) to analyze how price and output are determined under perfect competition. As explained in Chapter 1, the analysis of how price and output are determined in the market is a primary aim of microeconomic theory.

The chapter begins by identifying the various types of market structure and defining perfect competition. It then examines price determination in the market period, or the very short run, when the supply of the commodity is fixed. Subsequently, we discuss how the firm determines its best level of output in the short run at various commodity prices. In the process, we derive the short-run supply curve of the firm and industry, and show how the interaction of industry demand and supply curves determines the equilibrium price of the commodity. This was already demonstrated in Chapter 2, but now we know what lies behind the market demand and supply curves and how they are derived.

From the analysis of the market period and the short run, we go on to examine the long-run equilibrium of the firm and define constant, increasing, and decreasing cost industries. Subsequently, we consider the very significant effect of international competition on the domestic economy. The chapter concludes with an analysis of perfectly competitive markets. This analysis, together with the real-world examples presented in the theory sections, as well as the "At the Frontier" discussion of the auction of airwaves, highlights the great importance and relevance of the analytical tools developed in the chapter. In the optional appendix, the foreign exchange market and the dollar exchange rate are examined, and their importance to the operation of the firm in today's highly integrated world is discussed.

MARKET STRUCTURE: PERFECT COMPETITION

In economics, we usually identify four different types of market structure: perfect competition, monopoly, monopolistic competition, and oligopoly. This chapter examines perfect competition. The other three types of market organization are considered in the next three chapters (monopoly in Chapter 10 and monopolistic competition and oligopoly in Chapters 11 and 12). Chapter 13 then analyzes the efficiency implications of market imperfections and regulation.

Perfect competition refers to the type of market organization in which (1) there are many buyers and sellers of a commodity, each too small to affect the price of the commodity; (2) the commodity is homogeneous; (3) there is perfect mobility of resources; and (4) economic agents have perfect knowledge of market conditions (i.e., prices and costs). Let us now examine in detail the meaning of each of the four aspects of the definition.

First, in perfect competition, there are many buyers and sellers of the commodity, each of which is too small (or behaves as if he or she is too small) in relation to the market to have a perceptible effect on the price of the commodity. Under perfect competition, the equilibrium price and quantity of the commodity are determined at the intersection of the market demand and supply curves of the commodity. The equilibrium price will not be affected perceptibly if only one or a few consumers or producers change the quantity demanded or supplied of the commodity.

Second, the commodity is *homogeneous,* identical, or perfectly standardized, so that the output of each producer is indistinguishable from the output of others. An example of this might be grade A winter wheat. Thus, buyers are indifferent as to the output of which producer they purchase.

Third, resources are perfectly mobile. This means that resources or inputs are free to move (i.e., they can move at zero cost) among the various industries and locations within the market in response to monetary incentives. Firms can enter or leave the industry in the long run without much difficulty. That is, there are no artificial barriers (such as patents) or natural barriers (such as huge capital requirements) to entry into and exit from the industry.

Fourth, consumers, firms, and resource owners have perfect knowledge of all relevant prices and costs in the market. This ensures that the same price prevails in each part of the market for the commodity and for the inputs required in the production of the commodity.

Needless to say, these conditions have seldom if ever existed in any market. The closest we might come today to a perfectly competitive market is the stock market (see Example 9–1) and the foreign exchange market (in the absence of intervention by national monetary authorities) examined in the appendix. Another example might be U.S. agriculture at the turn of the century, when millions of small farmers raised wheat. Despite its rarity, the perfectly competitive model is extremely useful to analyze market situations that approximate perfect competition. More importantly, the perfectly competitive model provides the point of reference or standard against which to measure the economic cost or *inefficiency* of departures from perfect competition. These departures can take the form of monopoly, monopolistic competition, or oligopoly. In the case of monopoly, there is a *single* seller of a commodity for which there are no good substitutes. Under monopolistic competition, there are many sellers of a *differentiated* commodity.[1] In oligopoly, there are *few sellers* of

---

[1] An example of a differential commodity is the different brand names of the same commodity.

either a homogeneous or a differentiated commodity. Imperfectly competitive markets are examined in Part Four (Chapters 10–13).

The economist's definition of perfect competition is diametrically opposite to the everyday usage of the term. In economics, the term "perfect competition" stresses the *impersonality* of the market. One producer does not care and is not affected by what other producers are doing. The output of all producers is identical, and an individual producer can sell any quantity of the commodity at the given price without any need to advertise. On the other hand, in everyday usage, the term "competition" stresses the notion of *rivalry* among producers or sellers of the commodity. For example, GM managers speak of the fierce competition that their firm faces from other domestic and foreign auto producers with regard to style, mileage per gallon, price, and so on. Because of this, GM mounts elaborate and costly advertising campaigns to convince consumers of the superiority of its vehicles. This is not, however, what the economist means by competition.

Under perfect competition, the firm is a *price taker* and can sell any quantity of the commodity at the given market price. If the firm raised its price by the slightest amount, it would lose all of its consumers. On the other hand, there is no reason for the firm to reduce the commodity price since the firm can sell any quantity of the commodity at the given market price. Thus, the perfectly competitive firm faces a horizontal or infinitely elastic demand curve (as in Figure 5.7) at the price determined at the intersection of the market demand and supply curves for the commodity (as in Figure 2.5).

EXAMPLE 9–1

Competition in the New York Stock Market

The market for stocks traded on the New York and other major stock exchanges is as close as we come today to a perfectly competitive market. In most cases the price of a particular stock is determined by the market forces of demand and supply of the stock, and individual buyers and sellers of the stock have an insignificant effect on price (i.e., they are price takers). All stocks within each category are more or less homogeneous. The fact that a stock is bought and sold frequently is evidence that resources are mobile. Finally, information on prices and quantities traded is readily available.

In general, the price of a stock reflects all the publicly known information about the present and expected future profitability of the stock. This is known as the *efficient market hypothesis*. Funds flow into stocks, and resources flow into uses in which the rate of return, corrected for risk, is highest. Thus, stock prices provide the signals for the efficient allocation of investments in the economy. Despite the fact that the stock market is close to being a perfectly competitive market, imperfections occur even here. For example, the sale of $1 billion worth of stocks by IBM or any other large corporation will certainly affect (depress) the price of its stocks. Furthermore, stock prices can sometimes become grossly overvalued (i.e., we could have a "bubble market") and thus subject to a subsequent steep correction (fall). This is, in fact, what happened in the New York Stock Market at the end of the 1990s.

Today, more and more Americans trade foreign stocks, and more and more foreigners trade American stocks. This has been the result of a communications revolution that linked stock markets around the world into a huge global capital market and around-the-clock trading. While this provides immense new earning possibilities and sharply increased opportunities for portfolio diversification, it also creates the danger that a crisis in one market will very quickly spread to other markets around the world. This actually happened when the New York Stock Exchange collapse in October 1987 caused sharp declines in stock markets around the world and again 10 years later (in the fall of 1997), when the collapse of stock markets in Southeast Asia led to a sharp decline in the New York Stock Market and in stock markets in other nations. In 2002, history repeated itself when sharp declines in the New York stock market (as a result of low corporate profits and huge financial scandals) quickly spread to other stock markets around the world.

In recent years, the New York Stock Exchange seems to have lost some of its former ability to predict changing economic conditions and its importance as the central source of capital for corporate America, as the latter borrowed increasing amounts from banks for takeovers and mergers. Indeed, global markets for securities, featuring automated, round-the-world, round-the-clock trading could eventually eclipse Wall Street's capital-raising dominance.

Sources: New York Stock Exchange, *You and the Investment World* (New York: The New York Stock Exchange, 1998); "The Future of Wall Street," *Business Week,* November 5, 1990, pp. 119–124; "Luck or Logic? Debate Rages On Over 'Efficient Market Theory'," *The Wall Street Journal,* November 4, 1993, p. C1; "Worrying About World Markets," *Fortune,* July 24, 1995, pp. 43–45; "Unreality Check for the Bull Market," *The Wall Street Journal,* May 25, 1999, p. C1; and "Another Scandal, Another Scare," *The Economist,* June 29, 2002, pp. 67–69.

9.2   PRICE DETERMINATION IN THE MARKET PERIOD

The **market period,** or the very short run, refers to the time period during which no input can be varied (i.e., all costs are fixed) and so the market supply of a commodity is also fixed. The market period may be a day, a week, a month, or longer, depending on the industry. For example, if milk is delivered every morning to New York City, and no other deliveries can be arranged for the rest of the day, the market period is one day. For wheat, the market period extends from one harvest to the next. For Michelangelo's paintings, the length of the market period is infinite because the supply is fixed forever.

During the market period, costs of production are irrelevant in the determination of price, and the entire stock of a perishable commodity is put up for sale at whatever price it can fetch. Thus, with perfect competition among buyers and sellers, demand alone determines price, while supply alone determines quantity. This is shown in Figure 9.1.

In the figure, S is the fixed or zero-elastic market supply curve for 350 units of the commodity. With D as the market demand curve, the equilibrium price is $35. Only at this price does the quantity demanded equal the quantity supplied, and the market clears. At higher prices, there will be unsold quantities, and this will cause the price to fall to the

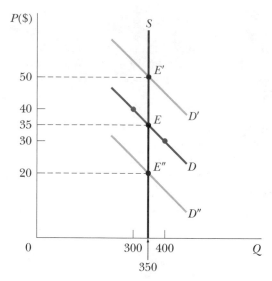

FIGURE 9.1   Price Determination in the Market Period   With the quantity supplied fixed at 350, the market supply curve of the commodity is S. With D as the market demand curve, the equilibrium price is $35. At prices higher than $35, there will be unsold quantities, and this will cause the price to fall to the equilibrium level. At prices below $35, the quantity demanded exceeds the quantity supplied, and the price will be bid up to $35. With D' as the demand curve, P = $50. With D", P = $20.

equilibrium level. For example, at the price of $40, only 300 units would be demanded (see the figure); hence, the quantity supplied would exceed the quantity demanded and the commodity price would fall. On the other hand, at lower than the equilibrium price, the quantity demanded exceeds the quantity supplied, and the price will be bid up to $35. For example, at the price of $30, 400 units of the commodity would be demanded; hence, the quantity demanded would exceed the quantity supplied and the price would be bid up to $35 (the equilibrium price at which the quantity demanded equals the quantity supplied). With D' as the demand curve, P = $50. With D", P = $20.

9.3   SHORT-RUN EQUILIBRIUM OF THE FIRM

Even though analysis of the market period is interesting, we are primarily interested in the short run and in the long run, when the quantity produced and sold of the commodity can be varied. In this section, we examine the determination of output by the firm in the short run. We first do so with the total approach and then with the marginal approach. Finally, we focus on the process of profit maximization or loss minimization by the firm.

Total Approach: Maximizing the Positive Difference between Total Revenue and Total Costs

We have seen in Section 7.1 that profit maximization provides the framework for the analysis of the firm. The equilibrium output of the firm is the output that maximizes the total profits of the firm. Total profits equal total revenue minus total costs. Thus, total profits are maximized when the positive difference between total revenue and total costs is largest. This is shown in Figure 9.2.

The short-run total cost (STC) curve in the top panel of Figure 9.2 is the one of Figure 8.1. The vertical intercept ($30) gives the fixed costs of the firm. Within the limits imposed by the given plant, the firm can vary its output by varying the quantity of the variable inputs it uses. This generates the STC curve of the firm. The STC curve shows the minimum total costs of producing the various levels of output in the short run. Past point W, the law of diminishing returns begins to operate and the STC curve faces upward or rises at an increasing rate (see Section 8.2).

The total revenue curve is a straight line through the origin because the firm can sell any quantity of the commodity at the given price (determined at the intersection of the market demand and supply curves of the commodity). With $P = \$35$, the total revenue ($TR$) of the firm is $35 if the firm sells one unit of output. The $TR = \$70$ if the firm sells two units of output, $TR = \$105$ with $Q = 3$, $TR = \$140$ with $Q = 4$, and so on. Put more succinctly, $TR = (\$35)(Q)$. Thus, the TR of the firm is a straight line through the origin with slope equal to the commodity price of $35 (see the top panel of Figure 9.2).

At zero output, $TR = 0$ while $STC = \$30$. Thus, the firm incurs a total loss of $30 equal to its fixed costs. This gives the negative intercept of $(-)\$30$ of the total profit curve in the bottom panel. At $Q = 1$, $TR = \$35$ and $STC = \$50$, so that total profits are $-\$15$. At $Q = 1.5$, $TR = STC = \$52.50$ (point W in the top panel), and total profits are zero (point W' in the bottom panel). This is called the **break-even point.** Between $Q = 1.5$ and $Q = 5$, TR exceeds STC and the firm earns a profit. Total profits equal the positive difference between TR and STC. Total profits are largest at $31.50 when $Q = 3.5$ (i.e., where the TR and the STC curves are parallel and the total profit curve has zero slope). At Q smaller than 3.5, say, $Q = 3$, $TR = \$105$ and $STC = \$75$, so that total profits are $30. At $Q = 4$, $TR = \$140$, $STC = \$110$, and total profits are again $30. At $Q = 5$, $TR = STC = \$175$, so that total profits are zero (points T and T', respectively). At Q greater than 5, TR is smaller than STC and the firm incurs a loss. Thus, the level of output at which the firm maximizes total profits is $Q = 3.5$ (point E and E' in the top and bottom panels, respectively). Figure 9.2 is summarized in Table 9.1.[2]

Marginal Approach: Equating Marginal Revenue and Marginal Cost[3]

Although the total approach to determine the equilibrium output of the firm is useful, the marginal approach is even more valuable and more widely used. This approach is shown in Figure 9.3. In the figure, the demand curve facing the firm (d) is horizontal or infinitely

---

[2] When the firm has no knowledge of the exact shape of its STC curve, it uses a break-even chart to determine the minimum sales volume to avoid losses (see Problem 4, with the answer at the end of the book).
[3] For a mathematical presentation of profit maximization using rudimentary calculus, see Section A.10 of the Mathematical Appendix at the end of the book.

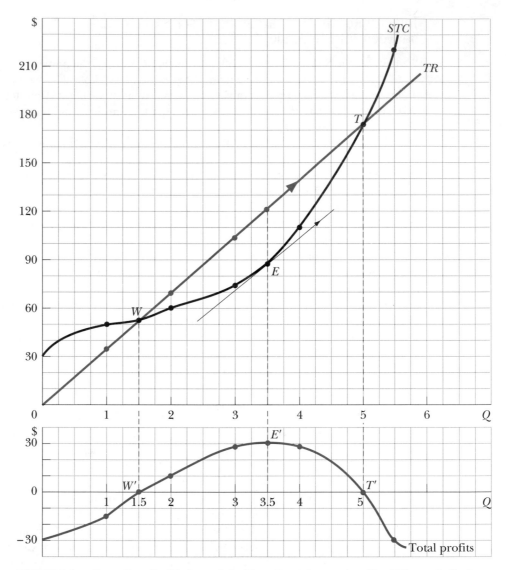

FIGURE 9.2   Short-Run Equilibrium of the Firm: Total Approach   The *STC* curve in the top panel is that of Figure 8.1. The *TR* curve is a straight line through the origin with slope of $P = \$35$. At $Q = 0$, $TR = 0$ and $STC = \$30$, so that total profits are $-\$30$ and equal the firm's *TFC* (see the bottom panel). At $Q = 1$, $TR = \$35$ and $STC = \$50$, so that total profits are $-\$15$. At $Q = 1.5$, $TR = STC = \$52.50$, and total profits are zero. This is the break–even point. Between $Q = 1.5$ and $Q = 5$, *TR* exceeds *STC* and the firm earns (positive) economic profits. Total profits are greatest at $\$31.50$ when $Q = 3.5$ (and the *TR* and the *STC* curves are parallel). At $Q = 5$, $TR = STC = \$175$ so that total profits are zero (points *T* and *T'*). At *Q* greater than 5, *TR* is smaller than *STC* and the firm incurs a loss.

TABLE 9.1   Total Revenue, Total Costs, and Total Profits

Quantity of Output	Price	Total Revenue	Total Costs	Total Profits
0	$35	$ 0	$ 30	$−30
1	35	35	50	−15
1.5	35	52.50	52.50	0
2	35	70	60	+10
3	35	105	75	+30
*3.5	35	122.50	91	+31.50
4	35	140	110	+30
5	35	175	175	0
5.5	35	192.50	220	−27.50

*Output at which firm maximizes total profits.

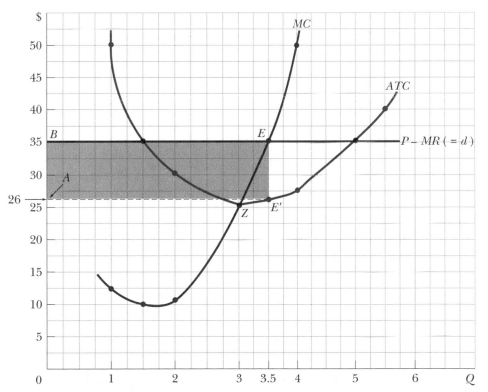

FIGURE 9.3   Short-Run Equilibrium of the Firm: Marginal Approach   The demand curve facing the firm (d) is horizontal or infinitely elastic at the given price of P = $35. Since P is constant, marginal revenue (MR) equals P. The firm maximizes total profits where P = MR = MC, and MC is rising. This occurs at Q = 3.5 (point E). At Q = 3.5, P = $35 and ATC = $26. Therefore, profit per unit is $9 (EE'), and total profits are $31.50 (shaded rectangle EE' AB).

elastic at the given price of $P = \$35$. That is, the perfectly competitive firm is a price taker and can sell any quantity of the commodity at $P = \$35$. Since marginal revenue (MR) is the change in total revenue per-unit change in output, and price (P) is constant, then $P = MR$ (see Section 5.6). For example, with $P = \$35$ and $Q = 1$, $TR = \$35$. With $P = \$35$ and $Q = 2$, $TR = \$70$. Thus, the change in TR per-unit change in output (the slope of the TR curve or marginal revenue) is $MR = P = \$35$ (see Figure 9.3).

The short-run marginal cost (MC) and the average total cost (ATC) curves of the firm in Figure 9.3 are those of Figure 8.2 (and derived from the STC curve of Figures 8.1 and 9.2). The $MC = \Delta STC / \Delta Q$, while $ATC = STC / Q$. As explained earlier, total profits are maximized where the TR and the STC curves are parallel and their slopes are equal. Since the slope of the TR curve is $MR = P$ and the slope of the STC curve is MC, this implies that when total profits are at a maximum, $P = MR = MC$. Furthermore, since the STC curve faces upward where profits are maximum, the MC curve must be rising. Thus, the firm is in short-run equilibrium or maximizes total profits by producing the output where $P = MR = MC$, and MC is rising.

For example, the best level of output for the firm in Figure 9.3 is $Q = 3.5$ (point E), and this is the same result as with the total approach. At $Q = 3.5$, $P = \$35$ and $ATC = \$26$. Therefore, profit per unit is 9 (EE' in the figure), and total profits are ($\$9$)(3.5) = $\$31.50$ (shaded rectangle $EE'AB$). Until point E, MR exceeds MC and so the firm earns higher profits by expanding output. On the other hand, past point E, MC exceeds MR and the firm earns higher profits by *reducing* output. This leaves point E as the profit-maximizing level of output. Note that at point E, P or $MR = MC$ and MC is rising so that the conditions for profit maximization are fulfilled.

Also note that profit per unit is largest ($\$10$) at point Z where $Q = 3$, $P = \$35$, and $ATC = \$25$. The firm, however, seeks to maximize total profits, not profit per unit, and this occurs at $Q = 3.5$, where total profits are $\$31.50$, as opposed to $\$30$ at $Q = 3$. The total profits of the firm at various levels of output with $P = \$35$ are summarized in Table 9.2. The MR, MC, and ATC values given in the table are read off Figure 9.3 at various output levels. For example, at $Q = 1$, $MR = \$35$, $MC = \$12.50$, and $ATC = \$50$. At $Q = 2$, $MR = \$35$, $MC = \$11$, and $ATC = \$30$, and so on.

| TABLE 9.2 | Profit Maximization for the Perfectly Competitive Firm: Per-Unit Approach | | | | | |

Q	P = MR	MC	ATC	Profit Per Unit	Total Profits	Relationship between MR and MC
1	$35	$12.50	$50	$−15	$−15	
1.50	35	10	35	0	0	MR > MC
2	35	11	30	+5	+10	
3	35	25	25	+10	+30	
*3.50	35	35	26	+9	+31.50	MR = MC
4	35	50	27.50	+7.50	+30	
5	35		35	0	0	MR < MC
5.5	35		40	−5	−27.50	

*Output at which firm maximizes total profits.

The rule that a firm maximizes profits at the output level at which the marginal revenue to the firm equals its marginal cost is a specific application of the general *marginal* concept that any activity should be pursued until the marginal benefit from the activity equals the marginal cost.

Profit Maximization or Loss Minimization?

We have seen that the best or optimum level of output of the firm is given at the point where *P* (or *MR*) equals *MC*, and *MC* is rising. At this level of output, however, the firm can either make a profit (as in Figure 9.3), break even, or incur a loss. In Figure 9.3, *P* was higher than the *ATC* at the best level of output, and the firm made a profit. If *P* were smaller than the *ATC* at the best level of output, the firm would incur a loss. However, as long as *P* exceeds the average *variable* cost (*AVC*), it pays for the firm to continue to produce, because by doing so it would *minimize its losses*. That is, the excess of *P* over the *AVC* can be used to partially cover the fixed costs of the firm. Were the firm to shut down, it would incur a greater loss equal to its total fixed costs. This is shown in Figure 9.4.

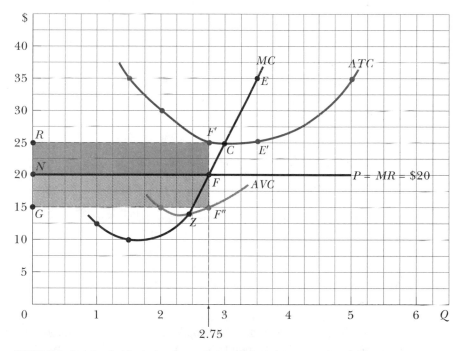

FIGURE 9.4   Profit Maximization or Loss Minimization   At *P* = $20, the best level of output of the firm is 2.75 units (point *F*, where *P* = *MR* = *MC*, and *MC* is rising). At *Q* = 2.75, average total cost (*ATC*) exceeds *P* and the firm will incur a loss of *F'F* (about $5.50) per unit, and a total loss equal to rectangle *F'FNR* (about $15). If, however, the firm were to shut down, it would incur the greater loss of $30 equal to its total fixed costs (the area of the larger rectangle *F'F"GR*). The shut down point (*Z*) is at *P* = *AVC*.

In the figure, the MC and the ATC curves are the same as in Figure 9.3. Figure 9.4 also includes the AVC curve of the firm (from Figure 8.2). In Figure 9.4, we assume that $P = MR = \$20$. The best level of output of the firm is then 2.75 units, given at point F, where $P = MR = MC = \$20$, and MC is rising. At $Q = 2.75$, ATC exceeds P and the firm incurs a loss equal to $F'F$ (about \$5.50) per unit, and a total loss equal to the area of rectangle $F'FNR$ (about \$15). Were the firm to shut down, it would incur the greater loss of \$30 (its total fixed costs, given by the area of the larger rectangle $F'F''GR$).

Put another way, by continuing to produce $Q = 2.75$ at $P = \$20$, the firm will cover FF'' (about \$5.50) of its fixed costs per unit and $FF''GN$ (about \$15) of its total fixed costs. Thus, it pays for the firm to stay in business even though it incurs a loss. That is, by remaining in business, the firm will incur losses that are smaller than its total fixed costs (which would be the firm's losses by shutting down). Only if P were smaller than the AVC at the best level of output would the firm minimize losses by shutting down. By doing so, the firm would limit its losses to an amount no larger than its total fixed costs. Finally, if $P = AVC$, the firm would be indifferent between producing or shutting down, because in either case it would incur a loss equal to its total fixed costs. The point where $P = AVC$ (point Z in the figure) is called the **shut down point.**[4]

9.4   SHORT-RUN SUPPLY CURVE AND EQUILIBRIUM

In this section, we derive the short-run supply curve of a perfectly competitive firm and industry. We also examine how the equilibrium price of the commodity is determined at the intersection of the market demand and supply curves for the commodity. This is the price at which the perfectly competitive firm can sell any quantity of the commodity.

Short-Run Supply Curve of the Firm and Industry

We have seen so far that a perfectly competitive firm always produces at the point where $P = MC$ and MC is rising, and this is so as long as $P > AVC$. As a result, the rising portion of the firm's MC curve above the AVC curve is the firm's short-run supply curve of the commodity. This is shown in the left panel of Figure 9.5.

The left panel of Figure 9.5 reproduces the firm's MC curve above point Z (the shutdown point) from Figure 9.4. This is the perfectly competitive firm's short-run supply curve (s) because it shows the quantity of the commodity that the firm would supply in the short run at various prices. For example, the firm supplies 3 units of the commodity at the price of \$25 (point C in the left panel). The reason is that at $P = \$25$, $P = MR = MC = \$25$, and MC is rising. At $P = \$35$, the firm supplies 3.5 units of the commodity (point E), while at $P = \$50$, it supplies 4 units (point T). The firm will supply no output at prices below the shutdown point (point Z in the figure). Thus, the rising portion of the firm's MC curve above

---

[4] Recall that $STC = TVC + TFC$ and total profits equal $TR - STC$. When $P = AVC$, $TR = TVC$, so that the firm's total losses would equal its TFC, whether it produces or shuts down. Thus, point Z, at which $P = AVC$ (and $TR = TVC$), is the firm's shut down point.

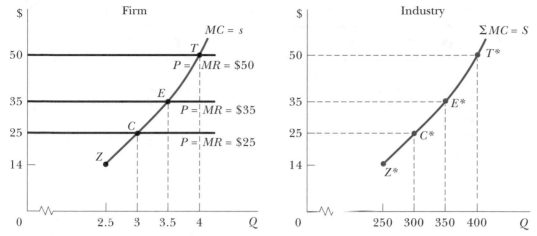

FIGURE 9.5   Short-Run Supply Curve of the Firm and Industry   The left panel reproduces the firm's *MC* curve above point *Z* (the shut down point) from Figure 8.4. This is the perfectly competitive firm's short-run supply curve *s*. For example, at $P = \$25$, $Q = 3$ (point *C*); at $P = \$35$, $Q = 3.5$ (point *E*); at $P = \$50$, $Q = 4$ (point *T*). The right panel shows the industry's short-run supply curve on the assumption that there are 100 identical firms in the industry and input prices are constant. This is given by the $\Sigma MC = S$ curve. Thus, at $P = \$25$, $Q = 300$ (point *C**); at $P = \$35$, $Q = 350$ (point *E**); at $P = \$50$, $Q = 400$ (point *T**).

the shutdown point is the firm's short-run supply curve of the commodity (*s* in the left panel of Figure 9.5). It shows the quantity of the commodity that the firm would supply in the short run at various prices. The firm's short-run supply curve is positively sloped because the *MC* curve is positively sloped, and the *MC* curve is positively sloped because of diminishing returns.

The horizontal summation of the supply curves of all firms in the industry then gives the industry short-run supply curve for the commodity. This is given by the $\Sigma MC = S$ curve in the right panel of Figure 9.5, where the symbol Σ refers to the "summation of." The perfectly competitive industry's short-run supply curve in the right panel is based on the assumption that there are 100 identical firms in the industry (and input prices do not vary with industry output). For example, at $P = \$25$, each firm supplies 3 units of the commodity (point *C* in the left panel) and the entire industry supplies 300 units (point *C** in the right panel). At $P = \$35$, each firm supplies 3.5 units (point *E* and the industry supplies 350 units (point *E**). At $P = \$50$, $Q = 4$ for the firm (point *T*) and $Q = 400$ for the industry (point *T**). Note that no output of the commodity is produced at prices below $P = \$14$ (points *Z* and *Z** in the figure).[5]

The derivation of the perfectly competitive industry short-run supply curve of the commodity as the horizontal summation of each firm's short-run supply curve is based on the assumption that input prices are constant regardless of the quantity of inputs that each firm and the industry demand. That is, it is based on the assumption that the firm is able to hire a

---

[5] Point *Z* in the left panel of Figure 9.5 corresponds to point *Z'* in Figure 8.2.

greater quantity of the inputs (to produce the larger output) at constant input prices. If input prices were to rise as firms demanded more of the inputs, the industry supply curve would be steeper or less elastic than indicated in the right panel of Figure 9.5. An increase in the commodity price will then result in a smaller increase in the quantity supplied of the commodity (see Problem 8, with the answer at the end of the book).

The responsiveness or sensitivity in the quantity supplied of a commodity to a change in its price can be measured by the **price elasticity of supply.** This is analogous to the price elasticity of demand and is given by the percentage change in the quantity supplied of the commodity divided by the percentage change in its price. That is, letting ϵ (the Greek letter epsilon) refer to the price elasticity of supply, we have

$$\epsilon = \frac{\Delta Q/Q}{\Delta P/P} = \frac{\Delta Q}{\Delta P} \cdot \frac{P}{Q} \qquad [9.1]$$

The only difference between the price elasticity of supply and that of demand is that in the numerator of the elasticity formula we now have the percentage change in the quantity *supplied* of the commodity rather than the percentage change in the quantity demanded. However, since quantity and price are usually directly related along the supply curve the price elasticity of supply is usually positive. Note that in the very short run or market period (when the supply curve is vertical), the price elasticity of supply is zero.[6] Example 9–2 examines the supply curve of petroleum from tar sands, while Example 9–3 shows how to derive the short-run world supply curve for copper.

EXAMPLE 9–2

The Supply Curve of Petroleum from Tar Sands

The industry supply curve of petroleum from tar sands (often called "synthetic fuel" or "shale oil") was estimated to be as indicated by curve S in Figure 9.6 in 1978. Large cost overruns, however, made actual production costs much higher, so that the supply curve looked like S' by 1984. Major technological breakthroughs since 1984, however, lowered costs as indicated by curve S'' in 2001, making petroleum extraction from tar sands more than competitive with petroleum from traditional wells.

The supply curve estimated in 1978 (S) showed that it would not be economical to produce oil from tar sands at prices below $10 per barrel. The quantity of oil supplied, in millions of barrels per day, would be 2 at the price of $10 per barrel, 6 at the price of $16 per barrel, and 16 at $18 per barrel. The maximum that would be supplied at any price would be about 16 million barrels per day, at a time when the international price of petroleum was $13 per barrel.

In 1980, Congress created the Synthetic Fuel Corporation to stimulate the production of oil from tar sands in Alaska and reduce American dependence on imported

---

[6] For a discussion of the price elasticity of supply using calculus, see Section A.5 of the Mathematical Appendix at the end of the book.

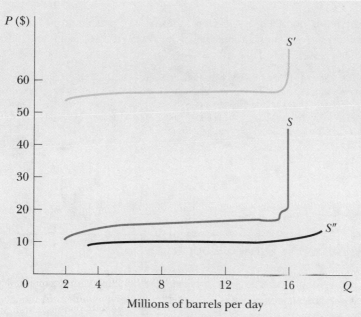

FIGURE 9.6   The Supply Curve of Oil from Tar Sands   The supply curve of oil from tar sands estimated in 1978 (*S*) roses gently up to 16 million barrels per day, where it becomes vertical. The actual supply curve *S′* in 1984 showed much higher costs per barrel, while actual supply curve *S″* in 2002 shows production costs to be about $9 per barrel in Alberta, Canada, and rising very gently as a result of major mining and extraction breakthroughs.

petroleum. By the end of 1984, $3 billion of federal subsidies had been spent on four projects. Because of large cost overruns, however, the actual cost of extracting petroleum from tar sands was found to be more than three times higher than anticipated and about double the price of $28 per barrel for imported oil (supply curve *S′* in Figure 9.6) in 1984. This led Exxon, one of the co-sponsors of the project, to withdraw from the project. The entire synthetic fuel project was abandoned at the end of 1985 when the U.S. government refused to provide further subsidies.

Major breakthroughs in the mining and extraction of petroleum from tar sands, however, sharply lowered costs, leading to supply curve *S″*. Supply curve *S″* indicates that petroleum can now (2002) be extracted from tar sands for about $9 per barrel in Canada's province of Alberta (compared with the international price of petroleum of about $20 per barrel at the beginning of 2002). Furthermore, extracting petroleum from tar sands can be expanded without incurring large increases in cost. To fully exploit this resource, however, will require several years and tens of billions of dollars in investments. But with more than 300 billion potential recoverable barrels of oil in Alberta alone and more in Alaska (as compared with 265 billion barrels in Saudi Arabia),

North America is not likely to develop a shortage of petroleum in the years to come. Extracting oil from Saudi Arabia wells, however, is far easier and cheaper—well below $1 per barrel.

Sources: N. Ericson and P. Morgan, "The Economic Feasibility of Shale Oil: An Activity Analysis," *Bell Journal of Economics*, August 1978; "Exxon Abandons Shale Oil Project," *New York Times*, May 3, 1982, p. 1; "Congressional Conferees End Financing of Synthetic Fuels Program," *New York Times*, December 17, 1985, p. B11; "Unlocking Oil in Canada's Tar Sands," *New York Times,* December 1994, p. D5; and "Digging for Oil: Canada Is Unlocking Petroleum from Sands," *New York Times,* January 23, 2001, p. 1.

EXAMPLE 9–3

The Short-Run World Supply Curve of Copper

Table 9.3 gives the production (in thousand metric tons) and the estimated marginal cost of production (in cents per pound) of the copper producers in the major copper-producing countries of the world. Summing up the production in the various countries

TABLE 9.3	Copper Production and Costs by Country in 2000 (in thousand metric tons and cents per pound)		
Country	Production	Cumulative Production	Cents Per Pound
1. Chile	4,500	4,500	54
2. Russia	520	5,020	54
3. Indonesia	850	5,870	60
4. China	510	6,380	60
5. Kazakhstan	380	6,760	60
6. Zambia	260	7,020	60
7. Australia	760	7,780	70
8. United States	1,450	9,230	76
9. Peru	530	9,760	76
10. Mexico	390	10,150	76
11. Canada	650	10,800	80
12. Poland	480	11,280	87
13. All Others	1,600	12,880	87

Sources: U.S. Geological Survey, *Mineral Commodity Summaries* and *Mineral Industry Surveys* (Washington, D.C.: U.S. Government Printing Office, 2001), 2001; and Daniel E. Eldstein, "Copper," *U.S. Geological Survey Mineral Yearbook* (Washington, D.C.: U.S. Government Printing Office, 2001), Chapter 10.

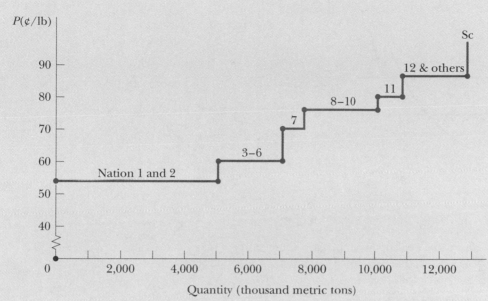

FIGURE 9.7   The Short-Run World Supply Curve of Copper   The short-run world supply curve of copper is obtained by summing up horizontally the marginal cost curve of the various countries. The short-run world supply curve of copper slopes up as countries facing higher marginal costs of production are included.

at the marginal cost of production in each country gives the short-run world supply curve of copper (Sc) shown in Figure 9.7. The supply curve slopes up as countries facing higher marginal costs of production are included.

Note that the short-run world supply curve of copper has a steplike appearance because we assume that all the producers in a country have the same marginal costs. The Sc curve would have a smoother shape if we knew the individual firm's marginal cost curve. The Sc curve shows that Chile and Russia are the low-cost producers (at 54 cents per pound), but their combined capacity is limited 5,020 thousand metric tons in the short run. The marginal costs of each producer vary because of differences in the ore content of individual mines and in labor, transportation, and other costs. The marginal cost of production is 60 cents per pound for Indonesia, China, Kazakhstan, and Zambia for a combined short-run output of 2,000 thousand metric tons. The marginal cost of production is 70 cents per pound for Australia, 76 cents for the United States (the world's second largest producer after Chile), Peru and Mexico, 80 cents for Canada, 87 cents for Poland and all other world's smaller producers. The maximum short-run world supply of copper is 12,880 thousand tons at which the Sc curve becomes vertical. Note that the Sc curve is very elastic at low copper prices and becomes progressively less so at higher prices.

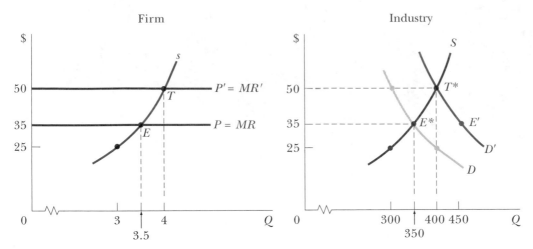

FIGURE 9.8   Short-Run Equilibrium of the Firm and Industry   With S (from Figure 9.5) and D in the right panel, $P = \$35$ and $Q = 350$ (point E^*), and the perfectly competitive firm would produce 3.5 units (point E in the left panel, as in Figure 9.3). If D shifted up to D', $P = \$50$ and $Q = 400$ (point T^*), and the firm would produce 4 units of output (point T in the left panel).

Short-Run Equilibrium of the Industry and Firm[7]

In Section 5.1, we showed how the market demand curve for a commodity was derived from the horizontal summation of the demand curves of all the individual consumers of the commodity in the market. We have now shown how to derive the industry or market supply curve of the commodity. In a perfectly competitive market, the equilibrium price of the commodity is determined at the intersection of the market demand curve and the market supply curve of the commodity. This was explained in Section 2.4. Thus, we have traveled a complete circle and returned to the point of departure. Now, however, we know what lies behind the market demand curve and the market supply curve of the commodity and how they are derived (i.e., we no longer simply assume these curves as given, as in Chapter 2).

Given the price of the commodity, the perfectly competitive firm can sell any quantity of the commodity at that price. As noted earlier, the firm will produce at the point where P or $MR = MC$, provided that MC is rising and $P \geq AVC$. This is shown in Figure 9.8.

The right panel of Figure 9.8 shows the short-run market supply curve S (from Figure 9.5) and hypothetical market demand curve D for the commodity. These curves intersect at point E^*, and result in the equilibrium price of \$35 and the equilibrium quantity of 350 units. At $P = \$25$, the quantity demanded (400 units) exceeds the quantity supplied (300 units), and the resulting shortage will drive the commodity price up to $P = \$35$. On the other hand, at $P = \$50$, the quantity supplied (400 units) exceeds the quantity demanded (300 units), and the resulting surplus will drive the price down to $P = \$35$. The left panel

---

[7] For a mathematical presentation of how equilibrium is determined in a perfectly competitive industry using rudimentary calculus, see Section A.11 of the Mathematical Appendix at the end of the book.

shows that at $P = \$35$, the perfectly competitive firm will produce 3.5 units (point E, as in Figure 9.3). Note that each firm produces 1/100 of the total industry or market output.

If the market demand curve then shifted up to D' (for example, as a result of an increase in consumers' incomes), there would be a shortage of 100 units of the commodity at $P = \$35$ (E^*E' in the right panel of Figure 9.8). This would cause the equilibrium price to rise to $50 and the equilibrium quantity to 400 units (point T^*). Then, at $P = \$50$, the perfectly competitive firm maximizes profits at point T by producing 4 units of output (see the left panel). This is based on the assumption that there are 100 identical firms in the perfectly competitive industry and that input prices remain constant.

<table><tr><td>9.5</td><td></td></tr></table>

LONG-RUN EQUILIBRIUM OF THE FIRM AND INDUSTRY

Having analyzed how equilibrium is reached in the market period and in the short run, we can now go on to examine how the perfectly competitive firm and industry reach equilibrium in the long run. This will set the stage for the analysis of constant, increasing, and decreasing cost industries in Section 9.6.

Long-Run Equilibrium of the Firm

In the long run, all inputs are variable and the firm can build the most efficient plant to produce the best or most profitable level of output. The *best (i.e., the profit-maximizing) level of output* of the firm in the long run is the one at which price or marginal revenue equals long-run marginal cost. The *most efficient plant* is the one that allows the firm to produce the best level of output at the lowest possible cost. This is the plant represented by the *SATC* curve tangent to the *LAC* curve of the firm at the best level of output, as shown in Figure 9.9.[8]

The *LAC* curve in Figure 9.9 is the one of Figure 8.11, and the $SATC_1$ curve is that of Figures 8.2, 8.11, and 9.3. At $P = MR = \$35$ in Figure 9.9, the firm is in *short-run* equilibrium at point E by producing 3.5 units of output. Note that *SMC* refers to the short-run *MC* to distinguish it from *LMC*. The firm makes a profit of $9 per unit (vertical distance EE') and $31.50 in total (as in Figure 9.3).

In the long run, the firm can increase its profits significantly by producing at point J', where P or $MR = LMC$ (and *LMC* is rising). The firm should build plant $SATC_5$ and operate it at point J (at $SATC = \$13$). Plant $SATC_5$ is the best plant (i.e., the one that allows the firm to produce the best level of output at the lowest *SATC*). In the long run, the firm will make profits of $22 ($J'J$) per unit and $286 in total ($22 times 13 units of output). This compares with total profits of $31.50 in the short run. Note that when the firm is in long-run equilibrium, it will also be in short-run equilibrium since P or $MR = SMC = LMC$ (see point J' in the figure).[9] This analysis assumes that input prices are constant.

---

[8] Since in the long run all costs are variable, the firm must at least cover all of its costs to remain in business.
[9] Note that $SMC_5 = LMC$ at $P = MR = \$35$ because the STC_5 curve is tangent to the LTC curve (neither curves shown in Figure 9.9) at $Q = 13$.

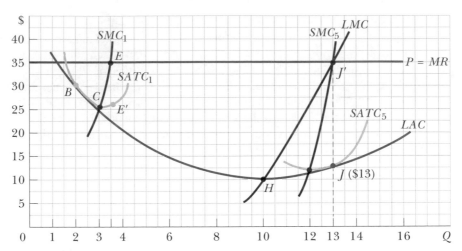

FIGURE 9.9   Long-Run Equilibrium of the Firm   At $P = MR = \$35$, the firm is in short-run equilibrium at point E (as in Figure 9.3). In the long run, the firm can increase its profits by producing at point J', where P or $MR = LMC$ (and LMC is rising), and operating plant $SATC_5$ at point J. In the long-run, the firm will make profits of $\$22$ ($J'J$) per unit and $\$286$ in total ($\$22$ times 13 units of output). Since at point J', $P = MR = SMC = LMC$, the firm is also in short-run equilibrium.

Long-Run Equilibrium of the Industry and Firm

Even though the firm would be in long-run equilibrium at point J' in Figure 9.9, the industry would not. This is because the large profits that this and other firms earn at point J' will attract more firms to the industry. As new firms enter the industry (entry is free and resources are mobile), aggregate output expands. This will shift the short-run industry supply curve to the right until it intersects the market demand curve at the commodity price at which all firms make zero economic profits (i.e., they earn only a normal return) in the long run. Then, and only then, will the industry (and the firm) be in equilibrium. In fact, the building of the best plant by the firm and the entrance of new firms into the industry will take place simultaneously in the long run. The final result (equilibrium) is shown in Figure 9.10.

In the figure, the industry (in the right panel) and the firm (in the left panel) are in long-run equilibrium at point H, where $P = MR = LMC = SMC = LAC = SATC = \$10$.[10] The firm produces at the lowest point on its LAC curve (operating optimal plant $SATC_4$ at point H) and earns zero economic profits. Zero economic profit means that the owner of the firm receives only a normal return on investment when the industry and firm are in long-run equilibrium. That is, the owner receives a return on the capital invested in the firm equal only to the amount that he or she would earn by investing the capital in a similarly risky venture.

---

[10] Note that the supply curve labeled S in the right panel of Figure 9.10 is much larger than the supply curve S in the right panel of Figure 9.8 because more firms have entered the industry in the long run and industry output is larger.

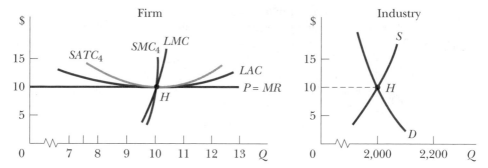

FIGURE 9.10   Long-Run Equilibrium of the Industry and Firm   The industry (in the right panel) and the firm (in the left panel) are in long-run equilibrium at point H, where $P = MR = SMC = LMC = SATC - LAC = \$10$. The firm produces at the lowest point on its LAC curve (operating optimal plant $SATC_4$ at point H) and earns zero profits.

If the owner manages the firm, zero economic profits also includes what he or she would earn in the best *alternative* occupation (i.e., managing a similar firm for someone else). Thus, zero profits in economics means that the total revenues of the firm just cover all costs (explicit and implicit).[11]

Efficiency Implications of Perfect Competition

We have seen that when the perfectly competitive industry is in long-run equilibrium, the firm not only earns zero profits but produces at the lowest point on its LAC curve (point H in the left panel of Figure 9.10). Thus, resources are used most efficiently to produce the goods and services most desired by society at the minimum cost. Since firms also earn zero profits, consumers purchase the commodity at the lowest possible price ($\$10$ at point H in the figure). In this sense, perfect competition is the most efficient form of market organization. This is to be contrasted to the situation under imperfect competition (discussed in the next four chapters), where we will see that firms seldom, if ever, produce at the lowest point on their LAC curve, and they charge a price that also usually includes a profit margin.

To summarize, when a perfectly competitive industry is in equilibrium, $P = LAC = LMC$ for each firm in the industry. Since $P = LAC$, the perfectly competitive firm earns zero economic profits, and so there is distributional efficiency. Since $P = LMC$, each firm produces at the lowest point on its LAC curve, and so there is production efficiency. Finally, since $P = LMC$, there is allocative efficiency in the sense that the amount of the commodity supplied represents the best use of the economy's resources.

We have seen so far that when a perfectly competitive firm earns (economic) profits, more firms will enter the industry in the long run and this will lower the commodity price until all firms just break even (i.e., earn zero economic profits). On the other hand, if the

---

[11] As pointed out in Section 7.1, the meaning of *profit* in economics is to be distinguished clearly from the everyday use of the term (which considers implicit costs as part of profits). In economics, profits always refer only to the excess of total revenue over total costs, and total costs include both explicit and implicit costs (see Section 8.1). In short, in economics, profits mean above-normal returns.

perfectly competitive firm incurs a loss in the short run and would continue to incur a loss in the long run even by constructing the best plant, some firms would leave the industry. This would shift the industry supply curve to the left until it intersected the industry demand curve at the (higher) commodity price at which the remaining firms made zero economic profits but incurred no losses. The final result would be as shown in Figure 9.10, except that there would now be fewer firms in the industry and the industry output would be smaller. As it is, Figure 9.10 indicates that if all firms had identical cost curves, there would be 200 identical firms in the industry when in long-run equilibrium. Each firm would produce 10 units of output and break even.

Perfectly competitive firms need not have identical cost curves (although we assume so for simplicity), but the *minimum point* on their *LAC* curves must occur at the same cost per unit. If some firms had more productive inputs and, thus, lower average costs than other firms in the industry, the more productive inputs would be able to extract from their employer higher rewards (payments) commensurate to their higher productivity, under the threat of leaving to work for others. As a result, their *LAC* curves would shift upward until the lowest point on the *LAC* curve of all firms is the same. Thus, competition in the input markets as well as in the commodity market will result in all firms having identical (minimum) average costs and zero economic profits when the industry is in the long-run equilibrium. Example 9–4 examines the long-run adjustment in the U.S. cotton textile industry.

EXAMPLE 9–4

Long-Run Adjustment in the U.S. Cotton Textile Industry

In a study of U.S. industries between the world wars, Lloyd Reynolds found that the U.S. cotton textile industry was the one that came closest to being perfectly competitive. Cotton textiles were practically homogeneous, there were many buyers and sellers of cotton cloth, each was too small to affect its price, and entry into and exit from the industry was easy. Reynolds found that the rate of return on investments in the cotton textile industry was about 6% in the South and 1% in the North (because of higher costs for raw cotton and labor in the North), as contrasted to an average rate of return of 8% for all other manufacturing industries in the United States over the same period of time.

Because of the lower returns, the perfectly competitive model would predict that firms would leave the textile industry in the long run and enter other industries. The model would also predict that because returns were lower in the North than in the South, a greater contraction of the textile industry would take place in the North than in the South. Reynolds found that both of these predictions were borne out by the facts. Capacity in the U.S. textile industry declined by over 33% between 1925 and 1938, with the decline being larger in the North than in the South. Thus, textile firms, cotton farms, and firms using cloth did seem to make use of this knowledge and did respond to these economic forces in their managerial decisions.

Most U.S. textile firms were able to remain in business after World War II only as a result of U.S. restrictions on cheaper textile imports and, subsequently, as a result of the introduction of labor-saving innovations that sharply cut their labor costs. But with the reduction in trade protection negotiated at the Uruguay Round (1986–1993) and with prospects of further reduction in protection during the current round of multilateral trade negotiations, U.S. textile firms are likely to come under renewed pressure from foreign competitors in the future.

Sources: L. Reynolds, "Competition in the Textile Industry," in W. Adams and T. Traywick, eds., *Readings in Economics* (New York: Macmillan, 1948), "Apparel Makes Last Stand," *The New York Times,* September 26, 1990, p. D2; W. McKibbin and D. Salvatore, "The Global Economic Consequences of the Uruguay Round," *Open Economies Review,* April 1995, pp. 111–129; and "Poor Nations Win Gains in Global Trade Deal, as U.S. Compromises," *Wall Street Journal,* November 15, 2001, p. A1.

9.6   CONSTANT, INCREASING, AND DECREASING COST INDUSTRIES

In the previous section, we examined how a perfectly competitive industry and firm reach equilibrium in the long run. Starting from a position of long-run equilibrium, we now examine how the perfectly competitive industry and firm adjust in the long run to an increase in the market demand for the commodity. This allows us to define constant, increasing, and decreasing cost industries and analyze their operation graphically.

Constant Cost Industries

Starting from the long-run equilibrium condition of the industry and the firm (point H) in Figure 9.10, if the market demand curve for the commodity increases, the equilibrium price will rise in the short run and firms earn economic profits (i.e., they receive above-normal returns). This will attract more firms into the industry, and the short-run industry or market supply curve of the commodity increases (shifts to the right). If input prices remain constant (as more inputs are demanded by the expanding industry), the new long-run equilibrium price for the commodity will be the same as before the increase in demand and supply. Then, the long-run industry supply curve (LS) for the commodity is horizontal at the minimum LAC. This is a **constant cost industry** and is shown in Figure 9.11.

In Figure 9.11, point H in the right and left panels shows the long-run equilibrium position of the perfectly competitive industry and firm, respectively (as in Figure 9.10), before the increase in demand (D) and supply (S). The increase in D to D' results in the short-run equilibrium price of \$20 (point H' in the right panel). At $P = \$20$, each of the 200 identical firms in the industry will produce $Q = 10.5$ (given by point H' in the left panel at which $P = SMC_4 = \$20$) for a total industry output of 2,100 units.

Because each firm earns profits at $P = \$20$ (see the left panel), more firms enter the industry in the long run, shifting S to the right. If input prices remain constant, S shifts to S', reestablishing the original equilibrium price of \$10 (point H'' in the right panel). At $P = \$10$, each firm produces at the lowest point on its LAC and earns zero economic profit (point H in the left panel). By joining points H and H'' in the right panel, we derive the long-run supply curve of the industry (LS). Since LS is horizontal, this is a constant cost industry (with 220 identical firms producing a total output of 2,200 units).

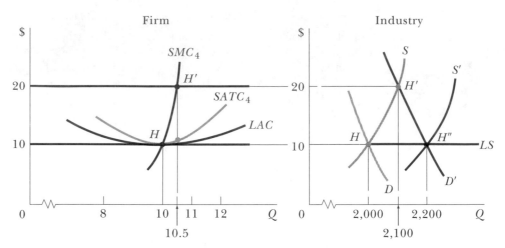

FIGURE 9.11   Constant Cost Industry   Point *H* is the original long-run equilibrium point of the industry and firm. An increase in *D* to *D'* results in *P* = $20, and all firms earn economic profits. As more firms enter the industry, *S* shifts to *S'* and *P* = $10 if input prices remain constant. By joining points *H* and *H''* in the right panel, we derive horizontal long-run supply curve *LS* for the (constant cost) industry.

Constant costs are more likely to result in industries that utilize general rather than specialized inputs and that account for only a small fraction of the total quantity demanded of the inputs in the economy. In these cases, the industry may be able to hire a greater quantity of the general inputs it uses without driving input prices upward.

Increasing Cost Industries

If input prices *rise* as more inputs are demanded by an expanding industry, the long-run industry supply curve for the commodity will be positively sloped and we have an **increasing cost industry.** This means that greater outputs of the commodity per time period will be supplied in the long run only at higher commodity prices (see Figure 9.12).

Starting from point *H* in the right and left panel of Figure 9.12, the increase in *D* to *D'* results in *P* = $20 (point *H'* in the right panel), at which all firms earn economic profits (point *H'* in the left panel). More firms enter the industry in the long run, and more inputs are demanded as industry output expands. *So far, this is identical to Figure 9.11.* If input prices now rise, each firm's per-unit cost curves shift up (as explained in the appendix to Chapter 8), and *S* shifts to the right to *S'* so as to establish equilibrium *P* = minimum *LAC'* = $15 (see point *H''* in both panels of Figure 9.12). All profits are squeezed out as costs rise and price falls. By joining points *H* and *H''* in the right panel, we get the long-run industry supply curve (*LS*). Since *LS* is positively sloped, the industry is an increasing cost industry (with 217.5 or 218 identical firms).

Increasing costs are more likely to result in industries that utilize some specialized input such as labor with unique skills (e.g., highly trained lab technicians to conduct experiments in genetics) or custom-made machinery to perform very special tasks (e.g., oil

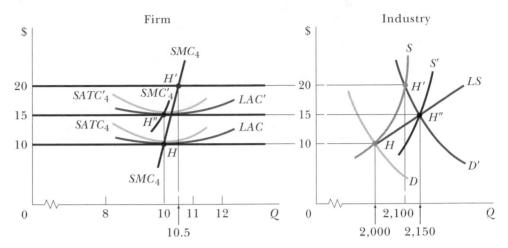

FIGURE 9.12   Increasing Cost Industry   Point *H* is the original long-run equilibrium point of the industry and firm. An increase in *D* to *D'* results in *P* = $20 and all firms earn economic profits. As more firms enter the industry, *S* shifts to *S'* and *P* = $15 if input prices rise. By joining points *H* and *H''* in the right panel, we derive positively sloped long-run supply curve *LS* for the (increasing cost) industry.

drilling platforms). These industries may have to pay higher prices to bring forth a greater supply of the specialized inputs they require, creating an increasing cost industry.

Decreasing Cost Industries

If input prices *fall* as more inputs are demanded by an expanding industry, the long-run industry supply curve for the commodity will be negatively sloped and we have a **decreasing cost industry.** This means that greater outputs of the commodity per time period will be supplied in the long run at lower commodity prices (see Figure 9.13).

The movement from point *H* to point *H'* in both panels of Figure 9.13 is the same as in Figures 9.11 and 9.12. Since at point *H'* firms earn profits, more firms enter the industry in the long run. Industry output expands, and more inputs are demanded. If input prices fall, each firm's per-unit cost curves shift down, and *S* shifts to the right to *S'* so as to establish equilibrium *P* = minimum *LAC'* = $5 (point *H''* in both panels). By joining points *H* and *H''* in the right panel, we derive *LS*, the industry long-run supply curve. Since *LS* is negatively sloped, we have a decreasing cost industry (with 230 identical firms).

Decreasing costs may result when the expansion of an industry leads to (1) the establishment of technical institutes to train labor for skills required by the industry at a lower cost than firms in the industry do; (2) the setting up of enterprises to supply some equipment used by the industry that was previously constructed by the firms in the industry for themselves at higher cost; (3) the exploitation of some cheaper natural resource that the industry can substitute for more expensive resources but which was not feasible to exploit when the demand for the natural resource was smaller.

In the real world, we have examples of constant, increasing, and decreasing cost industries. In fact, a particular industry could exhibit constant, increasing, or decreasing costs

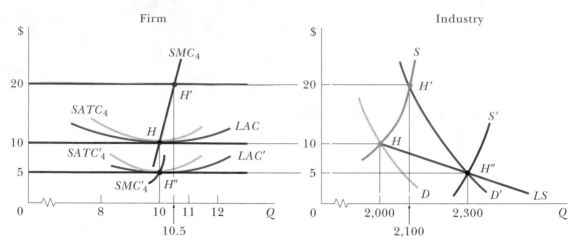

FIGURE 9.13 Decreasing Cost Industry Points *H* and *H'* are the same as in the preceding two figures. Starting from point *H'*, as more firms enter the industry, *S* shifts to *S'* and *P* = $5 if input prices fall. By joining points *H* and *H"* in the right panel, we derive the negatively sloped long-run supply curve *LS* for the (decreasing cost) industry.

over different time periods and at various levels of demand.[12] It should also be noted that the shifts in firms' per-unit cost curves in the left panel of Figures 9.12 and 9.13 were vertical (so that the lowest point on both the *LAC* and *LAC'* curves occurred at $Q = 10$). This is the case if the prices of all inputs change in the same proportion. Otherwise, per-unit cost curves would also shift to the right or to the left.

The *downward shift* in the firm's per-unit cost curves (due to a fall in input prices) as the *industry expands* is called an **external economy,** while the *upward shift* in the firm's per-unit cost curves (due to an increase in input prices) as the *industry expands* is called an **external diseconomy.** These terms are to be clearly distinguished from economies or diseconomies of scale, which are *internal* to the firm and refer instead to a downward or an upward *movement along* a given *LAC* curve (as the firm expands output and builds larger scales of plants). The assumption here is that as only a single firm expands output, input prices remain constant. External economies and diseconomies will be examined in detail in Chapter 18.

9.7 INTERNATIONAL COMPETITION IN THE DOMESTIC ECONOMY

Domestic firms in most industries face a great deal of competition from abroad. Most U.S.-made goods today compete with similar goods from abroad and in turn compete with foreign-made goods in foreign markets. Steel, textiles, cameras, wines, automobiles, television sets, computers, and aircraft are but a few of the domestic products that compete

---

[12] Of the three cases, increasing cost industries may be, perhaps, somewhat more common than the other two cases. Some important examples of decreasing cost industries are computers, VCRs, and many other consumer electronics products.

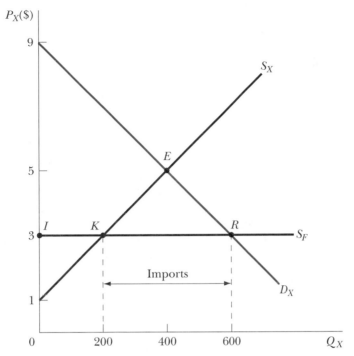

FIGURE 9.14   Consumption, Production, and Imports Under Free Trade   In the absence of trade, equilibrium is at point E, where D_X and S_X intersect, so that $P_X = \$5$ and $Q_X = 400$. With free trade at the world price of $P_X = \$3$, domestic consumers purchase $IR = 600X$, of which $IK = 200X$ are produced domestically and $KR = 400X$ are imported.

with foreign products for consumers' dollars in the U.S. economy today. Competition from imports allows domestic consumers to purchase more of a commodity at a lower price than in the absence of imports. This is shown by Figure 9.14.

In the figure, D_X and S_X refer to the domestic market demand and supply curves of commodity X. In the absence of trade, the equilibrium price is given by the intersection of the D_X and S_X at point E, so that domestic consumers purchase $400X$ (all of which is produced domestically) at $P_X = \$5$. With free trade at the world price of $P_X = \$3$, the price of commodity X to domestic consumers will fall to the world price. The foreign supply curve of this nation's imports of commodity X, S_F, is horizontal at $P_X = \$3$ *on the assumption that this nation's demand for imports of commodity X is small in relation to the foreign supply.* From the figure, we can then see that domestic consumers will purchase IR or $600X$ at $P_X = \$3$ with free trade (and no transportation costs), as compared with $400X$ at $P_X = \$5$ in the absence of trade (given by point E).

Figure 9.14 also shows that with free trade, domestic firms produce only IK or $200X$, so that KR or $400X$ are imported at $P_X = \$3$. Resources in the nation will then shift from the production of commodity X to the production of other commodities that the nation can produce relatively more efficiently (i.e., in which the nation has a comparative advantage). By doing this, the nation will be able to obtain more of commodity X through exchange than if it had used the same amount of domestic resources to produce commodity X domestically.[13]

In this section, we examine a number of important applications of the tools of analysis developed in this chapter. These include the definition and measurement of producer surplus, using consumers' and producers' surplus to further demonstrate the efficiency of perfect competition, and showing the effects of a per-unit tax and an import tariff. These applications, together with those from Chapter 2 (which presented an introductory overview of the perfectly competitive model) on rent control, U.S. farm-support programs, and the incidence of (i.e., who pays for) an excise tax, clearly demonstrate the great usefulness of the perfectly competitive model.

Producer Surplus

Producer surplus is a concept analogous to that of the consumer surplus examined in Section 4.5. Consumer surplus is the difference between what consumers are willing to pay for a commodity and what they actually pay, and it is measured by the area under the demand curve and above the commodity price. **Producer surplus** is defined as the excess of the commodity price over marginal cost, and it is measured by the area between the commodity price and the producer's marginal cost curve. This is shown in Figure 9.15.

Figure 9.15 shows that a perfectly competitive firm facing a price of $5 produces $4X$ (given by point E at which $d_X = MR_X = P_X = \$5 = MC_X$). This is derived from the optimization rule that a firm should expand production as long as price or marginal revenue exceeds marginal cost and until marginal revenue and marginal cost are equal. Since the firm sells all four units of commodity X at the market price of $5, but faces a marginal cost (or minimum price at which it will supply the first unit of the commodity) of only $2 on the first unit produced, the firm receives a surplus of $3 (given by the area of the first shaded rectangle in the figure) on the first unit sold. With $P_X = \$5$ but a marginal cost of $3 to produce the second unit of commodity X, the firm receives a surplus of $2 (the area of the second shaded rectangle) on the second unit sold. With $P_X = \$5$ and $MC = \$4$ on the third unit of commodity X produced, the firm receives a surplus of $1 (the area of the third shaded rectangle) on the third unit of X sold. Finally, since $P_X = MC_X = \$5$ on the fourth unit, producer surplus is zero on the fourth unit of X. The firm will not produce the fifth unit of commodity X because the marginal cost of producing the fifth unit ($6) exceeds the commodity price of $5 (see the figure).

---

[13] If the nation's demand for the imports of commodity X is large in relation to the total world supply of the exports of commodity X to the nation, then S_F would be positively sloped and intersect D_X at a higher price, so that the domestic production of commodity X would be higher while domestic consumption and imports would be smaller than indicated in Figure 9.14. Try to pencil in this change in Figure 9.14.

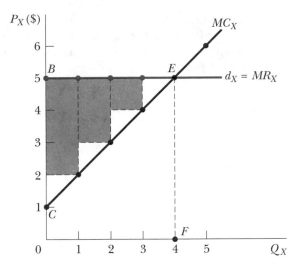

FIGURE 9.15   Producer Surplus   At $P_x = \$5$ the firm produces $4X$ (point E). Since the marginal cost is $2 on the first unit of X produced, the firm receives a surplus of $3 (given by the area of the first shaded rectangle). With $MC_x = \$3$ on the second unit of X, producer surplus is $2 (the area of the second shaded rectangle). With $MC_x = \$4$ on the third unit, producer surplus is $1 (the area of the third shaded rectangle). With $MC_x = \$5$ on the fourth unit, producer surplus is zero. Total producer surplus on $4X$ is $6. If commodity X were infinitesimally divisible, total producer surplus would be $8 (the area of triangle BEC).

By adding the producer surplus of $3 on the first unit of commodity X, $2 on the second unit, $1 on the third unit, and $0 on the fourth unit, we get the total producer surplus of $6 that the firm receives from the sale of $4X$. If commodity X could be produced and sold in infinitesimally small units, the total producer surplus would be given by the total area between the price of the commodity and the firm's marginal cost curve. This is the area of triangle BEC, which is equal to $8 (as compared with $6 found above). At the market price of $P_X = \$5$ and with output of $4X$, the total revenue of the firm is $20 (given by the area of rectangle $BEFO$ in the figure). Of this, $CEFO$ or $12 represents the opportunity cost of the variable inputs used or the minimum cost that the producer will incur to produce $4X$. The difference of $8 (the area of triangle BEC) thus represents the producer surplus or the amount that is not necessary for the producer to receive in order to induce him or her to supply $4X$.

If the market price of commodity X fell to $4, we can see from the figure that the best level of output of the firm would be $3X$ and the total producer's surplus would be $4.50 (given by the area of the triangle formed by $P_X = \$4$ and the MC_X curve). On the other hand, if the price of commodity X rose to $6, the best level of output of the firm would be $5X$ and the total producer's surplus would be $12.50 (given by the area of the triangle formed by $P_X = 6$ and the MC_X curve in Figure 9.15). This analysis applies to each producer in a perfectly competitive market. Indeed, the concepts of consumer and producer surplus are used in the next section to further demonstrate the efficiency of a perfectly competitive market and in the last two sections of this chapter to show the welfare effects of an excise tax and an import tariff.

Consumers' and Producers' Surplus, and the Efficiency of Perfect Competition

We have seen in Section 9.4 that in a perfectly competitive market, equilibrium occurs at the intersection of the industry or market demand and supply curves for the commodity. At this point, the marginal benefit to consumers from the last unit of the commodity purchased just matches the marginal cost to producers, and the combined consumers' and producers' surplus is at a maximum. This is another way of proving that perfect competition is the most efficient form of market structure, and is shown in Figure 9.16.

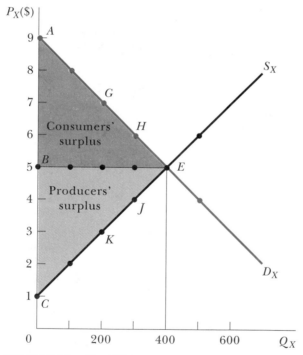

FIGURE 9.16   The Efficiency of Perfect Competition
Expanding output from 300X to 400X increases consumers'
plus producers' surplus by $HEJ = \$100$. Expanding output
past the competitive equilibrium output of 400X reduces the
total surplus, because the marginal benefit to consumers is
less than the marginal cost of producers. Thus, consumers'
plus producers' surplus is maximized when a perfectly
competitive market is in equilibrium.

In Figure 9.16, D_X and S_X refer, respectively, to the industry or market demand and supply curves for commodity X. The intersection of D_X and S_X defines equilibrium point E at which $P_X = \$5$ *and* $Q_X = 400$. The total consumers' surplus (the sum of the surpluses of all the consumers of commodity X in the market) is given by triangle AEB (the area under D_X and above P_X), which is equal to $\$800$. The total producers' surplus (the sum of the surpluses of all the producers of commodity X in the market) is given by triangle BEC (the area below P_X and above S_X), which is also $\$800$. Thus, the total combined consumers' and producers' surplus is given by area $AEC = \$1,600$.

We can use Figure 9.16 to show that when a perfectly competitive market is in equilibrium, consumers' plus producers' surplus is maximized. For example, expanding output from $200X$ to $300X$ leads to a combined increase of consumers' and producers' surplus equal to $GHJK = \$300$. The increase in consumers' and producers' surplus arises because the marginal benefit to consumers exceeds the marginal cost to producers for each additional unit produced and consumed. Expanding output from $300X$ to $400X$ leads to a further increase in consumers' plus producers' surplus of $HEJ = \$100$. If output expands past the equilibrium output of $400X$, the total surplus declines because consumers value the extra output at less than the marginal cost of producing it. Only at the competitive equilibrium output of $400X$ does the marginal benefit to consumers equal the marginal cost of producers and is the total combined consumers' and producers' surplus maximized. This can also be regarded as the benefit from exchange or trading (i.e., from buying and selling commodity X).

We will see in Part Four (Chapters 10–13) that imperfect competitors restrict output and charge a higher price so that the total combined consumers' and producers' surplus is smaller than under perfect competition. So important are the benefits of competition that market economies have been reducing the number and size of government regulations during the past decade. Even China has increasingly been relying on markets and less on planning.[14]

Welfare Effects of an Excise Tax

We will now use changes in consumers' and producers' surplus to measure the net loss in welfare resulting from an excise tax. The production and consumption effects of an excise tax as well as its incidence (i.e., who pays for the tax) were discussed in Section 2.7. Here, we expand that discussion to include a measurement of the loss in consumers' and producers' surplus resulting from the imposition of the tax. This is shown in Figure 9.17.

In Figure 9.17, D_X and S_X are, respectively, the market demand and supply curves for commodity X. The intersection of D_X and S_X defines the equilibrium price of $\$5$ and the equilibrium quantity of $400X$ (just as in Figure 9.16). A tax of $\$2$ per unit causes the S_X curve to shift up by $\$2$ to S_X' because producers must now pay the $\$2$ tax in addition to the previous marginal cost of producing each unit of commodity X shown by the S_X curve. This defines the new equilibrium point H at which $P_X = \$6$ to consumers and $Q_X = 300$. Producers, however, receive a net price of only $\$4$ after paying the tax of $\$2$ per unit. Thus, the tax raises the price to consumers from $\$5$ to $\$6$ and lowers the net price received by

---

[14] See "The Global March of Free Markets," *New York Times,* July 19, 1987, Section 3, p. 1; and "Support Is Growing in China for Shift to Free Markets," *New York Times,* June 28, 1992, p. 1.

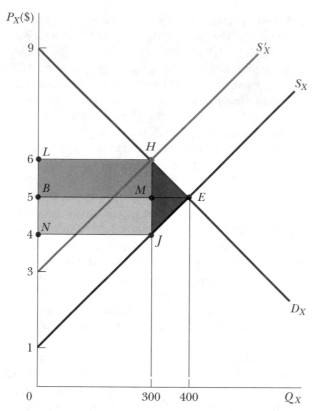

FIGURE 9.17   Welfare Effects of an Excise Tax   With D_x
and S_x, equilibrium is at point E at which $P_x = \$5$ and $Q_x = 400$.
A tax of \$2 per unit on commodity X shifts S_x up to S'_x and
defines new equilibrium point H at which $P_x = \$6$ to consumers,
$Q_x = 300$, and producers receive a net price of \$4 per unit.
The loss of consumers' surplus is $LHEB = \$350$, the loss of
producers' surplus is $BEJN = \$350$, for a combined loss of
$LHEJN = \$700$. Since tax revenues are $LHJN = \$600$ (\$2 per
unit on 300 units), there is a deadweight loss of $HEJ = \$100$.

producers from \$5 to \$4, so consumers and producers in this case share equally the burden
of the tax. So far, this is the same as in Section 2.7.

We can now go further, however, and measure the welfare effect of the tax by the
change in consumers' and producers' surplus resulting from the tax. From Figure 9.17 we
can see that the imposition of the tax leads to a reduction in consumers' surplus equal to
$LHEB = \$350$ and a reduction in producers' surplus equal to $BEJN = \$350$, for an overall
combined loss of consumers' and producers' surplus of \$700. Since the government col-
lects \$2 per unit on 300 units of the commodity, or a total of \$600 (the area of rectangle
$LHJN$), the tax results in a *net* loss of \$100 (the area of triangle HEJ) in consumers' and

producers' surplus. This **deadweight loss** remains even if the government were to return the entire amount of tax collected in the form of a general income subsidy to consumers. The loss results because of the distortions resulting from the tax. Specifically, some of society's resources shift from the production of commodity X to the production of other commodities that consumers value less. The provision of a per-unit production *subsidy* to producers would have the opposite effect of an excise tax (see Problem 11 at the end of this chapter).

Effects of an Import Tariff

We can show the effects of an import tariff using Figure 9.18. In Figure 9.18, D_X and S_X refer, respectively, to the domestic market demand and supply curves of commodity X. S_F is the foreign supply curve of exports of commodity X to the nation at the world price of $3 (on the assumption that the quantity demanded of imports of commodity X by the nation is very small in relation to the total foreign supply of exports of the commodity). With free trade at the world price of $P_X = \$3$, domestic consumers purchase $IR = 600X$, of which $IK = 200X$ are produced domestically and $KR = 400X$ are imported (so far this is the same as in Figure 9.14 in Section 9.7).

Suppose that from the free trade position, the nation imposes a 33% import tariff, or a tariff of $1 on each unit of commodity X imported. The new foreign supply curve for the nation's imports now becomes $S_F + T$, where T refers to the tariff. The price of commodity X to domestic consumers now becomes $4 (see Figure 9.18). At $P_X = \$4$, domestic consumers purchase $NU = 500X$, of which $NJ = 300X$ are produced domestically and $JU = 200X$ are imported. Thus, the consumption effect of the tariff (i.e., the reduction in domestic consumption resulting from the tariff) is $RW = -100X$, the production effect (i.e., the expansion of domestic production resulting from the tariff) is $KV = 100X$, the trade effect (i.e., the decline in imports) is $RW + KV = -200X$, and the revenue effect (i.e., the revenue collected by the government) is $JUWV = \$200$ ($JV = \$1$ on each of the $200X$ imported).

We can also measure the welfare effects of the tariff. From Figure 9.18, we see that the tariff leads to a reduction in consumers' surplus equal to $NURI = \$550$. Of this, $NJKI = \$250$ represents a transfer to producers in the form of an increase in producers' surplus, $JUWV = \$200$ is the tariff revenue collected by the nation's government, and the sum of triangles $URW = \$50$ and $JKV = \$50$ represents the protection cost or deadweight loss of the tariff. This results from the production and consumption distortions arising from the tariff.

Results would be similar if, starting from the free trade position in Figure 9.18, the nation imposed an import quota that directly restricted the *quantity* of imports of commodity X into the nation to $JU = 200X$. If the nation auctioned off import licenses to the highest bidder, it would collect the same revenue ($JUWV = \$200$) as with the 33% or $1 tariff on each unit of imports. If the nation does not auction off import licenses (as is often the case), the nation's importers or the foreign exporters would earn that much greater profits. This is exactly what happened when the United States negotiated an agreement with Japan during the 1980s under which Japan "voluntarily" reduced its automobile exports to the United States. Japanese automakers were, therefore, able to sell automobiles in the United States

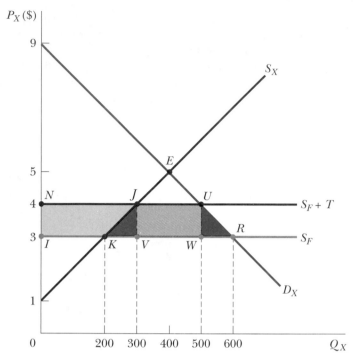

FIGURE 9.18   Effects of an Import Tariff D_X and S_X represent the domestic market demand and supply curves of commodity X. At the free trade price $P_X = \$3$, domestic consumers purchase $IR = 600X$, of which $IK = 200X$ are produced domestically and $KR = 400X$ are imported. With a $1 import tariff, P_X to domestic consumers rises to $4. At $P_X = \$4$, domestic consumers purchase $NU = 500X$, of which $NJ = 300X$ are produced domestically and $JU = 200X$ are imported. Thus, the consumption effect of the tariff is $RW = -100X$, the production effect is $KV = 100X$, the trade effect is $RW + KV = -200X$, and the revenue effect is $JUWV = \$200$. Consumers' surplus declines by $NURI = \$550$, of which $NJKI = \$250$ represents an increase in producers' surplus, $JUWV = \$200$ is the tariff revenue, and $URW = \$50$ plus $JKV = \$50$ represents the deadweight loss of the tariff.

at the world price plus the equivalent tariff (i.e., the tariff that would have reduced imports by the same amount as the quota) and earn huge profits. If trade restrictions were necessary to allow domestic automakers to improve quality and meet Japanese competition, then it would have been better for the United States to impose an equivalent import tariff and collect the tariff revenue.[15]

---

[15] See D. Salvatore, International Economics, 8th ed. (New York: John Wiley & Sons, 2003), Section 9.3a.

AT THE FRONTIER
Auctioning Airwaves

B etween December 5, 1994 and March 13, 1995, the U.S. government auctioned off to the highest bidder thousands of licenses to blanket the nation with new personal communications services (PCS) for the huge sum of $7.7 billion. The new generation of advanced wireless services involve voice, video, and data communications through small hand-held devices which, although similar to cellular phones, are more versatile, reliable, and cheaper. The Sprint Corporation, which formed a consortium with three of the nation's largest cable television companies, successfully bid $2.1 billion for licenses in 29 regional markets and metropolitan areas (including New York, San Francisco, Detroit, and Dallas–Forth Worth) with a total of 150 million people. In second place came the AT&T Corporation, which successfully bid $1.7 billion for 21 markets (including Chicago, Boston, Washington, and Philadelphia) with 107 million people. In third place came a consortium of three regional Bell companies, which bid $1.1 billion for licenses in 11 cities, including Chicago, Dallas, and Houston. The highest bid for a single market was $493.5 million that the Pacific Telesis Group paid for the license covering the region from Los Angeles to San Diego. The second highest single-market bid was $442 million that the Sprint coalition paid for a license to offer new wireless phone services in the New York metropolitan area. The third highest bid was $400 million that AT&T paid for each of two licenses to serve Chicago. Some licenses, such as that for American Samoa, sold for as little as $1 million, but overall this was an auction for big players and big money.

Although similar to an art auction—except that all licenses rather than a single license were up for bidding at the same time—auctioning airwaves licenses was unlike anything ever done before. In fact, since its creation in 1927, the Federal Communications Commission (FCC) had handed out airwaves (radio frequency) licenses free of charge either through lotteries or merit-based hearings, favoring local radio and TV stations, on the theory that they would be more attuned to community programming needs. The U.S. government has been raising money from leasing public lands to the private sector for the timber, mineral, and gas resources that they contained for more than a century. But from 1983 to 1993, the government awarded cellular telephone licenses through lotteries, free of charge, to many brokers who then sold the licenses to local wireless phone companies for over $1 billion.

During the 1980s, pressure began to mount to scrap the old system and allow market forces to allocate these scarce resources (airwaves). The pressure came from the need to cut the federal budget deficit, from the changed conditions brought about by the technological revolution in telecommunications which created an entirely new industry where private firms can make fortunes, and from the need to create much-needed competition in today's cellular telephone market.

Continued. . .

After a 10-year debate, Congress finally passed a law in 1993 that led to the recent auctioning of airwaves licenses.

The plan carved the nation into 51 regions and 492 subregions (metropolitan areas) and auctioned two licenses for each of the 51 regions and up to five licenses for each of the 492 subregions. A large company or group of companies could bid for a nationwide license by combining bids for a license for each region. Thus, each metropolitan area could have as many as seven new wireless services (five for the metropolitan area alone and another two from the region of which the metropolitan area is part), and each of these would compete with the one or two already established cellular telephone companies. For consumers this is likely to mean innovative services and lower prices. Traditional cellular telephone companies have the advantage of being already established, but are unable to provide the range of services that the new wireless companies offer at lower variable costs. Cellular telephone companies, however, were allowed and did bid for some of the new wireless licenses. Competition between cellular telephone companies and the new wireless companies will be intense during this decade.

Between 1995 and the end of 2001, 13 other auctions of wireless licenses were held, which netted the government an additional $40 billion, and more auctions were planned for the future. The auction held between December 2000 and January 2001 set aside licenses for small companies (those with revenues of less than $125 million in each of the previous two years) while others available to any buyer could be bought at deep discounts by small companies. More than 90% of these licenses, however, were in fact bought by large companies by striking alliances with small companies, thus triggering complaints of unfairness by the losing bidders that are likely to end up in federal court.

It is estimated that during this decade more than 100 million Americans will create a $100 billion-a-year industry for wireless services. Such large revenues are needed in order for the industry to recoup the original investments. These include the nearly $50 billion already paid for the licenses as well as the even larger investments that wireless companies are collectively making in order to set up the new digital transmission systems. Thus, it may take a decade before wireless companies can break even and possibly turn profitable. In the end, the difference between a profit and a loss could be the price of the license itself. Wireless companies may simply have paid too much for these licenses. This is referred to as the **winner's curse.**

The winner's curse arises because if the average for all the bids equals the true (but unknown) value of a license (based on the future stream of incomes that it is expected to generate), then the price paid by the highest bidder would exceed the average bid and the true value of the license. This is exactly what happened in the bidding for oil leases in the Gulf of Mexico during the 1950s and 1960s. The winner's curse can also arise when publishers bid for a novel. The most optimistic company is likely to be the highest bidder, and its bid will exceed the average bid and true value of the asset. The only way to avoid the winner's curse is for a company to adopt a prudent bidding approach and not overbid.

The winner's curse seems to have proven correct as evidenced by the fact that, starting in 1996, several of the less-known large bidders for the licenses started to default on payments. It seems that many successful bidders overpaid for the licenses in view of the strong competition that the sale of multiple licenses for each market generate. The government then re-auctioned these licenses. Thus far, the government collected only about half of the total sales bill, and it is not known if and when it will collect the other half.

Sources: "Disputed Phone Licenses Transferred to Big Carriers," *New York Times,* November 17, 2001, p. C2; "Clinton Orders a New Auction of Airwaves," *New York Times,* October 14, 2001, p. 1; "F.C.C. Auction Hit with Claims of Unfair Bids," *New York Times,* February 12, 2001, p. 1; "Airwave Auctions Falter as Source of Funds for U.S.," *New York Times,* April 3, 1997, p. 1; "Winners of Wireless Auctions to Pay $7 Billion," *New York Times,* March 14, 1995, p. D1; "Auction Fever," *The Economist,* December 3, 1994, p. 79; "The Sky's the Limit," *Washington Post,* June 5, 1994, p. 1; "U.S. Lays Out Rules for a Big Auction of Radio Airwaves," *New York Times,* September 24, 1993, p. 1; P. Milgrom, "Auctions and Bidding: A Primer," *Journal of Economic Perspectives,* Summer 1989; S. Thiel, "Some Evidence on the Winner's Curse," *American Economic Review,* December 1988; and J. H. Kagel and Dan Levin, "The Winner's Curve and Public Information," *American Economic Review,* December 1986.

SUMMARY

1. Economists identify four different types of market organization: perfect competition, monopoly, monopolistic competition, and oligopoly. In a perfectly competitive market, no buyer or seller affects (or behaves as if he or she affects) the price of a commodity, all units of the commodity are homogeneous or identical, resources are mobile, and knowledge of the market is perfect.

2. The market period, or the very short run, refers to the period of time during which the market supply of a commodity is fixed. During the market period, costs of production are irrelevant in the determination of the price of a perishable commodity and the entire supply of the commodity is put up for sale at whatever price it can fetch. Thus, demand alone determines price (while supply alone determines quantity).

3. The *TR* of a perfectly competitive firm is a straight line through the origin with slope of $MR = P$. The best or profit-maximizing level of output occurs where the positive difference between *TR* and *STC* is greatest. The same result is obtained where P or $MR = MC$ and *MC* is rising, provided that $P \geq AVC$. If P is smaller than *ATC* at the best level of output, the firm will incur a loss. As long as P exceeds *AVC*, it pays for the firm to continue to produce because it covers all variable costs and part of its fixed costs. If the firm were to shut down, it would incur a loss equal to its total fixed costs. The shut down point is where $P = AVC$.

4. The rising portion of the firm's *MC* curve above the *AVC* curve (the shut down point) is the firm's short-run supply curve for the commodity. The industry short-run supply curve is the horizontal summation of the firms' short-run supply curves. The equilibrium price is at the intersection of the market demand and supply curves of the commodity. The firm will then produce the output at which P or $MR = MC$, and *MC* is rising (as long as P exceeds *AVC*). With an increase in demand, the equilibrium price will rise and firms will expand their output. If input prices rise, the *MC* curve of each firm shifts up, and so the short-run supply curve of each firm and of the industry are less elastic.

5. In the long run, the industry and the firm are in long-run equilibrium where $P = MR = SMC = LMC = SATC = LAC$. Each firm operates at the lowest point on its *LAC* curve and earns zero profits. Competition in the input markets as well as in the commodity market will result in all firms having identical average costs and zero profits when the industry is in long-run equilibrium.

6. One of three possible cases can result as industry output expands and more inputs are demanded. If input prices remain constant, the industry long-run supply curve is horizontal and we have a constant cost industry. If input prices rise (external diseconomy), the industry long-run supply curve is positively sloped and we have an increasing cost industry. This may be more common than the former two cases. If input prices fall (external economy), the industry long-run supply curve is negatively sloped and we have a decreasing cost industry.

7. Domestic firms in most industries face a great deal of competition from imports. International trade leads to a decline in the domestic price of the commodity, and larger domestic consumption and lower domestic production of the commodity than in the absence of trade.

8. Producer surplus equals the excess of the commodity price over the producer's marginal cost of production. The combined consumers' and producers' surplus is maximized when a perfectly competitive market is in equilibrium. A tax leads to a deadweight loss. An import tariff increases the domestic price of the importable commodity, reduces domestic consumption and imports, increases domestic production, generates tax revenues, and leads to a deadweight loss.

9. Between December 1994 and the end of 2001, the U.S. Government auctioned off to the highest bidder thousands of licenses to offer new personal communications services (PCS) for nearly $50 billion. Some of the new wireless companies that purchased these licenses may have overpaid (and faced the winner's curse).

KEY TERMS

Perfect competition
Market period
Break-even point
Shutdown point
Price elasticity of supply
Constant cost industry

Increasing cost industry
Decreasing cost industry
External economy
External diseconomy
Producer surplus
Deadweight loss

Winner's curse
Foreign exchange market
Exchange rate
Depreciation
Appreciation

REVIEW QUESTIONS

1. If perfect competition is rare in the real world, why do we study it?

2. A firm's total revenue is $100, its total cost is $120, and its total fixed cost is $40. Should the firm stay in business? Why?

3. Why might a firm remain in business in the short run even if incurring a loss, but will always leave the industry if incurring a loss in the long run?

4. At what level of output is profit per unit maximized for a perfectly competitive firm? Why will the firm not produce this level of output?

5. Why would a firm enter a perfectly competitive industry if it knows that its profits will be zero in the long run?

6. Must a perfectly competitive industry be in long-run equilibrium if a perfectly competitive firm is in long-run equilibrium? Must each perfectly competitive firm be in equilibrium if the industry is in long-run equilibrium? Why?

7. Why should a nation trade if such trade benefits domestic consumers but harms domestic producers?

8. What is the difference between economic profit and producer surplus?

9. What is the combined consumers' and producers' surplus at the output level of 500X in Figure 9.15? Why is this not the best level of output?

10. Is the deadweight loss from an excise tax greater when the market demand and supply curves of the commodity are elastic or inelastic? Why?

11. What is the size of a prohibitive tariff in Figure 9.18? What would be the effects of such a prohibitive tariff?

12. What is meant by the winner's curse in an auction? How can this be avoided?

13. Assuming a two-currency world—the U.S. dollar and the British pound sterling—what does a depreciation of the dollar mean for the pound? Explain.

PROBLEMS

*1. Suppose that the market demand function of a perfectly competitive industry is given by $QD = 4{,}750 - 50P$ and the market supply function is given by $QS = 1{,}750 + 50P$, and P is expressed in dollars.
   a. Find the market equilibrium price.
   b. Find the quantity demanded and supplied in the market at $P = \$50, \$40, \$30, \$20,$ and $\$10$.
   c. Draw the market demand curve, the market supply curve, and the demand curve for one of 100 identical perfectly competitive firms in this industry.
   d. Write the equation of the demand curve of the firm.

2. a. If the market supply function of a commodity is $QS = 3{,}250$, are we in the market period, the short run, or the long run?
   b. If the market demand function is $QD = 4{,}750 - 50P$ and P is expressed in dollars, what is the market equilibrium price (P)?
   c. If the market demand increases to $QD' = 5{,}350 - 50P$, what is the equilibrium price?
   d. If the market demand decreases to $QD' = 4{,}150 - 50P$, what is the equilibrium price?
   e. Draw a figure showing parts (b), (c), and (d) of this problem.

3. Using the STC schedule provided in the table for Problem 2(a) in Chapter 8 and $P = \$26$ for a perfectly competitive firm,
   a. draw a figure similar to Figure 9.2 and determine the best level of output for the firm.
   b. construct a table similar to Table 9.1 showing TR, STC, and total profits at each level of output.

*4. Suppose that a perfectly competitive firm has no knowledge of the exact shape of its STC curve. It knows that its total fixed costs are $200, and it

assumes that its average variable costs are constant at $5.
   a. If the firm can sell any amount of the commodity at the price of $10 per unit, draw a figure and determine the sales volume at which the firm breaks even.
   b. How can an increase in the price of the commodity, in the total fixed costs of the firm, and in average variable costs, be shown in the figure of part (a) of this problem?
   c. What is an important shortcoming of this analysis?

*5. Using the per-unit cost schedules derived from the table for Problem 2(a) in Chapter 7 and $P = \$26$,
   a. draw a figure similar to Figure 9.3 and show the best level of output of the firm.
   b. construct a table similar to Table 9.2 showing $P, MR, ATC,$ and MC at each level of output.

6. For your figure in Problem 5a, determine the best level of output, the profit or loss per unit, total profit or losses, and whether the firm should continue to produce at
   a. $P = \$42$.
   b. $P = \$18$.
   c. $P = \$12.50$

7. Graph the quantity supplied (Q) at various prices (P) by firms 1, 2, and 3 given below, and derive the industry supply curve on the assumptions that the industry is composed only of these three firms and input prices remain constant.

Price and Quantity Supplied By Firms 1, 2, and 3

P	Q_1	Q_2	Q_3
$1	0	0	0
2	20	0	0
3	40	10	10
4	60	20	2

* = Answer provided at end of book.

*8. Starting from Figure 9.5, suppose that as each of the 100 identical firms in the perfectly competitive industry increases output (as a result of an increase in the market price of the commodity), input prices rise, causing the SMC curve of each firm to shift upward by $15. Draw a figure showing the original and the new MC curve and the quantity supplied by each firm and by the industry as a whole at the original price of $P = \$35$ and at $P = \$50$. On the same figure, show the supply curve of each firm and of the industry.

9. a. For the perfectly competitive firm of Problem 5, draw a figure similar to Figure 9.9 showing the short-run and long-run equilibrium on the assumption that the firm, but not the industry, is in long-run equilibrium. Assume $P = \$30$, the lowest $LAC = \$12.50$ at $Q = 8$, the best level of output is $Q = 10$, and $LAC = \$15$ with $SATC_5$ and $SMC_5 = LMC = \$30$ when the firm, but not the industry, is in long-run equilibrium.

b. Draw a figure similar to Figure 9.10 for the firm of part (a) showing the long-run equilibrium point for the firm and the industry.

*10. Starting from long-run equilibrium in a perfectly competitive increasing cost industry, show on one diagram the effect on price and quantity of an increase in demand in the market period, in the short run, and in the long run.

11. Starting with D_X and S_X in Figure 9.17, show all the effects of a production subsidy of $2 per unit given by the government to all producers of commodity X.

12. Starting with D_X and S_X in Figure 9.17, determine the effect of a price ceiling of $4 using the concepts of the consumers' and producers' surplus.

13. Starting with D_X and S_X of Figure 9.18, draw a figure similar to Figure 9.18 showing all the effects of a 100% import tariff on commodity X if the free trade price of commodity X is $2.

APPENDIX   THE FOREIGN EXCHANGE MARKET AND THE DOLLAR EXCHANGE RATE

A firm will import a commodity as long as the domestic currency price of the imported commodity is lower than the price of the identical or similar domestically produced commodity and until they are equal (in the absence of transportation costs, tariffs, or other obstructions to the flow of trade). In order to make the payment, the domestic importer will have to exchange the domestic currency for the foreign currency. Since the U.S. dollar is also used as an international currency, however, a U.S. importer could also pay in dollars. In that case, it is the foreign exporter that will have to exchange dollars into the local currency.

The market where one currency is exchanged for another is called the foreign exchange market. The **foreign exchange market** for any currency, say the U.S. dollar, is formed by all the locations (such as London, Tokyo, Frankfurt, and New York) where dollars are bought and sold for other currencies. These international monetary centers are connected by a telephone and telex network and are in constant contact with one another. The rate at which one currency is exchanged for another is called the **exchange rate.** This is the price of a unit of the foreign currency in terms of the domestic currency. For example, the exchange rate (R) between the U.S. dollar and the euro (€), the currency of the 12-nation European Monetary Union (Austria, Belgium, Finland, France, Germany, Greece, Ireland, Italy, Luxembourg, Netherlands, Portugal, and Spain), is the number of dollars required to purchase one euro. That is, $R = \$/€$. Thus, if $R = \$/€ = 1$, this means that one dollar is required to purchase one euro.

Under a flexible exchange rate system of the type we have today, the dollar price of the euro (R) is determined (just like the price of any other commodity in a competitive market)

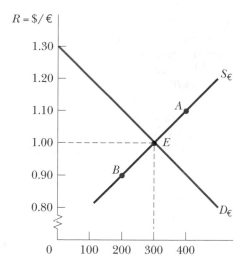

**FIGURE 9.19   The Foreign Exchange Market and the
Dollar Exchange Rate**   The vertical axis measures the
dollar price of euros ($R = \$/€$), and the horizontal axis
measures the quantity of euros. Under a flexible exchange
rate system, the equilibrium exchange rate is $R = 1$ and the
equilibrium quantity of euros bought and sold is €300 million
per day. This is given by point E, at which the U.S. demand
and supply curves for euros intersect.

by the intersection of the market demand and supply curves of euros. This is shown in Figure 9.19, where the vertical axis measures the dollar price of euros, or the exchange rate ($R = \$/€$), and the horizontal axis measures the quantity of euros. The market demand and supply curves for euros intersect at point E, defining the equilibrium exchange rate of $R = 1$, at which the quantity of euros demanded and the quantity of euros supplied are equal at €300 million per day. At a higher exchange rate, the quantity of euros supplied exceeds the quantity demanded, and the exchange rate will fall toward the equilibrium rate of $R = 1$. At an exchange rate lower than $R = 1$, the quantity of euros demanded exceeds the quantity supplied, and the exchange rate will be bid up toward the equilibrium rate of $R = 1$.

The U.S. demand for euros is negatively inclined, indicating that the lower the exchange rate (R), the greater the quantity of euros demanded by the United States. The reason is that the lower the exchange rate (i.e., the fewer the number of dollars required to purchase one euro), the cheaper it is for the United States to import from and invest in the European Monetary Union (EMU), and thus the greater the quantity of euros demanded by U.S. residents. On the other hand, the U.S. supply of euros is usually positively inclined, indicating that the higher the exchange rate (R), the greater the quantity of euros earned by or supplied to the United States. The reason is that at higher exchange rates, residents of the EMU receive more dollars for each of their euros. As a result, they find U.S. goods and investments cheaper and more attractive and spend more in the United States, thus supplying more euros to the United States.

If the U.S. demand curve for euros shifted up (for example, as a result of increased U.S. tastes for EMU's goods) and intersected the U.S. supply curve for euros at point *A* (see Figure 9.19), the equilibrium exchange rate would be $R = 1.10$, and the equilibrium quantity would be €400 million per day. The dollar is then said to have depreciated since it now requires $1.10 (instead of the previous $1.00) to purchase one euro. **Depreciation** thus refers to an increase in the domestic price of the foreign currency. On the other hand, if through time the U.S. demand for euros shifted down so as to intersect the U.S. supply curve of euros at point *B* (see Figure 9.19), the equilibrium exchange rate would fall to $R = 0.90$ and the dollar is said to have appreciated (because fewer dollars are now required to purchase one euro). An **appreciation** thus refers to a decline in the domestic price of the foreign currency. Shifts in the U.S. supply curve of euros through time would similarly affect the equilibrium exchange rate and equilibrium quantity of euros.

In the absence of interferences by national monetary authorities, the foreign exchange market operates just like any other competitive market, with the equilibrium price and quantity of the foreign currency determined at the intersection of the market demand and supply curves for the foreign currency. Sometimes, monetary authorities attempt to affect exchange rates by a coordinated purchase or sale of a currency on the foreign exchange market. For example, U.S. and foreign monetary authorities may sell dollars for foreign currencies to induce a dollar depreciation (which makes U.S. goods cheaper to foreigners) in order to reduce the U.S. trade deficit. These official foreign exchange market interventions are only of limited effectiveness, however, because the foreign exchange resources at the disposal of national monetary authorities are very small in relation to the size of daily transactions on the foreign exchange market (now estimated to be over $1 trillion per day!). Such huge volume of transactions has been made possible by sharp improvements in telecommunications and the coming into existence of a 24-hour foreign exchange market around the world.[16]

EXAMPLE 9–5

Foreign Exchange Quotations

Table 9.4 gives the exchange rate for various currencies with respect to the U.S. dollar for Tuesday, April 2, 2002 and for Monday April 1, 2002—defined first as the dollar price of the foreign currency (as in the text) and then, alternatively, as the foreign currency price of the dollar. For example, next to Europe, we find that the exchange rate of the euro (€) was $0.87890/€1 on Tuesday and $0.88050 on Monday. On the same line, we find that the euro price of the dollar was €1.1378/$ on Tuesday and €1.1357 on Monday. On the next two lines under Europe, we find the 30-day forward rate (i.e., the rate for a transaction entered upon today but with the foreign currency delivered in 30 days) and the 60-day and the 90-day forward rate. The 30-day forward rate of the euro is lower than the spot rate, meaning that the market expects the euro to be weaker

---

[16] See D. Salvatore, *International Economics,* 8th ed. (New York.: John Wiley & Sons, 2003), Chapter 13.

TABLE 9.4   Foreign Exchange Quotations

FOREIGN EXCHANGE

TUESDAY, APRIL 2, 2002

Currency	Foreign Currency in Dollars Tue.	Mon.	Dollars in Foreign Currency Tue.	Mon.	Currency	Foreign Currency in Dollars Tue.	Mon.	Dollars in Foreign Currency Tue.	Mon.
z-Argentina (Peso)	.3419	.3407	2.9250	2.9350	Kuwait (Dinar)	3.2563	3.2552	.3071	.3072
Australia (Dollar)	.5351	.5333	1.8688	1.8751	Lebanon (Pound)	.000660	.000660	1514.25	1514.25
Bahrain (Dinar)	2.6532	2.6532	.3769	.3769	Malaysia (Ringgit)	.2632	.2632	3.7995	3.7995
Brazil (Real)	.4340	.4295	2.3040	2.3285	z-Mexico (Peso)	.110797	.110988	9.0255	9.0100
Britain (Pound)	1.4365	1.4407	.6961	.6941	N. Zealand (Dollar)	.4420	.4415	2.2624	2.2650
30-day fwd	1.4339	1.4381	.6974	.6954	Norway (Krone)	.1141	.1135	8.7611	8.8090
60-day fwd	1.4314	1.4353	.6986	.6967	Pakistan (Rupee)	.0167	.0167	60.03	60.03
90-day fwd	1.4289	1.4329	.6998	.6979	y-Peru (New Sol)	.2899	.2904	3.450	3.444
Canada (Dollar)	.6277	.6255	1.5931	1.5986	z-Philpins (Peso)	.0196	.0196	50.91	50.91
30-day fwd	.6277	.6255	1.5931	1.5987	Poland (Zloty)	.2427	.2427	4.12	4.12
60-day fwd	.6275	.6253	1.5935	1.5992	a-Russia (Ruble)	.0321	.0321	31.2010	31.1900
90-day fwd	.6273	.6251	1.5942	1.5998	SDR (SDR)	1.24976	1.25150	.8002	.7990
y-Chile (Peso)	.001524	.001523	656.15	656.45	Saudi Arab (Riyal)	.2667	.2667	3.7502	3.7501
China (Yuan)	.1208	.1208	8.2774	8.2774	Singapore (Dollar)	.5414	.5413	1.8470	1.8473
Colombia (Peso)	.000443	.000440	2259.25	2273.00	SlovakRep (Koruna)	.0211	.0209	47.46	47.95
c-CzechRep (Koruna)	.0285	.0282	35.08	35.45	So. Africa (Rand)	.0889	.0879	11.2475	11.3750
Denmark (Krone)	.1184	.1176	8.4445	8.5053	So. Korea (Won)	.000753	.000753	1328.80	1327.20
Dominican (Peso)	.0575	.0575	17.40	17.40	Sweden (Krona)	.0974	.0977	10.2641	10.2345
d-Egypt (Pound)	.2159	.2159	4.6325	4.6325	Switzerlnd (Franc)	.6009	.6018	1.6642	1.6616
Europe (Euro)	.87890	.88050	1.1378	1.1357	30-day fwd	.6012	.6024	1.6633	1.6599
30-day fwd	.87740	.87950	1.1397	1.1370	60-day fwd	.6015	.6027	1.6626	1.6593
60-day fwd	.87640	.87840	1.1410	1.1384	90-day fwd	.6018	.6030	1.6618	1.6585
90-day fwd	.87540	.87740	1.1423	1.1397	Taiwan (Dollar)	.0286	.0286	35.00	34.99
Hong Kong (Dollar)	.1282	.1282	7.7994	7.7993	Thailand (Baht)	.02293	.02300	43.62	43.47
Hungary (Forint)	.0036	.0036	275.95	279.38	Turkey (Lira)	.000001	.000001	1340000	1347500
y-India (Rupee)	.0205	.0205	48.820	48.800	U.A.E. (Dirham)	.2723	.2723	3.6727	3.6728
Indnsia (Rupiah)	.000102	.000103	9767.50	9750.00	f-Uruguay (New Peso)	.0641	.0641	15.6000	15.6000
Israel (Shekel)	.2083	.2104	4.8000	4.7530	z-Venzuel (Bolivar)	.0011	.0011	906.0000	918.6250
Japan (Yen)	.007497	.007493	133.39	133.45					
30-day fwd	.007513	.007512	133.11	133.12					
60-day fwd	.007524	.007522	132.91	132.93					
90-day fwd	.007538	.007536	132.66	132.69					
Jordan (Dinar)	1.4104	1.4104	.70900	.70900					
Kenya (Shilling)	.0129	.0129	77.69	77.68					

a-Russian Central Bank rate.
c-commercial rate, d-free market rate, f-financial rate, y-official rate,
z-floating rate.
Prices as of 3:00 p.m. Eastern Time from Moneyline Telerate and
other sources.

Source: Reprinted by permission of *The New York Times*, © 2002. All rights reserved worldwide.

in 30 days (and still weaker in 60 and 90 days because the 60-day and the 90-day forward rate are smaller than the spot rate than the 30-day forward rate).

EXAMPLE 9–6

Depreciation of the U.S. Dollar and Profitability of U.S. Firms

A depreciation of the dollar, by making U.S. goods and services cheaper to foreigners in terms of their currency, allows U.S. firms to sell more abroad without lowering the dollar price of their products, and thus increases their profits and their share of foreign markets. U.S. firms also receive more dollars for their foreign-currency profits earned abroad. Against these benefits are the higher dollar prices that U.S. firms must pay for imported inputs. How much a U.S. firm gains from a depreciation of the dollar, therefore, depends on the amount of its foreign sales as opposed to its expenditures on imported inputs.

For example, the Black & Decker Corporation, a maker of power tools and appliances with about half of its sales abroad, found that the depreciation of the dollar during 1990 led to a 5% increase in its foreign sales and earnings. On the other hand, the Gillette Corporation, which has plants in many countries and uses almost exclusively local inputs to supply each market, benefited mostly through the repatriation of foreign profits. Merck & Company, which has plants in 19 nations and conducts most of its business in local currencies, was in a similar position. In between was Compaq, which found some of its price advantage abroad resulting from the depreciation of the dollar during 1990 eaten away by the higher cost of its imported disk drives and circuit-board parts.

On the other hand, the 20% appreciation of the dollar vis-à-vis the euro from the time of its launching at the beginning of 1999 until January 2002, meant that U.S. exporters received 20% fewer dollars per euro earned in Europe, while U.S. importers paid 20% less for imports from Europe. Thus, a change in the exchange rate benefits some and harms others, but affects all firms with foreign transactions and all individuals (Americans and foreigners) traveling abroad.

Sources: "How Dollar's Plunge Aids Some Companies, Does Little for Others," *Wall Street Journal,* October 22, 1990, p. A1; "Exporters in U.S. Confront a New Reality" *Wall Street Journal,* April 28, 1998, p. A2; "Euro Fails to Make Ground as Currency to Rival Dollar," *Financial Times,* November 20, 2001, p. 6; and D. Salvatore, "The Euro: Expectations and Performance," *Eastern Economic Journal,* January 2002.

INTERNET SITE ADDRESSES

For an excellent slide presentation of the perfectly competitive model, see:

> http://price.bus.okstate.edu/archive/Econ3113_963/Shows/Chapter8/index.htm

For information on the New York Stock Exchange, see:

> http://www.nyse.com

Petroleum production from tar sands is examined in:

> http://www.suncore.org/abouttar_sands.html

Information on the world supply of copper is found in:

> http://www.minerals.usgs.gov/minerals/pubs/commodity/copper
>
> http:/www.minecost.com/curves.htm

For a slide presentation and discussion of consumer surplus, see:

> http://price.bus.okstate.edu/archive/Econ3113_963/Shows/Chapter4/index.htm

For a discussion of the economic effects of an import tariff, see:

> http://www.public-policy.org/~ncpa/studies/s171/s171.html

On auctioning of the airwaves, see:

> http://news.cnet.com/news/0-1004-200-4606068.html
>
> http://www.zdnet.com/zdnn/stories/news/0,4586,2663083,00.html

PART FOUR

Imperfectly Competitive Markets

Part Four (Chapters 10–13) presents the theory of the firm in imperfectly competitive markets. It brings together the theory of consumer behavior and demand (from Part Two) and the theory of production and costs (from Chapters 7 and 8) to analyze how price and output are determined under various types of imperfectly competitive markets. Chapter 10 shows price and output determination under pure monopoly. Chapter 11 does the same for monopolistic competition and oligopoly. Chapter 12 describes how game theory is useful in analyzing oligopolistic behavior. Finally, Chapter 13 examines the efficiency implications of various market structures and regulation. As in previous parts of the text, the presentation of the theory is reinforced with many real-world examples and important applications, while the *At the Frontier* section in each chapter presents some new and important developments in the operation of imperfectly competitive markets.

CHAPTER 10

Price and Output Under Pure Monopoly

In this chapter, we bring together the theory of consumer behavior and demand (from Part Two) and the theory of production and costs (from Chapters 7 and 8) to analyze how price and output are determined under pure monopoly. Monopoly is the opposite extreme from perfect competition in the spectrum or range of market structure or organization. The monopoly model is useful for analyzing cases that approximate monopoly, and it provides insights into the operation of other imperfectly competitive markets (i.e., monopolistic competition and oligopoly).

The chapter begins by defining pure monopoly, describing the sources of monopoly, and explaining why the monopolist faces the market demand curve for the commodity. It then examines the determination of price and output in the short run and in the long run, and it compares the long-run equilibrium of the monopolist with that of a perfectly competitive firm and industry. Subsequently, we extend the monopoly model to examine how a monopolist (1) should allocate production among various plants to minimize production costs, and (2) can increase total profits by charging different prices for different quantities and in different markets at home and abroad. Finally, we discuss some other pricing practices that monopolists often use to increase their profits and present several important applications of the pure monopoly model. As in previous chapters, these applications, together with the real-world examples presented in the chapter, highlight the importance and relevance of the analytical tools developed in the chapter. The *At the Frontier* section examines the operation of one of the most talked-about near monopolies in the American economy today—Microsoft Corporation's Windows operating system.

10.1 PURE MONOPOLY—THE OPPOSITE EXTREME FROM PERFECT COMPETITION

In this section, we first define pure monopoly and discuss the sources of monopoly power. We then examine the shape of the demand and marginal revenue curves facing the monopolist and compare them with those of a perfectly competitive firm.

Definition and Sources of Monopoly

Pure monopoly is the form of market organization in which a *single firm* sells a commodity for which there are *no close substitutes*. Thus, the monopolist represents the industry and faces the industry's negatively sloped demand curve for the commodity. As opposed to a perfectly competitive firm, a monopolist can earn profits in the long run because *entry into the industry is blocked* or very difficult. Monopoly is at the opposite extreme from perfect competition in the spectrum or range of market organizations. Whereas the perfect competitor is a price taker and has no control over the price of the commodity it sells, the monopolist has complete control over price. The monopolist's ability to control or affect price is evidence of its monopoly power.

Monopoly can arise from several causes. First, a firm may own or control the entire supply of a raw material required in the production of a commodity, or the firm may possess some unique managerial talent. For example, until World War II, the Aluminum Company of America (Alcoa) controlled practically the entire supply of bauxite (the basic raw material necessary for the production of aluminum), giving it almost a complete monopoly in the production of aluminum in the United States (see Example 10–1).

Second, a firm may own a patent for the exclusive right to produce a commodity or to use a particular production process. Patents are granted by the government for 17 years as an incentive to inventors.[1] Some argue that if an invention could be copied freely (thus leaving little, if any, reward for the inventor), the flow of inventions and technical progress would be greatly reduced. Examples of monopolies that were originally based on patents are the Xerox Corporation for copying machines and Polaroid for instant cameras. An alternative to patents might be for the government to financially reward the inventor directly and allow inventions to be freely used. However, it is often difficult to determine the value of an invention: government archives are full of patents that found no commercial use.

Third, economies of scale may operate (i.e., the long-run average cost curve may fall) over a sufficiently large range of outputs so as to leave a single firm supplying the entire market. Such a firm is called a **natural monopoly.** Examples of natural monopolies are electrical, water, gas, and transportation companies. To have more than one firm supplying electricity, water, gas, and transportation services in a given market would lead to overlapping distribution systems and much higher per-unit costs.

Fourth, some monopolies are created by government franchise itself. For example, licenses are often required by local governments to start a radio or television station, to open a liquor store, to operate a taxi, to be a plumber, a barber, a funeral director, and so on. The purpose of these licenses is to ensure minimum standards of competency. Nevertheless, because the number of licenses issued (e.g., the number of taxi medallions issued in most metropolitan areas) is often restricted by the regulatory agency, licenses also protect present license holders from *new* competition (i.e., confer monopoly power to them as a group). In most cases, local governments turn the regulatory function (such as the issuance of licenses) over to the professional association involved. Examples include the medical and bar associations.

Aside from the few cases just mentioned and for public utilities, pure monopoly is rare in the United States today, and attempts to monopolize the market are forbidden by

---

[1] As opposed to copyrights, patents are not renewable. Improvement patents are available, however.

antitrust laws.[2] Nevertheless, the pure monopoly model is useful for analyzing situations that approach pure monopoly and for other types of imperfectly competitive markets (i.e., monopolistic competition and oligopoly).

A monopolist does not have unlimited market power, however, but faces many forms of direct and indirect competition. On a general level, a monopolist competes for the consumers' dollars with the sellers of all other commodities in the market. Furthermore, while *close* substitutes do not exist for the particular commodity supplied by the monopolist, imperfect substitutes are likely to exist. For example, although DuPont was the only producer of cellophane in the late 1940s, the company faced a great deal of competition from the producers of all other flexible packaging materials (waxed paper, aluminum foil, and so on). In addition, the market power of the monopolist (or the would-be monopolist) is sharply curtailed by fear of government antitrust prosecution, by the threat of potential competitors, and by international competition.

EXAMPLE 10-1

Barriers to Entry and Monopoly by Alcoa

The Aluminum Company of America (Alcoa) is a classic example of how a monopoly was created and maintained for almost 50 years. The monopoly was created in the late nineteenth century when Alcoa acquired a patent on the method to remove oxygen from bauxite to obtain aluminum. This patent expired in 1906, but in 1903, Alcoa had patented another more efficient method to produce aluminum. This patent expired in 1909. By that time, Alcoa had signed long-term contracts with producers of bauxite prohibiting them from selling bauxite to any other American firm. At the same time, Alcoa entered into agreements with foreign producers of aluminum not to export aluminum into each other's market. Alcoa even went as far as purchasing electricity only from those power companies that agreed not to sell energy for the production of aluminum to any other firm.

In 1912, the courts invalidated all of these contracts and agreements. Nevertheless, Alcoa retained monopoly power by always expanding productive capacity in anticipation of any increase in demand and by pricing aluminum in such a way as to discourage new entrants. The monopoly was finally broken after World War II, when Alcoa was not allowed to purchase government-financed aluminum plants built during the war. This is how Reynolds and Kaiser aluminum came into existence. During the 1960s, Reynolds diversified into plastics, gold, and consumer products, while Alcoa stuck to pure aluminum. But on May 3, 2000, Alcoa acquired Reynolds Metals Company, thus remaining the world's largest producer of aluminum, with 2001 revenues of $23 billion, 142,000 workers, operations in 37 countries and nearly 16% of the world aluminum market.

During the early 1990s, the world price of aluminum declined by almost 50% because of oversupply resulting in part from the sharp increase in aluminum exports by

---

[2] It should be noted that "monopoly" per se is not illegal; only "monopolizing" or "attempting to monopolize the market" are illegal under U.S. antitrust laws (Section 2, Sherman Antitrust Act, 1890).

Russia, as internal demand by its military–industrial complex vanished after the collapse of communism. In response to this price collapse, the representatives of 17 nations, including Russia, the European Union countries, the United States, and other major aluminum exporters, agreed in January 1994 to voluntarily cut production for two years, and this led to a partial recovery in aluminum prices. In agreeing to voluntarily cut production, the major exporting nations came very close to behaving like an international monopoly (cartel—cartels are examined in detail in Chapter 11). Despite the relatively high concentration in the aluminum market (e.g., Alcoa and Canadian-European APA, together, have a 27.4% share of the world market), prices rose and fell during the rest of the 1990s and early 2000s primarily because of demand and supply considerations.

Sources: R. Lanzilotti, "The Aluminum Industry," in W. Adams (ed.), *The Structure of American industry* (New York: Macmillan, 1961); "Reynolds Metals, Alcoa Split on Strategy," *Wall Street Journal,* November 7, 1990, p. A4; "Aluminum Pact Set to Curb World Output," *Wall Street Journal,* January 31, 1994; "Global Merger Could Steady Aluminum Market," *Wall Street Journal,* August 11, 1999, p. A13; and "Alcoa's Outlook Is Bright Due to Cost Cuts, Shortages," *Wall Street Journal,* January 1, 2000, p. B4.

The Monopolist Faces the Market Demand Curve for the Commodity[3]

Because a monopolist is the sole seller of a commodity for which there are no close substitutes, the monopolist faces the negatively sloped industry demand curve for the commodity. In other words, while the perfectly competitive firm is a price taker and faces a demand curve that is horizontal or infinitely elastic at the price determined by the intersection of the industry or market demand and supply curves for the commodity, the monopolist *is* the industry and, thus, it faces the negatively sloped industry demand curve for the commodity. This means that to sell more units of the commodity, the monopolist must lower the commodity price. As a result, marginal revenue (defined as the change in total revenue per-unit change in the quantity sold) is smaller than price, and the monopolist's marginal revenue curve lies below its demand curve (see Section 5.6).[4] This is shown in Table 10.1 and Figure 10.1.

The first two columns of Table 10.1 give a hypothetical market demand schedule for the commodity faced by a monopolist. In order to sell more of the commodity, the monopolist must lower the commodity price. Price times quantity gives total revenue (the third column of the table). The change in total revenue per-unit change in the quantity of the commodity sold gives the marginal revenue (the fourth column). For example, at $P = \$8$, the monopolist sells one unit of the commodity, so $TR = \$8$. To sell two units of the commodity, the monopolist must lower the price to $7 on both units of the commodity. TR is then $14. The change in TR resulting from selling the additional unit of the commodity is then $MR = \$14 - \$8 = \$6$. This equals the price of $7 for the second unit of the commodity sold minus the $1 reduction in price (from $8 to $7) on the first unit (since to sell two units of the commodity, the monopolist must lower the price of the commodity to $7 for both units).

[3] For the relationship between demand and marginal revenue for a monopolist in terms of calculus, see Section A.7 of the Mathematical Appendix at the end of the book.
[4] At this point, a review of the material in Section 5.6 may be helpful.

TABLE 10.1	Hypothetical Demand, Total Revenue, and Marginal Revenue Faced by a Monopolist		
P	Q	TR	MR
$9	0	$ 0	...
8	1	8	$ 8
7	2	14	6
6	3	18	4
5	4	20	2
4	5	20	0
3	6	18	−2
2	7	14	−4
1	8	8	−6
0	9	0	−8

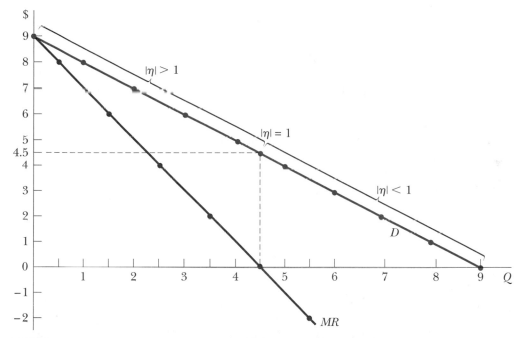

FIGURE 10.1   Hypothetical Demand and Marginal Revenue Curves of a Monopolist   Since *D* is negatively sloped, *MR* is lower than *P*. The *MR* values are plotted at the midpoint of each quantity interval. The *MR* curve starts at the same point as the *D* curve and at every point bisects the distance between *D* and the vertical axis. *MR* is positive when *D* is elastic. *MR* = 0 when *D* is unitary elastic and *TR* is at a maximum. *MR* is negative when *D* is inelastic.

The information contained in Table 10.1 is plotted in Figure 10.1. Since *MR* is defined as the change in *TR* per-unit change in *Q*, the *MR* revenue values are plotted at the midpoint of each quantity interval. Note that the *MR* curve starts at the same point on the vertical axis as the demand curve and at every point bisects (i.e., cuts in half) the distance between *D* and the vertical or price axis.[5] The *MR* is positive when *D* is elastic (i.e., in the top segment of the demand curve) because an increase in *Q* increases *TR*. *MR* = 0 when *D* is unitary elastic (i.e., at the geometric midpoint of *D*) because an increase in *Q* leaves *TR* unchanged (at its maximum level). *MR* is negative when *D* is inelastic (i.e., the bottom segment of *D*) because an increase in *Q* reduces *TR* (see Figure 10.1 and Section 5.6).

Contrast this situation with the case of a perfectly competitive firm (examined in Chapter 9), which faced a horizontal or infinitely elastic demand curve for the commodity at the price determined at the intersection of the market demand and supply curves for the commodity. Since the perfect competitor is a price taker and can sell any quantity of the commodity at the given price, price equals marginal revenue, and the demand and marginal revenue curves are horizontal and coincide.

The relationship between price, marginal revenue, and elasticity (η) can be examined with formula [5.8] introduced in Section 5.6:

$$MR = P(1 + 1/\eta) \qquad\qquad [5.8]$$

Using the formula, we see that since $\eta = -\infty$ for the perfect competitor, *MR* always equals *P*. That is, $MR = P(1 + 1/\infty) = P(1 + 0) = P$. Since $|\eta| < \infty$ (i.e., since the demand curve is not infinitely elastic) for the monopolist, $MR < P$. That is, for any value of $|\eta|$ smaller than infinity, *MR* will be smaller than *P*, and the *MR* curve will be below the market demand curve. Furthermore, we can see from the formula that when $\eta = -1$, $MR = 0$; when $|\eta| > 1$, $MR > 0$; and when $|\eta| < 1$, $MR < 0$. Since $MR < 0$ when $|\eta| < 1$, the monopolist can increase its *TR* by selling a *smaller* quantity of the commodity. Thus, the monopolist would never operate over the inelastic portion of the demand curve. By reducing output, the monopolist would increase total revenue, reduce total costs, and thus increase total profits. Example 10–2 examines how the De Beers Consolidated Mines diamond monopoly operated for over a century until 2001.

EXAMPLE 10–2

De Beers Abandons Its Diamond Monopoly

In 1887, Cecil Rhodes created the De Beers Consolidated Mines Company, which controlled about 90% of the total world supply of rough uncut diamonds with its South African mines. Until 2001, De Beers produced about half of the world's diamonds in its mines in South Africa, Botswana, and Namibia, and it marketed about 80% of the

---

[5] This is true only when, as in this case, the demand curve that the monopolist faces is a negatively sloped straight line.

world's diamonds through its London-based Central Selling Organization (CSO). Producers in Russia, Australia, Botswana, Angola, and other diamond-producing nations sold most of their production to De Beers, which then regulated the supply of cut and polished diamonds to final consumers on the world market so as to keep prices high. When there was a recession in the world's major markets and demand for diamonds was low, De Beers withheld diamonds from the market (i.e., stockpiled them) in order to avoid price declines until demand and prices rose. In short, De Beers acted as a monopolist and earned huge profits for itself and other producers by manipulating the world supply of diamonds. De Beers also advertised diamonds to drum up demand with the famous slogan "diamonds are forever" from the 1971 James Bond movie by the same name. In 2000, sales of uncut rough diamonds through De Beers amounted to $5.7 billion, and worldwide retail sales of diamond jewelry by De Beers and other firms exceeded $50 billion.

De Beers has had a monopoly in the marketing of diamonds since 1887 through wars, financial crisis, racial strife, hostile governments, and attempts by independent producers to circumvent the monopoly. When the former Soviet Union and Zaire started to sell large quantities of industrial diamonds on the world market outside the CSO in the early 1980s, De Beers immediately flooded the market from its own stockpiles (in excess of $5 billion in 2001), thereby driving prices sharply down and thus convincing the newcomers to join the cartel. And when large quantities of diamonds smuggled from Angola flooded Antwerp in 1992, De Beers purchased up to $400 to $500 million worth of these diamonds to prevent a collapse in prices. But faced with increased production by Russia (which sold only half of its diamonds through CSO) and new suppliers from Australia and Canada, and embarrassed by disclosures that to prop up prices it had bought "blood or conflict diamonds" from rebels in Angola, De Beers abandoned its cartel arrangement in 2001 and began concentrating instead on an advertising-driven strategy through its marketing arm, the Diamond Trading Company (DTC), to increase sales of its diamonds as branded luxuries. In 2001 De Beers also reorganized itself into a private company. It remains to be seen if this drastic change in strategy will work for De Beers.

Sources: "How De Beers Dominates the Diamonds," *The Economist,* February 23, 1980, pp. 101–102; "Can De Beers Hold to Its Own Hammerlock?" *Business Week,* September 21, 1992, pp. 45–46; "Disputes Are Forever," *The Economist,* September 17, 1994, p. 73; "The Rough Trade in Rough Stones," *Forbes,* March 27, 1995, pp. 47–48; "De Beers Halts Its Hoarding of Diamonds," *New York Times,* July 13, 2000, p. C1; "$17.6 Billion Deal to Make De Beers Private Company," *Financial Times,* February 16, 2001, p. W1; and "De Beers Upbeat Despite Profit Fall," *Financial Times,* February 16, 2002, p. 8.

10.2   SHORT-RUN EQUILIBRIUM PRICE AND OUTPUT

In this section, we examine the determination of price and output by a monopolist in the short run. We will do this first with the total approach and then with the marginal approach. We will also show that a monopolist, like a perfect competitor, can incur losses in the short run. Finally, we demonstrate that, unlike the case of the perfectly competitive firm, the monopolist's short-run supply curve cannot be derived from its short-run marginal cost curve.

Total Approach: Maximizing the Positive Difference between Total Revenue and Total Costs

As with the perfectly competitive firm, profit maximization provides the framework for the analysis of monopoly. The equilibrium price and output of a monopolist are the ones that maximize total profits. Total profits equal total revenue minus total costs. Total revenue is given by price times quantity. The total costs of the monopolist are similar to those discussed in Chapter 8 and need not differ from those of the perfectly competitive firm (if the monopolist does not affect input prices). Thus, except for the case of natural monopoly, the basic difference between monopoly and perfect competition lies on the demand side rather than on the production or cost side.

Table 10.2 gives the total revenue (TR), the short-run total costs (STC), and the total profits of a monopolist in the short run at various levels of output. The total revenue schedule is that of Table 10.1. As usual, short-run total costs rise slowly at first and then more rapidly (when the law of diminishing returns begins to operate). The best or optimum level of output for the monopolist in the short run is where total profits are maximized. For the monopolist of Table 10.2, this is at three units of output per time period. At this level of output, the monopolist charges the price of $6 and earns the maximum total profit of $4.50 per time period.

The data of Table 10.2 are plotted in Figure 10.2. The top panel shows that, unlike the case of a perfectly competitive firm, the monopolist's TR curve is not a straight line, but has the shape of an inverted U. The reason is that the monopolist must lower the price to sell additional units of the commodity. The monopolist's STC faces upward or increases at an increasing rate past $Q = 2$ because of diminishing returns.

Total profits are maximized at $Q = 3$, where the positive difference between the TR and the STC curves is greatest ($4.50). This is the point where the TR and the STC curves are parallel (see the top panel) and the total profits curve reaches its highest point (see the bottom panel). Total profits are positive between $Q = 1.5$ and $Q = 4.1$ and negative at other output levels. At $Q = 0$, $TR = 0$, while $STC = 6. Thus, by shutting down, the monopolist would incur the total loss of $6, which equals its total fixed costs. Note that the monopolist maximizes total profits at an output level smaller than the one at which TR is maximum (i.e., at $Q = 3$ rather than at $Q = 4.1$—see Figure 10.2).

TABLE 10.2 Total Revenue, Short-Run Total Costs, and Total Profits

Q	P	TR	STC	Total Profits
0	$9	$ 0	$ 6	$ −6
1	8	8	10	−2
2	7	14	12	2
*3	6	18	13.50	4.50
4	5	20	19	1
5	4	20	30	−10
6	3	18	48	−30

*Output at which firm maximizes total profit.

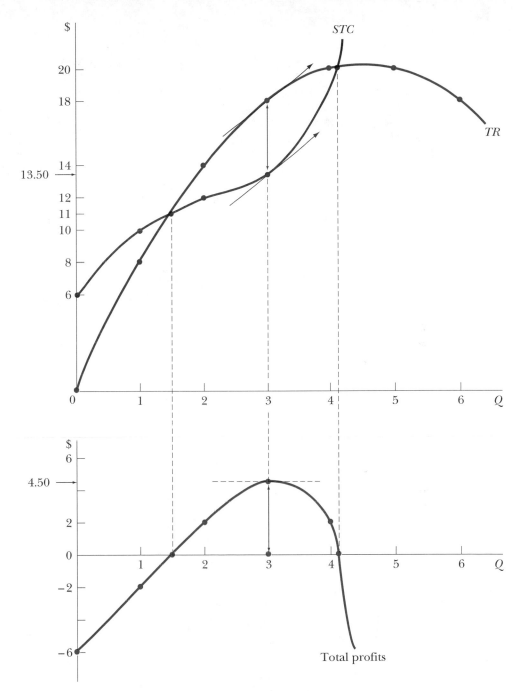

FIGURE 10.2 **Short-Run Equilibrium of the Monopolist: Total Approach** The monopolist's *TR* curve has the shape of an inverted U because the monopolist must lower the commodity price to sell additional units. The *STC* has the usual shape. Total profits are maximized at $Q = 3$, where the positive difference between *TR* and *STC* is greatest ($\$4.50$). This is the point where the *TR* and the *STC* curves are parallel (see the top panel) and the total profit curve is highest (see the bottom panel). Total profits are positive between $Q = 1.5$ and $Q = 4.1$ and negative at other output levels. At $Q = 0$, total loss is $\$6$ and equals total fixed costs.

Marginal Approach: Equating Marginal Revenue and Marginal Cost[6]

Although the total approach to determine the equilibrium price and output of the monopolist is useful, the marginal approach is even more valuable and widely used. According to the marginal approach, a monopolist maximizes total profits by producing the level of output at which *marginal revenue equals marginal cost*. The difference between the commodity price and the monopolist's average total cost at the best or optimum level of output gives the profit per unit. Profit per unit times output gives total profits. Thus, to be able to use the marginal approach and to determine the level of total profits, we must calculate the marginal cost and the average total cost of the monopolist.[7]

From the monopolist's short-run total cost schedule given in Table 10.2, we can derive the marginal cost and the average total cost schedules given in Table 10.3. Marginal cost equals the change in short-run total costs per-unit change in output. That is, $MC = \Delta STC/\Delta Q$. For example, at $Q = 1$, $STC = \$10$, while at $Q = 2$, $STC = \$12$. Therefore, $MC = (\$12 - \$10)/1 = \$2$. The other MC values in Table 10.3 are similarly obtained. On the other hand, average total costs equal short-run total costs divided by the level of output. That is, $ATC = STC/Q$. For example, at $Q = 1$, $STC = \$10$, and so $ATC = \$10/1 = \$10$. At $Q = 2$, $STC = \$12$, and so $ATC = \$12/2 = \$6$.

By plotting the monopolist's D and MR schedules of Table 10.1 and the MC and ATC schedules of Table 10.3 on the same set of axes, we get Figure 10.3. Note that MR and MC are plotted *between* the various levels of output, while D and ATC are plotted *at* the various output levels. In Figure 10.3, the best or optimum level of output of the monopolist is three units. This is given by point G, where $MR = MC$. At $Q = 3$, $P = \$6$ (point A on the demand curve), while $ATC = \$4.50$ (point B on the ATC curve). Thus, the monopolist earns \$1.50 (AB) per unit of output sold and \$4.50 in total (shaded area $ABCF$ in the figure). Note that at point G, the MC curve cuts the MR curve from below. This is always true for profit maximization, whether the MC curve is rising or falling at the point of intersection (see Section 10.8).

At outputs smaller than three units, MR exceeds MC (see the figure). Therefore, by expanding output, the monopolist would be adding more to TR than to STC, and total profits would rise. On the other hand, at outputs larger than three units, MC exceeds MR. A *reduction* in output would reduce STC more than TR and total profits would also rise. Thus, the monopolist must produce where $MR = MC$ (in this case three units of output) to maximize total profits. This is the same result obtained earlier by the total approach.

Table 10.4 summarizes the marginal approach numerically. Note that the MR and the MC values given in the table are read off Figure 10.3 *at* various output levels, just as P and ATC. For example, at $Q = 3$, $P = \$6$, $ATC = \$4.50$, and $MR = MC = \$3$. Table 10.4 shows that the monopolist maximizes total profits (equal to \$4.50) at $Q = 3$, where $MR = MC = \$3$ (as shown in Figure 10.3).

---

[6] For a mathematical presentation of profit maximization using rudimentary calculus, see Section A.10 of the Mathematical Appendix at the end of the book.

[7] Since we already know the monopolist's MR (see Figure 10.1), all we need to calculate now is the monopolist's marginal cost to determine the best or profit-maximizing level of output. This is given at the point where $MR = MC$. The average total cost is only required to measure the monopolist's profit at the best level of output.

TABLE 10.3	Short-Run Total Cost, Marginal Cost, and Average Total Cost		
Q	STC	MC	ATC
0	$ 6	. . .	. . .
1	10	$ 4	$10
2	12	2	6
3	13.50	1.50	4.50
4	19	5.50	4.75
5	30	11	6
6	48	18	8

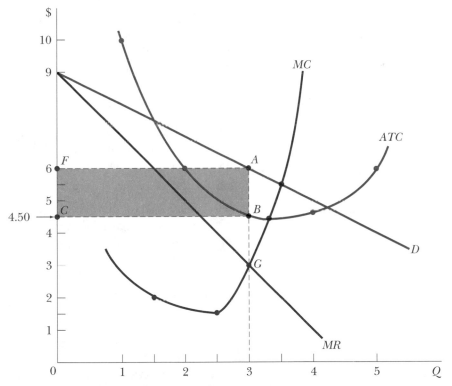

FIGURE 10.3   Short-Run Equilibrium of the Monopolist: Marginal Approach   The best or optimum level of output of the monopolist is three units. This is given by point G, where MR = MC (and the MC curve intersects the MR curve from below). At Q = 3, P = $6 (point A on the demand curve), ATC = $4.50 (point B on the ATC curve), and the monopolist earns $1.50 (AB) per unit of output sold and $4.50 in total (shaded area ABCF). At Q < 3, MR > MC and total profits rise by increasing Q. At Q > 3, MC > MR and total profits rise by reducing Q.

| TABLE 10.4 | Profit Maximization for the Monopolist: Marginal Approach | | | | | | |

Q	P	ATC	Profit Per Unit	Total Profits	MR	MC	Relationship of MR to MC
1	$8	$10	$−2	$ −2	$ 7	$ 3 ⎫	
2	7	6	1	2	5	1.50 ⎬	MR > MC
*3	6	4.50	1.50	4.50	3	3	MR = MC
4	5	4.75	0.25	1	1	8 ⎫	
5	4	6	−2	−10	−1	15 ⎬	MR < MC

*Output at which firm maximizes total profits.

Profit Maximization or Loss Minimization?

Like the perfect competitor, the monopolist can earn a profit, break even, or incur a loss in the short run. The monopolist will continue to produce in the short run (minimizing losses) as long as price exceeds the average variable cost at the best or optimum level of output. Were the monopolist to shut down, it would incur the higher loss equal to its total fixed costs (TFC).

To show this, assume that, for whatever reason, the monopolist's demand curve shifts down from its level in Figure 10.3 while its cost curves remain unchanged, so that $ATC > P$ at the best level of output. The monopolist will now incur losses at the best level of output. To determine whether the monopolist will minimize losses by continuing to produce, we now need to calculate the monopolist's average variable costs. Average variable costs (AVC) equal total variable costs (TVC) divided by output (Q). We can obtain the monopolist's total variable costs by subtracting its total *fixed* costs from its short-run *total* costs. That is, $TVC = STC - TFC$.

The monopolist's TVC and AVC are calculated in Table 10.5 from the STC of Tables 10.2 and 10.3. Specifically, since $STC = \$6$ at $Q = 0$ in Table 10.5, $TFC = \$6$. The TVC schedule is then obtained by subtracting TFC from STC at various output levels, and AVC is calculated by TVC/Q. For example, at $Q = 1$, $TVC = STC - TFC = \$10 - \$6 = \$4$ and $AVC = TVC/Q = \$4/1 = \$4$. At $Q = 2$, $TVC = \$12 - \$6 = \$6$ and $AVC = \$6/2 = \$3$. The other TVC and AVC values in Table 10.5 are calculated in a similar way.

In Figure 10.4, the MC and the ATC curves are those of Figure 10.3, and the AVC curve is obtained by plotting the AVC schedule given in Table 10.5. These per-unit *cost* curves are unchanged from Figure 10.3. The monopolist, however, now faces lower demand curve D' with marginal revenue curve MR'. The best or optimum level of output of the monopolist is now 2.5 units. This is given by point G', where $MR' = MC$ (the MC curve intersects the MR' curve from below in Figure 10.4). At $Q = 2.5$, $P = \$4$ (point A' on demand curve D') and $ATC = \$5$ (point B' on the ATC curve). Thus, the monopolist incurs a loss of $1 ($B'A'$) per unit of output sold and $2.50 in total (the area of rectangle $B'A'F'C'$).

At $Q = 2.5$, $AVC = \$2.60$ (point H' on the AVC curve). Since price ($4) exceeds average variable costs ($2.60) at the best level of output (2.5 units), the monopolist covers $1.40 ($A'H'$) of its fixed costs per unit and $3.50 (the area of rectangle $A'H'J'F'$) of its total fixed costs. If the monopolist were to shut down, it would incur the greater loss of $6

TABLE 10.5	Short-Run Total Cost, Total Fixed Costs, Total Variable Costs, and Average Variable Costs			
Q	STC	TFC	TVC	AVC
0	$ 6	$6	$ 0	. . .
1	10	6	4	$4
2	12	6	6	3
3	13.50	6	7.50	2.50
4	19	6	13	3.25

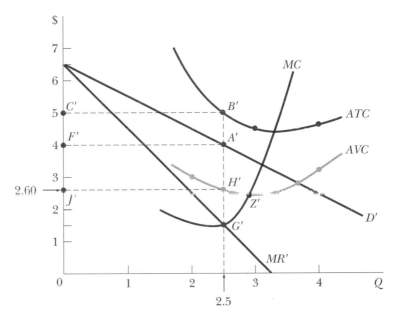

FIGURE 10.4   Profit Maximization or Loss Minimization   With D', the best or optimum level of output of the monopolist is $Q = 2.5$ (given by point G', where $MR' = MC$ and the MC curve intersects the MR' curve from below). At $Q = 2.5$, $ATC > P$, and the firm incurs a loss of $1 ($B'A'$) per unit and $2.50 in total (the area of rectangle $B'A'F'C'$). If, however, the firm were to shut down, it would incur the greater loss of $6 equal to its total fixed costs (the area of rectangle $B'H'J'C'$). The shut down point (Z') is at $P = AVC$.

(its total fixed costs, given by the area of rectangle $B'H'J'C'$). Only if P were smaller than AVC at the best level of output would the monopolist minimize total losses by shutting down (and incurring a loss equal only to its total fixed costs). At $P = AVC$, the monopolist would be indifferent between producing or shutting down because in either case it would incur a loss equal to its total fixed costs. Thus, the point where $P = AVC$ (point Z' in the figure) is the monopolist's shut down point.

Short-Run Marginal Cost and Supply

While the rising portion of the marginal cost curve over the average variable cost curve (the shut down point) is a perfect competitor's short-run supply curve (when input prices are constant), this is not the case for the monopolist. The reason is that the monopolist could supply the same quantity of a commodity at different prices depending on the price elasticity of demand. Thus, for the monopolist there is no unique relationship between price and quantity supplied, or no supply curve.

This is shown in Figure 10.5, where D is the original demand curve and D'' is an *alternative* and less elastic demand curve facing the monopolist. In the figure, MR is the marginal revenue curve for demand curve D, while MR'' is the marginal revenue curve for demand

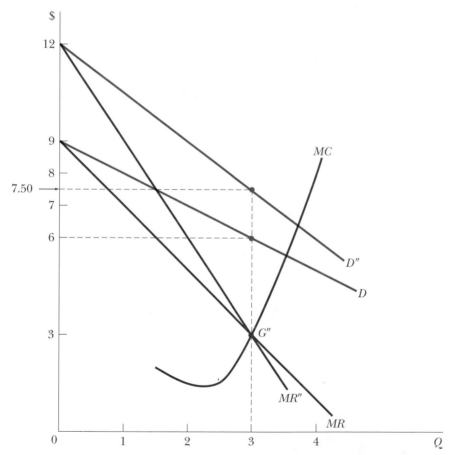

FIGURE 10.5   Short-Run Marginal Cost and Supply D is the original demand curve, and D'' is an alternative and less elastic demand curve facing the monopolist. Since the MC curve intersects the MR and MR'' curves from below at point G'', the best level of output is three units, whether the monopolist faces D or D''. However, with D, the monopolist charges $P = \$6$, whereas with D'', it would charge $P = \$7.50$. Thus, under monopoly, there is no unique relationship between price and output (i.e., the supply curve is undefined).

curve D''. Since the MC curve intersects the MR and MR'' curves from below at the same point (point G''), the best level of output is three units whether the monopolist faces D or D''. However, with D, the monopolist would sell the three units of output at $P = \$6$ (as in Figure 10.3), whereas with D'', the monopolist would sell the three units of output at $P = \$7.50$ (see Figure 10.5). Thus, the same quantity (i.e., $Q = 3$) can be supplied at two differ-ent prices (i.e., at $P = \$6$ or $P = \$7.50$) depending on the price elasticity of demand (i.e., depending on whether the monopolist faced demand curve D or D''). Therefore, under mo-nopoly, costs are related to the quantity supplied of the commodity, but there is no unique relationship between price and output (i.e., we cannot derive the monopolist's supply curve from its MC curve). Note that the monopolist would charge a higher price if it faced the less elastic demand curve (i.e., D'').

10.3   LONG-RUN EQUILIBRIUM PRICE AND OUTPUT

In this section, we analyze the behavior of the monopolist in the long run and compare it with the behavior of a perfectly competitive firm and industry. We also measure the welfare costs of monopoly.

Profit Maximization in the Long Run

In the long run, all inputs are variable and the monopolist can build the most efficient plant to produce the best level of output. The best or profit-maximizing level of output is given by the point where the monopolist's *long-run* marginal cost curve intersects the marginal revenue curve from below. The most efficient plant is the one that allows the monopolist to produce the best level of output at the lowest possible cost. This is the plant represented by the $SATC$ curve tangent to the LAC curve at the best level of output. As before, we assume that the monopolist does not affect input prices.

Figure 10.6 shows that the monopolist maximizes profits in the long run by producing $Q = 4$; this is given by point M, where the LMC curve intersects the MR curve from below. The monopolist should build plant $SATC_2$ and operate it at point N with $SATC = \$3.50$. Plant $SATC_2$ is the most efficient plant (i.e., the one that allows the monopolist to produce $Q = 4$ at the lowest $SATC$). In the long run, the monopolist will charge $P = \$5$ (point R), and earn a profit of $\$1.50$ (RN) per unit and $\$6$ in total (as opposed to $\$4.50$ in the short run with $SATC_1$—the same as Figure 10.3).

Even though profits will attract additional firms into the perfectly competitive industry until all firms just break even in the long run, the monopolist can continue to earn profits in the long run because of blocked entry. However, the value of these long-run profits will be capitalized into the market value of the firm. Thus, it is the original owner of the monopoly that directly benefits from the monopoly power. A purchaser of the firm would have to pay a price that reflected the present (discounted) value of the monopoly profits, and so would only break even in the long run. That is, monopoly profits become part of the opportunity costs of the original monopolist (see Example 10–3).

Note also that the monopolist, as opposed to a perfectly competitive firm, does not produce at the lowest point on its LAC curve (see Figure 10.6). Only if the monopolist's MR curve happened to go through the lowest point on its LAC would this be the case

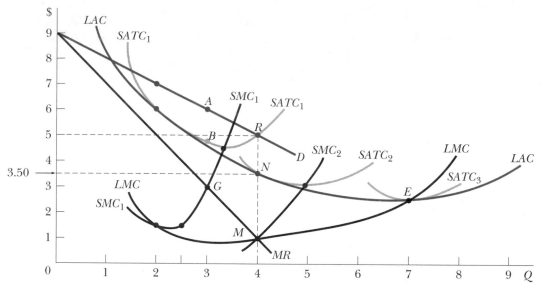

FIGURE 10.6   Long-Run Equilibrium of the Monopolist   In the long run, the monopolist maximizes profits by producing at point $M(Q = 4)$, where the *LMC* curve intersects the *MR* curve from below. The monopolist should build plant $SATC_2$, and operate it at point N at $SATC = \$3.50$. The monopolist will earn a profit of $\$1.50$ (*RN*) per unit and $\$6$ in total (as opposed to $\$4.50$ in the short run).

(see Problem 7 at the end of the chapter). Furthermore, a monopolist may earn long-run profits. Thus, as compared with a perfectly competitive firm when the industry is in long-run equilibrium (see Section 9.5), monopoly is inefficient because the monopolist is not likely to produce at the lowest point on its *LAC* curve and consumers are likely to pay a price that also usually includes a profit margin. In short, $P > LAC$ implies economic profits, and so there is distributional inefficiency; $LAC \neq LMC$ implies that *LAC* is not at a minimum, and so there is production inefficiency; and $P > LMC$ means that there is allocative inefficiency in the sense that the quantity of the commodity supplied does not represent the best use of the economy's resources. These social costs of monopoly are measured in the next subsection for a perfectly competitive industry that faces constant returns to scale and is subsequently monopolized.

EXAMPLE 10–3

Monopoly Profits in the New York City Taxi Industry

New York City, as most other municipalities (cities) in the United States, requires a license (medallion) to operate a taxi. Since medallions are limited in number, this confers a monopoly power (i.e., the ability to earn economic profits) to owners of medallions. The value of owning a medallion is equal to the present discounted value of the expected future stream of earnings from the ownership of a medallion—a process called *capitalization*. For example, the number of medallions in New York City remained at 11,787 from 1937 until 1996, when it was increased by only 400 to 12,187 and the value of a medallion rose from $10 in 1937 to $214,000 in May 2001, or by about 18% per year. The price of a medallion is lower (and sometimes much lower) in other cities, reflecting the lower earning power of a medallion in other cities. It is about $140,000 in Boston and over $50,000 in Chicago, where taxis are less scarce.

Proposals to increase the number of medallions in New York City have been successfully blocked by a powerful taxi industry lobby. Note that only the original owner benefits from the monopoly rights. A buyer of the rights would now have to pay a price that would fully reflect the future stream of earnings from the monopoly power, and so the buyer would only break even in the long run. The only way to prevent further windfall gains to present owners of the monopoly rights (medallions) is for the government to issue additional medallions. Were the city to freely grant a license to operate a taxi for the asking, the price of the medallion would drop to zero. While not doing that, New York City has allowed a sharp growth during the 1980s in the number of radio cabs, which can only respond to radio calls and cannot cruise the streets for passengers. This has sharply increased competition in the New York City taxi industry and reduced profits to taxi owners from 32% in 1993 to 11% in 2001.

Sources: "Owners Bewail Flood of Cabs in New York," *New York Times,* April 10, 1989, p. B1; "Panel Clears Plan to Enlarge Taxicab Fleet," *New York Times,* January 27, 1996, p. B1; "Medallion Financial Sees Growth in Taxi Tops," *Wall Street Journal,* July 19, 1999, p. B7A; and "Yellow Taxis Battle to Keep Livery Cabs Off Their Turf," *New York Times,* May 10, 2001, p. 1.

Comparison with Perfect Competition: The Social Cost of Monopoly

To measure the long-run social cost of monopoly, we assume that a perfectly competitive industry operating under constant returns to scale is suddenly monopolized and the market demand and cost curves remain unchanged. We will see that in that case output will be smaller and prices will be higher than under perfect competition. In addition, there will be a redistribution of income from consumers to the monopolist and a welfare loss due to less efficient resource use. These results are shown in Figure 10.7.

In Figure 10.7, D is the perfectly competitive industry market demand curve, and LS is the perfectly competitive industry long-run supply curve under constant costs. The long-run perfectly competitive equilibrium is at point E, where D intersects LS. At point E, $Q = 6$ and $P = $3. Consumers collectively would be willing to pay $LEI0$ ($36) for six units of the commodity, but need only pay $EI0C$ ($18). Thus, the consumers' surplus is LEC or $18 (see Section 9.8).

When the perfectly competitive industry is monopolized, the LS curve becomes the monopolist's LAC and LMC curves (the monopolist would simply operate the plants of the previously perfectly competitive firms).[8] The best level of output for the monopolist in

---

[8] Specifically, a perfectly competitive, constant-cost industry in long-run equilibrium has a horizontal LS curve at the minimum LAC of the individual firms (see Figure 9.11). A monopolist taking over the industry could change output by changing the number of plants previously operated by the independent firms at minimum LAC (where $LAC = LMC$). Thus, the horizontal LS supply curve of the competitive industry is the LAC and LMC curves of the monopolized industry. These curves show the constant LAC and LMC at which the monopolist can change output.

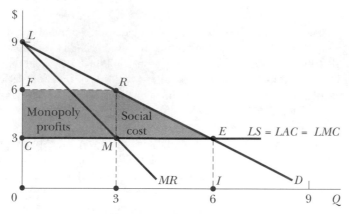

FIGURE 10.7   The Social Cost of Monopoly   With perfect competition, D is the market demand curve, and LS is the supply curve under constant costs. Equilibrium is at point E, where D intersects LS, and Q = 6 and P = $3. When the perfectly competitive industry is monopolized, the LS curve becomes the monopolist's LAC and LMC curve. Equilibrium is at point M, where MR = LMC. At point M, Q = 3, P = $6, total profits are RMCF, and REM is the social cost or deadweight loss to society due to the less efficient resource use under monopoly.

the long run is then given by point M, where $MR = LMC$. Thus, with monopoly, $Q = 3, P = 6 (which exceeds $LMC = 3), and the monopolist will earn total profits equal to $RMCF$ ($9). The consumers' surplus is now only LRF ($4.50), down from LEC ($18) under perfect competition. Of the $RECF$ ($13.50) reduction in the consumers' surplus, $RMCF$ ($9) represents a redistribution of income from consumers to the monopolist in the form of profits, and REM ($4.50) is the social cost or deadweight loss to society due to the less efficient resource use under monopoly.

Specifically, monopoly profits are not a net loss to society as a whole, because they represent simply a redistribution of income from consumers of the commodity to the monopolist producer. This redistribution is "bad" only to the extent that society "values" the welfare of consumers more than that of the monopolist. As we will see later, all of the monopolist's profits could be taxed away and redistributed to consumers of the commodity. On the other hand, the area of welfare triangle REM represents a true welfare or deadweight loss to society as a whole, which is inherent to monopoly and which society cannot avoid under monopoly.

Welfare triangle REM arises because the monopolist artificially restricts the output of the commodity so that some resources flow into the production of other commodities that society values less. Specifically, consumers pay $P = 6 for the third unit of the commodity produced by the monopolist. This is a measure of the social value or marginal benefit of this unit of the commodity to consumers. The marginal cost (MC) to produce this unit of the commodity, however, is only $3. This means that society forgoes one unit of the monopolized commodity valued at $6 for a unit of another commodity valued at $3. Thus, some of society's resources are used to produce less valuable commodities under monopoly. Since under perfect competition, production takes place at point *E*, where $P = LMC$ (see Figure 10.7), welfare triangle *REM* represents the social cost or welfare (deadweight) loss from the less efficient use of society's resources under monopoly.

EXAMPLE 10-4
Estimates of the Social Cost of Monopoly in the United States

In 1954, Harberger measured the area of the welfare triangle (*REM* in Figure 10.7) in each manufacturing industry in the United States on the assumption that the marginal cost was constant and that the price elasticity of the demand curve was 1. He found that the total social cost of monopoly was only about one-tenth of 1% of GNP. With some refinements of the estimating method, Scherer found that the social welfare loss from monopoly was between 0.5% and 2% of GNP, and most likely about 1%. The reason for these relatively low estimates is that there are few firms in the American economy with a great deal of monopoly power. In fact, Siegfried and Tiemann found that 44% of the total welfare loss due to monopoly power in the United States in 1963 came from the auto industry; the remainder of the loss was mostly due to a few other industries such as petroleum refining, plastics, and drugs.

There are, however, other losses resulting from monopoly power that are not included in the above estimates. One loss is that, in the absence of competition, monopolists do not keep their costs as low as possible, and they prefer the "quiet life" (*X*-inefficiency). For example, when U.S. steel firms started to face increased foreign competition during the 1970s and 1980s, they were able to sharply reduce costs. Another loss is that monopolists waste a lot of resources (from society's point of view) lobbying, engaging in legal battles, and advertising in the attempt to create and retain monopoly power, and to avoid regulation and prosecution under antitrust laws. These losses are sometimes referred to as the social costs of "rent seeking." In fact, some economists believe that these other social costs of monopoly are larger than those measured by the welfare triangle. The method of measurement and actual estimates of the size of these social costs are subject to a great deal of disagreement and controversy.

Sources: A. Harberger, "Monopoly and Resource Allocation," *American Economic Review,* May 1954; F. Scherer, *Industrial Market Structure and Economic Performance* (Chicago: Rand McNally, 1980), pp. 459–464; and J. Siegfried and T. Tiemann, "The Welfare Cost of Monopoly: An Interindustry Analysis," *Economic Inquiry,* June 1974. For the social costs of rent seeking, see W. Rogerson, "The Social Costs of Monopoly and Regulation: A Game-Theoretic Analysis," *Bell Journal of Economics* (now *The Rand Journal of Economics*), Autumn 1982; and F. Fisher, "The Social Costs of Monopoly and Regulation: Posner Reconsidered," *Journal of Political Economy,* April 1985; for more recent estimates of the social or welfare costs of food and tobacco oligopolies, see S. Bhuyan and R. A. Lopez, "What Determines Welfare Losses from Oligopoly Power in the Food and Tobacco Industries?," *Agricultural and Resource Economics Review,* October 1998.

328 PART FOUR Imperfectly Competitive Markets

10.4 PROFIT MAXIMIZATION BY THE MULTIPLANT MONOPOLIST

So far, the discussion has been based on the implicit assumption that the monopolist operated a single plant. This is not always or even usually the case. In this section, we examine how a multiplant monopolist should distribute its best level of output among its various plants, both in the short run and in the long run, to minimize its costs of production and maximize profits.

Short-Run Equilibrium

A multiplant monopolist will minimize the total cost of producing the best level of output in the short run when the marginal cost of the last unit of the commodity produced in each plant is equal to the marginal revenue from selling the combined output. This is shown in Figure 10.8, which refers to a two-plant monopolist.

The left and center panels of Figure 10.8 show the SMC curve of each of the two plants operated by the monopolist. The *horizontal* summation of SMC_1 and SMC_2 yields SMC in the right panel. The SMC curve shows the monopolist's minimum SMC of producing each additional unit of the commodity. Thus, the monopolist should produce the first and second unit of the commodity in plant 1 (at a SMC of \$2 and \$2.50, respectively), the third and fourth unit in plant 1 and plant 2 (one unit in each plant, at $SMC = \$3$), and so on.

If the monopolist were to produce all four units of the commodity in plant 1, it would incur a $SMC = \$4$ for the fourth unit (instead of a $SMC = \$3$ with plant 2). Thus, the monopolist should produce three units of the commodity in plant 1 and one unit in plant 2. By adding the three units of the commodity produced in plant 1 and the one unit produced in plant 2, we get point G on the SMC curve in the right panel of Figure 10.8. Thus, the SMC curve in the right panel is obtained from the horizontal summation of the SMC_1 and SMC_2

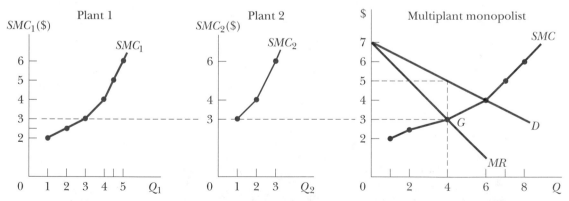

FIGURE 10.8 **Short-Run Equilibrium of the Multiplant Monopolist** The SMC curves of each of two plants of a monopolist are SMC_1 and SMC_2 in the left and center panels, respectively. The horizontal summation of SMC_1 and SMC_2 yields SMC in the right panel. SMC shows the monopolist's minimum SMC of producing each additional unit of the commodity. The best level of output is $Q = 4$, given by point G, where the SMC curve intersects the MR curve from below. To minimize STC, the monopolist should produce three units of the commodity in plant 1 and one unit in plant 2 so that $SMC_1 = SMC_2 = SMC = MR = \$3$.

curves in the left and center panels, respectively. The *SMC* shows the monopolist's mini-mum *SMC* of producing each additional unit of the commodity.

The best level of output for this monopolist is four units of the commodity and is given by point G, where the *SMC* curve intersects the *MR* curve from below. The monopolist should produce three units of the commodity in plant 1 and one unit of the commodity in plant 2 so that $SMC_1 = SMC_2 = SMC = MR = \$3$ (see the figure). This minimizes the total cost of producing the best level of output of four units at \$10.50 (\$2 + \$2.50 + \$3 + \$3) in the short run. If the monopolist were to produce all four units in plant 1, it would incur a $STC = \$11.50$ (\$2 + \$2.50 + \$3 + \$4). The *STC* would be even higher if the monopolist produced all four units in plant 2 (see the center panel of the figure).

Whether the monopolist earns a profit, breaks even, or incurs a loss by producing three units of the commodity in plant 1 and one unit of the commodity in plant 2 depends on the value of the *SATC* at $Q = 4$. Even if the monopolist were to incur a loss at its best level of output, it would pay to continue to produce in the short run as long as $P > AVC$ (see Section 10.2).

Long-Run Equilibrium

In the long run, a monopolist can build as many identical plants of optimal size (i.e., plants whose *SATC* curves form the lowest point of the *LAC* curve) as required to produce the best level of output. This is shown in Figure 10.9. The left panel shows one of the plants of the

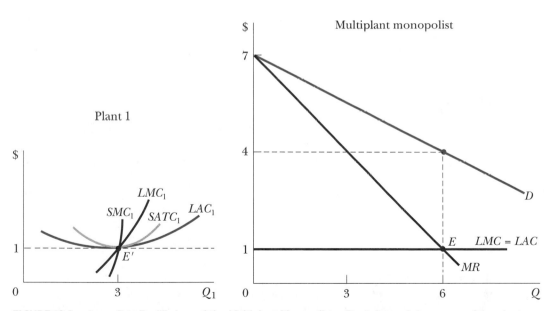

FIGURE 10.9   Long-Run Equilibrium of the Multiplant Monopolist   The left panel shows one of the plants of the monopolist. The monopolist will operate this plant at point E', where $LAC_1 = LMC_1 = \$1$ and $Q_1 = 3$. To produce larger outputs, the monopolist will build additional identical plants and run them at $Q = 3$. If input prices remain constant, the *LMC* curve of the monopolist is horizontal at $LMC = \$1$ (see the right panel). The best level of output is at point E, where the $LMC = MR = \$1$. At point E, $Q = 6$, $P = \$4$, $LAC = \$1$, and the monopolist earns a total profit of \$18 and operates two plants.

monopolist. The monopolist will operate this plant at point E', where $SATC_1 = SMC_1 = LAC_1 = LMC_1 = \$1$ and $Q = 3$. To produce larger outputs, the monopolist will build additional identical plants and run them at the optimal rate of output of $Q = 3$. If input prices remain constant, the LMC curve of the monopolist is horizontal at $LAC = LMC = \$1$ (see the right panel).

The best level of output of the monopolist in the long run is then given by point E, where $LMC = MR = \$1$ in the right panel. At point E, $Q = 6$, $P = \$4$, $LAC = \$1$, and the monopolist earns a profit of \$3 per unit and \$18 in total. The monopolist will produce three units of output in each of two identical plants (point E' in the left panel). If the best level of output is not a multiple of three, the monopolist will either have to run some plants at outputs greater than three units or build and run an extra plant at less than three units of output.

If input prices rise when the multiplant monopolist builds additional plants to increase output, then the LAC curve of each plant shifts upward (as in Figure 9.12) and the LMC curve of the monopolist will be upward sloping.

PRICE DISCRIMINATION—A MONOPOLIST'S METHOD OF INCREASING PROFITS

10.5

In this section, we examine various types of price discrimination. **Price discrimination** refers to the charging of different prices for different quantities of a commodity or in different markets which are not justified by cost differences. By practicing price discrimination, the monopolist can increase its total revenue and profits. We first examine the charging of different prices by the monopolist for different quantities sold and then the charging of different prices in different markets.

Charging Different Prices for Different Quantities

If a monopolist could sell each unit of the commodity separately and charge the highest price each consumer would be willing to pay for the commodity rather than go without it, the monopolist would be able to extract the entire consumers' surplus from consumers. This is called **first degree** or **perfect price discrimination.**

For example, in Figure 10.10, the consumer would be willing to pay $LRZO$ (\$22.50) for three units of the commodity. Since he or she only pays $RZOF$ (\$18), this consumer's surplus is LRF (\$4.50). If the monopolist, however, charged \$8.50 for the first unit (the highest price that this consumer would pay rather than forego entirely the consumption of the commodity), \$7.50 for the second unit of the commodity, and \$6.50 for the third unit, then the monopolist would receive \$22.50 (the sum of the areas of the rectangles above the first three units of the commodity), thereby extracting the entire consumer's surplus from this consumer.[9] The result would be the same if the monopolist made an all-or-nothing offer to the consumer either to purchase all three units of the commodity for \$22.50 or none at all.

---

[9] Note that the consumer is willing to pay an amount equal to the area under the demand curve between zero and one on the horizontal axis for the first unit of the commodity. This is equal to the area of the rectangle above the first unit of the commodity in Figure 10.10.

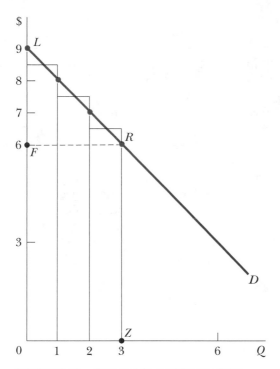

FIGURE 10.10   First and Second Degree Price Discrimination   Since the consumer is willing to pay $22.50 for three units of the commodity, but only pays $18, this consumer's surplus is $4.50. If the monopolist charged $8.50 for the first unit, $7.50 for the second, and $6.50 for the third, it would receive $22.50, thus extracting the entire consumer's surplus. This is first degree price discrimination. If the monopolist set $P = \$7$ for the first two units and $P = \$6$ for additional units, it would sell three units and extract $2 of the consumer's surplus. This is second degree price discrimination.

To be able to practice first degree price discrimination, however, the monopolist must (1) know the exact shape of each consumer's demand curve and be able to charge the highest price that each and every consumer would pay for each unit of the commodity, and (2) be able to prevent arbitrage or someone purchasing many units of the commodity at decreasing prices and reselling some of the units to others at higher prices. Even if this were possible, it would probably be prohibitively expensive to carry out. Thus, first degree price discrimination is not very common in the real world. Something close to first degree price discrimination is, however, used in making undergraduate financial-aid offers by American colleges (see Example 10–5).

EXAMPLE 10–5

First–Degree Price Discrimination in Undergraduate Financial Aid at American Colleges

It now costs over $100,000 for a four-year college education at many private colleges in the United States and close to $50,000 at public colleges. Financial aid is, however, available based on need. The greater the need, the higher is financial aid received. The way it works (as you may very well know) is as follows. In order to be considered for financial aid, students must provide information on their family's finances on the Free Application for Federal Student Aid (FAFSA) form. Using a government formula, the college then determines the Expected Family Contribution (EFC) toward college expenses. The lower the family's income and the higher the expenses of attending a particular college, the higher the financial aid offered to the student. By basing the amount of financial aid on a family's ability to pay, colleges thus practice something that comes very close to first-degree price discrimination. Many private colleges go well beyond this, however, in determining the aid package offered to each particular student and, in the process, have contributed to skyrocketing tuition costs.

Private colleges all over the country are now making financial aid offers to prospective students based not only on demonstrated family need but also on the particular student "price sensitivity" to college costs, calculated by statistical models using dozens of factors measuring how eager the student is to attend a particular college. The more eager the student, the lower the financial aid offered by the college. By offering less aid to more eager students, given their family's financial situation, the college is in effect charging a higher tuition and thus increasing its tuition revenue. This is referred to as "financial aid leveraging" and is similar to "yield management" used to price and fill airline seats and hotel rooms (discussed in "At the Frontier" section in Chapter 11). Thus, students who apply for early admission, those who go for on-campus interviews, or those who want to major in a very specific field are usually offered less financial aid (i.e., incur more of the college costs themselves). The National Center for Enrollment Management (NCEM), a consulting group that advises many colleges on financial-aid leveraging, estimated that its average college client's tuition revenue increased by about a half-million dollars. About 60% of the nation's 1,500 private four-year colleges now use some form of financial-aid leveraging.

Sources: "Colleges Manipulate Financial-Aid Offers, Shortcoming Many," *Wall Street Journal,* April 1996, p. A1; "Howls of Ivy," *Barron's,* March 1, 1999, p. 15; "Second Thoughts on Early Admission," *Business Week,* March 11, 2002, p. 96; and "Yale Seeks Shelter for pacts to End Early Admissions," *Wall Street Journal,* May 3, 2002, p. A2.

More practical and common is **second-degree** or **multipart price discrimination.** This refers to the charging of a uniform price per unit for a specific quantity of the commodity, a lower price per unit for an additional batch or block of the commodity, and so on. By doing so, the monopolist will be able to extract part, but not all, of the consumer's surplus. For example, in Figure 10.10, the monopolist could set the price of $7 per unit on the first two units

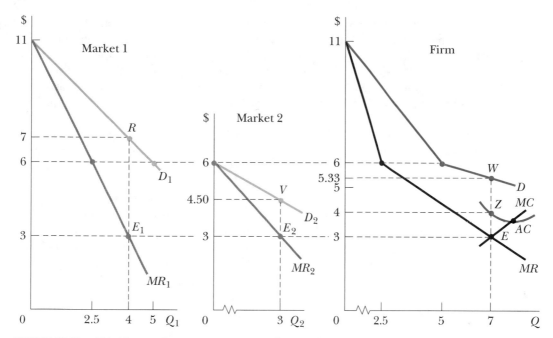

FIGURE 10.11   Third Degree Price Discrimination D_1 in the left panel is the demand curve faced by the monopolist in market 1 (with MR_1 as the corresponding marginal revenue curve). D_2 and MR_2, in the middle panel refer to market 2. By summing horizontally D_1 and D_2, and MR_1 and MR_2, we get the D and MR curves for the monopolist in the right panel. The best level of output is seven units, given where the MC curve intersects the MR curve from below. To maximize total profits the monopolist should sell $Q = 4$ at $P = \$7$ in market 1 and $Q = 3$ at $P = \$4.50$ in market 2, so that $MR_1 = MR_2 = MR = MC = \$3$. With $AC = \$4$ (point Z in the right panel), the monopolist's total profits are $13.50.

of the commodity and a price of $6 on additional units of the commodity. The monopolist would then sell three units of the commodity to this individual for $20 and extract $2 from the total consumer's surplus of $4.50. In general, this is also difficult to do because it requires that the monopolist be able to identify each consumer's demand curve and prevent arbitrage. Second-degree price discrimination is often practiced by public utilities, such as electrical power companies (this is examined in Example 10–6 at the end of the next section).

Charging Different Prices in Different Markets[10]

Charging a different price in different markets is called **third degree price discrimination.** For simplicity, we will assume that there are only two markets. To maximize profits, the monopolist must produce the best level of output and sell that output in the two markets in such a way that the marginal revenue of the last unit sold in each market is the same. This will require the monopolist to sell the commodity at a higher price in the market with the less elastic demand. This is shown in Figure 10.11.

---

[10] For a mathematical presentation of price discrimination using rudimentary calculus, see Section A.12 of the Mathematical Appendix at the end of the book.

The left panel of Figure 10.11 shows D_1 and MR_1, which are, respectively, the market demand and the corresponding marginal revenue curves faced by the monopolist in the first market. The middle panel shows the D_2 and MR_2 for the second market. From the horizontal summation of D_1 and D_2, and from MR_1 and MR_2, we get D and MR for the firm as a whole (monopolist) in the right panel. We sum horizontally D_1 and D_2, and MR_1 and MR_2, because the firm can sell the commodity in and obtain extra revenues from both markets. Note that until $Q = 2.5$, $MR_1 = MR$, and until $Q = 5$, $D_1 = D$.

The best level for output for the monopolist is seven units and is given by the point where the firm's marginal cost curve (MC) intersects the firm's total marginal revenue curve (MR) from below (point E in the right panel). To maximize total profits, the monopolist should then sell four units of the commodity in market 1 (given by point E_1 in the left panel) and the remaining three units in market 2 (given by point E_2 in the middle panel) so that $MR_1 = MR_2 = MR = MC = \$3$ (see the figure). If the MR for the last unit of the commodity sold in one market were different from the MR of the last unit sold in the other market, the monopolist could increase its total revenue and profits by redistributing sales from the market with the lower MR to the market with the higher MR until $MR_1 = MR_2$.

The monopolist should charge $P = \$7$ for each of the four units of the commodity sold in market 1 (point R on D_1) and $P = \$4.50$ for each of the three units of the commodity in market 2 (point V on D_2). This assumes that resale is not possible. Note that the price is higher in market 1, where demand is less elastic. The total revenue of the monopolist would be $\$41.50$ ($\$28$ from selling four units of the commodity at $P = \$7$ in market 1 plus $\$13.50$ from selling three units of the commodity at $P = \$4.50$ in market 2). With total costs of $\$28$ (seven units at $AC = \$4$, given by point Z in the right panel), the monopolist earns a profit of $\$13.50$ (the total revenue of $\$41.50$ minus the total costs of $\$28$). If the monopolist sold the best level of output of seven units at the price of $\$5.33$ (point W on D in the right panel) in both markets (i.e., if it did not practice third degree price discrimination), the monopolist would earn a profit of $WZ = \$1.33$ per unit (the price of $\$5.33$ minus the average cost of $\$4$) and $\$9.31$ in total (the $\$1.33$ profit per unit times the seven units sold) as compared with $\$13.50$ with third degree price discrimination. Any other output or distribution of sales between the two markets would similarly lead to lower total profits for the monopolist. This type of analysis is valid for the long run as well as for the short run.[11]

For a firm to be able to practice third degree price discrimination, three conditions must be met. First, the firm must have some monopoly power (i.e., the firm must not be a price taker). Second, the firm must be able to keep the two markets separate, so as to avoid arbitrage. Third, the price elasticity of demand for the commodity or service must be different in the two markets. All three conditions are met in the sale of electricity. For example, electrical power companies can set prices (subject to government regulation). The market for the industrial use of electricity is kept separate from that of household use by meters installed in each production plant and home. The price elasticity of demand for electricity for industrial use is higher than for household use because industrial users have better substitutes and more choices available (such as generating their own electricity) than

[11] If the monopolist knows the price elasticity of demand for the commodity in the two markets, it can determine the price to charge in each market to maximize total profits by utilizing formula [5.8]. See Problem 10, with the answer at the end of the book.

households. Thus, electrical power companies usually charge lower prices to industrial users than to households (see Example 10–6 at the end of this section).

Note that without market power the firm would be a price taker and could not practice any form of price discrimination. If the firm were unable to keep the markets separate, users in the lower-priced market could purchase more of the service than they needed and resell some of it in the higher-priced market (thus underselling the original supplier of the service). Finally, if the price elasticity of demand were the same in both markets, the best that the firm could do would be to charge the same price in both markets.

There are many other examples of third degree price discrimination: (1) the lower fees doctors usually charge low-income people than high-income people for basically identical services; (2) the lower prices that airlines, trains, and cinemas usually charge children and the elderly than other adults; (3) the lower postal rates for third-class mail than for equally heavy first-class mail; (4) the lower prices that producers usually charge abroad than at home for the same commodity, and so on.

Third-degree price discrimination is more likely to occur in service industries than in manufacturing industries because it is more difficult (often impossible) for a consumer to purchase a service in the low-price market and resell it at a higher price in the other market (thus undermining the monopolist's differential pricing in the two markets). For example, a low-income person could not possibly resell a doctor's visit at a higher fee to a high-income person. On the other hand, if an elderly person were charged a lower price for an automobile, he or she could certainly resell it at a higher price to other people. It is not clear that a supermarket's charging of $0.95 for two bars of soap and $0.50 for one bar is price discrimination, however, because the supermarket saves on clerks' time in marking the merchandise and on cashiers' time in ringing up customers' bills. That is, the charging of different prices to different consumers in different markets is not price discrimination if the different prices are based on different costs.

EXAMPLE 10–6
Price Discrimination by Con Edison

Table 10.6 gives the price per kilowatt-hour (kWh) that Con Edison charged residential and small commercial users for various quantities of electricity consumed in New York City in January and April 2002 (rates have been changing every month). Since Con Edison charged different rates for different categories of customers (i.e., residential and commercial) and for different quantities of electricity purchased, it is clear that Con Edison practiced both second- and third-degree price discrimination.

Note that charging higher rates for electricity during peak rather than off-peak hours, or *peak-load pricing,* is different from third-degree price discrimination because higher peak electricity rates are based on or reflect the higher costs of generating electricity at peak hours when older and less efficient plants and equipment have to be brought into operation to meet peak demand (peak-load pricing is examined in detail in Section 13.8).

TABLE 10.6	Electricity Rates Charged by Con Edison in 2002 (cents per kilowatt-hour)			
	kWh	Cents/kWh	kWh	Cents/kWh
Residential Rates (Single Residence)				
January	0–250	5.687	Above 250	5.298
April	0–250	6.534	Above 250	6.145
Commercial Rates (Small Business)				
January	0–900	6.62	Above 900	5.92
April	0–900	7.62	Above 900	6.92
Commercial Rates (Large Business)				
Low tension	0–15,000	1.82	Above 15,000	1.82
High tension	0–15,000	1.73	Above 15,000	1.73

Source: Con Edison, New York City, 2002.

Another way for a seller to practice third-degree price discrimination is by offering coupons to consumers for the purchase of some products (such as a box of breakfast cereal) at a discount. This allows a firm to sell the product at a lower price to only the 20% to 30% of consumers who bother to clip, save, and use coupons (these are the consumers who have a higher price elasticity of demand). In 2000, nearly $300 billion grocery coupons were distributed in the United States, but only a small percentage of them were redeemed. Offering coupons is a form of third-degree price discrimination that the firm can use to increase profits. Firms often also offer rebates, and airlines charge many different fares for a given trip for the same reason.

Sources: Con Edison, *Electric Rates,* New York 2002; C. Narasimhan, "A Price Discriminatory Theory of Coupons," *Marketing Science,* Spring 1984; and "The Art of Devising Air Fares," *New York Times,* March 8, 1987, p. D1.

10.6   INTERNATIONAL PRICE DISCRIMINATION AND DUMPING

Price discrimination can also be practiced between the domestic and the foreign market. International price discrimination is called **dumping.** Dumping refers to the charging of a lower price abroad than at home for the same commodity because of the greater price elasticity of demand in the foreign market. By so doing, the monopolist earns higher profits than by selling the best level of output at the same price in both markets. The price elasticity of demand for the monopolist's product abroad is higher than at home because of the competition from producers from other nations in the foreign market. Foreign competition is usually restricted at home by import tariffs or other trade barriers. These import restrictions serve to segment the market (i.e., keep the domestic market separate from the foreign market) and prevent the reexport of the commodity back to the monopolist's home country (which would undermine the monopolist's ability to sell the commodity at a higher price at home than abroad). International price discrimination can be viewed in Figure 10.11 if D_1 referred to the demand curve faced by the monopolist in the domestic market and D_2 referred to the demand curve that the monopolist faced in the foreign market.

Besides dumping resulting from international price discrimination (often referred to as *persistent dumping* to distinguish it from other types of dumping), there are two other forms of dumping. These are predatory dumping and sporadic dumping. *Predatory dumping* is the *temporary* sale of a commodity at below cost or at a lower price abroad in order to drive foreign producers out of business, after which prices are raised abroad to take advantage of the newly acquired monopoly power. *Sporadic dumping* is the *occasional* sale of the commodity at below cost or at a lower price abroad than domestically in order to unload an unforeseen and temporary surplus of a commodity without having to reduce domestic prices.

Trade restrictions to counteract *predatory* dumping are justified and allowed to protect domestic industries from unfair competition from abroad. These restrictions usually take the form of antidumping duties to offset price differentials. However, it is often difficult to determine the type of dumping, and domestic producers invariably demand protection against any form of dumping. In fact, the very threat of filing a dumping complaint discourages imports and leads to higher domestic production and profits. This is referred to as the "harassment thesis." Persistent and sporadic dumping benefit domestic consumers (by allowing them to purchase the commodity at a lower price), and these benefits may exceed the possible losses of domestic producers.

Over the past decades, Japan was accused of dumping steel, televisions, and computer chips in the United States, and Europeans of dumping cars, steel, and other products. Most industrial nations (especially those of the European Economic Community) have a tendency of persistently dumping surplus agricultural commodities arising from their farm-support programs. Export subsidies are also a form of dumping which, though illegal by international agreement, often occur in disguised forms. When dumping is proved, the violating firm usually chooses to raise its prices (as Volkswagen did in 1976 and Japanese TV exporters did in 1977) rather than face antidumping duties. Example 10–7 examines Kodak's antidumping court victory over Fuji.

EXAMPLE 10–7
Kodak Antidumping Victory Over Fuji—But Kodak Still Faces Competitive Problems

In August 1993, the Eastman Kodak Company of Rochester, New York, charged that the Fuji Photo Film Company of Japan had violated U.S. federal law by selling paper and chemicals for color-film processing in the United States at less than one-third of the price that it charged in Japan and that this had materially injured Kodak. Specifically, Kodak charged that Fuji used its excessive profits from its near monopoly in photographic supplies in Japan to dump photographic supplies in the United States in order to undermine the competitive position of Kodak and other U.S. competitors. By 1993, Fuji had captured more than 10% of the U.S. photographic supply market, mostly from Kodak. Kodak asked the U.S. Commerce Department to impose stiff tariffs on Fuji's imports of these products into the United States.

In August 1994, Fuji signed a five-year agreement under which it agreed to sell color paper and chemical components at or above a fair price determined quarterly by the U.S. Department of Commerce from Fuji cost of production figures in Japan and the Netherlands, where Fuji produces the photographic supplies exported to the United States. This "fair" price was about 50% higher than the pre-agreement price that Fuji charged in the United States. The immediate effect of the agreement was higher prices for photographic supplies for U.S. consumers.

In the face of continued loss of U.S. market share, Kodak again accused Fuji in 1995 of unfairly restricting its access to the Japanese market and again demanded the imposition of stiff tariffs on Fuji photographic exports to the United States. The World Trade Organization (the institution created in 1993 to regulate international trade and adjudicate trade disputes among its member nations), however, dismissed the case in 1997. Although Kodak retains nearly 70% of the U.S. photographic market (compared to Fuji's 19%), it has been steadily losing market share to Fuji over the past decade because of the latter's low-price policy.

In the meantime, Fuji has spent over $1 billion on new plants to produce photographic supplies in the United States, which makes Fuji a domestic supplier and, to a large extent, no longer subject to U.S. antidumping rules. Kodak, on the other hand, has gone through a deep restructuring during the past few years that cut its costs by $1 billion by eliminating 20,000 jobs or about 20% of its worldwide labor force and shifting to higher-end products (such as the Advanced Photo System cameras, which offer easier loading, panoramic shots, and other features) for which Fuji hasn't launched a price war, thus providing opportunities for higher profits. But problems persisted and Kodak undertook yet another restructuring plan at the end of 2001.

Sources: "Kodak Asks 25% Tariffs on Some Fuji Imports," *New York Times,* August 31, 1993, p. D1; "Fuji Photo Pact on U.S. Prices," *Wall Street Journal,* August 22, 1994, p. A4; "Kodak Is Loser in Trade Ruling on Fuji Dispute," *New York Times,* December 6, 1997, p. 1; "Can Kodak Refocus?" *US News & World Report,* November 9, 1998, pp. 47–50; "Kodak Losing Market U.S. Share to Fuji," *Wall Street Journal,* May 28, 1999, p. A3; and "Kodak Will Offer Its Staff a Chance to Upgrade Options," *Wall Street Journal,* November 11, 2001, p. B7.

10.7 TWO-PART TARIFFS, TYING, AND BUNDLING

In this section, we examine some other pricing practices by monopolists: two-part tariffs, tying, and bundling.

Two-Part Tariffs

A two-part tariff is another pricing practice that monopolists sometimes use to extract consumer surplus. It requires consumers to pay an initial fee for the right to purchase a product, as well as a usage fee or price for each unit of the product they purchase. An example of this is amusement parks where visitors are charged an admission fee as well as a fee or price for each ride they take. Other examples are telephone companies that charge a monthly fee plus a message-unit fee; computer companies that charge monthly rentals plus a usage fee for renting their mainframe computers; and golf and tennis clubs that charge an annual membership fee plus a fee for each round or game played. In each case, the monopolist wants to charge the initial fee and the usage fee that extracts as much of consumers' surplus as possible and thus maximizes total profits.

The monopolist maximizes total profits by charging a usage fee or per-unit price equal to its marginal cost and an initial or membership fee equal to the entire consumer surplus. To see this, assume that initially there is a single consumer in the market with demand curve D in the left panel of Figure 10.12. The monopolist should then charge the usage fee or price (P) equal to the marginal cost (MC) of $2 and an initial or membership fee of $8 (area AEB), which equals the entire consumer surplus at $P = \$2$. The monopolist would earn lower profits at any other price. For example, charging $P = \$3$ would provide the monopolist with a profit of $1 for each of the three units of the product or service that the monopolist would sell at $P = \$3$, but it would allow the monopolist to charge an initial or membership fee of only $4.50 (equal to the consumer surplus of $AE'B'$ for $P = \$3$). Thus, with $P = \$3$, the monopolist's total profit would be $7.50 ($3 from the sale of the three units of the product or service and $4.50 from the initial or membership fee) as compared with a profit of $8 (from the initial or membership fee for $P = MC = \$2$). On the other hand, with a usage fee or price of only $1, the monopolist would incur a loss of $1 on each of the five units of the product or service that it would sell at $P = \$1$, but it could charge an

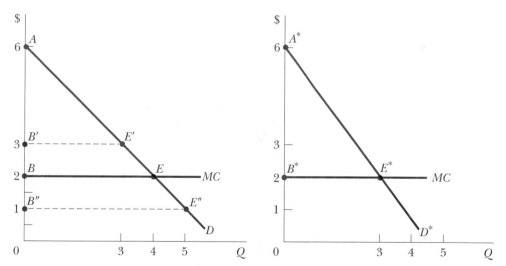

FIGURE 10.12   Two-Part Pricing by a Monopolist   With only one consumer in the market (left panel), the monopolist maximizes its total profits by charging $P = MC = \$2$ and the initial or membership fee of $AEB = \$8$. The monopolist can bring the consumer in the right panel into the market by lowering the initial or membership fee to $6 (equal to the surplus of $A^*E^*B^*$ of the second consumer at $P = MC = \$2$) for each consumer and earn a total profit of $12.

initial or membership fee of $12.50 (equal to the consumer surplus of $AE''B''$). This would leave the monopolist with a net profit of $7.50, which is also less than the total profit of $8 with $P = \$2$.

Suppose now that there was a second customer with demand curve D* in the right panel of Figure 10.12 who could be brought into the market. At $P = MC = \$2$, the consumer surplus for this second customer would be $6 ($A^*E^*B^*$ in the right panel of Figure 10.12), and this is as high an initial fee that the second consumer would be willing to pay. The monopolist would then have to lower the initial fee to $6 for both consumers to bring this second consumer into the market and thus earn the higher total profit of $12 (from the $6 initial fee from each consumer). This leaves $2 of consumer surplus to the first consumer. The monopolist could extract this remaining $2 surplus from the first consumer if it could somehow charge the first consumer a price higher than marginal cost. Another way would be to charge the first consumer an initial fee of $8 and provide a special discount membership of $6 for the second consumer. If both consumers were identical and faced the same demand curve, no such difficulty would arise and the monopolist would set $P = MC$ and charge each consumer an initial fee equal to their (identical) consumer surplus.[12]

Tying and Bundling

Tying refers to the requirement that a consumer who buys or leases a monopolist's product also purchase another product needed in the use of the first. For example, when the Xerox Corporation was the only producer of photocopiers in the 1950s, it required those leasing its machines to also purchase paper from Xerox. Similarly, until it was ordered by the court to discontinue the practice, IBM required by contract that the users of its computers purchase IBM punch cards. Sometimes tying of purchases is done to ensure that the correct supplies are used for the equipment to function properly or to ensure quality. More often, tying is used as a form of two-part tariff, whereby the monopolist can charge a price higher than marginal cost for supplies and thus extract more of the consumer surplus from the heavier users of the equipment (those who use more supplies). Often, the courts intervene to forbid these restrictions on competition. For example, McDonald's was forced to allow its franchises to purchase their materials and supplies from any McDonald's-approved supplier rather than only from McDonald's. This increased competition while still ensuring quality and protection of the brand name.[13]

Bundling is a common form of tying in which the monopolist requires customers buying or leasing one of its products or services to also buy or lease another product or service *when customers have different tastes* but the monopolist cannot price discriminate (as in tying). By selling or leasing the products or services as a package—a bundle—rather than separately, the monopolist can increase its total profits. A classic example of bundling is in movie leasing (see Example 10–8).

---

[12] For a more in-depth discussion of a two-part tariff, see W. Oi, "A Disneyland Dilemma: Two-Part Tariff for a Mickey Mouse Monopoly," *Quarterly Journal of Economics,* February 1971, pp. 77–96.

[13] See B. Klein and L. F. Saft, "The Law and Economics of Franchise Tying Contracts," *Journal of Law and Economics,* May 1985, pp. 345–361.

EXAMPLE 10–8

Bundling in the Leasing of Movies

Table 10.7 shows the prices that theater 1 and theater 2 would be willing to pay to lease movie A and movie B. If the film company cannot price discriminate and leases each movie separately to the two theaters, it will have to lease each movie at the lower of the two prices at which each theater is willing to lease each film. Specifically, the film company would have to charge $10,000 for movie A and $3,000 for movie B for a total of $13,000 to lease both movies to each theater (if the film company charged more for either movie, one of the theaters would not lease the movie). But theater 1 would have been willing to pay $15,000 to lease both movies and theater 2 would have been willing to pay $14,000 for both movies. The film company can thus lease both movies to both theaters as a package or a bundle for $14,000 (the lowest of the total amounts at which the two theaters are willing to lease the two movies) rather than individually for $13,000. Thus, by leasing the two movies together as a bundle rather than individually, the film company can extract some of the surplus from theater 1 without price discriminating between the two theaters.

TABLE 10.7	Maximum Price Each Theater Would Pay to Lease Each Film Separately and as Bundle	
	Theater 1	Theater 2
Movie A	$12,000	$10,000
Movie B	3,000	4,000

Such profitable bundling is possible only when one theater is willing to pay more for leasing one movie but less for leasing the other movie with respect to the other theater (i.e., when the *relative* valuation for the two movies differs between the two theaters or the demand for the two movies by each theater is negatively correlated). If, in our example, both theaters had been willing to pay only $9,000 to lease movie A, then the maximum price that the film company could charge either theater without price discrimination would be $12,000, whether it leased the movies as a bundle or separately. For bundling to be profitable, one theater must be willing to pay more for one movie and less for another movie with respect to the other theater. This occurs only if the two theaters serve different audiences with different tastes and have different relative valuations for the two movies.

Other examples of bundling are complete dinners versus à la carte pricing at restaurants, travel packages (which often include flights, hotel accommodations, and meals) and the sale of wire and wireless telephone services, Internet access and cable TV as a single package by telecommunications companies.

Sources: R. L. Schmalensee, "Commodity Bundling by Single-Product Monopolies," *Journal of Law and Economics,* April 1982, pp. 67–71; A. Lewbel, "Bundling of Substitutes or Complements," *International Journal of industrial Organization,* No. 3, 1985, pp. 101–107; and "The Benefits of Bundling," *Economic Intuition,* Winter 1999, pp. 6–7.

| 10.8 | ANALYSIS OF MONOPOLY MARKETS |

Now we will consider some analyses of monopoly markets. First, we will compare the effect of a per-unit tax on a monopolist and on a perfect competitor, then we will show that some commodities could only be supplied with price discrimination, and finally, we will answer the question of whether monopolists suppress inventions.

Per-Unit Tax: Perfect Competition and Monopoly Compared

One additional way to compare monopoly with perfect competition is with respect to the incidence of a per-unit tax. A per-unit excise tax (such as on cigarettes, gasoline, and liquor) will fall entirely on consumers if the industry is perfectly competitive and will fall only partly on consumers under monopoly, if both the monopolist and the perfectly competitive industry operate under constant costs.[14] For simplicity, we assume that the perfectly competitive industry and the monopolist face the same demand and cost conditions. Thus, S in Figure 10.13 refers to the long-run supply curve of the perfectly competitive industry and to the $LAC = LMC$ curve of the monopolist under constant costs.

Before the imposition of the per-unit tax, the perfectly competitive industry operates at point E, where D and S intersect, so that $Q = 6$ and $P = \$3$. If a tax of $\$2$ per unit is imposed, S shifts upward by $\$2$ to S'. The perfectly competitive industry would then operate at point E', where D and S' intersect, so that $Q = 4$ and $P = \$5$. Thus, when the industry is perfectly competitive and operates under constant costs, the entire amount of the per-unit tax ($\$2$ in this case) falls on consumers in the form of higher prices (so that $P = \$5$ instead of $\$3$).

The case is different under monopoly. Before the imposition of the tax, the monopolist produces at point M, where MR and S (the $LMC = LAC$ of the monopolist) intersect. $Q = 3$, $P = \$6$ (point R), $LAC = \$3$, and the monopolist earns a profit of $\$3$ (RM) per unit and $\$9$ in total. If the same tax of $\$2$ per unit is imposed on the monopolist, S shifts upward to S' ($= LMC' = LMC + 2 = LAC' = LAC + 2$). The monopolist would then operate at point M', where MR and S' intersect. At point M', $Q = 2$, $P = \$7$ (point R'), $LAC' = \$5$, and the monopolist earns $\$2$ per unit ($R'M'$) and $\$4$ in total. Thus, with monopoly, the price to consumers rises by only $\$1$ (one-half of the per-unit tax). The remaining half of the tax falls on the monopolist, so that it now only earns a profit of $\$2$, rather than $\$3$, per unit. Note also that with the tax, the decline in output under monopoly is half that with perfect competition (i.e., output falls from six to four units with perfect competition, but only from three to two units under monopoly).[15]

---

[14] The fact that a per-unit excise tax falls entirely on consumers under perfect competition but falls only partly on consumers with monopoly does not mean, however, that monopoly is "better" than perfect competition. When all inefficiencies associated with monopoly are considered, we would see that perfect competition leads to a higher level of social welfare than monopoly. Furthermore, the incidence of a per-unit tax is entirely on consumers only if the perfectly competitive industry operates under constant costs.

[15] From Figure 10.13, we can also see that the flatter or more elastic the market demand curve faced by the monopolist, the smaller the incidence or proportion of the tax paid by consumers.

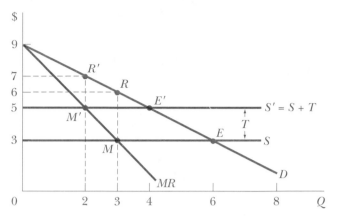

FIGURE 10.13   Per-Unit Tax: Perfect Competition and Monopoly Compared   Before the per-unit tax, the perfectly competitive industry operates at point E, where D and S intersect, so that $Q = 6$ and $P = \$3$. With a $\$2$ per-unit tax, S shifts up to S', and $Q = 4$ and $P = \$5$, so the tax falls entirely on consumers. Before the tax, the monopolist is in equilibrium at point M. $Q = 3$, $P = \$6$, and the monopolist earns a profit of $\$3$ (RM) per unit and $\$9$ in total. With a tax of $\$2$ per unit, $Q = 2, P = \$7$, and half of the per-unit tax falls on the monopolist.

Price Discrimination and the Existence of the Industry

Sometimes price discrimination is necessary for an industry to exist. For example, in Figure 10.14, D_1 is the demand curve for the commodity for one group of consumers (i.e., in market 1), while D_2 is the demand curve for another group (market 2). The horizontal summation of D_1 and D_2 yields D (ABC). Since the LAC curve is above D at every level of output, the commodity or service would not be supplied in the long run in the absence of price discrimination or a subsidy.

With third degree price discrimination (to the extent that the two markets can be kept separate), the firm could sell one unit of the commodity at $P = \$4$ in market 1 and sell three units of the commodity at $P = \$1.50$ in market 2. The total output would then be four units sold at the (weighted) average price of $\$2.13$, which equals the LAC of producing four units in the long run (point F in the figure).[16]

Do Monopolists Suppress Inventions?

A useful invention is one that allows the production of a given-quality product at lower cost or a higher-quality product at the same cost. Many people believe that a monopolist would suppress such inventions. Why, they argue, would a monopolist want to introduce a

---

[16] The weighted average price of $\$2.13$ is obtained by $[(1)(\$4) + (3)(\$1.50)]/4 = \$8.50/4$. The sale of $Q = 1$ in market 1 and $Q = 3$ in market 2 was obtained from inspection of the figure. This is the only output and distribution of sales (in whole units of the commodity) between the two markets by which this firm covers all costs.

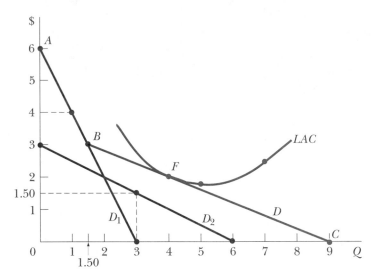

FIGURE 10.14   Price Discrimination and the Existence of an Industry
The demand curve is D_1 in market 1 and D_2 in market 2. The horizontal summation of D_1 and D_2 gives D (ABC). Since the LAC curve is above D at every output level, the commodity or service would not be supplied in the long run without price discrimination or a subsidy. With third degree price discrimination, the firm could sell $Q = 1$ at $P = \$4$ in market 1 and sell $Q = 3$ at $P = \$1.50$ in market 2 and break even (since at point F, the weighted average $P = \$2.13$ equals LAC).

longer-lasting light bulb that costs the same to produce when that would reduce the number of light bulbs sold, and the total revenue and profits of the monopolist? Such reasoning is wrong. We will see that the introduction of an invention usually increases rather than reduces profits, and so the monopolist has an economic incentive to introduce invention rather than to suppress it. This is shown in Figure 10.15.

The vertical axis of the figure measures the price of a kilowatt-hour (kWh) of electric light, and the horizontal axis measures the quantity (in thousands of hours) of kWhs provided either with original light bulbs or with new and longer-lasting light bulbs.[17] Thus, the axes do not refer to the price and quantity of light bulbs; instead they refer to the main attribute or characteristic of light bulbs, which is to provide light. D is the market demand curve for kWhs of light with either the original or new light bulbs, and MR is the corresponding marginal revenue curve. The $MC = AC$ curve shows the marginal and average cost of producing kWhs of light with the original light bulbs (produced under conditions of constant cost). The best level of output for the monopolist is 4 kWhs and is given by point M where $MC = MR$. At $Q = 4$ kWhs, $P = \$0.80$ per kWh, $AC = \$0.40$ per kWh, and the monopolist earns a profit of $\$0.40$ per kWh and $\$1.60$ in total. If each original light bulb provides or lasts 1/2 kWh, the monopolist sells eight of the original light bulbs at $P = \$0.40$ each.

---

[17] See "Bulb Lighted by Radio Waves May Last for up to 14 Years," *New York Times*, June 1, 1992, p. 1.

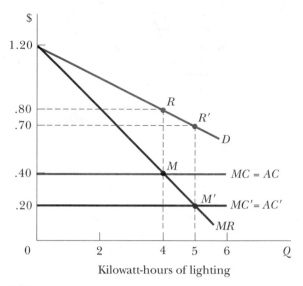

FIGURE 10.15   Monopoly and Inventions   The price per kilowatt-hour (kWh) of light is measured vertically and the quantity of kWhs horizontally. *D* is the market demand curve for kWhs of light. *MC* is the marginal cost of providing kWhs with the original bulbs and *MC'* with new bulbs (which last twice as long but cost the same to produce). With the original bulbs, $Q = 4$ kWhs, $P = \$0.80$ per kWh, $AC = \$0.40$, and profit is $\$0.40$ per kWh and $\$1.60$ in total. If original bulbs last $1/2$ kWh, the monopolist sells eight of them at $P = \$0.40$. With new bulbs, $Q = 5$ kWhs, $P = \$0.70$, $AC' = \$0.20$, and profit is $\$0.50$ per kWh and $\$2.50$ in total. The monopolist sells five new bulbs at $\$0.70$ each.

Suppose that the monopolist considers introducing a new light bulb that costs the same to produce but provides twice as many kWhs (i.e., lasts twice as long) as the original light bulbs. This is shown by the $MC' = AC'$ curve. This curve is half as high as the $MC = AC$ curve, indicating that each kWh of light could now be provided at half the cost. The best level of output for the monopolist is 5 kWhs and is given by point M' where $MC' = MR$. At $Q = 5$ kWhs, $P = \$0.70$ per kWh, $AC' = \$0.20$ per kWh, and the monopolist earns a profit of $\$0.50$ per kWh and $\$2.50$ in total (as compared with $\$1.60$ previously). Since each of the new light bulbs provides or lasts for 1 kWh (twice as much as the original light bulbs), the monopolist sells five light bulbs at $P = \$0.70$ each. Even though the monopolist sells fewer of the new light bulbs, it earns larger total profits, and so it has an economic incentive to introduce the invention. Consumers are also better off because after the invention they pay $\$0.70$ instead of $\$0.80$ per kWh of light and consume 5 kWh instead of 4 kWh.

Thus, the widespread belief that monopolists suppress inventions does not seem to be true.[18] This is a good example of how dispassionate economic analysis based on the

---

[18] This, however, does not mean that the monopolist innovates as much as competitive firms.

marginal principle can dispel some commonly held, yet incorrect, beliefs. Only when the monopolist is unsuccessful in patenting an invention and the introduction of the invention would lead to loss of monopoly power would the monopolist seek to suppress the invention.

AT THE FRONTIER
Windows 95—A Software Near Monopoly—Lands Microsoft in the Courts

Windows 95, the software operating system that controls the internal workings of personal computers (PC) that the Microsoft Corporation introduced on August 24, 1995, became almost as prominent as Coca-Cola in people's minds. There was one big difference, however. While Coca-Cola had about 40% of the U.S. soft drink market and faced stiff competition from its archrival, Pepsi, Microsoft's Windows 95 operating systems controlled almost 90% of the U.S. (and world) PC market and faced only weak competition from Apple Macintosh and IBM OS/2 operating systems. Windows 95 replaced Microsoft's MS-DOS and Windows 3.1 and made computing easier and more productive for the average nontechnical PC user. By fall 1995, every Intel Corp-based PC had Windows 95 as its main operating system, and so did 30 million new and old computers. By the end of 1996, that number had increased to nearly 100 million! Windows 95 was simply the most advertised, tested, and successful software program in the history of the personal computer business. In 20 years, Microsoft had become in software what IBM was in mainframes in the 1970s. Inevitably, the threat from Windows 95 gave rise to predictable cries of monopoly from competitors.

Not only did Microsoft have a near monopoly in the operating-system market, but it controlled more than 60% of the applications software business, such as word processors and spreadsheets. With the introduction of Windows 3.1 and its entrance into the applications software business in 1990, Microsoft's sales, revenues, and profits quadrupled, with two-thirds of them coming from applications. All of this led to charges of monopoly and monopolizing behavior. Specifically, Microsoft was accused of the following:

1. Preempting competitors' products by announcing products years before they were actually introduced, thus discouraging consumers from purchasing competing products (i.e., encouraging consumers to play it safe and wait for the market leader's product).
2. Using prior inside knowledge of the operating-system software that Microsoft planned to introduce allowed Microsoft's applications programmers to bring out better programs sooner than competitors.
3. Requiring PC manufacturers to pay Microsoft a fee for every PC they ship, whether or not they installed the Microsoft operating system, thus discouraging PC makers from using competing operating systems in their PCs (since this would mean paying double royalties).

4. Charging unfairly low prices for its application programs from the prof-
    its made on the sale of its operating software, on which Microsoft had a
    near monopoly.
5. Spreading fear and warning potential customers that competitors' soft-
    ware programs would not be around in a few years.
6. Stealing ideas and reworking competitors' programs, making them
    its own.

The introduction of Windows 95 put at risk especially small software companies that provided such specialized programs as hooking up to the Internet, retrieving lost files, turning the PC into a fax machine, and allocating memory inside the PC efficiently—since most of these programs were now provided as part
of Windows 95. This was good news for computer users but drove many small
software companies out of business, and may have reduced the level of program
innovations. The proper response of small software companies to this challenge
was to constantly introduce still better product that customers absolutely wanted,
but that was not easy to do.

In response to all these charges, in 1990 the Justice Department and the
Federal Trade Commission started to investigated Microsoft to determine if it engaged in unfair trade practices or violated antitrust laws. In May 1995, the Justice
Department prevented Microsoft from acquiring Intuit, the leading publisher of
personal finance management software, on the grounds that it could allow
Microsoft to dominate the on-line service business. A July 1995 consent agreement
with the Justice Department barred Microsoft from charging a licensing fee for
the company's operating system if the PC maker did not use Microsoft's operating system. Competitors, however, called this action only a slap on the wrist since
Microsoft already had a near operating-system monopoly. After 1995, the Justice
Department continued its investigation by focusing on whether the bundling of
access to the Microsoft Network (MSN) with Windows 95 gave Microsoft an unfair advantage over competitors in the on-line computer business and represented
an antitrust violation.

In fall 1998, the U.S. Justice Department sued Microsoft, accusing it of illegally using its Windows operating system near monopoly to overwhelm rivals
and hurt consumers. On April 4, 2000, the federal district judge trying the case
ruled that Microsoft had violated antitrust laws with predatory behavior and on
June 8, 2000 the same judge ordered the breakup of Microsoft. The company,
however, appealed and on November 9, 2001 the U.S. Justice Department and
Microsoft reached a settlement agreement that not only left Microsoft intact but
also continued to permit Microsoft's strategy of "bundling" applications with its
Windows operating system. Both represented substantial victories for Microsoft.
The settlement agreement only required Microsoft to (1) make technical disclosures on its software to potential rivals, (2) allow PC makers to add rivals' software to Windows operating system and delete Microsoft applications, and (3) license intellectual property to third parties. A three-person committee was set up
to ensure that Microsoft lived up to the agreement. The committee would remain

Continued. . .

in existence for five years unless Microsoft violated the terms of the agreement, in which case the committee's life would be extended to seven years. Competitors regarded the settlement agreement as nothing less than a sellout. In fact, with the introduction of Windows 98 in 1998 and Windows XP in 2001, Microsoft even increased its near monopoly position in software.

In January 2002, the Netscape Communications Corporation, the commercial pioneer in Web browsing software whose fortune faded as a result of the competition from Microsoft and that was acquired by AOL in 1999, filed a broad antitrust suit against Microsoft, charging that its decline had been the direct result of Microsoft's illegal tactics. This suit may last for years and could lead to billions of dollars in damages on Microsoft if it is found guilty.

Sources: "Is Microsoft Too Powerful?" *Business Week,* March 1, 1995, pp. 82–88; "Windows 95," *Business Week,* July 10, 1995, pp. 94–107; "U.S. Judge Says Microsoft Violated Antitrust Laws with Predatory Behavior," *New York Times,* April 4, 2000, p. 1; "Microsoft Breakup Ordered for Antitrust Law Violations," *New York Times,* June 8, 2000, p. 1; M. Whinston, "Exclusivity and Tying in U.S. vs. Microsoft," *Journal of Economic Perspectives,* Spring 2001, pp. 63–80; "Unsettling Settlement," *The Economist,* November 10, 2001, pp. 57–58; "Settlement or Sellout," *Business Week,* November 19, 2001, p. 114; and "An AOL Unit Sues Microsoft, Saying Tactics Were Illegal," *New York Times,* January 23, 2002, p. C1.

SUMMARY

1. A monopolist is a firm selling a commodity for which there are no close substitutes. Thus, the monopolist faces the industry's negatively sloped demand curve for the commodity, and marginal revenue is smaller than price. Monopoly can be based on control of the entire supply of a required raw material, a patent or government franchise, or declining long-run average costs over a sufficiently large range of outputs so as to leave a single firm supplying the entire market. In the real world, there are usually many forces that limit the monopolist's market power.

2. The best level of output for the monopolist in the short run is the one that maximizes total profits. This occurs where the positive difference between *TR* and *STC* is greatest. The same result is obtained where the *MC* curve intersects the *MR* curve from below. If *P* is smaller than *ATC*, the monopolist will incur a loss in the short run. However, if *P* exceeds *AVC*, it pays for the monopolist to continue to produce because production covers part of the fixed costs. There is no unique relationship between price and output or supply curve for the monopolist.

3. The best or profit-maximizing level of output for the monopolist in the long run is given by the point where the *LMC* curve intersects the *MR* curve from below. The best plant is the one whose *SATC* curve is tangent to the *LAC* at the best level of output. The monopolist can make long-run profits because of restricted entry and does not usually produce at the lowest point on the *LAC* curve. The long-run profits of the monopolist will be capitalized into the market value of the firm and benefit only the original owner of the monopoly. As compared with perfect competition, monopoly restricts output, results in a higher price, redistributes income from consumers to the monopolist, and leads to less efficient use of society's resources.

4. A multiplant monopolist minimizes the total cost of producing the best level of output in the short run when the marginal cost of the last unit of the commodity produced in each plant is

equal to the marginal revenue from selling the combined output. In the long run, a monopolist can build as many identical plants of optimal size (i.e., plants whose *SATC* curves form the lowest point of the *LAC* curve) as required to produce the best level of output.

5. Under first-degree price discrimination, the monopolist sells each unit of the commodity separately and charges the highest price that each consumer is willing to pay rather than go without the commodity. By doing so, the monopolist extracts the entire consumers' surplus. More practical and common is second-degree price discrimination. This refers to the charging of a lower price per unit of output for each additional batch or block of the commodity. By doing so, the monopolist will be able to extract part of the consumers' surplus. Third-degree price discrimination refers to the charging of a higher price for a commodity in the market with the less elastic demand in such a way as to equalize the *MR* of the last unit of the commodity sold in the two markets. To do this, the firm must have some control over prices, it must be able to keep the two markets separate, and the price elasticity of demand must be different in the two markets.

6. International price discrimination is called (persistent) dumping. Under this type of dumping, the monopolist sells the commodity at a higher price at home (where the market demand curve is less elastic) than abroad where the monopolist faces competition from other nations and the market demand curve for the monopolist's product is more elastic.

7. Two-part tariff is the pricing practice under which a monopolist maximizes total profits by charging a usage fee or price equal to its marginal cost and an initial or membership fee equal to the entire consumer surplus. Tying refers to the requirement that a consumer who buys or leases a monopolist's product also purchase another product needed in the use of the first. Bundling is a common form of tying in which the monopolist requires customers buying or leasing one of its products or services to also buy or lease another product or service when customers have different tastes but the monopolist cannot price discriminate (as in tying).

8. A per-unit excise tax will fall on consumers in its entirety under perfect competition, but only in part under monopoly with constant costs. Price discrimination may be necessary to permit the existence of an industry. The commonly held view that monopolists suppress inventions is not generally true. The introduction of Windows 95 by Microsoft is as close as we come today to a pure monopoly in a major U.S. industry.

KEY TERMS

Pure monopoly
Natural monopoly
Price discrimination
First-degree or perfect price
   discrimination

Second-degree or multipart
   price discrimination
Third-degree price
   discrimination
Dumping

Two-part tariff
Tying
Bundling

REVIEW QUESTIONS

1. a. What forces limit the monopolist's market power in the real world?
   b. Why would a monopolist advertise its product if it has a monopoly power over the product?

2. a. Why would a monopolist never operate in the inelastic range of its demand curve?

   b. What would be the best level of output for a monopolist that faced zero average and marginal costs?

3. a. How does the shape of the monopolist's total revenue curve differ from that of a perfectly competitive firm?

b. Why doesn't the monopolist produce where total revenue is maximum?

4. Suppose that a monopolist sells a commodity at the price of $10 per unit and that its marginal cost is also $10. Is the monopolist maximizing total profits? Why?

5. If the monopolist's total profits were entirely taxed away and redistributed to consumers, would any social cost of monopoly remain? Why?

6. If $LS = LAC = LMC = \$3$ in Figure 10.7 shifted upward to $5, what would be

   a. the consumers' surplus?

   b. the monopolist's total profits?

   c. the social cost of monopoly?

7. How could the government entirely eliminate the social cost of monopoly in Figure 10.7?

8. Under what condition would a multiplant monopolist keep some of its plants idle?

9. a. Will a monopolist's total revenue be larger with second-degree price discrimination when the batches on which it charges a uniform price are larger or smaller? Why?

   b. How does a two-part tariff differ from bundling?

10. If the monopolist of Figure 10.11 sold the best level of output at the same price in market 1 and market 2 (i.e., if the monopolist did not practice third-degree price discrimination), how much would it sell in each market?

11. Is persistent dumping good or bad for consumers in the importing country? Against what type of dumping would the nation want to protect itself? Why?

12. Assuming that everything is the same, will a per-unit tax reduce output more under perfect competition or under monopoly? Why?

PROBLEMS

1. Given that the demand function of a monopolist is $Q = 1/5(55 - P)$

   a. derive the monopolist's demand and marginal revenue schedules from $P = \$55$ to $P = \$20$, at $5 intervals.

   b. On the same set of axes, plot the monopolist's demand and marginal revenue curves, and show the range over which D is elastic and inelastic, and the point where D is unitary elastic.

   c. Using the formula relating marginal revenue, price, and elasticity, find the price elasticity of demand at $P = \$40$.

2. Using the TC schedule of Table 8.2 and the demand schedule of Problem 1

   a. construct a table similar to Table 10.2 showing TR, STC, and total profits at each level of output, and indicate by an asterisk the best level of output for the monopolist.

   b. draw a figure similar to Figure 10.2 and determine the best level of output for the monopolist.

3. Using the per-unit cost curves of Figure 8.2 and the demand and marginal revenue curves from Problem 1(b)

   a. draw a figure similar to Figure 10.3 and show the best level of output for the firm.

   b. From your figure in part (a), construct a table similar to Table 10.4 showing P, ATC, profit per unit, total profits, MR, and MC at each level of output.

*4. Suppose the demand curve facing the monopolist changes to $Q' = 1/5(30 - P)$, while cost curves remain unchanged.

   a. Draw a figure similar to Figure 10.4 showing the best level of output.

   b. Does the monopolist make a profit, break even, or incur a loss at the best level of output? Should the monopolist shut down? Why? Where is the monopolist's shut down point?

5. Suppose that the monopolist has unchanged cost curves but faces two alternative demand functions:

   $$Q = 1/5(55 - P) \text{ and } Q'' = 1/5(45 - P)$$

   a. Draw a figure similar to Figure 10.5 showing the best level of output with each demand function.

   b. Which of the two demand functions is more elastic? Where is the monopolist's supply curve?

---

* = Answer provided at end of book.

6. Starting with the cost curves in Figure 8.11 and the demand and marginal revenue curves of problem 1, draw a *SATC* curve (label it *SATC'*$_2$ and its associated *SMC* curve (label it *SMC'*$_2$) showing that the monopolist is in long-run equilibrium at $Q = 5$.

*7. Draw two figures and label the best level of output as $Q*$ and label per-unit profit as AB for a monopolist that

   a. produces at the lowest point on its *LAC* curve.

   b. overutilizes a plant larger than the one that forms the lowest point on its *LAC* curve.

8. Given that the market demand function facing a two-plant monopolist is $Q = 20 - 2P$ and the short-run marginal cost for plant 1 and plant 2 *at* various levels of output are

Q	0	1	2	3	4
SMC_1 (\$)	...	2	4	6	8
SMC_2 (\$)	...	2.50	3.50	4.50	5.50

draw a figure showing *D, MR, SMC*$_1$, *SMC*$_2$, and *MC* schedules of this monopolist. What is the best level of output for the monopolist? How much should the monopolist produce in plant 1 and how much in plant 2?

9. Given the following demand curve of a consumer for a monopolist's product

$$Q = 14 - 2P$$

   a. find the total revenue of the monopolist when it sells six units of the commodity without practicing any form of price discrimination. What is the value of the consumers' surplus?

   b. What would be the total revenue of the monopolist if it practiced first degree price discrimination? How much would the consumers' surplus be in this case?

   c. Answer part (a) if the monopolist charged $P = \$5.50$ for the first three units of the commodity and $P = \$4$ for the next three units. What type of price discrimination is this?

   d. With $MC = \$4$, what two-part tariff should the monopolist use to maximize total profits? What if $MC = 0$?

*10. With reference to Figure 10.11, use formula [5-8] to prove that if the monopolist charges $P = \$4.50$ in market 2, it must charge $P = \$7$ in market 1 to maximize total profits with third degree price discrimination.

11. With reference to Figure 10.13, compare the effect of a \$4 per-unit tax if the industry is perfectly competitive or a monopoly.

*12. Starting from Table 10.3 and Figure 10.3, construct a table and draw a figure showing

   a. how a lump-sum tax can be used to eliminate all of the monopolist's profits.

   b. what would happen if the government imposed a per-unit tax of \$2.50.

INTERNET SITE ADDRESSES

http://www.ci.chi.il.us/ConsumerServices/
auction2001.html

Third-degree price discrimination is examined in:

http://www.coned.com

http://www.supermarkets.com

http://www.coolsaving.com

On the antidumping case that Kodak brought against
Fuji, see:

http://www.gwu.edu/~trade/fairtrade/fairpapers/
ddaniels.html

http://www.euroeunio.org/news/press/1998-1/
pr10-98.htm

An excellent graphical presentation of price
discrimination, peak-load pricing, two-part
pricing, and bundling is found in:

http://pacific.commerce.ubc.cal/frank/comm295/
Oct22_2001.ppt-

The Microsoft antitrust cases are examined in:

http://www.usdoj.gov/cases/ms_index.htm

http://www.usdoj.gov.atr

## CHAPTER 11

Price and Output Under Monopolistic Competition and Oligopoly

I n this chapter, we bring together the theory of consumer behavior and demand (from Part Two) and the theory of production and costs (from Chapters 7 and 8) to analyze how price and output are determined under monopolistic competition and oligopoly. These fall between the two extremes of perfect competition and pure monopoly in the spectrum or range of market organizations, and, as such, they contain elements of both.

As with perfect competition and monopoly, the best level of output for a monopolistic competitor and oligopolist is where marginal revenue equals marginal cost. But, as in the case of monopoly, price exceeds marginal revenue and marginal cost. This means that monopolistically competitive and oligopolistic firms are able to somewhat restrict output and charge consumers a higher price than perfect competitors would, but their market power is not as great as that of the monopolist.

The chapter begins by examining the meaning and importance of monopolistic competition; it shows how the equilibrium price and quantity are determined in the short run and in the long run, and analyzes product variation and selling expenses. Then, after discussing the meaning and sources of oligopoly, we examine various models of oligopoly pricing and output. We will see that there is no general theory of oligopoly but a number of models of various degrees of realism. Subsequently, we discuss the long-run efficiency implications of oligopoly, review some other oligopolistic pricing practices, and examine the growth in the number and size of international oligopolists. In the next chapter, we will consider oligopolistic behavior with a novel approach called game theory. Chapter 13 deals with market structure, efficiency, and regulation.

MONOPOLISTIC COMPETITION: MANY SELLERS OF A DIFFERENTIATED PRODUCT

In Chapter 9 we defined perfect competition as the form of market organization in which there are many sellers of a homogeneous product. In Chapter 10 we defined pure monopoly as a single seller of a commodity for which there are no close substitutes. Between these two extreme forms of market organization lies **monopolistic competition.** This refers to the case in which there are many sellers of a heterogeneous or differentiated product, and entry into or exit from the industry is rather easy in the long run.

Differentiated products are products that are similar but not identical. The similarity of differentiated products arises from the fact that they satisfy the same basic consumption needs. Examples are the numerous brands of breakfast cereals, toothpaste, cigarettes, detergents, and cold medicines on the market today. The differentiation may be real (as in the case of the various breakfast cereals with various nutritional and sugar contents) or imaginary (as in the case of the different brands of aspirin, all of which contain the same ingredients). Product differentiation may also be based entirely on some sellers being more or less conveniently located or on the kind of service they provide (i.e., more or less friendly).

As the name implies, monopolistic competition is a blend of competition and monopoly. The competitive element arises because there are many sellers of the differentiated product, each of which is too small to affect the other sellers. Firms can also enter and leave a monopolistically competitive industry rather easily in the long run. The monopolistic element arises from product differentiation. That is, since the product of each seller is similar but not identical, each seller has a monopoly power over the *specific* product it sells. This monopoly power, however, is severely limited by the existence of close substitutes. Thus, if a seller of a particular brand of aspirin charged a price more than a few pennies higher than competitive brands, it would lose a great deal of its sales.

Monopolistic competition is most common in the retail and service sectors of the economy. Nationally, clothing, cotton textiles, and food processing are industries that come closest to monopolistic competition. Locally, the best examples of monopolistic competition are the many gasoline stations, barber shops, grocery stores, drug stores, newspaper stands, restaurants, pizzerias, and liquor stores, all located near one another. Each of these businesses has some monopoly power over its competitors due to the uniqueness of its product, better location, slightly lower prices, better service, greater range of products, and so on. Yet, this market power is very limited due to the availability of close substitutes.

Because each firm produces a somewhat different product under monopolistic competition, we cannot define the industry (which refers to the producers of an *identical* product). Chamberlin, who introduced the theory of monopolistic competition in the early 1930s, sought to overcome this difficulty by lumping all the sellers of *similar* products into a **product group.** For simplicity, we will continue to use the term "industry" here, but in this broader sense (i.e., to refer to all the sellers of the differentiated products in a product group). However, because of product differentiation, we cannot derive the industry demand and supply curves as we did under perfect competition, and we do not have a single equilibrium price for the differentiated product, but a cluster of prices. Thus, our graphic analysis will have to be confined to the "typical" or "representative" firm rather than to the industry. Under monopolistic competition, firms can affect the volume of their sales by changing the product price, by changing the characteristics of the product, or by varying their selling expenses (such as advertising). We will deal with each of these choice-related variables next.

11.2 MONOPOLISTIC COMPETITION: SHORT-RUN AND LONG-RUN ANALYSIS

In this section, we examine how a monopolistically competitive firm determines its best level of output and price in the short run and in the long run on the assumption that the firm has already decided on the characteristics of the product to produce and on the selling expenses to incur. Later, we examine product variation and selling expenses and evaluate the theory of monopolistic competition.

Price and Output Decisions Under Monopolistic Competition

Because a monopolistically competitive firm produces a differentiated product, the demand curve it faces is negatively sloped; but since there are many close substitutes for the product, the demand curve is highly price elastic. The price elasticity of demand is higher the smaller is the degree of product differentiation. As in the case of monopoly, since the demand curve facing a monopolistic competitor is negatively sloped, the corresponding marginal revenue curve is below it, with the same price intercept and twice the absolute slope. As for firms under any type of market structure, the best level of output for the monopolistically competitive firm in the short run is where marginal revenue equals marginal cost, provided that price exceeds the average variable cost. This is shown in the left panel of Figure 11.1.

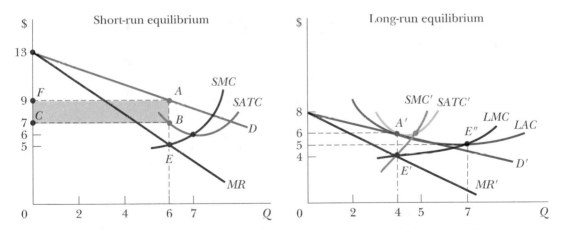

FIGURE 11.1   Short-Run and Long-Run Price and Output Determination Under Monopolistic Competition   The left panel shows that in the short run the firm produces six units, given by point *E*, where *MR = SMC*. At *Q* = 6, *P* = $9 (point *A* on the *D* curve) and *SATC* = $7 (point *B*), so that the firm maximizes profits of *AB* = $2 per unit and *ABCF* = $12 in total (the shaded area). The right panel shows that in the long run the firm produces four units, given by point *E'*, where *MR' = LMC = SMC'*. At *Q* = 4, *P* = *LAC* = *SATC'* = $6 (point *A'*), so that the firm breaks even. This compares to *Q* = 7, where *P* = lowest *LAC* = $5 (point *E''*) under long-run perfectly competitive equilibrium.

The left panel of Figure 11.1 shows that the best level of output for the typical or representative monopolistically competitive firm in the short run is six units and is given by point E, at which $MR = SMC$. At $Q < 6$, $MR > SMC$ and the total profits of the firm increase by expanding output. At $Q > 6$, $SMC > MR$ and the total profits of the firm increase by *reducing* output. To sell the best level of output (i.e., six units) the firm charges a price of $9 per unit (point A on the D curve). Since at $Q = 6$, $SATC = \$7$ (point B in the figure), the monopolistic competitor earns a profit of $AB = \$2$ per unit and $ABCF = \$12$ in total (the shaded area in the figure). As in the case of a perfectly competitive firm and monopolist, the monopolistic competitor can earn profits, break even, or incur losses in the short run. If at the best level of output, $P > SATC$, the firm earns a profit; if $P = SATC$, the firm breaks even; and if $P < SATC$, the firm incurs losses, but it minimizes losses by continuing to produce as long as $P > AVC$. Finally, since the demand curve facing a monopolistic competitor is negatively sloped, $MR = SMC < P$ at the best level of output, so that (as in the case of monopoly) the rising portion of the MC curve above the AVC curve does not represent the short-run supply curve of the monopolistic competitor.

Since the firm in the left panel of Figure 11.1 earns profits in the short run, more firms will enter the market in the long run because entry is easy. With more firms sharing the market, the demand curve facing each monopolistic competitor shifts to the left (as its market share decreases) until it becomes tangent to the firm's LAC curve. Thus, in the long run, all monopolistically competitive firms break even and produce on the negatively sloped portion of their LAC curve (rather than at the lowest point, as in the case of perfect competition). This is shown in the right panel of Figure 11.1.

In the right panel of Figure 11.1, D' is the new demand curve facing the monopolistically competitive firm in the long run. Demand curve D' is lower and more price elastic than demand curve D that the firm faced in the short run. This is because, as more firms enter the monopolistically competitive market in the long run (attracted by potential profits), the monopolistic competitor is left with a smaller share of the market and faces greater competition from the greater range of (differentiated) products that becomes available in the long run. Demand curve D' is tangent to the LAC and $SATC'$ curves at point A'—the output at which $MR' = LMC = SMC'$ (point E' in the figure). Thus, the monopolistic competitor sells four units of the product at the price of $6 per unit and breaks even in the long run (as compared to $Q = 6$ and $P = \$9$ and profits of $2 per unit and $12 in total in the short run). At any other price, the monopolistically competitive firm would incur losses in the long run, and with a different number of firms it would not break even.

The fact that the monopolistically competitive firm produces to the left of the lowest point on its LAC curve when in long-run equilibrium means that the average cost of production and price of the product under monopolistic competition are higher than under perfect competition ($6 at point A' as compared with $5 at point E'', respectively, in the right panel of Figure 11.1). This difference, however, is not large, because the demand curve faced by the monopolistic competitor is very elastic. In any event, the slightly higher LAC and P under monopolistic competition than under perfect competition can be regarded as the cost that consumers willingly pay for having a variety of differentiated products appealing to different consumer tastes, rather than a single undifferentiated product.

The difference between the level of output indicated by the lowest point on the LAC curve and the monopolistic competitor's output when in long-run equilibrium measures **excess capacity.** In the right panel of Figure 11.1, excess capacity is three units, given by $Q = 7$ at the lowest point on the LAC curve minus $Q = 4$ indicated by point A' on the

LAC curve at which the firm produces in the long run. Excess capacity permits more firms to exist (i.e., it leads to some overcrowding) in monopolistically competitive markets as compared with perfect competition. Consumers, however, seem to prefer that firms selling some services operate with some unused capacity (i.e., they are willing to pay a slightly higher price for getting a haircut, filling up on gasoline, checking out at a grocery store, and eating at a restaurant) so as to avoid waiting in long lines.

Product Variation and Selling Expenses

Under monopolistic competition, a firm can increase its expenditures on product variation and selling effort to increase the demand for its product and make it more price inelastic. **Product variation** refers to changes in some of the characteristics of the product that a monopolistic competitor undertakes in order to make its product more appealing to consumers. For example, producers may reduce the sugar and increase the fiber content of breakfast cereals. **Selling expenses** are all those expenses that the firm incurs to advertise the product, increase its sales force, provide better service for its product, and so on. Product variation and selling expenses can increase the firm's sales and profits, but they also lead to additional costs. A firm should spend more on product variation and selling effort as long as the *MR* from these efforts exceeds the *MC* and until $MR = MC$ (*see Example* 1–4). While spending more on product variation and selling effort (nonprice competition) can increase profits in the short run, monopolistically competitive firms will break even in the long run because of imitation and the entrance of new firms. This is shown in Figure 11.2.

In Figure 11.2, *D″* and *MR″* are demand and marginal revenue curves that are higher than *D′* and *MR′* in the right panel of Figure 11.1 as a result of greater product variation and selling expenses. The *LAC* curve is that of Figure 11.1, while *LAC** and *LMC** are the long-run average and marginal cost curves resulting from greater product variation and selling expenses. Note that the vertical distance between *LAC** and *LAC* increases on the (realistic) assumption that to sell greater quantities of the product requires larger expenses per unit on product variation and selling effort. While these efforts can lead to larger short-run profits, however, our typical or representative firm will break even in the long run because other firms can also increase product variation and selling expenses, and more firms can also enter the market in the long run. The long-run equilibrium of our representative firm is given by point *A** in Figure 11.2, at which $Q = 5$ and $P = LAC^* = \$8$ and $MR'' = LMC^*$ (point *E**). At point *A** the firm charges a higher price and sells a greater quantity than at point *A′* in the right panel of Figure 11.1, but the firm will nevertheless break even in the long run. If all firms selling similar products increase their expenses on product variation and selling effort, each firm may retain only its share of an expanding market in the long run.

Two important questions arise with respect to selling expenses in general and advertising in particular. First, is advertising manipulative, and does it create false needs? Second, does advertising increase or reduce the degree of competition in a market? The manipulative view that advertising creates false needs has been forcefully advanced by Galbraith.[1] Why, Galbraith asks, would firms keep spending millions on advertising if it didn't work? Recent studies on cigarette and beer consumption in the United States and Canada, however, have shown that although advertising does affect brand choices, it does not seem to be very effective in increasing the overall consumption of a product. With regard to the second

---

[1] J. K. Galbraith, The Affluent Society (Boston: Houghton Mifflin, 1958).

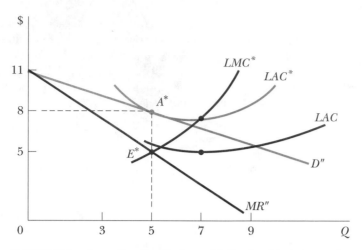

FIGURE 11.2   Long-Run Equilibrium with Product Variation and Selling Expenses   Curves D'' and MR'', as well as LAC^* and LMC^*, are higher than in the right panel of Figure 11.1 because of the firm's greater expenses on product variation and selling effort. While these efforts can increase the firm's profits in the short run, in the long run the firm breaks even. This is shown by point A^*, at which $Q = 5$ units and $P = LAC^* = \$8$, and $MR'' = LMC^*$ (point E^*). At point A^* the firm charges a higher price and sells a greater quantity than at point A' in the right panel of Figure 11.1, but the firm will nevertheless only break even in the long run.

question, a recent study has found that industries with higher-than-average advertising expenditures relative to sales had lower rates of price increases and higher rates of output increases than the average for 150 major U.S. industries studied from 1963 to 1977.[2] Thus, on balance (and as Example 11–1 clearly indicates), advertising seems to enhance, rather than restrict, competition. Even though some advertising is manipulative and can act as a barrier to entry, a great deal of it is informative and increases market competition. More will be said about advertising in Chapter 19, which deals with the economics of information.

EXAMPLE 11–1

Advertisers Are Taking on Competitors by Name . . . and Are Being Sued

Since 1981 when the National Association of Broadcasters abolished its guidelines against making disparaging remarks against competitors' products, advertisers have taken their gloves off and have begun to praise the superior qualities of their products,

---

[2] E. W. Eckard, "Advertising, Concentration Changes, and Consumer Welfare," *Review of Economics and Statistics,* May 1988, pp. 340–343; and "Cigarette Advertising and Competition," *The Margin,* March/April 1990, p. 22.

not compared to "brand X" as before 1981 but by identifying competitors' products by name. The Federal Trade Commission welcomed the change because it anticipated that this would increase competition and lead to better-quality products at lower prices. Some of these hopes have in fact been realized. For example, the price of eyeglasses was found to be much higher in states that prohibited advertising by optometrists and opticians than in states that allowed such advertising, without any increase in the probability of having the wrong eyeglass prescription. Similarly, the price of an uncontested divorce dropped from $350 to $150 in Phoenix, Arizona, after the Supreme Court allowed advertising for legal services.

Although less sportsmanlike and possibly resulting in legal suits, advertisers have been willing to take on competitors by name because the technique seems very effective. For example, Burger King sales soared when it began to attack McDonald's by name. However, Gillette has recently sued Wilkinson Sword, MCI sued AT&T, and Alpo Pet foods sued Ralston Purina over allegedly misleading ad claims. The stakes can be very high—just legal fees in battles between large companies can run as high as $200,000 per month! In the future, we are thus likely to see a return to comparison to "brand X" in many promotion campaigns, or at least to be much more careful in mentioning a competitor's product by name in advertising.

AT&T and MCI, however, do not seem ready for a truce in their long-running nasty campaign to take customers from each other for long-distance telephone service. In a recent TV ad, AT&T offered reason 117 for sticking with it rather than using MCI. MCI responded with an ad of its own in which it accused AT&T of either practicing deception or being lousy at math. Then AT&T lowered rates to 10 cents a minute for around-the-clock long distance calls, and MCI promptly responded with TV ads and direct telephone marketing advertising a five-cents-per-minute charge for long distance calls during off-peak hours. Consumers are thoroughly confused but are benefiting greatly from rapidly falling rates.

Sources: "Advertisers Remove the Cover from Brand X," *U.S. News & World Report,* December 19, 1983, pp. 75–76; L. Benham, "The Effect of Advertising on the Price of Eyeglasses," *Journal of Law and Economics,* October 1973, pp. 337–352; "Lawyers Are Facing Surge in Competition as Courts Drop Curbs," *The Wall Street Journal,* October 18, 1978, p. 1; "A Comeback May Be Ahead for Brand X," *Business Week,* December 1989, p. 35; "Long-Distance Risks of AT&T MCI War," *The Wall Street Journal,* April 14, 1993, p. B9; "MCI WorldCom Unveils Rate Reduction on Long Distance to Five Cents a Minute," *The Wall Street Journal,* August 9, 1999, p. A2; and "Marketers Increasingly Dispute Health Claims of Rivals' Products," *Wall Street Journal,* April 4, 2002, p. B1.

How Useful Is the Theory of Monopolistic Competition?

When the theory of monopolistic competition was introduced 70 years ago, it was hailed as a significant theoretical breakthrough. Today, economists have grown somewhat disenchanted with it. There are several reasons for this disenchantment.

First, it may be difficult to define the market and determine the firms and products to include in the theory. For example, should moist paper tissues be included with other paper tissues or with soaps? Are toothpaste, dental floss, toothpicks, and water picks part of the same market or product group?

Second, and more important, in markets where there are many small sellers, product differentiation has been found to be slight. As a result, the demand curve facing the monopolistic competitor is close to being horizontal. Under these circumstances, the perfectly competitive model provides a good approximation to the monopolistically competitive solution, and it is also much easier to use for analysis.[3]

Third, in many markets where there are strong brand preferences, it usually turns out that there are only a few producers, so that the market is oligopolistic rather than monopolistically competitive. For example, while there are numerous brands of breakfast cereals, cigarettes, toothpaste, detergents, soaps, and many other consumer products on the market today (so that the markets may seem to be monopolistically competitive), on closer examination we find that these products are produced by only four or five very large firms (so that the market is in fact oligopolistic). Millions of dollars are likely to be needed to develop and promote a new product in these markets, and this represents a significant barrier to entry into the market. In fact, only a handful of firms have been able to enter these markets during the past two decades.

Fourth (and related to the third point), even in a market where there are many small sellers of a product or service (say, gasoline stations), a change in price by one seller may have little or no effect on most other gasoline stations located far away from it, but the price change will have a significant impact on competitors in the immediate vicinity. These nearby stations are, therefore, likely to react to a reduction in price or to an increased promotional effort on the part of the nearby station. The nearby station is also likely to be aware of this fact and consider it in deciding to change its price or in undertaking a new promotional effort. In cases such as this, the oligopoly model is more appropriate than the model of monopolistic competition.

Despite these serious criticisms, the monopolistically competitive model does provide some important insights, such as the emphasis on product differentiation and selling expenses, which are also applicable to oligopolistic markets, to which we turn next.

11.3 OLIGOPOLY: INTERDEPENDENCE AMONG THE FEW PRODUCERS IN THE INDUSTRY

Oligopoly is the form of market organization in which there are few sellers of a homogeneous or differentiated product. If there are only two sellers, we have a **duopoly.** If the product is homogeneous, we have a **pure oligopoly.** If the product is differentiated, we have a **differentiated oligopoly.** Although entry into an oligopolistic industry is possible, it is not easy (as evidenced by the fact that there are only a few firms in the industry). While there are many firms selling a homogeneous product under perfect competition, many firms selling a differentiated product in monopolistic competition, and only a single firm selling a product with no good substitutes under monopoly, under oligopoly there are few sellers of a homogeneous or differentiated product.

---

[3] The short-run and long-run analysis of monopolistic competition presented here is a simplification of the full-fledged monopolistically competitive model introduced by Chamberlin in 1933 (see E. Chamberlin, *The Theory of Monopolistic Competition* (Cambridge, MA: Harvard University Press, 1933).

Oligopoly is the most prevalent form of market organization in the manufacturing sector of the United States and other industrial countries. Some oligopolistic industries in the United States are cigarettes, beer, aircraft, breakfast cereals, automobiles, tires, soap and detergents, office machinery, and many others. Some of the products (such as steel and aluminum) are homogeneous, whereas others (such as cigarettes, beer, breakfast cereals, and soaps and detergents) are differentiated. For simplicity, we will deal mostly with pure oligopolies (where products are homogeneous) in this chapter.

Because there are only a few firms selling a homogeneous or differentiated product in oligopolistic markets, the action of each firm affects the other firms in the industry, and vice versa. For example, when GM introduced zero-interest financing or price rebates in the sale of its automobiles, Ford and other car manufacturers selling on the American market immediately followed with zero-interest financing and price rebates of their own. Furthermore, since price competition can lead to ruinous price wars, oligopolists usually prefer to compete on the basis of product differentiation, advertising, and service. Yet, even here, if GM mounts a major advertising campaign, Ford and Chrysler are likely to soon respond in kind. Every time that Coca-Cola or Pepsi mounts a major advertising campaign, the other usually responds with a large advertising campaign of its own.

From what has been said, it is clear that the distinguishing characteristic of oligopoly is the *interdependence* or rivalry among firms in the industry. This interdependence is the natural result of fewness. Since an oligopolist knows that its own actions will have a significant impact on the other oligopolists in the industry, each oligopolist must consider the possible reaction of competitors in deciding its pricing policies, the degree of product differentiation to introduce, the level of advertising to undertake, the amount of service to provide, and so on. Because competitors can react in many different ways (depending on the nature of the industry, the type of product, etc.), we do not have a single oligopoly model but many—each based on the particular behavioral response of competitors to the actions of the first. Because of interdependence, policy decisions on the part of the firm are also much more complex under oligopoly than under other forms of market organization. In this chapter, we present some of the most important oligopoly models. We must keep in mind, however, that each model is usually applicable only to some specific situations, rather than generally, and that most models are more or less unrealistic.

The sources of oligopoly are generally the same as for monopoly: (1) economies of scale may operate over a sufficiently large range of outputs so as to leave only a few firms supplying the entire market; (2) huge capital investments and specialized inputs are usually required to enter an oligopolistic industry (say, automobiles, aluminum, steel, and similar industries), and this acts as an important natural barrier to entry; (3) a few firms may own a patent for the exclusive right to produce a commodity or to use a particular production process; (4) established firms might have a loyal following of customers based on product quality and service that new firms may find very difficult to match; (5) a few firms may own or control the entire supply of a raw material required in the production of the product; and (6) the government may award a franchise to only a few firms to operate in the market. These are not only the sources of oligopoly but also represent the barriers to other firms entering the market in the long run. If entry were not so restricted, the industry would not remain oligopolistic in the long run.

The degree by which an industry is dominated by a few large firms is measured by **concentration ratios,** which give the percentage of total industry sales of the 4, 8, or 12 largest firms in the industry (see Example 11–2). An industry in which the 4-firm concentration ratio is close to 100 is clearly oligopolistic, and industries where this ratio is higher than 50% or 60% are also likely to be oligopolistic. The 4-firm concentration ratio for most manufacturing industries in the United States is between 20% and 80%. As we will see, however, concentration ratios must be used and interpreted with great caution since they may greatly overestimate the market power of the largest firms in an industry.

EXAMPLE 11–2
Industrial Concentration in the United States

Table 11.1 gives the 4-firm and the 8-firm concentration ratios for various industries in the United States from the 1997 Census of Manufacturers (the latest available).

There are several reasons, however, for using these concentration ratios cautiously. First, in industries where imports are significant, concentration ratios may greatly overestimate the relative importance of the largest firms in the industry. For example, since

TABLE 11.1 Concentration Ratios in the United States, 1997

Industry	4-Firm Ratio	8-Firm Ratio
Cigarettes	99	D*
Breweries	90	93
Electric lamp bulbs and parts	89	94
Aircraft	85	96
Breakfast cereals	83	94
Motor vehicles	82	92
Tires	68	86
Soap and detergents	66	78
Office machines	53	68
Men's clothing	47	62
Soft drinks	46	54
Computers	45	69
Cement	34	52
Iron and steel mills	33	53
Pharmaceuticals and medicines	32	48
Book printing	32	45
Petroleum refining	29	49
Stationary	28	42
Canned fruits and vegetables	25	38
Women's dresses	14	24

D* = Data withheld to avoid disclosing company data.

Source: U.S. Bureau of Census, 1997 Census of Manufacturers, *Concentration Ratios in Manufacturing* (Washington, D.C.: U.S. Government Printing Office, June 2001), Table 2, pp. 7–16.

automobile imports represent about 11% of the U.S. auto sales, the real 4-firm concentration ratio in the automobile industry (which includes Nissan's U.S. output as the fourth largest U.S. producer) is not 82% (as indicated in the table) but 73% (i.e., 82% times 0.89). Second, concentration ratios refer to the nation as a whole, even though the relevant market may be local. For example, the 4-firm concentration ratio for the cement industry is 34%, but because of very high transportation costs, only two or three firms may actually compete in many local markets. Third, how broadly or narrowly a product is defined is also very important. For example, the concentration ratio in the office machines industry as a whole is smaller than that in the personal computer segment of the market. Fourth, concentration ratios do not give any indication of potential entrants into the market and of the degree of actual and potential competition in the industry. Indeed, as the *theory of contestable markets* discussed in Chapter 13 shows, vigorous competition can take place even among few sellers. In short, concentration ratios provide only one dimension of the degree of competition in the market, and, although useful, they must be used with great caution.

11.4   THE COURNOT AND THE KINKED-DEMAND CURVE MODELS

Now we examine two of the earliest and best known oligopoly models: the Cournot model and the kinked-demand curve model. In the Cournot model, oligopolists never recognize their interdependence or rivalry. As such, the Cournot model is quite unrealistic. Nevertheless, the model is useful in highlighting the interdependence that exists among oligopolistic firms (even though they do not actually recognize it). The Cournot model is also the forerunner of more realistic models. In the kinked-demand curve model, oligopolists do recognize their interdependence or rivalry. This model also faces many shortcomings, but it represents a step forward in the direction of greater realism in the analysis of oligopolistic behavior.

The Cournot Model: Interdependence Not Recognized[4]

The first formal oligopoly model was introduced by the French economist Augustin Cournot more than 160 years ago.[5] For simplicity, Cournot assumed that there were only two firms (duopoly) selling identical spring water. Consumers came to the springs with their own containers, so that the marginal cost of production was zero for the two firms. With these assumptions, the analysis is greatly simplified without losing the essence of the model.[6]

---

[4] A more advanced and complete treatment of the Cournot model, as well as an important extension of it (the Stackelberg model), is provided in the appendix to this chapter.

[5] A. Cournot, *Recherches sur les principes mathematiques de la theorie des richess* (Paris: 1838). English translation by N. Bacon, *Researches into the Mathematical Principles of the Theory of Wealth* (New York: Macmillan, 1897).

[6] The model, however, can be extended to deal with more than two firms and nonzero marginal costs.

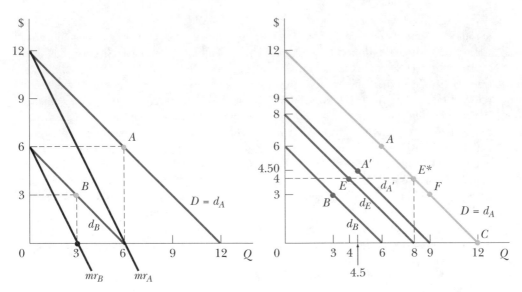

FIGURE 11.3 The Cournot Model In the left panel, D is the market demand curve for spring water. The marginal cost of production is assumed to be zero. When only firm A is the market, $D = d_A$ and the firm maximizes profits by selling $Q = 6$ at $P = \$6$ (point A, given by $mr_A = MC = 0$). When firm B enters the market, it will face d_B (given by shifting market demand curve D to the left by the six units sold by A). Firm B maximizes profits by selling $Q = 3$ at $P = \$3$ (point B, the midpoint of d_B at which $mr_B = MC = 0$). Duopolist A now faces d'_A (given by D minus 3 in the right panel) and maximizes profits by selling $Q = 4.5$ at $P = \$4.50$ (point A'). The process continues until each duopolist is at point E on d_E and sells $Q = 4$ at $P = \$4$.

The basic behavioral assumption made in the **Cournot model** is that each firm, while trying to maximize profits, assumes that the other duopolist holds its *output* constant at the existing level. The result is a cycle of moves and countermoves by the duopolists until each sells one-third of the total industry output. This is shown in Figure 11.3.

In the left panel of Figure 11.3, D is the market demand curve for spring water. Initially, firm A is the only firm in the market, and thus, it faces the total market demand curve. That is, $D = d_A$. The marginal revenue curve of firm A is then mr_A (see the figure). Since the marginal cost is zero, the MC curve coincides with the horizontal axis. Under these circumstances, firm A maximizes total profits where $mr_A = MC = 0$. Firm A sells six units of spring water at $P = \$6$ so that its total revenue (TR) is $36 (point A in the left panel). This is the monopoly solution. Note that point A is the midpoint of demand curve $D = d_A$, at which price elasticity is 1 and TR is maximum (see Section 5.6). With total costs equal to zero, total profits equal $TR = \$36$.

Next, assume that firm B enters the market and believes that firm A will continue to sell six units. The demand curve that firm B faces is then d_B in the left panel, which is obtained by subtracting the six units sold by firm A from market demand curve D (i.e., shifting D six units to the left). The marginal revenue curve of firm B is then mr_B. Firm B maximizes total profits where $mr_B = MC = 0$. Therefore, firm B sells three units at

$P = \$3$ (point B, the midpoint of d_B). This is also shown in the right panel of Figure 11.3. Assuming that firm B continues to sell three units, firm A reacts and faces d_A, in the right panel of Figure 11.3 (obtained by subtracting the three units supplied by firm B from market demand curve D). Firm A will then maximize profits by selling 4.5 units (point A', at the midpoint of $d_{A'}$ in the right panel). Firm B now reacts once again and maximizes profits on its new demand curve, which is obtained by shifting market demand curve D to the left by the 4.5 units supplied by firm A (not shown in the right panel of Figure 11.3).

The process continues until each duopolist faces demand curve d_E and maximizes profits by selling four units at $P = \$4$ (point E in the right panel of Figure 11.3).[7] This is equilibrium because whichever firm faces demand curve d_E and reaches point E first, the other will also face d_E (obtained by subtracting the 4 units sold by the first duopolist from market demand curve D) and maximize profits at point E. With each duopolist selling four units, a combined total of eight units will be sold in the market at $P = \$4$ (point E^* on D in the right panel of Figure 11.3). If the market had been organized along perfectly competitive lines, sales would have been twelve units, given by point C, where market demand curve D intercepts the horizontal axis. The reason for this is that since we have assumed costs to be zero, price will also have to be zero for each competitive firm to break even, as required, when the perfectly competitive industry is in long-run equilibrium.

Thus, the duopolists supply one-third or four units each (and two-thirds or eight units together) of the total perfectly competitive market quantity of twelve units. Note that the Cournot duopoly outcome of $P = \$4$ and $Q = 8$ lies between the monopoly equilibrium of $P = \$6$ and $Q = 6$ and the competitive equilibrium of $P = \$0$ and $Q = 12$. The final Cournot equilibrium reflects the interdependence between the duopolists, even though they (rather naively) do not recognize it.

In a more advanced treatment, we could show that with three oligopolists, each would supply one-fourth (i.e., three units) of the perfectly competitive market of twelve units and three-fourths (i.e., nine units) in total. Note that when $Q = 9$, $P = \$3$ on market demand curve D (point F in the right panel of Figure 11.3). Thus, as the number of firms increases, the total combined output of all the firms together increases and price falls (compare equilibrium point A with only firm A in the market, with equilibrium point E^* with firms A and B, and equilibrium point F with three firms). Eventually, as more firms enter, the market will no longer be oligopolistic. In the limit, with many firms, total output will approach twelve units and price will approach zero (the perfectly competitive solution—point C in the right panel of Figure 11.3).

The same result (i.e., zero profit) would occur even with only two firms (duopoly), if each firm assumed that the other kept its *price* rather than its quantity constant (as in the Cournot model). In that case, the first firm enters the market and maximizes its profits by producing 6 units at the price of $6. The second firm, assuming that the first will keep its price constant, will lower its price just a little and captures the entire market (because the product is homogeneous). The first firm will then react by lowering its price even more and recaptures the entire market. If the duopolists do not recognize their interdependence

---

[7] How this equilibrium is reached is shown in the appendix to this chapter. All that is important at this point is to show that when each duopolist faces demand curve d_E and sells four units at $P = \$4$ (i.e., is at point E), each duopolist and the market as a whole is in equilibrium.

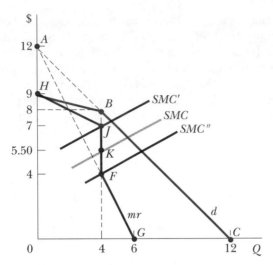

FIGURE 11.4   The Kinked-Demand Curve Model   The demand curve facing the oligopolist is *d* or *HBC* and has a "kink" at the prevailing price of $8 and $Q = 4$ (point *B*), on the assumption that competitors match price cuts but not price increases. The marginal revenue curve is *mr* or *HJKFG*. The oligopolist maximizes profits by selling $Q = 4$ at $P = $8 (given by point *K*, where the *SMC* curve intersects the discontinuous segment of the *mr* curve). Any shift between *SMC'* and *SMC"* will leave price and output unchanged.

(as in the Cournot model), the process will continue until each firm sells 6 units at zero price and makes zero profits. This is the **Bertrand model.**[8]

The Kinked-Demand Curve Model: Interdependence Recognized

The **kinked-demand curve model,** introduced by Paul Sweezy in 1939,[9] attempts to explain the price rigidity that is often observed in some oligopolistic markets. Sweezy postulated that if an oligopolist raised its price, it would lose most of its customers because the other firms in the industry would not match the price increase. On the other hand, an oligopolist could not increase its share of the market by lowering its price, since its competitors would immediately match the price reduction. As a result, according to Sweezy, oligopolists face a demand curve that is highly elastic for price increases and less elastic for price reductions. That is, the demand curve faced by oligopolists has a kink at the established price; and, because of this, oligopolists tend to keep prices constant even in the face of changed costs and demand conditions. This is shown in Figure 11.4.

[8] J. Bertrand, "Theorie Mathematiquede la Richesse Sociale," *Journal de Savantes,* 1983.

[9] P. Sweezy, "Demand under Conditions of Oligopoly," *Journal of Political Economy,* August 1939, pp. 568–573.

In Figure 11.4, the demand curve facing the oligopolist is *d* or *HBC* and has a "kink" at the prevailing price of $8 and $Q = 4$ (point *B*). The demand curve is much more elastic above than below the kink on the assumption that competitors will not match price increases but quickly match price cuts.[10] Thus, the oligopolist's marginal revenue curve is *mr* or *HJKFG*. Segment *HJ* of the *mr* curve corresponds to segment *HB* of the demand curve, and segment *FG* of the *mr* curve corresponds to segment *BC* of the demand curve (see the figure). The kink at point *B* on the demand curve results in discontinuity *JF* in the *mr* curve.

With *SMC* as the short-run marginal cost curve, the oligopolist will maximize profits by selling four units of output (given by point *K*, where the *SMC* curve intersects the discontinuous segment of the *mr* curve) at $P = \$8$. Any shift in the oligopolist's *SMC* curve that falls within the discontinuous segment of the *mr* curve will leave the oligopolist's price and output unchanged. That is, the oligopolist's best level of output will continue to be four units and price $8 for any shift in the *SMC* curve up to *SMC'* or down to *SMC''* (see the figure). Only if the *SMC* curve shifts above the *SMC'* curve will the oligopolist raise its price, and only if the *SMC* curve shifts below the *SMC''* curve will the oligopolist lower its price (see Problem 3). Similarly, a rightward or leftward shift in the demand curve will induce the oligopolist to increase or decrease output, respectively, but to keep its price unchanged if the kink remains at the same level (see Problem 4, with the answer at the end of the book). Note that the marginal principle postulating that the best level of output for the firm occurs where $MR = MC$ is still valid, even though the *MR* curve is discontinuous in this case.

When the kinked-demand curve model was first introduced, it was hailed by some economists as a general theory of oligopoly. Yet the model failed to live up to its expectations. For example, Stigler found no evidence that oligopolists were reluctant to match price increases as readily as price reductions, and thus he seriously questioned the existence of the kink.[11] Researchers in other oligopolistic industries found the same thing. Even more serious is the criticism that although the kinked-demand curve model can *rationalize* the existence of rigid prices where they occur, it cannot *explain* at what price the kink occurs in the first place. Since one of the major aims of microeconomic theory is to explain how prices are determined, this theory is, at best, incomplete.

11.5   COLLUSION: CARTELS AND PRICE LEADERSHIP MODELS

In the oligopoly models we have examined so far, oligopolists did not collude. In view of the interdependence in oligopolistic markets, however, there is a natural tendency to collude. With **collusion,** oligopolistic firms can avoid behavior that is detrimental to their general interest (for example, price wars) and adopt policies that increase their profits. Collusion can be overt (i.e., explicit), as in a centralized cartel, or tacit (i.e., implicit), as in

---

[10] That is, since competitors do not match price increases, the quantity demanded from the oligopolist that increases price *falls a great deal.* On the other hand, since competitors quickly match price reductions, the quantity demanded from the oligopolist that cuts price *does not increase very much.* This makes the demand curve faced by an oligopolist more elastic for price increases than for price reductions.

[11] G. Stigler, "The Kinky Oligopoly Demand Curve and Rigid Prices," *Journal of Political Economy,* October 1947, pp. 432–449.

price leadership models. In this section we examine oligopolistic models with collusion and provide several real-world examples. (Antitrust laws forbidding collusion in the United States are examined in Chapter 13.)

A Centralized Cartel Operates as a Monopolist

A **cartel** is a formal organization of producers of a commodity. Its purpose is to coordinate the policies of the member firms so as to increase profits. Cartels are illegal in the United States under the provision of the Sherman Antitrust Act passed in 1890 (see Section 13.4) but not in some other nations. Of the many types of cartels, the **centralized cartel** is at one extreme. The centralized cartel sets the monopoly price for the commodity, allocates the monopoly output among the member firms, and determines how the monopoly profits are to be shared. The centralized cartel is shown in Figure 11.5.

In Figure 11.5, D is the total market demand curve and MR is the corresponding marginal revenue curve for a homogeneous commodity produced by, say, four firms that have formed a centralized cartel. The ΣSMC curve for the cartel is obtained by summing

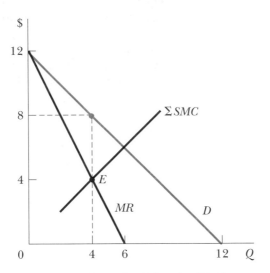

FIGURE 11.5   Centralized Cartel D is the market demand curve and MR is the corresponding marginal revenue curve for a homogeneous commodity produced by the four firms in centralized cartel. The ΣSMC curve for the cartel is obtained by summing horizontally the four firms' SMC curves on the assumption that input prices are constant. The centralized authority will set $P = \$8$ and $Q = 4$ (given by point E, where the ΣSMC curve intersects the MR curve from below). This is the monopoly solution.

horizontally the *SMC* curve of the four firms on the assumption that input prices remain constant. The centralized authority will set $P = \$8$ and sell $Q = 4$ (given by point E, where the ΣSMC curve intersects the *MR* curve from below). This is the monopoly solution. To minimize production costs, the centralized authority will have to allocate output among the four firms in such a way that the *SMC* of the last unit produced by each firm is equal. If the *SMC* of one firm is higher than for the other firms, the total costs of the cartel as a whole can be reduced by shifting some production from the firm with higher *SMC* to the other firms until the *SMC* of the last unit produced by all firms is equal. The cartel will also have to decide on the distribution of profits.

If all firms are the same size and have identical cost curves, then it is very likely that each firm will be allocated the same output and will share equally in the profits generated by the cartel. In Figure 11.5, each firm would be allocated one unit of output. The result would be the same if a monopolist acquired the four firms and operated them as a multiplant monopolist. If the firms in the cartel are different sizes and have different costs, it will be more difficult to agree on the share of output and profits. Then the allocation of output is likely to be based on past output, present capacity, and bargaining ability of each firm, rather than on the equalization of the *SMC* of the last unit of output produced by all member firms. Sometimes the market is divided among the firms in the industry as indicated in the next subsection.

Cartels often fail; there are several reasons for this. First, it is very difficult to organize all the producers of a commodity if there are more than a few producers. Second, as pointed out earlier, it is difficult to reach agreement among the member firms on how to allocate output and profits when firms face different cost curves. Third, there is a strong incentive for each firm to remain outside the cartel or cheat on the cartel by selling more than its quota at the high price resulting from the limited output of the other cartel members. Fourth, monopoly profits are likely to attract other firms into the industry and undermine the cartel agreement.

Even though cartels are illegal in the United States, many trade associations and professional associations perform many of the functions usually associated with cartels. Some cartellike associations are actually sanctioned by the government. An example of this was the American Medical Association, which, by rigidly restricting the number of students admitted to medical schools and forbidding advertising by physicians, ensured for many years very high doctors' fees and incomes. Another example is the New York Taxi and Limousine Commission, which restricts the number of taxis licensed, thus conferring monopoly profits to the original owners of the "medallions" (see Example 10–3). The best example of a successful international cartel is OPEC (the Organization of Petroleum Exporting Countries) during the 1970s and early 1980s (see Example 11–3, which follows).

EXAMPLE 11–3

The Organization of Petroleum Exporting Countries (OPEC) Cartel

It is often asserted that OPEC was able to sharply increase petroleum prices and profits for its members by restricting supply and behaving as a cartel. Eleven nations are presently members of OPEC: Algeria, Indonesia, Iran, Iraq, Kuwait, Libya, Nigeria,

Qatar, Saudi Arabia, the United Arab Emirates, and Venezuela (OPEC used to have 13 members, but Ecuador and Gabon left it).

As a result of supply shocks during the Arab–Israeli war in the fall of 1973 and the Iranian revolution during 1979–1980, OPEC was able to increase the price of petroleum from $2.50 per barrel in 1973 to more than $40 per barrel in 1980. This, however, stimulated conservation in developed nations (by lowering thermostats, switching to small, fuel-efficient automobiles, etc.), expanded exploration and production (by the United Kingdom and Norway in the North Sea, by the United States in Alaska, and by Mexico in newly discovered fields), and led to the switching to other energy sources (such as coal). As a result, from 1974 to 2001, OPEC's share of world oil production fell from 55% to about 37% and its share of world petroleum exports declined from more than 90% to 61%. Although OPEC meets regularly for the purpose of setting petroleum prices and production quotas, it has seldom succeeded in its effort under the conditions of excess supplies that have prevailed since 1980.

In general, the densely populated and low-petroleum reserve countries such as Indonesia, Nigeria, and Iran want to charge high prices to maximize short-run profits; in contrast, the sparsely populated and large-reserve countries such as Saudi Arabia and Kuwait prefer lower prices to discourage conservation and non-OPEC production so as to maximize long-run profits. Be that as it may, OPEC was unable to prevent a decline in petroleum prices to the $15 to $20 range and widespread cheating by its members during the 1980s. Thus, while OPEC is often given as the best example of a sometimes successful cartel, many economists are now convinced that OPEC never really controlled the world crude oil market. Under the conditions of tight supply that prevailed during the 1970s, OPEC was given credit for the sharp increase in petroleum prices; but when excess supplies arose, OPEC was unable to prevent almost equally sharp price declines. Even the mini oil shock resulting from Saddam Hussein's invasion of Kuwait in August 1990 was reversed with the quick end to the Persian Gulf War, so that by the middle of 1991 oil prices were as low as before the invasion of Kuwait.

Since 1997, oil prices have been very volatile, falling when demand fell (as, for example, during the financial and economic crisis in Southeast Asia in 1998 and the recession in 2001) and rising when demand rose (as, for example, during 1999 when growth resumed in Asia and Europe). The average price of a barrel of petroleum was $19 in 1997, it fell to $14 in 1998, it rose to $19 in 1999 and $28 in 2000 (peaking at $34 in March 2000—up from $11 in January 1999), but it then fell to $24 in 2001, and it was $26 in July 2002. Petroleum then started to increase again in spring 2002 as a result of increasing demand and political turmoil in the Middle East. How high petroleum prices will be in the future depend on how strong the world demand for petroleum will be, the political situation in the Middle East and in other petroleum-exporting countries, and on how successful OPEC (with the cooperation of other non-OPEC oil exporters, such as Russia, Mexico and Norway) will be in cutting supplies. Most of the time in the past,

OPEC did not succeed in controlling supply and petroleum prices reflected, for the most part, market conditions.

Sources: "OPEC's Painful Lessons," *New York Times,* December 29, 1985, p. F3; "OPEC Sets New Policy on Quota," *New York Times,* November 29, 1989, p. D1; "Gulf War: An Energy Defeat?," *New York Times,* June 18, 1991, p. D1; "OPEC Plan to Lift Oil Prices Goes Awry," *Wall Street Journal,* March 3, 1995, p. A2; and "Mideast and Venezuela Turmoil Sends Oil Prices into Wild Swing," *New York Times,* April 9, 2002, p. 1.

Market-Sharing Cartel

The difficulties encountered by the members of a centralized cartel (such as agreeing on the price to charge, allocating output and profits among members, and avoiding cheating) make a market-sharing cartel more likely to occur. In a **market-sharing cartel** the member firms agree only on how to share the market. Each firm then operates in only one area or region agreed upon without encroaching on the others' territories. An example is the agreement in the early part of this century between Du Pont (American) and Imperial Chemical (English) for the former to have exclusive selling rights for their products in North America (except for British colonies) and the latter in the British Empire. Under certain simplifying assumptions, a market-sharing cartel can also result in the monopoly solution. This is shown in Figure 11.6.

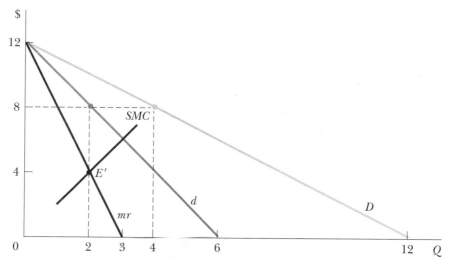

FIGURE 11.6   Market-Sharing Cartel   *D* is the total market demand for a homogeneous commodity, *d* is the half-share demand curve of each firm, and *mr* is the corresponding marginal revenue curve. If each duopolist also has the same *SMC* curve shown in the figure, each will sell two units of output at *P* = $8 (given by point *E'*, at which *mr* = *SMC*). Thus, the duopolists together will sell the monopolist output of four units at *P* = $8.

In Figure 11.6, we assume that there are two identical firms selling a homogeneous product and deciding to share the market equally. D is the total market demand for the commodity; d is the half-share demand curve of each firm, and mr is the corresponding marginal revenue curve. If each firm has the same SMC curve as shown in the figure, according to the marginal principle, each will sell two units of output at $P = \$8$ (given by point E', at which $mr = SMC$). Thus, the duopolists together will sell the monopolist output of four units at $P = \$8$ (see the figure). In the real world there may be more than two firms, each may have different cost curves, and the market may not be shared equally. Thus, we are not likely to have the neat monopoly solution shown above. The firm with greater capacity or operating in an inferior territory may demand a greater share of the market. The result will then depend on bargaining, and the possibility of incursions into each other's territory cannot be excluded.

The firms in a market-sharing cartel can also operate in the same geographic area by deciding which firm is to fill each particular contract. These market-sharing cartels are likely to be unstable due to cheating. Some loose market-sharing cartels are sanctioned by law. For example, local medical and bar associations essentially set the fees that doctors and lawyers are to charge. Similarly, many states had *fair trade laws* (until they became illegal in the mid-1970s), that allowed manufacturers to set the price each retailer was to charge for a product. The market was then shared by means other than price.

EXAMPLE 11–4

The Market-Sharing Ivy Cartel

For more than three decades prior to 1991, the presidents and top financial officers of the eight Ivy League colleges (Brown, Columbia, Cornell, Dartmouth, Harvard, Princeton, Yale, and the University of Pennsylvania), as well as the Massachusetts Institute of Technology (MIT), held yearly meetings at which they exchanged sensitive information about intended tuition increases, the amount of student financial aid packages, and increases in faculty salaries. The result was tuition increases, student financial aid packages, and faculty salary increases that were closely bunched together. For example, the charge for tuition, room, board, and fees at the eight Ivy League colleges and MIT ranged only from $16,841 to $17,100 for the 1988–1989 academic year. The same was true for increases in faculty salaries and for the amount of student aid packages. Specifically, the colleges agreed not to outbid each other in granting aid to top students who had been accepted to more than one school, thus leaving students and their families no reason to shop around for better financial aid packages. In 1986, this "Ivy League cartel" tried to bring Stanford University into the fold—an attempt that failed because (as court documents later showed) Stanford was worried that the Ivies were colluding illegally. Indeed, this is what the U.S. Justice Department subsequently charged.

In May 1991, the Ivy League colleges (while admitting no wrongdoing) signed a consent decree with the Justice Department to stop colluding on tuition, financial aid, and faculty salaries in order to avoid a costly trial, thereby putting an end to their cartel arrangement. The result was clear and immediate: Average increases in private-college tuition, which had soared fivefold between 1971–1972 and 1989–1990 in the face of only a tripling of consumer prices, subsided and were much smaller after 1990. MIT, however, refused to sign the consent decree and chose instead to fight the case in court, where it argued that antitrust laws did not apply to the noncommercial and charitable activities of universities. But in a ten-day trial in August 1992 that cost MIT $1 million, the court found MIT guilty of price fixing and restricting competition by reducing students' ability to get the best financial aid possible. In September 1993, however, a three-judge U.S. Court of Appeals panel reversed the lower court ruling, setting the stage for a settlement, reached in December 1993, under which the Ivy League Universities could meet to discuss their financial-aid policies, as long as they did not discuss individual grants to specific students and accepted students regardless of need (the so-called need-blind admission). As pointed out in Example 10–5, most private colleges not just the Ivies) today engage in "financial-aid leveraging."

Sources: "Ivy League Discussions on Finances Extended to Tuition and Salaries," *Wall Street Journal,* May 8, 1992, p. A1; "M.I.T. Ruled Guilty in Antitrust Case," *New York Times,* September 3, 1992, p. 1; "Antitrust Case Against MIT Dropped Allowing Limited Exchange of Aid Data," *Wall Street Journal,* December 12, 1993, p. A12; "Colleges Manipulate Financial-Aid Offers, Shortchanging Many," *Wall Street Journal,* April 1, 1996, p. A1; "Howls of Ivy," *Barron's,* March 1, 1999, p. 15; and "Second Thoughts on Early Admission," *Business Week,* March 11, 2002, p. 96; and "Yale Seeks Shelter for pacts to End Early Admissions," *Wall Street Journal,* May 3, 2002, p. A2.

Price Leadership

One way by which firms in an oligopolistic market can make necessary price adjustments without fear of starting a price war and without overt collusion is by **price leadership.** The firm generally recognized as the price leader starts the price change and the other firms in the industry quickly follow. The price leader is usually the dominant or largest firm in the industry. Sometimes, it is the low-cost firm (see Problem 9, with the answer at the end of the book) or any other firm (called the **barometric firm**) recognized as the true interpreter or barometer of changes in demand and cost conditions in the industry warranting a price change. In either case, an orderly price change is accomplished by other firms following the leader.

In the price leadership model by the dominant firm, the dominant firm sets the price for the commodity that maximizes its profits, allows all the other (small) firms in the industry to sell all they want at that price, and then comes in to fill the market. Thus, the small firms in the industry behave as perfect competitors or price takers, and the dominant firm acts as the residual supplier of the commodity. This is shown in Figure 11.7.

In the figure, D ($ABCFG$) is the market demand curve for the homogeneous commodity sold in the oligopolist market. Curve ΣSMC_s is the (horizontal) summation of the marginal cost curves of all the small firms in the industry. Since the small firms in the industry can sell all they want at the industry price set by the dominant firm (i.e., they are price takers), they behave as perfect competitors and always produce at the point where $P = \Sigma SMC_s$. Thus, the ΣSMC_s curve (above the average variable cost of the small firms) represents the

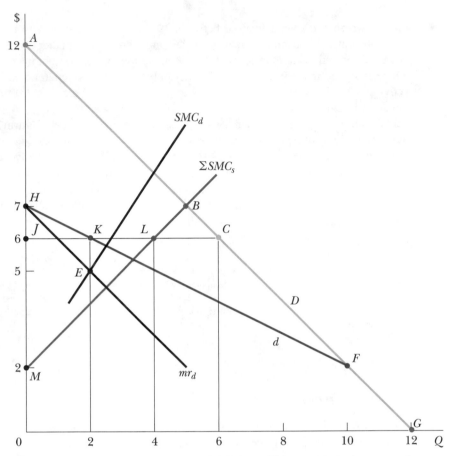

FIGURE 11.7   Price Leadership by the Dominant Firm   *D (ABCFG)* is the market demand curve and *ΣSMC_s* is the marginal cost curve of all the small firms in the industry. Since the small firms can sell all they want at the price set by the dominant firm, they behave as perfect competitors and produce where $P = ΣSMC_s$. The horizontal distance between the *D* and *ΣSMC_s* curves then gives the (residual) quantity supplied by the dominant firm at each price. Thus, the demand curve of the dominant firm (*d*) is *HKFG*, and the corresponding marginal revenue curve is *mr_d*. With *SMC_d*, the dominant firm will set $P = \$6$ (given by point *E*, where $mr_d = SMC_d$) to maximize its profits. At $P = \$6$, the small firms will supply four units of the commodity and the dominant firm $JK = LC$ or two units.

short-run supply curve of the commodity for all the small firms in the industry as a group (on the assumption that input prices remain constant).

The horizontal distance between *D* and *ΣSMC_s* at each price then gives the (residual) quantity of the commodity demanded from and supplied by the dominant firm at each price. For example, if the dominant firm set $P = \$7$, the small firms in the industry together supply *HB* or five units of the commodity, leaving nothing to be supplied by the dominant firm.

This gives the vertical intercept (point H) on the demand curve of the dominant firm (d). If the dominant firm set $P = \$6$, the small firms in the industry supply JL or four units of the commodity, leaving two units ($LC = JK$) to be supplied by the dominant firm (point K on the d curve). Finally, if the dominant firm set $P = \$2$, the small firms together supply zero units of the commodity (point M), leaving the entire market quantity demanded of MF or ten units to be supplied by the dominant firm. Thus, the demand curve of the dominant firm is d or $HKFG$.

With demand curve d, the marginal revenue curve of the dominant firm is mr_d (which bisects the distance from the vertical axis to the d curve). If the short-run marginal cost curve of the dominant firm is SMC_d, the dominant firm will set $P = \$6$ (given by point E, where $mr_d = SMC_d$) to maximize its profits. Note that the industry price set by the dominant firm is determined on the demand curve of the dominant firm (d), not on the market demand curve (D). At $P = \$6$, the small firms together will supply JL or four units of the commodity (see the figure). The dominant firm will then come in to fill the market by selling $JK = LC$ or two units of the commodity at $P = \$6$ which it set.

Among the firms that have operated as price leaders are Alcoa (in aluminum), American Tobacco, American Can, Chase Manhattan Bank (in setting the prime rate), GM, Goodyear Tire and Rubber, Gulf Oil, Kellogg (in breakfast cereals), U.S. Steel (now USX), and so on. Many of these industries are characterized by more than one large firm, and the role of the price leader has sometimes changed from one large firm to another. For example, Reynolds has also behaved at times as the price leader in tobacco products. Continental Can, Bethlehem and National Steel, and General Mills (in the breakfast cereals market) also behaved as the price leaders in their respective markets during some periods of time. Finally, note that one important advantage of price leadership is that it can be accomplished informally by tacit collusion, which is much more difficult to prove than overt or explicit collusion.

On the international level, Saudi Arabia was the dominant price leader for petroleum during the 1970s. Saudi Arabia set petroleum prices and satisfied only that portion of the world demand that was left unfilled by others. But with other petroleum exporting countries greatly exceeding their export quotas and cheating by selling oil at discount prices, Saudi Arabia's share of the world's export market shrunk considerably. As the holder of the world's largest proven petroleum reserves and largest exporter, Saudi Arabia threatened to flood the market if other petroleum exporting countries continued to exceed their export quotas and sell at a discount. In 1986, Saudi Arabia made good on its threat and sharply increased petroleum production and exports, which caused a collapse in world oil prices to below $10 a barrel. Some degree of price and production discipline was subsequently reestablished, so that the price of petroleum more than doubled (to $22 a barrel) in 1992. As discussed in Example 11–3 above, however, the price of petroleum has exhibited great volatility since then.[12]

---

[12] "Crude Oil Prices Fall Slightly on Traders' Belief that OPEC Again Failed to Set Output Strategy," *Wall Street Journal,* September 22, 1992, p. C14; "OPEC Plan to Lift Oil Prices Goes Awry," *Wall Street Journal,* March 3, 1995, p. A2; "Who's to Blame," *Business Week,* July 3, 2001, pp. 36–37; and "Breaking OPEC," *Fortune,* November 12, 2001, pp. 78–88.

| 11.6 | ## LONG-RUN ADJUSTMENTS AND EFFICIENCY IMPLICATIONS OF OLIGOPOLY |

Most of the analysis of oligopoly until this point has referred to the short run. In this section, we analyze the long-run adjustments and efficiency implications of oligopoly. We examine the long-run plant adjustments of existing firms and the entry prospects of other firms into the industry, we discuss nonprice competition, and we examine the long-run welfare effects of oligopoly.

Long-Run Adjustments in Oligopoly

As in other forms of market organization, oligopolistic firms can build the best plant to produce their anticipated best level of output in the long run. However, in view of the uncertainty generally surrounding oligopolistic industries, it is even more difficult than under other forms of market organization for firms to determine their best level of output and plant in the long run. An oligopolist would leave the industry in the long run if it would incur a loss even after building the best scale of plant. On the other hand, if existing firms earn profits, more firms will seek to enter the industry in the long run, and, unless entry is blocked or somehow restricted, industry output will expand until industry profits fall to zero. There may then be so many firms in the industry that the actions of each no longer affect the others. In that case, the industry would no longer be oligopolistic.[13]

For an industry to remain oligopolistic in the long run, entry must be somewhat restricted. This may result from many reasons, some natural and some artificial. These are generally the same barriers that led to the existence of the oligopoly in the first place. One of the most important natural barriers to entry is the smallness of the market in relation to the optimum size of the firm. For example, only three or four firms can most efficiently supply the entire national market for automobiles. Potential entrants know that by entering this market they would probably face huge losses and possibly also impose losses on the other established auto makers (see Problem 11).

Another important natural barrier to entry in oligopolistic markets are the usually huge investment and specialized inputs required (as, for example, to enter automobile, steel, aluminum, and similar industries). Many artificial barriers to entry may also exist. These include control over the source of an essential raw material (such as bauxite to produce aluminum) by the few firms already in the industry, unwillingness of existing firms to license potential competitors to use an essential industrial process on which they hold a patent, and the inability to obtain a government franchise (for example, to run a bus line or a taxi fleet). Still another artificial barrier to entry is **limit pricing,** whereby existing firms charge a price low enough to discourage entry into the industry.[14] By doing so, they voluntarily sacrifice some short-term profits to maximize their profits in the long run (see Section 11.7).

---

[13] As we will see in the theory of contestable markets discussed in Section 13.2, vigorous competition can take place even among few sellers.

[14] See J. Bain, *Industrial Organization,* rev. ed. (New York: John Wiley & Sons, 1967). Perhaps, more than an artificial barrier to entry, limit pricing is a practice that is designed to exploit barriers that do exist (e.g., economies of scale).

Nonprice Competition among Oligopolists

Most oligopoly models presented in this chapter predict infrequent price changes in oligopolistic markets. This conforms to what is often observed in the real world. To be sure, costly price wars do sometimes erupt as a result of miscalculations on the part of one of the oligopolists, but they usually last only short periods. To avoid the possibility of starting a price war, oligopolists prefer to leave price unchanged and compete instead on the basis of **nonprice competition** (advertising, product differentiation, and service). Only when demand and cost conditions make a price change absolutely essential will oligopolists change prices. An orderly price change is then usually accomplished by price leadership.

As pointed out in Section 11.2, a firm may use advertising to try to increase (i.e., to shift to the right) the demand curve for its product. If successful, the firm will then be able to sell a greater quantity of the product at an unchanged price. The problem is that other firms, upon losing sales, are likely to retaliate and also increase their advertising expenditures. The result may be simply to increase all firms' costs, with each firm retaining more or less its share of the market and earning less profits. For example, when the government banned cigarette advertising on television, all tobacco companies benefitted by spending less on advertising—a step that each firm alone was not willing to take before the ban. Although some advertising provides useful information to consumers on new or improved products and uses, a great deal does not. Examples might be the huge advertising expenditures (running in the hundreds of millions of dollars per year) of beer producers, automakers, and others.

The same is generally true for product differentiation. That is, producers often differentiate their product in order to increase sales, but this usually leads to retaliation and higher costs and prices. Sometimes product changes are simply cosmetic (e.g., the yearly automobile model changes). Other changes may truly improve the product, for example, when a new and longer-lasting razor blade is introduced at the same price. Some product differentiation is introduced to better serve particular segments of the market. Advertising, product differentiation, and market segmentation can be combined in many different ways and used with still other forms of nonprice competition in oligopolistic markets.

Welfare Effects of Oligopoly

We now turn to some of the long-run welfare effects of oligopoly. First, as in the case of monopoly and monopolistic competition, oligopolists usually do not produce at the lowest point on their LAC curve. This would only occur by sheer coincidence if the oligopolist's MR curve intersected the LAC curve at the lowest point of the latter. Only under perfect competition will firms produce at the lowest point on the LAC curve in the long run. Oligopoly, however, often results because of the smallness of the market in relation to the optimum size of the firm, and so it does not make much sense to compare oligopoly to perfect competition. Automobiles, steel, aluminum, and many other products could only be produced at prohibitive costs under perfectly competitive conditions.

Second, as in the case of monopoly, oligopolists can earn long-run profits, and so price can exceed LAC. This is to be contrasted with the case of perfect competition and monopolistic competition where $P = LAC$ in the long run. However, some economists believe that oligopolists utilize a great deal of their profits for research and development (R&D) to produce new and better products and to find cheaper production methods. These are the primary sources of growth in modern economies. These same economists point out that monopolists do not have as much incentive to engage in R&D, and perfect competitors and monopolistic competitors are too small and do not have the resources to do so on a large scale (more will be said on this in Section 13.3).

Third, as in imperfect competition in general, $P > LMC$ under oligopoly, and so there is underallocation of resources to the industry. Specifically, since the demand curve facing oligopolists is negatively sloped, $P > MR$. Thus, at the best level of output (given by the point where the LMC intersects the firm's MR curve from below), $P > LMC$. This means that society values an additional unit of the commodity more than the marginal cost of producing it. But again, $P = LMC$ only under perfect competition, and economies of scale may make perfect competition infeasible.

Fourth, while some advertising and product differentiation are useful because they provide information and satisfy the consumers' tastes for diversity, they are likely to be pushed beyond what is socially desirable in oligopolistic markets. It is difficult, however, to determine exactly how much advertising and product differentiation is socially desirable in the real world. For example, the cost of model changes equals about one-fourth of the price of a new automobile during many years.[15] To the extent that consumers purchase new automobiles and choose to have the options introduced into the new models, we can infer that most of the costs of model changes are wanted by consumers and do not represent a waste of resources. Nevertheless, the demand for some model changes and for some new options is surely created by advertising and may not represent true needs.

Turning to oligopoly theory itself, we can now see why we said earlier that there is no general theory of oligopoly. All the oligopoly models that we have examined are somewhat incomplete and unsatisfactory. This is unfortunate because oligopoly is the most prevalent form of market organization in production in all modern economies. Some progress in oligopoly theory is provided by game theory (examined in the next chapter).

EXAMPLE 11–5

Firm Size and Profitability

Do larger firms, because of their size and possible market power, earn larger profits than smaller firms? This question has been of great interest to both business and government and has been hotly debated over the years. To answer this question, we calculated the rank correlation between size (measured by sales) and profits in 2001 for the 20 largest U.S. corporations from the data shown in Table 11.2. The rank correlation, which can range from 0% to 100%, was found to be only 21%. Thus, profits were only

---

[15] See F. Fisher, Z. Griliches, and C. Kaysen, "The Cost of Automobile Model Changes Since 1949," *The Journal of Political Economy,* October 1962, pp. 433–451; and V. Bajic, "Automobiles and Implicit Markets: An Estimate of a Structural Demand Model for Automobile Characteristics," *Applied Economics,* April 1993, pp. 541–551.

| TABLE 11.2 | Sales and Profits for the 20 Largest U.S. Corporations in 2001 (in millions of dollars) | |

Company	Sales	Profits
Wal-Mart Stores	219,812	6,671
Exxon Mobil	191,581	15,320
General Motors	177,260	601
Ford Motor	162,412	−5,453
General Electric	125,913	13,684
Citigroup	112,020	14,126
Chevron Texaco	99,699	3,288
IBM	85,866	7,723
Philip Morris	72,944	8,560
Verizon Communications	67,190	389
American International Group	62,402	5,363
American Electric Power	61,257	971
Duke Energy	59,503	1,898
AT&T	59,142	7,715
Boeing	58,198	2,827
El Paso	57,475	93
Home Depot	53,553	3,044
Bank of America Corp.	52,641	6,792
Fannie Mae	50,803	5,894
J.P. Morgan Chase & Co.	50,429	5,727

Source: "Fortune 500 Largest U.S. Corporations," *Fortune,* April 15, 2002, pp. F-1 to F-20.

weakly associated with size in 2001 in the United States. It should be noted that life at the top is also slippery: 30 to 50 companies are displaced in a typical year from the *Fortune 500.*

11.7   OTHER OLIGOPOLISTIC PRICING PRACTICES

In this section, we examine two other pricing practices often used by oligopolists: limit pricing and cost-plus pricing.

Limit Pricing as a Barrier to Entry

Limit pricing was defined earlier as the charging of a price low enough to discourage entry into the industry. By doing so, existing firms voluntarily sacrifice some short-run profits to maximize their profits in the long run. We can show this with Figure 11.8.

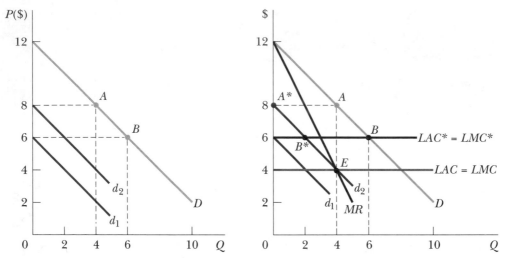

FIGURE 11.8   Limit Pricing   In the left panel, D is the total market demand curve for the commodity. The demand curve of a potential entrant is d_2 if existing firms sell $Q = 4$, and d_1 if they sell $Q = 6$. In the right panel, the $LAC = LMC$ curve refers to the constant costs of the established firms, while $LAC^* = LMC^*$ refers to the constant and higher costs of the potential entrant. Existing firms maximize profits by selling $Q = 4$ at $P = \$8$ (given by point E, at which $MR = LMC$). The demand curve facing the potential entrant is then d_2 and it could earn profits. To discourage entrance, existing firms can set the price at $6 so that d_1 lies everywhere below LAC^*.

In the left panel of Figure 11.8, D is the total market demand curve for the commodity. Suppose that existing firms are already selling four units of the commodity at $P = \$8$ (point A). The entrance of a new firm would increase industry output and cause the price to fall. That is, a potential entrant assumes that it faces the segment of demand curve D to the right of point A. Subtracting the four units of the commodity supplied by existing firms from the market demand curve (D) gives the potential entrant's demand curve (d_2). If, instead, existing firms were selling instead six units of the commodity at $P = \$6$ (point B), the potential entrant's demand curve would be d_1.

For simplicity, we assume that per-unit costs of existing firms and for the potential entrant are constant. We also assume (quite realistically) that the per-unit costs of the potential entrant are somewhat higher than for the established firms. These costs are shown in the right panel of Figure 11.8, where the horizontal $LAC = LMC$ curve refers to the constant costs of the established firms and the horizontal $LAC^* = LMC^*$ curve refers to the constant and higher costs of the potential entrant.

Existing firms maximize profits by selling $Q = 4$ at $P = \$8$ (given by point E, at which $LMC = MR$) and earn profits of AE or $4 per unit and $16 in total. The demand curve facing the potential entrant is then d_2. Since over the range A^*B^* of d_2, $P > LAC^*$, the potential entrant would find it profitable to enter the industry. However, this would increase industry output and lower price so that the profits of existing firms would fall. To avoid this, existing firms may choose to sell $Q = 6$ at $P = \$6$ so that the demand curve facing the potential entrant is d_1. Since d_1 lies everywhere below the LAC^* curve, the potential entrant would incur losses at all output levels and would not enter the industry. Therefore, $P = \$6$ is the entry-limit price. This is the highest price that existing firms can charge without inducing entry. By setting the limit price, existing firms sacrifice some profits in the short run (they now make a profit of $12 rather than $16) in order to maximize their profits in the long run.

Note that existing firms may only charge the limit price when they believe entry is imminent and will set their profit-maximizing price of $P = \$8$ at other times. Sometimes existing firms, faced with the entry of another firm, may voluntarily reduce their output to accommodate the new entrant and avoid a price reduction. Finally, note that limit pricing assumes some form of collusion (such as price leadership) on the part of existing firms.[16]

Cost-Plus Pricing: A Common Short-Cut Pricing Practice

In the real world, firms often lack exact information to set the price that maximizes their profits (given by the point where the firm's *MC* curve intersects its *MR* curve from below). In these cases, firms usually use **cost-plus pricing.** Here, the firm estimates the average variable cost for a "normal" output level (usually between 70% and 80% of capacity output) and then adds a certain percentage or **markup** over average variable cost to determine the price of the commodity. The markup is set sufficiently high to cover average variable and fixed costs and also provide a profit margin for the firm. The markup varies depending on the industry and demand conditions. For example, the markup is about 20% in the steel industry in general, but it is higher for products facing less elastic demand or in periods of high demand.

Cost-plus pricing is fairly common in oligopolistic industries, and, under certain conditions, it is not inconsistent with profit maximization. That is, to the extent that the markup is varied inversely with the elasticity of demand of the product, it leads to a price which is approximately the profit-maximizing price. This can be shown as follows:

$$m = \frac{P - AVC}{AVC} \qquad [11.1]$$

where P is price, AVC is average variable cost, and m is the markup over AVC, expressed as a percentage of AVC.

Solving for P, we get

$$m(AVC) = P - AVC$$
$$P = AVC + m(AVC) \qquad [11.2]$$
$$P = AVC(1 + m)$$

But from Section 5.6 we know that

$$MR = P(1 + 1/\eta) \qquad [11.3]$$

where MR is marginal revenue, P is price, and η is the price elasticity of demand.

---

[16] For more dynamic theories of limit pricing that predict that the limit price will be above existing firms' *LAC*, see R. T. Masson and J. Shaanan, "Stochastic-Dynamic Limiting Pricing: An Empirical Test," *The Review of Economics and Statistics,* August 1982, pp. 413–422.

Solving for P we get

$$P = \frac{MR}{1 + 1/\eta}$$

Since profits are maximized where $MR = MC$, we can substitute MC for MR in the above formula and get

$$P = \frac{MC}{1 + 1/\eta}$$

To the extent that the firm's MC is constant over a wide range of outputs, $MC = AVC$. Substituting AVC for MC in the above formula, we get

$$P = \frac{AVC}{1 + 1/\eta} \qquad [11.4]$$

Formula [11.4] for profit maximization equals formula [11.2] for the markup, if $1 + m = 1/(1 + (1/\eta))$ or if $m = -1/(\eta + 1)$. Thus, the firm will maximize profits if its markup is inversely related to the price elasticity of demand for the commodity. For example, when $\eta = -3$, m should be $1/2$, or 50%. For $\eta = -5$, $m = 1/4$, or 25%. This means that if $AVC = \$100$, P should equal $\$125$ (so that the markup is 25% of AVC) for the firm to cover all costs and maximize profits.

Cyert and March found that firms in the retailing sector adjusted prices on the basis of feedback from the market and did reduce the markup and price when the demand for a product declined and became more elastic.[17] Thus, using cost-plus pricing with a markup that varies inversely with the price elasticity of demand is consistent with profit maximization. In any event, those firms that choose a markup and price that is not near the profit-maximizing price are less likely to grow and may go out of business in the long run, as compared to firms that choose the appropriate markup. Cost-plus pricing is one of many *rules of thumb* that firms are forced to use in the real world because of the frequent lack of adequate data.

AT THE FRONTIER
The Art of Devising Air Fares

Introductory Comment: The following selection illustrates most of the concepts presented in this chapter as they are actually applied in the real world. It shows the importance of market structure in output and pricing decisions, price leadership, price discrimination, the pricing of multiple products, and how they are all interrelated to marginal analysis in pricing as it is actually conducted in a major oligopolistic industry today.

---

[17] R. M. Cyert and J. G. March, *A Behavioral Theory of the Firm* (Englewood Cliffs, N.J.: Prentice-Hall, 1963).

THE ART OF DEVISING AIR FARES

In the airline business, it is sometimes called the "dark science." The latest round of fare wars, however, has put the spot light on how carriers use state-of-the-art computer software, complex forecasting techniques, and a little intuition to devine how many seats and at what prices they will offer on any flight.

The aim of this inventory or yield management is to squeeze as many dollars as possible out of each seat and mile flown. This means trying to project just how many tickets to sell at a discount without running out of seats for the business traveler, who usually books at the last minute and therefore pays full fare. Too many wrong projections can lead to huge losses of revenue, or even worse. The inability of People Express (airline) to manage its inventory of seats properly, for example, was one of the major causes of its demise.

"It's a sophisticated guessing game," says Robert E. Martens, vice president of pricing and production planning at American Airlines, the carrier that has the most sophisticated technology for yield management, according to airline analysts and consultants. "You don't sell a seat to a guy for $69 when he is willing to pay $400."

With the industry now adopting very low discount but nonrefundable fares, the complex task of managing seat inventory may become easier because airlines will be better able to predict how many people will show up for a flight. Some airlines have already seen a reduction in their no-shows, which means that they can overbook less and spare more customers from being bumped. The nonrefundable fares could also enable carriers to sell more discount seats weeks before a flight, rather than putting them on sale at the last minute in an effort to fill up the plane.

American's inventory operations illustrate just how complicated the process can be. At the airline's corporate headquarters, 90 yield managers are linked by terminals to five International Business Machines mainframe computers in Tulsa, Oklahoma. The managers monitor and adjust the fare mixes on 1,600 daily flights as well as 528,000 future flights involving nearly 50 million passengers. Their work is hectic: A fare's average life span is two weeks, and industry-wide about 2,000 fares change daily.

Few Discounts on Fridays

American and other airlines base their forecasts largely on historical profiles on each flight. Business travelers, for example, book heavily on many Friday afternoon flights, but often not until the day of departure. The airlines reserve blocks of seats for those frequent fliers. Few, if any, discounts are made available. "Good luck on getting a 'Q fare' from New York to Chicago on Fridays afternoon," said James J. Hurtigan, president of United Airlines, using the industry parlance for the low-priced super saver ticket. "It's like winning the New York lottery." The same route on a midday on a Wednesday, however, begs for passengers, so the airline might discount more than 80% of its seats to draw leisure travelers and others with more flexible schedules.

Continued. . .

Passengers Angered

Many passengers, attracted by the advertisements trumpeting deep discounts but unaware that fare allocations change from flight to flight, have expressed anger at the carriers and travel agents when the cheap seats were unavailable. To help clear up the confusion, Continental Airlines is now running ads noting the relative demand for certain routes, thus giving some sense of the supply of discount seats. Overbooking, too, is based on the computerized history of flights and their no-shows and involves myriad factors that include destination, time of day, and cost of ticket.

The airlines have used inventory management for decades, but its importance in helping carriers to enhance their revenue coincides with new software developed in the past three of four years, analysts and airline executives said. Some of the software has been developed in-house; other systems have been from such companies as the Unis Corporation and the Control Data Corporation. "It's probably the No. 1 management tool required to compete properly in this highly competitive airline environment," said Lee R. Howard, executive vice president of Airline Economics, a Washington-based consulting firm.

Effective inventory management alone can improve an airline's revenues by 5% to 20% annually, analysts estimated. Mr. Martens said American's system was worth "hundreds of millions of dollars" a year to the airline. The airline's total sales exceeded $6 billion last year. "The revenue implications for yield management are enormous," said Julius Maltudis, airline analyst at Salomon Brothers. Inventory management improves a carrier's load factor, or ratio of seats filled. Every 1% increase in the load factor translates into $10 million in revenue for the typical major carrier, analysts said.

"Crystal-Ball Gazing"

As sophisticated as it is, however, yield management is still subject to variables beyond its control. "Yield management is about 70% technology and 30% crystal-ball gazing," said Robert W. Cuggin, assistant vice president of marketing development at Delta Airlines. Bad weather or a last-minute switch to a plane of a different size can wreak havoc with weeks of planning, he said.

At American, inventory management begins 330 days before departure. Yield managers use a profile of a flight's history to parcel out an alphabet soup of fares, rationing full-fare seats first, then moving down the price scale. In the following weeks, the computer alerts managers if sales in a particular fare class picked up unexpectedly. If a travel agent books a large group of passengers in advance, for example, the computer would flag the large order, and yield managers would restrict or expand the number of seats in that category. Otherwise, managers begin checking all fare mixes 180 days before departure, adding or subtracting seats in each according to demand.

The process continues right up to two hours before boarding, according to America's director of yield management, Dennis McKaige. Airlines typically put more discount seats on sale just before an advance purchase requirement expires, he said. Therefore, a new batch of cheap tickets that require a 30-day advance purchase might go on sale 31 days before departure. A cut-rate fare offered on Monday might be sold out by Wednesday, then suddenly reoffered hours before take off on Thursday if passengers projections based on previous flights fail to materialize, Mr. McKaige said.

There are some instances when an airline actually gives preference to discount travelers over customers paying full fare. American has recently developed software to increase the yield on flights through its hubs. American gives preference to a passenger flying on a discount fare from Austin, Texas, to London, through Dallas, over another passenger paying full fare from Austin to Shreveport, Louisiana, through Dallas. The London passenger, who pays $241 each way, is worth more to the airline than the passenger flying to Shreveport, who pays the full fare of $87 each way. For the bargain hunter, finding a discount will increasingly depend on the season, day and time of travel, the destination, and the length of stay.

The New Fare Cuts

Continental, a unit of Texas Air, ignited the latest round of rock-bottom fares in January with "Maxsaver tickets," which require a minimum two-day advance purchase and are nonrefundable. "The spread between our highest and lowest fares is much lower than other airlines," said James O'Donnel, vice president of marketing at Continental. "While our yield management job is no less important than other airlines', it is easier." Mr. O'Donnel said the carrier's system was more automated than those used by some of its competitors.

The two-day purchase requirement has siphoned off some business travelers who would otherwise have paid full fare. (American and several other airlines abandoned plans to raise their lowest discount fares and increase the advance purchase requirement on the cheapest tickets to 30 days, from 2. The airlines backed away from the change when support for the proposal collapsed.) Airline officials said that nonrefundable tickets were here to stay. Mr. Martens said that since the nonrefundable, Maxsaver-type fares were introduced, American's no-show rate has dropped "substantially below" the usual range of 12% to 15%. Passengers who are willing to commit themselves to a particular flight in exchange for lower prices allow yield managers to refine their operations by concentrating on the remaining coach seats.

Concluding Remarks: Yield management (i.e., the idea of selling as many tickets as possible at high fares and fill the rest of the seats at cut rates) is here to stay in the pricing of airline tickets and is constantly being refined with the use of ever more powerful computers and software. Indeed, yield management is considered the single most important technological improvement in airline management in the last decade and is often credited with making the difference between profit and loss for many airlines. For example, *The New York Times* found that on

Continued. . .

a single flight in 1997, the 33 passengers who held Chicago–Los Angeles tickets paid 27 different fares, ranging from $87 to $728. In 2001, a New York–Los Angeles roundtrip ticket might cost $287 to one flier and $2,247 to another.

The great variety and frequent changes in airfares is, however, creating great confusion and frustration for air travelers as they are routinely unable to book seats at the lowest advertised fares. This has led to increasing complaints of false advertisement, which the Transportation Department (the sole authority charged with regulating the airline industry since it was deregulated in 1978) has been regularly investigating since 1995. With the U.S. economy falling into recession in the second half of 2001 and the terrorist attack on the World Trade Center in New York, all types of air travel declined, and business travelers began rebelling against high full-fare ticket prices and demanding (and getting) discounts and more fare choices. Yield management may now come to haunt airlines, as more and more travelers use the increasing amount of price information available on the Internet to shop around for the lowest airfares available.

Sources: Eric Schmidt, "The Art of Devising Air Fares," *New York Times,* March 4, 1987, pp. D1–D2. Reprinted by permission of the New York Times Corporation. See also "Computers as Price Setters Complicate Travelers' Lives," *New York Times,* January 24, 1994, p. 1; "Special Offers by Airlines Come Under U.S. Review," *New York Times,* January 23, 1995, p. 10; "Why Airline Tickets Are Not Always a Bargain," *Wall Street Journal,* March 16, 1996, p. B1; "For Business Air Fares, The Sky's the Limit," *New York Times,* March 14, 1997, p. 1; "So, How Much Did You Pay for Your Ticket?" *New York Times,* April 12, 1998, Sect. 4, p. 2; and "Airlines Draw Flak Over Disparity Between Business, Discount Fares," *Wall Street Journal,* December 13, 2001, p. B1.

11.8 | THE MARCH OF GLOBAL OLIGOPOLISTS

During the past decade the trend toward the formation of global oligopolies has accelerated as the world's largest corporations have been getting bigger and bigger through internal growth and mergers. Indeed, in more and more industries and sectors the pressure to become one of the largest global players seems irresistible. No longer are corporations satisfied to be the largest or the next-to-the-largest national company in their industry or sector. More and more corporations operate on the belief that their very survival requires that they become one of a handful of world corporations or global oligopolists in their sector. Many smaller corporations are merging with larger ones in the belief that either they grow or they become a casualty of the sharply increased global competition. Strong impetus toward globalization has been provided by the revolution in telecommunications and transportation, the movement toward the globalization of tastes, and the reduction of barriers to international trade and investments.

The sector in which the size of the largest firm has grown the most during the past decades is international banking. From 1966 to 2001, the total deposits of the world's 10 largest banks grew from $87 billion to more than $7,000 billion. Even after accounting for the quadrupling of prices and exchange rate changes (to convert local currency values into dollar values), this meant that the size of the world's 10 largest banks increased by more than 16 times during the past three decades. It should also be pointed out that in

1966, six of the world's largest banks (including the first four) were American. By 1995, the largest eight banks were Japanese, the ninth was French, and the tenth was German. The largest American bank (Citicorp) was 29th! By 2001, the whole ranking had changed, and of the world's 10 largest banks three were American, two were Japanese, two German, and one each Swiss, British and French. It is often pointed out, however, that after a certain size, stability and profitability are more important than size per se. Nevertheless, the growth in the size of the world's largest banks has been nothing but spectacular (see Example 11–6).

Another sector where corporations have grown sharply in size and gone global has been in the entertainment and communication industry. The merger of Time Inc. with Warner Communications and its subsequent acquisition by America Online (AOL) for $110 billion, the acquisition by Viacom of CBS, and the acquisition by Walt Disney of Capital Cities formed, respectively, the world's first, second, and third largest communications company (all three American). Many mergers involved the purchase of American companies by foreigners: Japan's Sony Corporation's purchase of American Paramount Pictures and CBS Records, West Germany's Bertelsmann acquired RCA Records as well as Doubleday and Bantam Books, Ruppert Murdoch (from Australia but now residing in the United States) bought Harper & Row Publishers, Triangle Publications, and Twentieth-Century Fox, and Vivendi (French) acquired Seagram and US Networks. The industry is now dominated by AOL Time Warner, Walt Disney, Viacom CBS, the News Corporation (Australian), Bertlsmann (German), and Vivendi (French).

The reason given for most mergers in the entertainment and communications industry is to become more competitive globally. "Competitive," according to the current conventional wisdom, means being equipped to become one of the five to eight giant corporations expected to dominate the industry worldwide. These enterprises, the reasoning goes, will be able to produce and distribute information and entertainment in virtually any medium: books, magazines, news, television, movies, videos, cinemas, electronic data networks, and so on. This is expected to provide important synergies or cross benefits from joint operation.[18] The same merger fever has also caught the telecommunications industry (this is discussed in Example 13–1).

A similar move toward concentration and globalization has occurred in industry. The total sales in real terms (i.e., after taking inflation into account) of the world's 25 largest *industrial* corporations increased 70% faster than the combined index of real total industrial production in all industrial countries during the past 30 years. Thus, there has been a clear tendency for the largest industrial corporations to become relatively larger during the past three decades. The movement toward globalization is very clear in automobiles, where only a handful of global players are likely to survive. From 1997 to 2001, German Daimler-Benz acquired American Chrysler, Ford acquired British Jaguar and Rover and Swedish Volvo, French Renault bought Japanese Nissan, German Volkswagen acquired German Audi, British Rolls Royce, Spanish Seat, Czech Skoda, and Japanese Mazda and Mitsubishi, and General Motors formed an alliance with Italy's FIAT and Sweden's Saab. This left only a handful of viable global companies (General Motors with 2001 sales of

[18] "Media Mergers: An Urge to Get Bigger and More Global," *New York Times,* March 19, 1989, p. 7; "Corporations Dreams Converge in One Idea: It's Time to Do a Deal," *Wall Street Journal,* February 26, 1997, p. A1; and "The New Media Colossus," *Wall Street,* December 15, 2000, p. B1.

$177 billion—$230 billion with FIAT—Ford with $162 billion, Daimler Chrysler with $137 billion, Toyota with $121 billion, Renault-Nissan with $82 billion, and Volkswagen with $79 billion) and a few other companies, which are probably too small to survive as independent entities for much longer.[19] Globalization has proceeded even more rapidly in tires, where Bridgestone (Japanese), Michelin (French), and Goodyear (American) command more than half of the world's total sales, and further consolidation is expected. The retailing sector is also consolidating (discussed in Example 12–4).

The same type of globalization has been taking place in consumer products, food, drugs, electronics, and commercial aircraft. In 1990, Gillette introduced its new Sensor razor, which took 20 years and $300 million to develop, and captured an incredible 71% of the world razor market by 1999 when it introduced its Mach3. Nestlé, the world's largest food company, has production plants in 59 countries and sells its food products in more than 100 countries. America's Philip Morris, the world's largest tobacco and food company, Switzerland's Nestlé, and Britain's Unilever are among the world's 100 largest corporations. Coca-Cola has 40% of the U.S. market and an incredible 33% of the world's soft drink market. Despite the need to cater to local food tastes (Nestlé has more than 200 blends of Nescafé to cater to different local tastes), there is a clear trend toward global supermarkets. The same is true in chemicals, electronics, commercial aircraft, petroleum, and drugs (see Example 11–7), where a handful of huge corporations literally control the world market.

It no longer makes any sense to talk about or be concerned only with national rather than global competition in these sectors. A large corporation can even be a monopolist in the national market and face deadly competition from larger and more efficient global oligopolists. The ideal global corporation is today strongly decentralized to allow local units to develop products that fit into the local cultures and yet at its core is very centralized to coordinate activities around the globe.[20]

EXAMPLE 11–6

Rising Competition in Global Banking

This decade is likely to be an era of aggressively intensified competition in the high-stakes world of international banking, with less than 10 of the 40 to 45 large international banks now aspiring to become global powerhouses attaining their goal. From the 1950s through the 1970s world banking was dominated by U.S. banks, while in the 1980s Japanese banks made a run for the top.

American banks were weakened by soured loans on real estate and to developing countries during the 1980s and for highly leveraged takeovers during the 1990s. Japanese banks suffered from years of bad loans, low profits, and antiquated technology during the 1990s and were generally less competitive than European Banks and much less efficient

---

[19] See "The Fortune Global 500," *Fortune,* August 1970, May 1980, July 1990, and July 2002.
[20] "A View from the Top: Survival Tactics for the Global Business Arena," *Management Review,* October 1992, pp. 49–53; "The Fallout From Merger Mania," *Fortune,* March 2, 1998, pp. 26–27, and "Why the Sudden Rise in the Urge to Merge and Form Oligopolies, *Wall Street Journal,* February 25, 2002, p. A1.

than American banks. European banks entered into the 1990s in better shape than their American counterparts. They were better capitalized and made much fewer bad loans than American banks to developing countries, especially in Latin America, during the 1980s. They were also not restricted by law, as American Banks were until 1999, from entering the insurance and securities fields. European banks, however, generally lagged in technology and in the introduction of new financial instruments, such as derivatives, when compared with American banks. European banks were also much more exposed, and incurred much higher losses than, American banks from the financial and economic crisis in Southeast Asia during the latter part of the 1990s. The European banking sectors did start to consolidate since the mid-1990s, but mergers generally took place within countries rather than across countries because of persisting nationalism.

In 2001, the world's largest bank (with assets of $935 billion) was the Sumitomo Mitsui Banking Corporation and Citigroup (U.S.) was second (with $902 billion in assets). Of the world's top ten largest banks, three were American (Citigroup, J. P. Morgan Chase, and Bank of America), two Japanese, two German, and one each Swiss, British, and French. But size is not everything in banking, and once a bank is, say, one of the top 10 largest in the world, efficiency is then what matters the most. Size is important in banking because with deregulation, each bank must increasingly compete with foreign banks at home and abroad to be successful. Global banks must be able to meet the rising financial needs for lending, underwriting, currency and security trading, insurance, financial advice, and other financial services for customers and investors with increasingly global operations (i.e., they must provide one-stop banking for global corporations). Global banks must also be highly innovative and introduce new financial products and technologies to meet changing customer needs. Overcapacity—too many banks chasing too few customers—will also increase competition. Large U.S. banks are strong on innovations and with the repeal of the 1933 Glass–Steagal Act (which prevented them from entering the insurance and securities fields) are now able to compete with foreign banks more effectively at home and abroad.

Sources: "Competition Rises in Global Banking," *Wall Street Journal,* March 25, 1991, p. A1; "International Banking Survey," *The Economist,* April 30, 1994, pp. 1–42; "The Showdown in Global Banking," *Business Week,* October 2, 1995, pp. 96–100; "Congress Passes Wide-Ranging Bill Easing Bank Laws," *New York Times,* November 5, 1999, p. 1; "Banking in the 21st Century," *Global Finance,* January 2000, p. 41; and "The World's Largest Banks," *Global Finance,* October 2001, p. 83.

EXAMPLE 11–7

Globalization of the Pharmaceutical Industry

The past decade has witnessed more than a dozen huge mergers of large pharmaceutical companies—as well as many failed attempts. The largest merger was Pfizer's (the largest drug company in the world—American) acquisition of Pharmacia (the eighth largest, also American) for $60 billion in 2001. The merged company has annual sales of nearly $50 billion (twice GlaxoSmithKlein's, the second largest drug company in the world—British). Indeed, all but two of the world's 10 largest pharmaceutical companies in 2001 were the result of one or more mergers (Merck the third largest drug company in the world with 2001 sales of $20 billion and Johnson & Johnson, the seventh largest with sales of $15 billion) were not the result of major mergers. Still, the top 12 pharmaceutical companies control less than 50% of total world drug sales, and so there seem to be still a great deal of room for further mergers in the industry in the future.

There are three major reasons for the urge to merge in the pharmaceutical industry. The first and most important arises from the incredibly high cost of developing new drugs. It has been estimated that it now costs on the average about $500 million (including failures and lost opportunity costs) to bring a new commercial drug to market. Despite average profit rates of about 10% in the industry, these huge development costs are becoming out of reach of even the largest drug companies. Hence the need for further consolidation and globalization in the industry, even by today's largest industry players. The second reason is that management typically expects savings equivalent to 10% of the combined sales of the merged company. These can run in the billions of dollars per year for the largest companies. The third reason is that the combined sales force of the merged company can reach that many more doctors and hospitals and thus increase sales. Although making a great deal of sense theoretically, most mergers in the pharmaceutical industry did not deliver the benefits expected. In all cases the merged company lost market share and faced reduced profits after the merger, at the same time that Merck and Johnson & Johnson (the two American firms that were not involved in major mergers) increased theirs.

Because of price regulation (and thus lower profit margins) and fragmented national markets, European drug companies are losing international competitiveness to U.S. firms. Both face very strong competition from generic drugs as patents (usually granted for 20 years from the date the application is filed) expire on many blockbuster drugs. Generic drugs usually sell for as little as 10% of the price of the patented drug. By 1996, 43% of all prescriptions were filled by generic drugs (up from 20% in 1984) in the United States (saving consumers from $8 billion to $10 billion).

Sources: "Mergers Will Keep Reshuffling Rankings of Drug Makers," *The Wall Street Journal,* March 15, 1995, p. B4; "In a Drug's Journey to Market, Discovery Is Just the First of Many Steps," *The New York Times,* July 23, 2000, p. 15; "Price Controls in Europe Draw Drug Makers' Criticism," *The Wall Street Journal,* December 13, 2001, p. B4; and "A Risky Therapy," *Financial Times,* July 24, 2002, p. 14.

SUMMARY

1. Monopolistic competition is the form of market organization in which there are many sellers of a differentiated product, and entry into and exit from the industry are rather easy in the long run. Differentiated products are those that are similar but not identical and satisfy the same basic need. The competitive element arises from the many firms in the market. The monopoly element results from product differentiation. The monopoly power, however, is severely limited by the availability of many close substitutes. Monopolistic competition is most common in the retail sector of the economy. Because of product differentiation, we cannot derive the market demand curve and we have a cluster of prices. The choice-related

variables for a monopolistically competitive firm are product variation, selling expenses, and price.

2. Since a monopolistically competitive firm produces a differentiated product for which there are many close substitutes, the demand curve that the firm faces is negatively sloped but highly price elastic. The best level of output in the short run is given by the point at which $MR = SMC$, provided that $P > AVC$. If firms earn profits in the short run, more firms enter the market in the long run. This shifts the demand curve facing each firm to the left until all firms break even. Because of product differentiation, P and LAC are somewhat higher than if the market had been organized along perfectly competitive lines, there is excess capacity, and this allows more firms to exist in the market. A monopolistically competitive firm can increase the degree of product variation and selling expenses in an effort to increase the demand for its product and make it less elastic. The optimal level of these efforts is given by the point at which $MR = MC$. In the long run, however, the monopolistically competitive firm breaks even. Recently, economists have preferred to use the perfectly competitive and oligopoly models.

3. Oligopoly is the form of market organization in which there are few sellers of either a homogeneous or a differentiated product, and entry into or exit from the industry is possible but difficult. Oligopoly is the most prevalent form of market organization in the manufacturing sector of industrial countries, including the United States. The distinguishing characteristic of oligopoly is the interdependence or rivalry among the firms in the industry. The sources of oligopoly as well as the barriers to entry are economies of scale, the huge investments and specialized inputs required to enter the industry, patents and copyrights, the loyalty of customers to existing firms, control over the supply of a required raw material, and government franchise. The degree by which an industry is dominated by a few large firms is measured by concentration ratios. These ratios, however, can be very misleading as a measure of the degree of competition in the industry and must be used with great caution.

4. Cournot assumed that two firms sell identical spring water produced at zero marginal cost. Each duopolist, in its attempt to maximize profits, assumes the other will keep output constant at the existing level. The result is a sequence of moves and countermoves until each duopolist sells one-third of the total output that would be sold if the market were perfectly competitive. If each duopolist assumes that the other keeps its price (instead of its quantity) constant, then the price will fall to zero. This is the Bertrand model. In the kinked-demand or Sweezy model, it is assumed that oligopolists match the price reductions but not the price increases of competitors. Thus, the demand curve has a kink at the prevailing price. Oligopolists maintain the price as long as the SMC curve intersects the discontinuous segment of the MR curve. Some empirical studies do not support the existence of the kink, and the model does not explain how the price is set in the first place.

5. A centralized cartel is a formal organization of suppliers of a commodity that sets the price and allocates output and profits among its members so as to increase their joint profits. A market-sharing cartel is an organization of suppliers of a commodity that overtly or tacitly divides the market among its members. Cartels can result in the monopoly solution but are unstable and often fail. A looser form of collusion is price leadership by the dominant, the low-cost, or the barometric firm. Under price leadership by the dominant firm, the small firms are allowed to sell all they want at the price set by the dominant firm, and then the dominant firm comes in to fill the market.

6. In the long run, oligopolistic firms can build their best scale of plant and firms can leave the industry. Entry, however, has to be blocked or restricted if the industry is to remain oligopolistic. There can be several natural and artificial barriers to entry. Oligopolists seldom change prices for fear of starting a price war and prefer instead to compete on the basis of advertising, product differentiation, and service. In oligopolistic markets, production does not usually take place at the lowest point on the LAC curve, $P > LAC$, $P > LMC$, and too much

may be spent on advertising, product differentiation, and service. Oligopoly, however, may result from the limitation of the market, and it may lead to more research and development.

7. Limit pricing refers to existing firms charging a sufficiently low price to discourage entry into the industry. Cost-plus pricing refers to the setting of a price equal to average variable cost plus a markup. The pricing of airline tickets illustrates most of the concepts presented in this chapter as they are actually applied in a real-world oligopolistic market.

8. During the past decade, the trend toward the formation of global oligopolies has accelerated as the world's largest corporations have been getting even bigger through internal growth and mergers. More and more, corporations operate on the belief that their survival requires that they become one of a handful of world corporations, or global oligopolists, in their sector. This globalization of production and distribution has important implications for the concept of efficiency (to be explored in Section 13.3).

KEY TERMS

Monopolistic competition	Concentration ratios	Limit pricing
Differentiated products	Cournot model	Nonprice competition
Product group	Bertrand model	Cost-plus pricing
Excess capacity	Kinked-demand curve model	Markup
Product variation	Collusion	Reaction function
Selling expenses	Cartel	Cournot equilibrium
Oligopoly	Centralized cartel	Nash equilibrium
Duopoly	Market-sharing cartel	Stackelberg model
Pure oligopoly	Price leadership	
Differentiated oligopoly	Barometric firm	

REVIEW QUESTIONS

1. a. Why is it that we cannot define the industry in monopolistic competition?

   b. How can cross elasticities of demand help define a product group under monopolistic competition?

2. Can the short-run supply curve of a monopolistically competitive firm be derived? Why?

3. What effect will product variation and selling expenses have on

   a. the firm's demand and cost curves?

   b. short-run and long-run equilibrium?

4. a. What is the usefulness and cost of product variation?

   b. Is advertising good or bad for consumers? Why?

5. Why does excess capacity arise in monopolistic competition? What is its economic significance?

6. What is the distinction between interdependence and rivalry in oligopoly?

7. How much would be produced by each oligopolist and in total in Figure 11.3 if there were

   a. four firms in the market?

   b. five firms in the market?

8. What general conclusion can you draw from the results in the text and from your answer to Question 7 with regard to the proportion of the perfectly competitive total quantity sold by

   a. each oligopolist?

   b. all oligopolists together?

9. a. What is the usefulness of the kinked-demand curve model?

   b. What are its disadvantages?

10. Why do we study cartels and price leadership if they are illegal?

11. Why is there no general theory of oligopoly?

12. What are the advantages and disadvantages of oligopoly?

PROBLEMS

1. Suppose that *SATC* were $10 and *AVC* were $8 at the best level of output for the firm in the left panel of Figure 11.1.
   a. How much profit or loss per unit and in total would the firm have if it continued to produce?
   b. Should the firm continue to produce in the short run? Why?
   c. What would be the total loss of the firm if it stopped producing in the short run and if it didn't stop producing?

*2. Excess capacity is inversely related to the price elasticity of demand faced by a monopolistically competitive firm. True or false? Explain.

3. Starting with the assumptions of the Cournot model, explain what would happen if each duopolist assumed that the other kept its price rather than its output constant (as in the Cournot model).

4. Draw a figure showing the best level of output and price for the oligopolist of Figure 11.4 if its *SMC* curve shifts
   a. upward by $3.50;
   b. downward by $4.

5. Draw a figure showing the best level of output and price for the oligopolist of Figure 11.4 if the government sets a price ceiling of
   a. $8;
   b. $7.

*6. Draw a figure showing the best level of output and price for the oligopolist of Figure 11.4 if the demand curve it faces shifts
   a. upward by $0.50 but the kink remains at $P = \$8$.
   b. downward by $0.50 but the kink remains at $P = \$8$ and the *SMC* curve shifts up to *SMC'*.

7. Assume that (1) the four identical firms in a purely oligopolistic industry form a centralized cartel; (2) the total market demand function facing the cartel is $QD = 20 - 2P$, and P is given in dollars;

and (3) each firm's *SMC* function is given by $\$(1/4)Q$, and input prices are constant.
   a. Find the best level of output and price for this centralized cartel.
   b. How much should each firm produce if the cartel wants to minimize production costs?
   c. How much profit will the cartel make if the average total cost of each firm at the best level of output is $4?

8. Redraw Figure 11.6, and show on it the *MR* and the ΣSMC curves for the cartel as a whole. How are the best levels of output and price for the cartel as a whole determined? On the same figure, draw the *SATC* curve of one of the duopolists if $SATC = \$6$ at $Q = 2$ and $Q = 4$. How much profit does each duopolist earn?

*9. Start with Figure 11.6 where the duopolists share equally the market for a homogeneous product.
   a. Draw a figure such that duopolist 1's short-run marginal cost (SMC_1) is as shown in Figure 11.6 and duopolist 2's short-run marginal cost is given by $SMC_2 = 6 + 2Q$. What quantity of the commodity will each duopolist produce? What price would each like to charge? What is the actual result likely to be?
   b. If $SATC_1 = \$5$ at $Q = 2$ and $SATC_2 = \$8$ at $Q = 1$, how much profit will each duopolist earn?

10. Assume that (1) in a purely oligopolistic industry, there is one dominant firm and ten small identical firms; (2) the market demand curve for the commodity is $Q = 20 - 2P$, where P is given in dollars; (3) $SMC_d = 1.5 + Q/2$, while $SMC_s = 1 + Q/4$; and (4) input prices remain constant. Based on the above assumptions
   a. draw a figure similar to Figure 11.7 showing the market demand curve, SMC_d, SMC_s, and the demand curve that the dominant firm faces.
   b. What price will the dominant firm set? How much will the small firms supply together? How much will the dominant firm supply?

* = Answer provided at end of book.

11. Draw a figure showing that when two identical firms share the market equally for a homogeneous product they both earn profits, but if a third identical firm entered the industry, they would all face losses. How is this related to the existence of oligopoly?

*12. If an oligopolist knows that the price elasticity of demand of the product it sells (η) is -4 and its $AVC = \$10$, determine
   a. the markup that the oligopolist should use in pricing its product;
   b. the price the oligopolist should charge.

APPENDIX THE COURNOT AND STACKELBERG MODELS

This appendix is a more advanced and complete treatment of the Cournot model presented in Section 11.4, as well as an important extension of the model known as the Stackelberg model.

The Cournot Model—An Extended Treatment

We begin by writing the equation for market demand curve D shown in both panels of Figure 11.3 as

$$Q = 12 - P \qquad [11.5]$$

where Q is the total quantity of spring water sold in the market per unit of time (say, per week) and P is the market price. For example, applying formula [11.5], $Q = 0$ when $P = \$12$ (the vertical intercept of market demand curve D in the right panel of Figure 11.3, repeated below for ease of reference as the left panel of Figure 11.9). On the other hand, when $P = \$0$, $Q = 12$ (point C on market demand curve D in the left panel of Figure 11.9).

Given the quantity of spring water supplied by duopolist B (Q_B), duopolist A will supply one-half of the difference between 12 (the total that would be supplied to the market at $P = \$0$) and Q_B in order to maximize total profits. That is,

$$Q_A = \frac{12 - Q_B}{2} \qquad [11.6]$$

For example, when $Q_B = 0$, $Q_A = 12/2 = 6$ (point A on d_A in the left panel of Figure 11.9). On the other hand, when $Q_B = 3$, $Q_A = (12 - 3)/2 = 4.5$ (point A' on d_A in the left panel of Figure 11.9). With total costs equal to zero, duopolist A always maximizes total revenue and total profits by producing one-half of 12 minus the amount supplied by duopolist B (formula [11.6]). The reason is that (as shown in the left panel of Figure 11.3) this is the quantity at which $mr = MC = 0$.

Similarly, duopolist B maximizes total revenue and total profits by selling

$$Q_B = \frac{12 - Q_A}{2} \qquad [11.7]$$

For example, when $Q_A = 6$, $Q_B = (12 - 6)/2 = 3$ (point B on d_B in the left panel of Figure 11.9) because (as shown in the left panel of Figure 11.3) this is the quantity at which $mr = MC = 0$.

Equation [11.6] is duopolist A's **reaction function.** This shows how duopolist A reacts to duopolist B's action and is plotted in the right panel of Figure 11.9. It shows that if $Q_B = 0$, $Q_A = 6$ (given by point A at which duopolist A's reaction function crosses the horizontal or

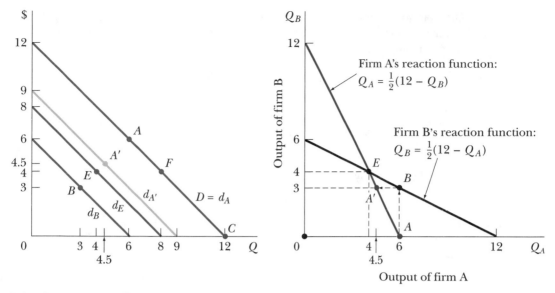

FIGURE 11.9   Duopolists' Demand Curves and Reaction Functions in the Cournot Model   The left panel shows the demand curves faced by duopolists A and B and the quantity sold by each, given the quantity sold by the other (exactly as in the right panel of Figure 11.3). The right panel shows duopolist A's and B's reaction functions. The intersection of the two reaction functions at point E gives the Cournot equilibrium of $Q_A = Q_B = 4$ (in the right panel), so that $Q_A + Q_B = 8$ and $P = \$4$ (point F in the left panel).

Q_A axis in the right panel of Figure 11.9) in order for duopolist A to maximize total revenue and total profits. If $Q_B = 3$, $Q_A = 4.5$ (point A' on duopolist A's reaction function).

Similarly, equation [11.7] is duopolist B's reaction function and is also plotted in the right panel of Figure 11.9. It shows that if $Q_A = 6$, $Q_B = 3$ (given by point B on duopolist B's reaction function in the right panel of Figure 11.9) in order for duopolist B to maximize total revenue and total profits. Thus, a duopolist's reaction function shows the quantity that the duopolist should sell to maximize its total profits, given the amount sold by the other duopolist.

The two reaction functions intersect at point E, giving the **Cournot equilibrium** of $Q_A = Q_B = 4$. That is, if $Q_B = 4$, then $Q_A = 4$ (point E on duopolist A's reaction function) for duopolist A to maximize total profits. Similarly, if $Q_A = 4$, then $Q_B = 4$ (point E on duopolist B's reaction function) for duopolist B to maximize total profits. Thus, point E (where the two reaction functions intersect) is the Cournot equilibrium point because there is no tendency for either duopolist to change the quantity it sells. A situation such as the Cournot equilibrium where each player's strategy is optimal, given the strategy chosen by the other player, is called a **Nash equilibrium.**

The right panel of Figure 11.9 can also be used to show the time path or movement toward equilibrium. With $Q_B = 0$, $Q_A = 6$ (point A on duopolist A's reaction function). With $Q_A = 6$, $Q_B = 3$ (point B on duopolist B's reaction function). With $Q_B = 3$, $Q_A = 4.5$ (point A' on duopolist A's reaction function). Note the direction of the arrows from point A to point B and from point B to point A' which move the duopolists toward the final Cournot equilibrium point E at the intersection of the two reaction functions.

The Cournot equilibrium point E can be obtained algebraically by substituting duopolist B's reaction function (i.e., equation [11.7]) into duopolist A's reaction function (equation [11.6]). Doing this, we get

$$Q_A = \frac{12 - (12 - Q_A)/2}{2}$$
$$= \frac{12 - 6 + Q_A/2}{2}$$
$$= 3 + Q_A/4 \qquad \text{[11.8]}$$

Multiplying both sides by 4, we get

$$4Q_A = 12 + Q_A$$

so that

$$3Q_A = 12$$

and

$$Q_A = 4 \qquad \text{[11.9]}$$

With $Q_A = 4$

$$Q_B = \frac{12 - 4}{2} \qquad \text{[11.10]}$$

so that

$$Q_A = 4 = Q_B \text{ (Cournot equilibrium)} \qquad \text{[11.11]}$$

and

$$Q = Q_A + Q_B = 4 + 4 = 8 \qquad \text{[11.12]}$$

Solving equation [11.5] for P, we get

$$P = 12 - Q \qquad \text{[11.13]}$$

With $Q = 8$ at Cournot equilibrium, the price at which each duopolist will sell spring water is

$$P = 12 - 8 = \$4 \qquad \text{[11.14]}$$

which is shown by point F in the left panel of Figure 11.9.

The Stackelberg Model

In 1934, the German economist Heinrich von Stackelberg made an important extension to the Cournot model. This became known as the **Stackelberg model.** Stackelberg assumed that one of the duopolists, say duopolist A, knows that duopolist B behaves in the naive Cournot fashion (i.e., A knows B's reaction function) and uses that knowledge in choosing its own output. Duopolist A is then called the *Stackelberg leader,* and duopolist B is referred to as the *Stackelberg follower.* All the other assumptions of the Cournot model hold

The Stackelberg model shows that duopolist A (the Stackelberg leader) will have higher profits than under the Cournot solution at the expense of duopolist B (the Stackelberg follower).

To examine the Stackelberg model, we begin by rewriting equation [11.5] for market demand function D:

$$Q = 12 - P \qquad [11.5]$$

Since Q refers to the total output of duopolists A and B, we can rewrite equation [11.5] as

$$Q_A + Q_B = 12 - P \qquad [11.15]$$

Because duopolist A knows duopolist B's reaction function, we can substitute equation [11.7] for Q_B into equation [11.15]. When we do this, we get

$$Q_A + (12 - Q_A)/2 = 12 - P \qquad [11.16]$$
$$Q_A + 6 - Q_A/2 = 12 - P$$
$$Q_A/2 = 6 - P$$
$$Q_A = 12 - 2P \qquad [11.17]$$

Equation [11.17] is now the demand function facing duopolist A when duopolist A knows duopolist B's reaction function and behavior. Plotting equation [11.17], we get the (residual) demand curve facing duopolist A, d_A^*, and its corresponding marginal revenue curve, mr_A^* (which, as usual, is twice as steep as the corresponding demand curve), as shown in Figure 11.10. Since marginal cost equals zero, duopolist A maximizes its total revenue and profits by selling six units of output (given by point E^* where $mr_A^* = MC = D$).

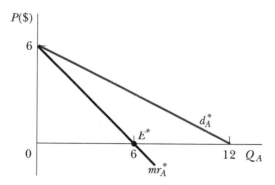

FIGURE 11.10   Demand and Marginal Revenue Curves of Stackelberg Duopolist A d_A^* and mr_A^* are, respectively, the demand curve and the marginal revenue curve facing Stackelberg duopolist A. Since $MC = 0$, duopolist A maximizes its total revenue and total profits by selling six units. This is given by point E^* where $mr_A^* = MC = 0$. Duopolist B would then sell three units. With $Q = 9, P = \$3$, duopolist A earns \$18 and duopolist B earns \$9.

With $Q_A = 6$, $Q_B = 3$ (according to B's reaction function given by equation [11.7]). With $Q = Q_A + Q_B = 6 + 3 = 9$, $P = 12 - Q = 12 - 9 = 3$. Thus, duopolist A earns a total revenue and total profit of $18 (six units at $P = \$3$), while duopolist B earns a total revenue and total profit of $9 (three units times $P = \$3$). This compares with the four units of output sold by each duopolist at $P = \$4$ (with each earning a total revenue and profit of $16) under the Cournot model. Thus, duopolist A (the Stackelberg leader) gains at the expense of duopolist B (the Stackelberg follower) with respect to the Cournot solution. Note, however, that what duopolist A gains is less than what duopolist B loses. Of course, if duopolist B were the Stackelberg leader and duopolist A were the Stackelberg follower, duopolist B would earn $18 and duopolist A would earn $9. By allowing one of the firms to behave strategically, the Stackelberg model is thus superior to the Cournot model.

When duopolist A is the Stackelberg leader, the solution is the same as point B on duopolist B's reaction function in Figure 11.9. However, while point B is not the Cournot equilibrium, it does represent the Stackelberg solution. Note that under the Stackelberg solution (whether duopolist A or B is the Stackelberg leader), the combined total revenue and profits of both firms would be $27 ($18 + $9). By colluding and operating as a centralized cartel or monopoly (see Section 11.5), the combined output of both firms could be cut from nine units in the Stackelberg solution to six units, which could be sold at $P = \$6$, so that the total combined revenue and profits that both firms could share would be $36 (rather than $27). This is sometimes referred to as the *Chamberlin model*.[21]

INTERNET SITE ADDRESSES

For an excellent slide presentation of monopolistic competition and oligopoly, see:

> http://price.bus.okstate.edu/archive/Econ3113_963/Shows/Chapter9/index.htm

For concentration ratios in U.S. manufacturing industries, see:

> http://www.census.gov/epcd/www/concentration.html and then click on manufacturing

For OPEC, see:

> http://www.opec.org

For the Fortune Global 500 companies, see:

> http://fortune.com/global500

For the Internet site of the companies discussed in this chapter, see:

> McDonald's: http://www.mcdonalds.com
> AT&T: http://www.att.com
> General Motors: http://www.gm.com
> Ford: http://www.ford.com
> Coca-Cola: http://www.coca-cola.com
> American Airline: http://www.aa.com
> Citigroup: http://www.citigroup.com
> J. P. Morgan Chase: http://www.jpmorganchase.com
> Merck: http://www.merck.com
> Johnson & Johnson: http://www.jj.com
> AOL Time Warner: http://www.aoltimewarner.com

---

[21] See D. Salvatore, Schaum's Outline, in *Microeconomic Theory*, 3rd ed. (New York: McGraw-Hill, 1992), pp. 262–263.

## CHAPTER 12

Game Theory and Oligopolistic Behavior

In this chapter, we extend our analysis of firm behavior in oligopolistic markets using game theory. As we will see, game theory offers many insights into oligopolistic interdependence and strategic behavior that could not be examined with the traditional tools of analysis presented in the previous chapter.

The chapter begins with an explanation of the basic concepts, objectives, and usefulness of game theory. It then defines a dominant strategy and a Nash equilibrium and examines their usefulness in the analysis of oligopolistic behavior. Next, the chapter describes the prisoners' dilemma and its applicability to the analysis of price and nonprice competition and cartel cheating. We conclude our discussion of game theory by analyzing multiple and strategic moves in domestic and international competition, with and without risk. The examples and applications presented in the chapter clearly highlight the importance of game theory to the understanding of many aspects of oligopolistic behavior that could not otherwise be explained. The "At the Frontier" section looks at the virtual corporation—the firm of the future—as the product of strategic alliances.

12.1 GAME THEORY: DEFINITION, OBJECTIVES, AND USEFULNESS

We have seen that oligopolists must consider the reactions of the other firms in the industry to their own actions. Some have likened the behavior of oligopolists to that of players in a game and to the strategic actions of warring factions. It is this crucial aspect of oligopolistic interdependence that game theory seeks to capture and explain (see Example 12–1).

Game theory was introduced by John von Neumann and Oskar Morgenstern in 1944, and it was soon hailed as a breakthrough in the study of oligopoly.[1] In general, **game theory** is concerned with the choice of an optimal strategy in conflict situations. Specifically, game theory can help an oligopolist choose the course of action (e.g., the best price to charge) that maximizes its benefits or profits after considering all possible reactions of its competitors. For example, game theory can help a firm determine (1) the conditions under which lowering its price would not trigger a ruinous price war; (2) whether the firm should build excess capacity to discourage entry into the industry, even though this lowers the firm's short-run profits; and (3) why cheating in a cartel usually leads to its collapse. Game theory can be of great use in the analysis of such conflict situations. In short, game theory shows how an oligopolistic firm can make strategic decisions to gain a competitive advantage over its rivals or how it can minimize the potential harm from a strategic move by a rival. Before we examine concrete examples, however, let us consider some of the common elements in all game theory.

Every game theory model includes players, strategies, and payoffs. The **players** are the decision makers (here, the managers of oligopolist firms) whose behavior we are trying to explain and predict. **Strategies** are the potential choices to change price, to develop new or differentiated products, to introduce a new or a different advertising campaign, to build excess capacity, and all other such actions that affect the sales and profitability of the firm and its rivals. The **payoff** is the outcome or consequence of each strategy. For each strategy adopted by a firm, there is usually a number of strategies (reactions) available to a rival firm. The payoff is the outcome or consequence of each *combination* of strategies by the two firms. The payoff is usually expressed in terms of the profits or losses of the firm that we are examining as a result of the firm's strategies and the rivals' responses. A table that gives the payoffs from all the strategies open to the firm and the rivals' responses is called the **payoff matrix.**

We must distinguish between zero-sum games and nonzero-sum games. A **zero-sum game** is one in which the gain of one player comes at the expense and is exactly equal to the loss of the other player. An example of this occurs if firm A increases its market share at the expense of firm B by increasing its advertising expenditures (in the face of unchanged advertising by firm B). But if firm B also increases its advertising expenditures, firm A might not gain any market share at all. On the other hand, if firm A increases its price and firm B does not match the price increase, firm A might lose market to firm B. Games of this nature, where the gains of one player equal the losses of the other (so that total gains plus total losses sum to zero) are called zero-sum games. If the gains or losses of one firm do not come at the expense of or provide equal benefit to the other firm, however, we have a **nonzero-sum game.** An example of this might arise if increased advertising leads to higher profits of both firms and we use profits rather than market share as the payoff. In this case we would have a *positive-sum game.* If increased advertising raises costs more than revenues and the profits of both firms decline, we have a *negative-sum game.*

---

[1] J. von Neumann and O. Morgenstern, *Theory of Games and Economic Behavior* (Princeton, NJ: Princeton University Press, 1944). A more recent and in-depth presentation of game theory with applications to economics is found in M. J. Osborne and A. Rubinstein, *A Course in Game Theory* (Cambridge, MA: MIT Press, 1994).

EXAMPLE 12-1
Military Strategy and Strategic Business Decisions

According to William E. Peackock, the president of two St. Louis companies and former assistant secretary of the army under President Carter, decision making in business has much in common with military strategy and can thus be profitably analyzed using game theory. Although business managers' actions are restricted by laws and regulations to prevent unfair practices and the objective of managers, of course, is not to literally destroy the competition, there is much that they can learn from military strategists. Peacock points out that throughout history, military conflicts have produced a set of basic Darwinian principles that can serve as an excellent guideline to business managers about how to compete in the marketplace. Neglecting these principles can make the difference between business success and failure.

In business as in war, it is crucial for the organization to have a clear objective and to explain this objective to all of its employees. The benefits of a simple marketing strategy that all employees can understand are clearly evidenced by the success of McDonald's. Both business and war also require the development of a strategy for attacking. Being aggressive is important because few competitions are ever won by being passive. Furthermore, both business and warfare require unity of command to pinpoint responsibility. Even in decentralized companies with informal lines of command, there are always key individuals who must make important decisions. Finally, in business as in war, the element of surprise and security (keeping your strategy secret) is crucial. For example, Lee Iacocca stunned the competition in 1964 by introducing the immensely successful (high payoff) Mustang. Finally, in business as in war, spying to discover a rival's plans or steal a rival's new technological breakthrough is becoming more common.

More than ever before, today's business leaders must learn how to tap employees' ideas and energy, manage large-scale rapid change, anticipate business conditions five or ten years down the road, and muster the courage to steer the firm in radical new directions when necessary. Above all, firms must think and act strategically in a world of increasing global competition. Game theory can be particularly useful and can offer important insights in the analysis of oligopolistic interdependence. Indeed, more and more firms are making use of war-games simulations in their decision making.

Sources: W. E. Peacock, *Corporate Combat* (New York: Facts on File Publication, 1984); "The Valley of Spies," *Forbes,* October 26, 1992, pp. 200–204; "Business War Games Attract Big Warriors," *Wall Street Journal,* December 22, 1994, p. B1; "The Right Game: Use Game Theory to Shape Strategy," *Harvard Business Review,* July–August 1995, pp. 57–71; "Spy vs. Spy: How Safe Are Your Company's Secrets?" *Fortune,* February 17, 1997, p. 136; "The Prying Game," *Fortune,* September 17, 2001, p. 235; and "The Return of von Clausewitz," *Economist,* March 2002, pp. 18–20.

12.2   DOMINANT STRATEGY AND NASH EQUILIBRIUM

In this section, we discuss the meaning of a dominant strategy and the Nash equilibrium and examine their usefulness in the analysis of oligopolistic interdependence.

TABLE 12.1 Payoff Matrix for the Advertising Game

		Firm B	
		Advertise	Don't Advertise
Firm A	Advertise	4, 3	5, 1
	Don't Advertise	2, 5	3, 2

Dominant Strategy

Let's begin with the simplest type of game with an industry (duopoly) composed of two firms, firm A and firm B, and a choice of two strategies for each—advertise or don't advertise. Firm A, of course, expects to earn higher profits if it advertises than if it doesn't. But the actual level of profits of firm A depends also on whether firm B advertises. Thus, each strategy by firm A (i.e., advertise or don't advertise) can be associated with each of firm B's strategies (also to advertise or not to advertise). The four possible outcomes from this simple game are illustrated by the payoff matrix in Table 12.1.

In the payoff matrix in Table 12.1, the first number in each of the four cells refers to the payoff (profit) for firm A, while the second is the payoff (profit) for firm B. From Table 12.1, we see that if both firms advertise, firm A will earn a profit of 4, and firm B will earn a profit of 3 (the top left cell of the payoff matrix).[2] The bottom left cell of the payoff matrix shows that if firm A doesn't advertise and firm B does, firm A will have a profit of 2, and firm B will have a profit of 5. The other payoffs in the second column of the table can be interpreted in the same way.

What strategy should each firm choose? Let's consider firm A first. If firm B does advertise (i.e., moving down the left column of Table 12.1), we see that firm A will earn a profit of 4 if it also advertises and 2 if it doesn't. Thus, firm A should advertise if firm B advertises. If firm B doesn't advertise (i.e., moving down the right column in Table 12.1), firm A would earn a profit of 5 if it advertises and 3 if it doesn't. Thus, firm A should advertise whether firm B advertises or not. Firm A's profits will always be greater if it advertises than if it doesn't, regardless of what firm B does. We can then say that advertising is the dominant strategy for firm A. The **dominant strategy** is the optimal choice for a player no matter what the opponent does.

The same is true for firm B. Whatever firm A does (i.e., whether firm A advertises or not), it will always pay for firm B to advertise. We can see this by moving across each row of Table 12.1. Specifically, if firm A advertises, firm B's profit would be 3 if it advertises and 1 if it does not. Similarly, if firm A does not advertise, firm B's profit would be 5 if it advertises and 2 if it doesn't. Thus, the dominant strategy for firm B is also to advertise.

In this case, both firm A and firm B have the dominant strategy of advertising and this will, therefore, be the final equilibrium. Both firm A and firm B will advertise regardless of what the other firm does and will earn a profit of 4 and 3, respectively (the top left cell in

---

[2] The profits of 4 and 3 could refer, for example, to $4 million and $3 million, respectively.

TABLE 12.2   Payoff Matrix for the Advertising Game

		Firm B	
		Advertise	Don't Advertise
Firm A	Advertise	4, 3	5, 1
	Don't Advertise	2, 5	6, 2

the payoff matrix in Table 12.1). The advertising solution or final equilibrium for both firms holds whether firm A or firm B chooses its strategy first or if both firms decide on their best strategy simultaneously.

Nash Equilibrium

Not all games have a dominant strategy for each player, however. An example of this is shown in the payoff matrix in Table 12.2. This table is the same as the payoff matrix in Table 12.1, except that the first number in the bottom right cell was changed from 3 to 6. Now firm B has a dominant strategy but firm A does not. The dominant strategy for firm B is to advertise whether firm A advertises or not, because the payoffs for firm B are the same as in Table 12.1. Firm A, however, has no dominant strategy now. If firm B advertises, firm A earns a profit of 4 if it advertises and 2 if it does not. Thus, if firm B advertises, firm A should also advertise. On the other hand, if firm B does not advertise, firm A earns a profit of 5 if it advertises and 6 if it does not.[3] Thus, firm A should advertise if firm B does, and it should not advertise if firm B doesn't. Firm A no longer has a dominant strategy. What firm A should do now depends on what firm B does.

In order for firm A to determine whether to advertise, firm A must first try to determine what firm B will do (and advertise if firm B does and not advertise if firm B does not). If firm A knows the payoff matrix, it can figure out that firm B has the dominant strategy of advertising. Therefore, the optimal strategy for firm A is also to advertise (because firm A will earn a profit of 4 by advertising and 2 by not advertising—see the first column of Table 12.2). This is the Nash equilibrium, named after John Nash, the Princeton University mathematician and 1994 Nobel prize winner who first formalized the notion in 1951.

The **Nash equilibrium** is a situation in which each player chooses an optimal strategy, *given the strategy chosen by the other player.* In our example, the high advertising strategy for firm A and firm B is the Nash equilibrium, because given that firm B chooses its dominant strategy of advertising, the optimal strategy for firm A is also to advertise. Note that when both firms had a dominant strategy, each firm was able to choose its optimal strategy regardless of the strategy adopted by its rival. Here, only firm B has a dominant strategy; firm A does not. As a result, firm A cannot choose its optimal strategy independently of firm B's strategy. Only when each player has chosen its optimal strategy given the strategy of

---

[3] This might result, for example, if firm A's advertisement is not effective or if advertising adds more to firm A's costs than to its revenues.

the other player do we have a Nash equilibrium. The Cournot equilibrium examined in Section 11.4 was an example of a Nash equilibrium. Not all games have a Nash equilibrium, and some games can have more than one Nash equilibrium (see Problem 3 with answer at end of book).

EXAMPLE 12–2

Dell Computers and Nash Equilibrium

Dell Computers of Austin, Texas, a company created by 27-year-old Michael Dell in 1984, ended the 2000 fiscal year with revenues of $38.9 billion, making it the fourth largest computer company in the nation (and largest seller of PCs in the United States and the world). By offering a 30-day money-back guarantee on next-day, free on-sight service through independent contractors for the first year of ownership, and unlimited calls to a toll-free technical support line, Dell established a solid reputation for reliability, thus taking the fear and uncertainty out of mail-order computers. Dell will even mail a $25 check to any customer that does not get a Dell technician within five minutes of calling Dell's technical support line! Ordering a computer from Dell by mail is now like ordering a Big Mac at MacDonald's—you know exactly what you will get. By eliminating retailers, Dell was also able to charge lower prices than its larger and more established competitors. For example, Dell's selling and administrative expenses were 14 cents for each dollar of sales, compared with 24 cents for Apple and 30 cents for IBM. Dell ships computers by mail by adding only a 2% shipping charge to the sale price. When receiving a mail order, Dell technicians simply pick up the now-standard components from the shelf to assemble the particular PC ordered. It is simple, quick, and inexpensive. Thus, Dell has developed a dominant strategy—one that is optimal regardless of what competitors do. By doing so, Dell has become a kind of high-tech Wal-Mart.

Until recently, traditional computer firms such as Compaq, IBM, Hewlett-Packard, Apple, and others always thought that customers were willing to pay a substantial retail markup for the privilege of being able to go to a store and feel and touch the machine before buying it. Some customers still do. But by reducing fears and uncertainty from ordering computers through the mail, Dell was able to convince a growing number of customers to bypass the retailers and order directly from Dell by mail at lower prices. Today, more than 20% of PCs are sold by mail in the United States. Given Dell's dominant and profitable strategy, Compaq, IBM, Hewlett-Packard, and Apple quickly followed and set up their own mail-order departments and 800 phone lines in 1993 and 1994. Their dominant strategy of selling exclusively through retail outlets was knocked out by Dell's new market strategy, and so we now can say that the computer industry is in Nash equilibrium. Given Dell's dominant strategy, the other major computer companies have decided to change their strategy and also sell by mail. Dell, however, is more apt at selling computers through the mail and retains almost 50% of the mail-order computer business. By 2002, Dell had 14% of the world PC market and

25% (and aiming at 40%) of the U.S. market, and it was growing and earning profits while other PC markers were shrinking and incurring losses. In fact, at the beginning of 2002, IBM announced that it was leaving the PC market.

Sources: "The Computer Is in the Mail (Really)," *Business Week,* January 23, 1995, pp. 76–77; "Michael Dell Turns the PC World Inside Out," *Fortune,* September 8, 1997, pp. 76–86; "IBM Plans to Stop Selling Its PC's in Retail Outlets," *New York Times,* October 20, 1999, p. C6; "Dell Domination," *Fortune,* January 21, 2002, pp. 71–75; and "Take No Prisoners," *U.S. News & World Report,*" January 14, 2002, pp. 36–38.

12.3 | THE PRISONERS' DILEMMA, PRICE AND NONPRICE COMPETITION, AND CARTEL CHEATING

In this section, we examine the meaning of the prisoners' dilemma and see how it can be applied to explain oligopolistic behavior in the form of price and nonprice competition and cartel cheating.

The Prisoners' Dilemma: Definition and Importance

Oligopolistic firms often face a problem called the **prisoners' dilemma.** This refers to a sit uation in which each firm adopts its dominant strategy, but each could do better (e.g., earn larger profits) by cooperating. Consider the following situation. Two suspects are arrested for armed robbery; if convicted, each could receive a maximum sentence of ten years imprisonment. Unless one or both suspects confess, however, the evidence is such that they could only be convicted of possessing stolen goods, which carries a maximum sentence of one year in prison. Each suspect is interrogated separately and no communication is allowed between the two suspects. The district attorney promises each suspect that by confessing, he or she will go free while the other suspect (who does not confess) will receive the full ten-year sentence. If both suspects confess, each gets a reduced sentence of five years imprisonment. The (negative) payoff matrix in terms of detention years is given in Table 12.3.

TABLE 12.3   Negative Payoff Matrix for Suspect A and Suspect B (years of detention)

		Suspect B	
		Confess	Don't Confess
Suspect A	Confess	5, 5	0, 10
	Don't Confess	10, 0	1, 1

From Table 12.3, we see that confessing is the best or dominant strategy for suspect A no matter what suspect B does. The reason is that if suspect B confesses, suspect A receives a five-year jail sentence if he also confesses and a ten-year sentence if he does not. Similarly, if suspect B does not confess, suspect A goes free if he confesses and receives a one-year sentence if he does not. Thus, the dominant strategy for suspect A is to confess. Confessing is also the best (and the dominant) strategy for suspect B. The reason is that if suspect A confesses, suspect B gets a five-year jail sentence if he also confesses and a ten-year jail sentence if he does not. Similarly, if suspect A does not confess, suspect B goes free if he confesses and gets one year if he does not. Thus, the dominant strategy for suspect B is also to confess.

With each suspect adopting his or her dominant strategy of confessing, each ends up receiving a five-year jail sentence. But if each suspect did not confess, each would get only a one-year jail sentence! Each suspect, however, is afraid that if he or she does not confess, the other will confess, and so he or she would end up receiving a ten-year jail sentence. Only if each suspect were sure that the other would not confess, and he or she does not confess, would each get only a one-year sentence. Because it is not possible to reach an agreement not to confess (remember, the suspects are already in jail and cannot communicate), each suspect adopts his or her dominant strategy to confess and receives a five-year jail sentence. Even if an agreement not to confess could be reached, the agreement could not be enforced. Therefore, each suspect will end up confessing and receiving a five-year jail sentence.

Price and Nonprice Competition, Cartel Cheating, and the Prisoners' Dilemma

The concept of the prisoners' dilemma can be used to analyze price and nonprice competition in oligopolistic markets, as well as the incentive to cheat in a cartel (i.e., the tendency to secretly cut prices or to sell more than the allocated quota). Oligopolistic price competition in the presence of the prisoners' dilemma can be examined with the payoff matrix in Table 12.4.

The payoff matrix of Table 12.4 shows that if firm B charged a low price (say, $6), firm A would earn a profit of 2 if it also charged the low price ($6) and 1 if it charged a high price (say, $8). Similarly, if firm B charged a high price ($8), firm A would earn a profit of 5 if it charged the low price and 3 if it charged the high price. Thus, firm A should adopt its

TABLE 12.4 Payoff Matrix for Pricing Game

		Firm B	
		Low Price	High Price
Firm A	Low Price	2, 2	5, 1
	High Price	1, 5	3, 3

dominant strategy of charging the low price. Turning to firm B, we see that if firm A charged the low price, firm B would earn a profit of 2 if it charged the low price and 1 if it charged the high price. Similarly, if firm A charged the high price, firm B would earn a profit of 5 if it charged the low price and 3 if it charged the high price. Thus, firm B should also adopt its dominant strategy of charging the low price. However, both firms could do better (i.e., earn the higher profit of 3) if they cooperated and both charged the high price (the bottom right cell).

Thus, the firms are in a prisoners' dilemma: each firm will charge the low price and earn a smaller profit because if it charges the high price, it cannot trust its rival to also charge the high price. Specifically, suppose that firm A charged the high price with the expectation that firm B would also charge the high price (so that each firm would earn a profit of 3). Given that firm A has charged the high price, however, firm B now has an incentive to charge the low price, because by doing so it can increase its profits to 5 (see the bottom left cell). The same is true if firm B started by charging the high price with the expectation that firm A would also do so. The net result is that each firm charges the low price and earns a profit of only 2. Only if the two firms cooperate and both charge the high price will they earn the higher profit of 3 (and overcome their dilemma).

Although the payoff matrix of Table 12.4 was used to examine oligopolistic price competition in the presence of the prisoners' dilemma, by simply changing the heading of the columns and rows of the payoff matrix we can use the same payoff matrix to examine nonprice competition and cartel cheating. For example, if we change the heading of "low price" to "advertise" and the heading of "high price" to "don't advertise" in Table 12.4, we can use the same matrix to analyze advertising as a form of nonprice competition in the presence of the prisoners' dilemma. We see that each firm would adopt its dominant strategy of advertising and (as in the case of charging a low price) would earn a profit of 2. Both firms, however, would do better by not advertising because they would then earn (as in the case of charging a high price) the higher profit of 3. The firms then face the prisoners' dilemma. Only by cooperating in not advertising would each increase its profits to 3. For example, when cigarette advertising on television was banned in 1971, all tobacco companies benefitted by spending less on advertising and earning higher profits. While the intended effect of the law was to encourage people not to smoke, the law had the unintended effect of solving the prisoners' dilemma for cigarette producers!

Similarly, if we now change the heading of "low price" or "advertise" to "cheat" and the heading of "high price" or "don't advertise" to "don't cheat" in the columns and rows of the payoff matrix of Table 12.4, we can use the same payoffs in the table to analyze the incentive for cartel members to cheat in the presence of the prisoners' dilemma. In this case, each firm adopts its dominant strategy of cheating and (as in the case of charging the low price or advertising) earns a profit of 2. But by not cheating, however, each member of the cartel would earn the higher profit of 3. The cartel members then face the prisoners' dilemma. Only if cartel members do not cheat will each share the higher cartel profits of 3. A cartel can prevent or reduce the probability of cheating by monitoring the sales of each member and punishing cheaters. However, the larger the cartel and the more differentiated the product, the more difficult it is for the cartel to do this and prevent cheating.

EXAMPLE 12–3

The Airlines' Fare War and the Prisoners' Dilemma

In April 1992, American Airlines, then the nation's largest carrier with 20% share of the domestic market, introduced a new simplified fare structure that included only four kinds of fares instead of 16, and it lowered prices for most business and leisure travelers. Coach fares were cut by an average of 38% and first class fares were lowered by 20% to 50%. Other domestic airlines quickly announced similar fare cuts. American and other carriers hoped that the increase in air travel resulting from the fare cuts would more than offset the price reductions and eventually turn losses into badly needed profits (during 1990 and 1991, domestic airlines lost more than $6 billion, Pan Am and Eastern Airlines went out of business, and Continental, TWA, and America West filed for bankruptcy protection).

Rather than establishing price discipline, however, American's new fare structure started a process of competitive fare cuts that led to another disastrous price war during the summer of 1992. It started when TWA, operating under protection from creditors and badly needing quick revenues, began to undercut American's fares by 10% to 20% as soon as they were announced. American and other airlines responded by matching TWA price cuts. Then, on May 26, 1992, Northwest, in an effort to stimulate summer leisure travel, announced that an adult and child could travel on the same flight within continental United States for the price of one ticket. The next day, American countered by cutting all fares by 50%. The other big carriers immediately matched American's 50% price cut for all summer travel. Another full-fledged price war had been unleashed.

Even though deep price cuts increased summer travel sharply, all airlines incurred losses (i.e., the low fares failed to cover the industry average cost). Three attempts to increase air fares by 30% above presale levels in the fall of 1992 failed when one or more of the carriers did not go along. Having become used to deep discounts, passengers were simply unwilling to pay higher fares, especially in a weak economy. Similar price wars erupted in summer 1993 and 1994. In short, U.S. airlines seemed to be in a prisoners' dilemma and, unable to cooperate, faced heavy losses. Only with the strong rebound in air travel in 1995 did airlines refrain from engaging in another disastrous price war and thus earned profits. But tranquility and profits did not last long. The reason is that the marginal cost of adding passengers to a flight after it has been scheduled is very low indeed, and so there is a great incentive for all airlines to cut fares to fill all seats on a flight. With the economy falling into recession in the second half of 2001 and the terrorist attack on the World Trade Center in September of that year, air travel fell sharply and airlines began to incur huge losses, prompting the U.S. Congress to extend $10 billion in loan guarantees to the nation's airlines to prevent their collapse.

Sources: "American Air Cuts Most Fares in Simplification of Rate System," *New York Times,* April 10, 1992, p. 1; "The Airlines Are Killing Each Other Again," *Business Week,* June 8, 1992, p. 32; "Airlines Cut Fares by up to 45%," *New York Times,* September 14, 1993, p. D1; "Come Fly the Unfriendly Skies," *The Economist,* November 5, 1994, pp. 61–62; "How High Can the Airlines Fly?," *Business Week,* August 7, 1995, pp. 24–25; "A New Sense of Urgency in Debating the Future of the Airlines," *New York Times,* December 17, 2001, p. C10.

12.4   REPEATED GAMES AND TIT-FOR-TAT STRATEGY

We have seen how two firms facing the prisoners' dilemma can increase their profits by co-operating. Such cooperation, however, is not likely to occur in the single-move prisoners' dilemma games discussed so far. Cooperation is more likely to occur in repeated or many-move games, which are more realistic in the real world. For example, oligopolists do not decide on their pricing strategy only once, but many times over many years. Axelrod found that in such **repeated games** the best strategy is that of tit-for-tat.[4] **Tit-for-tat** behavior can be summarized as follows: do to your opponent what he or she has just done to you. That is, begin by cooperating and continue to cooperate as long as your opponent cooperates. If he betrays you, the next time you betray him back. If he then cooperates, the next time you also cooperate. This strategy is retaliatory enough to discourage noncooperation but forgiving enough to allow a pattern of mutual cooperation to develop. In fact, Axelrod found through computer simulated experiments that tit-for-tat is the best strategy in repeated prisoners' dilemma games.

For an optimal tit-for-tat strategy, however, certain conditions must be met. First, a reasonably stable set of players is required. If the players change frequently, there is little chance for cooperative behavior to develop. Second, there must be a small number of players (otherwise, it becomes difficult to keep track of what each is doing). Third, it is assumed that each firm can quickly detect (and is willing and able to quickly retaliate for) cheating by other firms. Cheating that goes undetected for a long time encourages cheating. Fourth, demand and cost conditions must be relatively stable (for if they change rapidly, it is difficult to define what is cooperative behavior and what is not). Fifth, it must be assumed that the game is repeated indefinitely, or at least a very large and *uncertain* number of times. If the game is played for a finite number of times, each firm has an incentive not to cooperate in the final period because it cannot be harmed by retaliation. Each firm knows this and thus will not cooperate on the next-to-the-last move. Indeed, in an effort to gain a competitive advantage by being the first to start cheating, the entire situation will unravel and cheating begins from the first move.[5]

There are, of course, times when a firm finds it advantageous not to cooperate. For example, if a supplier is near bankruptcy, a firm may find every excuse for not paying its bills to the near-bankrupt firm (claiming, for example, that supplies were defective or did not meet specification) in the hope of avoiding payment altogether if the firm does go out of business. It is the necessity to deal with the same suppliers and customers in the future and their ability to retaliate for noncooperative behavior that often forces a firm to cooperate. With a tit-for-tat strategy, however, it is possible for firms to cooperate without actually resorting to collusion. As we will see in the next chapter, this can be a nightmare for antitrust officials.

---

[4] See R. Axelrod, *The Evolution of Cooperation* (New York: Basic Books, 1984).
[5] See D. Kreps, P. Milgron, J. Roberts, and R. Wilson, "Rational Cooperation in the Finitely Repeated Prisoners' Dilemma," *Journal of Economic Theory,* vol. 27, 1982, pp. 245–252.

12.5   STRATEGIC MOVES

In this section, we examine strategic games involving threats, commitments, credibility, and entry deterrence. In the next section, we discuss strategic games and international competitiveness, and in the final section we examine risk in game theory. These concepts greatly enrich game theory and provide an important element of realism and relevance.

Threats, Commitments, and Credibility

Oligopolistic firms often adopt strategies to gain a competitive advantage over their rivals, even if it means constraining their own behavior or temporarily reducing their own profits. For example, an oligopolist may threaten to lower its prices if its rivals lower theirs, even if this means reducing its own profits. This threat can be made credible, for example, by a written commitment to customers to match any lower price by competitors. Schelling defined such a **strategic move** as one that "influences the other person's choice in a manner favorable to one's self by affecting the other person's expectations of how one's self would behave."[6] There must be a *commitment* that the firm making the *threat* is ready carry it out for the threat to be *credible*.

For example, suppose that the payoff matrix of firms A and B is given by Table 12.5. This payoff matrix indicates that firm A has the dominant strategy of charging a high price. The reason is that if firm B charged a low price, firm A would earn a profit of 2 if it charged a low price and a profit of 3 if it charged a high price. Similarly, if firm B charged a high price, firm A would earn a profit of 2 if it charged a low price and a profit of 5 if it charged a high price. Therefore, firm A charges a high price regardless of what firm B does. Given that firm A charges a high price, firm B will want to charge a low price because by doing so it will earn a profit of 4 (instead of 3 with a high price). This is shown by the bottom left cell of Table 12.5. Now firm A can threaten to lower its price and also charge a low price. However, firm B does not believe this threat (i.e., the threat is not credible) because by lowering its price firm A would lower its profits from 3 (with a high price) to 2 with the low price (the top left cell in the table).

One way to make its threat credible is for firm A to develop a *reputation* for carrying out its threats, even at the expense of its profits. Although this may seem irrational, if firm A actually carried out its threat several times, it would earn a reputation for making credible threats. This is likely to induce firm B to also charge a high price, which would possibly lead to higher profits for firm A in the long run. In that case, firm A would earn a profit of 5 and firm B a profit of 3 (the bottom right cell) as opposed to a profit of 3 for firm A and 4 for firm B (the bottom left cell). Even if firm B earns a profit of 3 by charging the high price (as compared with a profit of 4 by charging the low price), the profit is still higher than the profit of 2 that it would earn if firm A carries out the threat of charging the low price if firm B does the same (see the top left cell of the table). By showing a commitment to carry out its threats, firm A makes its threats credible and increases its profits over time. The same result

---

[6] See T. Schelling, *The Strategy of Conflict* (New York: Oxford University Press, 1960). Another important volume examining strategic moves is M. Porter, *Competitive Strategy* (New York: Free Press, 1980).

TABLE 12.5	Payoff Matrix for Pricing Game with a Threat	
		Firm B	

		Low Price	High Price
Firm A	Low Price	2, 2	2, 1
	High Price	3, 4	5, 3

TABLE 12.6	Payoff Matrix without Credible Entry Deterrence	

| | | **Firm B** | |

		Enter	Don't Enter
Firm A	Low Price	4, −2	6, 0
	High Price	7, 2	10, 0

would follow if firm A develops a reputation for being irrational and charging a low price to deter entry into the industry—even if this means lower profits in the long run.

Entry Deterrence

One important strategy that an oligopolist can use to deter market entry is to threaten to lower its price and thereby impose a loss on the potential entrant. Such a threat, however, works only if it is credible. *Entry deterrence* can be examined with the payoff matrices of Tables 12.6 and 12.7.

The payoff matrix of Table 12.6 shows that firm A's threat to lower its price is not credible and does not discourage firm B from entering the market. The reason is that firm A earns a profit of 4 if it charges the low price and a profit of 7 if it charges the high price. Unless firm A makes a credible commitment to fight entry even at the expense of profits, it would not deter firm B from entering the market. Firm A could make a credible threat by expanding its capacity before it is needed (i.e., to build excess capacity). The new payoff matrix might then look like the one in Table 12.7.

The payoff matrix of Table 12.7 is the same as in Table 12.6, except that firm A's profits are now lower when it charges a high price because idle or excess capacity increases firm A's costs without increasing its sales. On the other hand, in the payoff matrix of Table 12.7, we assume that charging a low price would allow firm A to increase sales and utilize its newly built capacity, so that costs and revenues *increase* leaving firm A's profits the same as in Table 12.6 (i.e., the same as before firm A expanded capacity).[7] Building

---

[7] Revenues and profits need not increase exactly by the same amount, so that profits can change even when firm A charges a low price. The conclusion would remain the same, however (i.e., firm B would be deterred from entering the market), as long as firm A earns a higher profit with a low price than with a high price after increasing its capacity.

TABLE 12.7   Payoff Matrix with Credible Entry Deterrence

		Firm B	
		Enter	Don't Enter
Firm A	Low Price	4, −2	6, 0
	High Price	3, 2	8, 0

excess capacity in anticipation of future need now becomes a credible threat, because with excess capacity firm A will charge a low price and earn a profit of 4 instead of a profit of 3 if it charged the high price. By charging a low price now, however, firm B would incur a loss of 2 if it entered the market, and so firm B would stay out. Entry deterrence is now credible and effective. An alternative to building excess capacity could be for firm A to cultivate a reputation for irrationality in deterring entry by charging a low price even if this means earning lower profits indefinitely.[8]

EXAMPLE 12–4

Wal-Mart's Preemptive Expansion Marketing Strategy

Rapid expansion during the 1980s (from 153 stores in 1976 to more than 3,000 in 2001) propelled Wal-Mart, the discount retail-store chain started by Sam Walton in 1969, to become the nation's (and the world's) largest and most profitable retailer, at a time when most other retailers were making razor-thin profits or incurring losses as a result of stiff competition. How did Wal-Mart do it? By opening retail discount stores in small towns across America and adopting an everyday low-price strategy. The conventional wisdom had been that a discount retail outlet required a population base of at least 100,000 people to be profitable. Sam Walton showed otherwise: By relying on size, low costs, and high turnover, Wal-Mart earned high profits even in towns of only a few thousand people. Since a small town could support only one large discount store, Wal-Mart did not have to worry about competition from other national chains (which would drive prices and profit margins down). At the same time, Wal-Mart was able to easily undersell small local specialized stores out of existence (Wal-Mart has been labeled the "Merchant of Death" by local retailers), thereby establishing a virtual local retailing monopoly.

The success of Wal-Mart did not go unnoticed by other national discount retailers such as Kmart and Target, and so a frantic race started to open discount stores in rural America ahead of the competition. By adopting such an aggressive expansion or

---

[8] For a more detailed analysis of the use of excess capacity to deter entry, see J. Tirole, *The Theory of Industrial Organization* (Cambridge, MA: MIT Press, 1988).

preemptive investment strategy, Wal-Mart has continued to expand at breathtaking speed and to beat the competition most of the time. Sales at Wal-Mart increased from $80 billion in 1994 to $220 billion in 2001 (thus heading the list of the Fortune 500 companies) and are projected to continue its rise rapidly in the future. Pricier than Wal-Mart and dowdier than Target, Kmart, instead, filed for bankruptcy in January 2002.

Since 1992, Wal-Mart has also expanded abroad, first in Canada and Mexico (where it is already the largest retailer), then in Argentina, Brazil, China, Korea and Puerto Rico, and more recently in Germany, England and Japan. In 2001, Wal-Mart had 1,091 stores abroad, which generated 17% of its total revenue. Regarded as one of the most successful and aggressive retailers in the United States, Wal-Mart is now also shaking up the industry abroad in the nations in which it is operating by its winning low-price strategy, long store hours, friendly service, private-label brands, and a super-efficient distribution system. During the next few years, Europe is likely to be the fiercest battleground as Wal-Mart tries to expand across the continent and attempts to duplicate its American success. For example, Wal-Mart has yet to turn a profit in Germany. European retailers are responding by also consolidating. For example, in fall 1999, French retailer Carrefour and Promedes merged, creating Europe's biggest and the world's second largest retailer with annual sales of $60 billion and operating more than 9,000 stores in 31 countries.

Sources: "Big Discounters Duel Over Hot market," *Wall Street Journal,* August 23, 1995, p. A8; "Wal-Mart Casts Eye Northward," *New York Times,* February 16, 1999, p. C1; "French Retailers Create New Wall-Mart Rival," *Wall Street Journal,* August 31, 1999, p. A14; "How Well Does Wal-Mart Travel?" *Business Week,* September 3, 2001, pp. 82–84; "Wal-Mart Around the World," *The Economist,* December 8, 2001, pp. 55–57; "Kmart to File for Chapter 11 Bankruptcy," *Wall Street Journal,* January 23, 2002, p. A3; and "Wal-Mart Heads List of Fortune 500," *New York Times,* April 1, 2002, p. C3.

12.6   STRATEGIC MOVES AND INTERNATIONAL COMPETITIVENESS

Game theory can also be used to analyze the strategic trade and industrial policies that a nation could use to gain a competitive advantage over other nations, particularly in the field of high technology. This is best shown through an example.

Suppose that Boeing (the American commercial aircraft company) and Airbus Industrie (a consortium of German, French, English, and Spanish companies) are both deciding whether to produce a new aircraft. Suppose also that because of the huge cost of developing the new aircraft, a single producer would have to have the entire world market for itself to earn a profit, say of $100 million. If both firms produce the aircraft, each loses $10 million. This information is shown in Table 12.8. The case in which both firms produce the aircraft and each incurs a loss of $10 million is shown in the top left cell of the table. If only Boeing produces the aircraft, Boeing makes a profit of $100 million while Airbus makes a zero profit (the top right cell of the table). On the other hand, if Boeing does not produce the aircraft while Airbus does, Boeing makes zero profit while Airbus makes a profit of $100 million (the bottom left cell). Finally, if neither firm produces the aircraft, each makes a zero profit (the bottom right cell).

TABLE 12.8 Two-Firm Competition and Strategic Trade Policy

		Airbus	
		Produce	Don't Produce
Boeing	Produce	−10, −10	100, 0
	Don't Produce	0, 100	0, 0

Suppose that for whatever reason, Boeing enters the market first and earns a profit of $100 million (we might call this the first-mover advantage). Airbus is now locked out of the market because it could not earn a profit. This is the case shown in the top right cell of the table. If Airbus entered the market, both firms would incur a loss (and we would have the case shown in the top left column of the table). Suppose now that European governments give a subsidy of $15 million per year to Airbus. Airbus would then produce the aircraft even though Boeing is already producing the aircraft, because with the $15 million subsidy, Airbus would turn a loss of $10 million into a profit of $5 million. Without a subsidy, however, Boeing will go from making a profit of $100 million (without Airbus in the market) to incurring a loss of $10 million afterwards (we are still in the top left corner of the table, but with the Airbus entry changed from −10 without the subsidy to +5 with the subsidy). Because of its unsubsidized loss, Boeing will stop producing the aircraft, thereby leaving the entire market to Airbus, which will then make a profit of $100 million without any further subsidy (the bottom left cell of the table).[9]

The U.S. government could, of course, retaliate with a subsidy of its own to keep Boeing producing the aircraft. Except in cases of national defense, however, the U.S. government is much less disposed to grant subsidies to firms than European governments. Although the real world is certainly much more complex than this example, we can see how a nation could overcome a market disadvantage and acquire a strategic comparative advantage in a high-tech field by means of an industrial and strategic trade policy.

One serious shortcoming of the above analysis is that it is usually very difficult to accurately forecast the outcome of government industrial and trade policies (i.e., get the data to fill a table such as Table 12.8). Even a small change in the table could completely change the results. For example, suppose that if both Airbus and Boeing produce the aircraft, Airbus incurs a loss of $10 million (as before) but Boeing makes a profit of $10 million (without any subsidy), say, because of superior technology. Then, even if Airbus produces the aircraft with the subsidy, Boeing will remain in the market because it is able to earn a profit without any subsidy. Then, Airbus would require a subsidy indefinitely, year after year, in order to continue to produce the aircraft. In this case, giving a subsidy to Airbus does not seem to be such a good idea.[10] Thus, it is extremely difficult to carry out this type of analysis in the real world. Getting the analysis wrong, however, can be very harmful and may

---

[9] This type of analysis was first introduced into international trade by J. Brander and B. Spencer. See their "International R & D Rivalry and Industrial Strategy," *Review of Economic Studies,* October 1983, pp. 707–722. See also M. Porter, *The Competitive Advantage of Nations* (New York: The Free Press, 1990).

[10] See "A Paper Dart Against Boeing," *The Economist,* June 11, 1994, pp. 61–62.

even result in the firm's failure (see Example 12–5). This is the reason that most U.S. economists today are against industrial policy and still regard free trade as the best policy for the United States.[11]

Airbus did decide in 2000 to build its super-jumbo A380 capable of transporting 550 passengers and to be ready by 2006 at a cost of over $10 billion, and thus compete head-on with the Boeing 747 (which has been in service since 1969 and can carry up to 475 passengers). Boeing greeted Airbus' decisions to build its A380 by announcing in 2001 plans to build a new "sonic cruiser" jet that can transport, non-stop, up to 300 passengers to any point on earth at close to the speed of sound. Boeing believes that passengers prefer arriving at their destinations sooner and avoid congested hubs and the hassle and delays of intermediate stops. It remains to be seen as to which strategy turns out to be the winning or best one.[12]

EXAMPLE 12–5
Companies' Strategic Mistakes and Failures

Nearly 100,000 businesses failed in the United States during 1992 (a recession year) as compared with only about 35,000 in 2000 (the last year of the boom of the 1990s) and nearly 40,000 in 2001 (a recession year). Although the reasons businesses fail are many and the details differ from case to case, several general underlying causes can be identified. *First*, many business failures arise because senior executives do not fully understand the fundamentals of their business or core expertise and business of the firm. Then the company drifts (often through mergers and acquisitions) into lines of business about which it knows little. This, for example, happened to Kodak when it diversified from its core camera and film business into pharmaceuticals and consumer health products during the 1990s.

The *second* basic reason for business failures is lack of vision or the inability of top management to anticipate or foresee serious problems that the business may face down the road. For example, U.S. automakers (General Motors, Ford, and Chrysler) failed to understand early enough the seriousness of the competitive challenge coming from Japan and almost willingly ceded the small-car market to Japan (because of the low profits per car earned in that market) during the 1970s in the erroneous belief that Japan would never be able to compete effectively in the medium-range segment of the market (where profit per automobile was much higher and American automakers were stronger). This resulted in huge losses for American automakers during the second half of the 1980s and early 1990s and almost drove Chrysler out of business (this is examined in Example 13–6). Another example is provided by Sears, which was unable or

---

[11] "Remember Clinton's Industrial Policy? O.K. Now Forget It," *Business Week,* December 12, 1994, p. 53; and P. Krugman, "Is Free Trade Passé" *The Journal of Economic Perspectives,* Fall 1987, pp. 131–144.
[12] "The Birth of Giant," *Business Week,* July 10, 2000, pp. 170–176 and "Boeing Opts to Build New Class of "Sonic Cruiser" Jet," *Financial Times,* March 30, 2001, p. 1.

unwilling to understand the kind of change going on in consumer preferences, and this eventually propelled Wal-Mart to replace it as the nation's top marketeer. Most dangerous are latent or stealthy competitors, who as a result of some major and quick technological or market change can devastate the firm in its very core business. A clear example of this is IBM's inability to recognize early enough the importance and dramatic growth of the PC market in the mid-1980s and subsequent signing of Microsoft to develop the software and Intel to supply the chips for its PCs.

A *third* reason for business failures is the loading of the firm with a heavy debt burden (usually to carry out a program of merger and acquisitions, often at overpriced terms) which then robs the firm of its strength in a market downturn. This is precisely what happened (together with greed, deceit, and financial chicanery) to Enron (one of the world's largest energy traders), which filed the largest U.S. claim for bankruptcy in December 2001 (exceeded by WorldCom bankruptcy in July 2002).

Fourth, business failures arise when firms vainly try to recapture their past glories and become stuck on an obsolete strategies and are unable to respond to a new and major competitive challenges. This is, to some extent, what happened to General Motors and IBM during the past decade before the brutal forces of the market shook them out of their complacency. It is often more difficult to keep a business great than to build it in the first place. *Finally,* a company may fail as a result of strikes and hostilities from unhappy workers. This may happen to some of the nation's airlines during the next few years.

Sources: "Dinosaurs?," *Fortune,* May 3, 1994, pp. 36–42; "Why Companies Fail," *Fortune,* November 14, 1994, pp. 52–68; "How good Companies Go Bad," *Harvard Business Review,* July–August 1999, pp. 42–52; "Why Enron Went Bust," *Fortune,* December 24, 2001, pp. 58–68; "Enron: How Governance Rules Failed," *Business Week,* January 21, 2002, pp. 21–22; "WorldCom Files for Bankruptcy: Largest U.S. Case," *The New York Times,* July 22, 2002, p. 1; and "Why Companies Fail," *Business Week,* May 22, 2002, pp. 50–62.

AT THE FRONTIER
The Virtual Corporation

Today's joint ventures and strategic alliances provide a glimpse of the virtual corporation—the firm of the future. A **virtual corporation** is a temporary network of independent companies (suppliers, customers, and even rivals) coming together with each contributing its core competence to quickly take advantage of fast-changing opportunities. In today's world of fierce global competition, this window of opportunity is often so frustratingly brief that it is impossible for a single firm to have all the in-house expertise to quickly launch complex products in diverse markets. By acting strategically and temporarily banding together to take advantage of a specific market opportunity, and with each company bringing its speciality, the virtual firm is a "best-of-everything organization." Informational networks and electronic contracts will permit unusual partners to work together on a particular project and then disband when the opportunity has been fully exploited.

In a virtual firm, one of the partners may have the idea for a new product, another may design the product, another may produce it, and still another market it. For example, IBM, Apple Computer, and Motorola have come together to develop a new operating system and computer chip for a new generation of computers. MCI Communications has entered into partnerships with as many as 100 companies to provide a one-stop package of telecommunications hardware and services based on MCI competencies in network integration and software development, with the strength of other companies making all kinds of telecommunications equipment.

Although power, flexibility, and quickness are crucial advantages, the virtual corporation model does face two real risks. First, a company joining such a network may lose control of its core technology. Second, by abandoning manufacturing, the company may become "hollow" and become unable to resume the manufacturing of its traditional product in the future when the network dissolves. Some observers point out that IBM's desire to quickly enter the personal computer (PC) market in 1981 by relying on Intel for computer chips and Microsoft for the operating software left IBM without control of the market and encouraged hundreds of clone makers to eventually enter the market with lower prices and better products.

Thus, not everyone is sold on the virtual firm model. In order to work, the virtual firm (1) will have to be formed by partners that are dependable and are the best in their field, (2) the network must serve the interests of all partners in a win-win situation, (3) each company must put its best and brightest people in the network to show its partners that its link with them is important to the company, (4) the objective of the network must be clearly defined as well as what each partner is expected to gain, and (5) the network must build a common telecommunications network and other infrastructures so that each partner can be in constant touch with the other partners to anticipate problems and review progress. Creating and successfully operating a virtual firm is not easy but it may very well be the strategic way of the future.

Sources: "The Virtual Firm," *Business Week,* February 8, 1993, pp. 98–102; and "The Art of Managing Virtual Teams: Eight Key Lessons." *Harvard Management Review,* November 1998, pp. 4–5.

SUMMARY

1. Game theory is concerned with the choice of an optimal strategy in conflict situations. Every game theory model includes players, strategies, and payoffs. The players are the decision makers (here, the managers of oligopolist firms) whose behavior we are trying to explain and predict. The strategies are the potential choices that can be made by the players (firms). The payoff is the outcome or consequence of each combination of strategies

by the two players. The payoff matrix refers to all the outcomes of the players' strategies. A zero-sum game is one in which the gains or losses of one player equal the losses or gains of the other.

2. The dominant strategy is the optimal choice for a player, no matter what the opponent does. The Nash equilibrium occurs when each player has chosen his or her optimal strategy, given the strategy chosen by the other player. The Cournot solution is an example of a Nash equilibrium. Not all games have a Nash equilibrium and some games have more than one.

3. Oligopolistic firms often face a problem called the prisoners' dilemma. This refers to a situation in which each firm adopts its dominant strategy but could do better (i.e., earn larger profit) by cooperating. Oligopolistic firms deciding on their pricing or advertising strategy or on whether to cheat on a cartel face the prisoners' dilemma.

4. The best strategy for repeated or multiple-move prisoners' dilemma games is tit-for-tat. This strategy postulates that each firm should start by cooperating and continue to do so as long as the rival cooperates, but stop cooperating once the rival stops cooperating.

5. Oligopolists often make strategic moves. A strategic move is one in which a player constrains its own behavior in order to make a threat credible so as to gain a competitive advantage over a rival. The firm making the threat must be committed to carrying it out for the threat to be credible. This may involve accepting lower profits or building excess capacity.

6. Just like firms, nations can make strategic moves, such as subsidizing and providing export subsidies to a high-tech industry or adopting an industrial policy for the entire nation, to gain a competitive advantage over other nations. Industrial policies lead to waste if industries that are subsidized or otherwise supported do not become internationally competitive. Similarly, not knowing the exact payoff or outcome of the strategic moves open to it greatly complicates the development and conduct of business strategy by the firm. The virtual corporation is a temporary network of independent companies coming together with each contributing its core technology to quickly take advantage of fast-changing opportunities.

KEY TERMS

Game theory	Zero-sum game	Repeated games
Players	Nonzero-sum game	Tit-for-tat
Strategies	Dominant strategy	Strategic move
Payoff	Nash equilibrium	Virtual corporation
Payoff matrix	Prisoners' dilemma	

REVIEW QUESTIONS

1. In what way does game theory extend the analysis of oligopolistic behavior presented in Chapter 11?

2. a. Can game theory be used only for oligopolistic interdependence?

   b. In what way is game theory similar to playing chess?

3. Do we have a Nash equilibrium when each firm chooses its dominant strategy?

4. a. Why is the Cournot equilibrium a Nash equilibrium?

   b. In what way does the Cournot equilibrium differ from the Nash equilibrium given in Table 12.2?

5. In what way is the prisoners' dilemma related to the choice of dominant strategies by the players in a game and to the concept of Nash equilibrium?

6. How can the concept of the prisoners' dilemma be used to analyze price competition?

7. How can introducing yearly style changes lead to a prisoners' dilemma for automakers?

8. a. What is the incentive for the members of a cartel to cheat on the cartel?

   b. What can the cartel do to prevent cheating?

   c. Under what conditions is a cartel more likely to collapse?

9. Do the duopolists in a Cournot equilibrium face a prisoners' dilemma? Explain.

10. How did the 1971 law banning cigarette advertising on television solve the prisoners' dilemma for cigarette producers?

11. a. What is the meaning of "tit-for-tat" in game theory?

    b. What conditions are usually required for tit-for-tat strategy to be the best strategy?

12. a. How is a strategic move differentiated from a Nash equilibrium?

    b. What is a credible threat? When is a threat not credible?

PROBLEMS

1. From the following payoff matrix, where the payoffs are the profits or losses of the two firms, determine
   a. whether firm A has a dominant strategy.
   b. whether firm B has a dominant strategy.
   c. the optimal strategy for each firm.

		Firm B	
		Low Price	High Price
Firm A	Low Price	1, 1	3, −1
	High Price	−1, 3	2, 2

2. From the following payoff matrix, where the payoffs are the profits or losses of the two firms, determine
   a. whether firm A has a dominant strategy.
   b. whether firm B has a dominant strategy.
   c. the optimal strategy for each firm.
   d. the Nash equilibrium, if there is one.

		Firm B	
		Low Price	High Price
Firm A	Low Price	1, 1	3, −1
	High Price	−1, 3	4, 2

*3. From the following payoff matrix, where the payoffs are the profits or losses of the two firms, determine
   a. whether firm A has a dominant strategy.
   b. whether firm B has a dominant strategy.
   c. the optimal strategy for each firm.
   d. the Nash equilibrium.
   e. Under what conditions is the situation indicated in the payoff matrix likely to occur?

		Firm B	
		Small Cars	Large Cars
Firm A	Small Cars	4, 4	−2, −2
	Large Cars	−2, −2	4, 4

*4. Provide a hypothetical payoff matrix for example 12.2 in this chapter.

5. From the following payoff matrix, where the payoffs (the negative values) are the years of possible imprisonment for individuals A and B, determine
   a. whether individual A has a dominant strategy.
   b. whether individual B has a dominant strategy.

---

* = Answer provided at end of book.

c. the optimal strategy for each individual.

d. Do individuals A and B face a prisoners' dilemma?

		Individual B	
		Confess	Don't Confess
Individual A	Confess	−5, −5	−1, −10
	Don't Confess	−10, −1	−2, −2

6. Explain why the payoff matrix in Problem 1 indicates that firms A and B face the prisoners' dilemma.

7. Do firms A and B in Problem 2 face the prisoners' dilemma? Why?

*8. From the following payoff matrix, where the payoffs refer to the profits that firms A and B earn by cheating and not cheating in a cartel,

a. determine whether firms A and B face the prisoners' dilemma.

b. What would happen if we changed the payoff in the bottom left cell to (5, 5)?

		Firm B	
		Cheat	Don't Cheat
Firm A	Cheat	4, 3	8, 1
	Don't Cheat	2, 6	6, 5

*9. Starting with the payoff matrix of Problem 1, show what the tit-for-tat strategy would be for the first five of an infinite number of games if firm A starts by cooperating but firm B does not cooperate in the next period.

10. Given the following payoff matrix

a. indicate the best strategy for each firm.

b. Why is the entry-deterrent threat by firm A to lower price not credible to firm B?

c. What could firm A do to make its threat credible without building excess capacity?

		Firm B	
		Enter	Don't Enter
Firm A	Low Price	3, −1	3, 1
	High Price	4, 5	6, 3

11. Show how the payoff matrix in the table of Problem 10 might change for firm A to make a credible threat to lower price by building excess capacity to deter firm B from entering the market.

12. What strategic industrial or trade policy would be required (if any) in the United States and in Europe if the entries in the top left cell of the payoff matrix in Table 12.8 were changed to

a. 10, 10?

b. 5, 0?

c. 5, −10?

INTERNET SITE ADDRESSES

For an excellent presentation of game theory, see:
http://price.bus.okstate.edu/archive/Econ3113_963/Shows/Chapter9/index.htm
http://raven.stern.nyu.edu/networks/5.html

For the Fortune Global 500 companies, see:
http://fortune.com/global500

For competition in the computer industry, see;
Apple: http://www.apple.com
Compaq: http://www.compaq.com
Hewlett-Packard: http://www.hp.com
IBM: http://www.ibm.com
Dell: http://www.dell.com

For competition in airline industry, see:
American Airline: http://www.aa.com
America West Airline: http://www.americawest.com
Continental Airlines: http://www.continental.com
Delta Airline: http://www.delta.com
United Airline: http://www.ual.com

For competition in industry for commercial aircraft, see:
Airbus: http://www.airbus.com
Boeing: http://www.boeing.com
Lockheed: http://www.lockheedmartin.com

CHAPTER 13

Market Structure, Efficiency, and Regulation

"People of the same trade seldom meet together, even for merriment and diversion, but the conversation ends in a conspiracy against the public, or in some contrivance to raise prices."[1] This is one of the most famous quotations in economics, and it is as relevant today as two-and-a-quarter centuries ago when it was written. It explains in a nutshell why we are so interested in market structure, efficiency, antitrust, and regulation. In this chapter, we examine the relationship between these elements. We begin by reviewing why inefficiency and social costs arise in imperfect markets. We then consider how to measure market imperfections and ways to minimize, prevent, or overcome (through antitrust and regulation) the most serious social costs that arise from these market imperfections. The examples and applications in the chapter show the importance of the theory and its uses, while the "At the Frontier" section examines the relatively new field of experimental economics.

13.1 MARKET STRUCTURE AND EFFICIENCY

The concept and measure of **efficiency,** as well as the need for antitrust and regulation, is based on marginal analysis. Specifically, we have seen in previous chapters that the best level of output for a firm under any form of market organization (be it perfect competition, monopoly, monopolistic competition, or oligopoly) is where marginal revenue equals marginal cost. If marginal revenue exceeds marginal cost, it pays for the firm to expand output because by doing so the firm will add more to its total revenue than to

---

[1] A. Smith, The Wealth of Nations (Toronto: Random House, 1937), p. 128.

its total costs. On the other hand, if marginal cost exceeds marginal revenue, it pays for the firm to reduce output because by doing so its total costs will decline more than its total revenue. Thus, the best level of output is where marginal revenue equals marginal cost.

Chapter 9 showed that a perfectly competitive firm faces an infinitely elastic demand curve and so price equals marginal revenue. Thus, at the best level of output, $P = MR = MC$. Since price measures the marginal benefit that consumers receive for the last unit of the commodity consumed at the output where $MR = MC$, the marginal benefit to consumers equals the marginal cost to producers under perfect competition. If less of the commodity is produced, $P = MR > MC$, so that consumers' satisfaction would increase if firms produced more of the commodity. On the other hand, if more of the commodity is produced, $P = MR < MC$. This means that consumers would benefit if some inputs were shifted to the production of some other commodity. Thus, application of the $P = MR = MC$ rule by the firm leads to the highest consumer satisfaction when all markets are perfectly competitive. As pointed out in Figure 9.9, in long-run perfectly competitive equilibrium, consumers can purchase the commodity at the lowest possible price (i.e., at $P =$ lowest LAC).

In imperfectly competitive markets (monopoly, monopolistic competition, and oligopoly), however, the firm faces a negatively sloped demand curve, and so price exceeds marginal revenue. Thus, at the best level of output $P > MR = MC$. This means that the marginal benefit to consumers from the last unit of the commodity consumed exceeds the marginal cost that the firm incurs in producing it. Consumers want more of the commodity than is available, but producers have no incentive to produce more. As a result, consumers' satisfaction is not maximized. Furthermore, imperfect competitors do not usually produce at the lowest point on their LAC curve when in long-run equilibrium, and (except for monopolistic competitors) the price that they charge for the commodity may also include a profit margin. The social cost resulting when a constant-cost perfectly competitive industry is suddenly monopolized was shown in Figure 10.7. In the real world, we seldom if ever have (unregulated) monopoly, but firms in various industries have various degrees of monopoly power. Thus, it becomes important to examine ways to measure the degree of monopoly power in order to assess the social costs resulting from it. This topic is explored in Section 13.2. Section 13.3 then compares the social costs with the alleged dynamic benefits of monopoly power.

In many industries, however, technological conditions require such a large scale of production (to take advantage of economies of scale) that only one firm (natural monopoly) or a handful of firms (oligopoly) arise. For example, it would be inconceivable and highly inefficient to have numerous small producers of automobiles, steel, aircraft, and many other products. In the case of oligopolies, the government usually relies on the enforcement of antitrust laws aimed at attaining some degree of workable competition. This is examined in Section 13.4. In the case of natural monopoly, on the other hand, the single firm is usually allowed to operate, but with the government regulating the price and the quality of service. This is examined in Section 13.5. The rest of the chapter deals with the deregulation movement, the regulation of international competition, and price regulation. Table 13.1 summarizes and compares the various types of market structure that we have examined in previous chapters, from perfect competition to monopoly.

TABLE 13.1 Comparison of Market Structures

Type of Market	Number of Firms	Type of Product	Conditions of Entry	Firm's Influence Over Price	Interdependence Among Firms	Examples
Perfect competition	Many	Homogeneous	Easy	None	None	Some agricultural products and stock market
Monopolistic competition	Many	Differentiated	Easy	Little	None	Some retail trade and services
Oligopoly	Few	Homogeneous or differentiated	Difficult	Considerable	A great deal	Steel, automobiles
Monopoly	One	No good substitutes	Difficult or impossible	Substantial	No direct competitor	Local telephone service

13.2   MEASURING MONOPOLY POWER

In this section, we first define the Lerner index as a measure of the degree of a *firm's* monopoly power and the Herfindahl index as a measure of the degree of monopoly power in an *industry*. We then discuss how effective competition can occur even when there are only a few firms, according to the contestable market theory.

The Lerner Index as a Measure of Monopoly Power

We have seen in Chapter 9 that $P = MR = MC$ for a perfectly competitive firm but $P > MR = MC$ for an imperfectly competitive firm (i.e., for a monopolistic competitor, oligopolist, or monopolist). The greater the degree of monopoly power that a firm has, the more inelastic the demand curve for the product that it faces, and so the larger is the degree by which the commodity price exceeds the firm's marginal revenue and marginal cost. Thus, one way of measuring monopoly power is by the **Lerner index.** This is given by the ratio of the difference between price and marginal cost to price, as shown by formula [13.1].[2]

$$L = \frac{P - MC}{P} \qquad [13.1]$$

The Lerner index can have a value between zero and one. For a perfectly competitive firm, $P = MC$ and $L = 0$. On the other hand, the more price exceeds marginal cost (i.e., the greater the degree of monopoly power), the more the value of L approaches the value of one.

The Lerner index can also be expressed in terms of the price elasticity of the demand curve facing the firm. We can see this as follows. Since at the best level of output $MR = MC$, we can substitute MR for MC in [13.1]. But from [5.8], we know that $MR = P(1 + 1/\eta)$,

---

[2] A. P. Lerner, "The Concept of Monopoly and the Measurement of Monopoly Power," *Review of Economic Studies,* June 1934, pp. 157–175.

where η is the price elasticity of demand. Substituting this value of MR for MC in [13.1], we get

$$L = \frac{P - P(1 + 1/\eta)}{P}$$

Simplifying, we get

$$L = -1/\eta \qquad\qquad [13.2]$$

For a perfectly competitive firm, $\eta = \infty$ and $L = 0$. The fewer and the more imperfect are the substitutes available for the firm's product (i.e., the smaller is the absolute value of η), the larger is the value of L. For example, if $\eta = -4$, $L = 0.25$, but if $\eta = -2$, $L = 0.5$.[3] Note that a high value for L (implying a great deal of monopoly power) is not necessarily associated with high profits for the firm, because profits refer to the excess of price over *average* cost, and average costs can be high or low in relation to the commodity price at the output level where $MR = MC$ (see Problem 2, with the answer at the end of the book).

Some difficulties may arise, however, in using the Lerner index. For example, a firm with a great deal of monopoly power may keep its price low to avoid legal scrutiny or to deter entry into the industry (limit pricing). Furthermore, the Lerner index is applicable in a static context, but it is not very useful in a dynamic context when the firm's demand and cost functions shift over time.

Concentration and Monopoly Power: The Herfindahl Index

One method of estimating the degree of monopoly power *in an industry as a whole* is by the **Herfindahl index** (named after Orris Herfindahl, who introduced it). This is given by the sum of the squared values of the market sales shares of all the firms in the industry, as shown by

$$S = S_1^2 + S_2^2 + \cdots S_N^2 \qquad\qquad [13.3]$$

where S_1 is the market sales share of the largest firm in the industry, S_2 is the market sales share of the second largest firm in the industry, and so on, in such a way that the sum of the market sales shares of all firms in the industry totals 1 or 100%. In general, the greater the value of the Herfindahl index, the greater the degree of monopoly power in the industry.

For example, if we have a monopoly or a single firm in the industry, so that its market share is 100%, $H = (100)^2 = 10,000$. On the other hand, if there are 1,000 equal-sized firms in the (competitive) industry, each with 0.1% of the market, $H = 1,000(0.1)^2 = 10$. If there are 100 equal-sized firms in the (still competitive) industry, each with 1% of the market, $H = 100$. For an industry with 10 equal-sized firms, each with 10% market share, $H = 1,000$. But for an industry with 11 firms, one with 50% market share and the other 10 firms with 5% market share each, $H = 2,750$. This points to the advantage of the Herfindahl index over the concentration ratios discussed in Section 11.3. The Herfindahl index uses all the information and takes into account the size distribution of firms. Specifically, by squaring the market share of each firm, the Herfindahl index gives much more weight to larger firms in the industry than to smaller firms.

---

[3] If $\eta = -1$, then $L = 1$. This is the highest value for L because an imperfect competitor never produces in the inelastic portion of its demand curve (where $MR < 0$).

TABLE 13.2 Herfindahl Index for Selected U.S. Industries in 1997

Industry	Index*
Food	91.0
Sporting and athletic goods	161.1
Footwear	317.0
Pharmaceutical and medicines	446.3
Communications equipment	449.0
Computer and peripheral equipment	464.9
Aluminum	816.3
Office machinery	1,208.3
Tires	1,517.8
Breakfast cereals	2,445.9
Motor vehicles	2,505.8

*Index refers only to the largest 50 firms in each industry.

Source: U.S. Bureau of Census, 1997 Census of manufacturers, *Concentration Ratios in Manufacturing* (Washington, D.C.: U.S. Government Printing Office, June 2001, Table 2, pp. 7–16.

The Herfindahl index has become of great practical importance since 1982 when the Justice Department announced new guidelines (revised in 1984) for evaluating proposed mergers based on this index. According to these guidelines, if the postmerger Herfindahl index is 1,000 or less, the industry is regarded as relatively unconcentrated and a merger is unchallenged. On the other hand, an industry where the postmerger Herfindahl index is greater than 1,800 is regarded as highly concentrated and a merger is likely to be challenged (the full set of guidelines is given in Section 13.4). Table 13.2 shows the Herfindahl index (for the 50 largest firms rather than for all firms) in each of a selected number of industries in the United States in 1997. The table shows that for some industries, such as food and sporting goods, the Herfindahl index is very low; but for others, such as breakfast cereals and motor vehicles, the index is very high.

As with concentration ratios, however, the Herfindahl index must be used with caution. First, in industries where imports are significant (such as automobiles), the Herfindahl index greatly overestimates the relative importance of concentration in the domestic industry. Indeed, Raymond Vernon found that the Herfindahl index for the *world* automobiles, petroleum, aluminum-smelting, and pulp-and-paper industries declined sharply from 1950 to 1970, pointing to sharply increased international competition at home.[4] Second, the Herfindahl index for the nation as a whole may not be relevant when the market is local (as in the case of cement where transportation costs are very high). Third, how broadly or narrowly a product is defined is also very important. Fourth, the Herfindahl index does not give any indication of potential entrants into the market and of the degree of actual and potential competition in the industry. Indeed, as the *theory of contestable markets* discussed next shows, vigorous competition can take place even among few sellers.

---

[4] R. Vernon, "Competition Policy Toward Multinational Corporations," *American Economic Review,* May 1974, pp. 276–282.

Contestable Markets: Effective Competition Even with Few Firms

According to the **theory of contestable markets** developed during the 1980s, even if an industry has a single firm (monopoly) or only a few firms (oligopoly), the industry would still operate as if it were perfectly competitive if entry is "absolutely free" (i.e., if other firms can enter the industry and face exactly the same costs as existing firms) and if exit is "entirely costless" (i.e., if there are no sunk costs so that the firm can exit the industry without facing any loss of capital).[5] An example might be an airline that establishes a service between two cities already served by other airlines—*if* the new entrant faces the same costs as existing airlines and could subsequently leave the market by simply reassigning its planes to other routes without incurring any loss of capital.

When entry is absolutely free and exit is entirely costless, the market is contestable. Firms will then operate as if they were perfectly competitive and sell at a price that only covers their average costs (so that they earn zero economic profit) even if there is only one firm or a few firms in the market. In this view, competition within the market is less important than the potential competition for the market. This can be seen in Figure 13.1.

In Figure 13.1, D is the market demand curve, and AC and MC are the average and marginal cost curves, respectively, of each of two identical firms in the market. If the market is contestable (i.e., if entry is absolutely free and exit is entirely costless), each firm will sell 60 units of output at $P = AC = MC = \$6$ (point E in the figure) and behave as a perfect competitor facing horizontal demand curve AEE' and earn zero economic profits. The duopolists will not collude to charge a higher price and earn profits because they know that other firms would quickly enter the market and sell at a slightly lower price. This would lower price to equal marginal cost at the lowest average cost and quickly eliminate all profits. This is true whether the potential entrants are domestic or foreign.

The theory of contestable markets is similar to limit pricing (discussed in Section 11.7). With limit pricing, a firm charges a lower-than-the-profit-maximizing price to discourage potential entrants into the market. But whereas profits can still be earned with limit pricing (even though they are not maximized because the market is not entirely contestable), economic profits are zero in a contestable market because entry is absolutely free and exit is entirely costless. Even purely transitory profits will not be disregarded but result in entry-exit or hit-and-run behavior on the part of potential entrants into the industry until all profit opportunities are entirely exhausted.

The extreme assumptions on which the theory of contestable markets is based have been sharply criticized as unrealistic. That is, entry is seldom if ever absolutely free and exit is seldom if ever entirely costless in the real world, and so the theory is thought to be of limited applicability and usefulness.[6] Nevertheless, we have seen in Section 11.5 that a hypothesis need not be based on entirely realistic assumptions to be acceptable and useful. Thus, the theory of contestable markets can still be useful even if entry into and exit from the industry are only reasonably easy rather than absolutely free and costless. Perhaps the importance of the theory lies in cautioning us against uncritically accepting the view that a market with only one or a few firms must necessarily be noncompetitive and in suggesting that easy entry and exit can severely limit the exercise of monopoly power in contestable markets.

---

[5] See W. J. Baumol, "Contestable Markets: An Uprising in the Theory of Industrial Structure," *American Economic Review,* March 1982, pp. 1–5.

[6] W. G. Shepherd, "Contestability vs. Competition," *American Economic Review,* September 1984, pp. 572–587.

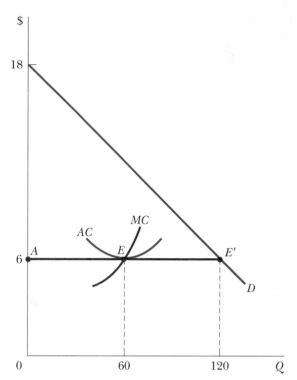

FIGURE 13.1   Two Firms in a Contestable Market
D is the market demand curve, and AC and MC are the average and marginal cost curves, respectively, of each of two identical firms in a contestable market. Each firm will sell 60 units of output at $P = AC = MC = \$6$ (point E in the figure) and behave as a perfect competitor facing horizontal demand curve AEE' and earn zero economic profits. Any higher price invites hit-and-run entrants.

AT THE FRONTIER
Functioning of Markets and Experimental Economics

E xperimental economics is a relatively new field of economics that uses laboratory experiments to understand how real-world markets actually work under
different institutional settings and levels of information. The field has already provided some interesting and important insights on the functioning of perfectly competitive markets, stock market behavior, monopoly profit maximization, oligopolistic

Continued. . .

behavior, bilateral monopoly (a monopolist in the product market facing a monopolist in the factor market), auction behavior, consumer response to price changes, and the effect of externalities (divergences between private and social costs and benefits).

According to Vernon Smith, one of the originators of the field, there are many important reasons for conducting experiments in economics. Some of these reasons include (1) to test a theory or discriminate between theories, (2) to explore the causes of a theory's failure, (3) to establish empirical regularities that can form the basis for a new theory, (4) to compare the effect of operating under different environmental and institutional conditions, (5) to evaluate policy proposals, and (6) to determine the effect of institutional changes.

The experiments are usually conducted with volunteers, often college students, who are given money to buy and sell a fictitious commodity within a simple specified institutional framework. The participants are allowed to keep some of the money that they earn by acting in an economically rational way. For example, participants are allowed to retain the profit from buying the commodity at a lower price from the experimenter or from other participants and reselling it at a higher price to others in the simulated market.

In a simple experiment, it was shown that under certain conditions, the commodity price quickly converges to the equilibrium price even when there are only a few buyers and sellers of the commodity. This would seem to confirm the conclusion of the theory of contestable markets, but from a completely different approach. Whereas the theory of contestable markets reached this conclusion in a purely deductive manner, experimental economics reaches the same conclusion by pure empirical evidence within a simple experimental framework. The results seem to suggest that the perfectly competitive model may have much wider applicability than previously thought. If so, this would go a long way toward overcoming the problems arising from the indeterminacy of oligopoly theory.

In another experiment, Vernon Smith handed out several thousand dollars of his own money to a group of students participating in a simulated stock market study. The study provided some interesting results. One conclusion is that stock market or speculative "bubbles" occur regularly within the experimental framework. Traders seem to be carried away in a rising market and continue to bid stock prices up far past the expected dividend and price-earnings ratio of the stock—inevitably leading to crash. Despite the very simple setting in which these experiments were conducted, their outcome closely mimics the actual stock market crash of 1987. Only after the participants have been through several boom-bust cycles do bubbles seem to disappear. As time passes, however, and the busts fade in investors' memories, great volatility in stock prices reappears.

In an attempt to eliminate the bubbles, Smith modified the experiment by adding futures trading (i.e., agreements to purchase or sell a stock at a specified price for delivery at a specified future time), margin buying (i.e., requiring a down payment when buying a stock on credit), and rules to stop trading when the market falls by a specified percentage. Smith's experiments showed that imposing limits on price declines only postpones the crash and makes it deeper when it comes. Only the availability of futures trading seemed to reduce the size and duration of speculative bubbles. These experimental results could have important practical implications in devising regulations to make the stock market less volatile in the real world.

Some of the other interesting results obtained by experimental economics are (1) auctions with large numbers of bidders (at least 6 or 7) produce more aggressive bidding than with small numbers (3 or 4) and result in negative profits (the winner's curse), (2) consumers more readily accept price increases resulting from rising costs of production than those that arise from higher profits, suggesting that firms' voluntary or mandated financial disclosures can influence consumer behavior, (3) providing subjects with complete information retards rather than speeds the convergence of a market to equilibrium, (4) participants come to have common expectations regarding the value of a stock by market experience, not by being given common information, and (5) market efficiency in buying and selling a commodity does not require the complete revelation of buyers' and sellers' preferences.

Despite its promising beginning, we must remember, however, that experimental economics is still in its infancy, and many economists remain skeptical of the usefulness of results obtained in simplistic institutional settings and of their applicability in devising regulatory policies in the real world. The number of converts is growing, however, and the field has boomed in recent years. An important new development that is likely to further stimulate the field is Internet-based experiments, which allow large number of participants in experiments at different sites and over longer periods of time as compared with experiments restricted to classroom laboratories.

Sources: "Experimental Economists Try to Fathom Behavior on Line," *Wall Street Journal,* October 2, 2000, p. B4; Sheryl B. Ball, "Research, Teaching, and Practice in Experimental Economics," Southern Economic Journal, January 1998, pp. 772–779; V. L. Smith, "Economics in the Laboratory," *Journal of Economic Perspectives,* Winter 1994, pp. 113–131; "Classroom Experimental Economics," Special Issue, *Journal of Economic Education,* Fall 1993; C. R. Plott, "Will Economics Become an Experimental Science?," *Southern Economic Journal,* April 1991, pp. 901–919; V. L. Smith, "Theory, Experiment and Economics," *The Journal of Economic Perspectives,* winter 1989, pp. 151–170, and C. R. Plott, "Industrial Organization and Experimental Economics," *Journal of Economic Literature,* December 1982, pp. 1485–1527.

13.3   SOCIAL COSTS AND DYNAMIC BENEFITS OF MONOPOLY POWER

We have seen that in imperfectly competitive markets the best level of output is where $P > MR = MC$. This means that the marginal benefit to consumers (as measured by the commodity price) from the last unit of the commodity consumed exceeds the marginal cost that the firm incurs in producing it. Consumers want more of the commodity than is available, but producers have no incentive to produce more. The social cost resulting when a constant-cost perfectly competitive industry is suddenly monopolized was shown by triangle *REM* in Figure 10.7. It was also pointed out in Section 10.3 that there are other losses or social costs resulting from monopoly power. The first of these is that monopolists do not have much incentive to keep their costs as low as possible and prefer instead the quiet life (X-inefficiency).[7] Second, monopolists waste a lot of resources lobbying and engaging in legal battles to avoid or defend themselves against regulation and antitrust prosecution, installing excess capacity to discourage entry into the industry, and advertising in an attempt to create and retain the monopoly power (i.e., engaging in rent-seeking activities). Some economists believe that these other social costs of monopoly are larger than those measured by the welfare triangle *REM* in Figure 10.7, but, as pointed out in Section 10.3, there is disagreement on the exact size of these social costs.[8]

Measuring the social costs of imperfect competition by comparing it with perfect competition begs the question, however, because the need for large-scale production often precludes the existence of perfect competition. We could not, for example, produce steel, automobiles, aluminum, aircraft, and most industrial products with numerous firms under perfect competition—except at exorbitant costs. The benefits that would result if cost conditions made perfect competition possible are thus irrelevant in these cases. Furthermore, there are many alleged benefits that result from large firm size (i.e., with firms with monopoly power) that just would not be possible under perfect competition. These were emphasized by Schumpeter 60 years ago and remain very controversial today.[9]

According to Schumpeter and others, perfect competition is not the market structure most conducive to long-run growth through technological change and innovations. Since long-run profits tend toward zero in perfectly competitive markets, firms will not have the necessary resources to undertake sufficient R&D to maximize growth. Furthermore, with free entry under perfect competition, a firm introducing a cost-reducing innovation or a new product would quickly lose its source of profits through imitation. Thus, Schumpeter argued that large firms with some degree of monopoly power are essential to provide the financial resources required for R&D and to protect the resulting source of profits. Although monopoly leads to some inefficiency at one point in time (static inefficiency), over time, it is likely to lead to much more technological change and innovation (dynamic efficiency) than perfect competition.[10]

In addition, according to Schumpeter, large firms with some monopoly power are not sheltered from competition. On the contrary, they face powerful competition from new products and new production techniques introduced by other large firms. For example, aluminum is replacing steel in many uses, and plastic is replacing aluminum. Such competition is much more dangerous and affects the very existence of the firm. This is the process of "creative destruction" as new products and technologies constantly lead to new investments

[7] See H. Leibenstein, "Allocative Efficiency vs. X-Inefficiency," *American Economic Review,* June 1966, pp. 392–415.

[8] The charge often heard that monopolists suppress inventions (e.g., that they would avoid introducing a longer-lasting light bulb) is not correct, however, since consumers would be willing to pay a higher price for such light bulbs and this could lead to higher profits for the monopolist. Only if the monopolist believed that the invention could not be patented and that this would result in loss of monopoly power would the monopolist suppress the invention. See Section 10.8.

[9] See J. Schumpeter, *Capitalism, Socialism, and Democracy* (New York: Harper & Row, 1942), p. 106; and Z. J. Acs and D. B. Audretsch, "Innovation in Large and Small Firms: An Empirical Analysis," *American Economic Review,* September 1988, pp. 678–690.

[10] The question of what is the institutional setting most conducive to technological change and innovations over time is a crucial one, because technological change and innovations are the forces responsible for most of the long-term growth in standards of living in modern societies.

and the obsolescence of some existing capital stock. In this process, the role of the entrepreneur is crucial. Indeed, the entrepreneur is the star performer in the dynamic process of creative destruction and growth in the economy.

Some economists disagree. They point out that it is not at all clear that monopoly power leads to more R&D and innovations and faster long-run growth than perfectly competitive markets. They also point out that a more decentralized market economy is more adaptable and flexible to changes and is much more consistent with individual freedom of choice than an economy characterized by great economic concentration. The challenge, according to these economists, is to devise policies that correct the most serious economic distortions in the economy resulting from monopoly power and encourage a high level of R&D, while retaining and encouraging a large degree of decentralization, equity, and individual freedoms.

After a careful review of the empirical evidence, Scherer and Ross conclude that Schumpeter was right in asserting that perfect competition cannot be the model for dynamic efficiency. But neither can powerful monopolies and tightly knit cartels. What is needed for rapid technical progress is a subtle blend of competition and monopoly, with more emphasis on the former than on the latter, especially in those industries in which technical progress is relatively rapid. In other words, although some monopoly power may be more conducive to innovation than perfect competition when technical progress is relatively slow, a great deal of monopoly power is likely to retard innovations and growth, especially when technical progress is rapid.[11]

13.4   CONTROLLING MONOPOLY POWER: ANTITRUST POLICY

Starting in 1890, a number of *antitrust laws* were passed in the United States which were aimed at preventing monopoly or undue concentration of economic power, protecting the public against the abuses and inefficiencies resulting from monopoly or the concentration of economic power, and maintaining a workable degree of competition in the economy. The two core antitrust laws were the Sherman Antitrust Act and the Clayton Act.

According to Section I of the **Sherman Antitrust Act** passed in 1890: "Every contract, combination . . . , or conspiracy in restraint of trade or commerce among the several states, or with foreign nations, is hereby declared to be illegal" in the United States. The Sherman Antitrust Act does not make monopoly, as such, illegal. What is illegal is collusion (i.e., formal or informal agreements or arrangements in restraint of trade). These agreements refer to all types of cartels, but also to informal understandings to share the market, price fixing, and price leadership. An illustration of collusion is provided by the market-sharing cartel of the Ivy League colleges in Example 11–4. What the courts did *not* rule as illegal is **conscious parallelism,** or the adoption of similar policies by oligopolists in view of their recognized interdependence. Specifically, the courts have ruled that parallel business behavior does not constitute proof of collusion or an offense under the Sherman Antitrust Act.

[11] F. M. Scherer and D. Ross, *Industrial Market Structure and Economic Performance* (Boston: Houghton Mifflin, 1990), pp. 644–660.

The most difficult part of applying Section I of the Sherman Antitrust Act is proving tacit or informal collusion. Sometimes the case is clear-cut. For example, in 1936, the U.S. Department of the Navy received 31 closed bids to supply a batch of steel, all of which quoting a price of $20,727.26. Also in 1936, the U.S. Engineer's Office received 11 closed bids to supply 6,000 barrels of cement, each quoting a price of $3.286854 per barrel! The probability of identical prices, down to the sixth decimal, occurring without some form of collusion is practically zero. Most antitrust cases are seldom so clear-cut, however.

Section II of the Sherman Antitrust Act makes attempts to monopolize the market illegal. The most famous of the recent court cases applying Section II of the Sherman Antitrust Act are those brought against AT&T (see Example 13–1) in 1982 and Microsoft in 1998 (see "At the Frontier" in Chapter 10). But monopolization can also occur through merger. Section 7 of the **Clayton Act** passed in 1914 (and amended by the Celler–Kefauver Act of 1950) prohibits mergers that "substantially lessen competition" or tend to lead to monopoly. According to its 1984 guidelines, the Justice Department would not usually challenge a horizontal merger (i.e., a merger of firms in the same product line) if the postmerger Herfindahl index was less than 1,000. If the postmerger index was between 1,000 and 1,800 and the increase in the index as a result of the merger was less than 100 points, the merger would usually also go unchallenged. But if the postmerger index was between 1,000 and 1,800 and the merger led to an increase in the index of more than 100 points, or if the postmerger index was more than 1,800 and the merger led to an increase in the index of more than 50 points, the Justice Department was likely to challenge the merger. Since the mid-1990s, these guidelines have been relaxed (see Example 13–5).

The Justice Department also considers other factors (besides the Herfindahl index) in horizontal mergers. These include the financial condition of the firm being acquired, the ease of entry into the industry, the degree of foreign competition, and the expected gains in efficiency that the merger would make possible. The Justice Department is more likely approve a horizontal merger if the merger would prevent the failure of the acquired firm, if entry into the industry is easy, if the degree of foreign competition is strong, and if the acquisition would lead to substantial economices of scale.[12] Less clear-cut are the guidelines on vertical and conglomerate mergers. As a result of relaxed guidelines and in the face of sharply increased foreign competition, the number and size of mergers and corporate acquisitions in the United States has increased sharply since the early 1980s.

Since antitrust laws are often broad and general, however, a great deal of judicial interpretation based on economic analysis has often been required in their enforcement. The problems of defining what is meant by "substantially lessening competition," defining the relevant product and geographic markets, and deciding when competition is "unfair" have not been easy to determine and often could not be resolved in a fully satisfactory and uncontroversial way. The fact that many antitrust cases last many years, involve thousands of pages of testimony, and cost millions of dollars to prosecute is ample evidence of their great complexity. Perhaps the most significant effect of the antitrust laws is deterring collusion rather than fighting it after it occurs.

---

[12] See "Symposium on Mergers and Antitrust," *Journal of Economic Perspectives,* Fall 1987, pp. 3–54; and W. E. Kovaric and Carl Shapiro, "Antitrust Policy: A Century of Economic and Legal Thinking," *Journal of Economic Perspectives,* winter 2000, pp. 43–60.

EXAMPLE 13–1

Antitrust Policy in Action—The Breakup of AT&T and the Creation of Competition in the Long-Distance Telephone Service

In 1974, the U.S. Justice Department filed suit (also under Section II of the Sherman Act) against AT&T for illegal practices aimed at eliminating competitors in the market for telephone equipment and in the market for long-distance telephone service. At the time, AT&T was the largest private firm in the world. After 8 years of litigation and a cost of $25 million to the government (and $360 million incurred by AT&T to defend itself), the case was settled on January 8, 1982. By consent decree, AT&T agreed to divest itself of the 22 local telephone companies (which represented two-thirds of its total assets) and lose its monopoly on long-distance telephone service. In return, AT&T was allowed to retain Bell Laboratories and its manufacturing arm, Western Electric, and it was allowed to enter the rapidly growing fields of cable TV, electronic data transmission, video-text communications, and computers. The settlement also led to an increase in local telephone charges (which had been subsidized by long-distance telephone service by AT&T) and a reduction in long-distance telephone rates.

By the end of 2001, WorldCom (which had acquired MCI Communications in 1999) and Sprint had captured more than 40% of the long-distance telephone market from AT&T. Furthermore, AT&T, WorldCom, and Sprint entered the local telephone market and the local Bell companies entered the long distance market. The sharp increase in competition and price wars resulted in much lower prices for local and long-distance telephone services for U.S. consumers. At the end of 2001, AT&T sold its cable-TV business to Comcast for $44 billion, thus ending its frenzied and costly three-year effort to transform itself into a telecommunications powerhouse and returning to being just a long-distance telephone company.

Sources: "Ma Bell's Big Breakup," *Newsweek,* January 18, 1982, pp. 58–63; "AT&T, MCI, Sprint Raise the Intensity of Their Endless War," *Wall Street Journal,* October 20, 1992, p. A1; "Congress Votes to Reshape the Communications Industry," *New York Times,* February 2, 1996, p. 1; "Bell Atlantic Long-Distance Bid May Spur Local-Phone Rivalry," *Wall Street Journal,* August 19, 1999, p. B6; "Telecoms in Trouble," *The Economist,* December 16, 2000, pp. 77–79; and "AT&T Long, Troubled Trip to Its Past," *Wall Street Journal,* December 21, 2001, p. B1.

EXAMPLE 13–2

Regulation and the Price of International Telephone Calls in Europe

Until the 1990s, state telephone monopolies ruled everywhere in Continental Europe and charged more than twice as much as AT&T charged its American customers for transatlantic telephone calls (and even more for local telephone services). During the 1990s, pressure mounted in Europe to dismantle the legal OPEC-like cartel by which national telecommunications companies cooperated to keep the price of international telephone calls very high and far above actual costs. With AT&T on this side of the Atlantic and British Telecom in Europe creeping into continental European markets with lower rates and with European corporations clamoring for rate reductions, the European Commission decided to open the international telephone market to competition throughout the 15-country European Union in 1998.

As a result, governments are privatizing their national telephone companies through stock sales (these exceeded $60 billion across Europe since the second half of the 1990s). At the same time, the major European telephone companies rushed to form alliances with other European and American telephone companies. Eventually, this could trigger massive consolidations around four or five telephone superpowers in the world. One alliance named "Concert" is led by AT&T and British Telecommunications, and another is led by WorldCom/Sprint. As these alliances take shape, price wars will be inevitable and are likely to result in sharply lower prices for telephone calls in Europe, just as occurred in the United States. Although still higher than in the United States, the price of local and international telephone calls in Europe has in fact already fallen sharply during the past few years.

Bigger and more frequent during the past few years have been mergers and acquisitions of cellular telephone companies by other wireless operators (such as England's Vodafone's acquisition of German Mannesmann) and by traditional telephone companies (such as France Telecom's acquisition of Orange P.L.C.—Britain's third largest wireless operator for $37 billion—and Deutsche Telekom's acquisition of American VoiceStream Wireless Corporation for $45 billion). With the convergence of telecommunications, information technology, and media services, the European Union's Parliament passed a law in December 2001 aimed at unifying and increasing competition in the entire telecommunication field in the European Union.

Sources: "An Unlikely Trustbuster," *Forbes,* February 18, 1991, pp. 100–104, "Sky-High Overseas Phone Bills May Drop," *Wall Street Journal,* September 20, 1994, p. B2; "European Phone Companies Reach Out for Partners," *Wall Street Journal,* November 30, 1994, p. B4; "Europe Begins Liberalizing Phone Sector," *Wall Street Journal,* December 5, 1994, p. A9F; "Who's on First?" *Wall Street Journal,* September 18, 2000, p. R2; and "Telephone Regulation Is Approved," *New York Times,* December 12, 2001, p. W1.

13.5   PUBLIC-UTILITY REGULATION

In this section, we consider the need for regulating natural monopolies (such as public utilities) and the dilemma faced by regulatory commissions in determining the appropriate method and degree of regulation.

Public Utilities as Natural Monopolies

As defined in Section 10.1, *natural monopoly* refers to the case in which a single firm can supply a service to the entire market more efficiently than a number of firms could. Natural monopoly arises when the firm's long-run average cost curve is still declining at the point where it intersects the market demand curve. Examples of natural monopolies are *public utilities* (local electrical, gas, water, and transportation companies). To have more than one such firm in a given market would lead to duplication of supply lines and to much higher costs per unit. To avoid this, local governments usually allow a single firm to operate in the market but regulate the price and quantity of the services provided so as to allow the firm only a normal rate of return (say, 10% to 12%) on its investment. This is shown in Figure 13.2.

In Figure 13.2, the *D* and *MR* curves are, respectively, the market demand and marginal revenue curves for the service faced by the public utility, while the *LAC* and *LMC* curves are its long-run average and marginal cost curves. The best level of output for the unregulated monopolist in the long run is 3 million units per time period and is given by

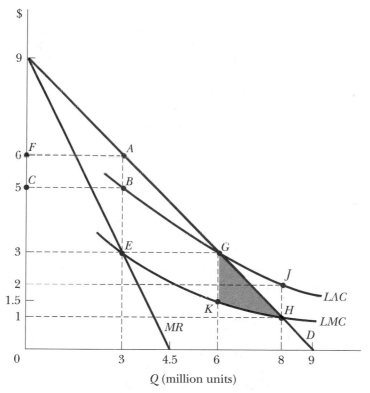

FIGURE 13.2   Natural Monopoly Regulation   A regularity commission usually sets $P = LAC = \$3$ (point *G*), at which output is 6 million units per time period and the public utility breaks even in the long run. This, however, would result in a welfare loss to society or social cost equal to about $1.50 million (the area of shaded triangle *GKH*), since only at point *H* is $P = LMC$. This cost could be avoided if the commission set $P = LMC = \$1$. But this would result in a loss of $1 (*JH*) per unit and $8 million in total for the company, and the public utility would not supply the service in the long run without a subsidy of $1 per unit.

point E, at which the LMC and MR curves intersect. For $Q = 3$ million units, the monopolist would charge the price of $6 (point A on the D curve) and incur a $LAC = \$5$ (point B on the LAC curve), thereby earning a profit of $1 ($AB$) per unit and $3 million (the area of rectangle $ABCF$) in total. Note that at $Q = 3$ million units, the LAC curve is still declining. Note also that at the output level of 3 million units, $P > LMC$, so that more of the service is desirable from society's point of view. There is, however, no incentive for the unregulated monopolist to expand output beyond $Q = 3$ million units per time period because its profits are maximized at $Q = 3$ million.

To ensure that the monopolist earns only a normal rate of return on its investment, the regulatory commission usually sets $P = LAC$. In Figure 13.2, this is given by point G, at which $P = LAC = \$3$ and output is 6 million units per time period. While the price is lower and the output is greater than at point A, $P > LMC$ at point G. Thus, consumers pay a price for the last unit of the service purchased which exceeds the LMC of producing it (see the figure). The welfare loss to society or social cost of setting $P = LAC = \$3$ is about $(0.5)(1.50)(2) = \$1.50$ million (the area of shaded triangle GKH). The only way to avoid this social cost is for the regulatory commission to set $P = LMC = \$1$ so that output is 8 million units per time period (point H in the figure). At $Q = 8$ million, however, the $LAC = \$2$ (point J on the LAC curve), and the public utility would incur a loss of $1 ($JH$) per unit and $8 million in total per time period. As a result, the public utility would not supply the service in the long run without a subsidy of $1 per unit. In general, regulatory commissions set $P = LAC$ (point G in Figure 13.2) so that the public utility breaks even in the long run without a subsidy.

Difficulties in Public-Utility Regulation

Although our discussion of public-utility regulation seems fairly simple and straightforward, the actual determination of prices (rates) for public-utility services by regulatory commissions (often called the *rate case*) is complex. For one thing, it is very difficult to determine the value of the plant or fixed assets on which to allow a normal rate of return. Should it be the original cost of the investment or the replacement cost? Usually regulatory commissions decide on the former. Furthermore, since public-utility companies supply the service to different classes of customers, each with different price elasticities of demand, many different rate schedules can be used to allow the public utility to break even. Even more troublesome is the fact that a public utility usually provides many services that are jointly produced, and so it is impossible to allocate costs in any rational way to the various services provided and customers served.

Regulation can also lead to inefficiencies. These result from the fact that, having been guaranteed a normal rate of return on investment, public-utility companies have little incentive to keep costs down. For example, managers may grant salary increases to themselves in excess of what they would get in their best alternative employment, and they may provide luxurious offices and large expense accounts for themselves. Regulatory commissions must, therefore, scrutinize costs to prevent such abuses. Regulated public utilities also have little incentive to introduce cost-saving innovations because they would not be able to keep the increased profits. An example of this is provided by the slowness with which AT&T introduced automatic switching equipment during the 1970s.

Other inefficiencies arise because if rates are set too high, public utilities will overinvest in fixed assets and use excessively capital-intensive production methods to avoid showing above-normal returns (which would lead to rate reductions). On the other hand, if public-utility rates are set too low, public-utility companies will underinvest in fixed assets (i.e., in plant and equipment) and overspend on variable inputs, such as labor and fuel, which tends to reduce the quality of services. Overinvestment or underinvestment in plant and equipment resulting from the wrong public-utility rates being set is known as the **Averch–Johnson (A–J) effect** (from Harvey Averch and Leland Johnson, who first identified this problem) and can lead to large inefficiencies.[13] And yet, it is difficult indeed for regulatory commissions to come up with correct utility rates in view of the difficulty of valuing the fixed assets of public utilities and because of the long planning and gestation period of public-utility investment projects.[14]

Finally, there is usually a lag of 9 to 12 months from the time the need for a rate change is recognized and the time it is granted. This *regulatory lag* results because public hearings must be conducted before a regulatory commission can approve a requested rate change. Since the members of the regulatory commissions are either political appointees or elected officials and are thus subject to political pressures from consumer groups, they usually postpone a rate increase as long as possible and tend to grant rate increases that are smaller than necessary. During inflationary periods, this leads to underinvestment in fixed assets and to the inefficiencies discussed above. To avoid these regulatory lags, rates are sometimes tied to fuel costs and are automatically adjusted as variable costs change. However, most public utilities are now in the process of deregulation (see Example 13–3).

EXAMPLE 13–3

Regulated Electricity Rates for Con Edison—A Thing of the Past

In February 1983, and after nearly six months of public hearings and deliberations, the New York Public Service Commission approved a 6.5% increase in electricity rates for the 2.7 million customers served by the Consolidated Edison Company. The increase in the monthly electricity charge was about half of the 12.4% that Con Edison had asked for because Con Edison's borrowing and operating costs had fallen sharply since it had made the request for a rate increase as the result of the decline in fuel costs, interest rates, and inflation.

Both Con Edison and consumer advocates immediately criticized the rate increase—the former as inadequate and the latter as too high. Because of even lower fuel costs, greater demand for electricity, and higher productivity increases than anticipated, the rate increase actually generated $267 million in additional revenues per year for Con Edison, which represented a 15.2% return on its investment. In 1986, the city administration threatened to sue Con Edison to have the excess profits returned to customers but dropped its plan when Con Edison agreed not to seek another rate increase until March 1987. In fact, Con Edison did

---

[13] H. Averch and L. Johnson, "Behavior of the Firm under Regulatory Constraint," *American Economic Review*, December 1962, pp. 1052–1069.

[14] Recently, regulatory commissions have begun to pay more attention to the structure of rates so as to avoid undue price discrimination against any class of customers.

not get another rate increase until 1992. The rate increases that it got from 1992 to 1995 were very small and from 1996 to 1999 rates actually declined slightly.

Con Edison and other electric utilities in New York State and in about one-third of the United States have now been deregulated, thus allowing customers to choose their power company and bargain for rates, just as they do for long-distance telephone services. Furthermore, while in the past, electric utility companies produced, delivered, metered, and billed for the electricity they sold, with the deregulation, these functions are being taken over (for the most part) by separate and more specialized companies. Deregulation is expected to increase the efficiency of the electric industry, but there is no guarantee that this will translate into lower rates for every type of user. In fact, deregulation brought blackouts and sharply higher electricity bills in California in 2000 and 2001, and this (together with the collapse of Enron, one of the world largest energy traders at the end of 2001) convinced many states to delay deregulation until enough generating capacity has been built to ensure ample supply with low and stable electricity rates.

Sources: "Con Edison Wins 6.5% Rise in Rates, Half of its Request," *The New York Times,* February 24, 1983, p. B4; "Con Edison Puts Freeze on Its Electricity Rates," *The New York Times,* January 13, 1986, p. B1; Paul L. Joskow, "Restructuring, Competition and Regulatory Reform in the U.S. Electric Sector," *Journal of Economic Perspectives,* Summer 1997, pp. 119–138; "California Moving Toward Re-regulating Energy," *New York Times,* September 21, 2001, p. 16; and "Collapse May Reshape the Battlefield of Deregulation," *New York Times,* December 4, 2001, p. C1.

13.6   THE DEREGULATION MOVEMENT

Regulation in the U.S. economy is not confined to cases of natural monopolies, where there is a single seller of a commodity or service, but extends to many other sectors, especially transportation, banking, and other financial services, where more than one firm operates. For example, airlines needed government approval to enter a market and change fares, railroads needed government approval to abandon a service or a line and change rates, the services that banks can provide and the interest that they can pay on deposits were also regulated, and so were the rates set by insurance companies and other financial institutions. Regulation was justified to ensure that industries operated in a manner consistent with the public interest, ensure a minimum standard of quality of services, and prevent the establishment of monopoly.

Many economists oppose regulation because it restricts competition, contributes to high prices, and reduces economic efficiency. One estimate put the social cost of regulation at more than $100 billion in the year 1979 (of which about 5% were administrative costs and the rest were the costs of compliance) and over $200 billion a year in the 1990s.[15] Even though these estimates have been challenged as grossly exaggerated,[16] compliance costs are surely very high, particularly in the area of social regulation (such as job safety), energy

---

[15] Murray Weidenbaum, "The High Cost of Government Regulation," *Challenge,* November–December 1979, pp. 32–39 and "A New Project Will Measure the Cost and Effect of Regulation," *New York Times,* March 30, 1998, p. D2.
[16] See William K. Tabb, "Government Regulation: Two Sides of the Story," *Challenge,* November–December 1980, pp. 40–48.

and the environment, and consumer safety and health. Regulation often leads to inefficiencies because regulators do not specify the desired result, but only the method of compliance (such as the type of pollution-abatement equipment to use), in the absence of adequate information and expertise. It is now generally agreed that it would be much better if regulators specified the results wanted and left to industry the task of determining the most efficient way to comply. In recent years, there has been a movement in this direction.

Since the 1970s, a growing **deregulation movement** has sprung up in the United States that led to deregulation of the air travel, trucking, railroads, banking, and telecommunications industries. The *Airline Deregulation Act of 1978* removed all restrictions on entry, scheduling, and pricing in domestic air travel in the United States, and so did the *Motor Carrier Act of 1980* in the trucking industry. The *Depository Institutions Deregulation and Monetary Control Act of 1980* allowed banks to pay interest on checking accounts and increased competition for business loans. The *Railroad Revitalization and Regulatory Reform Act of 1976* greatly increased the flexibility of railroads to set prices and to determine levels of service and areas of operation. The settlement of the *AT&T Antitrust Case in 1982* (see Example 13–1) opened competition in long-distance telephone service and in telecommunications. Natural gas pipelines and oil are now deregulated, and the banking and electric power industries are now in the process of being deregulated (see Example 13–3).

The general purpose of deregulation is to increase competition and efficiency in the affected industries and lead to lower prices without sacrificing the quality of service. Most observers would probably conclude that, on balance, the net effect has been positive. Competition has generally increased, and prices have fallen in industries that were deregulated. As expected, however, deregulation has also resulted in some difficulties and strains in the industries affected, to the point where some consumer groups and some firms in recently deregulated industries are asking Congress to re-regulate them. Nowhere is this more evident than in the airline industry (see Example 13–4). Deregulation has also encouraged and made possible the merger boom that has occurred in the United States since the early 1990s (see Example 13–5).

EXAMPLE 13–4
Deregulation of the Airline Industry: An Assessment

By 2002 all but one (America West) of the 16 air carriers that had been started since the 1978 deregulation had gone out of business or had merged with established carriers. Several mergers took place among large established carriers (such as American Airlines' acquisition of TWA in 2001), and Eastern Airline and Pan Am went out of business. The result was that at the beginning of 2002 seven carriers handled 93% of all domestic air travel in the United States (as compared with 11 carriers handling 87% of the traffic in 1978). Since 1985, the market share of the top five carriers jumped from 61% to 77%. Instead of a large number of small and highly competitive airlines envisioned by deregulation, the airline industry has become even more concentrated than it was before deregulation. Entry into the industry is increasingly being restricted by established airlines by (1) long-term leasing of the limited number of gates at most airports, (2) frequent flier programs that tie passengers to a given airline, (3) computerized reservations system that give a competitive advantage in attracting customers to the airlines owning the system, (4) the emergence of "hub and spoke" operations in which airlines funnel passengers through centrally located airports where one or two companies often dominate service, and (5) predatory pricing practices under which established airlines lower the price and increase flights to drive new entrants out.

It is true that airfares, after adjusting for inflation, have declined an average of 28% since deregulation and that this greatly stimulated domestic air travel (from about 250 million passengers in 1976 to over 600 million in 2000). But it is also true that airlines could not possibly have continued to charge fares as low as those charged during the latter part of the 1970s and the early part of the 1980s and continue to incur huge losses. Nevertheless, the sharp reduction in the number of airlines is beginning to worry even the strongest supporters of deregulation. Furthermore, while many small cities have not lost air service (as the opponents of deregulation had warned), delays at airports and passenger complaints about lost luggage, canceled flights, overbooking, and general declines in the quality of service have increased significantly since deregulation. These complaints are fueling demands to reimpose some type of regulation in the industry.

The economic recession and the terrorist attack on the World Trade Center on September 11, 2001 led to a sharp decline in air travel and huge losses for most American airlines, which were only partially covered by the $10 billion federal loan guarantees. This has led to suggestions that more consolidations are necessary in the industry. Opponents, however, point out that the enormous consolidation that has already taken place during the past two decades has not solved the problems of the industry, and further consolidation is likely to be detrimental to consumers. Most domestic airlines, however, did join one of the large international airline alliances. United Airlines joined Germany's Lufthansa and 10 other airlines in the Star Alliance, which accounts for over 21% of world air traffic; American Airlines joined British Air and other airlines in the Oneworld group with about 16% of traffic; Delta joined Air France and others in Skyteam with about 10% market share; and Northwest joined KLM in the Wings group with about 6% market share.

Sources: "Airline Deregulation," *Federal Reserve Bank of San Francisco Review,* March 9, 1990; "Air Travel Survey," *The Economist,* March 10, 2001, pp. 1–24; "Predatory Pricing: Cleared for Takeoff," *Business Week,* May 4, 2001, p. 50; "Airlines and Antitrust: A New World. Or Not," *New York Times,* November 18, 2001, p. 1, Section 3; and "A New Sense of Urgency in Debating the Future of Airlines," *New York Times,* December 12, 2001, p. C10.

EXAMPLE 13–5

Deregulation and the New Merger Boom

Since the early 1990s there has been a huge merger boom in the United States and abroad. The year 2000 was the biggest year for merger and acquisitions in history, with deals valued at more than $1.8 trillion. During the 1990s, megadeals occurred in telecommunications, defense, railroads, pharmaceuticals, retailing, health care, banking, entertainment, publishing, computers, consulting, and many other industries (see Section 11.8). The biggest merger in history was America Online's (AOL's) acquisition of Time Warner for $110 billion in 2000. There are several forces that fueled this urge to merger. The most important were massive technological changes, increased international competition, and deregulation. Firms are under strong pressure to reduce excessive capacity and cut costs and to become a major player in the global marketplace. Only with the U.S. recession in 2001 did the merger boom subside.

The merger wave since the early 1990s was also different from that of the 1980s and so has been the enforcement of antitrust laws. Whereas in the 1980s many mergers were among firms in unrelated industries (thus creating conglomerates) and raised few antitrust concerns, the merger wave since the early 1990s often involved the merger of competitors, potentially giving the combined companies the power to dominate their industries and, in theory, control prices and the availability of products. Starting from the second half of the 1990s, the enforcement of antitrust laws also changed its focus from the doctrine that bigness led to power and unfair behavior to that of protecting consumers, thus refusing to approve mergers that reduced competition and were likely to increase prices. In short, enforcement has become pro-competition and pro-consumer. For example, the Federal Trade Commission (FTC) did not approve the proposed merger of Staples and Office Depot, two chains of office-supply superstores, in 1997 because it found that Staples had lower prices in those locations where there was also an Office Depot outlet, thus concluding that their merger would very likely lead to higher consumer prices. Not approved for the same reason were many other proposed mergers, among which were WorldCom purchase of Sprint in 2000, United Airlines acquisition of American West, and General Electric acquisition of Honeywell in 2001 (which was blocked by the European Commission, even though the two companies are American and the merger had been cleared by the U.S. Justice Department).

Whether, in fact, the present merger boom leads companies to reduce costs and increase efficiency and revenue depends on the type of merger taking place. In the defense and the health care fields, the promise of reduced costs and increased efficiency has been or can be realized. In others sectors, it is not too certain. Often the acquiring company pays a premium over the market price because of synergies that the acquiring company's management sees but the market does not. When such synergies fail to materialize or do not live up to expectations, the acquiring company and its stockholders suffer, especially if the company took on huge debt loads to make the acquisitions.

Sources: "The New Merger Boom," *Fortune,* November 28, 1994, pp. 95–106; "Aiding Consumers Is Now the Thrust of Antitrust Push," *New York Times,* March 22, 1998, p. 1; "The Trustbusters' New Tools," *The Economist,* May 2, 1998, pp. 62–64; "Merger Wave Spurs New Scrutiny," *New York Times,* December 13, 1998, p. 4; "New Era in Washington Paves Way for This and Other Deals," *New York Times,* December 20, 2001, p. C8; "Corporate Governance and Merger Activity in the United States: Making Sense of the 1980s and 1990s," *Journal of Economic Perspectives,* Spring 2001, pp. 121–144; "Antitrust," Brookings Review, winter 2001, pp. 16–19; "Volatile Markets and Global Slowdown Cool Corporate Desire to Merge," *Wall Street Journal,* January 2, 2002, p. R10; and "They Shopped—Now They've Dropped," *Business Week,* February 25, 2002, pp. 36–37.

<table>
<tr><td>13.7</td><td></td></tr>
</table>

REGULATING INTERNATIONAL COMPETITION: VOLUNTARY EXPORT RESTRAINTS

Regulation affects not only domestic companies but also foreign firms. Consider **voluntary export restraints (VER).** These are some of the most important nontariff trade barriers and refer to cases in which an importing country induces another nation to reduce its exports of a commodity "voluntarily," under the threat of higher all-around trade restrictions, when these exports threaten an entire domestic industry.[17] Voluntary export restraints have been negotiated since the 1950s by the United States and other industrial countries to curtail textile exports from Japan, and more recently also to curb exports of automobiles, steel, shoes, and other commodities from Japan and other nations. These are the mature industries that faced sharp declines in employment in the industrial countries during the past two decades. Sometimes called "orderly marketing arrangements," these VERs have allowed the United States and other industrial nations making use of them to save at least the appearance of continued support for the principle of free trade.

When voluntary export restraints are successful, they have all the economic effects of equivalent import tariffs, except that they are administered by the exporting country, and so the revenue effect or monopoly profits are captured by foreign exporters. An example of this is provided by the "voluntary" restraint on Japanese automobile exports to the United States negotiated in 1981 (see Example 13–6).

Voluntary export restraints are likely to be less effective in limiting imports than import quotas, because the exporting nations agree only reluctantly to curb their exports. Foreign exporters are also likely to fill their quotas with higher-quality and higher-priced units of the product over time. This *product upgrading* was clearly evident in the case of the Japanese voluntary restraint on automobile exports to the United States. Furthermore, as a rule, only major supplier countries are involved, which leaves the door open for other nations to replace part of the exports of the major suppliers and also for trans-shipments through third countries.

EXAMPLE 13-6

Voluntary Export Restraints on Japanese Automobiles to the United States

From 1977 to 1981, U.S. automobile production fell by about one-third, the share of imports rose from 18% to 29%, and nearly 300,000 autoworkers in the United States lost their jobs. In 1980 the Big Three U.S. automakers suffered combined losses of $4 billion. As a result, the United States negotiated an agreement with Japan that limited Japanese automobile exports to the United States to 1.68 million units per year from 1981 to 1983 and to 1.85 million units for 1984 and 1985. Japan "agreed" to restrict its automobile exports out of fear of still more stringent import restrictions by the United States.

---

[17] The effects of an import tariff were examined in Section 9.8.

U.S. automakers generally used the time from 1981 to 1985 wisely to lower break-even points and improve quality, but the cost improvements were not passed on to consumers, and Detroit reaped profits of nearly $6 billion in 1983, $10 billion in 1984, and $8 billion in 1985. Japan gained by exporting higher-priced autos and earning higher profits. The big loser, of course, was the American public, which had to pay substantially higher prices for domestic and foreign automobiles. The U.S. International Trade Commission (USITC) estimated that the agreement resulted in a price $660 higher for U.S.-made automobiles and $1,300 higher for Japanese cars in 1984. The USITC also estimated that the total cost of the agreement to U.S. consumers was $15.7 billion from 1981 through 1984, and that 44,000 U.S. auto jobs were saved at a cost of more than $100,000 each. This was two to three times the yearly earnings of a U.S. autoworker.

Since 1985, the United States has not asked for a renewal of the VER agreement, but Japan unilaterally limited its auto exports (to 2.3 million from 1986 to 1991 and 1.65 million afterward) to avoid more trade friction with the United States. Since the late 1980s, however, Japan has invested heavily to produce automobiles in the United States in so-called transplant factories, and by 1996 it was producing more than 2 million cars in the United States had captured 23% of the U.S. auto market. During most of the 1990s, the increased efficiency of U.S. automakers halted the growth of the Japanese share of the U.S. market (but its growth resumed toward the end of the 1990s). By 2002, Japanese automakers had captured 26.6% of the U.S. market (between domestic production and imports), out of a total of 36.7% for all foreign automakers. Following the U.S. lead, Canada and Germany also negotiated restrictions on Japanese exports (France and Italy already had very stringent quotas). A 1991 agreement to limit the Japanese share of the European Union's automarket to 16% was to expire at the turn of the century, but did not.

Sources: U.S. International Trade Commission, *A Review of Recent Developments in the U.S. Automobile Industry Including an Assessment of the Japanese Voluntary Restraint Agreements* (Washington, D.C.: February 1985); Sparking a Revival," *U.S. News & World Report,* June 14, 1993, pp. 69–73; "Japanese Car Makers Plan Major Expansion of American Capacity," *Wall Street Journal,* September 1997, p. A1; and "Automakers' Big Sales Now May Cut Business Next Year," *New York Times,* December 17, 2001, p. C6.

13.8 | SOME APPLICATIONS OF MARKET STRUCTURE, EFFICIENCY, AND REGULATION

In this section, we discuss some important applications of the theory presented in this chapter: the regulation of monopoly price, peak-load pricing, and transfer pricing. These applications highlight the importance and relevance of the tools introduced in the chapter.

Regulating Monopoly Price

One way for the government to regulate a monopoly is to set a price below the price that the monopolist would charge in the absence of regulation. This leads to a larger output and lower profits for the monopolist, as shown in Figure 13.3.

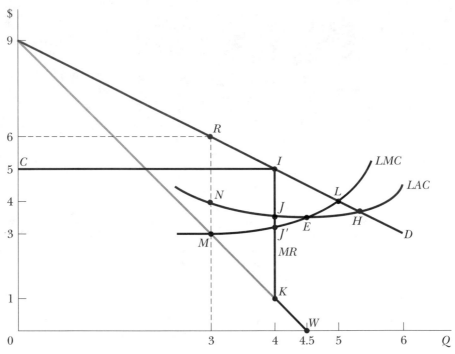

FIGURE 13.3   Regulating Monopoly Price   In the absence of regulation, $Q = 3, P = \$6$, $LAC = \$4$, and profits are \$2 per unit (RN) and \$6 in total. If the government set the maximum price at $P = \$5$, the demand curve becomes CID and the MR curve is $CIKW$. Then, $Q = 4, P = \$5, LAC = \$3.60$, and profits are \$1.40 per unit (IJ) and \$5.60 in total.

The figure shows that, in the absence of regulation, the best level of output of the monopolist is given by point M, where the LMC curve intersects the MR curve (the light blue line) from below. Thus, $Q = 3$, $P = \$6$ (point R), $LAC = \$4$ (point N), and profits are \$2 per unit (RN) and \$6 in total.

If the government now set the maximum price that the monopolist could charge at $P = \$5$, the demand curve facing the monopolist would become CID (see the figure). Thus, the monopolist's demand curve would be horizontal until $Q = 4$ (since the monopolist cannot charge a price higher than \$5) and would resume its usual downward shape at $Q > 4$ (since the monopolist can charge prices lower than \$5). As a result, the monopolist's MR curve is also horizontal and coincides with the demand curve until point I and resumes its usual downward shape when the demand curve does. That is, the monopolist's MR curve becomes $CIKW$. Note that the MR curve has a discontinuous (vertical) section at point I, where the demand curve has a kink.

With price set at $P = \$5$, the best level of output for the monopolist is given by point J', where $LMC = MR$. Thus, $Q = 4$, $P = \$5$ (point I), $LAC = \$3.60$ (point J), and profits are \$1.40 per unit and \$5.60 in total. Price is lower, output is larger, and the monopolist's profits are lower than without regulation.

If the government set the maximum price at point L, where the LMC curve intersects the D curve (so that $P = LMC = \$4$), the best level of output for the monopolist would be 5 units (see the figure). The monopolist would then earn a profit of $\$0.50$ per unit and $\$2.50$ in total. If the government, in an effort to eliminate all monopoly profits, were to set the lower price (about $\$3.50$) given by point H, where the monopolist's LAC curve intersects the D curve, a shortage of the commodity (and a black market) would arise. This is because consumers would demand nearly 5.5 units of the commodity while the monopolist would only produce about 4.5 units (given by the point where $P = LMC$ at about $\$3.50$ in the figure).

Regulation and Peak-Load Pricing

The demand for some services (such as electricity) is higher during some periods (such as in the evening and in the summer) than at other times (such as during the day or in the spring). Electricity is also a nonstorable service (i.e., it must be generated when it is needed). In order to satisfy peak demand, electrical power companies must bring into operation older and less efficient equipment and thus incur higher costs. Power companies should, therefore, charge a higher price during peak than during off-peak periods to reflect their higher marginal costs in the former than in the latter periods. Since such price differences would be based on cost differences, they are not technically price discrimination (nevertheless, they have sometimes been referred to as *intertemporal* price discrimination).

Before deregulation, regulatory commissions often did not permit the public utility to charge different prices during peak and off-peak periods, but required it to charge a constant given price that covered the average of the generating costs during both periods together. Such a constant price, in the face of different generating costs, did not represent the best pricing policy. Assuming that the public utility operated in the short run with a given plant and other equipment, the best pricing policy would be to charge the lower price equal to the lower marginal cost during off-peak periods and charge the higher price equal to the higher marginal cost in peak periods. By adopting such **peak-load pricing,** consumer welfare would be higher than by the policy of constant pricing during both off-peak and peak periods, and consumers generally would end up spending less on electricity for the peak and off-peak periods combined. This is shown in Figure 13.4.

In the figure, D_1 is the market demand curve for electricity during the off-peak period, and D_2 is the higher market demand curve for electricity during the peak period. The short-run marginal cost of the firm is given by SMC. The regulatory commission sets the price of 4 cents per kWh at all times to cover average total costs in both periods together. At $P = 4$ cents, the firm would sell 4 million kWh during the off-peak period (point A_1 on D_1) and 8 million kWh during the peak period (point A_2 on D_2). At point A_1, however, the marginal benefit to consumers from one additional kWh (given by the price of 4 cents per kWh) exceeds the marginal cost of generating the last unit of electricity produced (given by point B_1 on the SMC curve). From society's point of view, it would pay if the firm supplied more electricity until $P = SMC = 3$ cents (point E_1 at which D_1 and SMC intersect). The social benefit gained would be equal to the shaded triangle $A_1B_1E_1$.

On the other hand, at point A_2, the marginal benefit to consumers from one additional kWh (given by the price of 4 cents per kWh) is smaller than the marginal cost of generating the last unit of electricity produced (point B_2 on the SMC curve). From society's point

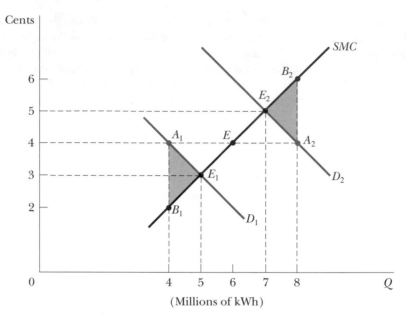

FIGURE 13.4   Peak-Load Pricing   At the constant price of 4 cents per kWh, the public utility sells 4 million kWh of electricity (point A_1) during the off-peak period and 8 million during the peak period (point A_2). But at A_1, $P > SMC$, while at A_2, $P < SMC$. With peak-load pricing, $P = SMC = 3$ cents (point E_1) in the off-peak period and $P = SMC = 5$ cents (point E_2) in the peak period. The gain in consumer welfare with peak-load pricing is thus given by the sum of the two shaded triangles.

of view, it would pay if the firm supplied less electricity until $P = SMC = 5$ cents (point E_2 at which D_2 and SMC intersect). The social benefit gained (by using the same resources to produce some other service that society values more) would be equal to the shaded triangle $B_2 A_2 E_2$. Charging $P = SMC = 3$ cents in the off-peak period (point E_1 in the figure) and $P = SMC = 5$ cents in the peak period (point E_2) would be the most efficient pricing policy.

With deregulation, peak-load or time-of-day pricing is in fact now being used by most electrical companies (telephone companies have been practicing second- and third-degree price discrimination for a long time). For example, in April 2002, Con Edison charged 7.89 cents per kWh for electricity from 10 A.M. to 10 P.M. and 0.70 cents from 10 P.M. to 10 A.M. and on weekends.[18] What is surprising is that it took so long for regulatory commissions to recognize peak-load pricing.

There are other effects from peak-load pricing, which are not shown in Figure 13.4. The first results from the substitution of electricity consumption from peak to off-peak periods to take advantage of the lower price during the off-peak period. This tends to reduce the benefit of peak-load pricing (see Problem 12, with the answer at the end of the book). Another effect also not shown in Figure 13.4 is that with peak-load pricing the scale of plant to meet

---

[18] See "Paying for Electricity by Time of Day," *New York Times*, June 9, 1990, p. 48; and Con Edison, 2002.

peak-load demand is smaller (7 million kWh with peak-load pricing as compared with 8 million kWh without peak-load pricing). Thus, in the long run, when the public utility needs to replace the present plant, it can do so with a smaller and more efficient one. One factor that militates against peak-load pricing is that it requires meters to measure consumption at different times of the day, week, or year, and these can be quite expensive to install.

Peak-load pricing is not confined to public utilities. It is equally applicable to such private enterprises as hotels, restaurants, airlines, movie theaters, and so on, which face a demand that fluctuates sharply and in a predictable way during peak and off-peak periods. These enterprises usually charge lower rates during off-season or in periods of naturally low demand (when marginal costs are lower) than during in-season or periods of high demand (when marginal costs are higher).

Regulation and Transfer Pricing

The rapid rise of modern large-scale enterprises has been accompanied by decentralization and the establishment of semi-autonomous profit centers. This occurred because of the need to contain the tendency toward increasing costs for communications and coordination among various divisions. Decentralization and the establishment of semi-autonomous profit centers also gave rise to the need for **transfer pricing,** or the need to determine the price of intermediate products sold by one semi-autonomous division of a large-scale enterprise and purchased by another semi-autonomous division of the same enterprise. The appropriate pricing of intermediate products or transfer pricing is of crucial importance to the efficient operation of the individual divisions as well as the enterprise as a whole. If the wrong transfer prices are set, the various divisions and the firm as a whole will not produce the optimum or profit-maximizing level of output and will not maximize total profits.

Transfer pricing has also been used by multinational corporations to increase their profits. Specifically, by artificially overpricing components shipped *to* an affiliate in a higher-tax nation and underpricing products shipped *from* the affiliate in the high-tax nation, the multinational corporation can minimize its tax bill and increase its profits. To overcome this problem, government regulators usually apply the "arm's length" test, under which the price of parts shipped from one affiliate of a multinational corporation in one country to another affiliate in another country is priced by regulators for taxing purposes according to the price that the same part would be sold to nonaffiliates.

For simplicity, we assume in our analysis that the firm has two divisions, a production division (indicated by the subscript p) and a marketing division (indicated by the subscript m). The production division sells the intermediate product only to the marketing division (i.e., there is no external market for the intermediate product). The marketing division purchases the intermediate product from the production division, completes the production process, and markets the final product for the firm. We further assume that one unit of the intermediate product is required to produce each unit of the final product.

In Figure 13.5, MC_p and MC_m are the marginal cost curves of the production and marketing divisions of the firm, respectively, while MC is the vertical summation of MC_p and MC_m and represents the total marginal cost curve for the firm as a whole. The figure also shows the external demand curve for the final product sold by the marketing division, D_m, and its corresponding marginal revenue curve, MR_m. The firm's best or profit-maximizing level of output for the final product is 40 units and is given by point

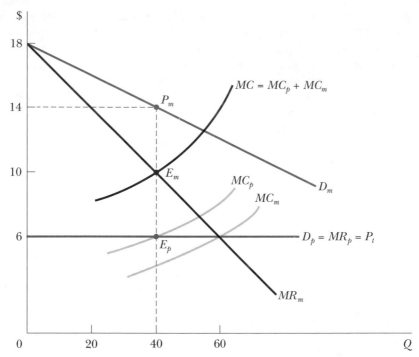

FIGURE 13.5   Transfer Pricing of the Intermediate Product with No External Market   The marginal cost of the firm, MC, is equal to the vertical summation of MC_P and MC_m, the marginal cost curves of the firm's production and marketing divisions. D_m is the external demand for the final product faced by the firm, and MR_m is the corresponding marginal revenue curve. The firm's best level of output is 40 units and is given by point E_m, at which $MR_m = MC$, so that $P_m = \$14$. Since each unit of the final product requires one unit of the intermediate product, the transfer price for the intermediate product, P_t, is set equal to MC_P at $Q_P = 40$ (point E_P). Thus, $P_t = \$6$.

E_m, at which $MR_m = MC$. Therefore, $P_m = \$14$. Since 40 units of the intermediate product are required to produce the 40 units of the final product, the transfer price for the intermediate product, P_t, is set equal to the marginal cost of the intermediate product (MC_p) at $Q_p = 40$. Thus, $P_t = \$6$ and is given by point E_p at which $Q_p = 40$. The demand and marginal revenue curves faced by the production division of the firm are then equal to the transfer price (i.e., $D_p = MR_p = P_t$). Note that $Q_p = 40$ is the best level of output of the intermediate product by the production division of the firm because at $Q_p = 40$, $D_p = MR_p = P_t = MC_p = \$6$. Thus, the correct transfer price for an intermediate product for which there is no external market is the marginal cost of production.[19]

---

[19] For a more detailed discussion of transfer pricing, including the case where there is an external market for the intermediate product of the firm, see D. Salvatore, *Managerial Economics in a Global Economy,* 4th ed. (Cincinnati: South-Western, 2001), Section, 11.4.

SUMMARY

1. In this chapter we have made use of the basic principle that any activity should be carried out until the marginal benefit equals the marginal cost to examine the relationship between market structure and efficiency, public-utility regulation, and antitrust.

2. The Lerner index measures the degree of a *firm's* monopoly power by the ratio of the difference between price and marginal cost to price. The Herfindahl index estimates the degree of monopoly power in an *industry* as a whole by the sum of the squared values of the market sales shares of all the firms in the industry. According to the theory of contestable markets, even if an industry has only one or a few firms, it would still operate as if it were perfectly competitive if entry into the industry is absolutely free and if exit is entirely costless. Experimental economics has been developing during the past two decades. This field seeks to determine how real markets work by using paid volunteers within a simple experimental institutional framework.

3. Static social costs of monopoly power arise because imperfect competitors produce where $P > MR = MC$ and also from rent-seeking activities. These must be balanced with the benefits of economies of scale resulting from large-scale production and the possibility that firms with monopoly power are more innovative than small firms without market power. A great deal of disagreement exists, however, about the alleged dynamic benefits that larger firms have over smaller ones.

4. Section I of the Sherman Antitrust Act passed in 1890 declared that "Every contract, combination . . . , or conspiracy in restraint of trade or commerce among the several states, or with foreign nations, is hereby declared to be illegal." This does not make monopoly as such, or conscious parallelism, illegal. What is illegal is collusion to restrain trade. Section II of the Sherman Antitrust Act makes attempts to monopolize the market illegal. Section VII of the Clayton Act passed in 1914 (and amended by the Celler–Kefauver Act of 1950) prohibits mergers that "substantially lessen competition" or tend to lead to monopoly.

5. Natural monopolies such as public utilities arise when the firm's LAC curve is still declining at the point where it intersects the market demand curve. The government then usually allows a single firm to operate but sets $P = LAC$ (so that the firm earns only a normal return on investment). Economic efficiency, however, requires that $P = LMC$, but this would result in a loss and the company would not supply the service in the long run without a subsidy. Therefore, P is usually set equal to LAC. Many difficulties arise in public-utility regulation, especially to ensure that the utilities keep costs as low as possible.

6. Since the mid-1970s, the government has deregulated airlines and trucking and reduced the level of regulation for financial institutions, telecommunications, and railroads in order to increase competition and avoid some of the heavy compliance costs of regulation. Even though the full impact of deregulation has yet to be felt, deregulation seems to have led to increased competition and lower prices, but it has also resulted in some problems such as deterioration in the quality of the services provided.

7. Voluntary export restraints (VER) refer to the case in which an importing country induces another nation to reduce its exports of a commodity "voluntarily" under the threat of higher all-around trade restrictions. When successful, the economic impact of voluntary export restraints is the same as that of an equivalent import tariff, except for the revenue effect, which is now captured by foreign suppliers. Voluntary export restraints have been negotiated to curtail exports of textiles, automobiles, steel, shoes, and other commodities to the United States and other industrial countries.

8. By setting price below the monopoly price, a monopolist can be induced to produce a larger output and have lower profits. Peak-load pricing refers to the charging of a price equal to

short-run marginal cost, both in the peak period when demand and marginal cost are higher and in the off-peak period when both are lower. The transfer price for an intermediate product for which there is no external market is the marginal cost of production.

KEY TERMS

Efficiency	Sherman Antitrust Act	Voluntary export restraints (VER)
Lerner index	Conscious parallelism	Peak-load pricing
Herfindahl index	Clayton Act	Transfer pricing
Theory of contestable markets	Averch–Johnson (A–J) effect	
Experimental economics	Deregulation movement	

REVIEW QUESTIONS

1. Under what conditions will an economy operate most efficiently? Why?

2. What can be done to increase efficiency if the price of the last unit consumed of a commodity exceeds the marginal cost of producing it?

3. What is the value of the Lerner index if $\eta = -5$? if $\eta = -3$?

4. What is the value of the Lerner index (L) if $P = \$10$ and $MR = \$5$?

5. What is the value of the Herfindahl index
   a. in a duopoly with one firm having 60% of the market?
   b. with 1,000 equal-sized firms?

6. What is the difference between limit pricing and the theory of contestable markets?

7. What are the most important
   a. social costs of monopoly power?
   b. benefits associated with monopoly power?

8. How does the government decide whether to subject a very large firm to antitrust action or regulation?

9. The settlement of the AT&T antitrust case in 1982 involved both good news and bad news for AT&T and its customers. What was
   a. the good news and bad news for AT&T?
   b. the good news and bad news for users of telephone services?

10. a. How could a regulatory commission induce a public-utility company to operate as a perfect competitor in the long run?
    b. To what difficulty would this lead?
    c. What compromise does a regulatory commission usually adopt?

11. Given the difficulties that the regulation of public utilities face, would it not be better to nationalize public utilities, as some European countries have done? Explain your answer.

12. Peak-load pricing can be regarded as an application of the marginal principle. True or false? Explain.

PROBLEMS

1. Explain why the value of the Lerner index can seldom if ever be equal to one (i.e., the value of L usually ranges from zero to smaller than one).

*2. Show with the use of a diagram that a given value of the Lerner index is consistent with different rates of profits for the firm.

3. In measuring the Herfindahl index, the market share of each firm in the industry is sometimes expressed in ratio form rather than in percentages (as in the text). Find the Herfindahl index if the market share of each firm is expressed as a ratio when
   a. there is a single firm in the industry.

* = Answer provided at end of book.

b. there is a duopoly with one firm having 0.6 of the total industry sales.

c. there is one firm with sales equal to 0.5 of total industry sales and ten other equal-sized firms.

d. there are ten equal-sized firms.

e. there are 100 equal-sized firms in the industry.

f. there are 1,000 equal-sized firms in the industry.

4. Starting with demand curve D in Figure 13.1, draw a figure showing three identical firms in the contestable market.

*5. Draw a figure similar to Figure 10.7 showing the net social losses of monopoly when the firm's marginal cost curve is rising, rather than horizontal as in Figure 10.7.

6. Determine if the Justice Department would challenge a merger between two firms in an industry with ten equal-sized firms, based on its Herfindahl-index guidelines only.

*7. Suppose that the market demand curve for the public-utility service shown in Figure 13.2 shifts to the right by 1 million units at each price level but the LAC and LMC curves remain unchanged. Draw a figure showing the price of the service that the public-utility commission would set and the quantity of the service that would be supplied to the market at that price.

8. Suppose that the market demand curve for the public-utility service shown in Figure 13.2 shifts

to the right by 1 million units at each price level, and, at the same time, the LAC curve of the public-utility company shifts upward by $1 throughout because of production inefficiencies that escape detection by the public-utility commission. Draw a figure showing the price of the service that the public-utility commission would set and the quantity of the service that would be supplied to the market at that price.

9. Compare the effects of a voluntary export restraint that restricts the export of commodity X to the nation to 200 units, with the effects of a $1 import tariff imposed by the nation on commodity X shown in Figure 9.17.

10. Draw a figure showing how a regulatory commission could induce the monopolist of Figure 13.3 to behave as a perfect competitor in the short run by setting the appropriate price.

11. Explain why the problems arising in public-utility regulation do not arise in the case of a monopoly that is not a natural monopoly.

*12. a. Starting from Figure 13.4, draw a figure showing peak-load pricing when substitution in consumption is taken into consideration.

b. Is the benefit of peak-load pricing greater or smaller when substitution in consumption is taken into consideration than when it is not? Why is this so?

INTERNET SITE ADDRESSES

For measures of concentration and monopoly power in the United States, see:

http://www.census.gov/epcd/www/concentration.html

Comprehensive antitrust links to the U.S. Department of Justice, the Federal Trade Commission, case summaries, journals, and so on, are found in:

http://www.antitrust.org

http://www.findlaw.com/01topics/01antitrust/index.html

For conditions, deregulation and antitrust cases in the airline industry, see:

American Airlines: http://www.aa.com

America West Airlines: http://www.americawest.com

Continental Airlines: http://www.continental.com

Delta Airlines: http://www.delta.com

TWA Airlines: http://www.twa.com

United Airlines: http://www.ual.com

The Internet site for the Energy Regulatory Commission is:

http://www.ferc.ed.us

For pricing by Con Edison, see:

http://www.conedison.com

Information on international trade regulations and rulings is found on the Internet site of the World Trade Organization at:

http://www.wto.org

PART FIVE

Pricing and Employment of Inputs

Part Five (Chapters 14–16) presents the theory of input pricing and employment. Until this point in the text, we have assumed input prices to be given. In this part, we examine how input prices and the level of their employment are determined in the market. Chapter 14 deals with input pricing and employment under perfect competition in the output and input markets. Chapter 15 examines input pricing and employment under imperfect competition in the output and/or input markets. Chapter 16 deals with financial microeconomics; that is, the allocation of inputs over time and the cost of capital. As in previous parts of the text, the presentation of theory is reinforced with many real-world examples and important applications, while the "At the Frontier" sections present some new and important developments in the analysis of input or factor markets.

CHAPTER 14

Input Price and Employment Under Perfect Competition

I n Chapters 7 and 8 we examined how firms combine inputs to minimize production costs on the assumption of given input prices. In Chapters 9 through 13 we dealt with the product market and examined the pricing and output of consumers' goods, again on the assumption of given input prices. We now turn our attention to the input market and examine how the price and employment of inputs are actually determined.

In many ways the determination of input prices and employment is similar to the pricing and output of commodities. That is, the price and employment of an input is generally determined by the interaction of the forces of market demand and supply for the input.

There are several important qualifications, however. First, whereas consumers demand commodities because of the utility or satisfaction they receive in consuming the commodities, firms demand inputs in order to produce the goods and services demanded by society. That is, the demand for an input is a "derived demand"; it is derived from the demand for the final commodities that the input is used in producing. Second, while consumers demand commodities, firms demand the *services* of inputs. That is, firms demand the *flow* of input services (e.g., labor time), not the stock of the inputs themselves. The same is generally true for the other inputs. Third, the analysis in this chapter and in the next deals with inputs in general; that is, it refers to all types of labor, capital, raw materials, and land inputs. However, since the various types of labor receive more than three-quarters of the national income, the discussion is couched in terms of labor.

We begin the chapter with a summary discussion of profit maximization and optimal input employment. Then we derive a firm's demand curve for an input. By adding the demand curves for the input of all firms, we get the market demand curve for the input. Next we discuss an individual's decision between work and leisure and the market supply curve of an input in general. The chapter then describes how the interaction of the market demand and supply of an input determines its price and employment under perfect competition (the case of imperfect competition is examined in the next chapter). Subsequently, the chapter shows the process by which input prices tend to be equalized among industries and regions of a country, and internationally among countries. A discussion of rent and quasi rent follows. This chapter concludes with several important applications and extensions of the theory. The "At the Frontier" section examines the effect of minimum wages on employment.

14.1   PROFIT MAXIMIZATION AND OPTIMAL INPUT EMPLOYMENT

In this section, we bring together and summarize the discussions of Chapters 7, 8, and 9 on the conditions for profit maximization and optimal input employment by firms operating under perfect competition. This is the first step in the derivation of the demand curve for an input by a firm.

In Section 8.3, we saw that the least-cost input combination of a firm was given by equation [8.5B], repeated below as [14.1]:

$$MP_L/w = MP_K/r \qquad [14.1]$$

where MP refers to the marginal (physical) product, L refers to labor, K to capital, w to wages or the price of labor time, and r to the interest rate or the rental price of capital. Equation [14.1] indicates that to minimize production costs, the extra output or marginal product per dollar spent on labor must be equal to the marginal product per dollar spent on capital. If $MP_L = 5$, $MP_K = 4$, and $w = r$, the firm would not be minimizing costs, because it is getting more extra output for a dollar spent on labor than on capital. To minimize costs, the firm would have to hire more labor and rent less capital. As the firm does this, the MP_L declines and the MP_K increases (because of diminishing returns). The process would have to continue until condition [14.1] held. If w were higher than r, the MP_L would have to be proportionately higher than the MP_K for condition [14.1] to hold. The same general condition would have to hold to minimize production costs, no matter how many inputs the firm uses. That is, the MP per dollar spent on each input would have to be the same for all inputs.

Going one step further, we can show that the reciprocal of each term (ratio) in equation [14.1] equals the marginal cost (MC) of the firm to produce an additional unit of output. That is,

$$w/MP_L = r/MP_K = MC \qquad [14.2]$$

Consider labor first. The wage rate (w) is the addition to the total costs of the firm from hiring one additional unit of labor, while MP_L is the resulting increase in the total output of the commodity of the firm. Thus, w/MP_L gives the change in total costs (in terms of labor) per unit increase in output. This is the definition of marginal cost. That is, $w/MP_L = MC$.[1] For example, if the hourly wage is $10 and the firm produces five additional units of the commodity with an additional hour of labor time, the marginal cost per unit of

---

[1] Specifically,

$$\frac{w}{MP_L} = \frac{\Delta TC/\Delta L}{\Delta Q/\Delta L} = \frac{\Delta TC}{\Delta L} \cdot \frac{\Delta L}{\Delta Q} = \frac{\Delta TC}{\Delta Q} = MC$$

output is \$2 ($w/MP_L = \$10/5 = \$2 = MC$). The same is true for capital. That is, $r/MP_K = MC$.[2]

To maximize profits, the firm must use the optimal or least-cost input combination to produce the *best level of output*. We saw in Section 9.3 that the best level of output for a perfectly competitive firm is the output at which marginal cost (MC) equals marginal revenue (MR) or price (P).[3] Thus, it follows that to maximize profits

$$w/MP_L = r/MP_K = MC = MR = P \qquad [14.3]$$

By cross multiplication and rearrangement of the terms, we get equations [14.4] and [14.5]:

$$MP_L \times MR = w \quad \text{or} \quad MP_L \times P = w \qquad [14.4]$$

$$MP_K \times MR = r \quad \text{or} \quad MP_K \times P = r \qquad [14.5]$$

Thus, the profit-maximizing rule is that the firm should hire labor until the marginal product of labor times the firm's marginal revenue or price of the commodity equals the wage rate. Similarly, the firm should rent capital until the marginal product of capital times the firm's marginal revenue or price of the commodity is equal to the interest rate. To maximize profits, the same rule would have to hold for all inputs that the firm uses. In the next section, we will see that this provides the basis for the firm's demand curve for an input.

14.2 | THE DEMAND CURVE OF A FIRM FOR AN INPUT

In this section, we build on the discussion of the last section and derive the demand curve of a firm for an input—first, when the input is the only variable input and then, when the input is one of two or more variable inputs.

The Demand Curve of a Firm for One Variable Input

We have stated earlier that a firm demands an input in order to produce a commodity demanded by consumers. Thus, the demand for an input is a **derived demand**—derived, that is, from the demand for the final commodities that the input is used in producing. The demand for an input by a firm shows the quantities of the input that the firm would hire at various alternative input prices. We begin by assuming that only one input is variable (i.e., the amount used of the other inputs is fixed and cannot be changed). This assumption will be relaxed in the next subsection.

According to the marginal concept, a profit-maximizing firm will hire an input as long as the extra income from the sale of the output produced by the input is larger than the extra cost of hiring the input. The extra income is given by the marginal product (MP) of the

---

[2] Specifically,

$$\frac{r}{MP_K} = \frac{\Delta TC/\Delta K}{\Delta Q/\Delta K} = \frac{\Delta TC}{\Delta K} \cdot \frac{\Delta K}{\Delta Q} = \frac{\Delta TC}{\Delta Q} = MC$$

[3] Remember that with perfect competition in the commodity market, $MR = P$.

input times the marginal revenue (*MR*) of the firm. This is called the **marginal revenue product (*MRP*).** That is,

$$MRP = MP \cdot MR \qquad [14.6]$$

When the firm is a perfect competitor in the product market, its marginal revenue is equal to the commodity price (*P*). In this case, the marginal revenue product is called the **value of the marginal product (*VMP*).** That is, when the firm is a perfect competitor in the product market (so that $MR = P$),

$$MRP = MP \cdot MR = MP \cdot P = VMP \qquad [14.6A]$$

If the variable input is labor, we have

$$MRP_L = MP_L \cdot MR = MP_L \cdot P = VMP_L \qquad [14.6B]$$

Thus, the MRP_L or VMP_L is the left-hand side of equation [14.4]. Similarly, the MRP_K or VMP_K is the left-hand side of equation [14.5].

The extra cost of hiring an input or **marginal expenditure (*ME*)** is equal to the price of the input if the firm is a perfect competitor in the input market. Perfect competition in the input market means that the firm demanding the input is too small, by itself, to affect the price of the input. In other words, each firm can hire any amount of the input (service) at the given market price for the input. Thus, the firm faces a horizontal or infinitely elastic *supply* curve for the input. For example, if the input is labor, this means that the firm can hire any quantity of labor time at the given wage rate. Thus, a profit-maximizing firm should hire labor as long as the marginal revenue product of labor exceeds the marginal expenditure on labor or wage rate and until $MRP_L = ME_L = w$, as indicated by equation [14.4]. Note that the $MRP = ME$ rule is entirely analogous to the $MR = MC$ profit-maximizing rule employed throughout our discussion of price and output determination in Chapters 9–13.

The actual derivation of a firm's demand schedule for labor, when labor is the only variable input (i.e., when capital and other inputs are fixed), is shown in Table 14.1. In Table 14.1, *L* refers to the number of workers hired by the firm per day. Q_X is the total output of commodity *X* produced by the firm by hiring various numbers of workers. The MP_L is the marginal or extra output generated by each additional worker hired. The MP_L is obtained by the change in Q_X per unit change in *L*. Note that the law of diminishing returns begins to operate

TABLE 14.1	Marginal Revenue Product of Labor as the Firm's Demand Schedule for Labor				
L	Q_X	MP_L	P_X	$MRP_L = VMP_L$	$ME_L = w$
0	0	. . .	$10	. . .	$40
1	12	12	10	$120	40
2	22	10	10	100	40
3	30	8	10	80	40
4	36	6	10	60	40
5	40	4	10	40	40
6	42	2	10	20	40

with the hiring of the second worker. P_X refers to the price of the final commodity, which is constant (at $10) because the firm is a perfect competitor in the product market. The marginal revenue product of labor (MRP_L) is obtained by multiplying the MP_L by MR_X (the marginal revenue from the sale of commodity X) and is equal to the value of the marginal product of labor (VMP_L) because $P_X = MR_X$.[4] The last column gives the marginal expenditure on labor (ME_L), which is equal to the constant wage rate (w) of $40 per day that the firm must pay to hire each additional worker (since the firm is a perfect competitor in the labor market).

Looking at Table 14.1, we see that the first worker contributes an extra $120 to the firm's revenue (i.e., $MRP_L = \$120$), while the firm incurs an extra expenditure of only $40 to hire this worker (i.e., $ME_L = w = \$40$). Thus, it pays for the firm to hire the first worker. The MRP_L of the second worker falls to $100 (because of diminishing returns), but this still greatly exceeds the daily wage of $40 that the firm must pay the second (and all) worker(s) hired. According to equation [14.4], the profit-maximizing firm should hire workers until the $MRP_L = ME_L = w$. Thus, this firm should hire five workers, at which $VMP_L = w = \$40$. The firm will not hire the sixth worker because he or she will contribute only an extra $20 to the firm's total revenue while adding an extra $40 to its total expenditures.

Thus, the MRP_L schedule gives the firm's demand schedule for labor. It indicates the number of workers that the firm would hire at various wage rates. For example, if $w = \$120$ per day, the firm would hire only one worker per day. If $w = \$100$, the firm would hire two workers. At $w = \$80$, the firm would hire three workers. At $w = \$40$, $L = 5$, and so on. If we plotted the MRP_L values of Table 14.1 on the vertical axis and L on the horizontal axis, we would get the firm's negatively sloped demand *curve* for labor when labor is the only variable input. This is shown next.

The Demand Curve of a Firm for One of Several Variable Inputs

We have seen that the declining MRP_L schedule given in Table 14.1 gives the firm's demand schedule for labor in the short run when labor is the only variable input. This is shown by the negatively sloped MRP_L curve in Figure 14.1 (on the assumption that labor is infinitesimally divisible or that workers can be hired for any part of a day). The MRP_L or demand for labor curve when labor is the only variable input shows that the firm will hire three workers at $w = \$80$ (point A in Figure 14.1) and five workers at $w = \$40$ (point B).

However, when labor is not the only variable input (i.e., when the firm can also change the quantity of capital and other inputs), the firm's demand curve for labor can be derived from the MRP_L curve, but it is not the MRP_L curve itself. Figure 14.1 shows the derivation of the demand curve for labor by a firm when both labor and capital are variable. As a first step, recall that at $w = \$80$, the profit-maximizing firm would hire three workers (point A on the MRP_L curve in Figure 14.1). This gives the first point on the firm's demand curve for labor when only labor is variable and when both labor and capital are variable. When the daily wage rate falls from $w = \$80$ to $w = \$40$, the firm does not move to point B on the given MRP_L curve and hire five workers (as shown before) if labor is not the only variable input.

---

[4] Note also that

$$MRP_L = MP_L \cdot MR = \frac{\Delta Q}{\Delta L} \cdot \frac{\Delta TR}{\Delta Q} = \frac{\Delta TR}{\Delta L}$$

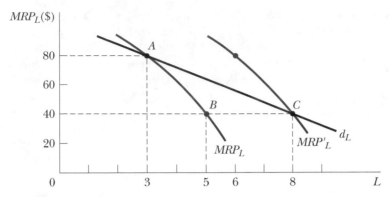

FIGURE 14.1   Demand Curve for Labor of a Firm with Labor and Capital Variable   At $w = \$80$, the firm will employ three workers per day (point A on the MRP_L curve). At $w = \$40$, the firm would employ five workers if labor were the only variable input (point B on the MRP_L curve). However, since capital is also variable and complementary to labor, as the firm hires more labor, the MRP_K shifts to the right and the firm also employs more capital (not shown in the figure). But as the firm employs more capital, the MRP_L curve shifts to the right to MRP'_L and the firm employs eight workers per day at $w = \$40$ (point C on MRP'_L). By joining point A and point C, we derive d_L (the firm's demand curve for labor).

To get another point on the firm's demand curve for labor when both labor and capital are variable, we should realize that labor and capital are usually **complementary inputs** in the sense that when the firm hires more labor, it will also employ more capital (e.g., rent more machinery). For example, when the firm hires more computer programmers, it will usually also pay for the firm to rent more computer terminals, and vice versa. Recall also that the MRP_L curve is drawn on the assumption that the quantity of capital used is fixed at a given level. Similarly, the MRP_K curve is drawn on the assumption of a given amount of labor being used. If the quantity of labor used with various amounts of capital increases (because of a reduction in wages), the entire MRP_K curve will shift outward or to the right. The reason for this is that with a greater amount of labor, each unit of capital will produce more output (see Section 7.3). Given the (unchanged) rental price of capital or interest rate, the profit-maximizing firm will then want to expand its use of capital.

But the increase in the quantity of capital used by the firm will, in turn, shift the entire MRP_L curve outward or to the right because each worker will have more capital with which to work (and produce more output). This is shown by the MRP'_L in Figure 14.1. Thus, when the daily wage rate falls to $w = \$40$, the profit-maximizing firm will hire eight workers (point C on the MRP'_L curve) rather than five workers (point B on the MRP_L curve). Thus, point C is another point on the firm's demand curve for labor when labor and capital are both variable. Other points can be similarly obtained. Joining point A and point C gives the firm's demand curve for labor (d_L in Figure 14.1) when labor and capital are both variable and complementary.

To summarize, when $w = \$80$, the firm will hire three workers (point A in Figure 14.1). Point A is a point on the firm's demand curve for labor, whether or not labor is the only variable input. When the wage rate falls to $w = \$40$, the firm will hire five workers (point B on the MRP_L curve) if labor is the only variable input. Thus, the MRP_L curve gives the firm's demand curve for labor when labor is the only variable input. If capital is also variable and complementary to labor, as the firm hires more labor because of the reduction in the wage rate, the MRP_K curve (not shown in Figure 14.1) shifts to the right and the firm uses more capital at the unchanged interest rate. However, as the firm uses more capital, its MRP_L curve shifts outward or to the right to MRP'_L and the firm hires not just five workers (point B on the MRP_L curve), but eight workers (point C on the MRP'_L curve). The reason is that only by hiring eight workers will $MRP'_L = w = \$40$. Joining points A and C gives the demand curve for labor of the firm d_L (see the figure) when labor and capital are both variable and complementary.

If capital or other inputs are substitutes for labor, the increase in the quantity of labor used by the firm as a result of a reduction in the wage rate will cause the MRP curves of these other inputs to shift to the *left* (as the utilization of more labor substitutes for, or replaces, some of these other inputs). This, in turn, will cause the MRP_L curve to shift outward and to the right as in Figure 14.1. Thus, whether other inputs are complements or substitutes for labor, the MRP_L shifts outward and to the right when the wage rate falls (and the price of these other inputs remains unchanged). As a result, the firm will hire more labor than indicated on its original MRP_L curve at the lower wage rate (see Figure 14.1).

Thus, the d_L curve is negatively sloped and generally more elastic than the MRP_L curve in the long run when all inputs are variable (whether the other inputs are complements or substitutes of labor, or both). In general, the better the complement and substitute inputs available for labor, the greater the outward shift of the MRP_L curve as a result of a decline in the wage rate, and the more elastic is d_L. The negative slope of the d_L curve means that when the wage rate falls, the profit-maximizing firm will hire more workers. The same is generally true for other inputs. That is, as the price of any input falls, the firm will hire more units of the input (i.e., the demand curve of the input of the firm is negatively sloped). In the process, however, the firm will also make marginal adjustments in the use of all complementary and substitute inputs.

14.3 THE MARKET DEMAND CURVE FOR AN INPUT AND ITS ELASTICITY

In this section, we examine how to derive the market demand curve for an input from the individual firms' demand curves for the input. The determination of the market demand curve for an input is important because the equilibrium price of the input is determined at the intersection of the market demand and supply curves of the input under perfect competition. After deriving the market demand curve for an input, we will discuss the determinants of the price elasticity of the demand for the input.

The Market Demand Curve for an Input

The market demand curve for an input is derived from the individual firms' demand curves for the input. Although the process is similar to the derivation of the market demand curve for a commodity from individuals' demand curves for the commodity, the market demand curve for an input is not simply the horizontal summation of the individual firms' demand curves for the input. The reason is that when the price of an input falls, not only this firm but all other firms will employ more of this and other (complementary) inputs, as explained in Section 14.2. Thus, the output of the *commodity* increases and its price falls. Since the *MRP* of an input is equal to the marginal product of the input times the marginal revenue (which is here equal to the commodity price), the reduction in the commodity price will cause each firm's *MRP* and demand curves of the input to shift down or to the left. The market demand curve for an input is then derived by the horizontal summation of the individual firms' demand curves for the input *after the effect of the reduction in the commodity price has been considered*. This is shown in Figure 14.2.

In the left panel of Figure 14.2, d_L is the individual firm's demand curve for labor time derived in Figure 14.1. The d_L curve was derived from the MRP_L of the firm, which itself depended on the marginal product of labor (i.e., MP_L) and the commodity price of $P_x = \$10$. The d_L curve shows that at the wage rate of $w = \$80$ per day the firm would hire three workers per day (point A on d_L). If there were 100 identical firms demanding labor, all firms together would employ 300 workers at $w = \$80$ (point A' in the right panel of Figure 14.2). Point A' is then one point on the market demand curve for labor.

When the wage rate falls to $w = \$40$, the firm would employ eight workers per day (point C on d_L). However, when we consider that all firms will be employing more labor (and capital) when the wage rate falls, they will produce more of the commodity, and the commodity price falls. The reduction in the commodity price will cause a leftward shift in d_L, say to d'_L in the left panel, so that when the wage rate falls to $w = \$40$, the firm will not hire eight workers per day but six workers (point E on d'_L). With 100 identical firms in the market, all firms together will employ 600 workers (point E' in the right panel). By joining points A'

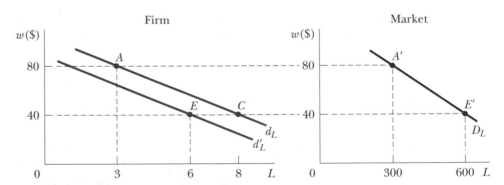

FIGURE 14.2   Derivation of the Market Demand Curve for Labor   In the left panel, d_L is the firm's demand curve for labor derived in Figure 14.1. At $w = \$80$ the firm hires three workers (point A on d_L). One hundred identical firms employ 300 workers (point A' in the right panel). Point A' is one point on the market demand curve for labor. When w falls to $w = \$40$, all firms employ more labor, the output of the commodity rises, and its price falls. Then d_L shifts to the left to d'_L, so that at $w = \$40$ the firm hires 6L (point E on d'_L), and all firms together will employ 600L (point E' in the right panel). By joining point A' and E', we get D_L.

and E' in the right panel, we get the market demand curve for labor, D_L. Note that D_L is less elastic than if it were obtained by the simple straightforward horizontal summation of the d_L curves. Example 14–1 examines the increase in the demand for temporary workers.

EXAMPLE 14–1

The Increase in the Demand for Temporary Workers

In recent years there has been a sharp increase in the demand for temporary workers not only for work in offices but also on factory floors around the country. The trend is evident not only in small local firms but also in such large leading multinational corporations as IBM, Microsoft, General Electric, and Johnson & Johnson, and it involves not only low-skilled workers but, increasingly, professionals such as lawyers, doctors, and scientists. With many corporations facing increasing competition from home and abroad, and having already pared their payrolls to the bone, skilled temporary workers are becoming increasingly common in computer labs, operating rooms, and even executive suites.

The tendency to hire temporary workers is strongest during economic downturns, but it persists even in times of strong demand. Some estimates indicate that as many as 30% of new jobs are now temporary, as compared with about 10% a decade ago. In 2001, temporary workers represented 2.2 of the nation's overall work force, double the level in 1991. Temporary workers usually earn significantly less than the permanent employees and can be laid off far more easily than regular employees. They also receive little in the way of nonwage benefits (health insurance, pension benefits, vacations, and so on). Although the lower labor costs make U.S. corporations more flexible and competitive on world markets, hiring temporary workers creates major problems for new entrants into the labor force and for older laid-off workers searching for a new job. Indeed, if the present trend toward hiring temporary workers continues, the traditional American job, with a 40-hour workweek, medical benefits, paid vacations, and a pension at 65, may become more and more rare.

Although some workers like the flexibility and diversity that temporary jobs provide, the vast majority would clearly prefer a more permanent job. This is also true for the many professionals who present themselves as consultants when they fail to secure a regular job. Temporary workers also have less loyalty to the firm than regular workers and can leave suddenly when they find a more permanent job or a better temporary occupation. Furthermore, temporary workers that are kept on a long time are likely to become grumpy and wonder why they are not hired more permanently. Finally, temporary workers create a strong need for society to provide a safety net separate from people's jobs to provide for their health care, pension, and job training.

Sources: "Temporary Workers Are on the Increase in the Nation's Factories," *New York Times,* July 6, 1993, p. 1; "New Jobs Lack the Old Security in a Time of 'Disposable' Workers," *New York Times,* March 3, 1993, p. 1; "In a Shaky Economy, Even Professionals Are 'Temps,'" *New York Times,* May 16, 1993, Section 3, p. 5; "Equal Work, Less-Equal Perks," *New York Times,* March 30, 1998, p. D1; "Regulators Probe U.S. Reliance on Temporary Workers," *Wall Street Journal,* August 7, 2000, p. A2; and "Temporary Work Is Sidestepping a Slowdown," *New York Times,* July 7, 2001, Section 3, p. 4.

Determinants of the Price Elasticity of Demand for an Input

In Section 5.2, we defined the price elasticity of demand for a commodity as the percentage change in the quantity demanded of the commodity resulting from a given percentage change in its price. The price elasticity of demand for an input can similarly be defined as the percentage change in the quantity demanded of the input resulting from a given percentage change in its price. The greater the percentage change in quantity resulting from a given percentage change in price, the greater is the price elasticity of demand. For example, if 2% more workers are employed as a result of a 1% reduction in the wage rate, the price (wage) elasticity of the market demand for labor is -2. If the quantity demanded of labor increased by only 1/2%, the wage elasticity of labor would be $-1/2$.

The determinants of the price elasticity of demand for an input are generally the same as the determinants of the price elasticity of demand for a commodity (discussed in Section 5.2). First, the price elasticity of demand for an input is larger the closer and the greater are the number of available substitutes for the input. For example, the price elasticity of demand for copper is greater than the price elasticity of demand for chromium (a metallic element used in alloys and in electroplating) because copper has better and more substitutes (silver, aluminum, and fiber glass) than chromium. Thus, the same percentage change in the price of copper and chromium elicits a larger percentage change in the quantity demanded of copper than of chromium.

Second, since the demand for an input is derived from the demand for the final commodity produced with the input, the price elasticity of demand for the input is greater the larger is the price elasticity of demand of the commodity. The reason is that (as we have seen in the previous section) a reduction in the price of an input results in a reduction in the price of the final commodity produced with the input. The more elastic is the demand for the final commodity, the greater is the increase in the quantity demanded of the commodity, and so the greater is the quantity demanded of the input used in the production of the commodity. For example, if the wage rate falls, the price of new homes also declines. If the price elasticity of demand for new homes is very high, then a price reduction for new homes greatly increases the quantity demanded of new homes and greatly increases the demand for labor and other inputs going into the production of new homes.

Third, the price elasticity of demand for an input, say aluminum, is greater the larger is the price elasticity of *supply* of other inputs for which aluminum is a very good substitute in production. The reason is as follows. A reduction in the price of aluminum will lead producers to substitute aluminum for these other inputs. This is the same as the first reason discussed above, but it is not the end of the story. If the supply curves of these other inputs are very elastic, the reduction (i.e., leftward shift) in their demand curves will not result in a large decline in their prices, and so a great deal of the original increase in the quantity demanded of aluminum as a result of a reduction in its price will persist. This makes the demand curve for aluminum price elastic (if aluminum is a good substitute for these other inputs). Had the supply of these other inputs been inelastic, a reduction in their demand would have reduced their price very much, and checked the increase in the quantity demanded (and the price elasticity of demand) for aluminum.

Fourth, the price elasticity of demand for an input is *lower* the smaller is the percentage of the total cost spent on the input. For example, if the percentage of the total cost of the firm spent on an input is only 1%, a doubling of the price of the input will only increase the total costs of the firm by 1%. In that case, a firm is not likely to make great efforts to economize on the use of the input. Therefore, the price elasticity of an input on which the firm spends only a small percentage of its costs is likely to be low. This is usually, but not always, the case.

Finally, the price elasticity of an input is greater the longer the period of time allowed for the adjustment to the change in the input price. For example, an increase in the wage of unskilled labor may not reduce employment very much in the short run because the firm must operate the given plant built to take advantage of the low wage of unskilled labor. In the long run, however, the firm can build a plant using more capital-intensive production techniques to save on the use of the now more expensive unskilled labor. Thus, the reduction in the employment (and the wage elasticity of the demand) of unskilled labor is likely to be greater in the long run than in the short run. In Figure 14.1, the d_L curve (which is the firm's demand curve for labor when labor and other inputs are variable) is more elastic than the MRP_L curve (which is the firm's short-run demand curve for labor when labor is the only variable input). Example 14–2 examines the price elasticity of the demand for inputs in some manufacturing industries.

EXAMPLE 14–2

Price Elasticity of Demand for Inputs in Manufacturing Industries

Table 14.2 presents the price elasticity of the demand for production labor, nonproduction labor, capital, and electricity in the textile, paper, chemicals, and metals industries in Alabama estimated from data on input quantities, input prices, and outputs over the 1971–1991 period. The data show that input demand is price inelastic, except for nonproduction labor in the textile industry, where it is about unitary elastic. This means that an increase in the price of an input reduces the quantity demanded of the input less than

TABLE 14.2	Price Elasticity of Input Demand for Manufacturing Industries			
	Production Labor	Nonproduction Labor	Capital	Energy
Textile	−0.50	−1.04	−0.41	−0.11
Paper	−0.62	−0.97	−0.29	−0.16
Chemicals	−0.75	−0.69	−0.12	−0.25
Metals	−0.41	−0.44	−0.91	−0.69

Source: A. H. Barnett, K. Reutter, and H. Thompson, "Electricity Substitution: Some Local Industrial Evidence," *Energy Economics,* 20, 1998, 411–419.

proportionately. For example, the table shows that a 10% increase in the wage of production workers tends to reduce the quantity demanded of production workers in the textile industry by 5%. A 10% increase in the price of capital reduces the quantity of capital demanded by the paper industry by 2.9%, while a 10% increase in the price of energy reduces the quantity demanded of that input by 1.1% in the textile industry (the lowest price elasticity shown in the table).

14.4 The Supply Curve of an Input

In this section, we first derive an individual's supply curve of labor. Then we examine the substitution and the income effects of a wage increase. Finally, we discuss the market supply curve of an input in general, and the market supply of labor in particular. In the following section, we will use the market supply curve examined in this section and the market demand curve derived in Section 14.3 to determine the equilibrium price of an input (the wage rate).

The Supply of Labor by an Individual

The short-run supply curve of an input (like the supply curve of a final commodity) is generally positively sloped, indicating that a greater quantity of the input is supplied per unit of time at higher input prices. For example, if the price of iron ore rises, mining firms will supply more iron ore per time period. The same is true for an **intermediate good** such as steel (produced with iron ore), which is itself used as an input in the production of many final commodities such as automobiles. That is, steel producers will supply more steel at higher steel prices. However, while natural resources (such as iron ore) and intermediate goods (such as steel) are supplied by firms, and their supply curves are generally positively sloped, labor is supplied by individuals and their supply curve may be backward-bending. That is, after some wage rate, higher wage rates may result in individuals demanding more leisure time and supplying fewer *hours* of work per day. This is shown in Figure 14.3.

The left panel of Figure 14.3 is used to derive the backward-bending supply curve of labor of an individual shown in the right panel. The movement from left to right on the horizontal axis of the figure in the left panel measures hours of leisure time for the individual (the top scale at the bottom of the figure). Subtracting hours of leisure from the 24 hours of the day, we get the hours worked by the individual per day (the bottom scale in the left panel). Hours of leisure plus hours of work always equal 24. On the other hand, the vertical axis in the left panel measures money income.

Indifference curves U_1, U_2, U_3, and U_4 in the left panel show the trade-off between leisure and income for the individual. They are similar to the individual's indifference curves between two commodities, discussed in Section 3.2. For example, the individual is indifferent between 14 hours of leisure (10 hours of work) and a daily income of $60 (point M

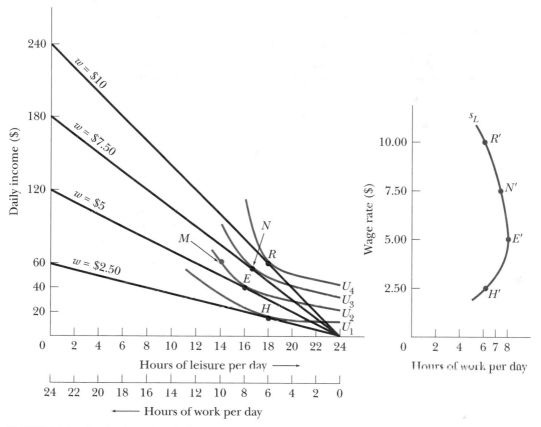

FIGURE 14.3   Derivation of an Individual's Supply Curve of Labor   In the left panel, U_1, U_2, U_3, and U_4 show the trade-off between leisure and income for the individual, while the straight budget lines show the trade-off between leisure and income in the market. The absolute slope of the budget lines gives the wage rates. The individual maximizes satisfaction at point H (with 18 hours of leisure per day and a daily income of $15) on U_1 with $w = \$2.50$, at point E (with 16 hours of leisure and income of $40) on U_2 with $w = \$5$, and so on. By plotting hours of work per day at various wage rates, we get the individual's backward-bending supply curve of labor (S_L) in the right panel.

on U_2) on the one hand, and 16 hours of leisure (8 hours of work) and a daily income of $40 (point E on U_2) on the other. Thus, the individual is willing to give up $20 of income to increase leisure time by 2 hours. Indifference curves U_3 and U_4 provide more utility or satisfaction to the individual than U_2, and U_2 provides more utility or satisfaction than U_1.

Given the wage rate, we can easily define the budget line of the individual. When the individual takes all 24 hours in leisure (i.e., works zero hours), the individual's income is zero regardless of the wage rate. Thus, any budget line of the individual starts at this point on the horizontal axis in the left panel. On the other hand, if the individual worked 24 hours per day, his or her income would be $60 if the wage rate were $2.50 (the lowest budget line), his or her income would be $120 if $w = \$5$ (the second budget line), $180 if

$w = \$7.50$ (the third budget line), and \$240 if $w = \$10$ (the highest budget line). Note that the wage rate is given by the absolute value of the slope of the budget line. Thus, $w = \$60/24$ hours $= \$2.50$/hour for the lowest budget line, $w = \$120/24$ hours $= \$5$ for the second budget line, $w = \$180/24$ hours $= \$7.50$ for the third budget line, and $w = \$240/24$ hours $= \$10$ for the highest budget line. These budget lines are similar to the individual's budget lines derived in Section 3.3.

As shown in Section 3.5, an individual maximizes utility or satisfaction by reaching the highest indifference curve possible with his or her budget line. Thus, if the wage rate is \$2.50, the individual will take 18 hours in leisure (i.e., work 6 hours) and earn an income of \$15 per day (point H on U_1 in the left panel of Figure 14.3). This gives point H' on the individual's supply curve of labor (s_L) in the right panel. With $w = \$5$, the individual takes 16 hours of leisure (i.e., works 8 hours) and earns an income of \$40 per day (point E on U_2 in the left panel). This gives point E' on s_L in the right panel. At $w = \$7.50$, the individual chooses 16.5 hours of leisure (works 7.5 hours) and has an income of \$56.25 per day (point N on U_3 and N' on s_L). Finally, at $w = \$10$, the individual chooses 18 hours of leisure (works 6 hours) and has an income of \$60 per day (point R on U_4 and R' on s_L).

Note that the individual's supply curve of labor (s_L in the right panel of Figure 14.3) is positively sloped until the wage rate of \$5, and it bends backward at higher wage rates. Thus, the individual works *more* hours (i.e., takes less leisure) until the wage rate of \$5 per hour and works *fewer* hours (i.e., takes more leisure) at higher wage rates.

Substitution and Income Effects of a Wage Increase

The reason that an individual's supply curve of labor may be backward-bending can be explained by separating the substitution effect from the income effect of the wage increase. That is, an increase in wages (just like an increase in a commodity price) gives rise to a substitution effect and an income effect. In the case of an increase in the price of a normal good, the substitution and the income effects work in the same direction (to reduce the quantity demanded of the commodity). On the other hand, in the case of an increase in the wage rate, the substitution and the income effects operate in opposite directions, and (as explained next) this may cause the individual's supply curve of labor to be backward-bending.

According to the substitution effect, an increase in the wage rate leads an individual to work more (i.e., to substitute work for leisure). That is, as the wage rate rises, the price of leisure increases and the individual takes less leisure (i.e., works more). Thus, the substitution effect of the wage increase always operates to make the individual's supply curve of labor *positively* sloped. However, an increase in the wage rate also raises the individual's income, and with a rise in income, the individual demands more of every normal good, including leisure (i.e., supplies fewer hours of work). Thus, the income effect of a wage increase, by itself, always operates to make the individual's supply curve *negatively* sloped.

The substitution and income effects operate over the entire length of the individual's supply curve of labor. Until the wage rate of $w = \$5$ in Figure 14.3, the substitution effect overwhelms the opposite income effect and the individual works more (i.e., his or her supply curve of labor is positively sloped). At $w = \$5$, the substitution effect is balanced by the income effect and S_L is vertical (point E' in the figure). At wage rates higher than $w = \$5$, the (positive) substitution effect is overwhelmed by the (negative) income effect and s_L bends backward. Note that theory does not tell us at what wage rate the bend occurs. It only says that at some sufficiently high wage rate this is likely to occur. Since individuals' tastes differ, the wage rate at which an individual's supply curve of labor bends backward is likely to differ from individual to individual.

Also note that although the substitution effect is usually greater than the income effect for a *commodity,* this is not the case for labor. The reason is that a consumer spends his or her income on many commodities, so that an increase in the price of any one commodity is not going to greatly reduce his or her real income (i.e., the income effect is small in relation to the substitution effect). On the other hand, since most individuals' incomes come primarily from wages, an increase in wages will greatly affect the individuals' incomes (so that the income effect may overwhelm the opposite substitution effect). At the wage rate at which this occurs, s_L will bend backward. The separation of the substitution and the income effects of a wage increase is shown graphically in Section 14.8.

It might be argued that individuals do not have a choice of the number of hours they work per day, and so the above analysis is irrelevant. Yet, this is not entirely true. For example, an individual may choose to work any number of hours on a part-time basis, may choose an occupation that requires six or seven hours of work per day instead of eight, may choose an occupation that allows more or less vacation time, and may or may not agree to work overtime (see Section 14.8), and so on. All that is required for the analysis to be relevant is for *some* occupations to require different hours of work per day and/or some flexibility in hours of work.

Note that as workers' wages and incomes have risen over time, the average work week (and the length of the average work day) has declined from ten hours per day for six days per week at the turn of the century to eight hours per day for five days per week, or even slightly less, today. However, the trend toward fewer hours of work per day and per week seems to have come to an end or to have considerably slowed down over the past half a century. Thus, the substitution and income effects of higher wages must have been more or less in balance in recent decades. Over the same period of time, however, the participation rate (i.e., the percentage of the population in the labor force) has increased, especially for married women (see Example 14–3).

EXAMPLE 14–3
Labor Force Participation Rates

Table 14.3 gives the labor force participation rates for the population as a whole, for males and females, and for married females in the United States in 1960, 1970, 1980, 1990, and 2000. The table shows that from 1960 to 2000 the labor force participation rate increased by about 13% for the population as a whole, it declined by about 10% for males, and it increased by about 60% for all females and 92% for married females.

Many reasons are responsible for the dramatic increase in labor force participation rate of married females in the United States over the 1960–2000 period. Some of these

TABLE 14.3	Labor Force Participation Rates in the United States (in percentages)			
Year	Total Population	Males	Females	Married Females
1960	59.4	83.3	37.7	31.9
1970	60.4	79.7	43.3	40.5
1980	63.8	77.4	51.5	49.9
1990	66.5	76.4	57.5	58.4
2000	67.2	74.7	60.2	61.3

Source: Statistical Abstract of the United States (Washington, D.C.: U.S. Government Printing Office, 2001), pp. 367, 372.

are changes in family income, child-rearing practices, rates of unemployment, and female educational levels. What must be true, however, is that the productivity of married women in "market" jobs must have increased much more than for work in the home during the past four decades, and so married females substituted a great deal of work outside the home for work in the home.

The Market Supply Curve for an Input

The market supply curve for an input is obtained from the straightforward horizontal summation of the supply curve of individual suppliers of the input, just as in the case of the supply curve of a final commodity (see Section 9.4). In the case of inputs of natural resources and intermediate goods, which are supplied by firms, the short-run market supply curve of the input is generally positively sloped (as is the firm's supply curve). The market supply curve of labor is usually also positively sloped, but it may bend backward at very high wages (see Example 14–4).

Figure 14.4 shows a hypothetical market supply curve of labor (S_L) measuring the *number* of workers on the horizontal axis and the *daily* wage rate on the vertical axis. The figure shows that at the wage of $20 per day, 400 people are willing to work in this market (point H). At $w = \$40$ per day, 600 people are willing to work (point E'). At $w = \$60$, 700 are willing to work (point G), and so on. Note that S_L is positively sloped over the range of daily wages shown in the figure but becomes less elastic at high wage rates (and may eventually bend backward at still higher wage rates).

The shape of S_L is also the net result of two opposing forces. Higher daily wages will, on one hand, induce some individuals to enter the labor market (to take advantage of the higher wages), but they will also result in some individuals leaving the job market as their spouse's wages and income rise (see Example 14–4). Note that the supply curve of labor is less likely to be backward-bending for a particular industry than for the economy as a whole, because workers can always be attracted to an industry from other industries by raising wages sufficiently.

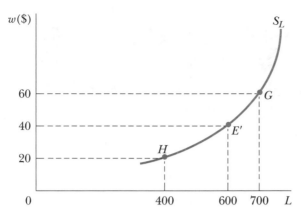

FIGURE 14.4   Market Supply Curve of Labor   Market supply curve of labor S_L shows that at the wage of $20 per day, 400 people are willing to work in this market (point H). At $w = 40 per day, 600 people are willing to work (point E'). At $w = 60, 700 are willing to work (point G), and so on. S_L is positively sloped over the range of daily wages shown but becomes less elastic at high wage rates (and may eventually bend backward at still higher wage rates).

EXAMPLE 14–4

Backward-Bending Supply Curve of Physicians' Services and Other Labor

The enactment of Medicare (a subsidy for the medical care of the elderly) and Medicaid (a subsidy for the medical care of the poor) in 1965, as well as the increased insurance coverage for physicians' bills, greatly increased the ability of broad segments of the population to pay for medical services and resulted in a sharp rise in medical fees. The rise in medical fees, however, seems to have led to a reduction, rather than to an increase, in the quantity supplied of physicians' services (i.e., the supply curve for physicians' services seems to be backward-bending).

Martin Feldstein found that the price elasticity of supply of physicians' services in the United States was between −0.67 and −0.91 over the 1948–1966 period. This means that a 10% increase in the price of physicians' services results in a *reduction* in the quantity supplied of services of between 6.7% and 9.1%. Thus, according to Feldstein's results, the sharp increase in the fees for physicians' services in recent years actually resulted in a reduction in the quantity of services supplied. Nurses also seem to have backward-bending supply curves and, more generally, so do the head of one-earner families with children and the head and the spouse of two-earner families, with or without children, as Table 14.4 shows.

From Table 14.4, we see that unmarried males and females with or without children, as well as one-earner families without children, operate on the upward-sloping portion of their labor supply curve, while all the others are on the backward bending

TABLE 14.4	Elasticities of Labor Supply (Hours Worked) with Respect to Wages		
	Head's Hours with Respect to Head's Wage	Spouse's Hours with Respect to Spouse's Wage	Head's Hours with Respect to Spouse's Wage
Unmarried males (no children)	0.026		
Unmarried females (no children)	0.011		
Unmarried females (with children)	0.106		
One-earner family (no children)	0.007		
One-earner family (with children)	−0.078		
Two-earner family (no children)	−0.107	−0.028	−0.059
Two-earner family (with children)	−0.002	−0.086	−0.004

Sources: M. Feldstein, "The Rising Price of Physicians' Services," *The Review of Economics and Statistics,* May 1970; D. Sullivan, "Monopsony Power in the Market for Nurses," *Journal of Law and Economics,* October 1989; and J. H. Kohlhase, "Labor Supply and Housing Demand for One- and Two-Earner Households," *Review of Economics and Statistics* 68, 1986.

portion of their labor supply curve. The price elasticities of supply of hours worked with respect to wages for all groups, whether positive or negative, are quite small, however (i.e., the labor supply curves are close to being vertical).

14.5   PRICING AND EMPLOYMENT OF AN INPUT

Just as in the case of a final commodity, the equilibrium price and employment of an input is given at the intersection of the market demand and the market supply curve of the input in a perfectly competitive market. The equilibrium price and level of employment for labor are shown in Figure 14.5.

In Figure 14.5, D_L is the market demand curve for labor (from the right panel of Figure 14.2), and S_L is the market supply curve of labor (from Figure 14.4). The intersection of D_L and S_L at point E' gives the equilibrium (daily) wage of $40 and level of employment of 600 workers per day. At the lower wage rate of $20 per day, firms would like to employ 800 workers per day, but only half that number are willing to work. Thus, there is a shortage of 400 workers per day (*HJ* in the figure), and the wage rate rises. At the high wage of $60 per day, 700 workers are willing to work, but firms would like to employ only 450. There is a surplus of 250 workers (*FG*), and the wage rate falls. Only at $w = 40 is the

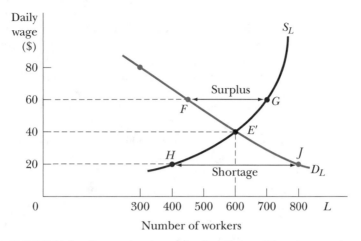

FIGURE 14.5   Determination of the Equilibrium Wage Rate and Level of Employment D_L is the market demand curve for labor (from the right panel of Figure 14.2), and S_L is the market supply curve of labor (from Figure 14.4). The intersection of D_L and S_L at point E' gives the equilibrium (daily) wage rate of $40 and the equilibrium level of employment of 600 workers per day.

number of workers who are willing to work equal to the number of workers that firms want to employ (600), and the market is in equilibrium.

Note that at the equilibrium daily wage of $40, each of the 100 identical firms in the market will employ six workers per day (point E on d_L' in the left panel of Figure 14.2). In a perfectly competitive input market, each firm is too small to perceptibly affect the wage rate (i.e., the firm can employ any number of workers per day at the equilibrium market wage rate of $40 per day). That is, the firm faces a horizontal or infinitely elastic supply curve of labor at the given wage rate. Since the price of an input equals its marginal revenue product (*MRP*), the theory of input pricing and employment has been called the **marginal productivity theory** (see Example 14–5).

Finally, note that we have implicitly assumed that all units of the input are identical (have the same productivity) and receive the same price. In the case of labor, the wages of all workers would be the same only if all occupations were equally attractive (or unattractive), if all workers had identical qualifications and productivity, and if there was no interference with the operation of the market. These topics are discussed in Section 14.8.

EXAMPLE 14–5

Labor Productivity and Total Compensation in the United States and Abroad

According to the marginal productivity theory, wages equal labor's marginal revenue product, and an increase in labor productivity should be reflected in an equal wage increase. From 1996 to 2000, however, real wages have increased by a total of 6.4% as compared with an increase in the productivity of U.S. labor of 9.2%. This is prompted a strong debate on whether the long-term link between productivity and wages has been broken. In fact, during the past 150 years, the share of GDP going to labor has remained remarkably stable at between 65% and 69% in all advanced economies. Has this strong regularity now been broken?

According to some economists, the present gap in the growth of real wages and productivity is the beginning of a long-run decline in labor's share of GDP. Others, however, believe that comparing real wages to labor productivity is not appropriate because the proportion of fringe benefits in total compensation has increased over time. In fact, the increase in total real compensation has been 9.0% over the 1996–2000 period—almost identical to the increase in total labor productivity of 9.2%. Using 1950 as the base, the increase in the real compensation of U.S. labor from 1950 to 2000 was 151.2% as compared with the increase in U.S. labor productivity of 154.1% over the same period. Thus, the historical regularity between wages and productivity has not been broken and persists. Furthermore, every time a gap arose between the growth in inflation-adjusted compensation and the growth of labor productivity in the United States, it invariably disappeared after a year or two.

The increase in labor productivity in the United States has been greater than in the other Group of Seven (G-7) leading industrial nations (Japan, Germany, France, Britain, Italy and Canada) during the second half of the 1990s, but not earlier. Specifically, labor productivity has increased at an annual average of 2.3% in the United States from 1996 to 2000, as compared to 1.4% for the other G-7 nations. From 1981 to 1995, however, labor productivity increased at an average 1.2% per year in the United States and 2.2% in the other G-7 nations. This has led to a great deal of wage convergence to the higher U.S. levels in the G-7 countries (see Example 14–6). The more rapid growth of labor productivity during the second half of the last decade in the United States than in the other G-7 countries has been attributed to more rapid spread of the "new economy" based on the new information technology and greater flexibility in labor markets and in the economy in general in the United States than abroad.

Sources: "Productivity Is All, But It Doesn't Pay Well," *New York Times,* June 25, 1995, Section E, p. 3; "As Worker's Pay Lags, Causes Spur a Debate," *Wall Street Journal,* July 31,1995, p. A1; and "Productivity Developments Abroad," *Federal Reserve Bulletin,* October 2000.

14.6 INPUT PRICE EQUALIZATION AMONG INDUSTRIES, REGIONS, AND COUNTRIES

In this section, we examine the process whereby input prices tend to be equalized through the movement of inputs among industries and regions, but through trade among countries. We deal specifically with the tendency of wage rates to equalize across industries, regions, and countries on the assumption that all labor is identical. The same price-equalizing process generally tends to operate for each type of labor and capital.

Input Price Equalization Among Industries and Regions of a Country

If the wage rate differs between two industries or regions of a country, some labor will leave the low-wage industry or region for the high-wage industry or region until the wage difference is eliminated. This is shown in Figure 14.6.

In Figure 14.6, the left panel refers to industry or region A, while the right panel refers to industry or region B. The vertical axes measure the daily wage, while the horizontal axes measure the number of workers. In the left panel, the intersection of the industry demand curve (D_A) and supply curve (S_A) at point E gives the equilibrium daily wage of $30 in industry or region A. On the other hand, the right panel shows that the equilibrium daily wage (given by point E at the intersection of D_B and S_B) in industry or region B is $50. Some workers will then leave industry or region A to take advantage of the higher wages in industry or region B. As this occurs, the supply of labor declines (i.e., the supply curve shifts to the left) in industry or region A and simultaneously increases (i.e., shifts to the right) in industry or region B. This continues until S_A has shifted to S'_A in the left panel and S_B has shifted to S'_B in the right panel, so that the wage rate is equal at $40 per day in both industries (see point E' where D_A and S'_A intersect in the left panel and where D_B and S'_B intersect in the right panel). In total, 1 million workers move from industry or region A to

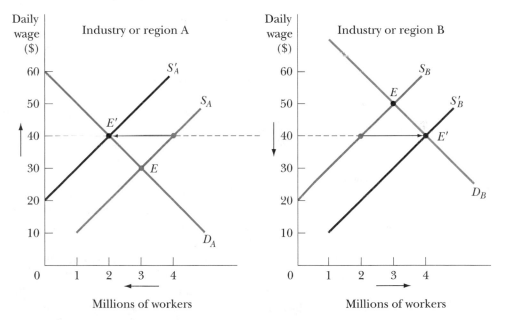

FIGURE 14.6   Wage-Equalizing Shifts in Domestic Supply   The left panel shows that D_A and S_A intersect at point E defining the equilibrium daily wage of $30 in industry or region A, while the right panel shows that D_B and S_B intersect at point E defining the equilibrium daily wage of $50 in industry or region B. As labor leaves industry or region A, attracted by the higher wage in region B, S_A shifts to the left to S'_A in the left panel while S_B shifts simultaneously to the right to S'_B in the right panel, so that the daily wage in the two industries or regions becomes equal at $40 (point E' in both panels).

industry or region B (see the direction and the length of the arrows on the quantity axes in both panels).

If there are obstructions to the movement of labor, or if workers—other things being equal—prefer working in industry or region A rather than in B, then less than 1 million workers will move from industry or region A to industry or region B, and wage differences will only be reduced rather than be entirely eliminated. What is important, however, is the process whereby changes or shifts in input supply in the two industries or regions reduce interindustry or interregional wage differences. The same is true for each particular type of labor and other mobile inputs. They always tend to flow or move to find employment in the industries or regions where returns or earnings are higher. In the process, they reduce interindustry and interregional differences in the returns to homogeneous factors or inputs (i.e., the earnings of inputs of the same quality and productivity). In fact, Bellante has found that when adjustment is made for regional differences in costs of living, North-South real wage differences for the same type of labor have been eliminated for the most part in the United States.[5]

Input Price Equalization Among Countries

The equalizing tendency in the returns or earnings of homogeneous inputs also operates internationally, but it occurs mostly through international trade rather than through the flow or migration of inputs from low- to high-return countries. The reason is that most countries impose serious restrictions on the international flow of some inputs, especially the migration of labor. Figure 14.7 shows how wage equalization occurs internationally through trade. For simplicity, we assume that we have only two homogeneous inputs, labor and capital.

The left panel shows that D_1 (the demand curve for labor in country 1) intersects S_1 (the supply curve of labor in country 1) at point E, giving the equilibrium daily wage of $20 in country 1 in the absence of trade. The right panel shows that D_2 and S_2 intersect at point E, giving the equilibrium daily wage of $40 in country 2 in the absence of trade. We assume that labor cannot migrate from country 1 to country 2. Wages can still tend to be equalized between the two countries through trade, however.

Because of lower wages, country 1 has a relative or comparative advantage in labor-intensive commodities (i.e., commodities that require a relative abundance of labor in production). Country 2 will then have a comparative advantage in capital-intensive commodities. With trade, country 1 will specialize in the production of and export labor-intensive commodities in exchange for capital-intensive commodities from country 2. The left panel shows that the demand curve for labor will then increase or shift to the right from D_1 to D_1' in country 1 and defines the new equilibrium daily wage of $30 at point E' (where D_1' intersects S_1). On the other hand, the right panel shows that the demand curve for labor will decrease or shift to the left from D_2 to D_2' in country 2 (as country 2 replaces some domestic production of labor-intensive commodities with imports from country 1) and defines the new equilibrium daily wage of $30 at point E' (where D_2' intersects S_2).

---

[5] See D. Bellante, "The North-South Wage Differential and the Migration of Heterogeneous Labor," *American Economic Review*, March 1979.

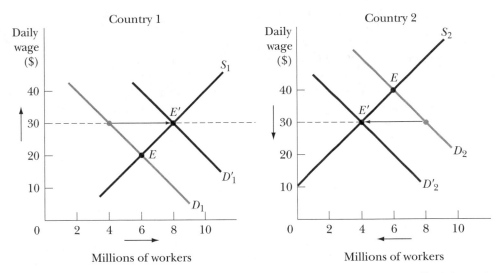

FIGURE 14.7   International Wage-Equalization Through International Trade   The left panel shows that in the absence of trade D_1 and S_1 intersect at point E, defining the equilibrium daily wage of $30 in country 1, while the right panel shows that D_2 and S_2 intersect at point E, defining the equilibrium daily wage of $40 in country 2. As country 1 specializes in the production of and exports labor-intensive commodities, D_1 shifts to the right to D'_1 and defines the new equilibrium daily wage of $30 at point E' in the left panel. On the other hand, as country 2 replaces some domestic production of labor-intensive commodities with imports from country 1, D_2 shifts to the left to D'_2 and defines the new equilibrium daily wage of $30 at point E' in the right panel.

Note that now wages have been equalized in the two countries through international trade without any migration of labor from country 1 to country 2. The reason for this is that as long as wages are lower in country 1, labor-intensive commodities will be cheaper in country 1 than in country 2, and country 1 will expand its exports of the labor-intensive commodity. But as trade expands, country 1 will demand more labor until D_1 has shifted all the way to the right to D'_1 (see the left panel). The demand for labor in country 2, on the other hand, will simultaneously decline until it reaches D'_2 (see the right panel), so that wages are equalized at $30 in both countries. Thus, international trade is a substitute for, or has the same effect on, wages as the international migration of labor (which is often seriously restricted). However, while trade operates on the demand for labor (i.e., shifts the demand curves for labor) in the two countries, international migration operates through the supply (i.e., shifts the supply curves) of labor in the two countries. This is true, how-ever, only in the absence of trade restrictions. If some labor is allowed to migrate from country 1 to country 2, this will reinforce the tendency of international trade to equalize wages in the two countries. Although we have dealt with labor in general, the same process would operate to equalize the wages of each particular type of labor and the price of each other type of input internationally. Example 14–6 shows that a great deal of conver-gence in real hourly compensation has in fact occurred during the past decades among the G-7 countries.

EXAMPLE 14-6

Convergence in Hourly Compensation in the Leading Industrial Countries

As predicted by theory, Table 14.5 shows that real hourly compensation (wages plus benefits) of production workers in manufacturing have indeed converged among the leading (G-7) industrial countries during the past four decades. It is true that many other forces (including international labor migration and capital flows) have contributed to this convergence, but international trade was certainly a major reason. The existence of transportation costs, trade restrictions, and other market imperfections prevented the complete equalization of hourly compensation internationally, however.

TABLE 14.5	Real Hourly Compensation of Production Workers in Manufacturing in the G-7 Countries as a Percentage of U.S. Compensation		
Country	1959	1983	2000
Japan	11	51	99
Italy	23	62	88
France	27	62	93
United Kingdom	29	53	94
Germany	29	84	149
Canada	42	75	91
Unweighted Average	27	65	102
United States	100	100	100

Sources: Calculated from indices from: IMF, *International Financial Statistics;* OECD, *Economic Outlook;* and U.S. Bureau of Labor Statistics, *Bulletin.*

One question remains unanswered. That is, if trade reduces wages in a higher-wage country, why should the higher-wage country trade with a lower-wage country? The reason (not shown in Figure 14.7) is that the higher-wage country will have a comparative advantage in capital-intensive commodities. As it specializes in the production of these commodities for export, the demand and returns on capital increase by more than wages fall. Some of the capital owners' gains from trade could then be taxed away and redistributed to labor in such a way that both labor and capital gain from trade.

14.7   ECONOMIC RENT: AN UNNECESSARY PAYMENT TO BRING FORTH THE SUPPLY OF AN INPUT

Economic rent differs from the everyday meaning of the term "rent," which is a payment made to lease an apartment, an automobile, or any other durable asset. Economic rent originally referred only to the payment made to landowners to lease their land (which was assumed to be in fixed supply). Today, **economic rent** is defined as that portion of the payment to the supplier of any input (not just land) that is in excess of the minimum amount necessary to retain the input in its present use. It is the excess payment to an input over its opportunity cost. If the market supply of an input is fixed, demand alone determines the input price and all of the payment made to the input is rent. If the market supply of an input is positively sloped, only the area above the supply curve and below the price of the input represents rent. This is shown in Figure 14.8.

In the left panel of Figure 14.8, the market supply of the input, say, land, is fixed at 600 acres (i.e., S is vertical). If the market demand curve is D, the (rental) price is $40 per acre (point E), and the entire payment of $24,000 ($40 times 600) per month made to the owners of land is economic rent. If the market demand were D', the rental price would be $60 (point E'), and rent $36,000 per month. If the market demand for the input were D'', the rental price would be $20 (point E''), and rent $12,000 per month. Note that regardless of the level of demand and price, the same quantity of land is supplied per month, even at an infinitesimally small rental price. Thus, all of the payments made to the landowners represent economic rent (since the opportunity cost of land is zero). This is true not only for land but for any input in fixed supply. For example, since the supply of Picasso paintings is fixed, they will be supplied (sold) at whatever price (including the retention or reservation price of present owners) they can fetch. Therefore, all payments made to purchase Picassos represent economic rent.

In the right panel, the supply of the input, say, labor, to an industry is positively sloped. This means that higher daily wages will induce more individuals to work in the industry. The equilibrium wage of $40 is determined at the intersection of D_L and S_L (point E in the figure, at which 600 workers are employed). Each of the 600 (identical) workers receives a wage of $40 per day. Yet, one worker could be found who would work for a wage of only

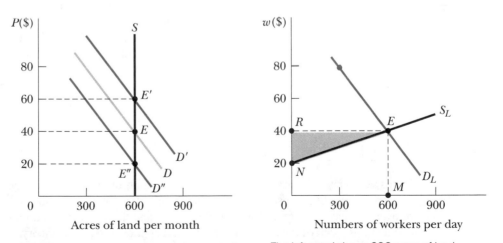

FIGURE 14.8   Measurement of Economic Rent   The left panel shows 600 acres of land supplied per month regardless of the rental price. With D, the price is $40 (point E) and the entire payment of $24,000 ($40 times 600) is rent. With D', $P = $60 (point E') and rent is $36,000. With D'', $P = $20 and rent is $12,000. In the right panel, S_L is positively sloped. With D_L, $w = $40 and 600 workers are employed (point E). Shaded area $ENR = $6,000 represents economic rent or a payment that is not needed to retain the 600 workers in the particular industry.

$20, and 300 workers would be willing to work at a daily wage of $30 each (see the S_L curve in the right panel). Thus, the shaded area above the supply curve and below the equilibrium wage of $40 represents economic rent. It is the workers' excess earnings over their next-best employment. That is, the 600 workers receive a total wage of $24,000 (the area of rectangle *EMOR*), but they only need to be paid *EMON* to be retained in the industry. Therefore, the area of shaded triangle *ENR* ($6,000) represents economic rent or the payment that need not be made by the particular industry to retain 600 workers in the long run.

Note that even land may not be fixed in supply to any industry, because some land could be bid away from other uses. Land may not even be fixed for the economy as a whole, since over time, land can be augmented through reclamation and drainage and depleted through erosion and loss of fertility. Thus, the payment to lease land, too, may be only partly rent. In general, the more inelastic is the supply curve of an input to the industry, the greater is the proportion of economic rent. In the extreme case, the supply curve is vertical and all the payment to the input is rent. The importance of this is that rent could all be taxed away without reducing the quantity supplied of the input. This is an excellent tax since it does not discourage work or reduce the supply of labor (or other inputs) even in the long run. Note that economic rent is analogous to the concept of *producer surplus* (see Section 9.8). Producer surplus was defined as the excess of the commodity price over the *marginal cost of producing a given level of the commodity*. Economic rent is the excess payment that an *input owner* receives over the minimum that he or she requires to continue to keep the input in its present use.

While all or some of the payment made by an industry to the suppliers of an input is rent, all payments made by an *individual firm* to employ an input are a *cost* to the firm, which the firm must pay to retain the use of the input. If the firm tried to pay less than the market price for the input, the firm would be unable to retain any unit of the input. For example, if a firm tried to employ workers at less than the $40 daily wage prevailing in the market, the firm would lose all of its workers to other firms. Finally, note that any payment made to *temporarily* fixed inputs is sometimes called **quasi rent.** Thus, the returns to fixed inputs in the short run are quasi rents (see Problem 8). These payments need not be made in order for these fixed inputs to be supplied in the short run. In the long run, however, all inputs are variable, and unless they receive a price equal to their next-best alternative, they will not be supplied. To the extent that they receive more than this, the inputs receive economic rent. In long-run, perfectly competitive equilibrium, all inputs receive payments equal to their marginal revenue product and the firm breaks even.

14.8 | ANALYSIS OF LABOR MARKETS UNDER PERFECT COMPETITION

In this section, we discuss some important applications of the theory presented in this chapter: separation of the substitution from the income effect of a change in wages, the analysis of overtime pay, the cause of wage differentials, and the effect of minimum wages. These applications clearly indicate the usefulness and applicability of the theory.

Substitution and Income Effects of a Wage Rate Change

We have seen in Section 14.4 that an increase in wages gives rise to a substitution effect and an income effect. That is, when the wage rate rises, on one hand, the individual tends to substitute work for leisure (since the price of leisure has increased). On the other hand, the increase in income resulting from the wage increase leads the individual to demand more of every normal good, including leisure (i.e., to work fewer hours). We can separate the substitution effect from the income effect as in Section 4.3. The separation is shown in Figure 14.9.

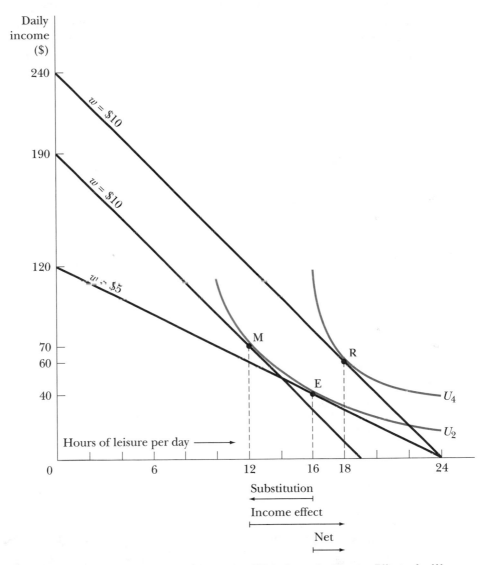

FIGURE 14.9   Separation of the Substitution Effect from the Income Effect of a Wage Increase   The movement from point E to point R is the combined substitution and income effects of the wage increase from $5 to $10 (as in Figure 14.3). We can isolate the substitution effect by shifting the highest budget line down parallel to itself until it is tangent to indifference curve U_2 at point M. The movement along U_2 from point E to point M measures the substitution effect of the wage increase. The shift from point M on U_2 to point R on U_4 is the income effect.

The movement from point E to point R in Figure 14.9 is the combined substitution and income effects of the wage increase from \$5 to \$10 (as in Figure 14.3). The substitution effect can be isolated by drawing the hypothetical budget line that is tangent to U_2 at point M with the slope reflecting the higher wage of \$10. Since the consumer is on original indifference curve U_2, his or her income is the same as before the wage increase, and the movement along U_2 from point E to point M measures the substitution effect. By itself, the substitution effect shows that when w rises from \$5 to \$10, the individual reduces leisure time from 16 to 12 hours (i.e., increases hours of work from 8 to 12 per day). The shift from point M on U_2 to point R on U_4 is the income effect of the wage increase. In this case, the increase in wages raises the individual's income by \$50 (\$240 − \$190; see the vertical axis of the figure). By itself, the income effect leads the individual to increase leisure from 12 to 18 hours (i.e., to work 6 hours less). The net result is that the individual increases leisure (works less) by 2 hours per day (ER).

Overtime Pay and the Supply of Labor Services

The hourly wage of many workers increases after a specific number of hours worked per day. This is called **overtime pay.** Figure 14.10 shows the additional number of hours worked per day by an individual as a result of overtime pay.

Initially, at the wage rate of \$5 per hour, the individual demands 16 hours of leisure (works eight hours per day) and earns an income of \$40 (point E on U_2, as in Figures 14.3 and 14.9). With an overtime pay of \$20 per hour (the slope of ET in Figure 14.10), the

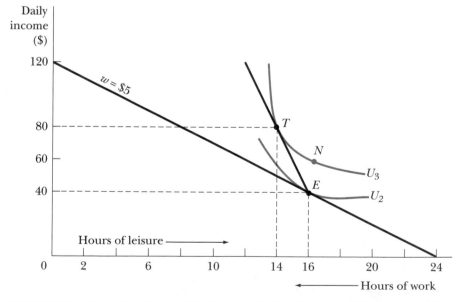

**FIGURE 14.10   Overtime Pay and the Supply of Labor Services   Initially, at $w = $5,$ the individual demands 16 hours of leisure (works 8 hours per day) and earns \$40 (point E on U_2, as in Figures 14.3 and 14.9). With overtime pay of $w = 20 per hour (the slope of ET), the individual will work 2 additional hours per day and have a total income of \$80 (point T on U_3).

individual can be induced to work two additional hours per day and have a total income of $80 per day (point T on higher indifference curve U_3). Thus, the substitution effect (which encourages work) exceeds the income effect (which discourages work), and the individual works more hours with overtime pay.[6]

Wage Differentials

Up to this point, we have generally assumed that all occupations are equally attractive and that all units of an input, say, labor, are homogeneous (i.e., have the same training and productivity), so that the wages of all workers are the same. If all jobs and workers were identical, wage differences could not persist among occupations or regions of a country under perfect competition. As pointed out in Section 14.6, workers would leave lower-wage occupations and regions for higher-wage occupations and regions until all wage differentials disappeared.

In the real world, jobs differ in attractiveness, workers have different qualifications and training, and markets may not be perfectly competitive. All of these factors can result in different wages for different occupations and for workers with different training and abilities. More formally, wages differ among different jobs and categories of workers because of (1) compensating differentials, (2) the existence of noncompeting groups, and (3) imperfect competition. We will now briefly examine each of these factors.

Compensating wage differentials are wage differences that compensate workers for the nonmonetary differences among jobs. Even though some jobs (such as garbage collection and being a porter in a hotel) may require equal qualifications, one job (garbage collection) may be more unpleasant than another (being a porter). Hence, the more unpleasant job must pay a higher wage to attract and retain workers. These wage differentials equalize or compensate for the nonmonetary differences among jobs and will persist in time. In the real world, many wage differences reflect nonmonetary factors.

For example, police officers' salaries are usually higher than fire fighters' salaries because of the alleged greater risk in being a police officer. Similarly, construction work generally pays more than garbage collection because the former offers less job security. Note that a particular individual may prefer being a police officer or a construction worker even if the salary were the same as (or lower than) that of a fire fighter or garbage collector, respectively. But it is the intersection of the *market* demand and supply curves of labor for each occupation that determines the equilibrium wage in the occupation and the compensating wage differentials among occupations that require the same general level of qualifications and training.

Noncompeting groups are occupations requiring different capacities, skills, education, and training, and, therefore, receive different wages. That is, labor in some occupations does not directly compete with labor in some other occupations. For example, physicians form one noncompeting group not in direct competition with lawyers (which form another noncompeting group). Other noncompeting groups are engineers, accountants, musicians, electricians, and so on. Engineers and electricians belong to different noncompeting groups because, although engineers could probably work easily as electricians, engineers' productivity and

---

[6] The entire overtime-pay system that was established during the Great Depression and which requires employers to pay a 50% premium to people working over 40 hours per week is now under attack, however, and may be relaxed or even abolished. See "Overtime-Pay System May Spark a Battle," *Wall Street Journal,* March 13, 1995.

wages are so much higher when working as engineers that they form a separate noncompeting group. On the other hand, electricians do not have the training and may not have the ability to be engineers.

Each noncompeting group has a particular wage structure as determined by the intersection of its demand and supply curves. Some mobility among noncompeting groups is possible (as, for example, when an electrician becomes an engineer by attending college at night), and this possibility is greater in the long run than in the short run. However, mobility among noncompeting groups is limited, even in the long run, especially if based on innate ability (e.g., not everyone can be a brain surgeon or an accomplished violinist).

An imperfect labor market can also result in wage differences for identical jobs requiring the same ability and level of training. A labor market is imperfect if workers lack information on wages and job opportunities in other occupations, if they are unwilling to move to other jobs and occupations, or if there are labor unions and large employers able to affect wages. These topics will be explored in detail in the next chapter.

Effect of Minimum Wages

In 1938, Congress passed the Fair Labor Standard Act, which established a minimum wage of $0.25 per hour. Since then, the minimum wage has been raised many times. The minimum wage was $3.35 in 1981 and $4.25 in 1991, and it has been $5.15 since 1997. In real terms (i.e., after taking into considerations the increase in the cost of living), the minimum wage in 2002 was where it stood in 1958. Coverage of the minimum wage was extended over the years, so that today 85% of all workers in the United States are covered. Since skilled workers generally have wages well above the minimum wage, they are not affected by it. Thus, most of the effect of minimum wages is on unskilled workers. We can analyze the effect of the minimum wage on unskilled workers (assuming for the moment that all unskilled workers are identical) with the aid of Figure 14.11.

In Figure 14.11, D_L is the market demand curve, and S_L is the market supply curve for unskilled workers. In a perfectly competitive labor market, the equilibrium wage would be $4.00 per hour ($24 per day with an 8-hour workday) and the equilibrium level of employment would be 4 million workers (point E in the figure). The imposition of a federal minimum wage of $5.15 per hour would result in firms hiring only 3.9 million workers (point M on D_L) as opposed to the 4.1 million workers (point N on S_L) willing to work at this minimum wage. Thus, the minimum wage of $5.15 per hour would lead to a total **unemployment gap** of 200,000 workers (MN) from the equilibrium rate of $4.00 per hour. This is composed of the 100,000 additional workers who would like to work at the minimum wage (the movement from point E to point N on the S_L curve) plus the **disemployment effect** of another 100,000 workers as firms employ fewer workers at the above-equilibrium minimum wage (the movement from point E to point M on the D_L curve). On the other hand, the increase in the minimum wage from $4.25 to $5.15 per hour increases the unemployment gap by 100,000 jobs (MN minus FG in Figure 14.11). While an increase of a minimum wage benefits those unskilled workers who remain employed, some unskilled workers would lose their jobs, and still more would like to work but could not find employment.

In 1998, 4.4 million workers of the 71.4 million Americans paid by the hour worked at or below the minimum wage (not all workers are covered by the legislation). Of these, 30% were teenagers and 62% were women. The U.S. Labor Department estimated that the

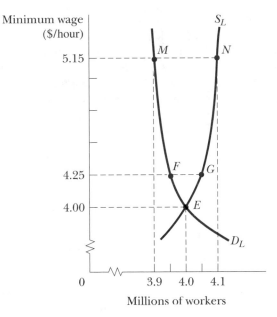

FIGURE 14.11   Effect of Minimum Wages D_L is the market demand curve, and S_L is the market supply curve for unskilled workers. The equilibrium wage is $4.00 per hour at which 4 million workers are employed (point E). A minimum wage of $5.15 results in 3.9 million workers being employed as opposed to 4.1 million willing to work, leaving an unemployment gap of 200,000 workers (MN). The disemployment effect is 100,000 workers (the movement from point E to point M on D_L). The increase in the minimum wage from $4.25 in 1991 to $5.15 in 1997 was estimated to increase the unemployment gap by 100,000 (MN minus FG).

increase in the minimum wage from $3.35 in 1981 to $4.25 in 1991 led to a loss of 100,000 jobs, mostly teenagers and women in two- or three-earner families, rather than bread-winners from poor families. Some researchers, however, question this estimate (see the "At the Frontier," which follows). Be that as it may, a moderate increase in the minimum wage can be expected to have only a modest and temporary effect on minimum-wage employment and poverty. A growing number of economists believe that higher minimum wages would force firms to purchase new equipment, improve productivity, and eventually create more jobs requiring higher skills and providing higher wages over time.[7]

---

[7] See C. Brown, "Minimum Wage Laws: Are They Overrated?," *Journal of Economic Perspectives,* summer 1988; "Forging New Insights on Minimum Wages and Jobs," *New York Times,* June 29, 1992, p. D1; "Higher Minimum Wage: Minimal Damage, *Business Week,* March 22, 1993, p. 92; and "As Officials Lost Faith in the Minimum Wage, Pat Williams Lives it," *Wall Street Journal,* July 19, 2001, p. 1.

There are other ways by which the imposition or the raising of a minimum wage rate can harm the very people it is supposed to help. An increase in the minimum wage may lead some employers to reduce or cut other fringe benefits (such as some health benefits, free or subsidized meals, free uniforms, and so on). Some employers may suspend apprenticeships and on-the-job training for unskilled workers whom they were hiring at a lower minimum wage. The harmful effect of an increase in the minimum wage is even greater in the long run, when employers have a greater opportunity to substitute more capital-intensive production techniques for unskilled labor. The problem can be addressed by providing more training to improve the skills of minimum-wage workers so that they can qualify for higher-paying jobs.

AT THE FRONTIER
Do Minimum Wages Really Reduce Employment?

As the above analysis shows, economists have traditionally believed that an increase in the minimum wage, by increasing the cost of unskilled labor, leads employers to hire fewer unskilled workers. This ingrained belief was temporarily shaken by new research by Princeton University's Professors David Card and Alan Krueger, who found that increasing minimum wages did not destroy jobs and sometimes even increased them.

In one study (see the first reference at the end of this section), Card found that the reduction in employment after the 1990 and 1991 federal minimum-wage increases was generally not bigger in states with a larger fraction of low-paid workers, such as teenagers (the group expected to be most adversely affected by an increases in the minimum wage) than in high-wage states. Thus, Card concluded that the reduction in employment must have been due to causes other than the increase in the minimum wage. In another study (see the second reference at the end), Card and Krueger found that the additional 19% increase in New Jersey's own minimum wage in April 1992 led to more, not fewer, jobs between February and December 1992 in the state's fast-food restaurants (which paid wages below the new minimum wage), as compared with other New Jersey restaurants that were already paying wages exceeding the new higher minimum wage and compared with fast-food restaurants in neighboring Pennsylvania, which did not raise its minimum wage in 1992. In short, the new research seemed to show that increasing the minimum wage did not destroy jobs, as previously believed, and may have created them.

Other economists, however, immediately attacked these revisionist studies as being seriously flawed. Donald Deere and Finis Welch of Texas A&M University and Kevin Murphy of the University of Chicago showed that the 27% increase in the federal minimum wage from $3.35 to $4.25 in 1990 and 1991 resulted in a reduction in teenage employment of 12% for males, 18% for females, and 6% for high-school dropouts (the groups expected to be most adversely affected by an increase in the minimum wage). Similarly, David Neumark of Michigan State University and William Wascher of the Federal Reserve, using payroll records (which are more accurate than the telephone poll data used by Card and Krueger in their New Jersey study), found that the 19% increase in New Jersey's minimum wages in April 1992 reduced employment in New Jersey's fast-food restaurants by 4.6% (rather than increased it, as reported by Card and Krueger). In another study, Neumark and Wascher also found that an increase in minimum wages was more likely to lead teenagers to leave school and to job losses for teenagers who had already left school.

More studies are likely to be undertaken in the future examining the effect of an increase in the minimum wage on employment. As of now, we can tentatively conclude that an increase in minimum wages is likely to reduce employment, but perhaps by not as much as it was previously thought, except when the minimum wage is already very high (as in some European countries, such as France, where the minimum wage is more than double the U.S. level and the unemployment rate is almost double the U.S. rate). We can also tentatively question the effectiveness of raising minimum wages as a way to reduce poverty in America. While apparently flawed, Card's and Krueger's research did, however, rekindle interest and research in this important field.

Sources: D. Card, "Using Regional Variation in Wages to Measure the Effects of the Federal Minimum Wage," *Industrial and Labor Relations Review,* October 1992, D. Card and A. Krueger, "Minimum Wages and Employment: A Case Study of the Fast-Food Industry in New Jersey and Pennsylvania," *American Economic Review,* September 1994; D. Card and A. Krueger, *Myth and Measurement: The New Economics of the Minimum Wage* (Princeton University Press, 1995); D. Deere, K. Murphy, and F. Welch, "Employment and the 1990–1991 Minimum-Wage Hike," *American Economic Review, Papers and Proceedings,* May 1995; D. Neumark and W. Wascher, "The Effect of New Jersey's Minimum Wage Increase on Fast-Food Employment: A Reevaluation Using Payroll Records," *Working Paper 5224,* National Bureau of Economic Research, September 1995; D. Neumark and W. Wascher, "Minimum Wage Effects on School and Work Transitions of Teenagers," *American Economic Review, Papers and Proceedings,* May 1995; J. Abowd, F. Kramarz, T. Lemieux, and D. Margolis, "Minimum Wage Reduces Jobs for Low-Wage Workers," *NBER Working Paper No. 6111,* July 1997; M. Zavodny, "Why Minimum Wage Hike May Not Reduce Unemployment," *Federal Reserve Bank of Atlanta Economic Review,* No. 2, 1998; "Prosperity Is Good for Living-Wage Drive," *Wall Street Journal,* December 20, 1999, p. A1; and "As Officials Lost Faith in the Minimum Wage, Pat Williams Lives it," *Wall Street Journal,* July 19, 2001, p. 1.

SUMMARY

1. To maximize profits a firm must produce the best level of output with the least-cost input combination. The optimal or least-cost input combination is the one at which the marginal product per dollar spent on each input is the same. The ratio of the input price to the marginal product of the input gives the marginal cost of the commodity. The best level of output of the commodity for a perfectly competitive firm is the output at which the firm's marginal cost equals its marginal revenue or price.

2. A profit-maximizing firm will employ an input only as long as the input adds more to its total revenue than to its total cost. If only one input is variable, the firm's demand curve for the input (d) is given by the marginal revenue product (*MRP*) curve of the input. The *MRP* equals the marginal product (*MP*) of the input times the marginal revenue (*MR*). If the firm is a perfect competitor in the product market (so that $MR = P$), then $MRP = VMP$ (the value of the marginal product). With more than one variable input, as the input price falls, the demand curve for the input is obtained by points on different *MRP* curves of the input and will be more elastic than the individual *MRP* curves.

3. When the price of an input falls, all firms will hire more of the input and produce more of the final commodity. This will reduce the commodity price and shift the individual firm's demand curves for the input to the left. This must be considered in summing the individual firm's demand curves for the input to obtain the market demand curve. The price elasticity of demand for an input is greater (1) the more and better are the available substitutes for the input, (2) the more elastic is the demand for the final commodity made with the input, (3) the more elastic is the supply of other inputs, and (4) the longer is the period of time under consideration.

4. The market supply curve of an input is obtained by the straightforward horizontal summation of the supply curves of the individual suppliers of the input. While natural resources and intermediate goods are supplied by firms and their supply curves are generally positively sloped, labor is supplied by individuals and their supply curves may be backward-bending. That is, as the wage rate rises, eventually the substitution effect (which, by itself, leads individuals to substitute work for leisure) may be overwhelmed by the opposite income effect, so that the individual's supply curve of labor may bend backward. The market supply curve of labor is usually positively sloped, but it may bend backward at very high wages.

5. Under perfect competition, the equilibrium price and the level of employment of an input are determined at the intersection of the market demand curve and the market supply curve of the input. Each firm can then employ any quantity of the input at the given market price of the input. Since each firm employs an input until the marginal revenue product equals its price, this theory is usually referred to as the marginal productivity theory. If all inputs were identical (and all occupations equally attractive for labor), all units of the same input would have the same price.

6. With perfect mobility of inputs among industries and regions of a country, input prices will be equalized by input flows (supply shifts) from the low-return to the high-return industries and regions. On the other hand, free trade in commodities and services among countries under perfect competition, with no transportation costs, would equalize input prices internationally by shifts in input demands resulting from trade.

7. Economic rent is that portion of the payment made to the supplier of an input that is in excess of the minimum amount necessary (opportunity cost) to retain the input in its present employment. When the supply of an input is fixed, demand alone determines its price and all the payment made to the input is rent. When the market supply curve of an input is positively sloped, the area above the supply curve and below the input price is rent. The return or payment to inputs that are fixed in the short run are sometimes called quasi rents.

8. By correcting for the income effect of an input-price change, we can graphically isolate the substitution effect as a movement along a consumer leisure-income indifference curve. The same type of analysis can also be used to show the additional number of hours an individual is willing to work per day with overtime pay. Wage differentials can be compensating, and they can be based on the existence of noncompeting groups and imperfect competition. Minimum wages lead to a disemployment effect and to an even greater unemployment gap.

KEY TERMS

Derived demand
Marginal Revenue Product (*MRP*)
Value of the Marginal
    Product (*VMP*)
Marginal Expense (ME)

Complementary inputs
Intermediate good
Marginal productivity theory
Economic rent
Quasi rent

Overtime pay
Compensating wage differentials
Noncompeting groups
Unemployment gap
Disemployment effect

REVIEW QUESTIONS

1. What is the function of input prices in the operation of a free-enterprise system?

2. Why is the marginal revenue product of a firm negatively sloped?

3. What happens to a firm's marginal revenue product of labor curve if the rental price of capital falls and capital is complementary to labor? If capital is a substitute for labor?

4. Why does the market price of a commodity fall with a reduction in the price of an input used in the production of the commodity?

5. What effect will a fall in a commodity price have on the firm's demand curve for an input used in the production of the commodity?

6. How can indifference curve analysis be used to explain an individual's supply curve of labor?

7. Under what condition will an individual's labor supply curve be backward-bending?

8. Interregional trade can be a substitute for interregional labor migration in reducing or eliminating interregional wage differences. True or false? Explain.

9. Mexican migrant or seasonal workers to the United States take away jobs from American workers, and so immigration should be stopped. Evaluate this statement.

10. How is a higher interest on capital in industry or region A than in industry or region B eliminated or reduced?

11. Can higher wages persist for technicians in nuclear plants as compared with technicians with the same qualifications and training working in aircraft-engine plants? Explain.

12. Why do we have minimum-wage laws if they increase unemployment among unskilled workers?

PROBLEMS

*1. a. Express in terms of equation [14.1] the condition for a firm utilizing too much labor or too little capital to minimize production costs. What is the graphic interpretation of this?

   b. What is the graphic interpretation of a firm utilizing the least-cost input combination but with its marginal cost exceeding its *MR*?

   c. Express in terms of equation [14.3] the condition for a firm minimizing the cost of producing an output that is too small to maximize profits. What is the graphic interpretation of this?

2. You are given the following production function of a firm, where *L* is the number of workers hired per day (the only variable input) and Q_X is the quantity

of the commodity produced per day, and the constant commodity price of $P_X = \$5$ is assumed:

L	0	1	2	3	4	5
Q_X	0	10	18	24	28	30

   a. Find the marginal revenue product of labor and plot it.

   b. How many workers per day will the firm hire if the wage rate is $50 per day? $40? $30? $20? $10? What is the firm's demand curve for labor?

3. Assume that (1) labor is infinitesimally divisible (i.e., workers can be hired for any part of the day)

---

* = Answer provided at end of book.

in the production function of the previous problem; (2) both labor and capital are variable and complementary; and (3) when the wage rate falls from $40 per day to $20 per day, the firm's value of the marginal product curve shifts to the right by two labor units. Derive the demand curve for labor of this firm. How many workers will the firm hire per day at the wage rate of $20 per day?

4. Derive the market demand curve for labor if there are 100 firms identical to the firm of Problem 3 demanding labor, and each individual firm's demand curve for labor shifts to the left by one unit when the wage rate falls from $w = 40 to $w = 20 per day.

*5. Assume that (1) U_1, U_2, U_3, and U_4 given in the following table are the indifference curves of an individual, where H refers to hours of leisure per day and Y to the daily income, and (2) the wage rate rises from $1 per hour of work to $2, $3, and then to $4.

U_1		U_2		U_3		U_4	
H	Y	H	Y	H	Y	H	Y
10	20	10	32	12	40	14	48
16	8	14	20	15	27	17	28
24	4	24	12	24	16	24	20

a. Derive the individual's supply curve of labor.

b. Why is the individual's supply curve of labor backward-bending?

6. Given that the market demand curve is the one derived in Problem 3 and that 400 individuals will work at $w = $10, 500 at $w = $20, and 600 at $w = $30, determine the equilibrium wage rate and the level of employment. What would happen if $w = $10? If $w = $30?

7. Given the industry demand function for labor, $D_L = 800 - 15w$, where w is given in dollars per day, draw a figure showing the equilibrium wage and find the amount of economic rent if the supply function of labor to the industry is $S_L = 500$, $S'_L = 25w$ or $S''_L = 50w - 500$.

8. Draw a figure for a perfectly competitive firm in the product and input markets, and label the price at which quasi rent is (1) negative as P_1, (2) zero as P_2, (3) smaller than total fixed costs as P_3, (4) equal to total fixed costs as P_4, and (5) exceeds total fixed costs as P_5. (Hint: See Figure 14.4.)

*9. Separate the substitution effect from the income effect of an increase in wages from $w = $2 to $w = $4 in Problem 5.

10. Starting with your answer to Problem 5 (also provided at the end of the book), draw a figure showing how many additional hours the individual will work and his or her total income (1) starting from $w = $1 and overtime $w = $4 and (2) starting from $w = $2 and overtime $w = $10.

*11. Starting from Figure 14.7, draw a figure showing the total demand and supply for labor in both industries or regions, the equilibrium wage rate, and the level of total employment.

12. Starting with Figure 14.7, draw a figure showing that wages will not be equalized when we take transportation costs into consideration.

INTERNET SITE ADDRESSES

A wealth of information on labor markets (employment, unemployment, productivity, earnings and others) is provided by the Bureau of Labor Statistics at:

http://stats.bls.gov

An excellent analysis of labor markets (including the effect of minimum wages) is found on the Website of the Labor Studies Program of George Washington University at:

http://www.gwu.edu/~labor/respurces.html#MW

For the backward bending supply curve of physicians'

services, see:

http://www.rmsdoctors.com/bulletin/92-1/10.htm

A comparison of hours of work and compensation in the United States, see:

http://www.cnn.com/2001/CAREER/trends/08/30/ilo.study

On economic rent, see:

http://www.economics.utoronto.ca/munro5/ECONRENT.pdf

CHAPTER 15

Input Price and Employment Under Imperfect Competition

I n the previous chapter, we analyzed the pricing and employment of inputs when the firm is a perfect competitor in both the product and input markets. In this chapter, we extend the discussion to the pricing and employment of inputs when the firm is (1) an imperfect competitor in the product market but a perfect competitor in the input market, and (2) an imperfect competitor in both the product and input markets. As in Chapter 14, the analysis deals with all inputs in general but is geared toward labor because of the greater importance of labor.

The presentation in this chapter proceeds along the same general lines as that of the previous chapter. We begin with a summary discussion of profit maximization and optimal input employment under imperfect competition in the product market. Then we derive the demand curve for an input by a firm and by the market as a whole, and we examine how the interaction of the forces of demand and supply determines the price and employment of the input under imperfect competition in the product market but perfect competition in the input market. We then turn to the case of imperfect competition in input markets and examine the pricing and employment of an input when only that input is variable and then when all inputs are variable. A discussion of international migration and the "brain drain" follows. Finally, the chapter presents several important applications of the theory. The "At the Frontier" section examines the effect of discrimination on gender and race wage differentials.

| 15.1 | PROFIT MAXIMIZATION AND OPTIMAL INPUT EMPLOYMENT |

In this section, we extend the discussion of profit maximization and optimal input employment of Section 14.1 to the case where the firm is an imperfect competitor in the product market but is still a perfect competitor in the input markets. A firm that is an imperfect competitor in the product market (a monopolist, an oligopolist, or a monopolistic competitor) faces a negatively sloped demand curve for the commodity it sells, and its marginal revenue is smaller than the commodity price. Such a firm, however, can still be one of many firms hiring inputs. That is, the firm can still be a perfect competitor in the input markets, so that it can hire any quantity of an input at the given market price of the input. This section and the next two sections of this chapter will examine this situation.

We have seen in Section 14.1 that to maximize profits, a firm must use the optimal or least-cost input combination to produce the best level of output. The profit maximizing condition was given by equation [14.3], which is repeated below as [15.1]:

$$w/MP_L = r/MP_K = MC = MR \qquad\qquad [15.1]$$

where w is the wage rate, r is the rental price of capital, MP is the marginal (physical) product, L refers to labor time, K refers to capital, MC is the marginal cost of the firm, and MR is its marginal revenue. The only difference between equations [14.3] and [15.1] is that equation [14.3] and the discussion in Section 14.1 referred to the case where the firm was a perfect competitor in both the product and input markets. Thus, the marginal revenue of the firm equaled the product price (P). Since the firm is now an imperfect competitor in the product market, $MR < P$ and equation [15.1] is the relevant condition for profit maximization.

By cross multiplying and rearranging the terms of equation [15.1], we get equations [15.2] and [15.3]:

$$MP_L \times MR = w \qquad\qquad [15.2]$$

$$MP_K \times MR = r \qquad\qquad [15.3]$$

Thus, the profit maximizing rule is that the firm should hire labor until the marginal product of labor times the firm's marginal revenue from the sale of the commodity equals the wage rate. Similarly, the firm should rent capital until the marginal product of capital times the firm's marginal revenue equals the rental price of capital. To maximize profits, the same rule would have to hold for all inputs that the firm uses. The condition is the same as when the firm is a perfect competitor in the product market, except that in that case, $MR = P$. In the next section, we will see that equation [15.2] provides the basis for the derivation of the firm's demand curve for labor.

15.2   THE DEMAND CURVE OF A FIRM FOR AN INPUT

We now extend the discussion of the last section and derive the demand curve of a firm for an input, first when the input is the only variable input and then when the input is one of two or more variable inputs.

The Demand Curve of a Firm for One Variable Input

We have seen in Section 14.2 that a profit-maximizing firm will hire more units of a variable input as long as the income from the sale of the extra output produced by the input is larger than the extra cost of hiring the input. When the firm is an imperfect competitor (say, a monopolist) in the product market, the extra income earned by the firm is called the **marginal revenue product (*MRP*)** and is equal to the marginal product of the input times the marginal revenue of the firm. That is,

$$MRP = MP \times MR \qquad\qquad [15.4]$$

If the variable input is labor, we have

$$MRP_L = MP_L \times MR \qquad\qquad [15.4A]$$

Thus, the MRP_L is the left-hand side of equation [15.2]. Similarly, the MRP_K is the left-hand side of equation [15.3]. Note that when the firm is a perfect competitor in the product market, the firm's marginal revenue equals the product price (i.e., $MR = P$) and the marginal revenue product equals the value of the marginal product (i.e., $MRP = VMP$). Since we are now dealing with a firm that is an imperfect competitor in the product market and $MR < P, MRP < VMP$.

Because the firm is a perfect competitor in the input market (i.e., faces a horizontal or infinitely elastic supply curve of the input), the extra cost or marginal expenditure (*ME*) of hiring each additional unit of the variable input is equal to the price of the input. If the variable input is labor, a profit-maximizing firm should hire labor as long as the marginal revenue product of labor exceeds the wage rate and until $MRP_L = w$, as indicated by equation [15.2].

The actual derivation of a firm's demand schedule for labor when labor is the only variable input (i.e., when capital and other inputs are fixed), and when the firm is an imperfect competitor (monopolist) in the product market but a perfect competitor in the labor market is shown with Table 15.1. In Table 15.1, L refers to the number of workers hired by the firm per day. Q_X is the total output of commodity X produced by the firm by hiring various numbers of workers. The MP_L is the marginal or extra output generated by each additional worker hired. The MP_L is obtained by the change in Q_X per unit change in L. Note that the law of diminishing returns begins to operate with the hiring of the second worker. P_X refers to the price for the final commodity, and it declines because the firm is an imperfect competitor (monopolist) in the product market. Total revenue (*TR$_X$*) is obtained by multiplying P_X by Q_X. The marginal revenue product of labor (*MRP$_L$*) is then given by the change in the firm's total revenue by selling the output of commodity X that results from the hiring of an additional worker. More briefly, $MRP_L = \Delta TR_X/\Delta L$. This is the same as MP_L times MR_X (not given in the table; see Problem 3, with the answer at the end of the text). The MRP_L

	The Marginal Revenue Product of Labor and the Firm's
TABLE 15.1	**Demand Schedule for Labor**

L	Q_x	MP_L	P_x	TR_x	MRP_L	$ME_L = w$
1	12	12	$13	$156	. . .	$40
2	22	10	12	264	$108	40
3	30	8	11	330	66	40
4	37	7	10	370	40	40
5	43	6	9	387	17	40
6	48	5	8	384	−3	40

declines because both the MP_L and MR_X decline. That is, as the firm hires more labor and produces more units of the commodity, the MP_L declines (because of diminishing returns) and MR_X also declines (because the firm must lower the commodity price to sell more units of the commodity). The last column of Table 15.1 gives the daily wage rate (w) that the firm must pay to hire each worker. Since the firm is a perfect competitor in the labor market, w is constant (at $40 per day) and is equal to the increase in the firm's total costs (the marginal expense) of hiring each additional worker.

Looking at Table 15.1, we see that the second worker contributes $108 extra revenue to the firm (i.e., $MRP_L = 108), while the firm incurs a cost of only $40 to hire this worker. Thus, it pays for the firm to hire the second worker. (Since the MRP of the first worker is even greater than the MRP of the second worker, the firm should certainly hire the first worker.) The MRP of the third worker falls to $66, but this still exceeds the daily wage of $40 that the firm must pay each worker. Thus, the firm should also hire the third worker. According to equation [15.2], the profit-maximizing firm should hire workers until the $MRP_L = w$. Thus, this firm should hire four workers, at which $MRP_L = w = 40. The firm will not hire the fifth worker because he or she will contribute only $17 to the firm's total revenue while adding $40 to its total costs.

The MRP_L schedule gives the firm's demand schedule for labor. It indicates the number of workers that the firm would hire at various wage rates. For example, if $w = $108 per day, the firm would hire only two workers per day. If $w = $66, the firm would hire three workers. At $w = $40, $L = 4$, and so on. If we plotted the MRP_L values of Table 15.1 on the vertical axis and L on the horizontal axis, we would get the firm's negatively sloped demand curve for labor when labor is the only variable input. This is shown in the next section.

Note that since the firm is a monopolist in the product market, the MRP_L is smaller than the VMP_L and the MRP_L curve lies below the VMP_L curve. As a result, the firm hires less labor and produces less of the commodity than if the firm were a perfect competitor in the product market. Joan Robinson called the excess of the VMP_L over the MRP_L at the point where $MRP_L = w$ (the level of employment) **monopolistic exploitation.**[1] Yet, this emotionally laden term is somewhat misleading, because the firm does not pocket the difference between the VMP_L and the MRP_L (see Problem 3, with the answer at the end of the text). That is, the last worker hired receives the entire increase in the total revenue of the firm (the MRP) that he or she contributes.

The Demand Curve of a Firm for One of Several Variable Inputs

We have seen that the declining MRP_L schedule given in Table 15.1 gives the firm's demand schedule for labor in the short run when labor is the only variable input. This is shown by the negatively sloped MRP_L curve in Figure 15.1 (on the assumption that labor is infinitesimally divisible or that workers can be hired for any part of a day). The MRP_L or demand for labor curve when labor is the only variable input shows that the firm will hire three workers at $w = $66 (point A in Figure 15.1) and four workers at $w = $40 (point B).

When labor is not the only variable input (i.e., when the firm can also change the quantity of capital and other inputs), the firm's demand curve for labor can be derived from the

---

[1] J. Robinson, *The Economics of Imperfect Competition* (London: Macmillan, 1933), Chapter 25.

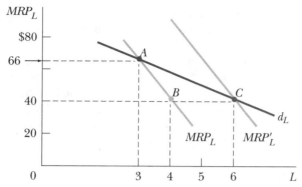

FIGURE 15.1   Demand Curve for Labor of a Monopolist with All Inputs Variable   As the wage rate falls and the firm hires more labor (i.e., moves down its MRP_L curve), the MRP curve of inputs that are complements to labor shifts to the right and the MRP curve of inputs that are substitutes for labor shifts to the left. Both of these shifts cause the MRP_L curve to shift to the right to MRP'_L. Thus, when the daily wage falls from $66 to $40, the firm increases the number of workers hired from three (point A on the MRP_L. curve) to six (point C on the MRP'_L curve). By joining points A and C, we get the firm's demand curve for labor (d_L).

MRP_L curve, but it is not the MRP_L curve itself. The derivation is basically the same as explained in Section 14.2 and is shown in Figure 15.1. That is, as the wage rate falls and the firm hires more labor (i.e., moves down its MRP_L curve), the MRP curve of inputs that are complements to labor shifts to the right, and the MRP curve of inputs that are substitutes for labor shifts to the left (exactly as explained in Section 14.2). Both of these shifts cause the MRP_L to shift to the right, say, from MRP_L to MRP'_L in Figure 15.1. Thus, when the daily wage falls from $66 to $40, the firm will increase the number of workers hired from three (point A on the MRP_L curve) to six (point C on the MRP'_L curve) rather than to four (point B on the original MRP_L curve). By joining points A and C, we get the firm's demand curve for labor (d_L in Figure 15.1) when other inputs besides labor are variable.

Note that the d_L curve is negatively sloped and generally more elastic than the MRP_L curve in the long run, when all inputs are variable. In general, the better the complementary and substitute inputs available for labor are, the greater is the outward shift of the MRP_L curve as a result of a decline in the wage rate, and the more elastic is d_L.

15.3   THE MARKET DEMAND CURVE, AND INPUT PRICE AND EMPLOYMENT

The market demand curve for an input is derived from the individual firms' demand curves for the input. If all the firms using the input are monopolists in their respective product markets, the market demand for the input is derived by the straightforward horizontal summation of the individual firms' demand curves for the input. The reason is that the reduction in the commodity price (as each monopolist produces and sells more of its commodity by hiring more inputs) has already been considered or incorporated in full into the calculation of the *MRP* of the input.

The case is different when a commodity market is composed of oligopolists and monopolistic competitors. That is, when all the oligopolists or monopolistic competitors in a product market hire more inputs and produce more of the commodity, the commodity price will decline. This decline in the price of the commodity causes a downward shift in each firm's demand curve for labor, exactly the same as when firms are perfect competitors in the product market (see Section 14.3). The market demand curve is obtained by adding the quantity demanded of each input on these downward shifting demand curves of the input of each firm. The process is identical to that shown in Figure 14.2 in Section 14.3, and it is not repeated here (see Problem 6).

The equilibrium price and employment of an input are then given at the intersection of the market demand and the market supply curves of the input, as described in Section 14.5. When all firms are perfect competitors in the input market, each firm can hire any quantity of the input at the given market price of the input. Each firm will then hire the input until the *MRP* of the input on the firm's demand curve for the input equals the *ME* or input price.

If, for whatever reason, the market demand curve for the input rises (i.e., shifts upward) from the equilibrium position, the market price and employment of the input will also increase until a new equilibrium price is reached at which the *MRP* of the input equals the *MRC* or input price. This usually does not occur instantaneously. During the adjustment period, there will be a temporary shortage of the input (see Example 15–1).

EXAMPLE 15–1

The Dynamics of the Engineers' Shortage

During the late 1950s and early 1960s a shortage of engineers existed in the United States, which might have endangered winning the "space race" with the former Soviet Union. This can be analyzed with the aid of Figure 15.2. The intersection of the hypothetical market demand curve for engineers D_G and the market supply curve of engineers S_G at point E determines the equilibrium daily wage of $40 for engineers. At $w =$ $40, the 600,000 engineers employed match the number of engineers demanded, and there is no shortage. In the late 1950s and early 1960s, the demand for engineers unexpectedly increased (i.e., shifted up, say, to D'_G) because of the space race. At the original equilibrium wage rate of $w =$ $40, there is a shortage of 500,000 (EF) engineers and engineers' wages rise. As this occurs, employers economize on the use of engineers, and more students enter engineering studies. Thus, the shortage is somewhat alleviated. For example, at $w =$ $50, the shortage declines to 250,000 (CM). Only after several years, as wages rise to $66 and enough new engineers are trained, is the shortage eliminated and new equilibrium point E' reached with 800,000 engineers employed.

If, over this time, the demand for engineers increases again, a new temporary shortage emerges. On the other hand, if the demand for engineers declines by the time an

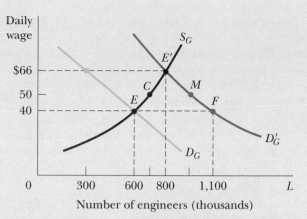

FIGURE 15.2   Dynamics of the Engineer Shortage
The intersection of D_G and S_G at point E determines the
equilibrium daily wage of $40 for engineers. There are
600,000 engineers employed, and there is no shortage. If
D_G shifts upward to D'_G, a temporary shortage of 500,000
(EF) results at $w = $40 and wages rise. As this occurs, the
shortage is somewhat alleviated. At $w = $50, the shortage
declines to 250,000 (CM). Only after the wage rises to $66
and enough new engineers are trained is the temporary
shortage eliminated and new equilibrium point E' reached.

increasing number of them graduate in response to higher wages, or if the supply response turns out to be excessive, a surplus of engineers develops. This is indeed what
occurred during the 1970s and 1980s. Because of the reduced pool of the college-age
population and high incomes in other occupations, the National Science Foundation
predicted that a shortfall of about half a million engineers and scientists would again develop by the end of the twentieth century in the United States. Indeed, a shortage of engineers of about 350,000 was estimated to exist in the United States in 2001. Thus, because of the lag in the supply response to a change in demand and possible subsequent
shifts in demand, alternating shortages or surpluses may arise rather than the market
moving smoothly toward long-run equilibrium.

The same type of dynamic disequilibrium exists in the market for nurses–with one
difference: The shortage of nurses seemed to be more or less chronic over the past three
decades and only fluctuated up and down. There were 2.7 million registered nurses in
the United States in 2000, up only from 2.6 million in 1996. Because of the sharp increase in the demand for nurses and the reduced supply (as the pool of 18- to 24-year-
olds declined, and a smaller percentage of them opted to become nurses because of increased job opportunities elsewhere), the percentage of full-time nursing positions that
are vacant is increasing. It seems that the average salary of $45,500 that a full-time reg-
istered nurse earned in 2002 was not sufficient to attract a sufficient number of them.

Hospitals around the country had 126,000 nursing vacancies in 2002 and experts predict the number could triple over the next decade as baby boomers age. As a delayed response to the surplus of Ph.D.s in the humanities (typified by the taxi driver who has a liberal arts Ph.D.) during the 1970s, a shortage of humanities Ph.D.s entering college teaching developed during the 1990s. Such dynamic market disequilibria are common in most occupations requiring long training periods, as in the case for nurses.

Sources: K. Arrow and W. Capron, "Dynamic Shortages and Price Rises: The Engineer-Scientist Case," *Quarterly Journal of Economics,* May 1959; C. Holden, "Supply and Demand for Scientists and Engineers: A National Crisis in the Making," *Science,* April 1990; "The Nurse Shortage," *Wall Street Journal,* December 15, 1992, p. A15; "Shortage of Nurses Spurs Bidding War in Hospital Industry," *New York Times,* May 28, 2002, p. C1; for the shortage of engineers, see http//www.newswise.com/articles/2001/3/ENGRCONF.STM.html; "Remember the Ph.D. Glut? Colleges Will Go Begging," *U.S. News and World Report,* September 25, 1989, p. 55; and American Association of University Professors (AAUP), *The Ph.D. Shortage: The Federal Role* (Washington, D.C.: AAUP, 1990).

15.4   MONOPSONY: A SINGLE FIRM HIRING AN INPUT

Until this point we have assumed that the firm is a perfect competitor in the input market. This means that the firm faces an infinitely elastic or horizontal supply curve of the input and that the firm can hire any quantity of the input at the given market price of the input. We now examine the case in which the firm is an imperfect competitor in the input market. When there is a single firm hiring an input, we have a **monopsony.** Thus, while *monopoly* refers to the single seller of a commodity, *monopsony* refers to the single buyer of an input. As such, the monopsonist faces the (usually) positively sloped *market* supply curve of the input. This means that to hire more units of the input, the monopsonist must pay a higher price per unit of the input.

An example of monopsony is provided by the "company towns" in nineteenth-century America, where a mining or textile firm was practically the sole employer of labor in many isolated communities. A present-day example of monopsony might be an automaker that is the sole buyer of some specialized automobile component or part, such as radiators, from a number of small local firms set up exclusively to supply these components or parts to the large firm (the automaker).

Monopsony arises when an input is specialized and thus much more productive to a particular firm or use than to any other firm or use. This allows the firm (in which the input is more productive) to pay a much higher price for the input than other firms and so become a monopsonist. Monopsony can also result from lack of geographic and occupational mobility. For example, people often become emotionally attached to a given locality because of family ties, friends, and so on, and are unwilling to move to other areas. Also, people may lack the information, the money, or the qualifications to move to other areas or occupations. In general, monopsony can be overcome by providing information about job opportunities elsewhere, by helping to pay for moving expenses, and by providing training for other occupations.

We have said that the monopsonist faces the usually positively sloped market supply curve of the input, so that it must pay a higher price to hire more units of the input. However, as all units of the input must be paid the same price, the monopsonist will have to pay a higher price, not only for the last unit hired, but for all units of the input it hires. As a result,

TABLE 15.2   Marginal Expenditure on Labor

L	w	TE_L	ME_L
1	$10	$10	—
2	20	40	$30
3	30	90	50
4	40	160	70
5	50	250	90

the **marginal expenditure (ME)** on the input exceeds the input price. This is shown in Table 15.2 for labor.

In Table 15.2, w is the daily wage rate that a monopsonist must pay to hire various numbers of workers (L). Thus, the first two columns of the table give the market supply schedule of labor faced by the monopsonist. TE_L is the total expenditure incurred by the monopsonist to hire various numbers of workers and is obtained by multiplying L by w. ME_L is the **marginal expenditure on labor** and gives the extra expenditure that the monopsonist faces to hire each additional worker. That is $ME_L = \Delta TC_L/\Delta L$.

Note that $ME_L > w$. For example, the monopsonist can hire one worker at the wage rate of $10 for a total cost of $10. To hire the second worker, the monopsonist must increase the wage rate from $10 to $20 and incur a total expenditure of $40. Thus, the increase in the total expenditure (i.e., the marginal expense) of hiring the second worker is $30 and exceeds the wage rate of $20 that the monopsonist must pay for each of the two workers.

Figure 15.3 gives the positively sloped market supply curve of labor (S_L) faced by the monopsonist (from columns 1 and 2 of Table 15.2) and the marginal expenditure curve (ME_L, from the first and the last columns of Table 15.2). Since the ME_L measures the changes in TE_L per unit change in L used, the ME_L values given in Table 15.2 are plotted between the various units of labor hired. Note also that the ME_L curve is everywhere above the S_L curve. Similarly, a firm that is the single renter of a particular type of specialized capital (i.e., a monopsonist in the capital market) faces the positively sloped market supply curve of capital, so that the firm's **marginal expenditure on capital (ME_K)** curve is above the supply curve of capital (S_K).[2]

Although our discussion has been exclusively in terms of monopsony, there are other forms of imperfect competition in input markets. Just as we have monopoly, oligopoly, and monopolistic competition in product markets, so we can have monopsony, oligopsony, and monopsonistic competition in input markets. **Oligopsony** refers to the case where there are only a few firms hiring a homogeneous or differentiated input. **Monopsonistic competition** refers to the case where there are many firms hiring a differentiated input. As for the monopsonist, oligopsonists and monopsonistic competitors must also pay higher prices to hire more units of an input, and so the marginal expenditure on the input exceeds the input price for them also.

---

[2] In Section A.14 of the Mathematical Appendix, we derive an important relationship among input price, marginal expenditure, and the price elasticity of input supply. This is analogous to the relationship among commodity price, marginal revenue, and the price elasticity of commodity demand derived in Section 5.5.

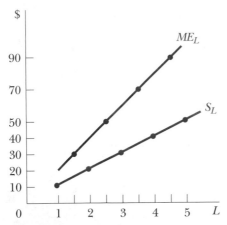

FIGURE 15.3   A Monopsonist's Supply and Marginal Expenditure on Labor Curves S_L is the positively sloped market supply curve of labor faced by the monopsonist (from columns 1 and 2 of Table 15.2) and ME_L is the marginal expenditure on labor curve (from the first and the last columns of Table 15.2). The ME_L values are plotted between the various units of L used, and the ME_L curve is everywhere above the S_L curve.

Finally, note that when the firm is a perfect competitor in the input market, the marginal expenditure on the input is equal to the input price, and the marginal expenditure curve is horizontal and coincides with the supply curve of the input that the firm faces. That is, since the firm hires such a small quantity of the input, the supply curve of the input that the firm faces is infinitely elastic, even though the market supply curve of the input is positively sloped. For example, if $w = \$10$ no matter how many workers a firm hires, then $ME_L = w = \$10$ and the ME_L curve is horizontal at $w = \$10$ and coincides with the S_L curve (the supply curve of labor faced by the firm). Example 15–2 examines the effect of occupational licensing on the functioning of labor markets.

EXAMPLE 15–2

Occupational Licensing, Mobility, and Imperfect Labor Markets

State governments require a license to engage in many professional activities. Occupational licensing now affects about 18% of the U.S. labor force, which is more than the workers affected by the minimum wage (about 10% of the U.S. labor force) or unionization (about 14% of the U.S. labor force), and it is increasing. There are now at least

800 occupations that are licenced in at least one state. Although occupational licensing is imposed to ensure quality of service, it invariably also restricts the flow of labor into the licensed occupations and increases the earnings of licensed labor.

Kleiner found that earnings are higher for licensed occupations that require more education and training (such as dentists and lawyers) than for those occupations that require less education and training (such as barbers and cosmetologists). Kleiner estimated that the earnings of dentists are about 30% higher and the earnings of lawyers are 10% higher than without licensing. These estimates are similar to those found for Canada.

Not only do most states require many occupations to be licensed, but many of them do not recognize the occupational license obtained in other states to pursue the occupation in their own state. This is often the case for dentists and lawyers. Invariably, these nonreciprocity regulations are the result of lobbying on the part of the professions involved as a way of restricting the possible competition that would arise from an inflow of professionals from other states. On theoretical grounds, we would expect that the income of professionals in states without reciprocity agreements would be higher than in states with reciprocity. In fact, Shepard found that the fees and income of dentists in the 35 states that have no reciprocity agreements were 12% to 15% higher than in states with reciprocity. If all states adopted reciprocity agreements, some lawyers and dentists in states with lower fees and incomes would migrate to those states with higher fees and incomes. This would reduce (and in the limit eliminate) all interstate differences in fees and incomes and increase the degree of competition in these labor markets.

Sources: M. M. Kleiner, "Occupational Licencing," *Journal of Economic Perspectives,* fall 2000; and L. Shepard, "Licensing Restrictions and the Cost of Dental Care," *Journal of Law and Economics,* October 1978.

15.5 | MONOPSONY PRICING AND EMPLOYMENT OF ONE VARIABLE INPUT

As pointed out in Section 14.2, a firm using only one variable input maximizes profits by hiring more units of the input until the extra revenue from the sale of the commodity equals the extra expenditure on hiring the input. This is a general marginal condition and applies whether the firm is a perfect or imperfect competitor in the product and/or input markets. If the variable input is labor and the firm is a monopsonist in the labor market, the monopsonist maximizes its total profits by hiring labor until the marginal revenue product of labor equals the marginal expenditure on labor. That is, the monopsonist should hire labor until equation [15.5] or, equivalently, equation [15.5A] holds:

$$MRP_L = ME_L \qquad\qquad [15.5]$$

$$MP_L \cdot MR = MRC_L \qquad\qquad [15.5A]$$

The wage rate paid by the monopsonist is then given by the corresponding point on the market supply curve of labor (S_L). This is shown in Figure 15.4.

In Figure 15.4, the S_L and the ME_L curves are those of Figure 15.3. With the firm's MRP_L curve shown in Figure 15.4, the monopsonist maximizes profits by hiring three

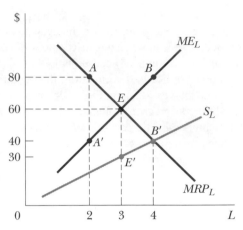

FIGURE 15.4   Optimal Employment of Labor and the Wage Rate Paid by a Monopsonist   The S_L and the ME_L curves are those of Figure 15.3. With MRP_L, the monopsonist maximizes profits by hiring three workers (given by point E, at which the MRP_L curve intersects the ME_L curve and $MRP_L = ME_L = \$60$). The monopsonist then pays $w = \$30$ to each worker (given by point E' on S_L). The excess of MRP_L over w ($EE' = \$30$) at $L = 3$ is called monopsonistic exploitation.

workers (given by point E, at which the MRP_L curve intersects the ME_L curve and $MRP_L = ME_L = \$60$). To prove this, consider that the second worker adds \$80 (point A) to the monopsonist's total revenue but only \$40 (point A') to its total expenditure. Thus, the monopsonist's profits rise (by $AA' = \$40$) by hiring the second worker. On the other hand, the monopsonist would not hire the fourth worker because he or she would add more to total expenditure (\$80, given by point B) than to total revenue (\$40, given by point B'), so that the monopsonist's total profits would fall by \$40 (BB' in the figure). Only at $L = 3$, $MRP_L = ME_L = \$60$ (point E) and the monopsonist maximizes total profits.

Figure 15.4 also shows that to hire three workers, the monopsonist must pay the wage of \$30. This is given by point E' on the S_L curve at $L = 3$. Thus, the intersection of the MRP_L and ME_L curves gives only the profit-maximizing number of workers that the firm should hire. The wage rate is then given by the amount that the firm must pay each worker, and this is given by the point on the market supply curve of labor at the level of employment. Note that $MRP_L = \$60$ (point E) exceeds $w = \$30$ (point E') at $L = 3$.

As noted earlier, Joan Robinson called the excess of the marginal revenue product of the variable input over the input price ($EE' = \$30$ at $L = 3$ in Figure 15.4) monopsonistic exploitation.[3] It arises because the monopsonist produces where the $MRP_L = ME_L$ in order to

---

[3] J. Robinson, *The Economics of Imperfect Competition* (London: Macmillan, 1933), Chapter 26.

maximize profits. Since the S_L curve is positively sloped, the ME_L curve is above it, and $ME_L > w$. The more inelastic the market supply curve that the monopsonist faces, the greater the degree of monopsonistic exploitation. If the firm in Figure 15.4 had been a perfect competitor in the labor market, it would have hired four workers (given by point B', at which $MRP_L = ME_L = w = \$40$). As we have seen, the monopsonist maximizes total profits by restricting output and employment and by hiring only three workers (point E). Example 15–3 examines monopsonistic exploitation in major league baseball. In Section 15.8, we will see how government regulation and/or union power can reduce or eliminate monopsonistic exploitation.

EXAMPLE 15–3

Monopsonistic Exploitation in Major League Baseball

Table 15.3 gives the net marginal revenue product (MRP) and the salary of mediocre, average, and star hitters and pitchers in major league baseball calculated by Scully for the year 1969. Scully found that the team's winning record increased attendance and revenues and that a team's performance depended primarily on the "slugging average" for hitters and on the ratio of "strikeouts to walks" for pitchers. Using these data, Scully calculated the net MRP or extra gate revenues and broadcast receipts resulting from each type of player's performance after subtracting the player's development cost. In 1969, development costs were as high as \$300,000 per player. Table 15.3 shows that for mediocre players, the net MRP was negative (−\$32,300 for hitters and −\$13,400 for pitchers). Of course, the team's scouts and managers could not precisely foresee which players would turn out to be mediocre, average, or stars. The table also shows the average players' salaries in each category.

Mediocre players reduced the team's profits. Average players received salaries far lower than their net MRP. Star players received salaries that were more than six times

TABLE 15.3	Net Marginal Revenue Product and Salaries in Major League Baseball, 1969 Average		
Type of Player	Quality of Player	Net *MRP*	Salary
Hitters	Mediocre	$–32,300	$15,200
	Average	129,500	28,000
	Star	313,900	47,700
Pitchers	Mediocre	$–13,400	$13,700
	Average	159,900	31,800
	Star	397,000	61,000

Source: G. Scully, "Pay and Performance in Major League Baseball," *American Economic Review,* December 1974, p. 928.

lower than their net *MRP*. Thus, monopsonistic exploitation was large for average players and very large for star players. On the other hand, mediocre players exploited their team! Note that even though star players received very large salaries (for 1969), they contributed so much more to the team's revenue (after subtracting the cost for their development) that they were greatly "exploited" by their teams. This exploitation was made possible by the "reserve clause," under which the player became the exclusive property of the team that first signed him. Aside from being traded, a player could only play for the team for whatever salary the team offered. Thus, the reserve clause practically eliminated all competition in hiring and remuneration and essentially established a cartel of employers (teams) for major league baseball players. As such, the cartel behaved much like a monopsonist and exploited players.

In 1975, the reserve clause was substantially weakened. After six years of playing for a team, players could declare themselves "free agents" and negotiate their salaries and the team for which they would play. As anticipated, competition resulted in startling increases in players' salaries and sharply reduced the monopsonistic power of baseball clubs. For example, Summers and Quinton found that free-agent star pitchers had an average marginal revenue product of nearly $300,000 and received salaries of nearly $258,000 in 1980. Even after adjusting for inflation, this represented a doubling of the 1969 salary of star pitchers. In an attempt to reduce these huge salaries and restore some of their previous monopsony power, in 1986 club owners did not sign any player that had become a free agent in 1985. The players' union filed a grievance in 1986, charging that the clubs had acted collusively and thus illegally. In fall 1987, an arbitrator for major league baseball ruled that the clubs had indeed conspired to destroy the free-agent market and that the affected players should be awarded financial damages. By 1991, players' salaries had shot up to more than $500,000 per year and were equal, on the average, to their marginal revenue product (thus essentially putting an end to exploitation in major league baseball). Thirty-five players earned $3 million or more per year, with Boston Red Sox pitcher Roger Clemens and New York Mets pitcher Dwight Gooden topping the list with earnings in excess of $5 million per year.

On August 12 1994, players went on strike as a result of the owners' decision to put a salary cap on multimillion dollar star players' salaries. The strike wiped out the last 52 days of the 1994 season as well as the World Series (for the first time in 90 years), and it also led to a three-week delay in the starting of the 1995 season. The strike was ended by a court injunction after the players agreed to some form of "luxury tax" on clubs paying very high star players' salaries (a partial victory for owners). This, however, is regarded as much too modest to equalize differences between the affluent and poor teams.

In December 2000, the nation's sporting establishment was left aghast by the $252-million, 10-year contract—the largest ever in any sport—that shortstop Alex Rodriguez signed with the Texas Rangers. This is more than Tom Hicks had paid for the entire team two years earlier and almost 10 times more than some teams' entire payroll. The Rangers reason: its desire to win. But experience shows that one player, by himself, cannot turn a team around no matter how great, and in 1999 the Rangers had the worst record in the League. Only the richest clubs can now pay star salaries, and they almost always win. This takes the competition—and some of the fun—out of baseball!

Sources: G. Scully, "Pay and Performance in Major League Baseball," *American Economic Review,* December 1974; P. M. Summers and N. Quinton, "Pay and Performance in Major League Baseball: The Case of the First Family of Free Agents," *Journal of Human Resources,* summer 1982; "Owners: 1, Players: 0," *Business Week,* April 17, 1995, pp. 32–33; "Bring Competition Back to Baseball," *New York Times,* April 5, 1999, p. 22; "Rodriguez Strikes It Rich in Texas," *New York Times,* December 12, 2000, p. D1; and "Good for A-Rod, Bad for Baseball," *Business Week,* December 25, 2000, p. 59.

15.6 | MONOPSONY PRICING AND EMPLOYMENT OF SEVERAL VARIABLE INPUTS

We have seen in Section 15.5 that when labor is the only variable input, a monopsonist maximizes profits by hiring labor until the marginal revenue product of labor equals the marginal expenditure on labor. This was given by equations [15.5] and [15.5A]. The same condition holds when there is more than one variable input. That is, the monopsonist maximizes profits by hiring each input until the marginal revenue product of the input equals the marginal expenditure on hiring it. With labor and capital as the variable inputs, the monopsonist should hire labor and capital until equations [15.6A] and [15.6B] hold:

$$MP_L \cdot MR = ME_L \qquad\qquad [15.6A]$$

$$MP_K \cdot MR = ME_K \qquad\qquad [15.6B]$$

Dividing both sides of equations [15.6A] and [15.6B] by MP_L and MP_K, respectively, and combining the results we get [15.7]

$$ME_L/MP_L = ME_K/MP_K = MC = MR \qquad\qquad [15.7]$$

This is identical to equation [15.1], except that w has been replaced by the ME_L and r has been replaced by the ME_K to reflect the fact that the firm is now a monopsonist in the labor and capital markets, and it must pay a higher wage and rental price to hire more labor and rent more capital, respectively. That is, the optimal input combination is now given by equation [15.7] rather than by equation [14.2], and each ratio in equation [15.7] equals the MC of the firm:

$$ME_L/MP_L = ME_K/MP_K = MC \qquad\qquad [15.8]$$

For example, if ME_L/MP_L is smaller than ME_K/MP_K, the monopsonist would not be minimizing production costs. The monopsonist can reduce the cost of producing any level of output by substituting labor for capital in production at the margin. As the monopsonist hires more labor, ME_L rises and MP_L declines, so that ME_L/MP_L rises. As the monopsonist rents less capital, ME_K falls and MP_K rises, so that ME_K/MP_K falls. To minimize the cost of producing any level of output, the monopsonist should continue to substitute labor for capital in production until equation [15.8] holds.

Note that the ME_L/MP_L and ME_K/MP_K measure the extra cost (in terms of labor and capital, respectively) to produce an extra unit of the commodity. This is the marginal cost of the firm. For example, if $ME_L = \$10$ and $MP_L = 5$, the marginal cost of the firm is $ME_L/MP_L = \$10/5 = \$2$. This means that it costs the monopsonist $2 extra to hire the additional labor to produce one extra unit of the commodity. The same is true for capital. That is, $ME_K/MP_K = MC$ or the marginal cost of the firm (in terms of capital). The best level of output is then given by the point where $MC = MR$ (see equation [15.7]).

EXAMPLE 15-4

Imperfect Competition in Labor Markets and the Pay of Top Executives

Table 15.4 gives the earnings of the 10 highest-paid chief executives in the United States in 2001. The total pay ranged from $706 million for Lawrence Ellison of Oracle to nearly $62 million for Tony White of Applied Biosystems Group. Even though all but the

TABLE 15.4	Earnings of the 10 Highest Paid CEOs in the United States in 2001 (in millions of dollars)		
Executive/ Company	Salary and Bonus	Long-Term Compensation #	Total Compensation
1. Lawrence Ellison Oracle	$0	$706.1	$706.1
2. Jozef Straus JDS Uniphase	0.5	150.3	150.8
3. Howard Solomon Forest Laboratories	1.2	147.3	148.5
4. Richard Fairbank Capital One Financial	0	142.2	142.2
5. Louis Gerstner* IBM	10.1	117.3	127.4
6. Richard Fuld, Jr. Lehman Brothers	4.8	100.4	105.2
7. James McDonald Scientific-Atlanta	2.1	84.7	86.8
8. Steve Jobs Apple Computer	43.5	40.5	84.0
9. Timothy Koogle** YAHOO!	0.2	64.4	64.6
10. Tony White Applied Biosystems Group	1.7	60.2	61.9

#Includes exercised options, restricted shares, and long-term incentive payments.
*Retired as CEO in March 2002.
**Stepped down as CEO in May 2001.

Source: "Executive Pay," Business Week, April 15, 2002, pp. 81–100.

first of these incomes are far smaller than the $550 million made in 1987 by junk-bond king Michael R. Milken of Drexel Burnham and Lambert, Inc., they do establish a new standard for chief executive officers' (CEOs') pay. Most of these incredible incomes resulted from stock option for CEOs (which are less visible to stockholders). While the average remuneration of CEOs was equal to 41 times the average pay for the factory worker in 1960, it was more than 100 times as large in 2001. Union leaders have denounced these multimillion-dollar yearly compensations as the "annual executive pig-out."

The question is, "Are these executives worth to their employer the huge compensation that they are paid?" One answer is that since firms voluntarily make these payments, the marginal revenue product of these top executives must be at least as high. These huge payments, however, also result because of a confluence of interests (collusion) between CEOs and compensation committees, and because the latter often have inadequate information or fail to comprehend how rapidly the payments from a complicated, long-term compensation package can escalate if all goes well.

15.7   INTERNATIONAL MIGRATION AND THE BRAIN DRAIN

International migration affects the supply of labor of the nations of emigration and immigration. Migration can take place for economic as well as for noneconomic reasons. Most of the international labor migration into the United States since the end of World War II has been motivated by the prospects of earning higher real wages and incomes in the United States than in the country of origin. Labor migration to the United States, however, is highly restricted (i.e., international labor markets are not perfectly competitive).

We can examine the effect of labor immigration on a nation with Figure 15.5. The figure is based on the assumption that the nation's output is produced under conditions of constant returns to scale with labor and capital inputs only. Before immigration, the nation employs 3 million workers at the daily wage of $60. The total value of output is, therefore, $0FAG = \$270$ million, of which $0HAG = \$180$ million goes to labor and the remainder, or $HFA = \$90$ million, goes to the owners of capital. With 1 million immigrants, the daily wage rate in the nation falls to $40 and the share of total output going to capital owners increases to $JFB = \$160$ million or by $HABJ = \$70$ million. Since the original workers' earnings decline by the area of rectangle $HACJ = \$60$ million, the nation as a whole gains a net amount equal to the area of triangle $ABC = \$10$ million. With income redistribution (i.e., with taxes on earnings of capital and subsidies to labor), both workers and owners of capital can gain from immigration.

This analysis is based on the implicit assumption that all labor is homogeneous and of average productivity. This is not the case in the real world. Some labor is much more productive because of better education and training. The immigration laws of the United States and other industrial countries favor the immigration of skilled labor (such as nurses and technicians) and professional people (doctors, engineers, scientists, etc.) and impose serious obstacles to the immigration of unskilled labor, except temporary migrants. The immigration of skilled workers and professionals is likely to provide even greater benefits to the country of immigration because it saves the nation the costs of education and training, but represents a **brain drain** for the nation of emigration (see Examples 15–5 and 15–6).

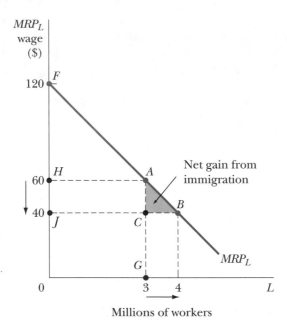

FIGURE 15.5   Effects of Immigration on the Earnings of Labor and Capital   Before immigration, the nation employs 3 million workers at the daily wage of $60. Total output is $OFAG = \$270$ million, of which $OHAG = \$180$ million goes to labor and $HFA = \$90$ million goes to the owners of capital. With 1 million immigrants, the wage falls to $40 and the share of total output going to capital increases to $JFB = \$160$ million, or by $HABJ = \$70$ million. Since the original workers' earnings decline by $HACJ = \$60$ million, the nation receives a net gain equal to the area of triangle $ABC = \$10$ million.

EXAMPLE 15–5

British and Russian Brain Drain Is U.S. Brain Gain

From 1983 to 1988 more than 200 well-known scholars in the fields of history, philosophy, political science, and physics left British universities to take positions in some of the top universities in the United States. Their departure resulted from a combination of "push and pull" forces. Among the push forces were the budget cuts that froze professors' salaries and left many vacancies unfilled, the abolishment of tenure and the suspension of promotions, and reductions in funds for libraries and assistants. The pull forces were U.S. salaries that often were more than three times higher than in Britain, as well as the availability of large research funds, assistants, and sophisticated laboratories. There was a time when it was almost impossible to induce a top scholar to leave Oxford or Cambridge University. In the late 1980s, on the other hand, a British scholar who had not received at least one attractive offer from an American university started even to question his reputation outside Britain.

With the collapse of communism in the Soviet Union in the late 1980s and early 1990s, a huge and growing exodus of top Russian scientists headed for the United States either permanently or on temporary work visas. This surpassed the earlier British exodus and became the largest brain drain to (and brain gain of) the United States since the end of World War II. Russia worried a great deal about losing many of its top scientists. Virtually the entire faculty of the University of Minnesota's Theoretical Physics Institute in the mid-1990s was from Russia. Many top Russian scientists flowed into the U.S. computer, biological, and chemical laboratories. As Russia struggles to restructure its economy, few if any funds are available for science. "For science, there is no money, no jobs, and no respect from the public," says one recent emigree. My productivity in America is 10 times more than in Russia," says another. He might have added that in the early 1990s his salary in the United States is also 100 times more than in Russia!

Another form of brain drain is given by the large number of foreign students getting advanced degrees in the United States and then choosing to remain. Today, more than 60% of the students receiving engineering doctorates in the United States are foreign born, and the percentage is almost as high in mathematics and computer science (it is 40% in economics). More than 70% of them chose to remain in the United States after getting their doctorate. Finally, the H1-B visa program established in 1990 allowed each year 65,000 educated foreigners (raised to 115,000 in 1998 and 195,000 in 2001) to fill specialized American jobs, largely in the high-tech industry for a period of six years (but requiring renewal after the first three years) if an employer petitions the U.S. Immigration and Naturalization Service on their behalf.

Sources: "British Brain Drain Enriches U.S. Colleges," *New York Times,* November 22, 1988, p. 1; "The Soviet Brain Drain Is the U.S. Brain Gain," *Business Week,* November 11, 1991, pp. 94–100; "Foreign Students Spur U.S. Brain Gain," *Wall Street Journal,* August 31, 1994, P. 9A; "Increase Seen in the Number of Foreign Students Here," *New York Times,* December 7, 1998, p. 23; "Congress Approves a Big Increase in Visas for Specialized Workers," *New York Times,* October 4, 2000, p. 1; and "Brain Circulation," *Brookings Review,* winter 2002, pp. 28–31.

EXAMPLE 15-6

The Debate Over U.S. Immigration Policy

In the year 2000, 28.4 million Americans were born elsewhere. This represented 10.1% of the entire population and it was higher than at any other time since 1940, when the percentage was 8.8% (the all-time high in modern times was 14.7% in 1910). The rapid increase in immigration in recent years has emerged as a hot issue, especially in California and New York, the states with the highest proportion of foreign born (25% and 16%, respectively). Indeed, an intense national debate is taking place on the nation's immigration policy.

The immigration of highly trained individuals and bright students coming to the United States to get higher degrees and then remaining is clearly of great benefit to the United States. Less clear is the case for immigration of uneducated and unskilled people. The U.S. Census data indicates that nearly 21% of recent immigrants over the age of 25 have bachelors degrees (as compared with about 15% for native Americans), but 36% do not have a high school diploma (as compared with 17% of those born in the United States). Thus, the majority of recent immigrants are either very educated or have little education.

In general immigration is good for the country. But, at least in the short run, native workers receive lower wages than without immigration while employers gain by being able to pay lower wages. This explains why labor is generally opposed to immigration while business favors it. The nation as a whole generally gains from immigration because employers' gains exceed labor's losses. With an appropriate redistribution policy, some of business' gains could be taxed away and used to compensate workers for their loss and also to provide workers with a share of the remaining gains. Borjas estimated that native workers who compete with immigrants for jobs lose about $133 billion (through lower wages) because of immigration, but firms gain about $140 billion, for a net gain of $7 billion. This, however, represents only 0.1% of U.S. GDP.

Sources: "Surprising Rise in Immigration Stirs Up Debate," *New York Times,* August 30, 1995, p. 1; George Borjas, "The Economic Benefits from Immigration," National Bureau of Economic Research, *Working Paper No. 4955,* July 1995; and "Foreign Workers at Highest Level in Seven Decades," *New York Times,* September 4, 2000, p. 1.

15.8   ANALYSIS OF IMPERFECT INPUT MARKETS

In this section, we discuss some important applications of the theory presented in the chapter: the regulation of monopsony, bilateral monopoly, the effect of unions on wages, and discrimination in employment. These applications clearly indicate the usefulness and applicability of the theory presented in this chapter.

Regulation of Monopsony

By setting a minimum price for an input at the point where the marginal revenue product curve of the input intersects the market supply curve of the input, the monopsonist can be made to behave as a perfect competitor in the input market, and monopsonistic exploitation is eliminated. If the input is labor, the minimum wage that would eliminate labor exploitation can be set by the government or negotiated by the union. This is shown in Figure 15.6.

In the absence of a minimum wage, the monopsonist of Figure 15.6 hires three workers (given by point E, where the MRP_L curve intersects the ME_L curve) and the daily wage is $30 (point E' on S_L) exactly as explained in Section 15.5 and Figure 15.4. Monopsonistic

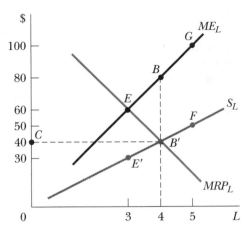

FIGURE 15.6   Regulation of Monopsony
By setting $w = \$40$, *CB'F* becomes the new supply of labor curve facing the monopsonist. The new ME_L curve is then *CB'BG*, with the vertical or discontinuous portion directly above and caused by the kink (at point B') on the new S_L curve. To maximize total profits, the monopsonist now hires four workers (given by point B', at which the MRP_L curve intersects the new ME_L curve) and $w = MRP_L = \$40$ (so that monopsonistic exploitation is zero).

exploitation of labor is given by the excess of the MRP_L over w at $L = 3$ and is equal to $30 per worker (*EE'* in the figure). If the daily wage is set at $40 (point B' in the figure, at which the MRP_L curve intersects S_L), *CB'F* becomes the new supply of labor curve facing the monopsonist. The new ME_L curve is then *CB'BG*, with the vertical or discontinuous portion directly above and caused by the kink (at point B') on the new S_L curve.

To maximize total profits when the minimum wage of $40 is imposed, the monopsonist hires four workers (given by point B', at which the MRP_L curve intersects the new ME_L curve) and $w = MRP_L = \$40$. Thus, the monopsonist behaves as a perfect competitor in the input market (operates at point B', where the MRP_L curve intersects S_L), and the monopsonistic exploitation of labor is entirely eliminated. With a daily wage between $30 and $40, the monopsonist will hire three or four workers per day and only part of the labor exploitation will be eliminated. Setting a wage above $40 will eliminate all labor exploitation, but the monopsonist will hire fewer than four workers (see Problem 9, with answer at end of the text). This neat result is often unreachable in the real world, however, because of lack of adequate data on the MRP_L and ME_L.

Bilateral Monopoly: A Monopsonistic Buyer Facing a Monopolistic Seller

Bilateral monopoly is said to exist when the single buyer of a product or input (the monopsonist) faces the single seller of the product or input (the monopolist). While this is a rare occurrence in the real world, it is approximated by the "one-mill town" of yesteryears facing the union of all of the town's workers; by some military contractors such as Boeing, which is the sole seller of the F-18, and the U.S. Navy, the sole purchaser; and (until 1982) by Western Electric, the sole producer of telephone equipment in the United States, and AT&T, the sole buyer of telephone equipment.

In bilateral monopoly, price and output are indeterminate, in the sense that they cannot be established by the profit-maximizing marginal calculations employed by economists. Rather, they are determined by the relative bargaining strength of the monopsonist buyer and the monopolist seller of the product or input. This is shown in Figure 15.7.

In the figure, D is the monopsonist's demand (MRP) curve for the product or input. Curve D is also the market demand curve faced by the monopolist seller of the product or input. Then MR is the corresponding marginal revenue curve of the monopolist. If the

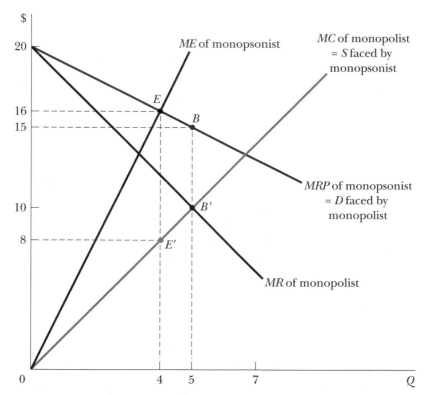

FIGURE 15.7   Bilateral Monopoly D is the monopsonist's demand (MRP) curve for the product or input that the monopolist seller faces. MR is the monopolist's marginal revenue curve. The monopolist maximizes profits at $Q=5$ (given by point B', where $MC = MR$) at $P = \$15$ (point B on the D curve). The monopolist's MC curve is the supply curve of the product that the monopsonist faces, and MF is its marginal expenditure curve. The monopsonist maximizes profits at $Q = 4$ (given by point E, where $MRP = ME$) and $P = \$8$ (given by point E' on the supply curve that the monopsonist faces). The solution is indeterminate and will be within area $E'B'BE$.

monopolist's marginal cost curve is as shown in the figure, the monopolist will maximize profits by selling five units of the product (given by point B', where its MC curve intersects its MR curve from below) at the price of $15 per unit (point B on its D curve).

To determine the monopsonist's profit-maximizing purchase of the product, we must realize that the monopolist's marginal cost curve is the supply curve of the product that the monopsonist faces. This curve shows the price at which the monopsonist can purchase various quantities of the product. Thus, the monopsonist's marginal expenditure curve for the product is higher, as indicated by the ME curve in the figure. To maximize profits, the monopsonist must buy four units of the product (given by point E, at which the monopsonist demand [D or MRP] curve intersects its ME of the product curve) and pay the price of $8 (given by point E' on the supply curve of the product that the monopsonist faces).

Thus, to maximize profits, the monopolist seller of the product wants to sell $Q = 5$ at $P = \$15$, while the monopsonist buyer of the product wants to purchase $Q = 4$ at $P = \$8$. The solution is indeterminate and depends on the relative bargaining strength of the two firms. All we can say is that the level of output and sales of the product will be between four and five units and the price will be between $8 and $16 (i.e., the solution will be within area $E'B'BE$). The greater the relative bargaining strength of the monopolist seller of the product, the closer output will be to five units and price to $15. The greater the relative bargaining strength of the monopsonist buyer of the product, the closer the purchase of the product will be to four units and the price to $8.

Effect of Labor Unions on Wages

A **labor union** is an organization of workers that seeks to increase the wages and the general welfare of union workers through collective bargaining with employers. The Wagner Act passed in 1935 prohibited firms from interfering with workers' rights to form unions. Union membership as a percentage of the nonagricultural labor force of the United States peaked at 35.5% in 1947, but it had declined to 13.5% in 2000. Among the reasons for the decline is the increase in the proportion of workers in service industries and women in the labor force, both of whom are less likely to join unions than male production workers. Workers are also less likely to join a union if the union does not have much bargaining clout or if workers lose their jobs when they strike. Furthermore, many workers feel that unions were needed when they started, but with more and more companies setting up work-involvement programs (to avoid unionization), unions are less needed now.

A labor union can try to increase the wages of its members by (1) restricting the supply of union labor that employers must hire, (2) bargaining for an above-equilibrium wage, or (3) increasing the demand for union labor. These strategies are shown in Figure 15.8. In each of the three panels in the figure, the intersection of the market demand curve for labor (D_L) and market supply curve of labor (S_L) at point E determines the equilibrium wage rate of $40 and the equilibrium level of employment of 600 workers in the absence of the union.

The left panel shows that if the union can reduce the supply of union labor that employers must hire from S_L to S'_L, the equilibrium daily wage will rise to $66, at which 300 workers are hired (point F, where S'_L intersects D_L). The union can restrict the number of union members by high initiation fees and by long apprenticeship periods. The center panel shows that the union can achieve the wage of $66 through bargaining with employers. The result is the same as if the government set the minimum wage of $66. Note that at

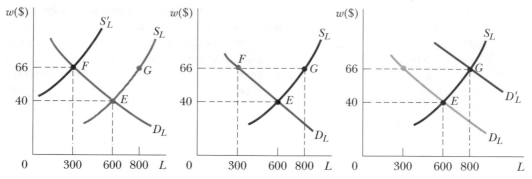

FIGURE 15.8   Methods by Which Labor Unions Can Increase Wages   The union can increase wages from $40 to $66 by reducing the supply of union labor from S_L to S'_L (the left panel), by bargaining with employers for $w = \$66$ (the center panel), or by increasing the demand for union labor from D_L to D'_L (the right panel). Employment falls from 600 workers to 300 workers with the first two methods (the left and center panels) and increases to 800 workers with the last method (the most difficult to accomplish).

$w = \$66$, 800 workers would like to work, but only 300 find employment. Thus, there is an unemployment gap of 500 workers (*FG* in the center panel), 300 of whom represent the disemployment effect (see Section 14.8).

Finally, the right panel of Figure 15.8 shows that by shifting D_L upward to D'_L, the union can increase wages to $66 and employment to 800 workers (given by point *G*, where D'_L intersects S_L). The union can increase the demand for union labor by advertising to buy "union labels" and by lobbying to restrict imports. Thus, trying to increase union wages by increasing the demand for union labor is the most advantageous method to raise wages from the point of view of union labor because it also increases employment. This, however, is also the most difficult for unions to accomplish.

There is a great deal of disagreement regarding the amount by which labor unions have increased the wages of their members. To be sure, unionized workers do receive, on the average, higher wages than nonunionized workers. At least to some extent, however, this is because unionized labor has traditionally been more skilled than nonunion labor, is employed in more efficient large-scale industries, and received higher wages even before unionization. On the other hand, wage differences between union and nonunion labor underestimate the effectiveness of labor unions in raising wages because nonunionized firms tend to increase wages when union wages rise in order to retain their workers and avoid unionization. Empirical studies seem to indicate that labor unions, on the average, have been able to increase union wages by 10% to 15% over what they would have been in the absence of unions, but this varies according to occupations, industry, race, and gender. Only during the 1970s and early 1980s were unions able to increase union-nonunion wage differentials to 20% to 30%. By the late 1980s, however, union-nonunion wage differentials returned to the traditional 10% to 15%.

In their actual negotiations with management, labor unions usually "demand" higher wage increases than they really expect to receive in order to leave room for bargaining. The wage increases in a few major industries, such as the automobile and steel industries, often set the pattern for wage demands in other industries. Union wage demands are also likely to be larger in periods of high profits and employment than in recessionary periods. In the final analysis, the actual wage settlement in a particular industry or firm depends on the relative bargaining strength of the union and the employer, along the lines of the bilateral monopoly model. In making wage demands, unions do take into account the effect of wage increases on employment. Labor unions also seem to have reduced wage differentials among union workers of different skills and among different regions of the country. By bargaining with management for higher wages, unions also tend to reduce monopsonistic exploitation.[4]

Economics of Discrimination in Employment

Discrimination in employment can take many forms, but in this Chapter we will consider only discrimination between male and female workers of equal productivity and its effect on their wages and employment. This is shown in Figure 15.9, where S_F and S_M are the supply curves of female and male labor to a particular industry, respectively; S_L is the total supply of female and male labor; and D_L is the total demand for labor by the industry. The figure shows that in the absence of gender discrimination, the equilibrium wage is $40 for males and females (given by point E, at which S_L intersects D_L), and 200 females (point A) and 400 males (point B) are employed.

However, if employers in the industry refused to hire females, the supply curve of labor to the industry would be only S_M, and 500 male workers would be hired at $w = \$50$ (point E', where S_M intersects D_L). No females would now be hired by the industry. Females would have to find employment in other industries that do not practice gender discrimination, and this would depress wages for all workers in these other industries. Thus, the gains of male workers from gender discrimination in the industry come at the expense of workers (both males and females) in other industries where there is no gender discrimination.

With a less extreme form of gender discrimination against females, employers in the industry may prefer to hire males over females at the same wage rate, but the employers' "taste for discrimination" is not absolute and can be overcome by a sufficiently lower wage for female labor than for male labor. For example, employers may also hire females if the wage of female workers is, say, $10 less than for male workers of the same productivity. Compared with the no-discrimination case, employers hire more males (and their wages rise) and fewer females (and their wages fall) until the male–female wage difference is $10. In Figure 15.9, employers hire 150 females at $w = \$35$ (point A') and 450 males at $w = \$45$ (point B'), compared with 200 females and 400 males at $40 (points A and B, respectively) without discrimination. Once again, males gain at the expense of females and other employees of this and other industries. The gain is larger the greater is the employers' taste for discrimination in the industry.

---

[4] For a discussion of labor unions and their effect on wages, see C. J. Parsley, "Labor Unions' Effects on Wage Gains: A Survey of Recent Literature," *Journal of Economic Literature,* March 1980; R. B. Freeman and J. L. Medoff, *What Do Unions Do?* (New York: Basic Books, 1984); R. Edwards and P. Swaim, "Union-Nonunion Earnings Differentials and the Decline of Private Sector Unionism," *American Economic Review,* May 1986; M. W. Reder, "The Rise and Fall of Unions: The Public Sector and the Private," *Journal of Economic Perspectives,* Spring 1988; "Unions' Woes Suggest How the Labor Force in the U.S. Is Shifting," *Wall Street Journal,* May 5, 1992, p. A1; and "Labor Unions Turn to Mergers in Pursuit of Growth," *Wall Street Journal,* September 1, 2000, p. A2.

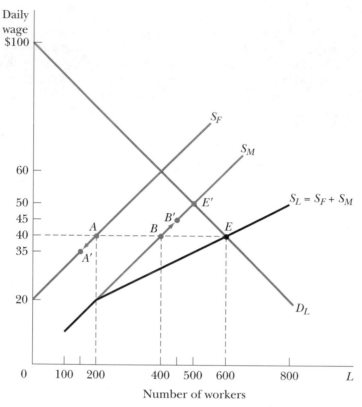

FIGURE 15.9   Effect of Gender Discrimination in Employment
Without discrimination, $w = \$40$ for males and females (given by point E, at which S_L intersects D_L), and 200 females (point A) and 400 males (point B) are employed. If employers refused to hire females, 500 males would be hired at $w = \$50$ (point E', where S_M intersects D_L). Females would have to find employment in other industries, and this would depress wages for all workers in these other industries. With a less extreme form of discrimination, employers may hire females if their wage is, say, $10 less than for males of the same productivity. Employers would then hire 150 females at $w = \$35$ (point A') and 450 males at $w = \$45$ (point B').

If only some employers in the industry discriminated against females, they would employ only male workers while nondiscriminating employers would employ mostly females. If there are enough nondiscriminating employers in the industry to employ all the female workers, no male–female wage differences need arise in the industry. Even if all employers in the industry discriminated against females so that female wages tended to be lower than the wages of male workers, more firms would enter the industry (attracted by the lower female wages), and this, once again, would tend to eliminate gender-based wage differences in the industry. Note that discrimination may also be practiced by employees and by customers.

AT THE FRONTIER
Discrimination, and Gender and Wage Differentials

Table 15.5 shows that in 2000, the median weekly earnings of white females were 75% that of white males (up from 67% in 1985). The median weekly earnings of black males were 75% that of white males (up from 73% in 1985), while the median weekly earnings of black females were 64% that of white males (up from 60% in 1985). Thus, females and blacks earned substantially less than white males in 2000, but the differential diminished over the 1985–2000 period. Table 15.6 shows that male–female wage differentials exist in all occupations indicated and are about of the same order of magnitude as the average difference

TABLE 15.5	Median Weekly Earnings for Full-Time Workers by Sex and Race in 1985 and 2000 (in dollars)			
	1985	As a Percentage of White Male Earnings	2000	As a Percentage of White Male Earnings
White Males	417	100	669	100
White Female	281	67	500	75
Black Males	304	73	503	75
Black Females	252	60	429	64

Source: Department of Commerce, Bureau of Census, *Statistical Abstract of the United States* (Washington, D.C.: U.S. Government Printing Office, 2002), p. 403.

TABLE 15.6	Median Weekly Earnings for Full-Time Workers by Sex and Occupation in 2000 (in dollars)		
	Median Earnings		Percent
Occupation	Males	Females	Females/Males
Manager	994	709	71
Technical	665	452	68
Service	414	316	76
Precision production	628	445	71
Operators	487	351	72
Farming, forestry, and fishing	347	294	85

Source: Department of Commerce, Bureau of Census, *Statistical Abstract of the United States* (Washington, D.C.: U.S. Government Printing Office, 2002), p. 403.

Continued. . .

in overall female–male and black–white differences in earnings, except in farming, forestry, and fishing, where it is less.

Empirical studies seem to indicate that most female–male and black–white wage differences are due to differences in productivity based on different levels of education, training, experience, age, hours of work, size of firm, and region of employment. Whether and to what extent the remaining difference is due to discrimination or to other still-unmeasured productivity factors has not yet been settled. The suspicion is that at least part of the unexplained difference is due to discrimination—despite the *Equal Pay Act of 1964,* which prohibits such discrimination.

An empirical study by Francine Blau and Marianne Ferber (see the references at the end) found that wage discrimination may account for as much as 10–12% of the lower female–male earnings, and occupational discrimination for another 5–9%. Thus, wage and occupational discrimination, together, may account for between 16% and 21% of female–male wage differentials. In addition, Francine Blau and Lawrence Kahn found that if black men had the same productive characteristics of white men, they would receive 89% of white men's earnings. Thus, the upper limit on the effect of race discrimination on black–white earnings differentials is about 11%.

To overcome possible discrimination, the **comparable-worth** doctrine proposes the evaluation of jobs in terms of the knowledge and skills required, working conditions, accountability, and the enforcement of equal pay for comparable jobs or "comparable worth." Many economists, however, consider this too difficult or impossible to do. For example, many of the male–female wage differences are due to fewer work interruptions and longer job tenure for males than for females of equal age and comparable training. Others, however, point out that these work choices themselves are the result of discrimination against females. The major push for comparable worth wages in the United States to date has come from state and local governments, but its effect on female–male wages differences has so far been small.

Sources: G. Becker, *The Economics of Discrimination,* 2nd ed. (Chicago: University of Chicago Press, 1971); F. D. Blau and M. A. Ferber, *The Economics of Men, Women, and Work* (Englewood Cliffs: Prentice-Hall, 1992); F. D. Blau and L. M. Kahn, "Gender Differences in Pay," *Journal of Economic Perspectives,* fall 2000; D. L. Costa, "From Mill Town to Board Room: The Rise of Women's Paid Labor," *Journal of Economic Perspectives,* fall 2000; and P. England, *Comparable Worth: Theory and Evidence* (New York: Aldine DeGruyter, 1993).

SUMMARY

1. A firm that is an imperfect competitor in the product market but a perfect competitor in the input market will maximize profits by hiring any input until the marginal product of the input times the firm's marginal revenue from the commodity equals the price of the input.

2. If only one input is variable and the firm is a monopolist in the product market but a perfect competitor in the input market, the firm's demand curve for the input is given by the marginal revenue product (*MRP*) curve of the input. *MRP* equals the marginal product (*MP*) of the input times the marginal revenue (*MR*) from the commodity. The excess of an input's *VMP* over

MRP at the level of utilization of the input is called monopolistic exploitation. When all inputs are variable, the demand curve of an input is obtained by points on different *MRP* curves of the input and will be more elastic than the *MRP* curves. A perfect competitor in an input market will employ the input until the input's *MRP* on its demand curve equals the input price.

3. When all firms hiring an input are monopolists in their respective product markets, the market demand curve of the input is obtained by the straightforward horizontal summation of all the firms' demand curves for the input. On the other hand, when the firms are oligopolists or monopolistic competitors in the product market, the market demand curve of the input is derived as in Section 14.3. The equilibrium price and employment of the input are then determined at the intersection of the market demand and the market supply curve of the input.

4. Monopsony refers to the case where there is a single buyer of an input. The monopsonist faces the positively sloped market supply curve of the input so that its marginal expenditures on the input exceeds the price of the input. Oligopsonists and monopsonistic competitors must also pay higher prices to hire more units of an input. Monopsony arises when an input is much more productive to a particular firm or use than to other firms or uses. It can also result from lack of geographic or occupational mobility.

5. A monopsonist hiring a single variable input maximizes profits by hiring the input until the marginal revenue product (*MRP*) of the input equals the marginal expenditure (*ME*) on the input. The price of the input is then determined by the corresponding point on the market supply curve of the input. A monopsonist hires less of the variable input and pays the input a lower price than would a perfectly competitive firm in the input market. The excess of the *MRP* over the price of the input at the point where *MRP* = *ME* is called monopsonistic exploitation.

6. To maximize profits a firm should hire any variable input until the marginal revenue product of the input equals the marginal expenditure on hiring it. If the firm is a perfect competitor in the product market, the marginal revenue product of the input is identical to the value of the marginal product of the input. If the firm is a perfect competitor in the input market, the marginal expenditure on the input equals the input price.

7. Immigration usually increases the earnings of capital and reduces those of labor. Since the former usually exceeds the latter, however, the nation of immigration as a whole receives a net gain. The emigration of skilled labor and professionals represents a brain drain on the nation of emigration and an even greater gain for the nation of immigration.

8. Monopsonistic exploitation can be eliminated by the government setting the minimum price of an input at the point where the *MRP* curve intersects the market supply curve of the input. Bilateral monopoly occurs when the monopsonist buyer of a product or input faces the monopolist seller of the product or input. Unions seem to have increased wages only slightly. Among the most important goals of unions are higher wages and greater employment of union labor. Discrimination in employment reduces the wages and/or the employment of the discriminated category. The marginal resource cost of an input is related to the price of the input and the price elasticity of the input supply.

KEY TERMS

Marginal revenue product (*MRP*)	Marginal expenditure on capital (*ME_K*)	Bilateral monopoly
Monopolistic exploitation		Labor Union
Monopsony	Oligopsony	Discrimination in employment
Marginal expenditure (*ME*)	Monopsonistic competition	Comparable worth
Marginal expenditure on labor (*ME_L*)	Monopsonistic exploitation	
	Brain drain	

REVIEW QUESTIONS

1. Why is the demand curve for an input less elastic when the firm is an imperfect rather than a perfect competitor in the product market?

2. Why are real average wages higher in the United States than in most other countries? Why have real wages in Germany and Japan been catching up with U.S. wages during the period after World War II?

3. Can a demand curve for an input be derived for a monopsonist? Why?

4. Monopsonistic exploitation is true exploitation while monopolistic exploitation is not. True or false? Explain.

5. What is the general rule for a firm to maximize profits in hiring an input? What does the rule become when the firm is a perfect competitor in the product market and/or in the input market?

6. A firm that is a perfect competitor in the product market hires more labor than a firm that is an imperfect competitor in the product market, everything else being equal. True or false? Explain.

7. How does immigration benefit the United States?

8. What trade alternative can the United States use to slow down the inflow of illegal aliens from Mexico?

9. Why are wages and employment indeterminate when a monopsonistic employer faces a monopolistic union?

10. Why might unionization in some industries lead to lower wages in other industries?

11. What are some of the ways by which labor unions can increase and reduce labor productivity?

12. What are the difficulties in establishing the existence and measuring the extent of discrimination in a labor market?

PROBLEMS

1. For a firm that is a monopolist in the product market but a perfect competitor in the input market, express the condition prevailing if the firm

   a. utilizes too much labor or too little capital at the best output level. What is the graphic interpretation of this?

   b. utilizes the least-cost input combination but with its marginal cost exceeding its MR. What is the graphic interpretation of this?

   c. minimizes the cost of producing an output that is too small to maximize profits. What is the graphic interpretation of this?

2. You are given the following data where L is the number of workers hired per day by a firm (the only variable input), Q_X is the quantity of the commodity produced per day, and P_X is the commodity price:

L	1	2	3	4	5
Q_X	10	20	28	34	38
P_X	$5.00	4.50	4.00	3.50	3.00

   a. Find the marginal revenue product of labor and plot it.

   b. How many workers per day will the firm hire if the wage rate is $40 per day? $22? $7? What is the firm's demand curve for labor?

*3. From Table 15.1 in the text

   a. find the MR_X, the MRP_L by multiplying MR_X by MP_L, and the VMP_L.

   b. Plot on the same graph, the VMP_L and the MRP_L on the assumption that labor is infinitesimally divisible. How many workers would the firm employ if it were a perfect competitor in the product market? What is the amount of monopolistic exploitation?

4. Repeat the procedure in Problem 3 for the data in Problem 2 and on the assumption that the daily wage is $22.

5. Assume that (1) labor is infinitesimally divisible (i.e., workers can be hired for any part of the day) in the production function of Problems 2 and 4, (2) all inputs are variable, and (3) when the wage rate falls from $40 to $22 per day, the firm's value of the marginal product curve shifts to the right by two labor units. Derive the demand curve for labor of this firm. How many workers will the firm hire per day at the daily wage rate of $22?

* = Answer provided at end of book.

6. a. Derive the market demand curve for labor if there are 100 monopolistically competitive firms identical to the firm of Problem 5 in the labor market and each individual firm's demand curve for labor shifts to the left by one unit when the wage rate falls from $w = \$40$ to $w = \$22$ per day.

   b. If 200 workers are willing to work at the daily wage of $10, and 600 are willing to work at the daily wage of $40, what is the equilibrium wage and level of employment? How many workers would each firm hire at the equilibrium wage?

7. a. From the following market supply schedule of labor faced by a monopsonist, derive the firm's marginal expenditures on labor schedule.

L	1	2	3	4	5
w	$10	11	16	40	100

   b. Plot on the same set of axes the firm's supply and marginal expenditures on labor schedules.

8. On your graph for Problem 7(b), superimpose the monopsonist's value of marginal product and marginal revenue product of labor curves from Problem 4. Assuming that labor is the only variable input, determine the number of workers that the firm hires, the wage rate, and the amount of monopolistic and monopsonistic exploitation if the firm is a monopolist in the product market and a monopsonist in the input market.

*9. Starting with Figure 15.4, explain what happens if the government sets the minimum wage at

   a. $35.

   b. $50.

*10. Assume that all workers in a town belong to the union and there is a single firm hiring labor in the town. Suppose that the supply for labor function of the firm (a monopsonist) is $S_L = 2w$ (where w refers to wages, measured in dollars per day) and the demand of labor function by the union (the monopolist seller of labor time) is $D_L = 120 - 2w$. Find the wage rate and number of workers that the firm would like to hire and the wage and level of employment that the union would seek if it behaved as a monopolist. What is the likely result?

*11. Draw a figure showing that an increase in union wages usually reduces employment in unionized industries and increases employment and lowers wages in nonunionized industries.

12. Given that (1) $ME_L = w(1 + 1/\epsilon_L)$ where ϵ_L is the price (wage) elasticity of the supply curve of labor (this formula is derived in Section A.15 of the Mathematical Appendix), and (2) S_L is a straight line through the origin, find the value of ME_L if

   a. $w = \$40$.

   b. $w = \$80$.

INTERNET SITE ADDRESSES

A wealth of information on labor markets (employment, unemployment, productivity, earnings, and others) is provided by the Bureau of Labor Statistics at:

   http://stats.bls.gov

An excellent analysis of labor markets is found on the Website of the Labor Studies Program of George Washington University at:

   http://www.edu/~labor/respurces.html#MW

For the shortage of engineers and nurses in the United States, see:

   http://www.cnn.com/2001/HEALTH/05/07/nursing.shortage.

   http://www.newswise.com/articles/2001/3/ENGRCONF.STM.html.

Monopsonistic exploitation in Major League Baseball is examined in:

   http://www.iesbs/com/pdf/sports_economics.pdf

For the pay of top executives, see:

   http://www.bls.gov/oco/ocos012.htm

The effect of immigration on labor markets is examined in:

   http://www.immigration-usa.com/debate.html

   http://www.ins.usdoj.gov/graphics/index.htm

On the economic effect of labor unions, see:

   http://papers.nber.org/jel/j5.html

   http://minneapolisfed.org/pubs/fedgaz/01-05/unions.html

Antidiscrimination laws and the effect of discrimination in labor markets are found in:

   http://papers.nber.org/jel/j7.html

   http://www.eeolaw.com/laws-us.html

## CHAPTER 16

Financial Microeconomics: Interest, Investment, and the Cost of Capital

I n this chapter, we consider intertemporal choices or the optimal allocation of resources *over time.* We examine the choice between consuming now or saving a portion of this year's income in order to consume more in the future. The alternative is borrowing against future income to increase present consumption. An individual's ability to exchange present income for future income or consumption (by lending or borrowing) enables the individual to maximize the total or joint satisfaction of present and future income and consumption. For example, people save during their working lives to provide for retirement, and by doing so, they maximize the lifetime satisfaction from their earnings. On the other hand, students often borrow against their future income (i.e., they dissave).

Another way by which present income can be exchanged for future income is to free some resources from the production of final commodities for present consumption (i.e., save) to produce more capital goods (i.e., invest in machinery, factories, and so on), which will lead to larger output and consumption in the future. The ability of individuals and firms to trade present for future income and output and vice versa (through lending and borrowing, saving and investing) is crucial in all societies. Indeed, a great deal of the increase in the standards of living in modern societies is the result of investments in physical capital (machinery, factories, etc.) and human capital (education, skills, health, and so on).

An individual usually requires a reward for postponing present consumption (i.e., saving) and lending a portion of this year's income. The reward takes the form of a repayment that exceeds the amount lent. This premium is the interest payment. The alternative would be the borrowing of a given sum today and the repaying of a larger sum in the future (the principal plus the interest). Similarly, individuals and firms will only invest in machinery, factories, or in acquiring or providing skills if they can expect a return on their investment in the form of higher future incomes or outputs than the amounts invested.

In this chapter, we examine the determination of the rate of interest that will balance the quantity of resources lent and borrowed and that equilibrates saving and investment. We also analyze the criteria used by individuals, business firms, and government agencies in their investment decisions. Subsequently, we discuss the reasons for differences in interest rates in the same nation, in different nations, and over time. The chapter also explains how to measure the cost of capital and describes the effects of foreign investments. Since capital is a crucial input, its cost is very important to a firm's production decisions. Finally, several important applications of the theory introduced in the chapter are presented. These range from investment in human capital to the pricing and management of renewable and nonrenewable resources. These applications, together with the numerous examples and the "At the Frontier" section on derivatives, add an important element of realism to the analysis.

16.1   LENDING–BORROWING EQUILIBRIUM

In this section, we examine how an individual maximizes the total or joint satisfaction from spending his or her present and future income by lending or borrowing. We also show how the equilibrium market rate of interest is determined at the level at which the total quantity demanded of loans (borrowings) equals the total quantity supplied of loans (lendings).

Lending

We begin by considering how a consumer can maximize satisfaction over time by lending. For simplicity, we assume that the consumer's income is measured in terms of the quantity of a commodity (say, corn) that he or she has or expects to receive. Also, to simplify matters, we will deal with only two time periods: this year and the next year. (This assumption is relaxed in Section 15.4.) We also begin by assuming that the consumer has an **endowment position,** or receives $Y_0 = 7.5$ units of corn this year and $Y_1 = 3$ units of corn next year (point A in the left panel of Figure 16.1).[1]

The consumer, however, is not bound to consume the $Y_0 = 7.5$ units of corn this year and the $Y_1 = 3$ units of corn next year, because he or she can lend part of this year's corn or borrow against next year's corn. The question is how should the consumer distribute consumption between this year and next so as to maximize the total or joint satisfaction over the two periods? This is analogous to the consumer's choice between hamburgers (commodity X) and soft drinks (commodity Y) examined in Section 3.5 and Figure 3.8. The only difference is that here the choice is between the consumption of corn this year or consumption the next.

In the left panel of Figure 16.1, the consumer's tastes between consumption this year and next are given by indifference curves U_1, U_2, and U_3. The consumer also faces budget

---

[1] Uncertainty is ruled out here so that the consumer knows exactly how much of the commodity he or she gets this year and next year. This assumption is relaxed in Section 16.4. In what follows, subscripts 0 and 1 denote, respectively, this year (or the present) and next year (or the future).

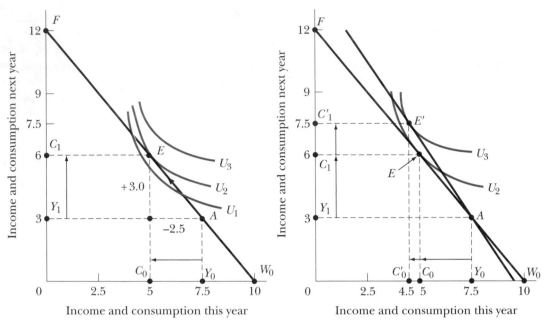

FIGURE 16.1   Lending   Starting from endowment A ($Y_0 = 7.5$ and $Y_1 = 3$), the consumer maximizes satisfaction at point E, where the budget line FW_0 is tangent to indifference curve U_2 in the left panel. The consumer reaches point E by lending $Y_0 - C_0 = 2.5$ units from this year's endowment and receiving 3 additional units next year. Thus, the slope of the budget line is $3/(-2.5) = -1.2$ or $-1(1 + 0.2)$ and the interest rate $r = 0.2$ or 20%. At $r = 50\%$, the optimal point is E' (in the right panel), where the steeper budget line through point A is tangent to indifference curve U_3. Point E' is reached by lending 3 units (instead of 2.5).

line FW_0. The latter shows the various combinations of present and future income and consumption available to the consumer. Starting from endowment position A ($Y_0 = 7.5$ and $Y_1 = 3$), the consumer can lend part of this year's corn endowment so that he or she will consume less this year and more next year. This is represented by an upward movement from point A along budget line FW_0. On the other hand, the consumer could increase consumption this year by borrowing against next year's endowment or income by moving downward from point A along FW_0.

The consumer maximizes satisfaction by reaching the highest indifference curve possible with his or her budget line. The optimal choice is given by point E, where budget line FW_0 is tangent to indifference curve U_2. At point E, the individual consumes $C_0 = 5$ units of corn this year and $C_1 = 6$ units next year (see the left panel of Figure 16.1). The consumer reaches point E by lending $Y_0 - C_0 = 2.5$ units of corn out of this year's endowment or output and by receiving 3 additional units next year.

The slope of the budget line gives the premium or the rate of interest that the lender receives. For example, the movement from point A to point E indicates that the consumer receives 3 units of the commodity next year by lending 2.5 units this year. Thus, the slope of the budget line is $3/(-2.5) = -1.2$ or $-1(1 + 0.2)$, so that the interest rate $r = 0.2$

or 20%. That is,

$$\frac{C_1 - Y_1}{C_0 - Y_0} = -(1 + r) = -(1 + 0.2) \qquad\qquad [16.1]$$

The negative sign reflects the downward-to-the-right inclination of the budget line. This simply means that for the consumer to be able to consume more next year, he or she will have to consume less this year. In this case, the consumer lends (i.e., reduces consumption by) 2.5 units this year and gets $2.5(1 + 0.2) = 3$ next year. If the consumer lends all of this year's income or endowment of $Y_0 = 7.5$ units at 20% interest, he or she will receive $7.5(1 + 0.2) = 9$ additional units next year (and reach point F on budget line FW_0). The consumer could do this, but does not, because he or she would not be maximizing satisfaction.

Returning to the slope of the budget line, we can say more generally that the **rate of interest (r)** is the premium received by an individual next year by lending \$1.00 today. Another way of stating this is that the rate of interest is the excess in the price next year (P_1) of \$1.00 this year (P_0). That is,

$$P_1 = P_0 (1 + r) \qquad\qquad [16.2]$$

The individual receives ($\$1)(1 + r)$ next year (P_1) by lending \$1.00 this year (P_0). If the interest rate r is 0.2 or 20%, the individual receives ($\$1)(1 + 0.2) = \$1.20$ next year by lending \$1.00 this year. Of course, the person who borrows \$1.00 today must repay \$1.20 next year if the rate of interest is 20%. Thus, the interest rate can be viewed as the excess in the price next year of \$1.00 lent or borrowed this year.

If the interest rate rises (i.e., if the budget line becomes steeper), lenders will usually lend more. For example, starting with endowment position A in the right panel of Figure 16.1, if the interest rate rises to 50% so that the slope of the budget line becomes $-(1 + 0.5)$, the optimal choice of the consumer is at point E', where the new steeper budget line through point A is tangent to higher indifference curve U_3. The consumer can reach point E' by lending $Y_0 - C_0' = 3$ units (instead of 2.5), for which he or she receives $C_1' - Y_1 = 4.5$ units next year. That is, by lending 3 units at 50% interest, the consumer receives $3(1 + 0.5) = 4.5$ units next year. Thus, the increase in the rate of interest from 20% to 50% leads this individual (the lender) to increase lending from 2.5 to 3 units.[2]

Borrowing

We will now show that if the endowment position of the consumer in the left panel of Figure 16.1 had been to the left of point E on budget line FW_0 (rather than at point A), the consumer would have been a borrower rather than a lender. This is shown in the left panel of Figure 16.2. Specifically, suppose the endowment position of the consumer had been at

---

[2] The increase in the rate of interest will usually, but not always, increase the amount of lending. The reason is that (as in the case of an increase in the wage rate), an increase in the rate of interest gives rise to a substitution effect and an income effect. According to the substitution effect, the increase in the rate of interest leads the individual to lend more. However, by increasing the future income of the individual, the increase in the rate of interest also gives rise to an income effect, which leads the individual to lend less. At a sufficiently high rate of interest, the negative income effect exceeds the positive substitution effect and the individual's supply curve of loans bends backward. This is examined in Problem 5(a), with the answer at the end of the text.

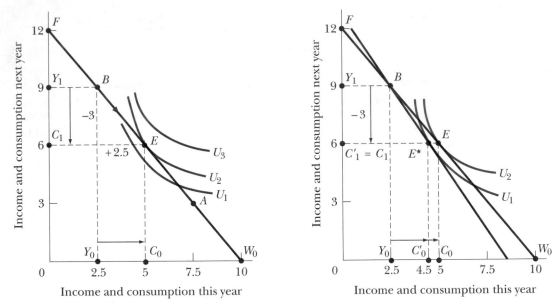

FIGURE 16.2   Borrowing   Starting from endowment B ($Y_0 = 2.5$ and $Y_1 = 9$), the consumer maximizes satisfaction at point E, where budget line FW_0 is tangent to indifference curve U_2 in the left panel. The consumer reaches point E by borrowing $C_0 - Y_0 = 2.5$ and repaying $Y_1 - C_1 = 3$ next year. Thus, the slope of the budget line is $-3/2 = -1.2$ or $-1(1 + 0.2)$ and the interest rate $r = 0.2$ or 20%. At $r = 50\%$, the optimal point is E^* in the right panel, where the steeper budget line through point B is tangent to indifference curve U_1. Point E^* is reached by borrowing 2 units (instead of 2.5).

point B ($Y_0 = 2.5$ and $Y_1 = 9$) on budget line FW_0. The consumer would maximize satisfaction at point E ($C_0 = 5$ and $C_1 = 6$), where budget line FW_0 is tangent to indifference curve U_2 (the highest the consumer can reach with budget line FW_0). To reach point E, the consumer would have to borrow $C_0 - Y_0 = 2.5$ units of the commodity this year and repay $Y_1 - C_1 = 3$ units next year.

Since $3/2.5 = 1.2$, the rate of interest $r = 0.2$ or 20%, as in the lending example. This means that in order to borrow 2.5 units this year, the individual must repay 3 units next year if the market rate of interest is 20%. That is, $2.5 = 3/(1 + 0.2)$. The reason for this is that 2.5 units this year will grow to 3 units next year at $r = 0.2$ or 20%. More generally, we can say that the price of \$1.00 today (P_0) is equal to \$1.00 next year (P_1) divided by $(1 + r)$. That is,

$$P_0 = P_1/(1 + r) \qquad\qquad [16.3]$$

This is obtained by dividing both sides of equation [16.2] by $(1 + r)$. For example, at $r = 20\%$, \$1.00 next year is equivalent to \$1/(1 + 0.2) = \$0.83 this year, because \$0.83 lent this year at 20% will grow to \$1.00 next year.

If the individual borrowed all of next year's income of $Y_1 = 9$, he or she could increase consumption this year by \$9/(1 + 0.2) = 7.5 and be at point $W_0 = 10$. Point $W_0 = 10$ gives the **wealth** of the individual. This is equal to the individual's income or endowment this year plus the present value of next year's income or endowment. That is, the consumer's wealth is given by

$$W_0 = Y_0 + [Y_1/(1 + r)] \tag{16.4}$$

In our example, the income this year is $Y_0 = 2.5$ and the present value of next year's income is $Y_1/(1 + r) = 9/(1 + 0.2) = 7.5$, resulting in the individual's wealth of 10. Graphically, the wealth of the individual or consumer is given by the intersection of the budget line with the horizontal axis. Thus, wealth plays the same role in intertemporal choice as the consumer's income plays in the consumer's choice between two commodities during the same year. An increase in wealth, like an increase in income, will shift the consumer's budget line outward and allows the consumer to purchase more of every normal good or to consume more, both this year and next.

   An increase in the rate of interest leads to a reduction in the amount the individual wants to borrow. Since present consumption becomes more expensive in terms of the future consumption that must be given up, the borrower will borrow less. This is shown in the right panel of Figure 16.2. Starting once again with endowment position B in the right panel of Figure 16.2, an increase in the rate of interest to 50% will result in a new budget line with a slope of $-(1 + 0.5)$. The optimal choice of the consumer is then at point E^*, where the steeper budget line through point B is tangent to lower indifference curve U_1. Indifference curve U_1 is the highest that the consumer can reach with his or her initial endowment position B and $r = 50\%$. To reach point E^* ($C_0' = 4.5$ and $C_1' = C_1 = 6$), the consumer will have to borrow $C_0' - Y_0 = 2$ units (instead of 2.5) this year, and will have to repay Y_1 $C_1' = 3$ units next year. That is, $2 = 3/(1 + 0.5)$. Thus, the increase in the rate of interest from 20% to 50% leads this individual to borrow less.[3]

The Market Rate of Interest with Borrowing and Lending

We now examine how the equilibrium rate of interest is determined in the market for borrowing and lending. For simplicity, we assume that we have only two individuals in the market for loans: individual B with endowment position B and individual A with endowment position A on budget line FW_0 (see the left panel of Figure 16.2). That is, instead of assuming as above that an individual has either endowment B (and is a borrower) or endowment A (and is a lender), we now assume that we have two individuals, one with endowment B (the borrower) and the other with endowment A (the lender) on FW_0. We also assume for now that both individuals have the same tastes or time preferences for present (this year) versus future (next year) consumption, as shown by indifference curves U_1, U_2, and U_3 in the left panel of Figure 16.2.

   As we can see from the left panel of Figure 16.2, the optimal choice for individual B is to move from point B to point E along budget line FW_0 by borrowing 2.5 units of the commodity this year at the rate of interest of 0.20 or 20% (so that he or she will have to repay 3 units next year). Thus, the quantity demanded of loans (borrowing) by individual B is 2.5 units at $r = 20\%$. On the other hand, the optimal choice of individual A is to move from

---

[3] As opposed to the supply curve of loans, which could bend backward at a sufficiently high rate of interest, the demand curve for loans is always negatively sloped (see Problem 5(b), with the answer at the end of the text).

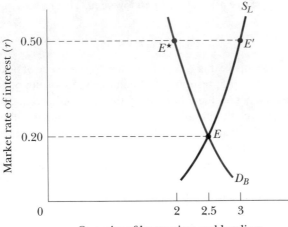

FIGURE 16.3   Borrowing-Lending Equilibrium
Borrowing–lending equilibrium occurs at point E, where the demand curve for borrowing (D_B) intersects the supply curve for lending (S_L). Point E shows that $r = 20\%$ and 2.5 units are borrowed and lent. At $r = 50\%$, the quantity supplied of lending of 3 units (point E') exceeds the quantity demanded of borrowing of 2 units (point E^*) and the interest rate falls to 20% (point E). The opposite is true at r lower than 20%.

point A to point E along budget line FW_0 by lending 2.5 units of the commodity this year at the rate of interest of 0.20 or 20% (so that he or she will receive an additional 3 units next year). Thus, the quantity supplied of loans (lending) by individual A is 2.5 units at $r = 20\%$.

Since we have assumed that A and B are the only two individuals in the market, the equilibrium market rate of interest is 0.20 or 20%. This is the only market rate of interest at which the desired quantity demanded of loans (borrowing) of 2.5 units equals the desired quantity supplied of loans (lending) of 2.5 units, and the market for loanable funds is in equilibrium. This is shown by point E in Figure 16.3, where the demand curve for borrowing (D_B) intersects the supply curve for lending (S_L). The figure also shows that at $r = 50\%$, individual B wants to borrow only 2 units (point E^* on D_B, from the right panel of Figure 16.2) and individual A wants to lend 3 units (point E' on D_L, from the right panel of Figure 16.1). The resulting excess in the quantity supplied over the quantity demanded of loans of 1 unit (E^*E') at $r = 50\%$ causes the rate of interest to fall to the equilibrium level of $r = 20\%$ (point E).

In the above analysis, we have assumed for simplicity that there are only two individuals, A and B, in the market and that both have identical tastes or time preferences.[4] In the real world, however, there are many individuals with different tastes. Yet, the process by which the equilibrium market rate of interest is determined is basically the same. That is, the equilibrium market rate of interest is the one at which the total or aggregate quantity

---

[4] The determination of the market rate of interest when consumers have different time preferences is examined in Problem 4 (with the answer at the end of the text).

demanded of borrowing matches the aggregate quantity supplied of lending. At a market rate of interest above the equilibrium rate, the supply of lending exceeds the demand for borrowing and the interest rate falls. On the other hand, at a market rate of interest below the equilibrium rate, the demand for borrowing exceeds the supply of lending and the market rate of interest rises toward equilibrium. Only at the equilibrium market rate of interest does the quantity demanded match the quantity supplied and there is no tendency for the interest rate to change. Example 16–1 gives examines data on personal savings and disposable personal income in the United States.

EXAMPLE 16–1

Personal Savings in the United States

Table 16.1 shows the total aggregate amount of personal savings (PS) and the level of disposable (i.e., after tax) personal income (DPI) in 1996 prices, and PS as a percentage of DPI in the United States for 1960, 1970, 1980, 1990, and 1995 through 2000. Personal savings were $120.0 billion in 1960, rose to a high of $390.4 billion in 1990, and fell to a low of $63.0 billion in 2000. As a percentage of GDP, personal savings were 7.2 in 1960, rose to 10.2 in 1980, and was only 1.0 in 2000. Americans are simply not saving much any more voluntarily.

Prior to the establishment of Social Security in 1935, individuals provided for their retirement by voluntarily saving a portion of their earnings during their working years. Social Security provided retirement income through a forced savings (Social Security tax) program, thus reducing the need for personal savings. If the government had saved the Social Security taxes it levied, net savings (personal plus government) would have been more or less unchanged. Because the government chose not to "fund" the system,

TABLE 16.1	Personal Savings and Disposable Personal Income (in billions of 1996 dollars)		
Year	PS	DPI	PS as a Percentage of DPI
1960	$120.0	$1,664.8	7.2
1970	248.2	2,630.0	9.4
1980	372.4	3,658.0	10.2
1990	390.4	5,014.2	7.8
1995	308.9	5,539.1	5.6
1996	272.1	5,677.7	4.8
1997	248.1	5,854.5	4.2
1998	292.6	6,168.6	4.7
1999	153.7	6,320.0	2.4
2000	63.0	6,539.2	1.0

Source: Council of Economic Advisors, *Economic Report of the President* (Washington, D.C.: U.S. Government Printing Office, 2002), pp. 357–358.

but to use Social Security taxes for current expenditures and pay future Social Security benefits out of future taxes, the nation's level of aggregate savings declined. Michael Darby estimated that the Social Security program reduced the nation's savings by 5% to 20% in the 1970s (and by much more in the 1990s).

Source: Michael R. Darby, *The Effects of Social Security on Income and Capital Stock* (Washington, D.C.: American Enterprise Institute, 1979).

16.2   SAVING–INVESTMENT EQUILIBRIUM

In Section 16.1 we analyzed borrowing–lending equilibrium. For simplicity, we assumed that no part of the current endowment or output was invested to increase future productive capacity. In this section, we begin with the opposite situation and examine saving–investment equilibrium without borrowing or lending. That is, we begin by examining the case in which an isolated individual (a Robinson Crusoe) consumes less than he or she produces in this period (saves) in order to have more seeds, or to produce a piece of equipment, to increase production in the next period (invests). Next, we relax the assumption that the individual is isolated and that he or she cannot borrow or lend and examine saving–investment equilibrium with borrowing and lending. Finally, we show how the equilibrium rate of interest is determined with saving and investment and with borrowing and lending.

Saving–Investment Equilibrium without Borrowing and Lending

Suppose that an individual lives alone on an island and produces and consumes a single commodity. This Robinson Crusoe has no possibility to borrow or lend (or trade) the commodity and can only consume what he produces. Suppose that under present conditions he can count on producing $Y_0 = 7.5$ units of the commodity during this year and $Y_1 = 3$ units next year. This is shown by point A on the production-possibilities curve FQ in Figure 16.4.

Production-possibilities curve FQ shows how much Crusoe can produce and consume next year by saving part of this year's output and investing it to increase next year's output. **Saving** refers to the act of refraining from present consumption. **Investment** refers to the formation of new capital assets. For example, Crusoe may use part of the year to construct a rudimentary net rather than catch fish with a spear. Since he is not catching fish while he is building the net, he is refraining from present consumption (saving). The net is an investment that will allow him to catch more fish in the future. In this case, the saving and the investment are done by the same person, and are one and the same thing.

Disregarding for the moment the indifference curves in Figure 16.4, we see that the FQ curve shows that if the individual consumes $C_0 = 6$ units of the commodity this year, he can produce and consume $C_1 = 6.5$ units of the commodity next year (point G on FQ). Starting from point A, this means that by saving and investing $Y_0 - C_0 = 7.5 - 6 = 1.5$ units of the commodity this year, the individual can increase output by $C_1 - Y_1 = 6.5 - 3 = 3.5$ units next year. Thus, the average yield or return on investment (in terms of next year's output) is $3.5/1.5 = 2.33 = (1 + 1.33)$ or 133%. Should the individual save and invest 3 units of the

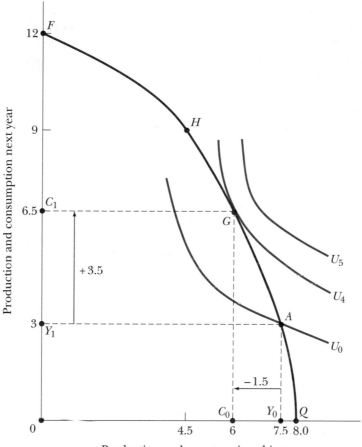

FIGURE 16.4   Saving-Investment Equilibrium without Borrowing or Lending   Production-possibilities curve *FQ* shows how much an isolated individual can produce and consume next year by saving and investing part of this year's output. Starting at point *A* on *FQ*, the optimal level of saving and investment is 1.5 units. This level allows the individual to reach point *G* on the highest indifference curve possible (U_4). Saving and investing 1.5 units this year allows the individual to produce and consume 3.5 more units next year. Thus, the average yield on investment is 133%.

commodity this year, his output will increase by 6 units next year (the movement from point *A* to point *H* on *FQ*), so that the average yield or rate of return would be $6/3 = 2 = (1 + 1)$ or 100%. Note that the larger the amount invested, the lower the rate of return (because of the operation of the law of diminishing returns).

Starting at point *A* on production-possibilities curve *FQ*, the question is, "What is the optimal amount of saving and investment for this individual?" The answer is 1.5 units. The reason is that this will permit the individual to reach point *G* on indifference curve U_4.

Indifference curve U_4 is the highest that Crusoe can reach with his production-possibilities curve. Note that indifference curves here show the trade-off or time preference between consumption this year and next. Thus, starting from point A, Crusoe should save and invest 1.5 units of this year's output so as to reach point G next year and maximize his total or joint utility or satisfaction over the two years.

Saving–Investment Equilibrium with Borrowing and Lending

Suppose that more people get stranded on Crusoe's island, and they also start producing and consuming the commodity. Now, borrowing and lending become possible. The optimal choice for Crusoe is now to save and invest, borrow or lend, so as to reach the highest indifference curve possible (higher than U_4).

To show this, we must realize that from every point of the production-possibilities curve there is a **market line,** the slope of which shows the rate at which the individual (Crusoe) can borrow or lend in the market. For example, starting at point A on the FQ curve in Figure 16.5, the individual can borrow or lend along market line FAW_0 at the rate of interest of $r = 20\%$ (as in the left panel of Figures 16.1 and 16.2). If starting from point A the individual only borrows or lends (or does neither), his wealth is $W_0 = 10$ (given by the intersection of market line FAW_0 with the horizontal axis).

However, with the possibility of saving and investment, and borrowing or lending now open, the optimal choice for Crusoe is to invest first (so as to maximize wealth) and then to borrow (so as to reach the highest indifference curve possible). Wealth is maximized by reaching the highest market line (with slope reflecting the market rate of interest) that is possible with the FQ curve. This is given by market line $HE''W_0'$, which is parallel to market line FAW_0 (so that $r = 20\%$) and tangent to production-possibilities curve FQ at point H. Market line $HE''W_0'$ shows that the maximum attainable wealth is $W_0' = 12$. Starting from point A on the FQ curve, the individual can attain market line $HE''W_0'$ and maximize wealth by investing $Y_0 - Q_0 = 3$ units of this year's output. This allows him to reach point H on this production-possibilities curve and produce $Q_1 = 9$ units of the commodity next year.

Having attained the highest wealth possible by investing 3 units of the commodity (point H on market line $HE''W_0'$), the individual can then borrow $C_0 - Q_0 = 2.5$ units (i.e., move to the right of point H on market line $HE''W_0'$) and reach point E'' on U_5. This is the highest indifference curve that the individual can reach with optimal investment and borrowing. Point E'' on indifference curve U_5 is superior to point A on U_0 (see Figure 16.4) without borrowing or investing, it is superior to borrowing alone (to the right of point A along budget line FEW_0), and it is superior to point G on U_4 (see Figure 16.4) with saving equal to investment and no borrowing.

To summarize, the optimal choice of the individual is to invest $Y_0 - Q_0 = 3$ units (i.e., to move from point A to point H on the FQ curve) in order to maximize wealth (at $W_0' = 12$) and to borrow $C_0 - Q_0 = 2.5$ units (the movement from point H to point E'' on indifference curve U_5) to maximize total or joint satisfaction or utility over both years. Of the total amount of $Y_0 - Q_0 = 3$ invested, the individual borrows $C_0 - Q_0 = 2.5$ and saves $Y_0 - C_0 = 0.5$. That is, the individual is saving a portion of his current output, but not enough to "finance" all of his investment. Therefore, other individuals must be saving

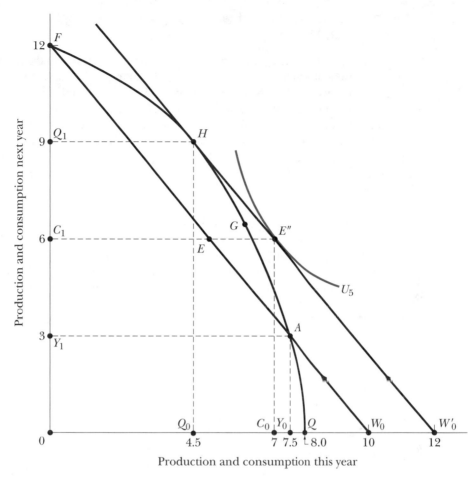

FIGURE 16.5   Saving-Investment Equilibrium with Borrowing and Lending   Starting from point A, the individual maximizes wealth (at $W_0' = 12$ units) by investing 3 units of the commodity and reaching point H, where market line $HE''W_0'$ (with slope reflecting the market rate of interest) is tangent to production-possibilities curve FQ. The individual then borrows 2.5 units (i.e., moves to the right of point H on market line $HE''W_0'$) and reaches point E'' on U_5 (the highest indifference curve possible). The individual invests 3 units, borrows 2.5, and saves 0.5.

2.5 units of the commodity more than they invest in order to lend this amount to our individual.

If the market rate of interest rises above $r = 20\%$, the market line becomes steeper and tangent to production-possibilities curve FQ to the right of point H, and the individual will invest less (see Figure 16.6 and Problem 6). If the individual borrows more than he invests, he will be dissaving (see Problem 7). If indifference curve U_5 had been tangent to market line HW_0' to the left of point H in Figure 16.5, the individual would have been investing and lending (rather than investing and borrowing) so that his saving would equal the sum of the two (see Problem 8).

The Market Rate of Interest with Saving and Investment, Borrowing and Lending

We now examine how the equilibrium rate of interest is determined in the market with saving and investment and borrowing and lending. For simplicity, we assume that only our individual, borrows and invests while all other individuals collectively only want to lend 2.5 units of the commodity at the rate of interest of $r = 20\%$. The equilibrium rate of interest is then 20% and is shown in Figure 16.6 in two different ways: (1) by point E, where the demand curve of borrowing of our individual (D_B) intersects the supply curve of lending of all other individuals (S_L) as in Figure 16.3, or equivalently, (2) by point E'', where the demand curve for investment of our individual (D_I) intersects the total supply curve of savings of this and other individuals (S_S).

At the equilibrium market rate of interest of $r = 20\%$, the quantity of desired borrowing of 2.5 units (done exclusively by our individual) equals the quantity of desired lending of 2.5 units (supplied by all other individuals). In addition, at $r = 20\%$, the total amount of desired savings of 3 units (2.5 units by other individuals and 0.5 units by our individual) matches the desired level of investment of 3 units (undertaken exclusively by our individual). That is, at equilibrium, desired borrowing equals desired lending (point E) and desired savings equals desired investment (point E''). Note that the excess between the saving-investment equilibrium and the borrowing-lending equilibrium refers to the amount of

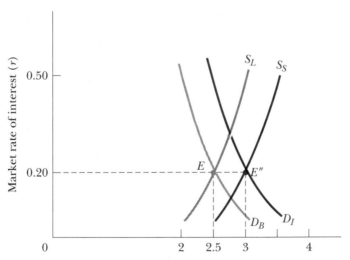

Quantity of borrowing and lending, investment and saving

FIGURE 16.6 Rate of Interest with Borrowing and Lending, Investment and Saving The equilibrium rate of interest is 20% and is shown (1) by point E, where the demand curve for borrowing (D_B) intersects the supply curve of lending (S_L), and (2) by point E'', where the demand curve for investment (D_I) intersects the total supply curve of savings (S_S). At $r > 20\%$, desired lending exceeds desired borrowing, and desired savings exceeds desired investments, and r falls. The opposite is true at $r < 20\%$.

investment that is self-financed from the investor's own savings rather than from borrowing in the market.[5]

At a rate of interest above equilibrium, there will be (1) an excess in the quantity supplied of lending over the quantity demanded of borrowing, and (2) an excess in the total quantity supplied of savings over the total quantity demanded of investment (see Figure 16.6). As a result, the interest rate will fall to the equilibrium level. The opposite is true at rates of interest below equilibrium. Of course, in the real world, there are many borrowers and many lenders, and many savers and investors, but the principles by which the equilibrium rate of interest is determined are the same (when capital markets are perfectly competitive). That is, at equilibrium, aggregate desired borrowing equals aggregate desired lending, and aggregate desired investment equals aggregate desired saving. Example 16–2 examines data on personal and business savings, and gross and net private domestic investment in the United States.

EXAMPLE 16-2

Personal and Business Savings, and Gross and Net Private Domestic Investment in the United States

Table 16.2 presents the total or aggregate amount of personal savings (PS), business savings (BS), gross private domestic investment (GPDI), and net private domestic

TABLE 16.2	Personal and Business Savings and Gross and Net Private Domestic Investment in the United States (in billions of 1996 dollars)					
Year	PS	BS	GPDI	NPDI	NNP	NPDI as a Percentage of NNP
1960	$120.0	$ 263.9	$ 272.8	$ 163.6	$2,154.9	7.6
1970	248.2	374.1	436.2	263.1	3,345.1	7.9
1980	372.4	601.3	655.3	348.7	4,499.0	7.8
1990	390.4	797.8	907.3	511.1	5,991.5	8.5
1995	308.9	982.9	1,140.6	694.3	6,639.3	10.5
1996	272.1	1,018.3	1,242.7	780.0	6,875.0	11.3
1997	248.1	1,069.0	1,393.3	910.2	7,165.9	12.7
1998	292.6	1,106.7	1,558.0	1,050.6	7,474.9	14.1
1999	153.7	1,133.7	1,660.1	1,124.6	7,745.4	14.5
2000	63.0	1,167.4	1,772.9	1,205.7	8,016.1	15.0

Source: Council of Economic Advisors, *Economic Report of the President* (Washington, D.C.: U.S. Government Printing Office, 2002), pp. 322, 338, 350, 358.

---

[5] Just as some people can borrow more than they invest so that they dissave, so some individuals can consume more than the sum of what they produce, borrow, and invest. Such individuals would be *disinvesting* or failing to maintain (i.e., not replacing depreciated) capital stock. To some extent, these individuals are "living off their capital." This may also be true for society as a whole during periods of war or natural disaster, or when it borrows abroad to increase present consumption.

investment (NPDI) in the United States in terms of 1996 prices for the years 1960, 1970, 1980, 1990, and 1995 through 2000. NPDI equals GPDI minus capital consumption allowances or depreciation resulting from the production of the given year's output. Table 16.2 also shows the level of real net national product (NNP) and NPDI as a percentage of NNP during the same years.

From the table, we see that business savings have steadily increased at the same time that personal savings have sharply declined. Net private domestic investment is the net addition to society's capital stock and is an important contributor to the growth of the economy and standards of living. Personal and business savings are required to provide for the replacement of the capital consumed during the course of producing current output and for the net additions to the capital stock of the country. Not included in the table are government savings and investments and foreign investments.

16.3 INVESTMENT DECISIONS

The previous discussion has important practical applications and is the basis for very valuable decision rules used by firms and government agencies in determining which investment project to undertake. For example, a bank may have to decide whether to purchase or rent a large computer, a government agency whether to build a dam, and a manufacturing firm whether it should purchase a more expensive machine that lasts longer or a cheaper one that lasts a shorter period of time. The decision rule to answer these questions and to rank various investment projects is called **capital budgeting.** Capital budgeting decisions require consideration of costs and returns that arise not only in the current period but also in the future and so we must find a way to compare future to present costs and returns. Our discussion of capital budgeting begins by considering a simple two-period time framework. We then extend and generalize the discussion to a multiperiod time horizon.

Net Present Value Rule for Investment Decisions: The Two-Period Case

An investment project involves a cost (to purchase the machinery, build the factory, acquire a skill, and so on) and a return in the form of an increase in output or income in the future. In a two-period framework, the cost is usually incurred in the current year and the return or benefit comes the following year. However, since one unit of a commodity or a dollar next year is worth less than a unit of the commodity or a dollar today, costs and benefits occurring at different times cannot simply be added together to determine whether to undertake the project.

For example, for a project that involves the expenditure of $1.00 this year and results in $1.50 return next year, we cannot simply add the −$1.00 of cost this year to the $1.50 return next year and say that the net value of the project is $0.50. The reason is that $1.50 next year is worth less than $1.50 today.[6] Specifically, if the rate of interest is 20%, $1.50 next

---

[6] We assume throughout this discussion that there is no price inflation. This assumption is relaxed in Section 16.4.

year is worth $\$1.50/(1.2) = \$1.25$ today. The reason is that $\$1.25$ today will grow to $\$1.50$ next year. That is, $\$1.25(1 + 0.2) = \$1.50$ if the interest rate or the rate of return is 20%. Thus, to determine the net return of an investment we must compare the cost incurred today with the value of the benefits *today*.

The **net present value (NPV)** of an investment is the value today of all the *net* cash flows of the investment. Expenditures or outflows are subtracted from revenues or inflows in each year to find the net cash flow. For a two-period time horizon, *NPV* is given by

$$NPV = -C + \frac{R_1}{1 + r} \qquad [16.5]$$

where C is the capital investment cost in the current year when the investment is made, R_1 is the net cash flow next year, and r is the rate of interest. For example, suppose that a firm purchases a machine this year for $\$100$, and this increases the firm's net income by $\$120$ next year. Suppose also that the rate of interest is 10%, and the machine has no salvage or scrap value at the end of the next year. The net present value of the machine (*NPV*) is

$$NPV = -\$100 + \frac{\$120}{(1 + 0.1)} = -\$100 + \$109.09 = \$9.09$$

This means that the purchase of the machine will increase the wealth of the firm by $\$9.09$.

Suppose the firm had to decide between the above project (with net present value of $\$9.09$) and another project that costs $\$150$ and generates a net income of $\$180$ next year. The firm should choose the second project because its net present value of $-\$150 + \$180/(1 + 0.1) = \$13.64$ exceeds the net present value of $\$9.09$ for the previous project. Such a choice arises because firms do not usually have or cannot usually borrow all of the resources required to undertake all of the projects that have a positive net present value.

We will see in the next section that the rule to undertake a project if its net present value is positive or to choose the project with the highest net present value is a general rule and applies to all projects, regardless of the number of periods or years over which the costs and returns of the project are spread. Furthermore, this rule is independent of the tastes or time preference of the investor. That is, regardless of the shape and location of the indifference curves of investors, the general investment or capital budgeting rule is to maximize the wealth of the firm. This is achieved by investing in projects with the highest (positive) net present value. The tastes of investors will then determine whether they will borrow or lend and how they will choose to use their (maximized) wealth. This means that if capital markets are perfect and costless (i.e., if borrowers and lenders are too small individually to affect the rate of interest and can borrow or lend at the same rate), then individuals' production and consumption decisions can be kept completely separate. This is sometimes called the **separation theorem.**

Net Present Value Rule for Investment Decisions: The Multiperiod Case

Most investment projects last longer than (i.e., give rise to net cash flows over more than) two periods. Thus, the investment rule given above must be extended to consider many periods (years). This can easily be done by "stretching" equation [16.5] to deal with many (n) years. This is given by

$$NPV = -C + \frac{R_1}{1+r} + \frac{R_2}{(1+r)^2} + \cdots + \frac{R_n}{(1+r)^n} \qquad [16.6]$$

where NPV is the net present value of the investment, C is the capital investment cost incurred this year when the investment is made, R_1 is the net cash flow from the investment next year, R_2 is the net cash flow in two years, R_n is the net cash flow in n years, and r is the rate of interest. Net cash flows refer to the revenue of the firm resulting from the investment during any given year minus the expenses or costs of the project during the same year. Thus, equation [16.5] is a special case of equation [16.6], applicable when there is no net cash flow after the first year.[7]

For example, suppose that a firm purchases a machine this year for $150, and this increases the firm's net income by $100 in each of the next two years. If the rate of interest is 10% and the machine has no salvage value after two years, the net present value of the machine (NPV) is

$$NPV = -C + \frac{R_1}{1+r} + \frac{R_2}{(1+r)^2} = -\$150 + \frac{\$100}{1+0.1} + \frac{\$100}{(1+0.1)^2}$$

$$= -\$150 + \$90.91 + \$82.64 = \$23.55$$

This means that the purchase of the machine will increase the wealth of the firm by $23.55. Specifically, $100 received next year is worth $100/(1 + 0.1) = $90.91 this year, because $90.91 this year grows to $100 next year at $r = 10\%$. On the other hand, $100 received two years from now is worth $100/(1 + 0.1)^2 = $82.64 this year because $82.64 this year grows to $90.91 next year at $r = 10\%$,[8] and the $90.91 next year grows to $100 the year after (i.e., two years from now) at $r = 10\%$. That is $82.64 today times $(1 + 0.1)^2$ or 1.21 equals $100 two years from now.

If the project generated a net cash flow of $100 in the third year also, this would be "worth" $100/(1 + 0.1)^3 = $100/(1.331) = $75.13 this year because $75.13 this year will grow to $100 (except for rounding errors) in three years at $r = 10\%$. Similarly, $100 in 10 years is worth $100/(1 + 0.1)^{10} = $38.55 this year because $38.55 this year will grow to $100 in 10 years at $r = 10\%$. Finally, $100 in n years (where n is any number of years) is worth $100/(1 + 0.1)^n$ this year because this sum today will grow to $100 in n years at $r = 10\%$.

The NPV for any net cash flow is inversely related to r. For example, if r had been 5% in the previous example, the net present value of the investment (NPV') would

[7] If we simply wanted to find the present discounted value (PDV) of a given sum (R) to be received in each of n years, starting with the next year, the equation would simply be

$$PDV = \frac{R}{(1+r)} + \frac{R}{(1+r)^2} + \cdots + \frac{R}{(1+r)^n}$$

If the given sum (R) were to be received in each year indefinitely or in perpetuity (an example of this is the British "consols"), then $PDV = R/r$ (see Section A.15 of the Mathematical Appendix).
[8] Actually, ($82.64)(1.1) equals $90.904 rather than $90.91 (as indicated) because of rounding errors.

have been

$$NPV' = -\$150 + \frac{\$100}{(1+0.05)^1} + \frac{\$100}{(1+0.05)^2}$$

$$= -\$150 + \$95.24 + \$90.70 = \$35.94$$

(as compared with the *NPV* of $23.55 with $r = 10\%$). On the other hand, if r had been 20%,

$$NPV'' = -\$150 + \frac{\$100}{(1+0.2)^1} + \frac{\$100}{(1+0.2)^2}$$

$$= -\$150 + \$83.33 + \$69.44 = \$2.77$$

The lower *NPV* when r is higher is due to the fact that with a higher r, the *net* cash flows from the project are "discounted" more heavily than the cost, because the net cash flows arise later in time than cost. Also note that the *net* cash flows should include the extra income generated by the machine minus the extra expense (such as maintenance and the higher cost of hiring more skilled workers) to operate the machine during each year. Similarly, the value today of the salvage value of the machine (if any) must also be included.

For example, suppose that the benefits and costs of an investment project (the purchase of a piece of machinery) are those given in Table 16.3. The table shows that the machine costs $1,000 to purchase this year and also gives rise to $200, $300, $300, and $400 maintenance and other expenses in each of the subsequent four years. The revenues from the investment are $600, $800, $800, and $800, and the salvage value of the machine is $200 at the end of the fourth year. The net revenue is the revenue from the investment minus the expenses in each year. The present value coefficient is $1/(1+0.1)^n$. For example, for the first year the present value coefficient is $1/(1+0.1)^1 = 0.909$. For the second year, it is $1/(1+0.1)^2 = 0.826$, and so on. The present value of the net revenue in each year is obtained by multiplying the net revenue (R) by the present value coefficient for that year.

TABLE 16.3 Benefit-Cost Analysis of an Investment Project

End of Year	Investment (Year 0) and Cost	Revenue	Net Revenue	Present Value Coefficient $1/(1+0.1)^n$	Present Value of Net Revenue
0	$1,000	. . .	−$1,000	. . .	−$1,000
1	200	$600	400	0.909	364
2	300	800	500	0.826	413
3	300	800	500	0.751	376
4	400	800	400	0.683	273
4	. . .	200*	200	0.683	137
					$563

*Salvage value.

By adding together all present values of the net revenues, we get the net present value of the project (V_0) of $563. Since *NPV* is positive, the firm should purchase the machine.

Sometimes, complications may arise in applying the net present value rule for investment decisions. First, projects may be interdependent, so that the stream of net cash flows from a project depends on whether other projects are undertaken at the same time. In such a case, the net present value of a group of projects may have to be evaluated together and compared with the net present value of other groups of projects. Second, it may sometimes be difficult to accurately forecast the future stream of net cash flows from a project. Third, the firm may not have the resources and may not be willing or able to borrow to undertake all of the projects that have a positive net present value. The firm should then choose those projects with the highest net present value.

EXAMPLE 16-3

Fields of Education and Higher Lifetime Earnings in the United States

Table 16.4 gives the present value of the higher lifetime earnings with a college degree in various fields in the United States in 2001. Present values were calculated by capitalizing (i.e., finding the present discounted value of) the difference between the higher yearly salaries with a bachelor's degree in the various fields over the average salary of workers with only a high school diploma. The interest rate used to find the present values was 5%. Only the benefits of going to college were included; the earnings foregone or opportunity costs and other costs (tuition, books, and so on) of going to college were not included. To be pointed out is that the higher earnings of the recipients of the bachelor's degree over the earnings of non-college graduates cannot be attributed entirely to college education. At least in part, the higher incomes of college graduates may be due to their higher level of intelligence, longer working hours, and more inherited wealth

TABLE 16.4 Present Values of Higher Lifetime Earnings with Bachelor's Degree in Various Fields, 2001

Field of Study	Higher Lifetime Earnings
Computer sciences	$579,740
Engineering	573,640
Business	400,720
Health sciences	362,020
Sciences	291,240
Agriculture & natural resources	202,180
Humanities & social sciences	190,320
Communications	150,740
Education	145,560

Source: Calculated from data reported in *Salary Survey,* National Association of Colleges and Employers, winter 2001.

than for non-college graduates. Earnings differentials with and without a college degree declined during the 1970s and increased during the 1980s and 1990s.

Source: "Soaring Payoff from Higher Education," *The Margin,* January/February 1990, p. 6; J. Bound and G. Johnson, "Changes in the Structure of Wages in the 1980s: An Evaluation of Alternative Explanations," *American Economic Review,* June 1992, pp. 371–392; "Technological Change Boosts Wage Gap," *The Margin,* Spring 1993, pp. 42–43; J. Mincer, "Investment in U.S. Education and Training," National Bureau of Economic Research, *Working Paper No. 4844,* October 1995; and "Making Sense of a Stubborn Education Gap," *New York Times,* July 23, 2000, p. 1.

16.4   DETERMINANTS OF THE MARKET RATES OF INTEREST

Until now we have discussed "the" interest rate; however, the rate of interest varies at different times and in different markets. Even at a given point in time and in a specific capital market, there is not a single rate of interest but many. That is, there is a different interest rate on different loans or investments depending on differences in (1) risk, (2) duration of the loan, (3) cost of administering the loan, and (4) tax treatment. We now briefly examine each of these in turn.

The major reason for differences in rates of interest at a given point in time and place is the risk of the loan. In general, the greater the risk, the higher the rate of interest. Two types of risk can be distinguished: default risk and variability risk. **Default risk** refers to the possibility that the loan will not be repaid. If the chance of default is 10%, the lender will usually charge a rate of interest 10% higher than on a loan with no risk of default, such as a government bond. Similarly, loans unsecured by collateral (such as installment credit) usually charge higher rates of interest than loans secured by collateral (such as home mortgages). **Variability risk** refers to the possibility that the yield or return on an investment, such as a stock, may vary considerably above or below the average. Given the usual aversion to risk, investors generally demand a premium or a higher yield for investments whose returns are more uncertain.

The second reason for differences in rates of interest is the duration of the loan. Loans for longer periods of time usually require higher rates of interest than loans for shorter durations. The reason is that the lender has less flexibility or liquidity with loans of longer duration, and so he or she will require a higher rate of interest. It is for this reason that savings deposits offer lower rates of interest than six-month certificates of deposit.[9]

The third reason for differences in rates of interest is the cost of administering the loan. Smaller loans and loans requiring frequent payments (such as installment loans) usually involve greater bookkeeping and service costs per dollar of the loan and, as a result, usually involve a higher interest charge. Finally, the tax treatment of interest and investment income can lead to differences in rates of interest among otherwise comparable loans and investments. For example, state and municipal bonds are exempted from federal income tax, and since investors look at the after-tax return, state and local governments can usually borrow at lower interest rates than corporations.

---

[9] Regulation may also account for part of the difference.

Thus, at a given point in time and in a given capital market there is a large number of interest rates depending on relative risk, term structure, administration costs, and tax treatment. Yet all of these rates of interest are related. If individuals and firms collectively decide to save less (a leftward shift in the aggregate supply curve of savings), interest rates will rise. Interest rates will also rise if the time preference of consumers shifts in favor of the present or if the net productivity or yield of capital increases. In addition, a rise in short-term rates will lead to higher long-term rates, and vice versa. Furthermore, higher interest rates for comparable instruments in one market than in another market will lead to an outflow of funds from the latter to the former. These flows of funds will reduce (and may eventually eliminate) interest rate differences between the two markets. Specifically, the supply curve of funds will shift to the left (i.e., the supply of funds decreases) and interest rates will rise in the market with lower rates of interest. The opposite occurs in the market with the higher rates of interest, causing interest rates to fall there.

Finally, a distinction must be made between real and nominal or money interest rates. Until this point, we have been discussing the **real rate of interest (r).** This refers to the premium on a unit of a commodity or real consumption income today compared to a unit of the commodity or real consumption income in the future. However, in the everyday usage of the term, the interest rate refers to the nominal or money rate of interest. The **nominal rate of interest (r')** refers to the premium on a unit of a monetary claim today compared to a unit of monetary claim in the future. The nominal rate of interest (r') is affected by the anticipated rate of price inflation (i), while the real rate of interest is not. Thus, the nominal rate of interest equals the real rate of interest plus the anticipated rate of price inflation. That is,

$$r' = r + i \qquad [16.7]$$

The reason for this is that during the period of the loan, the general price level may rise (i.e., inflation may occur) so that the loan is repaid with dollars of lower purchasing power than the dollars borrowed. Therefore, the nominal rate of interest must be sufficiently high to cover any increase in the price level (or in the price of real claims) during the loan period. It is primarily to avoid this complication (and to deal with the real rate of interest) that we chose to borrow and lend a *commodity* in Sections 16.1 and 16.2.

Anyone who borrows money now and repays in money in the future must expect to pay an additional monetary amount to cover any anticipated increase in the monetary price of real claims by the time of repayment. Only if anticipated inflation is zero will $r' = r$. Since some price inflation is always occurring, r' usually exceeds r. For example, if $r' = 11\%$ and $i = 6\%$, then $r = 5\%$. We have concentrated on the real rate of interest throughout most of the chapter because it is the real, and not the nominal, rate of interest that primarily affects incentives to borrow and lend, and to save and invest.

EXAMPLE 16-4

Nominal and Real Interest Rates in the United States: 1981–2001

Table 16.5 shows the nominal annual interest rates on three-month U.S. Treasury bills, the change in the Consumer Price Index, and the real interest rate (the difference between the nominal interest rate and the change in the Consumer Price Index) in the United

TABLE 16.5	Nominal and Real Interest Rates on Three-Month U.S. Treasury Bills: 1981–2001		
Year	Nominal Interest Rate	Change in Consumer Price Index	Real Interest Rate
1981	14.0	10.3	3.7
1982	10.7	6.2	4.5
1983	8.6	3.2	5.4
1984	9.6	4.3	5.3
1985	7.5	3.6	3.9
1986	6.0	1.9	4.1
1987	5.8	3.6	2.2
1988	6.7	4.1	2.6
1989	8.1	4.8	3.3
1990	7.5	5.4	2.1
1991	5.4	4.2	1.2
1992	3.5	3.0	0.5
1993	3.0	3.0	0.0
1994	4.3	2.6	1.7
1995	5.5	2.8	2.7
1996	5.0	3.0	2.0
1997	5.1	2.3	2.8
1998	4.8	1.6	3.2
1999	4.7	2.2	2.5
2000	5.9	3.4	2.5
2001	3.5	2.8	0.7

Source: Council of Economic Advisers, *Economic Report of the President* (Washington, D.C.: U.S. Government Printing Office, 2002), pp. 394, 406.

States from 1981 to 2001. The implicit assumption made here is that the anticipated rate of inflation is equal to the actual rate of inflation. Since the nominal interest rate was greater than the change in the Consumer Price Index (except for 1993, when it was equal), the real interest rate was positive (except for 1993, when it was zero). Note that, as expected, the nominal interest rate moved in the same direction as the change in the Consumer Price Index (except in 1986–1987, 1989–1990, 1995–1996, and 1998–2000).

EXAMPLE 16–5

Investment Risks and Returns in the United States

Table 16.6 shows that riskier assets, such as common stocks or long-term corporate bonds, have provided higher average real rates of returns than more liquid and less risky assets, such as U.S. (three-month) Treasury bills, in the United States over the period

	TABLE 16.6	**Investment Risks and Returns in the United States, 1926–2000**	

Asset	Real Rate of Return (%)	Risk (Standard Deviation, %)
Common stocks	9.8	20.2
Long-term corporate bonds	2.8	8.7
U.S. Treasury bills	0.7	3.2

Source: Ibbotson & Associates, *Stocks, Bonds, Bills, and Inflation, 2001 Yearbook* (Chicago, 2001), p. 14.

from 1926 to 2000. While corporate bonds can provide higher returns than stocks during some years, over many years, the reverse is usually true. Here risk is measured as the standard deviation of the real return as a percentage of the mean or average real return. Common stocks involve a great deal of variability risk while long-term corporate bonds involve a greater default risk and are less liquid (and therefore provide higher average real returns) than U.S. Treasury bills. Clearly, risk-averse investors must balance expected return against risk in their investment decisions.

16.5   THE COST OF CAPITAL

We now examine how a firm estimates the cost of raising capital to invest. This is an essential element of the capital budgeting process. The firm can raise investment funds internally (i.e., from undistributed profits) or externally (i.e., by borrowing and/or from selling stocks). The cost of using internal funds is the opportunity cost or foregone return on these funds outside the firm. The cost of external funds is the lowest rate of return that lenders and stockholders require to lend to or invest their funds in the firm. In this section, we examine how the cost of debt (i.e., the cost of raising capital by borrowing) and the cost of equity capital (i.e., the cost of raising capital by selling stocks) are determined. The estimation of the cost of debt is fairly straightforward. On the other hand, there are at least three methods of estimating the cost of equity capital: the risk-free rate plus premium, the dividend valuation model, and the capital asset pricing model (CAPM). These methods will be examined in turn.

Cost of Debt

The **cost of debt** is the return that lenders require to lend their funds to the firm. Since the interest payments made by the firm on borrowed funds are deductible from the firm's taxable income, the *after-tax* cost of borrowed funds to the firm (k_d) is given by the interest paid (r) multiplied by 1 minus the firm's marginal tax rate, t. That is,

$$k_d = r(1 - t)$$ [16.8]

For example, if the firm borrows at a 12.5% interest rate and faces a 40% marginal tax rate on its taxable income, the after-tax cost of debt capital to the firm is

$$k_d = 12.5\%(1 - 0.40) = 7.5\%$$

Cost of Equity Capital: The Risk-Free Rate Plus Premium

As pointed out earlier, the cost of equity capital is the rate of return that stockholders require to invest in the firm. The cost of raising equity capital externally usually exceeds the cost of raising equity capital internally by the flotation costs (i.e., the costs of issuing the stock). For simplicity, we disregard these costs in the following analysis and treat both types of equity capital together. Since dividends paid on stocks (as opposed to the interest paid on bonds) are not deductible as a business expense (i.e., dividends are paid out after corporate taxes have been paid), there is no tax adjustment in determining the equity cost of capital.

One method employed to estimate the cost of equity capital (k_e) is to use the risk-free rate (r_f) plus a risk premium (r_p). That is,

$$k_e = r_f + r_p \qquad [16.9]$$

The risk-free rate (r_f) is usually taken to be the six-month U.S. Treasury bill rate.[10] This is because the obligation to make payments of the interest and principal on government securities is assumed to occur with certainty. The risk premium (r_p) that must be paid in raising equity capital has two components. The first component results because of the greater risk that is involved in investing in a firm's securities (such as bonds) as opposed to investing in federal government securities. The second component is the additional risk resulting from purchasing the common stock rather than the bonds of the firm. Stocks involve a greater risk than bonds because dividends on stocks are paid only after the firm has met its contractual obligations to make interest and principal payments to bondholders. Because dividends vary with the firm's profits, stocks are more risky than bonds, so that their return must include an additional risk premium. If the premiums associated with these two types of risk are labeled p_1 and p_2, we can restate the formula for the cost of equity capital as

$$k_e = r_f + p_1 + p_2 \qquad [16.10]$$

The first type of risk (i.e., p_1) is usually measured by the excess of the rate of interest on the firm's bonds (r) over the rate of return on government bonds (r_f). The additional risk involved in purchasing the firm's stocks rather than bonds (i.e., p_2) is usually taken to be about four percentage points. This is the historical difference between the average yield (dividends plus capital gains) on stocks as opposed to the average yield on bonds issued by private companies. For example, if the risk-free rate of return on government securities is 8% and the firm's bonds yield 11%, the total risk premium (r_p) involved in purchasing the firm's stocks rather than government bonds is

$$r_p = p_1 + p_2 = (11\% - 8\%) + 4\% = 3\% + 4\% = 7\%$$

so that the firm's cost of equity capital is

$$k_e = r_f + p_1 + p_2 = 8\% + 3\% + 4\% = 15\%$$

---

[10] Some securities analysts prefer to use instead the long-term government bond rate for r_f.

Cost of Equity Capital: The Dividend Valuation Model

The equity cost of capital to a firm can also be estimated by the **dividend valuation model.** To derive this model, we begin by pointing out that, with perfect information, the value of a share of the common stock of a firm should be equal to the present value of all future dividends expected to be paid on the stock, discounted at the investor's required rate of return (k_e). If the dividend per share (D) paid to stockholders is expected to remain constant over time, the present value of a share of the common stock of the firm (P) is then

$$P = \sum_{t=1}^{\infty} \frac{D}{(1+k_e)^t} \qquad [16.11]$$

If dividends are assumed to remain constant over time and to be paid indefinitely, equation [16.11] can be rewritten as

$$P = \frac{D}{k_e} \qquad [16.12]$$

If dividends are instead expected to increase over time at the annual rate of g, the price of a share of the common stock of the firm will be greater and is given by

$$P = \frac{D}{k_e - g} \qquad [16.13]$$

Solving equation [16.13] for k_e, we get the following equation to measure the equity cost of capital to the firm:

$$k_e = \frac{D}{P} + g \qquad [16.14]$$

That is, the investor's required rate of return on equity is equal to the ratio of the dividend paid on a share of the common stock of the firm to the price of a share of the stock (the so-called dividend yield) plus the expected growth rate of dividend payments by the firm (g). The value of g is the firm's historic growth rate or the earnings growth forecasts of securities analysts (based on the expected sales, profit margins, and competitive position of the firm) published in *Business Week, Forbes,* and other business publications.

For example, if the firm pays a dividend of $20 per share on common stock that sells for $200 per share and the growth rate of dividend payments is expected to be 5% per year, the cost of equity capital for this firm is

$$k_e = \frac{\$20}{\$200} + 0.05 = 0.10 + 0.05 = 0.15 \text{ or } 15\%$$

Cost of Equity Capital: The Capital Asset Pricing Model (CAPM)

Another method commonly used to estimate the equity cost of capital is the **capital asset pricing model (CAPM).** This model considers not only the risk differential between common stocks and government securities but also the risk differential between the common stock of the firm and the average common stock of all firms, or broad-based market portfolio. The risk differential between common stocks and government securities is measured by ($k_m - r_f$), where k_m is the average return on all common stocks and r_f is the return on government securities.

The risk differential between the common stock of a particular firm and the common stock of all firms is called the **beta coefficient,** β. This is the ratio of the variability in the return of the common stock of the firm to the variability in the average return on the common stocks of all firms. Beta coefficients for individual stocks can be obtained from the *Value Line Investment Survey,* Merrill Lynch, or other brokerage firms.

A beta coefficient of 1 means that the variability in the returns on the common stock of the firm is the same as the variability in the returns on all stocks. Thus, investors holding the stock of the firm face the same risk as holding a broad-based market portfolio of all stocks. A beta coefficient of 2 means that the variability in the returns on (i.e., risk of holding) the stock of the firm is twice that of the average stock. On the other hand, holding a stock with a beta coefficient of 0.5 is half as risky as holding the average stock.

The cost of equity capital to the firm estimated by the capital asset pricing model (CAPM) is then measured by

$$k_e = r_f + \beta(k_m - r_f) \qquad\qquad [16.15]$$

where k_e is the cost of equity capital to the firm, r_f is the risk-free rate, β is the beta coefficient, and k_m is the average return on the stock of all firms. Thus, CAPM postulates that the cost of equity capital to the firm is equal to the sum of the risk-free rate plus the beta coefficient (β) times the risk premium on the average stock ($k_m - r_f$). Note that multiplying β by ($k_m - r_f$) gives the risk premium on holding the common stock of the particular firm.

For example, suppose that the risk-free rate (r_f) is 8%, the average return on common stocks (k_m) is 15%, and the beta coefficient (β) for the firm is 1. The cost of equity capital to the firm (k_e) is then

$$k_e = 8\% + 1(15\% - 8\%) = 15\%$$

That is, since a beta coefficient of 1 indicates that the stock of this firm is as risky as the average stock of all firms, the equity cost of capital to the firm is 15% (the same as the average return on all stocks). If $\beta = 1.5$ for the firm (so that the risk involved in holding the stock of the firm is 1.5 times larger than the risk on the average stock), the equity cost of capital to the firm would be

$$k_e = 8\% + 1.5(15\% - 8\%) = 18.5\%$$

On the other hand, if $\beta = 0.5$

$$k_e = 8\% + 0.5(15\% - 8\%) = 11.5\%$$

In this example, and in the examples using the risk-free rate plus premium and the dividend valuation model, the equity cost of capital was found to be the same (15%). This is seldom the case. That is, the different methods of estimating the equity cost of capital to a firm are likely to give somewhat different results. Firms are thus likely to use all three methods and then attempt to reconcile the differences to arrive at an equity cost of capital for the firm.

Weighted Cost of Capital

In general, a firm is likely to raise capital from undistributed profits, by borrowing, and by the sale of stocks, and so the marginal cost of capital to the firm is a weighted average of the cost of raising the various types of capital. Since the interest paid on borrowed funds is tax deductible while the dividends paid on stocks are not, the cost of debt is generally less than the cost of equity capital. The risk involved in raising funds by borrowing, how-ever, is greater than the risk on equity capital because the firm must regularly make pay-ments of the interest and principal on borrowed funds before paying dividends on stocks. Thus, firms do not generally raise funds only by borrowing but also by selling stock (as well as from undistributed profits).

Firms often try to maintain or achieve a particular long-term capital structure of debt to equity. For example, public utility companies may prefer a capital structure involving 60% debt and 40% equity, whereas auto manufacturers may prefer 30% debt and 70% equity. The particular debt-equity ratio that a firm prefers reflects the risk preference of its managers and stockholders and the nature of the firm's business. Public utilities accept the higher risk involved in a higher debt-to-equity ratio because of their more stable flow of earnings than automobile manufacturers. When a firm needs to raise investment capital, it borrows and sells stocks so as to maintain or achieve a desired debt-to-equity ratio.

The **composite cost of capital** to the firm (k_c) is then a weighted average of the cost of debt capital (k_d) and equity capital (k_e) as given by

$$k_c = w_d k_d + w_e k_e \qquad\qquad [16.16]$$

where w_d and w_e are, respectively, the proportion of debt and equity capital in the firm's capital structure. For example, if the (after-tax) cost of debt is 7.5%, the cost of equity cap-ital is 15%, and the firm wants to have a debt-to-equity ratio of 40:60, the composite or weighted marginal cost of capital to the firm is

$$k_c = (0.40)(7.5\%) + (0.60)(15\%) = 3\% + 9\% = 12\%$$

That is, the proportion of debt to equity that the firm seeks to achieve or maintain in the long run is not usually defined for individual projects but for all the investment projects that the firm is considering. Note that the marginal cost of capital eventually rises as the firm raises additional amounts of capital by borrowing and selling stocks because of the higher risk that lenders and investors face as the firm's debt-to-equity ratio increases.

AT THE FRONTIER
Derivatives: Useful but Dangerous

During the past decade, news about derivatives has been all over the financial and front pages of our newspapers. **Derivatives** are financial instruments or contracts whose value is derived from the price of such underlying financial as-sets as stocks, bonds, commodities, and currencies. Derivatives are offered by banks and brokerage firms to corporations and investors who wish to protect themselves against such risks as a decrease in the international value of the dollar, an increase in the price of a commodity, or an increase in interest rates. Used properly, derivatives can be a very useful risk-management tool; used without a clear understanding of all their implications, they can be very dangerous and can lead to huge losses. Despite the dangers and risks involved in their use, derivatives have been growing at a very rapid rate during the past decade and are clearly here to stay. The value of the underlying assets on which derivatives are based (called notional value) now exceeds $70 trillion (as compared with the $10 trillion of the U.S. gross domestic product or GDP in 2001).

Derivatives come in two basic categories: option-type contracts and forward-type contracts. These may be listed on the exchanges or negotiated privately between institutions (i.e., over the counter). *Options* give buyers the right, but not the obligation, to buy (a call) or sell (a put) an asset at a specific price over a given time period. The option price or premium is usually a small percentage of the price of the value of the underlying asset. Although the buyer can never lose more than the premium he or she paid for the option (by not exercising it), the seller's potential losses are unlimited. For example, you can buy a call on GE stock for a specified time, at a specified price, and for a specified premium. If within the specified time the price of the GE stock falls below the specified price, you do not exercise the call option to buy the stock and your losses are limited to the premium that you paid for the call. On the other hand, if the price of GE stock rises above the specified price, you exercise the call and buy the stock and gain the difference between the higher market price of the stock and the agreed call price.

Forward-type contracts, on the other hand, include forwards, futures, and swaps. *Forwards* commit both buyer and seller to trade a fixed amount of a given asset for a specific price at a specific on a future date. For example, a corporation that has to purchase a given amount of petroleum in three months faces the risk that the price of petroleum may be much higher in three months. The corporation can protect itself (i.e., hedge) this risk by entering today into a contract to purchase the quantity of petroleum that it will need at a price agreed upon today for delivery and payment in three months. In three months, the corporation will get the specified quantity of petroleum by paying the agreed price—whatever the price of petroleum is on that day.

Futures are standardized forward agreements to buy or sell a fixed amount of an asset (currency, bond, stock, or commodity) traded on an exchange. *Swaps* are agreements involving an exchange of streams of payments over time according to terms agreed today. The most common type is an interest rate swap, in which one party holding a fixed-interest rate mortgage and believing that interest rates will fall exchanges it for a flexible exchange rate mortgage owned by another party who believes that interest rates will rise. The first party will then pay the other's flexible rate mortgage in exchange for the second paying the fixed rate mortgage of the first.

Many derivatives are in the form of the simple options, forwards, futures, and swaps discussed above (called "plain vanilla" derivatives). They form the bread and butter of the derivatives market and are used mostly to hedge risks, but provide dealers only thin profit margins. Some of these derivatives, such as currency options and futures, have been used by U.S. and foreign corporations for decades and have been spared criticism. The derivatives that have caught most of the attention and criticism in recent years are the customized, over-the-counter, exotic derivatives whose dazzling growth to over $60 trillion since the late 1980s have

Continued. . .

provided huge profits for dealers and tremendous risks for users. Examples of exotic derivatives are options that depend on the amount by which one asset will outperform another, or that gamble that the price of oil will not fall below a specified price or that interest rates do rise above a given level. The list of derivatives products is very long and new ones are being created every day.

By allowing users to make big bets with little or no money down (i.e., by providing huge leverage), derivatives became very popular during the 1992–1993 bull market in bonds, when heavy bets were made that interest rates would continue to fall. As long as interest rates did fall, these derivatives provided huge profits for users and fat fees for providers. But when interest rates abruptly reversed course in early 1994, a number of companies that had invested heavily in these exotic derivatives faced huge losses. A fund managed by Orange County, California, lost more than $1.5 billion and was forced to declare bankruptcy. Similar losses by the use of derivatives were incurred by some large European and Asian corporations during the past decade. The most spectacular failure involving derivatives, however, was that of Long-Term Capital Management (LTCM) in September 1998, the Connecticut-based investment firm, which lost $3.6 billion as a result of massive speculative bets gone wrong. Investors in LTCM had little or no information on the Fund's investments strategy and no idea on its huge leverage (the ratio of borrowed funds used to the firm's capital).

Despite these spectacular failures, there are still little or no disclosure requirements in the United States and abroad on derivatives users. Most derivatives are treated as "off-balance-sheet" items and mentioned in footnotes in companies' financial statements. The systemic danger to which this gives rise is that a party to a derivative transaction may be unable to meet the terms of the transaction and lead to the insolvency of its counterparty (the other party of the derivative transaction), and that this may trigger a domino effect of defaults that could threaten the stability of the entire financial system. The Federal Reserve System and other regulators now face the delicate task of regulating the derivatives market without leading this very lucrative business for many U.S. banks (which are world leaders in this market) to relocate abroad. One proposal is for firms to report their derivatives profits or losses on their earnings statements, rather than carrying them on their books at cost, as they do now.

Sources: "The Risk That Won't Go Away," *Fortune,* March 7, 1994, pp. 40–60; "Untangling Derivatives Mess," *Fortune,* March 20, 1995, pp. 51–68; "Financiers Plan to Put Controls on Derivatives," *New York Times,* January 1, 1999, p. C1; and "Derivatives," *Financial Times,* September 25, 2001, pp. 1–4.

16.6 EFFECTS OF FOREIGN INVESTMENTS ON THE RECEIVING NATION

Foreign investments reduce the supply of investment funds in the investing nation and increase them in the receiving nation. Foreign investments flow from the nation where the rate of return on investment is lower to the nation where the rate of return is higher. During the 1980s, the United States was the recipient of a large net inflow of foreign investments

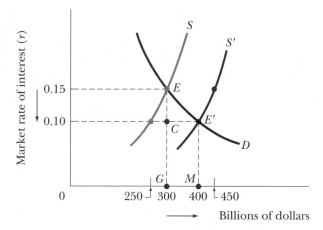

FIGURE 16.7   Effects of Foreign Investments on the Receiving Nation   *D* is the demand curve for and *S* is the supply curve of investment funds in the nation in the absence of foreign investments. *D* and *S* intersect at point *E*, defining the equilibrium rate of return (*r*) of 0.15 or 15% and level of investments of $300 billion. With $150 billion of foreign investments, *S* shifts to *S'*, defining the new equilibrium point of *E'*, at which total investments in the nation rise to $400 billion ($250 billion domestic and $150 billion foreign) and *r* falls to 0.10 or 10%. The $150 billion foreign investment increases the total output of the nation by *GEE'M* (about $12.5 billion), of which *GECE'M* — $10 billion is the return on foreign investments and *EE'C* (about $2.5 billion) is the net gain of the nation.

because of the higher rate of return on investments in the United States than abroad. We can examine the effect of foreign investments on the receiving nation with Figure 16.7. For simplicity, we assume that the rate of interest on borrowed capital is the same as the rate of return on both borrowed and equity capital in the nation.

In Figure 16.7, *D* is the nation's demand curve for investment funds, while *S* is the domestic supply curve of investment funds. *D* and *S* intersect at point *E* indicating that, in the absence of foreign investments, $300 billion is invested in the nation at the rate of return (*r*) of 0.15 or 15%. With $150 billion of foreign investment, the nation's supply curve shifts to the right to *S'*. The intersection of *D* and *S'* defines the new equilibrium point of *E'*, which indicates that total investments in the nation are $400 billion and the rate of return on domestic and foreign investments is 0.10 or 10%. Thus, foreign investments reduced the rate of return on domestic investments from 15% to 10% (and this led to a reduction in the quantity supplied of domestic investments to $250 billion).

The $150 billion foreign investment increases the total output of the receiving nation by *GEE'M* (about $12.5 billion), of which *GCE'M* = $10 billion is paid out to foreign investors as the return on their investment, and *EE'C* (about $2.5 billion) represents the net benefit or gain to the nation receiving the foreign investments. Some of this net benefit goes to domestic labor because the inflow of foreign investments increases the capital-labor ratio and thus the productivity and wages of domestic labor. Another benefit (not shown in the figure) accruing to the nation receiving the foreign investments is the taxes paid by foreigners on the income (the return on investments) earned in the nation.

In 1985, the United States changed from being a net creditor to being a net debtor nation (i.e., the amount that foreigners lent and invested in the United States began to exceed the amount that the United States lent and invested abroad) for the first time since 1914. Indeed, with a net foreign debt of about $2 trillion in 2000, the United States was by far the most indebted nation in the world. This large debt sparked a lively debate among economists, politicians, and government officials in the United States regarding the benefits, and risks of this recent development.

In terms of benefits, foreign investments allowed the United States to finance about half of its budget deficit without the need for still higher interest rates and more "crowding out" of private investments. To the extent that foreign investments went into directly productive activities and the return on this investment was greater than the interest and dividend payments flowing to foreign investors, this investment was beneficial to the United States.[11] To the extent, however, that foreign investments simply financed larger consumption expenditures in the United States, the interest and dividend payments flowing to foreign investors represent a real burden or drain on future consumption and growth in the United States. Some experts are concerned that a growing share of capital inflows to the United States since 1983 cannot be clearly identified as productive investments, and to that extent they may represent a real burden on the U.S. economy in the future.

There is also the danger that foreigners, for whatever reason, may suddenly withdraw their funds. This would lead to a financial crisis and much higher interest rates in the United States. Some economists and government officials also fear that foreign companies operating in the United States will transfer advanced American technology abroad. They further fear some loss of domestic control over political and economic matters. The irony is that these fears were precisely the complaints usually heard from Canada, smaller European nations, and developing countries with regard to the large American investments in their countries during the 1950s and 1960s. With the great concern often voiced in the United States today about the danger of foreign investments, the tables now seem to have turned.[12]

EXAMPLE 16-6

Fluctuations in the Flow of Foreign Direct Investments to the United States

Table 16.7 shows that the flow of foreign direct investments (FDI) to the United States was $12.2 billion in 1980. It declined to $8.1 billion 1983 before rising to $72.7 billion in 1988. Afterwards, it declined to $15.3 billion in 1992 and then rose to the all time

---

[11] Of course, the United States would have benefitted even more if it had financed its domestic investments entirely through domestic savings. But with inadequate domestic savings, the second best situation was to receive foreign investments and pay the return on investments to foreign investors.

[12] See "A Note on the United States as a Debtor Nation," *Survey of Current Business* (Washington, D.C.: U.S. Government Printing Office, 1985), p. 28.

TABLE 16.7	Foreign Direct Investment Flows to the United States 1980–2000 (billions of U.S. dollars)		
Year	FDI	Year	FDI
1980	$12.2	1990	$ 65.9
1981	23.2	1991	25.5
1982	10.8	1992	15.3
1983	8.1	1993	26.2
1984	15.2	1994	49.9
1985	23.1	1995	60.8
1986	39.2	1996	84.5
1987	40.3	1997	103.4
1988	72.7	1998	174.4
1989	71.2	1999	295.0
1990	65.9	2000	281.1

Source: U.S. Department of Commerce, *Survey of Current Business* (Washington, D.C.: U.S. Government Printing Office, Various Issues).

high of $295.0 billion in 1999, and it was $281.1 billion in 2000. Foreign direct investments include acquisitions, the formation of new businesses, and the construction of new plants. They do not include the purchase of stocks and bonds.

During the second half of the 1980s, many Americans became concerned that foreigners, particularly the Japanese, were "buying up" America. These fears subsided during the early 1990s, as slow growth and recession made FDI in the United States less attractive to foreigners. With the resumption of rapid growth in the United States since 1993, however, FDI in the United States shot up again to much higher levels than during the late 1980s (this time coming mostly form Europe instead of Japan), but with the United States doing much better in international competitiveness than in the 1980s (see "At the Frontier" in Chapter 7), the new upsurge in FDI did not cause much concern in the United States. At the same time, the flow of U.S. FDI abroad remained high and reached a high of $142.6 billion in 1999 and was $139.3 billion in 2000.

16.7   SOME APPLICATIONS OF FINANCIAL MICROECONOMICS

In this section, we discuss some important applications of the theory presented in the chapter. These applications include investment in human capital, the effect of investment in human capital on hours of work, the pricing of exhaustible resources, and the management of nonexhaustible resources. These applications clearly indicate the usefulness and applicability of the theory.

Investment in Human Capital

Investment in human capital is any activity on the part of a worker or potential worker that increases his or her productivity. It refers to expenditures on education, job training, health, migration to areas of better job opportunities, and so on. Like any other investment, investments in human capital involve costs and entail returns. For example, going to college involves explicit and implicit, or opportunity, costs. The explicit costs are tuition, books, fees, and all other out-of-pocket expenses of attending college. The implicit costs are the earnings or opportunities foregone while attending college (the individual could have worked or could have worked more by not attending college). As we have seen in the example in Section 9.1, the implicit costs of attending college are nearly as high as the explicit costs. The returns of attending college take the form of higher lifetime earnings with a college education than without a college education (see Example 16–3 in this chapter).

As with any other investment, we can find the present value of the stream of net cash flows from a college degree. Net cash flows are negative during the college years (because of the explicit and implicit or opportunity costs of attending college) and positive during the working life of the college graduate until retirement. The same is generally true for other investments in human capital. That is, they also lead to a stream of net cash flows and should be undertaken only if their net present value is positive or higher than the present value of other investments (such as the purchasing of a stock). Using this method, it was estimated that the return to a college education was about 10% to 15% per year during the 1950s and 1960s. This was substantially higher than the return on similarly risky investments (such as the purchasing of a stock). During the 1970s, and as a result of the sharp increases in tuition and relatively lower starting salaries, the returns to a college education declined to about 7% per year, but they increased during the 1980s and early 1990s.[13]

These studies, however, face a number of statistical problems. For example, not all expenditures for education represent an investment (as, for example, when a physics student takes a course in Shakespeare). In addition, at least part of the higher earnings of college graduates may be due to their being more intelligent or from working harder than noncollege graduates (see the next section). Nevertheless, there are benefits from a college education that cannot be easily measured. For example, college graduates seem to enjoy their jobs more than noncollege graduates, have happier marriages, and generally suffer less mental illness. In spite of these measurement difficulties, however, the concept of investment in human capital is very important and commonly used. Most differences in labor incomes can be explained by differences in human capital. Juries routinely determine the amount of damages to award injury victims (or their survivors, in cases of fatal accidents) on the basis of the human capital or income lost by the injured party. Developing countries complain about the brain drain or the emigration to rich nations of their young and skilled people (who embody a great deal of human capital), and so on.

---

[13] R. B. Freeman, "The Decline in the Economic Rewards to College Education, *The Review of Economics and Statistics,* February 1977, pp. 18–29; "The Soaring Payoff from Higher Education," *The Margin,* January/February, 1990, p. 6; "Technological Change Boosts Wage Gap," *The Margin,* spring 1993, pp. 42–43; J. Mincer, "Investment in U.S. Education and Training," National Bureau of Economic Research, *Working Paper No. 4844,* October 1995; "The New Math of Higher Education," *Business Week,* March 18, 1996, p. 39; and Alan B. Krueger and Michael Lindahl "Education for Growth: Why and for Whom," *Journal of Economic Literature,* December 2001, pp. 1101–1136.

Investment in Human Capital and Hours of Work

People may work more hours as a result of investment in human capital. This can be shown with the aid of Figure 16.8. In Figure 16.8, the movement from left to right on the horizontal axis measures hours of leisure per day. The movement from right to left measures the

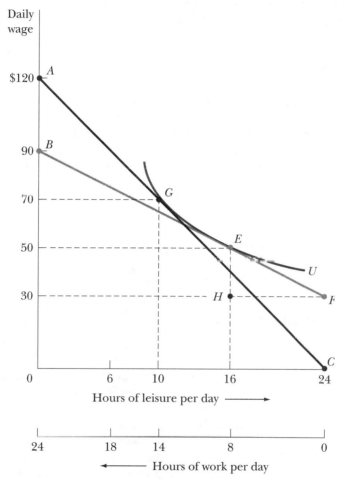

FIGURE 16.8   Education and Hours of Work   The individual has a daily property income of $FC = \$30$ and faces budget line FB (with the negative of the slope giving the wage of $2.50 per hour). The individual maximizes utility at point E, where indifference curve U is tangent to FB. The individual works 8 hours and has a daily income of $50 (of which $HE = \$20$ is labor income). Suppose the individual invests all property income in education and as a result earns $5 per hour. The budget line is now CA. The individual maximizes utility at point G, where U is tangent to CA, and works 14 hours for a daily income of $70.

hours of work. The sum of the hours of leisure and the hours of work always adds up to the 24 hours of the day. The vertical axis measures the daily income of the individual.

We begin by assuming that the individual portrayed in Figure 16.8 has a daily property income of *FC* ($30). If the hourly wage is $2.50, the individual's budget line is *FB* (so that the negative of the slope of the budget line gives the wage rate). Before investing in education, the individual maximizes utility or satisfaction at point *E*, where indifference curve *U* is tangent to budget line *FB*. The individual works 8 hours per day and has a daily income of $50 (*FC* or $30 from property income plus *HE* or $20 from working 8 hours at the wage rate of $2.50 per hour).

Suppose that now the individual decides to invest all of his or her endowed property income in education (i.e., sacrifice all of his or her nonhuman capital) and that as a result he or she can earn a wage rate of $5 per hour. With education, the budget line of the individual is now *CA* (see the figure), reflecting zero property income available for consumption and the wage of $5 per hour (the negative of the slope of budget line *CA*). Assuming that the individual's tastes remain unchanged as a result of the education, the individual will now maximize utility at point *G*, where indifference curve *U* is tangent to budget line *CA*. The individual now works 14 hours per day for a daily income of $70 (all of which is labor income).

Thus, education seems to induce individuals to work more hours (i.e., have fewer leisure hours) and earn higher incomes. Having made the investment in education, the individual will work more hours and earn a higher income to maximize utility. This seems to be confirmed in empirical studies. For example, Lindsay found that physicians work on average 62 hours per week, far more than the average worker.[14] The same seems to be true for other professionals as opposed to nonprofessionals.

Pricing of Exhaustible Resources

One of the great concerns of modern societies is that the world's resources will become depleted. Resources can generally be classified as exhaustible or nonexhaustible. **Exhaustible resources** are those, such as petroleum and other minerals, that are available in fixed quantities and are nonreplenishable. **Nonexhaustible resources** are those such as fertile land, forests, rivers, and fish, which can last forever if they are properly managed. We first examine the pricing of exhaustible or nonrenewable resources and then look at the pricing of nonexhaustible or renewable resources under proper management.

During the 1970s (and to a large extent as a result of the petroleum crisis), there was great concern that exhaustible resources would soon be depleted. Doomsday models were built that predicted when various exhaustible resources would run out, thereby threatening the living standard and the very future of humanity.[15] Economists, while not entirely shrugging off the danger, were skeptical for the most part. They pointed out that as the prices of

---

[14] C. M. Lindsay, "Real Returns to Medical Education," *Journal of Human Resources,* summer 1982, p. 338. See also "Wages and the Workday," *Economic Inquiry,* spring 2000, p. 15.

[15] See J. W. Forrester, *World Dynamics* (Cambridge, MA: Wright-Allen Press, 1971); D. H. Meadows et al., *The Limits to Growth: A Report for the Club of Rome's Project on the Predicament of Mankind* (New York: Universe Books, 1972); and M. Mesarovic and E. Pestel, *Mankind at the Turning Point: The Second Report to the Club of Rome* (New York: The American Library, 1974).

exhaustible resources tend to rise over time, this would lead to conservation and to the dis-covery of substitutes. Thus, doomsday models were not to be taken too seriously. Let us see why economists proved to be generally right.

We begin by pointing out that the owner of an exhaustible resource will keep it in the ground and available for future use if the present value of the resource in future use is greater than its current price. For example, suppose that the price of the resource is $100 per unit today, it is expected to be $120 next year, and the market rate of interest is 10% per year. The owner will sell the resource next year, since the present value of a unit of the resource sold next year is $120/(1 + 0.1) = $109.09 and this exceeds its price of $100 today.

In a perfectly competitive market, the net price of the resource (i.e., the price minus the cost of extraction) will rise at a rate equal to the market rate of interest, and this will spread available supplies over time. If the net price of a resource is expected to rise faster than the market rate of interest, more of the resource will be held off the market for future sale. This increases the current price and reduces the future price until the present value of the future net price is equal to the present net price. On the other hand, if the net price of the resource is expected to rise at a slower rate than the market rate of interest, more of the resource will be sold in the present. This will reduce the present price and increase the future price until the present value of the expected future net price equals the present net price. This is shown in Figure 16.9.

In the left panel of the figure, time is measured along the horizontal axis, and the price of the exhaustible resource and its average total cost (assumed to be constant, and thus equal to marginal cost) are measured along the vertical axis. The right panel shows the market

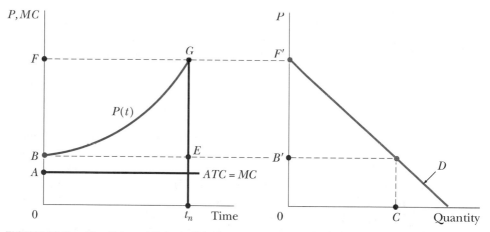

FIGURE 16.9   The Price of Exhaustible Resources   In the left panel, time is measured along the horizontal axis, and the price of the exhaustible resource and its average cost (assumed constant and equal to *MC*) is measured along the vertical axis. The right panel shows the demand curve for the resource. At $P = OB$, the net benefit is *AB* per unit and the quantity demanded is *OC*. Over time, the net benefit or net price rises at the same rate as the market rate of interest until at $P = OF$, the supply of the resource is exhausted (point *G* in the left panel), and the quantity demanded is zero (point *F'* in the right panel).

demand curve for the resource (input). The net price or benefit to the owners of the resource is given by the difference (*AB* at time zero) between the (gross) price of the resource and the assumed constant cost of extracting it. The owner can obtain these net benefits now or in the future (by leaving the resource in the ground). For the owner of the resource to be indifferent between extracting the resource now or in the future, the net benefit or net price of the resource must appreciate over time at a rate equal to the market rate of interest.

The right panel of Figure 16.9 shows that at the resource (gross) price $P = 0B'$, the quantity demanded of the resource is $0C$. Over time, the net price rises at the same rate as the market rate of interest (from AB to EG in the left panel) until at $P = 0F'$ the supply of the resource is exhausted (point G in the left panel) and the quantity demanded of the resource is zero (point F' in the right panel). Thus, in perfectly competitive markets, exhaustion of the resource coincides with zero quantity demanded. If exhaustion occurs before time t_n at $P = 0F$, owners of the resource could have sold the resource at a higher price (and net benefit) over time than indicated by line BG. On the other hand, if the resource is not exhausted by t_n at $P = 0F$, owners would have gained by selling the resource at a lower price over time.[16] In the real world, the net price of most resources increases at a smaller rate than the market rate of interest (and the net price of many resources actually falls) over time because of new discoveries, technological improvements in extraction, and conservation.

Management of Nonexhaustible Resources

Nonexhaustible or renewable resources such as forests and fish grow naturally over time. Unless the rate of utilization of the resource exceeds its rate of natural growth, the resource will never be depleted.[17] If the renewable resource is trees, the question is when should the trees be cut? The answer (as you might suspect by now) is that the trees should be allowed to grow as long as the rate of growth in the net value of the trees exceeds the market rate of interest. Cutting the trees when the rate of growth in their net value exceeds the market rate of interest would be equivalent to taking money out of a bank paying a higher rate of interest and depositing the money in another bank that pays a lower rate of interest. We can analyze this situation with the aid of Figure 16.10.

The top panel of Figure 16.10 shows the net value of the trees if harvested at time t. This is given by the $V(t)$ curve. The net value is the total market value of the trees minus the cost of harvesting them. We assume zero maintenance or management costs. The top panel shows that $V(t)$ grows at an increasing rate at first. At time $t = 3$ (point A), diminishing returns begin. $V(t)$ reaches the maximum value of $14 million at $t = 9$ (point B), after which disease, age, and decay set in.

When should the trees be cut? The answer is not at $t = 9$ when $V(t)$ is maximum. This would be the case only if the market rate of interest were zero. With a positive market

---

[16] See H. Hotelling, "The Economics of Exhaustible Resources, "*Journal of Political Economy*, April 1931, pp. 137–175.

[17] The term "renewable" is, perhaps, more appropriate than "nonexhaustible" because if the rate of utilization of the resource exceeds its natural growth rate, the resource can be exhausted. For example, if you cut all the trees or catch all the fish now, there will be no trees or fish in the future.

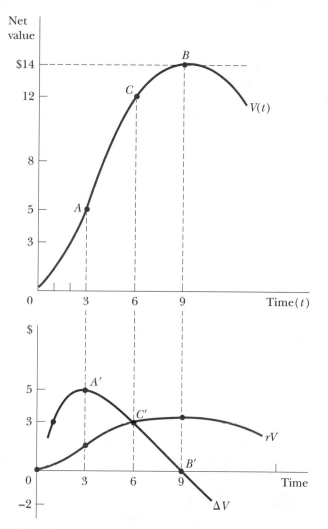

FIGURE 16.10   Optimal Management of a Standing Forest
The top panel shows the net value of the trees if harvested at
time t, $V(t)$. The trees should be cut when the growth in the net
value of the standing trees (ΔV) is equal to the growth in the net
receipts from cutting the trees and investing the proceeds at the
market rate of interest (rV). This equilibrium occurs at $t = 6$
when the ΔV or MV curve crosses the rV curve (point C' in the
bottom panel) and $\Delta V/V = r$.

rate of interest, the correct answer is to cut the trees when the growth in the net value
of the standing trees (ΔV) is equal to the growth of the net receipts from cutting the trees
and investing the proceeds at the market rate of interest (rV). That is, the trees should be
cut when

$$\Delta V = rV \qquad\qquad [16.17]$$

or

$$\Delta V/V = r \qquad\qquad [16.17A]$$

This says that trees should be cut when the *rate* of growth in the value of the standing trees ($\Delta V/V$) equals the market *rate* of interest (r).

In terms of Figure 16.10, the trees should be cut at $t = 6$ when the ΔV curve crosses the rV curve (point C' in the bottom panel). The ΔV curve (in the bottom panel) is the marginal value curve or slope of the $V(t)$ curve in the top panel (i.e., $\Delta V = MV$). The rV curve in the bottom panel is 0.25 or 25% of the $V(t)$ curve, at $r = 25\%$. To the left of point C', MV exceeds rV (i.e., $\Delta V/V > r$) and it pays for the firm to let the trees continue to grow. To the right of point C', MV is smaller than rV (i.e., $\Delta V/V < r$) and it pays for the firm to cut the trees. The optimal choice is to cut the trees at point $t = 6$ (point C', where $MV = rV$). This is the usual marginal rule applicable in all optimization decisions.

SUMMARY

1. Given the consumer's income or endowment for this year and the next, and the rate of interest, we can define the consumer's budget line. The rate of interest is the premium received next year for lending or borrowing one dollar this year. The optimal consumer's choice involves lending or borrowing so as to reach the highest possible indifference curve showing the consumer's time preference between present and future consumption. The wealth of an individual is given by the sum of the present income and the present value of future income. If the rate of interest rises, the borrower will borrow less and the lender will usually lend more. The equilibrium rate of interest is determined at the intersection of the market demand curve for borrowing and the market supply curve for lending.

2. For an isolated individual, optimal saving and investment is given by the point where the production-possibilities curve is tangent to an indifference curve. With saving and investment, and borrowing and lending, the optimal choice of the individual is first to maximize wealth (by reaching the market line that is tangent to the production-possibilities curve) and then to borrow or lend along the market line until the individual reaches the highest indifference curve possible. The equilibrium rate of interest is given by the intersection of (1) the aggregate demand curve for borrowing and the aggregate supply curve of lending, or (2) the aggregate demand curve for investment and the aggregate supply curve of savings.

3. A firm should undertake an investment only if the net present value of the investment is positive. The net present value (NPV) of the investment is the value today from the stream of the net cash flows (positive and negative) from the investment. In choosing between any two projects, the firm will maximize attained wealth by undertaking the project with the highest net present value. The separation theorem refers to the independence of the optimum production decision from the individual's preferences in perfect capital markets.

4. The rate of interest usually varies at different times and in different markets. Even at a given point in time and in a specific capital market, there is not a single rate of interest, but many. That is, there is a different interest rate on loans or investments depending on differences in (1) default and variability risks, (2) duration of the loan, (3) cost of administering the loan, and (4) tax treatment. Interest rates rise if society decides to save less or to borrow and invest more. The nominal rate of interest equals the real rate of interest plus the anticipated rate of price inflation.

5. The cost that a firm incurs for using internal funds is the foregone return on these funds invested outside the firm. The cost of external funds is the rate of return that lenders and stockholders require to lend or invest funds in the firm. The after-tax cost of borrowed funds

is given by the interest paid times $(1 - t)$, where t is the firm's marginal tax rate. The cost of equity capital can be measured by (1) the risk-free rate plus a risk premium, (2) the dividend valuation model, and (3) the capital asset pricing model (CAPM). The composite cost of capital is the weighted average of the cost of debt and equity capital.

6. Foreign investments result in a reduction in the rate of return on domestic investments but a net gain for the recipient nation. Labor in a nation receiving foreign investments shares in the gains through higher wages from the higher productivity resulting from an increased capital-labor ratio. The nation also collects taxes on foreign earnings. The United States is now the largest debtor nation in the world. Concern has been voiced on the dangers arising from a sudden withdrawal of foreign investments, technology transfer, and foreign domination. These dangers may be exaggerated.

7. Investment in human capital refers to expenditures on education, job training, health, or migration to areas of better job opportunities that increase the productivity of an individual. Like any other investment, investments in human capital involve costs and entail returns. Education seems to induce people to work more hours. The net price of exhaustible resources tends to rise at the same rate as the market rate of interest, and this spreads the available supply of the resource over time and stimulates the discovery of substitutes. A nonexhaustible resource should be harvested when the growth in its net value equals the market rate of interest.

KEY TERMS

Endowment position	Net present value (*NPV*)	Capital asset pricing model
Rate of interest (*r*)	Separation theorem	(CAPM)
Wealth	Default risk	Beta coefficient (β)
Production-possibilities curve	Variability risk	Composite cost of capital
Saving	Real rate of interest (*r*)	Derivatives
Investment	Nominal rate of interest (*r'*)	Investment in human capital
Market line	Cost of debt	Exhaustible resources
Capital budgeting	Dividend valuation model	Nonexhaustible resources

REVIEW QUESTIONS

1. How much interest must an individual be paid to save part of his or her income this year if his or her time preference is zero? What happens to the individual's satisfaction this year and next if the individual saves part of this year's income and spends it next year? What happens to the individual's combined satisfaction for this year and next if the individual saves part of this year's income and spends it next year?

2. In what way is intertemporal optimum consumer choice analogous or similar to optimum consumer choice at one point in time?

3. Is microeconomic theory concerned primarily with the real or with the nominal interest rate? Why?

4. What is the present discounted value of an inheritance of $10,000 to be paid in two years, if the market rate of interest is 10%?

5. Should you prefer $100 one year from today or $110 two years from today if the market rate of interest is 5% per year? Why?

6. What is the rate of interest or discount if an individual is indifferent between receiving $11,111.11 today or $1,000 at the end of each year in perpetuity?

7. Why is the cost of debt capital usually lower than the cost of equity capital for a firm?

8. What additional risks do the stockholders of a firm face in comparison to holders of government securities?

9. A corporation can sell bonds at an interest rate of 9%, and the interest rate on government securities is 7%. What is the cost of equity capital for this firm?

10. If labor and capital are the only inputs, what are the total gains of labor in Figure 16.7 when the nation receives $100 billion of foreign investments?

11. What are some of the benefits and costs of foreign investments not captured by Figure 16.7? When all benefits and costs are considered, can we still say that foreign investments are beneficial for the receiving nation?

12. Does a nation gain or lose from foreign investments when all benefits and costs from foreign investments are considered?

PROBLEMS

1. Suppose that an individual is endowed with $Y_0 = 7.5$ units of a commodity this year and $Y_1 = 2.75$ units next year. Draw a figure showing that the individual lends 2.5 units of this year's endowment for 2.75 units next year. What is the rate of interest? On the same figure show that the individual lends 3 units for 4.2 units. What would the rate of interest be then?

2. Suppose that an individual is endowed with $Y_0 = 2.5$ units of a commodity this year and $Y_1 = 8.25$ units next year. Draw a figure showing that the individual borrows 2.5 units this year and repays 2.75 units next year. What is the rate of interest? On the same figure, show that the individual borrows 2 units this year and repays 2.80 units next year. What would the rate of interest be then?

3. Assume that (1) the consumer of Problem 2 (call him or her individual B or the borrower) is a different individual from the consumer of Problem 1 (call him or her individual A or the lender), and that (2) both individual A and B have the same tastes or time preference. Draw a figure showing how the equilibrium rate of interest is determined if A and B are the only individuals in the market. What would happen at $r = 40\%$? At $r = 5\%$?

*4. Assume that (1) individuals A and B have identical endowments of a commodity of $Y_0 = 5$ this year and $Y_1 = 6$ next year, and that (2) the optimal choice for individual B is to borrow 2.5 units this year and repay 3 units next year, while the optimal choice for individual A is to lend 2.5 units this year and receive 3 units next year. Draw a figure similar to Figures 16.1 and 16.2 for the above. What is the equilibrium rate of interest if A and B are the only individuals in the market? On the same figure show that at $r = 50\%$, individual B wants to borrow 2 units instead of 2.5 this year and repay 3 units next year, while individual A wants to lend 3 units this year and receive 4.5 units next year. Why is $r = 50\%$ not the equilibrium rate of interest?

*5. a. Why does a lender's supply curve of loans (lending) bend backward at sufficiently high rates of interest?

b. Why is a borrower's demand curve for loans (borrowing) negatively sloped throughout?

6. Draw a figure similar to Figure 16.5 showing that a rise in the rate of interest will reduce the individual's level of investment and borrowing.

7. Starting from Figure 16.5, draw a figure showing that if indifference curve U_5 had been tangent to market line HW_0' to the right of point A, the individual would have been dissaving.

8. Starting from Figure 16.5, draw a figure showing that if indifference curve U_5 had been tangent to market line HW_0' to the left of point H, the individual would have been saving more than he or she invested.

*9. Reestimate the net present value of the project given in Table 16.4 for $r = 5\%$.

*10. A firm expects to earn $200 million after taxes for the current year. The company has a policy of paying out half of its net after-tax income to the holders of the company's 100 million shares of common stock. A share of the common stock of the company currently sells for eight times current earnings. Management and outside analysts expect the growth rate of earnings and dividends for the company to be 7.5% per year. Calculate the cost of equity capital to this firm.

11. A company pays the interest rate of 11% on its bonds, the marginal income tax rate that the firm faces is 40%, the rate on government bonds is 7.5%, the return on the average stock of all firms in the market is 11.55%, the estimated beta coefficient for the common stock of the firm is 2, and the firm wishes to raise 40% of its capital by borrowing. Determine:

    a. The cost of debt.

    b. The cost of equity capital.

    c. The composite cost of capital for this firm.

12. Draw a figure showing the effect of the following on the price of an exhaustible resource.

    a. A decrease in the market rate of interest.

    b. An increase in the demand for the resource.

INTERNET SITE ADDRESSES

Data and analyses of interest rates, savings and investments and the financial situation in the leading industrial nations is provided in *The Economic Report of the President,* The Federal Reserve Bank of St. Louis, the European Commission (EC), National Bureau of Economic Research (NBER), Institute for International Economics (IIE). The websites of these organizations are:

    http://www.gpo.ucop.edu/catalog/erp99.html

    http://www.stls.frb.org

    http://europa/eu.int

    http://nber.org

    http://www.iie.com

Information and data on emerging financial markets are found on the websites of the Bank for International Settlements (BIS), International Monetary Fund (IMF), and World Bank (WB) at:

    http://www.bis.org

    http://www.imf.org

    http://www.worldbank.org

Financial calculators that can be used to calculate present discounted values can be found at:

    http://www.pine-grove.com/SolveIt/ calculators.htm

    http://www.biznizportal.com/calculators/bus10/ java/BusinessValuation.html

For cost of capital analysis for over 300 industries, see the site of the Ibbotson Associates' *Cost of Capital Review* at:

    http://valuation.ibbotson.com

The data on foreign direct investments are published by the United Nations in the *World Investment Report* (yearly), the OECD in the *International Investment Statistics Yearbook,* and by the Bureau of Economic Analysis on the Websites indicated below.

    http://www.unctad.org/en/docs/wir99ove.pdf

    http://www.oecd.org

    http://bea.doc.gov/bea/di1.htm

PART SIX

General Equilibrium, Efficiency, and Public Goods

P art Six (Chapters 17–19) presents the theory of general equilibrium and welfare economics, examines the role of government, and deals with the economics of information. Chapter 17 describes general equilibrium theory and welfare economics. It examines the interdependence or relationship among all products and input markets and shows how the various individual markets (studied in Parts Two through Five) fit together to form an integrated economic system. The chapter also considers questions of equity in the distribution of income. Chapter 18 concentrates on externalities, public goods, and the role of government. It studies why externalities (such as pollution) and the existence of public goods (such as national defense) lead to economic inefficiencies and discusses policies that can be used to overcome these inefficiencies. It also presents the theory of public choice. Finally, Chapter 19 deals with the economics of information. It examines the economics of search and the problems arising from asymmetric information (i.e., the situation where one party to a transaction has more information than another) and moral hazard (i.e., the increased probability of a loss when an economic agent can shift some of its costs to others). As in previous parts of the text, the presentation of theory is reinforced with many real-world examples and important applications, while the *At the Frontier* sections present some new and important developments.

CHAPTER **17**

General Equilibrium and Welfare Economics

U
ntil this point we have examined the behavior of individual decision-making units (individuals as consumers of commodities and suppliers of inputs, and firms as employers of inputs and producers of commodities) and the workings of individual markets for commodities and inputs under various market structures. Generally missing from our presentation has been an examination of how the various individual pieces fit together to form an integrated economic system.

In this chapter, we take up the topic of interdependence or relationship among the various decision-making units and markets in the economy. This allows us to trace both the effect of a change in any part of the economic system on every other part of the system, and the repercussions from the latter on the former. We begin the chapter by distinguishing between partial equilibrium analysis and general equilibrium analysis and by examining the conditions under which each type of analysis is appropriate. Then, we discuss the conditions required for the economy to be in general equilibrium of exchange, production, and production and exchange simultaneously, and we examine their welfare implications. The numerous examples add realism to the presentation while the *At the Frontier* section examines the hot issue of growing income inequality in the United States today.

17.1 PARTIAL VERSUS GENERAL EQUILIBRIUM ANALYSIS

In Parts Two through Five (Chapters 3–16) we conducted **partial equilibrium analysis.** That is, we studied the behavior of individual decision-making units and individual markets *viewed in isolation.* We examined how an individual maximizes satisfaction subject to his or her income constraint (Part Two, Chapters 3–6), how a firm minimizes its costs of production (Part Three, Chapters 7–9) and maximizes profits under various market structures

567

(Part Four, Chapters 10–13), and how the price and employment of each type of input is determined (Part Five, Chapters 14–16). In doing so, we have abstracted from all the interconnections that exist between the market under study and the rest of the economy (the *ceteris paribus* assumption). In short, we have shown how demand and supply in each market determine the equilibrium price and quantity in that market *independently of other markets*.

However, a change in any market has spillover effects on other markets, and the change in these other markets will, in turn, have repercussions or feedback effects on the original market. These effects are studied by **general equilibrium analysis.** That is, general equilibrium analysis studies the **interdependence** or interconnections that exist among all markets and prices in the economy and attempts to give a complete, explicit, and simultaneous answer to the questions of what, how, and for whom to produce. In terms of Section 1.3 (examining the circular flow of economic activity), general equilibrium analysis examines simultaneously the links among all commodity and input markets, rather than studying each market in isolation.

For example, a change in the demand and price for new, domestically produced automobiles will immediately affect the demand and price of steel, glass, and rubber (the inputs of automobiles), as well as the demand, wages, and income of auto workers and of the workers in these other industries. The demand and price of gasoline and of public transportation (as well as the wages and income of workers in these industries) are also affected. These affected industries have spillover effects on still other industries, until the entire economic system is more or less involved, and all prices and quantities are affected. This is like throwing a rock in a pond and examining the ripples emanating in every direction until the stability of the entire pond is affected. The size of the ripples declines as they move farther and farther away from the point of impact. Similarly, industries further removed or less related to the automobile industry are less affected than more closely related industries.

What is important is that the effect that a change in the automobile industry has on the rest of the economy will have repercussions (through changes in relative prices and incomes) on the automobile industry itself. This is like the return or feedback effect of the ripples in the pond after reaching the shores. These repercussions or feedback effects are likely to significantly modify the original partial equilibrium conclusions (price and output) reached by analyzing the automobile industry in isolation (see Example 17–1).

When (as in the automobile example) the repercussions or feedback effects from the other industries are significant, partial equilibrium analysis is inappropriate. By measuring only the *impact* effect on price and output, partial equilibrium analysis provides a misleading measure of the total, final effect after all the repercussions or feedback effects from the original change have occurred. On the other hand, if the industry in which the original change occurs is small and the industry has few direct links with the rest of the economy (for example, the U.S. wristwatch industry), then partial equilibrium analysis provides a good first approximation to the results sought.

The logical question is why not use general equilibrium analysis all the time and immediately obtain the total, direct, and indirect results of a change on the industry (in which the change originated) as well as on all the other industries and markets in the economy? The answer is that general equilibrium analysis, dealing with each and all industries in the economy at the same time, is by its very nature difficult, time consuming, and expensive. Happily for the practical economist, partial equilibrium analysis often suffices. In any event, partial equilibrium analysis represents the appropriate point of departure, both for the relaxation of more and more of the *ceteris paribus* or "other things equal" assumptions, and for the inclusion of more and more industries in the analysis, as required.

The first and simplest general equilibrium model was introduced in 1874 by the great French economist, Léon Walras.[1] This model and subsequent general equilibrium models are necessarily mathematical in nature and include one equation for each commodity and input demanded and supplied in the economy, as well as market clearing equations.[2] More recently, economists have extended and refined the general equilibrium model theoretically and proved that under perfect competition, a general equilibrium solution of the model usually exists with all markets *simultaneously* in equilibrium.[3]

EXAMPLE 17–1

Effect of a Reduction in Demand for Domestically Produced Automobiles in the United States

With the sharp increase in the price of imported petroleum from 1973 to 1980, the demand for new, large domestically produced automobiles declined, as from D to D' in panel (a) of Figure 17.1, while the demand for small fuel-efficient, foreign-produced automobiles increased. This reduced the real (i.e., the inflation-adjusted) price and quantity of domestically produced automobiles, as from P to P' and from Q to Q', respectively, in panel (a). This impact effect is what partial equilibrium analysis measures. However, the reduction in the demand for the domestically produced automobiles had spillover effects that disturbed the equilibrium in the steel [panel (b)] industry and other industries that supply inputs to the domestic automobile industry, as well as in the petroleum industry [panel (c)]. The inflation-adjusted price and quantity of steel and other inputs fell, and part of the original increase in the price of gasoline was neutralized. Other industries related to these industries were also affected.

But this is not the end of the story. The demand for workers in the automobile industry [panel (d)] and other affected industries fell, and so did real wages, employment, and incomes. The reduction in real incomes reduced the demand, price, and quantity of steaks [panel (e)] and other normal goods purchased. To be sure, the demand for public transportation (buses, trains, and drivers and other attendants) and cheaper substitutes for steaks increased, but the net effect of the reduction in the demand for domestically produced cars was to reduce the demand and real income of labor. This, in turn, had feedback effects on the automobile industry, further reducing the demand, the inflation-adjusted price, and the output of domestically produced automobiles [panel (f)]. The same process continued throughout the 1980s and 1990s (long after the petroleum crisis ended),

---

[1] L. Walras, *Elements of Pure Economics,* translated by William Jaffé (Homewood, IL: Irwin, 1954).

[2] See Section A.16 of the Mathematical Appendix at the end of the text.

[3] K. J. Arrow and G. Debreu, "Existence of an Equilibrium for a Competitive Economy," *Econometrica,* July 1954, pp. 265–290; and L. W. McKenzie, "On the Existence of General Equilibrium for a Competitive Market," *Econometrica,* January 1959, pp. 54–71.

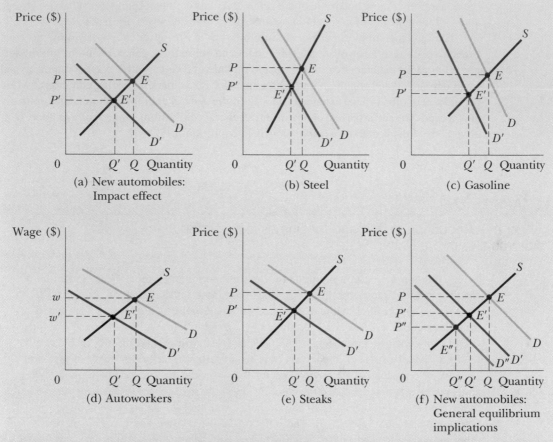

FIGURE 17.1   General Equilibrium Implications of a Reduction in the Demand for New Domestically Produced Automobiles   The impact or partial equilibrium effect of a reduction in the demand for new domestically produced automobiles is to reduce price from P to P' and quantity from Q to Q' [panel (a)]. This reduces the demand for (and price and quantity of) steel [panel (b)] and gasoline [panel (c)], and the demand for (and wages and employment of) workers in the automobile [panel (d)] and other affected industries. This, in turn, has spillover effects on the market for steaks [panel (e)] and other commodities, and feedback effects on the domestic automobile industry itself [panel (f)].

as Japanese automobile exports to and production in the United States displaced more and more domestic production by the big three U.S. automakers.

Panel (f) of Figure 17.1 shows that the feedback effects on the domestic automobile industry were significant. The inflation-adjusted price fell from P to P'' rather than to P', and quantity fell from Q to Q'' instead of falling only to Q'. Thus, partial equilibrium analysis gives only a rough first approximation to the final solution. Note that a first round of spillover and feedback effects (as shown in the above analysis) can be measured by the cross and income elasticities (see Sections 5.3 and 5.4), but these only carry us part of the way. The complete, final effects on the domestic automobile industry and on all other industries can only be measured through full-fledged general equilibrium analysis. This is necessarily mathematical in nature—words and graphs simply fail us.

Sources: "U.S. Giving Up on Making Small Cars," *U.S. News and Worm Report,* December 19, 1983, p. 56; "Auto Industry in U.S. Is Sliding Relentlessly into Japanese Hands," *Wall Street Journal,* February 16, 1990, p. A1; "Detroit Takes the Offensive," *Forbes,* September 28, 1992, pp. 108–112; "American Auto Makers Try to Redefine Their Brands," *Wall Street Journal,* October 30, 1995, p. B1; and "Detroit Fights Back," *Forbes,* September 17, 2001, pp. 76–78.

17.2   GENERAL EQUILIBRIUM OF EXCHANGE AND PRODUCTION

In this section, we examine separately general equilibrium of exchange and of production, and we derive the production-possibilities frontier. In the next section, we then examine how both equilibria are achieved *simultaneously* and the conditions for maximum economic efficiency.

General Equilibrium of Exchange

Let us begin by examining general equilibrium of exchange for a very simple economy composed of only two individuals (A and B), two commodities (X and Y), no production. This allows us to present the general equilibrium of exchange graphically.[4] The general equilibrium of exchange for this simple economy of two individuals, two commodities, and no production was presented earlier in Section 4.5. That analysis is now summarized and extended, and it will be used throughout the rest of the chapter.

The **Edgeworth box diagram for exchange** of Figure 17.2 is that of Figure 4.8, except that the indifference curves of individual A, convex to origin 0_A, are given by A_1, A_2, and A_3 (rather than by U_1, U_2, and U_3 as in Figure 4.8) and the indifference curves of individual B, convex to origin 0_B, are given by B_1, B_2, and B_3 (rather than by U_1', U_2', and U_3'). The dimensions of the box are given by the total amount of the two commodities ($10X$ and $8Y$) owned by the two individuals together.[5] Any point inside the box indicates how the total amount of the two commodities is distributed between the two individuals. For example, point C indicates that individual A has $3X$ and $6Y$, while individual B has $7X$ and $2Y$, for the combined total of $10X$ and $8Y$ (the dimensions of the box).

Suppose that point C does in fact represent the original distribution of commodities X and Y between individuals A and B. Since at point C, indifference curves A_1 and B_1 intersect,

---

[4] However, the analysis can be generalized mathematically to more than two individuals and more than two commodities. The graphic presentation in the text follows the well-known article by F. M. Bator, "The Simple Analytics of Welfare Maximization," *American Economic Review,* March 1957, pp. 22–59.

[5] As explained in Section 4.5, the Edgeworth box was obtained by rotating individual B's indifference curves diagram by 180 degrees (so that origin 0_B appears in the top right-hand corner) and superimposing it on individual A's indifference curves diagram (with origin at 0_A) in such a way that the size of the box refers to the combined amount of the X and Y owned by the two individuals together.

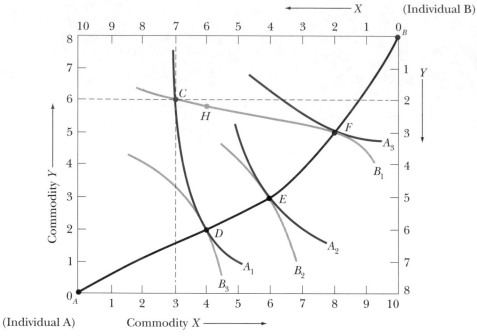

FIGURE 17.2   Edgeworth Box Diagram for Exchange   A point such as *C* indicates that individual A had 3*X* and 6*Y* (viewed from origin O_A), while individual B has 7*X* and 2*Y* (viewed from origin O_B) for a total of 10*X* and 8*Y* (the dimensions of the box). A's indifference curves (A_1, A_2, and A_3) are convex to O_A, while B's indifference curves (B_1, B_2, and B_3) are convex to O_B. Starting from point *C* where A_1 and B_1 intersect, individuals A and B can reach points on *DEF*, where one or both individuals gain. Curve $O_A DEFO_B$ is the contract curve for exchange. It is the locus of tangencies of the indifference curves (at which the MRS_{XY} are equal) for the two individuals and the economy is in general equilibrium of exchange.

their slope or marginal rate of substitution of commodity *X* for commodity *Y* (MRS_{XY}) differs. Starting at point *C*, individual A is willing to give up 4*Y* to get one additional unit of *X* (and move to point *D* on A_1), while individual B is willing to accept 0.2*Y* in exchange for one unit of *X* (and move to point *H* on B_1).[6] Because A is willing to give up much more *Y* than necessary to induce B to give up 1*X*, there is a basis for exchange that will benefit either or both individuals. This is true whenever, as at point *C*, the MRS_{XY} for the two individuals differs.

For example, starting from point *C*, if individual A exchanges 4*Y* for 1*X* with individual B, A moves from point *C* to point *D* along indifference curve A_1, while B moves from point *C* on B_1 to point *D* on B_3. Thus, individual B receives all of the gains from exchange while individual A gains or loses nothing (since A remains on A_1). At point *D*, A_1 and B_3 are tangent, so that their slopes (MRS_{XY}) are equal, and there is no further basis for exchange.[7]

_____

[6] That is, $MRS_{XY} = 4$ for A, and $MRS_{XY} = 0.2$ for B.

[7] At point *D*, the amount of *Y* that A is willing to give up for 1*X* is exactly equal to what B requires to give up 1*X*. Any further exchange would make either individual worse off than he or she is at point *D*.

Alternatively, if individual A exchanged $1Y$ for $5X$ with individual B, individual A would move from point C on A_1 to point F on A_3, while individual B would move from point C to point F along B_1. Then, A would reap all of the benefits from exchange while B would neither gain nor lose. At point F, MRS_{XY} for A equals MRS_{XY} for B and there is no further basis for exchange. Finally, if A exchanges $3Y$ for $3X$ with B and gets to point E, both individuals gain from exchange since point E is on A_2 and B_2. Thus, starting from point C, which is not on line DEF, both individuals can gain through exchange by getting to a point on line DEF between D and F. The greater A's bargaining strength, the closer the final equilibrium point of exchange will be to point F, and the greater will be the proportion of the total gains from exchange going to individual A (so that less will be left over for individual B).

Curve $0_A DEF 0_B$ is the **contract curve for exchange.** It is the locus of tangency points of the indifference curves of the two individuals.[8] That is, along the contract curve for exchange, the marginal rate of substitution of commodity X for commodity Y is the same for individuals A and B, and the economy is in general equilibrium of exchange. Thus, for equilibrium,

$$MRS_{XY}^A = MRS_{XY}^B \qquad [17.1]$$

Starting from any point not on the contract curve, both individuals can gain from exchange by getting to a point on the contract curve. *Once on the contract curve, one of the two individuals cannot be made better off without making the other worse off.* For example, a movement from point D (on A_1 and B_3) to point E (on A_2 and B_2) makes individual A better off but individual B worse off. Thus, the consumption contract curve is the locus of general equilibrium of exchange. For an economy composed of many consumers and many commodities, the general equilibrium of exchange occurs where the marginal rate of substitution between every pair of commodities is the same for all consumers consuming both commodities.

General Equilibrium of Production

Now that we have examined general equilibrium in a pure exchange economy with no production, we turn to general equilibrium of production in a simple economy in which no exchange takes place.

To examine general equilibrium of production, we deal with a very simple economy that produces only two commodities (X and Y) with only two inputs, labor (L) and capital (K). We construct an Edgeworth box diagram for production from the *isoquants* for commodities X and Y in a manner completely analogous to the Edgeworth box diagram for exchange of Figure 17.2. This is shown in Figure 17.3.

The **Edgeworth box diagram for production** shown in Figure 17.3 was obtained by rotating the isoquant diagram for commodity Y by 180 degrees (so that origin 0_Y appears in the top right-hand corner) and superimposing it on the isoquant diagram for commodity X (with origin 0_X) in such a way that the size of the box refers to the total amount of L and K available to the economy ($12L$ and $10K$). Any point inside the box indicates how the total amount of the two inputs is utilized in the production of the two commodities. For example,

---

[8] Such tangency points are assured because indifference curves are convex and the field is dense (i.e., there is an infinite number of indifference curves).

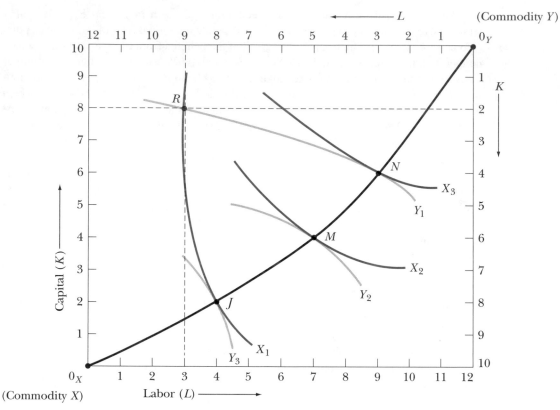

FIGURE 17.3   Edgeworth Box Diagram for Production   A point such as R indicates that $3L$ and $8K$ (viewed from origin 0_X) are used to produce X_1 of commodity X, and the remaining $9L$ and $2K$ (viewed from origin 0_Y) are used to produce Y_1 of Y. The isoquants for X (X_1, X_2, and X_3) are convex to 0_X, while the isoquants of Y (Y_1, Y_2, and Y_3) are convex to 0_Y. Starting from point R, where X_1 and Y_1 intersect, the economy can produce more of X, more of Y, or more of both by moving to a point on JMN. Curve $0_X JMN0_Y$ is the contract curve for production. It is the locus of tangencies of the isoquants (at which the $MRTS_{LK}$ are equal) for both commodities, and the economy is in general equilibrium of production.

point R indicates that $3L$ and $8K$ are used in the production of X_1 of commodity X, and the remaining $9L$ and $2K$ are used to produce Y_1 of Y. Three of X's isoquants (convex to origin 0_X) are X_1, X_2, and X_3. Three of Y's isoquants (convex to origin 0_Y) are Y_1, Y_2, and Y_3.

If this economy was initially at point R, it would not be maximizing its output of commodities X and Y because, at point R, the marginal rate of technical substitution of labor for capital ($MRTS_{LK}$) in the production of X (the absolute slope of X_1) exceeds the $MRTS_{LK}$ in the production of Y (the absolute slope of Y_1).[9] By simply transferring $6K$ from the production of X to the production of Y and $1L$ from the production of Y to the production of X, the economy can move from point R (on X_1 and Y_1) to point J (on X_1 and Y_3) and increase its output of Y without reducing its output of X.

---

[9] Review, if necessary, the definition and measurement of the marginal rate of technical substitution in Section 7.4.

Alternatively, this economy can move from point R to point N (and increase its output of X from X_1 to X_3 without reducing its output of Y_1) by transferring $2K$ from the production of X to the production of Y and $6L$ from Y to X. Or, by transferring $4K$ from the production of X to the production of Y and $4L$ from Y to X, this economy can move from point R (on X_1 and Y_1) to point M (on X_2 and Y_2), and increase its output of both X and Y. At points J, M, and N, an X isoquant is tangent to a Y isoquant so that the $MRTS_{LK}$ in the production of X equals $MRTS_{LK}$ in the production of Y.

Curve $0_X JMN 0_Y$ is the **contract curve for production.** It is the locus of tangency points of the isoquants for X and Y at which the marginal rate of technical substitution of labor for capital is the same in the production of X and Y. That is, the economy is in general equilibrium of production when

$$MRTS_{LK}^X = MRTS_{LK}^Y \qquad\qquad [17.2]$$

Thus, by simply transferring some of the given and fixed amounts of available L and K between the production of X and Y, this economy can move from a point not on the contract curve for production to a point on the curve and increase its output of either or both commodities. Once on its production contract curve, the economy can only increase the output of either commodity by reducing the output of the other. For example, by moving from point J (on X_1 and Y_3) to point M (on X_2 and Y_2), the economy increases its output of commodity X (by transferring $3L$ and $2K$ from the production of Y to the production of X), but its output of commodity Y falls. For an economy of many commodities and many inputs, the general equilibrium of production occurs where the marginal rate of technical substitution between any pair of inputs is the same for all commodities and producers using both inputs.

Derivation of the Production-Possibilities Frontier

From the production contract curve, we can derive the corresponding production-possibilities frontier or transformation curve by simply plotting the various combinations of outputs directly. For example, if isoquant X_1 in Figure 17.3 referred to an output of 4 units of commodity X and isoquant Y_3 referred to an output of 13 units of commodity Y, we can go from point J (X_1, Y_3) in Figure 17.3 to point J' $(4X, 13Y)$ in Figure 17.4. Similarly, if isoquant X_2 referred to an output of $10X$ and isoquant Y_2 to an output of $8Y$, we can go from point M (X_2, Y_2) in Figure 17.3 to point M' $(10X, 8Y)$ in Figure 17.4. Finally, if $X_3 = 12X$ and $Y_1 = 4Y$, we can plot point N (X_3, Y_1) from Figure 17.3 as point N' $(12X, 4Y)$ in Figure 17.4. By joining points $J'M'N'$ and other points similarly obtained, we derive the production-possibilities frontier or transformation curve of X for Y, TT, shown in Figure 17.4. Thus, the production-possibilities frontier is obtained by simply mapping or transferring the production contract curve from input space to output space.

The **production-possibilities frontier** or transformation curve shows the various combinations of commodities X and Y that the economy can produce by fully utilizing all of the fixed amounts of labor and capital with the best technology available. Since the production contract curve shows all points of general equilibrium of production, so does the production-possibilities frontier. That is, the production-possibilities frontier shows the maximum amount of either commodity that the economy can produce, given the amount of the other commodity that the economy is producing. For example, given that the economy

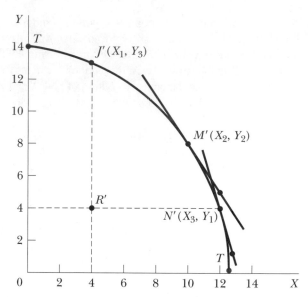

FIGURE 17.4   Production-Possibilities Frontier   The production–possibilities frontier or transformation curve *TT* is derived by mapping the production contract curve of Figure 17.3 from input to output space. Starting from point R', the economy could increase its output of *X* (point N'), of *Y* (point J'), or of both *X* and *Y* (point M'). The absolute slope or $MRT_{XY} = 3/2$ at point M' means that $3/2$ of *Y* must be given up to produce one additional unit of *X*. MRT_{XY} increases as we move down the frontier. Thus, at point N', $MRT_{XY} = 3$.

is producing $10X$, the maximum amount of commodity *Y* that the economy can produce is $8Y$ (point M' in Figure 17.4), and vice versa.

A point inside the production-possibilities frontier corresponds to a point off the production contract curve and indicates that the economy is not in general equilibrium of production, and it is not utilizing its inputs of labor and capital most efficiently. For example, point R', inside production-possibilities frontier *TT* in Figure 17.4, corresponds to point *R* in Figure 17.3, at which isoquant X_1 and Y_1 intersect. By simply reallocating some of the fixed labor and capital available between the production of *X* and *Y*, this economy can increase its output of *Y* only (and move from point R' to point J' in Figure 17.4), it can increase the output of *X* only (and move from point R' to point N'), or it can increase its output of both *X* and *Y* (the movement from point R' to point M'). On the other hand, a point outside the production-possibilities frontier cannot be achieved with the available inputs and technology.

Once on the production-possibilities frontier, the output of either commodity can be increased only by reducing the output of the other. For example, starting at point J' ($4X$ and $13Y$) on the production-possibilities frontier in Figure 17.4, the economy can move to point M' and produce $10X$ only by reducing the amount produced of *Y* by 5 units (i.e., to $8Y$).

The amount of commodity Y that the economy must give up, at a particular point on the production-possibilities frontier, so as to release just enough labor and capital to produce one additional unit of commodity X, is called the **marginal rate of transformation of X for Y (MRT_{XY}).** This is given by the absolute value of the slope of the production-possibilities frontier at that point. For example, at point M' on production-possibilities frontier TT in Figure 17.4, $MRT_{XY} = 3/2$ (the absolute value of the slope of the tangent to the production-possibilities frontier at point M').

The marginal rate of transformation of X for Y is also equal to the ratio of the marginal cost of X to the marginal cost of Y. That is, $MRT_{XY} = MC_X/MC_Y$. For example, at point M', $MRT_{XY} = 3/2$. This means that $3/2$ of Y must be given up to produce one additional unit of X. Thus, $MC_X = 3/2\ MC_Y$, and $MRT_{XY} = 3/2$. Another way of looking at this is that if $MC_Y = \$10$ and $MC_X = \$15$, this means that to produce one additional unit of X requires 1.5 or $3/2$ more units of labor and capital than to produce one additional unit of Y, so that $3/2$ of Y must be given up to produce one additional unit of X. This is exactly what the MRT_{XY} measures. Thus, at point M', $MRT_{XY} = MC_X/MC_Y = 3/2$.

As we move down the production-possibilities frontier (and produce more X and less Y), the MRT_{XY} increases, indicating that more and more Y must be given up to produce each additional unit of X. For example, at point N', the MRT_{XY} or absolute value of the slope of the production-possibilities frontier is 3 (up from $3/2$ at point M'). The reason for this is that, as the economy reduces its output of Y (in order to produce more of X), it releases labor and capital in combinations that become less and less suited for the production of more X. Thus, the economy incurs increasing MC_X in terms of Y. It is because of this imperfect input substitutability between the production of X and Y (and rising MC_X in terms of Y) that the production-possibilities frontier is concave to the origin.[10]

17.3 GENERAL EQUILIBRIUM OF PRODUCTION AND EXCHANGE AND PARETO OPTIMALITY

In this section, we examine general equilibrium of production and exchange and define the concept of Pareto optimality, which summarizes the marginal conditions for economic efficiency.

General Equilibrium of Production and Exchange Simultaneously

We now can use the production-possibilities frontier and the contract curve for exchange to examine how our very simple economy composed of two individuals (A and B), two commodities (X and Y), and two inputs (L and K) can reach *simultaneously* general equilibrium of production and exchange. This equilibrium is shown in Figure 17.5.

The production-possibilities frontier of Figure 17.5 is that of Figure 17.4, which was derived from the production contract curve of Figure 17.3. Thus, every point on production-possibilities frontier TT is a point of general equilibrium of production. Suppose that this

---

[10] If labor and capital were perfectly substitutable in the production of X and Y, MC_X would be constant in terms of Y, and the production-possibilities frontier would be a negatively-sloped straight line.

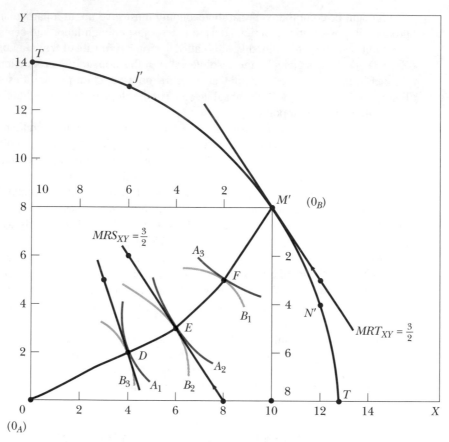

FIGURE 17.5   General Equilibrium of Production and Exchange   Production-possibilities frontier *TT* is that of Figure 17.4. Every point on *TT* is a point of general equilibrium of production. Starting from point *M'* (10*X*, 8*Y*) on the production-possibilities frontier, we constructed in Figure 17.4 the Edgeworth box diagram for exchange between individuals A and B shown in Figure 17.2. Every point on contract curve $0_A DEF0_B$ is a point of general equilibrium of exchange. Simultaneous general equilibrium of production and exchange is at point *E*, at which $MRT_{XY} = MRS_{XY}^A = MRS_{XY}^B = 3/2$.

economy produces 10*X* and 8*Y*, given by point *M'* on production-possibilities frontier *TT* in Figure 17.5.[11] By dropping perpendiculars from point *M'* to both axes, we can construct in Figure 17.5 the Edgeworth box diagram for exchange between individuals A and B of Figure 17.2. Note that the top right-hand corner of the Edgeworth box diagram for exchange of Figure 17.2 coincides with point *M'* on production-possibilities frontier *TT* in Figure 17.5. Given the indifference curves of individuals A and B and the output of 10*X* and 8*Y*, we derived contract curve $0_A DEF0_B$ for exchange in Figure 17.2. This curve is reproduced

---

[11] How this particular output level is determined is examined in Section 17.4.

in Figure 17.5. Every point on the contract curve for exchange in Figure 17.5 is a point of general equilibrium of exchange.

Thus, every point on production-possibilities frontier TT in Figure 17.5 is a point of general equilibrium of production, and every point on the contract curve for exchange is a point of general equilibrium of exchange. However, to be *simultaneously* in general equilibrium of production and exchange, the marginal rate of transformation of commodity X for commodity Y in production must be equal to the marginal rate of substitution of commodity X for commodity Y in consumption for individuals A and B. That is,

$$MRT_{XY} = MRS^A_{XY} = MRS^B_{XY} \qquad\qquad [17.3]$$

Geometrically, this equation corresponds to the point on the contract curve for exchange at which the common slope of an indifference curve of individual A and individual B equals the slope of production-possibilities frontier TT at the point of production. In Figure 17.5, this occurs at point E, where

$$MRS^A_{XY} = MRS^B_{XY} = MRT_{XY} = 3/2 \qquad\qquad [17.3A]$$

Thus, when producing $10X$ and $8Y$ (point M' on production-possibilities frontier TT), this economy is simultaneously in general equilibrium of production and exchange when individual A consumes $6X$ and $3Y$ (point E on his or her indifference curve A_2) and individual B consumes the remaining $4X$ and $5Y$ (point E on his or her indifference curve B_2).

If condition [17.3] did not hold, the economy would not be simultaneously in general equilibrium of production and exchange. For example, suppose that individuals A and B consumed at point D on the contract curve for exchange rather than at point E in Figure 17.5. At point D, the MRS_{XY} (the common absolute value of the slope of indifference curves A_1 and B_3) is 3. This means that individuals A and B are willing (indifferent) to give up $3Y$ to obtain one additional unit of X. Since in production only $3/2\ Y$ needs to be given up to produce an additional unit of X, society would have to produce more of X and less of Y to be simultaneously in general equilibrium of production and exchange. That is, if $MRS_{XY} = 3$, this society would not have chosen to produce at point M', but would have produced at point N' ($12X$ and $4Y$), where $MRS_{XY} = MRT_{XY} = 3$.

The opposite is true at point F. That is, at point F, $MRS_{XY} = 1/2$. Since $MRT_{XY} = 3/2$ at point M' (the point of production), more of Y needs to be given up in production to obtain one additional unit of X than individuals A and B are willing to give up in consumption. If this were the case, this society would have chosen to produce at point J' ($4X$ and $13Y$) where $MRS_{XY} = MRT_{XY} = 1/2$, rather than at point M'. Only by consuming at point E will $MRT_{XY} = MRS_{XY}$ for both individuals, and society will be simultaneously in general equilibrium of production and exchange when it produces at point M'.

We conclude the following about this simple economy when it is in general equilibrium of production and exchange: (1) it produces $10X$ and $8Y$ (point M' in Figure 17.5);[12] (2) individual A receives $6X$ and $3Y$, and individual B receives the remaining $4X$ and $5Y$ (point E in Figure 17.5); (3) to produce $10X$, $7L$ and $4K$ are used, while to produce $8Y$, the remaining $5L$ and $6K$ are used (see point M in Figure 17.3).[13]

---

[12] As pointed out in footnote 11, we will see how this level of output is determined in Section 17.4.

[13] In Section 17.4, we will also determine the relative price of commodity X (i.e., P_X/P_Y) and the relative price of labor time (i.e., P_L/P_K or w/r) for this simple economy when it is simultaneously in general equilibrium of production and exchange.

Marginal Conditions for Economic Efficiency and Pareto Optimality

With general equilibrium of production and exchange, **economic efficiency** is maximum and we have **Pareto optimality.**[14] According to this concept, *a distribution of inputs among commodities and of commodities among consumers is Pareto optimal or efficient if no reorganization of production and consumption is possible by which some individuals are made better off (in their own judgment) without making someone else worse off.* Any change that improves the well-being of some individuals without reducing the well-being of others clearly improves the welfare of society as a whole and should be undertaken. This will move society from a Pareto nonoptimal position to Pareto optimum. Once at Pareto optimum, no reorganization of production and exchange is possible that makes someone better off without, at the same time, making someone else worse off. To evaluate such changes requires interpersonal comparisons of utility, which are subjective and controversial.

In a very simple economy of two individuals, two commodities (X and Y), and no production, the contract curve for exchange (along which the MRS_{XY} is the same for both individuals) is the locus of Pareto optimum in exchange and consumption. As we have seen in Section 17.2, a movement from a point off the contract curve to a point on it improves the condition of either or both individuals, with the given quantities of the two commodities. Once on the contract curve, the economy is in general equilibrium or Pareto optimum in exchange, in the sense that either individual can be made better off only by making the other worse off. In an economy of many individuals and many commodities, Pareto optimum in exchange requires that the marginal rate of substitution between any pair of commodities be the same for all individuals consuming both commodities.

In a very simple economy of two commodities, two inputs (L and K), and no exchange, the production contract curve (along which the $MRTS_{LK}$ is the same for both commodities) is the locus of Pareto optimum in production. As we have seen in Section 17.2, a movement from a point off the production contract curve to a point on it makes it possible for the economy to produce more of either or both commodities, with the given inputs and technology. Once on the production contract curve, the economy is in general equilibrium or Pareto optimum in production in the sense that the economy can increase the output of either commodity only by reducing the output of the other. In an economy of many commodities and many inputs, Pareto optimum in production requires that the marginal rate of technical substitution between any pair of inputs be the same for all commodities and producers using both inputs.

Finally, Pareto optimum in production and exchange simultaneously in an economy of many inputs, many commodities, and many individuals requires that the marginal rate of transformation in production equals the marginal rate of substitution in consumption for every pair of commodities and for every pair of individuals consuming both commodities. In the case of a very simple economy composed of only two commodities and two individuals (A and B), Pareto optimality in production and consumption requires that

$$MRT_{XY} = MRS^A_{XY} = MRS^B_{XY}$$

---

[14] Vilfredo Pareto was the great Italian economist of the turn of the century who, in 1909, expressed the condition for maximum economic efficiency, which became known as Pareto optimality. See V. Pareto, *Manual of Political Economy,* translated by William Jaffé (New York: August Kelly, 1971).

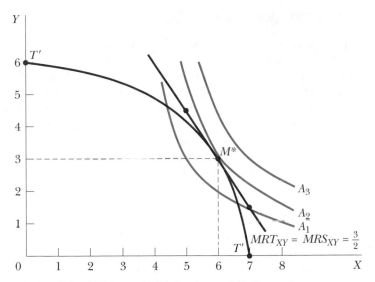

FIGURE 17.6   Efficiency in Production and Exchange in a "Robinson Crusoe" Economy   In a single-person economy, economic efficiency in production and exchange (and maximum social welfare) is achieved at point M^*, at which indifference curve A_2 for individual A (the only individual in society) is tangent to his or her production-possibilities frontier, $T'T'$. Output is $6X$ and $3Y$, and $MRT_{XY} = MRS_{XY} = 3/2$.

This was shown graphically in Figure 17.5 by the point on the contract curve for exchange at which the common slope of an indifference curve of individual A and individual B is equal to the slope of the production frontier at the point of production.

If we assume that there is only one individual (a Robinson Crusoe) in society, we achieve considerable graphic simplification in showing the point of economic efficiency in production and consumption.[15] This is given by point M^* in Figure 17.6, at which indifference curve A_2 for individual A (the only individual in society) is tangent to his or her production-possibilities frontier, $T'T'$. Any point on $T'T'$ represents a point of efficient production. Given $T'T'$, A_2 is the highest indifference curve that the individual can reach with his or her production-possibilities frontier. At point M^* (the tangency point of A_2 to $T'T'$), output is $6X$ and $3Y$, and $MRT_{XY} = MRS_{XY} = 3/2$. Production and consumption are economically efficient, and society (the individual) maximizes welfare.

17.4	PERFECT COMPETITION, ECONOMIC EFFICIENCY, AND EQUITY

In this section we show why perfect competition leads to economic efficiency or Pareto optimum, but not necessarily to equity.

---

[15] Since in this very special case there is no problem of interpersonal comparison of utility, the point of maximum economic efficiency in production and consumption also represents the point of maximum social welfare.

Perfect Competition and Economic Efficiency

With perfect competition in all input and commodity markets, the three marginal conditions for economic efficiency or Pareto optimum in production and exchange (Section 17.3) are automatically satisfied. This is the basic argument for perfect competition. We can easily prove that perfect competition leads to economic efficiency.

We have seen in Section 3.5 that a consumer maximizes utility or satisfaction when he or she reaches the highest indifference curve possible with his or her budget line. This occurs where an indifference curve is tangent to the budget line. At the tangency point, the slope of the indifference curve (the MRS_{XY}) is equal to the slope of the budget line (P_X/P_Y). Since P_X and P_Y, and thus P_X/P_Y, are the same for all consumers under perfect competition, the MRS_{XY} is also the same for all consumers consuming both commodities. This is the first marginal condition for economic efficiency or Pareto optimum in exchange. We can now also establish that for the simple economy examined in Section 17.3, $P_X/P_Y = 3/2$ (the absolute value of the slope of the common tangent to indifference curves A_2 and B_2 at point E in Figure 17.5).

We have also seen in Section 8.3 that efficiency in production requires that the $MRTS_{LK}$ (the absolute value of the slope of an isoquant) be equal to P_L/P_K or w/r (the ratio of the input prices given by the absolute value of the slope of the isocost line). Since P_L or w and P_K or r, and thus P_L/P_K or w/r, are the same for all producers under perfect competition, the $MRTS_{LK}$ is also the same for all producers using both inputs. This is the second marginal condition for economic efficiency or Pareto optimum in production. We can now also establish that for the simple economy examined in Section 17.3, P_L/P_K or $w/r = 2/3$ (the absolute value of the common tangent to isoquants X_2 and Y_2 at point M in Figure 17.3).[16]

Finally, we have seen in Section 17.3 that $MRT_{XY} = MC_X/MC_Y$, and in Section 9.3 that perfectly competitive firms produce where $MC_X = P_X$ and $MC_Y = P_Y$. Therefore, $MC_X/MC_Y = P_X/P_Y = MRT_{XY}$. Since we have also seen above that under perfect competition $MRT_{XY} = P_X/P_Y$ for all consumers consuming both commodities, we conclude that $MRT_{XY} = MRS_{XY}$ for all consumers consuming both commodities. This is the third marginal condition for economic efficiency and Pareto optimum in production and exchange. Thus, when the simple economy examined in Section 17.3 produces $10X$ and $8Y$ (point M' in Figure 17.5), $MRT_{XY} = MRS_{XY}^A = MRS_{XY}^B = 3/2$. Individual A should then consume $6X$ and $3Y$, and individual B should consume the remaining $4X$ and $5Y$ (point E in Figure 17.5) for the economy to be simultaneously at Pareto optimum in production and exchange.

The output of $10X$ and $8Y$ at point M' in Figure 17.5 is based on a particular distribution of inputs (income) between individuals A and B and on their tastes. A different distribution of income and/or tastes for individuals A and B would lead to a different combination of goods X and Y demanded. This would result in a different P_X/P_Y, different quantities of X and Y produced, and different levels of satisfaction for A and B. For example, suppose that individuals A and B demanded $12X$ and $4Y$ (point N' in Figure 17.5). Then, general

---

[16] Note that in microeconomic theory, we are only concerned with *relative,* not absolute, input and commodity prices. This means that proportionate changes in (e.g., doubling or halving) all input prices and/or all commodity prices do not change the solution to the general equilibrium model. If we want to get unique absolute (dollar) values for P_X, P_Y, P_L (or w), and P_K (or r), we would have to add a monetary equation, such as Fisher's "equation of exchange" to our model. This is done in a course in macroeconomic theory but is not needed in microeconomics.

equilibrium of production and exchange or Pareto optimality requires that $MRT_{XY} = P_X/P_Y = MRS^A_{XY} = MRS^B_{XY} = 3$ (the absolute slope of TT at point N'). This involves constructing an Edgeworth box diagram from point N' and retracing all the steps of the analysis in Section 17.3. In a purely exchange economy (i.e., one in which there is no production), the equilibrium P_X/P_Y is the one that exactly matches the desired quantity of X and Y that each individual wants to exchange. If B wants more of X for a given amount of Y than A is willing to exchange, then P_X/P_Y will rise until the demand for the quantities of X and Y to be exchanged match. Similarly, if B wants less of X for a given amount of Y than A is willing to exchange, P_X/P_Y will fall until equilibrium is reached.

Efficiency and Equity

The fact that perfect competition leads to optimum economic efficiency and Pareto optimum in production and exchange is no small achievement. It proves Adam Smith's famous **law of the invisible hand** stated more than 200 years ago. Smith's law postulates that in a free market economy, each individual by pursuing his or her own selfish interests is led, as if by an *invisible hand*, to promote the well-being of society more so than he or she intends or even understands.[17] This law leads to the **first theorem of welfare economics,** which postulates that *an equilibrium produced by competitive markets exhausts all possible gains from exchange,* or that *equilibrium in competitive markets is Pareto optimal.* There is also a **second theorem of welfare economics.** This postulates that *when indifference curves are convex to their origin, every efficient allocation (every point on the contract curve for exchange) is a competitive equilibrium for some initial allocation of goods or distribution of inputs (income).* The significance of the second welfare theorem is that the issue of equity in distribution is logically separable from the issue of efficiency in allocation. This means that whatever the redistribution of income that society wants would lead to the exhaustion of all possible gains from exchange under perfect competition. Pareto optimality does not, therefore, imply equity. Society can use taxes and subsidies to achieve what it considers to be a more equitable distribution of income. These may discourage work, however, and show that there is usually a trade-off between efficiency and equity (see Example 17–5).[18]

For economic efficiency and Pareto optimum to be reached, there should be no market failure. **Market failures** arise in the presence of imperfect competition, externalities, and public goods. *Externalities* and *public goods* will be examined in the next chapter. Here, we examine why imperfect competition in the product and input markets leads to economic inefficiency and Pareto nonoptimality.

To show that imperfect competition in the product market leads to economic inefficiency and Pareto nonoptimality, remember that in Part Four of the text it was shown that a profit-maximizing firm always produces where marginal revenue (MR) equals marginal cost (MC). If commodity Y is produced in a perfectly competitive market, $P_Y = MR_Y = MC_Y$.

---

[17] See A. Smith, *The Wealth of Nations* (Toronto: Random House, 1937), Book IV, Chapter 2, p. 423; and J. Persky, "Adam Smith's Invisible Hand," *Journal of Economic Perspectives,* fall 1989, pp. 195–201.

[18] See A. Okun, *Equality and Efficiency: The Big Tradeoff* (Washington, D.C.: Brookings Institution, 1975). We will return to questions of equity in Sections 17.6 and 17.7.

On the other hand, if commodity X is produced by a monopolist (or other imperfect competitor), $P_X > MR_X = MC_X$. Then,

$$MRT_{XY} = \frac{MC_X}{MC_Y} = \frac{MR_X}{MR_Y} < \frac{P_X}{P_Y} = MRS_{XY}$$

That is, $MRT_{XY} < MRS_{XY}$, so that the third condition for Pareto optimum and economic efficiency (discussed in Section 17.3) is violated.

To show that imperfect competition in the input market leads to economic inefficiency and Pareto nonoptimality, remember that in Part Five of the text it was shown that a profit-maximizing firm always produces where the marginal revenue product (MRP) of each input equals the marginal resource cost (MRC) for the input. If P is the price of the input, and the input market is perfectly competitive, $MRP = MRC = P$. Otherwise, $MRP = MRC > P$. Now suppose that all markets in the economy are perfectly competitive, except that the firm producing commodity X is a monopsonist in its labor market (i.e., it is the sole employer of labor in its labor market). Therefore, $MRP = MRC > P$ in the production of commodity X, while $MRP = MRC = P$ in the production of Y. That is, $MRTS_{LK}^X > MRTS_{LK}^Y$, so that the first of the conditions for Pareto optimum and economic efficiency (discussed in Section 17.4) is violated.

Finally, note that perfect competition leads to efficiency and Pareto optimum in production and exchange *at a particular point in time*. Over time, tastes, the supply of inputs, and technology change; what is most efficient at one point in time may not be most efficient over time. In short, perfect competition leads to *static, but not necessarily to dynamic, efficiency*. (This was discussed in Section 13.3.)

EXAMPLE 17–2

Watering Down Efficiency in the Pricing of Water

In some countries (Los Angeles, for example), the price of water is lower for irrigation than for most other purposes. This reduces economic efficiency because the marginal rate of technical substitution between water and other inputs differs in irrigation than in other uses. For example, suppose that the price of 1,000 cubic feet of water when used for irrigation is equal to the daily wage of an unskilled worker, but when used to wash cars it is twice the daily wage of the unskilled worker. So, a farmer will use water until the marginal rate of technical substitution between water and labor is equal to 1, but a car-washing firm will do so until $MRTS = 2$. Water and labor inputs are then utilized at a point (such as R in Figure 17.3) at which the isoquants intersect off the production contract curve, and production is inefficient. In this case, the farmer will use too much water and too little labor, whereas the car-washing firm will underutilize water and overutilize labor.

If the price of water were the same for both the farmer and the car-washing firm, economic efficiency in production would increase. Each producer would then use water and labor until the $MRTS$ between water and labor would be equal to the relative price of these two inputs. The result is that agricultural output declines and car-washing production increases, for a net increase in overall state output, with the given quantity of water and unskilled labor available. With the sharp increase in the demand for water in California as a result of rapid population growth, and with the reduced supply due to drought, the efficient use of scarce water resources became even more important in California since the early 1980s. This has generally meant an increase in the *relative* availability of water for nonirrigation purposes and an increase in the relative price of water in all uses. In the future, we are likely to see fewer golf courses built in the desert and, perhaps, less cotton and rice grown in California!

Sources: J. Hirschleifer, J. C. DeHaven, and W. J. Milliman, *Water Supply: Economics, Technology, and Policy* (Chicago: University of Chicago Press, 1960); "California Moves to Revitalize San Francisco Bay," *New York Times*, December 11, 1992, p. 28; Subcommittee on Water and Power, *Central Valley Project Improvement Act* (Washington, D.C.: U.S. Government Printing Office, 1992); and "The Coming Water Crisis," *U.S. News and World Report,* August 12, 2002, pp. 23–30.

17.5   GENERAL EQUILIBRIUM OF PRODUCTION AND EXCHANGE WITH INTERNATIONAL TRADE

An important example of general equilibrium of production and exchange is provided by international trade, say, between nations A and B. Suppose that nation A is endowed with an abundance of labor (L) relative to capital (K) with respect to nation B, and commodity X is labor intensive (i.e., the L/K ratio in the production of X is greater than in the production of Y). Given the same technology and tastes in the two nations, the cost (in terms of the amount of Y to be given up) of producing an additional unit of X (i.e., $MRT_{XY} = P_X/P_Y$) is lower in nation A than in nation B. We say that nation A has a **comparative advantage** in commodity X and nation B has a comparative advantage in commodity Y.

With trade, nation A specializes in the production of commodity X (i.e., it produces more of X than it demands for internal consumption) in order to exchange it for commodity Y from nation B. On the other hand, nation B specializes in the production of commodity Y (i.e., it produces more of Y than it demands for internal consumption) in order to exchange it for commodity X from nation A. With each nation specializing in the production of the commodity of its comparative advantage (nation A in commodity X and B in Y), the combined output of X and Y by the two nations is larger than without specialization. Both nations then share the increased output of X and Y through voluntary exchange (trade), and both are better off than without trade.

As each nation specializes in the production of the commodity of its comparative advantage, it will incur increasing opportunity costs. Specialization in production reaches the equilibrium level when $MRT_{XY} = P_X/P_Y$ is the same in both nations. The two nations are then simultaneously in general equilibrium of production and exchange (trade) when $MRT_{XY} = P_X/P_Y = MRS_{XY}^A = MRS_{XY}^B$.[19]

---

[19] See D. Salvatore, *International Economics,* 8th ed. (New York: John Wiley & Sons, 2003), Chapter 5.

EXAMPLE 17–3

The Basis and the Gains from International Trade

We can show general equilibrium of production and exchange and the gains from specialization in production and trade with the aid of Figure 17.7. The production-possibilities frontier is AA for nation A and BB for nation B. The different shapes of the two production-possibilities frontiers result from nation A having a relative abundance of labor and commodity X being the labor-intensive commodity, with nation B having a relative abundance of capital and commodity Y being the capital-intensive commodity. For simplicity, we assume that both technology and tastes are the same in both nations. Suppose that in the absence of trade, nation A is observed to be producing and consuming at point C, while nation B is observed to be at point C'.[20] Since $MRT_{XY} = P_X/P_Y$ (the

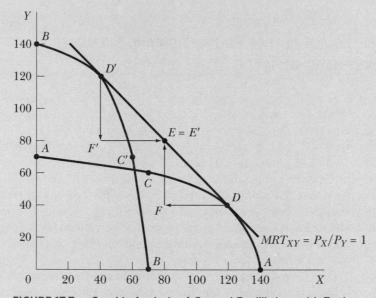

FIGURE 17.7   Graphic Analysis of General Equilibrium with Trade
The production–possibilities frontier is AA for nation A and BB for nation B. In the absence of trade, nation A is at point C and nation B is at point C'. Since $MRT_{XY} = P_X/P_Y$ (the absolute value of the slope of the production-possibilities frontier) is lower at point C than at point C', nation A has a comparative advantage in X while nation B has a comparative advantage in Y. With trade, A produces at point D, exchanges $40X$ for $40Y$ with B, and consumes at $E > C$. Nation B produces at point D', exchanges $40Y$ for $40X$ with A, and consumes at $E' > C'$.

---

[20] This means that $MRT_{XY} = MRS_{XY} = P_X/P_Y$ in each country, so that each country is simultaneously in equilibrium of production and exchange in isolation (i.e., in the absence of trade).

absolute slope of the production-possibilities frontier) is lower at point C for nation A than at point C' for nation B, nation A has a comparative advantage in commodity X, while nation B has a comparative advantage in commodity Y.

With the opening of trade, nation A specializes in the production of X (moves down its production-possibilities frontier from point C) and incurs increasing opportunity costs in the production of more X (i.e., the $MRT_{XY} = P_X/P_Y$ rises). Nation B specializes in the production of Y (moves up its production-possibilities frontier from point C') and incurs increasing opportunity costs in the production of more Y (i.e., the $MRT_{XY} = P_Y/P_X$ rises, which means that $MRT_{XY} = P_X/P_Y$ falls). Specialization in production proceeds until nation A has reached point D and nation B has reached point D', at which $MRT_{XY} = P_X/P_Y$ is the same in both nations. Nation A might then exchange $40X$ (DF) for $40Y$ (FE) with nation B and reach point E. At point E, nation A consumes $10X$ and $20Y$ more than at point C without trade. With trade, nation B consumes at point E' ($= E$) or $20X$ and $10Y$ more than at point C' without trade. Production and trade is in (general) equilibrium, and both nations gain.

Note that with trade, both nations consume $80X$ and $80Y$ (i.e., point E for nation A coincides with point E' for nation B). This would be true if both nations not only had the same technology and tastes but were also of equal size. These simplifying assumptions were made to simplify the graphic analysis. However, we can show comparative advantage (i.e., the basis for trade) and the gains from trade graphically even if the two nations have different technologies and tastes, and if they are unequal in size.[21]

17.6 | WELFARE ECONOMICS AND UTILITY-POSSIBILITIES FRONTIERS

Having completed our analysis of general equilibrium, we now move on to examine welfare economics. We begin by examining the meaning of welfare economics and then we will go on to derive the utility-possibilities frontier and the grand utility-possibilities frontier.

The Meaning of Welfare Economics

Welfare economics studies the conditions under which the solution to the general equilibrium model presented earlier in this chapter can be said to be optimal. It examines the conditions for economic efficiency in the production of output and in the exchange of commodities, and equity in the distribution of income. This is to be clearly distinguished from the everyday usage of the term "welfare," which refers mostly to government programs to aid low-income families. That topic is only a very small part of what welfare economics covers.

The maximization of society's well-being requires the optimal allocation of inputs among commodities and the optimal allocation of commodities (i.e., distribution of income) among consumers. The conditions for the optimal allocation of inputs among commodities and exchange of commodities among consumers have already been discussed.

---

[21] See D. Salvatore, *International Economics, op. cit.,* Chapter 3.

These are objective criteria devoid of ethical connotations or value judgments. On the other hand, it is impossible to objectively determine the optimal distribution of income. This necessarily requires interpersonal comparisons of utility and value judgments on the relative "deservingness" or merit of various members of society, and different people will inevitably have different opinions.

For example, taxing $100 away from individual A and giving it as a subsidy to individual B will certainly make B better off and A worse off. But who is to say that the society composed of both individuals is better or worse off as a whole? Determining this involves comparing the utility lost by individual A to the utility gained by individual B (i.e., making interpersonal comparison of utility). And even if A has a high income and B has a low income to begin with, different people will have different opinions on whether this increases social welfare, reduces it, or leaves it unchanged. Therefore, no entirely objective or scientific rule can be defined. The difficulty in making interpersonal comparisons of utility is clearly demonstrated in rationing hospital care, discussed in Example 17–4.

EXAMPLE 17–4

"The Painful Prescription: Rationing Hospital Care"

The great difficulty with interpersonal comparison of utility in making social choices is aptly exemplified by the need to ration hospital care. New therapeutic techniques (such as open-heart surgery) and new diagnostic devices (such as CAT scanners) have improved medical care but have greatly added to costs. For example, open-heart surgery costs tens of thousands of dollars and replaces the much cheaper (but somewhat less effective) use of drugs in treating patients with heart disease. This development raises difficult choices for society in general, and for physicians and hospitals in particular, as they try to contain the ever-rising costs of medical care. In England, only a handful of patients over the age of 55 with chronic kidney failure are referred for expensive dialysis; the others are simply allowed to die of chronic renal failure. The idea of rationing medical care is generally alien to Americans, accustomed as they are to expect the best care that can be medically provided. Nevertheless, ever-increasing medical costs have inevitably led to rationing in the use of some new and expensive techniques and diagnostic devices.

As pointed out by Fuchs, medical care has always been rationed in the United States and elsewhere, because "no nation is wealthy enough to provide all the care that is technically feasible and desirable. . . ." Therefore, the change is not between "no rationing and rationing, but rather in the way rationing takes place—who does the rationing and who is affected by it." The way hospital care (particularly the use of the more advanced and costly new diagnostic techniques) is to be rationed has given rise to a prolonged national debate in the United States. The introduction of "managed competition" with HMOs (see Example 1–1) during the last decade allows insurance companies to provide consumers with incentives to "price shop" when choosing doctors and hospitals as a way of keeping health-care costs down. The courts need also to redefine negligence so as to limit medical malpractice suits and higher physicians' insurance costs (which are then passed on to consumers in the form of higher costs of medical care). Be that as it may, health-care costs are likely to continue to rise as a proportion of GDP in the United States in the coming years. The same strain is experienced by government-financed health-care services in Canada, Britain, Germany, and Scandinavia, among other countries.

Sources: V. R. Fuchs, "The 'Rationing' of Medical Care," *The New England Journal of Medicine,* December 13, 1984, pp. 1572–1573; H. J. Aaron and W. B. Schwartz, *The Painful Prescription: Rationing Hospital Care* (Washington, D.C.: Brookings Institution, 1984); "How Managed Care Will Allow Market Forces to Solve the Problems," *New York Times,* August 13, 1995, p. 12; M. Feldstein, "The Economics of Health and Health Care: What Have We Learned? What Have I Learned?" *American Economic Review, Papers and Proceedings,* May 1995, pp. 28–31; "Medicine Isn't an Economic-Free Zone," *Wall Street Journal,* June 22, 2001, p. A14; "Canada Health Care Shows Strains," *New York Times,* October 11, 2001, p. 12; and "Propelled by Drugs and Hospital Costs, Health Spending Surged in 2000," *New York Times,* January 8, 2002, p. 14.

Utility-Possibilities Frontier

By assigning utility rankings to the indifference curves of individual A and individual B in Figure 17.5, we can map or transfer the contract curve for exchange of Figure 17.5 from output or commodity space to utility space, and thus derive utility-possibilities frontier $U_{M'}U_{M'}$ in Figure 17.8. Specifically, if indifference curve A_1 in Figure 17.5 refers to 200 units of utility for individual A (i.e., $U_A = 200$ utils) and B_3 refers to $U_B = 600$ utils, we can go from point D (on A_1 and B_3) in commodity space in Figure 17.5 to point D' in utility space in Figure 17.8. Similarly, if A_2 refers to $U_A = 400$ utils and B_2 refers to $U_B = 500$ utils, we can go from point E (on A_2 and B_2) in Figure 17.5 to point E' in Figure 17.8. Finally, if A_3 refers to $U_A = 500$ utils and B_1 refers to $U_B = 200$ utils, we can go from point F (on A_3 and B_1) in Figure 17.5 to point F' in Figure 17.8.[22] By joining points $D'E'F'$ and other points similarly obtained, we derive utility-possibilities frontier $U_{M'}U_{M'}$ in Figure 17.8. Thus, the utility-possibilities frontier is obtained by mapping or transferring the contract curve for exchange from output or commodity space into utility space.

The **utility-possibilities frontier** shows the various combinations of utilities received by individuals A and B (i.e., U_A and U_B) when this simple economy is in general equilibrium or Pareto optimum in exchange. It is the locus of maximum utility for one individual for any given level of utility for the other individual. For example, given that $U_A = 400$ utils, the maximum utility of individual B is $U_B = 500$ utils (point E'). A point such as C in Figure 17.2 (at which indifference curves A_1 and B_1 intersect off exchange contract curve $0_A DEF0_B$) corresponds to point C' inside utility-possibilities frontier $U_{M'}U_{M'}$ in

---

[22] Note that the scale along the horizontal axis refers only to individual A, while the scale along the vertical axis refers only to B. Thus, $U_A = 400$ utils is not necessarily smaller than $U_B = 500$ utils, since no interpersonal comparison of utility is implied. Furthermore, the scale along either axis is ordinal, not cardinal. That is, $U_A = 300$ utils is greater than $U_A = 200$ utils, but not necessarily 1.5 times larger. Note also that utility-possibilities frontier $U_{M'}U_{M'}$, is negatively sloped, but irregularly rather than smoothly shaped.

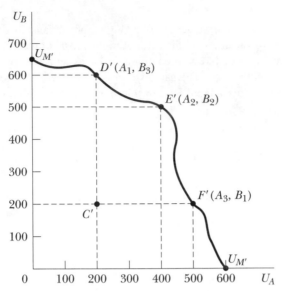

FIGURE 17.8   Utility-Possibilities Frontier
Utility-possibilities frontier $U_{M'}U_{M'}$ shows the various combinations of utilities received by individuals A and B (i.e., U_A and U_B) when the economy composed of individuals A and B is in general equilibrium or Pareto optimum in exchange. The frontier is obtained by mapping exchange contract curve $O_A DEF O_B$ in Figure 17.5 from output or commodity space to utility space. Specifically, if A_1 refers to $U_A = 200$ utils and B_3 to $U_B = 600$ utils, point D in Figure 17.5 can be plotted as point D' in this figure. Point E can be plotted as point E', and point F as F'. By joining points $D'E'F'$, we get utility-possibilities frontier $U_{M'}U_{M'}$.

Figure 17.8. By simply redistributing the $10X$ and $8Y$ available to the economy (point M' in Figure 17.5) between individuals A and B, the economy can move from point C' to point D' in Figure 17.8 and increase U_B, or to point F' and increase U_A, or to point E' and increase both U_A and U_B. A point outside the utility-possibilities frontier cannot be reached with the available amounts of commodities X and Y. Of all points of Pareto optimality in exchange along utility-possibilities frontier $U_{M'}U_{M'}$, in Figure 17.8, only point E' (which corresponds to point E in Figure 17.5) is also a point of Pareto optimality in production. That is, at point E', $MRS_{XY}^A = MRS_{XY}^B = MRT_{XY} = P_X/P_Y = 3/2$.

Grand Utility-Possibilities Frontier

We have seen that utility-possibilities frontier $U_{M'}, U_{M'}$, in Figure 17.8 (repeated in Figure 17.9) was derived from the contract curve for exchange drawn from point 0 to point M'

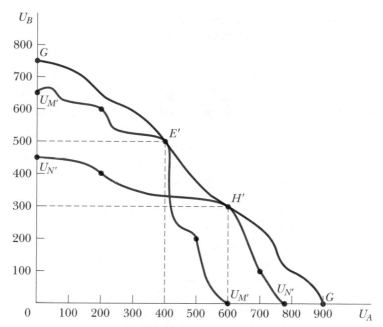

FIGURE 17.9   Grand Utility-Possibilities Frontier   Utility-possibilities frontier $U_{M'}U_{M'}$ is that of Figure 17.8. Utility-possibilities frontier $U_{N'}U_{N'}$ is derived from the contract curve for exchange in the Edgeworth box diagram constructed from point N' on the production-possibilities frontier of Figure 17.5. By joining E', H', and other Pareto optimum points of production and exchange similarly obtained, we get grand utility-possibilities frontier $GE'H'G$.

on the production-possibilities frontier in Figure 17.5. If we pick another point on the production-possibilities frontier of Figure 17.5, say, point N', we can construct another Edgeworth box diagram and get another contract curve for exchange, this one drawn from point 0 to point N' in Figure 17.5. From this different contract curve for exchange (not shown in Figure 17.5), we can derive another utility-possibilities frontier ($U_{N'}U_{N'}$ in Figure 17.9) and obtain another Pareto optimum point in production and exchange (point H' in Figure 17.9). By then joining points E', H', and other points similarly obtained, we can derive grand utility-possibilities frontier $GE'H'G$ in Figure 17.9).[23]

Thus, the **grand utility-possibilities frontier** is the envelope to the utility-possibilities frontiers at Pareto optimum points of production and exchange. The grand utility-possibilities frontier indicates that no reorganization of the production-exchange process is possible that makes someone better off without, at the same time, making someone else worse off. This is as far as objective analysis goes. To determine the Pareto optimum point in production and exchange at which social welfare is maximum, we need a social welfare function.

---

[23] Note that the various utility-possibilities frontiers and the grand utility-possibilities frontier derived from them are negatively sloped but are usually irregularly shaped (as in Figure 17.9).

However, since this is based on interpersonal comparisons of utility (which is not allowed), we cannot determine the point of maximum social welfare.

EXAMPLE 17–5
From Welfare to Work—The Success of Welfare Reform in the United States

A 1995 study by Tanner, Moore, and Hartman found that welfare payments provided welfare recipients with higher incomes than they would have received from many entry-level jobs, thus discouraging welfare recipients from finding work. The study measured the combined value of the benefits for a typical welfare family from various programs [such as Aid to Families with Dependent Children (AFDC), food stamps, Medicaid, and housing, nutrition, and energy assistance] and compared it with the income a worker would have to earn to get the same after-tax benefit as under the welfare program.

The study found that in the early 1990s in order to match the value of the welfare benefits, a mother of two children would have to earn as much as $36,000 in Hawaii (the state with the most generous welfare program) and $11,500 in Mississippi (the least generous state). Welfare paid the equivalent of $8 per hour in 40 states, $10 per hour in 17 states, and more than $12 per hour in Hawaii, Alaska, Massachusetts, Connecticut, Washington, D.C., New Work, New Jersey, and Rhode Island. Welfare benefits were even higher in large cities. For example, welfare provided the equivalent of an hourly pretax wage of $14.75 in New York City, $12.45 in Philadelphia, $11.35 in Baltimore, and $10.90 in Detroit. The study also found that welfare paid more than the entry-level salary for a computer programmer in 6 states, more than first-year salary of a teacher in 9 states, more than the average salary of a secretary in 29 states, and more than the salary of a janitor in 47 states. The study concluded that because of generous welfare benefits, welfare recipients were likely to choose welfare over work and become permanently dependent. Indeed, 70% of welfare recipients were found not to be looking for work. It is not difficult to see why: The typical untrained, uneducated welfare mother was not likely to find a job that paid $10 to $12 per hour (more than twice the minimum wage).

All of this changed with the Personal Responsibility and Work Opportunity Reconciliation Act of 1996 (PRWORA), otherwise known as welfare reform. This ended welfare as entitlements, available to all persons who qualified, and required recipients to look for work as a condition for continued assistance. Rather than simply disbursing payments to welfare recipients on demand, the Federal Government provided states with a block of funds to run this portion of the welfare program with the aim of getting welfare recipients off the welfare lists by encouraging them to find jobs. Welfare reform was a stunning success: It cut the number of welfare recipients from 12.2 million in 1996 to 5.8 million in 2000. The reform also led to an increase in the income of poor people, but at a slower rate than the reductions in welfare rolls. The rapidly growing economy helped, but most of the reduction in the number of welfare recipients was due to welfare reform. The proof? During periods of rapid economic expansion during the 1980s and early 1990s, welfare rolls generally increased. Since the welfare reform of 1996, they were cut by more than half. Welfare reform could be improved further by tidying up the food-stamps program, getting rid of the marriage penalty tax for the poor, and expanding the earned-income tax credit for the working poor.

Sources: M. Tanner, S. Moore, and D. Hartman, *The Work vs. Welfare Trade-Off* (Washington, D.C.: Cato Institute, 1995); "Rewriting the Social Contract," *Business Week,* November 20, 1995, pp. 120–134; "From Welfare to Work," *Brookings Review,* fall 1999, pp. 27–30; and "America's Great Achievement," *The Economist,* August 25, 2001, pp. 25–27.

17.7   SOCIAL POLICY CRITERIA

In this section we examine some very important criteria for measuring changes in social welfare and Arrow's impossibility theorem.

Measuring Changes in Social Welfare

There are four different criteria to determine whether a particular policy raises social welfare. The first is the **Pareto criterion,** discussed in Section 17.3 and accepted by nearly all economists. According to this criterion, a policy increases social welfare if it benefits some members of society (in their own judgment) without harming anyone. In terms of Figure 17.10, a movement from point C^*, inside grand utility-possibilities frontier GG, to points E', H', or any point between E' and H' (such as point V) on GG, benefits one or both individuals and harms none; thus, it passes the Pareto criterion. In contrast, a movement from point C^* to point Z on GG makes individual B much better off but individual A a little worse off, and so it does not pass the Pareto criterion. Because most policies will benefit some and harm others,[24] the Pareto criterion does not go very far, and it is biased in favor of the status quo.

To overcome this limitation of the Pareto criterion, Kaldor and Hicks introduced the second welfare criterion, which is based on the **compensation principle.**[25] According to the **Kaldor–Hicks criterion,** a change is an improvement if those who gain from the change can fully compensate the losers and still retain some gain. In terms of the movement from point C^* to point Z in Figure 17.10, individual B (the gainer) could fully compensate individual A for his or her loss, so that society could move from point C^* to point E' (instead of from point C^* to Z) on GG and we can determine that social welfare is higher.[26] Yet, this conclusion is not as clear-cut as it may seem.

First, it is possible (though unusual) for the Kaldor–Hicks criterion to indicate that a given policy increases social welfare but also to indicate that, after the change, a movement back to

---

[24] For example, a tax on high-income people to finance aid to low-income families benefits the latter but harms the former. Even the breakup of a monopoly harms someone (the monopolist who loses the source of profits).

[25] N. Kaldor, "Welfare Propositions in Economics and Interpersonal Comparisons of Utility," *Economic Journal,* December 1939, pp. 549–552; and J. R. Hicks, "The Foundations of Welfare Economics," *Economic Journal,* December 1939, pp. 696–712.

[26] One real-world example of actual compensation is given by the trade adjustment assistance provided since 1962 by the Trade Expansion Act for U.S. workers displaced by negotiated tariff reductions. This assistance was justified by the much greater benefits to society as a whole resulting from trade liberalization. See D. Salvatore, *International Economics, op. cit.,* Chapter 9.

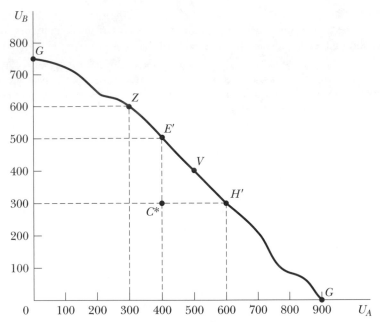

FIGURE 17.10   Measuring Changes in Social Welfare   A movement from point C^* to a point from E' to H' on grand utility-possibilities frontier GG benefits one or both individuals and harms no one. Thus, the movement increases social welfare according to the Pareto criterion. A movement from point C^* to point Z increases social welfare according to the Kaldor–Hicks criterion, since individual B could fully compensate individual A for his or her loss and still retain some gain. However, since this type of reasoning is based on interpersonal comparisons of utility, social welfare need not be higher.

the original position also increases social welfare. This limitation can be overcome with the third or **Scitovsky criterion.**[27] This is a double Kaldor–Hicks test. That is, according to Scitovsky, a change is an improvement if it satisfies the Kaldor–Hicks criterion, and, after the change, a movement back to the original position *does not* satisfy the Kaldor–Hicks criterion.

Another shortcoming of the Kaldor–Hicks criterion is more serious. It arises because the compensation principle measures the welfare changes of the gainers and losers in monetary units. For example, if a policy increases the income of individual B by \$100 but lowers the income of individual A by \$60, social welfare has increased according to the Kaldor–Hicks criterion (because individual B could transfer \$60 of his or her \$100 income gain to individual A and retain \$40).[28] Since compensation is not actually required, the Kaldor–Hicks criterion is based on the assumption that the gain in utility of individual B

---

[27] T. Scitovsky, "A Note on Welfare Propositions in Economics," *Review of Economics and Statistics,* November 1941, pp. 77–78.
[28] If compensation actually took place (something that is not required by the Kaldor–Hicks criterion), the Pareto criterion would suffice (since individual B is better off and individual A is not harmed), and the Kaldor–Hicks criterion would be superfluous.

(when his or her income rises by \$100) is greater than the loss of utility to individual A (when his or her income falls by \$60). Yet, this line of reasoning is based on interpersonal comparisons of utility, and social welfare need not be higher.

The only way to overcome this limitation of the Kaldor–Hicks criterion is to squarely face the problem of interpersonal comparison of utility. This leads us to the fourth welfare criterion, which is based on the construction of a **Bergson social welfare function** from the explicit value judgments of society.[29] A particular policy can then be said to increase social welfare if it puts society on a higher social indifference curve. However, as we will see in the next section, a social welfare function is extremely difficult or impossible to construct by democratic vote.

Arrow's Impossibility Theorem

Nobel laureate Kenneth Arrow proved that a social welfare function cannot be derived by democratic vote (i.e., reflect the preferences of all the individuals in society). This proof is known as **Arrow's impossibility theorem.**[30]

Arrow lists the following four conditions that he believes must hold for a social welfare function to reflect individual preferences:

1. Social welfare choices must be transitive. That is, if X is preferred to Y and Y is preferred to Z, then X must be preferred to Z.
2. Social welfare choices must not be responsive in the opposite direction to changes in individual preferences. That is, if choice X moves up in the ranking of one or more individuals and does not move down in the ranking of any other individual, then choice X cannot move down in the social welfare ranking.
3. Social welfare choices cannot be dictated by any one individual inside or outside the society.
4. Social choices must be independent of irrelevant alternatives. For example, if society prefers X to Y and Y to Z, then society must prefer X to Y even in the absence of alternative Z.

Arrow showed that a social welfare function cannot be obtained at by democratic voting without violating at least one of the four conditions. This can easily be proved for the first of the conditions. For example, suppose that Ann, Bob, and Charles (the three individuals in a society) rank alternatives X, Y, and Z as in Table 17.1.

Consider first the choice between alternatives X and Y. The majority (Ann and Charles) prefers X to Y. Now consider the choice between alternatives Y and Z. The majority (Ann and Bob) prefers Y to Z. It might then be concluded that since the majority prefers X to Y and Y to Z, the society composed of Ann, Bob, and Charles would prefer X to Z. However, from Table 17.1, we see that the majority (Bob and Charles) prefers Z to X. Therefore, the preference of the majority is inconsistent with the preferences of the individuals making up the majority. In short, this society cannot derive a social welfare function by democratic voting even if individual preferences are consistent. This is sometimes referred to as the "voting paradox."

---

[29] A. Bergson, "A Reformulation of Certain Aspects of Welfare Economics," *Quarterly Journal of Economics,* February 1938, pp. 310–334.

[30] K. J. Arrow, *Social Choice and Individual Values* (New York: Wiley, 1951).

TABLE 17.1	Rankings of Alternatives *X*, *Y*, and *Z* by Ann, Bob, and Charles		
	Alternative		
Individuals	*X*	*Y*	*Z*
Ann	1st	2nd	3rd
Bob	3rd	1st	2nd
Charles	2nd	3rd	1st

While disturbing, it must be noted that the above conclusion is based on considering only the rank and not the intensity with which various alternatives are preferred. Thus, if half of society *mildly* preferred more space exploration while the other half *strongly* preferred more aid to low-income families instead, the difference in the intensities of these preferences would have to be disregarded in the decision process according to Arrow.

AT THE FRONTIER
The Hot Issue of Income Inequality in the United States

W e have seen in Section 17.2 that once two individuals are on the contract curve for exchange, one of the two individuals cannot be made better off without making the other worse off. Thus, different points on the contract curve refer to different distributions of income between the two individuals. Income inequality has become a hotly debated issue in recent years—especially since the income gap between the rich and poor in the United States is wider than in other industrial countries and has increased somewhat during the past two decades.

The best known summary measure of income inequality is provided by the Lorenz curve and the Gini coefficients. A **Lorenz curve** shows the cumulative percentages of total income (from 0% to 100%) measured along the vertical axis, for various cumulative percentages of the population (also from 0% to 100%) measured along the horizontal axis. The Gini coefficient is calculated from the Lorenz curve as indicated below. An illustration of two Lorenz curves, obtained by plotting the data of Table 17.2, is given in Figure 17.11.

The table and the figure show that the 20% of the families with the lowest income received only 0.9% of the national income before all taxes and transfers to aid low-income families, but 4.8% of national income after all taxes and transfers. The 40% of the families with the lowest income received 8% of total income before taxes and transfers, but 15.5% afterwards, and so on, until 100% of the

TABLE 17.2	Distribution of Annual Family Income before and after Taxes and Transfers in the United States in 1993		
		Cumulative Percent of Total Income	
	Cumulative Percent of Families	Before Taxes and Transfers	After Taxes and Transfers
Lowest	20	0.9	4.8
	40	8.0	15.5
	60	22.6	31.6
	80	46.6	55.2
	100	100.0	100.0

Source: U.S. Bureau of the Census, *Current Population Survey* (Washington, D.C.).

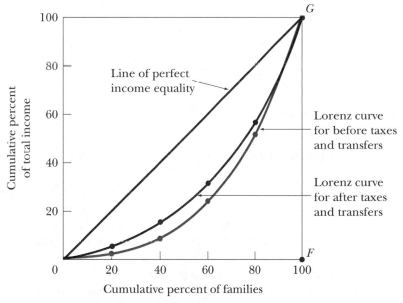

FIGURE 17.11   Lorenz Curves   A Lorenz curve gives the cumulative percentages of total income (measured along the vertical axis) for various cumulative percentages of the population or families (measured along the horizontal axis). The after-taxes and after-transfers Lorenz curve has a smaller curvature (or outward bulge from the diagonal) than the before-taxes and before-transfers Lorenz curve, indicating a smaller income inequality after taxes and transfers than before.

Continued...

families received the entire national income. Note that the after-taxes and after-transfers Lorenz curve has a smaller curvature than the before-taxes and before-transfers Lorenz curve, indicating a smaller income inequality after than before taxes and transfers.

If income were equally distributed, the Lorenz curve would coincide with the straight-line diagonal. On the other hand, if one family received the entire income of the nation, the Lorenz curve would be a right angle ($0FG$ in the figure). The **Gini coefficient** is given by the ratio of the area between the Lorenz curve and the straight-line diagonal to the total area of triangle $0FG$. The Gini coefficient can range from 0 with perfect equality (when the Lorenz curve coincides with the diagonal) to 1 with perfect inequality (when only one family receives all of the income and the Lorenz curve is given by $0FG$).

For the United States, the Gini coefficient in 1993 was 0.39 before all taxes and transfers and 0.36 afterwards, compared with 0.35 in 1975 and 0.37 in 1997 and the average of 0.34 for all industrial countries and 0.46 for developing nations in 1993. Thus, income inequality increased in the United States from 1975 to 1997 (the last year for which this coefficient was available and, on the average, it was higher in the United States than in other industrial countries but lower than in developing countries).

Sources: Organization for Economic Cooperation and development (OECD), *Income Distribution in OECD Countries* (Paris: OECD, October 1995); U.S. Bureau of Census, *Measuring the Effect and Benefits of Taxes on Income and Property: 1993, Current Population Report, Series P-60, No. 185RD* (Washington, D.C.: U.S. Government Printing Office, 1995); and "Income Inequality Measures," *Luxembourg Income Study* (Luxembourg: Centre for Population, Poverty and Policy 2001), pp. 1–3.

17.8 | TRADE PROTECTION AND ECONOMIC WELFARE

By increasing commodity prices, trade protection benefits domestic producers and harms domestic consumers (and usually the nation as a whole). However, since producers are few and stand to gain a great deal from protection, they have a strong incentive to lobby the government to adopt protectionist measures. On the other hand, since the losses are diffused among many consumers, each of whom loses very little from the protection, they are not likely to effectively organize to resist protectionist measures. Thus, there is a bias in favor of protectionism. For example, the sugar quota raises individual expenditures on sugar by only a few dollars per person per year in the United States. But with more than 280 million people in the United States, the quota generates nearly $1 billion in rents to the few thousand sugar producers.

In industrial countries, protection is more likely to be provided to labor-intensive industries employing unskilled, low-wage workers who would have great difficulty finding alternative employment if they lost their present jobs. Some empirical support has also been found for the *pressure-group* or *interest-group* theory, which postulates that industries that are highly organized (such as the automobile industry) receive more trade protection than less organized industries. An industry is more likely to be organized if it is composed of only a few firms. Also, industries that produce consumer products generally are able to obtain more protection than industries producing intermediate products used as inputs by other industries, because the latter industries can exercise *countervailing power* (i.e., apply opposing pressure) and block protection (since protection would increase the price of their inputs).

Furthermore, more protection seems to go to geographically decentralized industries that employ large numbers of workers than to industries that operate in only some regions and employ relatively few workers. The large number of workers have strong voting power to elect government officials who support protection for the industry. Decentralization ensures that elected officials from many regions support the trade protection. Another theory suggests that trade policies are biased in favor of maintaining the status quo. That is, it is more likely for an industry to be protected now if it was protected in the past. Governments also seem reluctant to adopt trade policies that result in large changes in the distribution of income, regardless of who gains and who loses. The most highly protected industries in the United States today are the textile and apparel, automobile, and steel. Example 17–6 provides estimates of the effect of removing protection to these industries.

EXAMPLE 17–6
Welfare Effects of Removing U.S. Trade Restrictions

Table 17.3 shows that removing all quantitative restrictions (QRs) on textile and apparel exports to the United States would result in a gain of $11.92 billion for the United States

TABLE 17.3 Welfare Benefits and Employment Effects of Removing Quantitative Restrictions (QRs) on Export of Textiles, Automobiles, and Steel to the United States

	Welfare Gain (billions of dollars)	Employment Change in Industry (1,000 worker-years)	Employment Change in Rest of Economy (1,000 worker-years)
Textile and apparel			
Remove QRs	11.92	−157.2	157.2
Capturing rents from foreigners	6.05	−3.1	28.4
Automobiles			
Remove QRs	7.50	−1.2	1.3
Capturing rents from foreigners	7.15	+1.3	37.2
Steel			
Remove QRs	0.86	−20.7	22.3
Capturing rents from foreigners	0.74	−0.1	3.5

Sources: J. de Melo and D. Tarr, A General Equilibrium Analysis of U.S. Foreign Trade Policy (Cambridge, MA: MIT Press, 1992); and H. J. Wall, "Using the Gravity Model to Estimate the Costs of Protection," *Federal Reserve Bank of St. Louis Review,* January/February 1999, pp. 211–244.

at 1984 prices. Retaining QRs but capturing the rents from foreigners (e.g., by auctioning off export quotas to foreign firms) would result instead in a gain of $6.05 billion for the United States. The gains are smaller for automobiles and much smaller for steel. Removing QRs also leads to employment losses in the industry losing the QRs, but these employment losses are matched or more than matched by economy-wide employment gains. Removing QRs on all three products leads to a total welfare gain of $20.28 ($11.92 + $7.50 + $0.86) billion for the United States. A more recent study by Wall (1999) found that the benefit removing all forms of trade protection on U.S. imports in 1996 was equal to $112 billion, which represented more than 15 percent of U.S. imports and more 1.9 percent of U.S. GDP in 1996.

SUMMARY

1. Partial equilibrium analysis studies the behavior of individual decision-making units and individual markets, viewed in isolation. General equilibrium analysis studies the interdependence that exists among all markets in the economy. Only when an industry is small and has few direct links with the rest of the economy is partial equilibrium analysis appropriate. The first general equilibrium model was introduced by Walras in 1874. Under perfect competition, a solution to the general equilibrium model usually exists.

2. A simple economy of two individuals (A and B), two commodities (X and Y), and two inputs (L and K) is in general equilibrium of exchange when the economy is on its contract curve for exchange. This is the locus of tangency points of the indifference curves (at which the MRS_{XY} are equal) for the two individuals. The economy is in general equilibrium of production when it is on its production contract curve. This is the locus of the tangency points of the isoquants (at which $MRTS_{LK}$ are equal) for the two commodities. By mapping or transferring the production contract curve from input to output space, we derive the corresponding production-possibilities frontier.

3. For the economy to be simultaneously in general equilibrium of production and exchange, the marginal rate of transformation of X for Y in production must be equal to the marginal rate of substitution of X for Y in consumption for individuals A and B. That is, $MRT_{XY} = MRS_{XY}^A = MRS_{XY}^B$. Geometrically, this corresponds to the point on the contract curve for exchange at which the common slope of the indifference curve of the two individuals equals the slope of the production-possibilities frontier at the point of production. A distribution of inputs among commodities and of commodities among consumers is Pareto optimal or efficient if no reorganization of production and consumption is possible by which some individuals are made better off without making someone else worse off. Thus, the conditions for Pareto optimality are the conditions for general equilibrium of production and exchange.

4. Under perfect competition in all input and output markets, all the conditions for Pareto optimum are automatically satisfied. This is the basic argument in favor of perfect competition and proof of Adam Smith's law of the invisible hand. The first theorem of welfare economics postulates that equilibrium in competitive markets is Pareto optimal. The second theorem of welfare economics postulates that equity in distribution is logically separable from efficiency in allocation. Perfect competition leads to maximum economic efficiency only in the absence of market failures (which arise from imperfect competition, externalities, and public goods). Perfect competition leads to static but not necessarily to dynamic efficiency.

5. Starting from the general equilibrium condition at which $MRT_{XY} = P_X/P_Y = MRS_{XY}$ in each country in the absence of trade, the country with the lower MRT_{XY} or P_X/P_Y will have a comparative advantage in commodity X. With trade, each nation will specialize in the production of the commodity of its comparative advantage until MRT_{XY} or P_X/P_Y becomes equal in both countries. Then each country will trade until $MRT_{XY} = P_X/P_Y = MRS_{XY}$ so as to be in general equilibrium once again. By specializing in production and trading, each country can consume more of both commodities than it can without trade.

6. Welfare economics studies the conditions under which the solution to the general equilibrium model can be said to the optimal. It examines the conditions for economic efficiency in the production of output and in the exchange of commodities, and for equity in the distribution of income. A utility-possibilities frontier is derived by mapping or transferring a contract curve for exchange from output or commodity space to utility space. It shows the various combinations of utilities received by two individuals at which the economy is in general equilibrium or Pareto optimum in exchange. We can construct an Edgeworth box and contract curve for exchange from each point on the production-possibilities frontier. From each contract curve for exchange, we can then construct the corresponding utility-possibilities frontier and determine on it the point of Pareto optimum in production and exchange. By joining points of Pareto optimality in production and exchange on each utility-possibilities frontier, we can derive the grand utility-possibilities frontier.

7. A change that benefits some but harms others can be evaluated with the Kaldor–Hicks–Scitovsky criterion. However, this is based on the compensation principle which measures the welfare changes of the gainers and the losers in monetary units. The only way to overcome this shortcoming is with a social welfare function. Arrow proved that a social welfare function cannot be derived by democratic vote. This is known as Arrow's impossibility theorem. Income inequality can be measured by the Lorenz curve and the Gini coefficient. These are higher in the United States than in other industrial countries and have increased since 1975.

8. By increasing the commodity price, trade protection benefits producers and harms consumers (and usually the nation as a whole). Protection is more likely to be provided to industries that (1) are labor-intensive and employ unskilled, low-wage workers, (2) are highly organized (such as the automobile industry), (3) produce consumer products rather than intermediate products, and (4) are geographically decentralized.

KEY TERMS

Partial equilibrium analysis
General equilibrium analysis
Interdependence
Edgeworth box diagram for exchange
Contract curve for exchange
Edgeworth box diagram for production
Contract curve for production
Production-possibilities frontier

Marginal rate of transformation of X for Y (MRT_{XY})
Economic efficiency
Pareto optimality
Law of the invisible hand
First theorem of welfare economics
Second theorem of welfare economics
Market failures
Comparative advantage

Welfare economics
Utility-possibilities frontier
Grand utility-possibilities frontier
Pareto criterion
Compensation principle
Kaldor–Hicks criterion
Scitovsky criterion
Bergson social welfare function
Arrow's impossibility theorem
Lorenz curve
Gini coefficient

REVIEW QUESTIONS

1. Are all points on the contract curve for exchange equally desirable from society's point of view? Why?

2. How will an increase in the quantity of labor available to society affect its Edgeworth box diagram for production? What effect will that have on the contract curve for production?

3. How can we show a 10% improvement in technology in the production of commodities X and Y in the Edgeworth diagram and production-possibilities frontier?

4. Why would the economy of Figure 17.5 not be at general equilibrium if production took place at point M' and consumption at point D?

5. If $MRT_{XY} = 3/2$ while $MRS_{XY} = 2$ for individuals A and B, should the economy produce more of X or more of Y to reach equilibrium of production and exchange simultaneously? Why?

6. What makes general equilibrium analysis objective while welfare economics is subjective?

7. Would the Robinson Crusoe of Figure 17.6 maximize utility or welfare by producing and consuming $5X$ and $4.5Y$? Why?

8. What is the relationship between Adam Smith's law of the invisible hand and Pareto optimum?

9. Why do market disequilibria lead to inefficiencies and non-Pareto optimum?

10. Perfect competition is the best form of market organization at one point in time but not over time. True or false? Explain.

11. What is meant by the "voting paradox?" How is this related to Arrow's impossibility theorem?

12. Why is international trade often restricted if it benefits few domestic producers but harms many domestic consumers?

PROBLEMS

1. Starting from a position of general equilibrium in the entire economy, if the supply curve of commodity X falls (i.e., S_X shifts up), examine what happens
   a. in the markets for commodity X, its substitutes, and complements.
   b. in the input markets.
   c. to the distribution of income.

*2. Suppose that the indifference curves of individuals A and B are given by A_1, A_2, A_3, and B_1, B_2, B_3, respectively, in the accompanying table. Suppose also that the total amount of commodities X and Y available to the two individuals together is $10X$ and $10Y$. Draw the Edgeworth box diagram for exchange, and show the contract curve for exchange.

A's Indifference Curves

A_1		A_2		A_3	
X	Y	X	Y	X	Y
3	7	5	6	6	7.5
4	3	6	4	8	6
6	1	8	3	9.5	5.5

B's Indifference Curves

B_1		B_2		B_3	
X	Y	X	Y	X	Y
7	2	6	4	8	4
2	3	4	5	6	6
1	4	3	7	5.5	8

3. For the Edgeworth box diagram of Problem 2 (shown in Appendix B at the end of the text):
   a. Explain how, starting from the point at which A_1 and B_1 intersect, mutually advantageous exchange can take place between individuals A and B.
   b. What is the value of the MRS_{XY} at points E, D, and F?

*4. Suppose that the isoquants for commodities X and Y are given by X_1, X_2, X_3, and Y_1, Y_2, Y_3, respectively, in the following table. Suppose also that a total of $14L$ and $9K$ are available to produce commodities X and Y. Draw the Edgeworth box

---

* = Answer provided at end of book.

diagram for exchange and show the production contract curve.

X's Isoquants

X_1		X_2		X_3	
L	K	L	K	L	K
5	7	8	5	10	7
6	2	9	3	11	5
7	1	11	2	13	4.5

Y's Isoquants

Y_1		Y_2		Y_3	
L	K	L	K	L	K
9	2	7	4	10	4
3	4	5	6	8	7
1	6	4	8	7.5	8.5

5. For the Edgeworth box diagram of Problem 4 (shown in Appendix B at the end of the text):

   a. Explain how, starting from the point at which X_1 and Y_1 intersect, the output of both commodities can be increased by simply reallocating some of the fixed amounts of L and K available between the production of X and Y.

   b. What is the value of the $MRTS_{LK}$ at points M, J, and N?

6. Suppose that in the figure in the answer to Problem 4, $X_1 = 4X$ and $Y_3 = 13Y$, $X_2 = 10X$ and $Y_2 = 9Y$, and $X_3 = 14X$ and $Y_1 = 4Y$. Derive the production-possibilities frontier corresponding to the production contract curve given in the figure in the answer to Problem 4. What does a point inside the production-possibilities frontier indicate? A point outside?

7. a. Find the MRT_{XY} at points J', M', and N' for the production-possibilities frontier of Problem 6.

b. If $MC_Y = \$100$ at point M', what is MC_X?

c. Why is the production-possibilities frontier concave to the origin?

d. When would the production-possibilities frontier be a straight line?

*8. Superimpose the Edgeworth box diagram for exchange of Problem 2 on the production-possibilities frontier of Problem 4 (both shown in Appendix B at the end of the text), and determine the general equilibrium of production and exchange.

9. Explain why the economy portrayed in the answer to Problem 8 would not be simultaneously in general equilibrium of production and exchange at points D and F.

10. Given that the economy of Problem 8 produces at point M' on its production-possibilities frontier, determine

   a. how much of commodities X and Y it produces.

   b. how this output is distributed between individuals A and B.

   c. how much labor (L) and capital (K) are used to produce commodities X and Y.

   d. What questions have been left unanswered in the model?

11. Suppose that the economy represented by the figure in the answer to Problem 8 (shown in Appendix B at the end of the text) grows over time and/or has available a more advanced technology. Explain how this affects the figure and general equilibrium analysis.

*12. Suppose that in the figure in the answer to Problem 8 (see Figure 17c in Appendix B), $A_1 = 100$ utils, $A_2 = 300$ utils, $A_3 = 450$ utils, and $B_1 = 200$ utils, $B_2 = 400$ utils, and $B_3 = 450$ utils.

   a. Derive the utility-possibilities frontier corresponding to contract curve $0_A DEF 0_B$ for exchange in Figure 17c in Appendix B.

   b. Derive the grand utility-possibilities frontier.

INTERNET SITE ADDRESSES

Information and data on the comparative advantage of nations, trade statistics by country and product group, and as specialization are published by the World Trade Organization (WTO) and the International Trade Center

(ITC) and can be found at:

   http://www.wto.org

   http://www.ita.doc.gov

Data on income inequality and the Gini coefficient are provided by the Centre for Population, Poverty and Policy Studies in Luxembourg and the U.S. Census Bureau at:

http://lisweb.ceps.lu/keyfigures/ineqtable.htm

http://www.census.gov/hhes/income/histinc/h04.html

On the efficiency and equity in the allocation of water to different uses in California, see:

http://www.monolake.org/waterpolicy/outsidebox.htm

http://agriculture.miningco.com/library/weekly/aa080101a.htm

http://www.nctimes.com/news/2001/20011128/52949.html

The rationing of health care in the United States and in Great Britain is examined in:

http://www.globalchange.com/rationin.htm

http://www.prospect.org/print/V11/13/stone-d.html

http://news.bbc.co.uk/hi/english/health/newsid_249000/249938.stm

## CHAPTER 18

Externalities, Public Goods, and the Role of Government

In this chapter, we examine why the existence of externalities and public goods leads to economic inefficiencies and to an allocation of inputs and commodities that is not Pareto optimum. We then consider how the government (through regulation, taxes, and subsidies) could attempt to overcome or at least reduce the negative impact of these distortions on economic efficiency. Because these distortions and government attempts to overcome them are fairly common in most societies, the importance of the topics presented in this chapter can hardly be overstated. The "At the Frontier" section examines the shift from equity to efficiency in tax reform in the United States. In this chapter, we also discuss the theory of public choice (i.e., how government decisions are made and implemented) and strategic trade policy (i.e., how comparative advantage can be created by subsidies, trade protection, and other government policies). We conclude by applying the tools of analysis developed in the chapter to the problem of environmental pollution.

18.1 EXTERNALITIES

In this section, we define externalities and examine why their existence prevents maximum economic efficiency or Pareto optimum, even under perfect competition.

Externalities Defined

In the course of producing and consuming some commodities, harmful or beneficial side effects arise that are borne by firms and people not directly involved in the production or consumption of the commodities. These side effects are called **externalities** because they are felt by economic units (firms and individuals) not directly involved with (i.e., that are external to or outside) the economic units that generate these side effects.[1] Externalities are called **external costs** when they are harmful and **external benefits** when they are beneficial. An example of an external cost is the air pollution that may accompany the production of a commodity. An example of an external benefit is the reduced chance of the spreading of a communicable disease when an individual is inoculated against it.

Externalities are classified into five different types. These are external diseconomies of production, external diseconomies of consumption, external economies of production, external economies of consumption, and technical externalities. Each of these will be examined in turn. **External diseconomies of production** are uncompensated costs imposed on others by the expansion of output by some firms. For example, the increased discharge of waste materials by some firms along a waterway may result in antipollution legislation that increases the cost of disposing of waste materials for all firms in the area. **External diseconomies of consumption** are uncompensated costs imposed on others by the consumption expenditures of some individuals. For example, the riding of a snowmobile by an individual imposes a cost (in the form of noise and smoke) on other individuals who are skiing, hiking, or ice fishing in the area.

On the other hand, **external economies of production** are uncompensated benefits conferred on others by the expansion of output by some firms. An example arises when some firms train more workers to increase output, and some of these workers go to work for other firms (which, therefore, save on training costs). **External economies of consumption** are uncompensated benefits conferred on others by the increased consumption of a commodity by some individual. For example, increased expenditures to maintain his or her lawn by a homeowner increase the value of the neighbor's house. Finally, **technical externalities** arise when declining long-run average costs as output expands lead to monopoly, so that price exceeds marginal cost. Not even regulation to achieve competitive marginal cost pricing is then viable (see Section 13.5).

Externalities and Market Failure

We have seen in Section 17.4 that perfect competition leads to maximum economic efficiency and Pareto optimum. However, this is true only when private costs equal social costs and when private benefits equal social benefits (i.e., in the absence of externalities). This was implicitly assumed to be the case until now. When externalities are present, the "invisible hand" is led astray and Pareto optimum is not achieved, even under perfect competition. This is shown in Figure 18.1.

We assume that commodity X in Figure 18.1 is produced by a competitive industry. The industry supply curve (S) is the horizontal summation (above minimum average variable costs) of the individual firm's marginal (private) cost curves (i.e., $S = \Sigma MPC$). Given market demand curve D for the commodity, the equilibrium price is \$12 and the equilibrium quantity is 6 million units per time period (given by the intersection of D and S at point E in the figure). Suppose that the production of commodity X involves rising external

---

[1] The presentation of this chapter follows F. M. Bator's "The Anatomy of Market Failure," *Quarterly Journal of Economics,* August 1958, pp. 351–379, which was drawn from the work of the great English economist Arthur Cecil Pigou (1877–1959).

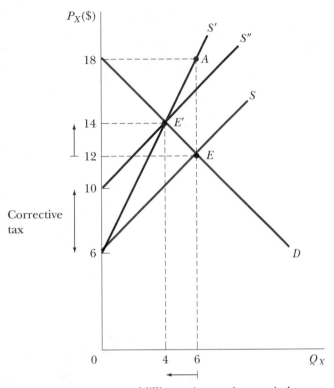

FIGURE 18.1   Competitive Overproduction with External Costs   With perfect competition, $P_X = \$12$ and $Q_X = 6$ million units (given by point E at which D and S intersect). S reflects only marginal private costs, while S' equals marginal private (internal) costs plus marginal external costs. Efficiency and Pareto optimality require that $P_X = \$14$ and $Q_X = 4$ million units (given by point E', at which D and S' intersect). This can be achieved with a $4 per-unit corrective tax on producers that shifts S to S''.

costs (in the form of air pollution, water pollution, traffic congestion, and so on) that the firms producing commodity X do not take into account. The industry supply curve that includes both the private and external costs might then be given by S' (see the figure). Curve S' shows that the marginal *social* cost (*MSC*) of producing 6 million units of commodity X exceeds the marginal private cost (*MPC*) of $12 by an amount equal to the marginal external cost (*MEC*) of $6 (*AE*) in the figure).

Thus, efficiency or Pareto optimality requires that $P_X = \$14$ and $Q_X = 4$ million (given by the intersection of D and S' at point E' in the figure). Only then would the commodity price reflect the full social cost of producing it. Starting with S (showing the *MPC*), this could be achieved with a $4 per-unit corrective tax on producers of commodity X, which shifts S upward to S'' and defines equilibrium point E' at the intersection of D and S''.[2] As we will see in the next Chapter, efficiency and Pareto optimality might also be achieved by the proper specification of property rights. Without any such corrective action, the perfectly competitive industry would charge too low a price and produce too much of commodity X (compare point E with E' in the figure).

Efficiency and Pareto optimality are not achieved whenever private and social costs or benefits differ. With external diseconomies of consumption, consumers do not pay the full marginal social cost of the commodity and consume too much of it. Corrective action would then require a tax on consumers rather than on producers. On the other hand, with external economies of production and consumption, the commodity price exceeds the marginal social cost of the commodity so that production and consumption fall short of the optimum level. Efficiency and Pareto optimum in production and in consumption would then require a subsidy (rather than a tax) on producers and on consumers, respectively (see Problem 5, with the answer at the end of the text). Finally, technical externalities (economies of large-scale production) over a sufficiently large range of outputs lead to the breakdown of competition (natural monopoly). In this case, marginal cost pricing is neither possible nor viable, and Pareto optimum cannot be achieved.

EXAMPLE 18–1

The Case for Government Support for Basic Research

Basic research refers to efforts to discover fundamental relationships in nature, such as natural laws. Often, these cannot be patented and do not have immediate commercial applications. It is also practically impossible for the firm that makes a discovery of this nature to take advantage of the full range of commercial applications that might result from its discovery. Thus, the social benefits from basic research greatly exceed private benefits. As a result, there is likely to be underinvestment in basic research by the private sector. Since technological change and innovations are the most important contributors to growth in modern societies, there is a strong case for government support for basic research. Indeed, past government expenditures in basic research, such as for space exploration, laid the foundations of many of today's most productive industries, from aerospace to computers.

The same arguments that apply to firms in a nation apply to nations in the world. That is, the government of a nation may support less than the optimal level of basic research because additions to fundamental knowledge made by a nation can easily be utilized by other nations. For example, until recently, Japan stressed the finding of commercial applications for basic discoveries made by other nations, mostly the United States, rather than doing basic research itself. Primarily to overcome this problem, since

---

[2] However, the marginal external costs created by firms in different areas of the market are likely to be different, so that different corrective per-unit taxes may be required to achieve Pareto optimality. Furthermore, MEC may be constant rather than rising. The corrective tax may also have some unintended side effects that lead to inefficiency (such as the utilization of a less efficient technology).

1990 the United States has been supporting generic and precompetitive technologies, such as superconductivity, that could have widespread industrial applications but which take many years to develop and commercialize. Many economists, however, believe that the government has no business picking "winners and losers"; that is, substituting its judgment for that of the market by selecting among technologies and firms may not lead to optimal results (see Example 18–5).

Sources: National Academy of Science, *Basic Research and National Goals* (Washington, D.C.: U.S. Government Printing Office, 1965); The MIT Commission on Industrial Productivity, *Made in America: Regaining the Productive Edge* (Cambridge, MA: The MIT Press, 1989), Chapter 5; "Basic Research Is Losing Out as Companies Stress Results," *New York Times,* October 8, 1996, p. 1; "How to Nurture a High-Technology Culture," *Financial Times,* September 14, 2001, p. 13; and C. Wessner, "The Advanced Technology Program: It Works," *Issues in Science and Technology,* Fall 2001, pp. 59–64.

18.2 | EXTERNALITIES AND PROPERTY RIGHTS

We have seen in the previous section that externalities, by driving a wedge between private and social costs or benefits, prevent economic efficiency and Pareto optimality. But why do externalities arise in some cases and not in others? Suppose you own a car. You have a clear property right in the car, and anyone ruining it is liable for damages. The courts will uphold your right to compensation. In this case there are no externalities. Private and social costs are one and the same thing. Compare this with the case of a firm polluting the air. Neither the firm nor the people living next to the firm own the air. That is, the air is **common property.** Since no resident owns the air, no one can sue the firm for damages resulting from the air pollution generated by the firm. The firm imposes an external (i.e., an uncompensated) cost on the individual. These two simple examples clearly demonstrate that externalities arise when property rights are not adequately specified. In the first case, you have a clear property right to the car and there are no externalities. In the second case, no one owns the air and externalities arise. This situation leads to the famous Coase theorem.[3]

The **Coase theorem** postulates that when property rights are clearly defined, perfect competition results in the internalization of externalities, regardless of how property rights are assigned among the parties (individuals or firms). For example, suppose that a brewery is located downstream from a paper mill that dumps waste into the stream. Suppose also that in order to filter and purify the water to make beer, the brewery incurs a cost of $1,000 per month, while the paper mill would incur a cost of $400 to dispose of its waste products by other means and not pollute the stream. If the brewery has the property right to clean water, the paper mill will incur the added cost of $400 per month to dispose of its waste without polluting the stream (lest the brewery sue it for damages of $1,000 per month). On the other hand, if the paper mill has the property right to the stream and can freely use it to dump its

---

[3] R. R. Coase, "The Problems of Social Cost," *Journal of Law and Economics,* October 1960, pp. 1–44. "A Nobel-Prize Winning Idea, Conceived in the 30's Is a Guide for Net Business," *New York Times,* October 2, 2000, p. C12; and "The Tragedy of the Commons," *Forbes,* September 10, 2001, pp. 61–63.

wastes in it, the brewery will pay the paper mill $400 per month not to pollute the stream (and thus avoid the larger cost of $1,000 to purify the water later).

The cost of avoiding the pollution is *internalized* by the paper mill in the first instance and by the brewery in the second. That is, the $400 cost per month of avoiding the pollution becomes a regular business expense of one party or the other and *no externalities result*. The socially optimal result of **internalizing external costs** and avoiding the pollution at $400 per month, rather than cleaning up afterwards at a cost of $1,000 per month, is achieved regardless of who has the property right to the use of the stream.[4] Thus, externalities are avoided (and economic efficiency and Pareto optimum achieved) under perfect competition, if property rights are clearly defined and transferable. Transaction costs must also be zero.[5]

Transaction costs are the legal, administrative, and informational expenses of drawing up, signing, and enforcing contracts. These expenses are small when the contracting parties are few (as in the above example). When the contracting parties are numerous (as in the case of a firm polluting the air for possibly millions of people in the area), it would be practically impossible or very expensive for the firm to sign a separate contract with each individual affected by the pollution it creates. Contracting costs are then very large, and externalities (and inefficiencies) arise. This is especially true in the case of environmental pollution (see Section 18.7).[6]

EXAMPLE 18-2

Commercial Fishing: Fewer Boats but Exclusive Rights?

As a response to catastrophic overfishing by foreigners during the 1960s, the United States passed the Fisheries Conservation and Management Act of 1976. The act extended the U.S. exclusive economic (fishing) zone from the traditional 3-mile limit to 200 miles and created eight U.S. regional councils dominated by local fishing interests to distribute exclusive rights to the catch. Economists strongly supported the plan to move from public to private ownership as the best method of preventing overfishing and preserving fisheries for future generations. However, strong disagreement as to who should benefit from the distribution of the rights to the catch (the government, current owners of fishing boats, or fishermen) has so far prevented the privatization plan from being implemented. As a result, the act has only eliminated overfishing by foreigners but not by Americans, so the catches have remained above biologically sustainable levels. Even though a small number of boats could catch the maximum sustainable yield at the lowest possible cost, there remains a strong incentive to overinvest in the industry as long as it is profitable to bring new boats into operation.

---

[4] Note that the cost of pollution abatement is minimized rather than entirely eliminated. The only way to completely avoid the cost of pollution is for the paper mill to stop production. But this would result in the greater social cost of the lost production. The above conclusion is also based on the assumption of a zero income effect on the demand curve for the use of the stream regardless of who has the property right of it.

[5] Even if neither the brewery nor the paper mill had a property right to the use of the stream, the conclusion would generally be the same as long as transaction costs are zero. That is, it pays for the brewery to pay the paper mill $400 per month not to pollute. This is equivalent to the paper mill having the right to the use of the stream.

[6] However, the development of class action lawsuits has greatly reduced transaction costs in these cases.

At present, the attempt to reduce overfishing takes the form of sharply reducing the length of the fishing seasons and the size of the catch. For example, off Alaska, the halibut season consists of only two or three days per year. A far more efficient way to curb overfishing would be to sell private harvesting rights to those who can fish most efficiently or cheaply. Owners of such rights would then have a strong incentive to prevent overfishing or pollution to protect the market value of their rights. Furthermore, if rights to the catch were sold so as to keep individual boats operating at full capacity, three-quarters of the boats could be retired, and this would lead to cost savings exceeding $1 billion per year for the Alaskan fisheries alone. These cost savings would be more than sufficient to compensate the loss of the owners of the boats to be retired. Thus, we see how the establishment of property rights would eliminate overfishing, reduce costs, and increase efficiency in U.S. fisheries.

Sources: "A Change in Commercial Fishing: Fewer Boats but Exclusive Rights," *New York Times,* April 2, 1991, p. 1; "Not Enough Fish in the Stormy Sea," *U.S. News & World Report,* August 15, 1994, pp. 55–56; "One Answer to Overfishing: Privatize the Fisheries," *New York Times,* May 11, 1995, p. D2; "In Deep Water," *Financial Times,* July 28, 2001, p. 7; and "Fish Stock Face Global Collapse," *Financial Times,* February 18, 2002, p. 5.

18.3 | Public Goods

We have seen in Section 17.4 that perfect competition leads to maximum economic efficiency and Pareto optimum in the absence of market failures. One type of market failure results from the existence of public goods. In this section, we examine the nature of public goods and their provision.

Nature of Public Goods

If consumption of a commodity by one individual does not reduce the amount available for others, the commodity is a public good. That is, once the good is provided for someone, others can also consume it at no extra cost. Examples of **public goods** are national defense, law enforcement, fire and police protection, and flood control (provided by the government), but also radio and TV broadcasting (which are provided by the private sector in many nations, including the United States).

The distinguishing characteristic of public goods is **nonrival consumption.** For example, when one individual watches a TV program, he or she does not interfere with the reception of others. This is to be contrasted with private goods, which are rival in consumption, in that if an individual consumes a particular quantity of a good, such as apples, these same apples are no longer available for others to consume.

Nonrival consumption must be distinguished for nonexclusion. **Nonexclusion** means that it is impossible or prohibitively expensive to confine the benefits of the consumption of a good (once produced) to selected people (such as only to those paying for it). Whereas nonrival consumption and nonexclusion often go hand in hand, a public good is defined in terms of nonrival consumption only. For example, since national defense and TV broadcasting are nonrival in consumption (i.e., the same amount can be consumed by more than one individual at the same time), they are both public goods. However, national defense also exhibits nonexclusion (i.e., when it is provided for some individuals, others cannot be excluded from also enjoying it), while TV broadcasting can be exclusive (e.g., only paying customers can view cable TV). We will see in the next section that public goods (i.e., goods that are nonrival in consumption) will not be provided in the optimal amount by the private sector under perfect competition, thus requiring government intervention. First, however, we must determine what is the optimal amount of a public good.

Because a given amount of a public good can be consumed by more than one individual at the same time, the aggregate or total amount of a public good is obtained by the vertical (rather than by the horizontal) summation of the demand curves of the various individuals who consume the public good. This is shown in Figure 18.2. In the figure, D_A is the

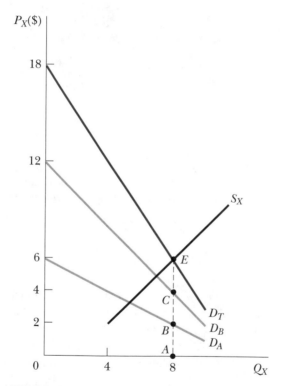

FIGURE 18.2   Optimal Amount of a Public Good
Aggregate demand curve D_T for public good X is obtained by the vertical summation of individual demand curves D_A and D_B. This is because each unit of public good X can be consumed by both individuals at the same time. Given market supply curve S_X, the optimal amount of X is 8 units per time period (given by the intersection of D_T and S_X at point E). At point E, the sum of the individuals' marginal benefits equals the marginal social costs (i.e., $AB + AC = AE$).

demand curve of Ann and D_B is the demand curve of Bob for public good X. If Ann and Bob are the only two individuals in the market, the aggregate demand curve for good X, D_T, is obtained by the vertical summation of D_A and D_B. The reason for this is that each unit of public good X can be consumed by both individuals at the same time.[7]

Given market supply curve S_X for public good X, the optimal amount of X is 8 units per time period (given by the intersection of D_T and S_X at point E in the figure). At point E, the sum of the individuals' marginal benefits or marginal social benefit equals the marginal social cost (i.e., $AB + AC = AE$). Thus, note once again that the marginal principle is at work. The problem is that, in general, less than the optimal amount of public good X will be supplied under perfect competition, and this prevents the attainment of maximum efficiency and Pareto optimum.

EXAMPLE 18–3
The Economics of a Lighthouse and Other Public Goods

A lighthouse is a good example of a public good. Once a lighthouse is built, it can send signals to ships during storms at practically zero extra cost. That is, lighthouse signals are nonrival in consumption. Lighthouse signals are not exclusive, however, as it was originally believed. That is, each user *can* be charged for the service. Indeed, historical research has shown that lighthouses were privately owned in England from 1700 to 1834, and that they must have been doing a good business because their number increased over the period. Lighthouse owners charged ships at dock (according to their tonnage) for their land-demarcation light signals during storms. Usually only one ship at a time was in sight of the lighthouse, and ships were identified by their flag. If a ship had not paid for the service, the light signals were not shown.

The lighthouse provides an example of a public good that is exclusive (so that users can be charged for the service). The same is true for the North Atlantic Treaty Organization (NATO), under which Western European nations and the United States contributed to provide for their mutual protection against past Soviet military threat. A similar public good is education. Entrepreneurs often show great ingenuity in making public goods exclusive. An example is the provision of in-place paying binoculars at Niagara Falls and other scenic sights. Another example is the placing of super-large TV screens in some bars. These and other similar services would not be provided if they were not, or if they could not be made, exclusive (i.e., if consumers could not be charged for them). Other examples of public goods that can be made exclusive are the findings of government-paid basic research and the use of advertising to pay for radio and TV broadcasts. Although any firm can make use of basic-research findings, the specific

---

[7] This is to be contrasted with the *market* demand curve for a private or rival good, which, as we have seen in Section 5.1, is obtained from the *horizontal* summation of the individuals' demand curves (see Problem 10, with the answer at the end of the text).

offshoots or commercial applications of basic research developed by a particular firm can be patented and thus made exclusive.

Sources: Ronald R. Coase, "The Lighthouse in Economics," *Journal of Law and Economics,* October 1974," pp. 357–376; "So, It's a Lighthouse. Now Leave Me alone," *New York Times,* April 18, 2002, p. 1; "Vast Sums for New Discoveries Pose Threat to Basic Science," *New York Times,* May 27, 1990, p. 1; "Do Firms Run Schools Well?" *U.S. News & World Report,* January 8, 1996, pp. 46–49; "Woes for Company Running Schools," New York Times, May 14, 2002, p. 1; and "Edison School Gets Reprieve: $40 Million in Financing," *New York Times,* June 5, 2002, p. C1.

Provision of Public Goods

We have seen that the optimal amount of a public good is the amount at which the sum of the marginal benefits of all the individuals consuming the good equals its marginal cost. Graphically, this is given by the point at which the aggregate demand curve for the good (obtained from the vertical summation of the individuals' demand curves) intersects the market supply curve of the good. However, less than this optimal amount of the public good is likely to be supplied by the private sector.

There are two related reasons for this. First, when the public good is nonexclusive (i.e., when those individuals not paying for it cannot be excluded from also consuming it), there is a tendency for each consumer to be a free rider. A **free-rider problem** arises because each consumer believes that the public good will be provided anyway, whether he or she contributes to its payment or not. That is, because there are many people sharing the cost of providing the public good, each individual feels that withdrawing his or her financial support will practically go unnoticed by others and will have little or no effect on the provision of the good. The problem is that since many individuals behave this way (i.e., behave as free riders), less than the optimal amount of the public good will be provided.[8] In general, as the group size increases, the free-rider problem becomes more acute. This problem can be and generally is overcome by the government taxing the general public to pay for the public good. A good example of this is national defense.[9] Sometimes governments go to great lengths to induce people to pay their fair share of taxes to provide public goods. For example, at the turn of the century, the government of China retained the right to purchase an individual's house to avoid the owner's incentive to undervalue it for tax purposes.

The second (related) problem cannot be resolved as satisfactorily by government intervention. This arises because each individual has no incentive to accurately reveal his or her preferences or demand for the public good. Therefore, it is practically impossible for the government to know exactly what is the optimal amount of the public good that it should provide or induce the private sector to provide. There is also the problem of possible government inefficiency in providing public goods and in otherwise intervening in the market (see Section 18.5).

---

[8] Note that even a private (rival) good leads to market failure if it is characterized by nonexclusion (i.e., if each individual consuming it cannot be adequately charged for it).

[9] Sometimes a free-rider problem can partially be resolved by the private sector. Examples are educational television stations, tenants' associations, and charitable associations such as the Salvation Army.

AT THE FRONTIER
Efficiency Versus Equity in the U.S. Tax System

T axpayers everywhere complain that they pay too much. Contrary to popular belief, however, taxes in the United States are lower than in all other major industrialized nations, except Japan. Table 18.1 shows that total tax receipts as a percentage of gross domestic product (GDP) were 31.6% in the United States in 2000 compared with an average of over 44.5% in the European Union. Another difference is that the United States raises most of its revenues from income and profit taxes, while European countries rely mostly on consumption taxes, such as the value added tax (which are taxes imposed on the value added at each stage of the production and distribution chain).

Although Europeans pay much higher taxes than Americans, they also get much greater benefits. Europeans have good free medical and nursing home care, nearly free college education, and generous pension and unemployment safety nets. They also have lower crime rates, cleaner streets, state-of-the-art mass transit, less income and wealth inequality, and less social instability, and this makes them more willing to accept higher taxes. In the United States, people do not see such a strong association between taxes and tangible benefits, and so there is a much greater resistance to higher taxes. The very strong welfare state in Europe where people rely on government for cradle-to-grave care has its shortcomings, however. For one thing, even with very high taxes, most European nations have huge budget deficits (much higher than in the United States as a percentage of GDP)

TABLE 18.1	Taxes as a Percentage of GDP in the Leading Industrialized Nations, 1985, 1990, 1995, 2000			
Country	1985	1990	1995	2000
Sweden	56.5	59.7	54.2	56.7
France	48.9	47.4	48.0	49.6
Belgium	46.8	43.7	45.8	46.7
Germany	44.5	41.8	43.0	44.4
Italy	37.4	41.2	43.5	44.1
Netherlands	47.9	43.7	43.6	43.8
Canada	36.7	39.9	39.7	40.9
United Kingdom	—	37.5	36.5	39.0
Spain	34.1	37.5	37.4	38.5
United States	28.7	29.3	29.8	31.6
Japan	28.8	32.4	30.2	30.0

Source: Organization for Economic Cooperation and Development (OECD), *Economic Outlook* (Paris, December 2001), p. 231.

Continued. . .

and are being forced to scale down welfare benefits. There is also much less labor mobility and much higher rates of unemployment, fewer patents, and much less entrepreneurship than in the United States, and these reduce European international competitiveness and future growth prospects.

Recent reform of the U.S. tax system further increased transatlantic differences. The drive to reduce Federal welfare programs and cut taxes represents a fundamental change in the U.S. tax system from the traditional emphasis on redistributing income from the well-off to the less well-off to making the economic system more efficient by encouraging investment and stimulating productivity growth. Bluntly, the equity or fairness argument in the U.S. tax system has, to some extent, given way to the efficiency and growth argument. This increased the international competitiveness of the U.S. economy during the past decade, but it has also increased income inequalities, both absolutely and relatively to other industrialized nations.

Tax reform proposals currently under discussion in the United States include (1) the proportional income tax, which would apply a single tax rate to all labor and capital income, with no exemptions or deductions; (2) the proportional consumption tax, which would permit 100% deduction for new investment; (3) the flat tax, which differs from the proportional consumption tax by including a standard deduction from wage income and for home mortgages; and (4) the X tax, which substitutes the flat tax's single-rate wage tax with a progressive wage tax. Each reform would broaden the tax base, thus permitting reductions in statutory marginal tax rates on wages and saving. Deciding which tax reform is better involves value judgments that go beyond economics. Reforms that attempt to prevent adverse distributional effects (such as the X tax) lead to lower rates of national growth than tax reforms that do not (such as the proportional income or consumption taxes).

Sources: "The Tax Code Heads Into the Operating Room," *New York Times,* September 3, 1995, Section 3, p. 1; "Gap in Wealth in U.S. Called Widest in West," *New York Times,* April 17, 1995, p. 1; "European Shrug as Taxes Go Up," *New York Times,* February 16, 1995, p. 10; "How Fair Are Our Taxes," *Wall Street Journal,* January 10, 1996, p. A12; M. Feldstein, "Tax Avoidance and the Deadweight Loss of the Income Tax," *Review of Economics and Statistics,* November 1999, pp. 674–680; D. Altig et al., "Simulating Fundamental Tax Reform in the United States," *American Economic Review,* June 2001, pp. 574–595; and D. Salvatore, "Relative Taxation and Competitiveness in the European Union: What the European Union Can Learn from the United States," *Journal of Policy Modeling,* May 2002, pp. 401–410.

18.4 BENEFIT–COST ANALYSIS

Governments play many roles in modern societies. These roles range from the provision of public goods, to the redistribution of income, the regulation of monopoly, and pollution control. In carrying out these functions, government agencies must constantly decide which projects to implement and which to reject. A useful procedure for determining the most worthwhile projects is **benefit–cost analysis.** This analysis compares the present value of the benefits of a project to the present value of the costs of a project. Government should carry out a project only if the present value of the social benefits from the project exceeds the present value of its social costs (i.e., if the benefit–cost ratio for the project exceeds 1). Often, the government does not have the resources (i.e., cannot raise taxes or borrow sufficiently) to undertake all the projects with a benefit–cost ratio exceeding 1. In such cases, government should rank all possible projects from the highest to the lowest (but exceeding 1) benefit–cost ratio, and starting at the top of the list, it should undertake all projects until its resources are fully utilized.

Although this sounds straightforward, a number of serious difficulties arise in the actual application of benefit–cost analysis, because it is often very difficult to correctly estimate the social benefits and the social costs of a project and to determine the appropriate rate of interest to use to calculate the present value of benefits and costs. First, since the benefits and the costs of most public projects (such as a dam, a highway, a training program, and so on) take place over many years, it is difficult to estimate them correctly so far into the future.

Second, benefits and costs are frequently estimated on the basis of current or projected prices, even though these prices may not reflect the true scarcity value or opportunity cost of the outputs resulting from or the inputs used in the project. For example, commodity prices under imperfectly competitive commodity markets exceed their marginal cost. Similarly, if a project results in the employment of otherwise unemployed labor, the real cost of hiring labor is zero, in spite of the positive wage paid to these workers. In other words, it is the real or opportunity value of the benefits and costs of the project that should be used in benefit–cost analysis. But it may be difficult to estimate them. Real costs may also rise as the project increases the demand for inputs.

Third, some of the benefits and costs of a project may not be quantifiable. For example, while it may be possible to estimate the rise in workers' income resulting from a training program, it is next to impossible to assign a value to their enhanced self-esteem and to their becoming more responsible citizens. Similarly, it is practically impossible to assign a value to the loss of scenery resulting from the construction of a dam. Yet, all of these social benefits and costs should be included in benefit–cost analysis for it to lead to appropriate public investment decisions.

The fourth and perhaps the most serious difficulty with benefit–cost analysis arises in the choice of the proper interest rate to be used to find the present value of the benefits and costs of the project. That is, since the benefits and costs of most projects occur over a number of years, they must be discounted to the present. For this a rate of interest must be used, as discussed in Section 16.3.[10] The question is *which* is the proper interest rate to use? As indicated in Section 16.4, there are a large number of rates of interest in the market (ranging from nearly zero to 40%) depending on the risk, duration, cost of administering, and the tax treatment of the loan. Since the use of resources by the government competes with private use, the interest (discount) rate to be used to find present values should reflect the opportunity cost of funds for a project of similar riskiness, duration, and administrative costs in the private sector. However, because different people may come up with a different rate

---

[10] In Section 16.3 we showed how to find the present value of a project. For benefit–cost analysis we need to find the present value of the benefits and costs of the project *separately*. The procedure, however, is the same. Note that a positive present value for a project is equivalent to a greater-than-one benefit–cost ratio.

of interest to use, benefit–cost analysis is usually prepared for a range of interest rates (from a low, to a medium, and a high one) rather than for a single interest rate. The lower the interest rate (or range of interest rates) used, the higher the benefit–cost ratio usually is and the greater the likelihood of the project being undertaken. The reason for this is that the benefits of a project usually arise later or over a longer period of time than its costs.

In spite of the great difficulties inherent in benefit–cost analysis, it is nevertheless a very valuable procedure for organizing our thoughts on the social benefits and the social costs of each project. If nothing else, it forces government officials to make explicit all the assumptions underlying the analysis. Scrutiny of the assumptions has sometimes led to decision reversals. For example, in 1971, the Federal Power Commission (now the Federal Energy Regulatory Commission) approved the construction of a hydroelectric dam on the Snake River, which flows from Oregon to Idaho and forms Hell's Canyon (the deepest in North America). The decision was based on a benefit–cost analysis that ignored some environmental costs. Because these costs were not accounted for, the Supreme Court, on appeal from the secretary of the interior, revoked the order to build the dam pending a new benefit–cost analysis that properly included *all* benefits and costs. Eventually, Congress passed a law prohibiting the construction of the dam.[11]

Although benefit–cost analysis is still more of an art than a science and is somewhat subjective, its usefulness has been proven in a wide variety of projects—water, transportation, health, education, and recreation. In fact, in 1965, the federal government formally began to introduce benefit–cost analysis for its budgetary procedures under the Planning-Programming-Budgeting System (PPBS). The practice has now spread to state and local governments as well. The process suffered a setback, however, when the Supreme Court ruled in February 2001 in Whitman v. American Trucking Associations Inc. that the EPA must consider only the requirements of public health and safety in setting national air quality standards and may not engage in cost–benefit analysis, as the American Trucking Associations Inc. had argued.[12]

EXAMPLE 18–4

Benefit–Cost Analysis and the SST

After a benefit–cost analysis, the development of the supersonic transport plane (SST) was abandoned by the United States in 1971. The benefits were simply not large enough to justify the costs. The French and British governments, however, jointly continued to pursue the project and built the Concorde at a huge cost. Today, there are only a handful of such planes operated exclusively by the British and French national airlines between

---

[11] J. V. Krutilla and A. C. Fisher, *The Economics of Natural Environments: Studies in the Valuation of Commodity and Amenity Resources* (Baltimore: Johns Hopkins University Press, 1975), pp. 101–103.
[12] "E.P.A.'s Right to Set Air Rules Wins Supreme Court Backing," *New York Times,* February 28, 2001, p. 1; and D. Clement, "Cost v. Benefit: Clearing the Air?" *The Region,* Federal Reserve Bank of Minneapolis, December 2001, pp. 19–57.

New York and Paris or London. With operating costs more than four times higher than the Boeing 747, the Concorde must be classified as a clear market failure. Specifically, a one-way seat from New York to London or Paris on the Concorde is priced at about $4,500 compared with less than $1,000 on the Boeing 747. This means that a passenger would be paying about $1,000 for each of the three-and-a-half hours he/she saves by flying the Concorde.

British Airways and Air France insist that the Concorde breaks even. Even so, the huge development cost of $8 billion was never recouped. And business on the Concorde is not brisk—British Airways and Air France are finding it increasingly difficult to fill the Concorde. It seems that in their benefit–cost analysis, the British and French greatly overestimated the benefits arising from building and operating the Concorde and grossly underestimated the costs. This is an example of how imprecise benefit–cost analysis (and how expensive national pride) can sometimes be.

Be that as it may, the Concorde is still, 30 years after its maiden voyage, a marvel of air travel with no rival in sight. A European project to build the "Concorde 2" with double the capacity of the present Concorde was scrapped in 1995. Similarly, a 10-year study on the feasibility of building an American supersonic passenger plane by the National Aeronautics and Space Administration and involving Boeing and engine makers General Electric and Pratt & Whitney that cost $1.8 billion was shut down in 1998. The problem is not technological but economic. It seems that there is no possibility of building a supersonic passenger aircraft that could be operated at a profit in the foreseeable future.

Sources: "The Concorde's Destination," *The New York Times,* September 28, 1979, p. 26; "Supersonic on the Back Burner," *The Economist,* March 6, 1999, p. 74; and "Concorde 'Successor' Faces Many Hurdles," *Financial Times,* December 12, 2001, p. V.

18.5   THE THEORY OF PUBLIC CHOICE

In this section we examine the meaning, importance, and policy implications of public-choice theory. Specifically, we explore the process by which government decisions are made and the reasons that these decisions might not increase social welfare.

Meaning and Importance of Public-Choice Theory

The **theory of public choice** is the study of how government decisions are made and implemented. It studies how the political process and government *actually* work rather than how they should work, and it recognizes the possibility of **government failures** or situations in which government policies do not reflect the public's interests and reduce rather than increase social welfare. The fact that markets do not operate efficiently does not necessarily mean that government policies will improve the situation; it is always possible that government intervention will make a bad situation worse. The opposite situation is also invalid. That is, the fact that government policies are inefficient does not necessarily mean that private markets can do better. For example, great waste in government defense expenditures does not mean that the provision of national defense can be left to private markets.

The theory of public choice is based on the premise that individuals attempt to further their own personal interests in the political arena just as they seek to further their own economic interests in the marketplace. According to the law of the invisible hand postulated by Adam Smith over two centuries ago, an individual who pursues his or her own selfish economic interests also and at the same time promotes the welfare of society as a whole. This was the basis for favoring and stimulating competition in the marketplace. The theory of public choice seeks to answer the question of whether such an invisible hand mechanism is also at work in the political system. That is, as each individual attempts to further his or her own interests in political activities, is he or she also and at the same time promoting society's welfare?

The Public-Choice Process

The theory of public choice examines how government decisions are made and implemented by analyzing the behavior of individuals within each of four broad groups or participants in the political process. These groups are voters, politicians, special-interest groups, and bureaucrats. Let us examine each in turn.

Voters   The voter in the political process can be regarded as the counterpart of the consumer in the marketplace. Rather than purchasing goods and services for himself or herself in the marketplace, the voter elects government representatives who make and enforce government policies and purchase goods and services for the community as a whole. Other things being equal, voters tend to vote for candidates who favor policies that will further their own individual interests. This is, in fact, the general process by which elected officials are responsive to the electorate.

According to public-choice theorists, however, voters are much less informed about political decisions than about their individual market decisions. This lack of information is often referred to as **rational ignorance.** There are three reasons for ignorance. First, with elected officials empowered to act as the purchasing agents for the community, there is less need for individual voters to be fully informed about public choices. Second, it is generally much more expensive for individuals to gather information about public choices than to become informed about individual market choices. For example, it is much more difficult for an individual to evaluate the full implications of a proposed national health insurance plan than to evaluate the implications of an individual insurance policy. Third, as a single individual, a voter feels—and, indeed, *is*—less influential in and less affected by public choices than by his or her own private market choices.

Politicians   Politicians are the counterpart in the political system of the entrepreneurs or managers of private firms in the market system. Both seek to maximize their personal benefit. While the entrepreneur or manager of a private firm seeks to maximize his or her interest by maximizing the firm's profits, the politician seeks to maximize chances of reelection. In doing so, politicians often respond to the desires of small, well-organized, well-informed, and well-funded special-interest groups. These include associations of farmers, importers, medical doctors, and many others. Faced with rational ignorance on the part of the majority of voters, politicians often support policies that greatly benefit small, vocal interest groups (who can contribute heavily to a candidate's reelection campaign) at the expense of the mostly silent and uninformed majority.

For example, in the early 1980s, U.S. automobile manufacturers were able to greatly increase their profits by having the U.S. government restrict auto imports from Japan (see the example in Section 13.7). The fact that politicians face reelection every few years may also lead politicians to pay undue attention to the short run, even when this leads to more serious long-run problems. For example, public policies are often adopted to reduce the rate of unemployment at election time in November, even though this might lead to higher inflation later. Such policies have led some to postulate the existence of a "political business cycle."

Special-Interest Groups   Perhaps the most maligned of the groups participating in the political process are special-interest groups. These pressure groups or organized lobbies seek to elect politicians who support their cause, and they actively support the passage of laws and regulations that further their interests. For example, for decades the American Medical Association succeeded in limiting admissions to medical schools, thereby increasing doctors' incomes; farmers' associations successfully lobbied the government to provide billions of dollars in subsidies each year; as pointed out earlier, U.S. automakers succeeded in having auto imports from Japan restricted in the early 1980s, thereby greatly increasing their profits. Even though not all lobbies are as successful as those mentioned here, thousands are in operation, and this, according to many, represents the worst aspects of our political system.[13]

The reason some of these special-interest groups are so influencial is that they are well organized and stand to benefit a great deal when their efforts are successful. Thus, they are very vocal and often can provide millions of dollars in financial support to politicians who advocate their cause. At the same time, most people are usually not aware of the costs (usually small) that they individually face from these laws and regulations. Furthermore, these laws and regulations are invariably rationalized in terms of the national interest. For example, import restrictions on shoes might only increase the price of shoes by $1 per pair while providing millions of dollars in extra profits to the few remaining shoe manufacturers in the nation. Supposedly, these import restrictions are temporary and are essential to give time to American producers to increase efficiency and be able to meet what is regarded as unfair foreign competition.

Bureaucrats   Bureaus are the government agencies that carry out the policies enacted by Congress. They do so by receiving annual lump-sum appropriations to cover the costs of providing the services that they are directed to provide. Bureaus often provide these services under conditions of monopoly (i.e., without any competition from other bureaus or private firms) and so have little incentive to promote internal efficiency. While it is difficult to compare the efficiency of government bureaus and private firms, there have been spectacular cost overruns in many defense projects. For example, the cost of the Lockheed C5A transport plane increased from an estimated $3.4 billion in 1965 to $5.3 billion in 1968.

According to public-choice theory, bureaucrats are not simply passive executors of adopted policies, but seek to influence such policies in order to further their own personal interests. They do so by constantly seeking to increase the scope of the bureau's activities

---

[13] In recent years, lobbying in Washington by foreign firms and nations (especially Japan) has increased sharply.

and the amount of funding, even when the raison d'être for the bureau no longer exists. This is because a top bureaucrat's career, income, power, prestige, and promotion are, in general, closely related to the size and growth of the bureau. In essence, the bureau often becomes a separate special-interest group within the government!

Policy Implications of Public-Choice Theory

The above characterization of the political process by public-choice theorists is, perhaps, excessively cynical. Voters elect only politicians who promote their individual interests, and are mostly ignorant and indifferent about most other public choices; politicians only seek to maximize their chances of reelection; special-interest groups only seek special advantages at the expense of the mostly silent and ignorant majority; and bureaucrats only seek to maximize their own interests by promoting the bureau's growth at the expense of efficiency.

Although there is some truth in all of this, we must also point out that many voters are well informed and often unselfish; many politicians have refused to compromise their principles simply to maximize their chances of reelection; many powerful special-interest groups have been unsuccessful in furthering their causes; and many bureaucracies have operated efficiently and sometimes even proposed their own abolition when their function was no longer required. For example, in the past, the majority of U.S. voters consistently voted for and supported most social welfare policies, even though these policies involved a redistribution of income to poor people; President Reagan refused to back away from large defense spending in spite of strong opposition in and out of Congress and the resulting huge budget deficits; the American Medical Association is no longer able to restrict admissions to medical schools as it did over many decades; and the CAB (the Civil Aeronautics Board) proposed its own abolition and is now no longer in existence.

These examples, however, do not necessarily represent contradictions of the theory of public choice. This theory seeks only to identify the forces that must be examined to properly analyze public choices. The theory concludes that while public policies can improve the functioning of the economic system in the presence of market failures, the government itself is subject to systematic forces that can lead to government failures. Public policies could then reduce, rather than increase, social welfare. More importantly, perhaps, the theory of public choice can be used to suggest specific institutional changes and to devise policies that can lead to improvements in public-sector performance.

One way that public-choice theory suggests for improving public-sector performance is to subject government bureaus or agencies to competition whenever feasible. One method of achieving this is by contracting out to private firms as many public services as possible. For example, market evidence suggests that garbage collection and fire protection can be provided more efficiently by private contractors than by public agencies. The same may be true for running school systems and jails.[14] Another method advocated by

---

[14] "Hartford Hires Group to Run School System," *New York Times,* October 4, 1994, p. B1; "For Privately Run Prisons, New Evidence of Success," *New York Times,* August 19, 1995, p. 7; M. Haririan and T. A. Bonomo, "Privatization and the Emergence of For-Profit Prisons," *Central Business Review,* winter 1996, pp. 11–15; "Do Firms Run Schools Well?" *U.S. News & World Report,* January 8, 1996, pp. 46–49; and "Pennsylvania Abandons Plan to Privatize School Offices," *New York Times,* November 21, 2001, p. 14.

public-choice theory to promote efficiency in public choices is to allow private firms to compete with government agencies in the provision of services that are not entirely public in nature.[15] For example, families could be given vouchers that they could use for public or private education. Giving parents the option and funding to choose private schools over public schools would stimulate public schools to provide better education and increase efficiency. Still another method of increasing efficiency in government is to encourage interagency competition. While streamlining government operations is likely to eliminate some duplication and waste, it also eliminates competition and incentives for efficient operation. For example, it has been estimated that the cost-effectiveness of the Department of Defense operations declined by one-third following the consolidation of the three branches of the armed forces within the department.

Public-choice theory also suggests at least two ways of reducing the influence of special-interest groups. One option would be to rely more on referenda to decide important political issues. Although the influence of special-interest groups is not entirely eliminated (since they can still spend a great deal of money on influencing the general public through advertisements), reverting from representative to direct democracy in deciding some important issues does overcome the interaction between special-interest groups and politicians. Today, referenda are much more common in European countries than in the United States. Another method of reducing the influence of special-interest groups is to specify the total amount of public funds budgeted for the year and encourage different groups to compete for government funding. Because the total amount of funds is fixed, one group can only gain at the expense of others. Each group is then likely to present its best case for funding while exposing the weaknesses in competitors' funding requests. In the process, a great deal of essential information is made available to government officials, who can therefore allocate funds more effectively. Many policies (such as import restrictions), however, do not involve direct public funding, and so this is not possible.

18.6   STRATEGIC TRADE POLICY

One qualified argument in favor of an activist government policy in the international arena is **strategic trade policy.** According to this argument, a nation can create a comparative advantage (through temporary trade protection, subsidies, tax benefits, and cooperative government-industry programs) in such fields as semiconductors, computers, telecommunications, and other industries that are deemed crucial to future growth in the nation. These high-tech industries are subject to high risks, require large-scale production to achieve economies of scale, and give rise to extensive external economies when successful. Strategic trade policy suggests that by encouraging such industries, a nation can reap the resulting large external economies and enhance its future growth prospects. Most nations encourage development in these industries. Indeed, some economists would go so far as to say that a great deal of the post-World War II industrial and technological success of Japan is due to its strategic industrial and trade policies.

---

[15] See "Public Services Are Found Better if Private Agencies Compete," *New York Times,* April 28, 1988, p. 1.

Examples of strategic trade and industrial policies can be found in the steel industry in the 1950s and in semiconductors in the 1970s and 1980s in Japan; in the development of the supersonic aircraft, the Concorde, in the 1970s (see Example 18–4); and in the Airbus aircraft in the 1980s in Europe. Semiconductors in Japan are usually given as the textbook case of successful strategic trade and industrial policy. The market for semiconductors (such as computer chips that are used in many products) was dominated by the United States in the 1970s. Starting in the mid-1970s, Japan's powerful Ministry of International Trade and Industry (MITI) targeted the development of this industry by financing research and development, granting tax advantages for investments in the industry, and fostering government-industry cooperation, while protecting the domestic market from foreign (especially U.S.) competition.

These policies are credited for Japan's success in challenging the United States' leading position in the semiconductor market in the mid-1980s. Most economists remain skeptical, however, and attribute Japan's stunning performance in this field primarily to other forces, such as greater educational emphasis on science and mathematics, higher rates of investment, and a willingness to take a long-run view of investments rather than stressing quarterly profits, as in the United States. In steel, the other targeted industry in Japan, the rate of return was lower than the average return for all Japanese industries during the postwar period. In Europe, the Concorde was a technological feat but a commercial disaster, and Airbus Industries would not have survived without continued heavy government subsidies.

While strategic trade policy can theoretically improve the market outcome in oligopolistic markets subject to extensive external economies and increase the nation's growth and welfare, even the originators and popularizers of this theory recognize the serious difficulties in implementing it. First, it is extremely difficult to pick winners (i.e., choose the industries that will provide large external economies in the future) and devise appropriate policies to successfully nurture them. Second, since most leading nations undertake strategic trade policies at the same time, efforts are largely neutralized, so that the potential benefits to each nation may be small. Third, when a country does achieve substantial success with strategic trade policy, this comes at the expense of other countries (i.e., it is a beggar-thy-neighbor policy), and so other countries are likely to retaliate. Faced with all these practical difficulties, even supporters of strategic trade policy grudgingly acknowledge that *free trade is still the best policy, after all.*

EXAMPLE 18–5
Strategic Trade and Industrial Policies in the United States

In the early 1980s, the U.S. government drew up a list of 26 generic and critical technologies which it was willing to support in a limited way. Among these were electronic materials, high-performance metals and alloys, flexible computer integrated manufacturing, software, high-performance computing networking, high-definition imaging displays, applied molecular biology, medical technology, aeronautics, and energy technologies. The best example of direct federal support for civilian technology is Semitech. This was an Austin-based consortium of 14 major U.S. semiconductor manufacturers which was established in 1987 with an annual budget of $225 million ($100 million from the government and the rest from the 14 member firms). Its aim was to help develop state-of-the-art manufacturing techniques for computer chips for its members and help firms producing equipment used in the manufacturing of computer chips develop and test more advanced equipment.

By 1991, Semitech claimed that, as a result of its efforts, U.S. computer chip companies had caught up with their Japanese competitors. Since then, Semitech has become entirely private (i.e., it no longer receives U.S. government financial support). In 1993, three of the original members of Semitech dropped out, leaving 11 members in the consortium, and in 1998 it created Semitech International, a wholly owned subsidiary, which included five foreign computer chip companies.

Despite being hailed as a successful model of government-industry cooperation in support of high-tech research and development (R&D) before it was privatized, a recent study found that participating in Semitech led firms to spend less on their own R&D than would have been expected, given the behavior of these firms prior to Semitech and given the behavior of U.S. computer chip firms that did not join Semitech. The study also found that the resurgence of the U.S. computer chip industry after 1987 was due more to the sharp depreciation of the U.S. dollar with respect to the Japanese yen (which made U.S.-made computer chips cheaper than Japanese ones) and the U.S.–Japanese computer chip agreement, which insulated U.S. computer chip firms against Japanese competition, than to Semitech.

Sources. D. Irwin and P. Klenow, "High Tech R & D Subsidies: Estimating the Effect of Semitech," *National Bureau of Economic Research, Working Paper No. 4974,* July 1995; and "When the State Picks Winners," *The Economist,* January 9, 1993, pp. 13–14; and C. Wessner, "The Advanced Technology Program: It Works," *Issues in Science and Technology,* Fall 2001, pp. 59–64.

18.7   GOVERNMENT CONTROL AND REGULATION OF ENVIRONMENTAL POLLUTION

Now we will use the tools of analysis developed in this chapter to analyze environmental pollution and the best way for government to control or regulate it.

Environmental Pollution

We have seen in Section 18.2 that externalities (and inefficiencies) may be eliminated by the clear definition of property rights if the parties involved are not very numerous. Otherwise, transaction costs are too high and externalities persist. This is precisely the case with **environmental pollution,** which refers to air pollution, water pollution, thermal pollution, pollution resulting from garbage disposal, and so on. Environmental pollution has become one of the major political and economic issues in recent decades. Environmental pollution results from and is an example of negative externalities.[16]

---

[16] See "Priority One: Rescue the Environment," *Science,* February 16, 1990, p. 777; M. L. Cropper and W. Oates, "Environmental Economics: A Survey," *Journal of Economic Literature,* June 1992, pp. 675–740; and "Where Money Is No Object," *Forbes,* March 5, 2001, p. 78.

Air pollution results mostly from automobile exhaust and smoke from factories and electrical generating plants through the combustion of fossil fuels, which releases particles into the air. While it is difficult to measure precisely the harmful effects of sulfur dioxide, carbon monoxide, and other air pollutants, they are known to cause damage to health (in the form of breathing illnesses and aggravating other diseases, such as circulatory problems) and to property (in the form of higher cleaning bills, and so on). *Water pollution* results from dumping raw (untreated) sewage, chemical waste products from factories and mines, and runoff of pesticides and fertilizers from farms into streams, lakes, and seashores. This reduces the supply of clean water for household uses (drinking, bathing, and so on) and recreational uses (swimming, boating, fishing, and so on). *Thermal pollution* results from the cooling off of electrical power plants and other machinery. This increases water temperature and kills fish. The disposal of garbage such as beer cans, newspapers, cigarette butts, and so on, spoils natural scenery, as do billboards and posters. To this visual pollution must be added noise pollution and many other forms of pollution.

Environmental pollution results whenever the environment is used (abused) as a convenient and cheap dumping ground for all types of waste products. It is convenient and cheap from the private point of view to use the environment in this manner because no one owns property rights to it. As a result, air and water users pay less than the full social cost of using these natural resources, and by so doing they impose serious external costs on society. In short, society produces and consumes too much of products that generate environmental pollution. Since property rights are ambiguous and the parties involved are numerous (often running into the millions), it is impossible and impractical (too costly) to identify and negotiate with individual agents. The external costs of environmental pollution cannot be internalized by the assignment of clear property rights and so government intervention is required. This intervention can take the form of regulation or taxation. However, appropriate corrective action on the part of the government requires knowledge of the exact cost of pollution.

Optimal Pollution Control

If a staunch environmentalist were asked how much environmental pollution society should tolerate, the answer would probably be zero. This would be the wrong answer. The optimal level of pollution is the level at which the marginal social cost of pollution equals the marginal social benefit (in the form of avoiding alternative and more expensive methods of waste disposal). Zero pollution is an ideal situation, but as long as pollution is the inevitable by-product of the production and consumption of commodities that we want, it is silly to advocate zero pollution. Economists advocate optimal pollution control instead. That is, we should be prepared to accept (as inevitable) that amount of pollution which, at the margin, balances the social costs and benefits of pollution. This is shown in Figure 18.3.

In Figure 18.3, the horizontal axis measures the quantity of pollution per year, and the vertical axis measures costs and gains in dollars. The *MC* curve, for example, could measure the value of the marginal loss of fish suffered by fishermen for various amounts of water pollution generated by a firm. The marginal loss (cost) increases with rising amounts of pollution. The *MB* curve would then measure the marginal benefit or saving that the polluting firm receives by being able to freely dump its waste into the water rather than disposing of it by the next-best alternative method (at a positive cost). The *MB* is negatively

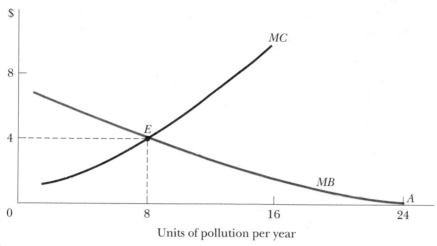

FIGURE 18.3   Optimal Pollution Control   The *MC* curve shows the rising marginal cost or loss to society from increasing amounts of pollution. The *MB* curve shows the declining marginal benefit to the polluter (and to society) by being able to freely dump increasing amounts of waste into the water rather than disposing of it by other costly alternatives. Since the firm does not pay for discharging its waste into the water, it will do so until *MB* = 0 (point *A*). From society's point of view, the optimal level of pollution for the firm is 8 units per year (point *E*, at which *MC* = *MB*).

sloped, indicating declining benefits for the firm for each additional unit of pollution that it discharges into the water.

When the firm does not incur any cost for discharging waste into the water, it will do so until the marginal benefit is zero (point *A* in the figure). That is, as long as the firm saves some cost by discharging its waste into the water, it will do so until the *MB* is zero. However, pollution does impose a cost on society as a whole. The optimal amount of pollution from society's point of view is 8 units, given by the intersection of the *MC* and the *MB* curves at point *E*. Only when pollution is 8 units per year is the marginal benefit to the individual and to society equal to the marginal social cost of pollution. To the left of point *E*, *MB* > *MC* and it pays for society to increase the level of pollution (see the figure). The opposite is true to the right of point *E*. As strange as it may have sounded earlier, we now know that the optimal level of pollution is not zero, but is positive.

Direct Regulation and Effluent Fees for Optimal Pollution Control

We have just seen that the optimal level of pollution from society's point of view is not zero, but is given by the level at which the marginal cost of pollution is equal to the private (and social) marginal benefit of disposing of waste by the cheapest method possible. Even though this prescription is theoretically precise, it is often very difficult to actually estimate the marginal social costs and benefits of pollution. Without government intervention, environmental pollution is certainly likely to be excessive (compare point *A* to point *E* in Figure 18.3).

There are generally two ways to achieve the optimal amount of pollution control: direct regulation and effluent fees. By direct regulation, government could legislate that the industry limit pollution to the optimal level (8 units per year in Figure 18.3) or install a particular pollution-abatement device. Alternatively, government could set the **effluent fee** that brings the private cost of pollution equal to its social cost. An effluent fee is a tax that a firm must pay to the government for discharging waste or otherwise polluting. For example, an effluent fee of $4 per unit of waste or pollution per year in Figure 18.3 results in the optimal level of pollution of 8 units per year. That is, an effluent fee of $4 per unit will make the marginal private (and social) cost of pollution equal to its marginal private (and social) benefit.

While direct regulation is sometimes necessary (as in the case of radioactive and other very dangerous waste materials), economists generally prefer effluent fees to achieve optimal pollution control. There are two reasons for this. First, effluent fees generally require less information on the part of the government than direct regulation. Second, and more importantly, effluent fees minimize the cost of optimal pollution control, whereas direct regulation does not. This is because with effluent fees, each polluter will pollute until the marginal benefit of pollution equals the effluent fee. Thus, the optimal amount of pollution is allocated to those firms that benefit the most from polluting. As a result, the social cost of pollution is minimized.

One way to use effluent fees to reduce pollution is by the *sale of pollution rights* by the government. Under such a system, the government determines the amount of pollution that it thinks is socially tolerable (based on the benefits that result from the activities that generate the pollution) and then auctions off licenses to firms that generate pollution up to the specified amount. Pollution costs are thus internalized (i.e., they are considered part of regular production costs) by firms and the allowed amount of pollution is utilized in activities in which it is most valuable (see Example 18–6).

EXAMPLE 18-6

The Market for Dumping Rights

A market for dumping rights came into existence in 1977 when the *Environmental Protection Agency (EPA)* issued the first transferrable permit for dumping. Under such a system, the EPA decides how much pollution it wants to allow and then issues marketable rights for that quantity of pollution. Since these dumping rights are marketable (i.e., can be bought and sold by firms), they are likely to be used in those activities in which they are most valuable. For example, suppose that the EPA has imposed specific dumping restrictions on two firms. If the cost of reducing emission by 1 unit (say, one ton of sulfur dioxide) is $10,000 for one firm and $50,000 for a second firm, the first firm could sell the right to dump that unit of emission to the second firm for a price between $10,000 and $50,000. The result would be that both firms (and society) would gain without any overall increase in pollution. In fact, the only way that a new firm can build a plant that pollutes the air in an area that does not meet federal air-quality standards is to purchase the right to a specific amount of pollution from an already existing and polluting firm in the area.

Since 1977, thousands of such market exchanges for pollution rights have been carried out. In fact, we now have pollution-rights banks, which act as brokers between firms that want to sell pollution rights and firms that want to purchase them. In 1980, the concept of marketable pollution rights was extended by the so-called bubble policy. Under this policy, a firm with several plants operating in single air pollution area is given a total permissible emission level for all of its plants rather than a limit for each one. This allows the firm to concentrate its emission reduction efforts in plants where it can be done more cheaply. The *Clean Air Act of 1990* required a phased reduction in overall pollution and established a generalized market for pollution permits. The establishment of a market for pollution permits represents a significant victory for economists (who have been advocating this for many years) and changes the direction of antipollution efforts in the United States for decades to come.

In 1992, the United Nations proposed the establishment of an international market where *nations* could purchase or sell pollution permits in order to cut the cost of reducing the greenhouse effect and resulting global warming. In July 2001, a historic accord that set targets for industrialized countries to cut emission of greenhouse gases that contribute to global warming was signed in 178 countries, thus keeping alive the *Kyoto Protocol* on climate change originally signed in 1997. The United States refused to sign the agreement calling its targets arbitrary and too costly for the United States to comply. When ratified by the participating countries, the agreement would stimulate the further development of a market for emission trading on a global scale, just as it developed in the United States since the late 1970s. In February 2002, President Bush unveiled the U.S. plan for slowing the build up of gases linked to climate changes, but environmentalists immediately critics attacked the plan because it would only slowdown but not halt the increase in this type of pollution.

Sources: "A Market Place for Pollution Rights," *U.S. News & World Report,* November 12, 1990, p. 79; "New Rules Harness the Power of Free Markets to Curb Air Pollution," *Wall Street Journal,* April 4, 1992, p. A1; "Cheapest Protection of Nature May Lie in Taxes, Not Laws," *New York Times,* November 24, 1992, p. C1; "Global Market for Pollution Rights Proposed by the U.N.," *Wall Street Journal,* January 30, 1992, p. C1; "178 Nations Reach a Climate Accord; U.S. Only Looks On," *New York Times,* July 24, 2001, p. 1; "How Much Is the Right to Pollute Worth?" *Wall Street Journal,* August 1, 2001, p. A15; and "Bush Outlines Plan to Counter Climate Change," *Financial Times,* February 15, 2002, p. 2.

SUMMARY

1. Externalities are harmful or beneficial side effects borne by those not directly involved in the production or consumption of a commodity. Externalities are classified into external economies or diseconomies of production or consumption, and technical externalities. With external diseconomies of production or consumption, the commodity price falls short of the full social cost of the commodity and too much of the commodity is produced or consumed. With external economies of production or consumption, the commodity price exceeds the full social cost of the commodity and too little of the commodity is produced and consumed. Technical externalities may prevent marginal cost pricing.

2. Externalities arise when property rights are not clearly defined and transaction costs are very high. The Coase theorem postulates that when property rights are clearly defined and transaction costs are zero, perfect competition results in the absence of externalities, regardless of how property rights are assigned among the parties involved.

3. Public goods are commodities that are nonrival in consumption. That is, consumption of a public good by some individual does not reduce the amount available for others (at zero marginal cost). Some public goods, such as national defense, exhibit nonexclusion. That is, once the good is produced, it is impossible to confine its use to only those paying for it. Other public goods, such as TV broadcasting, can exhibit exclusion. Because of the free-rider problem, public goods are usually underproduced and underconsumed.

4. Benefit–cost analysis is based on the government calculating the ratio of the present value of all the benefits to the present value of all the costs for each proposed public project. The projects are then ranked from the highest to the lowest in terms of benefit–cost ratios. Government should undertake those projects with the highest benefit–cost ratio (as long as the ratio exceeds 1) and until government resources are fully employed. There are many difficulties in estimating all benefits and costs of a project and in determining the interest rate to use to find the present value of the benefits and costs.

5. According to the theory of public choice, individuals vote for politicians who promote their individual interests; politicians seek to maximize their chances of reelection; special-interest groups seek special advantages for their group; and bureaucrats seek to promote the bureau's growth. The theory postulates that it is possible for government policies to reduce rather than increase social welfare (government failures). It proposes to increase efficiency by increasing competition in public choices and by relying more on referenda to decide important issues.

6. According to strategic trade policy, a nation can create a comparative advantage (through temporary trade protection, subsidies, tax benefits, etc.) in such fields as computers, that can give rise to extensive external economies, and which are deemed crucial to future growth in the nation. However, it is very difficult to determine which industry to promote, and other nations are likely to retaliate.

7. Environmental (air, water, thermal, scenic, and noise) pollution arises because of unclearly defined property rights and too-high transaction costs. The optimal level of pollution from society's point of view is not zero, but is given by the level at which the marginal cost of pollution to society is equal to the private (and social) marginal benefit of disposing of waste by the cheapest method available. Optimal pollution control can be achieved by direct regulation or effluent fees. Although direct regulation is sometimes necessary (as in the case of dangerous waste materials), economists generally prefer effluent fees and the establishment of a market for pollution permits because they are much more efficient.

KEY TERMS

Externalities
External costs
External benefits
External diseconomies
   of production
External diseconomies
   of consumption
External economies of production

External economies of consumption
Technical externalities
Common property
Coase theorem
Internalizing external costs
Public goods
Nonrival consumption
Nonexclusion

Free-rider problem
Benefit–cost analysis
Theory of public choice
Government failures
Rational ignorance
Strategic trade policy
Environmental pollution
Effluent fee

REVIEW QUESTIONS

1. How can typing a report late at night create a negative externality? How can this result in an externality that is mutually harmful?

2. Why is a public-housing project in a high-income neighborhood not likely to satisfy the Pareto optimality criterion?

3. Why does free access to a common resource usually lead to the overuse of the resource?

4. Why, during the Cold War period, did the knowledge that the United States would not have accepted a Soviet invasion of Europe lead to less defense expenditures in Western Europe?

5. What is the basic difference between using a subsidy to induce producers to install antipollution equipment and using a tax on producers who pollute?

6. How does the market demand for a public good differ from the market demand of a private good?

7. Why is it generally more difficult to estimate the benefits and the costs of a public than of a private project?

8. Everyone agrees that large federal budget deficits are bad. Why do budget deficits then persist?

9. What is the unifying concept by which public-choice theory analyzes individual behavior in the political process?

10. What policies does the theory of public choice prescribe (a) in order to increase efficiency in public choices and reduce government failures, and (b) to reduce the influence of special-interest groups?

11. Is there a conflict between the theory of comparative advantage and strategic trade policy?

12. When would direct regulation be better than effluent fees in pollution control?

PROBLEMS

1. Explain why
   a. in a system of private education (i.e., a system in which individuals pay for their own education), there is likely to be underinvestment in education.
   b. the discussion of external economies and diseconomies is in terms of marginal rather than total social costs and benefits.

2. Start with D and S as in Figure 18.1.
   a. Draw D' with the same vertical intercept as D but with twice the absolute value of its slope. Suppose that D' portrays the marginal social benefit of the public consuming various quantities of the commodity.
   b. Does D' indicate the existence of external economies of production or consumption?
   c. What is the marginal external benefit or cost and the marginal social benefit or cost at the competitive equilibrium point?
   d. What is the socially optimal price and consumption of the commodity?

*3. a. Draw a figure showing the corrective tax or subsidy that would induce society to consume the socially optimum amount of the commodity.
   b. What is the total value of the economic gain resulting from the imposition of the corrective tax or subsidy?

4. Start with D and S as in Figure 18.1.
   a. Draw S' with the same vertical intercept as S but with half of its slope. Suppose that S' portrays the marginal *social* costs of supplying various quantities of the commodity.
   b. Does S' indicate the existence of external economies or diseconomies of production or consumption?
   c. What is the marginal external cost or benefit and the marginal social cost at the competitive equilibrium point?
   d. What is the socially optimum price and output of the commodity?

---

* = Answer provided at end of book.

*5. a. Draw a figure showing the corrective tax or subsidy that would induce the industry to produce the socially optimal amount of the commodity.

   b. What is the total value of the economic inefficiency eliminated by the corrective tax or subsidy?

6. Start with D and S as in Figure 18.1.

   a. Draw D' with the same vertical intercept as D but with half the absolute value of its slope. Suppose that D' portrays the marginal social benefit of the public consuming various quantities of the commodity.

   b. Does D' indicate the existence of external economies or diseconomies of production or consumption?

   c. What is the marginal external benefit or cost and the marginal social benefit or cost at the equilibrium point?

   d. What is the socially optimum price and consumption of the commodity?

7. a. Draw a figure showing the corrective tax or subsidy that would induce the society to consume the socially optimal amount of the commodity.

   b. What is the total value of the economic gain resulting from the imposition of the corrective tax or subsidy?

8. Explain what would be the outcome if the cost of avoiding polluting the stream (with its waste products) by the paper mill of Section 18.2 was $1,200 rather than $400 per month, and property rights to the stream were assigned to the

   a. brewery.

   b. paper mill.

   c. When would the socially optimal solution be reached?

*9. Explain why, in each of the following cases, externalities arise and how they would be avoided or corrected when

   a. one individual owns an oil field next to another oil field owned by another individual.

   b. a firm develops a recreational site (golf, skiing, boating, or the like).

*10. a. Draw a figure showing the market demand curve for good X for Figure 18.2 if good X were a private rather than a public good.

   b. State the condition for the Pareto optimal output of commodity X when X is a private good and when it is a public good.

   c. What is the relationship between public goods and externalities?

11. Three possible solutions were proposed at the time of the severe water shortage experienced by New York City in 1949–1950. These solutions were (1) building a dam that would cost $1,000 per million gallons of water supplied, (2) sealing leaks in water mains, which would cost about $1.60 per million gallons of water gained, or (3) installing water meters that would cost $160 per million gallons of water saved. The city chose the first project. Was New York's choice the most efficient? If not, why might New York have made this choice?

12. With reference to Figure 18.3, calculate the total social gains by

   a. increasing the level of pollution from 4 to 8 units per year.

   b. reducing pollution from 12 to 8 units per year.

INTERNET SITE ADDRESSES

For externalities, see Chapter 4 in:

   http://www.humboldt.edu/~envecon/ppt/423/
   index.html

For law and economics and property rights, see:

   http://lawecon.lp.findlaw.com

   http://www.lincolninst.edu/landline/1997/march/
   common.html

   http://www.indiana.edu/~iascp

Public goods are examined at:

   http://www.magnolia.net/~leonf/sd/vpopg/
   vpog.html

For public choice theory, see:

   http://www.publichoicesoc.org/mtg2002.html

   http://www.magnolia.net/~leonf/sd/
   pub-choice/html

For government support of basic research and R&D in the United States and Japan, see the sites of the National Science Foundation and Sematech for the United States, as well as the site of the Statistics Center of the Management and Coordination Agency for Japan, respectively, at:

> http://www.nsf.gov/sbe/srs/fedfunds/start.htm
>
> http://www.sematech.org/public/index.htm
>
> http://www.stat.go.jp/1.htm

Benefit–cost analysis software is provided by Legacy Research System and presentation of benefit–cost analysis is provided in Chapter 6 by Steve Hackett, respectively, at:

> http://www.costbenefit.com/index.htm
>
> http://www.humboldt.edu/~envecon/ppt/423/index.html

For more information on the supersonic transport plane (SST), see the Internet site for British Airways and Air France, the only two airlines flying the Concorde, at:

> http://www.airfrance.fr.com
>
> http://www.british-airways.com

For U.S. strategic trade and commercial relations, see:

> http://www.ustr.gov/reports/tpa/2000/contents/html
>
> http://www.tufts.edu/departments/fletcher/multi/trade.html

Information on government control and regulation of environmental pollution as well as on the market for dumping rights and tradable permits is found at:

> http://www.natsource.com/enviroaction/index.htm
>
> http://www.epa.gov
>
> http://www.humboldt.edu/~envecon/ppt/423/index.html (Chapters 8 and 10)

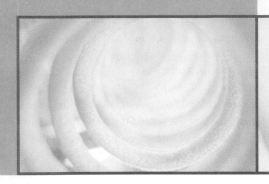

CHAPTER 19

The Economics of Information

In this chapter we study the economics of information. This field of study is becoming increasingly important in economics—and deservingly so. The chapter begins by examining the economics of search: search costs, the process of searching for the lowest price, and the informational content of advertising. The chapter goes on to discuss asymmetric information and the market for lemons (i.e., defective products), the insurance market and adverse selection, market signaling, moral hazard, and the principal-agent problem. The examples and applications of the theory provided in the chapter show the real-world importance and great relevance of the economics of information, while the *At the Frontier* section on the Internet and the information superhighway examines one of the most important and recent forms of the current worldwide information revolution.

19.1	THE ECONOMICS OF SEARCH

We begin our study by discussing search costs, outlining the process of searching for the lowest commodity price, and examining the informational content of advertising.[1]

Search Costs

One cost of purchasing a product is the time and money we spend seeking information about the product—what are the properties of the product, what are the alternatives, how good is the product, how safe, how much does the product cost in one store as opposed to another? **Search costs** include the time spent reading ads, telephoning, traveling, inspecting the product, and comparative shopping for the lowest price. Although the most important

---

[1] This discussion draws heavily on George J. Stigler, "The Economics of Information," *Journal of Political Economy,* June 1961, pp. 213–225; and Joseph E. Stiglitz, "The Contributions of the Economics of Information to Twentieth Century Economics," *Quarterly Journal of Economics,* November 2000, pp 1441–1478.

component of search costs is the time spent learning about the attributes of the product, consumers sometimes also spend money purchasing information to aid them in their search. They might purchase *Consumer Reports* magazine to check on the quality of a product, pay an impartial mechanic to evaluate a used car before deciding on purchasing it, or seek professional help from a financial advisor before making a major investment. In most cases, however, the major cost of search is the time required to learn about the product. Often the government provides a great deal of this information; for example, the government requires mileage disclosures for new automobiles, safety standards for some products, and weather forecasts, all of which greatly reduce uncertainty in the purchasing of many products.

One of the most important and time-consuming aspects of purchasing a product is comparison shopping for the lowest price. Even when a product is standardized and conditions of sale are identical (i.e., locational convenience, courteousness of service, availability of credit, returns policy, etc.), there will be a dispersion of prices in the absence of perfect information on the part of buyers. Since it takes time and money to gather information, and different consumers place different valuations on their time, some price dispersion will persist in the market even if the product is perfectly standardized and sales conditions are identical.

The general rule is that *a consumer should continue the search for lower prices as long as the marginal benefit from continuing the search exceeds the marginal cost, and until the marginal benefit equals the marginal cost.* The marginal benefit (*MB*) is equal to the degree by which a lower price is found as a result of each additional search times the number of units of the product purchased at the lower price. The marginal cost (*MC*) of continuing the search depends on the value that consumers place on their time (assuming that consumers do not find shopping itself pleasurable). Since the value that consumers place on their time differs for different consumers, the product will be purchased at different prices by different consumers when each consumer behaves according to the *MB* = *MC* rule. Specifically, those consumers forgoing higher wages when searching for lower prices will stop the search before consumers who face lower opportunity costs for their time, and thus will purchase the product at a higher price.[2] On the other hand, with the MC curve of search shifting down because of the Internet, consumers search more now than a decade ago.

Searching for the Lowest Price

At any time, there will be a dispersion of prices in the market even for a homogeneous product. A consumer can accept the price quoted by the first seller of the product he or she approaches, or the consumer can continue the search for lower prices. Unless the consumer knows that the price quoted by the first seller is the lowest price in the market, he or she should continue the search for lower prices as long as the marginal benefit from continuing the search exceeds the marginal cost of additional search. In general, the marginal benefit from searching declines as the time spent searching for lower prices continues. Even if the marginal cost of additional search is constant, a point is reached where *MB* = *MC*. At that point, the consumer should end the search.

---

[2] The same general rule applies in searching for a better-quality product. A consumer should continue the search as long as the *MB* exceeds the *MC* and until *MB* = *MC*. The actual application of this rule, however, is usually more difficult than in searching for lower product prices because it is difficult to assign higher monetary values correctly for better-quality products.

For example, suppose that a consumer wants to purchase a small portable TV of a given brand and knows the prices of different sellers range from $80 to $120. All sellers are identical in location, service, and so on, so that price is the only consideration. Suppose also that sellers are equally divided into five price classifications: Sellers of type I charge a price of $80 for the TV, type II sellers charge $90, type III charge $100, type IV charge $110, and type V charge $120. For a single search, the probability of each price is 1/5, and the expected price is the weighted average of all prices, or $100.[3] The consumer can now purchase the TV at the price of $100, or she can continue the search for lower prices. With each additional search the consumer will find a lower price, until the lowest price of $80 is found. The reduction in price with each search gives the marginal benefit of the search. How many searches the consumer conducts depends on the marginal cost that she faces. The consumer will end the search when the marginal benefit from the search equals the marginal cost.

We can use a simple formula to obtain the approximate lowest price expected with each additional search.[4] This is

$$\text{Expected Price} = \text{Lowest Price} + \frac{\text{Range of Prices}}{\text{Number of Searchers} + 1} \qquad [19.1]$$

For example, the lowest TV price expected from one search is

$$\text{Expected Price} = \$80 + \frac{\$40}{1+1} = \$100 \text{ (as found earlier)}$$

The approximate lowest expected price from two searches is $80 + ($40/3) = $93.33.[5] Thus, the approximate marginal benefit from the second search is $100 − $93.33 = $6.67. The lowest expected price with three searches is $80 + ($40/4) = $90, so that $MB = $3.33. The lowest expected price with four searches is $80 + ($40/5) = $88, so that $MB = $2. The lowest expected price with five searches is $80 + ($40/6) = $86.67, so that $MB = $1.33.

Note how the marginal benefit from each additional search declines. $MB = $6.67 for the second search, $3.33 for the third search, $2 for the fourth search, $1.33 for the fifth search, and so on. If the marginal cost of each additional search for the consumer is $2, the consumer should, therefore, conduct four searches, because only with the fourth search is the marginal benefit equal to the marginal cost. For fewer searches, $MB > MC$, and it pays for the consumer to continue the search. For more than four searches, $MB < MC$, and it does not pay for the consumer to conduct that many searches. Furthermore, the higher the price of the commodity, and the greater the range of product prices, the more searches a

---

[3] The expected price is equal to $80(1/5) + $90(1/5) + $100(1/5) + $110(1/5) + $120(1/5) = $16 + $18 + $20 + $22 + $24 = $100.

[4] The formula gives only an approximation of the lowest price found with each additional search, because prices are discrete rather than continuous variables (i.e., market prices are not infinitesimally divisible). Nevertheless, the formula provides a quick method of showing that the marginal benefit (in the form of lower prices) declines with each additional search. To calculate the precise lowest price for the second search, see Problem 1, with the answer at the end of the book.

[5] The *precise* expected price with two searches is $92 and is found with a much longer calculation, as shown in the answer to Problem 1 at the end of the book.

consumer will undertake. The reason for this is that the marginal benefit of each search is then greater (see Problem 3). Finally, note that because consumers face different marginal costs of search, they will end the search at different points and end up paying different prices for the product. This allows different producers to charge different prices. Producers selling the product at a higher price will sell only to those consumers who have less information because they stop searching for lower prices.

Search and Advertising

Even though most advertising contains an important manipulative component, it also provides a great deal of useful information to consumers on the availability of products, their use and properties, the firms selling particular products, retail outlets that carry the product, and product prices. Thus, advertising greatly reduces consumers' search costs. In most cases, it also reduces both price dispersion and average prices. For example, we saw in Section 11.2 that the price of eyeglasses was much higher in New York, which prohibits advertising by optometrists, than in New Jersey, which does not prohibit such advertising. Similarly, the price of an uncontested divorce dropped from $350 to $150 in Phoenix, Arizona, after the Supreme Court allowed advertising for legal services. Clearly, advertising often results in increased competition among sellers and lower product prices, and it provides very useful information to consumers.

In examining the role of advertising, Philip Nelson distinguishes between search goods and experience goods.[6] **Search goods** are those goods whose quality can be evaluated by inspection at the time of purchase. Examples of search goods are fresh fruits and vegetables, apparel, and greeting cards. **Experience goods,** on the other hand, are those which cannot be judged by inspection at the time of purchase but only after using them. Examples of experience goods are automobiles, TV sets, computers, canned foods, and laundry detergents. Some goods, of course, are borderline. For example, the content of a book or magazine can be partially gathered by quick inspection at the bookstore before purchasing it. But its quality can only be fully evaluated after reading it more carefully after the purchase.

Nelson points out that the advertisements of search goods must by necessity contain a large informational content. Any attempt on the part of the seller to misrepresent the product in any way would be easily detected by potential buyers before the purchase and would thus be self-defeating. The situation is different for experience goods, where the buyer cannot determine the true properties of the product before use. Nevertheless, the very fact that a large and established seller is willing to spend a great deal on advertising the product provides indirect support for the seller's claims. After all, a large seller that has been in business for a long time must have enjoyed repeated purchases from other satisfied customers.

In 2000, more than $236 billion was spent on advertising in the United States, of which 20.8% was in newspapers, 18.9% on direct mail, 8.3% on radio, 5.7% on Yellow Pages, 5.2% each on magazines and cable TV, and the rest in other forms of advertising.[7] Newspaper advertising was found to be the most informative, while TV advertising was found to

---

[6] P. Nelson, "Advertising as Information," *Journal of Political Economy,* July/August 1974, pp. 729–754.

[7] U.S. Department of Commerce, *Statistical Abstract of the United States* (Washington, D.C.: U.S. Government Printing Office, 2001), p. 777.

be the least informative among major forms of advertising.[8] Another study found that industries with higher-than-average advertising expenditures relative to sales had lower rates of price increases and higher rates of output increases than the average for 150 major industries.[9] From this, it can be inferred that advertising has a large informational content.

When the cost of gathering information is very high or when use of the product can be dangerous, the government usually steps in to provide the information (as in the case of gas mileage for automobiles) or regulates the use of the product (as in the case of prescription drugs). The spread of information is now growing by leaps and bounds as a result of the phenomenal growth of the Internet (see the "At the Frontier" section). Sometimes the seller announces the lowest possible price at which it will sell a product without bargaining in order to eliminate the need of searching for the lowest price by consumers. An example of this is the recent no-haggling value pricing introduced by General Motors (see Example 19–1).

EXAMPLE 19-1
No-Haggling Value Pricing in Car Buying

During the past decade, General Motors (GM) has been gradually moving toward no-haggling, value pricing for some of its cars. Other carmakers have also been experimenting with this policy in the United States. Although some Americans may find it stimulating, most consider the time-honored business of haggling over the price of a new car intimidating and even humiliating. One-price selling was first instituted at GM's Saturn division when it began building cars in 1990. Ford has also started experimenting with one-price selling on a few of its vehicles, and in 1999 Mercedes-Chrysler began to phase in its new N.F.P. policy (for negotiation-free process). Although no-haggle pricing in car buying may yet become the rule in the future, as of 1999, only the Saturn division of General Motors had successfully adopted the approach on a large scale. Dealers' great fear of one-price selling is that customers will simply take the offer elsewhere and use it to negotiate a better deal. Advocates of one-price selling respond that dealers can avoid being undercut by combining one-price selling with value pricing and accepting smaller profit margins. They believe that customers are not going to go to other dealers to haggle over $40 or $50 if they know that they are already getting good value for their money.

GM moved to value pricing for some of its cars (besides the Saturn) with the 1994 model year. This involved the selling of well-equipped 1994 cars at lower prices than similarly equipped 1993 models. For example, the 1994 Pontiac Grand Prix was offered at a lower price than the 1993 model even though the newer model had dual airbags while the 1993 model came with no airbags. GM's hope, of course, was to increase market share and profits. The strategy seemed to work. For example, by lowering the price of a well-equipped Buick LeSabre from $21,000 for the 1993 model to $18,995 for a similarly

---

[8] F. M. Scherer and D. Ross, *Industrial Market Structure and Economic Performance* (Boston: Houghton Mifflin, 1990), p. 572.
[9] E. W. Eckard, "Advertising, Concentration Changes, and Consumer Welfare," *Review of Economics and Statistics,* May 1988, pp. 340–343.

equipped 1994 model, GM boosted sales of the model by about 15%. But gross profit margins at GM fell to only 6.7% or $1,200 per new car sold in the United States in 1994, and net profit margins (after paying rent, commissions, and other selling costs) averaged only about $80 per new car sold. In 1999, profit margins at Mercedes were only 7% (down from 20% only a few years earlier) and dealers feared being squeezed even further in the future.

Sources: "GM Stresses Value Pricing for '94 Models," *Wall Street Journal,* July 12, 1993, p. A3; "Buying Without Haggling as Cars Get Fixed Prices," *New York Times,* February 1, 1994, p. 1; "At Car Dealers, a No-Haggle Policy Sets Off a Battle," *New York Times,* August 29, 1999, Section 3, p. 4; and "Meet Your Local GM Dealer: GM," *Business Week,* October 11, 1999, p. 48.

AT THE FRONTIER
The Internet and the Information Revolution

Information available to individuals, consumers, and firms is increasing by leaps and bounds as a result of the development of the Internet. The **Internet** or simply "the Net" is a collection of more than 100,000 computers throughout the world linked together in a service called the World Wide Web (www). In 2002, about 200 million people scattered throughout the world were connected through the Web, with hundreds of thousands of new individuals joining each week. Half of the on-line community is now outside the United States. In a few years, more than 1 billion people and 300 million PCs are expected to be connected to the Internet. In short, the entire globe is very rapidly becoming a single unified **information superhighway** through the Internet. The Internet has been around since the 1960s, but it is only during the last decade that its use has been greatly simplified and this led to massive growth.

This means that individuals, researchers, firms, and consumers could hook up with libraries, databases, and marketing information and have at their fingertips a vast amount of information as never before. Information technology is being applied to fields as diverse as science, manufacturing, finance, and marketing, and it is revolutionizing the way business is conducted. An individual can use the Internet to send electronic mail (e-mail) and examine thousands of multimedia documents from anywhere in the world, browse through a firm's catalogue, and be able (in an increasing number of cases) to click on a "buy" button and fill in an electronic order form, including shipping and credit-card information.

From 1997 to 2000, worldwide electronic commerce or e-commerce increased from less than $20 billion to over $300 billion and is expected to top $6 trillion in 2005. Over 80% of worldwide e-commerce took place in the United States in 2000, but this percentage is expected to fall to less than 50% in a few years because of its even more rapid growth outside the United States. About 90%

Continued. . .

of e-commerce is business-to-business sales, and the rest is business-to-consumer sales. Nearly half of business-to-business e-commerce is in the computer and electronics industries, while for business-to-consumer e-commerce the largest three categories are travel, PCs, and books. Even though e-commerce now accounts for only 15% of global gross domestic product (GDP), it is already having a significant effect on large economic sectors such as communications, finance, and retailing. For example, trading securities on the Web reached nearly one-third of all retail equity trades in the United States in 2001, from practically zero in 1995. Producers and sellers have found that on-line connections with consumers, on the one hand, and corporate customers and suppliers, on the other, have led to a dramatic fall in the cost of doing business, a cut in reaction times, and expansion of sales reach. For example, while the cost of processing a paper check by banks averages $1.20 and that of processing a credit card payment averages $0.50, the cost of processing an electronic payment is as low a $0.01

The Internet is not without problems, however. For one thing, even though the Web is making the Internet easier to use and hundreds of companies are developing software to make it easier still, finding what you want in the ocean of information available on the Internet can be maddening slow. Then there is the risk. For example, a file traveling on the Internet could be examined, copied, or altered without the intended recipient being aware of it. The Internet was simply not designed to ensure secure commerce. For example, in 1995 a hacker or computer expert tapped into Citibank computing system and transferred $10 million to various bank accounts throughout the world. Although this computer fraud was quickly discovered and only $400,000 was actually withdrawn, it vividly points out the danger of doing business on the Internet. All of this can be avoided by encrypting the data (i.e., transmitting the data in code) and then unencrypting it upon arrival by the intended recipient. But this still cannot be easily and conveniently done. The Internet also creates problems for publishers since any copyrighted material can easily be copied and transmitted, thus undermining copyright laws. It is very likely that all these problems will be overcome in time, but at present they present some thorny problems for Internet users.

Source: "An Information Superhighway," *Business Week,* February 1991, p. 28; "The Internet," *Business Week,* November 14, 1994, pp. 80–88; "Citibank Fraud Case Raises Computer Security Questions," *New York Times,* August 19, 1995, p. 31; "Putting the Internet in Perspective," *Wall Street Journal,* April 16, 1998, p. B12; "Business and the Internet," *The Economist,* June 26, 1999, pp. 1–40; B. Fraumeni, "E-Commerce: Measurement and Measurement Issues," *American Economic Review,* May 2001, pp. 318–322; D. Lucking-Reiley and D. F. Spulber, "Business-to-Business Electronic Commerce," *Journal of Economic Perspectives,* winter 2001, pp. 55–68; and "Online Shoppers Choose Price over Convenience," *Financial Times,* February 20, 2002, p. I.

19.2 ASYMMETRIC INFORMATION: THE MARKET FOR LEMONS AND ADVERSE SELECTION

We now discuss asymmetric information and the market for lemons, as well as the problem of adverse selection in the insurance market.

Asymmetric Information and the Market for Lemons

Often one party to a transaction (i.e., the seller or the buyer of a product or service) has more information than the other party regarding the quality of the product or service. This is a case of **asymmetric information.** An example of the problems created by asymmetric information is the market for "lemons" (i.e., a defective product, such as a used car, that will require a great deal of costly repairs and is not worth its price) discussed by Ackerlof.[10]

For example, sellers of used cars know exactly the quality of the cars that they are selling while prospective buyers do not. As a result, the market price for used cars will depend on the quality of the average used car available for sale. As such, the owners of "lemons" would then tend to receive a higher price than their cars are worth, while the owners of high-quality used cars would tend to get a lower price than their cars are worth. The owners of high-quality used cars would therefore withdraw their cars from the market, thus lowering the average quality and price of the remaining cars available for sale. Sellers of the now above-average quality cars withdraw their cars from the market, further reducing the quality and price of the remaining used cars offered for sale. The process continues until only the lowest-quality cars are sold in the market at the appropriate very low price. Thus, the end result is that low-quality cars drive high-quality cars out of the market. This is known as **adverse selection.**

The problem of adverse selection that arises from asymmetric information can be overcome or reduced by the acquisition of more information by the party lacking it. For example, in the used-car market, a prospective buyer can have the car evaluated at an independent automotive service center, or the used-car dealer can provide guarantees for the cars they sell. With more information on the quality of used cars, buyers would be willing to pay a higher price for higher-quality cars, and the problem of adverse selection can be reduced. More generally, brand names (such as Bayer aspirin), chain retailers (such as Sears, McDonald's, and Hilton), and professional licensing (of doctors, lawyers, beauticians, etc.) are important methods of ensuring the quality of products and services, and thus reduce the degree of asymmetric information and the resulting problem of adverse selection. Travelers are often willing to pay higher prices for nationally advertised products and services than for competitive local products, because they do not know the quality of local products and services. This is why tourists often pay more for products and services than residents. Sometimes, higher prices are themselves taken as an indication of higher quality.[11]

The Insurance Market and Adverse Selection

The problem of adverse selection arises not only in the market for used cars, but in any market characterized by asymmetric information. This is certainly the case for the insurance market. Here, the individual knows much more about the state of her health than an insurance company can ever find out, even with a medical examination. As a result, when

---

[10] G.A. Ackerlof, "The Market for 'Lemons': Qualitative Uncertainty and the Market Mechanism," *Quarterly Journal of Economics,* August 1970, pp. 488–500.

[11] See J. E. Stiglitz, "The Causes and Consequences of the Dependence of Quality on Price," *Journal of Economic Literature,* March 1987, pp. 1–48.

an insurance company sets the insurance premium for the average individual (i.e., an individual of average health), unhealthy people are more likely to purchase insurance than healthy people. Because of this adverse selection problem, the insurance company is forced to raise the insurance premium, thus making it even less advantageous for healthy individuals to purchase insurance. This increases even more the proportion of unhealthy people in the pool of insured people, thus requiring still higher insurance premiums. In the end, insurance premiums would have to be so high that even unhealthy people would stop buying insurance. Why buy insurance if the premium is as high as the cost of personally paying for an illness?

The problem of adverse selection arises in the market for any other type of insurance (i.e., for accidents, fire, floods, and so on). In each case, only above-average risk people buy insurance, and this forces insurance companies to raise their premiums. The worsening adverse selection problem can lead to insurance premiums being so high that in the end no one would buy insurance. The same occurs in the market for credit. Since credit card companies and banks must charge the same interest rate to all borrowers, they attract more low- than high-quality borrowers (i.e., more borrowers who either do not repay their debts or repay their debts late). This forces up the interest rate, which increases even more the proportion of low-quality borrowers, until interest rates would have to be so high that it would not pay even for low-quality borrowers to borrow.

Insurance companies try to overcome or reduce the problem of adverse selection by requiring medical checkups, charging different premiums for different age groups and occupations, and offering different rates of coinsurance, amounts of deductibility, length of contracts, and so on. These limit the variation in risk within each group and reduce the problem of adverse selection. Because there will always be some variability in risk within each group, however, the problem of adverse selection cannot be entirely eliminated in this way. The only way to avoid the problem entirely is to provide compulsory insurance to all the people in the group. Individuals facing somewhat lower risks than the group average will then get a slightly worse deal, while individuals facing somewhat higher risks will get a slightly better deal (in relation to the equal premium that each group member must pay). Indeed, this is an argument in favor of universal, government-provided, compulsory health insurance and no-fault auto insurance. On the other hand, credit companies significantly reduce the adverse selection problem that they face by sharing "credit histories" with other credit companies. Although such sharing of credit histories is justifiably attacked as an invasion of privacy, it does allow the credit market to operate and keep interest charges to acceptably low levels.

19.3   MARKET SIGNALING

The problem of adverse selection resulting from asymmetric information can be resolved or greatly reduced by **market signaling.**[12] If sellers of higher-quality products, lower-risk individuals, better-quality borrowers, or more-productive workers can somehow inform or

---

[12] A. M. Spence, *Market Signaling* (Cambridge, MA: Harvard University Press, 1974); and A. M. Spence, "Job Market Signaling," *Quarterly Journal of Economics,* August 1973, pp. 355–379.

send signals of their superior quality, lower risk, or greater productivity to potential buyers of the products, insurance companies, credit companies, and employers, then the problem of adverse selection can, for the most part, be overcome. Individuals would then be able to identify high-quality products; insurance and credit companies would be able to distinguish between low and high-risk individuals and firms; and firms would be able to identify higher-productivity workers. As a result, sellers of higher-quality products would be able to sell their products at commensurately higher prices; lower-risk individuals could be charged lower insurance premiums; better-quality borrowers would have more access to credit; and higher-productivity workers could be paid higher wages. Such market signaling can thus overcome the problem of adverse selection.

A firm can signal the higher quality of its products to potential customers by adopting brand names, by offering guarantees and warranties, and by a policy of exchanging defective items. A similar function is performed by franchising (such as McDonald's) and the existence of national retail outlets (such as Sears) that do not produce the goods they sell themselves, but select products from other firms and on which they put their brand name as an assurance of quality. The seller, in effect, is saying "I am so confident of the quality of my products that I am willing to put my name on them and guarantee them." The high rate of product returns and need to service low-quality merchandise would make it too costly for sellers of low-quality products to offer such guarantees and warranties. The acceptance of coinsurance and deductibles by an individual or firm similarly sends a powerful message to insurance companies indicating that they are good risks. The credit history of a potential borrower (indicating that he or she has repaid past debts in full and on time) also sends a strong signal to credit companies that he or she is a good credit risk.

Education serves as a powerful signaling device regarding the productivity of potential employees. That is, higher levels of educational accomplishments (such as years of schooling, degrees awarded, grade-point average achieved, etc.) not only represent an investment in human capital (see Section 16.7) but also serve as a powerful signal to an employer of the greater productivity of a potential employee. After all, the individual had the intelligence and perseverance to complete college. A less-intelligent and/or less-motivated person is usually not able to do so, or it might cost her so much more (for example, it may take five or six years rather than four years to get a college degree) as not to pay for her to get a college education even if she could. Thus, a college degree provides a powerful signal that its holder is in general a more productive individual than a person without a degree. Even if education did not in fact increase productivity, it would still serve as an important signal to employers of the greater *innate* ability and higher productivity of a potential employee.[13]

A firm could fire an employee if it subsequently found that the employee's productivity was too low. But this is usually difficult (the firm would have to show due cause) and expensive (the firm might have to give severance pay). In any event, it usually takes a great deal of on-the-job training before the firm can correctly evaluate the productivity of a new employee. Thus, firms are eager to determine as accurately as possible the productivity of a potential employee before he or she is hired. There is empirical evidence to suggest that education does in fact provide such an important signaling device. Liu and Wong found that while firms pay higher *initial* salaries to holders of educational certificates (such as college degrees)

[13] See K. J. Arrow, "Higher Education as a Filter," *Journal of Public Economics,* July 1973, pp. 193–216.

than to non-certificate holders, employees' salaries subsequently depend on their actual on-the-job productivity.[14] Thus, the firm relies on the market signal provided by education when it first hires an employee, for lack of a better signaling device, but then relies on actual performance after it has had adequate opportunity to determine the employee's true productivity on the job.

19.4   THE PROBLEM OF MORAL HAZARD

Another problem that arises in the insurance market is that of **moral hazard.** This refers to the increase in the probability of an illness, fire, or other accident when an individual is insured than when he or she is not. With insurance, the loss from an illness, fire, or other accident is shifted from the individual to the insurance company. Therefore, the individual will take fewer precautions to avoid the illness, fire, or other accident, and when a loss does occur he or she may tend to inflate the amount of the loss. For example, with medical insurance, an individual may spend less on preventive health care (thus increasing the probability of getting ill); and if he or she does become ill, will tend to spend more on treatment than if he or she had no insurance. With auto insurance, an individual may drive more recklessly (thus increasing the probability of a car accident) and then may be likely to exaggerate the injury and inflate the property damage suffered if the driver does get into an accident. Similarly, with fire insurance, a firm may take fewer reasonable precautions (such as the installation of a fire-detector system, thereby increasing the probability of a fire) than in the absence of fire insurance; and then the firm is likely to inflate the property damage suffered if a fire does occur. Indeed, the probability of a fire is high if the property is insured for an amount greater than the real value of the property.

If the problem of moral hazard is not reduced or somehow contained, it could lead to unacceptably high insurance rates and costs and thus defeat the very purpose of insurance. The socially valid purpose of insurance is to share *given* risks of a large loss among many economic units. But if the ability to buy insurance increases total risks and claimed losses, then insurance is no longer efficient and may not even be possible. One method by which insurance companies try to overcome the problem of moral hazard is by specifying the precautions that an individual or firm must take as a condition for buying insurance. For example, the insurance company might require yearly physical checkups as a condition for continuing to provide health insurance to an individual, increase insurance premiums for drivers involved in accidents, and require the installation of a fire detector before providing fire insurance to a firm. By doing this, the insurance company tries to limit the possibility of illness, accident, or fire, and thereby reduce the number and amount of possible claims it will face.

Another method used by insurance companies to overcome or reduce the problem of moral hazard is **coinsurance.** This refers to insuring only part of the possible loss or value of the property being insured. The idea is that if the individual or firm shares a significant portion of a potential loss with the insurance company, the individual or firm will be more

---

[14] P. W. Liu and C. Wong, "Educational Screening by Certificates: An Empirical Test," *Economic Inquiry,* January 1984, pp. 72–83.

prudent and will take more precautions to avoid losses from illness or accidents. Although we have examined moral hazard in connection with the insurance market, the problem of moral hazard arises whenever an externality is present (i.e., any time an economic agent can shift some of its costs to others). This is clearly shown in Examples 19–2 and 19–3.

EXAMPLE 19–2
Increased Disability Payments Reduce Labor-Force Participation

The Social Security program that pays disability benefits to individuals who are able to prove that they are unable to work is a socially useful program. Nevertheless, it may have resulted in a moral hazard problem by encouraging some individuals, who would otherwise be working despite their disability, to withdraw from the job market when receiving disability benefits. For example, an individual who is injured in a non-job-related accident and is unable to walk could train to be an accountant or to hold another sedentary occupation, but that individual may choose instead to remain unemployed and live on disability benefits. There are, of course, many forms of disability that would prevent an individual from doing *any* type of work, but this is not always the case.

Some indirect evidence exists that providing disability benefits since the early 1950s and raising them over time has led to a moral hazard problem. For example, the labor nonparticipation rate for men between the ages of 45 and 54 increased from nearly 4% in 1950 to more than 14% in 1993 at the same time that the Social Security disability-recipiency rate for men in the same age group increased from zero to about 5.3%. The nonparticipation rate refers to the proportion of people in a particular age group who are neither working nor seeking employment because of all causes (disability and other). On the other hand, the Social Security disability-recipiency rate refers to the proportion of people in a particular age group who are neither working nor seeking employment because of a disability.

Providing disability benefits and increasing them over time, thus, seems to have resulted in a moral hazard problem. There are, of course, other reasons besides disability that might have led to the large increase in the nonparticipation rate since the 1950s. However, the sharp and parallel increase in the two rates over time leads to the suspicion that a moral hazard problem was also at work. By providing disincentives for work, U.S. welfare programs also seem to have led to the same situation. In fact, when the welfare reform of 1996 ended welfare as entitlements, available to all persons who qualified, and required recipients to seek work as a condition for continued assistance, the number of people on welfare fell sharply (see Example 17–5).

Sources: Donald O. Parsons, "The Decline in Labor Force Participation," *Journal of Political Economy,* February 1980, pp. 117–134; "Disability Insurance and Male Labor-Force Participation," *Journal of Political Economy,* June 1984, pp. 542–549; Robert Moffitt, "Incentive Effects of the U.S. Welfare System: A Review," *Journal of Economic Literature,* March 1992, pp. 1–61; *U.S. Statistical Abstract* (Washington, D.C.: U.S. Government Printing Office, 2001), p. 351; "America's Great Achievement," *The Economist,* August 25, 2001, pp. 25–27; and "U.S. Disability Policy in a Changing World," *Journal of Economic Perspectives,* winter 2002, pp. 213–224.

EXAMPLE 19-3

Medicare and Medicaid and Moral Hazard

Medicare is a government program that covers most of the medical expenses of the elderly, while Medicaid covers practically all medical expenses of the poor. Both programs were enacted in the United States 1965. While socially useful, Medicare and Medicaid led to a moral hazard problem by encouraging more doctors' visits by the elderly and the poor, resulting in higher prices for medical services for the rest of the population. The effect of Medicare and Medicaid on the price and quantity of medical services consumed by people not covered by either program is analyzed in Figure 19.1. For simplicity, we assume that all medical costs of the elderly and the poor are covered by the programs and all medical services take the form of doctors' visits.

In the figure, D_c is the demand curve of medical services of the elderly and the poor before the subsidy or coverage under Medicare and Medicaid, while D_n is the demand curve of the rest of the population. $D_c + D_n = D_t$. The intersection of D_t and S (point E) defines the equilibrium price of \$15 per visit (and a total of 900 million visits) for the to-be covered group and for the noncovered group. At $P = \$15$, the elderly and the poor purchase 200 million doctors' visits per year, while the rest of the population consumes 700 million per year, for a total of 900 million visits for the entire population.

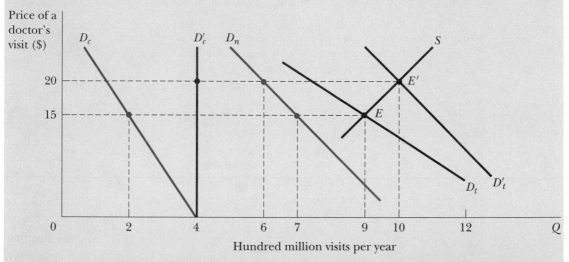

FIGURE 19.1   Medicare and Medicaid and the Price of Medical Services D_c is the demand curve of medical services of the elderly and the poor before the subsidy, while D_n is the demand curve of the rest of the population. $D_c + D_n = D_t$. With D_t and S, $P = \$15$ (point E). The to-be-covered group purchases 200 million visits and the others 700 million. When the government covers the entire cost of the doctors' visits of the elderly and the poor, their demand curve becomes D'_c. $D'_c + D_n = D'_t$. Then $P = \$20$ and $Q = 600$ million (point E') for the noncovered group.

When the government covers the entire cost of the doctors' visits of the elderly and the poor, their demand curve becomes D'_c. This is vertical at the quantity purchased at zero price. That is, the covered group will demand 400 million visits per year regardless of price. $D'_c + D_n = D'_t$. The intersection of D'_t and S (point E') defines the new equilibrium price of $20 for the noncovered group. The noncovered group now pays a higher price than before ($20 per visit instead of $15) and consumes a smaller quantity of medical services as indicated by D_n (600 million instead of the previous 700 million visits per year). The nonsubsidized group also pays the taxes to pay for the subsidy; the covered group, as well as doctors, receive the benefits. The conclusion of the foregoing analysis has been broadly borne out by the events that followed the adoption of Medicare and Medicaid. In short, Medicare and Medicaid led to a moral hazard problem.

19.5   THE PRINCIPAL–AGENT PROBLEM

A firm's managers act as the *agents* for the owners or stockholders (legally referred to as the *principals*) of the firm. Because of this separation of ownership from control in the modern corporation, a **principal-agent problem** arises.[15] This problem refers to the fact that while the owners of the firm want to maximize the total profits or the present value of the firm, the managers or agents want to maximize their own personal interests, such as their salaries, tenure, influence, and reputation.[16] The principal-agent problem often becomes evident in the case of takeover bids for a firm by another firm. Although the owners or stockholders of the firm may benefit from the takeover if it raises the value of the firm's stock, the managers may oppose it for fear of losing their jobs in the reorganization of the firm that may follow the takeover.

One way of overcoming the principal-agent problem and ensuring that the firm's managers act in the stockholders' interests is by providing managers with **golden parachutes.** These are large financial settlements paid out by a firm to its managers if they are forced out or choose to leave as a result of the firm being taken over. With golden parachutes, the firm is in essence buying the firm managers' approval for the takeover. Even though golden parachutes may cost a firm millions of dollars, they may be more than justified by the sharp increase in the value of the firm that might result from a takeover. Note that a principal-agent problem may also arise in the acquiring firm. Specifically, the agents or managers of a firm may initiate and carry out a takeover bid more for personal gain (in the form of higher salaries, more secure tenure, and the enhanced reputation and prestige in directing the resulting larger corporation) than to further the stockholders' interest. In fact, the managers of the acquiring firm may be carried away by their egos and bid too much for the firm being acquired.

---

[15] See E. F. Fama, "Agency Problems of the Theory of the Firm," *Journal of Political Economy,* April 1980, pp. 288–307.

[16] See W. Baumol, *Business Behavior, Value, and Growth* (New York: Harcourt-Brace, 1967); and O. Williamson, *Corporate Control and Business Behavior* (Englewood Cliffs, NJ: Prentice-Hall, 1964).

More generally (and independently of takeovers) a firm can overcome the principal-agent problem by offering big bonuses to its top managers based on the firm's long-term performance and profitability or a generous deferred-compensation package, which provides relatively low compensation at the beginning and very high compensation in the future. Such incentives would induce managers to stay with the firm and strive for its long-term success. In the case of public enterprises such as a public-transportation agency, or in a nonprofit enterprise such as a hospital, an inept manager can be voted out or removed.

As Example 19–4 shows, trying to overcome the principal-agent problem between owners or stockholders (principals) and managers (agents) with golden parachutes may not solve the principal-agent problem and may lead to abuses.

EXAMPLE 19–4

Do Golden Parachutes Reward Failure?

Some firms use golden parachutes to overcome their managers' objections to a takeover that might greatly increase the value of the firm. The proliferation and size of golden parachutes has sharply increased during the great wave of mergers that has taken place in the United States since the early 1980s. Some of the largest and most controversial golden parachutes (amounting to a total of nearly $100 million) were set up for ten of Primerica's executives for retiring as a result of its friendly merger with the Commercial Credit Corporation in 1988. These golden parachutes represented 6% of Primerica's $1.7 billion book value and cost stockholders $1.88 a share. Gerald Tsai, Jr., the chairman of Primerica, who arranged the merger, was to receive $19.2 million as severance pay, $8.6 million to defray the excise taxes resulting from the compensation agreement, and several other millions of dollars from Primerica's long-term incentive, life insurance, and retirement benefits program—for an overall total of nearly $30 million!

Even before the final approval of the merger in December 1988, some of Primerica's stockholders filed suit in New York State Supreme Court charging that Primerica's top executives had violated their fiduciary role and had acted in their own interest and against the stockholders' interests; they demanded that the termination agreements for the ten executives be canceled. The lawsuit pointed out that golden parachutes were originally set up in 1985 for six of Primerica's executives to cover only hostile takeovers; they were then extended to ten executives in 1987; and finally they were revised in 1988, three months after Primerica agreed to the merger, to also cover friendly takeovers.

It has been estimated that 15% of the nation's largest corporations offered golden parachutes to its top executives in 1981. This figure rose to 33% in 1985 and to nearly 50% in 1990. Indeed, golden parachutes are no longer confined to the corporation's top executives; they are offered farther and farther down the corporate ladder to middle-level management and sometimes even to all employees. This has resulted in a public outcry and has led the Securities and Exchange Commission to rule that a firm must hold a shareholder vote on its golden parachute plans. Until the early 1990s, corporations typically did not make public their offer of golden parachutes. Not only are they now required to do so, but some companies are even beginning to demand restitution.

The practice of giving golden parachutes, nevertheless, continues. Indeed, after observing huge severance packages given to CEOs who "were let go" in 2000, Dean Foust of *Business Week* (see the reference below) remarked "failure has never looked more lucrative." For example, in August 2000, Proctor & Gamble gave Durk Jager, its just-ousted CEO, a $9.5 million bonus even though he had been at P&G less than one-and-half years and P&G stock had fallen by 50% during his tenure. Also in 2000, Conseco Inc. gave a $49.3 million going-away gift to CEO Stephen Hilbert, who practically bankrupted the company with his ill-fated move into sub-prime lending. Similarly, Mattel gave a parachute package worth nearly $50 million in severance pay to Jill Barard, its departing CEO, and Ford gave Jacques Nasser, its ousted CEO, a compensation package worth $23 million in 2001 even though the company lost $5.5 billion that year. And this is not only an American problem. For example, Percy Barnevik's $87 million pension payment from ABB, the Swiss engineering group, was called into question in February 2002, especially after his admission of partial responsibility for ABB's worsening performance. In fact, ABB has now asked for restitution.

Sources: "Ten of Primerica Executives' Parachutes Gilded in $98.2 Million Severance Pay," *Wall Street Journal,* November 29, 1988, p. A3; "Primerica Holders File Lawsuit to Halt 'Golden Parachutes'," *Wall Street Journal,* December 2, 1988, p. A9; "Ruling by SEC May Threaten Parachute Plans," *Wall Street Journal,* January 1990, p. A3; "CEO Pay: Nothing Succeeds Like Failure," Business Week, September 11, 2000, p. 46; "When Bosses Get Rich from Selling the Company," *Business Week,* March 30, 1998, p. 33–34; "Golden Parachutes' Emerge in European Deals," *Wall Street Journal,* February 14, 2000, p. A17; "Ex-Ford Chief Receives $23 million in 2001," New York Times, April 10, 2002, p. C6; and "Barnevik's Role on GM Board to Be Reviewed," *Financial Times,* February 18, 2002, p. 17.

19.6 | THE EFFICIENCY WAGE THEORY

We have seen in Section 14.5 that in a perfectly competitive labor market, all workers who are willing to work find employment and the equilibrium wage rate reflects (i.e., is equal to) the marginal productivity of labor. In the real world, however, we often observe higher-than-equilibrium wages and a great deal of involuntary unemployment. Why then don't firms lower wages?

According to the **efficiency wage theory,** firms willingly pay higher than equilibrium wages to induce workers to avoid *shirking* or slacking off on the job.[17] The theory begins by pointing out that it is difficult or impossible for firms to accurately monitor workers' productivity (thus, firms face a principal-agent problem resulting from asymmetric information). If workers are paid the equilibrium wage, they are likely to shirk or slack off on the job because if fired, they can easily find another equally-paying job (remember, there is

---

[17] See J. L. Yellen, "Efficiency Wage Models of Unemployment," *American Economic Review,* May 1984, pp. 200–205; and J. E. Stiglitz, "The Causes and Consequences of the Dependence of Quality on Price," *Journal of Economic Literature,* March 1987, pp. 1–48.

no involuntary unemployment at the equilibrium wage, and in any event, it is not easy for a firm to catch a worker shirking). According to the *efficiency* wage theory, by paying a higher-than-equilibrium or efficiency wage the firm can induce employees to work more productively and not shirk, because the employees fear losing their high-paying jobs. Even if all firms paid efficiency wages, employees would not shirk and not risk being fired, because it is not easy to find another similarly rewarding job in view of the great deal of unemployment that exists at the efficiency wage.

The efficiency wage theory can be examined graphically with Figure 19.2. In the figure, D_L is the usual negatively sloped demand curve for labor of the firm, and S_L is the supply curve of labor (assumed to be fixed for simplicity) facing the firm. The intersection of D_L and S_L at point E determines the equilibrium wage of $10 per hour and equilibrium number of 600 workers hired by the firm. There are no unemployed workers and this wage is equal to the marginal productivity of labor.

But at this equilibrium wage, workers have an incentive to shirk. To induce workers not to shirk, the firm will have to pay a higher or efficiency wage. The efficiency wage is higher the smaller the level of unemployment, because workers can then more easily find another job at the efficiency wage (if fired from the present job because of shirking). This

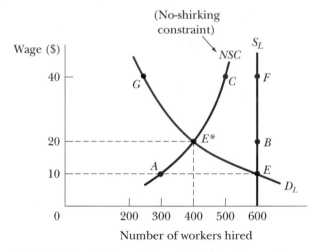

FIGURE 19.2 Efficiency Wage and Unemployment in a Shirking Model D_L and S_L are, respectively, the firm's demand and the supply curve for labor. Their intersection at point E determines the equilibrium wage of $10 per hour at which the firm employs 600 workers and there is no unemployment. Workers, however, have an incentive to shirk at this wage. The no-shirk constraint (*NSC*) curve is positively sloped and shows that the efficiency or minimum wage that the firm must pay to avoid shirking is higher the smaller the level of unemployment. The no-shirking equilibrium is determined at point E^* where D_L and *NSC* cross. The efficiency wage is $20 per hour and 200 workers (BE^*) are unemployed.

is shown by the no-shirking constraint (*NSC*) curve shown in the figure. The *NSC* curve shows the minimum wage that workers must be paid for each level of unemployment to avoid shirking. For example, the efficiency wage of $10 requires 300 workers (*EA*) to be unemployed. With 200 workers (*BE**) unemployed, the efficiency wage is $20, and with only 100 workers unemployed (*CF*) the efficiency wage will have to be $40. Note that the *NSC* curve is positively sloped (i.e., the efficiency wage is higher the smaller the level of unemployment) and gets closer and closer to the fixed S_L curve but never crosses it (i.e., there will always be some unemployment at the efficiency wage).

In Figure 19.2, the intersection of the D_L and *NSC* at point *E** determines the *efficiency wage* of $20 per hour. At this wage rate, the firm employs 400 workers and 200 workers are unemployed. The reason that $20 is the equilibrium efficiency wage is that only at this wage is the level of unemployment (*BE**) just enough to avoid shirking. For $10 to be the efficiency wage, 300 workers (*EA*) would have to be unemployed. But at the wage of $10 there is no unemployment (point *E*). Thus, *the equilibrium* efficiency wage must be higher. On the other hand, for $40 to be the efficiency wage, only 100 workers (*FE*) need to be unemployed. But at the wage of $40, 350 workers (*FG*) are unemployed. Thus, the equilibrium efficiency wage must be lower. The efficiency wage is $20 because only at this wage is the number of unemployed workers ($200 = BE*$) just right for workers not to shirk.

EXAMPLE 19–5

The Efficiency Wage at Ford

One example of the efficiency wage theory is provided by the decision by Henry Ford in January 1914 to reduce the length of the working day from nine to eight hours while increasing the minimum daily wage from $2.34 to $5 for assembly-line workers. What prompted Ford to adopt such a radical (for the time) wage decision was the low productivity and very high turnover of assembly-line workers at Ford's plants under the previous traditional wage system. For example, labor turnover at Ford was 380% in 1912 and nearly 1000% in 1913. This sharply increased costs and reduced profits. The paying of a wage much higher than the going wage by Ford did have the intended effect. Ford was able to attract more productive and loyal workers, absenteeism was cut in half, and productivity increased by more than 50%. In fact, the sharply reduced labor turnover and increased labor productivity was sufficient to actually reduce the cost of producing each automobile. The new wage system was also great publicity, which increased Ford's sales. Lower production costs and higher sales meant higher profits for Ford (Ford's profits rose from $30 million in 1914 to nearly $60 million in 1916). In short, what Ford did in 1914 was to pay the efficiency wage—and it took 70 years for economists to develop the theory to fit the facts!

Sources: J. R. Lee, "So-Called Profit Sharing System in the Ford Plant," *Annals of the American Academy of Political and Social Science,* May 1915, pp. 297–310; D. Raff and L. Summers, "Did Henry Ford Pay Efficiency Wages," *Journal of Labor Economics,* October 1987, pp. S57–S58; and G. A. Ackerlof and J. L. Yellen, (eds.), *Efficiency Wage Models of the Labor Market* (New York: Cambridge University Press, 1986).

SUMMARY

1. Search costs refer to the time and money we spend seeking information about a product. The general rule is to continue the search for lower prices, higher quality, and so on until the marginal benefit from the search equals the marginal cost. In most instances, advertising provides a great deal of information and greatly reduces consumers' search costs, especially for search goods. These are goods whose quality can be evaluated by inspection at the time of purchase (as opposed to experience goods, which can only be judged after using them).

2. When one party to a transaction has more information than the other on the quality of the product (i.e., in the case of asymmetric information), the low-quality product or "lemon" will drive the high-quality product out of the market. One way to overcome or reduce such a problem of adverse selection is for the buyer to get, or the seller to provide, more information on the quality of the product or service. Such is the function of brand names, chain retailers, professional licensing, and guarantees. Insurance companies try to overcome the problem of adverse selection by requiring medical checkups, charging different premiums for different age groups and occupations, and offering different rates of coinsurance, amounts of deductibility, and length of contracts. The only way to avoid the problem entirely is with universal compulsory health insurance. Credit companies reduce the adverse selection process that they face by sharing "credit histories" with other insurance companies.

3. The problem of adverse selection resulting from asymmetric information can also be resolved or greatly reduced by market signaling. Brand names, guarantees, and warranties are used as signals for higher-quality products, for which consumers are willing to pay higher prices. The willingness to accept coinsurance and deductibles signals low-risk individuals to whom insurance companies can charge lower premiums. Credit companies use good credit histories to make more credit available to good-quality borrowers, and firms use educational certificates to identify more-productive potential employees who may then receive higher salaries.

4. The insurance market also faces the problem of moral hazard, or the increase in the probability of an illness, fire, or other accident when an individual is insured than when he or she is not. If not contained, moral hazard could lead to unacceptably high insurance costs. Insurance companies try to overcome the problem of moral hazard by specifying the precautions that an individual or firm must take as a condition of insurance, and by coinsurance (i.e., insuring only part of the possible loss). The problem of moral hazard arises whenever an externality is present (i.e., any time an economic agent can shift some of its costs to others).

5. Because ownership is divorced from control in the modern corporation, a principal-agent problem arises. This refers to the fact that managers seek to maximize their own benefits rather than the owners' or principals' interests, which are to maximize the total profits or value of the firm. The firm may use golden parachutes (large financial payments to managers if they are forced out or choose to leave if the firm is taken over by another firm) to overcome the managers' objections to a takeover bid that sharply increases the value of the firm. The firm may also set up generous deferred-compensation schemes for its managers to reconcile their long-term interests with those of the firm.

6. According to the efficiency wage theory, firms willingly pay higher than equilibrium wages to induce workers to avoid shirking or slacking off on the job. The no-shirk constraint curve is positively sloped and shows that the efficiency or minimum wage that the firm must pay to

avoid shirking is higher the smaller the level of unemployment. The equilibrium efficiency wage is given by the intersection of the firm's demand curve for labor and the no-shirking constraint curve.

KEY TERMS

Search costs
Search goods
Experience goods
Internet
Information superhighway

Asymmetric information
Adverse selection
Market signaling
Moral hazard
Coinsurance

Principal-agent problem
Golden parachutes
Efficiency wage theory

REVIEW QUESTIONS

1. a. In which market structure was perfect information assumed on the part of all economic agents?

   b. If all consumers have perfect information, can a price dispersion for a given homogeneous product exist in the market if all conditions of the sale are identical? Why?

2. On which do you think consumers spend more time shopping for lower prices, sugar or coffee? Why?

3. Can you explain why the price dispersion for salt is much greater than the price dispersion for sugar?

4. Frozen vegetables are search goods because they are purchased frequently by consumers. True or false? Explain.

5. Most advertising is manipulative and provides very little information to consumers. True or false? Explain.

6. What is the relationship between speculation and the economics of information?

7. a. Adverse selection is the direct result of asymmetric information. True or false? Explain.

   b. How can the problem of adverse selection be overcome?

8. a. How do credit companies reduce the adverse selection problem that they face?

   b. What complaint does this give rise to?

9. a. What problem can arise for the Ford Corporation by providing a 50,000-mile guarantee for its new automobiles sold?

   b. How can Ford reduce this problem?

10. Should education be viewed as an investment in human capital or a market signaling device? Explain.

11. What is the relationship between moral hazard and externalities?

12. What is meant by the efficiency wage? What problem is this intended to solve?

PROBLEMS

*1. Determine the precise expected price for the TV from the second search in the problem discussed in the section on "Searching for the Lowest Price" without the use of equation [19.1].

2. Draw a figure showing the marginal benefit and the marginal cost of each additional search, and show the point of equilibrium for the TV problem using the information given in the text.

---

* = Answer provided at end of book.

*3. a. Suppose that type I sellers charged the price of $60 for the portable TV, type II sellers charged $80, type III sellers charged $100, type IV sellers charged $120, and type V sellers charged $140. Determine the expected lowest price for the TV from one, two, three, four, and five searches.

   b. Determine the marginal benefit from each additional search.

4. Using the data of Problem 3, indicate

   a. How many searches should a consumer undertake if the marginal cost of each additional search is $4?

   b. If it is $2?

   c. How many searches should a consumer undertake if the marginal cost of each additional search is $5.34 and the consumer plans to purchase two TV sets?

5. a. Suppose that type I sellers charged the price of $96 for the portable TV, type II sellers charged $98, type III sellers charged $100, type IV sellers charged $102, and type V sellers charged $104. Determine the expected lowest price for the TV from one, two, three, four, and five searches.

   b. Determine the marginal benefit from each additional search.

   c. How many searches should a consumer undertake if the marginal cost of each additional search is $1.00?

*6. Connect to the Internet from your computer or from any PC and go to http://www.priceline.com. What is Priceline.com?

7. Go to http://www.ebay.com and explain what it is.

*8. Suppose that there are only two types of used cars in the market: high-quality and low-quality, and all the high-quality cars are identical and all the low-quality cars are identical. With perfect information, the quantity demanded of high-quality used cars is zero at $16,000 and 100,000 at $12,000, while the quantity demanded of low-quality used cars is zero at $8,000 and 100,000 at $4,000. Suppose also that the supply curve for high-quality used cars is horizontal at $12,000, while the supply curve of low-quality used cars is horizontal at $4,000 in the relevant range. Draw a figure showing that with asymmetric information, no high-quality used cars will be sold and 100,000 low-quality used cars will be sold at the price of $4,000 each. Explain the precise sequence of events that leads to this result.

9. Draw another figure similar to the figure in the answer to Problem 8 but with the supply curves of high-quality and low-quality used cars positively sloped rather than horizontal. Assume further that used cars are of many different qualities rather than being simply of high-quality and low-quality. With reference to the figure, explain the precise sequence of events that leads to only cars of the lowest quality being sold.

10. Explain how franchising signals quality.

11. Suppose that the returns to education are 12% for an intelligent and motivated person but only 8% for a less-intelligent and less-motivated person (because it takes longer for the latter to get a college degree). Suppose also that the return on investing in stock is 10% and that such an investment is as risky as getting a college education. Suppose furthermore that getting a college education is viewed as a strictly investment undertaking (i.e., assume that there are no psychological benefits to getting a college education). Explain how a college education can serve as a market signaling device in this case.

12. An insurance company is considering providing fire insurance for $120,000, $100,000, or $80,000 to the owner of a house with a market value of $100,000.

   a. How much insurance is the company likely to sell for the house? Why?

   b. If the probability of a fire is 1 in 1,000, what would be the premium charged by the company?

INTERNET SITE ADDRESSES

For more information on the companies examined in this chapter, see:

   http://www.gm.com

   http://www.ford.com

   http://www.amazon.com

   http://www.barnesandnoble.com

   http://www.priceline.com

   http://www.ebay.com

For more information on e-commerce, see The Center for Research in Electronic Commerce at the University of Texas at Austin at:

>   http://cism.bus.utexas.edu

Asymmetric information is examined in:

>   http://www.nobel.se/economics/laureates/2001/ecoadv.pdf
>
>   http://economics.about.com/library/weekly/aa102301.htm

Market signaling is examined in:

>   http://citiseer.nj.nec.com/context/953248/0
>
>   http://www.berkeley.edu/berkeleyan/2001/10/17_asyme.html

For moral hazard, see:

>   http://www.economics.uni-linz.ac.at/members/winter/manager/Lecture9.pdf
>
>   http://www.rich.frb.org/pubs/eq/pdfs/winter1999/prescott.pdf

For the principal-agent problem, see:

>   http://www.chass.ncsu.edu/gason/pa765/agent.htm
>
>   http://www.jura.uni-hamburg.de/~le/disspr/riza.pdf

Efficiency wages are discussed in:

>   http://www.utdallas.edu/dept/socsci/working_papers/workingpaper15.pdf
>
>   http://www.nd.edu/~kellogg/WPS/153.pdf
>
>   http://www.econ.puc-rio.br/pdf/ribeiro.pdf

APPENDIX A

Mathematical Appendix

A.1 INDIFFERENCE CURVES

(Refers to Section 3.2, page 62)

Suppose that a consumer's purchases are limited to commodities X and Y, then

$$U = U(X, Y) \qquad [1A]$$

is a general utility function. Equation [1A] postulates that the utility or satisfaction that the consumer receives is a function of or depends on, the quantity of commodity X and commodity Y that he or she consumes. The more of X and Y the individual consumes, the greater the level of utility or satisfaction that he or she receives.

Using a subscript on u to specify a given level of utility or satisfaction, we can write

$$U_1 = U_1(X, Y) \qquad [2A]$$

This is the general equation for an indifference curve. Equation [2A] postulates that the individual can get U_1 of utility by various combinations of X and Y. Of course, the more of X the individual con-

sumes, the less of Y he or she will have to consume in order to remain on the same indifference curve. Higher subscripts refer to higher indifference curves. Thus, $U_2 > U_1$.

Taking the total differential of equation [1A], we get

$$dU = \frac{\partial U}{\partial X}dX + \frac{\partial U}{\partial Y}dY \qquad [3A]$$

Since a movement along an indifference curve leaves utility unchanged, we set $dU = 0$ and get

$$\frac{\partial U}{\partial X}dX + \frac{\partial U}{\partial Y}dY = 0 \qquad [4A]$$

so that

$$\frac{\partial U}{\partial X}dX = -\frac{\partial U}{\partial Y}dY \qquad [5A]$$

and

$$-\frac{dY}{dX} = \frac{\partial U/\partial X}{\partial U/\partial Y} = \frac{MU_X}{MU_Y} = MRS_{XY} \qquad [6A]$$

657

Equation [6A] indicates that the negative value of the slope of an indifference curve $(-dY/dX)$ is equal to the ratio of the marginal utility of X to the marginal utility of $Y (MU_X/MU_Y)$, which, in turn, equals the marginal rate of substitution of X for $Y (MRS_{XY})$.

A.2 UTILITY MAXIMIZATION

(Refers to Section 3.5, page 74)

We now wish to maximize utility (i.e., equation [1A]) subject to the budget constraint. The budget constraint of the consumer is

$$P_X X + P_Y Y = I \qquad [7A]$$

where P_X and P_Y are the price of commodity X and commodity Y, respectively, X and Y refer to the quantity X and commodity Y, and I is the consumer's income, which is given and fixed at a particular point in time.

To maximize equation [1A] subject to equation [7A], we form

$$V = U(X, Y) + \lambda(I - P_X X - P_Y Y) \qquad [8A]$$

where λ is the Lagrangian multiplier.

Taking the first partial derivative of V with respect to X and Y and setting them equal to zero gives

$$\frac{\partial V}{\partial X} = \frac{\partial U}{\partial X} - \lambda P_X = 0$$

$$\frac{\partial V}{\partial Y} = \frac{\partial U}{\partial Y} - \lambda P_Y = 0 \qquad [9A]$$

It follows that

$$\frac{\partial U}{\partial X} = \lambda P_X \quad \text{and} \quad \frac{\partial U}{\partial Y} = \lambda P_Y \qquad [10A]$$

Dividing, we get

$$\frac{\partial U/\partial X}{\partial U/\partial Y} = \frac{MU_X}{MU_Y} = MRS_{XY} = \frac{P_X}{P_Y} \qquad [11A]$$

Equation [11A] indicates that the consumer maximizes utility at the point utility at the point where the marginal rate of substitution of X for Y, $(\partial U/\partial X)/(\partial U/\partial Y')$, equals the ratio of the price of

X to the price of Y. Graphically, this occurs at the point where the budget line is tangent to the highest indifference curve possible (and their slopes are equal). Equation [11A] is only the first order condition for maximization (and minimization). The second order condition for maximization is that the indifference curves be convex to the origin.

A.3 CONSUMER SURPLUS

(Refers to Section 4.5, page 106)

In Section 4.5, we defined consumer surplus as the difference between what a consumer is willing to pay for a given quantity of a good and what he or she actually pays for it. Graphically, consumer surplus is given by the difference in the area under the demand curve and the area representing the total expenditures of the consumer for the given quantity of the good that he or she purchases.

Starting with $P = g(Q)$, g is the inverse of $Q = f(P)$. For a given price (P_1) and its associated quantity (Q_1),

$$\begin{matrix} \text{consumer} \\ \text{surplus} \end{matrix} = \int_0^{Q_1} g(Q)dQ - P_1 Q_1 \quad [12A]$$

where the integral sign ($\int$) represents the process of calculating the area under inverse demand function $P = g(Q)$ between zero quantity of the commodity and quantity Q_1, and $P_1 Q_1$ is the total expenditure of the consumer for Q_1 of the commodity.

A.4 SUBSTITUTION AND INCOME EFFECTS

(Refers to Section 4.3, page 98)

The substitution effect of a price change can be measured by a movement along a given indifference curve (so that utility or purchasing power is constant). With a change in the price of commodity X, we have

$$\text{substitution effect} = \frac{\partial X}{\partial P_X} \text{ with constant utility}(U) \qquad [13A]$$

The income effect can be measured by a shift to a different indifference curve (to reflect the change in utility or purchasing power) with prices constant. This is given by the change in the demand for X per dollar increase in income, weighed by the quantity of X purchased. That is,

$$\text{income effect} = X \left(\frac{\partial X}{\partial I} \right) \text{ with constant prices}$$

$$[14A]$$

When the price of X falls, the income effect tells us how much the consumer's income should be *reduced* in order to leave his or her purchasing power constant.

Combining the substitution and the income effects we get the Slutsky equation:

$$\frac{\partial X}{\partial P_X} = \underset{\text{for constant } U}{\frac{\partial X}{\partial P_X}} - \underset{\substack{\text{for constant} \\ \text{prices}}}{X \left(\frac{\partial X}{\partial I} \right)} \quad [15A]$$

The first term on the right side gives the substitution effect (shown by a movement along a given indifference curve). The second term gives the income effect (shown by a shift to a different indifference curve but with constant goods prices).

A.5 ELASTICITIES

(Refers to Section 5.2 to 5.4, pages 129–141)

In Chapter 5.2 we defined the *price elasticity of demand*, η, as the percentage change in the quantity demanded of a commodity divided by the percentage change in its price. That is, for $Q = f(P)$,

$$\eta = \frac{\Delta Q/Q}{\Delta P/P} = \frac{\Delta Q}{\Delta P} \frac{P}{Q} \quad [16A]$$

We also pointed out that since quantity and price move in opposite directions, the value of η is negative. Equation [16A] can be used to measure *are elasticity*. In that case, P and Q refer to the average price and the average quantity, respectively.

As the change in price approaches zero in the limit, we can measure *point elasticity* by

$$\eta = \frac{dQ}{dP} \frac{P}{Q} \quad [17A]$$

If the demand curve is linear and given by

$$Q = a + bP \quad [18A]$$

the slope of the demand curve is constant and is given by

$$\frac{dQ}{dP} = \frac{\Delta Q}{\Delta P} = b \quad [19A]$$

and

$$\eta = b \frac{P}{Q} \quad [20A]$$

For example, if $b = -2$ and $P/Q = 1$, then $\eta = -2$. Since P/Q is different at every point on the negatively sloped, straight-line demand curve, η varies at every point.

For a curvilinear demand curve of the form

$$Q = aP^b \quad [21A]$$

$$\frac{dQ}{dP} = abP^{b-1} \quad [22A]$$

and

$$\eta = abP^{b-1} \frac{P}{Q} = \frac{abP^b}{Q} = b \quad [23A]$$

since $aP^b = Q$. Thus, equation [21A] is a demand curve with a constant price elasticity equal to the exponent of P (i.e., $\eta = b$). Thus, if $b = -2$, $\eta = -2$ at every point on the demand curve. As pointed out in Chapter 5.2, demand is elastic if $|\eta| > 1$ and inelastic if $|\eta| < 1$.

The *income elasticity of demand*, η_I is defined as the ratio of the relative change in the quantity purchased (Q) to the relative change in income (I), other things remaining constant. That is, for $Q = f(I)$,

$$\eta_I = \frac{dQ}{dI} \frac{I}{Q} \quad [24A]$$

For the following linear income-demand function

$$Q = a + cI \quad [25A]$$

where $c > 0$, the derivative of Q with respect to I is

$$\frac{dQ}{dI} = c \qquad [26A]$$

Therefore,

$$\eta_I = c\left(\frac{I}{Q}\right) \qquad [27A]$$

For the following nonlinear income-demand function

$$Q = aI^c \qquad [28A]$$

the derivative of Q with respect to I is

$$\frac{dQ}{dI} = acI^{c-1} \qquad [29A]$$

Therefore,

$$\eta_1 = acI^{c-1}\frac{I}{Q} = \frac{acI^c}{Q} = c \qquad [30A]$$

As pointed out in Chapter 5.3, a commodity is normal if $\eta_I > 0$ and inferior if $\eta_I < 0$. A normal good is luxury if $\eta_I > 1$ and a necessity if η_I is between 0 and 1.

The *cross elasticity of demand* of commodity X for commodity Y, η_{XY}, is defined as the ratio of the relative change in the quantity purchased of commodity X (Q_X) to the relative change in the price of commodity Y (P_Y). That is,

$$\eta_{XY} = \frac{dQ_X/Q_X}{dP_Y/P_Y} = \frac{dQ_X}{dP_Y}\frac{P_Y}{Q_X} \qquad [31A]$$

Consider the following linear demand function for commodity X:

$$Q_X = a + bP_X + cP_Y \qquad [32A]$$

The above function indicates that Q_X depends on P_X and P_Y. The derivative of the function with respect to P_Y is

$$\frac{dQ_X}{dP_Y} = b\frac{dP_X}{dP_Y} + c \qquad [33A]$$

If the P_X remains unchanged when P_Y changes, then

$$\frac{dP_X}{dP_Y} = 0 \quad \text{while} \quad \frac{dQ_X}{dP_Y} = c \qquad [34A]$$

Therefore,

$$\eta_{XY} = c\frac{P_Y}{Q_X} \qquad [35A]$$

As pointed out in Chapter 5.4, commodities X and Y are substitutes if $\eta_{XY} > 0$ and complements if $\eta_{XY} < 0$.

The *price elasticity of supply,* ϵ, is defined as the ratio of the relative change in the quantity supplied of a commodity (Q_s) to the relative change in its price (P). That is, for $Q_s = f(P)$,

$$\epsilon = \frac{dQ_s/Q_s}{dP/P} = \frac{dQ_s}{dP}\frac{P}{Q_s} \qquad [36A]$$

Since the quantity supplied and price move in the same direction (i.e., supply curves are usually positively sloped), ϵ is positive.

For the following linear supply function

$$Q_s = a + bP \qquad [37A]$$

the derivative of Q_s with respect to P is

$$\frac{dQ_s}{dP} = b \qquad [38A]$$

Therefore,

$$\epsilon = b\frac{P}{Q_s} \qquad [39A]$$

Substituting equation [37A] for Q_s into equation [39A], we get

$$\epsilon = \frac{bP}{a + bP} \qquad [40A]$$

Thus, if $a = 0$ (so that the supply curve starts at the origin), $\epsilon = 1$ throughout the supply curve, regardless of the value of its slope (b). If $a > 0$ (so that the supply curve cuts the quantity axis), $\epsilon < 1$ throughout the supply curve. If $a < 0$ (so that the supply curve cuts the price axis, $\epsilon > 1$ throughout. When $a \neq 0$, ϵ varies with price.

A.6 RELATIONSHIP AMONG INCOME ELASTICITIES

*(Refers to Sections 5.2 and 5.3, pages **129–138**)*

If a consumer's income increases, say by 10% and the consumption of some commodities increases by less than 10%, the consumption of other commodities must increase by more than 10% for the entire increase in the consumer's income to be fully spent. This leads to the proposition that the income elasticity of demand must be unity, on the average, for all commodities. Assuming, for simplicity, that the entire consumer's income is spent on commodities X and Y, we can restate the above proposition mathematically as

$$K_X\eta_{IX} + K_Y\eta_{IY} \equiv 1 \qquad [41A]$$

where K_X is the proportion of the consumer's income (I) spent on commodity X (i.e., $K_X = P_X X/I$), η_{IX} is the income elasticity of demand for commodity X, K_Y is the proportion of income elasticity of demand for Y.

Starting with the consumer's budget constraint [7A]

$$I = P_X X + P_Y Y \qquad [7A]$$

we can prove proposition [41A] by differentiating equation [7A] with respect to income, while holding prices constant. This gives

$$\frac{dI}{dI} \equiv 1 \equiv P_X\frac{dX}{dI} + P_Y\frac{dY}{dI} \qquad [42A]$$

If we multiply the first term on the right-hand side by $(X/X)(I/I)$, which equals one, and the second term by $(Y/Y)(I/I)$, which equals one, the value of the expression will not change, and we get

$$1 \equiv P_X\frac{dX}{dI}\frac{X}{X}\frac{I}{I} + P_Y\frac{dY}{dI}\frac{Y}{Y}\frac{I}{I} \qquad [42A']$$

Rearranging equation [42A'], we get

$$\frac{P_x X}{I}\frac{dX}{dI}\frac{I}{X} + \frac{P_Y Y}{I}\frac{dY}{dI}\frac{I}{Y} \equiv 1 \qquad [43A]$$

Since $P_X X/I = K_X$, $(dX/dI)(I/X) = \eta_{IX}$, $P_Y Y/I = K_Y$, and $(dY/dI)(I/Y) = \eta_{IY}$, we have

$$K_X\eta_{IX} + K_Y\eta_{IY} \equiv 1 \qquad [41A]$$

That is, with the K's providing the weights, the weighted average of all income elasticities equals unity. Thus, the income elasticity of demand of a commodity on which the consumer spends a great proportion of his or her income cannot be

too different from unity (see Problem 12 in Chapter 5).

A.7 RELATIONSHIP AMONG MARGINAL REVENUE, PRICE, AND ELASTICITY

*(Refers to Section 5.6, page **143**)*

Let P and Q equal the price and the quantity of a commodity, respectively. Then the total revenue of the seller of the commodity (TR) is given by

$$TR = PQ \qquad [44A]$$

and the marginal revenue is

$$MR = \frac{d(TR)}{dQ} = P + Q\frac{dP}{dQ} \qquad [45A]$$

Manipulating expression [45A] mathematically, we get

$$MR = P\left(1 + \frac{Q}{P}\frac{dP}{dQ}\right) = P\left(1 + \frac{1}{\eta}\right) \qquad [46A]$$

where, η is the coefficient of price elasticity of demand. For example, if $P = \$12$ and $\eta = -3$, $MR = \$8$. If $\eta = -\infty$, $P = MR = \$12$.

A.8 ISOQUANTS

*(Refers to Sections 7.3 and 7.4, pages **198–207**)*

Suppose that there are two inputs, labor and capital. The

$$Q = Q(L, K) \qquad [47A]$$

is a general production function. Equation [47A] postulates that output (Q) is a function of, or depends on, the quantity of labor (L) and capital (K) used in production. The more L and K are used, the greater is Q.

Using a subscript on Q to specify a given level of output, we can write

$$Q_1 = Q_1(L, K) \qquad [48A]$$

This is the general equation for an isoquant. Equation [48A] postulates that output Q_1 can be produced with various combinations of L and K. The more L is used, the less K will be required to remain on the same isoquant. Higher subscripts refer to higher isoquants. Thus, $Q_2 > Q_1$.

Taking the total differential of equation [47A], we get

$$dQ = \frac{\partial Q}{\partial L}dL + \frac{\partial Q}{\partial K}dK \qquad [49A]$$

Since a movement along an isoquant leaves output unchanged, we set $dQ = 0$ and get

$$\frac{\partial Q}{\partial L}dL + \frac{\partial Q}{\partial K}dK = 0 \qquad [50A]$$

so that

$$\frac{\partial Q}{\partial K}dK = -\frac{\partial Q}{\partial L}dL \qquad [51A]$$

and

$$-\frac{dK}{dL} = \frac{\partial Q/\partial L}{\partial Q/\partial K} = \frac{MP_L}{MP_K} = MRTS_{LK} \qquad [52A]$$

Equation [52A] indicates that the negative value of the slope of an isoquant ($-dK/dL$) is equal to the ratio of the marginal product of L to the marginal product of K (MP_L/MP_K), which, in turn, equals the marginal rate of technical substitution of L for K ($MRTS_{LK}$).

A.9 COST MINIMIZATION

(Refers to Section 8.2, page 229)

A firm may wish to minimize the cost of producing a given level of output. The total cost of the firm (TC) is given by

$$TC = wL + rK \qquad [53A]$$

where w is the wage rate of labor and r is the rental price (per unit) of capital. A given level of output ($\overline{Q}$) can be produced with various combinations of L and K:

$$\overline{Q} = \overline{Q}(L, K) \qquad [54A]$$

To minimize equation [53A] subject to equation [54A], we form

$$Z = wL + rK + \lambda^*[\overline{Q} - \overline{Q}(L, K)] \qquad [55A]$$

where λ^* is the Lagrangian multiplier.

Taking the first partial derivative of Z with respect to L and K and setting them equal to zero gives

$$\frac{\partial Z}{\partial L} = w - \lambda^*\frac{\partial Q}{\partial L}$$

and

$$\frac{\partial Z}{\partial K} = r - \lambda^*\frac{\partial Q}{\partial K} \qquad [56A]$$

It follows that

$$w = \lambda^*\frac{\partial Q}{\partial L} \quad \text{and} \quad r = \lambda^*\frac{\partial Q}{\partial K} \qquad [57A]$$

Dividing, we get

$$\frac{w}{r} = \frac{\partial Q/\partial L}{\partial Q/\partial K} = MRTS_{LK} \qquad [58A]$$

Equation [58A] indicates that a firm minimizes the cost of producing a given level of output by hiring labor and capital up to the point where the ratio of the input prices (w/r) equals the ratio of the marginal products of labor and capital, $(\partial Q/\partial L)/(\partial Q/\partial K)$ which equals the marginal rate of technical substitution of labor for capital ($MRTS_{LK}$). Graphically, this occurs at the point where a given isoquant is tangent to an isocost line (and their slopes are equal). Equation [58A] is only the first order condition for minimization (and maximization). The second order condition for minimization is that the isoquant be convex to the origin.

A.10 PROFIT MAXIMIZATION

(Refers to Section 9.3, page 268)

A firm usually wants to produce the output that maximizes its total profits. Total profits (π) are equal to total revenue (TR) minus total cost (TC). That is,

$$\pi = TR - TC \qquad [59A]$$

where π, TR, and TC are all functions of output (Q).

Taking the first derivative of π with respect to Q and setting it equal to zero gives

$$\frac{d\pi}{dQ} = \frac{d(TR)}{dQ} - \frac{d(TC)}{dQ} = 0 \quad [60A]$$

so that

$$\frac{d(TR)}{dQ} = \frac{d(TC)}{dQ} \quad [61A]$$

and

$$MR = MC \quad [62A]$$

Equation [62A] indicates that in order to maximize profits, a firm must produce where marginal revenue (MR) equals marginal cost (MC).

Furthermore, since for a perfectly competitive firm P is constant and $d(TR)/dQ = MR = P$, the first order condition becomes

$$MR = P = MC \quad [63A]$$

Equation [61A] is only the first order condition for maximization (and minimization). The second order condition for profit maximization requires that the second derivative of π with respect to Q be negative. That is,

$$\frac{d^2\pi}{dQ^2} = \frac{d^2(TR)}{dQ^2} - \frac{d^2(TC)}{dQ^2} < 0 \quad [64A]$$

so that

$$\frac{d^2(TR)}{dQ^2} < \frac{d^2(TC)}{dQ^2} \quad [65A]$$

According to equation [65A], the algebraic value of the slope of the MC function must be greater than the algebraic value of the MR function. Under perfect competition, MR is constant (i.e., the MR curve of the firm is horizontal) so that equation [65A] requires that the MC curve be rising at the point where $MR = MC$ for the firm to maximize its total profits (or minimize its total losses).

Under imperfect competition, $P > MC$ and so the first order condition becomes simply

$$MR = MC \quad [63B]$$

The second order condition remains [65A], but with MR now declining, the second order condition

is for the MC curve to intersect the MR curve from below.

A.11 PRICE DETERMINATION

(Refers to Sections 9.4 and 10.2, pages 274 and 315)

At equilibrium, the quantity demanded of a commodity (Q_d) is equal to the quantity supplied of the commodity (Q_s). That is,

$$Q_d = Q_s \quad [66A]$$

The demand function can be written as

$$Q_d = a - bP(a, b > 0) \quad [67A]$$

where a is the positive quantity intercept, and $-b$ is the negative of the multiplicative inverse of the slope of the demand curve (so that when P rises, Q_d falls). The supply function can take the form of

$$Q_s = -c + dP(c, d > 0) \quad [68A]$$

where $-c$ refers to the negative quantity intercept (so that the supply curve crosses the price axis at a positive price), and d is the positive of the multiplicative inverse of the slope of the supply curve (so that when P rises, Q_s also rises).

Setting $Q_d = Q_s$ for equilibrium, we get

$$a - bP = -c + dP \quad [69A]$$

Solving for P, we have

$$\overline{P} = \frac{a + c}{b + d} \quad [70A]$$

where the bar on P refers to the equilibrium price. Since parameters $a, b, c,$ and d are all positive, $\overline{P}$ is also positive.

To find the equilibrium quantity ($\overline{Q}$) that corresponds to $\overline{P}$, we substitute equation [70A] into equation [67A] or [68A]. Substituting equation [70A] into equation [67A], we get

$$\overline{Q} = a - \frac{b(a + c)}{(b + d)}$$

$$= \frac{a(b + d) - b(a + c)}{b + d} = \frac{ad - bc}{b + d} \quad [71A]$$

Since the denominator of equation [71A], $(b + d)$, is positive, for $\overline{Q}$ to be positive (and for the model to be economically meaningful) the numerator, $(ad - bc)$, must also be positive. That is, $ad > bc$.

A.12 PRICE DISCRIMINATION

*(Refers to Section 10.5, page **330**)*

A monopolist selling a commodity in two separate markets must decide how much to sell in each market in order to maximize total profits. The total profits of the monopolist (π) are equal to the sum of the total revenue that it receives from selling the commodity in the two markets (i.e., $TR_1 + TR_2$) minus the total cost of producing the total output (TC). That is,

$$\pi = TR_1 + TR_2 - TC \qquad [72A]$$

Taking the first partial derivative of π with respect to Q_1 (the quantity sold in the first market) and Q_2 (the quantity sold *in* the second market), and setting them equal to zero, we get

$$\frac{\partial \pi}{\partial Q_1} = \frac{\partial(TR_1)}{\partial Q_1} - \frac{\partial(TC)}{\partial Q_1} = 0,$$

$$\frac{\partial \pi}{\partial Q_2} = \frac{\partial(TR_2)}{\partial Q_2} - \frac{\partial(TC)}{\partial Q_2} = 0 \qquad [73A]$$

or

$$MR_1 = MR_2 = MC \qquad [74A]$$

That is, in order to maximize its total profits, the monopolist must distribute its sales between the two markets in such a way that the marginal revenue is the same in both markets and equal to the common marginal cost. If $MR_1 > MR_2$, the monopolist could increase its total profits by redistributing sales from market 2 to market 1, until $MR_1 = MR_2$.

Equations [73A] and [74A] give the first order condition for profit maximization. The second order condition is given by

$$\frac{\partial^2 \pi}{\partial Q_1^2} < 0 \quad \text{and} \quad \frac{\partial^2 \pi}{\partial Q_2^2} < 0 \qquad [75A]$$

Since we know from equation [46A] that

$$MR = P(1 + 1/\eta) \qquad [46A]$$

profit maximization requires that

$$P_1(1 + 1/\eta_1) = P_2(1 + 1/\eta_2) \qquad [76A]$$

where P_1 and P_2 are the prices in market 1 and market 2, respectively, and η_1 and η_2 are the coefficients of price elasticity of demand in market 1 and market 2. If $|\eta_1| < |\eta_2|$, equation [76A] will hold only if $P_1 > P_2$. That is, in order to maximize total profits the monopolist must sell the commodity at a higher price in the market with the lower price elasticity of demand (see also Figure 9.11). For example, if $\eta_1 = -2$, $\eta_2 = -3$, and $P_2 = \$6$, then $P_1 = \$8$ (so that $MR_1 = MR_2 = \$4$).

A.13 EMPLOYMENT OF INPUTS

*(Refers to Section 14.5, page **472**)*

A firms employs the quantity of inputs that allows it to produce the profit-maximizing level of output. As indicated by equation [59A], total profits (π) are equal to total revenue (TR) minus total cost (TC). Total revenue is given by

$$TR = PQ \qquad [77A]$$

where P is the price of the commodity that the firm produces and Q is the output, such that $Q = Q(L, K)$. The total cost of the firm was defined by equation [53A]. Thus, the firm employs labor and capital so as to maximize:

$$\pi = PQ(L, K) - (wL + rK) \qquad [78A]$$

When P, w, and r are constant, the firm is a perfect competitor in the product and input markets.

Taking the first partial derivative of π with respect to L and K and setting them equal to zero gives

$$\frac{\partial \pi}{\partial L} = P\frac{\partial Q}{\partial L} - w = 0,$$

$$\frac{\partial \pi}{\partial K} = P\frac{\partial Q}{\partial K} - r = 0 \qquad [79A]$$

It follows that

$$P\frac{\partial Q}{\partial L} = w \quad \text{and} \quad P\frac{\partial Q}{\partial K} = r \quad [80A]$$

or

$$MRP_L = w \quad \text{and} \quad MRP_K = r \quad [81A]$$

Equation [81A] indicates that a firm maximizes profits by hiring labor and capital up to the point where the marginal revenue product of labor $[MRP_L = P(\partial Q/\partial L)]$ equals the wage rate (w) and the marginal revenue product of capital $[MRP_K = P(\partial Q/\partial K)]$ equals the rental price of capital (r). Geometrically, this occurs where the MRP_L curve intersects the (horizontal) supply curve of labor and the MRP_K curve intersects the (horizontal) supply curve of rental capital. Equation [81A] is only the first order condition for maximization. The second order condition is that the MRP_L and MRP_K curves be negatively sloped (i.e., that the firm produce in the area of diminishing returns).

A.14 INPUT PRICE, MARGINAL EXPENSE, AND THE PRICE ELASTICITY OF INPUT SUPPLY

*(Refers to Sections 15.4 and 15.5, pages **498** and **501**)*

The total cost (TC) of a firm hiring nly labor is given by

$$TC = wL \quad [82A]$$

where w is the wage rate and L is the number of workers hired.

If the firm is a monopsonist (i.e., the only employer of labor in the market), it will have to pay higher wages the more labor it wants to hire. That is, the wage rate is a function of or depends on the amount of labor the firm hires (and the amount of labor the firm hires depends on the wage rate).

The firm's marginal resource cost of labor (MRC_L) is then given by

$$MRC_L = \frac{dC}{dL} = w + L\frac{dw}{dL} \quad [83A]$$

Rearranging equation [83A], we get

$$MRC_L = w\left(1 + \frac{L}{w}\frac{dw}{dL}\right) \quad [84A]$$

Therefore,

$$MRC_L = w\left(1 + \frac{1}{\epsilon_L}\right) \quad [85A]$$

where ϵ_L is the price (wage) elasticity of the supply curve of labor. Graphically, this means that the MRC_L curve lies above the (positively sloped) S_L curve (see also Figure 15.3). The same would be true for capital or any other input for which the firm is the only employer in the market.

If the firm were a perfect competitor in the labor market, $\epsilon_L \to \infty$ and $MRC_L = w$ (i.e., the MRC_L curve would coincide with the horizontal S_L curve faced by the firm at the given level of w).

A.15 DERIVATION OF THE FORMULA TO FIND THE PRESENT VALUE OF AN INVESTMENT

*(Refers to Section 16.3, page **536**)*

We have seen in Section 16.3 that the present discounted value (PDV) of an investment that yields a constant stream of net cash flows in each future year is given by equation [86A]:

$$PDV = \frac{R}{r} \quad [86A]$$

where R is the constant net cash flow received the next year and in every subsequent year (i.e., in perpetuity), and r is the rate of interest.

To derive equation [86A], we start with

$$PDV = \frac{R}{(1+r)} + \frac{R}{(1+r)^2} + \cdots \frac{R}{(1+r)^n} \quad [87A]$$

which is similar to equation [15-6] in Chapter 15.3.

If we let $1/(1+r) = k$, then

$$PDV = R(k + k^2 + \cdots k^n) \quad [88A]$$

Multiplying both sides of equation [88A] by k, we get

$$kPDV = R(k^2 + k^3 + \cdots k^{n+1}) \quad [89A]$$

Subtracting equation [89A] from equation [88A] we have

$$PDV - kPDV = R(k - k^{n+1}) \quad [90A]$$

From equation [90A], we get

$$PDV = \frac{R(k - k^{n+1})}{1 - k} \quad [91A]$$

Since $k = 1/(1 + r)$ is smaller than 1, for n very large, k^{n+1} is very small and can be ignored. Thus, we are left with

$$PDV = R\left(\frac{k}{1 - k}\right) \quad [92A]$$

Substituting $1/(1 + r)$ for k into equation [92A], we get

$$PDV = R\left(\frac{\dfrac{1}{1+r}}{1 - \dfrac{1}{1+r}}\right)$$

$$= R\left(\frac{\dfrac{1}{1+r}}{\dfrac{1+r-1}{1+r}}\right)$$

$$= R\left(\frac{1}{1+r}\right)\left(\frac{1+r}{r}\right)$$

$$= \frac{R}{r} \quad [93A]$$

A.16 A MODEL OF GENERAL EQUILIBRIUM

*(Refers to Section 17.5, page **585**)*

In this section we outline the Walras-Cassel general equilibrium model.*

---

* The presentation is adapted from R. Dorfman, P.A. Samuelson, and R.M. Solow, *Linear Programming and Economic Analysis* (New York: McGraw-Hill, 1958), pp. 351–355.

Let $x_1, x_2, \ldots, x_n$ refer to the quantity of the n commodities in the economy, with prices p_1, $p_2, \ldots p_n$. Let $r_1, r_2, \ldots r_m$ refer to the quantity of the m resources or inputs in the economy, with prices $v_1, v_2, \ldots v_m$.

The market demand equations for the n commodities can be written as

$$x_1 = f_1(p_1, p_2, \ldots, p_n; v_1, v_2, \ldots, v_m)$$
$$x_2 = f_2(p_1, p_2, \ldots, p_n; v_1, v_2, \ldots, v_m) \quad [94A]$$
$$\cdots\cdots\cdots\cdots\cdots\cdots\cdots\cdots\cdots\cdots\cdots\cdots\cdots\cdots$$
$$x_n = f_n(p_1, p_2, \ldots p_n; v_1, v_2, \ldots, v_m)$$

The market demand for each commodity is the sum of the demand for the commodity by each consumer and is a function of, or depends on, the prices of all commodities and of all inputs. Input prices affect individuals' incomes and, thus, influence the demand for commodities.

Since in long-run perfectly competitive equilibrium, commodity prices equal their production costs, we have

$$a_{11}v_1 + a_{21}v_2 + \cdots + a_{m1}v_m = p_1$$
$$a_{12}v_1 + a_{22}v_2 + \cdots + a_{m2}v_m = p_2 \quad [95A]$$
$$\cdots\cdots\cdots\cdots\cdots\cdots\cdots\cdots\cdots\cdots\cdots\cdots$$
$$a_{1n}v_1 + a_{2n}v_2 + \cdots + a_{mn}v_m = p_n$$

where a_{11} refers to the quantity of input 1 required to produce one unit of commodity 1. Since v_1 is the price of input 1, $a_{11}v_1$ is then the dollar amount spent on input 1 to produce on unit of commodity 1. On the other hand, a_{21} refers to the quantity of input 2 required to produce one unit of commodity 1, so that $a_{21}v_2$ is the dollar amount spent on input 2 to produce one unit of commodity 1. Finally, a_{m1} is the amount of input m required to produce one unit of commodity 1, and $a_{m1}v_m$ is the expenditure on input m to produce one unit of commodity 1. Therefore, the left-hand side of equation [95A] refers to the total cost of producing one unit of commodity 1. This is equal to the unit price of commodity 1 (p_1). The second equation gives the expenditure on each input to produce one unit of commodity 2, and this is equal input to produce one unit of commodity 2, and this is equal to p_2. The same is true for each of the n commodities. The a'_{ij}s are called input or production coefficients, and they are assumed to be fixed in our simple model.

Setting the total demand for each resource or input (required to produce all commodities) equal to the total supply of the input, we have

$$a_{11}x_1 + a_{12}x_2 + \cdots + a_{1n}X_n = r_1$$
$$a_{21}x_1 + a_{22}X_2 + \cdots + a_{2n}X_n = r_2 \qquad [96A]$$
$$\cdots$$
$$a_{m1}x_1 + a_{m2}x_2 + \cdots + a_{mn}x_n = r_m$$

where $a_{11}x_1$ is the quantity of resource or input 1 required to produce x_1 units of commodity 1, $a_{12}x_2$ is the quantity of input 1 required to produce x_2 of commodity 2, and $a_{1n}x_n$ is the quantity of input 1 required to produce x_n of commodity n. Thus, the first equation sets the total quantity demanded of input 1 (required to produce x_1, x_2, to x_n) equal to the total supply of resource or input 1 (r_1). Similarly, the second equation sets the total quantity demanded of input 2 used in all commodities to equal the quantity supplied of input 2, and so on for each of the m resources of inputs.

The last step to close the model is to specify the set of equations that relate the supply of each resource or input to prices. This is given by

$$r_1 = g_1(p_1, p_2, \ldots, p_n; v_1, v_2, \ldots, v_m)$$
$$r_2 = g_2(p_1, p_2, \ldots, p_n; v_1, v_2, \ldots, v_m) \qquad [97A]$$
$$\cdots$$
$$r_m = g_m(p_1, p_2, \ldots, p_n; v_1, v_2, \ldots, v_m)$$

That is, the supply of each resource or input is a function of, or depends on, the price of all inputs (the v'_is) and the price of all commodities (the p'_js). For example, the supply of steel depends on the price of steel, the price of aluminum, the wages of auto workers, and other input prices. The price of steel also depends on the price of automobiles, washing machines, steaks, and other commodity prices. Therefore, a change in any part of the system affects every other part of the system.

Summing up, in equation [94A] to equation [97A] we have $2n + 2m$ equations and an equal number of unknowns (the x'_js, the p'_js, the v'_is, and the r'_is). However, according to Walras's law, equations [94A] and [97A] have only $n + m - 1$ independent equations, since if all but one of these $n + m$ equations are satisfied, the last one must also be satisfied. However, we can arbitrarily set any commodity price, say, $p_1 = 1$ and express all other prices in terms of p_1 (the *numéraire*). This reduces the number of unknowns in the system by 1, so as to equal the number of independent equations. The system may the have a unique solution (i.e., a set of prices and quantities that simultaneously satisfies all the equations of the model).

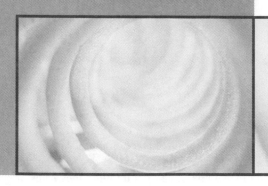

APPENDIX B

Answers to Selected Problems

Chapter 1

1. We study microeconomic theory to understand the economic behavior of individual consumers, resource owners, and business firms; to examine how individual commodity and resource prices are determined; and to understand the conditions for the efficient allocation of consumption and production in a free-enterprise economy. One cannot become an expert in any other field of economics without a thorough understanding of microeconomic theory.

6. a. With a price ceiling, consumers want to purchase more of the commodity than producers are willing to produce. This results in a shortage of the commodity, which leads to rationing and a black market.

   b. With a price floor, consumers want to purchase less of a commodity than producers are willing to produce. This results in a surplus of the commodity.

8. One way to measure the interdependence of the U.S. economy with the rest of the world is to calculate the percentage of U.S. imports and exports in relation to GNP. This percentage increased from about 8% in 1970 to almost 20% in 1996. Thus, U.S. interdependence has increased sharply during the past two decades.

12. a. The positive income aspects of positive analysis refer to such things as the shift in the kinds and quantities of goods and services produced and their effect on employment and incentives to work, on economic growth, and so on. All of these can be objectively measured or estimated.

   b. The normative aspects of income redistribution refer to the value-based disagreement on how much income should be redistributed.

Chapter 2

2. a.

P($)	8	7	6	5	4	3	2	1	0
QD'	0	10	20	30	40	50	60	70	80

b. See Figure 2a.

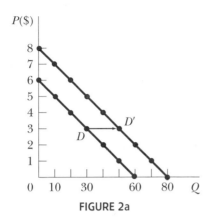

FIGURE 2a

c. D' represents an increase in demand because consumers demand more of the commodity at each and every price.

4. a.

**MARKET SUPPLY SCHEDULE, MARKET DEMAND
SCHEDULE, AND EQUILIBRIUM**

Price	Quantity Supplied	Quantity Demanded	Surplus (+) Deficit (−)	Pressure on Price
$6	60	0	60	Down
5	50	10	40	Down
4	40	20	20	Down
3	30	30	0	Equilibrium
2	20	40	−20	Up
1	10	50	−40	Up
0	0	60	−60	Up

b. See Figure 2b.

9. a. The demand for hamburgers increases,
resulting in a higher price and quantity.

b. The supply of hamburgers declines, resulting in an increase in the equilibrium price and
a reduction in the equilibrium quantity.

c. The supply of hamburgers increases, lowering the equilibrium price and increasing the
quantity purchased.

d. The demand for hamburgers increases,
causing the same effect as in part (a).

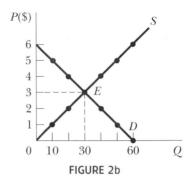

FIGURE 2b

e. A per-unit subsidy is the opposite of a per-
unit tax. The per-unit subsidy increases the
supply of hamburgers, causing the same effect
as in part (c).

12. a. See Figure 2c.

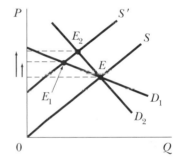

FIGURE 2c

b. See Figure 2d.

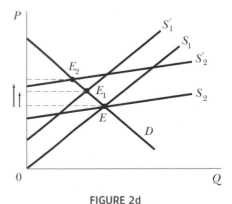

FIGURE 2d

Chapter 3

a. See Figure 3a.

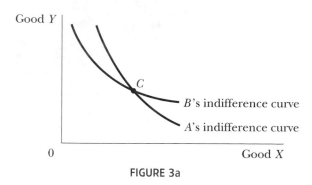

FIGURE 3a

b. Point C is the original equal endowment of good X and good Y of individual A and individual B. Since A prefers X to Y, A's indifference curve is steeper than B's indifference curve. That is, A is willing to give up more of Y for an additional unit of X, and MRS_{XY} for A at point C is greater than for B.

7. a. See Figure 3b.

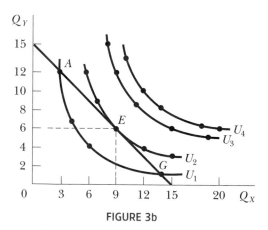

FIGURE 3b

b. The individual maximizes utility at point E, where U_2 is tangent to the budget line, by purchasing $9X$ and $6Y$. To maximize utility, the individual should spend all income in such a way that MRS_{XY} (the absolute slope of the indifference curve) equals P_X/P_Y (the absolute slope of the budget line).

c. Points A and G are on U_1 even though the individual spends all income.

d. The individual does not have sufficient income to reach U_3 and U_4.

9. a. The individual would spend $4 to purchase 4_X and the remaining $3 to purchase $3Y$.

b. $MU_X/P_X = MU_Y/P_Y = 6/\$1$ and $(\$1)(4X) + (\$1)(3Y) = \$7$.

c. The individual would receive 41 utils from consuming $4X$ (the sum of the MU_X up to $4X$) plus 27 utils from purchasing $3Y$ (the sum of the MU_Y up to $3Y$) for a total utility of 68 utils. If the individual spent all $7 on $7X$, he or she would get 49 utils (the sum of all MU_X). If the individual spent all income on $7Y$, he or she would get 38 utils (the sum of all MU_Y).

12. See Figure 3c. The vertical intercepts in the two figures measure the amount of material goods that each couple could enjoy without children. The slope of the budget lines measures the amount of material goods per year that each couple would have to give up per child. The couple portrayed in the top panel is at corner equilibrium A and chooses to have no children. The couple in the bottom panel is in equilibrium at point B by having one child. This couple is willing to give up the amount of material goods indicated on the vertical axis of the graph to have one child.

As the possibility for women to find high-paying jobs has increased in the United States and in other industrial countries since World War II, birth rates have declined because the opportunity costs of having children have increased. High-income people seem to have fewer children but tend to spend more on their education, health, and so on. It seems that high-income people have traded the number of children for a better quality of life for their children.

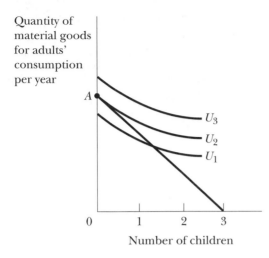

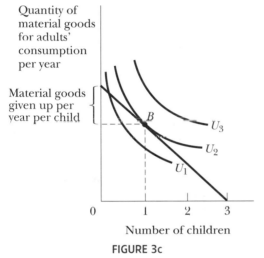

FIGURE 3c

Chapter 4

3. a. See Figure 4a.

b. At $P_X = \$0.50$, the consumer maximizes
utility at point G, where U_4 is tangent to budget line 3, by purchasing 14X. This gives point
G' in the bottom panel. With $P_X = \$1$, the op-
timum is at point E where U_2 is tangent to
budget line 2 and the consumer purchases 9X.
This gives point E' in the bottom panel.
Finally, with $P_X = \$2$, the consumer is at
optimum at point B where U_1 is tangent to
budget line 1 by buying 4X. This gives point

B' in the bottom panel. Joining points $G'E'B'$
in the bottom panel we derive d_X.

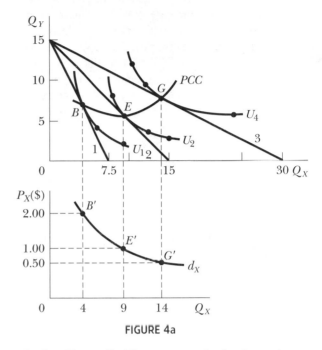

FIGURE 4a

5. See Figure 4b. The sequence in the figure is
from A to B to C.

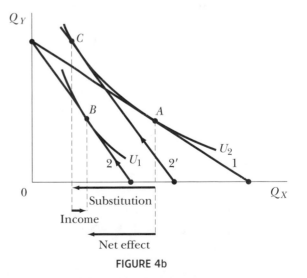

FIGURE 4b

7. In very poor Asian countries, people can purchase little else besides rice. If the price of rice

falls, the substitution effect tends to lead people to substitute rice for other goods. However, if rice is an inferior good in these nations, the increase in real income resulting from the decline in the price of rice leads people to purchase less rice. People spend most of their income on rice, so a decline in the price of rice will lead to a relatively large increase in purchasing power, which will allow people to purchase so much more of other goods that they need to purchase less rice.

That is, it is conceivable that the substitution effect (which leads people to purchase more rice when its price falls) could be overwhelmed by the opposite income effect. The net effect would then be that people purchase less rice when its price falls, so that the demand curve for rice would be positively sloped in these countries. However, there is no proof that this is indeed true.

9. See Figure 4c. The poor family is originally maximizing utility at point A where U_1 is tangent to budget line 1. With the government paying half of the family's food bill, we have budget line 2. With budget line 2, the poor family maximizes utility at point B on U_2. To get to point B, the family spends $2,000 of its income ($FG$). Without the subsidy the family would have to pay $4,000 ($FL$).

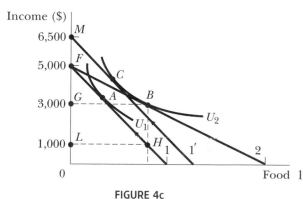

FIGURE 4c

Thus, the cost of the subsidy to the government is $2,000. The family, however, could

reach U_2 at point C with a cash subsidy of $1,500 ($FM$). The government may still prefer to subsidize the family's food consumption (even if more expensive) if one of its aims is to improve nutrition.

Chapter 5

4. a. When two demand curves are parallel, their slopes ($-\Delta P/\Delta Q$) and their inverse ($-\Delta Q/\Delta P$) are the same at every price. However, P/Q (the other component of the price elasticity formula) is smaller (since Q is larger) for the demand curve further to the right at every price. Therefore, the price elasticity of the demand curve further to the right is smaller.

   b. When two demand curves intersect, P/Q is the same for both demand curves at the point of intersection. However, $-\Delta Q/\Delta P$ is larger for the flatter demand curve. Therefore, the flatter demand curve is more elastic at the point where the demand curves intersect.

8. a. In a two-commodity world, both commodities cannot be luxuries because this would imply that a consumer could increase the quantity purchased of both commodities by a percentage larger than the percentage increase in his or her income. This is impossible if the consumer already spent all income on the two commodities before the increase in income (and does not borrow money).

   b. A 10% increase in income results in a 25% increase in the quantity of cars purchased if the income elasticity is 2.5. That is, since $2.5 = \%\Delta Q/10\%$, $(2.5)(10\%) = 25\%$.

10. a. Since $\eta = 0.13$ in the short run and 1.89 in the long run, the demand for electricity is inelastic in the short run and elastic in the long run. With a 10% increase in price, the quantity demanded of electricity will decline by

1.3% in the short run and by 18.9% in the long run.

b. Since the income elasticity of demand exceeds unity, electricity is a luxury. With a 10% increase in income, consumers would purchase 19.4% more electricity.

c. Since the cross elasticity of demand between electricity and natural gas is positive, natural gas is a substitute for electricity. However, a 10% increase in the price of natural gas increases electricity consumption by only 8%.

13. a. Since $K_X = 0.75$, K_Y must be 0.25. Thus,

$$(0.75)(0.90) + (0.25)(\eta_{IY}) = 1$$
$$0.25\eta_{IY} = 0.325$$
$$\eta_{IY} = 1.3$$

b. Commodity Y is a luxury, and commodity X is a necessity. For Y to be an inferior good, η_{IY} must be negative. For this to occur, $(0.75)(\eta_{IY})$ must be larger than 1, which means that η must exceed 1.33. Since most goods are normal, the income elasticity of demand of a commodity on which the consumer spends a great proportion of his or her income cannot be much higher than 1.

Chapter 6

1. a. The expected value of investment I is

$$(\$4,000)(0.6) + (\$6,000)(0.4)$$
$$= \$2,400 + \$2,400 = \$4,800$$

The expected value of investment II is

$$(\$3,000)(0.4) + (\$5,000)(0.3) + (\$7,000)(0.3)$$
$$= \$1,200 + \$1,500 + \$2,100 = \$4,800$$

b. The calculation of the standard deviation of each investment is shown in the following table.

c. Since both projects have the same expected value ($4,800) but the standard deviation of investment I is lower than that of investment II, a risk averse individual should choose investment I.

4. a. The expected value of project A is

$$(0.4)(-\$5) + (0.5)(\$35) + (0.1)(\$95)$$
$$= -\$2 + \$17.50 + \$9.50 = \$25$$

The expected value of project B is

$$(0.4)(-\$15) + (0.5)(\$45) + (0.1)(\$135)$$
$$= -\$6 + \$22.50 + \$13.50 = \$30$$

Project B is preferred.

Deviation from Expected Value	Deviation Squared	Probability	Deviation Squares Times Probability
	Investment I		
$4,000 − $4,800 = −$800	$640,000	0.6	$384,000
6,000 − 4,800 = 1,200	1,440,000	0.4	$576,000
	Sum of deviations squared = Variance = $960,000		
	Standard deviation = Square root of variance = $979.80		
	Investment II		
$3,000 − $4,800 = −$1,800	$3,240,000	0.4	$1,296,000
5,000 − 4,800 = 200	40,000	0.3	12,000
7,000 − 4,800 = 2,200	4,840,000	0.3	1,452,500
	Sum of deviations squared = Variance = $2,760,000		
	Standard deviation = Square root of variance = $1,661,000		

b. The standard deviation is the square root of the variance. The variance of project A is

$$(0.4)(-\$5 - \$25)^2 + (0.5)(\$35 - \$25)^2 + (0.1)(\$95 - \$25)^2$$

$$= (0.4)(-\$30^2) + (0.5)(10^2) + (0.1)(\$70^2)$$
$$= (0.4)(\$900) + (0.5)(\$100) + (0.1)(\$4,900)$$
$$= \$360 + \$50 + \$490 = \$900$$

So the standard deviation of the expected return to Project A is $30. The variance of project B is

$$(0.4)(-\$45^2) + (0.5)(\$15^2) + (0.1)(\$105^2)$$
$$= \$2,025$$

So the standard deviation of the expected return to Project A is $45.

(c) The expected value of project A ($25) is lower than the expected value of project B ($30), but the standard deviation of project A ($30) is also lower than the standard deviation of project B ($45). In this case the risk-verse individual should prefer the project with the highest expected value per dollar of standard deviation. This is $25/$30 = 0.83 for project A and $30/$45 = $0.66 for project B. Therefore, the individual should prefer project A.

7. a. Expected value of A = (0.4)($0) + (0.5)($16) + (0.1)($49) = $12.90
Expected value of B = (0.4)($4) + (0.5)($9) + (0.1)($49) = $11.00
Project A is preferred.

(b) Expected utility of A = (0.4)(0 utils) + (0.5)(4 utils) + (0.1)(7 utils) = 2.70 utils
Expected utility of B = (0.4)(2 utils) + (0.5)(3 utils) + (0.1)(7 utils) = 3.0 utils
Project B is preferred.

(c) The individual is risk averse because the utility function of profit increases at a decreasing rate or faces down so that the marginal utility of profit diminishes. Specifically, if profit were $1, the utility of the profit of $1 is the square root of 1, which is 1; if profit were

$2, the square root of $2 = 1.41, and if profit were $3, the square root of $3 is 1.732. If you plot profits of $1, $2, and $3 on the horizontal axis of a figure and the expected utility on the vertical axis, you will see that the expected utility of profit curve will be convex or increasing at a decreasing rate, thus making marginal utility diminishing and the individual risk averse.

*12. The U.S. importer can hedge his foreign-exchange risk with a forward purchase of £100,000 for $202,000 at today's three-month forward rate of $2.02/£1. In three months, the importer will pay $202,000 and obtain the £100,000 with which to pay for his imports.

The U.S. importer is usually willing to pay this extra $2,000 as the cost in insuring against having to pay much more in three months if the foreign currency appreciates (i.e., if the dollar depreciates) a great deal.

Chapter 7

7. See Figure 7. The right angle or L-shaped isoquant shows no possibility of substituting one input for the other in production. The straight-line isoquant shows that inputs are perfectly substitutable for each other in production (the $MRTS_{LK}$ is constant). That is, the given level of output could be produced with only labor or only capital.

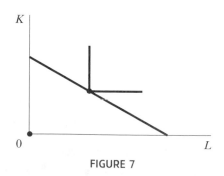

FIGURE 7

8. At 50 mph (point A), traveling the 600 miles requires 12 hours and 16 gallons of gasoline

for a total cost of (12)($6) + (16)($1.50) = $96. At 60 mph, the total cost is (10)($6) + (20)($1.50) = $90. At 66.7 mph, the total cost is (9)($6) + (30)($1.50) = $99. Thus, the cost of traveling the 600 miles is minimized at the speed of 60 mph.

10. a. The production function $Q = 10\sqrt{LK}$ exhibits constant returns to scale throughout. For example, when $L=1$ and $K=1$, $Q = 10\sqrt{1} = 10$. When $L=2$ and $K=2$, $Q = 10\sqrt{4} = 20$. When $L=3$ and $K=3$, $Q = 10\sqrt{9} = 30$. With $L=4$ and $K=4$, $Q = 10\sqrt{16} = 40$, and so on.

   b. The production function exhibits diminishing returns to capital and labor throughout. For example, holding capital constant at $K=1$ and increasing labor from $L=1$ to $L=2$ increases Q from 10 to $10\sqrt{2} = 14.14$. Therefore, the marginal product of labor (MPL) is 4.14. Increasing labor to $L=3$ results in $Q = 10\sqrt{3} = 17.32$. Thus, MPL declines to 3.18. The law of diminishing returns operates throughout, but MPL always remains positive. The same is true if labor is held constant and capital changes.

11. a. False. As long as returns are diminishing but positive, the student still benefits from additional hours of study.

   b. True. If economies of scale were present, larger and more efficient firms would drive smaller and less efficient firms out of business.

Chapter 8

1. a. The explicit costs are $10,000 + $30,000 + $15,000 = $55,000.

   b. The implicit costs are the foregone earnings of $15,000 in the previous occupation.

   c. The total costs are equal to the $55,000 of explicit costs plus the $15,000 of implicit costs, or $70,000. Since the total earnings or revenues are only $65,000, from the economist's point of view, the woman actually lost $5,000 for the year by being in business for herself.

4. a. Since electrical utility companies bring into operation older and less efficient equipment to expand output in the short run to meet peak electricity demand, their short-run marginal costs rise sharply.

   b. New generating equipment would have to be run around the clock, or nearly so, for AFC to be sufficiently low to make ATC lower than for older equipment. To meet only peak demand, older and *fully* depreciated equipment is cheaper.

9. a. The LTC curve would be a positively sloped straight line through the origin when constant returns to scale operate at all levels of output.

   b. The LAC and the LMC curves would coincide and be horizontal at the value of the constant slope of the LTC curve.

   c. Horizontal LAC and LMC curves are consistent with U-shaped SATC curves.

12. a. Rewriting learning curve equation $AC = 1,000Q^{-0.3}$ in double log form we get

$$\log(AC) = \log(1,000) - 0.3\log(Q)$$

Substituting the value of 100 for Q into the previous equation we get

$$\log(AC) = \log(1,000) - 0.3\log(100)$$

Substituting 3 for the log of 1,000 and 2 for the log of 100 (obtained by simply entering the numbers 1,000 and 100, respectively, in your calculator and pressing the "log" key), we get

$$\log(AC) = 3 - 0.3(2) = 2.4$$

Thus, AC equals the antilog of 2.4, which equals $251.19 (obtained by imply entering the log of 2.4 in your calculator and pressing the antilog key). The AC for the 100th unit of the product is $251.19.

   b. For $Q=200$, we have

$$\log(AC) = \log(1,000) - 0.3\log(200)$$
$$= 3 - 0.3(2.30103)$$
$$= 3 - 0.69039$$
$$= 2.309691$$

Thus, AC for the 200th unit of the product equals the antilog of 2.309691, which equals $204.03.

c. For $Q = 400$, we have

$$\log(AC) = \log(1,000) - 0.3 \log(400)$$
$$= 3 - 0.3(2.60206)$$
$$= 3 - 0.780618$$
$$= 2.219382$$

Thus, AC for the 400th unit of the product equals the antilog of 2.219382, which equals $165.72.

d. Figure 8 shows the figure for the learning curve estimated above.

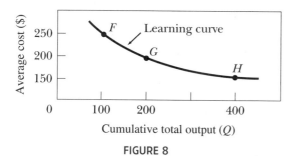

FIGURE 8

Chapter 9

1. a. $QD = QS$

$$4,750 - 50P = 1,750 + 50P$$
$$3,000 = 100P$$
$$P = \$30 \text{ (equilibrium price)}$$

b. See the following table.

MARKET DEMAND AND SUPPLY SCHEDULES

P($)	QD	QS
50	2,250	4,250
40	2,750	3,750
30	3,250	3,250
20	3,750	2,750
10	4,250	2,250

c. See Figure 9a.

d. $P = \$30$.

4. a. See Figure 9b. In Figure 9b, the slope of the TR curve refers to the constant price of $10 at which the perfectly competitive firm can sell its output. The TC curve indicates total fixed costs of $200 and a constant average variable

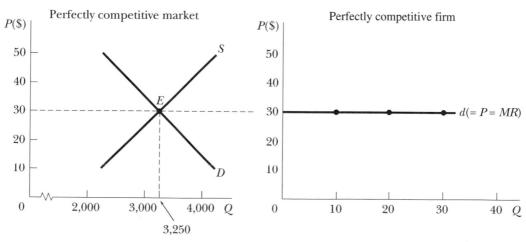

FIGURE 9a

cost of $5 (the slope of the *TC* curve). This is often the case for many firms for small changes in outputs. The firm breaks even at $Q = 40$ per time period (point *B* in the figure). The firm incurs a loss at smaller outputs and earns a profit at higher output levels. A figure such as Figure 9b is called a *break-even chart*.

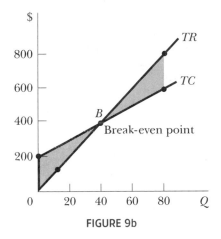

FIGURE 9b

b. An increase in the price of the commodity can be shown by increasing the slope of the *TR* curve; an increase in the total fixed costs of the firm can be shown by an increase in the vertical intercept of the *TC* curve, and an increase in average variable costs by an increase in the slope of the *TC* curve. The chart will

then show the change in the break-even point of the firm and the profits or losses at other output levels. Thus, the break-even chart is a flexible tool to analyze quickly the effect of changing conditions on the firm.

c. An important shortcoming of break-even charts is that they imply that firms will continue to earn larger and larger profits per time period with greater output levels. From our discussion in Chapter 9, we know that, eventually, the *TC* curve will begin to rise faster than *TR*, and total profits will fall. Thus, break-even charts must be used with caution. Nevertheless, under the appropriate set of circumstances, they can be a useful tool; they are being used extensively today by business executives, government agencies, and nonprofit organizations.

8. See Figure 9c.

10. See Figure 9d. The original long-run equilibrium point is *E* (where *D* crosses *S* and *LS*). If *D* shifts up to D', the equilibrium point is E' in the market period (where D' and *S* cross), E'' in the short run (where D' and S' cross), and E^* in the long run (where D' crosses *LS*). Thus, the adjustment to an increase in demand falls entirely on price in the market period, mostly on price in the short run, and mostly on output in the long run. With a constant cost

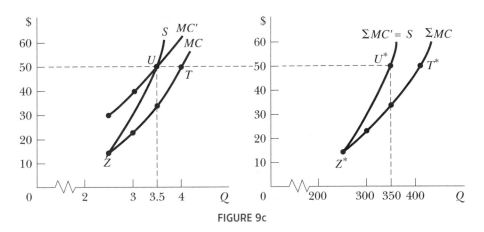

FIGURE 9c

industry, long-run adjustment would fall entirely on output.

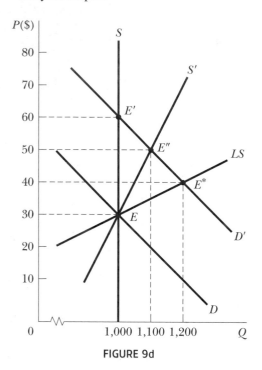

FIGURE 9d

Chapter 10

4. a. See Figure 10a. The best level of output is about $Q = 2$, where the MC curve intersects the MR' curve from below.

   b. Since at $Q = 2$, $P = \$20$ while $ATC = \$30$, the firm incurs a loss of $10 per unit and $20 in total. However, since $AVC = \$15$, the monopolist covers $10 out of its total fixed costs of $30. Were the monopolist to go out of business, it would incur a total loss equal to its $TFC = \$30$. The shut down point of the monopolist is at $Q = 2.5$, where $P = AVC = \$14$.

7. a. See Figure 10b.

   b. See Figure 10c.

10. With third degree price discrimination, $MR_1 = MR_2$. Also with formula [5-6], $MR_1 = P_1(1 + 1/\eta_1)$ and $MR_2 = P_2(1 + 1/\eta_2)$. Setting MR_1 equal to MR_2, we get

$$P_1(1 + 1/\eta_1) = P_2(1 + 1/\eta_2),$$

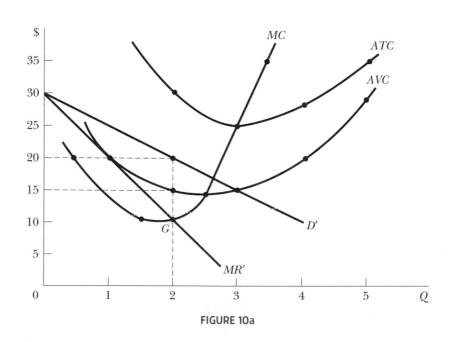

FIGURE 10a

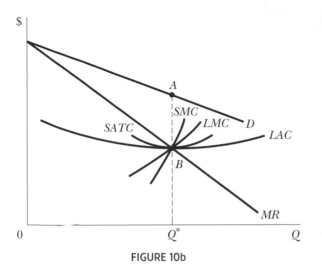

FIGURE 10b

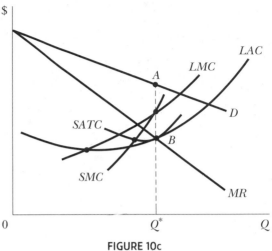

FIGURE 10c

so that

$$\frac{P_1}{P_2} = \frac{1 + 1/\eta_2}{1 + 1/\eta_1}$$

and

$$P_1 = \left(\frac{1 + 1/\eta_2}{1 + 1/\eta_1}\right) 4.5.$$

Since we were given $P_2 = \$4.50$, we need only to calculate η_1 and η_2 to prove that P_1 should be $\$7$. By extending D_1 to the horizontal axis and labeling H the intersection point at $Q = 11$ and also labeling J the point on the horizontal axis directly below point A, we get $\eta_1 = -JH/OJ = -7/4$. Doing the same for D_2, we get $\eta_2 = -3$. Substituting the η_1, η_2, and P_2 values into the formula for P_1 derived above, we get

$$P_1 = \left(\frac{1 - \dfrac{1}{3}}{1 - \dfrac{1}{4/7}}\right) 4.5 = \left(\frac{2/3}{1 - 7/4}\right) 4.5$$

$$= \left(\frac{2/3}{3/7}\right) 4.5 = \left(\frac{2}{3}\right)\left(\frac{7}{3}\right) 4.5 = 7.$$

12. a. See the following table and Figure 10d. The prime indicates the effect of the lump-sum tax of $\$4.50$.

Q	STC	MC	ATC	STC′	ATC′
0	$ 6	—	—	$10.50	—
1	10	$ 4	$10	14.50	$14.50
2	12	2	6	16.50	8.25
*3	13.50	1.50	4.50	18	6
4	19	5.50	4.75	23.50	5.88
5	30	11	6	34.50	6.90
6	48	18	8	52.50	8.75

The $STC′$ values are obtained by adding $\$4.50$ to the STC values.

$ATC′ = STC′/Q$. Since the lump-sum tax is like a fixed cost, it does not affect MC. Thus, the best level of output of the monopolist remains at three units, at which $P = \$6$, $ATC′ = \$6$, and the monopolist breaks even.

b. See the following table and Figure 10e, where the prime indicates the effect of a $\$2.50$ per-unit tax.

Q	STC	MC	ATC	STC′	MC′	ATC′
1	$10	$ 4	$10	$12.50	—	$12.50
2	12	2	6	17	$ 4.50	8.50
3	$13.50	1.50	4.50	21	4	7
4	19	5.50	4.75	29	8	7.25
5	30	$11	6	42.50	$13.50	8.50

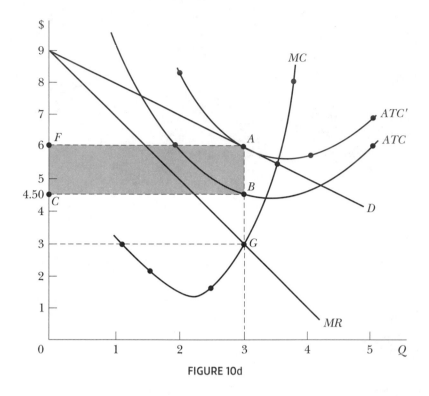

FIGURE 10d

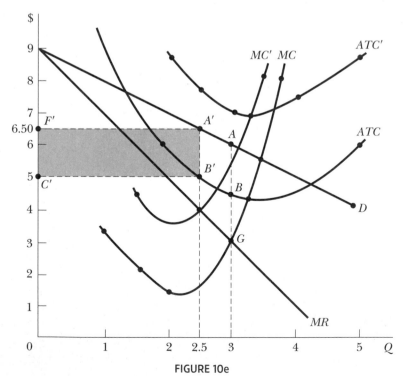

FIGURE 10e

The *STC'* values are obtained by adding $2.50 per unit of output to *STC*.

$$ATC' = STC'/Q. \; MC' = \Delta STC'/\Delta Q.$$

Since a per-unit tax is like a variable cost, both the *ATC* and the *MC* curves shift up to *ATC'* and *MC'*. The new equilibrium point is 2.5 units, given at point *G'* where the *MC'* curve intersects the *MR* curve from below. At $Q = 2.5$, $P = \$6.50$, $ATC' = \$7.50$, and the monopolist incurs a loss of $0.50 per unit and $1.25 in total (as opposed to a profit of $4.50 before the per-unit tax). Thus, the monopolist can shift part of the burden of the per-unit tax to consumers.

Chapter 11

2. The more price elastic the demand curve faced by a monopolistically competitive firm when in long-run equilibrium, the closer to the lowest point on its *LAC* curve will the firm be when in long-run equilibrium. Since excess capacity is measured by the distance between the two points, the more elastic the demand curve, the smaller the amount of excess capacity under monopolistic competition.

6. a. See Figure 11a. If the demand curve that the oligopolist faces shifts up by $0.50 but the kink remains at $P = \$8$, we get demand curve *d** or *H*B*C**. The marginal revenue curve is then *mr** or *H*K*F*G**. Since the *SMC* curve intersects the *mr** curve at point *K**, $Q = 6$ and price remains at $P = \$8$.

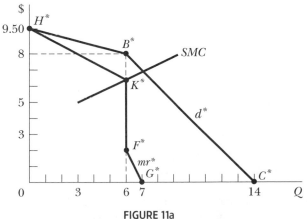

FIGURE 11a

b. See Figure 11b. If the demand curve that the oligopolist faces shifts down by $0.50 but the kink remains at $P = \$8$, we get demand curve *d*** or *H**B**C***. The marginal revenue curve is then *mr*** or *H**J**J*G***. Since the *SMC'* curve intersects the *mr*** curve at point *J**, $Q = 2$ and price remains at $P = \$8$.

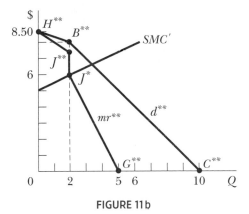

FIGURE 11b

9. a. See Figure 11c. Duopolist 1 (the low-cost duopolist) produces 2 units of the commodity and charges $P = \$8$ (given by point E_1, at which $SMC_1 = mr$, as in Figure 11.6). Duopolist 2 produces 1 unit of the commodity and would like to charge $P = \$10$ (given by point E_2, at which $SMC_2 = mr$). However, since the commodity is homogeneous, duopolist 2 (the high-cost duopolist) is forced to also sell at $P = \$8$ set by low-cost duopolist 1.

b. With $P = \$8$ and $SATC_1 = \$5$ at $Q = 2$, duopolist 1 earns a profit of $3 per unit and $6 in total. With $P = \$8$ and $SATC_2 = \$8$ at $Q = 1$, duopolist 2 breaks even. At $P = \$10$ duopolist 2 would have earned a profit of $2. Thus, only duopolist 1 maximizes profits.

If the high-cost duopolist would go out of business at the profit-maximizing price set by the low-cost duopolist, the latter would probably set a price sufficiently high to allow the high-cost duopolist to remain in the market and avoid possible prosecution under antitrust laws for monopolizing the market. In that case, the low-cost firm would not be maximizing profits.

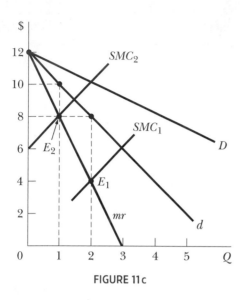

FIGURE 11c

12. a. The markup that the oligopolist should use in pricing its product is

$$m = -1/(\eta + 1)$$

$$= \frac{-1}{(-4+1)}$$

$$= \frac{1}{3} \text{ or } 33.33\%.$$

b. Since $AVC = \$10$ and the markup (m) equals 33.33%, the oligopolist should charge

$$P = AVC(1 + m)$$
$$= 10(1 + 0.3333)$$
$$= 10(1.3333)$$
$$= \$13.33$$

Chapter 12

3. a. If firm B produces small cars, firm A will earn a profit of 4 if it produces small cars and have a payoff of −2 (i.e., incurs a loss of 2) if it produces large cars. If firm B produces large cars, firm A will incur a loss of 2 if it also produces small cars and firm A earns a profit

of 4 if it produces large cars. Therefore, firm A does not have a dominant strategy.

b. If firm A produces large cars, firm B will earn a profit of 4 if it produces small cars and will have a payoff of −2 (i.e., incur a loss of 2) if it also produces large cars. If firm A produces small cars, firm B will incur a loss of 2 if it also produces small cars and will earn a profit of 4 if it produces large cars. Therefore, firm B does not have a dominant strategy.

c. The optimal strategy is for one firm to produce small cars and the other to produce large cars. In that case, each firm earns a profit of 4. If both firms produce either small cars or large cars, each incurs a loss of 2.

d. In this case we have *two* Nash equilibria: either firm A produces large cars and firm B produces small cars (the top left cell in the payoff matrix), or firm A produces small cars and firm B produces large cars (the bottom right cell in the payoff matrix).

e. A situation such as that indicated in the payoff matrix of this problem might arise if each firm does not have the resources to invest in the plant and equipment necessary to produce both large and small cars, and the demand for either small or large cars is not sufficient to justify the production of small or large cars by both firms. Specifically, if both firms produce the same type of car, the oversupply of that type of car will result in low car prices and losses for both firms.

4. The following table is a hypothetical payoff matrix for example 2 in Chapter 12.

		OTHER COMPUTER FIRMS	
		No Mail Orders	Mail Orders
Dell Computers	No Mail Orders	0, 1	0, 8
	Mail Orders	6, 2	4, 4

The payoff matrix in this table shows that when other computer companies do not sell computers through mail orders, Dell Computers earns zero profit if it also does not sell through the mail (since Dell was created specifically to sell only through the mail) but earns a profit of 6 if it does. Similarly, when other computer companies do sell through the mail, Dell earns zero profits if it does not sell through the mail and 4 if it does. Thus, Dell's dominant strategy is to sell computers through the mail, regardless of what the other computer companies do.

On the other hand, when Dell does not sell through the mail (i.e., when Dell is not in the market), other computer companies earn a profit of 1 if they do not sell through the mail and 8 if they do (at least that is what they believe). But if Dell is in the market and sells through the mail, other computer companies will earn 2 if they do not accept mail orders and 4 if they do. Thus, the other computer companies do not have a dominant strategy.

With Dell in the market and following its dominant strategy of selling through the mail, however, the other computer companies are also forced to enter the mail-order business. This is the Nash equilibrium.

8. a. Each firm adopts its dominant strategy of cheating (the top left cell) but could do better by cooperating not to cheat (the bottom right cell). Thus, the firms face the prisoners' dilemma.

b. If the payoff in the bottom right cell were changed to (5, 5), the firms would still face the prisoners' dilemma by cheating.

9. The tit-for-tat strategy for the first 5 of an infinite number of games for the payoff matrix of Problem 1, when firm A begins by cooperating but firm B does not cooperate in the next period, is given by the following table:

Period	Firm A	Firm B
1	2	2
2	−1	3
3	1	1
4	3	−1
5	2	2

The preceding table shows that in the first period, firm A sets a high price (i.e., cooperates) and so does firm B (so that each firm earns a profit of 2). If in the second period firm B does not cooperate and sets a low price, while firm A is still cooperating and setting a high price, firm B earns a profit of 3 and firm A incurs a loss of 1. In the third period, firm A retaliates and also sets a low price. As a result, each firm earns a profit of only 1 in period 3. In period 4, firm B cooperates again by setting a high price. With firm A still setting a low price, firm A earns a profit of 3 while firm B incurs a loss of 1. In the fifth period, firm A also cooperates again and sets a high price. Since both firms are now setting a high price, each earns a profit of 2.

Chapter 13

2. In Figure 13a, $P = \$8$ at the best level of output of $Q = 4$ given by point E at which $MR - MC = \$4$, so that $L = (8 − 4)/8 = 0.5$. This value of the Lerner index and the MC curve in Figure 12a is consistent with ATC_1 and ATC_2 and with profits of \$3 per unit and \$12 in total with ATC_1 and \$2 per unit and \$8 in total with

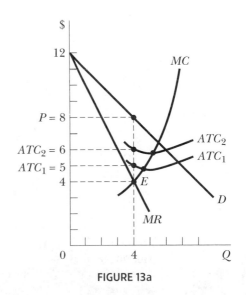

FIGURE 13a

ATC_2. All that is required is that both the ATC_1 and ATC_2 intersect the MC curve at the lowest points of the former. Thus, a high degree of monopoly power is consistent with high or low profits for the firm.

5. In Figure 13b, D is the market demand curve and MC is the positively sloped marginal cost curve faced by the monopolist. The demand curve shows the maximum price that consumers would be willing to pay and the marginal benefit that they would receive for various quantities of the commodity. On the other hand, the MC curve shows the opportunity cost (in terms of the commodities foregone that could have been produced with the same inputs) of producing various quantities of the commodity. The best level of output for the monopolist is Q^* at which $MR = MC$ (point E). The price of the commodity is then P^*. The excess of P^* over MC between outputs Q^* and Q' (shaded triangle P^*EE' in Figure 13b) measures the net social losses of monopoly. Other social losses arise from the rent-seeking activities of the monopolist.

7. In Figure 13c, D and D' are, respectively, the original and new market demand curves. With the new demand curve D' and the unchanged LAC curve, the regulatory commission would set $P' = LAC = \$2$ (point G') and the public-utility company would supply 8 million units of the service per time period (as compared with $P = LAC = \$3$ with $Q = 6$ million units per time period shown by point G on D). In either case, the public-utility company breaks even.

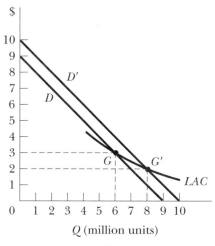

FIGURE 13c

12. a. When substitution in consumption is taken into account with peak-load pricing, the off-peak demand will be higher and the peak demand will be lower as compared with the case where substitution in consumption is not taken into account. This is shown by D_1' and D_2', respectively, in Figure 13d.

b. The gain in shifting from constant pricing to peak-load pricing (shown by the sum of the two shaded triangles in Figure 13d) is smaller when substitution in consumption is taken into account than when it is not. The reason is that the demand curves differ less with peak-load pricing when substitution in consumption is taken into account than when it is not.

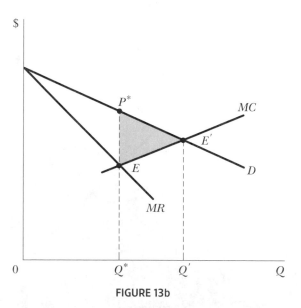

FIGURE 13b

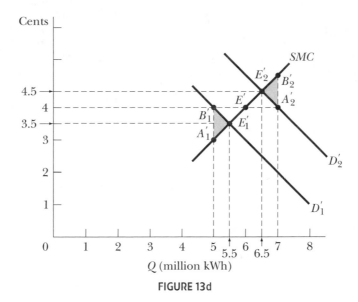

FIGURE 13d

Chapter 14

1. a. $MP_L/w < MP_K/r$. This means that the firm is above the *AVC* curve at the point where its *MC* curve intersects its *MR* curve.

   b. The firm is on its *AVC* cost curve to the right of the point of intersection of its *MC* and *MR* curves.

   c. $w/MP_L = r/MP_K = MC < MR$. The firm is on its *AVC* curve to the left of the intersection of its *MC* and *MR* curves.

5. a. See Figure 14a. The left panel of Figure 14a shows that the individual maximizes satisfaction at point *H* (with 16 hours of leisure per day, 8 hours of work, and a daily income of $8) on U_1 with $w = 1; at point *E* (with 14 hours of leisure, 10 hours of work, 8 and an income of $20) on U_2 with $w = 2; at point *N* (with 15 hours of leisure, 9 hours of work, and an income of $27) on U_3 with $w = 3; and at point *R* (with 17 hours of leisure, 7 hours of work, and an income of $28) on U_4 with $w = 4. Plotting the hours of work per day at various wage rates, we get

the individual's supply curve of labor (S_L) in the right panel. Note that S_L bends backward at the wage rate of $2 per hour.

   b. An increase in the wage rate, just like an increase in the price of a commodity, leads to a substitution effect and an income effect. The substitution effect leads individuals to substitute work for leisure when the wage rate (the price of leisure) increases. On the other hand, an increase in wages increases the individual's income, and when income rises, the individual demands more of every normal good, including leisure. Thus, the income effect, by itself, leads the individual to demand more leisure and work fewer hours.

   Up to $w = 2 (point *E'* on S_L in the right panel of Figure 14a), the substitution effect exceeds the opposite income effect and the individual supplies more hours of work (i.e., S_L is positively sloped). At $w = 2, the substitution effect and the opposite income effect are in balance and the individual supplies the same number of hours of work (S_L is vertical). Above $w = 2, the

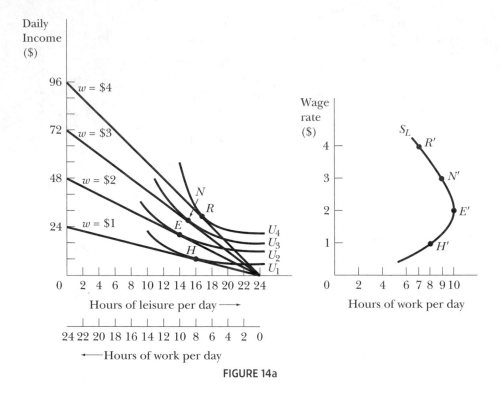

FIGURE 14a

substitution effect is smaller than the opposite income effect and the individual works fewer hours (i.e., S_L is negatively sloped or bends backward).

9. See Figure 14b. The movement from point E to point R is the combined substitution and income effects of the wage increase from $2 to $4 (as in Figure 14a). The substitution effect can be isolated by drawing the budget line with slope $w = \$4$ which is tangent to U_2 at point M. The movement along U_2 from point M to point E measures the substitution effect. By itself, it shows that the increase in w leads the individual to reduce leisure time and increase work by 4 hours per day.

The shift from point M on U_2 to point R on U_4 is the income effect of the wage increase. By itself, the income effect leads the individual to increase leisure and reduce work by 7 hours. The net result is that the individual increases leisure (works less) by 3 hours per day (ER).

11. See Figure 14c. In Figure 14c, D_T is the total demand for labor and S_T is the total supply of labor in both industries or regions. D_T is obtained from the horizontal summation of D_A and D_B, while S_A is obtained from the horizontal summation of S_A and S_B.

D_T and S_T intersect at point E, defining the equilibrium daily wage of $40 per day (the same as in both panels of Figure 14.6) and the equilibrium employment of labor of 6 million workers—the sum of the workers employed in industry or region A (the left panel in Figure 14.6) and industry or region B (the right panel of Figure 14.6).

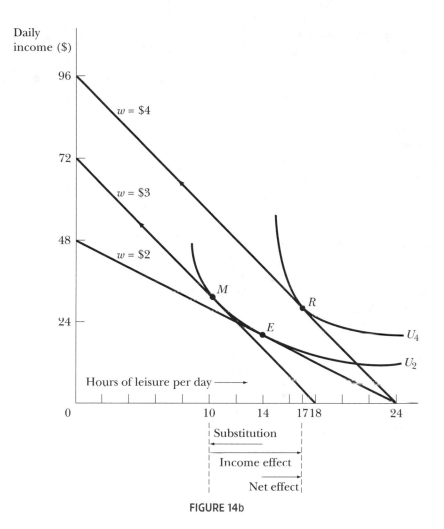

Daily income ($)

96

72

48

w = $4

w = $3

w = $2

24

M

E

R

U_4

U_2

Hours of leisure per day ⟶

0   10   14   1718   24

Substitution

Income effect

Net effect

FIGURE 14b

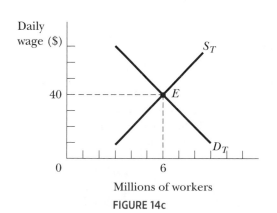

Daily wage ($)

S_T

40

E

D_T

0

6

Millions of workers

FIGURE 14c

Chapter 15

3. a. See the following table.

L	Q_X	MP_L	P_X	TR_X	MR_X	MRP_L	VMP_L	W
1	12	12	$13	$156	—	—	—	$40
2	22	10	12	264	$10.80	$108	$120	40
3	30	8	11	330	8.25	66	88	40
4	37	7	10	370	5.71	40	70	40
5	43	6	9	387	2.83	17	54	40
6	48	5	8	376	−1.80	−9	40	40

MR_X is obtained by the change in TR_X per unit change in the quantity of the commodity sold. That is, $MR_X = \Delta TR_X/\Delta Q_X = \Delta TR_X/MP_L$. For example, when the firm increases the number of workers it hires from one to two, Q_X rises from 12 to 22 units (i.e., $MP_L = 10$) and TR_X rises from \$156 to \$264 or by \$108. Thus, $MR_X = \$108/10 = \$10.80$. When the firm increases the number of workers it hires from two to three, TR_X increases by \$66 and Q_X increases by (i.e., MP_L equal to) eight units. Thus, $MR_X = \$66/8 = \$8.25$, and so on.

$MRP_L = (MP_L)(MR_X)$. For example, when the firm increases the number of workers hired from one to two workers, $MP_L = 10$ and $MR_X = \$10.80$. Thus, $MRP_L = (10)(\$10.80) = \$108$. This is equal to $\Delta TR_X/\Delta L$ or $\$108/1 = \$108$ (as found in the text).

$VMP_L = (MP_L)(P_X)$. For example, when the firm increases the number of workers it hires from one to two, $MP_L = 10$ and $P_X = \$12$, so that the $VMP_L = (10)(\$12) = \$120$.

b. See Figure 15a. If the firm were a perfect competitor in the product market as well as in the labor market, the firm would hire six workers (point E) because only by hiring six workers would $VMP_L = w = \$40$.

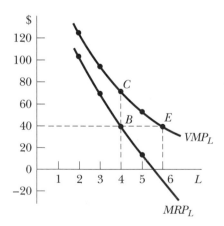

FIGURE 15a

Since the firm is a monopolist in the product market but a perfect competitor in

the labor market, it hires only four workers (point B) because only by hiring four workers would the $MRP_L = w = \$40$. The difference between the VMP_L and the MRP_L at $L = 4$ ($BC = \$30$ per worker and \$120 in total) is the amount of monopolistic exploitation.

9   a. See Figure 15b. The monopsonist's supply curve becomes HMB' and the ME_L curve becomes $HMNRB$. The monopsonist maximizes profits by hiring three workers on a full time basis and one worker on a half-time basis (given by point N, where the MRP_L curve intersects the vertical segment of the new ME_L curve). Monopsonistic exploitation is NM or \$15 per worker.

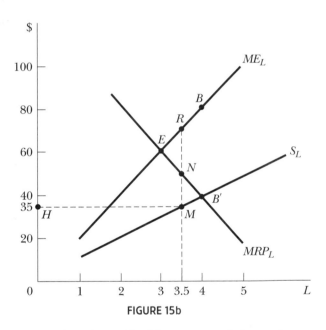

FIGURE 15b

b. See Figure 15c. The monopsonist's supply curve becomes TNF, and the ME_L curve becomes $TNFG$. The monopsonist maximizes profits by hiring three workers on a full time basis and one worker on a half-time basis (given by point N, where the MRP_L curve intersects the horizontal segment of the new ME_L curve). Now, $MRP_L = w = \$50$ at $L = 3.5$, and the monopsonistic exploitation of labor is zero.

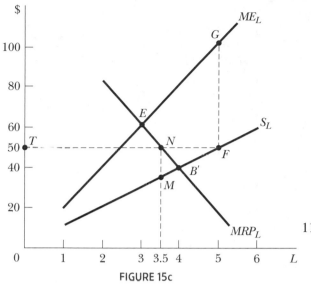

FIGURE 15c

10. See Figure 15d. The union (the monopolist seller of labor time) would like to have 40 workers employed (given by point E, where $MR = MC$) at the daily wage of $40 (point E' on D_L). The firm (the monopsonist employer of labor) would maximize profits by employing

40 workers (given by point E', where its D_L or MRP_L curve intersects its ME_L curve) at $w = $20 (point E on its S_L curve).

Thus, there is agreement between the union and the firm on the number of workers to be employed, but not on the wage. The greater the relative bargaining strength of the union, the closer the wage rate will be to $40. The greater the relative bargaining strength of the firm, the closer the wage rate will be to $20. Note that it is not certain that the union will behave entirely as a monopolist (see Section 15.8).

11. See Figure 15e. In the figure, the demand for union labor (D_U) plus the demand for nonunion labor (D_N) gives the total demand for labor (D_T). The intersection of D_T and S_T (the market supply of labor) at point E determines the equilibrium daily wage of $60 for union and nonunion labor (in the absence of any effect of unions on the wages). At $w = $60, 4 million union workers (point F') and 8 million nonunion workers (point E'') are employed.

If unions are now successful in raising union wages from $60 to $65, the employment

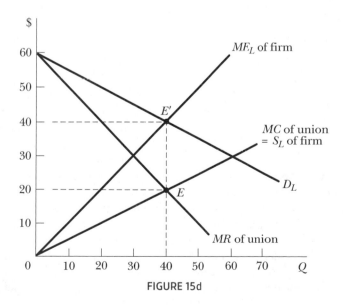

FIGURE 15d

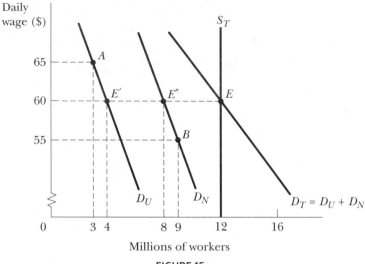

FIGURE 15e

of union labor falls from 4 to 3 million (point A on D_U). The 1 million workers who cannot find union employment will now have to find employment in the nonunion sector. This increases employment in the nonunion sector from 8 to 9 million workers. But 9 million workers can only be employed in the nonunion sector at $w = \$55$ (point B on D_N).

Thus, when unions increase wages in the unionized sector, employment in the unionized sector falls. More workers must find employment in the nonunionized sector and nonunion wages fall. Thus, what union workers gain comes mostly at the expense of nonunion workers.

Chapter 16

4. See Figure 16a. Starting at point B ($Y_0 = 5$ and $Y_1 = 6$) in the figure, individual B moves to point E (7.5, 3) on indifference curve U_2 by borrowing 2.5 units of the commodity at $r = 20\%$. On the other hand, starting from point A ($Y_0 = 5$ and $Y_1 = 6$) in the figure, individual A moves to point E' (2.5, 9) on indifference curve U_1' by lending 2.5 units of the commodity at

$r = 20\%$. Since at $r = 20\%$ desired borrowing equals desired lending, this is the equilibrium rate of interest.

On the other hand, at $r = 50\%$, individual B moves from point B to point E^* on U_1 by borrowing only 2 units of the commodity this year and repaying 3 units next year, while individual A moves from point A to point E'' on U_2' by lending 3 units this year for 4.5 units next year (so that $r = 50\%$). Since at $r = 50\%$ desired lending exceeds desired borrowing, $r = 50\%$ is higher than the equilibrium rate of interest and r will fall toward 20%.

5. a. The supply curve of loans (lending) is usually positively sloped, indicating that lenders will lend more at higher rates of interest. However, when the interest rate rises, the lender will face a substitution effect and an income or wealth effect (just as a worker does when the wage rate rises). The substitution effect induces the lender to substitute future for present consumption and lend more since the reward for lending has increased.

On the other hand, when the interest rate rises, the lender's wealth rises and he or she will want to consume more both in the present

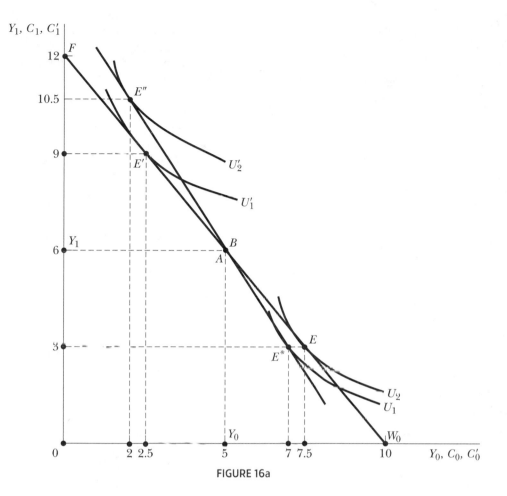

FIGURE 16a

(and lend less) and in the future. Thus, the substitution effect tends to lead the lender to lend more while the wealth effect leads the lender to lend less.

Up to a point, the substitution effect overwhelms the wealth effect and the lender will lend more at higher rates of interest. After a point, however, higher rates of interest will cause the wealth effect to exceed the opposite substitution effect so that the lender will lend less. Thus, at a sufficiently high rate of interest, the lender's supply curve will bend backward (as at r^* in Figure 16b).

b. For borrowers, both the substitution effect and the wealth effect operate to reduce the amount of desired borrowing when the rate of interest rises, so that the demand curve for borrowing is negatively sloped throughout. The substitution effect reduces the amount of borrowing as the rate of interest rises, because future consumption becomes more expensive in terms of the present consumption to be given up. The wealth effect also tends to reduce the amount of borrowing, because an increase in the rate of interest reduces the borrower's wealth.

9. See the following table. Note that the net present value of the project is higher with $r = 5\%$ than with $r = 10\%$.

BENEFIT–COST ANALYSIS OF AN INVESTMENT PROJECT

End of Year	Invest- ment (year 0) and Cost	Reve- nue	Net Reve- nue	Present Value Coefficient $1/(1 + 0.05)^n$	Present Value of Net Revenue
0	$1,000	—	-$1,000	—	-$1,000
1	200	$600	400	0.952	381
2	300	800	500	0.907	454
3	300	800	500	0.864	432
4	400	800	400	0.823	329
4	—	200*	200	0.823	165
					$761

*Salvage value

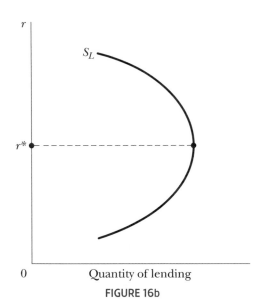

FIGURE 16b

10. The cost of equity capital for this firm (k_e) can be calculated with the dividend valuation model, as follows

$$k_e = D/P + g$$

where D is the amount of the yearly dividend paid per share of the common stock of the firm, P is the price of a share of the common stock of the firm, and g is the expected annual growth rate of dividend payments.

Since the company pays half of its expected $200 million in net after-tax earnings in dividends and there are 100 million shares of common stock of the firm, the dividend per share is $1. With a share of the common stock of the firm selling for eight times current earnings, the price of a share of the common stock of the firm is $8.

With the expected annual growth of earnings and dividends of the firm of 7.5%, the cost of equity capital for this firm is

$$k_e = \$1/\$8 + 0.075$$
$$= 0.125 + 0.075 = 0.20$$

or 20%.

Chapter 17

2. See Figure 17a. The Edgeworth box diagram of Figure 17a was obtained by rotating individual B's indifference curve diagram by 180 degrees (so that 0_B appears in the top right-hand corner) and superimposing it on individual A's indifference curve diagram (with origin 0_A) in such a way that the size of the box is $10X$ and $10Y$ (the combined amount of X and Y owned by individuals A and B). The contract curve for exchange is $0_A DEF 0_B$ and is given by the tangency points of the indifference curves (at which MRS_{XY} are equal) for the two individuals.

4. See Figure 17b. The Edgeworth box diagram of Figure 17b was obtained by rotating the isoquant diagram for commodity Y by 180 degrees (so that 0_Y appears in the top right-hand corner) and superimposing it on the isoquant diagram for commodity X (with origin 0_X) in such a way that the size of the box is $14L$ and $9K$ (the total amount of L and K available). The production contract curve is $0_X JMN 0_Y$ and is given by the tangency points of the isoquants (at which $MRTS_{LK}$ are equal) for commodities X and Y.

8. See Figure 17c. The simple economy portrayed in Figure 17c would be simultaneously

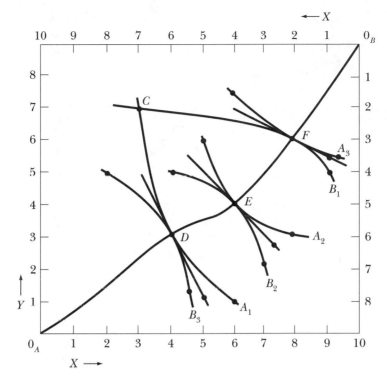

FIGURE 17a

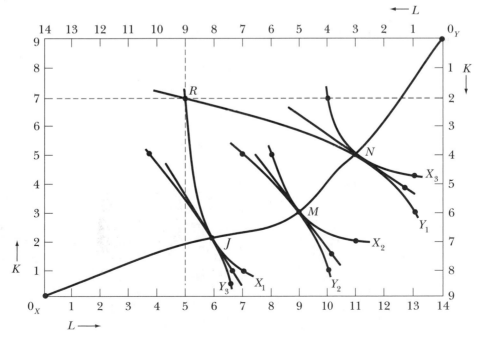

FIGURE 17b

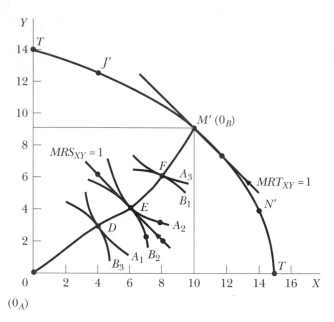

FIGURE 17c

in general equilibrium of production and exchange at point E, where

$$MRT_{XY} = MRS_{XY}^A = MRS_{XY}^B = 1$$

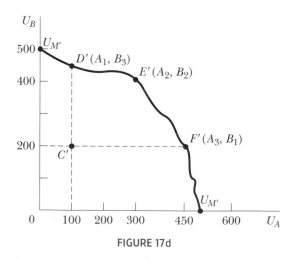

FIGURE 17d

12. a. See Figure 17d. Point D' in Figure 17d corresponds to point D (on A_1 and B_3) in

Figure 17a, point E' corresponds to point E (on A_2 and B_2), and point F' to point F (on A_3 and B_1). Other points can be similarly obtained. By joining these points, we get utility-possibilities frontier $U_{M'}U_{M'}$. This shows the various combinations of utilities received by individuals A and B at which this economy (composed of individuals A and B) is in general equilibrium and Pareto optimum in exchange. A point outside $U_{M'}U_{M'}$ cannot be reached with the available amount of commodities X and Y.

b. See Figure 17e. Utility-possibilities frontier $U_{M'}U_{M'}$ is that of part (a). Utility-possibilities frontier $U_{N'}U_{N'}$ is derived from the contract curve for exchange in the Edgeworth box diagram drawn from point N' on the production-possibilities frontier in Figure 17b (not shown in that figure). By joining E', H', and other Pareto optimum points of production and exchange, we get grand utility-possibilities frontier $GE'H'G$ in Figure 17e.

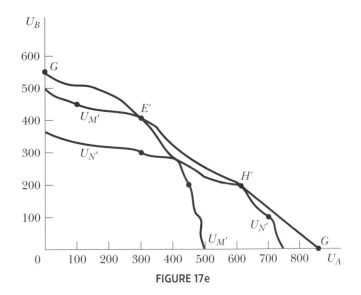

FIGURE 17e

Chapter 18

3. a. See Figure 18a. A corrective tax of $4 per unit imposed on the consumers of commodity X will make D'' the new industry demand curve. With D'', $P_X = \$10$ and $Q_X = 4$ million units per time period (given by the intersection of D'' and S at point E'). This is the socially optimum

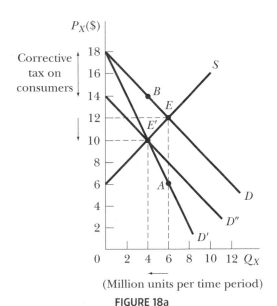

(Million units per time period)

FIGURE 18a

price and output. Consumers would now pay $P_X = \$10$ plus the $4 tax per unit ($E'B$) or a net $P_X = \$14$ (compared with $P_X = \$12$ under the previous competitive equilibrium at point E).

b. The total value of the economic gain resulting from the imposition of the corrective tax is equal to $6 million (given by area $EE'A$ in the figure). This is the excess of the MSC (shown by supply curve S) over MSB (shown by demand curve D') between $Q_X = 4$ and $Q_X = 6$ million units.

5. a. See Figure 18b. A corrective subsidy of $4 per unit given to producers of commodity X will make S'' the new industry supply curve. With S'', $P_X = \$10$ and $Q_X = 8$ million units per time period (given by the intersection of D and S'' at point E'). This is the socially optimum price and output. Producers would now receive $P_X = \$10$ plus the $4 subsidy per unit ($BE'$) for a total of $14 per unit.

b. The total value of the economic inefficiency eliminated by the corrective subsidy is equal to $3 million (given by area $EE'A$ in the figure). This is the excess of the marginal social value (shown by demand curve D) over

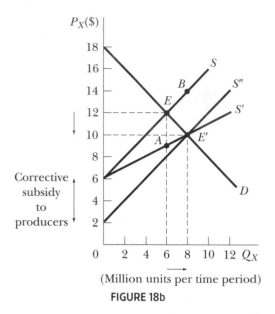

(Million units per time period)

FIGURE 18b

the *MSC* (shown by supply curve S') between $Q_X = 6$ and $Q_X = 8$ million units.

9. a. Each individual will drill more wells and pump oil faster than he or she would if no other oil field were located adjacent to his or hers in order to prevent some of the oil under his or her field to flow to the neighbor's field. The external diseconomies arise because oil is pumped faster than is socially desirable. The external diseconomies can be avoided by merging the two adjacent oil fields under joint ownership, by government regulation, or by taxation.

b. The development of a recreational site confers external benefits to owners of shops, gasoline stations, and motels in the area. In order to internalize the external benefits, the recreational site developer may also set up and operate establishments that provide these other services near the recreational site.

10. a. See Figure 18c. Market demand curve $D_X (CFEG)$ is obtained by the *horizontal* summation of demand curves D_A and D_B. D_X and S_X intersect at point E and define equilibrium price of $P_X = \$5.50$ and the equilibrium quantity of $Q_X = 7.5$, if the market for commodity X is perfectly competitive. Individual A consumes $1X$, and individual B consumes $6.5X$.

b. When X is a private good, the condition for Pareto optimal output is $MRT_{XY} = MRS_{XY}^A = MRS_{XY}^B$. That is, at the optimal output level, the marginal benefit that each consumer receives from an additional unit of commodity X equals its marginal cost. That is, $HJ = FR = EV$ in Figure 18c.

On the other hand, when X is a public good, the condition for the Pareto optimal output is $MRT_{XY} = MRS_{XY}^A + MRS_{XY}^B$. That is,

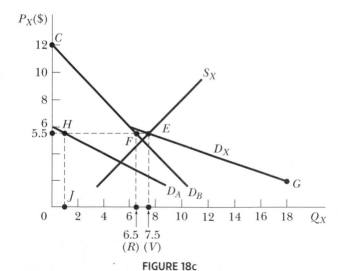

FIGURE 18c

since each consumer can consume the *same* quantity of commodity X when X is a public good, it is the sum of the marginal benefits that each consumer receives from the additional unit of commodity X that must equal its marginal cost (i.e., $AB + AC = AE$ in Figure 18.2).

c. Public goods that exhibit nonexclusion convey external economies of consumption on free riders (i.e., on the consumers not paying for the public goods).

Chapter 19

1. Because there is an equal number of five types of sellers, each price will be encountered one-fifth of the time on the first search.

  If search one yields the price of $120, four-fifths of the time search two will yield a lower price, averaging $95, and so the expected minimum price for search two is

$$\$120(1/5) + \$95(4/5) = \$24 + \$86$$
$$= \$100.$$

  If search one yields the price of $110, two-fifths of the time search two will yield a price of $120 or $110 (but in that case the price of $120 on search two would be disregarded), and three-fifths of the time search two will yield a lower price, averaging $90. Thus, the expected minimum price for search two in this case is

$$\$110(2/5) + \$90(3/5) = \$44 + \$54$$
$$= \$98.$$

  If search one yields the price of $100, three-fifths of the time search two will yield a price of $100 or higher (but in that case any price higher than $100 on search two would be disregarded), and two-fifths of the time search two will yield a lower price, averaging $85. Thus, the expected minimum price for search two in this case is

$$\$100(3/5) + \$85(2/5) = \$94.$$

  If search one yields the price of $90, four-fifths of the time search two will yield a price

of $90 or higher (but in that case any price higher than $90 on search two would be disregarded), and one-fifth of the time search two will yield a price of $80. Thus, the expected minimum price for search two in this case is $90(4/5) + $80(1/5) = $88.

  If search one yields the price of $80, the consumer will end the search because $80 is already the lowest price possible.

  The expected minimum price for the second search is then the average of the above expected minimum prices for the second search. That is, the *precise* minimum price on the second search is $100 + $98 + $94 + $88 + $80)/5 = $92 (compared with $93.33 found with the use of formula [19-1] in the text).

3. a. The formula for the lowest expected price for each search is

$$\text{Expected Price} = \text{Lowest Price}$$
$$+ \frac{\text{Range of Prices}}{\text{Number of Searches} + 1}$$

The lowest expected price with one search is

$$\$60 + \frac{\$80}{1+1} = \$100.00.$$

With two searches, the lowest expected price is

$$\$60 + \frac{\$80}{3} = \$86.67.$$

With three searches, the lowest expected price is

$$\$60 + \frac{\$80}{4} = \$80.00.$$

With four searches, the lowest expected price is

$$\$60 + \frac{\$80}{5} = \$76.00.$$

With five searches, the lowest expected price is

$$\$60 + \frac{\$80}{6} = \$73.33.$$

b. The marginal benefit from each search is measured by the reduction in the expected price resulting from the search. Thus, for the second search the marginal benefit (*MB*) is $100 − $86.67 = $13.37. For the third search, *MB* = $86.67 − $80.00 = $6.67. For the fourth search, *MB* = $80.00 − $76.00 = $4.00. For the fifth search, *MB* = $76.00 − $73.33 = $2.67.

Note that the marginal benefits of each additional search are now twice as large as those found in the text where the range of prices was half what they are in this problem.

6. Priceline is an Internet firm that allows buyers to name their own price for flights, hotel rooms, mortgages, cars, and, most recently, groceries. The only condition is that the buyer be flexible as to seller or brand name. For example, in the purchase of an airline ticket the buyer cannot specify the airline or the time of flight, but has to take what is offered by the carrier that accepts the bid. This allows airlines to sell empty seats without losing their regular customers. As customers gain experience and learn to make more realistic bids,

and as Priceline adds more airline and flights to the scheme, more and more bids are likely to be successful (they are now successful less than half of the time).

8. See Figure 19. In the figure, the subscripts H, L, and A refer, respectively, to high quality, low quality, and average quality. In the absence of perfect information (i.e., with asymmetric information), the demand for used cars will be the average of the demand curves for the high-quality and the low-quality used cars that would prevail in the market if all potential buyers had perfect information. As a result, the left panel of Figure 19 shows that no high-quality cars will be offered for sale at the price of $12,000.

But with all the high-quality cars withdrawn from the market, only the low-quality cars will be offered for sale. Thus, D_A will fall to D_L in the right panel and only the 100,000 low-quality cars will be sold in the market at $P_L = $4,000.

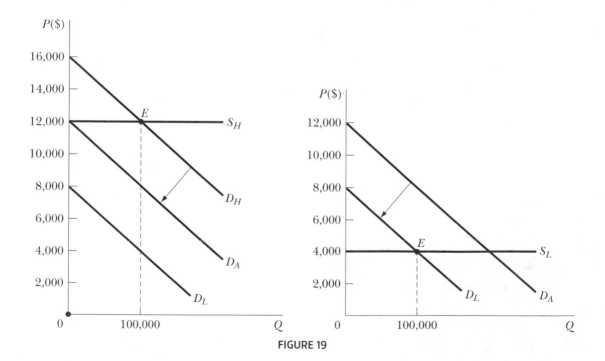

FIGURE 19

APPENDIX C

Glossary

Adverse selection The situation where low-quality products drive high-quality products out of the market as a result of the existence of asymmetric information between buyers and sellers.

Alternative or opportunity cost doctrine The doctrine that postulates that the cost to a firm in using any input (whether owned or hired) is what the input could earn in its best alternative use.

Appreciation A decrease in the domestic-currency price of the foreign currency.

Arbitrage The purchase of a commodity or currency where it is cheaper and its sale where it is more expensive.

Arc elasticity of demand The price elasticity of demand between two points on the demand curve; it uses the average price and the average quantity in calculating the percentage change in price and quantity.

Arrow's impossibility theorem The theorem that postulates that a social welfare function cannot be derived by democratic vote to reflect the preferences of all the individuals in society.

Asymmetric information The situation where one party to a transaction has more information on the quality of the product or service offered for sale than the other party.

Average fixed cost (AFC) Total fixed costs divided by output.

Average product (AP) The total product divided by the quantity of the variable input used.

Average revenue (AR) Total revenue divided by the quantity sold.

Average total cost (ATC) Total costs divided by output. Also equals $AFC + AVC$.

Average variable cost (AVC) Total variable costs divided by output.

Averch–Johnson (A–J) effect The overinvestments and underinvestments in plant and equipment resulting when public utility rates are set too high or too low, respectively.

Bad   An item of which less is preferred to more.

Bandwagon effect   The situation where some people demand a commodity because other people purchase it (i.e., in order to "keep up with the Jonesses" or because the commodity becomes more useful the more people buy it).

Barometric firm   An oligopolistic firm that is recognized as a true interpreter or barometer of changes in demand and cost conditions warranting a price change in the industry.

Benefit–cost analysis   A procedure for determining the most worthwhile public projects for the government to undertake. It prescribes that government should undertake those projects with the highest benefit-cost ratio, as long as that ratio exceeds 1, and until government resources are fully employed.

Bergson social welfare function   A social welfare function based on the explicit value judgments of society.

Bertrand model   The oligopoly model where each firm assumes that the other will keep its price constant. It leads to the perfectly competitive solution even with only two firms.

Beta coefficient (β)   The ratio of the variability of the return on the common stock of the firm to the variability of the average return on all stocks.

Bilateral monopoly   The case where the monopsonist buyer of a product or input faces the monopolist seller of the product or input.

Brain drain   The migration of highly skilled people from one nation to another. This benefits the receiving nation and harms the nations of emigration.

Break-even point   The point where total revenues equal total costs and profits are zero.

Budget constraint   The limitation on the amount of goods that a consumer can purchase imposed by

his or her limited income and the prices of the goods.

Budget line   A line showing the various combinations of two goods that a consumer can purchase by spending all income at the given prices of the two goods.

Bundling   A common form of tying in which the monopolist requires customers buying or leasing one of its products or services to also buy or lease another product or service when customers have different tastes but the monopolist cannot price discriminate.

Capital or investment goods   The machinery, factories, equipment, tools, inventories, irrigation, transportation, and communications networks that can be used to produce goods and services.

Capital asset pricing model (CAPM)   The method of measuring the equity cost of capital as the risk-free rate plus the beta coefficient (β) times the risk premium on the average stock.

Capital budgeting   The ranking of all investment projects from the highest present value to the lowest.

Cardinal utility   The ability to actually provide an index of utility from consuming various amounts of a good or baskets of goods.

Cartel   An organization of suppliers of a commodity aimed at restricting competition and increasing profits.

Centralized cartel   A formal agreement of the suppliers of a commodity that sets the price and allocates output and profits among its members so as to increase joint profits. It can result in the monopoly solution.

Certainty   The situation where there is only one possible outcome to a decision and this outcome is known precisely; risk-free.

Characteristics approach to consumer theory   The theory that postulates that a consumer demands a good because of the characteristics, properties, or attributes of the good, and it is these characteristics that give rise to utility.

Circular flow of economic activity   The flow of resources from households to business firms and the opposite flow of money incomes from business firms to households. Also, the flow of goods and services from business firms to households and the opposite flow of consumption expenditures from households to business firms.

Clayton Act   Prohibits mergers that "substantially lessen competition" or tend to lead to monopoly.

Coases theorem   Postulates that when property rights are clearly defined and transaction costs are zero, perfect competition results in the absence of externalities, regardless of how property rights are assigned among the parties involved.

Cobb–Douglas production function   The relationship between inputs and output expressed by $Q = AL^\alpha K^\beta$, where Q is output, L is labor, K is capital, and A, α, and β are positive parameters estimated from the data.

Coinsurance   Insurance that covers only a portion of a possible loss.

Collusion   A formal or informal agreement among the suppliers of a commodity to restrict competition.

Common property   Property, such as air, owned by no one.

Comparable worth   The evaluation of jobs in terms of the knowledge and skills required, working conditions, accountability, and the enforcement of equal pay for comparable jobs or "comparable worth."

Comparative advantage   The greater *relative* efficiency that an individual, firm, region, or nation has over another in the production of a good or service.

Comparative static analysis   The analysis of the effect of a change in demand and/or supply on the equilibrium price and output of a commodity.

Compensating wage differentials   Wage differences that compensate workers for the nonmonetary differences among jobs.

Compensation principle   The amount that gainers from a change could pay losers to fully compensate them for their losses.

Complementary inputs   Inputs related to one another in such a way that an increase in the employment of one input raises the marginal product of the other input.

Complements   Two commodities are complements if an increase in the price of one of them leads to less of the other being purchased.

Composite cost of capital   The weighted average of the cost of debt and equity capital to the firm.

Computer-aided design (CAD)   The process that allows research and development engineers to design a new product or component on a computer screen, quickly experiment with different alternative designs, and test each design's strength and reliability.

Computer-aided manufacturing (CAM)   The computer instructions to a network of integrated machine tools to produce a prototype of a new or changed product.

Concentration ratio   The percentage of total industry sales of the 4, 8, and 20 largest firms in the industry.

Concept of the margin   The central unifying theme in all of microeconomics, according to which the total net benefit is maximized when the marginal benefit is equal to the marginal cost.

Conscious parallelism   The adoption of similar policies by oligopolists in view of their recognized interdependence.

Constant cost industry   An industry with a horizontal long-run supply curve. It results if input prices remain constant as industry output expands.

Constant returns to scale   Output changes in the same proportion as inputs.

Constrained utility maximization   The process by which the consumer reaches the highest level of satisfaction given his or her income and the prices of goods. This occurs at the tangency of an indifference curve with the budget line.

Consumer equilibrium   Constrained utility maximization.

Consumer optimization   Constrained utility maximization.

Consumer surplus   The difference between what the consumer is willing to pay for a given quantity of a good and what he or she actually pays for it.

Contract curve for exchange   The locus of tangency points of the indifference curves (at which the *MRSXY* are equal) for the two individuals when the economy is in general equilibrium of exchange.

Contract curve for production   The locus of tangency points of the isoquants (at which the *MRTSLK* are equal) for the two commodities when the economy is in general equilibrium of production.

Corner solution   Constrained utility maximization with the consumer spending all of his or her income on only one or some goods.

Cost of debt   The net (after-tax) interest rate paid by a firm to borrow funds.

Cost-plus pricing   The setting of a price equal to average cost plus a markup.

Cournot equilibrium   The situation where there is no tendency for each of two duopolists to change the quantity each sells.

Cournot model   The oligopoly model in which each firm assumes that the other keeps output constant. With two firms, each will sell one-third of the perfectly competitive output.

Cross elasticity of demand (η_{XY})   The percentage change in the quantity purchased of a commodity divided by the percentage change in the price of another commodity.

Deadweight loss   The excess of the combined loss of consumers' and producers' surplus from a tax.

Decreasing cost industry   An industry with a negatively sloped long-run supply curve. It results if input prices fall as industry output expands.

Decreasing returns to scale   Output changes by a smaller proportion than inputs.

Default risk   The possibility that a loan will not be repaid.

Depreciation   An increase in the domestic-currency price of the foreign currency.

Deregulation movement   The reduction or elimination of many government regulations since the mid-1970s in order to increase competition and efficiency.

Derivatives   Financial instruments or contracts whose values are derived from the price of such underlying financial assets as stocks, bonds, commodities, and currencies.

Derived demand   The demand for an input that arises from the demand for the final commodities that the input is used in producing.

Differentiated oligopoly   An oligopoly where the product is differentiated.

Differentiated products   Products that are similar, but not identical, and satisfy the same basic need.

Diminishing marginal utility of money   The decline in the extra utility received from each dollar increase in income.

Discrimination in employment   The (illegal) unwillingness on the part of employers to hire some group of equally productive workers based on gender, color, religion, or national origin under any circumstances or at the same wage rate.

Diseconomies of scope   The higher costs that a firm can experience when it produces two or more products jointly rather than separate firms producing the products independently.

Disemployment effect The reduction in the number of workers employed as a result of an increase in the wage rate (as with the imposition of an effective minimum wage).

Diversification The spreading of risks.

Dividend valuation model The method of measuring the equity cost of capital to the firm with the ratio of the dividend per share of the stock to the price of the stock, plus the expected growth rate of dividend payments.

Division of labor The breaking up of a task into a number of smaller, more specialized tasks and assigning each of these tasks to different workers.

Dominant strategy The optimal strategy for a player no matter what the other player does.

Dumping International price discrimination or the sale of the commodity at a lower price abroad than at home.

Duopoly An oligopoly of two firms.

Economic efficiency The situation in which the marginal rate of transformation in production equals the marginal rate of substitution in consumption for every pair of commodities and for every pair of individuals consuming both commodities.

Economic growth The increase in resources, commodities, and incomes, and the improvements in technology over time.

Economic rent That portion of a payment made to the supplier of an input that is in excess of what is necessary to retain the input in its present employment in the long run.

Economic resources Resources that are limited in supply or scarce and thus command a price.

Economics A field of study that deals with the allocation of scarce resources among alternative uses to satisfy human wants.

Economies of scope The lowering of costs that a firm often experiences when it produces two or more products jointly rather than separate firms producing the products independently.

Edgeworth box diagram A diagram constructed from the indifference map diagrams of two individuals, which can be used to analyze voluntary exchange.

Edgeworth box diagram for exchange A diagram constructed from the indifference curves diagram of two individuals, which can be used to analyze voluntary exchange.

Edgeworth box diagram for production A diagram constructed from the isoquants diagram of the two commodities, which can be used to analyze general equilibrium of production.

Efficiency The situation where the price of a commodity (which measures the marginal benefit to consumers) equals the marginal cost of producing the commodity.

Efficiency wage theory Postulates that firms willingly pay higher than equilibrium wages to induce workers to avoid *shirking* or slacking off on the job.

Effluent fee A tax that a firm must pay for discharging waste or polluting.

Endowment position The quantity of a commodity that the consumer receives in each year.

Engel curve Shows the amount of a good that a consumer would purchase at various income levels.

Engel's law The proportion of total expenditures on food declines as family incomes rise.

Entrepreneurship The introduction of new technologies and products to exploit perceived profit opportunities.

Environmental pollution The lowering of air, water, scenic, and noise qualities of the world around us that results from the dumping of waste products. It arises because of unclearly defined property rights and too-high transaction costs.

Equilibrium The condition that, once achieved, tends to persist. It occurs when the quantity demanded of a commodity equals the quantity supplied and the market clears.

Equilibrium price The price at which the quantity demanded equals the quantity supplied of a good or service.

Excess capacity The difference between the output indicated by the lowest point on the *LAC* curve and the output actually produced by a monopolistically competitive firm when in long-run equilibrium.

Excess demand The amount by which the quantity demanded of a commodity is larger than the quantity supplied of the commodity at below-equilibrium prices; with a tradable commodity, it gives the quantity demanded of imports of the commodity.

Excess supply The amount by which the quantity supplied of a commodity is larger than the quantity demanded of the commodity at above-equilibrium prices; for a tradable commodity, it gives the quantity supplied of exports of the commodity.

Exchange The trade of one good for another through the medium of money.

Exchange rate The price of a unit of the foreign currency in terms of the domestic currency.

Excise tax A tax on each unit of the commodity.

Exhaustible resources Nonrenewable resources, such as petroleum and other minerals, which are available in fixed quantities and are nonreplenishable.

Expansion path The line joining the origin with the points of tangency of isoquants and isocost lines with input prices held constant. It shows the least-cost input combination to produce various output levels.

Expected income ($\bar{I}$) The probability of one level of income (p) times that income level plus the probability of an alternative income ($1 - p$) times that alternative income level.

Expected utility The sum of the product of the utility of each possible outcome of a decision or strategy and the probability of its occurrence.

Expected value The sum of the products of each possible outcome of a decision or strategy and the probability of its occurrence.

Expected value of money The sum of the product of the amount of money involved from each possible outcome of a decision or strategy and the probability of its occurrence.

Experience goods Goods whose quality can only be judged after using them.

Experimental economics The newly developing field of economics that seeks to determine how real markets operate by examining how paid volunteers behave within a simple experimental institutional framework.

Explicit costs The actual expenditures of the firm to purchase or hire inputs.

External benefits Beneficial side effects received by those not directly involved in the production or consumption of a commodity.

External costs Harmful side effects borne by those not directly involved in the production or consumption of a commodity.

External diseconomies of consumption Uncompensated costs borne by those not directly involved in the consumption of a commodity.

External diseconomies of production Uncompensated costs borne by those not directly involved in the production of a commodity.

External diseconomy An upward shift in all firms' per-unit cost curves, resulting from an increase in input prices as the industry expands.

External economies of consumption Uncompensated benefits received by those not directly involved in the consumption of a commodity.

External economies of production Uncompensated benefits received by those not directly involved in the production of a commodity.

External economy A downward shift in all firms' per-unit cost curves resulting from a decline in input prices as the industry expands.

Externalities   Harmful or beneficial side effects borne by those not directly involved in the production or consumption of a commodity.

Firm   An organization that combines and organizes resources for the purpose of producing goods and services for sale at a profit.

First-degree price discrimination   The charging of the highest price for each unit of a commodity that each consumer is willing to pay rather than go without it.

First theorem of welfare economics   Postulates that equilibrium in competitive markets is Pareto optimum.

Fixed inputs   The resources that cannot be varied or can be varied only with excessive cost during the time period under consideration.

Food stamp program   A federal program under which eligible low-income families receive free food stamps to purchase food.

For whom to produce   The way that output is distributed among the members of society.

Foreign exchange market   The market where national currencies are bought and sold.

Foreign exchange rate   The price of a unit of a foreign currency in terms of the domestic currency.

Forward contract   An agreement to purchase or sell a specific amount of a foreign currency at a rate specified today for delivery at a specified future date.

Forward or futures transaction   The purchase and sale of a commodity or currency for future delivery at a price agreed upon today.

Forward or futures market   The market where forward transactions take place.

Forward or futures price or rate   The price or rate at which a commodity or currency is bought and sold in the forward market.

Free-enterprise system   The form of market organization where economic decisions are made by individuals and firms.

Free-rider problem   The problem that arises when an individual does not contribute to the payment of a public good in the belief that it will be provided anyway.

Fringe benefits   Goods and services provided to employees and paid by employers.

Futures contract   A standardized forward contract for predetermined quantities of the currency and selected calendar dates.

Gambler   An individual who is willing to pay a small sum of money in order to have the small probability of a large gain or win; a risk seeker or lover.

Game theory   The theory that examines the choice of optimal strategies in conflict situations.

General equilibrium analysis   Studies the interdependence that exists among all markets in the economy.

Giffen good   An inferior good for which the positive substitution effect is smaller than the negative income effect, so that less of the good is purchased when its price falls.

Gini coefficient   A measure of income inequality calculated from the Lorenz curve and ranging from 0 (for perfect equality) to 1 (for perfect inequality).

Globalization of economic activity   The increasing proportion of consumer goods, and parts and components of manufactured goods imported from abroad; the increasing share of domestic production exported; and the rising repercussions of domestic policies on other nations.

Golden parachute   A large financial settlement paid out by a firm to its managers if they are forced or choose to leave as a result of a takeover that greatly increases the value of the firm.

Good   A commodity of which more is preferred to less.

Government failures   Situations where government policies do not reflect the public's interests and reduce rather than increase social welfare.

Grand utility-possibilities frontier   The envelope to utility-possibilities frontiers at Pareto optimum points of production and exchange.

Hedging   The covering of risks arising from changes in future commodity and currency prices.

Herfindahl index   A measure of the degree of monopoly power in an industry, which is given by the sum of the squared values of the market sales shares of all the firms in the industry.

Homogeneous of degree 1   In production, it refers to constant returns to scale.

How to produce   The way resources or inputs are combined to produce the goods and services that consumers want.

Human wants   All the goods, services, and the conditions of life that individuals desire, which provide the driving force for economic activity.

Identification problem   The difficulty sometimes encountered in estimating the market demand or supply curve of a commodity from quantity-price observations.

Implicit costs   The value of the inputs owned and used by the firm; value is imputed from the best alternative use of the inputs.

Import tariff   A per-unit tax on the imported commodity.

Incidence of tax   The relative burden of the tax on buyers and sellers.

Income–consumption curve   The locus of consumer optimum points resulting when only the consumer's income varies.

Income effect   The increase in the quantity purchased of a good resulting only from the increase in real income that accompanies a price decline.

Income elasticity of demand (η_I)   The percentage change in the quantity purchased of a commodity over a specific period of time divided by the percentage change in consumers' income.

Income elasticity of demand for imports   The percentage change in the demand for imports by a nation over a specific period of time divided by the percentage change in the income of the nation.

Income elasticity of demand for exports   The percentage change in the demand for the exports of a nation over a specific period of time divided by the percentage change in the income of other nations.

Income or expenditure index (E)   The ratio of period 1 to base period money income or expenditures.

Increasing cost industry   An industry with a positively sloped long-run supply curve. It results if input prices rise as industry output expands.

Increasing returns to scale   Output changes by a larger proportion than inputs.

Indifference curve   The curve showing the various combinations of two commodities that give the consumer equal satisfaction and among which the consumer is indifferent.

Indifference map   The entire set of indifference curves reflecting the consumer's tastes and preferences.

Individual's demand curve   Shows the quantity that the individual would purchase of the good per unit of time at various alternative prices of the good, while keeping everything else constant.

Inferior good   A good of which a consumer purchases less with an increase in income.

Information superhighway   The ability of researchers, firms, and consumers to hook up with libraries, databases, and marketing information through a national high-speed computer network and have at their fingertips a vast amount of information as never before.

Inputs   The resources or factors of production used to produce goods and services.

Insurer   An individual who is willing to pay a small sum of money in order to ensure against the small probability of a large loss; a risk averter.

Interdependence   The relationship among all markets in the economy, such that a change in any of them affects all the others.

Intermediate good   The output of a firm or industry that is the input of another firm or industry producing final commodities.

Internalizing external costs   The process whereby an external cost becomes part of the regular business expense of the firm.

International economies of scale   The lower costs resulting from the firm's integration of its entire system of manufacturing operations around the world.

Internationalization of economic activity   The trend toward producing and distributing goods throughout the world.

Internet   A collection of thousands of computers, businesses, and millions of people throughout the world linked together in a service called World Wide Web.

Intraindustry trade   The international trade in the differentiated products of the same industry or broad product group.

Investment   The formation of new capital assets.

Investment in human capital   Any activity, such as education and training, that increases an individual's productivity.

Isocost line   Shows the various combinations of two inputs that the firm can hire with a given total cost outlay.

Isoquant   A curve showing the various combinations of two inputs that can be used to produce a specific level of output.

Kaldor–Hicks criterion   Postulates that a change is an improvement if those who gain from the change can fully compensate the losers and still retain some of the gain.

Kinked-demand curve model   The model that seeks to explain price rigidity by postulating a demand curve with a kink at the prevailing price.

Labor or human resources   The different types of skilled and unskilled workers that can be used in the production of goods and services.

Labor union   An organization of workers devoted to increasing the wages and welfare of its members through bargaining with employers.

Land or natural resources   The land, its fertility, mineral deposits, and forests that can be used to produce goods and services.

Laspeyres price index (L)   The ratio of the cost of purchasing base period quantities at period 1 prices relative to base period prices.

Law of demand   The inverse price-quantity relationship illustrated by the negative slope of the demand curve.

Law of diminishing marginal utility   Each additional unit of a good eventually gives less and less extra utility.

Law of diminishing returns   After a point, the marginal product of the variable input declines.

Law of the invisible hand   The law stated by Adam Smith over 200 years ago that postulates that in a free market economy, each individual by pursuing his or her own selfish interests is led, as if by an invisible hand, to promote the welfare of society more so than he or she intends or even understands.

Learning curve   The curve showing the decline in average costs with rising cumulative total outputs over time.

Least-cost input combination   The condition where the marginal product per dollar spent on each input is equal. Graphically, it is the point where an isoquant is tangent to an isocost line.

Lerner index   A measure of the degree of a firm's monopoly power which is given by the ratio of the difference between price and marginal cost to price.

Limit pricing   The charging of a sufficiently low price by existing firms to discourage entry into the industry.

Long run   The time period when all inputs can be varied.

Long-run average cost (*LAC*) The minimum per-unit cost of producing any level of output when the firm can build any desired scale of plant. It equals long-run total cost divided by output.

Long-run marginal cost (*LMC*) The change in long-run total costs per-unit change in output; the slope of the *LTC* curve.

Long-run total cost (*LTC*) The minimum total costs of producing various levels of output when the firm can build any desired scale of plant.

Lorenz curve A curve showing income inequality by measuring cumulative percentages of total income along the vertical axis, for various cumulative percentages of the population (from the lowest to the highest income) measured along the horizontal axis.

Luxury A commodity with income elasticity of demand greater than 1.

Macroeconomic theory The study of the total or *aggregate* level of output, national income, national employment, consumption, investment, and prices for the economy *viewed as a whole.*

Marginal analysis The analysis based on the application of the marginal concept according to which net benefits increase as long as the marginal benefit exceeds the marginal cost and until they are equal.

Marginal benefit The change in the total benefit, or extra benefit, resulting from an economic action.

Marginal cost The change in the total cost, or extra cost, resulting from an economic action.

Marginal product (*MP*) The change in total product per-unit change in the variable input used.

Marginal productivity theory The theory according to which each input is paid a price equal to its marginal productivity.

Marginal rate of substitution (*MRS*) The amount of a good that a consumer is willing to give up for an additional unit of another good while remaining on the same indifference curve.

Marginal rate of technical substitution (*MRTS*) The absolute value of the slope of the isoquant. It also equals the ratio of the marginal product of the two inputs.

Marginal rate of transformation of *X* for *Y* (*MRT_{XY}*) The amount of *Y* that must be given up to release just enough labor and capital to produce one additional unit of *X*. It is equal to the absolute value of the slope of the production-possibilities frontier and to the ratio of the marginal cost of *X* to the marginal cost of *Y*.

Marginal expenditure (ME) The extra expenditure or cost of hiring an additional unit of the input.

Marginal expenditure on capital (ME_K) The extra expenditure or cost of hiring an additional unit of capital.

Marginal expenditure on labor (ME_L) The extra expenditure or cost of hiring an additional unit of labor.

Marginal revenue (*MR*) The change in total revenue per-unit change in the quantity sold.

Marginal revenue product (*MRP*) The marginal physical product of the input (*MP*) multiplied by the marginal revenue of the commodity (*MR*).

Marginal utility (*MU*) The extra utility received from consuming one additional unit of a good.

Market An institutional arrangement under which buyers and sellers can exchange some quantity of a good or service at a mutually agreeable price.

Market demand curve Shows the quantity demanded of a commodity in the market per time period at various alternative prices of the commodity, while holding everything else constant.

Market demand schedule A table showing the quantity of a commodity that consumers are willing and able to purchase during a given period of time at each price of the commodity, while holding constant all other relevant economic variables on which demand depends.

Market failures   The existence of monopoly, monopsony, price controls, externalities, and public goods that prevent the attainment of economic efficiency or Pareto optimum.

Market line   A line from any point on the production-possibilities curve showing the various amounts of a commodity that the individual can consume in each period by borrowing or lending.

Market period   The time period during which the market supply of a commodity is fixed. Also called the very short run.

Market-sharing cartel   An organization of suppliers of a commodity that overtly or tacitly divides the market among its members.

Market signaling   Signals that convey product quality, good insurance or credit risks, and high productivity.

Market supply curve   The graphic representation of the market supply schedule showing the quantity supplied of a commodity per time period at each commodity price, while holding constant all other relevant economic variables on which supply depends.

Marketing research approaches to demand estimation   The estimation of consumer demand for a product or service by consumer surveys, consumer clinics, or market experiments.

Markup   The percentage over average cost in cost-plus pricing.

Maximum social welfare   The point at which a social indifference curve is tangent to the grand utility-possibilities frontier; also called constrained bliss.

Methodology of economics   The proposition that a model is tested by its predictive ability, the consistency of its assumptions, and the logic with which the predictions follow from the assumptions.

Microeconomic theory   The study of the economic behavior of *individual* decision-making units such as individual consumers, resource owners, and

business firms, and the operation of individual markets in a free-enterprise economy.

Micromarketing   Narrowing a marketing strategy to the individual store or consumer.

Minimal income maintenance   The transfer or subsidy going to families that have no other income under a negative income-tax program.

Minimum efficient scale (MES)   The smallest quantity at which the LAC curve reaches its minimum.

Mixed economy   An economy, such as that in the United States, characterized by private enterprise and government actions and regulations.

Mixed strategy   The best strategy for each player in a non-strictly determined game.

Model   Another name for theory, or the set of assumptions from which the result of an event is deduced or predicted.

Monopolistic competition   The form of market organization in which there are many sellers of a differentiated product, and entry into or exit from the market is rather easy in the long run.

Monopolistic exploitation   The excess of an input's value of marginal product over its marginal revenue product at the level of utilization of the input.

Monopsonistic competition   One of many firms hiring a differentiated input.

Monopsonistic exploitation   The excess of the marginal revenue product of an input over the price of the input at the level of utilization of the input.

Monopsony   A single buyer of an input.

Moral hazard   The increased probability of a loss when an economic agent can shift some of its costs to others.

Multiple regression   A statistical technique that allows the economist to disentangle the independent effect of the various determinants of demand, so as to identify from the data the average market demand curve for the commodity.

Nash equilibrium   The situation when each player has chosen his or her optimal strategy, *given the strategy chosen by the other player.*

Natural monopoly   The case of declining long-run average costs over a sufficiently large range of outputs so as to leave a single firm supplying the entire market.

Necessity   A commodity with income elasticity of demand between 0 and 1.

Negative income tax (*NIT*)   A type of welfare program involving declining cash transfers to low-income families as the family's earned income rises.

Net present value (*NPV*)   The value today from the stream of net cash flows (positive and negative) from an investment project.

Neuter   A commodity of which an individual is indifferent between having more or less.

Nominal rate of interest (*r′*)   The real rate of interest plus the anticipated rate of price inflation.

Nonclearing markets theory   Theories that seek to explain the persistence of surpluses and shortages in some real-world markets.

Noncompeting groups   Occupations requiring different capacities, skills, education, and training, and, therefore, receiving different wages.

Nonexclusion   The situation in which it is impossible or prohibitively expensive to confine the benefit or the consumption of a good (once produced) to selected people (such as only to those paying for it).

Nonexhaustible resources   Renewable resources, such as fertile land, forests, rivers, and fish, which need never be depleted if they are properly managed.

Nonprice competition   Competition based on advertising and product differentiation rather than on price.

Nonrival consumption   The distinguishing characteristic of a public good whereby its consumption by some individuals does not reduce the amount available to others.

Nonzero-sum game   A game where the gains of one player do not come at the expense of or are not equal to the losses of the other player.

Normal good   A good of which the consumer purchases more with an increase in income.

Normative analysis   The study of what *ought* to be or how the basic economic functions *should* be performed. It is based both on positive economics and value judgments.

Oligopoly   The form of market organization in which there are few firms selling either a homogeneous or a differentiated product.

Oligopsony   The form of market organization in which there are few firms hiring either a homogeneous or a differentiated input.

Opportunity cost   What an input could earn in its best alternative use.

Ordinal utility   The rankings of the utility received by an individual from consuming various amounts of a good or various baskets of goods.

Output elasticity of capital   The percentage increase in output resulting from a 1% increase in the quantity of capital used. For the Cobb-Douglas production function, this is given by the exponent of K.

Output elasticity of labor   The percentage increase in output resulting from a 1% increase in the quantity of labor used. For the Cobb-Douglas production function, this is given by the exponent of L.

Overtime pay   The higher hourly wage of many workers for working additional hours after the regular work day.

Paasche price index (*P*)   The ratio of the cost of purchasing period 1 quantities at period 1 prices relative to base period prices.

Pareto criterion   Postulates that a change increases social welfare if it benefits some members of society (in their own judgment) without harming anyone.

Pareto optimality   The situation in which no reorganization of production and consumption is possible by which some individuals are made better off without making someone else worse off.

Pareto optimum   The situation in which no reorganization of production or consumption can lead to an increase in the welfare of some without, at the same time, reducing the welfare of others.

Partial equilibrium analysis   Studies the behavior of individual decision-making units and individual markets, viewed in isolation.

Payoff   The outcome or consequence of each combination of strategies by the players in game theory.

Payoff matrix   The table of all the outcomes of the players' strategies.

Peak-load pricing   Refers to the charging of a price equal to short-run marginal cost, both in the peak period when demand and marginal cost are higher and in the off-peak period when both are lower.

Perfectly competitive market   A market where no buyer or seller can affect the price of the product, all units of the product are homogeneous, resources are mobile, and knowledge of the market is perfect.

Planning horizon   The time period when the firm can build any desired scale of plant; the long run.

Players   The decision makers in the theory of games (here, the oligopolistic firm or its managers) whose behavior we are trying to explain and predict.

Point elasticity of demand   The price elasticity of demand at a specific point on the demand curve.

Positive analysis   The study of what *is* or how the economic system performs the basic economic functions. It is entirely statistical in nature and devoid of ethical or value judgments.

Price ceiling   The maximum price allowed for a commodity. If the price ceiling is below the equilibrium price, it leads to a shortage of the commodity.

Price-consumption curve   The locus of consumer optimum points resulting when only the price of a good varies.

Price discrimination   Charging different prices (for different quantities of a commodity or in different markets) that are not justified by cost differences.

Price elasticity of demand (η)   The percentage change in the quantity demanded of a commodity during a specific period of time divided by the percentage change in its price.

Price elasticity of demand for imports   The percentage change in the quantity purchased of imports by a nation divided by the percentage change in their prices.

Price elasticity of demand for exports   The percentage change in the quantity purchased of a nation's exports divided by the percentage change in the price of the nation's exports.

Price elasticity of supply (ϵ)   The percentage change in the quantity supplied of a commodity during a specific period of time divided by the percentage change in its price.

Price floor   A minimum price for a commodity. If the price floor is above the equilibrium price, it leads to a surplus of the commodity.

Price leadership   The form of market collusion in oligopolistic markets whereby the firm that serves as the price leader initiates a price change and the other firms in the industry soon match it.

Price system   The system whereby the organization and coordination of economic activity is determined by commodity and resource prices.

Price theory   Another name for microeconomic theory that stresses the importance of prices in the determination of what goods are produced and in what quantities, the organization of production, and the distribution of output or income.

Principal-agent problem The fact that the agents (managers and workers) of a firm seek to maximize their own benefits (such as salaries) rather than the total profits or value of the firm, which is the owners' or principals' interest.

Prisoners' dilemma The situation where each player adopts his or her dominant strategy but could do better by cooperating.

Private costs The costs incurred by individuals and firms.

Probability The chance or odds that an event will occur.

Probability distribution The list of all possible outcomes of a decision or strategy and the probability attached to each.

Producer surplus The excess of the market price of the commodity over the marginal cost of production.

Product group The sellers of a differentiated product.

Product cycle model The introduction of new products by firms in an advanced nation, which are then copied and produced by firms in lower-wage countries.

Product innovation The introduction of new or improved products.

Process innovation The introduction of new or improved production processes.

Production The transformation of resources or inputs into outputs of goods and services.

Production function The unique relationship between inputs and outputs represented by a table, graph, or equation showing the maximum output of a commodity that can be produced per period of time with each set of inputs.

Production-possibilities frontier or transformation curve Shows the alternative combinations of commodities that a nation can produce by fully utilizing all of its resources with the best technology available to it.

Product variation Differences in some of the characteristics of differentiated products.

Public goods Commodities for which consumption by some individuals does not reduce the amount available for others. That is, once the good is provided for someone, others can consume it at no additional cost.

Pure monopoly The form of market organization in which there is a single seller of a commodity for which there are no close substitutes.

Pure oligopoly An oligopoly in which the product of the firms in the industry is homogeneous.

Quasi rent The return or payment to inputs that are fixed in the short run (i.e., $TR - TVC$).

Rate of interest (r) The premium received in one year for lending one dollar this year.

Rational consumer An individual who seeks to maximize utility or satisfaction in spending his or her income.

Rational ignorance The condition whereby voters are much less informed about political decisions than about their individual market decisions because of the higher costs of obtaining information and the smaller direct benefits that they obtain from the former than from the latter.

Rationing Quantitative restrictions imposed by the government on the amount of a good that an individual can purchase per unit of time.

Rationing over time The allocation of a given amount of a commodity over time.

Reaction function shows how a duopolist reacts to the other duopolist's action.

Real rate of interest (r) The premium on a unit of a commodity or real consumption income today compared to a unit of the commodity or real consumption income in the future.

Relative price   The price of a good in terms of another.

Repeated games   Prisoners' dilemma games of more than one move.

Ridge lines   The lines that separate the relevant (i.e., the negatively sloped) from the irrelevant (or the positively sloped) portions of the isoquants.

Risk   The situation where there is more than one possible outcome to a decision and the probability of each possible outcome is known or can be estimated.

Risk averter   An individual for whom the marginal utility of money diminishes; he or she would not accept a fair bet.

Risk neutral   An individual for whom the marginal utility of money is constant; he or she is indifferent to a fair bet.

Risk premium   The maximum amount that a risk-averse individual would be willing to pay to avoid a risk.

Risk–return indifference curve   A curve showing the various risk–return combinations among which a manager or investor is indifferent.

Risk seeker or lover   An individual for whom the marginal utility of money increases; he or she would accept a fair bet and even some unfair bets.

Saddle point   The solution or outcome of a strictly determined game.

Saving   The refraining from present consumption.

Scitovsky criterion   Postulates that a change is an improvement if it satisfies the Kaldor–Hicks criterion and, if, after the change, a movement back to the original position does not satisfy the Kaldor-Hicks criterion.

Search costs   The time and money spent seeking information about a product.

Search goods   Goods whose quality can be evaluated by inspection at the time of purchase.

Second-degree price discrimination   Charging a lower price for each additional batch or block of the commodity.

Second theorem of welfare economics   Postulates that equity in distribution is logically separable from efficiency in allocation.

Selling expenses   Expenditures (such as advertising) that the firm incurs to induce consumers to purchase more of its product.

Separation theorem   The independence of the optimum investment decision from the individual's preferences.

Sherman Antitrust Act   Prohibits all contracts and combinations in restraint of trade and all attempts to monopolize the market.

Shortage   The excess quantity demanded of a commodity at lower than equilibrium prices.

Short run   The time period when at least one input is fixed.

Shutdown point   The output level at which price equals average variable cost and losses equal total fixed costs, whether the firm produces or not. Also, the lowest point on the AVC curve at which $MC = AVC$.

Snob effect   The situation where some people demand a smaller quantity of a commodity as more people consume it in order to be different and exclusive.

Social costs   The costs incurred by society as a whole.

Specialization   The use of labor and other resources to perform those tasks in which each resource is most efficient.

Speculator   An individual or firm that buys a commodity or currency when it expects the price to rise, and sells the commodity or currency if it expects the price to fall.

Spot market   The market where spot transactions take place.

Spot price or rate The price or rate of a commodity or currency in the spot market.

Spot transaction The purchase and sale of a commodity or currency for immediate delivery and payment.

Stackelberg model The extension of the Cournot model in which one duopolist knows how the other behaves and, by using this information, earns higher profits than in the Cournot solution at the expense of the other duopolist.

Standard deviation (sd) A measure of the dispersion of possible outcomes from the expected value of a distribution; the square root of the variance.

Strategies The potential choices that can be made by the players (firms) in the theory of games.

Strategic move A player's strategy of constraining his or her own behavior to make a threat credible so as to gain a competitive advantage.

Strategic trade policy The attempt by a nation to create a comparative advantage in some high-tech field through temporary trade protection, subsidies, tax benefits, and cooperative government-industry programs.

Substitutes Two commodities are substitutes if an increase in the price of one of them leads to more of the other being purchased.

Substitution effect The increase in the quantity demanded of a good when its price falls, resulting only from the relative price decline and independent of the change in real income.

Surplus The excess quantity supplied of a commodity at higher than equilibrium prices.

Technical externalities Economies of scale.

Technological progress Refers to the development of new and better production techniques to make a given, improved, or an entirely new product.

Theory of contestable markets The theory that postulates that even if an industry has only one or a few firms, it would still operate as if it were perfectly competitive if entry into the industry is absolutely free and if exit is entirely costless.

Theory of public choice The study of how government decisions are made and implemented.

Theory of revealed preference The theory that postulates that a consumer's indifference curve can be derived from the consumer's market behavior and without any need to inquire directly into his or her preferences.

Third degree price discrimination Charging a higher price for a commodity in the market with the less elastic demand in such a way as to equalize the MR of the last unit of the commodity sold in the two markets.

Tit-for-tat The best strategy in repeated prisoners' dilemma games which postulates "do to your opponent what he or she has just done to you."

Time budget line A line showing the various combinations of two goods that an individual can obtain with his or her available time.

Total costs (TC) TFC plus TVC.

Total fixed costs (TFC) The total obligations of the firm per time period for all fixed inputs.

Total product (TP) Total output.

Total revenue (TR) The price of the commodity times the quantity sold of the commodity.

Total utility (TU) The aggregate amount of satisfaction received from consuming various amounts of a good or baskets of goods.

Total variable costs (TVC) The total obligations of the firm per time period for all the variable inputs the firm uses.

Transfer pricing The determination of the price of intermediate products sold by one semiautonomous division of the firm to another semiautonomous division of the same enterprise.

Two-part tariff The pricing practice whereby a monopolist maximizes its total profits by charging a usage fee or price equal to its marginal cost and an initial or membership fee equal to the entire consumer surplus.

Tying   The requirement that a consumer who buys or leases a monopolist's product also puchase another product needed in the use of the first.

Uncertainty   The situation where there is more than one possible outcome to a decision and the probability of each specific outcome is not known or even meaningful.

Unemployment gap   The excess in the quantity supplied over the quantity demanded of labor at above equilibrium wages.

Util   The arbitrary unit of measure of utility.

Utility   The ability of a good to satisfy a want.

Utility-possibilities frontier   Shows the various combinations of utilities received by two individuals at which the economy (composed of the two individuals) is in general equilibrium or Pareto optimum in exchange.

Value of the marginal product (*VMP*)   The marginal (physical) product of the input (*MP*) multiplied by the commodity price (*P*).

Variability risk   The possibility that the return on an investment, such as on a stock, may vary considerably above or below the average.

Variable inputs   The resources that can be varied easily and on short notice during the time period under consideration.

Veblen effect   The situation in which some people purchase more of certain commodities the more expensive they are; also called conspicuous consumption.

Virtual corporation   A temporary network of independent companies coming together with each contributing its core technology to quickly take advantage of fast-changing opportunities.

Voluntary export restraints (*VER*)   The situation in which an importing country induces another nation to reduce its exports of a commodity "voluntarily" under the threat of higher all-around trade restrictions.

Water–diamond paradox   The question of why water, which is essential to life, is so cheap while diamonds, which are not essential, are so expensive.

Wealth   The individual's income this year plus the present value of future income.

Welfare economics   Examines the conditions for economic efficiency in the production of output and in the exchange of commodities, and for equity in the distribution of income.

What to produce   Which goods and services a society chooses to produce and in what quantities.

Winner's curse   The overbidding or the paying of a price higher than the true (but unknown) value of an asset by the highest bidder at an auction.

Zero-sum game   A game where the gains of one player equal the losses of the other (so that total gains plus total losses sum to zero).

NAME INDEX

SUBJECT INDEX

The Visualization Toolkit

An Object-Oriented Approach to 3D Graphics

The Visualization Toolkit

2nd Edition

Will Schroeder
Ken Martin
Bill Lorensen

with special contributors:
Lisa Sobierajski Avila, Rick Avila, C. Charles Law

To join a Prentice Hall PTR internet mailing list, point to
http://www.prenhall.com/mail_lists/

Prentice Hall PTR
Upper Saddle River, NJ 07458
http://www.prenhall.com

ISBN 0-13-954694-4

90000

9 780139 546945

Library of Congress Cataloging-in-Publication Data

Schroeder, Will.
  The visualization toolkit / William Schroeder, Kenneth Martin, William Lorensen. -- 2nd ed.
     p.   cm.
  Includes bibliographical references and index.
  ISBN 0-13-954694-4
  1. Object-oriented programming (Computer science) 2. Computer graphics. I. Martin,
Kenneth W. (Kenneth William). 1952-   II. Lorensen, Bill.   Title.
QA76.64.S36   1997
003',3666--DC21   97-40620
                                                                CIP

Editorial/Production Supervision: *Kathleen M. Caren*
Acquisitions Editor: *Mary Franz*
Cover Design Director: *Jerry Votta*
Cover Design: *Design Source*
Manufacturing Manager: *Alexis R. Heydt*
Marketing Manager: *Miles Williams*
Editorial Assistant: *Noreen Regina*

© 1998 Prentice Hall PTR
Prentice-Hall, Inc.
A Simon & Schuster Company
Upper Saddle River, New Jersey 07458

Prentice Hall books are widely used by corporations and government agencies
for training, marketing, and resale.
The publisher offers discounts on this book when ordered in bulk quantities.
For more information, contact: Corporate Sales Department, Phone: 800-382-3419;
FAX: 201-236-7141; E-mail: corpsales@prenhall.com
Or write: Corp. Sales Dept., Prentice Hall PTR, 1 Lake Street, Upper Saddle River, NJ   07458

Printed in the United States of America
10 9 8 7 6 5 4 3 2

ISBN 0-13-954694-4

Prentice-Hall International (UK) Limited, *London*
Prentice-Hall of Australia Pty. Limited, *Sydney*
Prentice-Hall Canada Inc., *Toronto*
Prentice-Hall Hispanoamericana, S.A., *Mexico*
Prentice-Hall of India Private Limited, *New Delhi*
Prentice-Hall of Japan, Inc., *Tokyo*
Simon & Schuster Asia Pte. Ltd., *Singapore*
Editora Prentice-Hall do Brasil, Ltda., *Rio de Janeiro*

To Susan and Z,
— Will

To Michelle and my parents,
— Ken

To Terri,
— Bill

To Linette and my parents,
— Lisa

To my parents,
— Rick

To Mia and Preston,
— Charles

Contents

Chapter 5   Basic Data Representation   115

Preface

Visualization is a great field to work in these days. Advances in computer hardware and software have brought this technology into the reach of nearly every computer system. Even the ubiquitous personal computer now offers specialized 3D graphics hardware. And with the release of Windows95 and OpenGL, there is an API for 3D graphics as well.

We view visualization and visual computing as nothing less than a new form of communication. All of us have long known the power of images to convey information, ideas, and feelings. Recent trends have brought us 2D images and graphics as evidenced by the variety of graphical user interfaces and business plotting software. But 3D images have been used sparingly, and often by specialists using specialized systems. Now this is changing. We believe we are entering a new era where 3D images, visualizations, and animations will begin to extend, and in some cases, replace the current communication paradigm based on words, mathematical symbols, and 2D images. Our hope is that along the way the human imagination will be freed like never before.

This text and companion software offers one view of visualization. The field is broad, including elements of computer graphics, imaging, computer science, computational geometry, numerical analysis, statistical methods, data analysis, and studies in human perception. We certainly do not pretend to cover the field in its entirety. However, we feel that this text does offer you a great opportunity to learn about the fundamentals of visualization. Not only can you learn from the written word and companion images, but the included software will allow you to *practice* visualization. You can start by using the sample data we have provided here, and then move on to your own data and applications. We believe that you will soon appreciate visualization as much as we do.

In this, the second edition of *Visualization Toolkit* and **vtk** version 2.0, we have added several new features since the first edition. Volume rendering is now fully supported, including the ability to combine opaque surface graphics with volumes. We have added an extensive image processing pipeline that integrates conventional 3D visualization and graphics with imaging. Besides several new filters such as clipping, smoothing, 2D/3D Delaunay triangulation, and a new decimation algorithm, we have added several readers and writers, and better support net-based tools such as Java and VRML. Finally, our PC support has greatly improved, including a nice tool for managing the compile process.

The additions of these features necessitated the addition of three special contributors to the text: Lisa Sobierajski Avila, Rick Avila, and C. Charles Law. Rick and Lisa worked hard to create an object-oriented design for volume rendering, and to insure that the design and software is fully compatible with the surface-based rendering system. Charles is the principle architect and implementor for the imaging pipeline. We are proud of the streaming and caching capability of the architecture: It allows us to handle large data sets despite limited memory resources.

Especially satisfying has been the response from users of the text and software. Not only have we received a warm welcome from these wonderful people, but many of them have contributed code, bug fixes, data, and ideas that greatly improved the system. In fact, it would be best to categorize these people as co-developers rather than users of the system. We would like to encourage anyone else who is interested in sharing their ideas, code, or data to contact the **vtk** user community, or one of the authors. We would very much welcome any contributions you have to make. Contact us at http://www.kitware.com.

Acknowledgments

During the creation of the *Visualization Toolkit* we were fortunate to have the help of many people. Without their aid this book and the associated educational software might never have existed. Their contributions included performing book reviews, discussing software ideas, creating a supportive environment, and providing key suggestions for some of our algorithms and software implementations.

We would like to first thank our management at the General Electric Corporate R&D Center who allowed us to pursue this project and utilize company facilities: Peter Meenan, Manager of the Computer Graphics and Systems Program, and Kirby Vosburgh, Manager of the Electronic Systems Laboratory. We would also like to thank management at GE Medical Systems who worked with us on the public versus proprietary issues. This includes John Lalonde, John Heinen, and Steve Roehm.

We thank our co-workers at the R&D Center who have all been supportive: Matt Turek, for proof reading much of the second edition; also Majeid Alyassin, Russell Blue, Jeanette Bruno, Shane Chang, Nelson Corby, Rich Hammond, Margaret Kelliher, Tim Kelliher, Joyce Langan, Paul Miller, Chris Nafis, Bob Tatar, Chris Volpe, Boris Yamrom, Bill Hoffman, Harvey Cline and Siegwalt Ludke. We thank former co-workers Skip Montanaro (who created a FAQ for us), Dan McLachlan and Michelle Barry. We'd also like to thank our friends and co-workers at GE Medical Systems: Ted Hudacko (who is managing the **vtk** users mailing list), Darin Okerlund, and John Skinner. Many ideas, helpful hints, and suggestions to improve the system came from this delightful group of people.

Many of the bug fixes and improvements found in the second edition came from talented people from around the world. Some of these people are acknowledged in the software and elsewhere in the text, but most of them have contributed their time, knowledge, code, and data without regard for recognition and acknowledgment. It is this exchange of ideas and information with people like this that makes the *Visualization Toolkit* such a fun and exciting project to work on. Thank you very much.

A special thanks to the software and text reviewers who spent their own time to track down some nasty bugs, provide examples, and offer suggestions and improvements. Thank you Tom Citriniti, Mark Miller, George Petras, Hansong Zhang, Penny Rheingans, Paul Hinker, Richard Ellson, and Roger Crawfis. We'd also like to mention that Tom Citriniti at RPI, and Penny Rheingans at the University of Mississippi were the first faculty members to teach from early versions of this text. Thank you Penny and Tom for your feedback and extra effort.

We'd especially like to thank Mary Franz, Noreen Regina, Kathleen Caren, Ann Sullivan, and the rest of the folks at Prentice Hall who helped turn our dreams into reality. These are some of the most enthusiastic people we've ever worked with, an invaluable quality when it seems as if things will never end. We'd also like to thank John Nelson at Corporate Graphics Resources who helped us format and arrange the color plates.

Most importantly we would like to thank our friends and loved ones who supported us patiently during this project. We know that you shouldered extra load for us. You certainly saw a lot less of us! But we're happy to say that we're back. Thank you.

Introduction

Visualization — "2: the act or process of interpreting in visual terms or of putting into visual form," *Webster's Ninth New Collegiate Dictionary.*

1.1 What Is Visualization?

Visualization is a part of our everyday life. From weather maps to the exciting computer graphics of the entertainment industry, examples of visualization abound. But what is visualization? Informally, visualization is the transformation of data or information into pictures. Visualization engages the primary human sensory apparatus, *vision,* as well as the processing power of the human mind. The result is a simple and effective medium for communicating complex and/or voluminous information.

Terminology

Different terminology is used to describe visualization. *Scientific visualization* is the formal name given to the field in computer science that encompasses user interface, data representation and processing algorithms, visual representations, and other sensory presentation such as sound or touch [McCormick87]. The term *data visualization* is another phrase used to describe visualization. Data visualization is generally interpreted to be more general than scientific visualization, since it implies treatment of data sources beyond the sciences and engineering. Such data sources include financial, marketing, or business data. In addition, the term data visualization is broad enough to include application of statistical methods and other standard data analysis techniques [Rosenblum94]. Another recently emerging term is *information visualization*. This field endeavors to visualize abstract information such as hyper-text documents on the World Wide Web, directory/file structures on a computer, or abstract data structures [InfoVis95]. A major challenge facing information visualization researchers is to develop coordinate systems, transformation methods, or structures that meaningfully organize and represent data.

In this text we use the term data visualization instead of the more specific terms scientific visualization or information visualization. We feel that scientific visualization is too narrow a description of the field, since visualization techniques have moved beyond the scientific domain and into areas of business, social science, demographics, and information management in general. We also feel that the term data visualization is broad enough to encompass the term information visualization.

Examples of Visualization

Perhaps the best definition of visualization is offered by example. In many cases visualization is influencing peoples' lives and performing feats that a few years ago would have been unimaginable. A prime example of this is its application to modern medicine.

Computer imaging techniques have become an important diagnostic tool in the practice of modern medicine. These include techniques such as X-ray *Computed Tomography* (CT) and *Magnetic Resonance Imaging* (MRI). These techniques use a sampling or data acquisition process to capture information about the internal anatomy of a living patient. This information is in the form of *slice-planes* or cross-sectional images of a patient, similar to conventional photographic X-rays. CT imaging uses many pencil thin X-rays to acquire the data, while MRI combines large magnetic fields with pulsed radio waves. Sophisticated mathematical techniques are used to reconstruct the slice-planes. Typically, many such closely spaced slices are gathered together into a *volume* of data to complete the study.

As acquired from the imaging system, a slice is a series of numbers representing the attenuation of X-rays (CT) or the relaxation of nuclear spin magnetization (MRI) [Krestel90]. On any given slice these numbers are arranged in a matrix, or regular array. The amount of data is large, so large that it is not possible to understand the data in its raw form. However, by assigning to these numbers a gray scale value, and then displaying the data on a computer screen, structure emerges. This structure results from the interaction of the human visual system with the spatial organization of the data and the gray-scale values we have chosen. What the computer represents as a series of numbers, we see as a cross section through the human body: skin, bone, and muscle. Even more impressive results are possible when we extend these techniques into three dimensions. Image slices can be gathered into volumes and the volumes can be processed to reveal complete anatomical structures. Using modern techniques, we can view the entire brain, skeletal system, and vascular system on a living patient without interventional surgery. Such capability has revolutionized modern medical diagnostics, and will increase in importance as imaging and visualization technology matures.

Another everyday application of visualization is in the entertainment industry. Movie and television producers routinely use computer graphics and visualization to create entire worlds that we could never visit in our physical bodies. In these cases we are visualizing other worlds as we imagine them, or past worlds we suppose existed. It's hard to watch the movies such as *Jurassic Park* and *Toy Story* and not gain a deeper appreciation for the awesome Tyrannosaurus Rex, or to be charmed by *Toy Story*'s heroic Buzz Lightyear.

Morphing is another popular visualization technique widely used in the entertainment industry. Morphing is a smooth blending of one object into another. One common application is to morph between two faces. Morphing has also been used effectively to illustrate car design changes from one year to the next. While this may seem like an esoteric application, visualization techniques are used routinely to present the daily weather report. The use of isovalue, or contour, lines to display areas of constant temperature, rainfall, and barometric pressure has become a standard tool in the daily weather report.

Many early uses of visualization were in the engineering and scientific community. From its inception the computer has been used as a tool to simulate physical processes such as ballistic trajectories, fluid flow, and structural mechanics. As the size of the computer simulations grew, it became necessary to transform the resulting calculations into pictures. The amount of data overwhelmed the ability of the human to assimilate and understand it. In fact, pictures were so important that early visualizations were created by manually plotting data. Today, we can take advantage of advances in computer graphics and computer hardware. But, whatever the technology, the application of visualization is the same: to display the results of simulations, experiments, measured data, and fantasy; and to use these pictures to communicate, understand, and entertain.

1.2 Why Visualize?

Visualization is a necessary tool to make sense of the flood of information in today's world of computers. Satellites, supercomputers, laser digitizing systems, and digital data acquisition systems acquire, generate, and transmit data at prodigious rates. The Earth-Orbiting Satellite (EOS) transmits terabytes of data every day. Laser scanning systems generate over 500,000 points in a 15 second scan [Waters91]. Supercomputers model weather patterns over the entire earth [Chen93]. In the first four months of 1995, the New York Stock Exchange processed, on average, 333 million transactions per day [NYTimes]. Without visualization, most of this data would sit unseen on computer disks and tapes. Visualization offers some hope that we can extract the important information hidden within the data.

There is another important element to visualization: It takes advantage of the natural abilities of the human vision system. Our vision system is a complex and powerful part of our bodies. We use it and rely on it in almost everything we do. Given the environment in which our ancestors lived, it is not surprising that certain senses developed to help them survive. As we described earlier in the example of a 2D MRI scan, visual representations are easier to work with. Not only do we have strong 2D visual abilities, but also we are adept at integrating different viewpoints and other visual clues into a mental image of a 3D object or plot. This leads to interactive visualization, where we can manipulate our viewpoint. Rotating about the object helps to achieve a better understanding. Likewise, we have a talent for recognizing temporal changes in an image. Given an animation consisting of hundreds of frames, we have an uncanny ability to recognize trends and spot areas of rapid change.

With the introduction of computers and the ability to generate enormous amounts of data, visualization offers the technology to make the best use of our highly developed visual senses. Certainly other technologies such as statistical analysis, artificial intelligence, mathematical filtering, and sampling theory will play a role in large-scale data processing. However, because visualization directly engages the vision system and human brain, it remains an unequaled technology for understanding and communicating data.

Visualization offers significant financial advantages as well. In today's competitive markets, computer simulation teamed with visualization can reduce product cost and improve time to market. A large cost of product design has been the expense and time required to create and test design prototypes. Current design methods strive to eliminate these physical prototypes, and replace them with digital equivalents. This digital prototyping requires the ability to create and manipulate product geometry, simulate the design under a variety of operating conditions, develop manufacturing techniques, demonstrate product maintenance and service procedures, and even train operators on the proper use of the product before it is built. Visualization plays a role in each case. Already CAD systems are used routinely to model product geometry and design manufacturing procedures. Visualization enables us to view the geometry, and see special characteristics such as surface curvature. For instance, analysis techniques such as finite element, finite difference, and boundary element techniques are used to simulate product performance; and visualization is used to view the results. Recently, human ergonomics and anthropometry are being analyzed using computer techniques in combination with visualization [MDHMS]. Three-dimensional graphics and visualization are being used to create training sequences. Often these are incorporated into a hypertext document or World Wide Web (WWW) pages. Another practical use of graphics and visualization has been in-flight simulators. This has been shown to be a significant cost-savings as compared to flying real airplanes and is an effective training method.

1.3 Imaging, Computer Graphics, and Visualization

There is confusion surrounding the difference between imaging, computer graphics, and visualization. We offer these definitions.

- *Imaging*, or image processing, is the study of 2D pictures, or images. This includes techniques to transform (e.g., rotate, scale, shear), extract information from, analyze, and enhance images.

- *Computer graphics* is the process of creating images using a computer. This includes both 2D paint-and-draw techniques as well as more sophisticated 3D drawing (or rendering) techniques.

- *Visualization* is the process of exploring, transforming, and viewing data as images (or other sensory forms) to gain understanding and insight into the data.

Based on these definitions we see that there is overlap between these fields. The output of computer graphics is an image, while the output of visualization is often produced using computer graphics. Sometimes visualization data is in the form of an image, or we wish to visualize object geometry using realistic rendering techniques from computer graphics.

Generally speaking we distinguish visualization from computer graphics and image processing in three ways.

1. The dimensionality of data is three dimensions or greater. Many well-known methods are available for data of two dimensions or less; visualization serves best when applied to data of higher dimension.

2. Visualization concerns itself with data transformation. That is, information is repeatedly created and modified to enhance the meaning of the data.

3. Visualization is naturally interactive, including the human directly in the process of creating, transforming, and viewing data.

Another perspective is that visualization is an activity that encompasses the process of exploring and understanding data. This includes both imaging and computer graphics as well as data processing and filtering, user interface methodology, computational techniques, and software design. Figure 1–1 depicts this process.

As this figure illustrates we see that the visualization process focuses on data. In the first step data is acquired from some source. Next, the data is transformed by various methods, and then mapped to a form appropriate for presentation to the user. Finally, the data is rendered or displayed, completing the process. Often, the process repeats as the data is better understood or new models are developed. Sometimes the results of the visualization can directly control the generation of the data. This is often referred to as *analysis steering*. Analysis steering is an important goal of visualization because it enhances the interactivity of the overall process.

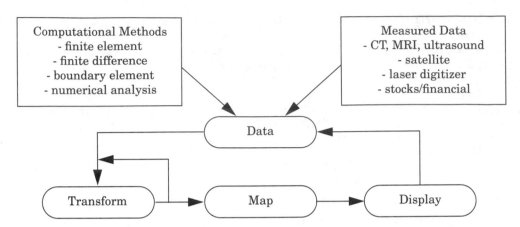

Figure 1–1 The visualization process. Data from various sources is repeatedly transformed to extract, derive, and enhance information. The resulting data is mapped to a graphics system for display.

1.4 Origins of Data Visualization

The origin of visualization as a formal discipline dates to the 1987 NSF report *Visualization in Scientific Computing* [McCormick87]. That report coined the term *scientific visualization*. Since then the field has grown rapidly with major conferences, such as IEEE Visualization, becoming well established. Many large computer graphics conferences, for example ACM SIGGRAPH, devote large portions of their program to visualization technology.

Of course, data visualization technology had existed for many years before the 1987 report referenced [Tufte83]. The first practitioners recognized the value of presenting data as images. Early pictorial data representations were created during the eighteenth century with the arrival of statistical graphics. It was only with the arrival of the digital computer and the development of the field of computer graphics, that visualization became a practicable discipline.

The future of data visualization and graphics appears to be explosive. Just a few decades ago, the field of data visualization did not exist and computer graphics was viewed as an offshoot of the more formal discipline of computer science. As techniques were created and computer power increased, engineers, scientists, and other researchers began to use graphics to understand and communicate data. At the same time, user interface tools were being developed. These forces have now converged to the point where we expect computers to adapt to humans rather than the other way around. As such, computer graphics and data visualization serve as the window into the computer, and more importantly, into the data that computers manipulate. Now, with the visualization window, we can extract information from data and analyze, understand, and manage more complex systems than ever before.

Dr. Fred Brooks, Kenan Professor of Computer Science at the University of North Carolina at Chapel Hill and recipient of the John von Neumann Medal of the IEEE, puts it another way. At the award presentation at the ACM SIG-GRAPH '94, Dr. Brooks stated that computer graphics and visualization offer "intelligence amplification" (IA) as compared to artificial intelligence (AI). Besides the deeper philosophical issues surrounding this issue (e.g., human before computer), it is a pragmatic observation. While the long-term goal of AI has been to develop computer systems that could replace humans in certain applications, the lack of real progress in this area has lead some researchers to view the role of computers as amplifiers and assistants to humans. In this view, computer graphics and visualization play a significant role, since arguably the most effective human/computer interface is visual. Recent gains in computer power and memory are only accelerating this trend, since it is the interface between the human and the computer that often is the obstacle to the effective application of the computer.

1.5 Purpose of This Book

There currently exist texts that define and describe data visualization, many of them using case studies to illustrate techniques and typical applications. Some provide high-level descriptions of algorithms or visualization system architectures. Detailed descriptions are left to academic journals or conference proceedings. What these texts lack is a way to *practice* visualization. Our aim in this text is to go beyond descriptions and provide tools to learn about and apply visualization to your own application area. In short, the purpose of the book is fourfold.

1. Describe visualization algorithms and architectures in detail.

2. Demonstrate the application of data visualization to a broad selection of case studies.

3. Provide a working architecture and software design for application of data visualization to real-world problems.

4. Provide effective software tools packaged in a C++ class library. We also provide a prototyping library in the interpreted language Tcl.

Taken together, we refer to the text and software as the *Visualization Toolkit*, or **vtk** for short. Our hope is that you can use the text to learn about the fundamental concepts of visualization, and then adapt the computer code to your own applications and data.

1.6 What This Book Is Not

The purpose of this book is not to provide a rigorous academic treatise on data visualization. Nor do we intend to include an exhaustive survey of visualization technology. Our goal is to bridge the formal discipline of data visualization with practical application, and to provide a solid technical overview of this emerging technology. In many cases we refer you to the included software to understand implementation details. You may also wish to refer to the appropriate references for further information.

1.7 Intended Audience

Our primary audience is computer users who create, analyze, quantify, and/or process data. We assume a minimal level of programming skill. If you can write simple computer code to import data and know how to run a computer program, you can practice data visualization with the software accompanying this book.

As we wrote this book we also had in mind educators and students of introductory computer graphics and visualization courses. In more advanced courses this text may not be rigorous enough to serve as asole reference. In these instances, this book will serve well as a companion text, and the software is well suited as a foundation for programming projects and class exercises.

Educators and students in other disciplines may also find the text and software to be valuable tools for presenting results. Courses in numerical analysis, computer science, business simulation, chemistry, dynamic systems, and engineering simulations, to name a few, often require large-scale programming projects that create large amounts of data. The software tools provided here are easy to learn and readily adapted to different data sources. Students can incorporate this software into their work to display and analyze their results.

1.8 How to Use This Book

There are a number of approaches you can take to make effective use of this book. The particular approach depends on your skill level and goals. Three likely paths are as follows:

> *Novice.* You're a novice if you lack basic knowledge of graphics, visualization, or object-oriented principles. Start by reading Chapter 2 if you are unfamiliar with object-oriented principles, Chapter 3 if you are unfamiliar with computer graphics, and Chapter 4 if you are unfamiliar with visualization. Continue by reading the case studies in Chapter 13. You can then move on to the CD-ROM and try out some programming examples. Leave the more detailed treatment of algorithms and data representation until you are familiar with the basics and plan to develop your own applications.

Hacker. You're a hacker if you are comfortable writing your own code and editing other's. Review the examples in Chapters 3, 4, and 13. Read the "Software Conventions" in Appendix A to get an understanding of how we have organized the software. Then retrieve the examples from the CD-ROM and start practicing.

Researcher/Educator. You're a researcher if you develop computer graphics and/or visualization algorithms or if you are actively involved in using and evaluating such systems. You're an educator if you cover aspects of computer graphics and/or visualization within your courses. Start by reading Chapters 2, 3, and 4. Select appropriate algorithms from the text and examine the associated source code. If you wish to extend the system, you will need to read the "Software Conventions" and "Development Guide" in Appendix A.

1.9 Software Considerations

In writing this book we have attempted to strike a balance between practice and theory. We did not want the book to become a user manual, yet we did want a strong correspondence between algorithmic presentation and software implementation. As a result, we have adopted the following approach:

Application versus Design. The book's focus is the application of visualization techniques to real-world problems. We devote less attention to software design issues. Some of these important design issues include: memory management, deriving new classes, shallow versus deep object copy, single versus multiple inheritance, and interfaces to other graphics libraries. While Appendix A covers some of these design issues in detail, we did not want to distract you from the focus of this book.

Theory versus Implementation. Whenever possible, we separate the theory of data visualization from our implementation of it. We felt that the book would serve best as a reference tool if the theory sections were independent of software issues and terminology. Toward the end of each chapter there are separate implementation or example sections that are implementation specific. Earlier sections are implementation free.

Documentation. Appendix A contains documentation considered essential to understanding the software architecture. This includes object diagrams and condensed object descriptions. More extensive documentation of object methods and data members is embedded in the software and as help documentation and manual pages on the CD-ROM. You should also check out the reference pages in the latter half of this book. Appendix A also describes conventions used during implementation of the software.

We use a number of conventions in this text. Computer code including variable, class, and method names is denoted with a typewriter font. For example,

`Foo`, `vtkObject`, and `Execute()` are examples of a variable, class name, and method. To avoid conflict with other C++ class libraries, all class names in **vtk** begin with the "vtk" prefix. Methods are differentiated from variables with the addition of the "()" postfix. (Other conventions are listed in Appendix A.)

All images in this text have been created using the *Visualization Toolkit* software and data on the CD-ROM. In addition, every image has source code (sometimes in C++ and sometimes a Tcl script). We decided against using images from other researchers because we wanted you to be able to practice visualization with every example we present. Each computer generated image indicates the originating file. Files ending in .cxx are C++ code, files ending in .tcl are Tcl scripts. (See Chapter 11 for more information on Tcl.) Hopefully these examples can serve as a starting point for you to create your own applications.

1.10 Chapter-by-Chapter Overview

Chapter 2: Object-Oriented Design

This chapter discusses some of the problems with developing large and/or complex software systems and describes how object-oriented design addresses many of these problems. This chapter defines the key terms used in object-oriented modelling and design and works through a real-world example. The chapter concludes with a brief look at some object-oriented languages and some of the issues associated with object-oriented visualization.

Chapter 3: Computer Graphics Primer

Computer graphics is the means by which our visualizations are created. This chapter covers the fundamental concepts of computer graphics from an application viewpoint. Common graphical entities such as cameras, lights, and geometric primitives are described along with some of the underlying physical equations that govern lighting and image generation. Issues related to currently available graphics hardware are presented, as they affect how and what we choose to render.

Chapter 4: The Visualization Pipeline

This chapter explains our methodology for transforming raw data into a meaningful representation that can than be rendered by the graphics system. We introduce the notion of a visualization pipeline, which is similar to a data flow diagram from software engineering. The differences between process objects and data objects are covered, as well as how we resolved issues between performance and memory usage. We explain the advantages to a pipeline network topology regarding execution ordering, result caching, and reference counting.

Chapter 5: Basic Data Representation

There are many types of data produced by the variety of fields that apply visualization. This chapter describes the data objects that we use to represent and access such data. A flexible design is introduced where the programmer can interact with most any type of data using one consistent interface. The three high level components of data (structure, cells, and data attributes) are introduced, and their specific subclasses and components are discussed.

Chapter 6: Fundamental Algorithms

Where the preceding chapter deals with data objects, this one introduces process objects. These objects encompass the algorithms that transform and manipulate data. This chapter looks at commonly used techniques for isocontour extraction, scalar generation, color mapping, and vector field display, among others. The emphasis of this chapter is to provide the reader with a basic understanding of the more common and important visualization algorithms.

Chapter 7: Advanced Computer Graphics

This chapter covers advanced topics in computer graphics. The chapter begins by introducing transparency and texture mapping, two topics important to the main thrust of the chapter: volume rendering. Volume rendering is a powerful technique to see inside of 3D objects, and is used to visualize volumetric data. We conclude the chapter with other advanced topics such as stereoscopic rendering and special camera effects.

Chapter 8: Advanced Data Representation

Part of the function of a data object is to store the data. The first chapter on data representation discusses this aspect of data objects. This chapter focuses on basic geometric and topological access methods, and computational operations implemented by the various data objects. The chapter covers such methods as coordinate transformations for data sets, interpolation functions, derivative calculations, topological adjacency operations, and geometric operations such as line intersection and searching.

Chapter 9: Advanced Algorithms

This chapter is a continuation of *Fundamental Algorithms* and covers algorithms that are either more complex or less widely used. Scalar algorithms such as dividing cubes are covered along with vector algorithms such as stream ribbons. A large collection of modelling algorithms is discussed, including triangle strip generation, polygon decimation, feature extraction, and implicit modelling. We conclude with a look at some visualization algorithms that utilize texture mapping.

Chapter 10: Image Processing

While 3D graphics and visualization is the focus of the book, image processing is an important tool for pre-processing and manipulating data. In this chapter we focus on several important image processing algorithms, as well as describe how we use a streaming data representation to process large datasets.

Chapter 11: Interpreters and Tcl/Tk

Most of this book assumes that you will be doing development in C++, a compiled language. There are some advantages and disadvantages to using an interpreted language for data visualization. This chapter discusses some of these trade-offs and describes an implementation of **vtk** that is integrated with the Tcl interpreted language. The basic syntax of Tcl is described along with some sample programs.

Chapter 12: Visualization on the Web

The Web is one of the best places to share your visualizations. In this chapter we show you how to write Java-based visualization applications, and how to create VRML (Virtual Reality Modelling Language) data files for inclusion in your own Web content.

Chapter 13: Applications

In this chapter we tie the previous chapters together by working through a series of case studies from a variety of application areas. For each case, we briefly describe the application and what information we expect to obtain through the use of visualization. Then, we walk through the design and resulting source code to demonstrate the use of the tools described earlier in the text.

Appendices

Two appendices serve as a valuable resource if you are creating computer code using the *Visualization Toolkit* software. Appendix A gives an overview of coding conventions and techniques, as well as tips and suggestions on how to create classes and read and write data files. Appendix B describes the contents of the CD-ROM, and offers suggestions on retrieving the source code, data, and additional reference information.

1.11 Legal Considerations

We make no warranties, expressly or implied, that the computer code contained in this text is free of error or will meet your requirements for any particular application. Do not use this code in any application where coding errors could result in injury to a person or loss of property. If you do use the code in this way, it is at your own risk. The authors and publisher disclaim all liability for direct or consequential damages resulting from your use of this code.

The computer code contained in this text is copyrighted. We grant permission for you to use, copy, and distribute this software for any purpose. However, you may not modify and then redistribute the software. Some of the algorithms presented here are implementations of patented software. If you plan to use this software for commercial purposes, please insure that applicable patent laws are observed. See the README file in the patented directory for more information.

Some of the data on the CD-ROM may be freely distributed or used (with appropriate acknowledgment). Refer to the local README files or other documentation for details.

Several registered trademarks are used in this text. UNIX is a trademark of UNIX System Laboratories. Sun Workstation and XGL are trademarks of Sun Microsystems, Inc. Microsoft, MS, MS-DOS, and Windows are trademarks of Microsoft Corporation. The X Window System is a trademark of the Massachusetts Institute of Technology. Starbase and HP are trademarks of Hewlett-Packard Inc. Silicon Graphics and OpenGL, are trademarks of Silicon Graphics, Inc. Macintosh is a trademark of Apple Computer. RenderMan is a trademark of Pixar.

1.12 Bibliographic Notes

A number of visualization texts are available. The first six texts listed in the reference section are good general references ([Nielson90], [Patrikalakis91], [Brodlie92], [Wolff93], [Rosenblum94], and [Gallagher95]). Gallagher [Gallagher95] is particularly valuable if you are from a computational background. Wolff and Yaeger [Wolff93] contains many beautiful images and is oriented towards Apple Macintosh users. The text includes a CD-ROM with images and software.

You may also wish to learn more about computer graphics and imaging. Foley and van Dam [FoleyVanDam90] is the basic reference for computer graphics. Another recommended text is [BurgerGillies89]. Suggested reference books on computer imaging are [Pavlidis82] and [Wolberg90].

Two texts by Tufte [Tufte83] [Tufte90] are particularly impressive. Not only are the graphics superbly done, but the fundamental philosophy of data visualization is articulated. He also describes the essence of good and bad visualization techniques.

Another interesting text is available from Siemens, a large company offering medical imaging systems [Krestel90]. This text describes the basic concepts of imaging technology, including MRI and CT. This text is only for those users with a strong mathematical background. A less mathematical overview of MRI is available from [SmithRanallo89].

1.13 References

[Brodlie92]
  K. W. Brodlie et al. *Scientific Visualization Techniques and Applications.*
  Springer-Verlag, Berlin, 1992.

[BurgerGillies89]
  P. Burger and D. Gillies. *Interactive Computer Graphics Functional, Procedural and Device-Level Methods.* Addison-Wesley Publishing Company, Reading, MA, 1989.

[Chen93]
  P. C. Chen. "A Climate Simulation Case Study." In *Proceedings of Visualization '93.* pp. 397–401, IEEE Computer Society Press, Los Alamitos, CA, 1993.

[FoleyVanDam90]
  J. D. Foley, A. van Dam, S. K. Feiner, and J. F. Hughes. *Computer Graphics Principles and Practice (2d Ed).* Addison-Wesley, Reading, MA, 1990.

[Gallagher95]
  R. S. Gallagher (ed). *Computer Visualization Graphics Techniques for Scientific and Engineering Analysis.* CRC Press, Boca Raton, FL, 1995.

[Krestel90]
  E. Krestel (ed). *Imaging Systems for Medical Diagnostics.* Siemens-Aktienges, Munich, 1990.

[InfoVis95]
  The First Information Visualization Symposium. IEEE Computer Society Press, Los Alamitos, CA, 1995.

[McCormick87]
  B. H. McCormick, T. A. DeFanti, and M. D. Brown. "Visualization in Scientific Computing." Report of the NSF Advisory Panel on Graphics, Image Processing and Workstations, 1987.

[MDHMS]
  McDonnell Douglas Human Modeling System Reference Manual. Report MDC 93K0281. McDonnell Douglas Corporation, Human Factors Technology, Version 2.1, July 1993.

[Nielson90]
  G. M. Nielson and B. Shriver (eds). *Visualization in Scientific Computing.* IEEE Computer Society Press, Los Alamitos, CA, 1990.

[NYTimes]
  The New York Times Business Day, Tuesday, May 2, 1995.

[Patrikalakis91]
  N. M. Patrikalakis (ed). *Scientific Visualization of Physical Phenomena.* Springer-Verlag, Berlin, 1991.

[Pavlidis82]
  T. Pavlidis. *Graphics and Image Processing.* Computer Science Press, Rockville, MD, 1982.

[Rosenblum94]
  L. Rosenblum et al. *Scientific Visualization Advances and Challenges.* Harcourt Brace & Company, London, 1994.

[SmithRanallo89]

H. J. Smith and F. N. Ranallo. *A Non-Mathematical Approach to Basic MRI*.
Medical Physics Publishing Corporation, Madison, WI, 1989.

[Tufte83]

E. R. Tufte. *The Visual Display of Quantitative Information*. Graphics Press,
Cheshire, CT, 1990.

[Tufte90]

E. R. Tufte. *Envisioning Information*. Graphics Press, Cheshire, CT, 1990.

[Waters91]

K. Waters and D. Terzopoulos. "Modeling and Animating Faces Using Scanned
Data." *Visualization and Computer Animation*. 2:123–128, 1991.

[Wolberg90]

G. Wolberg. *Digital Image Warping*. IEEE Computer Society Press, Los Alamitos, CA, 1990.

[Wolff93]

R. S. Wolff and L. Yaeger. *Visualization of Natural Phenomena*. TELOS,
Springer-Verlag, Santa Clara, CA, 1993.

## CHAPTER 2

Object-Oriented Design

*O*bject-oriented systems are becoming widespread in the computer industry for good reason. Object-oriented systems are more modular, easier to maintain, and easier to describe than traditional procedural systems. Since the *Visualization Toolkit* has been designed and implemented using object-oriented design, we devote this chapter to summarizing the concepts and practice of object-oriented design and implementation.

2.1 Introduction

Today's software systems try to solve complex, real-world problems. A rigorous software design and implementation methodology can ease the burden of this complexity. Without such a methodology, software developers can find it difficult to meet a system's specifications. Furthermore, as specifications change and grow, a software system that does not have a solid, underlying architecture and design will have difficulty adapting to these expanding requirements.

Our visualization system is a good example of complex software that needs to be designed with extensibility in mind. Data visualization is a rapidly expanding field, with visualization techniques being introduced each year. Any system that hopes to incorporate future innovations must have an underlying design that supports the addition of new material without a significant impact on the existing system.

Object-oriented design is a software engineering methodology that deals comfortably with complexity and provides a framework for later changes and additions. The object-oriented design process attempts to divide a complex task into small and simple pieces called objects. The objects are computer abstractions that model physical or abstract pieces of the system being simulated. Object-oriented design methodologies provide mechanisms to identify the abstractions that exist within a system and to model the behavior of the objects.

2.2 Goals of Good Software Design

The quality of a software design is difficult to measure, but some qualitative aspects can guide us. A good software design should be robust, understandable, extendible, modular, maintainable, and reusable.

A robust system handles exceptional conditions gracefully and behaves consistently. Robustness gives software developers confidence that the underlying components of the system will behave as expected, even when the system is used under different circumstances than the original implementor intended.

An understandable system can be used by someone other than the original implementor. The use of the system should seem logical and sensible. The names of the components of the system should be derived from the problem domain.

Extendable systems accept new tasks while still doing the tasks they were originally intended to perform. A system should accept new forms of data and new algorithms without disrupting existing software. Adding a new primitive to the system should not cause large portions of the system to be modified. Experience shows that the more existing code that is modified in a system, the more likely errors will be introduced.

Modular software systems minimize the number of relationships that exist between components of a system. System components that are tightly coupled should be grouped together logically and obey common naming conventions and protocols.

Software maintenance is often ignored during system design. Nevertheless, the total cost of a system includes maintenance as well as the original development. A software system is maintainable if problems are easily isolated and the repair of one problem does not introduce problems in unrelated parts of the system.

Finally, the economics of software development require that we leverage as much of our past work as possible. In an ideal world, the implementation of a new technique in an existing system should be a simple task. This is seldom the case in software systems. Creation of reusable software components can reduce duplication of effort and promote consistent interfaces within a system. However, as we see throughout this book, creating software that can be reused often takes extra effort. A short-term view of productivity by one individual conflicts with the long-term view of the productivity of a software development organization.

2.3 Object-Oriented Concepts

Objects are the dominating concepts in object-oriented systems. Objects are abstractions that encapsulate the properties and behavior of the entities within a system. Each object has an identity that distinguishes it from other objects in the system. Often, the distinguishable aspects of an object are obvious. For example, a difference in color, location on a screen, size, or contents distinguishes one window from another on a computer desktop. But, appearances can be deceiving, and even two objects that share all the same characteristics may still have different identities. Two automobiles may have the same manufacturer, model, options and colors, but remain two different cars. The real world distinguishes the two cars by a vehicle identification number. Likewise, programming systems that deal with multiple entities need an identity mechanism. A pointer to allocated memory or a variable name in a system-managed symbol table are often used to distinguish objects in a system. In a database system, a set of identifier keys (called an *n*-tuple) identifies an entity in a system.

But, how do object-oriented systems differ from conventional, procedural programming systems? The major difference is in the way the two approaches treat data abstraction. Conventional systems limit abstraction to data typing, while object-oriented systems create abstractions for both the data and the operations that can be applied to the data. In fact, an object-oriented system keeps the data and operations together in one programming construct called an object. Together, the data and operations comprise an object's *properties*. When an operation is applied to an object, the programming language's dynamic-binding mechanism executes the procedure that is appropriate for that object. This is not the case in procedure-oriented systems. The programmer must supply logic to decide which procedure to call. Systems that handle multiple types are often littered with case statements to select the appropriate procedure for an operation. As new types are added to these systems, the code that dispatches operations based on data type must be extended to handle the new type. For example, in a program to display different types of primitives, the following pseudo code shows how a procedure-oriented system differs from an object-oriented system.

Procedure oriented (in C):

```
Primitive *aPrim;
...
DrawPrimitive (aPrim)
...
procedure DrawPrimitive (aPrim)
{
  if (aPrim->type == TRIANGLE) then DrawTriangle (aPrim)
  else if (aPrim->type == SQUARE) then DrawSquare (aPrim)
  else if (aPrim->type == CIRCLE) then DrawCircle (aPrim)
...
}
```

Object-oriented (in C++):

```
...
aPrim->Draw ();
...
```

Later in this project's existence, someone may want to add a new primitive, let's say a quadratic. The person assigned with such a formidable task must search the existing system for all occurrences of the if statements in the first example and add a test for the new quadratic type. Of course, a good programmer will have isolated the code in one location, as we have done here, so the task is easier. Nevertheless, that programmer must first realize that the original programmer was skilled enough to modularize the drawing code, then find the code (without necessarily knowing the procedure name) and modify the code. To complicate matters, a system built by more than one programmer will undoubtedly be under a configuration management system, requiring a check-out, edit, and check-in cycle.

The object-oriented programmer has an easier task. Consulting the design document that defines the object properties for a primitive, this programmer adds a draw operation to the quadratic object. The new primitive is available to the system without changing any existing code! Of course, this is an oversimplified example. But think about past programs you have written and remember how hard it was to add a new data type. Were your changes isolated to the new code you added? Did you have to edit code that you did not write and maybe did not understand? Keep this example in mind as you read our object-oriented implementation of a data visualization library.

Before describing object-oriented design and programming in more detail, we provide an observation and prediction. Over the several years that we have designed and implemented software using an object-oriented methodology, we have observed that newcomers to the technique will say, "But this is how I already write programs. My systems are modular; they're robust; I can easily add to them." If you still feel that way after reading this book, do not fault the object-oriented approach. Rather, we have failed as authors. However, such a negative response is unlikely. In our experience, users become comfortable with this approach in a short time. Especially when they are introduced to objects through an existing, well-designed object-oriented system. You will reach the "aha" stage, after which it will be difficult to begin a software project without looking for the objects in the problem.

2.4 Object-Oriented Terminology

As with any software engineering design methodology, object-oriented design has its own terminology. Unfortunately, not everyone agrees on what that is. We adopt much of our terminology from Rumbaugh [Rumbaugh91] and, since the *Visualization Toolkit* is written in C++, from Stroustrup [Stroustrup84]. For the

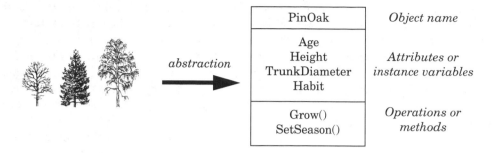

PinOak	*Object name*
Age Height TrunkDiameter Habit	*Attributes or instance variables*
Grow() SetSeason()	*Operations or methods*

Figure 2–1 Mapping a real-world object into an object abstraction. The real-world objects are various types of trees. One of these objects (a pin oak tree) is mapped into the computer object we call PinOak.

most part, Rumbaugh's terminology is independent of programming language, while Stroustrup is specific to implementation in C++. The transition from design to programming will be painless though, and the mappings between the two terminologies are mostly obvious. Where we think there might be confusion, we will point out the correspondences.

What Is an Object?

An *object* is an abstraction that models the state and behavior of entities in a system. Abstraction is a mental process that extracts the essential aspects of a situation for a particular purpose. Entities are things in the system that have identity. Chairs, airplanes, and cameras are objects that correspond to physical entities in the real world. Binary trees, symbol tables, and ordered collections are objects that exist only within the world of computer science.

Figure **2–1** is an example of the abstraction that occurs when we map the state and behavior of a system component to an object. Here, the object is a particular type of tree: a pin oak. In this application we desire to simulate the growth of various types of trees over the course of a season. For our purpose we have decided that the important state variables are the tree's age, trunk diameter, height, and habit (i.e., growing form). To capture the behavior of the pin oak we have methods to simulate growth and seasonal effects corresponding to spring, summer, fall, and winter. There are also methods (not shown) for setting and getting current state variables.

We call the state of an object its *attributes* (also called *instance variables*) and define its behavior by the *operations* that can be applied to it. Attributes have a name, a data type, and a data value. The data type of an attribute may be a primitive type in the programming language (such as a char or float in C++), or another object. For example, the vtkTransform object in our visualization system has an attribute of type vtkMatrix4x4, another object. vtkMatrix4x4 in turn has attributes that are an array of primitive values declared as float values in C++.

Operations are functions or transformations that can be applied to an object. Operations define the behavior of the object. The operations for a particular object are implemented in procedures we call *methods*.

Together, the attributes and operations of an object comprise its *properties*. A two-dimensional line graph could have attributes that include an x and y axis, a legend, and a connected set of points. This graph has methods that draw the graph in a window. It also has methods that let a user specify the axes, data to draw, and legend to use.

Objects that share the same properties can be grouped using the process of *classification*. An object class, usually just called a class, specifies the properties that all objects in the class have. The class only specifies the names of the properties, not their specific values. Different classes can (and usually do) have properties with names that exist in other classes. Many classes in our visualization system have an attribute named `Position`. Although both a camera and actor in our visualization system have this attribute, the effect on each is different because they are different classes. Attribute names are shared by all objects in a given class, but separate storage is allocated for each object's attribute values.

When an operation with the same name is applied to objects of different classes we call the operation *polymorphic*. For example, our visualization system has an operation named `Render()` that can be applied to many different objects. The implementation of an operation for a particular class is called a method. The print operation for a `vtkMatrix4x4` object is implemented in its print method. That is, there exists code that knows how to print objects of class `vtkMatrix4x4` and not objects of other classes. Objects know which method to use because they are kept within each object's data structure. In most systems the code for the methods is shared by all objects in the same class. Some programming languages, including C++, define a method by combining an operation name with its argument types. This process is called overloading an operation and is a powerful technique that permits the same name to be used for logically similar operations. For example, the class definition below defines three methods for calculating the square of a number. Even though these methods have the same operation name, they are unique because C++ uses both the operation name and the operations argument types.

```
class math
{
float square(float x);
int square(int x);
double square(double x);
}
```

To use a member of a class for some purpose, we create an instance of the class (the process of *instantiation*). Instance creation establishes the identity of the instance including specifying its initial state. The instance's class serves as a template for the instance during creation, defining the names of each of its attributes and operations. Creation establishes the similarities and differences between this instance and other instances of the same class. The similarities are the names and type of its attributes and the methods that implement its operations. The differences are the specific values of the attributes. The details of how one creates an instance of a class vary from programming language to programming language. In C++, a program creates an instance using a declarative form such as

```
vtkActor aBall;
```

which creates an object from the program stack, or by applying the new operation

```
vtkActor *aBall = new vtkActor;
```

which creates the object from the program heap.

Inheritance

Inheritance is a programming mechanism that simplifies adding new classes to a system when they differ in small ways from currently existing classes. The notion of inheritance is adopted from the observation that most systems can be specified using a hierarchical classification system. A fine example of a classification system is the phyla of life on earth.

Earlier we created an object corresponding to a pin oak tree. The properties of the tree can be more thoroughly described using inheritance (Figure **2–2**). The classification shown here is based on the five kingdom system of Margulis and Schwartz [Margulis88]. In this system, biota is classified as belonging to one of the five kingdoms Prokaryotae (bacteria), Protoctista (algae, protozoans and slime molds), Fungi (mushrooms, molds, lichens), Plantae (mosses, ferns, cone-bearing, and flowering plants), and Animalia (animals with and without backbones). Below this level we have the classifications division, class, order, family, genus, and species. The figure shows the kingdom, division, class, genus, and species of the pin oak.

Organizing objects into an inheritance hierarchy provides many benefits. Properties of a general classification are also properties of its subclassification. For example, we know that all species of genus *Quercus* form acorns. From the software point of view this means any instance variables and methods of a *superclass* are automatically inherited by its *subclass*. This allows us to make changes to a number of objects simultaneously by modifying their superclass. Furthermore, if we desire to add a new class (say a red oak tree) to the hierarchy we can do so without duplicating existing functionality. We need only differentiate the new class from the others by adding new instance variables or overloading existing methods.

The ability to quickly add new classes that are slightly different from currently existing classes promotes the extensibility of a system. Inheritance can be derived top-down using a process called *specialization*, or it can be created bot-

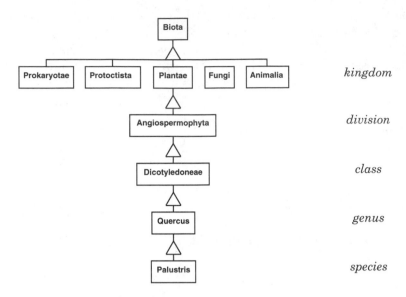

Figure 2–2 Inheritance hierarchy for pin oak tree.

tom-up, combining similar classes during a process called *generalization*. The use of inheritance implies a class hierarchy with one or more classes being the superclasses of one or more subclasses. A subclass inherits the operations and attributes of its superclasses. In C++, subclasses are called *derived* classes and superclasses are called *base* classes. A subclass can add additional operations and attributes that modify the properties it inherited from its superclasses. Through this inheritance, an object can exhibit its superclass's behavior plus any additional behavior it wishes. It can also restrict, or override, operations implemented by its superclass.

Classes that exist only to act as superclasses for their subclasses are called *abstract* classes. Instance creation of an abstract class is generally prohibited. Abstract classes are useful for gathering attributes and methods that all subclasses will use. They can also define protocols for behavior for their subclasses. This is a powerful use of inheritance that will show up in the design of our visualization system. Abstract classes can enforce complex sequence, control protocols, and ensure uniform behavior. They remove the responsibility of complex protocols from the individual subclasses and isolate the protocol in the superclass.

An example of a simple plotting package illustrates the power of abstract classes. Consider a data presentation application that allows for a variety of two-dimensional plotting. This application must support line charts and horizontal and vertical bar charts. The design process identifies properties common to all plots including title, axes, and legend. We then create an abstract class called

TwoDPlot to contain these common attributes. Common behavior can also be captured in TwoDPlot within its plot method:

```
Method Plot
{
Draw the border
Scale the data
Draw the axes
Draw the data
Draw the title
Draw the legend
}
```

An abstract class may or may not provide default behavior for each operation. In this example, default behavior for border and title drawing might be provided. Then subclasses of TwoDPlot would define their own functions for the other methods. The protocol specification explicitly spells out what methods a subclass of TwoDPlot should respond to. In the above example, subclasses will need to define their own methods for drawing the axis, data, and legend. Some subclasses might use TwoDPlot's methods for drawing the border, others might require their own version of this method. The abstract interface defined in TwoDPlot makes it easier to add new classes of 2D plots and the resulting subclasses tend to be more uniform and consistent.

Another mechanism, *delegation*, is useful for isolating and reusing behavior. Using delegation, an object applies operations to one of its attributes that is an object. As an example, in the *Visualization Toolkit* the vtkTransform object delegates its Identity() operation to its vtkMatrix4x4 attribute. This instance of vtkMatrix4x4 then performs the operation. There are many more useful object-oriented concepts, but for the time being we have enough information to describe how we can use objects to design a system.

2.5 Object-Oriented Modelling and Design

The design of any large software system is a formidable task and the first steps in system design are often the most challenging. No matter what design technique we choose, we must have a thorough understanding of the system's application domain. It would be difficult to see how one could design a fly-by-wire airplane control system without a detailed knowledge of the underlying hardware control systems. Of course, all flight system software is not designed by aeronautical engineers, so some form of system specification must exist. The depth of information in the specifications varies from application to application.

Object-oriented system design begins with a modelling step that extracts objects and their relationships with other objects from a problem statement or software requirement specification. First, the designer must completely understand the problem being solved. This often requires an in-depth knowledge of the problem domain or access to detailed specifications of the problem being solved.

Then, major abstractions must be identified within the system. The abstractions will become, at this high level of design, the first set of objects. For example, a system that keeps track of an investment portfolio will need objects such as stocks, bonds, and mutual funds. In a computer animation system we might need actors, cameras, and lights. A medical computed tomography system will have a table, X-ray source, detectors, and gantry. Our visualization system will have models, isosurfaces, streamlines, and cut planes. During this modelling step, we search the problem domain for objects, properties, and relationships. Later, during multiple passes through the design, the model will be expanded.

Modelling is a step in most design processes regardless of whether we are designing a ship, house, electronics system, or software. Each discipline follows a methodology that uses techniques specifically created to make the design process efficient and worthwhile. These techniques are so-called "tools of the trade." An electrical engineer uses schematics and logic diagrams, an architect uses drawings and mock-ups, and a ship builder uses scale models. Likewise, software designers need tools that can help create a model of the system. The software tools should have enough expressive power to help the software designer evaluate a design against a specification and help communicate that design to others on the software team.

We use the Object Modeling Technique (OMT) developed at GE by Jim Rumbaugh and his colleagues [Rumbaugh91]. OMT uses three models to specify an object-oriented design: an object model, a dynamic model, and a functional model. Each model describes a different aspect of the system and each has a corresponding diagramming technique that helps us analyze, design, and implement software systems.

The Object Model

The object model identifies each object in the system, its properties, and its relationships to other objects in the system. For most software systems, the object model dominates the design. The OMT graphical technique uses rectangles to depict object classes, and a variety of connectors to depict inheritance and other object-object relations. Object classes are represented as solid rectangles. Instances are represented as dotted rectangles. The name of the class or instance occupies the top of the rectangle. A line separates the class name from the next section that contains the attributes; a third section describes the methods. Relationships between objects are shown with line segments connecting the two related objects. In OMT, relationships are called associations and they can have various cardinalities: one-to-one, one-to-many, and many-to-many. Special associations that represent containers of other objects are called aggregations. Associations can be labeled with roles. (Roles are names given to associations and are used to further describe the nature of the association.) OMT represents inheritance with a triangle, with the superclass attached to the apex, and subclasses attached to the base of the triangle. Figure **2–3** shows an object model for locator devices in a virtual reality system.

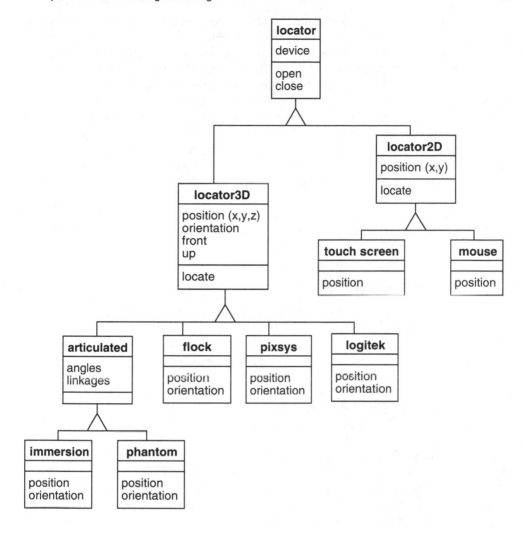

Figure 2–3 Object model for locator devices.

The first object in the class hierarchy is `locator`. This abstract class specifies common attributes and methods for all locators. The subclasses of `locator`
are `locator2D` and `locator3D`. In the current rendition of this object model,
the `locator` only has one attribute, a `device` and two methods, `open()` and
`close()`. The two subclasses of `locator`, `locator2D` and `locator3D` are also
abstract classes, containing attributes and methods that distinguish them from
each other based on their spatial dimensionality. For example, `locator3D` has
an *x, y, z* position while `locator2D` has an *x, y* position. Both locators have a
`locate()` method that updates the current position. In the 3D locator class,
`locate()` also updates the orientation. The subclasses of `locator3D` include

hardware from three different manufacturers: `flock`, `pixsys`, and `logitek`, as well as an `articulated` positioner abstract class. The three object classes for the hardware contain methods specific to each device. Each method knows how to convert the hardware specific codes returned by the device. They know that to be considered a `locator3D` subclass, they must implement a position and orientation operation that will provide *x, y, z* coordinates and three angular rotations that can be composed into a transformation matrix. The object model also shows us that the articulated locator has `angles` and `linkages`. Two specific articulated locators are `immersion` and `phantom`. An object model diagrammed in this fashion serves as a starting point for design and discussion. It reveals common methods and attributes as well as the distinguishing characteristics of each class.

Later, during implementation, we will convert these object models into software objects. The particular computer language we choose for implementation will dictate the details of the conversion.

The Dynamic Model

The object model describes the static portion of a system while the dynamic model details the sequences of events and time dependencies of the system. OMT uses state diagrams to model system dynamics. Dynamic models are frequently used to design control systems and user interfaces. Our visualization system has limited sequence and control aspects, so we will not dwell on state diagrams. But, if we were designing a user-friendly interface for a digital wristwatch, the state diagram in Figure **2–4** would be useful.

The ovals in the diagram show a state; the arrows show a transition from one state to another; and the labels on the arrows show an event that causes the state transition. This example shows three display states and multiple setting states. The event `b1` means button one is pressed. This watch has three buttons. The diagram shows what happens in each state when any of the three buttons is pressed. The diagram clearly shows that `b1` is used to move between display modes for time, date, and alarm. `B2` changes from display mode into setting mode or selects the field to change in a given mode. `B3` increments the selected field by one unit. The state diagram also shows what happens when illegal buttons are pressed. If the watch is displaying time and button 3 is pressed, nothing happens. If button 3 is pressed when the watch is displaying the alarm, the alarm on/off is toggled.

The Functional Model

The functional model shows how data flows through the system and how processes and algorithms transform the data. It also shows functional dependencies between processes. Exposing these relationships will affect the associations in the object model. The major components of a data flow diagram (DFD) are data sources, data sinks, and processes. Data sources and sinks are represented as rectangles. Ellipses show processes. Data stores are shown within two horizontal

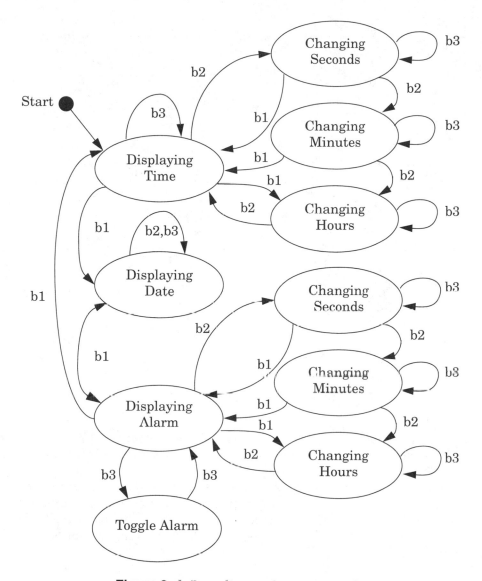

Figure 2–4 State diagram for a wristwatch.

lines. DFDs are useful to describe the overall flow in the system. They can also be used to describe any process that transforms one data representation into another. Processes identified in the DFD during function modelling may turn up as operations or objects in the object model.

Figure **2–5** shows a data flow diagram for a 3D medical imaging system. The diagram shows the data acquisition on the computed tomography (CT) or magnetic resonance imaging (MRI) scanner. The series of cross-sectional slices provided by the scanner is first processed by image processing filters to enhance

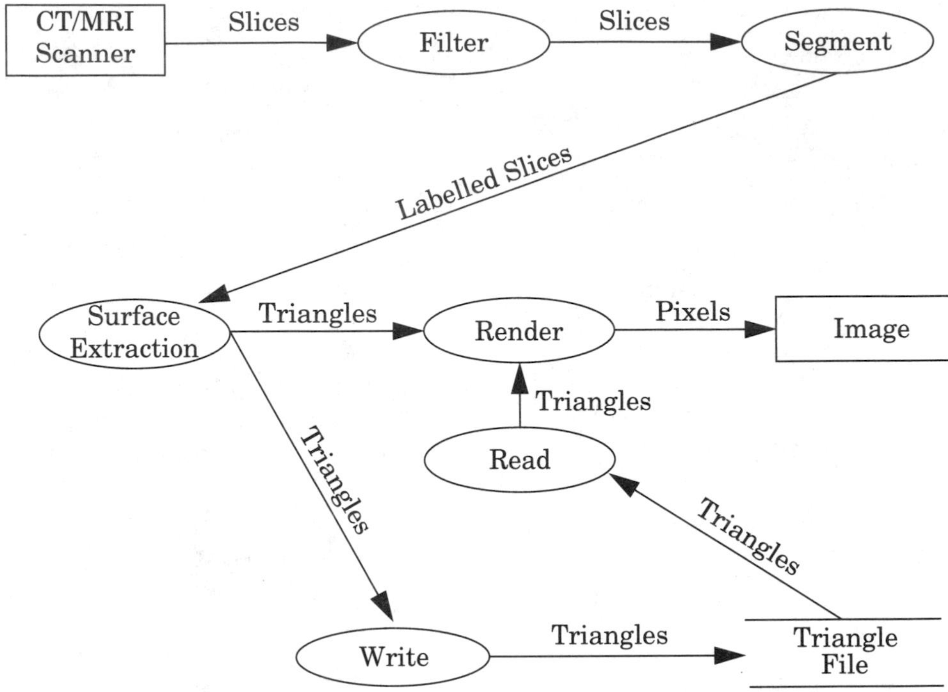

Figure 2–5 Data flow diagram.

features in the gray scale slices. A segment process identifies tissues and produces labels for the various tissues present in the slices. These labeled slices are then passed through a surface extraction process to create triangles that lie on the surface of each tissue. The render process transforms the geometry into an image. Alternatively, the write process stores the triangles in a file. Later, the triangles can be read and rendered into an image. We defer the decision whether to make the processes objects or operations until later. Chapter 4 uses DFDs to model the visualization pipeline.

2.6 Object-Oriented Programming Languages

The choice of computer programming language is a religious issue. Every computer language has its evangelists and followers. Most of our experience in object-oriented languages is with C and C++. C itself does not have object-oriented facilities, but an object-oriented methodology and strict coding guidelines permit the development of object-oriented code. We chose C++ for the *Visualization Toolkit* because it has built-in support for the notion of classes, dynamic binding of methods to objects, and inheritance. C++ is also widely available on many UNIX platforms and personal computers.

Simula [Birtwistle79] is usually acknowledged as the first object-oriented language, but Smalltalk [Goldberg83] is probably the best-known language. Smalltalk was developed at the Xerox Palo Alto Research Center (PARC) in the seventies and eighties. Well before its time, Smalltalk provided not just a language, but also an operating system and programming environment built with objects. When you use Smalltalk, you live and breathe objects. For the object-oriented purist, there is no substitute. Smalltalk spin-offs include window systems, workstations, and the desktop paradigm. Both Apple Computer and Microsoft acknowledge the influence that Smalltalk and Xerox PARC had on the Macintosh and Windows. Smalltalk was probably conceived 10 years too early for widespread commercial acceptance. During Smalltalk's infancy and adolescence, the complexity of software was much lower than today's systems. FORTRAN served the scientific and engineering community, COBOL was the choice for business applications and the computer science community embraced C. The use of abstractions was limited to mathematicians and other abstract thinkers. Programming was considered an art form and programmers concentrated on clever implementations of algorithms. Each new task often required a new program. Technical programmers did use numerical libraries for common mathematical operations, but any notions of common abstractions at a higher level were relatively few.

2.7 Object-Oriented Visualization

Don't underestimate the investment required to design a system. Although object-oriented technologies have tremendous potential to produce good software designs, these techniques do not guarantee a good design. The visualization system we present in this text has its roots in an animation [Lorensen89] and visualization system [Schroeder92] that we developed over a 10-year period. The initial design, which identified 25 classes for computer animation of industrial applications, took four software professionals 10 months (almost 3.5 person years) to complete. During this design stage the developers produced zero (!) lines of code. The subsequent implementation took one month, or ten percent of the effort. This system still serves our visualization group even after 20 other software developers have added over 500 classes to the system. The original 25 classes still exist in the system today.

As a reader, we hope that you can benefit from our experience in visualization system design. We have tried to assist you by describing the properties (attributes and methods) of many of the *Visualization Toolkit* classes in each chapter's "Putting It All Together" section. We also include a series of object diagrams in Appendix A that will give you a quick overview of object relationships such as superclass and subclass. And of course, it will be helpful if you supplement this information with the examples in the text/code and on CD-ROM. In the next chapter we will also explain the decisions we made to design our object-oriented toolkit.

2.8 Chapter Summary

This chapter introduced object-oriented concepts and terminology. The emphasis was on dealing with complexity and how object-oriented technology provides mechanisms to reduce the complexity of software.

Model building is an important part of any design methodology. We introduced three models and notations. The object model describes the objects in a system and their static relationships, attributes, and methods. Object diagrams succinctly present this static information. The dynamic model focuses on the time dependent aspects of the system. State transition diagrams are used to model the sequence and control portions of the system. The functional model shows how objects in the system transform data or other objects. The data flow diagram is a convenient notation for showing functional dependencies.

There are several choices available today for object-oriented implementations. Although it is possible to implement an object-oriented system in a non-object-oriented language such as C, the methodology is best served by an object-oriented language. We have chosen C++ to implement the *Visualization Toolkit*.

The emphasis in this book is on architecture, data structure design, and algorithms. The object-oriented aspects of the system are important, but what the system does is far more important.

2.9 Bibliographic Notes

There are several excellent textbooks on object-oriented design. Both [Rumbaugh91] and [Birtwistle79] present language-independent design methodologies. Both books emphasize modelling and diagramming as key aspects of design. [Meyer88] also describes the OO design process in the context of Eiffel, an OO language. Another popular book has been authored by Booch [Booch91].

Anyone who wants to be a serious user of object-oriented design and implementation should read the books on Smalltalk [Goldberg83][Goldberg84] by the developers of Smalltalk at Xerox Parc. In another early object-oriented programming book, [Cox86] describes OO techniques and the programming language Objective-C. Objective-C is a mix of C and Smalltalk and was used by Next Computer in the implementation of their operating system and user interface.

There are many texts on object-oriented languages. CLOS [Keene89] describes the Common List Object System. Eiffel, a strongly typed OO language is described by [Meyer88]. Objective-C [Cox86] is a weakly typed language.

Although C++ has become a popular programming language, there are few class libraries available for use in applications. [Gorlen90] describes an extensive class library for collections and arrays modeled after the Smalltalk classes described in [Goldberg83]. [Stepanov94] and [Musser94] describe the Standard Template Library, a framework of data structures and algorithms that is now a part of the ANSI C++ standard.

C++ texts abound. The original description by the author of C++ [Stroustrup84] is a must for any serious C++ programmer. Another book

[Ellis90] describes standard extensions to the language. Check with your colleagues for their favorite C++ book.

To keep in touch with new developments there are conferences, journals, and Web sites. The strongest technical conference on object-oriented topics is the annual Object-Oriented Programming Systems, Languages, and Applications (*OOPSLA*) conference. This is where researchers in the field describe, teach and debate the latest techniques in object-oriented technology. The bi-monthly *Journal of Object-Oriented Programming* (JOOP) published by SIGS Publications, NY, presents technical papers, columns, and tutorials on the field. Resources on the World Wide Web include the Usenet newsgroups *comp.object* and *comp.lang.c++*.

2.10 References

[Birtwistle79]
> G. M. Birtwistle, O. Dahl, B. Myhrhaug, and K. Nygaard. *Simula Begin*. Chartwell-Bratt Ltd, England, 1979.

[Booch91]
> G. Booch. *Object-Oriented Design with Applications*. Benjamin/Cummings Publishing Co., Redwood City, CA, 1991.

[Cox86]
> B. J. Cox. *Object-Oriented Programming: An Evolutionary Approach*. Addison-Wesley, Reading, MA, 1986.

[Ellis90]
> M. Ellis and B. Stroustrup. *The Annotated C++ Reference Manual*. Addison-Wesley, Reading, MA, 1990.

[Goldberg83]
> A. Goldberg, D. Robson. *Smalltalk-80: The Language and Its Implementation*. Addison-Wesley, Reading, MA, 1983.

[Goldberg84]
> A. Goldberg. *Smalltalk-80: The Interactive Programming Environment*. Addison-Wesley, Reading, MA, 1984.

[Gorlen90]
> K. Gorlen, S. Orlow, and P. Plexico. *Data Abstraction and Object-Oriented Programming*. John Wiley & Sons, Ltd., Chichester, England, 1990.

[Keene89]
> S. Keene. *Object-Oriented Programming in Common Lisp: A Programmer's Guide to CLOS*. Addison-Wesley, Reading, MA, 1989.

[Lorensen89]
> W. E. Lorensen, B. Yamrom. "Object-Oriented Computer Animation." *Proceedings of IEEE NAECON*, 2:588-595, Dayton, Ohio, May 1989.

[Margulis88]
> L. Margulis and K. V. Schwartz. *Five Kingdoms an Illustrated Guide to the Phyla of Life on Earth*. W. H. Freeman & Co., New York, 1988.

[Meyer88]
B. Meyer. *Object-Oriented Software Construction*. Prentice Hall International, Hertfordshire, England, 1988.

[Musser94]
D. Musser and A. Stepanov. "Algorithm-Oriented Generic Libraries." *Software Practice and Experience*. 24(7):623–642, July 1994.

[Rumbaugh91]
J. Rumbaugh, M. Blaha, W. Premerlani, F. Eddy, and W. Lorensen. *Object-Oriented Modeling and Design*. Prentice Hall, Englewood Cliffs, NJ, 1991.

[Schroeder92]
W. J. Schroeder, W. E. Lorensen, G. Montanaro, and C. Volpe. "Visage: An Object-Oriented Scientific Visualization System." In *Proceedings of Visualization '92*. pp. 219–226, IEEE Computer Society Press, Los Alamitos, CA, October 1992.

[Stepanov94]
A. Stepanov and M. Lee. *The Standard Template Library*. ISO Programming Language C++ Project. Doc. No. X3J16/94-0095, WG21/N0482, May 1994.

[Stroustrup84]
B. Stroustrup. *The C++ Programming Language*. Addison-Wesley, Reading, MA, 1986.

2.11 Exercises

2.1 Answer the following questions about a program you have written.
a) How much time did you spend on design and implementation?
b) What methodology, if any, did you use?
c) Could you easily extend the system?
d) Could anyone extend the system?

2.2 Identify the major objects and operations for the following applications.
a) An airline reservation system.
b) An adventure game.
c) A 2D plotting package.
d) An automatic teller machine.

2.3 Draw an object diagram for each example in Exercise 2.2.

2.4 Computer animation uses concepts from graphics and movie making. Identify the major objects and operations in a computer animation system.

2.5 For the animation system in Exercise 2.4, design control and looping objects that will allow flexible control of the properties of the actors in the system. If we call these control and looping objects scenes and cues, how would you expect them to look?

2.6 Draw a state diagram for your wristwatch using Figure 2–4 as an example.

2.7 Draw a data flow diagram for calculating the surface area and volume of a sphere and cylinder.

Computer Graphics Primer

*C*omputer graphics is the foundation of data visualization. Practically speaking, we can say that visualization is the process that transforms data into a set of graphics primitives. The methods of computer graphics are then used to convert these primitives into pictures or animations. This chapter discusses basic computer graphics principles. We begin by describing how lights and physical objects interact to form what we see. Then we examine how to simulate these interactions using computer graphics techniques. Hardware issues play an important role here since modern computers have built-in hardware support for graphics. The chapter concludes with a series of examples that illustrate our object-oriented model for 3D computer graphics.

3.1 Introduction

Computer graphics is the process of generating images using computers. We call this process *rendering*. There are many types of rendering processes, ranging from 2D paint programs to sophisticated 3D techniques. In this chapter we focus on basic 3D techniques for visualization.

We can view rendering as the process of converting graphical data into an image. In data visualization our goal is to transform data into graphical data, or *graphics primitives*, that are then rendered. The goal of our rendering is not so much image realism as it is information content. We also strive for interactive

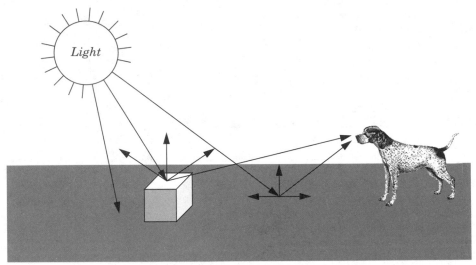

Figure 3–1 Physical generation of an image.

graphical displays so we can interact with the data. This chapter explains the process of rendering an image from graphical data. We begin by looking at the way lights, cameras, and objects (or actors) interact in the world around us. From this foundation we explain how to simulate this process on a computer.

A Physical Description of Rendering

Figure **3–1** presents a simplified view of what happens when we look at an object, in this case a cube. Rays of light are emitted from a light source in all directions. (In this example we assume that the light source is the sun.) Some of these rays happen to strike the cube whose surface absorbs some of the incident light and reflects the rest of it. Some of this reflected light may head towards us and enter our eyes. If this happens, then we "see" the object. Likewise, some of the light from the sun will strike the ground and some small percentage of it will be reflected into our eyes.

As you can imagine, the chances of a ray of light traveling from the sun through space to hit a small object on a relatively small planet are low. This is compounded by the slim odds that the ray of light will reflect off the object and into our eyes. The only reason we can see is that the sun produces such an enormous amount of light that it overwhelms the odds. While this may work in real life, trying to simulate it with a computer can be difficult. Fortunately, there are other ways to look at this problem.

A common and effective technique for 3D computer graphics is called *ray-tracing* or *ray-casting*. Ray-tracing simulates the interaction of light with objects by following the path of each light ray. Typically, we follow the ray backwards from the viewer's eyes and into the world to determine what the ray strikes. The direction of the ray is in the direction we are looking (i.e., the view direction) including effects of perspective (if desired). When a ray intersects an object, we can determine if that point is being lit by our light source. This is done by tracing a ray from the point of intersection towards the light. If the ray intersects the light, then the point is being lit. If the ray intersects something else before it gets to the light, then that light will not contribute to illuminating the point. For multiple light sources we just repeat this process for each light source. The total contributions from all the light sources, plus any ambient scattered light, will determine the total lighting or shadow for that point. By following the light's path backwards, ray-tracing only looks at rays that end up entering the viewer's eyes. This dramatically reduces the number of rays that must be computed by a simulation program.

Having described ray-tracing as a rendering process, it may be surprising that many members of the graphics community do not use it. This is because ray-tracing is a relatively slow image generation method since it is typically implemented in software. Other graphics techniques have been developed that generate images using dedicated computer hardware. To understand why this situation has emerged, it is instructive to briefly examine the taxonomy and history of computer graphics.

Image-Order and Object-Order Methods

Rendering processes can be broken into two categories: *image-order* and *object-order*. Ray-tracing is an image-order process. It works by determining what happens to each ray of light, one at a time. An object-order process works by rendering each object, one at a time. In the above example, an object-order technique would proceed by first rendering the ground and then the cube.

To look at it another way consider painting a picture of a barn. Using an image-order algorithm you would start at the upper left corner of the canvas and put down a drop of the correct color paint. (Each paint drop is called a picture element or *pixel*.) Then you would move a little to the right and put down another drop of paint. You would continue until you reached the right edge of the canvas, then you would move down a little and start on the next row. Each time you put down a drop of paint you make certain it is the correct color for each pixel on the canvas. When you are done you will have a painting of a barn.

An alternative approach is based on the more natural (at least for many people) object-order process. We work by painting the different objects in our scene, independent of where the objects actually are located on the scene. We may paint from back-to-front, front-to-back, or in arbitrary order. For example, we could start by painting the sky and then add in the ground. After these two objects were painted we would then add in the barn. In the image-order process we worked on the canvas in a very orderly fashion; left to right, top to bottom. With an object-order process we tend to jump from one part of the canvas to another, depending on what object we are drawing.

The field of computer graphics started out using object-order processes. Much of the early work was closely tied to the hardware display device, initially a vector display. This was little more than an oscilloscope, but it encouraged graphical data to be drawn as a series of line segments. As the original vector displays gave way to the currently ubiquitous raster displays, the notion of representing graphical data as a series of objects to be drawn was preserved. Much of the early work pioneered by Bresenham [Bresenham65] at IBM focused on how to properly convert line segments into a form that would be suitable for line plotters. The same work was applied to the task of rendering lines onto the raster displays that replaced the oscilloscope. Since then the hardware has become more powerful and capable of displaying much more complex primitives than lines.

It wasn't until the early 1980s that a paper by Turner Whitted [Whitted80] prompted many people to look at rendering from a more physical perspective. Eventually ray-tracing became a serious competitor to the traditional object-order rendering techniques, due in part to the highly realistic images it can produce. Object-order rendering has maintained its popularity because there is a wealth of graphics hardware designed to quickly render objects. Ray-tracing tends to be done without any specialized hardware and therefore is a time-consuming process.

Surface versus Volume Rendering

The discussion to this point in the text has tacitly assumed that when we render an object, we are viewing the surfaces of objects and their interactions with light. However, common objects such as clouds, water, and fog, are translucent, or scatter light that passes through them. Such objects cannot be rendered using a model based exclusively on surface interactions. Instead, we need to consider the changing properties inside the object to properly render them. We refer to these two rendering models as *surface rendering* (i.e., render the surfaces of an object) and *volume rendering* (i.e., render the surface and interior of an object).

Generally speaking, when we render an object using surface rendering techniques, we mathematically model the object with a surface description such as points, lines, triangles, polygons, or 2D and 3D splines. The interior of the object is not described, or only implicitly represented from the surface representation (i.e., surface is the boundary of the volume). Although techniques do exist that allow us to make the surface transparent or translucent, there are still many phenomena that cannot be simulated using surface rendering techniques alone (e.g., scattering or light emission). This is particularly true if we are trying to render data interior to an object, such as X-ray intensity from a CT scan.

Volume rendering techniques allow us to see the inhomogeneity inside objects. In the prior CT example, we can realistically reproduce X-ray images by considering the intensity values from both the surface and interior of the data. Although it is premature to describe this process at this point in the text, you can imagine extending our ray-tracing example from the previous section. Thus rays not only interact with the surface of an object, they also interact with the interior.

In this chapter we focus on surface rendering techniques. While not as powerful as volume rendering, surface rendering is widely used because it is relatively fast compared to volume rendering, and allows us to create images for a wide variety of data and objects. Chapter 7 describes volume rendering in more detail.

Visualization Not Graphics

Although the authors would enjoy providing a thorough treatise on computer graphics, such a discourse is beyond the scope of this text. Instead we make the distinction between visualization (exploring, transforming, and mapping data) and computer graphics (mapping and rendering). The focus will be on the principles and practice of visualization, and not on 3D computer graphics. In this chapter and Chapter 7 we introduce basic concepts and provide a working knowledge of 3D computer graphics. For those more interested in this field, we refer you to the texts recommended in the "Bibliographic Notes" on page 80 at the end of this chapter.

One of the regrets we have regarding this posture is that certain rendering techniques are essentially visualization techniques. We see this hinted at in the previous paragraph, where we use the term "mapping" to describe both visualization and computer graphics. There is not currently and will likely never be a firm distinction between visualization and graphics. For example, many researchers consider volume rendering to be squarely in the field of visualization because it addresses one of the most important forms of visualization data. Our distinction is mostly for our own convenience, and offers us the opportunity to finish this text. We recommend that a serious student of visualization supplement the material presented here with deeper books on computer graphics and volume rendering.

In the next few pages we describe the rendering process in more detail. We start by describing several color models. Then we examine the primary components of the rendering process. There are sources of light such as the sun, objects we wish to render such as a cube or sphere (we refer to these objects as *actors*), and there is a camera that looks out into the world. These terms are taken from the movie industry and tend to be familiar to most people. Actors represent graphical data or objects, lights illuminate the actors, and the camera constructs a picture by projecting the actors onto a view plane. We call the combination of lights, camera, and actors the *scene*, and refer to the rendering process as rendering the scene.

3.2 Color

The electromagnetic spectrum visible to humans contains wavelengths ranging from about 400 to 700 nanometers. This light that enters our eyes consists of dif-

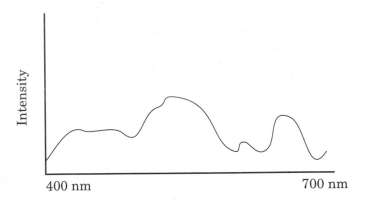

Figure 3–2 Wavelength intensity plot.

ferent *intensities* of these wavelengths, an example of which is shown in Figure **3–2**. This intensity plot defines the color of the light, a different plot results in a different color. Unfortunately, we may not notice the difference since the human eye throws out most of this information. There are three types of color receptors in the human eye. Each type responds to a subset of the 400 to 700 nanometer wavelength range as in Figure **3–3**. Any color we see gets coded by our eyes into these three overlapping responses. This is a great reduction from the amount of information that actually comes into our eyes. As a result, the human eye is incapable of recognizing differences in any colors whose intensity curves, when applied to the human eye's response curves, result in the same triplet of responses. This also implies that we can store and represent colors in a computer using a simplified form without the human eye being able to recognize the difference.

The two simplified component systems that we use to describe colors are RGB and HSV color systems. The RGB system represents colors based on their red, green, and blue intensities. This can be thought of as a three dimensional space with the axes being red, green, and blue. Some common colors and their RGB components are shown in Figure **3–4**.

The HSV system represents colors based on their hue, saturation, and value. The value component is also known as the brightness or intensity component, and represents how much light is in the color. A value of 0.0 will always give you black and a value of 1.0 will give you something bright. The hue represents the dominant wavelength of the color. Hue is often illustrated using a circle as in Figure **3–5**. Each location on the circumference of this circle represents a different hue and can be specified using an angle. When we specify a hue we use the range from zero to one, where zero corresponds to zero degrees on the hue circle and one corresponds to 360 degrees. The saturation indicates how much of the hue is mixed into the color. For example, we can set the value to one, which gives us a bright color, and the hue to 0.66, to give us a dominant wavelength of

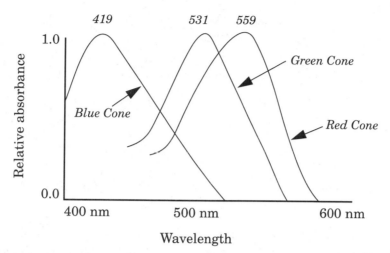

Figure 3–3 Relative absorbance of light by the three types of cones in the human retina [Dartnall83].

Color	RGB	HSV
Black	0,0,0	*,*,0
White	1,1,1	*,0,1
Red	1,0,0	0,1,1
Green	0,1,0	1/3,1,1
Blue	0,0,1	2/3,1,1
Yellow	1,1,0	1/6,1,1
Cyan	0,1,1	1/2,1,1
Magenta	1,0,1	5/6,1,1
Sky Blue	1/2,1/2,1	2/3,1/2,1

Figure 3–4 Common colors in RGB and HSV space.

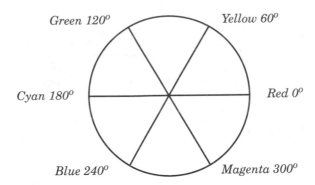

Figure 3–5 Circular representation of hue. (See Color Plate 11.)

blue. Now if we set the saturation to one, the color will be a bright primary blue.
If we set the saturation to 0.5, the color will be sky blue, a blue with more white
mixed in. If we set the saturation to zero, this indicates that there is no more of
the dominant wavelength (hue) in the color than any other wavelength. As a
result, the final color will be white (regardless of hue value). Figure **3–4** lists
HSV values for some common colors.

3.3 Lights

One of the major factors controlling the rendering process is the interaction of
light with the actors in the scene. If there are no lights, the resulting image will
be black and rather uninformative. To a great extent it is the interaction
between the emitted light and the surface (and in some cases the interior) of the
actors in the scene that defines what we see. Once rays of light interact with the
actors in a scene, we have something for our camera to view.

Of the many different types of lights used in computer graphics, we will discuss the simplest, the infinitely distant, point light source. This is a simplified
model compared to the lights we use at home and work. The light sources that
we are accustomed to typically radiate from a region in space (a filament in an
incandescent bulb, or a light-emitting gas in a fluorescent light). The point
source lighting model assumes that the light is emitted in all directions from a
single point in space. For an infinite light source, we assume that it is positioned
infinitely far away from what it is illuminating. This is significant because it
implies that the incoming rays from such a source will be parallel to each other.
The emissions of a local light source, such as a lamp in a room, are not parallel.
Figure **3–6** illustrates the differences between a local light source with a finite
volume, versus an infinite point light source. The intensity of the light emitted
by our infinite light sources also remains constant as it travels, in contrast to the
actual $1/\text{distance}^2$ relationship physical lights obey. As you can see this is a great
simplification, which later will allow us to use less complex lighting equations.

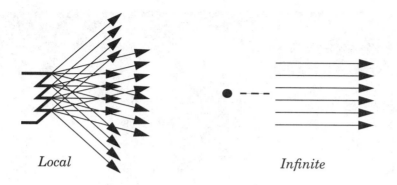

Local   *Infinite*

Figure 3–6 Local light source with a finite volume versus an infinite point light source.

3.4 Surface Properties

As rays of light travel through space, some of them intersect our actors. When this happens, the rays of light interact with the surface of the actor to produce a color. Part of this resulting color is actually not due to direct light, but rather from *ambient* light that is being reflected or scattered from other objects. An ambient lighting model accounts for this. It applies the intensity curve of the light source to the color of the object, also expressed as an intensity curve. The result is the color of the light we see when we look at that object. With such a model, it is important to realize that a white light shining on a blue ball is indistinguishable from a blue light shining on a white ball. The ambient lighting equation is

$$R_c = L_c \cdot O_c \qquad \qquad \textbf{(3-1)}$$

where R_c is the resulting intensity curve, L_c is the intensity curve of the light, and O_c is the color curve of the object. To help keep the equations simple we assume that all of the direction vectors are normalized (i.e., have a magnitude of one).

Two components of the resulting color depend on direct lighting. *Diffuse lighting*, which is also known as Lambertian reflection, takes into account the angle of incidence of the light onto an object. Figure **3–7** shows the image of a cylinder that becomes darker as you move laterally from its center. The cylinder's color is constant; the amount of light hitting the surface of the cylinder changes. At the center, where the incoming light is nearly perpendicular to the surface of the cylinder, it receives more rays of light per surface area. As we move towards the side, this drops until finally the incoming light is parallel to the side of the

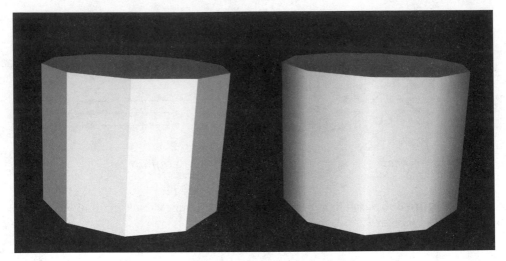

Figure 3–7 Flat and Gouraud shaded cylinders.

cylinder and the resulting intensity is zero. The contribution from diffuse lighting is expressed in Equation **3-2** and illustrated in Figure **3–9**.

$$R_c = L_c O_c [\vec{O}_n \cdot (-\vec{L}_n)]$$ (3-2)

where R_c is the resulting intensity curve, L_c is the intensity curve for the light, and O_c is the color curve for the object. Notice that the diffuse light is a function of the relative angle between incident light vector $\vec{L}_n$ and the surface normal of the object $\vec{O}_n$. As a result diffuse lighting is independent of viewer position.

Specular lighting represents direct reflections of a light source off a shiny object. Figure **3–10** shows a diffusely lit ball with increasing amounts of specular reflection. There is an additional factor, O_{sp}, the specular power. This indicates how shiny an object is, more specifically it indicates how quickly specular reflections diminish as the reflection angles deviate from a perfect reflection. Higher values indicate a faster dropoff, and therefore a shinier surface. Figure **3–11** shows the effects of the specular power. Referring to Figure **3–9**, the equation for specular lighting is

$$R_c = L_c O_c [\vec{S} \cdot (-\vec{C}_n)]^{O_{sp}}$$

$$\vec{S} = 2[\vec{O}_n \cdot (-\vec{L}_n)]\vec{O}_n + \vec{L}_n$$ (3-3)

where $\vec{C}_n$ is the direction of projection for the camera and $\vec{S}$ is the direction of specular reflection.

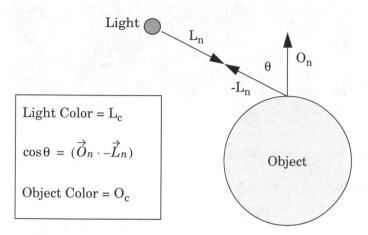

Figure 3–8 Diffuse lighting.

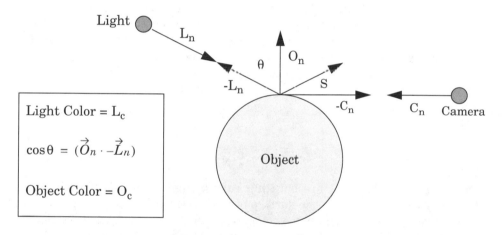

Figure 3–9 Specular lighting.

Figure 3–10 A diffuse lit ball with increasing amounts of specular reflection.

Figure 3–11 Effects of specular power, O_{sp} = (5,10,20,80,200).

We have presented the equations for the different lighting models independently. We can apply all lighting models simultaneously or in combination. Equation **3-4** combines ambient, diffuse and specular lighting into one equation.

$$R_c = O_{ai}O_{ac}L_c - O_{di}O_{dc}L_c(\vec{O}_n \cdot \vec{L}_n) + O_{si}O_{sc}L_c[\vec{S} \cdot (-\vec{C}_n)]^{O_{sp}} \qquad \textbf{(3-4)}$$

The result is a color at a point on the surface of the object. The constants O_{ai}, O_{di}, and O_{si} control the relative amounts of ambient, diffuse and specular lighting for an object. The constants O_{ac}, O_{dc}, and O_{sc} specify the colors to be used for each type of lighting. These six constants along with the specular power are part of the surface material properties. (Other properties such as transparency will be covered in later sections of the text.) Different combinations of these property values can simulate dull plastic and polished metal. The equation assumes an infinite point light source as described in "Lights" on page 42. However the equation can be easily modified to incorporate other types of directional lighting.

3.5 Cameras

We have light sources that are emitting rays of light and actors with surface properties. At every point on the surface of our actors this interaction results in some composite color (i.e., combined color from light, object surface, specular, and ambient effects). All we need now to render the scene is a camera. There are a number of important factors that determine how a 3D scene gets projected onto a plane to form a 2D image (see Figure **3–12**). These are the position, orientation, and focal point of the camera, the method of camera *projection*, and the location of the camera *clipping planes*.

The position and focal point of the camera define the location of the camera and where it points. The vector defined from the camera position to the focal point is called the *direction of projection*. The camera image plane is located at the focal point and is typically perpendicular to the projection vector. The camera orientation is controlled by the position and focal point plus the camera *view-up* vector. Together these completely define the camera view.

The method of projection controls how the actors are mapped to the image plane. *Orthographic projection* is a parallel mapping process. In orthographic

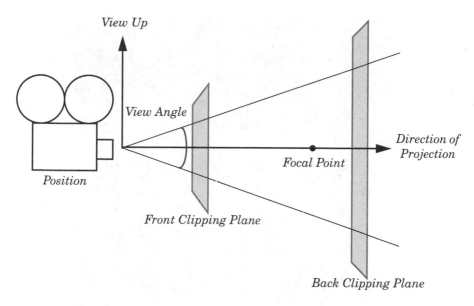

Figure 3–12 Camera attributes.

projection (or parallel projection) all rays of light entering the camera are parallel to the projection vector. *Perspective projection* occurs when all light rays go through a common point (i.e., the viewpoint or center of projection). To apply perspective projection we must specify a perspective angle or camera view angle.

The front and back *clipping planes* intersect the projection vector, and are usually perpendicular to it. The clipping planes are used to eliminate data either too close to the camera or too far away. As a result only actors or portions of actors within the clipping planes are (potentially) visible. Clipping planes are typically perpendicular to the direction of projection. Their locations can be set using the cameras clipping range. The location of the planes are measured from the camera's position along the direction of projection. The front clipping plane is at the minimum range value, and the back clipping plane is at the maximum range value. Later on in Chapter 7, when we discuss stereo rendering, we will see examples of clipping planes that are not perpendicular to the direction of projection.

Taken together these camera parameters define a rectangular pyramid, with its apex at the camera's position and extending along the direction of projection. The pyramid is truncated at the top with the front clipping plane and at the bottom by the back clipping plane. The resulting *view frustum* defines the region of 3D space visible to the camera.

While a camera can be manipulated by directly setting the attributes mentioned above, there are some common operations that make the job easier. Figure **3–13** and Figure **3–14** will help illustrate these operations. Changing the *azimuth* of a camera rotates its position around its view up vector, centered at the focal point. Think of this as moving the camera to the left or right while

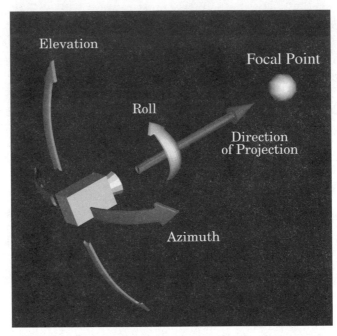

Figure 3–13 Camera movements around focal point (`camera.tcl`).

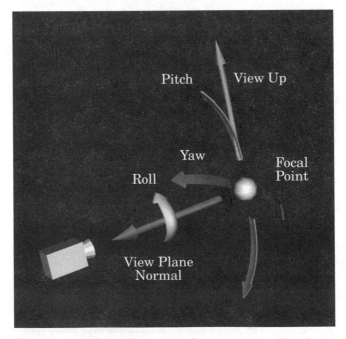

Figure 3–14 Camera movements centered at camera position (`camera2.tcl`).

always keeping the distance to the focal point constant. Changing a camera's *elevation* rotates its position around the cross product of its direction of projection and view up centered at the focal point. This corresponds to moving the camera up and down. To *roll* the camera, we rotate the view up vector about the view plane normal. Roll is sometimes called twist.

The next two motions keep the camera's position constant and instead modify the focal point. Changing the *yaw* rotates the focal point about the view up centered at the camera's position. This is like an azimuth, except that the focal point moves instead of the position. Changes in *pitch* rotate the focal point about the cross product of the direction of projection and view up centered at the camera's position. *Dollying* in and out moves the camera's position along the direction of projection, either closer or farther from the focal point. This operation is specified as the ratio of its current distance to its new distance. A value greater than one will dolly in, while a value less than one will dolly out. Finally, *zooming* changes the camera's view angle, so that more or less of the scene falls within the view frustum.

Once we have the camera situated, we can generate our 2D image. Some of the rays of light traveling through our 3D space will pass through the lens on the camera. These rays then strike a flat surface to produce an image. This effectively projects our 3D scene into a 2D image. The camera's position and other properties determine which rays of light get captured and projected. More specifically, only rays of light that intersect the camera's position, and are within its viewing frustum, will affect the resulting 2D image.

This concludes our brief rendering overview. The light has traveled from its sources to the actors, where it is reflected and scattered. Some of this light gets captured by the camera and produces a 2D image. Now we will look at some of the details of this process.

3.6 Coordinate Systems

There are four coordinate systems commonly used in computer graphics and two different ways of representing points within them (Figure **3–15**). While this may seem excessive, each one serves a purpose. The four coordinate systems we use are: *model*, *world*, *view*, and *display*.

The model coordinate system is the coordinate system in which the model is defined in, typically a local Cartesian coordinate system. If one of our actors represents a football, it will be based on a coordinate system natural to the football geometry (e.g., a cylindrical system). This model has an inherent coordinate system determined by the decisions of whoever generated it. They may have used inches or meters as their units, and the football may have been modeled with any arbitrary axis as its major axis.

The world coordinate system is the 3D space in which the actors are positioned. One of the actor's responsibilities is to convert from the model's coordinates into world coordinates. Each model may have its own coordinate system but there is only one world coordinate system. Each actor must scale, rotate, and

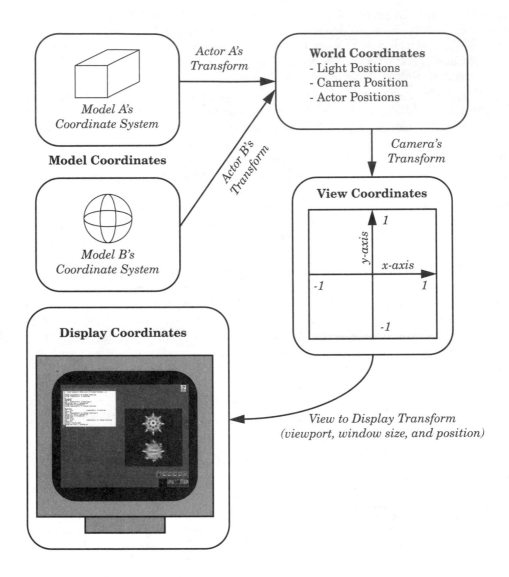

Figure 3–15 Modelling, world, view, and display coordinate systems.

translate its model into the world coordinate system. (It may also be necessary for the modeller to transform from its natural coordinate system into a local Cartesian system. This is because actors typically assume that the model coordinate system is a local Cartesian system.) The world coordinate system is also the system in which the position and orientation of cameras and lights are specified.

The view coordinate system represents what is visible to the camera. This consists of a pair of x and y values, ranging between $(-1,1)$, and a z depth coordinate. The x, y values specify location in the image plane, while the z coordinate represents the distance, or range, from the camera. The camera's properties are represented by a four by four transformation matrix (to be described shortly), which is used to convert from world coordinates into view coordinates. This is where the perspective effects of a camera are introduced.

The display coordinate system uses the same basis as the view coordinate system, but instead of using negative one to one as the range, the coordinates are actual x, y pixel locations on the image plane. Factors such as the window's size on the display determine how the view coordinate range of (-1,1) is mapped into pixel locations. This is also where the *viewport* comes into effect. You may want to render two different scenes, but display them in the same window. This can be done by dividing the window into rectangular viewports. Then, each renderer can be told what portion of the window it should use for rendering. The viewport ranges from (0,1) in both the x and y axis. Similar to the view coordinate system, the z-value in the display coordinate system also represents depth into the window. The meaning of this z-value will be further described in the section titled "Z-Buffer" on page 61.

3.7 Coordinate Transformation

When we create images with computer graphics, we project objects defined in three dimensions onto a two-dimensional image plane. As we saw earlier, this projection naturally includes perspective. To include projection effects such as vanishing points we use a special coordinate system called *homogeneous coordinates*.

The usual way of representing a point in 3D is the three element Cartesian vector (x, y, z). Homogeneous coordinates are represented by a four element vector (x_h, y_h, z_h, w_h). The conversion between Cartesian coordinates and homogeneous coordinates is given by:

$$x = \frac{x_h}{w_h} \qquad y = \frac{y_h}{w_h} \qquad z = \frac{z_h}{w_h} \qquad \text{(3-5)}$$

Using homogeneous coordinates we can represent an infinite point by setting w_h to zero. This capability is used by the camera for perspective transformations. The transformations are applied by using a 4×4 *transformation matrix*. Transformation matrices are widely used in computer graphics because they allow us to perform translation, scaling, and rotation of objects by repeated matrix multiplication. Such operations are not easily performed using a 3×3 matrix.

For example, suppose we wanted to create a transformation matrix that translates a point (x, y, z) in Cartesian space by the vector (t_x, t_y, t_z). We need only construct the translation matrix given by

$$T_T = \begin{bmatrix} 1 & 0 & 0 & t_x \\ 0 & 1 & 0 & t_y \\ 0 & 0 & 1 & t_z \\ 0 & 0 & 0 & 1 \end{bmatrix}$$ (3-6)

and then postmultiply it with the homogeneous coordinate (x_h, y_h, z_h, w_h). To carry this example through, we construct the homogeneous coordinate from the Cartesian coordinate (x, y, z) by setting $w_h = 1$ to yield $(x, y, z, 1)$. Then, to determine the translated point (x', y', z') we premultiply the current position by the transformation matrix T_T to yield the translated coordinate. Substituting into Equation **3-6** we have the result

$$\begin{bmatrix} x' \\ y' \\ z' \\ w' \end{bmatrix} = \begin{bmatrix} 1 & 0 & 0 & t_x \\ 0 & 1 & 0 & t_y \\ 0 & 0 & 1 & t_z \\ 0 & 0 & 0 & 1 \end{bmatrix} \cdot \begin{bmatrix} x \\ y \\ z \\ 1 \end{bmatrix}$$ (3-7)

Converting back to Cartesian coordinates via Equation **3-5** we have the expected solution

$$x' = x + t_x$$
$$y' = y + t_y$$ (3-8)
$$z' = z + t_z$$

The same procedure is used to scale or rotate an object. To scale an object we use the transformation matrix

$$T_S = \begin{bmatrix} s_x & 0 & 0 & 0 \\ 0 & s_y & 0 & 0 \\ 0 & 0 & s_z & 0 \\ 0 & 0 & 0 & 1 \end{bmatrix}$$ (3-9)

where the parameters s_x, s_y, and s_z are scale factors along the x, y, and z axes. Similarly, we can rotate an object around the x axes by angle θ using the matrix

$$T_{R_x} = \begin{bmatrix} 1 & 0 & 0 & 0 \\ 0 & \cos\theta & -\sin\theta & 0 \\ 0 & \sin\theta & \cos\theta & 0 \\ 0 & 0 & 0 & 1 \end{bmatrix}$$ (3-10)

Around the y axis we use

$$T_{R_y} = \begin{bmatrix} \cos\theta & 0 & \sin\theta & 0 \\ 0 & 1 & 0 & 0 \\ -\sin\theta & 0 & \cos\theta & 0 \\ 0 & 0 & 0 & 1 \end{bmatrix} \qquad (3\text{-}11)$$

and around the z axis we use

$$T_{R_z} = \begin{bmatrix} \cos\theta & -\sin\theta & 0 & 0 \\ \sin\theta & \cos\theta & 0 & 0 \\ 0 & 0 & 1 & 0 \\ 0 & 0 & 0 & 1 \end{bmatrix} \qquad (3\text{-}12)$$

Another useful rotation matrix is used to transform one coordinate axes $x - y - z$ to another coordinate axes $x' - y' - z'$. To derive the transformation matrix we assume that the unit x' axis makes the angles $(\theta_{x'x}, \theta_{x'y}, \theta_{x'z})$ around the $x - y - z$ axes (these are called direction cosines). Similarly, the unit y' axis makes the angles $(\theta_{y'x}, \theta_{y'y}, \theta_{y'z})$ and the unit z' axis makes the angles $(\theta_{z'x}, \theta_{z'y}, \theta_{z'z})$. The resulting rotation matrix is formed by placing the direction cosines along the rows of the transformation matrix as follows

$$T_R = \begin{bmatrix} \cos\theta_{x'x} & \cos\theta_{x'y} & \cos\theta_{x'z} & 0 \\ \cos\theta_{y'x} & \cos\theta_{y'y} & \cos\theta_{y'z} & 0 \\ \cos\theta_{z'x} & \cos\theta_{z'y} & \cos\theta_{z'z} & 0 \\ 0 & 0 & 0 & 1 \end{bmatrix} \qquad (3\text{-}13)$$

Rotations occur about the coordinate origin. It is often more convenient to rotate around the center of the object (or a user-specified point). Assume that we call this point the object's center O_c. To rotate around O_c we must first translate the object from O_c to the origin, apply rotations, and then translate the object back to O_c.

Transformation matrices can be combined by matrix multiplication to achieve combinations of translation, rotation, and scaling. It is possible for a single transformation matrix to represent all types of transformation simultaneously. This matrix is the result of repeated matrix multiplications. A word of warning: The order of the multiplication is important. For example, multiplying a translation matrix by a rotation matrix will not yield the same result as multiplying the rotation matrix by the translation matrix.

3.8 Actor Geometry

We have seen how lighting properties control the appearance of an actor, and how the camera in combination with transformation matrices is used to project an actor to the image plane. What is left to define is the geometry of the actor, and how we position it in the world coordinate system.

Modelling

A major topic in the study of computer graphics is modelling or representing the geometry of physical objects. Various mathematical techniques have been applied including combinations of points, lines, polygons, curves, and splines of various forms, and even implicit mathematical functions. This topic is beyond the scope of the text. The important point here is that there is an underlying geometric model that specifies where an object is located in the model coordinate system.

In data visualization, modelling takes a different role. Instead of directly creating geometry to represent an object, visualization algorithms *compute* these forms. Often the geometry is abstract (like a contour line) and has little relationship to real world geometry. We will see how these models are computed when we describe visualization algorithms in Chapters 6 and 9.

The representation of geometry for data visualization tends to be simple, even though computing the representations is not. These forms are most often primitives like points, lines, and polygons, or visualization data such as volume data. We use simple forms because we desire high performance and interactive systems. Thus we take advantage of computer hardware (to be covered in "Graphics Hardware" on page 55) or special rendering techniques like volume rendering (see "Volume Rendering" on page 216).

Actor Location and Orientation

Every actor has a transformation matrix that controls its location and scaling in world space. The actor's geometry is defined by a model in model coordinates. We specify the actor's location using orientation, position, and scale factors along the coordinate axes. In addition, we can define an origin around which the actor rotates. This feature is useful because we can rotate the actor around its center or some other meaningful point.

The orientation of an actor is determined by rotations stored in an orientation vector (O_x, O_y, O_z). This vector defines a series of rotational transformation matrices. As we saw in the previous section on transformation matrices, the order of application of the transformations is not arbitrary. We have chosen a fixed order based on what we think is natural to users. The order of transformation is a rotation by O_y around the y axis, then by O_x around the x axis, and finally by O_z around the z axis. This ordering is arbitrary and is based on the standard camera operations. These operations (in order) are a camera azimuth, followed by an elevation, and then a roll (Figure **3–16**).

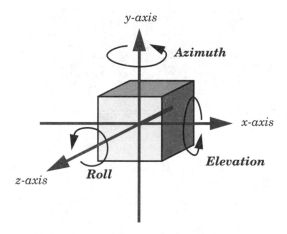

Figure 3–16 Actor coordinate system.

All of these rotations take place around the origin of the actor. Typically this is set to the center of its bounding box, but it can be set to any convenient point. There are many different methods for changing an actor's orientation. `RotateX()`, `RotateY()`, and `RotateZ()` are common methods that rotate about their respective axes. Many systems also include a method to rotate about a user-defined axis. In the *Visualization Toolkit* the `RotateXYZ()` method is used to rotate around an arbitrary vector passing through the origin.

3.9 Graphics Hardware

Earlier we mentioned that advances in graphics hardware have had a large impact on how rendering is performed. Now that we have covered the fundamentals of rendering a scene, we look at some of the hardware issues. First, we discuss raster devices that have replaced vector displays as the primary output device. Then, we look at how our programs communicate to the graphics hardware. We also examine the different coordinate systems used in computer graphics, hidden line/surface removal, and z-buffering.

Raster Devices

Usually, we see computer graphics in a printed picture or displayed on a computer monitor. Occasionally, we see something on TV or in a movie. All of these mediums are raster devices. A raster device represents an image using a two dimensional array of picture elements called pixels. For example, the word "hello" can be represented as an array of pixels.

In Figure **3–17**, the word "hello" is written within a pixel array that is twenty-five pixels wide and ten pixels high. Each pixel stores one bit of information, whether it is black or white. This is how a black and white laser printer

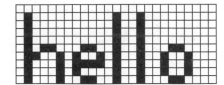

Figure 3–17 A pixel array for the word hello.

works, for each point on the paper it either prints a black dot or leaves it the color of the paper. Due to hardware limitations, raster devices such as laser printers and computer monitors do not actually draw accurate square pixels like those in Figure **3–17**. Instead, they tend to be slightly blurred and overlapping. Another hardware limitation of raster devices is their resolution. This is what causes a 300 dpi (dots per inch) laser printer to produce more detailed output than a nine pin dot matrix printer. A 300 dpi laser printer has a resolution of 300 pixels per inch compared to roughly 50 dpi for the dot matrix printer.

Color computer monitors typically have a resolution of about 80 pixels per inch, making the screen a pixel array roughly one thousand pixels in width and height. This results in over one million pixels, each with a value that indicates what color it should be. Since the hardware in color monitors uses the RGB system, it makes sense to use that to describe the colors in the pixels. Unfortunately, having over one million pixels, each with a red, green, and blue component, can take up a lot of memory. This is part of what differentiates the variety of graphics hardware on the market. Some companies use 24 bits of storage per pixel, others use eight, some advanced systems use more than 100 bits of storage per pixel. Typically, the more bits per pixel the more accurate the colors will be.

One way to work around color limitations in the graphics hardware is by using a technique called *dithering*. Say, for example, that you want to use some different shades of gray, but your graphics hardware only supports black and white. Dithering lets you approximate shades of gray by using a mixture of both black and white pixels. In Figure **3–18**, seven gray squares are drawn using a mixture of black and white pixels. From a distance the seven squares look like different shades of gray even though up close, it's clear that they are just different mixtures of black and white pixels. This same technique works just as well for other colors. For example, if your graphics hardware supports primary blue, primary green, and white but not a pastel sea green, you can approximate this color by dithering the green, blue, and white that the hardware does support.

Interfacing to the Hardware

Now that we have covered the basics of display hardware, the good news is that you rarely need to worry about them. Most graphics programming is done using higher-level primitives than individual pixels. Figure **3–19** shows a typical

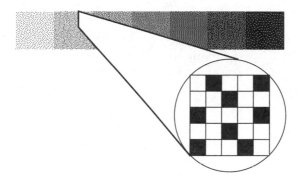

Figure 3–18 Black and white dithering.

arrangement for a visualization program. At the bottom of the hierarchy is the display hardware that we already discussed; chances are your programs will not interact directly with it. The top three layers above the hardware are the layers you may need to be concerned with.

Many programs take advantage of application libraries as a high-level interface to the graphics capabilities of a system. The *Visualization Toolkit* accompanying this book is a prime example of this. It allows you to display a complex object or graph using just a few commands. It also can interface to a number of different graphics libraries, since different libraries are supported on different hardware platforms.

The graphics library and graphics hardware layers both perform similar functions. They are responsible for taking high-level commands from an application library or program, and executing them. This makes programming much easier by providing more complex primitives to work with. Instead of drawing

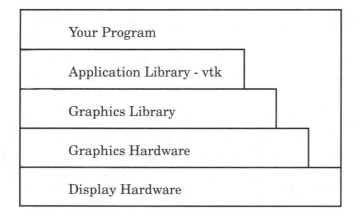

Figure 3–19 Typical graphics interface hierarchy.

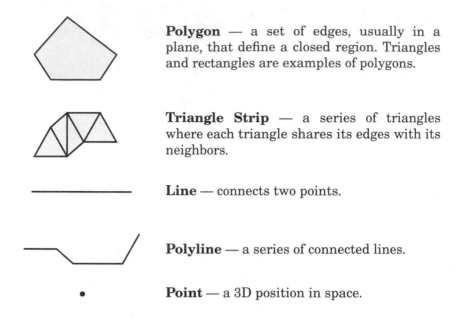

Polygon — a set of edges, usually in a plane, that define a closed region. Triangles and rectangles are examples of polygons.

Triangle Strip — a series of triangles where each triangle shares its edges with its neighbors.

Line — connects two points.

Polyline — a series of connected lines.

Point — a 3D position in space.

Figure 3–20 Graphics primitives.

pixels one at a time, we can draw primitives like polygons, triangles, and lines, without worrying about the details of which pixels are being set to which colors. Figure **3–20** illustrates some high-level primitives that all mainstream graphics libraries support.

This functionality is broken into two different layers because different machines may have vastly different graphics hardware. If you write a program that draws a red polygon, either the graphics library or the graphics hardware must be able to execute that command. On high-end systems, this may be done in the graphics hardware, on others it will be done by the graphics library in software. So the same commands can be used with a wide variety of machines, without worrying about the underlying graphics hardware.

The fundamental building block of the primitives in Figure **3–20** is a point (or vertex). A vertex has a position, normal, and color, each of which is a three element vector. The position specifies where the vertex is located, its normal specifies which direction the vertex is facing, and its color specifies the vertex's red, green, and blue components. A polygon is built by connecting a series of points or vertices as shown in Figure **3–21**. You may be wondering why each vertex has a normal, instead of having just one normal for the entire polygon. A planar polygon can only be facing one direction regardless of what the normals of its vertices indicate. The reason is that sometimes a polygon is used as an approximation of something else, like a curve. Figure **3–22** shows a top-down view of a cylinder. As you can see, it's not really a cylinder but rather a polygonal approxi-

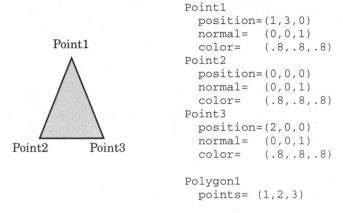

```
Point1
  position=(1,3,0)
  normal=  (0,0,1)
  color=   (.8,.8,.8)
Point2
  position=(0,0,0)
  normal=  (0,0,1)
  color=   (.8,.8,.8)
Point3
  position=(2,0,0)
  normal=  (0,0,1)
  color=   (.8,.8,.8)

Polygon1
  points= (1,2,3)
```

Figure 3–21 An example polygon.

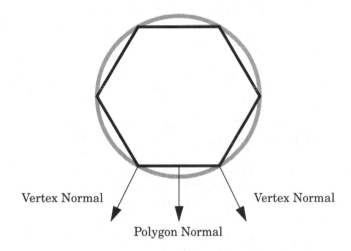

Figure 3–22 Vertex and polygon normals.

mation of the cylinder drawn in gray. Each vertex is shared by two polygons and the correct normal for the vertex is not the same as the normal for the polygon. Similar logic explains why each vertex has a color instead of just having one color for an entire polygon.

When you limit yourself to the types of primitives described above, there are some additional properties that many graphics systems support. Edge color and edge visibility can be used to highlight the polygon primitives that make up an actor. Another way to do this is by adjusting the representation from *surface* to *wireframe* or *points*. This replaces surfaces such as polygons with either their boundary edges or points respectively. While this may not make much sense from a physical perspective, it can help in some illustrations. Using edge visibility when rendering a CAD model can help to show the different pieces that comprise the model.

Rasterization

At this point in the text we have described how to represent graphics data using rendering primitives, and we have described how to represent images using raster display devices. The question remains, how do we convert graphics primitives into a raster image? This is the topic we address in this section. Although a thorough treatise on this topic is beyond the scope of this text, we will do our best to provide a high-level overview.

The process of converting a geometric representation into a raster image is called *rasterization*. This process is also called *scan conversion*. In the description that follows we assume that the graphics primitives are triangle polygons. This is not as limiting as you might think, because any general polygon can be tessellated into a set of triangles. Moreover, other surface representations such as splines are usually tessellated by the graphics system into triangles or polygons. (The method described here is actually applicable to convex polygons.)

Most of today's hardware is based on object-order rasterization techniques. As we saw earlier in this chapter, this means processing our actors in order. And since our actors are represented by polygon primitives, we process polygons one at a time. So although we describe the processing of one polygon, bear in mind that many polygons and possibly many actors are processed.

The first step is to transform the polygon using the appropriate transformation matrix. We also project the polygon to the image plane using either parallel or orthographic projection. Part of this process involves clipping the polygons. Not only do we use the front and back clipping planes to clip polygons too close or too far, but we must also clip polygons crossing the boundaries of the image plane. Clipping polygons that cross the boundary of the view frustum means we have to generate new polygon boundaries.

With the polygon clipped and projected to the image plane, we can begin scan-line processing (Figure **3–23**). The first step identifies the initial scan-line intersected by the projected polygon. This is found by sorting the vertex's y values. We then find the two edges joining the vertex on the left and right sides. Using the slopes of the edges along with the data values we compute delta data values. These data are typically the R, G, and B color components. Other data values include transparency values and z depth values. (The z values are necessary if we are using a z-buffer, described in the next section.) The row of pixels within the polygon (i.e., starting at the left and right edges) is called a *span*. Data values are interpolated from the edges on either side of the span to compute the internal pixel values. This process continues span-by-span, until the entire polygon is filled. Note that as new vertices are encountered, it is necessary to recompute the delta data values.

The shading of the polygon (i.e., color interpolation across the polygon) varies depending on the actor's interpolation attribute. There are three possibilities:

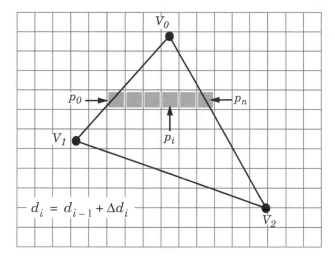

Figure 3–23 Rasterizing a convex polygon. Pixels are processed in horizontal spans (or scan-lines) in the image plane. Data values d_i at point p_i are interpolated along the edges and then along the scan-line using delta data values. Typical data values are RGB components of color.

flat, Gouraud, or *Phong shading.* Figure **3–7** illustrates the difference between flat and Gouraud interpolation. Flat shading calculates the color of a polygon by applying the lighting equations to just one normal (typically the surface normal) of the polygon. Gouraud shading calculates the color of a polygon at all of its vertices using the vertices' normals and the standard lighting equations. The interior and edges of the polygon are then filled in by applying the scan-line interpolation process. Phong shading is the most realistic of the three. It calculates a normal at every location on the polygon by interpolating the vertex normals. These are then used in the lighting equations to determine the resulting pixel colors. Both flat and Gouraud shading are commonly used methods. The complexity of Phong shading has prevented it from being widely supported in hardware.

Z-Buffer

In our earlier description of the rendering process, we followed rays of light from our eye through a pixel in the image plane to the actors and back to the light source. A nice side effect of ray tracing is that viewing rays strike the first actor they encounter and ignore any actors that are hidden behind it. When rendering actors using the polygonal methods described above, we have no such method of computing which polygons are hidden and which are not. We cannot generally count on the polygons being ordered correctly. Instead, we can use a number of hidden-line methods for polygon rendering.

One method is to sort all of our polygons from back to front and then render them in that order. This is called the painter's algorithm or painter's sort, and

Figure 3–24 Problem with Painter's algorithm.

has one major weakness illustrated in Figure **3–24**. Regardless of the order in which we draw these three triangles, we cannot obtain the desired result, since each triangle is both in front of, and behind, another triangle. There are algorithms that sort and split polygons as necessary to treat such a situation [Carlson85]. This requires more initial processing to perform the sorting and splitting. If the geometric primitives change between images or the camera view changes, then this processing must be performed before each render.

Another hidden surface algorithm, z-buffering, takes care of this problem and does not require sorting. Z-buffering takes advantage of the z-value (i.e., depth value along direction of projection) in the view coordinate system. Before a new pixel is drawn, its z-value is compared against the current z-value for that pixel location. If the new pixel would be in front of the current pixel, then it is drawn and the z-value for that pixel location is updated. Otherwise the current pixel remains and the new pixel is ignored.

Z-buffering has been widely implemented in hardware because of its simplicity and robustness. The downside to z-buffering is that it requires a large amount of memory, called a z-buffer, to store a z-value of every pixel. Most systems use a z-buffer with a depth of 24 or 32 bits. For a 1000 by 1000 display that translates into three to four megabytes just for the z-buffer. Another problem with z-buffering is that its accuracy is limited depending on its depth. A 24-bit z-buffer yields a precision of one part in 16,777,216 over the height of the viewing frustum. This resolution is often insufficient if objects are close together. If you do run into situations with z-buffering accuracy, make sure that the front and back clipping planes are as close to the visible geometry as possible.

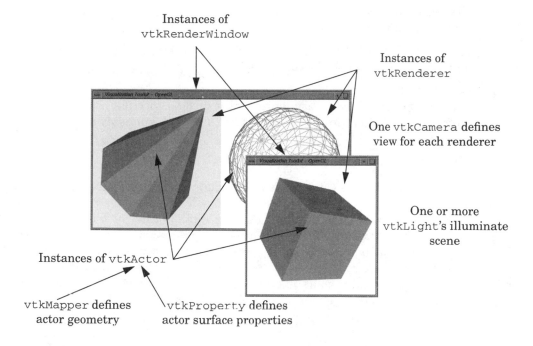

Figure 3–25 Illustrative diagram of graphics objects (Model cxx)

3.10 Putting It All Together

This section provides an overview of the graphics objects and how to use them in the *Visualization Toolkit*.

The Graphics Model

We have discussed many of the objects that play a part in the rendering of a scene. Now it's time to put them together into a comprehensive object model for graphics and visualization.

In the *Visualization Toolkit* there are seven basic objects that we use to render a scene. There are many more objects behind the scenes, but these seven are the ones we use most frequently. The objects are listed in the following and illustrated in Figure **3–25**.

1. vtkRenderWindow — manages a window on the display device; one or more renderers draw into an instance of vtkRenderWindow.

2. vtkRenderer — coordinates the rendering process involving lights, cameras, and actors.

3. vtkLight — a source of light to illuminate the scene.

4. `vtkCamera` — defines the view position, focal point, and other viewing properties of the scene.

5. `vtkActor` — represents an object rendered in the scene, both its properties and position in the world coordinate system.

6. `vtkProperty` — defines the appearance properties of an actor including color, transparency, and lighting properties such as specular and diffuse. Also representational properties like wireframe and solid surface.

7. `vtkMapper` — the geometric representation for an actor. More than one actor may refer to the same mapper.

The class `vtkRenderWindow` ties the rendering process together. It is responsible for managing a window on the display device. For PCs running Windows '95 or NT, this will be a Microsoft display window, and for UNIX systems this will be an X window. In **vtk**, instances of `vtkRenderWindow` are device independent. This means that you do not need to be concerned about what underlying graphics hardware or software is being used, the software automatically adapts to your computer as instances of `vtkRenderWindow` are created. (See "Achieving Device Independence" on page 66 for more information.)

In addition to window management, `vtkRenderWindow` objects are used to manage renderers and store graphics specific characteristics such as size, position, window title, *window depth*, and the *double buffering* flag. The depth of a window indicates how many bits are allocated per pixel. Double buffering is a technique where a window is logically divided into two buffers. At any given time one buffer is currently visible to the user. Meanwhile, the second buffer can be used to draw the next image in an animation. Once the rendering is complete, the two buffers can be swapped so that the new image is visible. This common technique allows animations to be displayed without the user seeing the actual rendering of the primitives. High-end graphics systems perform double buffering in hardware. A typical system would have a rendering window with a depth of 72 bits. The first 24 bits are used to store the red, green, and blue (RGB) pixel components for the front buffer. The next 24 bits store the RGB values for the back buffer. The last 24 bits are used as a z-buffer.

The class `vtkRenderer` is responsible for coordinating its lights, camera, and actors to produce an image. Each instance maintains a list of the actors, lights, and an active camera in a particular scene. At least one actor must be defined, but if lights and a camera are not defined, they will be created automatically by the renderer. In such a case the actors are centered in the image and the default camera view is down the z-axis. Instances of the class `vtkRenderer` also provide methods to specify the background and ambient lighting colors. Methods are also available to convert to and from world, view, and display coordinate systems.

One important aspect of a renderer is that it must be associated with an instance of the `vtkRenderWindow` class into which it is to draw, and the area in the render window into which it draws must be defined by a rectangular *viewport*. The viewport is defined by normalized coordinates (0,1) in both the x and y

image coordinate axes. By default, the renderer draws into the full extent of the rendering window (viewpoint coordinates (0,0,1,1)). It is possible to specify a smaller viewport. and to have more than one renderer draw into the same rendering window.

Instances of the class `vtkLight` illuminate the scene. Various instance variables for orienting and positioning the light are available. It is also possible to turn on/off lights and set the color of the light. Normally at least one light is "on" to illuminate the scene. If no lights are defined and turned on, the renderer constructs a light automatically. Lights in **vtk** can be either positional or infinite. Positional lights have an associated cone angle and attenuation factors. Infinite lights project light rays parallel to one another.

Cameras are constructed by the class `vtkCamera`. Important parameters include camera position, focal point, location of front and back clipping planes, view up vector, and field of view. Cameras also have special methods to simplify manipulation. These include elevation, azimuth, zoom, and roll. Similar to `vtkLight`, an instance of `vtkCamera` will be created automatically by the renderer if none is defined.

Instances of the class `vtkActor` represent objects in the scene. In particular, `vtkActor` combines object properties (color, shading type, etc.), geometric definition, and orientation in the world coordinate system. This is implemented behind the scenes by maintaining instance variables that refer to instances of `vtkProperty`, `vtkMapper`, and `vtkTransform`. Normally you need not create properties or transformations explicitly, since these are automatically created and manipulated using `vtkActor`'s methods. You do need to create an instance of `vtkMapper` (or one of its subclasses). The mapper ties the data visualization pipeline to the graphics device. (We will say more about the pipeline in the next chapter.)

There are other classes of actors with specialized behavior, implemented as subclasses of `vtkActor`. One example is `vtkFollower`. Instances of this class always face the active camera. This is useful when designing signs or text that must be readable from any camera position in the scene.

Instances of the class `vtkProperty` affect the rendered appearance of an actor. When actors are created, a property instance is automatically created with them. It is also possible to create property objects directly and then associate the property object with one or more actors. In this way actors can share common properties.

Finally, `vtkMapper` (and its subclasses) defines object geometry and, optionally, vertex colors. We will examine the mapping process in more detail in "Mapper Design" on page 191. For now assume that `vtkMapper` is an object that represents geometry and other types of visualization data. In addition, `vtkMapper` refers to a table of colors (i.e., `vtkLookupTable`) that are used to color vertices. (We discuss mapping of data to colors in "Color Mapping" on page 155.)

There is another important object, `vtkRenderWindowInteractor`, that captures events for a renderer in the rendering window. `vtkRenderWindowInteractor` captures these events and then triggers certain operations like camera dolly, pan, and rotate, actor picking, into/out of stereo mode, and so on.

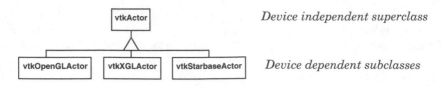

(a) Inheritance of device classes

```
vtkActor *vtkActor::New()
{
  char *temp = vtkRenderWindow::GetRenderLibrary();
...
  if ( !strcmp("OpenGL",temp)) return vtkOpenGLActor::New();
...
}
```

(b) Code fragment from `vtkActor::New()`

Figure 3–26 Achieving device independence using (a) inheritance and (b) object factories.

Instances of this class are associated with a rendering window using the `Set-RenderWindow()` method.

Achieving Device Independence

A desirable property of applications built with **vtk** is that they are device independent. This means that computer code that runs on one operating system with a particular software/hardware configuration runs unchanged on a different operating system and software/hardware configuration. The advantage of this is that the programmer does not need to expend effort porting an application between different computer systems. Also, existing applications do not need to be rewritten to take advantage of new developments in hardware or software technology. Instead, **vtk** handles this transparently by a combination of inheritance and a technique known as *object factories*.

Figure **3–26**(a) illustrates the use of inheritance to achieve device independence. Certain classes like `vtkActor` are broken into two parts: a device independent superclass and a device dependent subclass. The trick here is that the user creates a device dependent subclass by invoking the special constructor `New()` in the device independent superclass. For example we would use (in C++)

```
vtkActor *anActor = vtkActor::New()
```

to create a device dependent instance of `vtkActor`. The user sees no device dependent code, but in actuality `anActor` is a pointer to a device dependent subclass of `vtkActor`. Figure **3–26**(b) is a code fragment of the constructor method `New()`. (Note that in this example `vtkOpenGLActor::New()` is a simple constructor returning an instance of itself using `{return new vtkOpenGLActor;}`. It is possible that even this method could be tailored to a specific implementation of the graphics library OpenGL.)

The use of object factories as implemented using the `New()` method allows us to create device independent code that can move from computer to computer and adapt to changing technology. For example, if a new graphics library became available, we would only have to create a new device dependent subclass, and then modify the `New()` method from the device independent superclass to instantiate the subclass based on environment variables or other system information. This extension would be localized and only done once, and all applications based on these object factories would be automatically ported without change.

Examples

This section works through some simple applications implemented with **vtk** graphics objects. The focus is on the basics: how to create renderers, lights, cameras, and actors. Later chapters tie together these basic principles to create applications for data visualization.

Render a Cone. The following C++ code uses most of the objects introduced in this section to create an image of a cone. The `vtkConeSource` generates a polygonal representation of a cone and `vtkPolyDataMapper` maps the geometry (in conjunction with the actor) to the graphics library. (The source code to this example can be found in `Cone.cxx`.)

```
#include "vtk.h"

main ()
{
  char a;

  // create a rendering window and renderer
  vtkRenderer *ren = vtkRenderer::New();
  vtkRenderWindow *renWindow = vtkRenderWindow::New();
    renWindow->AddRenderer(ren);

  // create an actor and give it cone geometry
  vtkConeSource *cone = vtkConeSource::New();
    cone->SetResolution(8);
  vtkPolyDataMapper *coneMapper = vtkPolyDataMapper::New();
    coneMapper->SetInput(cone->GetOutput());
```

```
vtkActor *coneActor = vtkActor::New();
  coneActor->SetMapper(coneMapper);

// assign our actor to the renderer
ren->AddActor(coneActor);

// draw the resulting scene
renWindow->Render();

// loop until key is pressed
cout << "Press any key followed by <Enter> to exit>> ";
cin >> a;

// Clean up
ren->Delete();
renWindow->Delete();
cone->Delete();
coneMapper->Delete();
coneActor->Delete();
}
```

Some words about this example. The include file vtk.h includes class definitions for all objects in **vtk**. (This is a convenience to the user; you may want to include only the particular classes you're interested in to speed up compilation.) We use the constructor New() to create the objects in this example, and the method Delete() to destroy the objects. In **vtk** the use of New() and Delete() is recommended to insure device independence and properly manage reference counting. (See "Creating, Deleting, and Reference Counting Objects" on page 562.) In this example the use of Delete() is really not necessary because the objects are automatically deleted upon program termination. But generally speaking, you should always use a Delete() for every invocation of New(). (Future examples will not show the Delete() methods in the scope of the main() program to conserve space.)

The data in this example is created by linking together a series of objects into a *pipeline* (which is the topic of the next chapter). First a polygonal representation of the cone is created serving as input to the data mapper. The Set-Mapper() method associates the mapper's data with the coneActor. The next line adds coneActor to our renderer's list of actors. And finally we tell renWindow to render itself. This in turn causes the renderer instance ren to render itself. We conclude this example by waiting for a keyboard stroke before exiting. Since there are no cameras or lights defined in the above example, **vtk** automatically generates a default light and camera as a convenience to the user.

Creating Multiple Renderers. The next example is a bit more complex and uses multiple renderers that share a single rendering window. We use viewports to define where the renderers should draw. (This C++ code can be found in Cone2.cxx.)

```
#include "vtk.h"

main ()
{
  int i;

  // create a rendering window and both renderers
  vtkRenderer *ren1 = vtkRenderer::New();
  vtkRenderWindow *renWindow = vtkRenderWindow::New();
    renWindow->AddRenderer(ren1);
  vtkRenderer *ren2 = vtkRenderer::New();
    renWindow->AddRenderer(ren2);
  // create an actor and give it cone geometry
  vtkConeSource *cone = vtkConeSource::New();
    cone->SetResolution(8);
  vtkPolyDataMapper *coneMapper = vtkPolyDataMapper::New();
    coneMapper->SetInput(cone->GetOutput());
  vtkActor *coneActor = vtkActor::New();
    coneActor->SetMapper(coneMapper);

  // assign our actor to both renderers
  ren1->AddActor(coneActor);
  ren2->AddActor(coneActor);

  // set the size of our window
  renWindow->SetSize(400,200);

  // set the viewports and background of the renderers
  ren1->SetViewport(0,0,0.5,1);
  ren1->SetBackground(0.2,0.3,0.5);
  ren2->SetViewport(0.5,0,1,1);
  ren2->SetBackground(0.2,0.5,0.3);

  // draw the resulting scene
  renWindow->Render();

  // make one view 90 degrees from other
  ren1->GetActiveCamera()->Azimuth(90);

  // do a azimuth of the cameras 9 degrees per iteration
  for (i = 0; i < 360; i += 9)
    {
    ren1->GetActiveCamera()->Azimuth(9);
    ren2->GetActiveCamera()->Azimuth(9);
    renWindow->Render();
    }
}
```

As you can see, much of the code is the same as the previous example. The first difference is that we create two renderers instead of one. We assign the

Figure 3–27 Four frames of output from Cone2.cxx.

same actor to both renderers, but set each renderer's background to a different color. We set the viewport of the two renderers so that one is on the left half of the rendering window and the other is on the right. The rendering window's size is specified as 400 by 200 pixels, which results in each renderer drawing into a viewport of 200 by 200 pixels.

A good application of multiple renderers is to display different views of the same world as demonstrated in this example. Here we adjust the first renderer's camera with a 90 degree azimuth. We then start a loop that rotates the two cameras around the cone. Figure **3–27** shows four frames from this animation.

Introducing vtkRenderWindowInteractor. The previous examples are limited in that it is not possible to directly interact with the data without modifying and recompiling the C++ code. One common type of interaction is to change camera position so that we can view our scene from different vantage points. In the *Visualization Toolkit* we have provided a convenient object to do this: vtkRenderWindowInteractor.

Instances of the class vtkRenderWindowInteractor capture mouse and keyboard events in the rendering window, and perform operations depending on the particular event. For example, we can perform camera dolly, pan, and rotation with vtkRenderWindowInteractor. The following example shows how to instantiate and use this object. The example is the same as our first example with the addition of the interactor. The example C++ code is in Cone3.cxx.

```
#include "vtk.h"

main ()
{
  // create a rendering window and renderer
  vtkRenderer *ren = vtkRenderer::New();
  vtkRenderWindow *renWindow = vtkRenderWindow::New();
    renWindow->AddRenderer(ren);
  vtkRenderWindowInteractor *iren =
                          vtkRenderWindowInteractor::New();
```

```
        iren->SetRenderWindow(renWindow);

    // create an actor and give it cone geometry
    vtkConeSource *cone = vtkConeSource::New();
      cone->SetResolution(8);
    vtkPolyDataMapper *coneMapper = vtkPolyDataMapper::New();
      coneMapper->SetInput(cone->GetOutput());
    vtkActor *coneActor = vtkActor::New();
      coneActor->SetMapper(coneMapper);

    // assign our actor to the renderer
    ren->AddActor(coneActor);

    // draw the resulting scene
    renWindow->Render();

    //  Begin mouse interaction
    iren->Start();
}
```

After the interactor is created using its `New()` method, we must tell it what render window to capture events in using the `SetRenderWindow()` method. In order to use the interactor we have to execute its `Start()` method, which works with the event loop of the windowing system to begin to catch events. Some of the more useful events include the "w" key, which draws all actors in wireframe; the "s" key, which draws the actors in surface form; the "3" key, which toggles in and out of 3D stereo for those systems that support this; the "r" key, which resets camera view; and the "e" key, which exits the application. In addition, the mouse buttons rotate, pan, and dolly about the camera's focal point. Two advanced features are the "u" key, which executes a user-defined function; and the "p" key, which picks the actor under the mouse pointer.

Properties and Transformations. The previous examples did not explicitly create property or transformation objects or apply actor methods that affect these objects. Instead, we accepted default instance variable values. This procedure is typical of **vtk** applications. Most instance variables have been preset to generate acceptable results, but methods are always available for you to override the default values.

This example creates an image of two cones of different colors and specular properties. In addition, we transform one of the objects to lay next to the other. The C++ source code for this example can be found in `Cone4.cxx`.

```
    #include "vtk.h"

main ()
{
    char a;
```

```
// create a rendering window and renderer
vtkRenderer *ren = vtkRenderer::New();
vtkRenderWindow *renWindow = vtkRenderWindow::New();
  renWindow->AddRenderer(ren);
vtkRenderWindowInteractor *iren =
    vtkRenderWindowInteractor::New();
  iren->SetRenderWindow(renWindow);

// create an actor and give it cone geometry
vtkConeSource *cone = vtkConeSource::New();
  cone->SetResolution(8);
vtkPolyDataMapper *coneMapper = vtkPolyDataMapper::New();
  coneMapper->SetInput(cone->GetOutput());
vtkActor *cone1 = vtkActor::New();
  cone1->SetMapper(coneMapper);
  cone1->GetProperty()->SetColor(0.2000,0.6300,0.7900);
  cone1->GetProperty()->SetDiffuse(0.7);
  cone1->GetProperty()->SetSpecular(0.4);
  cone1->GetProperty()->SetSpecularPower(20);

vtkProperty *prop = vtkProperty::New();
  prop->SetColor(1.0000, 0.3882, 0.2784);
  prop->SetDiffuse(0.7);
  prop->SetSpecular(0.4);
  prop->SetSpecularPower(20);

vtkActor *cone2 = vtkActor::New();
  cone2->SetMapper(coneMapper);
  cone2->SetProperty(prop);
  cone2->SetPosition(0,2,0);

// assign our actor to the renderer
ren->AddActor(cone1);
ren->AddActor(cone2);

// draw the resulting scene
renWindow->Render();

//  Begin mouse interaction
iren->Start();
}
```

We set the actor cone1 properties by modifying the property object automatically created by the actor. This differs from actor cone2, where we create a property directly and then assign it to the actor. Cone2 is moved from its default position by applying the SetPosition() method. This method affects the transformation matrix that is an instance variable of the actor. The resulting image is shown in Figure **3–28**.

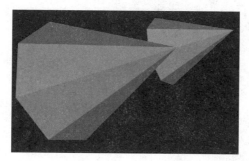

Figure 3–28 Modifying properties and transformation matrix (Cone4.cxx).

Interpreted Code. In an earlier example we saw how to create an interactor object that allows us to manipulate the camera (among other things). Although this provides flexibility and interactivity for a large number of applications, there are examples throughout this text where we want to modify other parameters. These parameters range from actor properties, such as color, to the name of an input file. Of course we can always write or modify C++ code to do this, but in many cases the turn-around time between change and result is too long. To improve overall interactivity we use an interpreted system. Interpreted systems allow us to modify objects and immediately see the result, without the need to recompile and relink source code. Chapter 11 discusses interpreters in more depth.

The *Visualization Toolkit* uses Tcl as one of its interpreted languages (other interpreters will be or are available — see "Interpreters and Tcl/Tk" on page 457). There is a one-to-one mapping between C++ methods and Tcl functions for most objects in the system. The following example repeats our third example but is implemented using a Tcl script. (The script can be found in Cone.tcl.)

```
catch {load vtktcl}
# user interface command widget
source ../../examplesTcl/vtkInt.tcl

# create a rendering window and renderer
vtkRenderer ren1
vtkRenderWindow renWin
    renWin AddRenderer ren1
vtkRenderWindowInteractor iren
    iren SetRenderWindow renWin

# create an actor and give it cone geometry
vtkConeSource cone
  cone SetResolution 8
```

Figure 3–29 Using Tcl and Tk to build an interpreted application (`Cone.tcl`).

```
vtkPolyDataMapper coneMapper
   coneMapper SetInput [cone GetOutput]
vtkActor coneActor
   coneActor SetMapper coneMapper

# assign our actor to the renderer
ren1 AddActor coneActor

# enable user-interface interactor
iren SetUserMethod {wm deiconify .vtkInteract}
iren Initialize

# prevent the tk window from showing up then start the event loop
wm withdraw .
```

As we can see from this example, the number of lines of code is less for the Tcl example than for equivalent C++ code. Also, many of the complexities of C++ are hidden using the interpreted language. Most importantly, we extend the interactor so that when a "u" keystroke is entered into the window (i.e., the user function key), a Tcl/Tk command widget appears (Figure **3–29**). (Tk is a computer independent graphical user-interface widget set that is part of Tcl.) Using this user-interface tool we can create, modify, and delete objects, and modify their instance variables. The resulting changes appear as soon as a `Render()` method is applied or mouse events in the rendering window cause a render to occur. We encourage you to use Tcl (or other interpreter) for rapid creation of graphics and visualization examples. C++ is best used when you desire higher performing applications.

Transformation Matrices

Transformation matrices are used throughout *Visualization Toolkit*. Actors use them to position and orient themselves. Various filters, including `vtkGlyph3D` and vtkTransformFilter, use transformation matrices to implement their own functionality. As a user you may never use transformation matrices directly, but understanding them is important to successful use of many **vtk** classes.

The most important aspect to applying transformation matrices is to understand the order in which the transformations are applied. If you break down a complex series of transformations into simple combinations of translation, scaling, and rotation, and keep careful track of the order of application, you will have gone a long way to mastering their use.

A good demonstration example of transformation matrices is to examine how vtkActor uses its internal matrix. vtkActor has an internal instance variable Transform to which it delegates many of its methods or uses the matrix to implement its methods. For example, the RotateX(), RotateY(), and RotateZ() methods are all delegated to Transform. The method SetOrientation() uses Transform to orient the actor.

The vtkActor class applies transformations in an order that we feel is natural to most users. As a convenience, we have created instance variables that abstract the transformation matrices. The Origin (o_x, o_y, o_z) specifies the point that is the center of rotation and scaling. The Position (p_x, p_y, p_z) specifies a final translation of the object. Orientation (r_x, r_y, r_z) defines the rotations about the x, y and z axes. Scale (s_x, s_y, s_z) defines scale factors for the x, y, and z axes. Internally, the actor uses these instance variables to create the following sequence of transformations (see Equation **3-6**, Equation **3-9**, Equation **3-13**).

$$T = T_T(p_x + o_x, p_y + o_y, p_z + o_z) T_{R_z} T_{R_x} T_{R_y} T_S T_T(-o_x, -o_y, -o_z) \qquad \textbf{(3-14)}$$

The term $T_T(x, y, z)$ denotes the translations in the x, y, and z directions. Recall that we premultiply the transformation matrix times the position vector. This means the transformations are read from right to left. In other words, Equation **3-14** proceeds as follows:

1. Translate the actor to its origin. Scaling and rotation will occur about this point. The initial translation will be countered by a translation in the opposite direction after scaling and rotations are applied.

2. Scale the geometry.

3. Rotate the actor about the y, then x, and then z axes.

4. Undo the translation of step 1 and move the actor to its final location.

The order of the transformations is important. In **vtk** the rotations are ordered to what is natural in most cases. We recommend that you spend some time with the software to learn how these transformations work with your own data.

Probably the most confusing aspect of transformations are rotations and their effect on the Orientation instance variable. Generally orientations are not set directly by the user, and most users will prefer to specify rotations with the RotateX(), RotateY(), and RotateZ() methods. These methods perform rotations about the x, y, and z axes in an order specified by the user. New rotations are applied to the right of the rotation transformation. If you need to rotate your actor about a single axis, the actor will rotate exactly as you expect it will, and the resulting orientation vector will be as expected. For example, the operation RotateY(20) will produce an orientation of (0,20,0) and a RotateZ(20) will produce (0,0,20). However, a RotateY(20) followed by a RotateZ(20) will not produce (0,20,20) but produce an orientation of (6.71771, 18.8817, 18.8817)! This is because the rotation portion of Equation **3-14** is built from the rotation order z, then x, and then y. To verify this, a RotateZ(20) followed by a RotateY(20) does produce an orientation of (0,20,20). Adding a third rotation can be even more confusing.

A good rule of thumb is to only use the SetOrientation() method to either reset the orientation to (0,0,0) or to set just one of the rotations. The RotateX(), RotateY(), and RotateZ() methods are preferred to SetOrientation() when multiple angles are needed. Remember that these rotations are applied in reverse order. Figure **3–30** illustrates the use of the rotation methods. We turn off the erase between frames using the render window's EraseOff() method so we can see the effects of the rotations. Note that in the fourth image the cow still rotates about her own y axis even though an x axis rotation preceded the y rotation.

We have seen that **vtk** hides some of the complexities of matrix transformations by using instance variables that are more natural than a transformation matrix. But there will be times when the predefined order of transformations performed by the actor will not be sufficient. vtkActor has an instance variable UserMatrix that contains a 4 x 4 transformation matrix. This matrix is applied before the transformation composed by the actor. As you become more comfortable with 4 x 4 transformation matrices you may want to build your own matrix. The object vtkTransform creates and manipulates these matrices. Unlike an actor, an instance of vtkTransform does not have an instance variable for position, scale, origin, etc. You control the composition of the matrix directly. The following statements create an identical 4 x 4 matrix that the actor creates:

```
vtkTransform *myTrans = vtkTransform::New ();
myTrans->Translate (position[0],position[1],position[2]);
myTrans->Translate (origin[0],origin[1],origin[2]);
myTrans->RotateZ (orientation[2]);
myTrans->RotateX (orientation[0]);
myTrans->RotateZ (orientation[1]);
myTrans->Scale (scale[0],scale[1],scale[2]);
myTrans->Translate (-origin[0],-origin[1],-origin[2]);
```

Compare this sequence of operations on the transform with the transformation in Equation **3-14**.

Our final example shows how the transform built with vtkTransform compares with a transform built by vtkActor. In this example, we will transform our cow so that she rotates about the world coordinate origin (0,0,0). She will

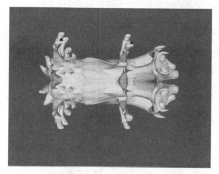

(a) Six rotations about the x axis.

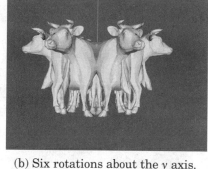

(b) Six rotations about the y axis.

(c) Six rotations about the z axis.

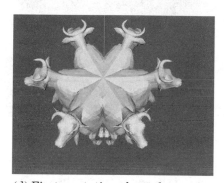

(d) First a rotation about the x axis, then six rotations about the y axis.

Figure 3–30 Rotations of a cow about her axes. In this model, the x axis is from the left to right; the y axis is from bottom to top; and the z axis emerges from the image. The camera location is the same in all four images (`rotations.tcl`).

appear to be walking around the origin. We accomplish this in two ways: one using `vtkTransform` and the actor's `UserMatrix`, then using the actor's instance variables.

First, we will move the cow five feet along the z axis then rotate her about the origin. We always specify transformations in the reverse order of their application:

```
vtkTransform *walk = vtkTransform::New();
  walk->RotateY(0,20,0);
  walk->Translate(0,0,5);
vtkActor *cow=vtkActor::New();
  cow->SetUserMatrix(walk->GetMatrix());
```

These operations produce the transformation sequence:

$$T = T_{R_y} T_S T_T (0, 0, 5)$$

(3-15)

Figure 3–31 The cow "walking" around the global origin (`walkCow.tcl`).

Now we do the same using the cow's instance variables:

```
vtkActor *cow=vtkActor::New();
  cow->SetOrigin(0,0,-5);
  cow->RotateY(20);
  cow->SetPosition(0,0,5);
```

When the actor builds its transform it will be:

$$T = T_T(0, 0, 5 - (-5))T_{R_y}T_S T_T(0, 0, -(-5)) \qquad \textbf{(3-16)}$$

Canceling the minus signs in the right-most translation matrix and combining the position and origin translation produce the equivalent transform that we built with `vtkTranform`. Figure **3–31** shows the cow rotating with the specified transformation order. Your preference is a matter of taste and how comfortable you are with matrix transformations. As you become more skilled (and your demands are greater) you may prefer to always build your transformations. **vtk** gives you the choice.

There is one final and powerful operation that affects an actor's orientation. You can rotate an actor about an arbitrary vector positioned at the actor's origin. This is done with the actor's (and transform's) `RotateWXYZ()` method. The first argument of the operation specifies the number of degrees to rotate about the vector specified by the next three arguments. Figure **3–32** shows how to rotate

Figure 3–32 The cow rotating about a vector passing through her nose. (a) With origin (0,0,0). (b) With origin at (6.1,1.3,.02). (`walkCow.tcl`).

the cow about a vector passing through her nose. At first, we leave the origin at (0,0,0). This is obviously not what we wanted. The second figure shows the rotation when we change the cow's rotation origin to the tip of her nose.

If all of this transformation talk seems confusing, rest assured that for the most part you won't need to master transformations. For those of you that will master transformations, the *Visualization Toolkit* transformation capabilities has enough flexibility for you to meet your needs.

3.11 Chapter Summary

The process of generating an image using a computer is called rendering. Computer graphics is the field of study that encompasses rendering techniques. Computer graphics forms the foundation of data visualization.

Three-dimensional rendering techniques simulate the interaction of lights and cameras with objects, or actors, to generate images. A scene consists of a combination of lights, cameras, and actors. Object-order rendering techniques generate images by rendering actors in a scene in order. Image-order techniques render the image one pixel at a time. Polygon-based graphics hardware is based on object-order techniques. Ray-tracing or ray-casting is an image-order technique.

Lighting models require a specification of color. We saw both the RGB (red-green-blue) and HSV (hue-saturation-value) color models. The HSV model is a more natural model than the RGB model for most users. Lighting models also include effects due to ambient, diffuse, and specular lighting.

There are four important coordinate systems in computer graphics. The model system is the 3D coordinate system where our geometry is defined. The world system is the global Cartesian system. All modeled data is eventually transformed into the world system. The view coordinate system represents what is visible to the camera. It is a 2D system scaled from (-1,1). The display coordinate system uses actual pixel locations on the computer display.

Homogeneous coordinates are a 4D coordinate system in which we can include the effects of perspective transformation. Transformation matrices are 4×4 matrices that operate on homogeneous coordinates. Transformation matrices can represent the effects of translation, scaling, and rotation of an actor. These matrices can be multiplied together to give combined transformations.

Graphics programming is usually implemented using higher-level graphics libraries or hardware systems. These dedicated systems offer better performance and easier implementation of graphics applications. Common techniques implemented in these systems include dithering and z-buffering. Dithering is a technique to simulate colors by mixing combinations of available colors. Z-buffering is a technique to perform hidden-line and hidden-surface removal.

The *Visualization Toolkit* uses a graphics model based on lights, cameras, actors, and renderers. The renderers draw into rendering windows. Actor properties are represented by a property object and their geometry by a mapper object.

3.12 Bibliographic Notes

This chapter provides the reader with enough information to understand the basic issues and terms used in computer graphics. There are a number of good text books that cover computer graphics in more detail and are recommended to readers who would like a more thorough understanding. The bible of computer graphics is [FoleyVanDam90]. For those wishing for less intimidating books [BurgerGillies89] and [Watt93] are useful references. You also may wish to peruse proceedings of the ACM SIGGRAPH conferences. These include papers and references to other papers for some of the most important work in computer graphics. [Carlson85] provides a good introduction for those who wish to learn more about the human vision system.

3.13 References

[Bresenham65]
     J. E. Bresenham. "Algorithm for Computer Control of a Digital Plotter." *IBM Systems Journal*, 4(1): 25–30, January 1965.

[BurgerGillies89]
     P. Burger and D. Gillies. *Interactive Compute Graphics Functional, Procedural and Device-Level Methods*. Addison-Wesley, Reading, MA, 1989.

[Carlson85]
     N. R. Carlson. *Physiology of Behaviour (3d Edition)*. Allyn and Bacon Inc., Newton, MA, 1985.

[Dartnall83]
     H. J. A. Dartnall, J. K. Bowmaker, and J. D. Mollon. "Human Visual Pigments: Microspectrophotometric Results from the Eyes of Seven Persons." *Proceedings of the Royal Society,* London, 1983.

[FoleyVanDam90]

J. D. Foley, A. van Dam, S. K. Feiner, and J. F. Hughes. *Computer Graphics Principles and Practice (2d Edition)*. Addison-Wesley, Reading, MA, 1990.

[Fuchs80]

H. Fuchs, Z. M. Kedem, and B. F. Naylor. "On Visible Surface Generation By A Priori Tree Structure." *Computer Graphics (SIGGRAPH '80)*, 14(3):124–133, 1980.

[Watt93]

A. Watt. *3D Computer Graphics (2d Edition)*. Addison-Wesley, Reading, MA, 1993.

[Whitted80]

T. Whitted. "An Improved Illumination Model for Shaded Display." *Communications of the ACM*, 23(6):343–349, 1980.

3.14 Exercises

3.1   Estimate the odds of a ray of light being emitted from the sun, traveling to earth and hitting a one meter square picnic blanket. You can assume that the sun is a point light source that emits light uniformly in all directions. The approximate distance from the sun to the earth is 150,000,000 km.
a) What are the odds when the sun is directly overhead?
b) What are the odds when the sun is inclined 45 degrees relative to the surface normal of the picnic blanket?
c) What assumptions or approximations did you make?

3.2   Proceeding from your result of Exercise 3.1, what are the difficulties in determining the odds of a ray of light traveling from the sun to hit the picnic blanket and then entering a viewer's eye?

3.3   The color cyan can be represented in both the HSV and RGB color spaces as shown in Figure **3–4**. These two representations for cyan do not yield the same wavelength intensity plots. How do they differ?

3.4   The `vtkSphereSource` class generates a polygonal model of a sphere. Using the examples at the end of this chapter as starting points, create a program to display a white sphere. Set the ambient and diffuse intensities to 0.5. Then add a `for`-loop to this program that adjusts the ambient and diffuse color of this sphere so that as the loop progresses, the diffuse color goes from red to blue, and the ambient color goes from blue to green. You might also try adjusting other lighting parameters such as specular color, ambient, diffuse, and specular intensity.

3.5   Using the `vtkSphereSource` as described in Exercise 3.4, create a program to display the sphere with a light source positioned at (1,1,1). Then extend this program by adding a `for`-loop that will adjust the active camera's clipping range so that increasing portions of the interior of the sphere can be seen. By increasing the first value of the clipping range, you will be adjusting the position of the front clipping plane. Once the front clipping plane starts intersecting the sphere, you should be able to see inside of it. The default radius of the vtkSphereSource is 0.5, so make sure that you adjust the clipping range in increments less than 1.0.

3.6 Modify the program presented in "Render a Cone" on page 67 so that the user can enter in a world coordinate in homogenous coordinates and the program will print out the resulting display coordinate. Refer to the reference page for vtkRenderer for some useful methods.
a) Are there any world coordinates that you would expect to be undefined in display coordinates?
b) What happens when the world coordinates are behind the camera?

3.7 Consider rasterizing a ten by ten pixel square. Contrast the approximate difference in the number of arithmetic operations that would need to be done for the cases where it is flat, Gouraud, or Phong shaded.

3.8 When using a z-buffer, we must also interpolate the z-values (or depth) when rasterizing a primitive. Working from Exercise 3.7, what is the additional burden of computing z-buffer values while rasterizing our square?

3.9 vtkTransform has a method GetOrientation() that looks at the resulting transformation matrix built from a series of rotations and provides the single x, y, and z rotations that will reproduce the matrix. Specify a series of rotations in a variety of orders and request the orientation with GetOrientation(). Then apply the rotations in the same order that vtkActor does and verify that the resulting 4 x 4 transformation matrix is the same.

3.10 vtkTransform, by default, applies new transformations at the right of the current transformation. The method PostMultiply() changes the behavior so that the transformations are applied to the left.
a) Use vtkTransform to create a transform using a variety of transformation operators including Scale(), RotateXYZ(), and Translate(). Then create the same matrix with PostMultiplyOn().
b) Applying rotations at the right of a series of transformations in effect rotates the object about its own coordinate system. Use the rotations.tcl script to verify this. Can you explain this?
c) Applying rotations at the left of a series of transformations in effect rotates the object about the world coordinate system. Modify the rotations.tcl script to illustrate this. (Hint: you will have to create an explicit transform with vtkTransform and set the actor's transform with SetUserMatrix().)

The Visualization Pipeline

*I*n the previous chapter we created graphical images using simple mathematical models for lighting, viewing, and geometry. The lighting model included ambient, diffuse, and specular effects. Viewing included the effects of perspective and projection. Geometry was defined as a static collection of graphics primitives such as points and polygons. In order to describe the process of visualization we need to extend our understanding of geometry to include more complex forms. We will see that the visualization process transforms data into graphics primitives. This chapter examines the process of data transformation and develops a model of data flow for visualization systems.

4.1 Overview

Visualization transforms data into images that efficiently and accurately represent information about the data. Hence, visualization deals with the issues of *transformation* and *representation*.

Transformation is the process of converting data from its original form into graphics primitives, and eventually into computer images. This is our working definition of the visualization process. An example of such a transformation is the process of extracting stock prices and creating an x-y plot depicting stock price as a function of time.

Representation includes both the internal data structures used to depict the data and the graphics primitives used to display the data. In the previous example, an array of stock prices and an array of times are the computational representation of the data, while the x-y plot is the graphical representation. Visualization transforms a computational form into a graphical form.

From an object-oriented viewpoint, transformations are processes in the functional model, while representations are the objects in the object model. Therefore, we characterize the visualization model with both functional models and object models.

A Data Visualization Example

A simple mathematical function for a quadric will clarify these concepts. The function

$$F(x, y, z) = a_0x^2 + a_1y^2 + a_2z^2 + a_3xy + a_4yz + a_5xz + a_6x + a_7y + a_8z + a_9 \quad \textbf{(4-1)}$$

is the mathematical representation of a quadric. Figure **4–1**(a) shows a visualization of Equation **4-1** in the region $-1 \leq x, y, z \leq 1$. The visualization process is as follows. We sample the data on a regular grid at a resolution of $50 \times 50 \times 50$. Three different visualization techniques are then used. On the left, we generate 3D surfaces corresponding to the function $F(x, y, z) = c$ where c is an arbitrary constant (i.e., the isosurface value). In the center, we show three different planes that cut through the data and are colored by function value. On the right we show the same three planes that have been contoured with constant valued lines. Around each we place a wireframe outline.

The Functional Model

The functional model in Figure **4–1**(b) illustrates the steps to create the visualization. The oval blocks indicate operations (processes) we performed on the data, and the rectangular blocks represent data stores (objects) that represent and provide access to data. Arrows indicate the direction of data movement. Arrows that point into a block are inputs; data flowing out of a block indicate outputs. The blocks also may have local parameters that serve as additional input. Processes that create data with no input are called data *source* objects, or simply sources. Processes that consume data with no output are called *sinks*. Processes with both an input and an output are called *filters*.

The functional model shows how data flows through the system. It also describes the dependency of the various parts upon one another. For any given process to execute correctly, all the inputs must be up to date. This suggests that functional models require a synchronization mechanism to insure that the correct output will be generated.

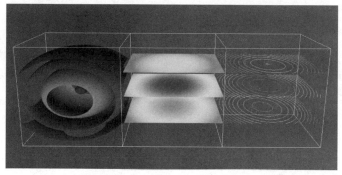

(a) Quadric visualization (`Sample.cxx`)

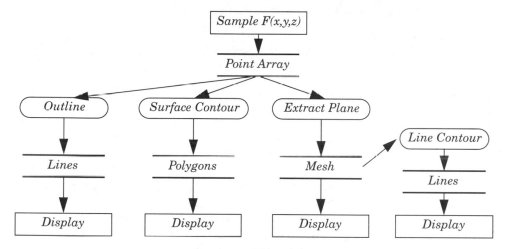

(b) Functional model

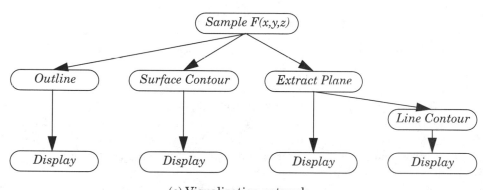

(c) Visualization network

Figure 4–1 Visualizing a quadric function $F(x,y,z) = c$.

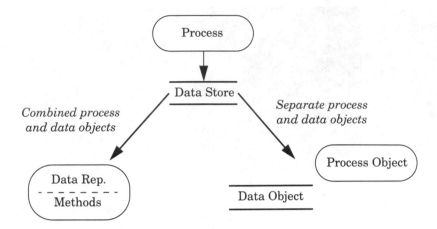

Figure 4–2 Object model design choices. One basic choice is to combine processes and data stores into a single object. This is the usual object-oriented choice. Another choice creates separate data objects and process objects.

The Visualization Model

In the examples that follow we will frequently use a simplified representation of the functional model to describe visualization processes (Figure **4–1**(c)). We will not explicitly distinguish between sources, sinks, data stores, and process objects. Sources and sinks are implied based on the number of inputs or outputs. Sources will be process objects with no input. Sinks will be process objects with no output. Filters will be process objects with at least one input and one output. Intermediate data stores will not be represented. Instead we will assume that they exist as necessary to support the data flow. Thus, as Figure **4–1**(c) shows, the *Lines* data store that the *Outline* object generates (Figure **4–1**(b)) are combined into the single object *Outline*. We use oval shapes to represent objects in the visualization model.

The Object Model

The functional model describes the flow of data in our visualization, the object model describes which modules operate on it. But what *are* the objects in the system? At first glance, we have two choices (Figure **4–2**).

The first choice combines data stores (object attributes) with processes (object methods) into a single object. In the second choice we use separate objects for data stores and processes. There is actually a third alternative: a hybrid combination of these two choices.

The conventional object-oriented approach (our first choice above) combines data stores and processes into a single object. This view follows the standard definition that objects contain a data representation combined with procedures to operate on the data. One advantage of this approach is that the processes, which are the data visualization algorithms, have complete access to the data structures, resulting in good computational performance. But this choice suffers from several drawbacks.

- From a user's perspective, processes are often viewed as independent of data representation. In other words, processes are naturally viewed as objects in the system. For example, we often say we want to "contour" data, meaning creating lines or surfaces corresponding to a constant data value. To the user it is convenient to have a single contour object to operate on different data representations.

- We must duplicate algorithm implementation. As in the previous contouring example, if we bind data stores and processes into a single object, the contour operation must be recreated for each data type. This results in duplicating code even though the implementations of an algorithm may be functionally and structurally similar. Modifying such algorithms also means modifying a large amount of code, since they are implemented across many objects.

- Binding data stores and algorithms together results in complex, data dependent code. Some algorithms may be much more complex than the data they operate on, with large numbers of instance variables and elaborate data structures. By combining many such algorithms with a data store, the complexity of the object greatly increases, and the simple meaning of the object becomes lost.

The second choice separates the data stores and processes. That is, one set of objects represents and provides access to the data, while another set of objects implements all operations on the data. Our experience shows that this is natural to users, although it may be considered unconventional to the object-oriented purist. We also have found that the resulting code is simple, modular, and easy for developers to understand, maintain, and extend.

One disadvantage to the second choice is that the interface between data representation and process is more formal. Thus the interface must be carefully designed to insure good performance and flexibility. Another disadvantage is that strong separation of data and process results in duplicate code. That is, we may implement operations that duplicate algorithms and that cannot be considered strictly data access methods. One example of such a situation is computing data derivatives. This operation is more than simple data access, so strictly speaking it doesn't belong in the data object methods. So to compute derivatives we would have to duplicate the code each time we needed derivatives computed. (Or create a procedural library of functions or macros!)

As a result of these concerns we use the hybrid approach in the *Visualization Toolkit*. Our approach is closest to the second choice described above, but we have selected a small set of critical operations that we implement within the data objects. These operations have been identified based on our experience implementing visualization algorithms. This effectively combines the first two choices to receive the maximum benefit and fewest disadvantages of each.

4.2 The Visualization Pipeline

In the context of data visualization, the functional model of Figure **4–1**(c) is referred to as the *visualization pipeline* or *visualization network*. The pipeline consists of objects to represent data (data objects), objects to operate on data (process objects), and an indicated direction of data flow (arrow connections between objects). In the text that follows, we will frequently use visualization networks to describe the implementation of a particular visualization technique.

Data Objects

Data objects represent information. Data objects also provide methods to create, access, and delete this information. Direct modification of the data represented by the data objects is not allowed except through formal object methods. This capability is reserved for process objects. Additional methods are also available to obtain characteristic features of the data. This includes determining the minimum and maximum data values, or determining the size or the number of data values in the object.

Data objects differ depending upon their internal representation. The internal representation has significant impact on the access methods to the data, as well as on the storage efficiency or computational performance of process objects that interact with the data object. Hence, different data objects may be used to represent the same data depending on demands for efficiency and process generality.

Process Objects

Process objects operate on input data to generate output data. A process object either derives new data from its inputs, or transforms the input data into a new form. For example, a process object might derive pressure gradient data from a pressure field or transform the pressure field into constant value pressure contours. The input to a process object includes both one or more data objects as well as local parameters to control its operation. Local parameters include both instance variables or associations and references to other objects. For example, the center and radius are local parameters to control the generation of sphere primitives.

Process objects are further characterized as *source objects*, *filter objects*, or *mapper objects*. This categorization is based on whether the objects initiate, maintain, or terminate visualization data flow.

Source objects interface to external data sources or generate data from local parameters. Source objects that generate data from local parameters are called *procedural* objects. The previous example of Figure **4–1** uses a procedural object to generate function values for the quadric function of Equation **4-1**. Source objects that interface to external data are called *reader* objects since the external file must be read and converted to an internal form. Source objects may also interface to external data communication ports and devices. Possible examples include simulation or modelling programs, or data acquisition systems to measure temperature, pressure, or other similar physical attributes.

Filter objects require one or more input data objects and generate one or more output data objects. Local parameters control the operation of the process object. Computing weekly stock market averages, representing a data value as a scaled icon, or performing union set operations on two input data sources are typical example processes of filter objects.

Mapper objects correspond to the sinks in the functional model. Mapper objects require one or more input data objects and terminate the visualization pipeline data flow. Usually mapper objects are used to convert data into graphical primitives, but they may write out data to a file or interface with another software system or devices. Mapper objects that write data to a computer file are termed *writer* objects.

4.3 Pipeline Topology

In this section we describe how to connect data and process objects to form visualization networks.

Pipeline Connections

The elements of the pipeline (sources, filters, and mappers) can be connected in a variety of ways to create visualization networks. However, there are two important issues that arise when we try to assemble these networks: *type* and *multiplicity*.

Type means the form or type of data that process objects take as input or generate as output. For example, a sphere source object may generate as output a polygonal or faceted representation, an implicit representation (e.g., parameters of a conic equation), or a set of occupancy values in a discretized representation of 3D space. Mapper objects might take as input polygonal, triangle strip, line, or point geometric representations. The input to a process object must be specified correctly for successful operation.

There are two general approaches to maintain proper input type. One approach is to design with type-less or single-type systems. That is, create a single type of data object and create filters that operate only on this one type (Figure **4–3**(a)). For example, we could design a general *DataSet* that represents any form of data that we're interested in, and the process objects would only input *DataSets* and generate *DataSets*. This approach is simple and elegant, but inflexible. Often, particularly useful algorithms (i.e., process objects) will operate only on specific types of data and to generalize them results in large inefficiencies in representation or data access. A typical example is a data object that represents structured data such as pixmaps or 3D volumes. Because the data is structured it can easily be accessed as planes or lines. However, a general representation will not include this capability because typically data is not structured.

Another approach to maintain proper input type is to design typed systems

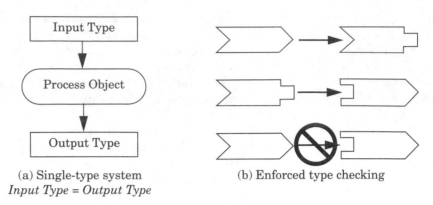

(a) Single-type system
Input Type = Output Type

(b) Enforced type checking

Figure 4–3 Maintaining compatible data type. (a) Single-type systems require no type checking. (b) In multiple-type systems only compatible types can be connected together.

(Figure **4–3**(b)). In typed systems only objects of compatible type are allowed to be connected together. That is, more than one type is designed, but type checking is performed on the input to insure proper connection. Depending on the particular computer language, type checking can be performed at compile, link, or run time. Although type checking does insure correct input type, this approach often suffers from an explosion of types. If not careful, the designers of a visualization system may create too many types, resulting in a fragmented, hard to use and understand system. In addition, the system may require a large number of *type-converter* filters. (Type-converter filters serve only to transform data from one form to another.) Carried to extremes, excessive type conversion results in computationally and memory wasteful systems.

The issue of multiplicity deals with the number of input data objects allowed, and the number of output data objects created during the operation of a process object (Figure **4–4**). We know that all filter and mapper objects require at minimum one input data object, but in general these filters can operate sequentially across a list of input. Some filters may naturally require a specific number of inputs. A filter implementing boolean operations is one example. Boolean operations such as union or intersection are implemented on data values two at a time. However, even here more than two inputs may be defined as a recursive application of the operation to each input.

We need to distinguish what is meant by multiplicity of output. Most sources and filters generate a single output. *Multiple fan-out* occurs when an object generates an output that is used for input by more than one object. This would occur, for example, when a source object is used to read a data file, and the resulting data is used to generate a wireframe outline of the data, plus contours of the data (e.g., Figure **4–1**(a)). *Multiple output* occurs when an object generates two or more output data objects. An example of multiple output is generating x, y, and z components of a gradient function as distinct data objects. Combinations of multiple fan-out and multiple output are possible.

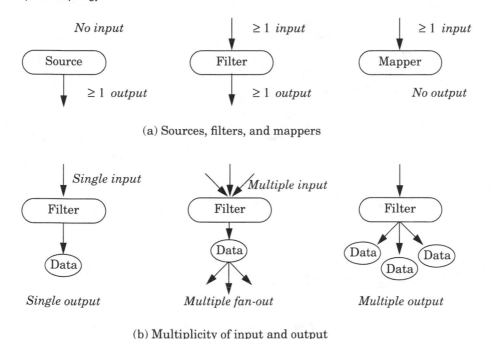

(a) Sources, filters, and mappers

(b) Multiplicity of input and output

Figure 4–4 Multiplicity of input and output. (a) Definition of source, filter, and mapper objects. (b) Various types of input and output.

Loops

In the examples described so far, the visualization networks have been free of cycles. In graph theory these are termed directed, acyclic graphs. However, in some cases it is desirable to introduce feedback loops into our visualization networks. Feedback loops in a visualization network allow us to direct the output of a process object upstream to affect its input.

Figure **4–5** shows an example of a feedback loop in a visualization network. We seed a velocity field with an initial set of random points. A probe filter is used to determine the velocity (and possibly other data) at each point. Each point is then repositioned in the direction of its associated vector value, possibly using a scale factor to control the magnitude of motion. The process continues until the points exit the data set or until a maximum iteration count is exceeded.

We will discuss the control and execution of visualization networks in the next section. However, loops pose no special problem in visualization networks. We need only make sure that the combined operation of the filters in the loop does not enter an infinite loop or nonterminating recursive state. Typically, we limit the number of executions of the loop in order to view intermediate results. However, it is possible to execute the loop repeatedly to process data as required.

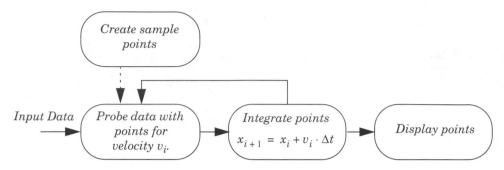

Figure 4–5 Looping in a visualization network. This example implements linear integration. The sample points are created to initialize the looping process. The output of the integration filter is used in place of the sample points once the process begins.

4.4 Executing the Pipeline

So far we have seen the basic elements of the visualization network and ways to connect these elements together. In this section we discuss how to control the execution of the network.

To be useful, a visualization network must process data to generate a desired result. The complete process of causing each process object to operate is called the *execution* of the network.

Most often the visualization network is executed more than once. For example, we may change the parameters of, or the input to, a process object. This is typically due to user interaction: The user may be exploring or methodically varying input to observe results. After one or more changes to the process object or its input, we must execute the network to generate up-to-date results.

For highest performance, the process objects in the visualization network must execute *only* if a change occurs to their input. In some networks, as shown in Figure **4–6**, we may have parallel branches that need not execute if objects are modified local to a particular branch. In this figure, we see that object D and the downstream objects E and F must execute because D's input parameter is changed, and objects E and F depend on D for their input. The other objects need not execute because there is no change to their input.

We can control the execution of the network using either a *demand-driven* or *event-driven* approach. In the demand-driven approach, we execute the network only when output is requested, and only that portion of the network affecting the result. In the event-driven approach, every change to a process object or its input causes the network to reexecute. The advantage of the event-driven approach is that the output is always up to date (except during short periods of computation). The advantage of the demand driven approach is that large numbers of changes can be accumulated without intermediate computation. The demand-driven approach minimizes computation and results in more interactive visualization networks.

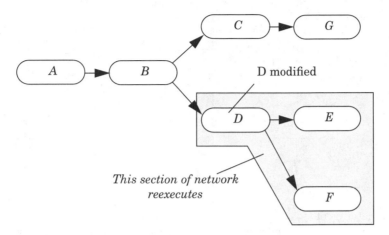

Figure 4–6 Network execution. Parallel branches need not execute if changes are local to a particular branch.

The execution of the network requires synchronization between process objects. We want to execute a process object only when all of its input objects are up to date. There are generally two ways to synchronize network execution: explicit or implicit control (Figure **4–7**).

Explicit Execution

Explicit control means directly tracking the changes to the network, and then directly controlling the execution of the process objects based on an explicit dependency analysis. The major characteristic of this approach is that a centralized *executive* is used to coordinate network execution. This executive must track changes to the parameters and inputs of each object, including subsequent changes to the network topology (Figure **4–7**(a)).

The advantage of this approach is that synchronization analysis and update methods are local to the single executive object. In addition, we can create dependency graphs and perform analysis of data flow each time output is requested. This capability is particularly important if we wish to decompose the network for parallel computing or to distribute execution across a network of computers.

The disadvantage of the explicit approach is that each process object becomes dependent upon the executive, since the executive must be notified of any change. Also, the executive cannot easily control execution if the network execution is conditional, since whether to execute or not depends on the local results of one or more process objects.

The explicit approach may be either demand-driven or event-driven. In the event-driven approach, the executive is notified whenever a change to an object occurs (typically in response to a user-interface event), and the network is imme-

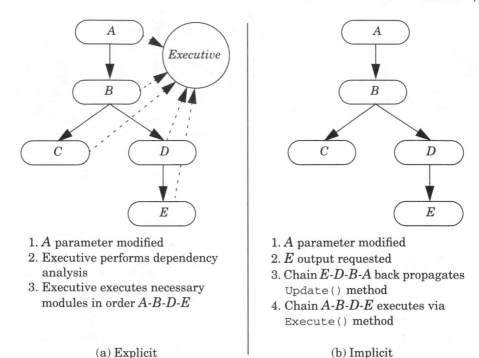

1. *A* parameter modified
2. Executive performs dependency
   analysis
3. Executive executes necessary
   modules in order *A-B-D-E*

1. *A* parameter modified
2. *E* output requested
3. Chain *E-D-B-A* back propagates
   Update() method
4. Chain *A-B-D-E* executes via
   Execute() method

(a) Explicit   (b) Implicit

Figure 4–7 Explicit and implicit network execution.

diately executed. In the demand-driven approach, the executive accumulates changes to object inputs and executes the network based on explicit user demand.

The explicit approach with a central executive is typical of many commercial visualization systems such as AVS, Irix Explorer, and IBM Data Explorer. Typically these systems use a visual-programming interface to construct the visualization network. Often these systems are implemented on parallel computers, and the ability to distribute computation is essential.

Implicit Execution

Implicit control means that a process object executes only if its local input or parameters change (Figure **4–7**(b)). Implicit control is implemented using a two-pass process. First, when output is requested from a particular object, that object requests input from its input objects. This process is recursively repeated until source objects are encountered. The source objects then execute if they have changed or their external inputs have changed. Then the recursion unwinds as each process object examines its inputs and determines whether to execute. This procedure repeats until the initial requesting object executes and terminates the process. These two steps are called the *update* and *execution* passes.

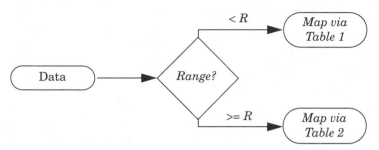

Figure 4–8 Examples of conditional execution. Depending upon range, data is mapped through different color lookup tables.

Implicit network execution is naturally implemented using *demand-driven* control. Here network execution occurs only when output data is requested. Implicit network execution may also be event-driven if we simply request output each time an appropriate event is encountered (such as change to object parameter).

The primary advantage of the implicit control scheme is its simplicity. Each object only need keep track of its internal modification time. When output is requested, the object compares its modification time with that of its inputs, and executes if out of date. Furthermore, process objects need only know about their direct input, so no global knowledge of other objects (such as a network executive) is required.

The disadvantage of implicit control is that it is harder to distribute network execution across computers or to implement sophisticated execution strategies. One simple approach is to create a queue that executes process objects in order of network execution (possibly in a distributed fashion). Of course, once a central object is introduced back into the system, the lines between implicit and explicit control are blurred.

Conditional Execution

Another important capability of visualization networks is conditional execution. For example, we may wish to map data through different color lookup tables depending upon the variation of range in the data. Small variations can be amplified by assigning more colors within the data range, while we may compress our color display by assigning a small number of colors to the data range (Figure **4–8**).

The conditional execution of visualization models (such as that shown Figure **4–1**(c)) can be realized in principle. However, in practice we must supplement the visualization network with a conditional language to express the rules for network execution. Hence, conditional execution of visualization networks is a function of implementation language. Many visualization systems are programmed using the visual programming style. This approach is basically a visual editor to construct data flow diagrams directly. It is difficult to express conditional execution of networks using this approach. Alternatively, in a procedural programming language, conditional execution of networks is straightforward. We defer discussion of this topic until "Putting It All Together" on page 101.

4.5 Memory and Computation Trade-off

Visualization is a demanding application, both in terms of computer memory and computational requirement. Data streams on the order of 1 to 100 megabytes are not uncommon. Many visualization algorithms are computationally expensive, in part due to input size, but also due to the inherent algorithm complexity. In order to create applications that have reasonable performance, most visualization systems have various mechanisms to trade off memory and computation costs.

Static and Dynamic Memory Models

Memory and computation trade-offs are important performance issues when executing visualization networks. In the networks presented thus far, the output of a process object is assumed to be available to downstream process objects at all times. Thus, network computation is minimized. However, the computer memory requirement to preserve object output can be huge. Networks of only a few objects can tie up extensive computer memory resources.

An alternative approach is to save intermediate results only as long as they are needed by other objects. Once these objects finish processing, the intermediate result can be discarded. This approach results in extra computation each time output is requested. The memory resources required are greatly reduced at the expense of increased computation. Like all trade-offs, the proper solution depends upon the particular application and the nature of the computer system executing the visualization network.

We term these two approaches as *static* and *dynamic* memory models. In the static model intermediate data is saved to reduce overall computation. In the dynamic model intermediate data is discarded when it is no longer needed. The static model serves best when small, variable portions of the network reexecute, and when the data sizes are manageable by the computer system. The dynamic model serves best when the data flows are large, or the same part of the network executes each time. Often, it is desirable to combine both the static and dynamic models into the same network. If an entire leg of the network must execute each time, it makes no sense to store intermediate results, since they are never used. On the other hand, we may wish to save an intermediate result at a branch point in the network, since the data will more likely be reused. A comparison of the static and dynamic memory model for a specific network is shown in Figure **4–9**.

As this figure shows, the static model executes each process object only once, storing intermediate results. In the dynamic model, each process object releases memory after downstream objects complete execution. Depending upon the implementation of the dynamic model, process object B may execute once or

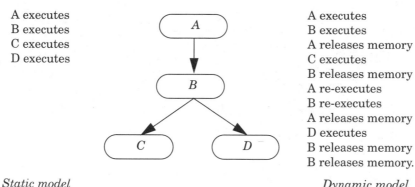

A executes
B executes
C executes
D executes

A executes
B executes
A releases memory
C executes
B releases memory
A re-executes
B re-executes
A releases memory
D executes
B releases memory
B releases memory.

Static model   *Dynamic model*

Figure 4–9 Comparison of static versus dynamic memory models for typical network. Execution begins when output is requested from objects C and D. In more complex dynamic models, we can prevent B from executing twice by performing a more thorough dependency analysis.

twice. If a thorough dependency analysis is performed, process B will release memory only after both objects C and D execute. In a simpler implementation, object B will release memory after C and subsequently, D executes.

Reference Counting

Another valuable tool to minimize memory cost is to share storage using reference counting. To use reference counting, we allow more than one process object to refer to the same data object. For example, assume that we have three objects A, B, and C that form a portion of a visualization network as shown in Figure **4–10**. Also assume that these objects modify only part of their input data, leaving the data object that specifies x-y-z coordinate position unchanged. Then to conserve memory resources we can allow the output of each process object to refer to the single data object representing these points. Data that is changed remains local to each filter and is not shared.

4.6 Programming Models

Visualization systems are by their very nature designed for human interaction. As a result they must be easy to use. On the other hand, visualization systems must readily adapt to new data, and must be flexible enough to allow rapid data exploration. To meet these demands, a variety of programming models have been developed.

Visualization Models

At the highest level are applications. Visualization applications have finely tailored user-interfaces that are specific to an application area, e.g., stock market or

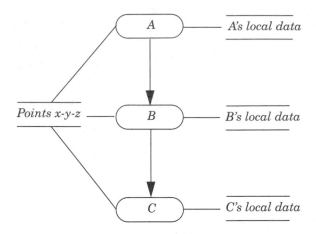

Figure 4–10 Reference counting to conserve memory resource. Each filter A, B, and C shares a common point representation. Other data is local to each object.

fluid flow visualization. Applications are the easiest to use, but are the least flexible. It is very difficult or impossible for the user to extend applications into a new domain because of inherent logistical issues. Commercial turn-key visualization software is generally considered to be application software.

At the opposite end of the spectrum are programming libraries. A conventional programming library is a collection of procedures that operate on a library-specific data structure. Often these libraries are written in conventional programming languages such as C or FORTRAN. These offer great flexibility and can be easily combined with other programming tools and techniques. Programming libraries can be extended or modified by the addition of user-written code. Unfortunately, the effective use of programming libraries requires skilled programmers. Furthermore, non graphics/visualization experts cannot easily use programming libraries because there is no notion of how to fit (or order) the procedures together correctly. These libraries also require extensive synchronization schemes to control execution as input parameters are varied.

Most commercial systems lie between these two extremes. These typically use a *visual programming* approach to construct visualization networks. The basic idea is to provide graphical tools and libraries of modules or process objects. Modules may be connected subject to input/output type constraints, using simple graphical layout tools. In addition, user interface tools allow association of interface widgets with object input parameters. System execution is generally transparent to the user by way of an internal execution executive.

Alternative Visual Programming Models

There are two other graphics and visualization programming models that bear mentioning. These are *scene graphs* and the *spreadsheet* model.

Scene graphs are typically found in 3D graphics systems such as OpenInventor [Wernecke94]. Scene graphs are acyclic tree-structures that represent objects, or nodes, in an order defined by the tree layout. The nodes may be geometry (called shape nodes), graphics properties, transformations, manipulators, lights, cameras, and so forth, that define a complete scene. The parent/child relationship controls how properties and transformations are applied to the nodes as they are rendered, or how the objects relate to other objects in the scene (e.g., which objects the lights shine on). Scene graphs are not used to control the execution of a visualization pipeline, rather they are used to control the rendering process. Scene graphs and visualization pipelines may be used together in the same application. In such a case the visualization pipeline is the generator of the shape nodes, and the scene graph controls the rendering of the scene including the shapes.

Scene graphs have found wide use in the graphics community because of their ability to compactly and graphically represent a scene. In addition, scene graphs have been popularized by their recent use in Web tools such as VRML and Java3D. See Chapter 12 for more information.

Another recently introduced technique for visual programming is the spreadsheet technique of Levoy [Levoy94]. In the spreadsheet model, we arrange operations on a regular grid similar to the common electronic accounting spreadsheets. The grid consists of rows and columns of cells, where each cell is expressed as a computational combination of other cells. The combination is expressed for each cell by using a simple programming language to add, subtract, or perform other more complex operations. The result of the computation (i.e., a visual output) is displayed in the cell.

Although visual programming systems are widely successful, they suffer two drawbacks. First, they are not as tailored as an application and require extensive programming, albeit visual, to be so. Second, visual programming is too limited for detailed control, so constructing complex low-level algorithms and user-interfaces is not feasible. What is required is a visualization system that provides the "modularity" and automatic execution control of a visual system, and the low-level programming capability of a programming library. Object-oriented systems have the potential to provide these capabilities. Carefully crafted object libraries provide the ease of use of visual systems with the control of programming libraries. That is a major goal of the *Visualization Toolkit (vtk)* described in this text.

4.7 Data Interface Issues

At this point in the text you may be wondering how to apply a visualization pipeline towards your own data. The answer depends on the type of data you have, preferences in programming style, and required complexity. Although we have not described particular types of data (we will in the next chapter), there are three general approaches you may wish to consider when interfacing your data to a visualization system.

Programming Interface

The most powerful and flexible approach is to directly program your application to read, write, and process data. There is almost no limit to what you can achieve using this approach. Unfortunately, in a complex system like **vtk** this requires a level of expertise that may be beyond your time budget to obtain. (If you are interested in this approach using **vtk**, you'll have to become familiar with the objects in the system. You will also want to refer to Appendix A, and see the examples in the next chapter that describe how to construct data objects.)

Typical applications requiring a programming interface are interfacing to data files that are not currently supported by the system or generating synthetic data (e.g., from a mathematical relationship) where no data file is available. Also, sometimes it is useful to directly code your data in the form of a program, and then execute the program to visualize the results. (This is exactly what many of the **vtk** examples do.)

File Interface (Readers / Writers)

In this chapter we saw that readers are source objects, and writers are mappers. What this means from a practical point of view is that readers will ingest data from a file, create a data object, and then pass the object down the pipeline for processing. Similarly, writers ingest a data object and then write the data object to a file. Thus, readers and writers will interface to your data well if **vtk** supports your format, *and* you only need to read or write a *single* data object. If your data file format is not supported by the system, you will need to interface to your data via the programming interface. Or, if you wish to interface to a collection of objects, you will probably want to see whether an exporter or importer object (described in the next section) exists to support your application.

Examples of readers include vtkSTLReader (read stereo-lithography files) and vtkBYUReader (read MOVIE.BYU format data files). Similarly the objects vtkSTLWriter and vtkBYUWriter can be used to write data files. To see which readers and writers are supported by **vtk**, see "Object Synopsis" on page 564. You may also want to check the Web pages at http://www.kitware.com for the current manual pages.

System Interface (Importers / Exporters)

Importers and *exporters* are objects in the system that read or write data files consisting of more than one object. Typically importers and exporters are used to save or restore an entire scene (i.e., lights, cameras, actors, data, transformations, etc.). When an importer is executed, it reads one or more files and may create several objects. For example, in **vtk** the vtk3DSImporter imports a *3D Studio* file and creates a rendering window, renderer, lights, cameras, and actors. Similarly, the vtkVRMLExporter creates a VRML file given a **vtk** render window. The VRML file contains cameras, lights, actors, geometry, transformations, and the like, indirectly referred to by the rendering window provided.

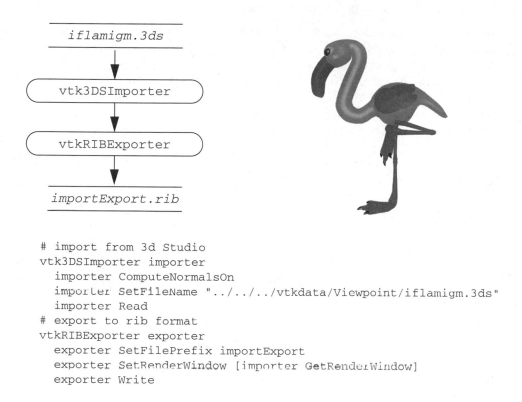

```
# import from 3d Studio
vtk3DSImporter importer
   importer ComputeNormalsOn
   importer SetFileName "../../../vtkdata/Viewpoint/iflamigm.3ds"
   importer Read
# export to rib format
vtkRIBExporter exporter
   exporter SetFilePrefix importExport
   exporter SetRenderWindow [importer GetRenderWindow]
   exporter Write
```

Figure 4–11 Importing and exporting files in **vtk**. An importer creates a vtkRender-Window that describes the scene. Exporters use an instance of vtkRenderWindow to obtain a description of the scene (3dsToRIB.tcl and flamingo.tcl).

In the *Visualization Toolkit*, there are several importers and exporters. To see which importers and exporters are supported by **vtk**, see "Object Synopsis" on page 564. You may also want to check the Web pages at http://www.kitware.com for current manual pages. If the exporter you are looking for does not exist, you will have to develop your own using the programming interface. Figure **4–11** shows an image created from a *3D Studio* model and saved as a *Renderman* RIB file.

4.8 Putting It All Together

In the previous sections we have treated a variety of topics relating to the visualization model. In this section we describe the particular implementation details that we have adopted in the *Visualization Toolkit*.

Procedural Language Implementation

The *Visualization Toolkit* is implemented in the procedural language C++. A class library containing data and process objects facilitates visualization application building. Supporting abstract objects are available to derive new objects. The visualization pipeline is designed to connect directly to the graphics subsystem described in the previous chapter.

A visual programming interface could be implemented using the class library provided. However, for real-world applications the procedural language implementation provides several advantages. This includes straightforward implementation of conditional network execution and looping, and simple interfacing to other systems such as graphical user-interfaces.

Strongly Typed

With the choice of C++ as the implementation language, strong type checking is mandatory. Most type checking is performed at compile time by the C++ compiler. There is one case where the type checking occurs at run time. This occurs when there is one or more special requirements on input data type.

In this case we find that there are certain filters that operate on a special part of their input data. An example of such a case is the tube filter vtkTube-Filter. This filter creates a tube around any lines found in its input data. Lines are represented using the type vtkPolyData, which represents the graphics primitives we saw in the previous chapter (i.e., points, lines, polygons, and triangle strips). Sometimes the input data will not contain lines. At run time vtk-TubeFilter will detect this and issue an error. So even though the compiler is satisfied, there are additional run-time checks that are not.

We would like to mention that one solution to this case is to create more data types. Instead of creating a single type that consists of points, lines, polygons, and triangle strips, we could create four different types of points, lines, polygons, and triangle strips. This certainly is a viable solution, but in our opinion the result is that too many data types are introduced into the system. The result is that the system is harder to understand and use and is less efficient.

Implicit Control of Execution

We have implemented implicit control of visualization network execution. Execution of the network occurs when output is requested from an object (i.e., demand-driven). This approach is simple to implement, is nearly transparent to the user of the system, and accommodates conditional execution and looping. On parallel computers or other special hardware, implicit control can be used in conjunction with an explicit load-balancing scheme by breaking the network into smaller subnetworks.

Our implementation is based on two key methods: Update() and Execute(). If you understand these methods, then you understand the basis for the implicit execution techniques found in **vtk**.

The `Update()` method is generally initiated when the user requests the system to render a scene. As part of the process the actors send a `Render()` method to their mappers. At this point network execution begins. The mapper invokes the `Update()` method on its input(s). These in turn recursively invoke the `Update()` method on their input(s). This process continues until a source object is encountered. At this point the source object compares its modified time to the last time it executed. If it has been modified more recently than executed, it re-executes via the `Execute()` method. The recursion then unwinds with each filter comparing its input time to its execution time. `Execute()` is called where appropriate. The process terminates when control is returned to the mapper.

This process is extremely simple, but depends upon keeping track of modified time and execution time properly. If you create a filter or source and fail to keep track of modification time correctly, you will encounter cases where your pipeline does not execute properly.

Multiple Input / Output

The *Visualization Toolkit* pipeline architecture has been designed to support multiple inputs and outputs. In practice, you will find that most filters and sources actually generate a single output and filters accept a single input. This is because most algorithms (which sources and filters represent) tend to be single input/output in nature. There are exceptions and we will describe some of these shortly.

The visualization pipeline architecture is depicted in Figure **4–12**. This figure shows how filters and data objects are connected together to form a visualization network. For the case shown here (i.e., objects with single input/output) the input data is represented by the `Input` instance variable and is set using the `SetInput()` method. The output data is represented by the `Output` instance variable and is accessed using the `GetOutput()` method. To connect filters together we generally use the C++ statement

```
filter2->SetInput(filter1->GetOutput());
```

where `filter1` and `filter2` are filter objects of compatible type. (The C++ compiler will enforce proper type.)

The trick to this architecture is that data objects know which filters "own" them. That is, if a filter creates an output data object, the data object knows which filter created it. This allows us to delegate certain messages from a filter through the data object to the connected filter. For example, if `filter2` receives an `Update()` method, it forwards it to its input data object, which in turn forwards it to its owning filter (if any). In this case `filter1` is the owning filter of the data object. This process continues until a source object is reached, where the propagation of the `Update()` method terminates.

You probably already have seen how this approach can be extended to multiple inputs and multiple outputs. The difference is that when a filter receives a message to be forwarded (e.g., `Update()`), it sends it to all its inputs. Also, when

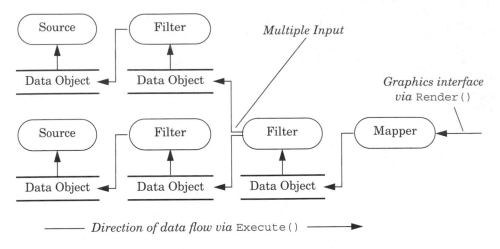

Figure 4–12   Description of implicit execution process implemented in **vtk**. The `Update()` method is initiated via the `Render()` method from the actor. Data flows back to mapper via `Execute()` method. Arrows connecting objects indicate direction of `Update()` process.

a filter executes, it must update all its outputs. Let's look at some concrete examples.

    `vtkGlyph3D` is an example of a filter that accepts multiple inputs and generates a single output. The inputs to `vtkGlyph3D` are represented by the `Input` and `Source` instance variables. The purpose of `vtkGlyph3D` is to copy the geometry defined by the data in `Source` to each point defined by `Input`. The geometry is modified according to the `Source` data values (e.g., scalars and vectors). (For more information about glyphs see "Glyphs" on page 185.) If you study the source code for this object carefully, you will see that the object implements its own `Update()` method (overloading its superclass method). To use the `vtkGlyph3D` object in C++ code you would do something like

```
glyph = vtkGlyph3D::New();
  glyph->SetInput(foo->GetOutput());
  glyph->SetSource(bar->GetOutput());
  . . .
```

where `foo` and `bar` are filters returning the appropriate type of output.

    The class `vtkExtractVectorComponents` is an example of a filter with a single input and multiple outputs. This filter extracts the three components of a 3D vector into separate scalar components. Its three outputs are named `VxComponent`, `VyComponent`, and `VzComponent`. An example use of the filter follows:

```
vz = vtkExtractVectorComponents::New();
foo = vtkDataSetMapper::New();
```

```
foo->SetInput(vz->GetVzComponent());
...
```

Several other special objects having multiple inputs or outputs are also available. Some of the more notable classes are `vtkMergeFilter`, `vtkAppend-Filter`, and `vtkAppendPolyData`. These filters combine multiple pipeline streams and generate a single output. The class `vtkProbeFilter` takes two inputs. The first input is the data we wish to probe. The second input supplies a set of points that are used as probe points. Some process objects take a list of input data. The `vtkBooleanStructuredPoints` object performs set operations on volume datasets. The first data item in the list is used to initialize the set operation. Each subsequent item in the list is combined with the result of previous operations using a boolean operation specified by the user.

For more details regarding the object design of filters and data objects, please see Chapters 5 and 6.

Support of Looping and Conditional Execution

Our implementation supports network looping and conditional execution. Each loop executes only once each time the network is updated. Multiple loop executions can be effected by updating the network multiple times.

Conditional execution is implemented by using the conditional constructs of the C++ language in conjunction with a local update method available to each process object.

Flexible Computation / Memory Trade-off

By default, networks constructed using the *Visualization Toolkit* store intermediate computational results (i.e., favor computation). However, a single class variable can be set to discard intermediate data when they are no longer needed (i.e., favor memory). In addition, a local parameter can be set within each process object to control this trade-off at object level.

This global variable is set as follows. Given the data object O, (or the output of a filter obtained using `O=filter->GetOutput()`), invoke `O->SetGlobal-ReleaseDataFlagOn()` to enable data release. To enable data release for a particular object use `O->SetReleaseDataFlagOn()`. Appropriate methods exist to disable memory release as well.

High-Level Object Design

At this point in the text it is premature to describe design details. However, there are two important classes that affect many of the objects in the text. These are the classes `vtkObject` and `vtkReferenceCount`.

`vtkObject` is the base object for many inheritance hierarchies. It provides methods and instance variables to control run-time debugging and printing, and maintains internal object modification time. In particular, the method `Modi-`

fied() is used to update the modification time, and the method GetMTime() is used to retrieve it.

vtkReferenceCount implements data object reference counting (See "Reference Counting" on page 97.) Subclasses of vtkReferenceCount may be shared by other objects, without duplicating memory.

Note that we do not always include vtkObject and vtkReferenceCount in object diagrams to conserve space. Refer to the source code for a definitive statement.

Examples

We will now demonstrate some of the features of the visualization pipeline with four examples. Some of the objects used here will be unfamiliar to you. Please overlook missing details until we cover the information later in the book. The goal here is to provide a flavor and familiarity with the software architecture and its use.

Simple Sphere. The first example demonstrates a simple visualization pipeline. A polygonal representation of a sphere is created with the source object (vtk-SphereSource). The sphere is passed through a filter (vtkElevationFilter) that computes the height of each point of the sphere above a plane. The plane is perpendicular to the z-axis, and passes through the point (0,0,-1). The data is finally mapped (vtkDataSetMapper) through a lookup table. The mapping process converts height value into colors, and interfaces the sphere geometry to the rendering library. The mapper is assigned to an actor, and then the actor is displayed. The visualization network, a portion of code, and output image are shown in Figure **4–13**.

The execution of the pipeline occurs implicitly when we render the actor. Each actor asks its mapper to update itself. The mapper in turn asks its input to update itself. This process continues until a source object is encountered. Then the source will execute if modified since the last render. Then the system walks through the network and executes each object if its input or instance variables are out of date. When completed, the actor's mapper is up to date and an image is generated.

Now let's reexamine the same process of pipeline execution by following method invocation. The process begins when the actor receives a Render() message from a renderer. The actor in turn sends a Render() message to its mapper. The mapper begins network execution by asking its input to update itself via the Update() operation. This causes a cascade of Update() methods as each filter in turn asks its input to update itself. If branching in the pipeline is present, the update method will branch as well. Finally, the cascade terminates when a source object is encountered. If the source object is out of date, it will send itself an Execute() command. Each filter will send itself an Execute() as necessary to bring itself up to date. Finally, the mapper will perform operations to transform its input data into rendering primitives.

In the *Visualization Toolkit*, the Update() method is public while the Exe-

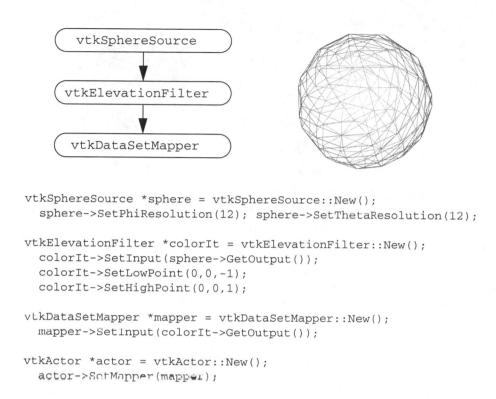

```
vtkSphereSource *sphere = vtkSphereSource::New();
  sphere->SetPhiResolution(12); sphere->SetThetaResolution(12);

vtkElevationFilter *colorIt = vtkElevationFilter::New();
  colorIt->SetInput(sphere->GetOutput());
  colorIt->SetLowPoint(0,0,-1);
  colorIt->SetHighPoint(0,0,1);

vtkDataSetMapper *mapper = vtkDataSetMapper::New();
  mapper->SetInput(colorIt->GetOutput());

vtkActor *actor = vtkActor::New();
  actor->SetMapper(mapper);
```

Figure 4–13 A simple sphere example (`ColorSph.cxx`).

cute() method is protected. Thus, you can manually cause network execution to occur by invoking the Update() operation. This can be useful when you want to set instance variables in the network based on the results of upstream execution, but do not want the whole network to update. The Execute() method is protected because it requires a certain object state to exist. The Update() method insures that this state exists.

One final note. The indentation of the code serves to indicate where objects are instantiated and modified. The first line (i.e., the New() operator) is where the object is created. The indented lines that follow indicate that various operations are being performed on the object. We encourage you to use a similar indenting scheme in your own work.

Warped Sphere. This example extends the pipeline of the previous example and shows the effects of type checking on the connectivity of process objects. We add a transform filter (vtkTransformFilter) to nonuniformly scale the sphere in the *x-y-z* directions.

The transform filter only operates on objects with explicit point coordinate representation (i.e., a subclass of vtkPointSet). However, the elevation filter

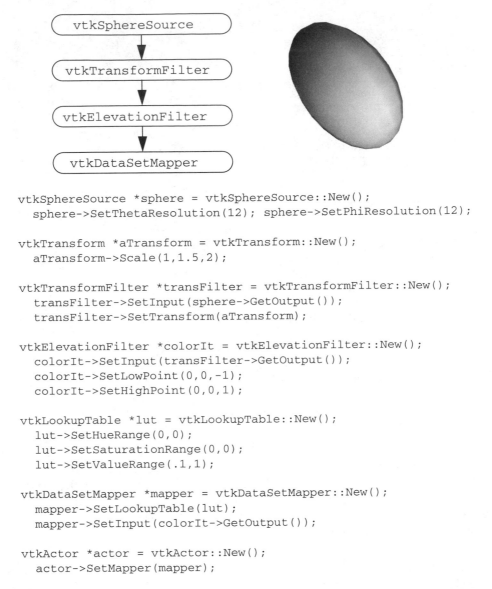

```
vtkSphereSource *sphere = vtkSphereSource::New();
  sphere->SetThetaResolution(12); sphere->SetPhiResolution(12);

vtkTransform *aTransform = vtkTransform::New();
  aTransform->Scale(1,1.5,2);

vtkTransformFilter *transFilter = vtkTransformFilter::New();
  transFilter->SetInput(sphere->GetOutput());
  transFilter->SetTransform(aTransform);

vtkElevationFilter *colorIt = vtkElevationFilter::New();
  colorIt->SetInput(transFilter->GetOutput());
  colorIt->SetLowPoint(0,0,-1);
  colorIt->SetHighPoint(0,0,1);

vtkLookupTable *lut = vtkLookupTable::New();
  lut->SetHueRange(0,0);
  lut->SetSaturationRange(0,0);
  lut->SetValueRange(.1,1);

vtkDataSetMapper *mapper = vtkDataSetMapper::New();
  mapper->SetLookupTable(lut);
  mapper->SetInput(colorIt->GetOutput());

vtkActor *actor = vtkActor::New();
  actor->SetMapper(mapper);
```

Figure 4–14 The addition of a transform filter to the previous example (StrSph.cxx).

generates the more general form vtkDataSet as output. Hence we cannot connect the transform filter to the elevation filter. But we can connect the transform filter to the sphere source, and then the elevation filter to the transform filter. The result is shown in Figure **4–14**. (Note: an alternative method is to use vtk-CastToConcrete to perform run-time casting.)

The C++ compiler enforces the proper connections of sources, filters, and mappers. To decide which objects are compatible, we check the type specification

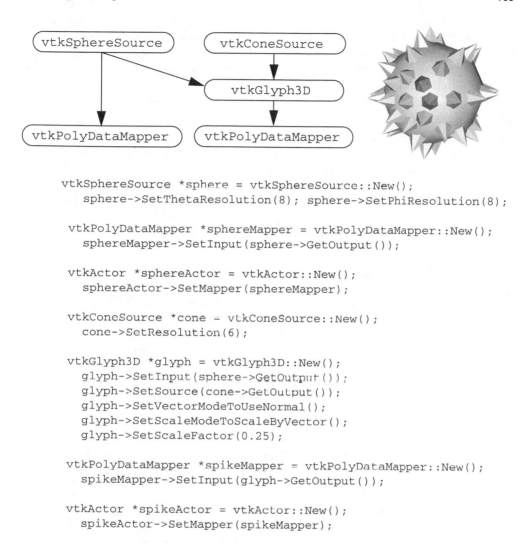

```
vtkSphereSource *sphere = vtkSphereSource::New();
   sphere->SetThetaResolution(8); sphere->SetPhiResolution(8);

vtkPolyDataMapper *sphereMapper = vtkPolyDataMapper::New();
   sphereMapper->SetInput(sphere->GetOutput());

vtkActor *sphereActor = vtkActor::New();
   sphereActor->SetMapper(sphereMapper);

vtkConeSource *cone = vtkConeSource::New();
   cone->SetResolution(6);

vtkGlyph3D *glyph = vtkGlyph3D::New();
   glyph->SetInput(sphere->GetOutput());
   glyph->SetSource(cone->GetOutput());
   glyph->SetVectorModeToUseNormal();
   glyph->SetScaleModeToScaleByVector();
   glyph->SetScaleFactor(0.25);

vtkPolyDataMapper *spikeMapper = vtkPolyDataMapper::New();
   spikeMapper->SetInput(glyph->GetOutput());

vtkActor *spikeActor = vtkActor::New();
   spikeActor->SetMapper(spikeMapper);
```

Figure 4–15 An example of multiple inputs and outputs (Mace.cxx).

of the SetInput() method. If the input object returns an output object or a sub-class of that type, the two objects are compatible and may be connected.

Generating Oriented Glyphs. This example demonstrates the use of an object with multiple inputs. vtkGlyph3D places 3D icons or glyphs (i.e., any polygonal geometry) at every input point. The icon geometry is specified with the instance variable Source, and the input points are obtained from the Input instance variable. Each glyph may be oriented and scaled in a variety of ways, depending upon the input and instance variables. In our example we place cones oriented in the direction of the point normals (Figure **4–14**).

The visualization network branches at vtkGlyph3D. If either branch is modified, then this filter will reexecute. Network updates must branch in both directions, and both branches must be up to date when vtkGlyph3D executes. These requirements are enforced by the Update() method, and pose no problem to the implicit execution method.

Disappearing Sphere. In our last example we construct a visualization network with a feedback loop, and show how we can use procedural programming to change the topology of the network. The network consists of four objects: vtk-SphereSource to create an initial polygonal geometry, vtkShrinkFilter to shrink the polygons and create a gap or space between neighbors, vtkEleva-tionFilter to color the geometry according to height above the x-y plane, and vtkDataSetMapper to map the data through a lookup table and interface to the rendering library. The network topology, a portion of the C++ code, and output are shown in Figure **4–14**.

After vtkSphereSource generates an initial geometry (in response to a render request), the input of vtkShrinkFilter is changed to the output of the vtkElevationFilter. Because of the feedback loop, vtkShrinkFilter will always reexecute. Thus, the behavior of the network is to reexecute each time a render is performed. Because the shrink filter is reapplied to the same data, the polygons become smaller and smaller and eventually disappear.

4.9 Chapter Summary

The visualization process is naturally modelled using a combination of functional and object models. The functional model can be simplified and used to describe visualization networks. The object model specifies the components of the visualization network.

Visualization networks consist of process objects and data objects. Data objects represent information; process objects transform the data from one form to another. There are three types of process objects — sources have no input and at least one output; filters have at least one input and output; sinks, or mappers, terminate the visualization network.

The execution of the network can be controlled implicitly or explicitly. Implicit control means that each object must insure its input is up to date, thereby distributing the control mechanism. Explicit control means that there is a centralized executive to coordinate the execution of each object.

Many techniques are available to program visualization networks. Direct visual programming is most common in commercial systems. At a higher level, applications provide tailored but more rigid interfaces to visualize information. At the lowest level, subroutine or object libraries provide the greatest flexibility. The *Visualization Toolkit* contains an object library implemented in C++ for constructing visualization networks.

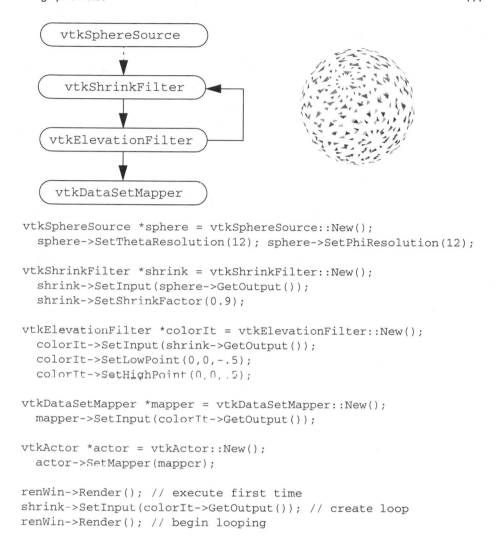

```
vtkSphereSource *sphere = vtkSphereSource::New();
   sphere->SetThetaResolution(12); sphere->SetPhiResolution(12);

vtkShrinkFilter *shrink = vtkShrinkFilter::New();
   shrink->SetInput(sphere->GetOutput());
   shrink->SetShrinkFactor(0.9);

vtkElevationFilter *colorIt = vtkElevationFilter::New();
   colorIt->SetInput(shrink->GetOutput());
   colorIt->SetLowPoint(0,0,-.5);
   colorIt->SetHighPoint(0,0,.5);

vtkDataSetMapper *mapper = vtkDataSetMapper::New();
   mapper->SetInput(colorIt->GetOutput());

vtkActor *actor = vtkActor::New();
   actor->SetMapper(mapper);

renWin->Render(); // execute first time
shrink->SetInput(colorIt->GetOutput()); // create loop
renWin->Render(); // begin looping
```

Figure 4–16 A network with a loop (LoopShrk.cxx).

4.10 Bibliographic Notes

The practical way to learn about the visualization process is to study commercially available systems. These systems can be categorized as either direct visual programming environments or as applications. Common visual programming systems include AVS [AVS89], Iris Explorer [IrisExplorer], IBM Data Explorer [DataExplorer], aPE [aPE90], and Khoros [Rasure91]. Application systems generally provide less flexibility than visual programming systems, but are better tailored to a particular problem domain. PLOT3D [PLOT3D] is an early example of a tool for CFD visualization. This has since been superseded by FAST [FAST90]. FieldView is another popular CFD visualizer [FieldView91]. VISUAL3 [VISUAL3] is a general tool for unstructured or structured grid visualization. PV-WAVE [Charal90] can be considered a hybrid system, since it has both simple visual programming techniques to interface to data files as well as a more structured user-interface than the visual programming environments. Wavefront's DataVisualizer [DataVisualizer] is a general-purpose visualization tool. It is unique in that it is part of a powerful rendering and animation package. A nice system for visualizing 3D gridded data (such as that produced by numerical weather models) is VIS5D. Find out more at the VIS5D Web site http://www.ssec.wisc.edu/~billh/vis5d.html.

Although many visualization systems claim to be object-oriented, this is often more in appearance than implementation. Little has been written on object-oriented design issues for visualization. VISAGE [VISAGE92] presents an architecture similar to that described in this chapter. Favre [Favre94] describes a more conventional object-oriented approach. His dataset classes are based on topological dimension and both data and methods are combined into classes.

4.11 References

[aPE90]
D. S. Dyer. "A Dataflow Toolkit For Visualization." *IEEE Computer Graphics and Applications*. 10(4):60–69, July 1990.

[AVS89]
C. Upson, T. Faulhaber Jr., D. Kamins and others. "The Application Visualization System: A Computational Environment for Scientific Visualization." *IEEE Computer Graphics and Applications*. 9(4):30–42, July 1989.

[Charal90]
S. Charalamides. "New Wave Technical Graphics Is Welcome." *DEC USER*, August 1990.

[DataExplorer]
Data Explorer Reference Manual. IBM Corp, Armonk, NY, 1991.

[DataVisualizer]
Data Visualizer User Manual. Wavefront Technologies, Santa Barbara, CA, 1990.

[FAST90]
G. V. Bancroft, F. J. Merritt, T. C. Plessell, P. G. Kelaita, R. K. McCabe, and A. Globus. "FAST: A Multi-Processed Environment for Visualization." In *Proceedings of Visualization '90*. pp. 14–27, IEEE Computer Society Press, Los Alamitos, CA, 1990.

[Favre94]
J. M. Favre and J. Hahn. "An Object-Oriented Design for the Visualization of Multi-Variate Data Objects." In *Proceedings of Visualization '94*. pp. 319–325, IEEE Computer Society Press, Los Alamitos, CA, 1994.

[FieldView91]
S. M. Legensky. "Advanced Visualization on Desktop Workstations." In *Proceedings of Visualization '91*. pp. 372–378, IEEE Computer Society Press, Los Alamitos, CA, 1991.

[Haeberli88]
P. E. Haeberli. "ConMan: A Visual Programming Language for Interactive Graphics." *Computer Graphics (SIGGRAPH '88)*. 22(4):103–11, 1988.

[IrisExplorer]
Iris Explorer User's Guide. Silicon Graphics Inc., Mountain View, CA, 1991.

[Levoy94]
M. Levoy. "Spreadsheets for Images." In *Proceedings of SIGGRAPH '94*. pp. 139–146, 1994.

[PLOT3D]
P. P. Walatka and P. G. Buning. *PLOT3D User's Manual*. NASA Fluid Dynamics Division, 1988.

[Rasure91]
J. Rasure, D. Argiro, T. Sauer, and C. Williams. "A Visual Language and Software Development Environment for Image Processing." *International Journal of Imaging Systems and Technology*. 1991.

[VISAGE92]
W. J. Schroeder, W. E. Lorensen, G. D. Montanaro, and C. R. Volpe. "VISAGE: An Object-Oriented Visualization System." In *Proceedings of Visualization '92*. pp. 219–226, IEEE Computer Society Press, Los Alamitos, CA, 1992.

[VISUAL3]
R. Haimes and M. Giles. "VISUAL3: Interactive Unsteady Unstructured 3D Visualization." AIAA Report No. AIAA-91-0794. January 1991.

[Wernecke94]
J. Wernecke. *The Inventor Mentor*. Addison-Wesley Publishing Company, ISBN 0-201-62495-8, 1994.

4.12 Exercises

4.1 Consider the following 2D visualization techniques: x-y plotting, bar charts, and pie charts. For each technique:
a) Construct functional models.
b) Construct object models.

4.2 A *height field* is a regular array of 2D points $h = f(x, y)$ where h is an altitude above the point (x,y). Height fields are often used to represent terrain data. Design an object-oriented system to visualize height fields.
a) How would you represent the height field?
b) What methods would you use to access this data?
c) Develop one process object (i.e., visualization technique) to visualize a height field. Describe the methods used by the object to access and manipulate the height field.

4.3 Describe how you would implement an explicit control mechanism for network execution.

a) How do process objects register their input data with the executive?

b) How is the executive notified of object modification?

c) By what method is the executive notified that network execution is necessary?

d) Describe an approach for network dependency analysis. How does the executive invoke execution of the process objects?

4.4 Visual programming environments enable the user to construct visualization applications by graphically connecting process objects.

a) Design a graphical notation to represent process objects, their input and output, and data flow direction.

b) How would you modify instance variables of process objects (using a graphical technique)?

c) By what mechanism would network execution be initiated?

d) How would you control conditional execution and looping in your network?

e) How would you take advantage of parallel computing?

f) How would you distribute network execution across two or more computers sharing a network connection?

4.5 Place oriented cylinders (instead of cones) on the mace in Figure **4–14**. (*Hint:* use `vtkCylinderSource`.)

4.6 The implicit update method for the visualization network used by **vtk** is simple to implement and understand. However, it is prone to a common programming error. What is this error?

4.7 Experiment with the transformation object in Figure **4–14**.

a) Translate the actor with `vtkTransform`'s `Translate()` method.

b) Rotate the actor with the `RotateX()`, `RotateY()`, and `RotateZ()` methods.

c) Scale the actor with the `Scale()` method.

d) Try combinations of these methods. Does the actor transform in ways that you expect?

4.8 Visualize the following functions. (*Hint:* use `vtkSampleFunction` and refer to Figure **4–1**.)

a) $F(x, y, z) = x^2$

b) $F(x, y, z) = x + 2y + 3z + 1$

c) $F(x, y, z) = x^2 + y^2 - (\cos z + 1)$

Basic Data Representation

*I*n Chapter 4 we developed a working definition of the visualization process: mapping information into graphics primitives. We saw how this mapping proceeds through one or more steps, each step transforming data from one form, or data representation, into another. In this chapter we examine common data forms for visualization. The goal is to familiarize you with these forms, so that you can visualize your own data using the tools and techniques provided in this text.

5.1 Introduction

To design representational schemes for data we need to know something about the data we might encounter. We also need to keep in mind design goals, so that we can design efficient data structures and access methods. The next two sections address these issues.

Characterizing Visualization Data

Since our aim is to visualize data, clearly we need to know something about the character of the data. This knowledge will help us create useful data models and powerful visualization systems. Without a clear understanding of the data, we risk designing inflexible and limited visualization systems. In the following we describe important characteristics of data. These characteristics are the discrete nature of data, whether it is regular or irregular, and its topological dimension.

First, visualization data is *discrete*. This is because we use digital computers to acquire, analyze, and represent our data, and typically measure or sample information at a finite number of points. Hence, all information is necessarily represented in discrete form.

Consider visualizing the simple continuous function $y = x^2$. If we are using a conventional digital computer, we must discretize this equation to operate on the data it represents (we are ignoring symbolic/analog computers and methods). For example, to plot this equation we would sample the function in some interval, say (-1,1), and then compute the value y of the function at a series of discrete points $x = x_i$ in this interval. The resulting points $((x_0,y_0), (x_1,y_1), (x_2,y_2), \ldots (x_n,y_n))$ connect the points with straight line segments. Thus, our (continuous) data is represented by a discrete sampling.

Because of the discrete character of the data we do not know anything about regions in between data values. In our previous example, we know that data is generated from the function $y = x^2$, but, generally speaking, when we measure and even compute data, we cannot infer data values between points. This poses a serious problem, because an important visualization activity is to determine data values at arbitrary positions. For example, we might probe our data and desire data values even though the probe position does not fall on a known point.

There is an obvious solution to this problem: interpolation. We presume a relationship between neighboring data values. Often this is a linear function, but we can use quadratic, cubic, spline, or other interpolation functions. Chapter 8 discusses interpolation functions in greater detail, but for now suffice it to say that interpolation functions generate data values in between known points.

A second important characteristic of visualization data is that its structure may be *regular* or *irregular* (alternatively, *structured* or *unstructured*). Regular data has an inherent relationship between data points. For example, if we sample on an evenly spaced set of points, we do not need to store all the point coordinates, only the beginning position of the interval, the spacing between points, and the total number of points. The point positions are then known implicitly, which we can take advantage of to save computer memory.

Data that is not regular is Irregular data. The advantage of irregular data is that we can represent information more densely where it changes quickly and less densely where the change is not so great. Thus, irregular data allows us to create adaptive representational forms, which can be beneficial given limited computing resources.

Characterizing data as regular or irregular allows us to make useful assumptions about the data. As we saw a moment ago, we can store regular data more compactly. Typically, we can also compute with regular data more efficiently relative to irregular data. On the other hand, irregular data gives us more freedom in representing data and can represent data that has no regular patterns.

Finally, data has a topological *dimension*. In our example $y = x^2$, the dimension of the data is one, since we have the single independent variable x. Data is potentially of any dimension from 0D points, to 1D curves, 2D surfaces, 3D volumes, and even higher dimensional regions.

The dimension of the data is important because it implies appropriate methods for visualization and data representation. For example, in 1D we naturally use *x-y* plots, bar charts, or pie charts, and store the data as a 1D list of values. For 2D data we might store the data in a matrix, and visualize it with a deformed surface plot (i.e., a *height field* — see Exercise 4.2).

In this chapter and Chapter 8, we show how these characteristics: discrete, regular/irregular, and data dimension, shape our model of visualization data. Keep these features in mind as you read these chapters.

Design Criterion

Visualizing data involves interfacing to external data, mapping into internal form, processing the data, and generating images on a computer display device. We pose the question: What form or forms should we use to represent data? Certainly many choices are available to us. The choice of representation is important because it affects the ability to interface to external data and the performance of the overall visualization system. To decide this issue we use the following design criteria:

Compact. Visualization data tends to be large, so we need compact storage schemes to minimize computer memory requirements.

Efficient. Data must be computationally accessible. We want to retrieve and store data in constant time (i.e., independent of data size). This requirement offers us the opportunity to develop algorithms that are linear, or $O(n)$, in time complexity.

Mappable. There are two types of mappings. First, data representations need to efficiently map into graphics primitives. This ensures fast, interactive display of our data. Second, we must be able to easily convert external data into internal visualization data structures. Otherwise, we suffer the burden of complex conversion processes or inflexible software.

Minimal Coverage. A single data representation cannot efficiently describe all possible data types. Nor do we want different data representations for every data type we encounter. Therefore, we need a minimal set of data representations that balances efficiency against the number of data types.

Simple. A major lesson of applied computation is that simple designs are preferable to complex designs. Simple designs are easier to understand, and therefore, optimize. The value of simplicity cannot be overemphasized. Many of the algorithms and data representations in this text assign high priority to this design criterion.

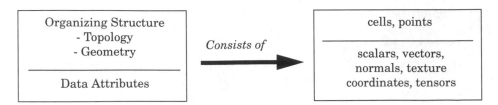

Figure 5–1 The architecture of a dataset. A dataset consists of an organizing structure, with both topological and geometric properties, and attribute data associated with the structure.

The remainder of this chapter describes common visualization data forms based on these design criteria. Our basic abstraction is the dataset, a general term for the various concrete visualization data types.

5.2 The Dataset

Data objects in the visualization pipeline are called *datasets*. The dataset is an abstract form; we leave the representation and implementation to its concrete subclasses.

A dataset consists of two pieces: an organizing *structure* and supplemental data *attributes* associated with the structure (Figure **5–1**).

The structure has two parts: *topology* and *geometry*. Topology is the set of properties invariant under certain geometric transformations [Weiler86]. Here we consider the transformations: rotation, translation, and nonuniform scaling. Geometry is the instantiation of the topology, the specification of position in 3D space. For example, saying that a polygon is a "triangle", specifies topology. By providing point coordinates, we specify geometry.

Dataset attributes are supplemental information associated with geometry and/or topology. This information might be a temperature value at a point or the inertial mass of a cell.

Our model of a dataset assumes that the structure consists of *cells* and *points*. The cells specify the topology, while the points specify the geometry. Typical attributes include scalars, vectors, normals, texture coordinates, tensors, and user-defined data.

The definition of the structure of a dataset as a collection of cells and points is a direct consequence of the discrete nature of our data. Points are located where data is known and the cells allow us to interpolate between points. We give detailed descriptions of dataset structure and attributes in the following sections.

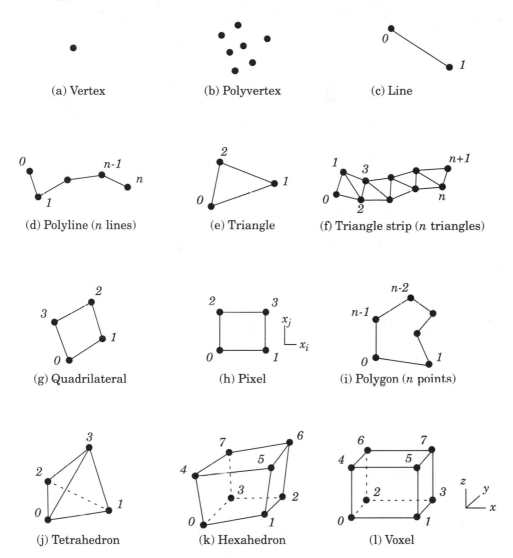

Figure 5–2 Cell types. Numbers define ordering of the defining points.

5.3 Cell Types

A dataset consists of one or more cells (Figure **5–2**). Cells are the fundamental building blocks of visualization systems. Cells are defined by specifying a *type* in combination with an ordered list of points. The ordered list, often referred to as the *connectivity list*, combined with the type specification, implicitly defines the topology of the cell. The *x-y-z* point coordinates define the cell geometry.

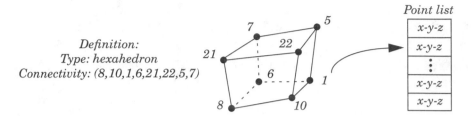

Figure 5–3 Example of a hexahedron cell. The topology is implicitly defined by the ordering of the point list.

Figure **5–3** shows one cell type, a hexahedron. The ordered list is a sequence of point ids that index into a point coordinate list. The topology of this cell is implicitly known: we know that (8,10) is one of the 12 edges of the hexahedron, and that (8,10,22,21) is one of its six faces.

Mathematically, we represent a cell by the symbol C_i. Then the cell is an ordered sequence of points $C_i = \{p_1, p_2, ..., p_n\}$ with $p_i \in P$, where P is a set of n-dimensional points (here $n=3$). The type of cell determines the sequence of points, or cell topology. The number of points n defining the cell is the *size* of the cell. A cell C_i "uses" a point p_i when $p_i \in C_i$. Hence the "use set" $U(p_i)$ is the collection of all cells using p_i:

$$U(p_i) = \{C_i : p_i \in C_i\} \qquad \textbf{(5-1)}$$

The importance of "uses" and "use sets" will become evident in Chapter 8 when we explore the topology of datasets.

Although we define points in three dimensions, cells may vary in topological dimension. Vertices, lines, triangles, and tetrahedron are examples of 0, 1, 2, and three-dimensional cells embedded in three-dimensional space. Cells can also be primary or composite. Composite cells consist of one or more primary cells, while primary cells cannot be decomposed into combinations of other primary cell types. A triangle strip, for example, consists of one or more triangles arranged in compact form. The triangle strip is a composite cell because it can be broken down into triangles, which are primary cells.

Certainly there are an infinite variety of possible cell types. In the *Visualization Toolkit* each cell type has been chosen based on application need. We have seen how some cell types: vertex, line, polygon, and triangle strip (Figure **3–20**) are used to represent geometry to the graphics subsystem or library. Other cell types such as the tetrahedron and hexahedron are common in numerical simulation. The utility of each cell type will become evident through the practice of visualization throughout this book. A description of the cell types found in the *Visualization Toolkit* is given in the following sections.

Vertex

The vertex is a primary zero-dimensional cell. It is defined by a single point.

Polyvertex

The polyvertex is a composite zero-dimensional cell. The polyvertex is defined by an arbitrarily ordered list of points.

Line

The line is a primary one-dimensional cell. It is defined by two points. The direction along the line is from the first point to the second point.

Polyline

The polyline is a composite one-dimensional cell consisting of one or more connected lines. The polyline is defined by an ordered list of $n+1$ points, where n is the number of lines in the polyline. Each pair of points $(i, i+1)$ defines a line.

Triangle

The triangle is a primary two-dimensional cell. The triangle is defined by a counter-clockwise ordered list of three points. The order of the points specifies the direction of the surface normal using the right-hand rule.

Triangle Strip

The triangle strip is a composite two-dimensional cell consisting of one or more triangles. The points defining the triangle strip need not lie in a plane. The triangle strip is defined by an ordered list of $n+2$ points, where n is the number of triangles. The ordering of the points is such that each set of three points $(i, i+1, i+2)$ with $0 \leq i \leq n$ defines a triangle.

Quadrilateral

The quadrilateral is a primary two-dimensional cell. It is defined by an ordered list of four points lying in a plane. The quadrilateral is convex and its edges must not intersect. The points are ordered counterclockwise around the quadrilateral, defining a surface normal using the right-hand rule.

Pixel

The pixel is a primary two-dimensional cell defined by an ordered list of four points. The cell is topologically equivalent to the quadrilateral with the addition of geometric constraints. Each edge of the pixel is perpendicular to its adjacent edges, and lies parallel to one of the coordinate axes *x-y-z*. Hence, the normal to the pixel is also parallel to one of the coordinate axes.

The ordering of the points defining the pixel is different from the quadrilateral cell. The points are ordered in the direction of increasing axis coordinate, starting with *x*, then *y*, then *z*. The pixel is a special case of the quadrilateral and is used to improve computational performance.

One important note is that the definition of the pixel cell given here is different from the usual definition for a pixel. Normally pixels are thought of as constant-valued "picture-elements" in an image (see "Graphics Hardware" on page 55). The definition given here implies that four picture-elements form the four corner points of the pixel cell. We normally use the term pixel to describe a pixel cell, but the meaning of the term will vary depending on context.

Polygon

The polygon is a primary two-dimensional cell. The polygon is defined by an ordered list of three or more points lying in a plane. The polygon normal is implicitly defined by a counterclockwise ordering of its points using the right-hand rule.

The polygon may be nonconvex, but may not have internal loops, and it cannot self-intersect. The polygon has *n* edges, where *n* is the number of points in the polygon.

Tetrahedron

The tetrahedron is a primary three-dimensional cell. The tetrahedron is defined by a list of four nonplanar points. The tetrahedron has six edges and four triangular faces.

Hexahedron

The hexahedron is a primary three-dimensional cell consisting of six quadrilateral faces, twelve edges, and eight vertices. The hexahedron is defined by an ordered list of eight points as shown in Figure **5–2**. The faces and edges must not intersect any other faces and edges, and the hexahedron must be convex.

Voxel

The voxel is a primary three-dimensional cell. The voxel is topologically equivalent to the hexahedron with additional geometric constraints. Each face of the voxel is perpendicular to one of the coordinate *x-y-z* axes. The defining point list is ordered in the direction of increasing coordinate value as shown in Figure **5–2**. The voxel is a special case of the hexahedron and is used to improve computational performance.

Similar to pixels, our definition of a voxel cell differs from the conventional definition of the term voxel. Typically, a voxel is referred to as a constant-valued

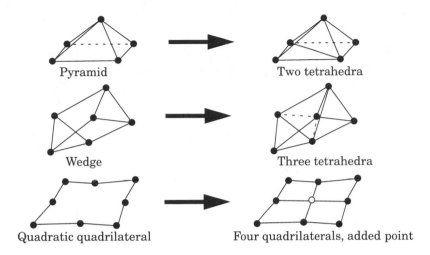

Figure 5–4 Decomposing cells into simpler forms.

"volume element". Using our definition, eight volume elements form the eight corner points of the voxel cell. We normally use the term voxel to describe a voxel cell, but the meaning of the term will vary depending on the context.

Other Types

We have implemented the previous twelve cell types in the *Visualization Toolkit*. In addition, there is one other type used as a place holder during data traversal. (The name of this cell type is vtkEmptyCell.) This cell type has no points or topological structure; it is only used to mark the existence of a deleted cell.

Besides these twelve types (and the empty cell type), many other potential cell types exist. You may add new types to the library (Appendix A), but an alternative is to decompose your cell type into combinations of the twelve described earlier. For example, the cell types pyramid, wedge, and quadratic quadrilateral can be decomposed as follows (Figure **5–4**).

- Pyramid — decompose into two tetrahedra.

- Wedge — decompose into three tetrahedra.

- Quadratic quadrilateral (e.g., higher order finite element) — decompose into four quadrilaterals by introducing a midpoint vertex.

There are many problems when decomposing cells. Interpolation errors arise when artificial cell boundaries (vertices, edges, and faces) are introduced. Also, the internal cell variation (interpolation functions) of the decomposed cells may be markedly different from those of the original cell. To avoid these difficulties we recommend that you derive your own cell type. (See Appendix A.)

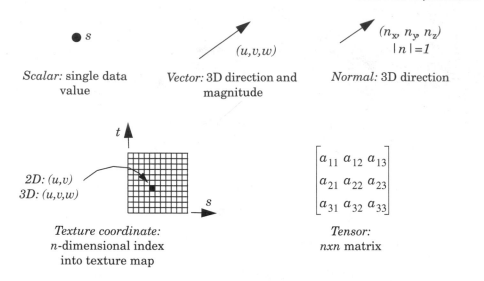

Figure 5–5 Attribute data.

5.4 Attribute Data

Attribute data is information associated with the structure of the dataset. This structure includes both the dataset geometry and topology. Most often, attribute data is associated with dataset points or cells, but sometimes attribute data may be assigned to cell components such as edges or faces. Attribute data may also be assigned across the entire dataset, or across a group of cells or points. We refer to this information as attribute data because it is an attribute to the structure of the dataset. Typical examples include temperature or velocity at a point, mass of a cell, or heat flux into and out of a cell face.

Attribute data is often categorized into specific types of data. These categories have been created in response to common data forms. Visualization algorithms are also categorized according to the type of data they operate on.

Single-valued functions, such as temperature or pressure, are examples of scalar data, which is one attribute type. More generally, attribute data can be treated as n-dimensional data arrays. For example, the single-valued function temperature can be treated as a 1×1 array, while velocity can be treated as a 3×1 array of components in the x, y, and z directions. This abstract model for data attribute can be extended throughout the visualization system. Some systems extend this model to include the structure of the data. For example, a structured point set (i.e., a volume) can be represented as a 3D array of $l \times m \times n$ data values. Unstructured data can be represented as a 3D vector of position, plus an array of connectivity. We refer to this general approach as the hyperdata model for visualization data (see "Other Data Abstractions" on page 130).

In the following sections we describe data attributes using the simpler type-specific model (Figure **5–5**). We also limit ourselves to three-dimensional structure, since the dataset structure and graphics are assumed to be three-dimensional.

Scalars

Scalar data is data that is single valued at each location in a dataset. Examples of scalar data are temperature, pressure, density, elevation, and stock price. Scalar data is the simplest and most common form of visualization data.

Vectors

Vector data is data with a magnitude and direction. In three dimensions this is represented as a triplet of values (u, v, w). Examples of vector data include flow velocity, particle trajectory, wind motion, and gradient function.

Normals

Normals are direction vectors: that is, they are vectors of magnitude $|n|=1$. Normals are often used by the graphics system to control the shading of objects. Normals also may be used by some algorithms to control the orientation or generation of cell primitives, such as creating ribbons from oriented lines.

Texture Coordinates

Texture coordinates are used to map a point from Cartesian space into a 1-, 2-, or 3-dimensional texture space. The texture space is usually referred to as a *texture map*. Texture maps are regular arrays of color, intensity, and/or transparency values that provide extra detail to rendered objects. One application of texturing in two dimensions is to "paste" a photograph onto one or more polygons, yielding a detailed image without a large number of graphics primitives. (Texture mapping is covered in more detail in Chapter 7.)

Tensors

Tensors are complex mathematical generalizations of vectors and matrices. A tensor of rank k can be considered a k-dimensional table. A tensor of rank 0 is a scalar, rank 1 is a vector, rank 2 is a matrix, and a tensor of rank 3 is a three-dimensional rectangular array. Tensors of higher rank are k-dimensional rectangular arrays.

General tensor visualization is an area of current research. Efforts thus far have been focused on two-dimensional, rank 2 tensors, which are 3×3 matrices. The most common form of such tensors are the stress and strain tensors, which represent the stress and strain at a point in an object under load. **vtk** only treats real-valued, symmetric 3×3 tensors.

user-Defined

Most visualization data can be mapped into the attribute data described previously. However, you may develop visualization techniques for a special application. In that case, you will have to develop your own representational form. We refer to such data as *user-defined* data.

5.5 Types of Datasets

A dataset consists of an organizing structure plus associated attribute data. The structure has both topological and geometric properties and is composed of one or more points and cells. The type of a dataset is derived from the organizing structure, and specifies the relationship that the cells and points have with one another. Common dataset types are shown in Figure **5–6**.

A dataset is characterized according to whether its structure is regular or irregular. A dataset is regular if there is a single mathematical relationship within the composing points and cells. If the points are regular, then the geometry of the dataset is regular. If the topological relationship of cells is regular, then the topology of the dataset is regular. Regular (or structured) data can be implicitly represented, at great savings in memory and computation. Irregular (or unstructured) data must be explicitly represented, since there is no inherent pattern that can be compactly described. Unstructured data tends to be more general, but requires greater memory and computational resources.

Polygonal Data

We have already seen how graphics libraries are designed to render such geometric primitives as lines and polygons. These primitives also are frequently generated or consumed by computational geometry and visualization algorithms. In the *Visualization Toolkit*, we call this collection of graphics primitives *polygonal data*. The polygonal dataset consists of vertices, polyvertices, lines, polylines, polygons, and triangle strips. The topology and geometry of polygonal data is unstructured, and the cells that compose that dataset vary in topological dimension. The polygonal dataset forms a bridge between data, algorithms, and high-speed computer graphics.

Vertices, lines, and polygons form a minimal set of primitives to represent 0-, 1-, and 2-dimensional geometry. We have included polyvertex, polyline, and triangle strip cells for convenience, compactness, and performance. Triangle strips in particular are high-performing primitives. To represent n triangles with a triangle strip requires just $n+2$ points, compared to the $3n$ points for conventional representations. In addition, many graphics libraries can render triangle strips at higher speeds than triangle polygons.

Our minimal selection of cells is based on common application and performance, representing a subset of the cells available in some graphics libraries. Other types include quadrilateral meshes, Bezier curves and surfaces, and other

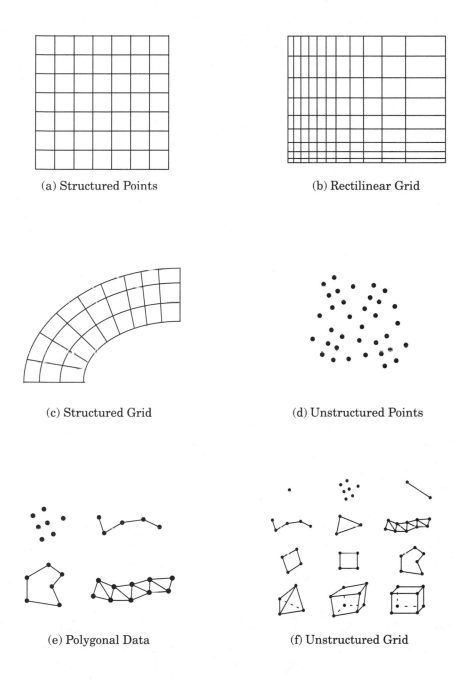

(a) Structured Points

(b) Rectilinear Grid

(c) Structured Grid

(d) Unstructured Points

(e) Polygonal Data

(f) Unstructured Grid

Figure 5–6 Dataset types. The unstructured grid consists of all cell types.

spline types such as NURBS (Non-Uniform Rational B-Splines) [Mortenson85]. Spline surfaces are generally used to accurately model and visualize geometry. Few visualization algorithms (other than geometry visualization) have been developed that require spline surfaces.

Structured Points

A structured points dataset is a collection of points and cells arranged on a regular, rectangular lattice. The rows, columns, and planes of the lattice are parallel to the global x-y-z coordinate system. If the points and cells are arranged on a plane (i.e., two-dimensional) the dataset is referred to as a pixmap, bitmap, or image. If the points and cells are arranged as stacked planes (i.e., three-dimensional) the dataset is referred to as a volume. We use the more general term structured points because we can refer to images, volumes, or one-dimensional point arrays collectively. Note that some authors have referred to structured points as uniform grids.

Structured points consist of line elements (1D), pixels (2D), or voxels (3D). Structured points are regular in both geometry and topology and can be implicitly represented. The representational scheme requires only data dimensions, an origin point, and the data spacing. The dimension of the data is a 3-vector (n_x, n_y, n_z), specifying the number of points in the x, y, and z directions. The origin point is the position in three-dimensional space of the minimum x-y-z point. Each pixel (2D) or voxel (3D) in a structured point dataset is identical in shape, the spacing specifying the length in the x-y-z directions.

The regular nature of the topology and geometry of the structured points dataset suggests a natural i-j-k coordinate system. The number of points in the dataset is $n_x \times n_y \times n_z$ while the number of cells is $(n_x - 1) \times (n_y - 1) \times (n_z - 1)$. A particular point or cell can be selected by specifying the three indices i-j-k. Similarly, a line is defined by specifying two out of three indices, and a plane by specifying a single index.

The simplicity and compactness of representation are desirable features of structured points. It is an efficient structure to traverse and compute with. For this reason structured points are rivaled only by polygonal data as the most common form of visualization dataset. The major disadvantage with structured points is the so-called "curse of dimensionality". To obtain greater data resolution we must increase the dimensions of the dataset. Increasing the dimensions of an image results in an $O(n^2)$ increase in memory requirement, while volumes require an $O(n^3)$ increase. Therefore, to resolve a small feature using structured points may require more disk space or computer memory than is available.

Structured point datasets are often used in imaging and computer graphics. Volumes are frequently generated from medical imaging technologies such as Computed Tomography (CT) and Magnetic Resonance Imaging (MRI). Sometimes volumes are used to sample mathematical functions or numerical solutions.

Rectilinear Grid

The rectilinear grid dataset is a collection of points and cells arranged on a regular lattice. The rows, columns, and planes of the lattice are parallel to the global *x-y-z* coordinate system. While the topology of the dataset is regular, the geometry is only partially regular. That is, the points are aligned along the coordinate axis, but the spacing between points may vary.

Like the structured points dataset, rectilinear grids consist of pixels (2D) or voxels (3D). The topology is represented implicitly by specifying grid dimensions. The geometry is represented by maintaining a list of separate *x*, *y*, and *z* coordinates. To obtain the coordinates of a particular point, values from each of the three lists must be appropriately combined.

Structured Grid

A structured grid is a dataset with regular topology and irregular geometry. The grid may be warped into any configuration in which the cells do not overlap or self-intersect.

The topology of the structured grid is represented implicitly by specifying a 3-vector of dimensions (n_x, n_y, n_z). The geometry is explicitly represented by maintaining an array of point coordinates. The composing cells of a structured grid are quadrilaterals (2D) or hexahedron (3D). Like structured points, the structured grid has a natural coordinate system that allows us to refer to a particular point or cell using topological *i-j-k* coordinates.

Structured points are commonly found in finite difference analysis. Finite difference is a numerical analysis technique to approximate the solution to partial differential equations. Typical applications include fluid flow, heat transfer, and combustion.

Unstructured Points

Unstructured points are points irregularly located in space. There is no topology in an unstructured point dataset, and the geometry is completely unstructured. The vertex and polyvertex cells are used to represent unstructured points.

Unstructured points are a simple but important type of dataset. Often data has no inherent structure, and part of the visualization task is to discover or create it. For example, consider a piston in a car instrumented with temperature gauges. The number of gauges and their location is chosen at a finite set of points, resulting in temperature values at "unrelated" (at least in terms of visualization topology) positions on the surface of the piston. To visualize the surface temperature, we have to create an interpolation surface and scheme to fill in intermediate values.

Unstructured points serve to represent such unstructured data. Typically, this data form is transformed into another more structured form for the purposes of visualization. Algorithms for transforming unstructured points into other forms are described in "Visualizing Unstructured Points" on page 394.

Unstructured Grid

The most general form of dataset is the unstructured grid. Both the topology and geometry are completely unstructured. Any cell type can be combined in arbitrary combinations in an unstructured grid. Hence the topology of the cells ranges from 0D (vertex, polyvertex) to 3D (tetrahedron, hexahedron, voxel). In the *Visualization Toolkit* any dataset type can be expressed as an unstructured grid. We typically use unstructured grids to represent data only when absolutely necessary, because this dataset type requires the most memory and computational resources to represent and operate on.

Unstructured grids are found in fields such as finite element analysis, computational geometry, and geometric modelling. Finite element analysis is a numerical solution technique for partial differential equations (PDEs). Applications of finite element analysis include structural design, vibration, dynamics, and heat transfer. (This compares to finite difference analysis for PDEs. One advantage of finite element analysis is that the constraint on regular topology is removed. Hence complex domains can be more easily meshed.)

5.6 Other Data Abstractions

Other data models have been proposed besides the dataset model presented here. We briefly examine two other models that have been applied successfully. These are the AVS field model and the model of Haber, Lucas, and Collins, adapted in modified form by the commercial IBM Data Explorer system. The section concludes with a brief comparison between these two models and **vtk**'s data model.

The Application Visualization System

AVS (the Application Visualization System) was the first large-scale, commercial visualization system [AVS89]. Much of the early growth, visibility, and successful application of visualization technology was achieved because of the direct application of AVS or the influence of AVS on other researchers. AVS is a data-flow visualization system with a crisp user interface to create, edit, and manipulate visualization networks. Using an explicit executive to control execution of networks, AVS can run distributed and parallel visualization applications. Since the AVS architecture is open, researchers and developers can and have donated filters for use by others.

The AVS data model consists of primitive data and aggregate data. Primitive data are fundamental representations of data such as byte, integer, real, and string. Aggregate types are complex organizations of primitive types and include fields, colormaps, geometries, and pixel maps. Fields can be considered AVS' fundamental data type, and will be described in detail shortly. Colormaps are used to map functional values (i.e., scalar values) into color and transparency values. Geometries consist of graphics primitives such as points, lines, and polygons, and are used by the geometric renderer to display objects. A pixel map is the rendered image, or output, of a visualization.

The field is the most interesting part of the AVS data model. In general, it is an n-dimensional array with scalar or vector data at each point. A scalar is a single value, while a vector is two or more values (not necessarily three). The field array can have any number of dimensions, and the dimensions can be of any size. There is no implicit structure to the field, instead, a *mapping* function is defined. That is, either an implicit or explicit relationship from data elements to coordinate points is specified. Thus a field is a mapping between two kinds of space: the *computational space* of the field data and the *coordinate* space, which is typically the global coordinate system. AVS supports three types of mappings: uniform (i.e., structured), rectilinear, and irregular (i.e., unstructured).

The Data Explorer

The data model of Haber, Lucas, and Collins [Haber91] is based on the mathematics of fiber bundles. The goal of their work is to create a general model for piecewise representations of fields on regular and irregular grids. They refer to their model as the *field data model*, but their definition of the word *field* is different from the AVS model. A field is an object composed of a *base* and *dependent data*. Informally, the base is a manifold whose coordinates are the independent variables for the field, and the dependent data relate the values of dependent variables to the independent variables of the base. Visualization data consists of *field elements* that describe the base and dependent variables over a local region.

The Visualization Toolkit

There are similarities and differences between these data models and **vtk**'s dataset model. The greatest difference is that these other models are more abstract. They are capable of representing a wider range of data and are more flexible. In particular, the AVS field model is capable of representing arbitrary streams of numbers in a simple and elegant manner. The field data model of Haber et al. is also powerful: The authors show how this data representation can be used to exploit regularity in data to obtain compact representations. On the other hand, all these models (including **vtk**'s) share the notion of structure versus data. The AVS field model introduces structure by using a mapping function. The field data of the Haber et al. model resembles **vtk**'s dataset model, in that the base is equivalent to **vtk**'s cells, and the field data model's dependent data is analogous to **vtk**'s attribute data.

The difference in level of abstraction raises important issues in the design of visualization systems. In the following discussion we will refer to data models as abstract or concrete, where the relative level of abstraction is lower in concrete models. In general, abstract and concrete classes compare as follows:

- Abstract models are more flexible and capable of representing a wider range of data forms than concrete models.

- Abstract models lend themselves to compact computer code.

- Concrete models are easier to describe, interface, and implement than abstract models.

- The level of abstraction influences the computer code and/or database interface to the data model. Abstract models result in abstract code and data representations; concrete models result in concrete code and data representations.

- The complexity of abstract models can be hidden by creating simpler, application-specific interfaces. However, this requires extra effort. Concrete models, on the other hand, cannot be made more abstract by modifying interfaces.

The design of computer systems demands careful attention to the balance between abstract and concrete systems. Visualization systems, in particular, must be carefully designed because they interface to other systems and data models. Models that are too abstract can result in confusing computer code and interfaces, and can be misused because of user misunderstanding. On the other hand, concrete models are limited in flexibility and capability, but tend to be easier to learn and apply.

In the design of the *Visualization Toolkit*, we chose to use a more concrete data model relative to the AVS and field data models. Our decision was based on the premise that the system was to be informative as well as functional, and we wanted to clearly demonstrate basic concepts. On the other hand, **vtk**'s data model is general enough to support our practice of visualization. Our experience with users also has shown us that **vtk**'s data model is easier for the casual visualization user to understand than the more abstract models. If you decide to design your own system, we recommend that you examine other data models. However, we feel that the clarity of code manifested in the *Visualization Toolkit* is an example of a well-balanced trade-off between design abstraction and simplicity.

5.7 Putting It All Together

In this section we will describe the implementation details of the dataset types covered previously. We will also show you how to create these datasets through a variety of C++ examples.

Memory Allocation

Because of the size and scope of data, memory must be carefully managed to create efficient visualization systems. In the *Visualization Toolkit*, we use contiguous data arrays as the basis for most data structures. Contiguous arrays can be

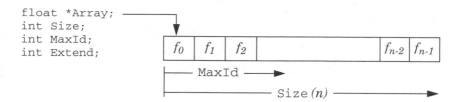

Figure 5–7 Implementation of contiguous array. This example is a fragment of the class definition vtkFloatArray.

created, deleted, and traversed faster than alternative data structures, such as linked lists or arrays of pointers to structures.

Contiguous arrays also can be easily transported across a network, particularly if the information in the array is independent of computer memory address. Memory independence avoids the overhead of mapping information from one memory location to another. Therefore, in **vtk** we access information based on an "id", an integer index into an array-like object. Data arrays are 0-offset just like C++ arrays. That is, given n data values, we successively access these values using the ids $(0, 1, 2, ..., n-1)$.

An important design decision was not to represent data using arrays of objects (e.g., cells or points). Our experience has shown that such designs severely impact performance. Instead, we focus on designing objects at a higher level of abstraction. From the perspective of performance, the object-oriented approach serves best at the application level, not at the level of implementation.

The class vtkFloatArray is an example of a contiguous array. We will use this class to describe how contiguous arrays are implemented in **vtk**. As shown in Figure **5–7**, the instance variable Array is a pointer to memory of type float. The allocated length of the array is given by Size. The array is dynamic, so an attempt to insert data beyond the allocated size automatically generates a Resize() operation. The Extend field specifies the amount of additional memory that is requested during a resize operation. The MaxId field is an integer offset defining the end of inserted data. If no data has been inserted, then MaxId is equal to -1. Otherwise, MaxId is an integer value where $0 \leq \text{MaxId} < \text{Size}$.

Abstract/Concrete Data Array Objects

Visualization data comes in many forms: floating point, integer, byte, and double precision, to name a few simple types. More complex types such as character strings or multidimensional identifiers also are possible. Given this variety of types, how do we represent and manipulate such data using the representation model presented in this chapter? The answer is to use abstract data objects.

Abstract data objects are objects that provide uniform methods to create, manipulate, and delete data using dynamic binding. In C++ we use the virtual keyword to declare methods as dynamically bound. Dynamic binding allows us to

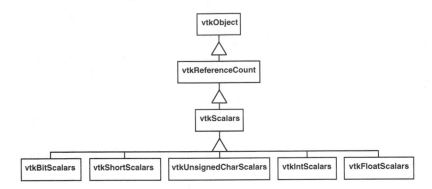

Figure 5–8 Scalar object diagram. vtkScalar is an abstract base class. Subclasses of vtkScalar implement type specific representation and operations.

execute a method belonging to a concrete object by manipulating that object's abstract superclass.

Consider the abstract class vtkScalars. We can access the scalar value at point id 129 by executing the method float s = GetScalar(129). Since the virtual GetScalar() method returns a floating-point scalar value, each subclass of vtkScalars must also return a floating-point value. Although the subclass is free to represent data in any possible form, it must transform its data representation into a floating-point value. This process may be as simple as a cast from a built-in type to floating-point value, or it may be a complex mapping of data. For example, if our scalar data consists of character strings, we could create an alphabetical list and map the string into a location in the list, and then cast the location into a float value.

vtk uses abstract data array objects for point coordinates, scalars, vectors, normals, texture coordinates, and tensors. Typically, we provide concrete subclasses based on the built-in types char, short, int, and float, but other types may be easily added.

Figure **5–8** shows the object diagram for scalar data. Similar object models exist for points, vectors, normals, texture coordinates, and tensors. The abstract class vtkScalars is a subclass of vtkReferenceCount and vtkObject, while the concrete classes vtkBitScalars, vtkUnsignedCharScalars, vtkInt-Scalars, vtkShortScalars, and vtkFloatScalars are subclasses of vtk-Scalars. These classes represent scalars of type packed bit (0/1 values), unsigned char, int, short, and float, respectively.

Dataset Representation

Five datasets are implemented in **vtk**: vtkPolyData, vtkStructuredPoints, vtkStructuredGrid, vtkRectilinearGrid, and vtkUnstructuredGrid. The unstructured points dataset is not implemented, but can be represented using either vtkPolyData or vtkUnstructuredGrid.

We use a different internal data representation for each dataset type. By using different representations we minimize data structure memory requirements and implement efficient access methods. It would have been possible to use `vtkUnstructuredGrid` to represent all dataset types, but the memory and computational overhead are unacceptable for large data. The following sections describe how we represent the dataset.

vtkStructuredPoints. The simplest and most compact representation is `vtk-StructuredPoints`. Both the dataset points and cells are represented implicitly by specifying the dimensions, data spacing, and origin. The dimensions define the topology of the dataset, while the origin and spacing specify the geometry.

There is an implicit ordering of both the points and cells composing `vtk-StructuredPoints`. Both the cells and points are numbered in the direction of increasing x, then y, then z. The total number of points is $n_x \times n_y \times n_z$ where n_x, n_y, and n_z are the dimensions of `vtkStructuredPoints`. The total number of cells is $(n_x - 1) \times (n_y - 1) \times (n_z - 1)$.

vtkRectilinearGrid. While the topology of `vtkRectilinearGrid` is regular, the geometry can be described as "semi-regular". The topology is implicitly represented by specifying data dimensions along the x, y, and z coordinate axes. The geometry is defined using three arrays of coordinate values along these axes. These three coordinate arrays can be combined to determine the coordinates of any point in the dataset. In **vtk**, we represent the arrays using three instances of `vtkScalar`. The numbering of points and cells is implicit in exactly the same way as described for `vtkStructuredPoints`.

vtkStructuredGrid. Like `vtkStructuredPoints`, the topology of `vtkStructuredGrid` is regular and is defined by specifying dimensions in the topological *i-j-k* coordinate system. However, the geometry of `vtkStructuredGrid` is realized by specifying point coordinates in the global *x-y-z* coordinate system.

The abstract data class `vtkPoints` and its concrete subclasses (e.g., `vtk-FloatPoints`) are used to represent the point coordinates. These are implemented as arrays. A particular point coordinate may be retrieved or inserted by specifying a particular point id. The numbering of the points and cells is implicit in the same fashion as `vtkStructuredPoints`. Care must be taken to insure that the number of points in the data array is the same as that implied by the dimensions of the grid.

vtkPolyData. Unlike `vtkStructuredPoints` and `vtkStructuredGrid`, the topology of `vtkPolyData` is not regular, so both the topology and geometry of the dataset must be explicitly represented. The point data in `vtkPolyData` is represented using the `vtkPoints` class (and subclasses), just the same as in `vtk-StructuredGrid`.

The *Visualization Toolkit* uses the class `vtkCellArray` to explicitly represent cell topology. This class is a list of connectivity for each cell. The structure of the list is a sequence of integer numbers (Figure **5–9**). The first number in the list is a count (the number of points in the cell connectivity), and the next series of numbers is the cell connectivity. (Each number in the connectivity list is an index into an instance of a point coordinate list.) Sequences of count followed by the connectivity list are repeated until each cell is enumerated. Additional information such as the number of cells in the list and current position in the list (for traversal purposes) is also maintained by vtkCellArray.

Notice that type information is not directly represented in this structure. Instead, vtkPolyData maintains four separate lists to vertices, lines, polygons, and triangle strips. The vertex list represents cells of type vtkVertex and vtk-PolyVertex. The lines list represents cells of type vtkLine and vtkPolyLine. The polygon list represents cells of type vtkTriangle, vtkQuad, and vtkPoly-gon. The triangle strip list represents cells of the single type vtkTrian-gleStrip. As a result, the cell type is known from the particular list the cell is defined in, plus the number of points that define the cell.

Our design of the vtkPolyData class is based on two important requirements. First, we want an efficient interface to external graphics libraries. Second, we wish to aggregate cells according to topology. The four separate lists provide efficient interface because graphics libraries have separate vertex, line, polygon, and triangle strip primitives. As a result, in **vtk** no run-time checking is required to match the different cell types with the appropriate "load primitive" function, since the type is known from the list in which the primitive resides. The four lists also separate cells into 0-, 1-, and 2-dimensional types. This is useful because visualization algorithms often treat data of varying topological order differently.

vtkUnstructuredGrid. The dataset type vtkUnstructuredGrid is the most general in terms of its ability to represent topological and geometric structure. Both points and cells are explicitly represented using derived classes of vtkPoints and vtkCellArray. The class vtkUnstructuredGrid is similar to vtkPoly-Data except that vtkUnstructuredGrid must be capable of representing all cell types, not just the limited graphics types (i.e., vertices, lines, polygons, and triangle strips) of vtkPolyData.

Another distinguishing characteristic of vtkUnstructuredGrid is that we represent type information differently. In vtkPolyData we categorized cells into four separate lists, thereby representing cell type indirectly. In vtkUnstruc-turedGrid we add the additional class vtkCellTypes to represent cell type explicitly.

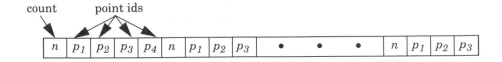

Figure 5–9 vtkCellArray structure to represent cell topology.

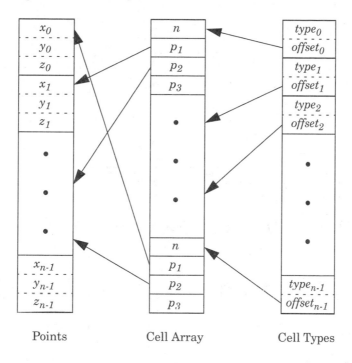

Figure 5–10 The vtkUnstructuredGrid data structure. (This is a subset of the complete structure. See Chapter 8 for the complete representation.)

The vtkCellTypes is an array of supplemental information. For each cell, an integer flag defines the cell type. Another variable is used to record the location of the cell definition in the corresponding vtkCellArray (Figure **5–10**).

Besides representing cell type, this design also enables random access to cells. Because the length of a cell connectivity list varies, the vtkCellArray class cannot locate a particular cell without traversing its data structure from the origin. With the added class vtkCellTypes, however, it is possible to directly access a cell with a single dereference (i.e., using the offset value).

The vtkCellTypes may also be added to the vtkPolyData data representation — and indeed it has. However, our reasons for this addition are not to represent type explicitly, but rather to provide random access to the cells and enable many topological operations. We will expand on this idea in Chapter 8.

Object Model. The five datasets are implemented as shown in Figure **5–11**. As this object diagram illustrates, these concrete datasets are subclasses of the abstract class vtkDataSet. Two additional classes are introduced as well. The class vtkStructuredData contributes instance variables and methods for structured data. vtkStructuredData is not in an inheritance relationship with the datasets; rather the structured datasets shown delegate to it in order to

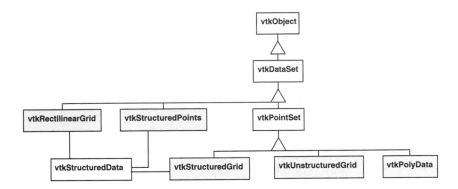

Figure 5–11 Dataset object diagram. The five datasets (shaded) are implemented in **vtk**.

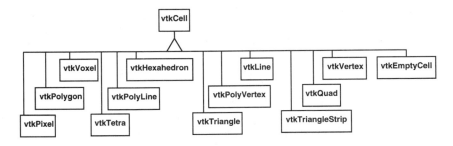

Figure 5–12 Object diagram for twelve cell types (plus the empty cell type) in **vtk**.

implement some of their methods. (This was done to avoid multiple inheritance.) Subclasses of the class vtkPointSet represent their points explicitly, that is, through an instance of vtkPoints or its subclasses. vtkPointSet provides methods and instance variables to manipulate the point data, as well as a general searching capability to find points and cells. (See "Searching" on page 331.)

Cell Representation

In the *Visualization Toolkit* each cell type has been implemented by creating specific classes. Each cell is a subclass of the abstract type vtkCell. Cell topology is represented by a list of ordered point ids, and cell geometry is represented by a list of point coordinates. The object diagram for vtkCell and its subclasses is shown in Figure 5–12.

The abstract class vtkCell specifies methods that each cell must implement. These methods provide a defined interface to the cell's geometry and topology. Additional methods perform computation on the cell. These methods will be discussed in detail in Chapter 8.

Data Attributes

Data attributes are associated with the structure of a dataset. The dataset model is built on points and cells, so it is natural to associate data attributes with points and cells as well. Intermediate structure features, such as cell edges or faces, are not explicitly represented so we cannot easily associate data attributes with them.

In **vtk** we have chosen to associate data attributes with the points. There is no association of data attributes to cells. (Here we refer to data attributes associated with points as *point attributes*, and data attributes associated with cells as *cell attributes*.) Our design choice is based on the following rationale.

- Point attributes are representationally complete. We can represent cell attributes by assigning cell values to each of the cell's points. Sometimes this may require duplication of points. For example, to represent a cell with constant data value, we need to duplicate each point and assign each point the cell data value.

- Point attributes are more common than cell attributes. Of course, this varies by application, but our experience suggests this to be generally true.

- Coding and implementation is greatly simplified. There is no need to introduce further complexity to maintain dual data representation.

- Inconsistencies in the data are avoided. If both point and cell attributes coexist, data values may not be consistent. For example, if a cell's scalar value is 0.5, and its points have scalar values other than 0.5, which is the correct value? Priority schemes can be devised to resolve such situations. However, we feel that this capability is not worth the additional complexity.

To represent point attributes we use the organizing class `vtkPointData` and the data specific classes `vtkScalars`, `vtkVectors`, `vtkNormals`, `vtkTCoords`, `vtkTensors`, and `vtkUserDefined`. `vtkPointData` serves to coordinate the movement of data from one process object to the next. It provides methods for copying, interpolating, and moving data between input and output. The data-specific classes represent and provide access to data. As with `vtkPoints`, the data-specific classes are abstract and depend on concrete subclasses to represent specific types of data (e.g., `float`, `char`, `int`).

There is a one-to-one correspondence between each dataset point and its attribute data. Point attributes are accessed by way of the point id. For example, to access the scalar value of point id 129 in the dataset instance `aDataSet`, we use

```
aDataSet->GetPointData()->GetScalars()->GetScalar(129);
```

This statement assumes that the scalar data has been defined for this dataset and is non-NULL.

The class `vtkPointData` provides important capabilities. When a filter object executes, attribute data from its input is operated on and passed on to its output. These operations are typically copying input data from one point to an output point, interpolating input data to generate output data, or passing entire data objects from input to output. When we perform these operations, the filters are designed to be as independent of the attribute data as possible. That is, we would like the filters to operate on the point data generically, without knowledge of the types of data associated with each point. Such capabilities simplify the coding of filters, and avoid the need to recode them if the representation of the point data changes.

Examples

In the examples that follow we show manual creation and manipulation of datasets. Typically, these operations are not performed directly by users of **vtk**. Instead, source objects are used to read data files or generate data. This is more convenient than the manual techniques shown here and should be used whenever possible.

Creation of datasets is a two step process. First the geometry and topology of the dataset must be defined. Depending on the type of dataset, the geometry and topology definition will proceed differently. Then the point attribute data is created and associated with the dataset. Remember that there is a one-to-one relationship between the attribute data and the points in the dataset.

Create a Polygonal Dataset. In our first example we create a polygonal representation of a cube. The cube is defined by eight points and six quadrilateral faces. We also create eight scalar values associated with the eight vertices of the cube. Figure **5–13** shows the key C++ code fragments used to create the data, and the resulting image.

The geometry of the cube is defined using an instance of the class vtk-FloatPoints. The topology of the cube (i.e., polygons) is defined with an instance of the class vtkCellArray. These define the points and polygons of the cube, respectively. Scalar data is represented by an instance of the class vtkIntScalars.

As this example shows, polygonal data is created by constructing pieces (e.g., points, cells, and point attribute data), and then assembling the pieces to form the complete dataset. If the name of the instance of vtkPolyData is cube, we can summarize these three steps as follows:

1. Create instance of subclass of vtkPoints to define geometry. Use the operator cube->SetPoints() to associate the points with the dataset.

2. Create instances of vtkCellArray to define topology for vertices, lines, polygons, and triangle strips. Use the operators cube->SetVerts(), cube->SetLines(), cube->SetPolys(), and cube->SetStrips() to associate the cells with the dataset.

3. Create point attribute data. Every dataset has an attribute that is an instance of vtkPointData. Use the operator pd=cube->GetPointData() to retrieve the pointer to the point attribute data. Associate the attribute

```
vtkPolyData *cube = vtkPolyData::New();
vtkFloatPoints *points = vtkFloatPoints::New();
vtkCellArray *polys = vtkCellArray::New();
vtkIntScalars *scalars = vtkIntScalars::New();

for (i=0; i<8; i++) points->InsertPoint(i,x[i]);
for (i=0; i<6; i++) polys->InsertNextCell(4,pts[i]);
for (i=0; i<8; i++) scalars->InsertScalar(i,i);

cube->SetPoints(points);
points->Delete();
cube->SetPolys(polys);
polys->Delete();
cube->GetPointData()->SetScalars(scalars);
scalars->Delete();
```

Figure 5–13 Creation of polygonal cube (Cube.cxx).

data with the dataset using the operators pd->SetScalars(), pd->Set-Vectors(), pd->SetNormals(), pd->SetTensors(), pd->SetT-Coords(), and pd->SetUserDefined().

Polygonal data supports the following cell types: vertices, polyvertices, lines, polylines, triangles, quadrilaterals, polygons, and triangle strips. Point attribute data does not need to be defined — you can create none, some, or all of the point attributes in any combination.

The most confusing aspect of this example is the Delete() method. To prevent memory leaks we must use a Delete() method (**vtk**'s destructor) after every New() method. It is apparent from the example that the instance's points, polys, and scalars are referred to by another object (e.g., cube). So doesn't invocation of the Delete() method pose a problem?

The answer is no. Certain data objects in **vtk** are reference counted to conserve memory resources (i.e., subclasses of vtkReferenceCount). That means they can be shared between objects. For most objects the Delete() will invoke the destructor. Reference counted objects act a little differently. The `Delete()` method simply decrements the reference count. This may or may not destroy the object depending on whether it is being used by another object. In this example the `points`, `polys`, and `scalars` are used by the polygonal dataset `cube`, so they are not deleted when `Delete()` is invoked. They will be freed once we free the dataset cube, that is, when their reference count drops to zero. (See "Creating, Deleting, and Reference Counting Objects" on page 562 of Appendix A.)

Create a Structured Points Dataset. In this example, we create a structured points dataset (i.e., an instance of `vtkStructuredPoints`). The topology of the dataset is defined by specifying the data dimensions. The geometry is defined by the data spacing and origin. The spacing specifies the length, width, and height of each voxel. The origin specifies the position in 3D space of the "lower-left" corner of the data. In our example we set the origin and spacing of the dataset so that its center lies at the origin, and the bounds of the dataset are (-0.5,0.5, -0.5,0.5, -0.5,0.5).

In this example we create scalar data along with the structured points dataset. The scalar values are computed from the implicit function for a sphere

$$F(x, y, z) = (x^2 + y^2 + z^2) - R^2 \qquad\qquad \textbf{(5-2)}$$

with the radius $R = 0.4$. The scalar data is stored in an instance of `vtkFloatScalars` and assigned to the point attribute data of the dataset.

To complete this example, a contour filter is used to generate a surface of scalar value $F(x, y, z) = 0$. Note that this functionality (in a more general form) is available from the source object `vtkSampleFunction` in combination with `vtkSphere`. Figure **5–14** shows the key C++ code fragment used to create the data and contour the scalar field, and the resulting image.

Structured points datasets are easy to construct because both the geometry and topology are implicitly defined. If the name of the instance of `vtkStructuredPoints` is `vol`, we can summarize the steps to create the dataset as follows:

1. Define the topology of the dataset using the operator `vol->SetDimensions()`.

2. Define the geometry of the dataset using the operators `vol->SetOrigin()` and `vol->SetSpacing()`.

3. Create point attribute data and associate it with the dataset.

You do not need to specify origin and data spacing. By default the data spacing is (1,1,1) in the x-y-z directions, and the origin is (0,0,0). Thus if the dimensions of the dataset are $n_x \times n_y \times n_z$, the default length, width, and height of the dataset will be $(n_x - 1, n_y - 1, n_z - 1)$.

The topological dimension of the dataset is implicitly known from its instance variables. For example, if any of the dimensions (n_x, n_y, n_z) is equal to one (and the other two are greater than one), the topological dimension of the dataset is two.

Create a Structured Grid Dataset. In the next example we create a vtkStructuredGrid dataset. Topology is implicitly defined from the dimensions of the dataset. The geometry is explicitly defined by providing an object to represent the point coordinates. In this example we use an instance of vtkFloatPoints and assume that the structured grid is warped according to the equation for a cylinder

$$x = r_i \cos\theta$$

$$y = r_i \sin\theta \qquad\qquad (5\text{-}3)$$

$$z = z_i$$

We arbitrarily choose the number of points in the tangential direction to be thirteen, the number of points in the radial direction to be eleven, and the number of points in the axis direction to be eleven (i.e., dimensions are $13 \times 11 \times 11$).

Vectors are generated tangential to the cylinder and of magnitude proportional to the radius. To display the data we draw small, oriented lines at each point as shown in Figure **5–15**. (This technique is called a *hedgehog*. See "Hedgehogs and Oriented Glyphs" on page 167.)

The creation of a structured grid dataset is partially explicit and partially implicit. Geometry is created explicitly be creating an instance of vtkPoints, while the topology is created implicitly by specifying dataset dimensions. If the name of the instance of vtkStructuredGrid is sgrid, the following three steps are used to create it.

1. Specify the dataset geometry by creating an instance of vtkPoints. Use the operator sgrid->SetPoints() to associate the points with the dataset.

2. The dataset topology is specified using the operator sgrid->SetDimensions(). Make sure the number of points created in item number 1 above is equal to the implied number of points $n_x \cdot n_y \cdot n_z$.

3. Create point attribute data and associate it with the dataset.

The topological dimension of the dataset is implied by the specified dimensions. For example, if any of the dimensions (n_x, n_y, n_z) is equal to one, the topological dimension of the dataset is two. If two of the three dimensions (n_x, n_y, n_z) are equal to one, the topological dimension of the dataset is one.

Create a Rectilinear Grid Dataset. A rectilinear grid is regular in topology and semi-regular in geometry. Similar to a structured grid or structured points dataset, topology is implicitly represented by specifying grid dimensions. Because the grid is axis-aligned but the point coordinates along each axis may

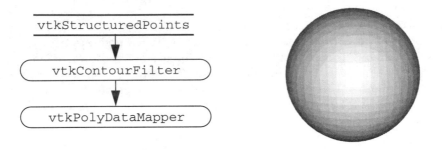

```
vtkStructuredPoints *vol = vtkStructuredPoints::New();
  vol->SetDimensions(26,26,26);
  vol->SetOrigin(-0.5,-0.5,-0.5);
  sp = 1.0/25.0;
  vol->SetSpacing(sp, sp, sp);

vtkFloatScalars *scalars = vtkFloatScalars(26*26*26)::New()
for (k=0; k<26; k++)
  {
  z = -0.5 + k*ar;
  kOffset = k * 26 * 26;
  for (j=0; j<26; j++)
     {
     y = -0.5 + j*ar;
     jOffset = j * 26;
     for (i=0; i<26; i++)
       {
       x = -0.5 + i*ar;
       s = x*x + y*y + z*z - (0.4*0.4);
       offset = i + jOffset + kOffset;
       scalars->InsertScalar(offset,s);
       }
     }
  }
  vol->GetPointData()->SetScalars(scalars);
  scalars->Delete();
```

Figure 5–14 Creating a structured points dataset. Scalar data is generated from the equation for a sphere. Volume dimensions are 26^3 (Vol.cxx).

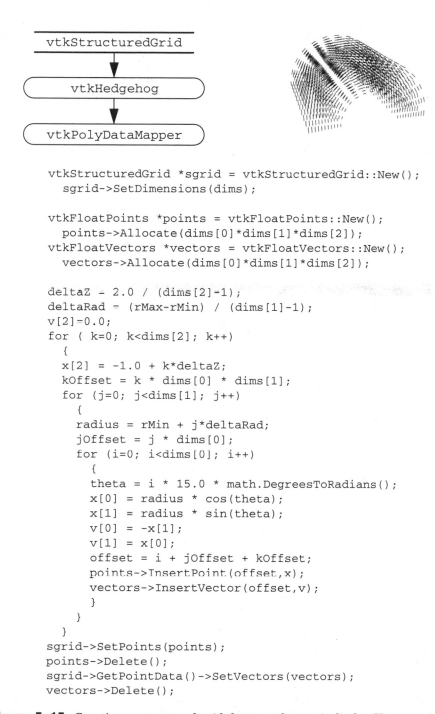

```
vtkStructuredGrid *sgrid = vtkStructuredGrid::New();
  sgrid->SetDimensions(dims);

vtkFloatPoints *points = vtkFloatPoints::New();
  points->Allocate(dims[0]*dims[1]*dims[2]);
vtkFloatVectors *vectors = vtkFloatVectors::New();
  vectors->Allocate(dims[0]*dims[1]*dims[2]);

deltaZ = 2.0 / (dims[2]-1);
deltaRad = (rMax-rMin) / (dims[1]-1);
v[2]=0.0;
for ( k=0; k<dims[2]; k++)
  {
  x[2] = -1.0 + k*deltaZ;
  kOffset = k * dims[0] * dims[1];
  for (j=0; j<dims[1]; j++)
    {
    radius = rMin + j*deltaRad;
    jOffset = j * dims[0];
    for (i=0; i<dims[0]; i++)
      {
      theta = i * 15.0 * math.DegreesToRadians();
      x[0] = radius * cos(theta);
      x[1] = radius * sin(theta);
      v[0] = -x[1];
      v[1] = x[0];
      offset = i + jOffset + kOffset;
      points->InsertPoint(offset,x);
      vectors->InsertVector(offset,v);
      }
    }
  }
sgrid->SetPoints(points);
points->Delete();
sgrid->GetPointData()->SetVectors(vectors);
vectors->Delete();
```

Figure 5–15 Creating a structured grid dataset of a semicylinder. Vectors are created whose magnitude is proportional to radius and oriented in tangential direction (SGrid.cxx).

vary, we need three arrays to represent the geometry of the dataset, one array for each of the *x-y-z* axes. Note that the cell types of the rectilinear dataset are pixels and voxels.

For maximum flexibility when creating rectilinear grids, in **vtk** we use three vtkScalar objects to define the axes arrays. This means that different native data type (e.g., unsigned char, int, float, and so on) can be used for each axes.

To summarize the process of creating an instance of vtkRectilinear-Grid, we follow four steps. In this example (shown in Figure **5–16**), we assume that the name of the vtkRectilinearGrid instance is rgrid.

1. Create the dataset geometry by creating three instance of vtkScalars (or one of its subclasses), one for each of the *x-y-z* coordinate axes. We will assume that the number of values in each scalar is n_x, n_y, and n_z.

2. Each of the three instances is assigned to the *x*, *y*, and *z* axes using the rgrid->SetXCoordinates(), rgrid->SetYCoordinates(), and rgrid->SetZCoordinates() methods, respectively.

3. The dataset topology is specified using the operator rgrid->SetDimensions(). Make sure the number of points created in item number 1 above is equal to the implied number of points $n_x \cdot n_y \cdot n_z$.

4. Create point attribute data and associate it with the dataset.

The topological dimension of the dataset is implied by the specified dimensions. For example, if any of the dimensions (n_x, n_y, n_z) is equal to one, the topological dimension of the dataset is two. If two of the three dimensions (n_x, n_y, n_z) are equal to one, the topological dimension of the dataset is one.

Create an Unstructured Grid Dataset. Unstructured grid datasets are the most general dataset type in both topology and geometry. In this example we "artificially" create an unstructured grid using an instance of vtkUnstructuredGrid (Figure **5–17**). The grid contains examples of each cell type except for pixels and voxels. (Pixels and voxels are generally used internally to process structured points datasets. They can be explicitly created and manipulated as long as the required relationship of point geometry is observed.) Creating the dataset structure requires creating points to define the geometry and various cells to define the topology. (Note that in the finite element world we would refer to these as *nodes* and *elements*.)

To summarize the process of creating an instance of vtkUnstructuredGrid, we follow five steps. We assume the name of vtkUnstructuredGrid instance is ugrid.

1. Allocate memory for the dataset. Use the operator ugrid->Allocate(). This operator takes two optional parameters related to the size of the data. The first is the size of the connectivity list, and the second is the amount to extend storage (if necessary). As a rule of thumb, use the number of cells

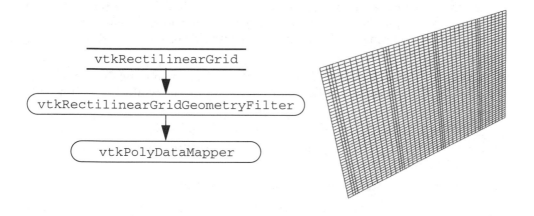

```
vtkFloatScalars *xCoords = vtkFloatScalars::New();
for (i=0; i<47; i++) xCoords->InsertScalar(i,x[i]);

vtkFloatScalars *yCoords = vtkFloatScalars::New();
for (i=0; i<33; i++) yCoords->InsertScalar(i,y[i]);

vtkFloatScalars *zCoords = vtkFloatScalars::New();
for (i=0; i<44; i++) zCoords->InsertScalar(i,z[i]);

vtkRectilinearGrid *rgrid = vtkRectilinearGrid::New();
  rgrid->SetDimensions(47,33,44);
  rgrid->SetXCoordinates(xCoords);
  rgrid->SetYCoordinates(yCoords);
  rgrid->SetZCoordinates(zCoords);

vtkRectilinearGridGeometryFilter *plane =
      vtkRectilinearGridGeometryFilter::New();
  plane->SetInput(rgrid);
  plane->SetExtent(0,46, 16,16, 0,43);

vtkPolyDataMapper *rgridMapper = vtkPolyDataMapper::New();
  rgridMapper->SetInput(plane->GetOutput());

vtkActor *wireActor = vtkActor::New();
  wireActor->SetMapper(rgridMapper);
  wireActor->GetProperty()->SetRepresentationToWireframe();
  wireActor->GetProperty()->SetColor(0,0,0);
```

Figure 5–16 Creating a rectilinear grid dataset. The coordinates along each axis are defined using an instance of vtkScalar (RGrid.cxx).

times the average number of points defining each cell for both parameters. Exact values for these parameters are not important, although the choice may affect performance. If you fail to execute this operation before inserting data, the software will break.

2. Create an instance of a subclass of `vtkPoints` to define the dataset geometry. Use the operator `ugrid->SetPoints()` to associate the points with the dataset.

3. Create the dataset topology on a cell by cell basis by using the cell insertion operator `ugrid->InsertNextCell()`. There are various flavors of this operator, use the appropriate one.

4. Create point attribute data and associate it with the dataset.

5. Complete the creation process by executing the `ugrid->Squeeze()` operator. This operator reclaims any extra memory consumed by the data structures. Although this step is not required, it will return memory resource back to the computer system.

The creation of unstructured grid datasets is somewhat different from the creation of the other dataset types. This is because of the unstructured nature of the data, and the complex nature of the internal data structures.

5.8 Chapter Summary

A dataset represents visualization data. The dataset has an organizing structure, with topological and geometric components, and associated attribute data. The structure of a dataset consists of cells (topology) and points (geometry). An important characteristic of the structure is whether its geometry and topology are regular or irregular (or equivalently, structured or unstructured). Regular data is more compact and usually more computationally efficient than irregular data. However, irregular data is more flexible in representation capability than regular data.

Important dataset types include polygonal data, rectilinear grid, structured points, structured grids, and unstructured grids. The polygonal dataset type is used to represent graphics data, as well as many kinds of visualization data. The unstructured grid is the most general type, consisting of arbitrary combinations of all possible cell types.

Attribute data consists of scalars, vectors, tensors, texture coordinates, normals, and user-defined data. In the *Visualization Toolkit*, attribute data is associated with the dataset points.

5.9 Bibliographic Notes

A variety of representation schemes have been proposed for each dataset type described here. These schemes vary depending on design goals. For example,

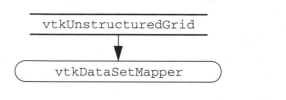

```
vtkFloatPoints *points = vtkFloatPoints::New();
for (i=0; i<27; i++) points->InsertPoint(i,x[i]);

vtkUnstructuredGrid *ugrid = vtkUnstructuredGrid::New();
  ugrid->Allocate(100);
  ugrid->InsertNextCell(VTK_HEXAHEDRON, 8, pts[0]);
  ugrid->InsertNextCell(VTK_HEXAHEDRON, 8, pts[1]);
  ugrid->InsertNextCell(VTK_TETRA, 4, pts[2]);
  ugrid->InsertNextCell(VTK_TETRA, 4, pts[3]);
  ugrid->InsertNextCell(VTK_POLYGON, 6, pts[4]);
  ugrid->InsertNextCell(VTK_TRIANGLE_STRIP, 6, pts[5]);
  ugrid->InsertNextCell(VTK_QUAD, 4, pts[6]);
  ugrid->InsertNextCell(VTK_TRIANGLE, 3, pts[7]);
  ugrid->InsertNextCell(VTK_TRIANGLE, 3, pts[8]);
  ugrid->InsertNextCell(VTK_LINE, 2, pts[9]);
  ugrid->InsertNextCell(VTK_LINE, 2, pts[10]);
  ugrid->InsertNextCell(VTK_VERTEX, 1, pts[11]);

ugrid->SetPoints(points);
points->Delete();
```

Figure 5–17 Creation of an unstructured grid (UGrid.cxx).

even the simple volume representation has been implemented with other more complex schemes such as run-length encoding and octrees [Bloomenthal88]. A description of more general representation schemes is available in [Haber91], the AVS field model [AVS89], and the compact cell structure [Schroeder94]. An overview of dataset types can be found in [Gelberg90]. Some structures for those mathematically oriented can be found in [Brisson90] and [Poluzzi93]. Haimes [VISUAL3] describes an efficient data structure for unstructured grid visualization.

If you are interested in more details on finite element methods see the classic Zienkiewicz [Zienkiewicz87] or [Gallagher75]. Information about both finite difference and finite element methods is available in [Lapidus82].

5.10 References

[AVS89]
  C. Upson, T. Faulhaber, Jr., D. Kamins, and others. "The Application Visualiza-
  tion System: A Computational Environment for Scientific Visualization." *IEEE
  Computer Graphics and Applications*. 9(4):30–42, July 1989.

[Bloomenthal88]
  J. Bloomenthal. "Polygonization of Implicit Surfaces." *Computer Aided Geometric Design*. 5(4):341–355, November 1988.

[Brisson90]
  E. Brisson. "Representing Geometric Structures in *d*-Dimensions: Topology
  and Order." *ACM Symposium on Computational Geometry*. ACM Press, NY,
  1989.

[Gallagher75]
  R. H. Gallagher. *Finite Element Analysis: Fundamentals*. Prentice Hall, Upper
  Saddle River, NJ, 1975.

[Gelberg90]
  L. Gelberg, D. Kamins, D. Parker, and J. Stacks. "Visualization Techniques for
  Structured and Unstructured Scientific Data." *SIGGRAPH '90 Course Notes for
  State of the Art Data Visualization*. August 1990.

[Haber91]
  R. B. Haber, B. Lucas, N. Collins. "A Data Model for Scientific Visualization
  with Provisions for Regular and Irregular Grids." In *Proceedings of Visualization '91*. pp. 298–395, IEEE Computer Society Press, Los Alamitos, CA, 1991.

[Lapidus82]
  L. Lapidus and G. F. Pinder. *Numerical Solution of Partial Differential Equations in Science and Engineering*. John Wiley and Sons, New York, 1987.

[Mortenson85]
  M. E. Mortenson. *Geometric Modeling*. John Wiley and Sons, New York, 1985.

[Poluzzi93]
  A. Paoluzzi, F. Bernardini, C. Cattani, and V. Ferrucci. "Dimension-Indepen-
  dent Modeling with Simplicial Complexes." *ACM Transactions on Graphics*.
  12(1):56–102, 1993.

[Schroeder94]
  W. J. Schroeder and B. Yamrom. "A Compact Cell Structure for Scientific Visu-
  alization." *SIGGRAPH '93 and '94 Course Notes for Advanced Techniques for
  Scientific Visualization*.

[VISUAL3]
  R. Haimes and M. Giles. "VISUAL3: Interactive Unsteady Unstructured 3D Visualization." AIAA Report No. AIAA-91-0794. January 1991.

[Weiler86]
  K. J. Weiler. *Topological Structures for Geometric Modeling*. PhD thesis, Rens-
  selaer Polytechnic Institute, Troy, NY, May 1986.

[Zienkiewicz87]
  O. C. Zienkiewicz and R. L. Taylor. *The Finite Element Method, vol. 1*. McGraw-
  Hill Book Co., New York, 4th ed. 1987.

5.11 Exercises

5.1 Consider a pixmap of dimensions 100^2. Compare the memory requirements to represent this data using:
a) a structured point dataset,
b) a structured grid dataset,
c) a polygonal mesh of quadrilaterals,
d) an unstructured grid of quadrilateral cells,
e) and a triangle strip mesh of 100 strips of 200 triangles each.

5.2 Consider a volume of dimensions 100^3. Compare the memory requirements to represent this data using:
a) a structured point dataset,
b) a structured grid dataset,
c) and an unstructured grid of hexahedral cells.

5.3 Develop a representational scheme for a rectilinear grid. How does this compare (in memory requirement) to a structured grid?

5.4 Consider a volume of dimensions 100^3. Compute the memory requirements for the following point attribute types:
a) unsigned character scalars (1 byte per scalar),
b) float scalars (4 bytes per scalar),
c) float vectors,
d) and double-precision tensors (3x3 tensors).

5.5 List three examples of scalar data.

5.6 List three examples of vector data.

5.7 List three examples of tensor data.

5.8 List three examples of user-defined data.

5.9 A common method to represent cell connectivity is to list point ids with the last id negated. For example, triangle (8,7,3) would be represented (8,7,-3). The negative index represents end of cell definition. What are the advantages and disadvantages of this scheme as compared to the **vtk** cell array structure?

5.10 How many different ways can a hexahedral cell be decomposed into tetrahedron? Are there compatibility issues between neighboring hexahedra?

5.11 Write a program to create and display a structured grid in the form of a hollow cylinder (i.e., cylinder with a hole through it).

5.12 Write a program to create and display an unstructured grid in the form of a hollow cylinder.

5.13 Write a program to create and display a polygonal octahedron.

## CHAPTER 6

Fundamental Algorithms

We have seen how to represent basic types of visualization data such as structured points and grids, unstructured grids, and polygonal data. This chapter explores methods to transform this data to and from these various representations, eventually generating graphics primitives that we can render. These methods are called *algorithms*, and are of special interest to those working in the field of visualization. Algorithms are the verbs that allow us to express our data in visual form. By combining these verbs appropriately, we can reduce complex data into simple, readily comprehensible sentences that are the power of data visualization.

6.1 Introduction

The algorithms that transform data are the heart of data visualization. To describe the various transformations available, we need to categorize algorithms according to the *structure* and *type* of transformation. By structure we mean the effects that transformation has on the topology and geometry of the dataset. By type we mean the type of dataset that the algorithm operates on.

Structural transformations can be classified in four ways, depending on how they affect the geometry, topology, and attributes of a dataset.

- *Geometric transformations* alter input geometry but do not change the topology of the dataset. For example, if we translate, rotate, and/or scale the points of a polygonal dataset, the topology does not change, but the point coordinates, and therefore the geometry, does.

- *Topological transformations* alter input topology but do not change geometry and attribute data. Converting a dataset type from polygonal data to unstructured grid data, or from structured points to unstructured grid, changes the topology but not the geometry. More often, however, the geometry changes whenever the topology does, so topological transformation is uncommon.

- *Attribute transformations* convert data attributes from one form to another, or create new attributes from the input data. The structure of the dataset remains unaffected. Computing vector magnitude or creating scalars based on elevation are data attribute transformations.

- *Combined transformations* change both dataset structure and attribute data. For example, computing contour lines or surfaces is a combined transformation.

We also may classify algorithms according to the type of data they operate on, or the type of data they generate. By type, we most often mean the type of attribute data, such as scalars or vectors. Typical categories include:

- *Scalar algorithms* operate on scalar data. For example, the generation of contour lines of temperature on a weather map.

- *Vector algorithms* operate on vector data. Showing oriented arrows of airflow (direction and magnitude) is an example of vector visualization.

- *Tensor algorithms* operate on tensor matrices. An example of a tensor algorithm is to show the components of stress or strain in a material using oriented icons.

- *Modelling algorithms* generate dataset topology or geometry, or surface normals or texture data. Modelling algorithms tend to be the catch-all category for many algorithms, since some do not fit neatly into any single category mentioned above. For example, generating glyphs oriented according to the vector direction and then scaled according to the scalar value, is a combined scalar/vector algorithm. For convenience we classify such an algorithm as a modelling algorithm, because it does not fit squarely into any other category.

Algorithms also can be classified according to the type of data they process. This is the most common scheme found in the visualization literature. However, this scheme is not without its problems. Often the categories overlap, resulting in confusion. For example, a category (not mentioned above) is *volume visualization*, which refers to the visualization of volume data (or in our terminology, structured points). This category was initially created to describe the visualization of scalar data arranged on a volume, but more recently, vector (and even tensor) data has been visualized on a volume. Hence, we have to qualify our techniques to *volume vector visualization*, or other potentially confusing combinations.

In the text that follows, we will use the attribute type classification scheme: scalar, vector, tensor, and modelling. In cases where the algorithms operate on a particular dataset type, we place them in the appropriate category according to our best judgment. Be forewarned, though, that alternative classification schemes do exist, and may be better suited to describing the true nature of the algorithm.

Generality Versus Efficiency

Most algorithms can be written specifically for a particular dataset type, or more generally, treating any dataset type. The advantage of a specific algorithm is that it is usually faster than a comparable general algorithm. (See "Other Data Abstractions" on page 130 where we discussed the trade-off between abstract and concrete forms.) An implementation of a specific algorithm also may be more memory efficient and its implementation may better reflect the relationship between the algorithm and the dataset type it operates on.

One example of this is contour surface creation. Algorithms for extracting contour surfaces were originally developed for volume data, mainly for medical applications. The regularity of volumes lends itself to efficient algorithms. However, the specialization of volume-based algorithms precludes their use for more general datasets such as structured or unstructured grids. Although the contour algorithms can be adapted to these other dataset types, they are less efficient than those for volume datasets.

Our presentation of algorithms favors the more general implementations. In some special cases we will describe performance improving techniques for particular dataset types. Refer to the bibliography at the end of each chapter for detailed descriptions of specialized algorithms.

6.2 Scalar Algorithms

Scalars are single data values associated with each point and/or cell of a dataset. (Recall that in the *Visualization Toolkit* we associate data with points.) Because scalar data is commonly found in real-world applications, and because scalar data is so easy to work with, there are many different algorithms to visualize it.

Color Mapping

Color mapping is a common scalar visualization technique that maps scalar data to colors, and displays the colors on the computer system. The scalar mapping is implemented by indexing into a *color lookup table*. Scalar values serve as indices into the lookup table.

The mapping proceeds as follows. The lookup table holds an array of colors (e.g., red, green, blue components or other comparable representations). Associ-

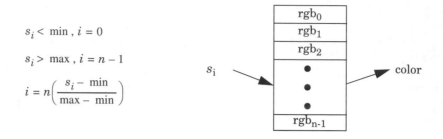

$$s_i < \min , i = 0$$

$$s_i > \max , i = n - 1$$

$$i = n \left(\frac{s_i - \min}{\max - \min} \right)$$

Figure 6–1 Mapping scalars to colors via a lookup table.

ated with the table is a minimum and maximum *scalar range (min, max)* into which the scalar values are mapped. Scalar values greater than the maximum range are clamped to the maximum color, scalar values less than the minimum range are clamped to the minimum color value. Then, for each scalar value s_i, the index i into the color table with n entries (and 0-offset) is given by Figure **6–1**.

A more general form of the lookup table is called a *transfer function*. A transfer function is any expression that maps scalar value into a color specification. For example, Figure **6–2** maps scalar values into separate intensity values for the red, green, and blue color components. We can also use transfer functions to map scalar data into other information such as local transparency. (Transfer functions are discussed in more detail in "Transparency and Alpha Values" on page 212 and "Volume Rendering" on page 216.) A lookup table is a discrete sampling of a transfer function. We can create a lookup table from any transfer function by sampling the transfer function at a set of discrete points.

Color mapping is a one-dimensional visualization technique. It maps one piece of information (i.e., a scalar value) into a color specification. However, the display of color information is not limited to one-dimensional displays. Often we

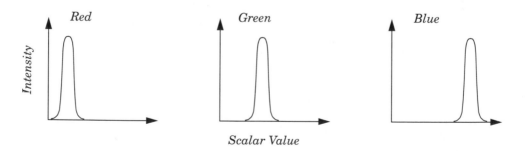

Figure 6–2 Transfer function for color components red, green, and blue as a function of scalar value.

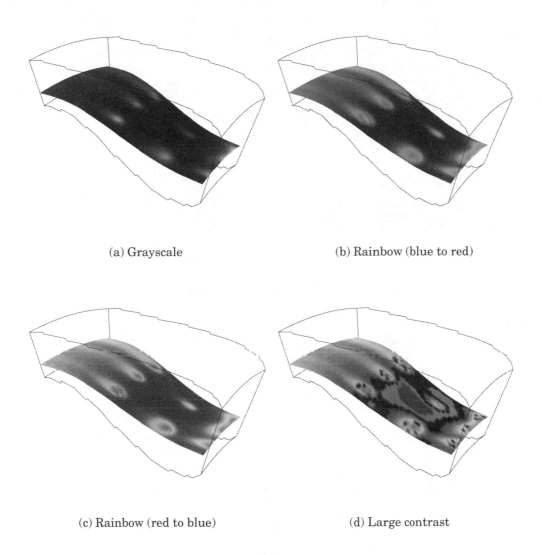

(a) Grayscale   (b) Rainbow (blue to red)

(c) Rainbow (red to blue)   (d) Large contrast

Figure 6–3 Flow density colored with different lookup tables: (a) Grayscale, (b) Rainbow (blue to red), (c) Rainbow (red to blue), (d) Large contrast (`rainbow.tcl`).

use color information mapped onto 1D, 2D, or 3D objects. This is a simple way to increase the information content of our visualizations.

The key to color mapping for scalar visualization is to choose the lookup table entries carefully. Figure **6–3** shows four different lookup tables used to visualize gas density as fluid flows through a combustion chamber. The first lookup table is grayscale. Grayscale tables often provide better structural detail to the eye. The other three images in Figure **6–3** use different color lookup tables. The second uses rainbow hues from blue to red. The third uses rainbow hues arranged from red to blue. The last table uses a table designed to enhance contrast. Careful use of colors can often enhance important features of a dataset. However, any type of lookup table can exaggerate unimportant details or create visual artifacts because of unforeseen interactions between data, color choice, and human physiology.

Designing lookup tables is as much art as it is science. From a practical point of view, tables should accentuate important features, while minimizing less important or extraneous details. It is also desirable to use palettes that inherently contain scaling information. For example, a color rainbow scale from blue to red is often used to represent temperature scale, since many people associate "blue" with cold temperatures, and "red" with hot temperatures. However, even this scale is problematic: a physicist would say that blue is hotter than red, since hotter objects emit more blue light (i.e., shorter wavelength) than red. Also, there is no need to limit ourselves to "linear" lookup tables. Even though the mapping of scalars into colors has been presented as a linear operation (Figure **6–1**), the table itself need not be linear. That is, tables can be designed to enhance small variations in scalar value using logarithmic or other schemes.

There is another element to visualization that is the artistic, or aesthetic, quality. Good visualizations represent a balance between effective communication of information and aesthetically pleasing presentation. While it is true in this day of mass media that information is often sacrificed for the sake of image, improving the comfort level and engaging the human observer more deeply in the presentation of data improves the effectiveness of communication.

Contouring

A natural extension to color mapping is *contouring*. When we see a surface colored with data values, the eye often separates similarly colored areas into distinct regions. When we contour data, we are effectively constructing the boundary between these regions. These boundaries correspond to contour lines (2D) or surfaces (3D) of constant scalar value.

Examples of 2D contour displays include weather maps annotated with lines of constant temperature (isotherms), or topological maps drawn with lines of constant elevation. Three-dimensional contours are called *isosurfaces*, and can be approximated by many polygonal primitives. Examples of isosurfaces include constant medical image intensity corresponding to body tissues such as skin, bone, or other organs. Other abstract isosurfaces such as surfaces of constant pressure or temperature in fluid flow also may be created.

Consider the 2D structured grid shown in Figure **6–4**. Scalar values are shown next to the points that define the grid. Contouring always begins by selecting a scalar value, or contour value, that corresponds to the contour lines or surfaces generated. To generate the contours, some form of interpolation must be used. This is because we have scalar values at a finite set of points in the dataset, and our contour value may lie between the point values. Since the most common interpolation technique is linear, we generate points on the contour sur-

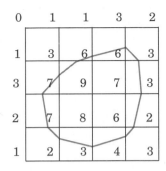

Figure 6–4 Contouring a 2D structured grid with contour line value = 5.

face by linear interpolation along the edges. If an edge has scalar values 10 and 0 at its two end points, and if we are trying to generate a contour line of value 5, then edge interpolation computes that the contour passes through the midpoint of the edge.

Once the points on cell edges are generated, we can connect these points into contours using a few different approaches. One approach detects an edge intersection (i.e., the contour passes through an edge) and then "tracks" this contour as it moves across cell boundaries. We know that if a contour edge enters a cell, it must exit a cell as well. The contour is tracked until it closes back on itself, or exits a dataset boundary. If it is known that only a single contour exists, then the process stops. Otherwise, every edge in the dataset must be checked to see whether other contour lines exist.

Another approach uses a divide and conquer technique, treating cells independently. This is the *marching squares* algorithm in 2D, and *marching cubes* [Lorensen87] in 3D. The basic assumption of these techniques is that a contour can only pass through a cell in a finite number of ways. A case table is constructed that enumerates all possible topological *states* of a cell, given combinations of scalar values at the cell points. The number of topological states depends on the number of cell vertices, and the number of inside / outside relationships a vertex can have with respect to the contour value. A vertex is considered inside a contour if its scalar value is larger than the scalar value of the contour line. Vertices with scalar values less than the contour value are said to be outside the contour. For example, if a cell has four vertices and each vertex can be either inside or outside the contour, there are $2^4 = 16$ possible ways that the contour passes through the cell. In the case table we are not interested in where the contour passes through the cell (e.g., geometric intersection), just how it passes through the cell (i.e., topology of the contour in the cell).

Figure **6–5** shows the sixteen combinations for a square cell. An index into the case table can be computed by encoding the state of each vertex as a binary digit. For 2D data represented on a rectangular grid, we can represent the 16 cases with 4 bit index. Once the proper case is selected, the location of the contour line / cell edge intersection can be calculated using interpolation. The algo-

rithm processes a cell and then moves, or *marches t*o the next cell. After all cells
are visited, the contour will be completed. In summary, the marching algorithms
proceed as follows:

1. Select a cell.

2. Calculate the inside / outside state of each vertex of the cell.

3. Create an index by storing the binary state of each vertex in a separate bit.

4. Use the index to look up the topological state of the cell in a case table.

5. Calculate the contour location (via interpolation) for each edge in the case
   table.

This procedure will construct independent geometric primitives in each cell. At
the cell boundaries duplicate vertices and edges may be created. These duplicates can be eliminated by using a special coincident point-merging operation.
Note that interpolation along each edge should be done in the same direction. If
not, numerical round-off will likely cause points to be generated that are not precisely coincident, and will not merge properly.

There are advantages and disadvantages to both the edge-tracking and
marching cubes approaches. The marching squares algorithm is easy to implement. This is particularly important when we extend the technique into three
dimensions, where isosurface tracking becomes much more difficult. On the
other hand, the algorithm creates disconnected line segments and points, and
the required merging operation requires extra computation resources. The tracking algorithm can be implemented to generate a single polyline per contour line,
avoiding the need to merge coincident points.

As mentioned previously, the 3D analogy of marching squares is marching
cubes. Here, there are 256 different combinations of scalar value, given that
there are eight points in a cubical cell (i.e., 2^8 combinations). Figure **6–6** shows
these combinations reduced to 15 cases by using arguments of symmetry. We use
combinations of rotation and mirroring to produce topologically equivalent cases.

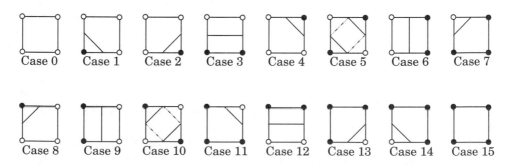

Figure 6–5 Sixteen different marching squares cases. Dark vertices indicate scalar
value is above contour value. Cases 5 and 10 are ambiguous.

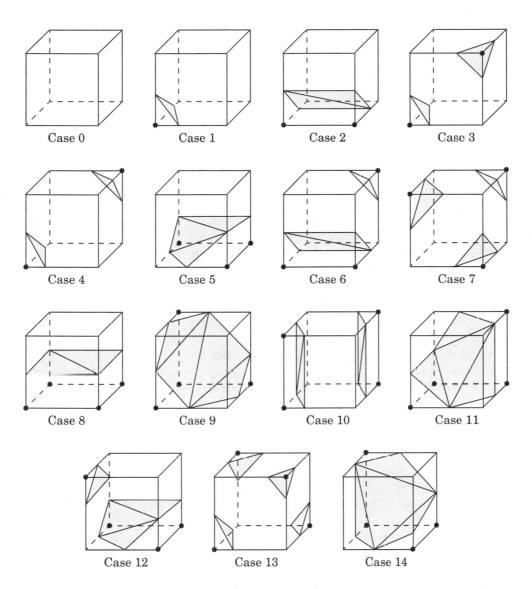

Figure 6–6 Marching cubes cases for 3D isosurface generation. The 256 possible cases have been reduced to 15 cases using symmetry. Dark vertices are greater than the selected isosurface value.

An important issue is *contouring ambiguity*. Careful observation of marching squares cases numbered 5 and 10 and marching cubes cases numbered 3, 6, 7, 10, 12, and 13 show that there are configurations where a cell can be contoured in more than one way. (This ambiguity also exists when using an edge tracking approach to contouring.) Contouring ambiguity arises on a 2D square or

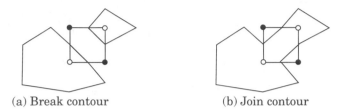

(a) Break contour   (b) Join contour

Figure 6–7 Choosing a particular contour case will break (a) or join (b) the current contour. Case shown is marching squares case 10.

the face of a 3D cube when adjacent edge points are in different states, but diagonal vertices are in the same state.

In two dimensions, contour ambiguity is simple to treat: for each ambiguous case we implement one of the two possible cases. The choice for a particular case is independent of all other choices. Depending on the choice, the contour may either extend or break the current contour as illustrated in Figure **6–7**. Either choice is acceptable since the resulting contour lines will be continuous and closed (or will end at the dataset boundary).

In three dimensions the problem is more complex. We cannot simply choose an ambiguous case independent of all other ambiguous cases. For example Figure **6–8** shows what happens if we carelessly implement two cases independent of one another. In this figure we have used the usual case 3 but replaced case 6 with its *complementary* case. Complementary cases are formed by exchanging the "dark" vertices with "light" vertices. (This is equivalent to swapping vertex scalar value from above the isosurface value to below the isosurface value, and vice versa.) The result of pairing these two cases is that a hole is left in the isosurface.

Several different approaches have been taken to remedy this problem. One approach tessellates the cubes with tetrahedron, and uses a *marching tetrahedra* technique. This works because the marching tetrahedra exhibit no ambiguous cases. Unfortunately, the marching tetrahedra algorithm generates isosurfaces consisting of more triangles, and the tessellation of a cube with tetrahedra requires making a choice regarding the orientation of the tetrahedra. This choice may result in artificial "bumps" in the isosurface because of interpolation along the face diagonals as shown in Figure **6–9**. Another approach evaluates the asymptotic behavior of the surface, and then chooses the cases to either join or break the contour. Nielson and Hamann [Nielson91] have developed a technique based on this approach they call the *asymptotic decider*. It is based on an analysis of the variation of the scalar variable across an ambiguous face. The analysis determines how the edges of isosurface polygons should be connected.

A simple and effective solution extends the original 15 marching cubes cases by adding additional complementary cases. These cases are designed to be compatible with neighboring cases and prevent the creation of holes in the isosurface. There are six complementary cases required, corresponding to the

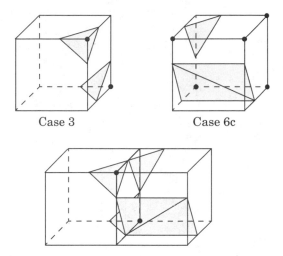

Case 3   Case 6c

Figure 6–8 Arbitrarily choosing marching cubes cases leads to holes in the isosurface.

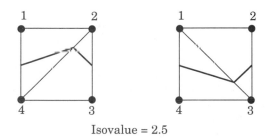

Isovalue = 2.5

Figure 6–9 Using marching triangles or marching tetrahedra to resolve ambiguous cases on rectangular lattice (only face of cube is shown). Choice of diagonal orientation may result in "bumps" in contour surface. In 2D, diagonal orientation can be chosen arbitrarily, but in 3D diagonal is constrained by neighbor.

marching cubes cases 3, 6, 7, 10, 12, and 13. The complementary marching cubes cases are shown in Figure **6–10**.

We can extend the general approach of marching squares and marching cubes to other topological types. In **vtk** we use marching lines, triangles, and tetrahedra to contour cells of these types (or composite cells that are composed of these types). In addition, although we speak of regular types such as squares and cubes, marching cubes can be applied to any cell type topologically equivalent to a cube (e.g., hexahedron or noncubical voxel).

Figure **6–11** shows four applications of contouring. In Figure **6–11**(a) we see 2D contour lines of CT density value corresponding to different tissue types. These lines were generated using marching squares. Figure **6–11**(b) through

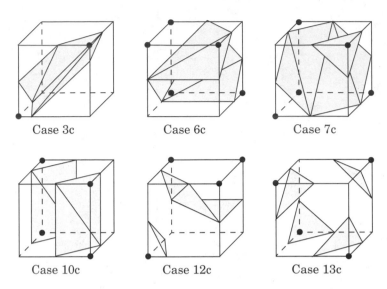

Figure 6–10 Marching cubes complementary cases.

Figure **6–11**(d) are isosurfaces created by marching cubes. Figure **6–11**(b) is a surface of constant image intensity from a computed tomography (CT) X-ray imaging system. (Figure **6–11**(a) is a 2D subset of this data.) The intensity level corresponds to human bone. Figure **6–11**(c) is an isosurface of constant flow density. Figure **6–11**(d) is an isosurface of electron potential of an iron protein molecule. The image shown in Figure **6–11**(b) is immediately recognizable because of our familiarity with human anatomy. However, for those practitioners in the fields of computational fluid dynamics and molecular biology, Figure **6–11**(c) and Figure **6–11**(d) are equally familiar. As these examples show, methods for contouring are powerful yet general techniques for visualizing data from a variety of fields.

Scalar Generation

The two visualization techniques presented thus far, color mapping and contouring, are simple, effective methods to display scalar information. It is natural to turn to these techniques first when visualizing data. However, often our data is not in a form convenient to these techniques. The data may not be single-valued (i.e., a scalar), or it may be a mathematical or other complex relationship. That is part of the fun and creative challenge of visualization: We must tap our creative resources to convert data into a form we can visualize.

For example, consider terrain data. We assume that the data is x-y-z coordinates, where x and y represent the coordinates in the plane, and z represents the elevation above sea level. Our desired visualization is to color the terrain according to elevation. This requires creating a colormap — possibly using white for

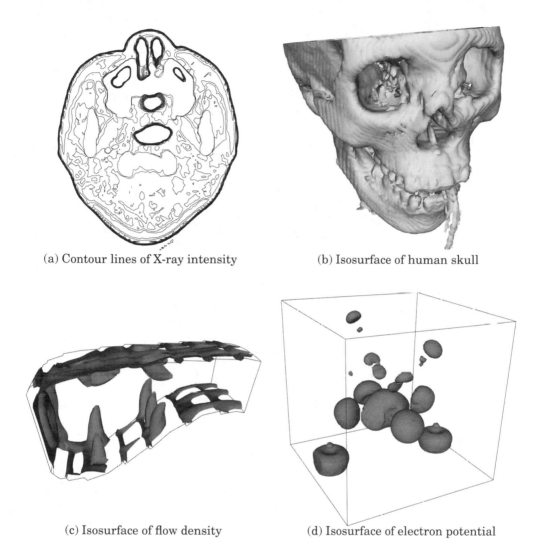

(a) Contour lines of X-ray intensity

(b) Isosurface of human skull

(c) Isosurface of flow density

(d) Isosurface of electron potential

Figure 6–11 Contouring examples. (a) Marching squares used to generate contour lines (hcadSlic.tcl); (b) Marching cubes surface of human bone (headBone.tcl); (c) Marching cubes surface of flow density (combIso.tcl); (d) Marching cubes surface of iron-protein (ironPIso.tcl).

high altitudes, blue for sea level and below, and various shades of green and brown corresponding to elevation between sea level and high altitude. We also need scalars to index into the colormap. The obvious choice here is to extract the z coordinate. That is, scalars are simply the z-coordinate value.

This example can be made more interesting by generalizing the problem. Although we could easily create a filter to extract the z-coordinate, we can create

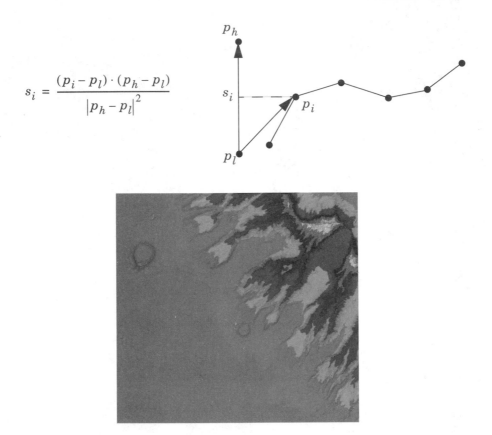

$$s_i = \frac{(p_i - p_l) \cdot (p_h - p_l)}{\left| p_h - p_l \right|^2}$$

Figure 6–12 Computing scalars using normalized dot product. Bottom half of figure illustrates technique applied to terrain data from Honolulu, Hawaii (`hawaii.tcl`).

a filter that produces elevation scalar values where the elevation is measured along any axis. Given an oriented line starting at the (low) point p_l (e.g., sea level) and ending at the (high) point p_h (e.g., mountain top), we compute the elevation scalar s_i at point $p_i = (x_i, y_i, z_i)$ using the dot product as shown in Figure **6–12**. The scalar is normalized using the magnitude of the oriented line, and may be clamped between minimum and maximum scalar values (if necessary). The bottom half of this figure shows the results of applying this technique to a terrain model of Honolulu, Hawaii. A lookup table of 256 ranging from deep blue (water) to yellow-white (mountain top) is used to color map this figure.

Part of the creative practice of visualization is selecting the best technique for given data from the palette of available techniques. Often this requires creative mapping by the user of the visualization system. In particular, to use scalar visualization techniques we need only to create a relationship to generate a unique scalar value. Other examples of scalar mapping include an index value into a list of data, computing vector magnitude or matrix determinate, evaluating surface curvature, or determining distance between points. Scalar genera-

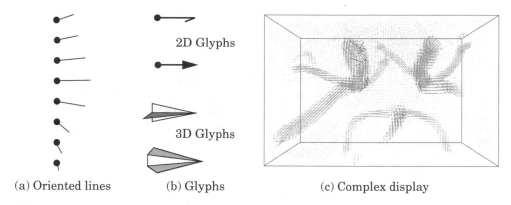

(a) Oriented lines   (b) Glyphs   (c) Complex display

Figure 6–13 Vector visualization techniques: (a) oriented lines; (b) using oriented glyphs; (c) complex vector visualization (`complexV.tcl`).

tion, when coupled with color mapping or contouring, is a simple, yet effective, technique for visualizing many types of data.

6.3 Vector Algorithms

Vector data is a three-dimensional representation of direction and magnitude. Vector data often results from the study of fluid flow, or when examining derivatives (i.e., rate of change) of some quantity.

Hedgehogs and Oriented Glyphs

A natural vector visualization technique is to draw an oriented, scaled line for each vector (Figure **6–13**(a)). The line begins at the point with which the vector is associated and is oriented in the direction of the vector components (v_x, v_y, v_z). Typically, the resulting line must be scaled up or down to control the size of its visual representation. This technique is often referred to as a *hedgehog* because of the bristly result.

There are many variations of this technique (Figure **6–13**(b)). Arrows may be added to indicate the direction of the line. The lines may be colored according to vector magnitude, or some other scalar quantity (e.g., pressure or temperature). Also, instead of using a line, oriented "glyphs" can be used. By glyph we mean any 2D or 3D geometric representation such as an oriented triangle or cone.

Care should be used in applying these techniques. In 3D it is often difficult to understand the position and orientation of a vector because of its projection into a 2D image. Also, using large numbers of vectors can clutter the display to the point where the visualization becomes meaningless. Figure **6–13**(c) shows

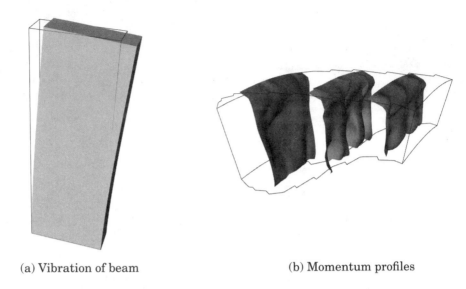

(a) Vibration of beam   (b) Momentum profiles

Figure 6–14 Warping geometry to show vector field; (a) Beam displacement (`vib.tcl`); (b) Flow momentum (`velProf.tcl`).

167,000 3D vectors (using oriented and scaled lines) in the region of the human carotid artery. The larger vectors lie inside the arteries, the smaller vectors lie outside the arteries and are randomly oriented (measurement error) but small in magnitude. Clearly the details of the vector field are not discernible from this image.

Scaling glyphs also poses interesting problems. In what Tufte has termed a "visualization lie," [Tufte83] scaling a 2D or 3D glyph results in nonlinear differences in appearance. The surface area of an object increases with the square of its scale factor, so two vectors differing by a factor of two in magnitude may appear up to four times different based on surface area. Such scaling issues are common in data visualization, and great care must be taken to avoiding misleading viewers.

Warping

Vector data is often associated with "motion." The motion is in the form of velocity or displacement. An effective technique for displaying such vector data is to "warp" or deform geometry according to the vector field. For example, imagine representing the displacement of a structure under load by deforming the structure. Or if we are visualizing the flow of fluid, we can create a flow profile by distorting a straight line inserted perpendicular to the flow.

Figure **6–14** shows two examples of vector warping. In the first example the motion of a vibrating beam is shown. The original undeformed outline is shown in wireframe. The second example shows warped planes in a structured grid dataset. The planes are warped according to flow momentum. The relative back and forward flow are clearly visible in the deformation of the planes.

Typically, we must scale the vector field to control geometric distortion. Too small a distortion may not be visible, while too large a distortion can cause the structure to turn inside out or self-intersect. In such a case the viewer of the visualization is likely to lose context, and the visualization will become ineffective.

Displacement Plots

Vector displacement on the surface of an object can be visualized with displacement plots. A displacement plot shows the motion of an object in the direction perpendicular to its surface. The object motion is caused by an applied vector field. In a typical application the vector field is a displacement or strain field.

Vector displacement plots draw on the ideas in "Scalar Generation" on page 164. Vectors are converted to scalars by computing the dot product between the surface normal and vector at each point (Figure **6–15**(a)). If positive values result, the motion at the point is in the direction of the surface normal (i.e., positive displacement). Negative values indicate that the motion is opposite the surface normal (i.e., negative displacement).

A useful application of this technique is the study of vibration. In vibration analysis, we are interested in the eigenvalues (i.e., natural resonant frequencies) and eigenvectors (i.e., mode shapes) of a structure. To understand mode shapes we can use displacement plots to indicate regions of motion. There are special regions in the structure where positive displacement changes to negative displacement. These are regions of zero displacement. When plotted on the surface of the structure, these regions appear as the so-called *modal* lines of vibration. The study of modal lines has long been an important visualization tool for understanding mode shapes.

Figure **6–15**(b) shows modal lines for a vibrating rectangular beam. The vibration mode in this figure is the second torsional mode, clearly indicated by the crossing modal lines. (The aliasing in the figure is because of the coarseness of the analysis mesh.) To create the figure we combined the procedure of Figure **6–15**(a) with a special lookup table. The lookup table was arranged with dark areas in the center (i.e., corresponds to zero dot product) and bright areas at the beginning and end of the table (corresponds to 1 or -1 dot product). As a result, regions of large normal displacement are bright and regions near the modal lines are dark.

Time Animation

Some of the techniques described so far can be thought of as moving a point or object over a small time step. The hedgehog line is an approximation of a point's

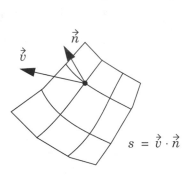
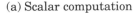

(a) Scalar computation   (b) Displacement plot

Figure 6–15 Vector displacement plots. (a) Vector converted to scalar via dot product computation; (b) Surface plot of vibrating plate. Dark areas show nodal lines. Bright areas show maximum motion (dispPlot.tcl).

motion over a time period whose duration is given by the scale factor. In other words, if velocity $\vec{V} = dx/dt$, then the displacement of a point is

$$dx = \vec{V}\, dt \qquad\qquad \textbf{(6-1)}$$

This suggests an extension to our previous techniques: repeatedly displace points over many time steps. Figure **6–16** shows such an approach. Beginning with a sphere S centered about some point C, we move S repeatedly to generate the bubbles shown. The eye tends to trace out a path by connecting the bubbles, giving the observer a qualitative understanding of the fluid flow in that area. The bubbles may be displayed as an animation over time (giving the illusion of motion) or as a multiple exposure sequence (giving the appearance of a path).

Such an approach can be misused. For one thing, the velocity at a point is instantaneous. Once we move away from the point the velocity is likely to change. Using Equation **6-1** above assumes that the velocity is constant over the entire step. By taking large steps we are likely to jump over changes in the velocity. Using smaller steps we will end in a different position. Thus the choice of step size is a critical parameter in constructing accurate visualization of particle paths in a vector field.

Initial position

Instantaneous
velocity

Final position

Figure 6–16 Time animation of a point C. Although the spacing between points varies, the time increment between each point is constant.

To evaluate Equation **6-1** we can express it as an integral:

$$\vec{x}(t) = \int_t \vec{V} dt \tag{6-2}$$

Although this form cannot be solved analytically for most real world data, its solution can be approximated using numerical integration techniques. Accurate numerical integration is a topic beyond the scope of this book, but it is known that the accuracy of the integration is a function of the step size dt. Since the path is an integration throughout the dataset, the accuracy of the cell interpolation functions, as well as the accuracy of the original vector data, plays an important role in realizing accurate solutions. No definitive study is yet available that relates cell size or interpolation function characteristics to visualization error. But the lesson is clear: the result of numerical integration must be examined carefully, especially in regions of large vector field gradient. However, as with many other visualization algorithms, the insight gained by using vector integration techniques is qualitatively beneficial, despite the unavoidable numerical errors.

The simplest form of numerical integration is Euler's method,

$$\vec{x}_{i+1} = \vec{x}_i + \vec{V}_i \Delta t \tag{6-3}$$

where the position at time $\vec{x}_{i+1}$ is the vector sum of the previous position plus the instantaneous velocity times the incremental time step Δt.

Euler's method has error on the order of $O(\Delta t^2)$, which is not accurate enough for some applications. One such example is shown in Figure **6–17**. The velocity field describes perfect rotation about a central point. Using Euler's method we find that we will always diverge and, instead of generating circles, will generate spirals instead.

In this text we will use the Runge-Kutta technique of order 2 [Conte72]. This is given by the expression

$$\vec{x}_{i+1} = \vec{x}_i + \frac{\Delta t}{2}(\vec{V}_i + \vec{V}_{i+1}) \tag{6-4}$$

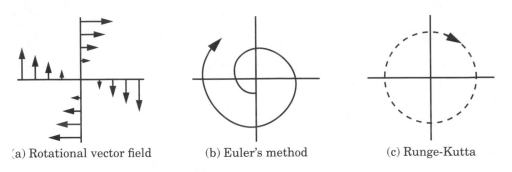

(a) Rotational vector field   (b) Euler's method   (c) Runge-Kutta

Figure 6–17 Euler's integration (b) and Runge-Kutta integration of order 2 (c) applied to uniform rotational vector field (a). Euler's method will always diverge.

where the velocity $\vec{V}_{i+1}$ is computed using Euler's method. The error of this method is $O(\Delta t^3)$. Compared to Euler's method, the Runge-Kutta technique allows us to take a larger integration step at the expense of one additional function evaluation. Generally this trade-off is beneficial, but like any numerical technique, the best method to use depends on the particular nature of the data. Higher-order techniques are also available, but generally not necessary, because the higher accuracy is countered by error in interpolation function or inherent in the data values. If you are interested in other integration formulas, please check the references at the end of the chapter.

One final note about accuracy concerns. The errors involved in either perception or computation of visualizations is an open research area. The discussion in the preceding paragraph is a good example of this. There we characterized the error in streamline integration using conventional numerical integration arguments. But there is a problem with this argument. In visualization applications, we are integrating across cells whose function values are continuous, but whose derivatives are not. As the streamline crosses the cell boundary, subtle effects may occur that are not treated by the standard numerical analysis. Thus the standard arguments need to be extended for visualization applications.

Integration formulas require repeated transformation from global to local coordinates. Consider moving a point through a dataset under the influence of a vector field. The first step is to identify the cell that contains the point. This operation is a search (see "Searching" on page 325), plus a conversion to local coordinates. Once the cell is found, then the next step is to compute the velocity at that point by interpolating the velocity from the cell points. The point is then incrementally repositioned (using the integration formula Equation **6-4**). The process is then repeated until the point exits the dataset or the distance or time traversed exceeds some specified value.

This process can be computationally demanding. There are two important steps we can take to improve performance.

- *Improving search procedures.* There are two distinct types of searches. Initially, the starting location of the particle must be determined by a global search procedure. Once the initial location of the point is determined in the dataset, an incremental search procedure can then be used. Incremental searching is efficient because the motion of the point is limited within a single cell, or at most across a cell boundary. Thus, the search space is greatly limited, and the incremental search is faster relative to the global search.

- *Coordinate transformation.* The cost of a coordinate transformation from global to local coordinates can be reduced if either of the following conditions are true: the local and global coordinate systems are identical with one another (or vary by *x-y-z* translation), or if the vector field is transformed from global space to local coordinate space. The structured point coordinate system is an example of parallel coordinates, and global to local coordinate transformation can be greatly accelerated. If the vector field is transformed into local coordinates (either as a preprocessing step or on a cell-by-cell basis), then the integration can proceed completely in local space. Once the integration path is computed, selected points along the path can be transformed into global space for the sake of visualization.

Streamlines

A natural extension of the previous time animation techniques is to connect the point position $\vec{x}(t)$ over many time steps. The result is a numerical approximation to a particle trace represented as a line.

Borrowing terminology from the study of fluid flow, we can define three related line representation schemes for vector fields.

- *Particle traces* are trajectories traced by fluid particles over time.

- *Streaklines* are the set of particle traces at a particular time t_i that have previously passed through a specified point x_i.

- *Streamlines* are integral curves along a curve s satisfying the equation

$$s = \int_t \vec{V}\, ds, \text{ with } s = s(x, \bar{t}) \tag{6-5}$$

for a particular time $\bar{t}$.

Streamlines, streaklines, and particle traces are equivalent to one another if the flow is steady. In time-varying flow, a given streamline exists only at one moment in time. Visualization systems generally provide facilities to compute particle traces. However, if time is fixed, the same facility can be used to compute streamlines. In general, we will use the term streamline to refer to the method of tracing trajectories in a vector field. Please bear in mind the differences in these representations if the flow is time-varying.

Figure **6–18** shows forty streamlines in a small kitchen. The room has two windows, a door (with air leakage), and a cooking area with a hot stove. The air leakage and temperature variation combine to produce air convection currents

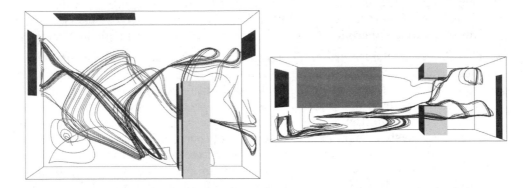

Figure 6–18 Flow velocity computed for a small kitchen (top and side view). Forty streamlines start along the rake positioned under the window. Some eventually travel over the hot stove and are convected upwards (`Kitchen.cxx`).

throughout the kitchen. The starting positions of the streamlines were defined by creating a *rake*, or curve (and its associated points). Here the rake was a straight line. These streamlines clearly show features of the flow field. By releasing many streamlines simultaneously we obtain even more information, as the eye tends to assemble nearby streamlines into a "global" understanding of flow field features.

Many enhancements of streamline visualization exist. Lines can be colored according to velocity magnitude to indicate speed of flow. Other scalar quantities such as temperature or pressure also may be used to color the lines. We also may create constant time dashed lines. Each dash represents a constant time increment. Thus, in areas of high velocity, the length of the dash will be greater relative to regions of lower velocity. These techniques are illustrated in Figure **6–19** for airflow around a blunt fin. This example consists of a wall with half a rounded fin projecting into the fluid flow. (Using arguments of symmetry, only half of the domain was modeled.) Twenty-five streamlines are released upstream of the fin. The boundary layer effects near the junction of the fin and wall are clearly evident from the streamlines. In this area, flow recirculation is apparent, as well as the reduced flow speed.

6.4 Tensor Algorithms

As we mentioned earlier, tensor visualization is an active area of research. However there are a few simple techniques that we can use to visualize 3×3 real symmetric tensors. Such tensors are used to describe the state of displacement or

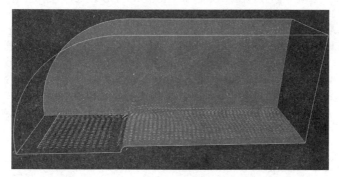

Figure 6–19 Dashed streamlines around a blunt fin. Each dash is a constant time increment. Fast moving particles create longer dashes than slower moving particles. The streamlines also are colored by flow density scalar (`bluntStr.cxx`).

$$
\begin{bmatrix}
\sigma_x & \tau_{xy} & \tau_{xz} \\
\tau_{yx} & \sigma_y & \tau_{yz} \\
\tau_{zx} & \tau_{zy} & \sigma_z
\end{bmatrix}
$$

(a) Stress tensor

$$
\begin{bmatrix}
\dfrac{\partial u}{\partial x} & \left(\dfrac{\partial u}{\partial y}+\dfrac{\partial v}{\partial z}\right) & \left(\dfrac{\partial u}{\partial z}+\dfrac{\partial w}{\partial x}\right) \\[2ex]
\left(\dfrac{\partial u}{\partial y}+\dfrac{\partial v}{\partial z}\right) & \dfrac{\partial v}{\partial y} & \left(\dfrac{\partial v}{\partial z}+\dfrac{\partial w}{\partial y}\right) \\[2ex]
\left(\dfrac{\partial u}{\partial z}+\dfrac{\partial w}{\partial x}\right) & \left(\dfrac{\partial v}{\partial z}+\dfrac{\partial w}{\partial y}\right) & \dfrac{\partial w}{\partial z}
\end{bmatrix}
$$

(b) Strain tensor

Figure 6–20 Stress and strain tensors. Normal stresses in the x-y-z coordinate directions indicated as $\sigma_x, \sigma_y, \sigma_z$, shear stresses indicated as τ_{ij}. Material displacement represented by u, v, w components.

stress in a 3D material. The stress and strain tensors for an elastic material are shown in Figure **6–20**.

In these tensors the diagonal coefficients are the so-called normal stresses and strains, and the off-diagonal terms are the shear stresses and strains. Normal stresses and strains act perpendicular to a specified surface, while shear stresses and strains act tangentially to the surface. Normal stress is either compression or tension, depending on the sign of the coefficient.

A 3×3 real symmetric matrix can be characterized by three vectors in 3D called the eigenvectors, and three numbers called the eigenvalues of the matrix. The eigenvectors form a 3D coordinate system whose axes are mutually perpendicular. In some applications, particularly the study of materials, these axes also are referred to as the principle axes of the tensor and are physically significant. For example, if the tensor is a stress tensor, then the principle axes are the directions of normal stress and no shear stress. Associated with each eigenvector is an eigenvalue. The eigenvalues are often physically significant as well. In the study of vibration, eigenvalues correspond to the resonant frequencies of a structure, and the eigenvectors are the associated mode shapes.

Mathematically we can represent eigenvalues and eigenvectors as follows. Given a matrix $\mathbf{A}$, the eigenvector $\vec{x}$ and eigenvalue λ must satisfy the relation

$$A \cdot \vec{x} = \lambda \vec{x} \tag{6-6}$$

For Equation **6-6** to hold, the matrix determinate must satisfy

$$\det|A - \lambda I| = 0 \tag{6-7}$$

Expanding this equation yields a nth degree polynomial in λ whose roots are the eigenvalues. Thus, there are always n eigenvalues, although they may not be distinct. In general, Equation **6-7** is not solved using polynomial root searching because of poor computational performance. (For matrices of order 3 root searching is acceptable because we can solve for the eigenvalues analytically.) Once we determine the eigenvalues, we can substitute each into Equation **6-7** to solve for the associated eigenvectors.

We can express the eigenvectors of the 3×3 system as

$$\vec{v}_i = \lambda_i \vec{e}_i, \text{ with } i = 1, 2, 3 \tag{6-8}$$

with $\vec{e}_i$ a unit vector in the direction of the eigenvalue, and λ_i the eigenvalues of the system. If we order eigenvalues such that

$$\lambda_1 \geq \lambda_2 \geq \lambda_3 \tag{6-9}$$

then we refer to the corresponding eigenvectors $\vec{v}_1$, $\vec{v}_2$, and $\vec{v}_3$ as the *major*, *medium*, and *minor* eigenvectors.

Tensor Ellipsoids

This leads us to the tensor ellipsoid technique for the visualization of real, symmetric 3×3 matrices. The first step is to extract eigenvalues and eigenvectors as described in the previous section. Since eigenvectors are known to be orthogonal, the eigenvectors form a local coordinate system. These axes can be taken as the *minor*, *medium*, and *major* axes of an ellipsoid. Thus, the shape and orientation of the ellipsoid represent the relative size of the eigenvalues and the orientation of the eigenvectors.

To form the ellipsoid we begin by positioning a sphere at the tensor location. The sphere is then rotated around its origin using the eigenvectors, which in the form of Equation **6-8** are direction cosines. The eigenvalues are used to scale the sphere. Using 4×4 transformation matrices and referring to

Equation **3-6**, Equation **3-9**, and Equation **3-13**, we form the ellipsoid by transforming the sphere centered at the origin using the matrix T

$$T = T_T \cdot T_R \cdot T_S \qquad \qquad \textbf{(6-10)}$$

(remember to read right-to-left). The eigenvectors can be directly plugged in to create the rotation matrix, while the point coordinates x-y-z and eigenvalues $\lambda_1 \geq \lambda_2 \geq \lambda_3$ are inserted into the translation and scaling matrices. A concatenation of these matrices forms the final transformation matrix T.

Figure **6–21**(a) depicts the tensor ellipsoid technique. In Figure **6–21**(b) we show this technique to visualize material stress near a point load on the surface of a semi-infinite domain. (This is the so-called Boussinesq's problem.) From Saada [Saada74] we have the analytic expression for the stress components in Cartesian coordinates shown in Figure **6–21**(c). Note that the z-direction is defined as the axis originating at the point of application of the force P. The variable ρ is the distance from the point of load application to a point x-y-z. The orientation of the x and y axes are in the plane perpendicular to the z axis. (The rotation in the plane of these axes is unimportant since the solution is symmetric around the z axis.) (The parameter ν is Poisson's ratio which is a property of the material. Poisson's ratio relates the lateral contraction of a material to axial elongation under a uniaxial stress condition. See [Saada74] or [Timoshenko70] for more information.)

In Figure **6–22** we visualize the analytical results of Boussinesq's problem from Saada. The left-hand portion of the figure shows the results by displaying the scaled and oriented principal axes of the stress tensor. (These are called *tensor axes*.) In the right-hand portion we use tensor ellipsoids to show the same result. Tensor ellipsoids and tensor axes are a form of *glyph* (see "Glyphs" on page 185) specialized to tensor visualization.

A certain amount of care must be taken to visualize this result since there is a stress singularity at the point of contact of the load. In a real application loads are applied over a small area and not at a single point. Also, plastic behavior prevents stress levels from exceeding a certain point. The results of the visualization, as with any computer process, are only as good as the underlying model.

6.5 Modelling Algorithms

Modelling algorithms are the catch-all category for our taxonomy of visualization techniques. Modelling algorithms have one thing in common: They create or change dataset geometry or topology.

Source Objects

As we have seen in previous examples, source objects begin the visualization pipeline. Source objects are used to create geometry such as spheres, cones, or

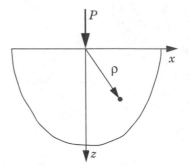

(a) Tensor ellipsoid   (b) Point load on semiinfinite domain

$$\sigma_x = -\frac{P}{2\pi\rho^2}\left(\frac{3zx^2}{\rho^3} - (1-2\nu)\left(\frac{z}{\rho} - \frac{\rho}{\rho+z} + \frac{x^2(2\rho+z)}{\rho(\rho+z)^2}\right)\right)$$

$$\sigma_y = -\frac{P}{2\pi\rho^2}\left(\frac{3zy^2}{\rho^3} - (1-2\nu)\left(\frac{z}{\rho} - \frac{\rho}{\rho+z} + \frac{y^2(2\rho+z)}{\rho(\rho+z)^2}\right)\right)$$

$$\sigma_z = -\frac{3Pz^3}{2\pi\rho^5}$$

$$\tau_{xy} = \tau_{yx} = -\frac{P}{2\pi\rho^2}\left(\frac{3xyz}{\rho^3} - (1-2\nu)\left(\frac{xy(2\rho+z)}{\rho(\rho+z)^2}\right)\right)$$

$$\tau_{xz} = \tau_{zx} = -\frac{3Pxz^2}{2\pi\rho^5}$$

$$\tau_{yz} = \tau_{zy} = -\frac{3Pyz^2}{2\pi\rho^5}$$

c) Analytic solution

Figure 6–21 Tensor ellipsoids. (a) Ellipsoid oriented along eigenvalues (i.e., principle axes) of tensor; (b) Pictorial description of Boussinesq's problem; (c) Analytic results according to Saada.

cubes to support visualization context or are used to read in data files. Source objects also may be used to create dataset attributes. Some examples of source objects and their use are as follows.

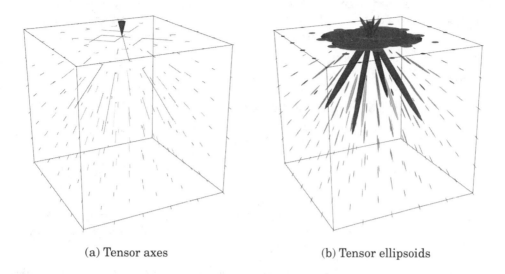

(a) Tensor axes   (b) Tensor ellipsoids

Figure 6–22 Tensor visualization techniques; (a) Tensor axes (`TenAxes.tcl`);
(b) Tensor ellipsoids (`TenEllip.tcl`).

Modelling Simple Geometry. Spheres, cones, cubes, and other simple geometric objects can be used alone or in combination to model geometry. Often we visualize real-world applications such as air flow in a room and need to show real-world objects such as furniture, windows, or doors. Real-world objects often can be represented using these simple geometric representations. These source objects generate their data procedurally. Alternatively, we may use reader objects to access geometric data defined in data files. These data files may contain more complex geometry such as that produced by a 3D CAD (Computer-Aided Design) system.

Supporting Geometry. During the visualization process we may use source objects to create supporting geometry. This may be as simple as three lines to represent a coordinate axis or as complex as tubes wrapped around line segments to thicken and enhance their appearance. Another common use is as supplemental input to objects such as streamlines or probe filters. These filters take a second input that defines a set of points. For streamlines, the points determine the initial positions for generating the streamlines. The probe filter uses the points as the position to compute attribute values such as scalars, vectors, or tensors.

Data Attribute Creation. Source objects can be used as procedures to create data attributes. For example, we can procedurally create textures and texture coordinates. Another use is to create scalar values over a uniform grid. If the scalar values are generated from a mathematical function, then we can use the visualization techniques described here to visualize the function. In fact, this leads us to a very important class of source objects: implicit functions.

Implicit Functions

Implicit functions are functions of the form

$$F(x, y, z) = c \qquad\qquad\qquad \textbf{(6-11)}$$

where c is an arbitrary constant. Implicit functions have three important properties.

- *Simple geometric description.* Implicit functions are convenient tools to describe common geometric shapes. This includes planes, spheres, cylinders, cones, ellipsoids, and quadrics.

- *Region separation.* Implicit functions separate 3D Euclidean space into three distinct regions. These regions are inside, on, and outside the implicit function. These regions are defined as $F(x, y, z) < 0$, $F(x, y, z) = 0$, and $F(x, y, z) > 0$, respectively.

- *Scalar generation.* Implicit functions convert a position in space into a scalar value. That is, given an implicit function we can sample it at a point (x_i, y_i, z_i) to generate a scalar value c_i.

An example of an implicit function is the equation for a sphere of radius R

$$F(x, y, z) = x^2 + y^2 + z^2 - R^2 \qquad\qquad \textbf{(6-12)}$$

This simple relationship defines the three regions $F(x, y, z) = 0$ (on the surface of the sphere), $F(x, y, z) < 0$ (inside the sphere), and $F(x, y, z) > 0$ (outside the sphere). Any point may be classified inside, on, or outside the sphere simply by evaluating Equation **6-12**.

Implicit functions have a variety of uses. This includes geometric modelling, selecting data, and visualizing complex mathematical descriptions.

Modelling Objects. Implicit functions can be used alone or in combination to model geometric objects. For example, to model a surface described by an implicit function, we sample F on a dataset and generate an isosurface at a contour value c_i. The result is a polygonal representation of the function. Figure **6–23**(b) shows an isosurface for a sphere of radius=1 sampled on a volume. Note that we can choose nonzero contour values to generate a family of offset surfaces. This is useful for creating blending functions and other special effects.

Implicit functions can be combined to create complex objects using the boolean operators union, intersection, and difference. The union operation $F \cup G$

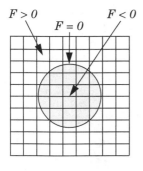  

(a) Sphere sampling   (b) Isosurface of sphere   (c) Boolean combinations

Figure 6–23 Sampling functions: (a) 2D depiction of sphere sampling; (b) Isosurface of sampled sphere; (c) Boolean combination of two spheres, a cone, and two planes. (One sphere intersects the other, the planes clip the cone.) (Refer to `sphere.tcl` and `iceCream.tcl`.)

between two functions $F(x, y, z)$ and $G(x, y, z)$ at a point (x_0, y_0, z_0) is the minimum value

$$F \cup G = min(F(x_0, y_0, z_0), G(x_0, y_0, z_0)) \tag{6-13}$$

The intersection between two implicit functions is given by

$$F \cap G = max(F(x_0, y_0, z_0), G(x_0, y_0, z_0)) \tag{6-14}$$

The difference of two implicit functions is given by

$$F - G = max(F(x_0, y_0, z_0), -G(x_0, y_0, z_0)) \tag{6-15}$$

Figure **6–23**(c) shows a combination of simple implicit functions to create an ice-cream cone. The cone is created by clipping the (infinite) cone function with two planes. The ice cream is constructed by performing a difference operation on a larger sphere with a smaller offset sphere to create the "bite." The resulting surface was extracted using surface contouring with isosurface value 0.0.

Selecting Data. We can take advantage of the properties of implicit functions to select and cut data. In particular we will use the region separation property to select data. (We defer the discussion on cutting to "Cutting" on page 187.)

Selecting or extracting data with an implicit function means choosing cells and points (and associated attribute data) that lie within a particular region of the function. To determine whether a point x-y-z lies within a region, we simply evaluate the point and examine the sign of the result. A cell lies in a region if all its points lie in the region.

Figure **6–24**(a) shows a 2D implicit function, here an ellipse, used to select the data (i.e., points, cells, and data attributes) contained within it. Boolean com-

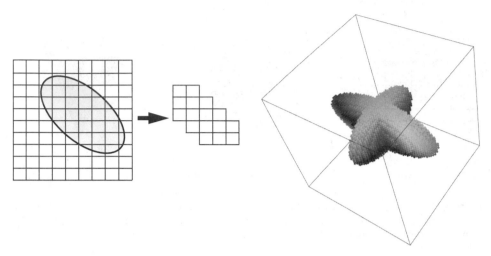

(a) Selecting data with implicit function   (b) Selecting data with boolean combination

Figure 6–24 Implicit functions used to select data: (a) 2D cells lying in ellipse are selected; (b) Two ellipsoids combined using the union operation used to select voxels from a volume. Voxels shrunk 50 percent (`extractD.tcl`).

binations also can be used to create complex selection regions as illustrated in Figure **6–24**(b). Here, two ellipses are used in combination to select voxels within a volume dataset. Note that extracting data often changes the structure of the dataset. In Figure **6–24** the input type is a structured points dataset, while the output type is an unstructured grid dataset.

Visualizing Mathematical Descriptions. Some functions, often discrete or probabilistic in nature, cannot be cast into the form of Equation **6-11**. However, by applying some creative thinking we can often generate scalar values that can be visualized. An interesting example of this is the so-called *strange attractor*.

Strange attractors arise in the study of nonlinear dynamics and chaotic systems. In these systems, the usual types of dynamic motion — equilibrium, periodic motion, or quasi-periodic motion — are not present. Instead, the system exhibits chaotic motion. The resulting behavior of the system can change radically as a result of small perturbations in its initial conditions.

A classical strange attractor was developed by Lorenz in 1963 [Lorenz63]. Lorenz developed a simple model for thermally induced fluid convection in the atmosphere. Convection causes rings of rotating fluid and can be developed from

Figure 6–25 Visualizing a Lorenz strange attractor by integrating the Lorenz equations in a volume. The number of visits in each voxel is recorded as a scalar function. The surface is extracted via marching cubes using a visit value of 50. The number of integration steps is 10 million, in a volume of dimensions 200^3. The surface roughness is caused by the discrete nature of the evaluation function (`Lorenz.cxx`).

the general Navier-Stokes partial differential equations for fluid flow. The Lorenz equations can be expressed in nondimensional form as

$$\frac{dx}{dt} = \sigma(y - x)$$

$$\frac{dy}{dt} = \rho x - y - xz \qquad\qquad \textbf{(6-16)}$$

$$\frac{dz}{dt} = xy - \beta z$$

where x is proportional to the fluid velocity in the fluid ring, y and z measure the fluid temperature in the plane of the ring, the parameters σ and ρ are related to the Prandtl number and Raleigh number, respectively, and β is a geometric factor.

Certainly these equations are not in the implicit form of Equation **6-11**, so how do we visualize them? Our solution is to treat the variables x, y, and z as the coordinates of a three-dimensional space, and integrate Equation **6-16** to generate the system "trajectory", that is, the state of the system through time. The integration is carried out within a volume and scalars are created by counting the number of times each voxel is visited. By integrating long enough, we can create a volume representing the "surface" of the strange attractor, Figure **6–25**. The surface of the strange attractor is extracted by using marching cubes and a scalar value specifying the number of visits in a voxel.

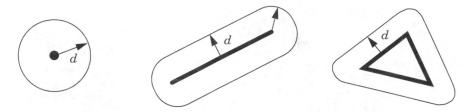

Figure 6–26 Distance functions to a point, line, and triangle.

Implicit Modelling

In the previous section we saw how implicit functions, or boolean combinations of implicit functions, could be used to model geometric objects. The basic approach is to evaluate these functions on a regular array of points, or volume, and then to generate scalar values at each point in the volume. Then either volume rendering (see "Volume Rendering" on page 216), or isosurface generation in combination with surface rendering, is used to display the model.

An extension of this approach, called implicit modeling, is similar to modeling with implicit functions. The difference lies in the fact that scalars are generated using a distance function instead of the usual implicit function. The distance function is computed as a Euclidean distance to a set of generating primitives such as points, lines, or polygons. For example, Figure **6–26** shows the distance functions to a point, line, and triangle. Because distance functions are well-behaved monotonic functions, we can define a series of offset surfaces by specifying different isosurface values, where the value is the distance to the generating primitive. The isosurfaces form approximations to the true offset surfaces, but using high volume resolution we can achieve satisfactory results.

Used alone the generating primitives are limited in their ability to model complex geometry. By using boolean combinations of the primitives, however, complex geometry can be easily modeled. The boolean operations union, intersection, and difference (Equation **6-13**, Equation **6-14**, and Equation **6-15**, respectively) are illustrated in Figure **6–27**. Figure **6–28** shows the application of implicit modeling to "thicken" the line segments in the text symbol "HELLO". The isosurface is generated on a $110 \times 40 \times 20$ volume at a distance offset of 0.25 units. The generating primitives were combined using the boolean union operator. Although Euclidean distance is always a nonnegative value, it is possible to use a signed distance function for objects that have an outside and an inside. A negative distance is the negated distance of a point inside the object to the surface of the object. Using a signed distance function allows us to create offset surfaces that are contained within the actual surface.

Another interesting feature of implicit modeling is that when isosurfaces are generated, more than one connected surface can result. These situations occur when the generating primitives form concave features. Figure **6–29** illus-

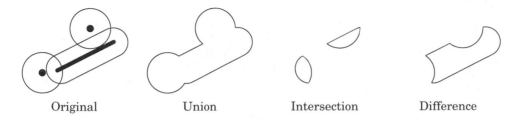

| Original | Union | Intersection | Difference |

Figure 6–27 Boolean operations using points and lines as generating primitives.

Figure 6–28 Implicit modelling used to thicken a stroked font. Original lines can be seen within the translucent implicit surface (`hello.tcl`).

trates this situation. If desired, multiple surfaces can be separated by using the connectivity algorithm described in "Connectivity" on page 377.

Glyphs

Glyphs, sometimes referred to as icons, are a versatile technique to visualize data of every type. A glyph is an "object" that is affected by its input data. This object may be geometry, a dataset, or a graphical image. The glyph may orient, scale, translate, deform, or somehow alter the appearance of the object in response to data. We have already seen a simple form of glyph: hedgehogs are lines that are oriented, translated and scaled according to the position and vector value of a point. A variation of this is to use oriented cones or arrows. (See "Hedgehogs and Oriented Glyphs" on page 167.)

More elaborate glyphs are possible. In one creative visualization technique Chernoff [Chernoff73] tied data values to an iconic representation of the human face. Eyebrows, nose, mouth, and other features were modified according to financial data values. This interesting technique built on the human capability to recognize facial expression. By tying appropriate data values to facial characteristics, rapid identification of important data points is possible.

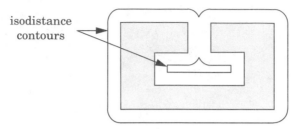

isodistance
contours

Figure 6–29 Concave features can result in multiple contour lines/surfaces.

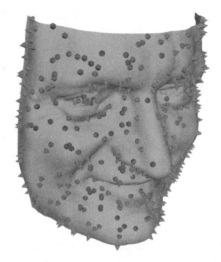

Figure 6–30 Glyphs indicate surface normals on model of human face. Glyph positions are randomly selected (`spikeF.tcl`).

In a sense, glyphs represent the fundamental result of the visualization process. Moreover, all the visualization techniques we present can be treated as concrete representations of an abstract glyph class. For example, while hedge-hogs are an obvious manifestation of a vector glyph, isosurfaces can be considered a topologically two-dimensional glyph for scalar data. Delmarcelle and Hesselink [Delmarcelle95] have developed a unified framework for flow visualization based on types of glyphs. They classify glyphs according to one of three categories.

- *Elementary icons* represent their data across the extent of their spatial domain. For example, an oriented arrow can be used to represent surface normal.

- *Local icons* represent elementary information plus a local distribution of the values around the spatial domain. A surface normal vector colored by local curvature is one example of a local icon, since local data beyond the elementary information is encoded.

- *Global icons* show the structure of the complete dataset. An isosurface is an example of a global icon.

This classification scheme can be extended to other visualization techniques such as vector and tensor data, or even to nonvisual forms such as sound or tactile feedback. We have found this classification scheme to be helpful when designing visualizations or creating visualization techniques. Often it gives insight into ways of representing data that can be overlooked.

Figure **6–30** is an example of glyphing. Small 3D cones are oriented on a surface to indicate the direction of the surface normal. A similar approach could be used to show other surface properties such as curvature or anatomical key-points.

Cutting

Often we want to cut through a dataset with a surface and then display the interpolated data values on the surface. We refer to this technique as *data cutting* or simply *cutting*. The data cutting operation requires two pieces of information: a definition for the surface and a dataset to cut. We will assume that the cutting surface is defined by an implicit function. A typical application of cutting is to slice through a dataset with a plane, and color map the scalar data and/or warp the plane according to vector value.

A property of implicit functions is to convert a position into a scalar value (see "Implicit Functions" on page 180). We can use this property in combination with a contouring algorithm (e.g., marching cubes) to generate cut surfaces. The basic idea is to generate scalars for each point of each cell of a dataset (using the implicit cut function), and then contour the surface value $F(x, y, z) = 0$.

The cutting algorithm proceeds as follows. For each cell, function values are generated by evaluating $F(x, y, z)$ for each cell point. If all the points evaluate positive or negative, then the surface does not cut the cell. However, if the points evaluate positive and negative, then the surface passes through the cell. We can use the cell contouring operation to generate the isosurface $F(x, y, z) = 0$. Data attribute values can then be computed by interpolating along cut edges.

Figure **6–31** illustrates a plane cut through a structured grid dataset. The plane passes through the center of the dataset with normal (–0.287, 0, 0.9579). For comparison purposes a portion of the grid geometry is also shown. The grid geometry is the grid surface $k=9$ (shown in wireframe). A benefit of cut surfaces is that we can view data on (nearly) arbitrary surfaces. Thus, the structure of the dataset does not constrain how we view the data.

We can easily make multiple planar cuts through a structured grid dataset by specifying multiple isovalues for the cutting algorithm. Figure **6–32** shows 100 cut planes generated perpendicular to the camera's view plane normal. Rendering the planes from back to front with an opacity of 0.05 produces a simulation of volume rendering. (See "Volume Rendering" on page 216.)

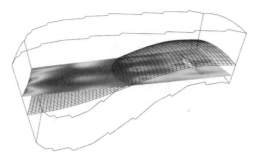

Figure 6–31 Cut through structured grid with plane. The cut plane is shown solid shaded. A computational plane of constant k value is shown in wireframe for comparison (cut.tcl).

This example illustrates that cutting the volumetric data in a structured grid dataset produced polygonal cells. Similarly, cutting polygonal data produces lines. Using a single plane equation, we can extract "contour lines" from a surface model defined with polygons. Figure **6–33** shows contours extracted from a surface model of the skin. At each vertex in the surface model we evaluate the equation of the plane $F(x, y, z) = c$ and store the value of the function as a scalar value. Cutting the data with 46 isovalues from 1.5 to 136.5 produces contour lines that are 3 units apart.

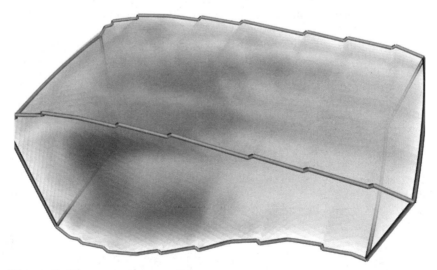

Figure 6–32 100 cut planes with opacity of 0.05. Rendered back to front to simulate volume rendering (combVol.tcl).

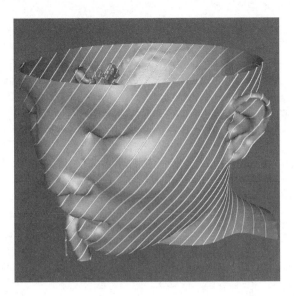

Figure 6–33 Cutting a surface model of the skin with a series of planes produces contour lines (cutModel.tcl). Lines are wrapped with tubes for visual clarity.

6.6 Putting It All Together

Process Object Design

Algorithms are implemented in the *Visualization Toolkit* as process objects. These objects may be either sources, filters, or mappers (See "The Visualization Pipeline" on page 88.) In this section we will describe how these objects are implemented.

Source Design. Source objects have no visualization data for input and one or more outputs, Figure **6–34**. To create a source object, inheritance is used to specify the type of dataset that the process object creates for output. Figure **6–34** illustrates this for the concrete source object vtkSphereSource. This class inherits from vtkSource, indicating that it is a source object, and vtkPoly-Data, indicating that it creates polygonal data on output.

The convenience object vtkPolyDataSource has been created to simplify subclass derivation. For example, vtkBYUReader is also of type vtkPolyData-Source. The major difference between vtkSphereSource and vtkBYUReader is the implementation of the virtual method Execute(). This method actually creates its output data. If you derive a source object you do not need to make it a subclass of any convenience object (e.g., vtkPolyDataSource) but you should

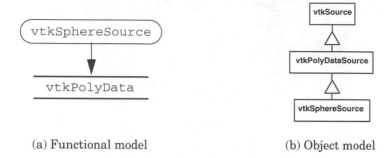

(a) Functional model   (b) Object model

Figure 6–34 Source object design. Example shown is a source object that creates a polygonal representation of a sphere.

are created, since no convenience classes exist expressly for derivation in this case.

Filter Design. Filter objects have one or more inputs and one or more outputs as shown in Figure **6–35**. (You may also refer to "Multiple Input / Output" on page 103.) To create a filter object, inheritance is used to specify the type of input and output data objects. Figure **6–35** illustrates this for the concrete source object vtkContourFilter (which implements marching cubes and other contouring techniques). It is worth examining this object diagram in detail since it is the basis for the architecture of the visualization pipeline.

The superclasses of vtkContourFilter are vtkSource, vtkFilter, vtkDataSetFilter, and vtkDataSetToPolyDataFilter. Although the inheritance of vtkContourFilter from vtkSource may be confusing at first glance, the meaning is this: the filter is a source of visualization data. Similarly, inheritance from vtkFilter means that vtkContourFilter has at least one input. The class vtkDataSetFilter specifies the type of data vtkContourFilter takes as input (i.e., a dataset), while vtkDataSetToPolyDataFilter specifies the type of output (i.e., polygonal data). Note that inheritance from vtkDataSetFilter and vtkDataSetToPolyDataFilter is optional – this functionality could be implemented directly in vtkContourFilter. These optional objects are simply convenience objects to make class derivation a little easier.

What is left for vtkContourFilter to implement is its Execute() method (as well as constructor, print method, and any other methods special to this class). Thus the primary difference between classes with equivalent inheritance hierarchies is the implementation of the Execute() method.

As we mentioned a moment ago, the class vtkDataSetFilter enforces filter input type with the type checking features of the C++ compiler. It accepts type vtkDataSet (or subclasses). Since vtkDataSet is a base class for all data types, this filter will accept any type as input. Specialized filters are derived from other classes. For example, filters that accept polygonal data are derived from

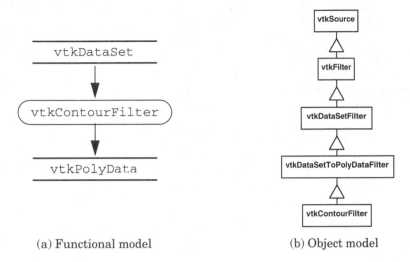

(a) Functional model   (b) Object model

Figure 6–35 Filter object design. The example shown is for an object that receives a general dataset as input and creates polygonal data on output.

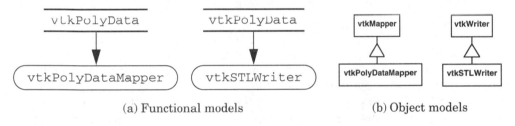

(a) Functional models   (b) Object models

Figure 6–36 Mapper object design. Graphics mapper shown (e.g., vtkPolyDataMapper) maps polygonal data through graphics library primitives. Writer shown (e.g., vtkSTLWriter) writes polygonal data to stereo lithography format.

vtkPolyDataFilter, and filters that accept structured point datasets are derived from vtkStructuredPointsFilter.

We encourage you to examine the source code carefully (included on the CD-ROM) for a few filter and source objects. The architecture is simple enough that you can grasp it quickly.

Mapper Design. Mapper objects have one or more inputs and no visualization data output, Figure **6–36**. Two different types of mappers are available in the *Visualization Toolkit*: graphics mappers and writers. Graphics mappers interface geometric structure and data attributes to the graphics library; writers write datasets to disk or other I/O devices.

Since mappers take datasets as input, type enforcement is required. Each mapper implements this functionality directly. For example, both classes vtk-PolyDataMapper and vtkSTLWriter implement a SetInput() method to enforce the input to be of type vtkPolyData. Other mappers and writers enforce input type as appropriate.

Although writers and mappers do not create visualization data, they both have methods similar to the Execute() method of the sources and filters. Each subclass of vtkMapper must implement the Render() method. This method is exchanged by the graphics system actors and its associated mappers during the rendering process. The effect of the method is to map its input dataset to the appropriate rendering library/system. Subclasses of the class vtkWriter must implement the WriteData() method. This method causes the writer to write its input dataset to disk (or other I/O device).

Color Maps

Color maps are created in the *Visualization Toolkit* using instances of the class vtkLookupTable. This class allows you to create a lookup table using HSVA (e.g., hue, saturation, value, and alpha opacity value) specification. Although we discussed the HSV color system in Chapter 3, we haven't yet defined alpha opacity. We shall do so in Chapter 7, but until then consider the alpha value to be the opacity of an object. Alpha values of one indicate that the object is opaque, while alpha values of zero indicate that the object is transparent.

The procedure for generating lookup table entries is to define pairs of values for HSVA. These pairs define a linear ramp for hue, saturation, value, and opacity. When the Build() method is invoked, these linear ramps are used to generate a table with the number of table entries requested. Alternatively, vtk-LookupTable also enables you to load colors directly into the table. Thus, you build custom tables that cannot be simply expressed as linear ramps of HSVA values.

To demonstrate this procedure, we specify a starting and ending value for each of the components of HSVA, then we will create a rainbow lookup table from blue to red by using the following C++ code.

```
vtkLookupTable *lut=vtkLookupTable::New();
    lut->SetHueRange(0.6667, 0.0);
    lut->SetSaturationRange(1.0, 1.0);
    lut->SetValueRange(1.0, 1.0);
    lut->SetAlphaRange(1.0, 1.0);
    lut->SetNumberOfColors(256);
    lut->Build();
```

Since the default values for SaturationRange, ValueRange, AlphaRange, and the number of lookup table colors are (1,1), (1,1), (1,1), and 256, respectively, we can simplify this process to the following

```
vtkLookupTable *lut=vtkLookupTable::New();
    lut->SetHueRange(0.6667, 0.0);
    lut->Build();
```

(The default values for `HueRange` are (0.0, 0.6667) — a red to blue color table.
To build a black and white lookup table of 256 entries we use

```
vtkLookupTable *lut=vtkLookupTable::New();
    lut->SetHueRange(0.0, 0.0);
    lut->SetSaturationRange(0.0, 0.0);
    lut->SetValueRange(0.0, 1.0)
```

In some cases you may want to specify colors directly. You can do this by
specifying the number of colors, building the table, and then inserting new colors. When you insert colors, the RGBA color description system is used. For
example, to create a lookup table of the three colors red, green, and blue, use the
following C++ code.

```
vtkLookupTable *lut=vtkLookupTable::New();
    lut->SetNumberOfColors(3);
    lut->Build();
    lut->SetTableValue(0, 1.0, 0.0, 0.0, 1.0);
    lut->SetTableValue(0, 0.0, 1.0, 0.0, 1.0);
    lut->SetTableValue(0, 0.0, 0.0, 1.0, 1.0);
```

Lookup tables in the *Visualization Toolkit* are associated with the graphics
mappers. Mappers will automatically create a red to blue lookup table if no table
is specified, but if you want to create your own, use the `mapper->SetLookup-
Table(lut)` operation where `mapper` is an instance of `vtkMapper` or its sub-
classes.

A few final notes on using lookup tables.

- Mappers use their lookup table to map scalar values to colors. If no scalars
  are present, the mappers and their lookup tables do not control the color of
  the object. Instead the `vtkProperty` object associated with the `vtkActor`
  class does. Use the method `actor->GetProperty()->SetColor(r,g,b)`
  where r, g, and b are floating-point values specifying color.

- If you want to prevent scalars from coloring your object, use the method
  `mapper->ScalarVisibilityOff()` to turn off color mapping. Then the
  actor's color will control the color of the object.

- The scalar range (i.e., the range into which the colors are mapped) is specified with the mapper. Use the method `mapper->SetScalarRange(min,
  max)`.

You can also derive your own lookup table types. Look at `vtkLogLookup-
Table` for an example. This particular lookup table inherits from `vtkLookup-`

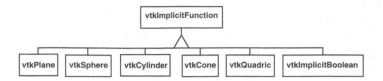

Figure 6–37 Inheritance hierarchy of `vtkImplicitFunction` and subclasses.

`Table`. It performs logarithmic mapping of scalar value to table entry, a useful capability when scalar values span many orders of magnitude.

Implicit Functions

As we have seen, implicit functions can be used for visualizing functions, creating geometry, and cutting or selecting datasets. **vtk** includes several implicit functions including a single plane (`vtkPlane`), multiple convex planes (`vtkPlanes`), spheres (`vtkSphere`), cones (`vtkCone`), cylinders (`vtkCylinder`), and the general quadric (`vtkQuadric`). The class `vtkImplicitBoolean` allows you to create boolean combinations of these implicit function primitives. Other implicit functions can be added to **vtk** by deriving from the abstract base class `vtkImplicitFunction`.

The existing inheritance hierarchy for implicit functions is shown in Figure **6–37**. Subclasses of `vtkImplicitFunction` must implement the two methods `Evaluate()` and `Gradient()`. The method `Evaluate()` returns the value of the function at point (x,y,z), while the method `Gradient()` returns the gradient vector to the function at point (x,y,z).

Contouring

Scalar contouring is implemented in the *Visualization Toolkit* with `vtkContourFilter`. This filter object accepts as input any dataset type. Thus, `vtkContourFilter` treats every cell type and each cell type must provide a method for contouring itself.

Contouring in **vtk** is implemented using variations of the marching cubes algorithm presented earlier. That is, a contour case table is associated with each cell type, so each cell will generate contouring primitives as appropriate. For example, the tetrahedron cell type implements "marching tetrahedron" and creates triangle primitives, while the triangle cell type implements "marching triangles" and generates lines segments.

The implication of this arrangement is that `vtkContourFilter` will generate point, line, and surface contouring primitives depending on the combination of input cell types. Thus `vtkContourFilter` is completely general. We have created another contour filter, `vtkMarchingCubes`, that is specific to the dataset type structured points (in particular, 3D volumes). These two filters allow us to compare (at least for this one algorithm) the cost of generality.

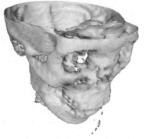
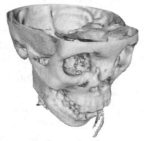
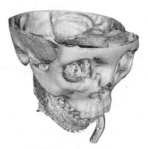

(a) Quarter resolution   (b) Half resolution   (c) Full resolution

Resolution	Specific (w/ normals)	General (no normals)	Factor	General (w/ normals)	Factor
64 x 64 x 93	1.000	2.889	2.889	7.131	7.131
128 x 128 x 93	5.058	11.810	2.330	23.260	4.600
256 x 256 x 93	37.169	51.620	1.390	87.230	2.350

Figure 6–38 The cost of generality. Isosurface generation of three volumes of different sizes are compared. The results show normalized execution times for two different implementations of the marching-cubes isosurface algorithm. The specialized filter is vtkMarchingCubes. The general algorithms are first vtkContourFilter and then in combination with vtkPolyDataNormals.

Recall from "Generality Versus Efficiency" on page 155 the issues regarding the trade-offs between general and specific algorithms. Figure **6–38** shows a comparison of CPU times for a volume dataset at $64 \times 64 \times 93$, $128 \times 128 \times 93$, and $256 \times 256 \times 93$ resolution. The volume is a CT dataset of a human head. Three cases were run. In the first case the vtkMarchingCubes object was used. The output of this filter is triangles plus point normals. In the second case vtkContourFilter was run. The output of this filter is just triangles. In the last case vtkContourFilter was combined with vtkPolyDataNormals (to generate point normals). The output of the combined filters is also triangles plus point normals.

The execution times are normalized to the smallest dataset using the vtkMarchingCubes object. The results are clear: The specific object outperforms the general object by a factor of 1.4 to 7, depending on data size and whether normals are computed. The larger differences occur on the smaller datasets. This is because the ratio of voxel cells containing the isosurface to the total number of voxels is larger for smaller datasets. (Generally the total number of voxels increases as the resolution cubed, while the voxels containing the isosurface increase as the resolution squared.) As a result, more voxels are processed in the smaller datasets relative to the total number of voxels than in the larger datasets. When the datasets become larger, more voxels are "empty" and are not processed.

Although these results do not represent all implementations or the behavior of other algorithms, they do point to the cost of generality. Of course, there is a cost to specialization as well. This cost is typically in programmer time, since the programmer must rewrite code to adapt to new circumstances and data. Like all trade-offs, resolution of this issue requires knowledge of the application.

An example use of `vtkContourFilter` is shown in Figure **6–39**. This example is taken from Figure **4–1**, which is a visualization of a quadric function. The class `vtkSampleFunction` samples the implicit quadric function using the `vtkQuadric` class. Although `vtkQuadric` does not participate in the pipeline in terms of data flow, it is used to define and evaluate the quadric function. It is possible to generate one or more isolines/isosurfaces simultaneously using `vtkContourFilter`. As Figure **6–39** shows, we use the `GenerateValues()` method to specify a scalar range, and the number of contours within this range (including the initial and final scalar values). `vtkContourFilter` generates duplicate vertices, so we can use `vtkCleanPolyData` to remove them. To improve the rendered appearance of the isosurface, we use `vtkPolyDataNormals` to create surface normals. (We describe surface normal generation in Chapter 9.)

Cutting

`vtkCutter` performs cutting of all **vtk** cell types. The `SetValue()` and `GenerateValues()` methods permit the user to specify which multiple scalar values to use for the cutting. `vtkCutter` requires an implicit function that will be evaluated at each point in the dataset. Then each cell is cut using the cell's `Contour` method. Any point attributes are interpolated to the resulting cut vertices. The sorting order for the generated polygonal data can be controlled with the `SortBy` method. The default sorting order, `SortByValue()`, processes cells in the inner loop for each contour value. `SortByCell()` processes the cutting value in the inner loop and produces polygonal data that is suitable for back-to-front rendering (see Figure **6–32**). (The sorting order is useful when rendering with opacity as discussed in Chapter 7.) Notice the similarity of this filter to the `vtkContourFilter`. Both of these objects contour datasets with multiple isovalues. `vtkCutter` uses an implicit function to calculate scalar values while `vtkContourFilter` uses the scalar data associated with the dataset's point data.

Glyphs

The `vtkGlyph3D` class provides a simple, yet powerful glyph capability in the *Visualization Toolkit*. `vtkGlyph3D` is an example of an object that takes multiple inputs (Figure **6–40**). One input, specified with the `SetInput()` method, defines a set of points and possible attribute data at those points. The second input, specified with the `SetSource()` method, defines a geometry to be copied to every point in the input dataset. The source is of type `vtkPolyData`. Hence, any

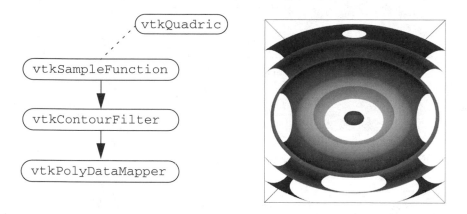

```
// Define implicit function
vtkQuadric *quadric = vtkQuadric::New();
  quadric->SetCoefficients(.5,1,.2,0,.1,0,0,.2,0,0);
vtkSampleFunction *sample = vtkSampleFunction::New();
  sample->SetSampleDimensions(50,50,50);
  sample->SetImplicitFunction(quadric);
vtkContourFilter *contour = vtkContourFilter::New();
  contour->SetInput(sample->GetOutput());
  contour->GenerateValues(5,0,1.2);
vtkPolyDataMapper *contourMapper = vtkPolyDataMapper::New();
  contourMapper->SetInput(contour->GetOutput());
  contourMapper->SetScalarRange(0,1.2);
vtkActor *contourActor = vtkActor::New();
  contourActor->SetMapper(contourMapper);

// Create outline
vtkOutlineFilter *outline = vtkOutlineFilter::New();
  outline->SetInput(sample->GetOutput());
vtkPolyDataMapper *outlineMapper = vtkPolyDataMapper::New();
  outlineMapper->SetInput(outline->GetOutput());
vtkActor *outlineActor = vtkActor::New();
  outlineActor->SetMapper(outlineMapper);
  outlineActor->GetProperty()->SetColor(0,0,0);
```

Figure 6–39 Contouring quadric function. Pipeline topology, C++ code, and resulting image are shown (contQuad.cxx).

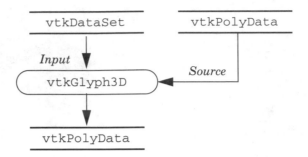

Figure 6–40 Data flow into and out of the vtkGlyph3D class.

filter, sequence of filters creating polygonal data, or a polygonal dataset may be used to describe the glyph's geometry.

The behavior of an instance of vtkGlyph3D depends on the nature of the input data and the value of its instance variables. Generally, the input Source geometry will be copied to each point of the Input dataset. The geometry will be aligned along the input vector data and scaled according to the magnitude of the vector or the scalar value. In some cases, the point normal is used rather than the vector. Also, scaling can be turned on or off.

We saw how to use vtkGlyph3D in the example given in Figure **4–14**. Cones were used as the glyph and were located at each point on the sphere, oriented along the sphere's surface normal.

Streamlines

Streamlines and particle motion require numerical integration to guide a point through the vector field. Vector visualization algorithms that we will see in later chapters also require numerical integration. As a result, we designed an object hierarchy that isolates the numerical integration process into a single base class. The base class is vtkStreamer and it is responsible for generating a particle path through a vector field of specified length (expressed as elapsed time). Each derived class of vtkStreamer takes advantage of this capability to move through the vector field but implements its own particular representational technique to depict particle motion. Streamlines (vtkStreamLine) draw connected lines while particle motion is shown by combining the output of vtkStream-Points with the vtkGlyph3D object. Using vtkGlyph3D we can place spheres or oriented objects such as cones or arrows at points on the particle path created by vtkStreamPoints. The inheritance hierarchy for vtkStreamer and subclasses is shown in Figure **6–41**.

The integration method in vtkStreamer is implemented as a virtual function. Thus it can be overloaded as necessary. Possible reasons for overloading include implementing an integration technique of higher or lower accuracy, or creating a technique specialized to a particular dataset type. For example, the

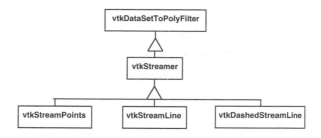

Figure 6–41 Inheritance hierarchy for `vtkStreamer` and subclasses.

search process in a volume is much faster than it is for other dataset types, therefore, highly efficient vector integration techniques can be constructed.

The vector integration technique in **vtk** will accommodate any cell type. Thus, integration through cells of any topological dimension is possible. If the cells are of topological dimension 2 or less, the integration process constrains particle motion to the surface (2D) or line (1D). The particle may only leave a cell by passing through the cell boundary, and traveling to a neighboring cell, or exiting the dataset.

Abstract Filters

Attribute transformations create or modify data attributes without changing the topology or geometry of a dataset. Hence filters that implement attribute transformation (e.g., `vtkElevationFilter`) can accept any dataset type as input, and may generate any dataset type on output. Unfortunately, because filters must specialize the particular type of data they output, at first glance it appears that filters that create general dataset types on output are not feasible. This is because the type `vtkDataSet` is an abstract type and must be specialized to allow instantiation.

Fortunately, there is a a solution to this dilemma. The solution is to use the "virtual constructor" `MakeObject()`. Although C++ does not allow virtual constructors, we can simulate it by creating a special virtual function that constructs a copy of the object that it is invoked on. For example, if this function is applied to a dataset instance of type `vtkPolyData`, the result will be a copy of that instance (Figure **6–42**). (Note that we use reference counting to make copies and avoid duplicating memory.) The virtual constructor function `MakeObject()` is implemented in a number of **vtk** classes including datasets and cells.

Using the virtual constructor we can construct filters that output abstract data types like `vtkDataSet`. We simply apply `MakeObject()` to the input of the filter. This will then return a pointer to a concrete object that is the output of the filter. The result is a general filter object that can accept any dataset type for input and creates the general `vtkDataSet` type as output. In **vtk**, this function-

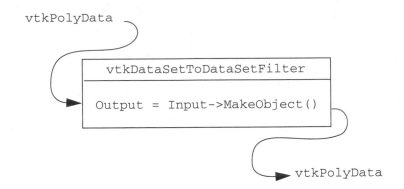

Figure 6–42 Depiction of data flow for abstract filter output. The output object type is the same as the input type.

ality has been implemented in the abstract class `vtkDataSetToDataSetFilter`.

There are other filters that implement variations of this delegation technique. The class `vtkPointSetToPointSetFilter` is similar to `vtkDataSetToDataSetFilter`. This class takes as input any dataset whose geometry is explicitly defined via an instance of `vtkPoints` (or subclass), and generates on output an object of the same type (i.e., `vtkPointSet`). The class `vtkMergeFilter` combines dataset structure and point attributes from one or more input datasets. For example, you can read multiple files and combine the geometry/ topology from one file with different scalars, vectors, and normals from other files.

One difficulty using abstract filter types is that the output type may not match with the input type of a downstream filter. For example, the output of `vtkElevationFilter` is specified as `vtkDataSet` even though the input may be of type `vtkPolyData`, and we know from the previous discussion that the actual output type will be `vtkPolyData`. This difficulty is removed by using the filter `vtkCastToConcrete`, which allows you to run-time cast to the appropriate output type. In this case we would use the `GetPolyDataOutput()` from `vtkCastToConcrete`. After checking the validity of the cast, this method returns a dataset cast to `vtkPolyData`. Of course, this process requires that the input to `vtkCastToConcrete` be set before the output is requested.

Visualizing Blood Flow

In this example we'll combine a few different techniques to visualize blood flow in the human carotid arteries. Our data contains both vectors that represent the velocity of blood and scalars that are proportional to the magnitude of the velocity (i.e., speed).

We can provide context for the visualization by creating an isosurface of speed. This isosurface shows regions of fastest blood flow, and is similar to, but not the same as, the actual surface of the arteries. However, it provides us with a visual cue to the structure of the arteries.

The first vector visualization technique we'll use is to generate vector glyphs (Figure **6–43**). Unfortunately, we cannot just create glyphs at each point because of the number of points (over 167,000 points). To do so would result in a confusing mess, and the interactive speed would be poor. Instead, we'll use two filters to select a subset of the available points. These filters are `vtkThreshold-Points` and `vtkMaskPoints`.

`vtkThresholdPoints` allows us to extract points that satisfy a certain threshold criterion. In our example, we choose points whose speed is greater than a specified value. This eliminates a large number of points, since most points lie outside the arteries and have a small speed value.

The filter `vtkMaskPoints` allows us to select a subset of the available points. We specify the subset with the `OnRatio` instance variable. This instance variable indicates that every `OnRatio` point is to be selected. Thus, if the `OnRatio` is equal to one, all points will be selected, and if the `OnRatio` is equal to ten, every tenth point will be selected. This selection can be either uniform or random. Random point selection is set using the `RandomModeOn()` and `Random-ModeOff()` methods.

After selecting a subset of the original points, we can use the `vtkGlyph3D` filter in the usual way. A cone's orientation indicates blood flow direction, and its size and color correspond to the velocity magnitude. Figure **6–43** shows the pipeline, sample code, and a resulting image from this visualization. Note that we've implemented the example using the interpreted language Tcl. See Chapter 11 if you want more information about Tcl.

In the next part of this example we'll generate streamtubes of blood velocity. Again we use an isosurface of speed to provide us with context. The starting positions for the streamtubes were determined by experimenting with the data. Because of the way the data was measured and the resolution of the velocity field, many streamers travel outside the artery. This is because the boundary layer of the blood flow is not captured due to limitations in data resolution. Consequently, as the blood flows around curves, there is a component of the velocity field that directs the streamtube outside the artery. As a result it is hard to find starting positions for the streamtubes that yield interesting results. We use the source object `vtkPointSource` in combination with `vtkThresholdPoints` to work around this problem. `vtkPointSource` generates random points centered around a sphere of a specified radius. We need only find an approximate position for the starting points of the streamtubes and then generate a cloud of random seed points. `vtkThresholdPoints` is used to cull points that may be generated outside the regions of high flow velocity.

Figure **6–44** shows the pipeline, sample Tcl code, and a resulting image from the visualization. Notice that the isosurface is shown in wireframe. This provides context, yet allows us to see the streamtubes within the isosurface.

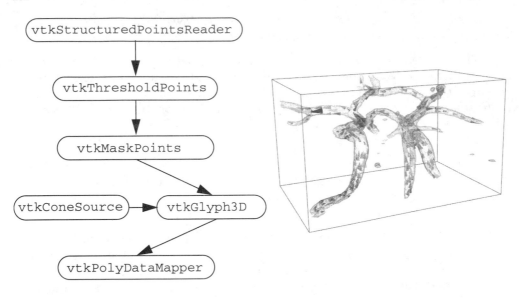

```
vtkStructuredPointsReader reader
    reader SetFileName "../../../vtkdata/carotid.vtk"
    reader DebugOn
vtkThresholdPoints threshold
    threshold SetInput [reader GetOutput]
    threshold ThresholdByUpper 200
vtkMaskPoints mask
    mask SetInput [Threshold GetOutput]
    mask SetOnRatio 10
vtkConeSource cone
    cone SetResolution 3
    cone SetHeight 1
    cone SetRadius 0.25
vtkGlyph3D cones
    cones SetInput [mask GetOutput]
    cones SetSource [cone GetOutput]
    cones SetScaleFactor 0.005
    cones SetScaleModeToScaleByVector
vtkPolyDataMapper vecMapper
    vecMapper SetInput [cones GetOutput]
    vecMapper SetScalarRange 2 10
```

Figure 6–43 Visualizing blood flow in human carotid arteries. Cone glyphs indicate flow direction and magnitude. The code fragment shown is from the Tcl script thrshldV.tcl and shows creation of vector glyphs.

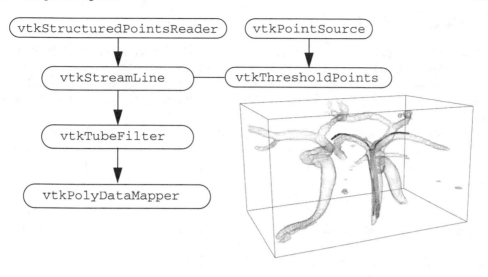

```
vtkStructuredPointsReader reader
    reader SetFileName "../../../vtkdata/carotid.vtk"
vtkPointSource source
    source SetNumberOfPoints 25
    source SetCenter 133.1 116.3 5.0
    source SetRadius 2.0
vtkThresholdPoints threshold
    threshold SetInput [reader GetOutput]
    threshold ThresholdByUpper 275
vtkStreamLine streamers
    streamers SetInput [reader GetOutput]
    streamers SetSource [source GetOutput]
    streamers SetMaximumPropagationTime 100.0
    streamers SetIntegrationStepLength 0.2
    streamers SpeedScalarsOn
    streamers SetTerminalSpeed .1
vtkTubeFilter tubes
    tubes SetInput [streamers GetOutput]
    tubes SetRadius 0.3
    tubes SetNumberOfSides 6
    tubes SetVaryRadiusToVaryRadiusOff
vtkPolyDataMapper streamerMapper
    streamerMapper SetInput [tubes GetOutput]
    streamerMapper SetScalarRange 2 10
```

Figure 6–44 Visualizing blood flow in the human carotid arteries. Streamtubes of flow vectors (streamV.tcl).

6.7 Chapter Summary

Visualization algorithms transform data from one form to another. These transformations can change or create new structure and/or attributes of a dataset. Structural transformations change either the topology or geometry of a dataset. Attribute transformations change dataset attributes such as scalars, vectors, normals, or texture coordinates.

Algorithms are classified according to the type of data they operate on. Scalar, vector, and tensor algorithms operate on scalar, vector, and tensor data, respectively. Modelling algorithms operate on dataset geometry or topology, texture coordinates, or normals. Modelling algorithms also may include complex techniques that may represent combinations of different data types.

Algorithms can be designed and implemented for general types of data or specialized for a specific type. General algorithms are typically less efficient than their specialized counterparts. Conversely, general algorithms are more flexible and do not require rewriting as new dataset types are introduced.

Important scalar algorithms include color mapping and contouring. Color maps are used to map scalar values to color values. Contouring algorithms create isosurfaces or isolines to indicate areas of constant scalar value.

Glyphs such as hedgehogs are useful for visualizing vector data. These techniques are limited by the number of glyphs that can be displayed at one time. Particle traces or streamlines are another important algorithm for vector field visualization. Collections of particle traces can convey something of the structure of a vector field.

Real, symmetric 3×3 tensors can be characterized by their eigenvalues and eigenvectors. Tensors can be visualized using tensor ellipsoids or oriented axes.

Implicit functions and sampling techniques can be used to make geometry, cut data, and visualize complex mathematical descriptions. Glyphs are objects whose appearance is associated with a particular data value. Glyphs are flexible and can be created to visualize a variety of data.

6.8 Bibliographic Notes

Color mapping is a widely studied topic in imaging, computer graphics, visualization, and human factors. References [Durrett87] [Ware88] [Rheingans92] provide samples of the available literature. You also may want to learn about the physiological and psychological effects of color on perception. The text by Wyszecki and Stiles [Wyszecki82] serves as an introductory reference.

Contouring is a widely studied technique in visualization because of its importance and popularity. Early techniques were developed for 2D data [Watson92]. Three dimensional techniques were developed initially as contour connecting methods [Fuchs77] — that is, given a series of 2D contours on evenly spaced planes, connect the contours to create a closed surface. Since the introduction of marching cubes, many other techniques have been implemented. (A few of these include [Nielson91] [Montani94] and [Durst88]). A particularly interesting reference is given by Livnat et al. [Livnat96]. They show a contouring method with the addition of a preprocessing step that generates isocontours in near optimal time.

Although we barely touched the topic, the study of chaos and chaotic vibrations is a delightfully interesting topic. Besides the original paper by Lorenz [Lorenz63], the book by Moon [Moon87] is a good place to start.

Two- and three-dimensional vector plots have been used by computer analysts for many years [Fuller80]. Streamlines and streamribbons also have been applied to the visualization of complex flows [Volpe89]. Good general references on vector visualization techniques are given in [Helman90] and [Richter90].

Tensor visualization techniques are relatively few in number. Most techniques are glyph oriented [Haber90] [deLeeuw93]. We will see a few more techniques in Chapter 9.

Blinn [Blinn82], Bloomental [Bloomenthal88] [Bloomenthal97] and Wyvill [Wyvill86] have been important contributors to implicit modeling. Implicit modeling is currently popular in computer graphics for modeling "soft" or "blobby" objects. These techniques are simple, powerful, and are becoming widely used for advanced computer graphics modeling.

6.9 References

[Abraham85]
> R. H. Abraham and Christopher D. Shaw. *Dynamics The Geometry of Behavior.* Aerial Press, Santa Cruz, CA, 1985.

[Blinn82]
> J. F. Blinn. "A Generalization of Algebraic Surface Drawing." *ACM Transactions on Graphics.* 1(3):235–256, July 1982.

[Bloomenthal88]
> J. Bloomenthal. "Polygonization of Implicit Surfaces." *Computer Aided Geometric Design.* 5(4):341–355, November 1982.

[Bloomenthal97]
> J. Bloomenthal, editor. *Introduction to Implicit Surfaces.* Morgan Kaufmann Publishers, Inc., San Francisco, CA., 1997.

[Chernoff73]
> H. Chernoff. "Using Faces to Represent Pints in K-Dimensional Space Graphically." *J. American Statistical Association.* 68:361–368, 1973.

[Cline93]
> H. Cline, W. Lorensen, and W. Schroeder. "3D Phase Contrast MRI of Cerebral Blood FLow and Surface Anatomy." *Journal of Computer Assisted Tomography.* 17(2):173–177, March/April 1993.

[Conte72]
> S. D. Conte and C. de Boor. *Elementary Numerical Analysis.* McGraw-Hill Book Company, 1972.

[deLeeuw93]

W. C. de Leeuw and J. J. van Wijk. "A Probe for Local Flow Field Visualization." In *Proceedings of Visualization '93*. pp. 39–45, IEEE Computer Society Press, Los Alamitos, CA, 1993.

[Delmarcelle95]

T. Delmarcelle and L. Hesselink. "A Unified Framework for Flow Visualization." In *Computer Visualization Graphics Techniques for Scientific and Engineering Analysis*. R. S. Gallagher, ed. CRC Press, Boca Raton, FL, 1995.

[Durrett87]

H. J. Durrett, ed. *Color and the Computer.* Academic Press, Boston, MA, 1987.

[Durst88]

M. J. Durst. "Additional Reference to Marching Cubes." *Computer Graphics.* 22(2):72–73, 1988.

[Fuchs77]

H. Fuchs, Z. M. Kedem, and S. P. Uselton. "Optimal Surface Reconstruction from Planar Contours." *Communications of the ACM*. 20(10):693–702, 1977.

[Fuller80]

A. J. Fuller and M.L.X. dosSantos. "Computer Generated Display of 3D Vector Fields." *Computer Aided Design*. 12(2):61–66, 1980.

[Haber90]

R. B. Haber and D. A. McNabb. "Visualization Idioms: A Conceptual Model to Scientific Visualization Systems." *Visualization in Scientific Computing,* G. M. Nielson, B. Shriver, L. J. Rosenblum, ed. IEEE Computer Society Press, pp. 61–73, 1990.

[Helman90]

J. Helman and L. Hesselink. "Representation and Display of Vector Field Topology in Fluid Flow Data Sets." *Visualization in Scientific Computing*. G. M. Nielson, B. Shriver, L. J. Rosenblum, eds. IEEE Computer Society Press, pp. 61–73, 1990.

[Livnat96]

Y. Livnat, H. W. Shen, C. R. Johnson. "A Near Optimal Isosurface Extraction Algorithm for Structured and Unstructured Grids." *IEEE Transactions on Visualization and Computer Graphics*. Vol. 2, No. 1, March 1996.

[Lorensen87]

W. E. Lorensen and H. E. Cline. "Marching Cubes: A High Resolution 3D Surface Construction Algorithm." *Computer Graphics*. 21(3):163–169, July 1987.

[Lorenz63]

E. N. Lorenz. "Deterministic Non-Periodic Flow." *Journal of Atmospheric Science*. 20:130–141, 1963.

[Montani94]

C. Montani, R. Scateni, and R. Scopigno. "A Modified Look-Up Table for Implicit Disambiguation of Marching Cubes." *Visual Computer.* (10):353–355, 1994.

[Moon87]

— F. C. Moon. *Chaotic Vibrations.* Wiley-Interscience, New York, NY, 1987.

[Nielson91]
G. M. Nielson and B. Hamann. "The Asymptotic Decider: Resolving the Ambiguity in Marching Cubes." In *Proceedings of Visualization '91*. pp. 83–91, IEEE Computer Society Press, Los Alamitos, CA, 1991.

[Rheingans92]
P. Rheingans. "Color, Change, and Control for Quantitative Data Display." In *Proceedings of Visualization '92*. pp. 252–259, IEEE Computer Society Press, Los Alamitos, CA, 1992.

[Richter90]
R. Richter, J. B. Vos, A. Bottaro, and S. Gavrilakis. "Visualization of Flow Simulations." *Scientific Visualization and Graphics Simulation*. D. Thalmann editor, pp. 161–171, John Wiley and Sons, 1990.

[Saada74]
A. S. Saada. *Elasticity Theory and Applications*. Pergamon Press, Inc., New York, NY, 1974.

[Timoshenko70]
S. P. Timoshenko and J. N. Goodier. *Theory of Elasticity, 3d Edition*. McGraw-Hill Book Company, New York, NY, 1970.

[Tufte83]
E. R. Tufte. *The Visual Display of Quantitative Information*. Graphics Press, Cheshire, CT, 1990.

[Volpe89]
G. Volpe. "Streamlines and Streamribbons in Aerodynamics." Technical Report AIAA-89-0140, 27th Aerospace Sciences Meeting, 1989.

[Ware88]
C. Ware. "Color Sequences for Univariate Maps: Theory, Experiments and Principles." *IEEE Computer Graphics and Applications*. 8(5):41–49, 1988.

[Watson92]
D. F. Watson. *Contouring: A Guide to the Analysis and Display of Spatial Data*. Pergamon Press, 1992.

[Wyszecki82]
G. Wyszecki and W. Stiles. *Color Science: Concepts and Methods, Quantitative Data and Formulae*. John Wiley and Sons, 1982.

[Wyvill86]
G. Wyvill, C. McPheeters, B. Wyvill. "Data Structure for Soft Objects." *Visual Computer*. 2(4):227–234, 1986.

6.10 Exercises

6.1 Sketch contour cases for marching triangles. How many cases are there?

6.2 Sketch contour cases for marching tetrahedron. How many cases are there?

6.3 A common visualization technique is to animate isosurface value. The procedure is to smoothly vary isosurface value over a specified range.
a) Create an animation sequence for the quadric example (Figure **4–1**).
b) Create an animation sequence for the head sequence (Figure **6–11**(b)).

6.4   Marching cubes visits each cell during algorithm execution. Many of these cells do not contain the isosurface. Describe a technique to improve the performance of isosurface extraction by eliminating visits to cells not containing isosurface. (*Hint:* use a preprocessing step to analyze data. Assume that many isosurfaces will be extracted and that the preprocessing step will not count against execution time.)

6.5   Scan-line rasterization proceeds along horizontal spans in graphics hardware (see "Rasterization" on page 60). Interpolation of color occurs along horizontal spans as well.
a) Show how the orientation of a polygon affects interpolated color.
b) Discuss potential problems caused by orientation dependent viewing of visualizations.

6.6   Write a program to simulate beam vibration. Use the code associated with Figure **6–14**(a) as your starting point.

6.7   Using the filters `vtkStreamLine`, `vtkMaskPoints`, and `vtkGlyph3D`, create a visualization consisting of oriented glyphs along a streamline.

6.8   Visualize the following functions.
a) Scalar $S(x, y, z) = \sin(xy)$, for x,y between 0 and π .
b) The effective stress field (a scalar field) from Figure **6–21**.
c) The vector field described in the combustor data (i.e., `combq.bin` and `combxyz.bin`).

6.9   Tensor ellipsoids are based on an ellipsoidal glyph. Describe two other glyphs that you might use.

6.10 Write a source object to generate a polygonal representation of a torus.

6.11 Design a glyph to convey airplane heading, speed, and altitude, and proximity (i.e., distance) to other planes.

6.12 Morphing is a process to smoothly blend images (2D) or geometry (3D) between two known images or geometry. Using an implicit modeling approach, how would you morph a torus into a cube?

6.13 Describe a technique to visualize vector information by animating a color map. (*Hint:* By choosing a map carefully, you can give the illusion of motion across a surface.)

6.14 Isoline contours of different values are typically shown together in one image.
a) Describe the advantages and disadvantages of displaying isosurfaces simultaneously.
b) What two graphics properties might you adjust to improve the display of multiple isosurfaces?

6.15 Describe a parallel algorithm for marching cubes. Use a parallel architecture of your choice.

6.16 Decomposition can greatly increase the speed of an operation.

a) Prove that 3D Gaussian smoothing can be decomposed into three 1D operations.

b) Give the complexity of the decomposed filter and the same filter implemented as a 3D convolution.

c) Under what conditions can constant smoothing be decomposed into 1D operations.

## CHAPTER 7

Advanced Computer Graphics

Chapter 3 introduced fundamental concepts of computer graphics. A major topic in that chapter was how to represent and render geometry using surface primitives such as points, lines, and polygons. In this chapter our primary focus is on volume graphics. Compared to surface graphics, volume graphics has a greater expressive range in its ability to render inhomogeneous materials, and is a dominant technique for visualizing structured points datasets.

We begin the chapter by describing two techniques that are important to both surface and volume graphics. These are simulating object transparency using simple blending functions, and using texture maps to add realism without excessive computational cost. We also describe various problems and challenges inherent to these techniques. We then follow with a focused discussion on volume graphics, including both object-order and image-order techniques, illumination models, approaches to mixing surface and volume graphics, and methods to improve performance. Finally, the chapter concludes with an assortment of important techniques for creating more realistic visualizations. These techniques include stereo viewing, antialiasing, and advanced camera techniques such as motion blur, focal blur, and camera motion.

7.1 Transparency and Alpha Values

Up to this point in the text we have focused on rendering opaque objects — that is, we have assumed that objects reflect, scatter, or absorb light at their surface, and no light is transmitted through to their interior. Although rendering opaque objects is certainly useful, there are many applications that can benefit from the ability to render objects that transmit light. One important application of transparency is volume rendering, which we will explore in greater detail later in the chapter. Another simple example makes objects translucent so that we can see inside of the region bounded by the surface, as shown in Color Plate 54. As demonstrated in this example, by making the skin semitransparent, it becomes possible to see the internal organs.

Transparency and its complement, opacity, are often referred to as *alpha* in computer graphics. For example, a polygon that is 50 percent opaque will have an alpha value of 0.5 on a scale from zero to one. An alpha value of one represents an opaque object and zero represents a completely transparent object. Frequently, alpha is specified as a property for the entire actor, but it also can be done on a vertex basis just like colors. In such cases, the RGB specification of a color is extended to RGBA where A represents the alpha component. On many graphics cards the frame buffer will store the alpha value along with the RGB values.

Unfortunately, having transparent actors introduces some complications into the rendering process. If you think back to the process of ray tracing, viewing rays are projected from the camera out into the world, where they intersect the first actor they come to. With an opaque actor, the lighting equations are applied and the resulting color is drawn to the screen. With a semitransparent actor we must solve the lighting equations for this actor, and then continue projecting the ray farther to see if it intersects any other actors. The resulting color is a composite of all the actors it has intersected. For each surface intersection this can be expressed as Equation **7-1**.

$$R = A_s R_s + (1 - A_s)R_b$$
$$G = A_s G_s + (1 - A_s)G_b$$
$$B = A_s B_s + (1 - A_s)B_b \qquad \text{(7-1)}$$
$$A = A_s + (1 - A_s)A_b$$

In this equation subscript s refers to the surface of the actor, while subscript b refers to what is behind the actor. The term $1 - A_s$ is called the transmissivity, and represents the amount of light that is transmitted through the actor. As an example, consider starting with three polygons colored red, green, and blue each with a transparency of 0.5. If the red polygon is in the front and the background is black, the resulting RGBA color will be (0.4, 0.2, 0.1, 0.875) on a scale from zero to one (Figure **7–1**).

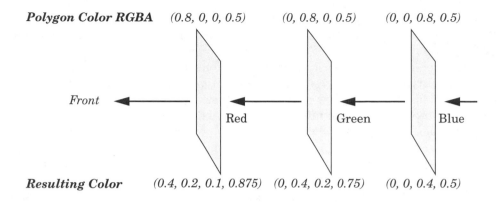

Figure 7–1 Alpha compositing.

It is important to note that if we switch the ordering of the polygons, the resulting color will change. This underlies a major technical problem in using transparency. If we ray-trace a scene, we will intersect the surfaces in a well-defined manner — from front to back. Using this knowledge we can trace a ray back to the last surface it intersects, and then composite the color by applying Equation **7-1** to all the surfaces in reverse order (i.e., from back to front). In object-order rendering methods, this compositing is commonly supported in hardware, but unfortunately we are not guaranteed to render the polygons in any specific order. Even though our polygons are situated as in Figure **7–1**, the order in which the polygons are rendered might be the blue polygon, followed by the red, and finally the green polygon. Consequently, the resulting color is incorrect.

If we look at the RGBA value for one pixel we can see the problem. When the blue polygon is rendered, the frame buffer and z-buffer are empty, so the RGBA quad (0,0,0.8,0.5) is stored along with the its z-buffer value. When the red polygon is rendered, a comparison of its z-value and the current z-buffer indicates that it is in front of the previous pixel entry. So Equation **7-1** is applied using the frame buffer's RGBA value. This results in the RGBA value (0.4,0,0.2,0.75) being written to the buffer. Now, the green polygon is rendered and the z comparison indicates that it is behind the current pixel's value. Again this equation is applied, this time using the frame buffer's RGBA value for the surface and the polygon's values from behind. This results in a final pixel color of (0.3,0.2, 0.175,0.875), which is different from what we previously calculated. Once the red and blue polygons have been composited and written to the frame buffer, there is no way to insert the final green polygon into the middle where it belongs.

One solution to this problem is to sort the polygons from back to front and then render them in this order. Typically, this must be done in software requiring additional computational overhead. Sorting also interferes with actor properties (such as specular power), which are typically sent to the graphics engine just before rendering the actor's polygons. Once we start mixing up the polygons of different actors, we must make sure that the correct actor properties are set for each polygon rendered.

Another solution is to store more than one set of RGBAZ values in the frame buffer. This is costly because of the additional memory requirements, and is still limited by the number of RGBAZ values you can store. Some new techniques use a combination of multiple RGBAZ value storage and multipass rendering to yield correct results with a minimum performance hit [Hodges92].

The second technical problem with rendering transparent objects occurs less frequently, but can still have disastrous effects. In certain applications, such as volume rendering, it is desirable to have thousands of polygons with small alpha values. If the RGBA quad is stored in the frame buffer as four eight-bit values, then the round-off can accumulate over many polygons, resulting in gross errors in the output image. Some of the newer systems solve this by using more bits for storing the RGBA values.

7.2 Texture Mapping

Texture mapping is a technique to add detail to an image without requiring modelling detail. Texture mapping can be thought of as pasting a picture to the surface of an object. The use of texture mapping requires two pieces of information: a *texture map* and *texture coordinates*. The texture map is the picture we paste, and the texture coordinates specify the location where the picture is pasted. More generally, texture mapping is a table lookup for color, intensity, and/or transparency that is applied to an object as it is rendered. Textures maps and coordinates are most often two-dimensional, but three-dimensional texture maps and coordinates are becoming more common.

The value of texture mapping can be shown through the simple example of rendering a wooden table. The basic geometry of a table can be easily created, but achieving the wood grain details is difficult. Coloring the table brown is a good start, but the image is still unrealistic. To simulate the wood grain we need to have many small color changes across the surface of the table. Using vertex colors would require us to have millions of extra vertices just to get the small color changes. The solution to this is to apply a wood grain texture map to the original polygons. This is like applying an oak veneer onto inexpensive particleboard.

There are several ways in which we can apply texture data. For each pixel in the texture map (commonly called a *texel* for texture element), there may be one to four components that affect how the texture map is pasted onto the surface of the underlying geometry. A texture map with one component is called an *intensity map*. Applying an intensity map results in changes to the intensity (or value in HSV) of the resulting pixels. If we took a gray scale image of wood grain, and then texture-mapped it onto a brown polygon, we would have a reasonable looking table. The hue and saturation of the polygon would still be determined by the brown color, but the intensity would be determined from the texture map. A better looking table could be obtained by using a color image of the wood. This is a three-component texture map, where each texel is represented as a RGB triplet. Using an RGB map allows us to obtain more realistic images, since we would have more than just the intensity changes of the wood.

By adding alpha values to an intensity map we get two components. We can do the same to an RGB texture map to get an RGBA texture map. In these cases, the alpha value can be used to make parts of the underlying geometry transparent. A common trick in computer graphics is to use RGBA textures to render trees. Instead of trying to model the complex geometry of a tree, we just render a rectangle with an RGBA texture map applied to it. Where there are leaves or branches, the alpha is one, where there are gaps and open space, the alpha is zero. As a result, we can see through portions of the rectangle, giving the illusion of viewing through the branches and leaves of a tree.

Besides the different ways in which a texture map can be defined, there are options in how it interacts with the original color of the object. A common option for RGB and RGBA maps is to ignore the original color; that is, just apply the texture color as specified. Another option is to modulate the original color by the texture map color (or intensity) to produce the final color.

While we have been focusing on 2D texture maps, they can be of any dimension, though the most common are 2D and 3D. Three-dimensional texture maps are used for textures that are a function of 3D space, such as wood grain, stone, or X-ray intensity (i.e., CT scan). In fact, a structured point dataset is essentially a 3D texture. We can perform high-speed volume rendering by passing planes through a 3D texture and compositing them using translucent alpha values in the correct order. Techniques for performing volume rendering using texture mapping hardware will be discussed later in this chapter.

A fundamental step in the texture mapping process is determining how to map the texture onto the geometry. To accomplish this, each vertex has an associated texture coordinate in addition to its position, surface normal, color, and other point attributes. The texture coordinate maps the vertex into the texture map as shown in Figure **7–2**. The texture coordinate system uses the parameters (u,v) and (u,v,t) or equivalently (r,s) or (r,s,t) for specifying 2D and 3D texture values. Points between the vertices are linearly interpolated to determine texture map values.

Another approach to texture mapping uses procedural texture definitions instead of a texture map. In this approach, as geometry is rendered, a procedure is called for each pixel to calculate a texel value. Instead of using the (u,v,t) texture coordinates to index into an image, they are passed as arguments to the procedural texture that uses them to calculate its result. This method provides almost limitless flexibility in the design of a texture; therefore, it is almost impossible to implement in dedicated hardware. Most commonly, procedural textures are used with software rendering systems that do not make heavy use of existing graphics hardware.

While texture maps are generally used to add detail to rendered images, there are important visualization applications.

3D Polygonal Model   2D Texture Map

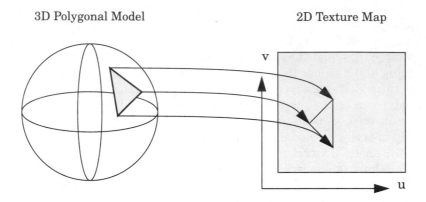

Figure 7–2 Vertex texture coordinates.

- Texture maps can be generated procedurally as a function of data. One example is to change the appearance of a surface based on local data value.

- Texture coordinates can be generated procedurally as a function of data. For example, we can *threshold* geometry by creating a special texture map and then setting texture coordinates based on local data value. The texture map consists of two entries: fully transparent ($\alpha = 0$) and fully opaque ($\alpha = 1$). The texture coordinate is then set to index into the transparent portion of the map if the scalar value is less than some threshold, or into the opaque portion otherwise.

- Texture maps can be animated as a function of time. By choosing a texture map whose intensity varies monotonically from dark to light, and then "moving" the texture along an object, the object appears to crawl in the direction of the texture map motion. We can use this technique to add apparent motion to things like hedgehogs to show vector magnitude. Figure **7–3** is an example of a texture map animation used to simulate vector field motion.

These techniques will be covered in greater detail in Chapter 9. (See "Texture Algorithms" on page 402.)

7.3 Volume Rendering

Until now we have concentrated on the visualization of data through the use of geometric primitives such as points, lines, and polygons. For many applications such as architectural walk-throughs or terrain visualization, this is obviously the most efficient and effective representation for the data. In contrast, some applications require us to visualize data that is inherently volumetric (which we

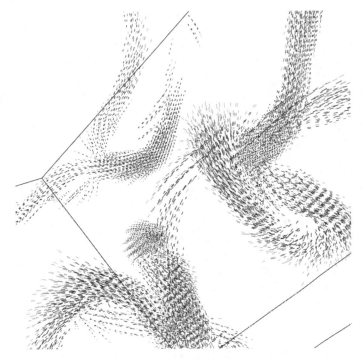

Figure 7–3 One frame from a vector field animation using texture maps.

refer to as structure points datasets). For example, in biomedical imaging we may need to visualize data obtained from an MR or CT scanner, a confocal microscope, or an ultrasound study. Weather analysis and other simulations also produce large quantities of volumetric data in three or more dimensions that require effective visualization techniques. As a result of the popularity and usefulness of volume data over the last several decades, a broad class of rendering techniques known as volume rendering has emerged. The purpose of volume rendering is to effectively convey information within volumetric data.

In the past, researchers have attempted to define volume rendering as a process that operates directly on the dataset to produce an image without generating an intermediate geometric representation. With recent advances in graphics hardware and clever implementations, developers have been able to use geometric primitives to produce images that are identical to those generated by direct volume rendering techniques. Due to these new techniques, it is nearly impossible to define volume rendering in a manner that is clearly distinct from geometric rendering. Therefore, we choose a broad definition of volume rendering as any method that operates on volumetric data to produce an image.

The next several sections cover a variety of volume rendering methods that use direct rendering techniques, geometric primitive rendering techniques, or a combination of these two methods, to produce an image. Some of the direct volume rendering techniques discussed in this chapter generate images that are nearly identical to those produced by geometric rendering techniques discussed in earlier chapters. For example, using a ray-casting method to produce an isosurface image is similar, though not truly equivalent, to rendering geometric primitives that were extracted with the marching cubes contouring technique described in Chapter 6.

The two basic surface rendering approaches described in Chapter 3, image-order and object-order, apply to volume rendering techniques as well. In an image-order method, rays are cast for each pixel in the image plane through the volume to compute pixel values, while in an object-order method the volume is traversed, typically in a front to back or back to front order, with each voxel processed to determine its contribution to the image. In addition, there are other volume rendering techniques that cannot easily be classified as image-order or object-order. For example, a volume rendering technique may traverse both the image and the volume simultaneously, or the image may be computed in the frequency domain rather than the spatial domain.

Since volume rendering is typically used to generate images that represent an entire 3D dataset in a 2D image, several new challenges are introduced. Classification must be performed to assign color and opacity to regions within the volume, and volumetric illumination models must be defined to support shading. Furthermore, efficiency and compactness are of great importance due to the complexity of volume rendering methods and the size of typical volumetric datasets. A geometric model that consists of one million primitives is generally considered large, while a volumetric dataset with one million voxels is quite small. Typical volumes contain between ten and one hundred million voxels, with datasets of a billion or more voxels becoming more common. Clearly care must be taken when deciding to store auxiliary information at each voxel or to increase the time required to process each voxel.

7.4 Image-Order Volume Rendering

Image-order volume rendering is often referred to as ray casting or ray tracing. The basic idea is that we determine the value of each pixel in the image by sending a ray through the pixel into the scene according to the current camera parameters. We then evaluate the data encountered along the ray using some specified function in order to compute the pixel value. As we will demonstrate throughout this chapter, ray casting is a flexible technique that can be used to render any structured points dataset, and can produce a variety images. Also, it is relatively easy to extend a basic ray-casting technique designed for structured points to work on rectilinear or structured grids. Unfortunately, basic ray casting is also fairly slow; therefore, later in this chapter we will discuss a number of acceleration methods that can be used to improve performance, though often with some additional memory requirements or loss in flexibility.

The ray-casting process is illustrated in Figure **7–4**. This example uses a standard orthographic camera projection; consequently, all rays are parallel to each other and perpendicular to the view plane. The data values along each ray

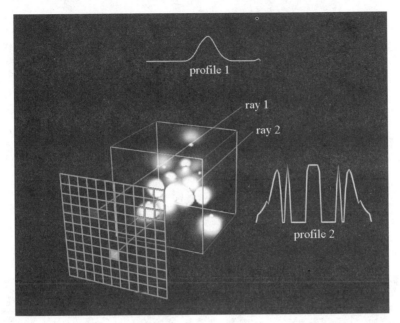

Figure 7–4 Image-order volume rendering. High potential iron protein data courtesy of Scripps Clinic, La Jolla, CA.

are processed according to the ray function, which in this case determines the maximum value along the ray and converts it to a gray scale pixel value where the minimum scalar value in the volume maps to transparent black, and the maximum scalar value maps to opaque white.

The two main steps of ray casting are determining the values encountered along the ray, and then processing these values according to a ray function. Although in implementation these two steps are typically combined, we will treat them independently for the moment. Since the specific ray function often determines the method used to extract values along the ray, we will begin by considering some of the basic ray function types.

Figure **7–5** shows the data value profile of a ray as it passes through 8 bit volumetric data where the data values can range between 0 and 255. The x-axis of the profile indicates distance from the view plane while the y-axis represents data value. The results obtained from four different simple ray functions are shown below the profile. For display purposes we convert the raw result values to gray scale values using a method similar to the one in the previous example.

The first two ray functions, maximum value and average value, are basic operations on the scalar values themselves. The third ray function computes the distance along the ray at which a scalar value at or above 30 is first encountered, while the fourth uses an alpha compositing technique, treating the values along the ray as samples of opacity accumulated per unit distance. Unlike the first three ray functions, the result of the compositing technique is not a scalar value or distance that can be represented on the ray profile.

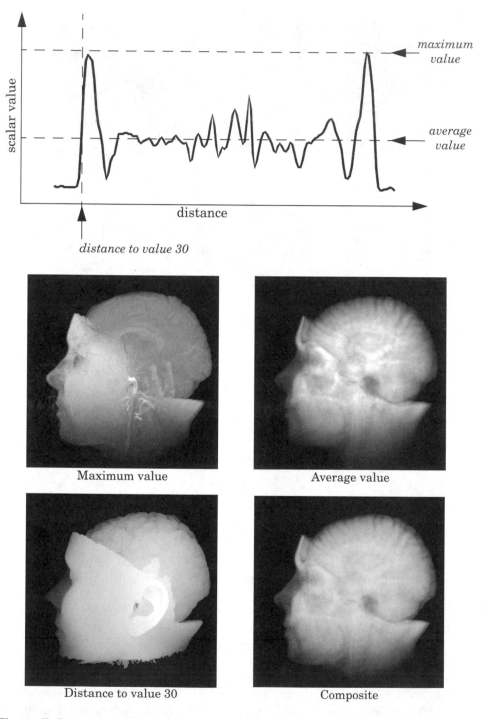

Figure 7–5 A ray profile and four example ray functions. MRI head data courtesy of Siemens Medical Systems, Inc., Iselin, NJ.

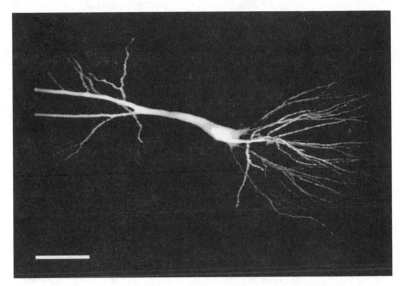

Figure 7–6 A maximum intensity projection created with a ray-casting technique. Confocal microscopy data courtesy of Howard Hughes Medical Institute, SUNY Stony Brook.

The maximum intensity projection, or MIP, is probably the most common way to visualize volumetric data. This technique is fairly forgiving when it comes to noisy data, and produces images that provide an intuitive understanding of the underlying data. One problem with this method is that it is not possible to tell from a still image where the maximum value occurred along the ray. For example, consider the image of a nerve cell shown in Figure **7–6**. We are unable to fully understand the structure of the cell from this still image since we cannot determine whether some branch of the cell is in front of or behind some other branch. This problem can be solved by generating a small sequence of images showing the data rotating, although for parallel camera projections even this animation will be ambiguous. This is due to the fact that two images generated from cameras that view the data from opposite directions will be identical except for a reflection about the Y axis of the image.

Later in this chapter, during the classification and illumination discussions, we will consider more complex ray functions. Although the colorful, shaded images produced by the new methods may contain more information, they may also be more difficult to interpret, and often easier to misinterpret, than the simple images of the previous examples. For that reason, it is beneficial to use multiple techniques to visualize your volumetric data.

A volume is represented as a 3D structured points dataset where scalar values are defined at the points of the regular grid, yet in ray casting we often need to sample the volume at arbitrary locations. To do this we must define an interpolation function that can return a scalar value for any location between grid points. The simplest interpolation function, which is called zero-order, constant,

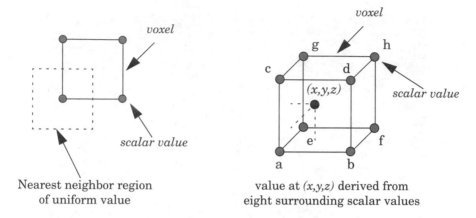

Nearest neighbor region
of uniform value

value at *(x,y,z)* derived from
eight surrounding scalar values

Figure 7–7 A 2D example of nearest neighbor interpolation (left) and a 3D example of trilinear interpolation (right).

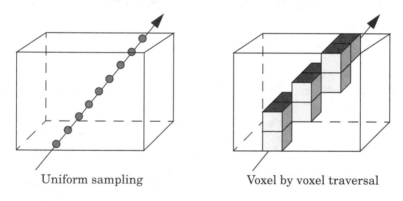

Uniform sampling

Voxel by voxel traversal

Figure 7–8 Two basic ray traversal methods for volume rendering.

or nearest neighbor interpolation, returns the value of the closest grid point. This function defines a grid of identical rectangular boxes of uniform value centered on grid points, as illustrated in 2D on the left side of Figure **7–7**. In the image on the right we see an example of trilinear interpolation where the value at some location is defined by using linear interpolation based on distance along each of the three axes. In general, we refer to the region defined by eight neighboring grid points as a voxel. In the special case where a discrete algorithm is used in conjunction with nearest neighbor interpolation, we may instead refer to the constant-valued regions as voxels.

To traverse the data along a ray, we could sample the volume at uniform intervals or we could traverse a discrete representation of the ray through the volume, examining each voxel encountered, as illustrated in Figure **7–8**. The selection of a method depends upon factors such as the interpolation technique, the ray function, and the desired trade-off between image accuracy and speed.

The ray is typically represented in parametric form as

$$(x, y, z) = (x_0, y_0, z_0) + (a, b, c)t \qquad\qquad \textbf{(7-2)}$$

where (x_0, y_0, z_0) is the origin of the ray (either the camera position for perspective viewing transformations or a pixel on the view plane for parallel viewing transformations), and (a, b, c) is the normalized ray direction vector. If t1 and t2 represent the distances where the ray enters and exits the volume respectively, and delta_t indicates the step size, then we can use the following code fragment to perform uniform distance sampling:

```
t = t1;
v = undefined;
while ( t < t2 )
   {
   x = x0 + a * t;
   y = y0 + b * t;
   z = z0 + c * t;
   v = EvaluateRayFunction( v, t );
   t = t + delta_t;
   }
```

One difficulty with the uniform distance sampling method is selecting the step size. If the step size is too large, then our sampling might miss features in the data, yet if we select a small step size, we will significantly increase the amount of time required to render the image. This problem is illustrated in Figure **7–9** using a volumetric dataset with grid points that are one unit apart along the X, Y, and Z axes. The images were generated using step sizes of 2.0, 1.0, and 0.1 units, where the 0.1 step-size image took nearly 10 times as long to generate as the 1.0 step-size image, which in turn took twice as long to render as the 2.0 step-size image. A compositing method was used to generate the images, where the scalar values within the dataset transition sharply from transparent black to opaque white. If the step size is too large, a banding effect appears in the image highlighting regions of the volume equidistant from the ray origin along the viewing rays. To reduce this effect when a larger step size is desired for performance reasons, the origin of each ray can be bumped forward along the viewing direction by some small random offset, which will produce a more pleasing image by eliminating the regular pattern of the aliasing.

In some cases it may make more sense to examine each voxel along the ray rather than taking samples. For example, if we are visualizing our data using a nearest neighbor interpolation method, then we may be able to implement a more efficient algorithm using discrete ray traversal and integer arithmetic. Another reason for examining voxels may be to obtain better accuracy on certain ray functions. We can easily compute the exact maximum value encountered along a ray within each voxel when using trilinear interpolation by taking the

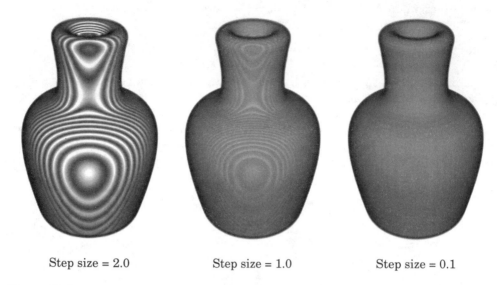

Step size = 2.0   Step size = 1.0   Step size = 0.1

Figure 7–9 Images generated using a ray-casting method with three different step sizes.Vase data courtesy of SUNY Stony Brook.

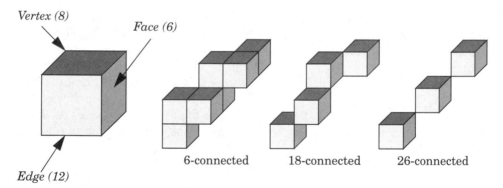

Figure 7–10 Discrete ray classification.

first derivative of the interpolation function along the ray and solving the result-ing equation to compute the extrema. Similarly, we can find the exact location along the ray where a selected value is first encountered to produce better images of isovalue surfaces within the volume.

A 3D scan conversion technique, such as a modified Bresenham method, can be used to transform the continuous ray into a discrete representation. The discrete ray is an ordered sequence of voxels v_1, v_2, ... v_n, and can be classified as 6-connected, 18-connected, or 26-connected as shown in Figure **7–10**. Each voxel contains 6 faces, 12 edges, and 8 vertices. If each pair of voxels v_i,

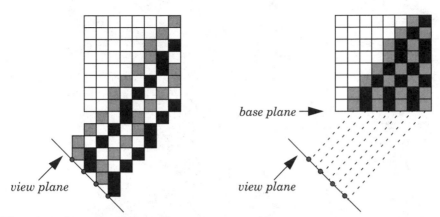

Figure 7–11 Ray casting with templated discrete rays. If the rays originate from the image plane (left) then voxels are missed in the volume. If instead the rays originate from a base plane of the volume (right), each voxel is visited exactly once.

v_{i+1} along the ray share a face then the ray is 6-connected, if they share a face or an edge the ray is 18-connected, and if they share a face, an edge, or a vertex the ray is 26-connected. Scan converting and traversing a 26-connected ray requires less time than a 6-connected ray but is more likely to miss small features in the volume dataset.

If we are using a parallel viewing transformation and our ray function can be efficiently computed using a voxel by voxel traversal method, then we can employ a templated ray-casting technique [Yagel92b] with 26-connected rays to generate the image. All rays are identical in direction; therefore, we only need to scan convert once, using this "template" for every ray. When these rays are cast from pixels on the image plane, as shown in the left image of Figure **7–11**, then some voxels in the dataset will not contribute to the image. If instead we cast the rays from the voxels in the base plane of the volume that is most parallel to the image plane, as shown in the right image, then the rays fit together snugly such that every voxel in the dataset is visited exactly once. The image will appear warped because it is generated from the base plane, so a final resampling step is required to project this image back onto the image plane.

7.5 Object-Order Volume Rendering

Object-order volume rendering methods process samples in the volume based on the organization of the voxels in the dataset and the current camera parameters. When an alpha compositing method is used, the voxels must be traversed in either a front to back or back to front order to obtain correct results. This process is analogous to sorting translucent polygons before each projection in order to ensure correct blending. When graphics hardware is employed for compositing, a

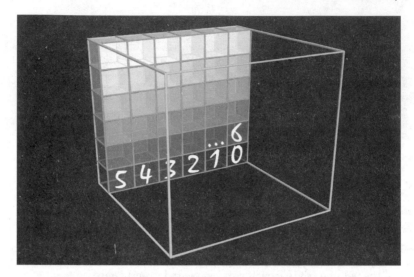

Figure 7–12 Object-order, back to front volume rendering.

back to front ordering is typically preferred since it is then possible to perform alpha blending without the need for alpha bitplanes in the frame buffer. If a software compositing method is used, a front to back ordering is more common since partial image results are more visually meaningful, and can be used to avoid additional processing when a pixel reaches full opacity. Voxel ordering based on distance to the view plane is not always necessary since some volume rendering operations, such as MIP or average, can be processed in any order and still yield correct results.

Figure **7–12** illustrates a simple object-order, back to front approach to projecting the voxels in a volume for an orthographic projection. Voxel traversal starts at the voxel that is furthest from the view plane and then continues progressively to closer voxels until all voxels have been visited. This is done within a triple nested loop where, from the outer to the inner loop, the planes in the volume are traversed, the rows in a plane are processed, and finally the voxels along a row are visited. Figure **7–12** shows an ordered labeling of the first seven voxels as the volume is projected. Processing voxels in this manner does not yield a strict ordering from the furthest to the closest voxel. However, it is sufficient for orthographic projections since it does ensure that the voxels that project to a single pixel are processed in the correct order.

When a voxel is processed, its projected position on the view plane is determined and an operation is performed at that pixel location using the voxel and image information. This operator is similar to the ray function used in image-order ray-casting techniques. Although this approach to projecting voxels is both fast and efficient, it often yields image artifacts due to the discrete selection of the projected image pixel. For instance, as we move the camera closer to the volume in a perspective projection, neighboring voxels will project to increasingly distant pixels on the view plane, resulting in distracting "holes" in the image.

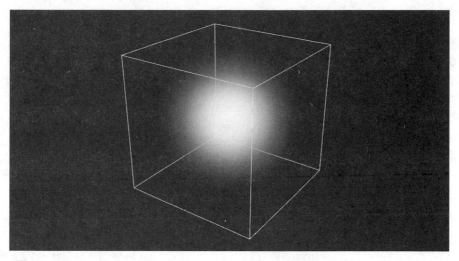

Figure 7–13 A Gaussian kernel is projected onto the view plane to produce a splat footprint.

A volume rendering technique, called splatting, addresses this problem by distributing the energy of a voxel across many pixels. Splatting is an object-order volume rendering technique proposed by Westover [Westover90] and, as its name implies, it projects the energy of a voxel onto the image plane one splat, or footprint, at a time. A kernel with finite extent is placed around each data sample. The footprint is the projected contribution of this sample onto the image plane, and is computed by integrating the kernel along the viewing direction and storing the results in a 2D footprint table. Figure **7–13** illustrates the projection of a Gaussian kernel onto the image plane that may then be used as a splatting footprint. For a parallel viewing transform and a spherically symmetric kernel, the footprint of every voxel is identical except for an image space offset. Therefore, the evaluation of the footprint table and the image space extent of a sample can be performed once as a preprocessing step to volume rendering. Splatting is more difficult for perspective volume rendering since the image space extent is not identical for all samples. Accurately correcting for perspective effects in a splatting approach would make the algorithm far less efficient. However, with a small loss of accuracy we can still use the generic footprint table if we approximate the image plane extent of an ellipsoid with an ellipse.

There are several important considerations when utilizing a splatting approach for volume rendering. The type of kernel, the radius of the kernel, and the resolution of the footprint table will all impact the appearance of the final image. For example, a kernel radius that is smaller than the distance between neighboring samples may lead to gaps in the image, while a larger radius will lead to a blurry image. Also, a low resolution footprint table is faster to precompute, but a high resolution table allows us to use nearest neighbor sampling for faster rendering times without a significant loss in image accuracy.

Texture mapping as described earlier in this chapter was originally developed to provide the appearance of high surface complexity when rendering geometric surfaces. As texture mapping methods matured and found their way into standard graphics hardware, researchers began utilizing these new capabilities to perform volume rendering [Cabral94]. There are two main texture-mapped volume rendering techniques based on the two main types of texture hardware currently available. Two-dimensional texture-mapped volume rendering makes use of 2D texture mapping hardware whereas 3D texture-mapped volume rendering makes use less commonly available 3D texture mapping graphics hardware.

We can decompose texture-mapped volume rendering into two basic steps. The first is a sampling step where the data samples are extracted from the volume using some form of interpolation. Depending on the type of texture hardware available, this may be nearest neighbor, bilinear, or trilinear interpolation and may be performed exclusively in hardware or through a combination of both software and hardware techniques. The second step is a blending step where the sampled values are combined with the current image in the frame buffer. This may be a simple maximum operator or it may be a more complex alpha compositing operator.

Texture-mapped volume renderers sample and blend a volume to produce an image by projecting a set of texture-mapped polygons that span the entire volume. In 2D texture-mapped volume rendering the dataset is decomposed into a set of orthographic slices along the axis of the volume most parallel to the viewing direction. The basic rendering algorithm consists of a loop over the orthogonal slices in a back to front order, where for each slice, a 2D texture is downloaded into texture memory. Each slice, which is a rectangular polygon, is projected to show the entire 2D texture. If neighboring slices are far apart relative to the image size, then it may be necessary to use a software bilinear interpolation method to extract additional slices from the volume in order to achieve a desired image accuracy. The image on the left side of Figure **7–14** illustrates the orthogonal slices that are rendered using a 2D texture mapping approach. Several example images generated using 2D texture-mapped volume rendering are shown in Figure **7–15**.

The performance of this algorithm can be decomposed into the software sampling rate, the texture download rate, and the texture-mapped polygon scan conversion rate. The software sampling step is required to create the texture image, and is typically dependent on view direction due to cache locality when accessing volumetric data stored in a linear array. Some implementations minimize the software sampling cost at the expense of memory by precomputing and saving images for the three major volume orientations. The texture download rate is the rate at which this image can be transferred from main memory to texture mapping memory. The scan conversion of the polygon is usually limited by the rate at which the graphics hardware can process pixels in the image, or the pixel fill rate. For a given hardware implementation, the download time for a volume is fixed and will not change based on viewing parameters. However, reducing the relative size of the projected volume will reduce the number of samples

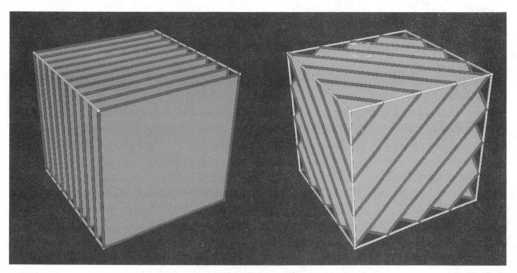

Figure 7–14 Volume rendering using a 2D (left) and 3D (right) texture mapping technique.

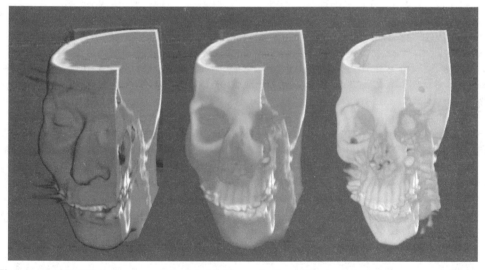

Figure 7–15 2D texture-mapped volume rendering. The images were generated using three different mappings of scalar value to opacity. CT data courtesy of North Carolina Memorial Hospital.

processed by the graphics hardware that, in turn, will increase volume rendering rates at the expense of image quality.

Unlike 2D hardware, 3D texture hardware is capable of loading and interpolating between multiple slices in a volume by utilizing 3D interpolation techniques such as trilinear interpolation. If the texture memory is large enough to hold the entire volume, then the rendering algorithm is simple. The entire volume is downloaded into texture memory once as a preprocessing step. To render an image, a set of equally spaced planes along the viewing direction and parallel to the image plane is clipped against the volume. The resulting polygons, illustrated in the image on the right side of Figure **7–14**, are then projected in back to front order with the appropriate 3D texture coordinates.

In practice, it is generally not possible to load the entire volume into 3D texture memory. The solution to this problem is to break the dataset into small enough subvolumes, or bricks, so that each brick will fit in texture memory. The bricks must then be processed in back to front order while computing the appropriately clipped polygon vertices inside the bricks. Special care must be taken to ensure that boundaries between bricks do not result in image artifacts.

Similar to a 2D texture mapping method, the 3D algorithm is limited by both the texture download and pixel fill rates of the machine. However, 3D texture mapping is superior to the 2D version in its ability to sample the volume, generally yielding higher quality images with fewer artifacts. Since it is capable of performing trilinear interpolation, we are able to sample at any location within the volume. For instance, a 3D texture mapping algorithm can sample along polygons representing concentric spheres rather than the more common view-aligned planes.

In theory, a 3D texture-mapped volume renderer and a ray-casting volume renderer perform the same computations, have the same complexity, $O(n^3)$, and produce identical images. Both sample the entire volume using either nearest neighbor or trilinear interpolation, and combine the samples to form a pixel value using, for example, a maximum value or compositing function. Therefore, we can view 3D texture mapping and standard ray-casting methods as functionally equivalent. The main advantage to using a texture mapping approach is the ability to utilize relatively fast graphics hardware to perform the sampling and blending operations. However, there are currently several drawbacks to using graphics hardware for volume rendering. Hardware texture-mapped volume renderings tend to have more artifacts than software ray-casting techniques due to limited precision within the frame buffer for storing partial results at each pixel during blending. In addition, only a few ray functions are supported by the hardware, and advanced techniques such as shading are more difficult to achieve. However, over time most of these limitations will likely disappear as texture mapping hardware evolves.

7.6 Other Volume Rendering Methods

Not all volume rendering methods fall cleanly into the image-order or object-order categories. For example, the shear-warp method [Lacroute94] of volume rendering traverses both image and object space at the same time. The basic idea behind this method is similar to that of templated ray casting. If we cast rays from the base plane of the volume for an orthographic projection, then it is possible to shear the volume such that the rays become perpendicular to the base

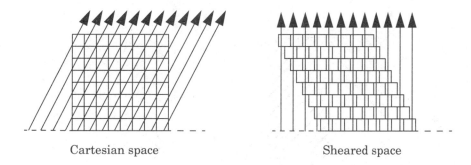

Cartesian space   Sheared space

Figure 7–16 On the left, orthographic rays are cast from the base plane of the volume. In the right image the volume is sheared such that these rays become perpendicular to the base plane.

plane, as shown in Figure **7–16**. Looking at the problem this way, it is clear to see that if all rays originate from the same place within the voxels on the base plane, then these rays intersect the voxels on each subsequent plane of the volume at consistent locations. Using bilinear interpolation on the 2D planes of the dataset, we can precompute one set of interpolation weights for each plane. Instead of traversing the volume by evaluating samples along each ray, an object-order traversal method can be used to visit voxels along each row in each plane in a front to back order through the volume. There is a one-to-one correspondence between samples in a plane of the volume and pixels on the image plane, making it possible to traverse both the samples and the pixels simultaneously. As in templated ray casting, a final resampling (warping) operation must be performed to transform the image from sheared space on the base plane to cartesian space on the image plane.

Shear-warp volume rendering is essentially an efficient variant of ray casting. The correspondence between samples and pixels allows us to take advantage of a standard ray-casting technique known as early ray termination. When we have determined that a pixel has reached full opacity during compositing, we no longer need to consider the remaining samples that project onto this pixel since they do not contribute to the final pixel value. The biggest efficiency improvement in shear-warp volume rendering comes from run-length encoding the volume. This compression method removes all empty voxels from the dataset, leaving only voxels that can potentially contribute to the image. Depending on the classification of the data, it is possible to achieve a greater than 10:1 reduction in voxels. As we step through the compressed volume, the number of voxels skipped due to run-length encoding also indicates the number of pixels to skip in the image. One drawback to this method is that it requires three copies of the compressed volume to allow for front to back traversal from all view directions. In addition, if we wish to use a perspective viewing transformation then we may need to traverse all three compressed copies of the volume in order to achieve the correct traversal order.

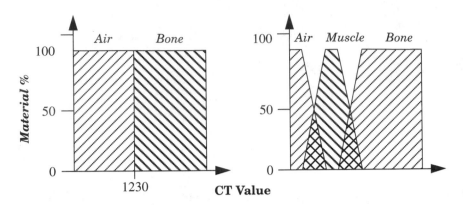

Figure 7–17 Transfer functions that classify CT densities into material percentages. A simple binary classification used to define a bone isosurface (left) and a gradual transition from air to muscle to bone (right) is shown.

Volume rendering can also be performed using the Fourier slice projection theorem [Totsuka92] that states that if we extract a slice of the volume in the frequency domain that contains the center and is parallel to the image plane, then the 2D spectrum of that slice is equivalent to the 2D image obtained by taking line integrals through the volume from the pixels on the image plane. Therefore we can volume render the dataset by extracting the appropriate slice from the 3D Fourier volume, then computing the 2D inverse Fourier transform of this slice. This allows us to render the image in $O(n^2 \log n)$ time as opposed to the $O(n^3)$ complexity required by most other volume rendering algorithms.

Two problems that must be addressed when implementing a frequency domain volume renderer are the high cost of interpolation when extracting a slice from the Fourier volume, and the high memory requirements (usually two double precision floating-point values per sample) required to store the Fourier volume. Although some shading and depth cues can be provided with this method, occlusion is not possible.

7.7 Volume Classification

Classifying the relevant objects of interest within a dataset is a critical step in producing a volume rendered image. This information is used to determine the contribution of an object to the image as well as the object's material properties and appearance. For example, a simple binary classification of whether a data sample corresponds to bone within a CT dataset is often performed by specifying a density threshold. When the scalar value at a voxel is greater than this threshold, it is classified as bone, otherwise it is considered air. This essentially specifies an isosurface in the volume at the transition between air and bone. If we plot this operation over all possible scalar values we will get the binary step function shown on the left in Figure **7–17**. In volume rendering we refer to this function

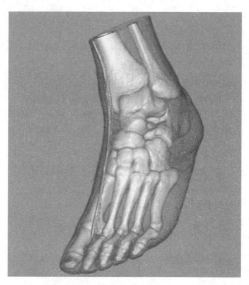

Figure 7–18 Volume rendering using a gradient magnitude opacity transfer function. The Visible Man CT data is courtesy of The National Library of Medicine.

as a transfer function. A transfer function is responsible for mapping the information at a voxel location into different values such as material, color, or opacity. The strength of volume rendering is that it can handle transfer functions of much greater complexity than a binary step function. This is often necessary since datasets contain multiple materials and classification methods cannot always assign a single material to a sample with 100 percent probability. Referring back to our CT example, we can now specify a material percentage transfer function that defines a gradual transition from air to muscle, then from muscle to bone, as shown on the right in Figure **7–17**.

In addition to material percentage transfer functions, we can define four independent transfer functions that map scalar values into red, green, blue, and opacity values for each material in the dataset. For simplicity, these sets of transfer functions are typically preprocessed into one function each for red, green, blue and opacity at the end of the classification phase. During rendering we must decide how to perform interpolation to compute the opacity and color at an arbitrary location in the volume. We could interpolate scalar value then evaluate the transfer functions, or we could evaluate the transfer functions at the grid points then interpolate the resulting opacities and colors. These two methods will produce different image results. It is generally considered more accurate to classify at the grid points then interpolate to obtain color and opacity; although if we interpolate then classify, the image often appears more pleasing since high frequencies may be removed by the interpolation.

Classifying a volume based on scalar value alone is often not capable of isolating an object of interest. A technique introduced by Levoy [Levoy88] adds a gradient magnitude dimension to the specification of a transfer function. With this technique we can specify an object in the volume based on a combination of scalar value and the gradient magnitude. This allows us to define an opacity transfer function that can target voxels with scalar values in a range of densities and gradients within a range of gradient magnitudes. This is useful for avoiding the selection of homogeneous regions in a volume and highlighting fast-changing regions. Figure **7–18** shows a CT scan of a human foot. The sharp changes in the volume, such as the transition from air to skin and flesh to bone, are shown. However, the homogeneous regions, such as the internal muscle, are mostly transparent.

If we are using a higher-order interpolation function such as tri-cubic interpolation then we can analytically compute the gradient vector at any location in the dataset by evaluating the first derivative of the interpolation function. Although we can use this approach for trilinear interpolation, it may produce undesirable artifacts since trilinear interpolation is not continuous in its first derivative across voxel boundaries. An alternative approach is to employ a finite differences technique to approximate the gradient vector:

$$g_x = \frac{f(x + \Delta x, y, z) - f(x - \Delta x, y, z)}{2\Delta x}$$

$$g_y = \frac{f(x, y + \Delta y, z) - f(x, y - \Delta y, z)}{2\Delta y} \qquad \textbf{(7-3)}$$

$$g_z = \frac{f(x, y, z + \Delta z) - f(x, y, z - \Delta z)}{2\Delta z}$$

where $f(x, y, z)$ represents the scalar value at location (x, y, z) in the dataset according to the interpolation function, and g_x, g_y, and g_z are the partial derivatives of this function along the x, y, and z axes respectively. The magnitude of the gradient at (x, y, z) is the length of the resulting vector (g_x, g_y, g_z). This vector can also be normalized to produce a unit normal vector. The choice of Δx, Δy, and Δz are critical as shown in Figure **7–19**. If these values are too small, then the gradient vector field derived from Equation **7-3** may contain high frequencies, yet if these values are too large we will lose small features in the dataset.

It is often the case that transfer functions based on scalar value and even gradient magnitude are not capable of fully classifying a volume. Ultrasound data is an example of particularly difficult data that does not perform well with simple segmentation techniques. While no one technique exists that is universally applicable, there exists a wide variety of techniques that produce classification information at each sample. For instance, [Kikinis96] provides techniques for classifying the human brain. In order to properly handle this information a volume renderer must access the original volume and a classification volume. The classification volume usually contains material percentages for each sample, with a set of color and opacity transfer functions for each material used to define appearance.

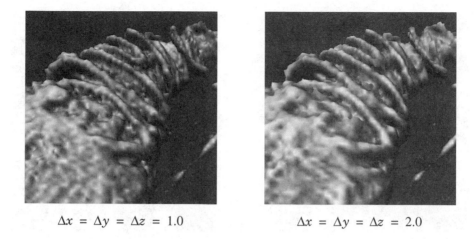

$$\Delta x \ = \ \Delta y \ = \ \Delta z \ = \ 1.0 \qquad\qquad \Delta x \ = \ \Delta y \ = \ \Delta z \ = \ 2.0$$

Figure 7–19 A comparison of shaded images with two different step sizes used during normal estimation. Confocal microscopy data courtesy of Howard Hughes Medical Institute, SUNY Stony Brook.

7.8 Volumetric Illumination

The volume rendered images that we have shown so far in this chapter do not include any lighting effects. Scientist sometimes prefer to visualize their volumes using these simpler methods because they fear that adding lighting effects to the image will interfere with their interpretation. For example, in a maximum intensity projection, a dark region in the image clearly indicates the lack of high opacity values in the corresponding region of the volume, while a dark feature in a shaded image may indicate either low opacity values or values with gradient directions that point away from the light source.

There are several advantages to lighting that can often justify the additional complexity in the image. First, consider the fact that volume rendering is a process of creating a 2D image from 3D data. The person viewing that data would like to be able to understand the 3D structure of the volume from that image. Of course, if you were to look at a photograph of a skeleton it would be easy to understand its structure from the 2D representation. The two main clues that you received from the picture are occlusion and lighting effects. If you were to view a video of the skeleton, you would receive the additional clue of motion parallax. A static image showing a maximum intensity projection does not include occlusion or lighting effects, making it difficult to understand structure. An image generated with a compositing technique does include occlusion, and the compositing ray function can be modified to include shading as well. A comparison of these three methods is shown in Figure **7–20** for a CT scan of a human foot.

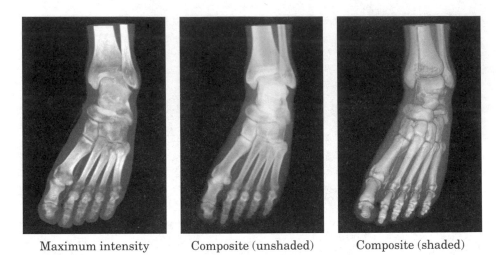

| Maximum intensity | Composite (unshaded) | Composite (shaded) |

Figure 7–20 A comparison of three volume rendering techniques. A maximum intensity projection does not include occlusion or shading. A composite image includes occlusion and can include shading.

To accurately capture lighting effects, we could use a transport theory illumination model [Krueger91] that describes the intensity of light I arriving at a pixel by the path integral along the ray:

$$I(t_0,\vec{\omega}) = \int_{t_0}^{\infty} Q(t)e^{-\int_{t_0}^{t}\sigma_a(t') + \sigma_{sc}(t')dt'} dt \qquad \textbf{(7-4)}$$

If we are using camera clipping planes, then t_0 and ∞ would be replaced by the distance to the near clip plane t_{near} and the distance to the far clip plane t_{far} respectively. The contribution $Q(t)$ from each sample at a distance t along the ray $\vec{\omega}$ is attenuated according to how much intensity is lost on the way from t to t_0 due to absorption $\sigma_a(t')$ and scattering $\sigma_{sc}(t')$. The contribution at t can be defined as:

$$Q(t) = E(t) + \sigma_{sc}(t)\int_{4\pi} \rho_{sc}(\vec{\omega}' \to \vec{\omega})I(l, \vec{\omega}')d\vec{\omega}' \qquad \textbf{(7-5)}$$

The contribution consists of the amount of light directly emitted by the sample $E(t)$, plus the amount of light coming from all directions that is scattered by this sample back along the ray. The fraction of light arriving from the $\vec{\omega}'$ direction that is scattered into the $\vec{\omega}$ direction is defined by the scattering function

$\rho_{sc}(\vec{\omega}' \to \vec{\omega})$. To compute the light arriving from all directions due to multiple bounce scattering, we must recursively compute the illumination function.

If scattering is accurately modelled, then basing the ray function on the transport theory illumination model will produce images with realistic lighting effects. Unfortunately, this illumination model is too complex to evaluate, therefore approximations are necessary for a practical implementation. One of the simplest approximations is to ignore scattering completely, yielding the following intensity equation:

$$I(t_0, \vec{\omega}) = \int_{t_0}^{\infty} E(t)e^{-\int_{t_0}^{t}\sigma_a(t')dt'} dt \qquad (7\text{-}6)$$

We can further simplify this equation by allowing $\alpha(t)$ to represent both the amount of light emitted per unit length and the amount of light absorbed per unit length along the ray. The outer integral can be replaced by a summation over samples along the ray within some clipping range, while the inner integral can be approximated using an over operator:

$$I(t_{near}, \vec{\omega}) = \sum_{t=t_{near}}^{t \leq t_{far}} \alpha(t) \prod_{t'=t_{near}}^{t'<t} (1-a(t')) \qquad (7\text{-}7)$$

This equation is typically expressed in its recursive form:

$$I(t_n, \vec{\omega}) = \alpha(t_n) + (1-\alpha(t_n))I(t_{n+1}, \vec{\omega}) \qquad (7\text{-}8)$$

which is equivalent to the simple compositing method using the over operator that was described previously. Clearly in this case we have simplified the illumination model to the point that this ray function does not produce images that appear to be realistic.

If we are visualizing an isosurface within the volumetric data, then we can employ the surface illumination model described in Chapter 3 to capture ambient and diffuse lighting as well as specular highlights. There are a variety of techniques for estimating the surface normal needed to evaluate the shading equation. If the image that is produced as a result of volume rendering contains the distance from the view plane to the surface for every pixel, then we can post-process the image with a 2D gradient estimator to obtain surface normals. The

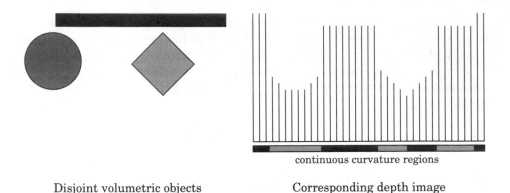

continuous curvature regions

Disjoint volumetric objects   Corresponding depth image

Figure 7–21 A scene (left) and the corresponding depth image (right) used in 2D gradient estimation.

gradient at some pixel (x_p, y_p) can be estimated with a central difference technique by:

$$\frac{\partial Z}{\partial x} = \frac{Z(x_p + \Delta x, y_p) - Z(x_p - \Delta x, y_p)}{2\Delta x}$$

$$\frac{\partial Z}{\partial y} = \frac{Z(x_p, y_p + \Delta y) - Z(x_p, y_p - \Delta y)}{2\Delta y} \qquad\qquad \textbf{(7-9)}$$

$$\frac{\partial Z}{\partial z} = 1$$

The results are normalized to produce a unit normal vector. As with the 3D finite differences gradient estimator given in Equation **7-3**, care must be taken when selecting Δx and Δy. Typically, these values are simply the pixel spacing in x and y so that neighboring pixel values are used to estimate the gradient, although larger values can be used to smooth the image.

One problem with the 2D gradient estimation technique described above is that normals are computed from depth values that may represent disjoint regions in the volume, as shown in Figure **7–21**. This may lead to a blurring of sharp features on the edges of objects. To reduce this effect, we can locate regions of continuous curvature in the depth image, then estimate the normal for a pixel using only other pixel values that fall within the same curvature region [Yagel92a]. This may require reducing our Δx and Δy values, or using an off-centered differences technique to estimate the components of the gradient. For example, the x component of the gradient could be computed with a forward difference:

$$\frac{\partial Z}{\partial x} = \frac{Z(x_p + \Delta x, y_p) - Z(x_p, y_p)}{\Delta x} \qquad \textbf{(7-10)}$$

or a backward difference:

$$\frac{\partial Z}{\partial x} = \frac{Z(x_p, y_p) - Z(x_p - \Delta x, y_p)}{\Delta x} \qquad \textbf{(7-11)}$$

Although 2D gradient estimation is not as accurate as the 3D version, it is generally faster and allows for quick lighting and surface property changes without requiring us to recompute the depth image. However, if we wish to include shading effects in an image computed with a compositing technique, we need to estimate gradients at many locations within the volume for each pixel. A 3D gradient estimation technique is more suitable for this purpose. An illumination equation for compositing could be written as:

$$I(t_{near}, \vec{\omega}) = \sum_{t = t_{near}}^{t \le t_{far}} \alpha(t)(I_a + I_d + I_s) \prod_{t' = t_{near}}^{t' < t} (1 - a(t'))　\qquad \textbf{(7-12)}$$

where the ambient illumination I_a, the diffuse illumination I_d, and the specular illumination I_s are computed as in surface shading using the estimated volume gradient in place of the surface normal. In this equation, $\alpha(t)$ represents the amount of light reflected per unit length along the ray, with $1 - \alpha(t)$ indicating the fraction of light transmitted per unit length.

As in classification, we have to make a decision about whether to directly compute illumination at an arbitrary location in the volume, or to compute illumination at the grid points and then interpolate. This is not a difficult decision to make on the basis of accuracy since it is clearly better to estimate the gradient at the desired location rather than interpolate from neighboring estimations. On the other hand, if we do interpolate from the grid points then we can precompute the gradients for the entire dataset once, and use this to increase rendering performance for both classification and illumination. The main problem is the amount of memory required to store the precomputed gradients. A naive implementation would store a floating-point value (typically four bytes) per component of the gradient per scalar value. For a dataset with 256^3 one-byte scalars, this would increase the storage requirement from 16 Mbytes to 218 Mbytes.

In order to reduce the storage requirements, we could quantize the precomputed gradients by using some number of bits to represent the magnitude of the vector, and some other number of bits to encode the direction of the vector. Quantization works well for storing the magnitude of the gradient, but does not pro-

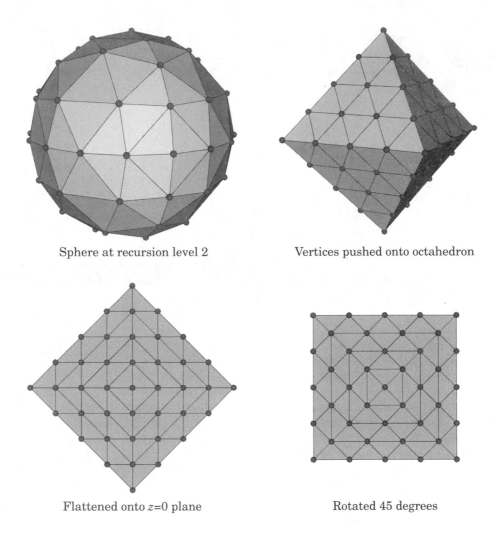

Sphere at recursion level 2   Vertices pushed onto octahedron

Flattened onto $z=0$ plane   Rotated 45 degrees

Figure 7–22 Gradient direction encoding.

vide a good distribution of directions if we simply divide the bits among the three components of the vector. A better solution is to use the uniform fractal subdivision of an octahedron into a sphere as the basis of the direction encoding, as shown in Figure **7–22**. The top left image shows the results obtained after the recursive replacement of each triangle with four new triangles, with a recursion depth of two. The vector directions encoded in this representation are all directions formed by creating a ray originating at the sphere's center and passing through a vertex of the sphere. The remaining images in this figure illustrate how these directions are mapped into an index. First we push all vertices back onto the original faces of the octahedron, then we flatten this sphere onto the $z = 0$ plane. Finally, we rotate the resulting grid by $45°$. We label the vertices in the grid with indices starting at 0 at the top left vertex and continue across the rows then down the columns to index 40 at the lower right vertex. These indices represent only half of the encoded normals because when we flattened the octahedron, we placed two vertices on top of each other on all but the edge locations. Thus, we can use indices 41 through 81 to represent vectors with a negative z component. Vertices on the edges represent vectors with out a z component, and although we could represent them with a single index, using two keeps the indexing scheme more consistent and, therefore, easier to implement.

The simple example above requires only 82 values to encode the 66 unique vector directions. If we use an unsigned short to store the encoded direction, then we can use a recursion depth of 6 when generating the vertices. This leads to 16,642 indices representing 16,386 unique directions.

Once the gradients have been encoded for our volume, we need only compute the illumination once for each possible index and store the results in a table. Since data samples with the same encoded gradient direction may have different colors, this illumination value represents the portion of the shading equation that is independent of color. Each scalar value may have separate colors defined for ambient, diffuse, and specular illumination; therefore, the precomputed illumination is typically an array of values.

Although using a shading table leads to faster rendering times, there are some limitations to this method. Only infinite light sources can be supported accurately since positional light sources would result in different light vectors for data samples with the same gradient due to their different positions in the volume. In addition, specular highlights are only captured accurately for orthographic viewing directions where the view vector does not vary based on sample position. In practice, positional light sources are often approximated by infinite light sources, and a single view direction is used for computing specular highlights since the need for fast rendering often outweighs the need for accurate illumination.

7.9 Regions of Interest

One difficulty in visualizing volumetric data with the methods presented thus far is that in order to study some feature in the center of the volume we must look through other features in the dataset. For example, if we are visualizing a tomato dataset, then we will be unable to see the seeds within the tomato using a maximum intensity projection because the seeds have lower intensity than the surrounding pulp. Even using a compositing technique, it is difficult to visualize the seeds since full opacity may be obtained before reaching this area of the dataset.

We can solve the problem of visualizing internal features by defining a region of interest within our volume, and rendering only this portion of the dataset as shown in Figure **7–23**. There are many techniques for defining a

Full tomato   Tomato wedge

Figure 7–23 Volume rendering with regions of interest. MR tomato data courtesy of Lawrence Berkeley Laboratory.

region of interest. We could use the near and far clipping planes of the camera to exclude portions of the volume. Alternatively, we could use six orthographic clipping planes that would define a rectangular subvolume; we could use a set of arbitrarily oriented half-space clipping planes; or we could define the region of interest as the portion of the volume contained within some set of closed geometric objects. Another approach would be to create an auxiliary structured points dataset with binary scalar values that define a mask indicating which values in the volume should be considered during rendering.

All of these region of interest methods are fairly simple to implement using an image-order ray-casting approach. As a preprocessing step to ray casting, the ray is clipped against all geometric region definitions. The ray function is then evaluated only along segments of the ray that are within the region of interest. The mask values are consulted at each sample to determine if its contribution should be included or excluded.

For object-order methods we must determine for each sample whether or not it is within the region of interest before incorporating its contribution into the image. If the underlying graphics hardware is being utilized for the object-order volume rendering as is the case with a texture mapping approach, hardware clipping planes may be available to help support regions of interest.

7.10 Intermixing Volumes and Geometry

Although the volume is typically the focus of the image in volume visualization, it is often helpful to add geometric objects to the scene. For example, showing the bounding box of the dataset or the position and orientation of cut planes can improve the viewer's understanding of the volumetric data. Also, it can be useful to visualize volumetric data using both geometric and volumetric methods

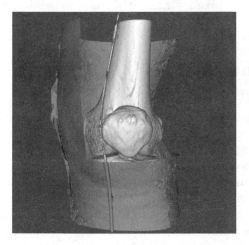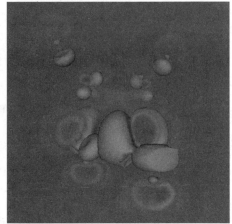

Figure 7–24 Two volumes rendered with both geometric and volumetric techniques. The Visible Woman CT data is courtesy of The National Library of Medicine.

within the same image. The left image in Figure **7–24** shows a CT scan of a human knee where a contouring method is used to extract the skin isosurface. This isosurface is rendered as triangles using standard graphics hardware. The upper-right portion of the skin is cut to reveal the bone beneath, which is rendered using a software ray-casting technique with a compositing ray function. In the right image, the wave function values of an iron protein are visualized using both geometric isosurface and volume rendering techniques.

When using graphics hardware to perform volume rendering, as is the case with a texture mapping approach, intermixing opaque geometry in the scene is trivial. All opaque geometry is rendered first, then the semitransparent texture-mapped polygons are blended in a back to front order into the image. If we wish to include semitransparent geometry in the scene, then this geometry and the texture-mapped polygons must be sorted before rendering. Similar to a purely geometric scene, this may involve splitting polygons to obtain a sorted order.

If a software volume rendering approach is used, such as an object-order splatting method or an image-order ray-casting method, opaque geometry can be incorporated into the image by rendering the geometry, capturing the results stored in the hardware depth buffer, and then using these results during the volume rendering phase. For ray casting, we would simply convert the depth value for a pixel into a distance along the view ray and use this to bound the segment of the ray that we consider during volume rendering. The final color computed for a pixel during volume rendering is then blended with the color produced by geometric rendering using the over operator. In an object-order method, we must consider the depth of every sample and compare this to the value stored in the depth buffer at each pixel within the image extent of this sample. We accumulate this sample's contribution to the volume rendered image at each pixel only if the sample is in front of the geometry for that pixel. Finally, the volume rendered image is blended over the geometric image.

7.11 Efficient Volume Rendering

Rendering a volumetric dataset is a computationally intensive task. If n is the size of the volume on all three dimensions and we visit every voxel once during a projection, the complexity of volume rendering is $O(n^3)$. Even a highly optimized software algorithm will have great difficulty projecting a moderately sized volume of $512 \times 512 \times 128$ or approximately 32 million voxels at interactive rates. If every voxel in the volume contributes in some way to the final image and we are unwilling to compromise image quality, our options for efficiency improvements are limited. However, it has been observed that many volumetric datasets contain large regions of empty or uninteresting data that are assigned opacity values of 0 during classification. In addition, those areas that contain interesting data may be occupied by coherent or nearly homogeneous regions. There have been many techniques developed that take advantage of these observations.

Space leaping refers to a general class of efficiency improvement techniques that attempt to avoid processing regions of a volume that will not contribute to the final image. One technique often used is to build an octree data structure which hierarchically contains all of the important regions in the volume. The root node of the octree contains the entire volume and has eight child nodes, each of which represents 1/8 of the volume. These eight subregions are created by dividing the volume in half along the x, y, and z axes. This subdivision continues recursively until a node in the octree represents a homogeneous region of the volume. With an object-order rendering technique, only the nonempty leaf nodes of the octree would be traversed during rendering thereby avoiding all empty regions while efficiently processing all contributing homogeneous regions. Similarly, an image-order ray-casting technique would cast rays through the leaf nodes, with the regular structure of the octree allowing us to quickly step over empty nodes.

A hybrid space leaping technique [Sobierajski95] makes use of graphics hardware to skip some of the empty regions of the volume during software ray casting. First, a polygonal representation is created that completely contains or encloses all important regions in the volume. This polygonal representation is then projected twice — first using the usual less than operator on the depth buffer and the second time using a greater than operator on the depth buffer. This produces two depth images that contain the closest and farthest distance to relevant data for every pixel in the image. These distances are then used to clip the rays during ray casting.

An alternate space-leaping technique for ray casting involves the use of an auxiliary distance volume [Zuiderveld92], with each value indicating the closest distance to a nontransparent sample in the dataset. These distance values are used to take larger steps in empty regions of the volume while ensuring that we do not step over any nontransparent features in the volume. Unfortunately, the distance volume is computationally expensive to compute accurately, requires additional storage, and must be recomputed every time the classification of the volume is modified.

One difficulty with these space-leaping techniques is that they are highly data dependent. On a largely empty volume with a small amount of coherent data we can speed up volume rendering by a substantial amount. However, when a dataset is encountered that is entirely made up of high-frequency information such as a typical ultrasound dataset, these techniques break down and will usually cause rendering times to increase rather than decrease.

7.12 Interactive Volume Rendering

Generating a volume rendered image may take anywhere from a fraction of a second to tens of minutes depending on a variety of factors including the hardware platform, image size, data size, and rendering technique. If we are generating the image for the purpose of medical diagnostics we clearly would like to produce a high quality image. On the other hand, if the image is produced during an interactive session then it may be more important to achieve a desired rendering update rate. Therefore, it is clear that we need to be able to trade off quality for speed as necessary based on application. As opposed to our discussion on efficiency improvements, the techniques described here do not preserve image quality. Instead, they allow a controlled degradation in quality in order to achieve speed.

Since the time required for image-order ray casting depends mostly on the size of the image in pixels and the number of samples taken along the ray, we can adjust these two values to achieve a desired update rate. The full-size image can be generated from the reduced resolution image using either a nearest neighbor or bilinear interpolation method. If bilinear interpolation is used, the number of rays cast can often be reduced by a factor of two along each image dimension during interaction, resulting in a four-times speed-up, without a noticeable decrease in image quality. Further speed-ups can be achieved with larger reductions, but at the cost of blurry, less detailed images.

We can implement a progressive refinement method for ray casting if we do not reduce the number of samples taken along each ray. During interaction we can compute only every n^{th} ray along each image dimension and use interpolation to fill in the remaining pixels. When the user stops interacting with the scene the interpolated pixels are progressively filled in with their actual values.

There are several object-order techniques available for achieving interactive rendering rates at the expense of image quality. If a splatting algorithm is used, then the rendering speed is dependent on the number of voxels in the dataset. Reduced resolution versions of the data can be precomputed, and a level of resolution can be selected during interaction based on the desired frame rate. If we use a splatting method based on an octree representation, then we can include an approximate scalar value and an error value in each parent node where the error value indicates how much the scalar values in the child nodes deviate from the approximate value in the parent node. Hierarchical splatting [Laur91] can be performed by descending the octree only until a node with less than a given error tolerance is encountered. The contribution of this region of the volume on the image can be approximated by rendering geometric primitives for the splat [Shirley90], [Wilhelms91]. Increasing the allowed error will decrease the time required to render the data by allowing larger regions to be approximated at a higher level in the octree.

When using a texture mapping approach for volume rendering, faster rendering speeds can be achieved by reducing the number of texture-mapped polygons used to represent the volume. This is essentially equivalent to reducing the number of samples taken along the ray in an image-order ray-casting method. Also, if texture download rates are a bottleneck, then a reduced resolution version of the volume can be loaded into texture memory for interaction. This is similar to reducing both the number of rays cast and the number of samples taken along a ray in an image-order method.

7.13 Volume Rendering Future

In the past decade, volume rendering has evolved from a research topic with algorithms that required many minutes to generate an image on a high-end workstation to an area of active development with commercial software available for home computers. Yet as the demand for volume rendering increases, so do the challenges. The number of voxels in a typical dataset is growing, both due to advances in acquisition hardware and increased popularity of volume rendering in areas such as simulation and volume graphics [Kaufman93]. New methods are needed in order to satisfy the conflicting needs of high quality images and interactivity on these large datasets. In addition, time dependent datasets that contain volumetric data sampled at discrete time intervals present new challenges for interpolation, image accuracy, and interactivity while providing new opportunities in classification and interpolation methods.

Most of the volume rendering discussion in this chapter focused on structured points datasets. Although it is clearly possible to extend most ray casting and object-order methods to visualize rectilinear grid, structured grid, and even irregular data, in practice it is difficult to provide both high quality images and interactivity with these methods. Rendering techniques for these data types continues to be an area of active research in volume visualization [Cignoni96], [Silva96], [Wilhelms96].

7.14 Stereo Rendering

In our practice of computer graphics so far, we have used a number of techniques to simulate 3D graphics on a 2D display device. These techniques include the use of perspective and scale, shading to confer depth, and motion/animation to see all sides of an object. However, one of the most effective techniques to simulate 3D viewing is *binocular parallax*.

Binocular parallax is a result of viewing 3D objects with our two eyes. Since each eye sees a slightly different picture, our mind interprets these differences to determine the depth of objects in our view. There have been a number of "3D" movies produced that take advantage of our binocular parallax. Typically, these involve wearing a set of special glasses while watching the movie.

This effect can be valuable in our efforts to visualize complex datasets and CAD models. The additional depth cues provided by stereo viewing aid us in determining the relative positions of scene geometry as well as forming a mental image of the scene. There are several different methods for introducing binocular parallax into renderings. We will refer to the overall process as *stereo rendering*, since at some point in the process a stereo pair of images is involved.

To generate correct left and right eye images, we need information beyond the camera parameters that we introduced in Chapter 3. The first piece of information we need is the separation distance between the eyes. The amount of parallax generated can be controlled by adjusting this distance. We also need to know if the resulting images will be viewed on one or two displays. For systems that use two displays (and hence two view planes), the parallax can be correctly produced by performing camera azimuths to reach the left and right eye positions. Head mounted displays and booms are examples of two display systems. Unfortunately, this doesn't work as well for systems that have only one view plane. If you try to display both the left and right views on a single display, they are forced to share the same view plane as in Figure **7–25**. Our earlier camera model assumed that the view plane was perpendicular to the direction of projection. To handle this nonperpendicular case, we must translate and shear the camera's viewing frustum. Hodges provides some of the details of this operation as well as a good overview on stereo rendering [Hodges92].

Now let's look at some of the different methods for presenting stereoscopic images to the user. Most methods are based on one of two main categories: *time multiplexed* and *time parallel* techniques. Time multiplexed methods work by alternating between the left and right eye images. Time parallel methods display both images at once in combination with a process to extract left and right eye views. Some methods can be implemented as either a time multiplexed or a time parallel technique.

Time multiplexed techniques are most commonly found in single display systems, since they rely on alternating images. Typically this is combined with a method for also alternating which eye views the image. One cost-effective time multiplexed technique takes advantage of existing television standards such as NTSC and PAL. Both of these standards use interlacing, which means that first the even lines are drawn on the screen and then the odd. By rendering the left eye image to the even lines of the screen and the right eye image to the odd, we can generate a stereo video stream that is suitable for display on a standard television. When this is viewed with both eyes, it appears as one image that keeps jumping from left to right. A special set of glasses must be worn so that when the left eye image is being displayed, the user's left eye can see and similarly for the

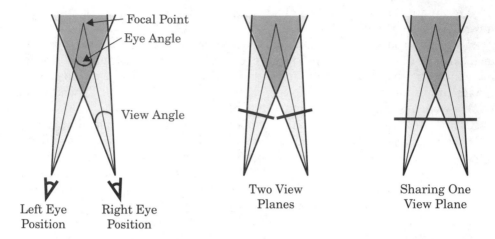

Left Eye   Right Eye   Two View   Sharing One
Position   Position   Planes   View Plane

Figure 7–25 Stereo rendering and binocular parallax.

right eye. The glasses are designed so that each lens consists of a liquid crystal shutter that can either be transparent or opaque, depending on what voltage is applied to it. By shuttering the glasses at the same rate as the television is interlacing, we can assure that the correct eye is viewing the correct image.

There are a couple of disadvantages to this system. The resolutions of NTSC and PAL are both low compared to a computer monitor. The refresh rate of NTSC (60 Hz) and PAL (50 Hz) produces a fair amount of flicker, especially when you consider that each eye is updated at half this rate. Also, this method requires viewing your images on a television, not the monitor connected to your computer.

To overcome these difficulties, some computer manufacturers offer stereo ready graphics cards. These systems use liquid crystal shuttered glasses to directly view the computer monitor. To obtain the alternating stereo images, the left eye image is rendered to the top half of the screen and the right eye image to the bottom. Then the graphics card enters a special stereo mode where it doubles the refresh rate of the monitor. So a monitor that initially displays both images at 60Hz begins to alternate between the left and right eye at a rate of 120Hz. This results in each eye getting updated at 60Hz, with its original horizontal resolution and half of its original vertical resolution. For this process to work, your application must take up the entire screen while rendering.

Some more recent graphics cards have a left image buffer and a right image buffer for stereo rendering. While this requires either more memory or a lower resolution, it does provide for stereo rendering without having to take over the entire screen. For such a card, double buffering combined with stereo rendering results in quad buffering, which can result in a large number of bits per pixel. For example: 24 bits for an RGB color, another 24 bits for the back buffer's color, plus 24 bits for the z-buffer results in 72 bits per pixel. Now double that for the

Figure 7–26 Single image random dot stereogram of a tetrahedron.

two different views and you have 144 bits per pixel or 18 megabytes for a 1K by 1K display.

Time parallel techniques display both images at the same time. Head-mounted displays and booms have two separate screens, one for each eye. To generate the two video streams requires either two graphics cards or one that can generate two separate outputs. The rendering process then involves just rendering each eye to the correct graphics card or output. Currently, the biggest disadvantage to this approach is the cost of the hardware required.

In contrast, SIRDS (Single Image Random Dot Stereograms) require no special hardware. Both views are displayed in a single image, as in Figure **7–26**. To view such an image the user must focus either in front of, or behind, the image. When the user's focal point is correct, the two triangular cutouts in the top of the image will appear as one and the image should appear focused. This works because dot patterns repeat at certain intervals. Here, only the depth information is present in the resulting image. This is incorporated by changing the interval between patterns just as our ocular disparity changes with depth.

The next two techniques for stereo rendering can be implemented using either the time parallel or time multiplexed methods. The distinction is slightly blurred because most of the time parallel methods can be multiplexed, though typically there is no advantage to it. Both of these methods have been used by the movie industry to produce "3D" movies. The first is commonly called red-blue (or red-green or red-cyan) stereo and requires the user to wear a pair of glasses that filter entering light. The left eye can only see the image through a red filter, the right through a blue filter. The rendering process typically involves generating images for the two views, converting their RGB values into intensity, and then creating a resulting image. This image's red values are taken from the left eye image intensities. Likewise the blue values (a mixture of blue and green) are taken from the right eye image intensities. The resulting image has none of the original hue or saturation, but it does contain both original images' intensities. (An additional note: red-green methods are also used because the human eye is more sensitive to green than blue.) The benefits of this technique are that the resulting images can be displayed on a monitor, paper, or film, and all one needs to view them is an inexpensive pair of glasses.

The second technique is similar to the first but it preserves all the color information from the original images. It separates the different views by using polarized light. Normally, the light we see has a mixture of polarization angles, but there are lenses that can filter out a subset of these angles. If we project a color image through a vertical polarizing filter, and then view it through another vertical filter, we will see the original image, just slightly dimmer because we've filtered out all the horizontally polarized light. If we place a horizontal filter and a vertical filter together, all the light is blocked. Polarized stereo rendering typically projects one eye's image through a vertical filter and the other through a horizontal filter. The user wears a pair of glasses containing a vertical filter over one eye and a horizontal filter over the other. This way each eye views the correct image.

All the methods we have discussed for stereo rendering have their advantages and disadvantages, typically revolving around cost and image quality. At the end of this chapter we will look at an example program that renders stereo images using the red-blue technique.

7.15 Aliasing

At one point or another most computer users have run into aliasing problems. This "stair-stepping" occurs because we represent continuous surface geometry with discrete pixels. In computer graphics the most common aliasing problem is jagged edges when rendering lines or surface boundaries, as in Figure **7–27**.

The aliasing problem stems from the rasterization process as the graphics system converts primitives, such as line segments, into pixels on the screen. For example, the quickest way to rasterize a line is to use an all or nothing strategy.

Figure 7–27 Wireframe image and antialiased equivalent.

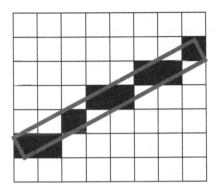 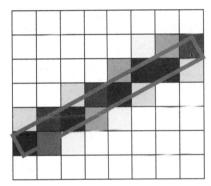

Figure 7–28 A one pixel wide line (outlined in gray) draw using a winner take all approach (left) and a coverage approach (right).

If the line passes through the pixel, then the pixel is set to the line's color; otherwise, it is not altered. As can be seen in Figure **7–28**, this results in the stairstepped appearance.

There are several techniques for handling aliasing problems, and they are collectively known as *antialiasing* techniques. One approach to antialiasing is to change how the graphics system rasterizes primitives. Instead of rasterizing a line using an all or nothing approach, we look at how much of the pixel the line occupies. The resulting color for that pixel is a mixture of its original color and the line's color. The ratio of these two colors is determined by the line's occupancy. This works especially well when working primarily with wireframe models. A similar approach breaks each pixel down into smaller subpixels. Primitives are rendered using an all or nothing strategy, but at subpixel resolutions. Then the subpixels are averaged to determine the resulting pixel's color. This tends to require much more memory.

A good result can be obtained by breaking each pixel into 10 subpixels, which requires about 10 times the memory and rendering time. If you don't have access to hardware subpixel rendering, you can approximate it by rendering a large image and then scaling it down. Using a program such as pnmscale, which does bilinear interpolation, you can take a 1000 by 1000 pixel image and scale it down to a 500 by 500 antialiased image. If you have a graphics library that can render into memory instead of the screen, large images such as 6000 by 6000 pixels can be scaled down into high quality results, still at high resolutions such as 2000 by 2000. This may seem like overkill, but on a good 300dpi color printer this would result in a picture roughly seven inches on a side.

The last method of antialiasing we will look at uses an accumulation buffer to average a few possibly aliased images together to produce one antialiased result. An accumulation buffer is just a segment of memory that is set aside for performing image operations and storage. The following fragment of C++ code illustrates this process.

```
for (imageNum = 0; imageNum < imageTotal; imageNum++)
  {
  // Jitter the camera and focal point by less than one pixel
  // Render an image
  // add the image to the accumulation buffer
  }
// Divide the accumulation buffer by imageTotal
// Display the resulting antialiased image
```

Instead of using one image with eight subpixels per pixel, we can use eight images without subpixels. The antialiasing is achieved by slightly translating the camera's position and focal point between each image. The amount of translation should be within one pixel of magnitude and perpendicular to the direction of projection. Of course, the camera's position is specified in world coordinates not pixels, but Equation **7-13** will do the trick. We calculate the new camera position and focal point (i.e., p_{new} and f_{new}) from the offset to avoid difficulties surrounding the transformation matrix at the camera's position.

$$f_{new} = (fM_{WD} + O_p)M_{DW}$$
$$O_w = f_{new} - f \qquad\qquad (7\text{-}13)$$
$$p_{new} = p + O_w$$

In this equation O_p is the offset in pixel coordinates, O_w is the offset in world coordinates, f is the camera focal point, p is the camera position, and the transformation matrices M_{WD} and M_{DW} transform from world coordinates to display coordinates and from display coordinates to world coordinates, respectively.

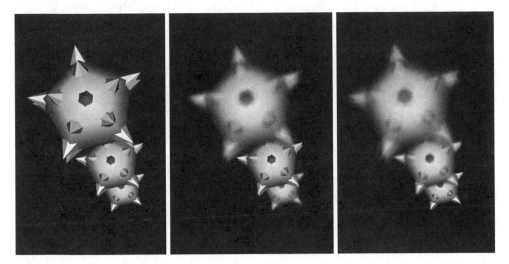

Figure 7–29 Three images showing focal depth. The first has no focal depth, the second is focused on the center object, the third image is focused on the farthest object.

7.16 Camera Tricks

In the previous section we saw how to combine an accumulation buffer and small camera translations to produce an antialiased image. In this section we will cover a few other camera techniques of interest. You may have noticed that with computer generated images all actors are in focus. With a real camera you have to set the focal depth to match the distance of the object you are photographing. Anything that is closer or farther than your focal depth will appear out of focus. This is because a real camera has a lens that lets light pass through a finite area. The camera model we have introduced has a point lens, where all the light travels through at exactly the same point. (See Figure **7–29** for a comparison.)

We can simulate a finite camera lens by rendering many images, each with a slightly different camera position but the same focal point. Then we accumulate these images and take the average. The resulting image simulates a camera lens with focal depth. The different camera positions are determined by selecting random points from the lens you are trying to simulate. Larger diameter lenses will produce more distortion and vice versa. Increasing the number of random points will improve the precision of your result. Typically 10 to 30 samples is desirable. The images in Figure **7–29** were created using 30 sample points.

Another difference between a real camera and a computer camera is in the shutter speed. Our model generates an image for a single moment in time; in contrast, a photograph captures what the camera views while its shutter is open. Fast moving objects appear blurred because of changes in their position during the small time that the shutter is open. This effect, known as *motion blur*, can also be simulated with our camera model. Instead of rendering one image and displaying it, we render a few subframes that are accumulated, averaged, and

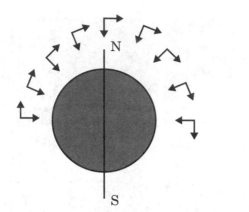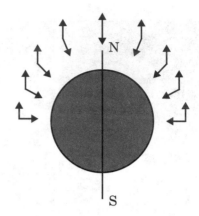

Figure 7–30 Rotations using an orthogonalized view-up vector (left) and a constant view-up vector (right).

finally displayed. This is similar to the antialiasing and focal depth techniques we just discussed. In both of those techniques, the camera is jittered while the actors remain fixed in time. To implement motion blur we don't jitter the camera; we increment the scene's time between each subframe. Moving objects or camera movements will result in differences between each subframe. The resulting image approximates the effects of photographing moving objects over a finite time.

7.17 Mouse-Based Interaction

There's no doubt that being able to interactively view an object aids in understanding and recognizing its important features. Using a pointing device (e.g., a mouse or trackball) is certainly the most common method for controlling such movements. The software that accompanies this book contains the vtkRender-WindowInteractor object that translates mouse and keyboard events into modifications to the camera and actors. For example, while the user holds the left mouse button down, the vtkRenderWindowInteractor rotates the camera towards the current pointer position. The farther the pointer is from the center of the window, the faster the camera rotates.

Most of these interactions are straightforward, but there are a few issues associated with rotations. When rotating around an object, one must decide what to do with the view-up vector. We can keep it perpendicular to the direction of projection as we rotate, or we can leave it unchanged. This results in two different types of rotations. If we keep our view-up vector orthogonal to the direction of projection, we will rotate all around the object much like a plane flying around the globe. This is shown in the left half of Figure **7–30**. If we leave the view-up vector unchanged, our plane will start flying backwards at the north and south poles, as shown in the right half of Figure **7–30**.

The advantage of a constant view-up vector is that some objects have a natural sense of up and down (e.g., terrain). Elevation and azimuth operations remain consistent as we move around the object. On the other hand, there are singular points where the view-up vector and direction of projection become parallel. In these cases the camera viewing transformation matrix is undefined. Then we have to modify the view-up vector or use the perpendicular view-up / direction of projection method to handle this situation. If the data you are working with has a well-defined up and down, then it probably makes sense to leave the view-up constant during rotations; otherwise, it makes sense to keep it orthogonal to the direction of projection.

7.18 Putting It All Together

This chapter has covered a wide variety of topics. In this section we demonstrate applications of each topic to some simple problems.

Texture Mapping

Figure **7–31** shows the complete source code for a simple texture mapping example. You will notice that most of the code is similar to what we used in the preceding examples. The key step here is the creation of a vtkTexture object. This object interfaces between its data input and the texture mapping functions of the graphics library. The vtkTexture instance is associated with an actor. More than one texture instance may be shared between multiple actors. For texture mapping to function properly, texture coordinates must be defined by the actor's modeller.

One interesting note regarding the vtkTexture object. Instances of this class are mappers that have an Input instance variable that is updated during each render. The input type is a vtkStructuredPoints dataset type. Thus, a visualization pipeline can be constructed to read, process, and/or generate the texture map. This includes using the object vtkRendererSource, which converts the renderer's image into a structured point dataset. The input texture map can be either 2D (a pixmap) or 3D (a volume).

A few words of warning when using textures. Some renderers only support 2D texture, or may not support alpha textures. Also, some rendering systems require that each dimension of the structured point dataset is an exact power of two. (At the time of printing this was true of OpenGL.)

Volume Rendering

This example focuses on volume rendering. The source code shown in example Figure **7–32** begins by creating the usual objects. Then we use a vtkStructuredPointsReader to read in a volume dataset for a high potential iron protein. We create a vtkPiecewiseFunction object to map the scalar values in the volume dataset to opacity, and another vtkPiecewiseFunction object to

```
#include "vtk.h"

main ()
{
  vtkRenderer *ren1 = vtkRenderer::New();
  vtkRenderWindow *renWin = vtkRenderWindow::New();
    renWin->AddRenderer(ren1);
  vtkRenderWindowInteractor *iren =
            vtkRenderWindowInteractor::New();
    iren->SetRenderWindow(renWin);

  // load the texture map
  vtkPNMReader *pnm = vtkPNMReader::New();
    pnm->SetFileName("../../../vtkdata/masonry.ppm");
  vtkTexture *atext = vtkTexture::New();
    atext->SetInput(pnm->GetOutput());
    atext->InterpolateOn();

  vtkPlaneSource *plane = vtkPlaneSource::New();
  vtkPolyDataMapper *planeMapper = vtkPolyDataMapper::New();
    planeMapper->SetInput(plane->GetOutput());
  vtkActor *planeActor = vtkActor::New();
    planeActor->SetMapper(planeMapper);
    planeActor->SetTexture(atext);

  ren1->AddActor(planeActor);
  ren1->SetBackground(0.2,0.3,0.4);
  renWin->SetSize(500,500);

  // interact with data
  renWin->Render();

  ren1->GetActiveCamera()->Zoom(1.4);
  renWin->Render();

  iren->Start();
}
```

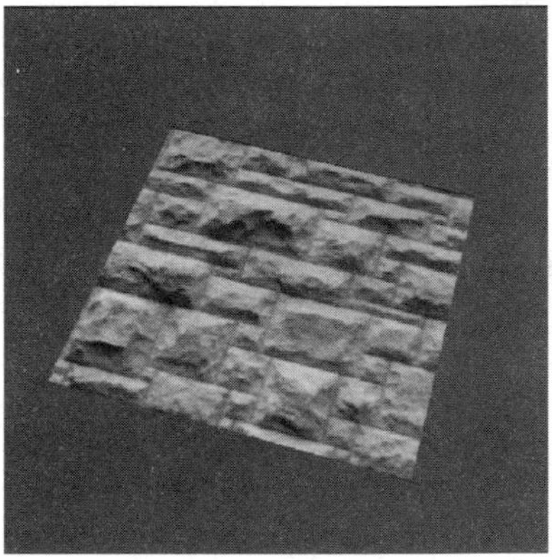

Figure 7–31 Example of texture mapping (TPlane.cxx).

map the scalar values to color. These two transfer functions are referenced from the vtkVolumeProperty object. In addition, we use the ShadeOn() method of vtkVolumeProperty to enable shading for this volume, and the SetInterpolationTypeToLinear() method to request trilinear interpolation. Since we are using a ray-casting approach, we need to create a ray function. In this example we use a vtkVolumeRayCastCompositeFunction object for this purpose. The output of the reader is given to the vtkVolumeRayCastMapper as the scalar input, and the SetVolumeRayCastFunction() method is used to assign the ray function. The vtkVolume object is quite similar to a vtkActor, and the SetVolumeMapper() and SetVolumeProperty() methods are used just like

```
main ()
{
  vtkRenderer *ren1 = vtkRenderer::New();
  vtkRenderWindow *renWin = vtkRenderWindow::New();
    renWin->AddRenderer(ren1);
  vtkRenderWindowInteractor *iren =
              vtkRenderWindowInteractor::New();
    iren->SetRenderWindow(renWin);

  vtkStructuredPointsReader *reader =
              vtkStructuredPointsReader::New();
    reader->SetFileName("../../../vtkdata/ironProt.vtk");
    reader->Update();

  vtkPiecewiseFunction *oTFun = vtkPiecewiseFunction::New();
    oTFun->AddSegment(80, 0.0, 255, 1.0);
  vtkPiecewiseFunction *gTFun = vtkPiecewiseFunction::New();
    gTFun->AddSegment(0, 1.0, 255, 1.0);

  vtkVolumeProperty *volProperty = vtkVolumeProperty::New();
    volProperty->SetColor(gTFun);
    volProperty->SetOpacity(oTFun);
    volProperty->SetInterpolationTypeToLinear();
    volProperty->ShadeOn();

  vtkVolumeRayCastCompositeFunction *compositeFunction =
              vtkVolumeRayCastCompositeFunction::New();

  vtkVolumeRayCastMapper *volMapper =
              vtkVolumeRayCastMapper::New();
    volMapper->SetScalarInput(reader->GetOutput());
    volMapper->SetVolumeRayCastFunction(compositeFunction);

  vtkVolume *vol = vtkVolume::New();
    vol->SetVolumeMapper(volMapper);
    vol->SetVolumeProperty(volProperty);

  ren1->AddVolume(vol);
  ren1->GetActiveCamera()->Azimuth(20);
  ren1->GetActiveCamera()->Dolly(1.65);

  iren->SetDesiredUpdateRate(3.0);
  iren->Start();
}
```

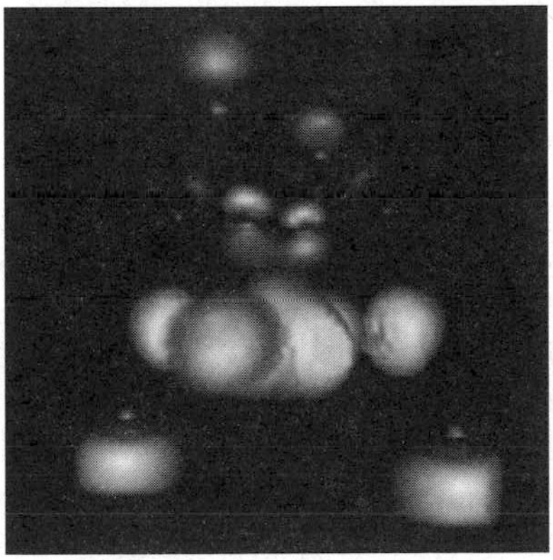

Figure 7–32 Volume rendering of a high potential iron protein (`vol.cxx`).

the `SetMapper()` and `SetProperty()` methods of `vtkActor`. Finally, we add this volume to the renderer, adjust the camera, set the desired image update rate and start the interactor.

In Figure **7–32** a `vtkPiecewiseFunction` is used to map scalar value to color, resulting in a grayscale image. We could instead use the code fragment

```
vtkColorTransferFunction *cTFun =
    vtkColorTransferFunction::New();
cTFun->AddRedSegment( 0, 0.0, 64, 1.0 );
cTFun->AddRedSegment( 64, 1.0, 128, 0.0 );
cTFun->AddBlueSegment( 64, 0.0, 128, 1.0 );
cTFun->AddBlueSegment( 128, 1.0, 192, 0.0 );
cTFun->AddGreenSegment( 128, 0.0, 192, 1.0 );
cTFun->AddGreenSegment( 192, 1.0, 255, 0.0 );
```

to define a color transfer function ranging from red through blue to green. To produce a maximum intensity projection, we would simply change the type of the ray function to a `vtkVolumeRayCastMIPFunction`. We could also produce a surface image using a `vtkVolumeRayCastIsosurfaceFunction` where the `IsoValue` instance variable would be set to define the surface.

Red-Blue Stereo

In our first example, we will be looking at using red-blue stereo rendering. We start off with the example shown in Figure **7–33**, which renders something akin to a mace. Then, in Figure **7–33** we add in red-blue stereo rendering by adding two lines near the bottom that invoke the `StereoRenderOn()` and `SetStereo-Type()` methods. Once these two methods have been invoked, further rendering will be done in stereo. The picture in the upper right corner displays a grayscale version of the resulting image.

Motion Blur

In our second example, we show how to simulate motion blur using the *Visualization Toolkit*. As shown in Figure **7–34**, we begin with our previous example. We then remove the two lines controlling stereo rendering and add a few lines to create another mace. We position the first mace in the top of the rendering window and the second mace at the bottom. We then use the `SetSubFrames()` method to start performing subframe accumulation. Here, we will perform 21 renders to produce the final image. For motion blur to be noticeable, something must be moving, so we set up a loop to rotate the bottom mace by two degrees between each subframe. Over the 21 subframes it will rotate 40 degrees from its initial position. It is important to remember that the resulting image is not displayed until the required number of subframes have been rendered.

```
#include "vtk.h"

main ()
{
  // create the rendering objects
  vtkRenderer *ren1 = vtkRenderer::New();
  vtkRenderWindow *renWin =
      vtkRenderWindow::New();
    renWin->AddRenderer(ren1);
  vtkRenderWindowInteractor *iren =
       vtkRenderWindowInteractor::New();
    iren->SetRenderWindow(renWin);

  // create the pipeline, ball and spikes
  vtkSphereSource *sphere = vtkSphereSource::New();
    sphere->SetThetaResolution(7); sphere->SetPhiResolution(7);
  vtkPolyDataMapper *sphereMapper = vtkPolyDataMapper::New();
    sphereMapper->SetInput(sphere->GetOutput());
  vtkActor *sphereActor = vtkActor::New();
    sphereActor->SetMapper(sphereMapper);

  vtkConeSource *cone = vtkConeSource::New();
    cone->SetResolution(5);
  vtkGlyph3D *glyph = vtkGlyph3D::New();
    glyph->SetInput(sphere->GetOutput());
    glyph->SetSource(cone->GetOutput());
    glyph->SetVectorModeToUseNormal();
    glyph->SetScaleModeToScaleByVector();
    glyph->SetScaleFactor(0.25);
  vtkPolyDataMapper *spikeMapper = vtkPolyDataMapper::New();
    spikeMapper->SetInput(glyph->GetOutput());
  vtkActor *spikeActor = vtkActor::New();
    spikeActor->SetMapper(spikeMapper);

  ren1->AddActor(sphereActor);
  ren1->AddActor(spikeActor);
  ren1->SetBackground(0.2,0.3,0.4);
  renWin->SetSize(400,400);

  // do the first render and then zoom in a little
  renWin->Render();
  ren1->GetActiveCamera()->Zoom(1.4);
  renWin->StereoRenderOn();
  renWin->SetStereoTypeToRedBlue();
  renWin->Render();
}
```

Figure 7–33 An example of red-blue stereo rendering (Mace3.cxx).

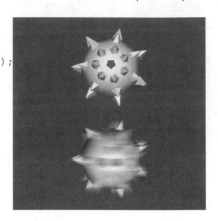

```
// changes and additions to the
// preceding example's source
vtkActor *spikeActor2 = vtkActor::New();
  spikeActor2->SetMapper(spikeMapper);

spikeActor2->SetPosition(0,-0.7,0);
sphereActor2->SetPosition(0,-0.7,0);

ren1->AddActor(sphereActor2);
ren1->AddActor(spikeActor2);

// zoom in a little
ren1->GetActiveCamera()->Zoom(1.5);

renWin->SetSubFrames(21);

for (i = 0; i <= 1.0; i = i + 0.05)
  {
  spikeActor2->RotateY(2);
  sphereActor2->RotateY(2);
  renWin->Render();
  }

iren->Start();
```

Figure 7–34 Example of motion blur (`MotBlur.cxx`).

Focal Depth

Now we will change the previous example to illustrate focal depth. First, we change the position of the bottom mace, moving it farther away from us. Since it is farther away it will appear smaller, so we scale it by a factor of two to maintain reasonable image size. We then remove the code for rendering the subframes and instead set the number of frames for focal depth rendering. We also set the camera's focal point and focal disk to appropriate values. The resulting image and the required changes to the source code are shown in Figure **7–35**.

7.19 Chapter Summary

Alpha opacity is a graphics method to simulate transparent objects. Compositing is the process of blending translucent samples in order. Alpha compositing requires the data to be ordered properly.

  Texture mapping is a powerful technique to introduce additional detail into an image without extensive geometric modelling. Applying 2D texture maps to

```
// changes and additions to the
// preceding example's source

// set the actors position and scale
spikeActor->SetPosition(0,0.7,0);
sphereActor->SetPosition(0,0.7,0);
spikeActor2->SetPosition(0,-0.7,-10);
sphereActor2->SetPosition(0,-0.7,-10);
spikeActor2->SetScale(2,2,2);
sphereActor2->SetScale(2,2,2);
```

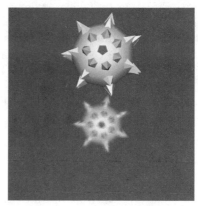

```
// zoom in a little
ren1->GetActiveCamera()->SetFocalPoint(0,0,0);
ren1->GetActiveCamera()->Zoom(4);
ren1->GetActiveCamera()->SetFocalDisk(0.05);

renWin->SetFDFrames(11);
renWin->Render();

iren->Start();
```

Figure 7–35 Example of a scene rendered with focal depth (`CamBlur.cxx`).

the surface of an object is analogous to pasting a picture. The location of the texture map is specified via texture coordinates.

Volume rendering is a powerful rendering technique to view the interior of inhomogeneous objects. Typically volume rendering is applied to structured point datasets. Volume rendering is broad in both its implementation and applications. Both image-order and object-order techniques are practiced, as well as the use of texture mapping.

Stereo rendering techniques create two separate views for the right and left eyes. This simulates binocular parallax and allows us to see depth in the image. Time multiplexed techniques alternate left and right eye views in rapid succession. Time parallel techniques display both images at the same time.

Raster devices often suffer from aliasing effects. Antialiasing techniques are used to minimize the effects of aliasing. These techniques create blended images that soften the boundary of hard edges.

By using an accumulation buffer we can create interesting effects, including motion blur and camera focus. In motion blurring we accumulate multiple renders as the actors move. To simulate camera depth, we jitter the camera position and hold its focal point constant.

Volume rendering is a powerful technique for directly viewing 3D datasets. Most volume rendering techniques can be classified as image-order or object-order, although some are a combination of the two while others do not fall into either category. Object-order techniques generally composite voxels in front to back or back to front order. Image-order techniques cast rays through pixels in the image plane to sample the volume. Other methods may traverse both the image and the volume at the same time or may operate in the frequency domain. For effective visualization of volumetric data, classification and shading are important considerations. Regions of interest may be used to reduce the amount of data visible in an image. Due to the complexity of volume rendering algorithms, efficiency and methods that allow for interactivity are critical.

7.20 Bibliographic Notes

An overview of volume rendering and volume visualization techniques can be found in a tutorial by Kaufman [Kaufman91]. Many of the volume rendering techniques discussed in this chapter are also accessible from research institutions as source code. The shear-warp algorithm is provided within the VolPack rendering library and is available on the Web at `http://www-graphics.stanford.edu/software/volpack/`. SUNY Stony Brook offers a turnkey volume visualization system called VolVis to nonprofit and government organizations. Source code and executable versions are available at `http://www.cs.sunysb.edu/~volvis`. In addition, an application called Vis5D is available that applies volume visualization techniques to time varying atmospheric weather data. Vis5D may be obtained from the Web location `http://www.ssec.wisc.edu/~billh/vis5d.html`.

For more in-depth coverage of the various computer graphics topics described in this chapter we refer you to the references in our earlier chapter on computer graphics (Chapter 3). Since these topics tend to be more obscure you will probably find that relevant papers may be more valuable.

7.21 References

[Cabral94]
B. Cabral, N. Cam, J. Foran. "Accelerated Volume Rendering and Tomographic Reconstruction Using Texture Mapping Hardware." In *Proceedings of 1994 Symposium on Volume Visualization*. pp. 91–98, October 1994.

[Cignoni96]
P. Cignoni, C. Montani, E. Puppo, R. Scopigno. "Optimal Isosurface Extraction from Irregular Volume Data." In *Proceedings of 1996 Symposium on Volume Visualization*. pp. 31–38, IEEE Computer Society Press, Los Alamitos, CA, October 1996.

[Hodges92]
L. F. Hodges. "Tutorial: Time-Multiplexed Stereoscopic Computer Graphics." *IEEE Computer Graphics & Applications*. March 1992.

[Kaufman91]
A. Kaufman (ed.). *Volume Visualization*. IEEE Computer Society Press, Los Alamitos, CA, 1991.

[Kaufman93]
A. Kaufman, R. Yagel, D. Cohen. "Volume Graphics." *IEEE Computer.* 26(7):51–64, July 1993.

[Kelly94]
M. Kelly, K. Gould, S. Winner, A. Yen. "Hardware Accelerated Rendering of CSG and Transparency." *Computer Graphics (SIGGRAPH '94).* pp. 177-184.

[Kikinis96]
R. Kikinis, M. Shenton, D. Iosifescu, R. McCarley, P. Saiviroonporn, H. Hokama, A. Robatino, D. Metcalf, C. Wible, C. Portas, R. Donnino, F. Jolesz. "A Digital Brain Atlas for Surgical Planning, Model Driven Segmentation and Teaching." *IEEE Transactions on Visualization and Computer Graphics.* 2(3), September 1996.

[Krueger91]
W. Krueger. "The Application of Transport Theory to Visualization of 3D Scalar Data Fields." *Computers in Physics.* pp. 397–406, July/August 1994.

[Lacroute94]
P. Lacroute and M. Levoy. "Fast Volume Rendering Using a Shear-Warp Factorization of the Viewing Transformation." In *Proceedings of SIGGRAPH '94.* pp. 451-458, Addison-Wesley, Reading, MA, 1994.

[Laur91]
D. Laur and P. Hanrahan. "Hierarchical Splatting: A Progressive Refinement Algorithm for Volume Rendering." In *Proceedings of SIGGRAPH '91.* 25:285–288, 1991.

[Levoy88]
M. Levoy. "Display of Surfaces from Volumetric Data." *IEEE Computer Graphics & Applications.* 8(3), pp. 29–37, May 1988.

[Shirley90]
P. Shirley and A. Tuchman. "A Polygonal Approximation to Direct Volume Rendering." *Computer Graphics.* 24(5):63–70, 1990.

[Silva96]
C. Silva, J. S. B. Mitchell, A. E. Kaufman. "Fast Rendering of Irregular Grids." In *Proceedings of 1996 Symposium on Volume Visualization.* pp. 15–22, IEEE Computer Society Press, Los Alamitos, CA, October 1996.

[Sobierajski95]
L. Sobierajski and R. Avila. "A Hardware Acceleration Method for Volumetric Ray Tracing." In *Proceedings of Visualization '95.* pp. 27–34, IEEE Computer Society Press, Los Alamitos, CA, October 1995.

[Totsuka92]
T. Totsuka and M. Levoy. "Frequency Domain Volume Rendering." *Computer Graphics (SIGGRAPH '93).* pp. 271–278, August 1993.

[Westover90]
L. Westover. "Footprint Evaluation for Volume Rendering." *Computer Graphics (SIGGRAPH '90).* 24(4):36, 1990.

[Wilhelms91]
J. Wilhelms and A. Van Gelder. "A Coherent Projection Approach for Direct Volume Rendering." *Computer Graphics (SIGGRAPH '91).* 25(4):275–284, 1991.

[Wilhelms96]
    J. P. Wilhelms, A. Van Gelder, P. Tarantino, J. Gibbs. "Hierarchical and Paral-
    lelizable Direct Volume Rendering for Irregular and Multiple Grids." In *Pro-
    ceedings of Visualization '96*. pp. 73ê80, IEEE Computer Society Press, Los
    Alamitos, CA, October 1996.

[Yagel92a]
    R. Yagel, D. Cohen, and A. Kaufman. "Normal Estimation in 3D Discrete
    Space." *The Visual Computer.* pp. 278–291, 1992.

[Yagel92b]
    R. Yagel and A. Kaufman. "Template-based Volume Viewing." In *Proceedings of
    Eurographics '92*. pp. 153–167, September 1992.

[Zuiderveld92]
    K. J. Zuiderveld, A. h. j. Koning, and M. A. Viergever. "Acceleration of Ray-Cast-
    ing Using 3D Distance Transforms." In *Proceedings of Visualization and Bio-
    medical Computing*, pp. 324–335, October 1992.

7.22 Exercises

7.1 In astronomy, photographs can be taken that show the movements of the
stars over a period of time by keeping the camera's shutter open. Without
accounting for the rotation of the earth, these photographs display a swirl
of circular arcs all centered about a common point. Such time lapse photog-
raphy is essentially capturing motion blur. If we tried to simulate these
images using the motion blur technique described in this chapter, they
would look different from the photographs. Why is this? How could you
change the simple motion blur algorithm to correct this?

7.2 In Figure **7–25** we show the difference between stereo rendering with two
or one view planes. If you were viewing a rectangle head-on (its surface normal parallel to your direction), what artifacts would be introduced by rendering onto one view plane while using the equations for two planes?

7.3 On some graphics systems transparent objects are rendered using a technique called screen door transparency. Basically, every pixel is either completely opaque or completely transparent. Any value in between is
approximated using dithering. So a polygon that was 50 percent opaque
would be rendered by drawing only half of the pixels. What visual artifacts
does this introduce? What blending problems can arise in using such a technique?

7.4 In this chapter we describe a few different techniques for antialiased rendering. One technique involved rendering a large image and then scaling it
down to the desired size using bilinear interpolation. Another technique
involved rendering multiple images at the desired size using small camera
movements and then accumulating them into a final image. When rendering a model with a surface representation, these two techniques will produce roughly the same result. When rendering a model with a wireframe

representation there will be significant differences. Why is this?

7.5   You need to create a small image of a volume dataset to include on your web page. The dataset contains 512^3 voxels, and the desired image size is 100^2 pixels. You can use a software object-order method that projects each voxel onto the image, or a software ray-casting method that casts one ray for each pixel. Assuming that identical images are created, which method would you select, and why?

7.6   Two software developers implement volume rendering methods. The first developer uses a software ray-casting approach, while the second uses a graphics hardware texture mapping approach. The grayscale images are generated and displayed on a workstation with an 8 bit frame buffer (256 levels of gray). They both use the same interpolation method and the same compositing scheme, yet the two methods produce different images even though the same number of samples from identical locations were used to generate the images. Why is this?

7.7   In the classification of some medical dataset, scalar values from 100 to 200 represent skin, 200 to 300 represent muscle and 300 to 400 represent bone. The color transfer functions define skin as tan, muscle as red, and bone as white. If we interpolate scalar value and then perform classification, what classification artifacts may appear in the image?

7.8   The normal encoding example illustrated in Figure **7–22** produced 82 indices at a recursion depth of two, which would require seven bits of storage. If we instead use a recursion depth of three, how many indices are there? How many unique vector directions does this represent? How many bits of storage does this require?

7.9   Writing an object-order back to front projection algorithm is more difficult for a perspective viewing transformation than a parallel viewing transformation. Explain why this is and draw a 2D diagram of the volume and the viewing frustum that illustrates the issues.

Color Plates

*I*n the following pages we have collected many of the black and white images in this text and reproduced them in color. Our goals are to provide you with an overview of the most common visualization algorithms, and to demonstrate their practical application.

The color plates have been organized according to the categories listed below. For each category we have included a series of color plates demonstrating important visualization concepts or techniques. These categories are as follows:

- *Computer Graphics*. In this section we demonstrate various concepts in computer graphics including surface properties, shading methods, and rendering techniques.

- *Scalar Visualization*. We show how to visualize single-valued scalar data using color mapping, a variety of contouring techniques, carpet plots, and scalar generation.

- *Vector Visualization*. Vectors are data consisting of a magnitude and direction. In this section we show how to visualize vectors using hedgehogs, warping, displacement plots, time animation, and streamlines.

- *Tensor Visualization*. Tensors can be described as n-dimensional tables. We show how to visualize 3×3 real-valued, symmetric tensors. Methods described include tensor ellipsoids and hyperstreamlines.

- *Image Processing.* Image processing is used to improve the quality of 3D visualizations. Techniques such as data smoothing, noise reduction, and segmentation are used.

- *Volume Visualization.* Three-dimensional structured datasets are often referred to as volumes. In this section we show the basic volume rendering techniques, and demonstrate important volume visualization concepts such as classification, illumination, regions of interest, and intermixing of volumes and geometry.

- *Modelling.* Modelling is a catchall category for many visualization, dataset transformation, and geometric construction algorithms. In this section we describe techniques for modelling geometry; specialized visualization methods like resampling, probing, and glyphing; operations on datasets; texture-based algorithms; and multi-dimensional visualization.

- *Applications.* Here we've collected images from the applications chapter (Chapter 13), and a few other spots throughout the text.

If any of these concepts are unfamiliar to you, or you would like additional information, please refer to the text proper. The computer graphics images are from Chapters 3 and 7. The algorithms are described in the two chapters on visualization algorithms, Chapters 6 and 9.

Part of the fun of practicing visualization is the sheer aesthetic pleasure of the image. Unlike computer graphics, the purpose of visualization is to convey information – visualizations are not necessarily physically realistic or artful. But despite this quality, visualizations are beautiful anyway, mostly due to the fact that they are eminently useful. To better appreciate these images, you may wish to reflect on the size and complexity of the underlying data. The true value of these images is based on their ability to communicate information in a clear and simple manner.

We hope you enjoy these images.

Computer Graphics. Computer graphics is the foundation of data visualization. From a practical point of view, visualization techniques transform data into graphics primitives. The methods of computer graphics are then used to create the final images.

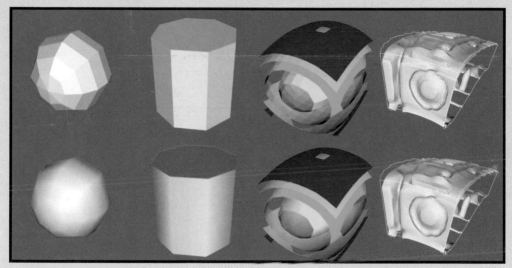

Plate 1   Flat and Gouraud shading. Different shading methods can dramatically improve the look of an object represented with polygons. On the top, flat shading uses a constant surface normal across each polygon. On the bottom, Gouraud shading interpolates colors from polygon vertices to give a smoother look.

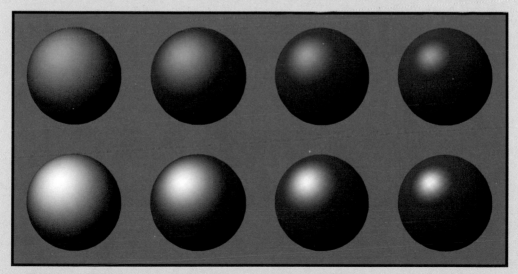

Plate 2   Effects of specular coefficients. Specular coefficients control the apparent "shininess" of objects. The top row has a specular intensity value of 0.5; the bottom row 1.0. Along the horizontal direction the specular power changes. The values (from left to right) are 5, 10, 20, and 40.

Plate 3   Camera movement centered at the focal point. The plate to the right shows some common camera movements. Azimuth is rotation around the view up vector. Elevation is rotation around the vector defined as the cross product between the projection and view up vectors. Roll is a rotation around the view plane normal, which is typically parallel to the projection vector.

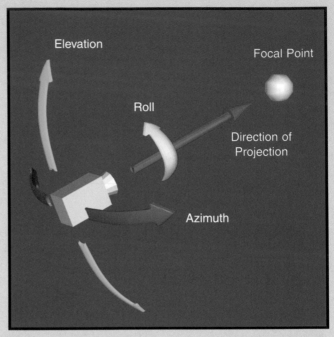

Plate 4   Camera movement centered at the camera position. Yaw is a rotation of the camera around the view up vector. Roll is a rotation around the view plane normal. Pitch is a rotation around the vector defined by the cross product between the view up vector and view plane normal.

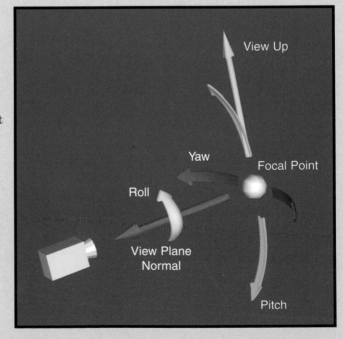

Plate 5 Simulating motion blur. Rapidly moving objects appear blurry when recorded on film or video-tape. This effect is due to object motion in the brief instant that the image is recorded. To simulate motion blur with a computer camera, multiple images (or subframes) can be accumulated and averaged. This figure was generated by accumulating 21 subframes.

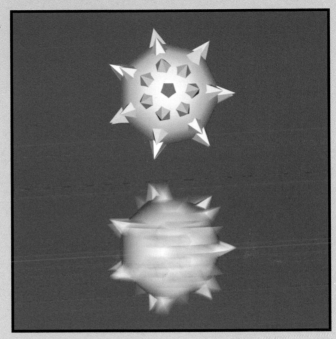

Plate 6 Simulating focal blur. Another common camera effect is blurring due to focal depth. This can be simulated with a computer camera by accumulating many subframes while the camera is jittered about its focal point. (These motions are small combinations of elevation and azimuth.) In this image the focal point is fixed on the near object, and 11 frames are accumulated. As a result, the far object appears out of focus.

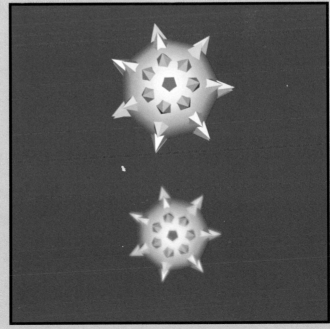

Plate 7   Texture mapping. Texture mapping is a simple but highly effective method of introducing image detail without the complexity of geometric modelling. A texture map can be thought of as a photograph pasted on the surface of an object. The location and orientation of the texture map is controlled by assigning texture coordinates at the vertices defining the surface. In this image a masonry texture map is applied to a single polygon to yield the detailed image shown.

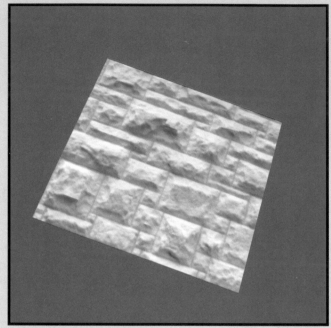

Plate 8   Red-blue stereo pair. The principle of stereo imaging is that each eye is presented with a slightly different view of the same object. (The idea is to simulate the parallax we naturally experience when looking through our two eyes.) To see this object in stereo, you must have a pair of special glasses with the left lens red and the right lens blue. The colored lenses act as filters so that the left and right eyes see only a portion of the image. The visual system then assembles the view into a stereo image.

Instances of `vtkRenderWindow`

Instances of `vtkRenderer`

One `vtkCamera` defines the view for each renderer

One or more `vtkLight`'s illuminate the scene

Instances of `vtkActor`

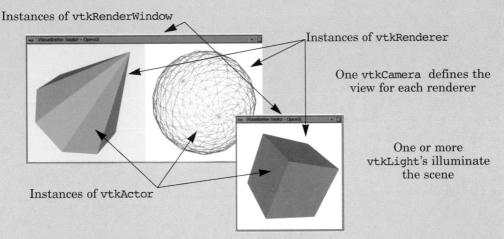

Plate 9   The **vtk** graphics model is intuitive for most users. One or more renderers draw into a rendering window. Actors, lights, and a camera are associated with each renderer. Actors refer to mappers, which represent and map geometry into the graphics hardware. Actors also refer to a transformation matrix and property object. One important feature of the graphics model is that it is independent of the underlying graphics hardware and windowing system; thus an application can be easily ported to other systems.

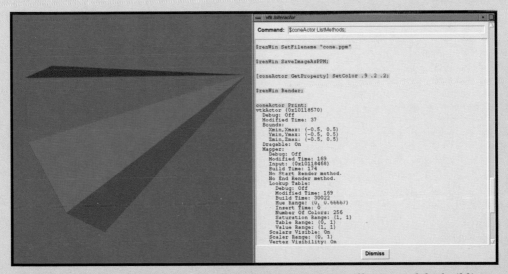

Plate 10   Tcl interpreter. The **vtk** C++ class library is an effective tool for building compiled software applications. However, interpreted languages such as Tcl offer the advantage of rapid application development since no compilation or object linking is required. The *Visualization Toolkit* includes a Tcl/Tk interpreted application. Tk is a simple language for creating user interfaces. A simple example with a rendering window and interpreter user interface is shown above.

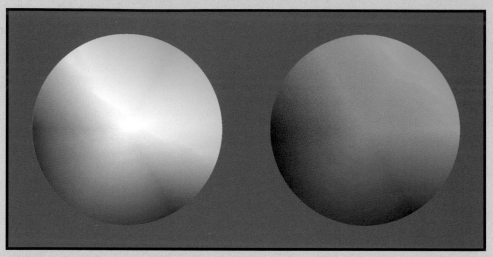

Plate 11   HSV (Hue-Saturation-Value) color space. Two slices through the HSV color space are shown. In both disks, the distance from the center corresponds to saturation, ranging from zero to one. The angle of rotation represents the hue, with red along the x-axis and increasing counterclockwise. Each disk has a fixed color value. The disk on the left has a value of one; the disk on the right has a value of 0.5.

Plate 12   Colors used to indicate elevation. This terrain data in the vicinity of Honolulu, Hawaii, has been color-coded to show change in elevation. This is an example of a simple but effective scalar visualization technique called color mapping. In this case the scalar we are visualizing is the height above sea level. This example points to an important difference between computer graphics and visualization. In visualization we associate features of the image with data values. In graphics, we create images based on a specification for geometry, surface properties, lighting, and camera position.

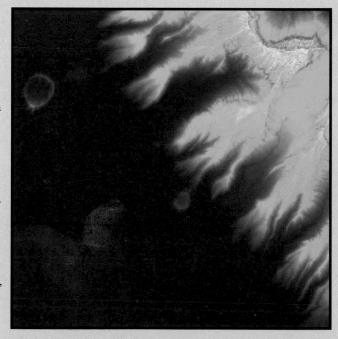

Scalar Visualization. Scalars are single-valued data items. Examples of scalar data include pressure, temperature, or X-ray intensity. Scalar data is the simplest and most common form of visualization data.

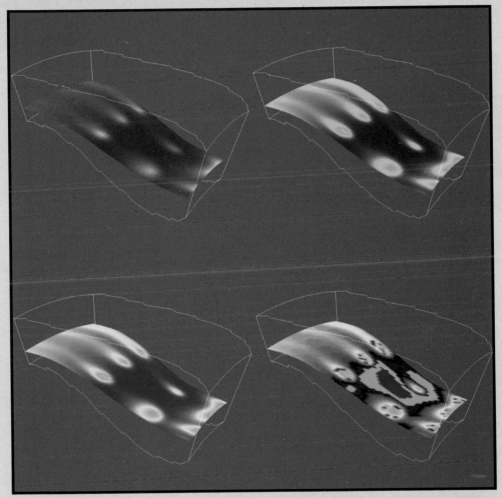

Plate 13   Comparison of four color maps in a combustion chamber. Effective color mapping requires careful selection of a color lookup table or transfer function. This selection requires sensitivity to the qualities of human perception, plus any special features in the data itself. The image in the upper left uses a gray-scale lookup table. The image in the upper right uses a blue to red rainbow table. The lower left image uses a red to blue table. The final image uses a special table designed to accentuate transitions in the data. The data shown is flow density.

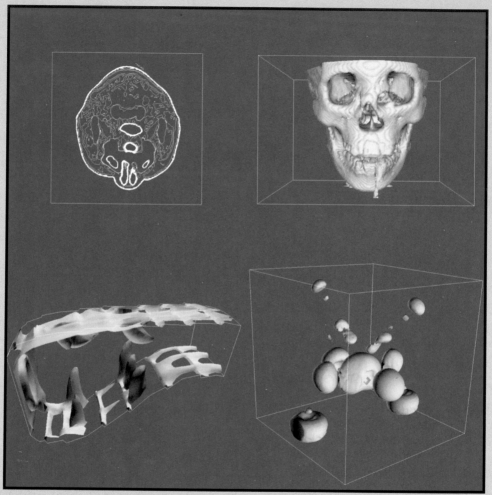

Plate 14   Applications of contouring. Contouring is one of the most important and widely used visualization techniques. Contouring is used to generate lines of constant scalar value in 2D (isolines) and isosurfaces in 3D. The contour lines in the upper left were generated from medical slice data. The isosurface in the upper right was generated from a series of slices (i.e., a volume) using the marching cubes isosurface algorithm. The lower left image shows an isosurface of flow density. The lower right image is an isosurface from a high potential iron protein molecule.

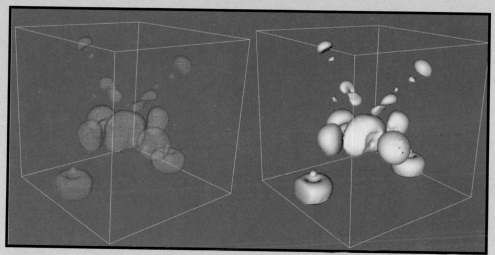

Plate 15 Dividing cubes. Dividing cubes is a contouring algorithm that represents isocontours with dense point clouds. As long as the points are generated at display resolution, the point clouds appear solid. The left image consists of 154,857 points; the right image consists of 1,917,900 points.

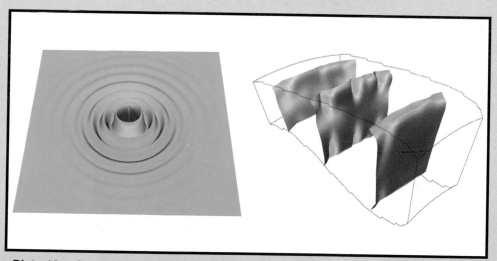

Plate 16 Carpet plots are another important visualization technique. These plots are typically used to visualize functions of the form $F(x,y) = z$. A plane (in the x-y plane) is distorted according to z function value. Color mapping is often used to introduce another variable into the visualization. The left image above shows the function $F(x,y) = e^{-r} \cos(10r)$. The colors indicate derivative values. The right image shows displacement of planes with flow energy. The colors also correspond to flow energy.

Vector Visualization. Vectors are data items with both a magnitude and direction. Typical examples of 3D vectors are velocity, displacement, and momentum. Vector data is especially important in computational fluid dynamics (CFD). CFD is the study of fluid flow using computers.

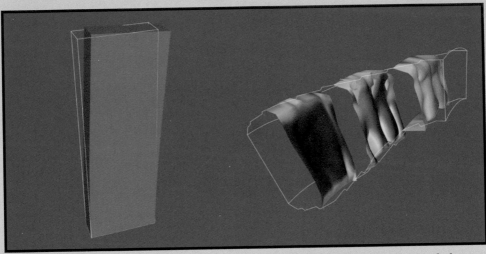

Plate 17   Warping geometry with vector data. The left image shows a simple beam deformed with displacement vectors. The wireframe outline represents the undeformed configuration. On the right, planes are deformed with flow velocity. The color map depicts flow density.

Plate 18   Displacement plot in combination with vector warping to visualize vibration. A displacement plot is created by computing the dot product between the vector and surface normal at each vertex. The resulting scalar value is color mapped to indicate relative surface motion. Red areas are moving in the direction of the surface normal – blue areas in the opposite direction. Black areas indicate little or no motion in the direction of the surface normal. These black regions are similar to nodal lines used to visualize modes of vibration. The vibration mode shown here is the second torsional.

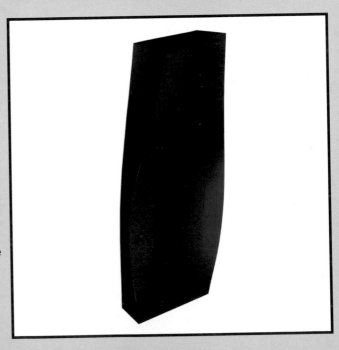

Plate 19 Hedgehogs of blood flow in the human carotid arteries. Hedgehogs are created by placing a line in the direction of the vector at a particular point. The line is also scaled proportionally to the vector magnitude. Scalar data is often used to color the line. In 2D and for small numbers of 3D vectors, hedgehogs are quite effective. For greater numbers of vectors, such as the image shown here, it is difficult to see which direction the line is pointing and to distinguish information in the resulting visual clutter. This MRI data has been specially acquired to determine tissue density as well as blood velocity.

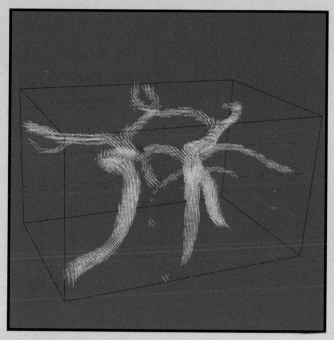

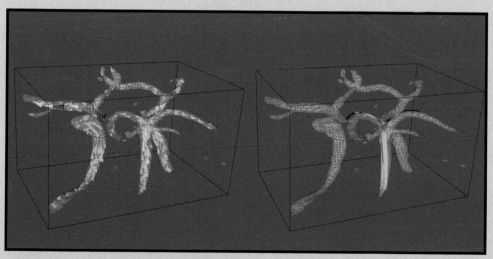

Plate 20 3D vector glyphs and streamtubes in the human carotid arteries. The cone glyphs in the left image clearly indicate vector direction, but small numbers must be used for visual clarity. A natural extension of hedgehogs is to connect the line segments (via a numerical integration technique) into extended lines, or as shown on the right, thick lines or tubes.

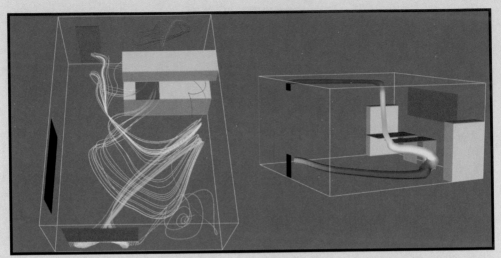

Plate 21 Examples of streamlines and streamtubes. On the left, streamlines are computed from a CFD analysis of ventilation in a small kitchen. The streamlines are color mapped with air pressure data. Thirty streamlines are initiated under a window and allowed to travel through the kitchen. On the right, a single streamtube is initiated in an office near a ventilation duct. The streamtube travels through the office and exits through an exhaust duct at top. The radius of the tube varies according to flow velocity. Slower speeds result in fatter tubes; larger speeds result in thinner tubes. (Data courtesy Dr. L. Besse, ETH, Zurich.)

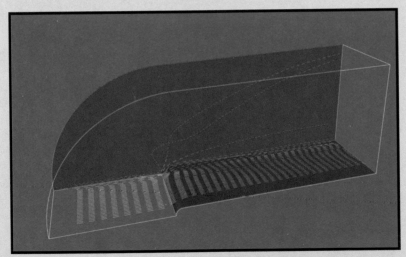

Plate 22 Dashed streamlines. More than two dozen streamlines are initiated upstream of a blunt fin projecting into a moving air stream. Each dash is of equal length measured in units of time. As a result, longer dashes are in regions of higher velocity.

Tensor Visualization. General tensors can be described as *n*-dimensional tables. Recent research has focused on visualizing 3 x 3 real-valued, symmetric matrices. These types of tensors are found in the study of materials (both solid and liquid). Examples include strain and stress tensors.

Plate 23   Tensor ellipsoids. The eigenvectors of a 3 x 3 real symmetric matrix define the axes of an ellipsoid. The length of the axes is determined by the eigenvalues. In stress analysis, these axes are the principle axes of stress. In this example a single point load is applied to an elastic material, resulting in singular stress and strain values. At the surface of the material the ellipsoids flatten because there is no stress perpendicular to the surface. Near the singularity the ellipsoids elongate and point in the direction of the load point.

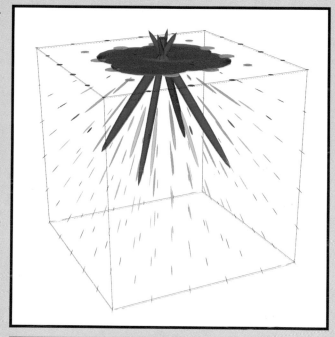

Plate 24   Hyperstreamlines. The tensor eigenvectors define three perpendicular vector fields corresponding to the major, medium, and minor eigenvalues. One of these fields is used to generate a streamline. The other two fields control the cross-section of an ellipse that is swept along the streamline. In this example, the hyperstreamlines flare as they approach the stress singularity. A plane is also shown to show the symmetric nature of the stress field. The plane is colored by effective stress and uses a different lookup table then the hyperstreamlines.

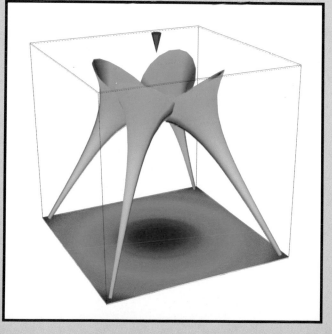

Image Processing. Image processing is typically used to improve the appearance of or to extract information from an image. In visualization, imaging is applied to remove noise, smooth data, identify segmented regions, and perform morphological operations such as erosion and dilation.

Plate 25 Image processing algorithms used to highlight regions of high gradient magnitude. In this CT cross section of the human head, color saturation represents the magnitude of the gradient, and color hue represents gradient direction. The color value is constant.

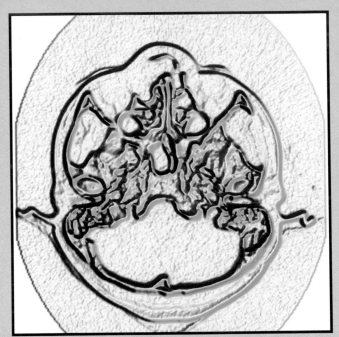

Plate 26 Image algorithms used to smooth data. On the left, contouring is applied to create an isosurface of a frog brain. Because of the segmentation and sampling interval of the original physical slice data, the isosurface is highly aliased. On the right, image smoothing has been applied prior to isosurfacing. (Data courtesy Lawrence Berkeley Labs.)

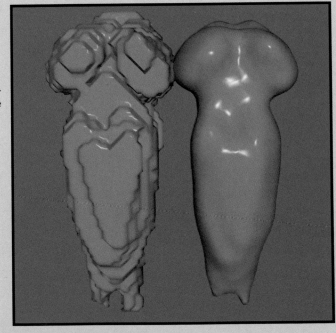

Volume Visualization. Volume rendering is a process of generating a 2D image from 3D data. The two most common volume rendering types are image-order rendering where the image is computed pixel by pixel, and object-order rendering where the volume is processed voxel by voxel to produce an image. Effective visualization of volumetric data requires a classification phase during which material properties such as color and opacity are assigned to the scalar samples within the dataset. A blending operation and an illumination model are used during rendering to combine the many samples that contribute to a single pixel in the image. Both geometry and volumes can be incorporated into an image, with clipping operations and regions of interest used to visualize internal structures.

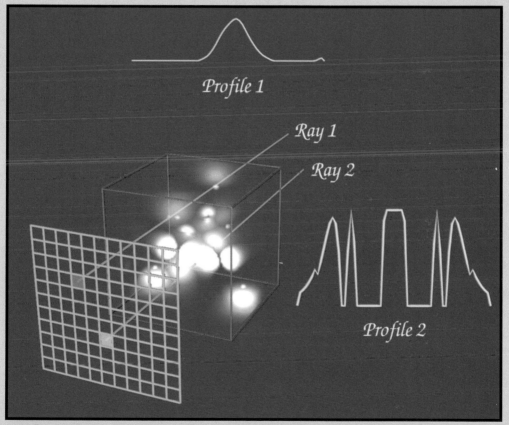

Plate 27   In image-order volume rendering rays are cast from the pixels on the image plane. The volume is sampled along the ray, and the resulting ray profile is processed by the ray function to produce a pixel value. In the above example, the ray function is a maximum intensity function that maps the highest possible value to opaque white and the lowest possible value to transparent black. Image-order ray casting is a flexible technique that can be used to visualize nearly any type of structured data. The complexity, and therefore the rendering time, for a ray casting method is dependent on the number of rays cast and the processing performed along each ray.

Plate 28   Object-order volume rendering is performed by processing the voxels within the dataset to produce an image. Graphics hardware may be utilized to improve performance. For example, if two-dimensional texture hardware is available, then axis-aligned slices of the dataset can be extracted and mapped onto polygons that are then rendered in a back-to-front order. Blending is performed in the frame buffer, and opaque geometry can easily be included in the image. Currently, precision within the frame buffer and the limited number of blending operations provided in hardware may present problems, but these will likely be improved in future hardware releases. In the example images on the right, two-dimensional texture mapped volume rendering is used to render a 256 x 256 x 225 voxel data set containing a CT scan of a human head. In the image on the top, color and opacity transfer functions are defined in order to visualize the transition from air to skin. The color transfer functions range from dark tan to light tan within the scalar values defined as soft tissue, and white within the bone. Even though no shading calculations are being performed, the darker colors specified at the lower visible scalar values of the soft tissue provide a false sense of shading in the image. Two cut planes reveal the internal structure present within this volumetric dataset. Modifying the opacity transfer function allows us to make the soft tissue more transparent, partially revealing the skull in the middle image. Further modification of the transfer functions almost entirely eliminates the soft tissue, allowing us to clearly visualize the skull in the image on the bottom.

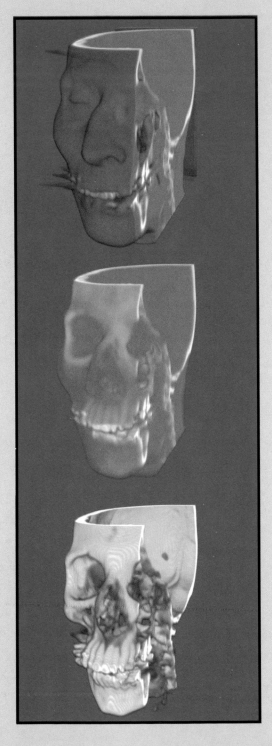

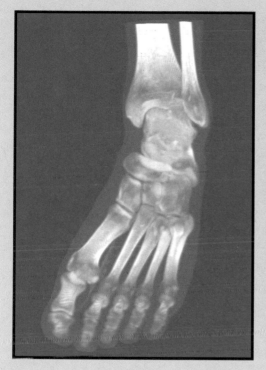

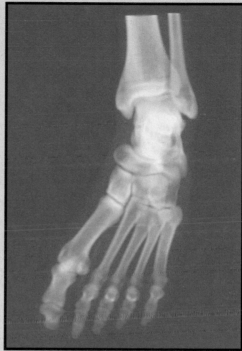

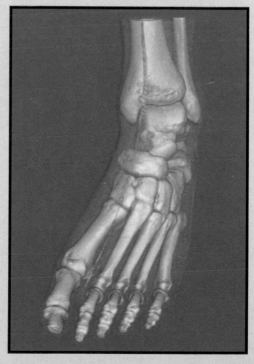

Plate 29 Scientists often visualize data using nonrealistic blending functions such as the maximum intensity projection (MIP) shown in the upper left image. This blending method has the advantage in that values in the image correspond directly to values in the volume. An alternative blending operation, alpha compositing, is shown in the upper right image. Compositing provides occlusion cues that can help in understanding the structure of the dataset. An illumination model can be defined in order to provide shading effects, as shown in the lower right image. Volume gradients are used in place of surface normals for the lighting calculations. Three-dimensional shape information can be obtained from volume rendered images that incorporate shading. To effectively visualize volumetric data, multiple techniques should be used. For example, the upper left image indicates that the smaller leg bone contains higher CT values, while the lower right image shows that this smaller bone is behind the larger leg bone.

Plate 30   Classification methods can be used to segment the dataset into different materials. In this example, the skin is defined with an isosurface within the volume while color and opacity transfer functions are used to specify a range of scalar values that represent bone. The skin isosurface is extracted using a contouring technique, and is rendered as geometry. An alpha compositing ray casting method is used to render the bone, and an illumination model capturing ambient, diffuse, and specular lighting is employed. The skin isosurface is cut to reveal the bone.

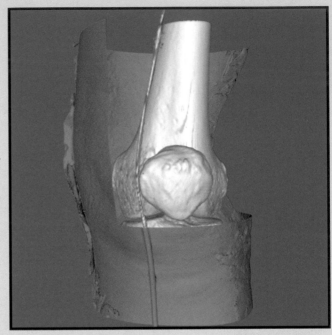

Plate 31   Color transfer functions can be used to reveal the internal distribution of scalar values within a volumetric dataset. In this example, a color transfer function that transitions from red through blue to green is used to visualize the positive wave function values in a high potential iron protein dataset. An isosurface within the negative wave function values is extracted using a contouring method and rendered using geometric primitives. The geometric isosurface is rendered with shading, while the ray casting is performed with a simple alpha compositing technique.

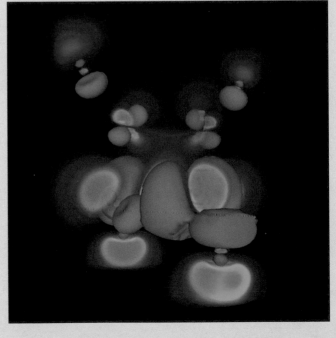

Modelling. Many visualization techniques cannot be easily classified as scalar, vector, or tensor techniques. We categorize these as modelling techniques. Examples include glyphing, resampling, and texture methods. Other algorithms are used to generate geometry or operate on data. Implicit modelling, calculating surface normals, polygon reduction, and data extraction are typical examples. We also classify these as modelling techniques.

Plate 32 Examples of source objects that procedurally generate polygonal models. These nine images represent some of the capability of the *Visualization Toolkit*. From upper left in reading order: sphere, cone, cylinder, cube, plane, text, random point cloud, disk (with or without holes), and line source. More complex geometry can be read from CAD or other modelling systems via reader objects.

Plate 33 Implicit modelling used to construct geometric objects. Implicit modelling employs functions of the form $F(x,y,z) = c$, where c is a constant. These so-called implicit functions can be sampled on a regular grid (i.e., a volume) and then rendered with surface or volume rendering techniques. Moreover, it is easy to combine these functions using boolean operations such as union, intersection, and difference. This ice cream cone was generated using a cone clipped with two planes and a sphere intersected with another sphere. An isosurface was then extracted with marching cubes by choosing a value for the constant c.

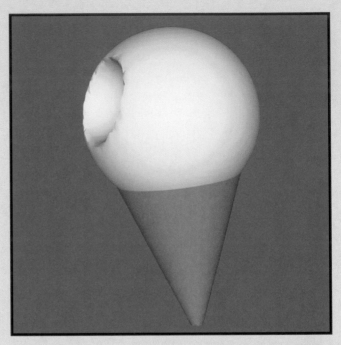

Plate 34 Implicit functions can also be used to select data. In this example, two ellipsoidal quadric functions are joined in a boolean operation and then used to select a subsample of the original volume data. The extracted voxel data (shown colored and slightly shrunk) is much smaller in size than the original dataset. Thus, data in important regions can be selected and processed much faster than if the whole dataset was processed.

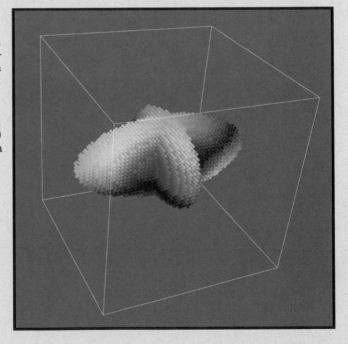

Plate 35   Implicit modelling based on distance function. Implicit models can be created by methods other than implicit functions. In this example, the lines (shown in purple) spell the word "HELLO." Then, for each point in a volume, a distance function to the line segments are computed. An offset surface at a specified distance from the lines is then extracted using marching cubes. The offset surface is shown in translucent red.

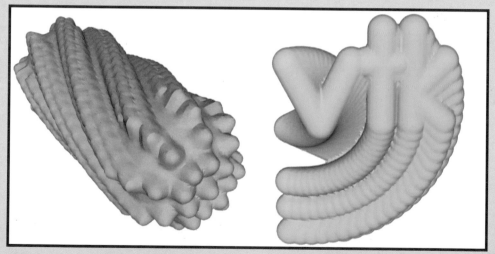

Plate 36   Implicit modelling used to create swept surfaces. The method described in the previous plate is combined with the boolean union operation as a part moves through a volume. In the left image, a mace is translated and rotated to create the swept surface shown. In the right, the letters "vtk" are rotated and translated to create the swept **vtk**. The bumps in the surface can be eliminated by choosing a smaller step size.

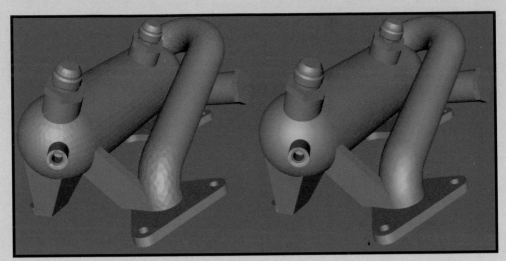

Plate 37   Generating surface normals. Geometry in graphics systems is often represented with polygons. To achieve smooth shading (compared to a faceted look), surface normals at the vertices of polygons are required. These images show how computed surface normals improve the rendered appearance.

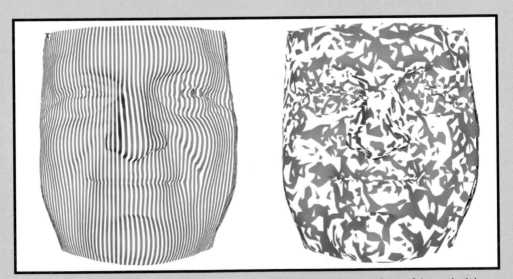

Plate 38   Creating triangle strips. Triangle strips are a type of graphics primitive that can be compactly stored in memory and are often faster to render. The image on the left shows a selected set of triangle strips (every other strip turned off) generated from a structured dataset. The image on the right shows a selected subset of triangle strips generated from an unstructured dataset.

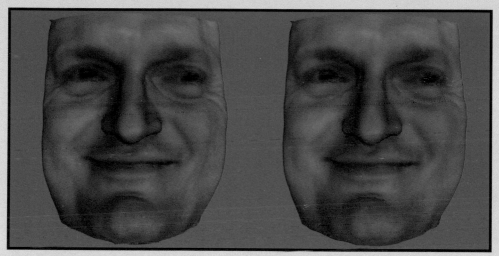

Plate 39   Decimation of a triangle mesh. Decimation is one of a family of polygon reduction techniques. These techniques aim at reducing the size of a polygonal mesh while preserving a good approximation to the original data. This example compares two triangle meshes. The one on the right has been reduced 90 percent.

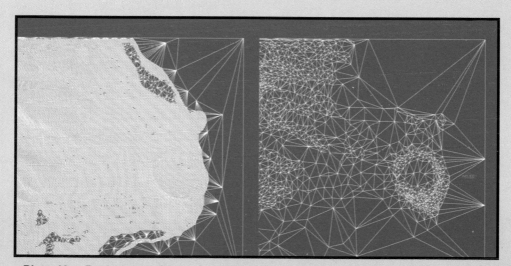

Plate 40   Decimation of digital elevation data from Honolulu, Hawaii. The mesh on the left has been reduced 31.1 percent by removing co-planar triangles (from 403,680 to 277,952 triangles). A portion of the shoreline is shown. On the right, the same area with total reduction 92.6 percent (29,525 triangles remaining). Data source Lee Moore, Webster Research Center, Xerox Corporation.

Plate 41 Glyphs used to indicate surface normals. Glyphing is one of the most versatile visualization techniques. Glyphs are often designed to show many variables simultaneously. The secret to good glyph design is a simple and intuitive relationship between data variable(s) and glyph features.

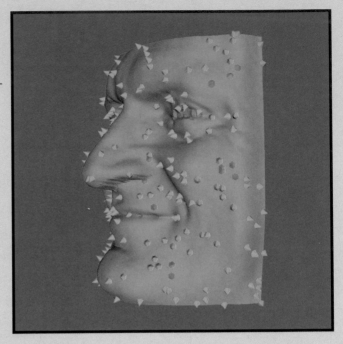

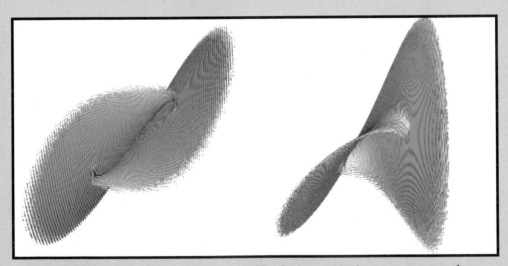

Plate 42 The Lorenz strange attractor. The Lorenz equations are expressed as a system of differential equations. These equations are numerically integrated to form a trajectory. To generate the isosurface shown, we count the number of times the trajectory passes through the voxels of a volume dataset. The isosurface value is a user-specified count value.

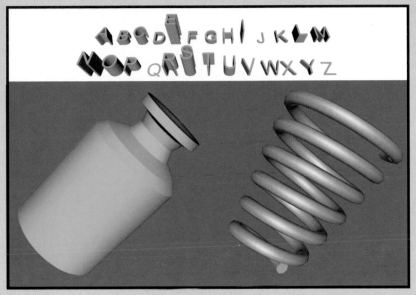

Plate 43 Linear and rotational extrusion. On the top, linear extrusion is tied to the frequency of occurrence of letters in a text document. On the bottom left, an axisymmetric bottle is created by sweeping a profile curve. On the bottom right, a spring is created by sweeping a circle while varying its sweep radius and translating it at the same time.

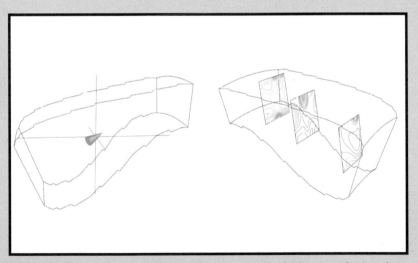

Plate 44 Probing datasets. Probing is a method of interpolating data values at one or more points. The left image shows a cone glyph oriented and sized according to vector and scalar data. The position of the cone is at the focus of the 3D cursor (shown in red). Probing is also used to resample data on a set of points. In the right image, three planes are used as probes in the original data. Contour lines (of flow density) are then generated on the sampled planes

Plate 45 Cut plane through a dataset. Cutting allows us to view data on surfaces that "pass through," or cut, a dataset. In this image, a computational surface of the structured grid dataset is shown in wireframe. A cut plane (shown as colored surface) is then used to cut through the dataset at an arbitrary position and orientation. The colors correspond to flow density. Cutting surfaces are not necessarily planes: implicit functions such as spheres, cylinders, and quadrics can also be used.

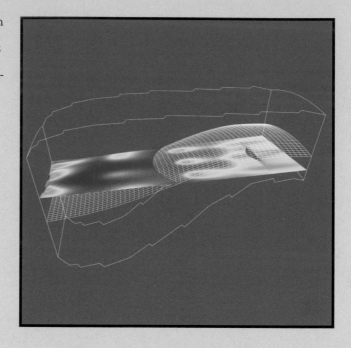

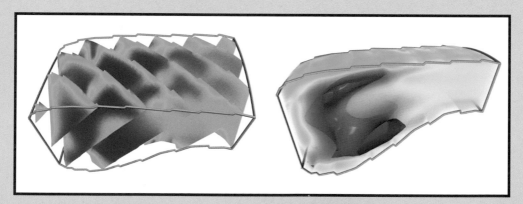

Plate 46 Unstructured volume rendering using multiple cut planes. The left figure shows eight cut planes extracted from a computational fluid dynamics dataset of a jet engine combustor. The right figure shows the effect of using 200 cut planes extracted perpendicular to the camera's view plane normal. Rendering the planes from back to front with a low opacity produces a volume rendering of the scalar field. An opaque isosurface of the density is also shown.

Plate 47 Combined contouring, clipping, cutting, and volume rendering. In the bottom figure, the CT volume is used to generate isosurfaces of the skin and bone. A sphere is used to clip away the skin to reveal the bone, and a sphere cutter is used to reveal internal structure on the surface of the cut sphere. Volume rendering is performed within the clipping sphere in the bottom pair of images. In the lower right figure, cutting is used to generate contour lines which are then wrapped with tubes. In the top two figures, clipping is used to reveal the bone structure of the human foot. In one figure, a sphere is used to clip; in the other, a set of planes. The foot data is from the Visible Human project at the National Library of Medicine. The data shown is from the Visible Woman.

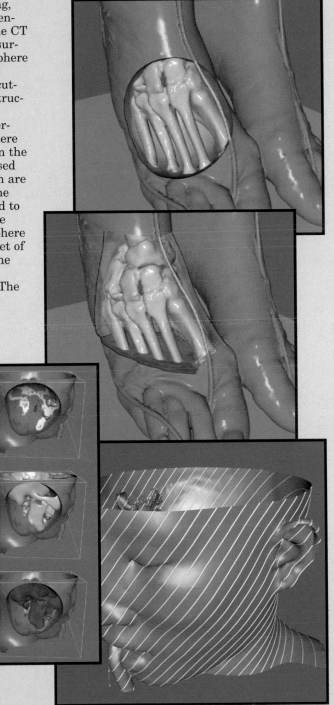

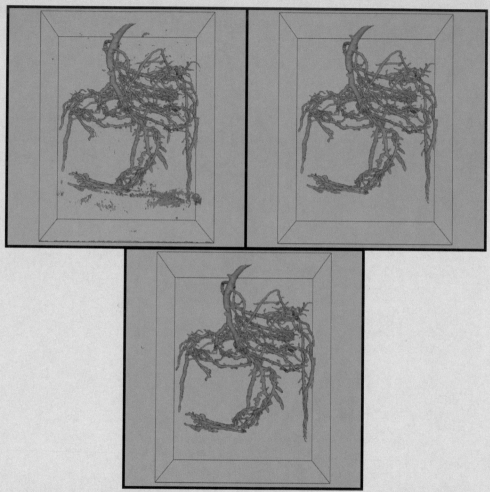

Plate 48   Connectivity and decimation used to select and reduce data. The original isosurface is generated from a 256^3 volume and consists of 351,118 triangles (shown upper left). The next image (shown upper right) has been modified by extracting the largest, topologically connected surface, resulting in 299,480 triangles. In the bottom image, decimation has been applied to reduce the mesh size to a final count of 81,111 triangles. (Data origin: J. McFall at the Center for In Vivo Microscopy at Duke University.)

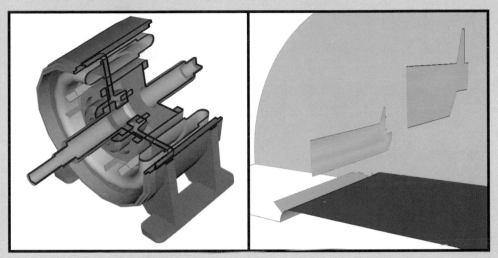

Plate 49 Texture mapping techniques. Texture maps can be used to accentuate important data characteristics or to reveal features. In the left image, the outer portions of a motor are cut away using transparent texture. In the right image, scalar data controls the application of a texture map. Portions of three planes are set transparent when their scalar values are less than a specified threshold.

Plate 50 Boolean textures. Texture maps can be subdivided into separate regions, each region corresponding to a particular data range. In this example, a 2D texture map is created consisting of opaque, transition (shown in black), and transparent regions along both the s and t texture axes. Implicit functions are used to associate a part of the sphere surface with the texture map. Different results are obtained depending on the combination of opacity and transparency for each texture map. This shows the 16 possible combinations applied to a sphere.

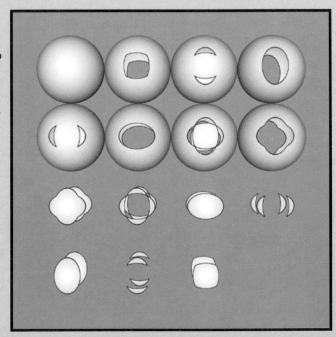

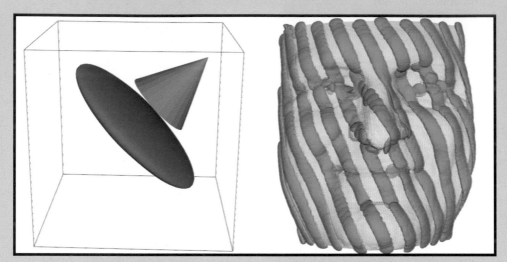

Plate 51 Splatting data to build topological structure. Each splat is a fuzzy ellipse that influences nearby regions with an exponential function. The shape of the ellipse can be controlled by vector or normal data. The size of the splat can be controlled by scalar magnitude. The left image shows a single elliptical splat (in blue) modified by a vector (shown as a cone). The right image shows a regular subsampling of points used to reconstruct a surface. The original surface is shown as a teal, wireframe mesh.

Plate 52 Visualization of multidimensional data. The splatting technique shown in the previous plate is used to visualize financial data. This data is from over 3,000 loan accounts. For each account there are six different variables. The axes in this example are monthly payment, interest rate, and loan amount. The grayish surface shows the total population, while the red surfaces indicate accounts that are delinquent on loan payments. This information could be used to characterize bad credit risks.

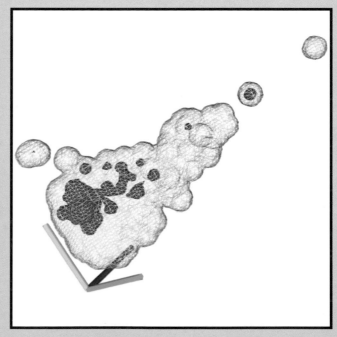

Applications. These examples represent but a few of the many possible application areas of visualization. These applications draw on many of the concepts and visualization techniques presented earlier.

Plate 53 Medical imaging. Two isosurfaces are shown corresponding to the human skin and bone. Data is from CT scan with 94 slice planes at 128^2 resolution.

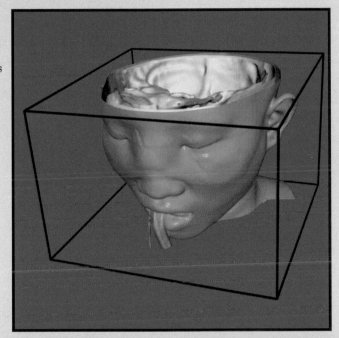

Plate 54 Medical imaging. This image shows an isosurface of the human skin plus additional image planes. Each plane is colored with a different color lookup table. The skin is rendered translucent.

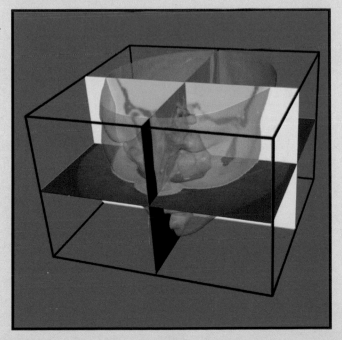

Plate 55 Visualization techniques can be used for sophisticated modeling and image generation. This image has three elements: a cow, grass and a background image. The cow was read as geometry. The grass was created by generating 100 random points on a plane and placing a geometric model of ferns with a glyph filter. A random scalar controls the height of the grass clumps. The foreground model was exported to the Renderman photo-realistic rendering system. A procedural texture generated the spots on the cow. The final foreground image was composited over a background image.

Plate 56 Photo-realistic rendering. Visualization can be used to produce models that can be rendered by sophisticated rendering systems. The bone isosurfaces were extracted from the Visible Woman's CT data. The polygonal data was exported into a Render-Man RIB file and rendered using a procedural displacement shader.

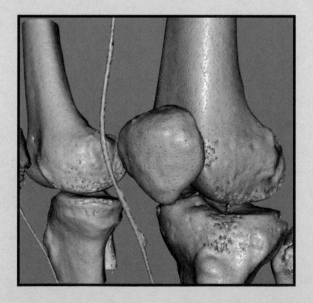

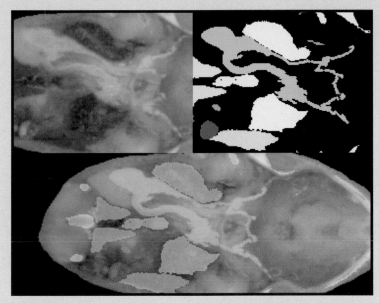

Plate 57   A segmentation map from a frog. This composite shows the original photographic image, a segmented slice, and the two slices overlayed. The data is one of 136 slices from the Virtual Frog. The data and segmentation are courtesy of Lawrence Berkeley Labs.

Plate 58   Visualization combined with photo-realistic rendering. Visualization algorithms were used to create the frog models. These models were then rendered using the RenderMan photo-realistic rendering system. The effects of the spots were created by using four different procedural shaders. A variety of effects are available using more sophisticated shaders. Procedural shaders calculate colors and shade on a pixel by pixel basis.

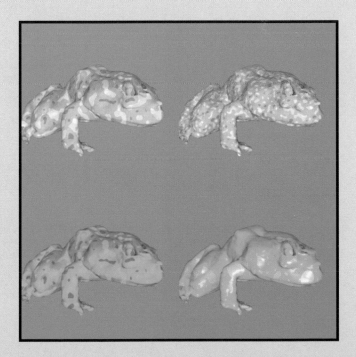

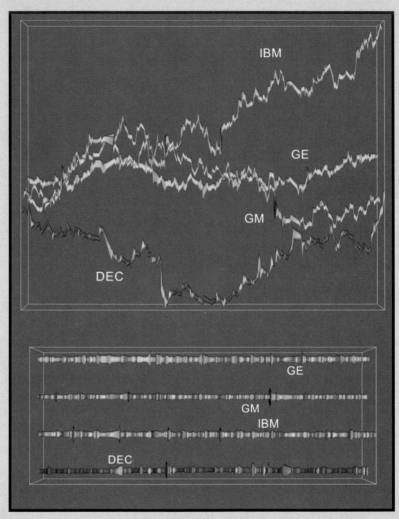

Plate 59   Financial visualization of stock market data. Typical stock value plot is extended using the third dimension. Lines have been wrapped with variable-radius tubes. Radius of tube and color correspond to trade volume. Images show front and top views.

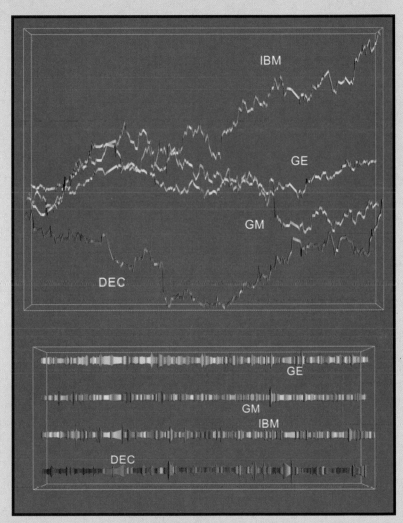

Plate 60   Financial visualization. The previous example was modified to use a constant-width ribbon (width of each plot is constant in front view). Ribbon is extruded in third direction to represent stock trade volume (shown top view).

Plate 61   Computational fluid dynamics (CFD) visualization. Portions of grid (corresponding to physical boundaries) are colored with velocity magnitude. This analysis simulates the flow of liquid oxygen over a post projecting from a flat surface. The post promotes mixing of liquid oxygen. The mesh grid lines were wrapped with tubes and the final image was generated with the RenderMan photorealistic renderer.

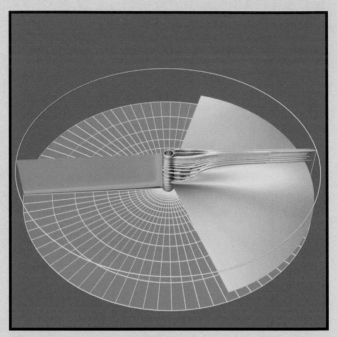

Plate 62   CFD visualization. Portions of grid are used to seed streamtubes. Notice flow vortices around post. Shadows created using RenderMan add a nice touch.

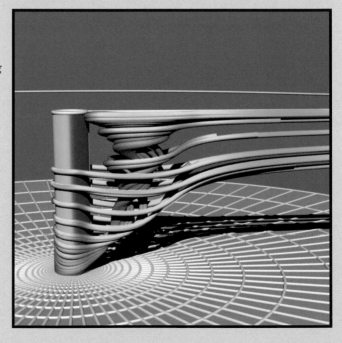

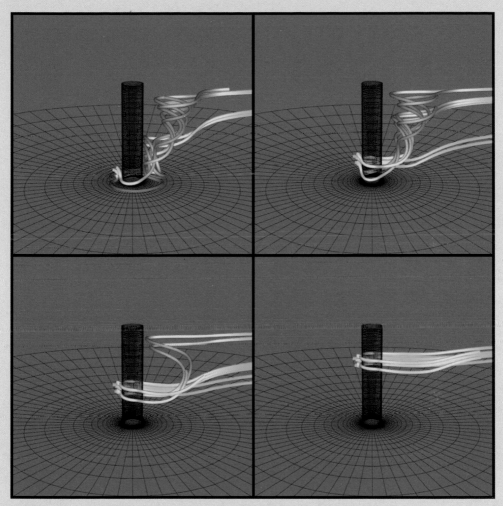

Plate 63   CFD Visualization of a vertical post in fluid flow. Four images form a sequence of streamline generation. A spherical cloud of points is used to generate the streamlines. The seed cloud is moved up along the front of the post.

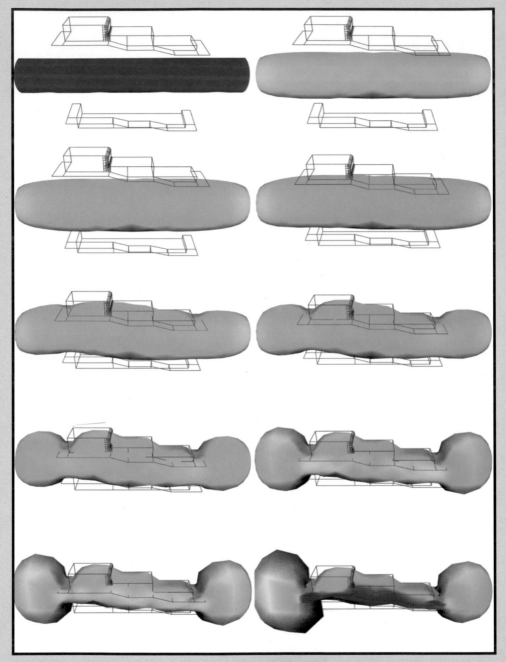

Plate 64   Finite element visualization. Ten frames from a simulated blow molding process are shown. A balloon-like plastic parison is simultaneously inflated and pressed with a die (shown in wireframe). The red color indicates thin walls; blue indicates thicker walls.

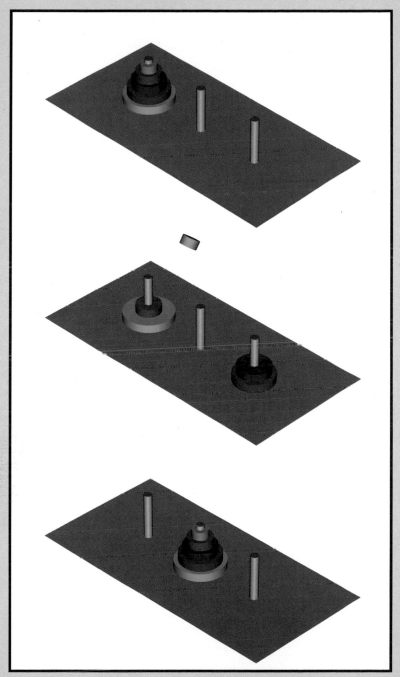

Plate 65   Algorithm visualization. Three images from "Towers of Hanoi" simulation are shown. The top image shows the starting configuration; the middle image shows an intermediate configuration; and the bottom image shows the final configuration.

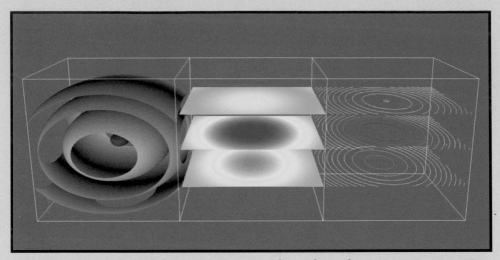

Plate 66   Visualizing the quadric $F(x,y,z) = x^2 + 2y^2 + 3z^2 + yz$ in three parts. The left part of the image shows isosurfaces $F(x,y,z) = c$. In the middle part, color mapped planes indicate function value. In the right part, contour lines illustrate regions of constant function value.

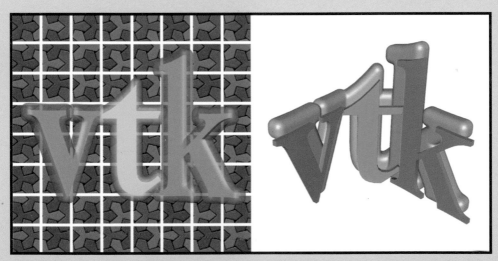

Plate 67   Implicit modelling to create stylistic logo. The original letters "v," "t," and "k" (shown in reddish hue in right image) are represented with a polygonal mesh. A structured point dataset is used to sample the distance from these letters, and an isosurface technique extracts the blobby "vtk" at a specified distance value. The left image shows a different version of the logo with a texture mapped plane whose cells have been passed through a shrink filter.

Advanced Data Representation

This chapter examines advanced topics in data representation. Topics include topological and geometric relationships and computational methods for cells and datasets.

8.1 Coordinate Systems

We will examine three different coordinate systems: the global, dataset, and structured coordinate systems. Figure **8–1** shows the relationship between the global and dataset coordinate systems, and depicts the structured coordinate system.

Global Coordinate System

The global coordinate system is a Cartesian, three-dimensional space. Each point is expressed as a triplet of values (x,y,z) along the x, y, and z axes. This is the same system that was described in Chapter 3 (see "Coordinate Systems" on page 49).

The global coordinate system is always used to specify dataset geometry (i.e., the point coordinates), and data attributes such as normals and vectors. We will use the word "position" to indicate that we are using global coordinates.

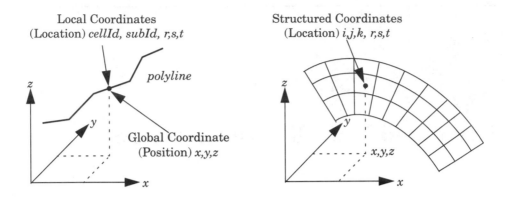

Figure 8–1 Local and global coordinate systems.

Dataset Coordinate System

The dataset, or local, coordinate system is based on combined topological and geometric coordinates. The topological coordinate is used to identify a particular cell (or possibly a subcell), and the geometric coordinate is used to identify a particular location within the cell. Together they uniquely specify a location in the dataset. Here we will use the word "location" to refer to local or dataset coordinates.

The topological coordinate is an "id": a unique, nonnegative integer number referring to either a dataset point or cell. For a composite cell, we use an additional "sub-id" to refer to a particular primary cell that composes the composite cell. The sub-id is also unique and nonnegative. The id and sub-id together select a particular primary cell.

To specify a location within the primary cell, we use geometric coordinates. These geometric coordinates, or *parametric coordinates*, are coordinates "natural" or canonical to the particular topology and dimension of a cell.

We can best explain local coordinates by referring to an example. If we consider the polyline cell type shown in Figure **8–1**, we can specify the position of a point by indicating 1) the polyline cell id, 2) the primary cell (i.e., line) sub-id and 3) the parametric coordinate of the line. Because the line is one-dimensional, the natural or parametric coordinate is based on the one-dimensional parameter r. Then any point *along* the line is given by a linear combination of the two end points of the line x_i and x_{i+1}

$$x(r) = (1-r)x_i + rx_{i+1} \tag{8-1}$$

where the parametric coordinate r is constrained between (0,1). In this equation we are assuming that the sub-id is equal to i.

The number of parametric coordinates corresponds to the topological dimension of the cell. Three-dimensional cells will be characterized by the three parametric coordinates *(r, s, t)*. For cells of topological order less than three, we will ignore the last *(3 − n)* parametric coordinates, where *n* is the topological order of the cell. For convenience and consistency, we also will constrain each parametric coordinate to range between *(0,1)*.

Every cell type will have its own parametric coordinate system. Later in this chapter we will describe the parametric coordinate systems in detail. But first we will examine another coordinate system, the *structured coordinate system*.

Structured Coordinate System

Many dataset types are structured. This includes structured points and structured grids. Because of their inherent structure, they have their own natural coordinate system. This coordinate system is based on the *i-j-k* indexing scheme that we touched on in Chapter 5 (see "Structured Points" on page 128).

The structured coordinate system is a natural way to describe components of a structured dataset. By fixing some indices, and allowing the others to vary within a limited range, we can specify points, lines, surfaces, and volumes. For example, by fixing the *i* index $i = i_0$, and allowing the *j* and *k* indices to range between their minimum and maximum values, we specify a surface. If we fix three indices, we specify a point, if we fix two indices, we specify a line, and if we allow three indices to vary, we specify a volume (or sub-volume). The structured coordinate system is generally used to specify a *region of interest* (or ROI). The region of interest is an area that we want to visualize, or to operate on.

There is a simple relationship between the point and cell id of the dataset coordinate system and the structured coordinate system. To obtain a point id p_{id} given the indices (i_p, j_p, k_p) and dimensions (n_x, n_y, n_z) we use

$$p_{id} = i_p + j_p n_x + k_p n_x n_y \qquad \text{(8-2)}$$

with $0 \le i_p < n_x, 0 \le j_p < n_y, 0 \le k_p < n_z$. (We can use this id to index into an array of points or point attribute data.) This equation implicitly assumes an ordering of the points in topological space. Points along the *i* axis vary fastest, followed by the *j* and then the *k* axes. A similar relationship exists for cell id's

$$cell_{id} = i_p + j_p(n_x - 1) + k_p(n_x - 1)(n_y - 1) \qquad \text{(8-3)}$$

Here we've taken into account that there are one fewer cells along each topological axes than there are points.

8.2 Interpolation Functions

Computer visualization deals with discrete data. The data is either supplied at a finite number of points or created by sampling continuous data at a finite number of points. But we often need information at positions other than these discrete point locations. This may be for rendering or for subsampling the data during algorithm execution. We need to interpolate data from known points to some intermediate point using *interpolation functions*.

Interpolation functions relate the values at cell points to the interior of the cell. Thus, we assume that information is defined at cell points, and that we must interpolate from these points. We can express the result as a weighted average of the data values at each cell point.

General Form

To interpolate data from the cell points p_i to a point p that is inside the cell, we need three pieces of information:

1. the data values at each cell point,

2. the parametric coordinates of the point p within the cell, and

3. the cell type including interpolation functions.

Given this information, the interpolation functions are a linear combination of the data values at the cell points

$$d = \sum_{i=0}^{n-1} W_i \cdot d_i \tag{8-4}$$

where d is the data value at the interior cell location (r,s,t), d_i is the data value at the ith cell point, and W_i is a weight at the ith cell point. The interpolation weights are functions of the parametric coordinates $W_i = W(r,s,t)$. In addition, because we want $d = d_i$ when the interior point coincides with a cell point, we can place additional constraints on the weights

$$W_i = 1, W_j = 0 \text{ when } p = p_i \text{ and } i \neq j \tag{8-5}$$

We also desire the interpolated data value d to be no smaller than the minimum d_i and no larger than the maximum d_i. Thus the weights should also satisfy

$$\sum_i W_i = 1, \quad 0 \leq W_i \leq 1 \tag{8-6}$$

The interpolation functions are of a characteristic shape. They reach their maximum value $W_i = 1$ at cell point p_i, and are zero at all other points. Examining Equation **8-1**, we draw Figure **8–2** and see that each interpolation function has the shape of a peaked "hat," and that interpolation is a linear combination of these hat functions, scaled by the data value at each point.

Equation **8-4** is the general form for cell interpolation. It is used to interpolate any data value defined at the cell points to any other point within the cell. We have only to define the specific interpolation functions W_i for each cell type.

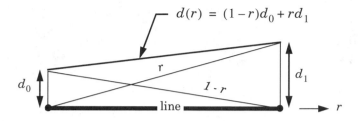

$$d(r) = (1-r)d_0 + rd_1$$

Figure 8–2 Interpolation is a linear combination of local interpolation functions. Interpolation functions are scaled by data values at cell points.

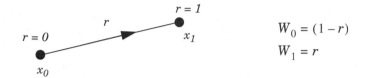

Figure 8–3 Parametric coordinate system and interpolation functions for a line.

Specific Forms

Each cell type has its own interpolation functions. The weights W_i are functions of the parametric coordinates r, s, and t. In this section we will define the parametric coordinate system and interpolation function for each primary cell type. Composite cells use the interpolation functions and parametric coordinates of their composing primary cells. The only difference in coordinate system specification between primary and composite cells is that composite cells use the additional sub-id to specify a particular primary cell.

Vertex. Vertex cells do not require parametric coordinates or interpolation functions since they are zero-dimensional. The single weighting function is $W_0 = 1$.

Line. Figure **8–3** shows the parametric coordinate system and interpolation functions for a line. The line is described using the single parametric coordinate r.

Pixel. Figure **8–4** shows the parametric coordinate system and interpolation functions for a pixel cell type. The pixel is described using the two parametric coordinates (r,s). Note that the pixel edges are constrained to lie parallel to the global coordinate axes. These are often referred to as *bilinear interpolation* functions.

Quadrilateral. Figure **8–5** shows the parametric coordinate system and interpolation functions for a quadrilateral cell type. The quadrilateral is described using the two parametric coordinates (r,s).

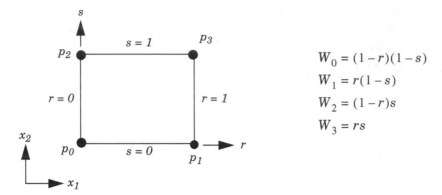

Figure 8–4 Parametric coordinate system and interpolation functions for a pixel.

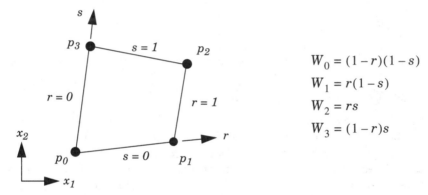

Figure 8–5 Parametric coordinate system and interpolation functions for a quadrilateral.

Triangle. Figure **8–6** shows the parametric coordinate system and interpolation functions for a triangle cell type. The triangle is characterized using the two parametric coordinates (r,s).

Polygon. Figure **8–7** shows the parametric coordinate system and interpolation functions for a polygon cell type. The polygon is characterized using the two parametric coordinates (r,s). The parametric coordinate system is defined by creating a rectangle oriented along the first edge of the polygon. The rectangle also must bound the polygon.

The polygon poses a special problem since we do not know how many vertices define the polygon. As a result, it is not possible to create general interpolation functions in the fashion of the previous functions we have seen. Instead, we use a function based on weighted distance squared from each polygon vertex.

The weighted distance squared interpolation functions work well in practice. However, there are certain rare cases where points topologically distant

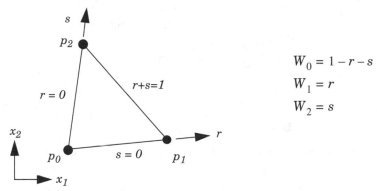

Figure 8–6 Parametric coordinate system and interpolation functions for a triangle.

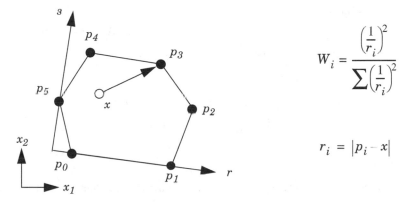

Figure 8–7 Parametric coordinate system and interpolation functions for a polygon.

from the interior of a polygon have an undue effect on the polygon interior (Figure **8–8**). These situations occur only if the polygon is concave and wraps around on itself.

Tetrahedron. Figure **8–9** shows the parametric coordinate system and interpolation functions for a tetrahedron cell type. The tetrahedron is described using the three parametric coordinates (r,s,t).

Voxel. Figure **8–10** shows the parametric coordinate system and interpolation functions for a voxel cell type. The voxel is described using the three parametric coordinates (r,s,t). Note that the voxel edges are constrained to lie parallel to the global coordinate axes. These are often referred to as *trilinear interpolation* functions.

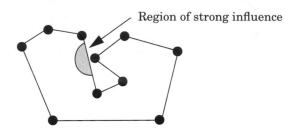

Figure 8–8 Potential problem with distance-based interpolation functions.

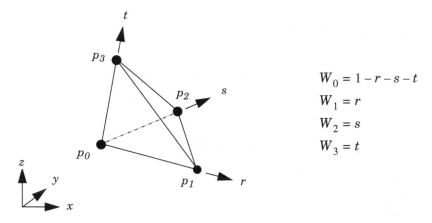

$$W_0 = 1 - r - s - t$$
$$W_1 = r$$
$$W_2 = s$$
$$W_3 = t$$

Figure 8–9 Parametric coordinate system and interpolation functions for a tetrahedron.

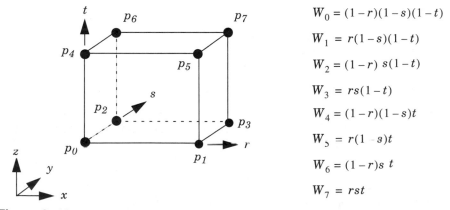

$$W_0 = (1-r)(1-s)(1-t)$$
$$W_1 = r(1-s)(1-t)$$
$$W_2 = (1-r)\,s(1-t)$$
$$W_3 = rs(1-t)$$
$$W_4 = (1-r)(1-s)t$$
$$W_5 = r(1-s)t$$
$$W_6 = (1-r)s\,t$$
$$W_7 = rst$$

Figure 8–10 Parametric coordinate system and interpolation functions for a voxel.

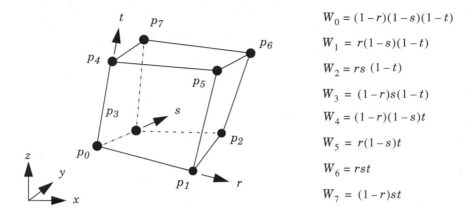

$$W_0 = (1-r)(1-s)(1-t)$$

$$W_1 = r(1-s)(1-t)$$

$$W_2 = rs\,(1-t)$$

$$W_3 = (1-r)s(1-t)$$

$$W_4 = (1-r)(1-s)t$$

$$W_5 = r(1-s)t$$

$$W_6 = rst$$

$$W_7 = (1-r)st$$

Figure 8–11 Parametric coordinate system and interpolation functions for a hexahedron.

Hexahedron. Figure **8–11** shows the parametric coordinate system and interpolation functions for a hexahedron cell type. The hexahedron is described using the three parametric coordinates (r,s,t).

8.3 Coordinate Transformation

Coordinate transformation is a common visualization operation. This may be either transformation from dataset coordinates to global coordinates, or global coordinates to dataset coordinates.

Dataset to Global Coordinates

Transforming between dataset coordinates and global coordinates is straightforward. We start by identifying a primary cell using the cell id and sub-id. Then the global coordinates are generated from the parametric coordinates by using the interpolation functions of Equation **8-4**. Given cell points $p_i = p_i(x_i, y_i, z_i)$ the global coordinate p is simply

$$p = \sum_{i=0}^{n-1} W_i(r_0, s_0, t_0)p_i \tag{8-7}$$

where the interpolation weights W_i are evaluated at the parametric coordinate (r_0, s_0, t_0).

 In the formulation presented here, we have used the same order interpolation functions for both data and cell geometry. (By order we mean the polynomial degree of the interpolating polynomials.) This is termed *iso-parametric* interpolation. It is possible to use different interpolation functions for geometry and data. *Super-parametric* interpolation is used when the order of the interpolation functions for geometry is greater than those used for data. *Sub-parametric* interpolation is used when the order of the interpolation functions for geometry is less than those used for data. Using different interpolation functions is commonly used in numerical analysis techniques such as the finite element method. We will always use the iso-parametric interpolation for visualization applications.

Global to Dataset Coordinates

Global to dataset coordinate transformations are expensive compared to dataset to global transformations. There are two reasons for this. First, we must identify the particular cell C_i that contains the global point p. Second, we must solve Equation **8-4** for the parametric coordinates of p.

To identify the cell C_i means doing some form of searching. A simple but inefficient approach is to visit every cell in a dataset and determine whether p lies inside any cell. If so, then we have found the correct cell and stop the search. Otherwise, we check the next cell in the list.

This simple technique is not fast enough for large data. Instead, we use accelerated search techniques. These are based on spatially organizing structures such as an octree or three-dimensional hash table. The idea is as follows: we create a number of "buckets," or data place holders, that are accessed by their location in global space. Inside each bucket we tag all the points or cells that are partially or completely inside the bucket. Then, to find a particular cell that contains point p, we find the bucket that contains p, and obtain all the cells associated with the bucket. We then evaluate inside/outside for this abbreviated cell list to find the single cell containing p. (See "Searching" on page 325 for a more detailed description.)

The second reason that global to dataset coordinate transformation is expensive is because we must solve the interpolation function for the parametric coordinates of p. Sometimes we can do this analytically, but in other cases we must solve for the parametric coordinates using numerical techniques.

Consider the interpolation functions for a line (Figure **8–2**). We can solve this equation exactly and find that

$$r = \frac{(x - x_0)}{(x_1 - x_0)} = \frac{(y - y_0)}{(y_1 - y_0)} = \frac{(z - z_0)}{(z_1 - z_0)} \qquad \textbf{(8-8)}$$

Similar relations exist for any cell whose interpolation functions are linear combinations of parametric coordinates. This includes vertices, lines, triangles, and tetrahedra. The quadrilateral and hexahedron interpolation functions are nonlinear because they are products of linear expressions for the parametric coordinates. As a result, we must resort to numerical techniques to compute global to dataset coordinate transformations. The interpolation functions for pixels and voxels are nonlinear as well, but because of their special orientation with respect to the *x, y,* and *z* coordinate axes, we can solve them exactly. (We will treat pixel and voxel types in greater depth in "Special Techniques for Structured Points" on page 329.)

To solve the interpolation functions for parametric coordinates we must use nonlinear techniques for the solution of a system of equations. A simple and effective technique is Newton's method [Conte72].

To use Newton's method we begin by defining three functions for the known global coordinate $p = p(x,y,z)$ in terms of the interpolation functions $W_i = W_i(r,s,t)$

$$
\begin{aligned}
f(r, s, t) &= 0 = x - \sum_i W_i x_i \\
g(r, s, t) &= 0 = y - \sum_i W_i y_i \\
h(r, s, t) &= 0 = z - \sum_i W_i z_i
\end{aligned}
\tag{8-9}
$$

and then, expanding the functions using a Taylor's series approximation,

$$
\begin{aligned}
f &= 0 = f_0 + \frac{\partial f}{\partial r}(r - r_0) + \frac{\partial f}{\partial s}(s - s_0) + \frac{\partial f}{\partial t}(t - t_0) + \dots \\
g &= 0 = g_0 + \frac{\partial g}{\partial r}(r - r_0) + \frac{\partial g}{\partial s}(s - s_0) + \frac{\partial g}{\partial t}(t - t_0) + \dots \\
h &= 0 = h_0 + \frac{\partial h}{\partial r}(r - r_0) + \frac{\partial h}{\partial s}(s - s_0) + \frac{\partial h}{\partial t}(t - t_0) + \dots
\end{aligned}
\tag{8-10}
$$

we can develop an iterative procedure to solve for the parametric coordinates. This yields the general form

$$
\begin{bmatrix} r_{i+1} \\ s_{i+1} \\ t_{i+1} \end{bmatrix}
=
\begin{bmatrix} r_i \\ s_i \\ t_i \end{bmatrix}
-
\begin{bmatrix}
\dfrac{\partial f}{\partial r} & \dfrac{\partial f}{\partial s} & \dfrac{\partial f}{\partial t} \\[2mm]
\dfrac{\partial g}{\partial r} & \dfrac{\partial g}{\partial s} & \dfrac{\partial g}{\partial t} \\[2mm]
\dfrac{\partial h}{\partial r} & \dfrac{\partial h}{\partial s} & \dfrac{\partial h}{\partial t}
\end{bmatrix}^{-1}
\begin{bmatrix} f_i \\ g_i \\ h_i \end{bmatrix}
\tag{8-11}
$$

Fortunately, Newton's method converges quadratically (if it converges) and the interpolation functions that we have presented here are well behaved. In practice, Equation **8-11** converges in just a few iterations.

8.4 Computing Derivatives

Interpolation functions enable us to compute data values at arbitrary locations within a cell. They also allow us to compute the rate of change, or derivatives, of data values. For example, given displacements at cell points we can compute cell strains and stresses — or, given pressure values, we can compute the pressure gradient at a specified location.

To introduce this process, we will begin by examining the simplest case:

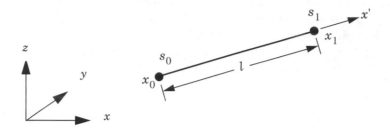

Figure 8–12 Computing derivatives in an 1D line cell.

computing derivatives in a 1D line (Figure **8–12**). Using geometric arguments, we can compute the derivatives in the r parametric space according to

$$\frac{ds}{dr} = \frac{(s_1 - s_0)}{1} = (s_1 - s_0) \tag{8-12}$$

where s_i is the data value at point i. In the local coordinate system x', which is parallel to the r coordinate system (that is, it lies along the vector $\vec{x}_1 - \vec{x}_0$), the derivative is

$$\frac{ds}{dx'} = \frac{(s_1 - s_0)}{l} \tag{8-13}$$

where l is the length of the line.

Another way to derive Equation **8-13** is to use the interpolation functions of Figure **8–3** and the chain rule for derivatives. The chain rule

$$\frac{d}{dr} = \frac{d}{dx'} \cdot \frac{d}{dr}x' \tag{8-14}$$

allows us to compute the derivative d/dx' using

$$\frac{d}{dx'} = \left(\frac{d}{dr}\right)\Big/\frac{d}{dr}x' \tag{8-15}$$

With the interpolation functions we can compute the x' derivatives with respect to r as

$$\frac{d}{dr}x' = \frac{d}{dr}\left(\sum_{i=0}^{1} W_i \cdot x'_i\right) = -x_0' + x_1' = l \tag{8-16}$$

which, when combined with Equation **8-15** and Equation **8-12** for the s derivatives, yields Equation **8-13**.

One final step remains. The derivatives in the $\vec{x}$ coordinate system must be converted to the global x-y-z system. We can do this by creating a unit vector $\vec{v}$

as

$$\vec{v} = \frac{(\vec{x}_1 - \vec{x}_0)}{|x_1 - x_0|} \tag{8-17}$$

where $\vec{x}_0$ and $\vec{x}_1$ are the locations of the two end points of the line. Then the derivatives in the x, y, and z directions can be computed by taking the dot products along the axes.

$$\frac{ds}{dx} = \left(\frac{s_1 - s_0}{l}\right)\vec{v} \cdot (1, 0, 0)$$

$$\frac{ds}{dy} = \left(\frac{s_1 - s_0}{l}\right)\vec{v} \cdot (0, 1, 0) \tag{8-18}$$

$$\frac{ds}{dz} = \left(\frac{s_1 - s_0}{l}\right)\vec{v} \cdot (0, 0, 1)$$

To summarize this process, derivatives are computed in the local r-s-t parametric space using cell interpolation. These are then transformed into a local $x' - y' - z'$ Cartesian system. Then, if the $x' - y' - z'$ system is not aligned with the global $x - y - z$ coordinate system, another transformation is required to generate the result.

We can generalize this process to three dimensions. From the chain rule for partial derivatives

$$\frac{\partial}{\partial x} = \frac{\partial}{\partial r}\frac{\partial r}{\partial x} + \frac{\partial}{\partial s}\frac{\partial s}{\partial x} + \frac{\partial}{\partial t}\frac{\partial t}{\partial x}$$

$$\frac{\partial}{\partial y} = \frac{\partial}{\partial r}\frac{\partial r}{\partial y} + \frac{\partial}{\partial s}\frac{\partial s}{\partial y} + \frac{\partial}{\partial t}\frac{\partial t}{\partial y} \tag{8-19}$$

$$\frac{\partial}{\partial z} = \frac{\partial}{\partial r}\frac{\partial r}{\partial z} + \frac{\partial}{\partial s}\frac{\partial s}{\partial z} + \frac{\partial}{\partial t}\frac{\partial t}{\partial z}$$

or after rearranging

$$\begin{bmatrix} \dfrac{\partial}{\partial r} \\[2mm] \dfrac{\partial}{\partial s} \\[2mm] \dfrac{\partial}{\partial t} \end{bmatrix} = \begin{bmatrix} \dfrac{\partial x}{\partial r} & \dfrac{\partial y}{\partial r} & \dfrac{\partial z}{\partial r} \\[2mm] \dfrac{\partial x}{\partial s} & \dfrac{\partial y}{\partial s} & \dfrac{\partial z}{\partial s} \\[2mm] \dfrac{\partial x}{\partial t} & \dfrac{\partial y}{\partial t} & \dfrac{\partial z}{\partial t} \end{bmatrix} \begin{bmatrix} \dfrac{\partial}{\partial x} \\[2mm] \dfrac{\partial}{\partial y} \\[2mm] \dfrac{\partial}{\partial z} \end{bmatrix} = J \begin{bmatrix} \dfrac{\partial}{\partial x} \\[2mm] \dfrac{\partial}{\partial y} \\[2mm] \dfrac{\partial}{\partial z} \end{bmatrix} \tag{8-20}$$

The 3×3 matrix J is called the Jacobian matrix, and it relates the parametric coordinate derivatives to the global coordinate derivatives. We can rewrite

Equation **8-20** into more compact form

$$\frac{\partial}{\partial r_i} = J \frac{\partial}{\partial x_i} \qquad\qquad (8\text{-}21)$$

and solve for the global derivatives by taking the inverse of the Jacobian matrix

$$\frac{\partial}{\partial x_i} = J^{-1} \frac{\partial}{\partial r_i} \qquad\qquad (8\text{-}22)$$

The inverse of the Jacobian always exists as long as there is a one-to-one correspondence between the parametric and global coordinate systems. This means that for any *(r, s, t)* coordinate, there corresponds only one *(x, y, z)* coordinate. This holds true for any of the parametric coordinate systems presented here, as long as pathological conditions such as cell self-intersection or a cell folding in on itself are avoided. (An example of cell folding is when a quadrilateral becomes nonconvex.)

In our one-dimensional example, the derivatives along the line were constant. However, other interpolation functions (e.g., Figure **8–5**) may yield nonconstant derivatives. Here, the Jacobian is a function of position in the cell and must be evaluated at a particular *(r, s, t)* coordinate value.

8.5 Topological Operations

Many visualization algorithms require information about the topology of a cell or dataset. Operations that provide such information are called *topological operations*. Examples of these operations include obtaining the topological dimension of a cell, or accessing neighboring cells that share common edges or faces. We might use these operations to decide whether to render a cell (e.g., render only one-dimensional lines) or to propagate particles through a flow field (e.g., traversing cells across common boundaries).

Before proceeding we need to define some terms from topology. *Manifold topology* describes a region surrounding a point that is topologically connected. That is, a region around the point is topologically equivalent to a small "disk" (in two-dimensions) or "ball" (in three-dimensions). Topology that is not manifold is termed *nonmanifold*. Examples of manifold and nonmanifold geometry are shown in Figure **8–13**.

There are some simple rules we can use to decide whether a surface or region approximated with cells is manifold or nonmanifold. In two dimensions, if every edge of a two-dimensional cell is used by exactly one other cell, than the surface is locally manifold. In three dimensions, if every face of a three-dimensional cell is used by exactly one other cell, than the region is locally manifold.

We also will use the term *simplex* on some occasions. A simplex of dimension n is the convex region defined by a set of $n+1$ independent points. A vertex, line, triangle, and tetrahedron are simplices of dimension 0, 1, 2, and 3, respectively. These are shown in Figure **8–14**.

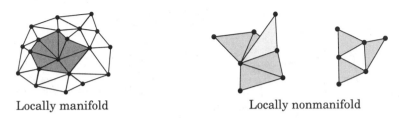

Locally manifold   Locally nonmanifold

Figure 8–13 Manifold and nonmanifold surface topology. If the local neighborhood around a vertex is topologically a 2D disk (i.e., a small disk can be placed on the surface without tearing or overlapping), then the surface is manifold at that vertex.

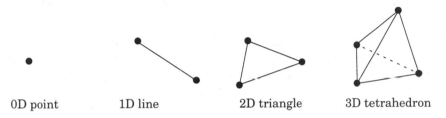

0D point   1D line   2D triangle   3D tetrahedron

Figure 8–14 Simplices of dimension three and lower.

Cell Operations

Cell operations return information about the topology of a cell. Typically, we want to know the topological order of the cell or the topology of the cell boundary.

Given a cell C_i of topological dimension d, the cell is (implicitly) composed of boundary cells of topological order $d\text{-}1$ and lower. For example, a tetrahedron is composed of four two-dimensional triangles, six one-dimensional edges, and four zero-dimensional vertices. Cell operations return information about the number of boundary cells of a particular topological dimension, as well as the ordered list of points that define each bounding cell.

Another useful cell operation returns the closest boundary cell of dimension $d\text{-}1$ given the parametric coordinates of the cell. This operation ties the geometry to the topology of the cell, as compared to the parametric coordinate system, which ties the topology to the geometry. The closest boundary cell operation is implemented by partitioning each cell into various regions, as illustrated in Figure **8–15**. To determine the closest boundary cell we need only to identify the parametric region that the point lies in, and then return the appropriate boundary cell.

Another useful cell operation is cell decomposition into simplices. Every cell can be decomposed into a collection of simplices. By doing so, and by operating on the simplex decomposition rather than the cell itself, we can create algorithms that are independent of cell type. For example, if we want to intersect two

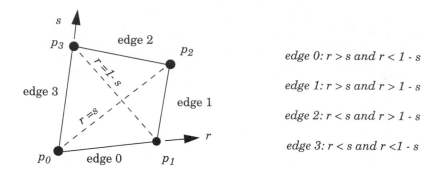

Figure 8–15 Closest boundary cell operation for quadrilateral cell.

datasets of varied cell type, without simplex decomposition we would have to create methods to intersect every possible combination of cells. With simplex decomposition, we can create a single intersection operation that operates on only the limited set of simplices. The significant advantage of this approach is that as new cells are added to the visualization system, only the cell object (including its method for simplex decomposition) must be implemented, and no other objects need be modified.

Dataset Operations

Dataset operations return information about the topology of a dataset or topological information about the adjacency of cells. Typical operations include determining the neighbors of a cell or returning a list of all cells that use a particular point.

We can formalize the adjacency operations by continuing the discussion of "Cell Types" on page 119. Adjacency methods are used to obtain information about the neighbors of a cell. A neighbor of a particular cell C_i is simply a cell that shares one or more points in common with C_i. A vertex neighbor is a neighbor that shares one or more vertices. An edge neighbor is a neighbor that shares one or more edges. A face neighbor is a cell that shares vertices that define one of the faces of the cell. Note that a face neighbor is also an edge neighbor, and an edge neighbor is also a vertex neighbor.

The adjacency operators are simple set operations. For a particular cell C_i defined by points

$$C_i = \{p_1, p_2, ..., p_n\} = P \qquad\qquad \textbf{(8-23)}$$

and a point list $\bar{P} = (\bar{p}_1, \bar{p}_2, ..., \bar{p}_n)$ with $\bar{P} \subset P$, where $\bar{P}$ typically corresponds to the points defining a boundary cell of C_i; the neighbors of C_i are the adjacency set $A(\bar{C}, \bar{P})$. The adjacency set is simply the intersection of the use sets for each point, excluding the cell C_i.

$$A(C_i, \overline{P}) = \left(\bigcap_{i=1}^{n} U(\overline{p}_i) \right) - C_i \qquad \text{(8-24)}$$

The adjacency set represents a variety of useful information. In a manifold object represented by a polyhedra, for example, each polygon must have exactly one edge neighbor for each of its edges. Edges that have no neighbors are boundary edges; edges that have more than one edge neighbor represent nonmanifold topology. Datasets that consist of three-dimensional cells (e.g., unstructured grids) are topologically consistent only if, for each cell, there is exactly one face neighbor for each face. Faces that have no neighbors are on the boundary of the dataset. More than one face neighbor implies that the neighbors are self-intersecting (in 3D space).

8.6 Searching

Searching is an operation to find the cell containing a specified point p, or to locate cells or points in a region surrounding p. Algorithms requiring this operation include streamline generation, where we need to find the starting location within a cell; probing, where the data values at a point are interpolated from the containing cell; or collision detection, where cells in a certain region must be evaluated for intersection. Sometimes (e.g., structured point datasets), searching is a simple operation because of the regularity of data. However, in less structured data, the searching operation is more complex.

To find the cell containing p, we can use the following naive search procedure. Traverse all cells in the dataset, finding the one (if any) that contains p. To determine whether a cell contains a point, the cell interpolation functions are evaluated for the parametric coordinates (r,s,t). If these coordinates lie within the cell, then p lies in the cell. The basic assumption here is that cells do not overlap, so that at most a single cell contains the given point p. To determine cells or points lying in the region surrounding p, we can traverse cells or points to see whether they lie within the region around p. For example, we can choose to define the region as a sphere centered at p. Then, if a point or the points composing a cell lie in the sphere, the point or cell is considered to be in the region surrounding p.

These naive procedures are unacceptable for all but the smallest datasets, since they are of order $O(n)$, where n is the number of cells or points. To improve the performance of searching, we need to introduce supplemental data structures to support spatial searching. Such structures are well-known and include MIP maps, octrees, kd-trees, and binary sphere trees (see "Bibliographic Notes" on page 350 at the end of this chapter).

The basic idea behind these spatial search structures is that the search space is subdivided into smaller parts, or buckets. Each bucket contains a list of the points or cells that lie within it. Buckets are organized in structured fashion so that constant or logarithmic time access to any bucket is possible. For example, if we assign a portion of 2D Euclidean space into a grid of n by m buckets, the location of p in a particular bucket can be determined with two subtractions and two divisions: a constant time access. Similarly, the location of p in a non-uniformly subdivided octree is determined in logarithmic time, since recursive insertion into octant children is required. Once the bucket is found, the search is then limited to the points or cells contained within it. In a properly designed spatial search structure, the number of points or cells in a bucket is a small portion of the total number of cells and less then a fixed value. Thus, the time to search within a bucket can be bounded by a fixed constant. The result is that introducing spatial search structures reduces search times to a maximum $O(log\ n)$, or better yet $O(n)$.

We have two options when applying spatial search structures. We may insert points into the search structure, or we may insert cells, depending on the application. There are advantages and disadvantages to both approaches. Inserting cells into buckets is not a trivial operation. In general, cells are arbitrarily oriented and shaped, and will not fit completely into a single bucket. As a result, cells often span multiple buckets. To reliably determine whether a cell is in a bucket requires geometric intersection tests, a costly operation. Another approach is to use the *bounding box* of a cell to decide which bucket(s) a cell belongs in. We only need to intersect the bounding box with a bucket to determine whether the cell may belong in the bucket. Unfortunately, even though this operation is generally fast, often cells are associated with buckets even though they may not actually lie inside them, wasting (in large models) memory resources and extra processing time.

Inserting points into a search structure is easier because points can be uniquely placed into a bucket. Inserting points also allows us to search for both points *and* cells. Cells can be found by using p to index into the appropriate bucket. The closest point(s) p_i to p are then located. Using the topological adjacency operator to retrieve the cells using points p_i, we can then search these cells for the cell containing p. This procedure must be used with caution, however, since the closest points may not be used by the cells containing p (Figure **8–16**).

8.7 Cell / Line Intersection

An important geometric operation is intersection of a line with a cell. This operation can be used to interactively select a cell from the rendering window, to perform ray-casting for rendering, or to geometrically query data.

In the *Visualization Toolkit* each cell must be capable of intersecting itself against a line. Figure **8–17** summarizes these operations for the nine primitive cell types supported by **vtk**. (Intersections on composite cells are implemented by intersecting each primitive cell in turn.)

Line/cell intersection for 0D, 1D, and 2D cells follows standard approaches. Intersection against 3D cells is difficult. This is because the surfaces of these cells are described parametrically and are not necessarily planar. For example, to

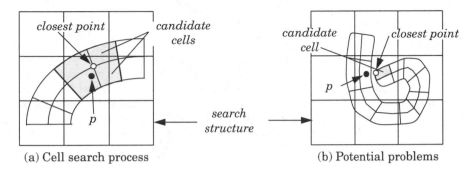

(a) Cell search process   (b) Potential problems

Figure 8–16 Using search structure (containing points) to find cells. (a) Points are associated with appropriate bucket. Point p is used to index into bucket, and closest point(s) p_i is found. Cells using p_i are evaluated for the cell containing p. (b) Sometimes closest points p_i are not used by cells containing p.

intersect a line with a tetrahedron, we can intersect the line against the four triangular faces of the tetrahedron. Hexahedron, however, may have nonplanar faces. Thus, we cannot intersect the line against six quadrilateral, planar faces. Instead, we use line/face intersection as an initial guess, and project the intersection point onto the surface of the cell. This produces an approximate result, but is accurate enough for most applications.

8.8 Scalars and Colors

There is a close correspondence between scalar data and colors. We saw this in "Color Mapping" on page 155, where we saw how to use a color table to map scalar values into a color specification (i.e., red, green, and blue, or *RGB*). There are cases, however, when we want to circumvent this mapping process. Such cases occur when color data is supplied instead of scalar data.

A common example occurs in imaging. Recall that an image is a regular, two-dimensional array of points. The points define pixels, which in turn form a two-dimensional structured points dataset. Images are frequently stored as a pair of dimensions along with data values. The data values may be one of black and white (e.g., a bitmap), grayscale, or color (e.g., a pixmap). Bitmaps and grayscale images can be directly cast into the form of single-values scalar data, and we can use our earlier approach. Pixmaps, however, consist of (at a minimum) three values per pixel of red, green, and blue. (Sometimes, a fourth alpha opacity value may also be included.) Thus, pixmaps cannot be directly cast into scalar form.

To accommodate color data, special types of scalar objects need to be created. Each class must act as if it were a scalar: that is, a request for data at a particular point must return a *single* scalar value. This allows us to use standard scalar visualization techniques such as contouring or warping. Thus a mapping

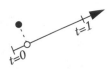 

Vertex	Line	Triangle
• project point onto ray	• 3D line intersection	• line/plane intersection
• distance to line must be within tolerance	• distance between lines must be within tolerance	• intersection point must lie in triangle
• t must lie between [0,1]	• s,t must lie between [0,1]	• t must lie between [0,1]

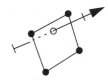 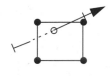 

Quadrilateral	Pixel	Polygon
• line/plane intersection	• line/plane intersection	• line/plane intersection
• intersection point must lie in quadrilateral	• intersection point must lie in pixel (uses efficient in/out test)	• intersection point must lie in polygon (uses ray casting for polygon in/out)
• t must lie between [0,1]	• t must lie between [0,1]	• t must lie between [0,1]

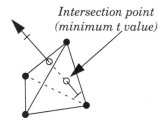 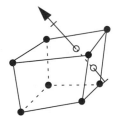 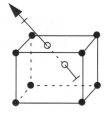

Intersection point (minimum t value)

Tetrahedron	Hexahedron	Voxel
• intersect each (triangle) face	• intersect each (quadrilateral) face	• intersect each (pixel) face
• t must lie between [0,1]	• since face may be non-planar, project previous result onto hexahedron surface	• t must lie between [0,1]
	• t must lie between [0,1]	

Figure 8–17 Summary of line/cell intersection operations for nine primitive cell types. Line is assumed normalized in parametric coordinate t with $0 \leq t \leq 1$.

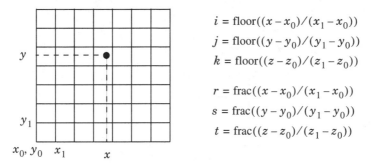

Figure 8–18 is accompanied by the following equations:

$$i = \mathrm{floor}((x - x_0)/(x_1 - x_0))$$
$$j = \mathrm{floor}((y - y_0)/(y_1 - y_0))$$
$$k = \mathrm{floor}((z - z_0)/(z_1 - z_0))$$

$$r = \mathrm{frac}((x - x_0)/(x_1 - x_0))$$
$$s = \mathrm{frac}((y - y_0)/(y_1 - y_0))$$
$$t = \mathrm{frac}((z - z_0)/(z_1 - z_0))$$

Figure 8–18 Structured point coordinate transformation.

from *RGB* or *RGBA* color coordinates to a single scalar value is required.

One simple mapping returns the *luminance Y* of a color. Given three components, *RGB*, the luminance is

$$Y = 0.30R + 0.59G + 0.11B \tag{8-25}$$

If the color includes transparency, *RGBA*, the luminance is

$$Y = A(0.30R + 0.59G + 0.11B) \tag{8-26}$$

Using this abstraction allows us to treat single-valued scalars and scalars consisting of multivalued colors the same. The end result is that we can mix both types of scalar data into our visualization networks.

8.9 Special Techniques for Structured Points

A significant attraction of the structured points dataset is the speed and simplicity of computation. In this section, we will explore specific techniques that exploit the special regular topology and geometry of structured point datasets.

Coordinate Transformation

Given a point p we can find the structured coordinates by performing three division operations (Figure **8–18**). Taking the integer `floor` function yields the structured coordinates. Taking the fractional part of the result yields the parametric coordinates of the cell. We can then use Equation **8-3** to convert to dataset coordinates.

Derivative Computation

Because the structured point dataset is oriented parallel to the coordinate x, y, and z axes, and because the spacing of points in each of these directions is regu-

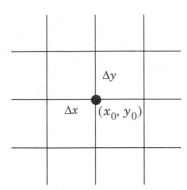

Figure 8–19 Using finite differences to compute derivatives on structured points dataset.

lar, finite difference schemes can be used to compute partial derivatives at the cell points. Referring to Figure **8–19**, we see that central differences can be used in each of the three directions according to

$$
\begin{aligned}
g_x &= \frac{d(x_0 + \Delta x, y_0, z_0) - d(x_0 - \Delta x, y_0, z_0)}{2\Delta x} \\[2mm]
g_y &= \frac{d(x_0, y_0 + \Delta y, z_0) - d(x_0, y_0 - \Delta y, z_0)}{2\Delta y} \\[2mm]
g_z &= \frac{d(x_0, y_0, z_0 + \Delta z) - d(x_0, y_0, z_0 - \Delta z)}{2\Delta z}
\end{aligned}
\tag{8-27}
$$

(Note that at the boundary of the dataset, one-sided differences may be used.) We can use these equations to compute derivatives within the cell as well. We simply compute the derivatives at each cell point from Equation **8-27**, and then use the cell interpolation functions to compute the derivative at the point inside the cell.

Topology

Structured datasets lend themselves to efficient topological operations (i.e., both structured points and structured grids). Given a cell id, it is possible to determine vertex, edge, or face neighbors using simple constant time operations. First, given the cell id in a three-dimensional structured dataset, we use a combination of division and modulo arithmetic to compute the structured coordinates

$$
\begin{aligned}
i &= id \ \text{modulo} \ (n_x - 1) \\
j &= (id/(n_x - 1)) \ \text{modulo} \ (n_y - 1) \\
k &= id/((n_x - 1)(n_y - 1))
\end{aligned}
\tag{8-28}
$$

Face neighbors are determined by incrementing one of the i, j, or k indices. Edge neighbors are determined by incrementing any two indices, while vertex neighbors are found by incrementing all three indices. Care must be taken while incrementing to insure that the indices fall in the range

$$0 \leq i < (n_x - 1)$$
$$0 \leq j < (n_y - 1) \tag{8-29}$$
$$0 \leq k < (n_z - 1)$$

An attempt to index outside these ranges indicates that the neighbor in question does not exist.

Searching

Given a point $p = (x, y, z)$ we can determine the cell containing p by using the equations given in Figure **8–18**. These equations generate the structured coordinates (i, j, k), which can then be converted to cell id (i.e., dataset coordinates) using Equation **8-3**.

To find the closest point to p, we compute the structured coordinates by rounding to the nearest integer value (instead of using the floor function). Thus,

$$\iota = \text{int}((x - x_0)/(x_1 - x_0))$$
$$j = \text{int}((y - y_0)/(y_1 - y_0)) \tag{8-30}$$
$$k = \text{int}((z - z_0)/(z_1 - z_0))$$

8.10 Putting It All Together

In this section we will finish our earlier description of an implementation for unstructured data. We also define a high-level, abstract interface for cells and datasets. This interface allows us to implement the general (i.e., dataset specific) algorithms in the *Visualization Toolkit*. We also describe implementations for color scalars, searching and picking, and conclude with a series of examples to demonstrate some of these concepts.

Unstructured Topology

In Chapter 5 we described data representations for the unstructured dataset types vtkPolyData and vtkUnstructuredGrid. Close examination of this data structure reveals that operations to retrieve topological adjacency are inefficient. In fact, to implement any operation to retrieve vertex, edge, or face neighbors requires a search of the cell array, resulting in $O(n)$ time complexity. This is unacceptable for all but the smallest applications, since any algorithm travers-

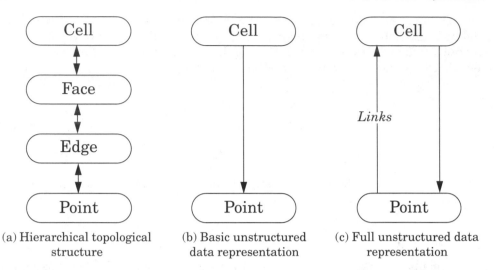

(a) Hierarchical topological   (b) Basic unstructured   (c) Full unstructured data
       structure   data representation   representation

Figure 8–20 Enhancing hierarchical unstructured data representation. (a) Conventional topological hierarchy for geometric model. (b) Basic unstructured data hierarchy. (c) Full unstructured data hierarchy. By introducing upward references from points to cells, the unstructured data hierarchy may be efficiently traversed in both directions, and is more compact than conventional topological hierarchies.

ing the cell array and retrieving adjacency information is at a minimum $O(n^2)$.

The reason for this inefficiency is that the data representation is a "downward" hierarchy (Figure **8–20**(b)). That is, given a cell we can quickly determine the topological features lower in the topological hierarchy such as faces, edges, and points. However, given a face, edge, or point we must search the cell array to determine the owning cells. To improve the efficiency of this data representation, we must introduce additional information into the hierarchy that allows "upward" hierarchy traversal (similar to that shown in Figure **8–20**(a)).

The solution to this problem is to extend the unstructured data structure with *cell links*. The cell links array is a list of lists of cells that use each point and corresponds to the upward links of Figure **8–20**(c). The cell links array transforms the hierarchical structure of Figure **5–10** into a ring structure. Cells reference their composing points, and points in turn reference the cells that use them. The full unstructured data structure is shown in Figure **8–21**.

The cell links array is in fact an implementation of the use sets of Equation **5-1**. We can use this equation to compute adjacency operation in constant time, if the maximum number of cells using a point is much smaller than the number of points in a dataset. To see this, we refer to Equation **8-24** and see that the adjacency operations consist of a finite number of set intersections. Each operation is an intersection of the link lists for each point. If the number of cells in each link list is "small," then the intersection operation can be bounded by a fixed constant in time, and the total operation can be considered a constant time operation.

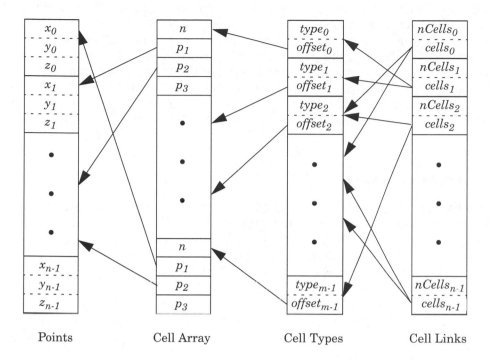

Figure 8–21 Complete unstructured data representation including link lists. There are m cells and n points. The n structures in the link list are lists of cells that use each vertex. Each link list is variable in length.

There are several important characteristics of this data representation.

- The cell links array is an extension of the basic unstructured data representation. As a result, we can defer the construction of the cell links until they are required. Often the cell links are never needed and require no computer resources to compute or store.

- Building the cell links is a linear $O(n)$ operation. Each cell is traversed and for every point that the cell uses, the list of using cells for that point is extended to include the current cell. Building the cell links is only needed once as an initialization step.

- The data representation is compact relative to other topology representation schemes (e.g., the winged-edge structure and the radial-edge structures [Baumgart74] [Weiler88]). These other data structures contain explicit representation of intermediate topology such as edges, loops, faces, or special adjacency information such as adjacent edges (winged-edge structure) or extensive "use" descriptions (radial-edge structure). The compactness of representation is particularly important for visualization, since the data size is typically large.

The unstructured data structure in the *Visualization Toolkit* is implemented using the four classes vtkPoints (and subclasses), vtkCellArray, vtk-CellTypes, and vtkCellLinks. The building of this data structure is incremental. At a minimum, the points and cells are represented using vtkPoints and vtkCellArray. If random access or extra type information is required, then the object vtkCellTypes is used. If adjacency information is required, an instance of the class vtkCellLinks is created. These operations are carried out behind the scenes, and generally do not require extra knowledge by the application programmer.

Abstract Interfaces

With the completion of Chapters 5 and 8, we can summarize the abstract interface for cells, datasets, and the point data attributes. These pseudo-code descriptions encapsulate the core functionality of the classes vtkDataSet, vtkCell, and vtkPointData, and their subclasses. All algorithms presented in this text can be implemented using combinations of these methods.

Dataset Abstraction. The dataset is the central data representation in **vtk**. Datasets are composed of one or more cells and points. Associated with the points are attribute data consisting of scalars, vectors, normals, texture coordinates, and user-defined data.

type = GetDataType()
    Return the type of dataset (e.g., vtkPolyData, vtkStructured-Points, vtkStructuredGrid, vtkRectilinearGrid, or vtkUnstructuredGrid).

numPoints = GetNumberOfPoints()
    Return the number of points in the dataset.

numCells = GetNumberOfCells()
    Return the number of cells in the dataset.

GetPoint(ptId, x)
    Given a point id, return the *(x,y,z)* coordinates of the point.

cell = GetCell(cellId)
    Given a cell id, return a pointer to a cell object.

type = GetCellType(cellId)
    Return the type of the cell given by cell id.

GetCellTypes(types)
    Return a list of types of cells that compose the dataset.

cells = GetPointCells(ptId)
    Given a point id, return the cells that use this point.

GetCellPoints(cellId, ptIds)
>   Given a cell id, return the point ids (e.g., connectivity list) defining the cell.

GetCellNeighbors(cellId, ptIds, neighbors)
>   Given a cell id and a list of points composing a boundary face of the cell, return the neighbors of that cell sharing the points.

cellId = FindCell(x, cell, cellId, tol2, subId, pcoords, weights)
>   Given a coordinate value x, an initial search cell defined by cell and cellId, and a tolerance measure (squared), return the cell id and sub-id of the cell containing the point and its interpolation function weights. The initial search cell is used to speed up the search process when the position x is known to be near the cell. If no cell is found, cellId < 0 is returned.

pointData = GetPointData()
>   Return a pointer to the object maintaining point attribute data. This includes scalars, vectors, normals, tensors, texture coordinates, and user-defined data.

bounds = GetBounds()
>   Get the bounding box of the dataset.

length = GetLength()
>   Return the length of the diagonal of the bounding box of the dataset.

center = GetCenter()
>   Get the center of the bounding box of the dataset.

range = GetScalarRange()
>   A convenience method to return the (minimum, maximum) range of the scalar attribute data associated with the dataset.

dataSet = MakeObject()
>   Make a copy of the current dataset. A "virtual" constructor. (Typically, reference counting methods are used to copy data.)

CopyStructure(dataSet)
>   Update the current structure definition (i.e., geometry and topology) with the supplied dataset.

Cell Abstraction. Cells are the atomic structures of **vtk**. Cells consist of a topology, defined by a sequence of ordered point ids, and a geometry, defined by point coordinates. The cell coordinate consists of a cell id, a subcell id, and a parametric coordinate. The subid specifies a primary cell that lies within a composite cell such as a triangle strip. Cell edges and faces are defined implicitly from the topology of the cell.

`type = GetCellType()`
> Return the type of the cell. Must be one of the twelve **vtk** cell types (or the empty cell type).

`dim = GetCellDimension()`
> Return the topological definition of the cell.

`order = GetInterpolationOrder()`
> Return the degree of the interpolating polynomial of the cell. (The twelve cell types are all degree 1; cells added in the future may be of higher-order.)

`numberPoints = GetNumberOfPoints()`
> Return the number of points that define the cell.

`points = GetPoints()`
> Return a list of point ids defining the cell.

`numberEdges = GetNumberOfEdges()`
> Return the number of edges in the cell.

`edge = GetEdge(i)`
> Given an edge id ($0 \leq i <$ numberEdges) return a pointer to a cell that represents an edge of the cell.

`numberFaces = GetNumberOfFaces()`
> Return the number of faces in a cell.

`face = GetFace(i)`
> Given an face id ($0 \leq i <$ numberFaces) return a pointer to a cell that represents a face of the cell.

`inOutStatus = CellBoundary(subId, pcoords, poindIds)`
> Given a cell subid and parametric coordinates, return a list of point ids that define the closest boundary face of the cell. Also return whether the point is actually in the cell.

`inOutStatus = EvaluatePosition(x, closestPoint, subId, pcoords, weights, dist2)`
> Given a point coordinate x, return the sub-id, parametric coordinates, and interpolation weights of the cell if x lies inside the cell. The position `closestPoint` is the closest point on the cell to x (may be the same) and `dist2` is the squared distance between them. The method returns an `inOutStatus` indicating whether x is *topologically* inside or outside the cell. That is, the point may satisfy parametric coordinate conditions but may lie off the surface of the cell (e.g., point lies above polygon). Use both `inOutStatus` and `dist2` to determine whether point is both topologically and geometrically in the cell.

EvaluateLocation(subId, pcoords, x, weights)
> Given a point location (i.e., sub-id and parametric coordinates), return the position x of the point and the interpolation weights.

Contour(value, cellScalars, locator, verts, lines, polys, inputPointData, outputPointData)
> Given a contour value and scalar values at the cell points, generate contour primitives (vertices, lines, or polygons with associated points and attribute data values). The points are placed in a locator object (see "Searching" on page 331) which merges coincident points, and the attribute data values are interpolated (along the cell edge) from the inputPointData to the outputPointData.

Clip(value, cellScalars, locator, cells, inputPointData, outputPointData, insideOut)
> Given a contour value and scalar values at the cell points, clip the cell to generate new cells of the same topological dimension as the original cell. The points are placed in a locator object (see "Searching" on page 331) which merges coincident points, and the attribute data values are interpolated (or copied) from the inputPointData to the outputPointData. The clipped cells are placed in the cells list.

Derivatives(subId, pcoords, values, dim, derivs)
> Given a cell location (i.e., subid and parametric coordinates) and data values at the cell points, return dim*3 derivatives (i.e., corresponds to the x, y, and z directions times dimension of data).

inOutStatus = IntersectWithLine(p1, p2, tol, t, x, pcoords, subId)
> Given a finite line defined by the two points p1 and p2 and an intersection tolerance, return the point of intersection x. The parametric coordinate t along the line and cell location at the point of intersection is also returned. Returns a nonzero if intersection occurs.

Triangulate(index, ptIds, points)
> Decompose the cell into simplices of dimension equal to the topological cell dimension. The index is an integer that controls the triangulation if more than one triangulation is possible. The simplices are defined by an ordered list of point ids and their corresponding coordinates.

bounds = GetBounds()
> Return the bounding box of the cell.

Point Attribute Abstraction. Point attribute data is information associated with the points of a cell/dataset. This information consists of scalars, vectors, normals, tensors, texture coordinates, and/or user-defined data. There is a one-to-one relationship between the points in a dataset and the attribute data. For example, scalar value at location 100 is associated with point id 100.

Many of the methods described below deal with moving data from the input to the output of a filter. Since the possibility exists that new types of attribute data could be added in the future, the details of moving data is hidden as much as possible (i.e., minimize the knowledge that the filter has about specific attribute types). Thus, generic functions like `CopyData()` allow for copying data from the input to the output without knowing what this data is.

`CopyScalarsOn() / CopyScalarsOff()`
> Turn on/off boolean flag controlling copying of scalar data from input to output of filter.

`CopyVectorsOn() / CopyVectorsOff()`
> Turn on/off boolean flag controlling copying of vector data from input to output of filter.

`CopyNormalsOn() / CopyNormalsOff()`
> Turn on/off boolean flag controlling copying of normal data from input to output of filter.

`CopyTensorsOn() / CopyTensorsOff()`
> Turn on/off boolean flag controlling copying of tensor data from input to output of filter.

`CopyTextureCoordsOn() / CopyTextureCoordsOff()`
> Turn on/off boolean flag controlling copying of texture coordinates data from input to output of filter.

`CopyUserDefinedOn() / CopyUserDefinedOff()`
> Turn on/off boolean flag controlling copying of user-defined data from input to output of filter.

`CopyAllOn() / CopyAllOff()`
> Turn on/off all boolean flags controlling copying of data from input to output of filter.

`PassData(pointData)`
> Transfer all point attribute data (`pointData`) to the output according to the copy flags listed previously.

`CopyAllocate(pointData)`
> Initialize and allocate storage for point-by-point copy process.

`CopyData(pointData, fromId, toId)`
> Given point data and a specific point id, copy the point attribute data (`pointData`) to the output point.

`InterpolateAllocate(pointData)`
> Initialize and allocate storage for point-by-point interpolation process.

`InterpolatePoint(pointData, toId, ptIds, weights)`
> Given input point data (`pointData`) and a list of points and their interpolation weights, interpolate data to the specified output point.

```
InterpolateEdge(pointData, toId, p1, p2, t)
```
From an edge defined by the two points `p1` and `p2`, interpolate the `pointData` at the edge parametric coordinate `t` and copy the interpolated attribute data to the output point `ptId`.

```
NullPoint(int ptId)
```
Set the data value(s) of the specified output point id to a null value.

```
SetScalars() / GetScalars()
```
Set / return scalar data. The `GetScalars()` method may return a `NULL` value, in which case the scalars are not defined.

```
SetVectors() / GetVectors()
```
Set / return vector data. The `GetVectors()` method may return a `NULL` value, in which case the vectors are not defined.

```
SetNormals() / GetNormals()
```
Set / return normal data. The `GetNormals()` method may return a `NULL` value, in which case the normals are not defined.

```
SetTensors() / GetTensors()
```
Set / return tensor data. The `GetTensors()` method may return a `NULL` value, in which case the tensors are not defined.

```
SetTextureCoords() / GetTextureCoords()
```
Set / return texture coordinate data. The `GetTextureCoords()` method may return a `NULL` value, in which case the texture coordinates are not defined.

```
SetUserDefined() / GetUserDefined()
```
Set / return user-defined data. The `GetUserDefined()` method may return a `NULL` value, in which case user-defined data is not defined.

Traversing Intermediate Topology

The dataset abstraction implemented by **vtk** provides simple techniques to traverse points and cells. Sometimes we want to traverse intermediate topology such as edges or faces. For example, to identify boundary edges in a triangular mesh we must traverse each edge, counting the number of triangles that use each edge. (Recall that boundary edges are used by just one triangle.) Unfortunately, there is no obvious way to traverse edges. The same problem holds true if we want to traverse the faces of a dataset containing 3D cells.

A simple solution is to traverse each cell and then obtain the edges (or faces) that compose the cell. The problem with this approach is that edges and faces are generally used by more than one cell, resulting in multiple visits to the same face or edge. This may be acceptable in some algorithms, but usually we count on visiting each edge or face only once.

A better solution to this problem is to traverse each cell as before, but only process intermediate topology if the current cell has the smallest cell id. (The

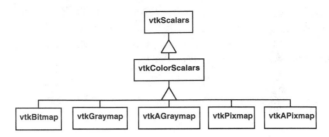

Figure 8–22 Color scalars object model.

current cell is the cell being visited in the traversal process.) To determine whether the current cell has the smallest cell id, we obtain all cells using the intermediate topology. This information can be obtained using the topological adjacency operators described earlier (e.g., Equation **8-24**).

To illustrate this process consider visiting the edges of a triangle mesh. We begin by visiting the first triangle, t, and then its edges. For each edge we determine the adjacent triangle(s) (if any) that use the edge. If the id of the adjacent triangle(s) is greater than triangle t's id, or there are no adjacent triangles, then we know to process the current edge. (Of course the first triangle will always have the smallest id — but this will change as the traversal proceeds.) We then continue traversing the triangle list for new t's. In this way all the edges of the mesh will be visited.

Color Scalar Data

Multivalued scalar data, or scalars represented by various color representations, are a special type in the *Visualization Toolkit*. These classes are of generic type vtkColorScalars, which is in turn a subclass of vtkScalars (Figure **8–22**).

vtkColorScalars is an abstract class that specifies a uniform interface to its concrete subclasses, as well as implementing the methods required by vtk-Scalars. Special features of this class are as follows.

- Subclasses of vtkColorScalars operate on color specification in the RGBA (i.e., red-green-blue-alpha transparency) format. The internal representation of data may be different, but must be converted to this form to satisfy the abstract interface. For example, vtkGraymap, which represents data as a single unsigned char value, converts its value to RGBA by setting its alpha value $\alpha = 1$ and each color component to the gray value $R = G = B = \text{gray}$.

- To satisfy the abstract interface specified by vtkScalars, subclasses of vtkColorScalars must also be capable of converting their multivalued color values into a single value. Equation **8-25** and Equation **8-26** are used.

- Special methods provide information about the type of scalar, either SingleValued or ColorScalar, and the number of data values per scalar

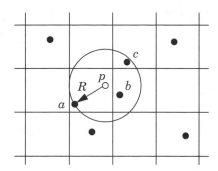

Figure 8–23 Determining closest point to p in vtkPointLocator. Initial search in bucket results in point a. Search must extend beyond local bucket as a function of search radius R, resulting in point b.

(i.e., GetScalarType() and GetNumberOfValuesPerScalar()). This information allows us to differentiate between general types of scalar and to perform special operations like texture mapping and writing data to disk.

- Every subclass of vtkColorScalars must be capable of returning an array of unsigned char values. The array consists of 1–4 values per scalar (depending on the number of values per scalar). This operation is used for high-performance texture and imaging operations.

Searching

The *Visualization Toolkit* provides two classes to perform searches for dataset points and cells. These are vtkPointLocator and vtkCellLocator. (Both of these classes are subclasses of vtkLocator, which is an abstract base class for spatial search objects.) vtkPointLocator is used to search for points and, if used with the topological dataset operator GetPointCells(), to search for cells as well. vtkCellLocator is used to search for cells.

vtkPointLocator is implemented as a regular grid of buckets (i.e., same topology and geometry as a structured point set). The number of buckets can be user-specified, or more conveniently, automatically computed based on the number of dataset points. On average, vtkPointLocator provides constant time access to points. However, in cases where the point distribution is not uniform, the number of points in a bucket may vary widely, giving $O(n)$ worst-case behavior. In practice this is rarely a problem, but adaptive spatial search structures (e.g., an octree) may sometimes be a better choice.

Determining closest point to a point p using vtkPointLocator (as well as other spatial search structures) is a three-step process. In the first step, the bucket containing p is found using the appropriate insertion scheme. (For vtkPointLocator this is three divisions to determine bucket indices (i, j, k).) Next, the list of points in this bucket is searched to determine the closest point. How-

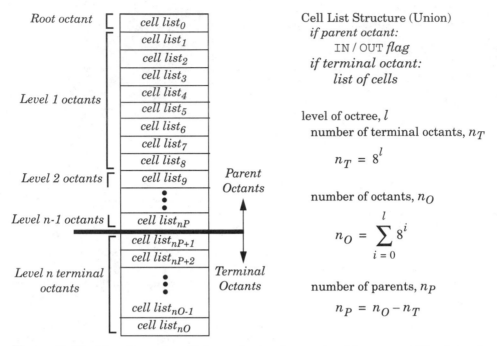

Figure 8–24 Structure of spatial search structure `vtkCellLocator`. The data structure represents a uniformly subdivided octree.

ever, as Figure **8–23** shows, this may not be the true closest point, since points in neighboring buckets may be closer. Consequently, a final search of neighboring buckets is necessary. The search distance is a function of the distance to the current closest point. Once all neighbors within this distance are searched, the closest point is returned.

vtkCellLocator is implemented as a uniformly subdivided octree with some peculiar characteristics (Figure **8–24**). Conventional octree representations use upward parent and downward children pointers to track parent and children octants. Besides the required list of entities (i.e., points or cells) in each octant, additional information about octant level, center, and size may also be maintained. This results in a flexible structure with significant overhead. The overhead is the memory resources to maintain pointers, plus the cost to allocate and delete memory.

In contrast, vtkCellLocator uses a single array to represent the octree. The array is divided into two parts. The first part contains a list of parent octants, ordered according to level and octant child number. In the second part are the terminal, or leaf octants. The terminal octants are ordered on a regular array of buckets, just the same as vtkLocator. The terminal octants contain a list of the entities inside the octant. The parent octants maintain a value indicating whether the octant is empty, or whether something is inside it. (Both types of information are represented in the same portion of the octant structure.)

(a) Original data   (b) Selected cells

```
  sphereActor->SetPosition(picker->GetPickPosition());

  if ( picker->GetPointId() >= 0 )
    {
    cout << "Point id: " << picker->GetPointId() << "\n";
    cellsActor->VisibilityOn();
    plateActor->VisibilityOff();
    cells->Initialize();
    cells->Allocate(100);
    cells->SetPoints(plateOutput->GetPoints());

    plateOutput->GetPointCells(picker->GetPointId(), cellIds);
    for (i=0; i < cellIds.GetNumberOfIds(); i++)
      {
      cellId = cellIds.GetId(i);
      plateOutput->GetCellPoints(cellId, ptIds);
      cells->InsertNextCell(plateOutput->GetCellType(cellId), ptIds
      }
    }
  else
    {
    cellsActor->VisibilityOff();
    plateActor->VisibilityOn();
    }
renWin->Render();
```

(c) C++ code (pickCells.cxx)

Figure 8–28 Selecting group of cells sharing a common point. (a) Original data.
(b) Selected cells sharing point on corner. Cells shrunk for clarity. The small
sphere indicates the selected point. (c) C++ code fragment in pick routine.

tion point must be specified in pixel coordinates. The `vtkPointPicker` converts these coordinates into world and then dataset coordinates using the renderer in which the pick occurred. (The renderer uses the transformation matrix of its active camera to perform coordinate transformation.)

The picking process is conveniently managed in `vtkRenderWindowInteractor`. This object allows the specification of functions to execute just before picking and just after picking (i.e., `StartPickMethod()` and `EndPickMethod()`). Using this facility we can define a postpicking function to retrieve the point id and then execute the `GetPointCells()` operation. This process is shown in Figure **8–28**.

Point Probe. In this example we will show how to build a point probe using the dataset and cell operations described in this chapter. A point probe is defined as follows. Given a *(x,y,z)* point coordinate, find the cell coordinates (i.e., cell id, subcell id, and parametric coordinates) and the interpolation weights. Once the interpolation weights are found, we can then compute local data values at *(x,y,z)*.

The point probe is implemented using the dataset operation `FindCell()`. This method requires a point specified in global coordinates (our *(x,y,z)* value) and a tolerance. The tolerance is often necessary because of numerical precision or when picking near the surface of 3D cells, or on 0D, 1D, and 2D cells. The `FindCell()` operation returns the information we require, plus the interpolation weights of the cell containing our point probe. To determine the data value at our probe point, we need to retrieve the data values on the cell points. We can then use the interpolation functions of Equation **8-4** to determine the probe scalar value.

Figure **8–29** depicts this process and includes C++ code. In the example we use the combustor dataset with the objects `vtkCursor3D`, `vtkProbeFilter`, and `vtkGlyph3D`. The purpose of the cursor is to control the position of the probe point. The class `vtkProbeFilter` performs the probing operation just described. (This filter has been generalized so that it can handle more than one input point.) `vtkGlyph3D` is used to place an oriented, scaled cone at the cursor focal point. This gives us visual feedback about the scalar and vector quantities at the probe. Of course, we can extract numeric values and display them to the user if this is important.

8.11 Chapter Summary

Three important visualization coordinate systems are the world, dataset, and structured coordinate systems. The world coordinate system is an x y-z Cartesian three-dimensional space. The dataset coordinate system consists of a cell id, subcell id, and parametric coordinates. The structured coordinate system consists of (i,j,k) integer indices into a rectangular topological domain.

Visualization data is generally in discrete form. Interpolation functions are used to obtain data at points between the known data values. Interpolation functions vary depending on the particular cell type. The form of the interpolation

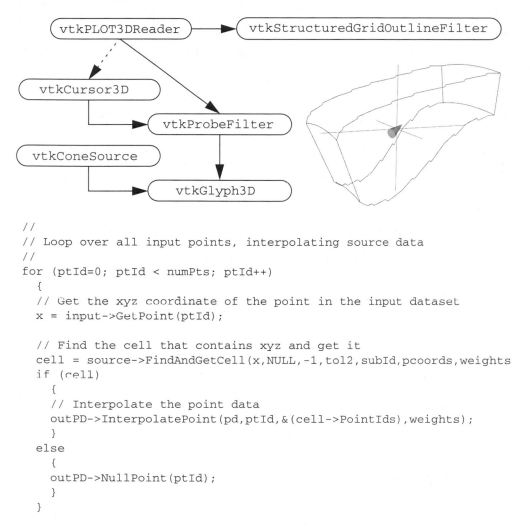

```
//
// Loop over all input points, interpolating source data
//
for (ptId=0; ptId < numPts; ptId++)
  {
  // Get the xyz coordinate of the point in the input dataset
  x = input->GetPoint(ptId);

  // Find the cell that contains xyz and get it
  cell = source->FindAndGetCell(x,NULL,-1,tol2,subId,pcoords,weights
  if (cell)
    {
    // Interpolate the point data
    outPD->InterpolatePoint(pd,ptId,&(cell->PointIds),weights);
    }
  else
    {
    outPD->NullPoint(ptId);
    }
  }
```

Figure 8–29 Creating a point probe. Visualization network shown in diagram above. C++ code shows inner loop of vtkProbeFilter and resulting image for combustor data (probe.cxx).

functions are weighting values located at each of the cells points. The interpolations functions form the basis for conversion from dataset to global coordinates and vice versa. The interpolation functions also are used to compute data derivatives.

Topological operators provide information about the topology of a cell or dataset. Obtaining neighboring cells to a particular cell is an important visualization operation. This operation can be used to determine whether cell boundaries are on the boundary of a dataset or to traverse datasets on a cell-by-cell basis.

Because of the inherent regularity of structured point datasets, operations can be efficiently implemented compared to other dataset types. These operations include coordinate transformation, derivative computation, topological query, and searching.

8.12 Bibliographic Notes

Interpolation functions are employed in a number of numerical techniques. The finite element method, in particular, depends on interpolation functions. If you want more information about interpolation functions refer to the finite element references suggested below [Cook89] [Gallagher75] [Zienkiewicz87]. These texts also discuss derivative computation in the context of interpolation functions.

Basic topology references are available from a number of sources. Two good descriptions of topological data structures are available from Weiler [Weiler86] [Weiler88] and Baumgart [Baumgart74]. Weiler describes the radial-edge structure. This data structure can represent manifold and nonmanifold geometry. The winged-edge structure described by Baumgart is widely known. It is used to represent manifold geometry. Shephard [Shephard88] describes general finite element data structures — these are similar to visualization structures but with extra information related to analysis and geometric modelling.

There are extensive references regarding spatial search structures. Samet [Samet90] provides a general overview of some. Octrees were originally developed by Meagher [Meagher82] for 3D imaging. See [Williams83], [Bentley75], and [Quinlan94] for information about MIP maps, kd-trees, and binary sphere trees, respectively.

8.13 References

[Baumgart74]
   B. G. Baumgart. "Geometric Modeling for Computer Vision." Ph.D. thesis, Stanford University, Palo Alto, CA, 1974.

[Bentley75]
   J. L. Bentley. "Multidimensional Binary Search Trees Used for Associative Search." *Communications of the ACM*. 18(9):509–516, 1975.

[Conte72]
   S. D. Conte and C. de Boor. *Elementary Numerical Analysis*. McGraw-Hill Book Company, 1972.

[Cook89]
   R. D. Cook, D. S. Malkus, and M. E. Plesha. *Concepts and Applications of Finite Element Analysis*. John Wiley and Sons, New York, 1989.

[Gallagher75]
   R. H. Gallagher. *Finite Element Analysis: Fundamentals*. Prentice Hall, Upper Saddle River, NJ, 1975.

Advanced Algorithms

We return again to visualization algorithms. This chapter describes algorithms that are either more complex to implement, or less widely used for 3D visualization applications. We retain the classification of algorithms as either scalar, vector, tensor, or modelling algorithms.

9.1 Scalar Algorithms

As we have seen, scalar algorithms often involve mapping scalar values through a lookup table, or creating contour lines or surfaces. In this section, we examine another contouring algorithm, *dividing cubes*, which generates contour surfaces using dense point clouds. We also describe carpet plots. Carpet plots are not true 3D visualization techniques, but are widely used to visualize many types of scalar data. Finally, clipping is another important algorithm related to contouring, where cells are cut into pieces as a function of scalar value.

Dividing Cubes

Dividing cubes is a contouring algorithm similar to marching cubes [Cline88]. Unlike marching cubes, dividing cubes generates point primitives as compared to triangles (3D) or lines (2D). If the number of points on the contour surface is

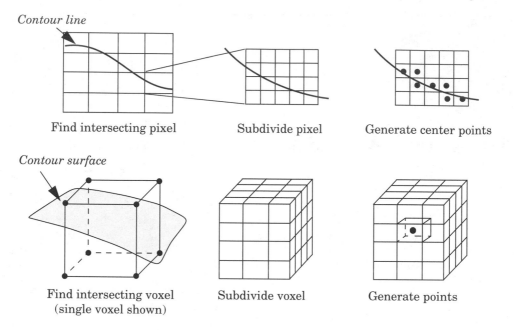

Contour line

Find intersecting pixel   Subdivide pixel   Generate center points

Contour surface

Find intersecting voxel   Subdivide voxel   Generate points
(single voxel shown)

Figure 9–1 Overview of the dividing cubes algorithm. Voxels through which the contour passes are subdivided into subvoxels at less than screen resolution. If the contour passes through a subvoxel, a center point is generated.

large, the rendered appearance of the contour surface appears "solid." To achieve this solid appearance, the density of the points must be at or greater than screen resolution. (Also, the points must be rendered using the standard lighting and shading equations used in surface rendering.)

The motivation for dividing cubes is that rendering points is much faster than rendering polygons. This varies depending upon rendering hardware/software. Special purpose hardware has been developed to render shaded points at high speed. In other systems, greater attention has been placed on polygon rendering, and the rendering speed differences are not so great. Also, certain geometric operations such as clipping and merging data are simple operations with points. Comparable operations with polygons are much more difficult to implement.

One disadvantage of creating contours with dense point clouds is that magnification of the surface (via camera zooming, for example) reveals the disconnected nature of the surface. Thus, the point set must be constructed for maximum zoom, or constructed dynamically based on the relative relationship between the camera and contour.

Although dividing cubes was originally developed for volume datasets, it is possible to adapt the algorithm to other dataset types by subdividing in parametric coordinates. Our presentation assumes that we are working with volumes.

Figure **9–1** provides an overview of the dividing cubes algorithm. Like other

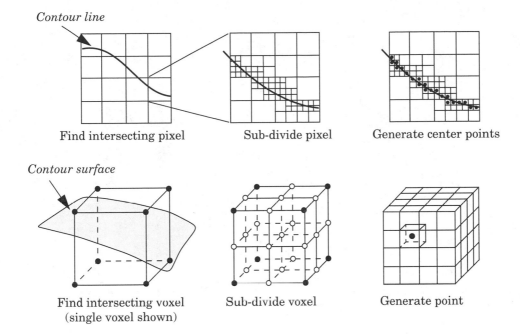

Figure 9–2 Recursive dividing cubes algorithm. Top half of figure shows algorithm depicted in two dimensions. Lower half depicts algorithm in three dimensions.

contouring algorithms, we first choose a contour value. We begin by visiting each voxel and select those through which the isosurface passes. (The isosurface passes through a voxel when there are scalar values both above and below the contour value.) We also compute the gradient at each voxel point for use in computing point normals.

After selecting a voxel that the isosurface passes through, the voxel is subdivided into a regular grid of $n_1 \times n_2 \times n_3$ subvoxels. The number of divisions is controlled by the width of a voxel w_i in combination with screen resolution R. The screen resolution is defined as the distance between adjacent pixels in world coordinates. We can express the number of divisions n_i along the coordinate axes x_i as

$$n_i = \frac{w_i}{R} \tag{9-1}$$

where the quotient is rounded up to the nearest integer. The scalar values at the subpoints are generated using the interpolation functions for a voxel (see Figure **8–10**). Then we determine whether the contour passes through each subvoxel. If it does, we simply generate a point at the center of the subvoxel and compute its normal using the standard interpolation functions.

An interesting variation on this algorithm is a recursive implementation as shown in Figure **9–2**. Instead of subdividing the voxel directly (i.e., procedurally)

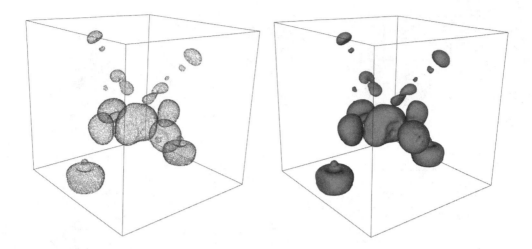

Figure 9–3 Examples of dividing cubes isosurface. The left image consists of 50,078 points, and the right image consists of 2,506,989 points (dcubes.tcl).

into a regular grid we recursively divide the voxel (similar to octree decomposition). The voxel is subdivided regularly creating eight subvoxels and 19 new points (12 midedge points, 6 midface points, and 1 midvoxel point). The scalar values at the new points are interpolated from the original voxel using the trilinear interpolation functions. The process repeats for each subvoxel if the isosurface passes through it. This process continues until the size of the subvoxel is less than or equal to screen resolution. In this case, a point is generated at the center of the subvoxel. The collection of all such points composes the dividing cubes' isosurface.

The advantage of the recursive implementation is that the subdivision process terminates prematurely in those regions of the voxel where the contour cannot pass. On the other hand, the recursive subdivision requires that the voxel subdivision occurs in powers of two. This can generate far more points than the procedural implementation.

Figure **9–3** shows two examples of dividing cubes isosurfaces. The contour surface on the left consists of 50,078 points. Because the points are not generated at display resolution, it is possible to see through the contour surface. The second contour surface on the right is composed of 2,506,989 points. The points are generated at display resolution, and as a result the contour surface appears solid.

As Figure **9–1** and Figure **9–2** show, the points generated by dividing cubes do not lie exactly on the contour surface. We can determine the maximum error by examining the size of the terminal subvoxels. Assume that a terminal subvoxel is a cube, and that the length of the side of the cube is given by l. Then the maximum error is half the length of the cube diagonal, or $l\sqrt{3}/2$.

9.2 Vector Algorithms

In Chapter 6 we showed how to create simple vector glyphs and how to integrate particles through a vector field to create streamlines. In this section we extend these concepts to create streamribbons and streampolygons. In addition, we introduce the concept of vector field topology, and show how to characterize a vector field using topological constructs.

Streamribbons and Streamsurfaces

Streamlines depict particle paths in a vector field. By coloring these lines, or creating local glyphs (such as dashed lines or oriented cones), we can represent additional scalar and temporal information. However, these techniques can convey only elementary information about the vector field. Local information (e.g., flow rotation or derivatives) and global information (e.g., structure of a field such as vortex tubes) is not represented. Streamribbons and streamsurfaces are two techniques used to represent local and global information.

A natural extension of the streamline technique widens the line to create a ribbon. The ribbon can be constructed by generating two adjacent streamlines and then bridging the lines with a polygonal mesh. This technique works well as long as the streamlines remain relatively close to one another. If separation occurs, so that the streamlines diverge, the resulting ribbon will not accurately represent the flow, because we expect the surface of the ribbon to be everywhere tangent to the vector field (i.e., definition of streamline). The ruled surface connecting two widely separated streamlines does not generally satisfy this requirement.

The streamribbon provides information about important flow parameters: the vector vorticity and flow divergence. *Vorticity* $\vec{\omega}$ is the measure of rotation of the vector field, expressed as a vector quantity: a direction (axis of rotation) and magnitude (amount of rotation). *Streamwise vorticity* Ω is the projection of $\vec{\omega}$ along the instantaneous velocity vector, $\vec{v}$. Said another way, streamwise vorticity is the rotation of the vector field around the streamline defined as follows.

$$\Omega = \frac{\vec{v} \cdot \vec{\omega}}{|\vec{v}||\vec{\omega}|} \tag{9-3}$$

The amount of twisting of the streamribbon approximates the streamwise vorticity. Flow *divergence* is a measure of the "spread" of the flow. The changing width of the streamribbon is proportional to the cross-flow divergence of the flow.

A streamsurface is a collection of an infinite number of streamlines passing through a *base curve*. The base curve, or *rake*, defines the starting points for the streamlines. If the base curve is closed (e.g., a circle) the surface is closed and a streamtube results. Thus, streamribbons are specialized types of streamsurfaces with a narrow width compared to length.

Compared to vector icons or streamlines, streamsurfaces provide additional information about the structure of the vector field. Any point on the streamsurface is tangent to the velocity vector. Consequently, taking an example from fluid flow, no fluid can pass through the surface. Streamtubes are then representations of constant mass flux. Streamsurfaces show vector field structure better than streamlines or vector glyphs because they do not require visual interpolation across icons.

Streamsurfaces can be computed by generating a set of streamlines from a user-specified rake. A polygonal mesh is then constructed by connecting adjacent streamlines. One difficulty with this approach is that local vector field divergence can cause streamlines to separate. Separation can introduce large errors into the surface, or possibly cause self-intersection, which is not physically possible.

Another approach to computing streamsurfaces has been taken by Hultquist [Hultquist92]. The streamsurface is a collection of streamribbons connected along their edges. In this approach, the computation of the streamlines and tiling of the streamsurface is carried out concurrently. This allows streamlines to be added or removed as the flow separates or converges. The tiling can also be controlled to prevent the generation of long, skinny triangles. The surface may also be "torn", i.e., ribbons separated, if the divergence of the flow becomes too high.

Stream Polygon

The techniques described so far provide approximate measures of vector field quantities such as streamwise vorticity and divergence. However, vector fields contain more information than these techniques can convey. As a result, other techniques have been devised to visualize this information. One such technique is the *stream polygon* [Schroeder91], which serves as the basis for a number of advanced vector and tensor visualization methods. The stream polygon is used to visualize local properties of strain, displacement, and rotation. We begin by describing the effects of a vector field on the local state of strain.

Nonuniform vector fields give rise to local deformation in the region where they occur. If the vector field is displacement in a physical medium such as a fluid or a solid, the deformation consists of local strain (i.e., local distortion) and rigid body motion. To mathematically describe the deformation, we examine a 3D vector $\vec{v} = (u, v, w)$ at a specified point $\vec{x} = (x, y, z)$. Using a first order Taylor's series expansion about $\vec{x}$, we can express the local deformation e_{ij} as

$$e_{ij} = \varepsilon_{ij} + \omega_{ij} \qquad \text{(9-4)}$$

where ε_{ij} is the local strain and ω_{ij} is the local rotation. Note that these variables are expressed as 3×3 tensors. (Compare this equation to that given in Figure **6–20**. Note that this equation and the following Equation **9-5** differ in their off-diagonal terms by a factor of 1/2. This is because Figure **6–20** expresses *engineering shear strain* which is used in the study of elasticity. Equation **9-5** expresses a tensor quantity and is mathematically consistent.)

The local strain is expressed as a combination of the partial derivatives at

$\vec{x}$ as follows.

$$
\varepsilon_{ij} = \begin{bmatrix}
\dfrac{\partial u}{\partial x} & \dfrac{1}{2}\left(\dfrac{\partial u}{\partial y} + \dfrac{\partial v}{\partial x}\right) & \dfrac{1}{2}\left(\dfrac{\partial u}{\partial z} + \dfrac{\partial w}{\partial x}\right) \\[2ex]
\dfrac{1}{2}\left(\dfrac{\partial u}{\partial y} + \dfrac{\partial v}{\partial x}\right) & \dfrac{\partial v}{\partial y} & \dfrac{1}{2}\left(\dfrac{\partial v}{\partial z} + \dfrac{\partial w}{\partial y}\right) \\[2ex]
\dfrac{1}{2}\left(\dfrac{\partial u}{\partial z} + \dfrac{\partial w}{\partial x}\right) & \dfrac{1}{2}\left(\dfrac{\partial v}{\partial z} + \dfrac{\partial w}{\partial y}\right) & \dfrac{\partial w}{\partial z}
\end{bmatrix}
\tag{9-5}
$$

The terms on the diagonal of ε_{ij} are the normal components of strain. The off-diagonal terms are the shear strain. The local rigid-body rotation is given by

$$
\omega_{ij} = \begin{bmatrix}
0 & \dfrac{1}{2}\left(\dfrac{\partial u}{\partial y} - \dfrac{\partial v}{\partial x}\right) & \dfrac{1}{2}\left(\dfrac{\partial u}{\partial z} - \dfrac{\partial w}{\partial x}\right) \\[2ex]
\dfrac{1}{2}\left(\dfrac{\partial v}{\partial x} - \dfrac{\partial u}{\partial y}\right) & 0 & \dfrac{1}{2}\left(\dfrac{\partial v}{\partial z} - \dfrac{\partial w}{\partial y}\right) \\[2ex]
\dfrac{1}{2}\left(\dfrac{\partial w}{\partial x} - \dfrac{\partial u}{\partial z}\right) & \dfrac{1}{2}\left(\dfrac{\partial w}{\partial y} - \dfrac{\partial v}{\partial z}\right) & 0
\end{bmatrix}
\tag{9-6}
$$

Equation **9-6** can also be represented using tensor notation as

$$
\omega_{ij} = -\frac{1}{2}\varepsilon_{ijk}\vec{\omega}
\tag{9-7}
$$

where $\vec{\omega}$ is the vorticity vector referred to in the previous section. The vorticity, or local rigid body rotation is then

$$
\vec{\omega} = \begin{bmatrix}
\dfrac{\partial w}{\partial y} - \dfrac{\partial v}{\partial z} \\[2ex]
\dfrac{\partial u}{\partial z} - \dfrac{\partial w}{\partial x} \\[2ex]
\dfrac{\partial v}{\partial x} - \dfrac{\partial u}{\partial y}
\end{bmatrix}
\tag{9-8}
$$

For the reader unfamiliar with tensor notation, this presentation is certainly less than complete. However, the matrices in Equation **9-5** and Equation **9-6** directly translate into visual form, which will help clarify the concepts presented here. Referring to Figure **9–11**, the normal strain, shear strain, and rigid body motion create distinct deformation modes. These modes combine to produce the total deformation. Modes of normal strain cause compression or extension in the direction perpendicular to a surface, while shear strains cause angular distortions. These strains combined with rigid body rotation around an axis yield the total strain at a point.

The essence of the stream polygon technique is to show these modes of

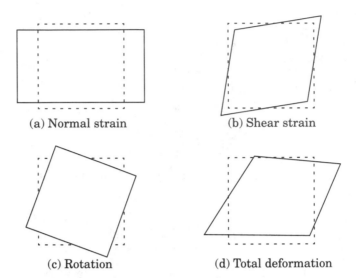

(a) Normal strain   (b) Shear strain

(c) Rotation   (d) Total deformation

Figure 9–11 Components of local deformation due to vector field. Dotted line shows initially undeformed object.

deformation. A regular n-sided polygon (Figure **9–12**) is placed into a vector field at a specified point and then deformed according to the local strain. The components of strain may be shown separately or in combination. The orientation of the normal of the polygon is arbitrary. However, it is convenient to align the normal with the local vector. Then the rigid body rotation about the vector is the streamwise vorticity, and the effects of normal and shear strain are in the plane perpendicular to a streamline passing through the point.

The stream polygon offers other interesting possibilities. The stream polygon may be swept along a trajectory, typically a streamline, to generate tubes. The radius of the tube r can be modified according to some scalar function. One application is to visualize fluid flow. In incompressible flow with no shear, the radius of the tube can vary according to the scalar function vector magnitude. Then the equation

$$r(\vec{v}) = r_{max}\sqrt{\frac{|\vec{v}_{min}|}{|\vec{v}|}}$$ (9-9)

represents an area of constant mass flow. As a result, the tube will thicken as the flow slows and narrow as the velocity increases. Each of the n sides of the tube can be colored with a different scalar function, although for visual clarity, at most, one or two functions should be used.

The streamtubes generated by the streampolygon and the streamtubes we described in the previous section are not the same. The streampolygon does not necessarily lie along a streamline. If it does, the streampolygon represents infor-

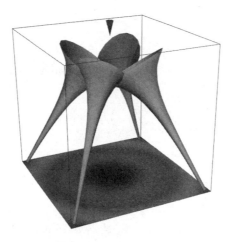

Figure 9–15 Example of hyperstreamlines (`Hyper.tcl`). The four hyperstreamlines shown are integrated along the minor principle stress axis. A plane (colored with a different lookup table) is also shown.

9.4 Modelling Algorithms

Visualizing Geometry

One of the most common applications of visualization is to view geometry. We may have a geometric representation of a part or complex assembly (perhaps designed on a CAD system) and want to view the part or assembly before it is manufactured. While viewing geometry is better addressed in a text on computer graphics, often there is dataset structure we wish to view in the same way. For example, we may want to see data mapped on a particular portion of the dataset, or view the structure of the dataset itself (e.g., view a finite element mesh).

Three-dimensional datasets have a surface and interior. Typically we want to visualize the surface of the dataset or perhaps a portion of the interior. (Note: volume rendering is a different matter — see "Volume Rendering" on page 216.) To visualize the dataset we must extract a portion of the dataset topology/geometry (and associated data) as some form of surface primitives such as polygons. If the surface of the dataset is opaque, we may also wish to eliminate occluded interior detail.

We have already seen how structured datasets, such as structured points or structured grids, have a natural *i-j-k* coordinate system that allow extraction of points, lines, and planes from the interior of the dataset (see "Structured Coordinate System" on page 311). For example, to extract the fifth *i*-plane from a struc-

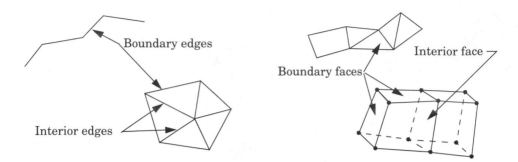

Figure 9–16 Boundary edges and faces.

tured grid of dimensions (i_m, j_m, k_m), we specify the data extents using $(4, 4, 0, (j_m - 1), 0, (k_m - 1))$ (assuming zero-offset addressing).

More generally, we can extract boundary edges and faces from a dataset. A boundary edge is an 1D cell type (e.g., line or polyline), or the edge of a 2D cell used by only that single cell. Similarly, a boundary face is a 2D cell type (e.g., polygon, triangle strip) or the face of a 3D cell used by only that single cell (Figure **9–16**). We can obtain this information using the topological operators of the previous chapter. Cells of dimensions two or less are extracted as is, while boundary edges and faces are determined by counting the number of cell neighbors for a particular topological boundary (i.e., edge or face neighbors). If there are no neighbors, the edge or face is a boundary edge or face, and is extracted.

Using these techniques we can view the structure of our dataset. However, there are also situations where we want more control in the selection of the data. We call this *data extraction*.

Data Extraction

Often we want to extract portions of data from a dataset. This may be because we want to reduce the size of the data, or because we are interested in visualizing only a portion of it.

Reducing dataset size is an important practical capability, because visualization data size can be huge. By reducing data size, reductions in computation and memory requirements can be realized. This results in better interactive response.

We also may need to reduce data size in order to visualize the important features of a large dataset. This can be used to reduce image clutter and improve the effectiveness of the visualization. Smaller data size also enables the visualization user to navigate through and inspect data more quickly relative to larger datasets. Next we describe two techniques to extract data. One is based on *geometry extraction*, and the other is based on *data thresholding*, or *thresholding*.

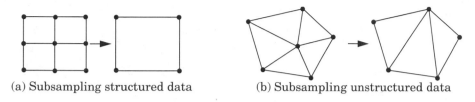

(a) Subsampling structured data   (b) Subsampling unstructured data

Figure 9–17 Subsampling data. (a) Structured data can be subsampled by choosing every nth point. (b) Subsampling unstructured data requires local retriangulation.

Geometry Extraction. Geometry extraction selects data based on geometric or topological characteristics. A common extraction technique selects a set of points and cells that lie within a specified range of ids. A typical example is selecting all cells having ids between 0–100, or all cells using point ids 250–500. Finite element analysts use this method frequently to isolate the visualization to just a few key regions.

Another useful technique called *spatial extraction*, selects dataset structure and associated data attributes lying within a specified region in space. For example, a point and radius can be used to select (or deselect) data within an enclosing sphere. Implicit functions are particularly useful tools for describing these regions. Points that evaluate negative are inside the region, while points outside the region evaluate positive; thus, cells whose points are all positive are outside the region, and cells whose points are all negative are inside the region.

Subsampling (Figure **9–17**) is a method that reduces data size by selecting a subset of the original data. The subset is specified by choosing a parameter n, specifying that every nth data point is to be extracted. For example, in structured datasets such as structured points and grids, selecting every nth point produces the results shown in Figure **9–17**(a).

Subsampling modifies the topology of a dataset. When points or cells are not selected, this leaves a topological "hole." Dataset topology must be modified to fill the hole. In structured data, this is simply a uniform selection across the structured i-j-k coordinates. In unstructured data (Figure **9–17**(b)), the hole must be filled in by using triangulation or other complex tessellation schemes. Subsampling is not typically performed on unstructured data because of its inherent complexity.

A related technique is *data masking*. In data masking we select every nth cell that at a minimum leaves one or more topological "holes" in the dataset. Masking also may change the topology of the dataset, since partial selections of cells from structured datasets can only be represented using unstructured grids. Masking is typically used to improve interactive performance or to quickly process portions of data.

Thresholding. Thresholding extracts portions of a dataset data based on attribute values. For example, we may select all cells having a point with scalar

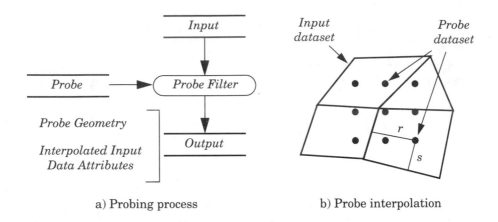

a) Probing process   b) Probe interpolation

Figure 9–18 Probing data. The geometry of one dataset *(Probe)* is used to extract dataset attributes from another dataset *(Input)*.

value between $(0,1)$ or all points having a velocity magnitude greater than 1.0.

Scalar thresholding is easily implemented. The threshold is either a single value that scalar values are greater than or less than, or a range of values. Cells or points whose associated scalar values satisfy the threshold criteria can be extracted. Other dataset attribute types such as vectors, normals, or tensors can be extracted in similar fashion by converting the type to a single scalar value. For example, vectors can be extracted using vector magnitude, and tensors using matrix determinate.

A problem with both geometry extraction and thresholding is that the approaches presented thus far extract "atomic" pieces of data, that is, a complete cell. Sometimes the cell may lie across the boundary of the threshold. In this case the cell must be clipped (see "Clipping With Scalar Fields" on page 360) and only a portion of the cell is extracted.

Probing

Probing obtains dataset attributes by sampling one dataset (the input) with a set of points (the probe) as shown in Figure **9–18**(a). Probing is also called "resampling." Examples include probing an input dataset with a sequence of points along a line, on a plane, or in a volume. The result of the probing is a new dataset (the output) with the topological and geometric structure of the probe dataset, and point attributes interpolated from the input dataset. Once the probing operation is completed, the output dataset can be visualized with any of the appropriate techniques described in this text.

Figure **9–18**(b) illustrates the details of the probing process. For every point in the probe dataset, the location in the input dataset (i.e., cell, subcell, and parametric coordinates) and interpolation weights are determined. Then the data

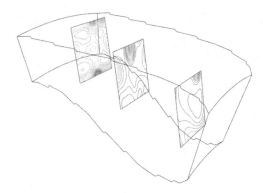

Figure 9–19 Probing data in a combustor. Probes are regular array of 50^2 points that are then passed through a contouring filter (probeComb.tcl).

values from the cell are interpolated to the probe point. Probe points that are outside the input dataset are assigned a nil (or appropriate) value. This process repeats for all points in the probe dataset.

Probing can be used to reduce data or to view data in a particular fashion.

- Data is reduced when the probe operation is limited to a subregion of the input dataset, or the number of probe points is less than the number of input points.

- Data can be viewed in a particular fashion by sampling on specially selected datasets. Using a probe dataset consisting of a line enables x-y plotting along a line, or using a plane allows surface color mapping or line contouring.

Probing must be used carefully or errors may be introduced. Under-sampling data in a region can miss important high-frequency information or localized data variations. Oversampling data, while not creating error, can give false confidence in the accuracy of the data. Thus the sampling frequency should have a similar density as the input dataset, or if higher density, the visualization should be carefully annotated as to the original data frequency.

One important application of probing converts irregular or unstructured data to structured form using a volume of appropriate resolution as a probe to sample the unstructured data. This is useful if we use volume rendering or other volume visualization techniques to view our data.

Figure **9–19** shows an example of three probes. The probes sample flow density in a structured grid. The output of the probes is passed through a contour filter to generate contour lines. As this figure illustrates, we can be selective with the location and extent of the probe, allowing us to focus on important regions in the data.

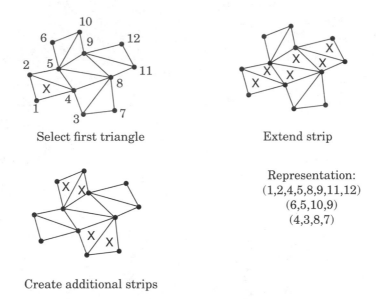

Select first triangle   Extend strip

Representation:
(1,2,4,5,8,9,11,12)
(6,5,10,9)
(4,3,8,7)

Create additional strips

Figure 9–20 Creating triangle strips.

Triangle Strip Generation

Triangle strips are compact representations of triangle polygons as described in "Triangle Strip" on page 121. Many rendering libraries include triangle strips as graphics primitives because they are a high-performance alternative to general polygon rendering.

Visualization and graphics data is often represented with triangles. Marching cubes, for example, generates thousands and potentially millions of triangles to represent an isosurface. To achieve greater performance in our visualizations, we can convert triangle polygons into triangle strips. Or, if data is represented using polygons, we can first triangulate the polygons and then create triangle strips.

A simple method to generate triangle strips uses greedy gathering of triangles into a strip (Figure **9–20**). The method proceeds as follows. An "unmarked" triangle is found to initialize the strip — unmarked triangles are triangles that have not yet been gathered into a triangle strip. Starting with the initial triangle, the strip may grow in one of three directions, corresponding to the three edges of the triangle. We choose to grow the strip in the direction of the first unmarked neighbor triangle we encounter. If there are no unmarked neighbors the triangle strip is complete; otherwise, the strip is extended by adding triangles to the list that satisfy triangle strip topology. The strip is grown until no unmarked neighbor can be found. Additional strips are then created using the same procedure until every triangle is marked.

The length of the triangle strips varies greatly depending on the structure

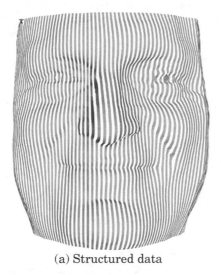 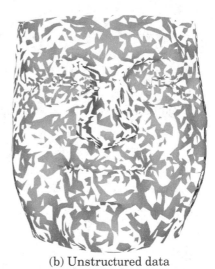

(a) Structured data (b) Unstructured data

Figure 9–21 Triangle strip examples. (a) Structured triangle mesh consisting of 134 strips each of 390 triangles (`stripF.tcl`). (b) Unstructured triangle mesh consisting of 2227 strips of average length 3.94, longest strip 101 triangles. Images are generated by displaying every other triangle strip (`uStripeF.tcl`).

of the triangle mesh. Figure **9–21**(a) shows triangle strips each of 390 triangles in length from a dataset that was originally structured. Such a case is an exception: unstructured triangle meshes typically average about 5–6 triangles per strip (Figure **9–21**(b)). Even so, the memory savings are impressive. A triangle strip of length 6 requires 8 points to represent, while 8 triangles require 24 points, for a memory savings of 66.7 percent. Rendering speed may be greatly affected, too, depending upon the capabilities of the rendering system.

Connectivity

Intercell connectivity is a topological property of datasets. Cells are topologically connected when they share boundary features such as points, edges, or faces (Figure **9–22**). Connectivity is useful in a number of modeling applications, particularly when we want to separate out "parts" of a dataset.

One application of connectivity extracts a meaningful portion of an isosurface. If the isosurface is generated from measured data such as an MRI or CT scan, it likely contains "noise" or unimportant anatomical structure. Using connectivity algorithms, we can separate out the part of the isosurface that we desire, either by eliminating noise or undesirable anatomical structure. Figure **9–23** is an example where a 2D surface of interest (e.g., an isocontour) is extracted from a noisy signal.

Connectivity algorithms can be implemented using a recursive visit

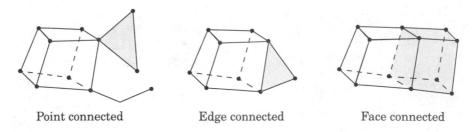

Point connected   Edge connected   Face connected

Figure 9–22 Connected cells.

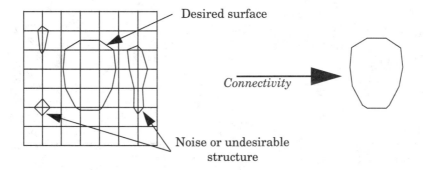

Figure 9–23 Extracting portion of isosurface of interest using connectivity.

method. We begin by choosing an arbitrary cell and mark it "visited". Then, depending upon the type of connectivity desired (i.e., point, edge, face), we gather the appropriate neighbors and mark them visited. This process repeats recursively until all connected cells are visited. We generally refer to such a set of connected cells as a connected "surface" even though the cells may be of a topological dimension other than two.

To identify additional connected surfaces we locate another unvisited cell and repeat the processes described previously. We continue to identify connected surfaces until every cell in the dataset is visited. As each connected surface is identified, it is assigned a surface number. We can use this number to specify the surfaces to extract or we can specify "seed" points or cells and extract the surfaces connected to them.

In some cases the recursion depth of the connectivity algorithm becomes larger than the computer system can manage. In this case, we can specify a maximum recursion depth. When this depth is exceeded, recursion is terminated and the current cells in the recursion are used as seeds to restart the recursion.

Polygon Normal Generation

Gouraud and Phong shading (see Chapter 3) can improve the appearance of rendered polygons. Both techniques require point normals. Unfortunately polygonal meshes do not always contain point normals, or data file formats may not support point normals. Examples include the marching cubes algorithm for general datasets (which typically will not generate surface normals) and the stereo lithography file format (does not support point normals). Figure **9–24**(a) shows a model defined from stereo-lithography format. The faceting of the model is clearly evident.

To address this situation we can compute surface normals from the polygonal mesh. A simple approach follows. First, polygon normals are computed around a common point. These normals are then averaged at the point, and the normal is renormalized (i.e., $|n| = 1$) and associated with the point. This approach works well under two conditions.

1. The orientation of all polygons surrounding the point are consistent as shown in Figure **9–24**(b). A polygon is oriented consistently if the order of defining polygon points is consistent with its edge neighbors. That is, if polygon p is defined by points *(1,2,3)*, then the polygon edge neighbor p_{23} must use the edge *(2,3)* in the direction *(3,2)*. If not consistent, then the average point normal may be zero or not accurately represent the orientation of the surface. This is because the polygon normal is computed from a cross product of the edges formed by its defining points.

2. The angular difference in surface normals between adjacent polygons is small. Otherwise, sharp corners or edges will have a washed out appearance when rendered, resulting in an unsatisfactory image (Figure **9–24**(c)).

To avoid these problems we adopt a more complex polygon normal generation algorithm. This approach includes steps to insure that polygons are oriented consistently, and an edge-splitting scheme that duplicates points across sharp edges.

To orient edges consistently we use a recursive neighbor traversal. An initial polygon is selected and marked "consistent." For each edge neighbor of the initial polygon, the ordering of the neighbor polygon points is checked — if not consistent, the ordering is reversed. The neighbor polygon is then marked "consistent." This process repeats recursively for each edge neighbor until all neighbors are marked "consistent". In some cases there may be more than one connected surface, so that the process may have to be repeated until all polygons are visited.

A similar traversal method splits sharp edges. A sharp edge is an edge shared by two polygons whose normals vary by a user-specified *feature angle*. The feature angle between two polygons is the angle between their normals (Figure **9–25**(a)). When sharp edges are encountered during the recursive traversal, the points along the edge are duplicated, effectively disconnecting the mesh along that edge (Figure **9–25**(b)). Then, when shared polygon normals are computed later in the process, contributions to the average normal across sharp edges is prevented.

On some computers limitations on recursion depth may become a problem. Polygonal surfaces can consist of millions of polygons, resulting in large recur-

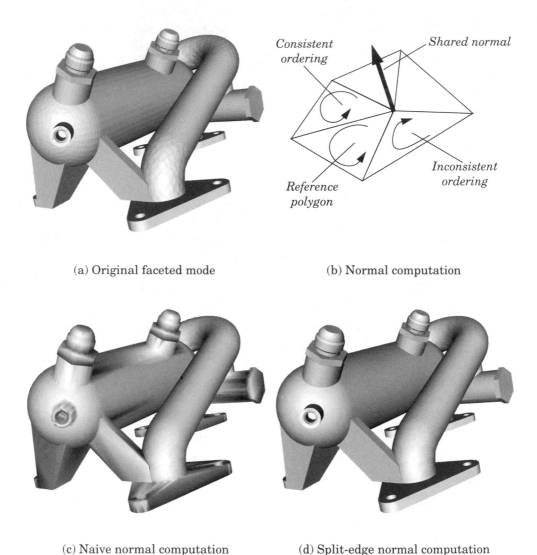

(a) Original faceted mode   (b) Normal computation

(c) Naive normal computation   (d) Split-edge normal computation

Figure 9–24 Surface normal generation. (a) Faceted model without normals. (b) Polygons must be consistently oriented to accurately compute normals. (c) Sharp edges are poorly represented using shared normals as shown on the corners of this cube. (d) Normal generation with sharp edges split (Normals.cxx).

sion depth. As a result, the depth of recursion can be specified by the user. If recursion depth exceeds the specified value, the recursion halts and the polygons on the boundary of the recursion become seeds to begin the process again.

Figure **9–24**(d) shows the result of the advanced normal generation tech-

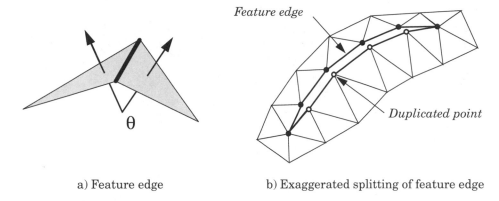

a) Feature edge   b) Exaggerated splitting of feature edge

Figure 9–25 Computing feature angles (a) and splitting edges (b).

nique with a feature angle of 60 degrees. Sharp edges are well defined and curved areas lack the faceting evident in the original model. The figure is shown with Gouraud shading.

Decimation

Various data compression techniques have been developed in response to large data size. The UNIX utilities `compress/uncompress` and the PC utility `zip` compress data files. The MPEG compression algorithm compresses video sequences. These techniques may be loss-less, meaning that no data is lost between the compression/decompression steps, or lossy, meaning that data is lost during compression. The utilities `compress/uncompress` and `zip` are loss-less, while MPEG is lossy.

In graphics, data compression techniques have been developed as well. The subsampling methods we saw earlier in this chapter are an example of simple data compression techniques for visualization data. Another emerging area of graphics data compression is polygon reduction techniques.

Polygon reduction techniques reduce the number of polygons required to model an object. The size of models, in terms of polygon count, has grown tremendously over the last few years. This is because many models are created using digital measuring devices such as laser scanners or satellites. These devices can generate data at tremendous rates. For example, a laser digitizer can generate on the order of 500,000 triangles in a 15-second scan. Visualization algorithms such as marching cubes also generate large numbers of polygons: one to three million triangles from a 512^3 volume is typical.

One polygon reduction technique is the decimation algorithm [Schroeder92a]. The goal of the decimation algorithm is to reduce the total number of triangles in a triangle mesh, preserving the original topology and forming a good approximation to the original geometry. A triangle mesh is a special form of a polygonal mesh, where each polygon is a triangle. If need be, a polygon mesh

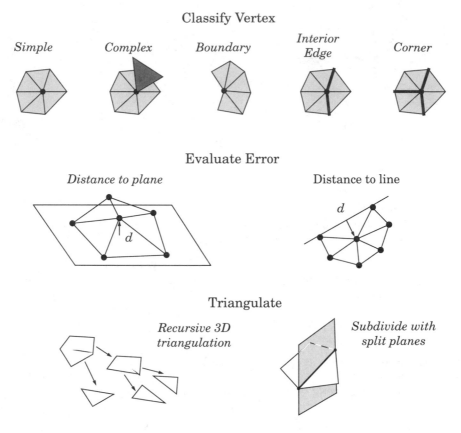

Figure 9–26 Overview of decimation algorithm.

can be converted to a triangle mesh using standard polygon triangulation methods.

Decimation is related to the subsampling technique for unstructured meshes described in Figure **9–17**(b). The differences are that

- decimation treats only triangle meshes not arbitrary unstructured grids;

- the choice of which points to delete is a function of a *decimation criterion*, a measure of the local error introduced by deleting a point; and

- the triangulation of the hole created by deleting the point is carried out in a way as to preserve edges or other important features.

Decimation proceeds by iteratively visiting each point in a triangle mesh. For each point, three basic steps are carried out (Figure **9–26**). The first step classifies the local geometry and topology in the neighborhood of the point. The classification yields one of the five categories shown in the figure: simple, boundary, complex, edge, and corner point. Based on this classification, the second step uses a local error measure (i.e., the decimation criterion) to determine whether the point can be deleted. If the criterion is satisfied, the third step deletes the point (along with associated triangles), and triangulates the resulting hole. A more detailed description of each of these steps and example applications follow.

Point Classification. The first step of the decimation algorithm characterizes the local geometry and topology for a given point. The outcome of classification determines whether the vertex is a potential candidate for deletion, and if it is, which criteria to use.

Each point may be assigned one of five possible classifications: simple, complex, boundary, interior edge, or corner vertex. Examples of each type are shown in Figure **9–26**.

A *simple point* is surrounded by a complete cycle of triangles, and each edge that uses the point is used by exactly two triangles. If the edge is not used by two triangles, or if the point is used by a triangle not in the cycle of triangles, then the point is *complex*. These are nonmanifold cases.

A point that is on the boundary of a mesh, that is, within a semicycle of triangles, is a *boundary point*.

A simple point can be further classified as an *interior edge* or *corner point*. These classifications are based on the local mesh geometry. If the surface normal angle between two adjacent triangles is greater than a specified *feature angle*, then a *feature edge* exists (see Figure **9–25**(a)). When a point is used by two feature edges, the point is an interior edge point. If one, three, or more feature edges use the point, the point is a *corner point*.

Complex and corner vertices are not deleted from the triangle mesh; all other vertices become candidates for deletion.

Decimation Criterion. Once we have a candidate point for deletion, we estimate the error that would result by deleting the point and then replacing it (and its associated triangles) with another triangulation. There are a number of possible error measures; but the simplest are based on distance measures of local planarity or local colinearity (Figure **9–26**).

In the local region surrounding a simple point, the mesh is considered nearly "flat," since there are by definition no feature edges. Hence, simple points use an error measure based on distance to plane. The plane passing through the local region can be computed either using a least-squares plane or by computing an area-averaged plane.

Points classified as boundary or interior edge are considered to lay on an edge, and use a distance to edge error measure. That is, we compute the distance that the candidate point is from the new edge formed during the triangulation process.

A point satisfies the decimation criterion d if its distance measure is less than d. The point can then be deleted. All triangles using the point are deleted as well, leaving a "hole" in the mesh. This hole is patched using a local triangulation process.

Triangulation. After deleting a point, the resulting hole must be retriangulated. Although the hole, defined by a loop of edges, is topologically two dimensional, it is generally non-planar, and therefore general purpose 2D triangulation techniques cannot be used. Instead, we use a special recursive 3D divide-and-conquer technique to triangulate the loop.

Triangulation proceeds as follows. An initial split plane is chosen to divide the loop in half and create two subloops. If all the points in each subloop lie on opposite sides of the plane, then the split is a valid one. In addition, an *aspect ratio* check insures that the loop is not too long and skinny, thereby resulting in needle-like triangles. The aspect ratio is the ratio between the length of the split line to the minimum distance of a point in the subloop to the split plane. If the candidate split plane is not valid or does not satisfy the aspect ratio criterion, then another candidate split plane is evaluated. Once a split plane is found, then the subdivision of each subloop continues recursively until a subloop consists of three edges. In this case, the subloop generates a triangle and halts the recursion.

Occasionally, triangulation fails because no split plane can be found. In this case, the candidate point is not deleted and the mesh is left in its original state. This poses no problem to the algorithm and decimation continues by visiting the next point in the dataset.

Results. Typical compression rates for the decimation algorithm range from 2:1 to 100:1, with 10:1 a nominal figure for "large" (i.e., 10^5 triangles) datasets. The results vary greatly depending upon the type of data. CAD models typically reduce the least because these models have many sharp edges and other detailed features, and the CAD modellers usually produce minimal triangulations. Terrain data, especially if relatively flat regions are present, may reduce at rates of 100:1.

Figure **9–27** shows two applications of decimation to laser digitized data and to a terrain model of Honolulu, Hawaii. In both cases the reduction was on the order of 90 percent for a 10:1 compression ratio. Wireframe images are shown to accentuate the density of the polygonal meshes. The left-hand image in each pair is the original data; the right-hand image is the decimated mesh. Notice the gradations in the decimated mesh around features of high curvature. The advantage of decimation, as compared to subsampling techniques, is that the mesh is adaptively modified to retain more details in areas of high curvature.

Advanced Techniques. Polygon reduction is an active field of research. Many powerful algorithms beyond the decimation algorithm have been presented (see "Bibliographic Notes" on page 421). Although we cannot cover the field in its entirety in this section, there are two notable trends worth addressing. First, progressive schemes [Hoppe96] allow incremental transmission and reconstruction of triangle meshes — this is especially important for Web-based geometry visualization. Second, recent algorithms modify the topology of the mesh [He96] [Popovic97] [Schroeder97]. This feature is essential towards obtaining arbitrary levels of mesh reduction.

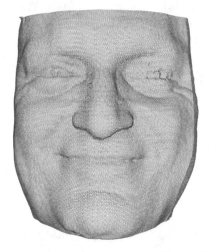 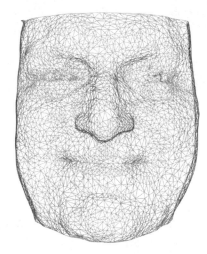

(a) Decimation of laser digitizer data (`deciFran.tcl`).

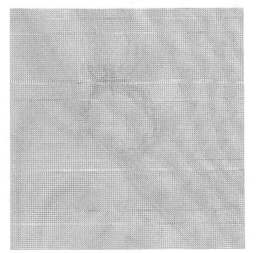 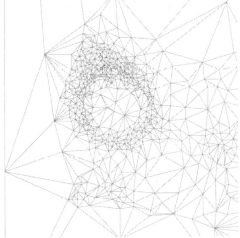

(b) Decimation of terrain data (`deciHawa.tcl`).

Figure 9–27 Examples of decimation algorithm. Triangle meshes are shown in wireframe.

A *progressive mesh* is a series of triangle meshes M^i related by the operations

$$(\hat{M} = M^n) \to M^{n-1} \to \dots \to M^1 \to M^0 \tag{9-14}$$

where M and M^n represent the mesh at full resolution, and M^0 is a simplified base mesh. The critical characteristic of progressive meshes is that is possible to choose the mesh operations in such a way to make them invertible. Then the operations can be applied in reverse order (starting with the base mesh M^0)

$$M^0 \rightarrow M^1 \rightarrow ... \rightarrow M^{n-1} \rightarrow M^n \qquad \text{(9-15)}$$

to obtain a mesh of desired reduction level (assuming that the reduction level is *less than* the base mesh M^0).

One such invertible operator is an edge collapse and its inverse is the edge split shown in Figure **9–28**(a). Each collapse of an interior mesh edge results in the elimination of two triangles (or one triangle if the collapsed vertex is on a boundary). The operation is represented by five values

$$\text{Edge Collapse/Split } (v_s, v_t, v_l, v_r, A) \qquad \text{(9-16)}$$

where v_s is the vertex to collapse/split, v_t is the vertex being collapsed to / split from, and v_l and v_r are two additional vertices to the left and right of the split edge. These two vertices in conjunction with v_s and v_t define the two triangles deleted or added. A represents vertex attribute information, which at a minimum contains the coordinates x of the collapsed / split vertex v_s. (Note: in the context of the decimation algorithm, the edge collapse operator replaces the recursive triangulation process.)

While progressive meshes allow us to compactly store and transmit triangle meshes, the problem remains that the size of the base mesh is often larger than desired reduction level. Since in some applications we wish to realize *any* given level, we want the base mesh to contain no triangles

$$(\hat{M} = M^n) \rightarrow M^{n-1} \rightarrow ... \rightarrow M^1 \rightarrow (M^0 = M(V, \varnothing)) \qquad \text{(9-17)}$$

(some vertices are necessary to initiate the edge split operations). To address this problem, the invertible edge collapse/split operator — which is topology preserving — is extended with a vertex split/merge operator. The vertex split/merge operator modifies the topology of the mesh and allows arbitrary levels of reduction.

A mesh split occurs when we replace vertex v_s with vertex v_t in the connectivity list of one or more triangles that originally used vertex v_s (Figure **9–28**(b)). The new vertex v_t is given exactly the same coordinate value as v_s. Splits introduce a "crack" or "hole" into the mesh. We prefer not to split the mesh, but at high decimation rates this relieves topological constraint and enables further decimation. Splitting is only invoked when a valid edge collapse is not available, or when a vertex cannot be triangulated (e.g., a nonmanifold vertex). Once the split operation occurs, the vertices v_s and v_t are re-inserted into the priority queue.

Different splitting strategies are used depending on the classification of the vertex (Figure **9–28**(c)). Interior edge vertices are split along the feature edges, as are corner vertices. Nonmanifold vertices are split into separate manifold pieces. In any other type of vertex splitting occurs by arbitrarily separating the loop into two pieces. For example, if a simple vertex cannot be deleted because a

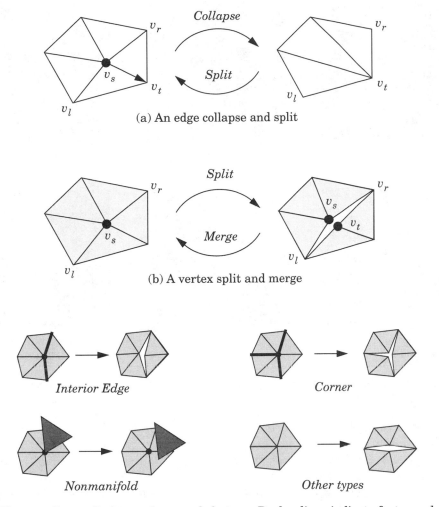

(a) An edge collapse and split

(b) A vertex split and merge

Interior Edge   *Corner*

Nonmanifold   *Other types*

(c) Vertex splits applied to various mesh features.Darker lines indicate feature edges.

Figure 9–28 Progressive mesh operators edge collapse/split and vertex split/merge.

valid edge collapse is not available, the loop of triangles will be arbitrarily divided in half (possibly in a recursive process).

Like the edge collapse/split, the vertex split/merge can also be represented as a compact operation. A vertex split/merge operation can be represented with four values

$$\text{Vertex Split/Merge } (v_s, v_t, v_l, v_r) \tag{9-18}$$

The vertices v_l and v_r define a sweep of triangles (from v_r to v_l) that are to be

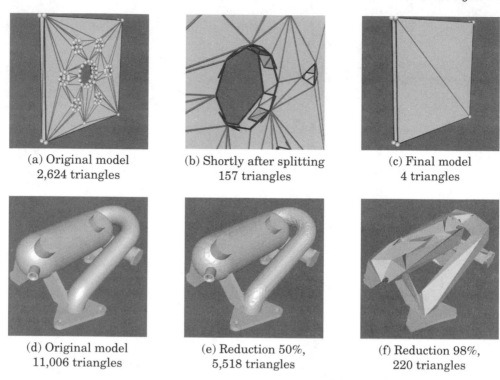

(a) Original model
2,624 triangles

(b) Shortly after splitting
157 triangles

(c) Final model
4 triangles

(d) Original model
11,006 triangles

(e) Reduction 50%,
5,518 triangles

(f) Reduction 98%,
220 triangles

Figure 9–29 Results of topology modifying progressive mesh algorithm.

separated from the original vertex v_s (we adopt a counter-clockwise ordering convention to uniquely define the sweep of triangles).

Figure **9–29** shows the results of applying the topology modifying progressive mesh algorithm to two sets of data. In Figure **9–29**(a-c), a thin plate with holes is decimated (the darker lines show split edges). The middle image in the sequence shows the limits of topology on the algorithm. It is only when the topology of the mesh is allowed to be modified that the final level of reduction is possible. Figure **9–29**(d-f) shows the same algorithm applied to CAD data.

Mesh Smoothing

Mesh smoothing is a technique that adjusts the point coordinates of a dataset. The purpose of mesh smoothing is to improve the appearance of a mesh, and/or improve the shape of dataset cells. During smoothing the topology of the dataset is not modified, only the geometry. Applications of mesh smoothing include improving the appearance of isosurfaces, or as a modelling tool to remove surface noise. The appearance of models can be dramatically improved by applying mesh smoothing. Figure **9–30** is an example of smoothing applied to analytic surface (a semicylinder) with a random surface distortion (smoothCyl.tcl).

A simple, yet effective technique is Laplacian smoothing. The Laplacian

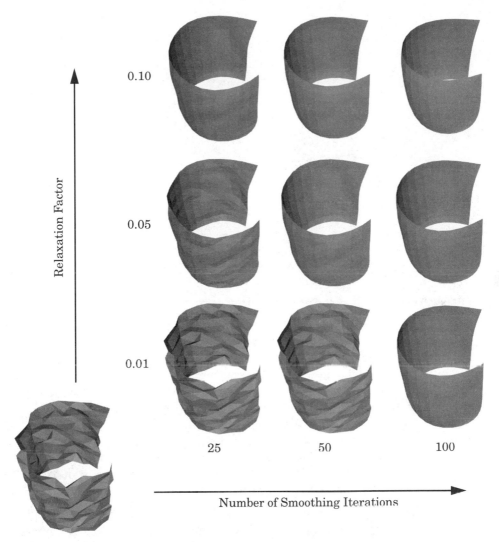

Figure 9–30 Mesh smoothing applied to a semicylinder. Lower left image is the original model. On the x-axis the number of smoothing iterations is modified. On the y-axis the relaxation factor is modified.

smoothing equation for a point p_i at position $\vec{x}_i$ is given by

$$\vec{x}_{i+1} = \vec{x}_i + \lambda \vec{V}_{ij} = \vec{x}_i + \lambda \sum (\vec{x}_j - \vec{x}_i) \quad \forall j : 0 \le j < n \tag{9-19}$$

where $\vec{x}_{i+1}$ is the new coordinate position, and $\vec{x}_j$ are the positions of points p_j "connected" to p_i, and λ is a user-specified weight. Geometrically this relation is depicted in Figure **9–31**(a). Here the vertex p_i is connected to the surrounding points p_j via edges. The equation expresses that the new position $\vec{x}_{i+1}$ is offset

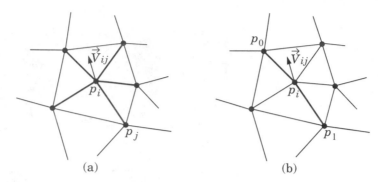

Figure 9–31 Mesh smoothing. (a) Motion of point. (b) Smoothing a point on an edge. Bold lines indicate connectivity.

from the original position $\vec{x}_i$ plus the average vector $\vec{V}_{ij}$ multiplied by λ. Typically, the factor λ is a small number (e.g., 0.01), and the process is executed repeatedly (e.g., 50-100 iterations). Notice that the overall effect of smoothing is to reduce the high frequency surface information. The algorithm will reduce surface curvature and tend to flatten the surface.

Besides adjusting the number of iterations and smoothing factor, smoothing can be controlled by modifying the connections between p_i and its surrounding points p_j. For example, if p_i lies along a fold or sharp edge in the mesh, we may want to only use the two edge end points to compute the smoothing vector $\vec{V}_{ij}$, limiting the motion of p_i along the edge (Figure **9–31**(b)). We can also anchor p_i to prevent any motion. Anchoring is useful for points that are located on "corners" or other special features such as nonmanifold attachments. One benefit of anchoring and controlling point connectivity is that we can limit the amount of shrinkage in the mesh. It also tends to produce better overall results. (In Figure **9–30** the boundary points of the surface are constrained to move along the boundary, while the points at sharp corners are anchored.)

Although Laplacian smoothing works well in most cases, there are applications of Laplacian smoothing that can badly damage the mesh. Large numbers of smoothing iterations, or large smoothing factors, can cause excessive shrinkage and surface distortion. Some objects, like spheres or the cylinder shown in Figure **9–30**, will lose volume with each iteration, and can even shrink to a point. In rare cases it is possible for the mesh to pull itself "inside-out." Situations like this occur when the average vector moves p_i across a mesh boundary, causing some of the attached triangles to overlap or intersect.

Mesh smoothing is particularly useful when creating models that do not require high accuracy. As we have seen, smoothing modifies point coordinates and, therefore, surface geometry. Use smoothing to improve the appearance of models, but characterize error carefully if you are going to measure from a smoothed surface. Alternatively, you may want to design your own smoothing algorithms that better fit the underlying data.

Swept Volumes and Surfaces

Consider moving an object (e.g., your hand) over some path (e.g., raise your hand). How can we visualize this motion? The obvious answer is to form a time-animation sequence as the hand is moved. But what if we wish to statically represent the motion as well as the space that is traversed by the hand? Then we can use *swept surfaces* and *swept volumes*.

A swept volume is the volume of space occupied by an object as it moves through space along an arbitrary trajectory. A swept surface is the surface of the swept volume. Together, swept volumes and swept surfaces can statically represent the motion of objects.

Past efforts at creating swept surfaces and volumes have focused on analytical techniques. The mathematical representation of various 3D geometric primitives (e.g., lines, polygons, splines) was extended to include a fourth dimension of time (the path). Unfortunately, these approaches have never been practically successful, partly due to mathematical complexity and partly due to problem degeneracies.

Degeneracies occur when an n-dimensional object moves in such a way that its representation becomes $(n-1)$-dimensional. For example, moving a plane in the direction of its normal, sweeps out a 3D "cubical" volume. Sweeping the plane in a direction perpendicular to its normal, however, results in a degenerate condition, since the plane sweeps out a 2D "rectangle."

Instead of creating swept surfaces analytically, numerical approximation techniques can be used [Schroeder94]. Implicit modeling provides the basis for an effective technique to visualize object motion via swept surfaces and volumes. The technique is immune to degeneracies and can treat any geometric representation for which a distance function can be computed, such as the **vtk** cell types.

The technique to generate swept surfaces and volumes using an implicit modeling approach proceeds as follows. The geometric model, or part, and a path describing the parts motion, or sweep trajectory ST, must be defined. Then we use the following steps as depicted in Figure **9–32**.

1. Generate an implicit model from the part. This results in an implicit representation in the form of a volume. We call this the implicit model V_I.

2. Construct another volume, the workspace volume V_W, that strictly bounds V_I as it moves along the path ST. Then sweep V_I through V_W by moving in small steps, Δx, along ST. At each step, s, sample V_I with the workspace volume V_W. We use a boolean union operation to perform the sampling.

3. Extract isosurface, or offset surface(s) from V_W using a contouring algorithm such as marching cubes.

4. Step 3 may create multiple connected surfaces. If a single surface is desired, use connectivity to extract the single "largest" surface (in terms of number of triangles). This surface is an approximation to the swept surface, and the volume it encloses is an approximation to the swept volume.

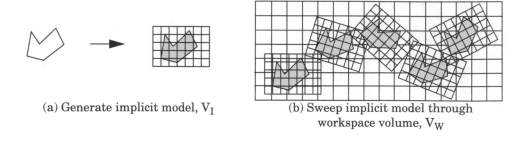

(a) Generate implicit model, V_I

(b) Sweep implicit model through workspace volume, V_W

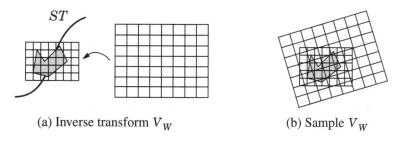

(c) Generate swept surface via isosurface extraction.
Use connectivity to extract single surface.

Figure 9–32 Overview of swept surface technique.

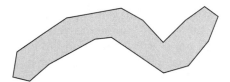

(a) Inverse transform V_W

(b) Sample V_W

Figure 9–33 Generating workspace volume by sampling implicit volume.

There are a few points that require additional explanation. This algorithm uses two volumes, the implicit model and the workspace volume. Both are implicit models, but the workspace volume is used to accumulate the part as it moves along the sweep trajectory. In theory, the part could be sampled directly into the workspace volume to create the implicit model of the swept surface. Performance issues dictate that the implicit model is sampled into the workspace volume. This is because it is much faster to sample the implicit model of the part rather than the part itself, since computing the distance function from a part that may consist of tens of thousands of cells is relatively time-consuming, compared to sampling the implicit model V_I.

Sampling V_I is depicted in Figure **9–33**. The sweep trajectory is defined by

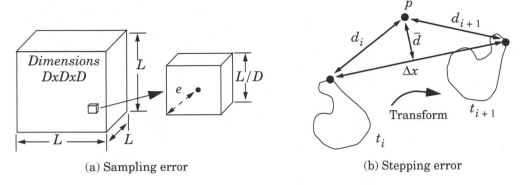

(a) Sampling error   (b) Stepping error

Figure 9–34 Computing sampling and stepping error.

a series of transformation matrices $ST = \{t_1, t_2, ..., t_m\}$. As the part moves along ST, interpolation is used to compute an inbetween transformation matrix t. Sampling is achieved by inverse transforming V_W into the local space of V_I using t. Then, similar to the probe operation described in "Probing" on page 374, the points of V_W are transformed by the inverse of the transformation matrix t^{-1}, and used to interpolate the distance values from the implicit model V_I.

Because we are dealing with an implicit modeling technique, parts with concave features can generate multiple surfaces. As discussed in "Connectivity" on page 377, the connectivity algorithm is used to separate out the swept surface. This final surface is an approximation to the actual swept surface, since we are sampling the actual geometric representation on an array of points (i.e., the implicit model), and then sampling the implicit model on another volume (i.e., the workspace volume). Also, stepping along the sweep trajectory generates errors proportional to the step size Δx.

These errors can be characterized as follows (Figure **9–34**). Given a voxel size L/D, where L is the edge length of the volume, and D is the dimension of the volume (assumed uniform for convenience), the maximum sampling error is

$$e \le \frac{\sqrt{3}}{2}\left(\frac{L}{D}\right) \tag{9-20}$$

The error due to stepping, which includes both translation and rotational components, is bounded by $\Delta x/2$, where Δx is the maximum displacement of any point on the implicit model at any given translational step. Combining these terms for sampling both volumes and the error due to stepping, the total error is

$$e_{\text{tot}} \le \frac{\sqrt{3}}{2}\left(\frac{L_I}{D_I} + \frac{L_W}{D_W}\right) + \frac{\Delta x}{2} \tag{9-21}$$

where the subscripts I and W refer to the implicit model and workspace volume, respectively.

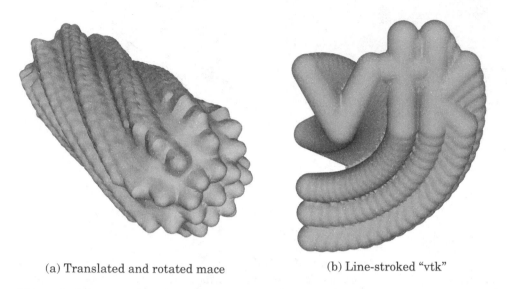

(a) Translated and rotated mace   (b) Line-stroked "vtk"

Figure 9–35 Swept surfaces. (a) Swept mace sampled at 25 locations (`sweptMac.cxx`). (b) Swept vtk sampled at 21 locations (`sweptVtk.tcl`).

To show the application of this algorithm, we have generated swept surfaces for the letters "**vtk**" and the "mace" model as shown in Figure **9–35**. We have purposely chosen a step size to exaggerate the stepping error. Using more steps would smooth out the surface "bumps" due to stepping. Also, the appearance of the surface varies greatly with the selected isosurface value. Larger values give rounder, smoother surfaces. If you use small values near zero (assuming positive distance function) the surface may break up. To correct this you need to use a higher resolution workspace or compute negative distances. Negative distances are computed during the implicit modeling step by negating all points *inside* the original geometry. Negative distances allow us to use a zero isosurface value or to generate internal offset surfaces. Negative distances can only be computed for closed (i.e., manifold) objects.

Visualizing Unstructured Points

Unstructured point datasets consist of points at irregular positions in 3D space. The relationship between points is arbitrary. Examples of unstructured point datasets are visualizing temperature distribution from an array of (arbitrarily) placed thermocouples, or rainfall level measured at scattered positions over a geographic region.

Unlike structured points and grids, or even unstructured grids, unstructured point dataset have no topological component relating one point to another. For these reasons unstructured points are simple to represent but difficult to visualize. They are difficult to visualize because there is no inherent "structure"

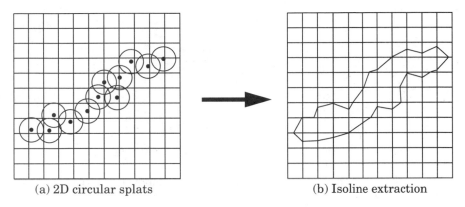

(a) 2D circular splats   (b) Isoline extraction

Figure 9–36 Splatting techniques depicted in 2D. (a) Injecting points into structured point dataset (circular splats). (b) Visualizing structured point dataset via contouring.

to which we can apply our library of visualization techniques. Beyond just displaying points (possibly colored with scalar value, or using oriented vector glyphs) none of the techniques discussed thus far can be used. Thus, to visualize unstructured points we have to build structure to which we can apply our visualization techniques.

There are several approaches available to build topological structure given a random set of points. One common approach samples unstructured points with a structured point set, and then visualizes the data using standard volume or surface-based rendering techniques. Another approach creates n-dimensional triangulations from the unstructured points, thereby creating topological structure. These and other common techniques are described in the following sections.

Splatting Techniques. Splatting techniques build topological structure by sampling unstructured points with a structured point set (Figure **9–36**). The sampling is performed by creating special influence, or splatting, functions $SF(x,y,z)$ that distribute the data value of each unstructured point over the surrounding region. To sample the unstructured points, each point is inserted into a structured point dataset SP, and the data values are distributed through SP using the splatting functions $SF(x,y,z)$. Once the topological structure is built, any structured point visualization technique can be used (including volume rendering).

A common splatting function is a uniform Gaussian distribution centered at a point p_i. The function is conveniently cast into the form

$$SF(x, y, z) = se^{-f(r/R)^2} \qquad\qquad \textbf{(9-22)}$$

where s is a scale factor that multiplies the exponential, f is the exponent scale factor $f \geq 0$, r is the distance between any point and the Gaussian center point (i.e., the splat point) $r = \|p - p_i\|$, and R is the radius of influence of the Gaussian, where $r \leq R$.

The Gaussian function (Figure **9–37**(a)) becomes a circle in cross section in

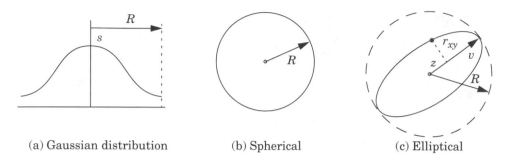

(a) Gaussian distribution   (b) Spherical   (c) Elliptical

Figure 9–37 Gaussian splatting functions. (a) one-dimensional, (b) 2D spherical, and (c) 2D elliptical.

two dimensions (Figure **9–37**(b)) and a sphere in three dimensions. Since the value of the function is maximum when $r = 0$, the maximum value is given by the scale factor s. The parameter f controls the rate of decay of the splat. Scalar values can be used to set the value of s, so that relatively large scalar values create bigger splats than smaller values.

Splats may be accumulated using the standard implicit modeling boolean operations (Equation **6-13**, Equation **6-14**, and Equation **6-15**). That is, we may choose to form a union, intersection, or difference of the splats. The union and intersection operators are used most frequently.

Another interesting variation modifies the shape of the splat according to a vector quantity such as surface normal or vector data. Figure **9–37**(c) shows an example where the splat shape is elongated in the direction parallel to a vector. Thus, if we have a set of points and normals, we can create a polygonal surface by combining splatting with isosurface extraction.

To generate oriented splats, we modify Equation **9-22** by introducing an eccentricity factor E and the vector $\vec{v}$.

$$SF(x, y, z) = se^{-f\left(\frac{\left(\frac{r_{xy}}{E}\right)^2 + z^2}{R^2}\right)} \qquad \textbf{(9-23)}$$

where z and r_{xy} are computed from

$$z = \vec{v} \cdot (p - p_i), \text{ with } |\vec{v}| = 1$$
$$r_{xy} = r^2 - z^2 \qquad \textbf{(9-24)}$$

The parameter z is the distance along the vector $\vec{v}$, and the parameter r_{xy} is the distance perpendicular to v to the point p. The eccentricity factor controls the shape of the splat. A value $E = 1$ results in spherical splats, whereas $E > 1$ yields flattened splats and $E < 1$ yields elongated splats in the direction of the vector v.

Figure **9–38**(a) shows an elliptical splat with $E = 10$. (The splat surface is created by using isosurface extraction.) As expected, the splat is an ellipsoid. Figure **9–38**(b) is an application of elliptical splatting used to reconstruct a surface from an unstructured set of points. The advantage of using an elliptical splat is that we can flatten the splat in the plane perpendicular to the point normal. This tends to bridge the space between the point samples. The surface itself is extracted using a standard isosurface extraction algorithm.

Interpolation Techniques. Interpolation techniques construct a function to smoothly interpolate a set of unstructured points. That is, given a set of n points $p_i = (x_i, y_i, z_i)$ and function values $F_i(p_i)$, a new function $F(p)$ is created that interpolates the points p_i. Once the interpolation function is constructed, we can build topological structure from the unstructured points by sampling $F(p)$ over a structured point dataset. We can then visualize the structured point dataset using the various techniques presented throughout the text.

Shepard's method is an inverse distance weighted interpolation technique [Wixom78]. The interpolation functions can be written

$$F(p) = \frac{\displaystyle\sum_{i=1}^{n} \frac{F_i}{|p - p_i|^2}}{\displaystyle\sum_{i=1}^{n} \frac{1}{|p - p_i|^2}} \tag{9-25}$$

where $F(p_i) = F_i$. Shepard's method is easy to implement, but has the undesirable property that limits its usefulness for most practical applications. The interpolation functions generate a local "flat spot" at each point p_i since the derivatives are zero

$$\frac{\partial F}{\partial x} = \frac{\partial F}{\partial y} = \frac{\partial F}{\partial z} = 0 \tag{9-26}$$

As a result, Shepard's method is overly constrained in the region around each point.

Shepard's method is an example of a basis function method. That is, the interpolation function $F(p)$ consists of a sum of functions centered at each data point, p_i. Other basis function methods have been developed as described by Nielson [Nielson91]. They vary in localization of the basis functions and the sophistication of the interpolation function. Localization of basis functions means that their effect is isolated to a small region. Examples of more sophisticated basis functions include quadratic polynomials and cubic splines. Please see the references for more information.

Triangulation Techniques. Triangulation techniques build topology directly from unstructured points. The points are *triangulated* to create a topological structure

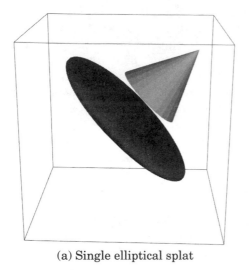

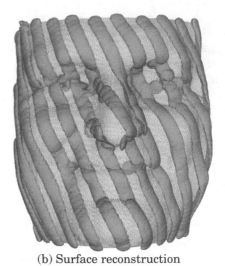

(a) Single elliptical splat   (b) Surface reconstruction

Figure 9–38   Elliptical splatting. (a) Single elliptical splat with eccentricity $E=10$. Cone shows orientation of vector (`singleSplat.cxx`). (b) Surface reconstructed using elliptical splats into 100^3 volume followed by isosurface extraction. Points regularly subsampled and overlayed on original mesh (`splatFace.tcl`).

consisting of n-dimensional simplices that completely bound the points and linear combinations of the points (the so-called *convex hull*). The result of triangulation is a set of triangles (2D) or tetrahedra (3D), depending upon the dimension of the input data [Lawson86].

An n-dimensional triangulation of a point set $P = (p_1, p_2, p_3, ..., p_n)$ is a collection of n-dimensional simplices whose defining points lie in P. The simplices do not intersect one another and share only boundary features such as edges or faces. The Delaunay triangulation is a particularly important form [Bowyer81] [Watson81]. It has the property that the circumsphere of any n-dimensional simplex contains no other points of P except the $n+1$ defining points of the simplex (Figure **9–39**(a)).

The Delaunay triangulation has many interesting properties. In two dimensions, the Delaunay triangulation has been shown to be the optimal triangulation. That is, the minimum interior angle of a triangle in a Delaunay triangulation is greater than or equal to the minimum interior angle of any other possible triangulation. The Delaunay triangulation is the dual of the Dirichlet tessellation (Figure **9–39**(b)), another important construction in computational geometry. The Dirichlet tessellation, also known as the Voronoi tessellation, is a tiling of space where each tile represents the space closest to a point p_i. (The tiles are called Voronoi cells.) An n-dimensional Delaunay triangulation can be constructed from the Dirichlet tessellation by creating edges between Voronoi cells that share common $n-1$ boundaries (e.g., faces in 3D and edges in 2D). Conversely, the vertices of the Dirichlet tessellation are located at the circumcenters

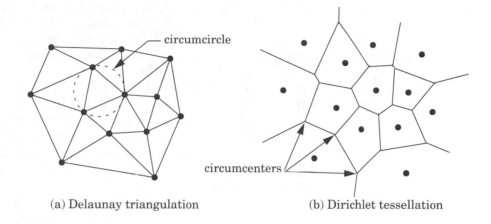

(a) Delaunay triangulation   (b) Dirichlet tessellation

Figure 9–39 The Delaunay triangulation (a) and Dirichlet tessellation (b). The circumcircle of each triangle in a Delaunay triangulation contains no other points but the three vertices of the triangle. The region surrounding each point p_i in a Dirichlet tessellation is the set of points closest to p_i.

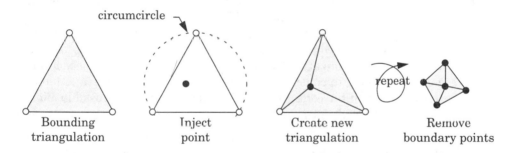

Bounding   Inject   Create new   Remove
triangulation   point   triangulation   boundary points

Figure 9–40 Computing the Delaunay triangulation using technique of Watson and Boyer. Points are injected into triangulation forming new Delaunay triangulations. In the final step, the initial bounding points are removed to reveal final triangulation.

of the Delaunay circumcircles.

The Delaunay triangulation can be computed using a variety of techniques. We describe a particularly elegant technique introduced independently by Watson [Watson81] and Bowyer [Bowyer81] (Figure **9–40**). The algorithm begins by constructing an initial Delaunay triangulation that strictly bounds the point set P, the so-called bounding triangulation. This bounding triangulation can be as simple as a single triangle (2D) or tetrahedron (3D). Then, each point of P is injected one by one into the current triangulation. If the injected point lies within the circumcircle of any simplex, then the simplex is deleted, leaving a "hole" in the triangulation. After deleting all simplices, the *n–1* dimensional faces on the boundary of the hole, along with the injected point, are used to construct a modified triangulation. This is a Delaunay triangulation, and the process continues until all points are injected into the triangulation. The last step removes the simplices connecting the points forming the initial bounding triangulation to reveal the completed Delaunay triangulation.

This simplistic presentation of triangulation techniques has shown how to create topological structure from a set of unstructured points. We have ignored some difficult issues such as degeneracies and numerical problems. Degeneracies occur when points in a Delaunay triangulation lie in such a way that the triangulation is not unique. For example, the points lying at the vertices of a square, rectangle, or hexagon are degenerate because they can be triangulated in more than one way, where each triangulation is equivalent (in terms of Delaunay criterion) to the other. Numerical problems occur when we attempt to compute circumcenters, especially in higher-dimensional triangulations, or when simplices of poor aspect ratio are present.

Despite these problems, triangulation methods are a powerful tool for visualizing unstructured points. Once we convert the data into a triangulation (or in our terminology, an unstructured grid), we can directly visualize our data using standard unstructured grid techniques.

Hybrid Techniques. Recent work has focused on combining triangulation and basis function techniques for interpolating 2D bivariate data. The basic idea is as follows. A triangulation of P is constructed. Then an interpolating network of curves is defined over the edges of the triangulation. These curves are constructed with certain minimization properties of interpolating splines. Finally, the curve network is used to construct a series of triangular basis functions, or surface patches, that exhibit continuity in function value, and possibly higher order derivatives. (See [Nielson91] for more information.)

Multidimensional Visualization

The treatment of multidimensional datasets is an important data visualization issue. Each point in a dataset is described by an n-dimensional coordinate, where $n \geq 3$. Here we assume that each coordinate is an independent variable, and that we wish to visualize a single dependent variable. (Multidimensional visualization of vectors and tensors is an open research area.) An application of multidimensional data is financial visualization, where we might want to visualize return on investment as a function of interest rate, initial investment, investment period, and income, to name just a few possibilities.

There are two fundamental problems that we must address when applying multidimensional visualization. These are the problems of *projection* and *understanding*.

The problem of projection is that in using computer graphics we have two dimensions in which to present our data, or possibly three or four if we use specialized methods. Using 3D graphics we can give the illusion of three dimensions, or we can use stereo viewing techniques to achieve three dimensions. We can also

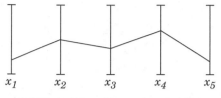

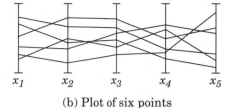

(a) Plot of five-dimensional point   (b) Plot of six points

Figure 9–41 Plotting a five-dimensional point using parallel coordinates. (a) plot of single point, (b) plot of many points.

use time as a fourth dimension by animating images. However, except for these limited situations, general n-dimensional data cannot be represented on a 2D computer screen.

The problem of understanding is that humans do not easily comprehend more than three dimensions, or possibly three dimensions plus time. Thus, even if we could create a technique to display data of many dimensions, the difficulty in understanding the data would impair the usefulness of the technique.

Most multidimensional visualization techniques work with some form of dimension mapping, where n dimensions are mapped to three dimensions and then displayed with 3D computer graphics techniques. The mapping is achieved by fixing all variables except three, and then applying the visualization techniques described throughout the text to the resulting data. For maximum benefit, the process of fixing independent variables, mapping to three dimensions, and then generating visualization must be interactive. This improves the effectiveness of the visualization process, allowing the user to build an internal model of the data by manipulating different parts of the data.

One novel approach to multidimensional visualization has been proposed by Inselberg and Dimsdale [Inselberg87]. This approach uses *parallel coordinate systems*. Instead of plotting points on orthogonal axes, the ith dimensional coordinate of each point is plotted along separate, parallel axes. This is shown in Figure **9–41** for a five-dimensional point. In parallel coordinate plots, points appear as lines. As a result, plots of n-dimensional points appear as sequences of line segments that may intersect or group to form complex fan patterns. In so doing, the human pattern recognition capability is engaged. Unfortunately, if the number of points becomes large, and the data is not strongly correlated, the resulting plots can become a solid mass of black, and any data trends are drowned in the visual display.

Another useful multivariable technique uses glyphs. This technique associates a portion of the glyph with each variable. Although glyphs cannot generally be designed for arbitrary n-dimensional data, in many applications we can create glyphs to convey the information we are interested in. Refer to "Glyphs" on page 185 for more information about glyphs.

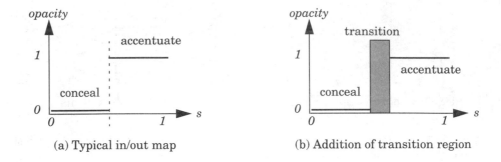

Figure 9–42 1D texture map. (a) In/out map. (b) Addition of transition region to in/out map.

Texture Algorithms

Texturing is a common tool in computer graphics used to introduce detail without the high cost of graphics primitives. As we suggested in Chapter 7, texture mapping can also be used to visualize data. We explore a few techniques in the following sections.

Texture Thresholding. We saw earlier how to threshold data based on scalar values (see "Thresholding" on page 373). We refer to this approach as *geometric thresholding* because structural components of a dataset (e.g., points and cells) are extracted based on data value. In contrast, we can use texture mapping techniques to achieve similar results. We call this technique *texture thresholding*.

Texture thresholding conceals features we do not want to see and accentuates features that we want to see. There are many variations on this theme. A feature can be concealed by making it transparent or translucent, by reducing its intensity, or using muted colors. A feature can be accentuated by making it opaque, increasing its intensity, or adding bright color. In the following paragraphs we describe a technique that combines intensity and transparency.

Texture thresholding requires two pieces of information: a texture map and an index into the map, or texture coordinate. In the simplest case we can devise a texture map that consists of two distinct regions as shown in Figure **9–42**(a). The first region is alternatively referred to as "conceal," "off," or "outside." The second region is referred to as "accentuate," "on," or "inside." (These different labels are used depending upon the particular application.) With this texture map in hand we can texture threshold by computing an appropriate texture coordinate. Areas that we wish to accentuate are assigned a coordinate to map into the "accentuate" portion of the texture map. Areas that we want to conceal are assigned a coordinate to map into the "conceal" portion of the texture map.

One texture threshold technique uses transparency. We can conceal a region by setting its alpha opacity value to zero (transparent), and accentuate it by setting the alpha value to one (opaque). Thus, the texture map consists of two

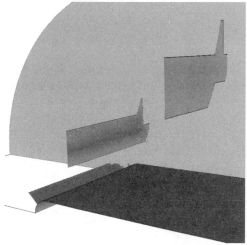 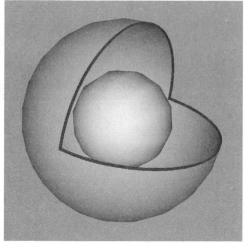

(a) Thresholding data with texture   (b) Sphere cut with transparent texture

Figure 9–43 Examples of texture thresholding. (a) Using scalar threshold to show values of flow density on plane above value of 1.5 (texThresh.tcl). (b) Boolean combination of two planes to cut nested spheres (tcutSph.cxx).

regions: a concealed region with $\alpha = 0$ and an accentuated region with $\alpha = 1$. Of course, the effect can be softened by using intermediate alpha values to create translucent images.

An extension of this technique introduces a third region into the texture map: a transition region (Figure **9–42**(b)). The transition region is the region between the concealed and accentuated regions. We can use the transition region to draw a border around the accentuated region, further highlighting the region.

To construct the texture map we use *intensity-alpha,* or $I\alpha$ values. The intensity modulates the underlying color, while the alpha value controls transparency (as described previously). In the accentuated region, the intensity and opacity values are set high. In the concealed region, the intensity value can be set to any value (if $\alpha = 0$) or to a lower value (if $\alpha \neq 0$). The transition region can use various combinations of α and intensity. A nice combination produces a black, opaque transition region (i.e., $I = 0$ and $\alpha = 1$).

To visualize information with the thresholding technique, we must map data to texture coordinates. As we saw previously, we can use scalar values in combination with a threshold specification to map data into the concealed, transition, and accentuated regions of the texture map. Figure **9–43**(a) shows an example of texture thresholding applied to scalar data from a simulation of fluid flow. A scalar threshold s_T is set to show only data with scalar value greater than or equal to s_T.

Another useful texture thresholding application uses implicit functions to map point position to texture coordinate. This is similar in effect to geometric

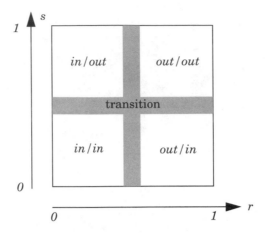

Figure 9–44 2D Boolean texture.

clipping (see "Clipping With Scalar Fields" on page 360). As we saw in "Implicit Functions" on page 180, implicit functions naturally map a (x, y, z) coordinate value into three regions: $F(x, y, z) < 0$, $F(x, y, z) = 0$, and $F(x, y, z) > 0$; or equivalently, the concealed, transition, and accentuated regions of the texture map. Using boolean combinations of implicit functions, we can create complex cuts of our data as illustrated in Figure **9–43**(b). This figure shows two nested spheres. The outer sphere is cut by a boolean combination of two planes to show the inner sphere.

Boolean Textures. Texture thresholding can be extended into higher dimensions. That is, 2D or 3D texture coordinates can be used to map two or three data variables into a texture map. One such technique is *boolean textures*, a method to clip geometry using a 2D texture map and two implicit functions [Lorensen93].

Boolean textures extend texture thresholding for geometric clipping from 1D to 2D. Instead of using a single implicit function to label regions "in" or "out", two implicit functions are used. This results in four different regions corresponding to all possible combinations of "in" and "out." The boolean texture map is modified to reflect this as shown in Figure **9–44**. As with 1D texture thresholding, transition regions can be created to separate the four regions.

The boolean texture map can be created with combinations of intensity and transparency values to achieve a variety of effects. By combining the four combinations of in/out (i.e., four regions of Figure **9–44**) with the two combinations of "conceal" and "accentuate," sixteen different boolean textures are possible. Figure **9–45**(a) illustrates these combinations expressed as boolean combinations of two implicit functions A and B. The "inside" of the implicit functions is indicated with subscript i, while the outside is indicated with subscript o. The boolean expressions indicate the regions that we wish to conceal, as shown by open circles. The darkened circles are the regions that are accentuated. We can see in Figure **9–45**(b) the effects of applying these different boolean textures to a

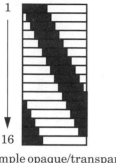

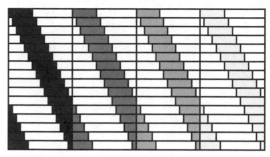

(a) Simple opaque/transparent variation

(b) Feathered opaque/transparent variation

Figure 9–46 Texture maps for vector animation. Sixteen textures applied in succession create effect of motion along a vector. (a) Simple map. (b) Varying intensity "feathers" effect of motion.

sphere. The implicit functions in this figure are two elliptical cylinders sharing a common axis, and rotated 90 degrees from one another. In addition, transition regions have been defined with $I = 0$ to generate the dark cut edges shown. All 16 spheres share the same texture coordinates; only the texture map changes.

Texture Animation. Time-based animation techniques can illustrate motion or temporal data variations. This process often requires relatively large amounts of computer resource to read, process, and display the data. As a result, techniques to reduce computer resources are desirable when animating data.

Texture mapping can be used to animate certain types of data. In these techniques, the data is not regenerated frame by frame, instead a time-varying texture map is used to change the visual appearance of the data. An example of this approach is texture animation of vector fields [Yamrom95].

As we saw in "Hedgehogs and Oriented Glyphs" on page 167, vector fields can be represented as oriented and scaled lines. Texture animation can transform this static representational scheme into a dynamic representation. The key is to construct a series of 1D texture maps that when applied rapidly in sequence create the illusion of motion. Figure **9–46**(a) shows a series of sixteen such texture maps. The maps consist of intensity-alpha ($I\alpha$) values. A portion of the texture map is set fully opaque with full intensity ($I = 1,\ \alpha = 1$). This is shown as the "dark" pattern in Figure **9–46**(a). The remainder of the map is set fully transparent with arbitrary intensity ($I = 1,\ \alpha = 0$) shown as the "white" portion. As is evidenced by the figure, the sequence of 16 texture maps scanned top to bottom generate the appearance of motion from left to right. Notice also how the texture maps are designed to wrap around to form a continuous pattern.

Along with the 1D texture map, the texture coordinate s must also be generated — on a line this is straightforward. The line origin receives texture coordinate $s = 0$, while the line terminus receives texture coordinate value $s = 1$. Any intermediate points (if the vector is a polyline) are parameterized in monotonic

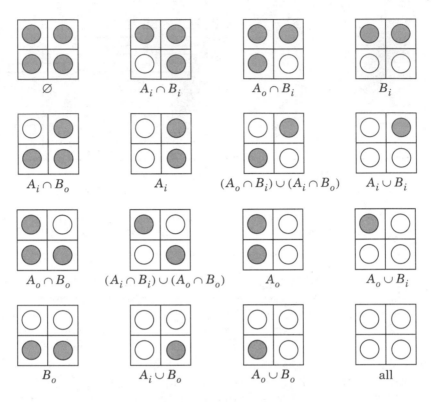

(a) Combinations of 2D in/out textures

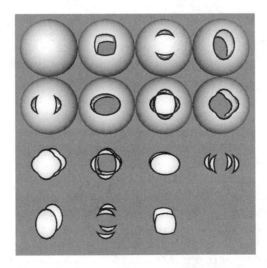

(b) Sixteen boolean textures (from above) applied to sphere (`quadricCut.cxx`)

Figure 9–45 Sixteen boolean textures. (a) Sixteen combinations of in/out. (b) Textures applied to sphere using two elliptical cylinder implicit functions.

fashion in the interval (0,1). Texture coordinates need only be generated once. Only the texture map is varied to generate the vector animation.

Other effects are possible by modifying the texture map. Figure **9–46**(b) shows a texture map with a repeating sequence of opaque/transparent regions. In each opaque region the intensity is gradually reduced from left to right. The result is that this tends to "feather" the appearance of the vector motion. The resulting image is more pleasing to the eye.

9.5 Putting It All Together

With the conclusion of this chapter we have provided an overview of the basics of data visualization. In this section we show you how to use some of the advanced algorithms as implemented in the *Visualization Toolkit*.

Dividing Cubes / Point Generation

Dividing cubes is implemented in **vtk** with the class vtkDividingCubes. It has been specialized to operate with structured point datasets. Besides specifying the contour value, you must specify a separation distance between points (using the method SetDistance()). If you desire a solid appearance, pick a distance that is less than or equal to display resolution.

The separation distance controls the accuracy of point generation. It is possible to generate points that appear to form a solid surface when rendered, but are not accurately located on the contour surface. Although this usually is not an issue when viewing contour surfaces, if the accuracy of the point positions is important, the distance value must be set smaller. However, this can result in huge numbers of points. To reduce the number of points, you can use the Set-Increment() method, which specifies that every *n*th point is to be generated. Using this approach, you can obtain good accuracy and control the total number of points. An example where point positions are important is when the points are used to locate glyphs or as seed points for streamline generation.

The *Visualization Toolkit* provides other point generation techniques. The source object vtkPointSource generates a user-specified number of points within a spherical region. The point positions are random within the sphere. (Note that there is a natural tendency for higher point density near the center of the sphere because the points are randomly generated along the radius and spherical angles ϕ and θ.)

Figure **9–47** is an example use of vtkPointSource to generate streamlines. The dataset is a structured grid of dimensions $21 \times 20 \times 20$ with flow velocity and a scalar pressure field. The dataset is a CFD simulation of flow in a small office. As this picture shows, there are a couple of bookcases, desks, a window, and an inlet and outlet for the ventilation system. On one of the desks is a small, intense heat source (e.g., a cigarette). In the left image 25 streamlines are started near the inlet using a vtkPointSource point generator. The second image shows what happens when we move the point source slightly to the left.

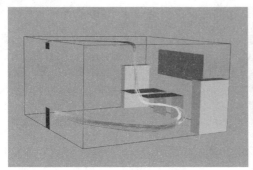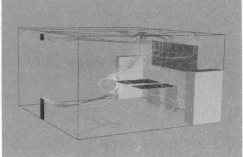

Figure 9–47 Using random point seeds to create streamlines (office.tcl).

By adjusting a single parameter (e.g., the center of the point source) it is possible to quickly explore our simulation data.

Another convenient object for point generation is the class vtkEdge-Points. vtkEdgePoints generates points on an isosurface. The points are generated by locating cell edges whose points are both above and below the isosurface value. Linear interpolation is used to generate the point. Since vtkEdgePoints operates on any cell type, this filter's input type is any dataset type (e.g., vtkDataSet). Unlike vtkDividingCubes this filter will not typically generate dense point clouds that appear solid.

Clipping with Scalar Fields

Clipping is implemented in vtkClipPolyData. Each polygonal data primitive implements the operation in its Clip() method using cases tables derived in a manner similar to that of triangles described on Page 360. vtkClipPolyData has methods to control whether an implicit function provides the scalar data or whether the dataset's scalar data will be used. ComputeScalarDataOn() uses the implicit function and ComputeScalarDataOff() uses the dataset's scalar data. Two output polygonal datasets are produced. These are accessed with GetOutput() and GetClippedOutput() methods. GetOutput() returns the polygonal data that is "inside" the clipping region while GetClippedOutput() returns polygonal data that is "outside" the region. (Note that Generate-ClippedOutputOn() must be enabled if you are to get the clipped output.) The meaning of inside and outside can be reversed using the InsideOutOn() method. Figure **9–48** shows a plane of quadrilaterals clipped with a boolean implicit function.

Currently **vtk** supports clipping for all polygonal data cell types (vertices, polyvertices, line, polylines, polygons and triangle strips). Derivation of the cases for volumetric cell types like hexahedra are complex and require more research.

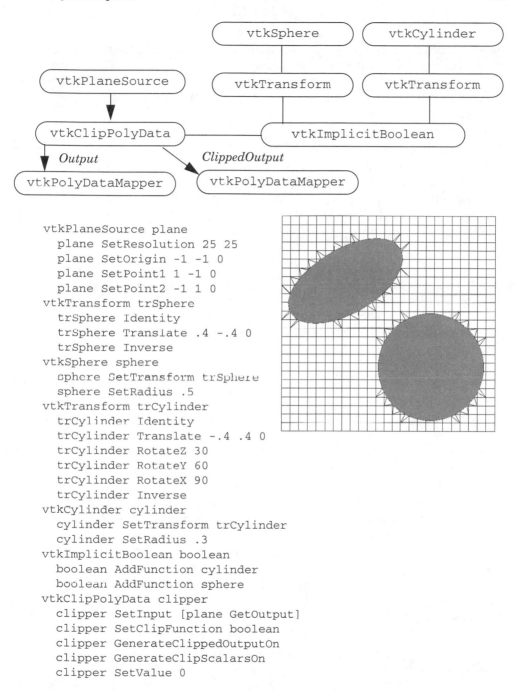

```
vtkPlaneSource plane
   plane SetResolution 25 25
   plane SetOrigin -1 -1 0
   plane SetPoint1 1 -1 0
   plane SetPoint2 -1 1 0
vtkTransform trSphere
   trSphere Identity
   trSphere Translate .4 -.4 0
   trSphere Inverse
vtkSphere sphere
   sphere SetTransform trSphere
   sphere SetRadius .5
vtkTransform trCylinder
   trCylinder Identity
   trCylinder Translate -.4 .4 0
   trCylinder RotateZ 30
   trCylinder RotateY 60
   trCylinder RotateX 90
   trCylinder Inverse
vtkCylinder cylinder
   cylinder SetTransform trCylinder
   cylinder SetRadius .3
vtkImplicitBoolean boolean
   boolean AddFunction cylinder
   boolean AddFunction sphere
vtkClipPolyData clipper
   clipper SetInput [plane GetOutput]
   clipper SetClipFunction boolean
   clipper GenerateClippedOutputOn
   clipper GenerateClipScalarsOn
   clipper SetValue 0
```

Figure 9–48 A plane clipped with a sphere and an ellipse. The two transforms place each implicit function into the appropriate position. Two outputs are generated by the clipper. (clipSphCyl.tcl).

Swept Volumes and Surfaces

Swept surfaces can be applied in two interesting ways. First, they can be used as a modelling tool to create unusual shapes and forms. In this sense, swept surfaces are an advanced implicit modelling technique. Second, swept surfaces can be used to statically represent object motion. This is an important visualization technique in itself and has many important applications. One of these applications is design for maintainability.

When a complex mechanical system like a car engine is designed, it is important to design proper access to critical engine components. These components, like spark plugs, require higher levels of service and maintenance. It is important that these components can be easily reached by a mechanic. We've read horror stories of how it is necessary to remove an engine to change a spark plug. Insuring ready access to critical engine parts prevents situations like this from occurring.

Swept surface can assist in the design of part access. We simply define a path to remove the part (early in the design process), and then generate a swept surface. This surface (sometimes referred to as a maintenance access solid or MAS) is then placed back into the CAD system. From this point on, the design of surrounding components such as fuel lines or wiring harnesses must avoid the MAS. As long as the MAS is not violated, the part can be removed. If the MAS is violated, a reevaluation of the removal path or redesign of the part or surrounding components is necessary.

Figure **9–49** shows how to create a swept surface from a simple geometric representation. The geometry is simply a line-stroked **vtk**. The next step is to define a motion path. This path is defined by creating a list of transformation matrices. Linear interpolation is used to generate intermediate points along the path if necessary.

In Figure **9–49** we also see the basic procedure to construct the swept surface. First, we must construct an implicit representation of the part by using `vtkImplictModeller`. This is then provided as input to `vtkSweptSurface`. It is important that the resolution of the implicit model is greater than or equal to that of `vtkSweptSurface`. This will minimize errors when we construct the surface. A bounding box surrounding the part and its motion can be defined, or it will be computed automatically. For proper results, this box must strictly contain the part as its moves. We also can set the number of interpolation steps, or allow this to be computed automatically as well. In the figure, we have chosen a small number to better illustrate the stepping of the algorithm.

Once `vtkSweptSurface` executes, we extract the swept surface using an isosurfacing algorithm. The isosurface value is an offset distance; thus we can create surfaces that take into account geometry tolerance. (This is particularly important if we are designing mechanical systems.) The implementation of the implicit modeller in **vtk** uses a positive distance function; so the isosurface value should always be positive. To create swept surfaces of zero and negative value requires a modification to the implicit modeller.

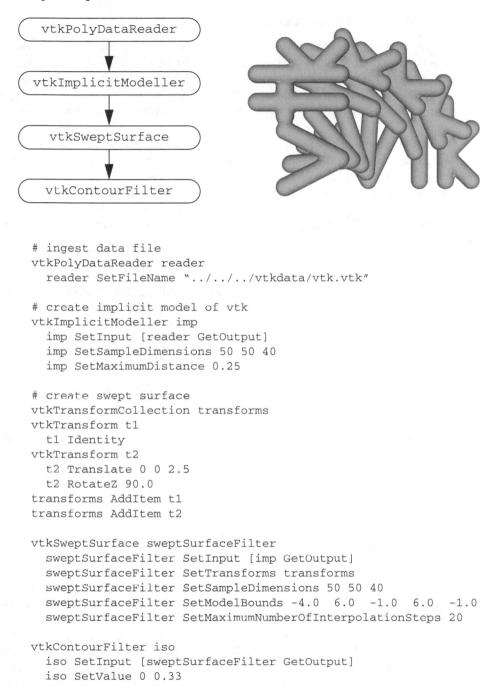

```
# ingest data file
vtkPolyDataReader reader
  reader SetFileName "../../../vtkdata/vtk.vtk"

# create implicit model of vtk
vtkImplicitModeller imp
  imp SetInput [reader GetOutput]
  imp SetSampleDimensions 50 50 40
  imp SetMaximumDistance 0.25

# create swept surface
vtkTransformCollection transforms
vtkTransform t1
  t1 Identity
vtkTransform t2
  t2 Translate 0 0 2.5
  t2 RotateZ 90.0
transforms AddItem t1
transforms AddItem t2

vtkSweptSurface sweptSurfaceFilter
  sweptSurfaceFilter SetInput [imp GetOutput]
  sweptSurfaceFilter SetTransforms transforms
  sweptSurfaceFilter SetSampleDimensions 50 50 40
  sweptSurfaceFilter SetModelBounds -4.0  6.0  -1.0  6.0  -1.0
  sweptSurfaceFilter SetMaximumNumberOfInterpolationSteps 20

vtkContourFilter iso
  iso SetInput [sweptSurfaceFilter GetOutput]
  iso SetValue 0 0.33
```

Figure 9–49 Generating swept surface from line-stroked "vtk" (sweptVtk.tcl).

Multidimensional Visualization

An important characteristic of multidimensional datasets is that they cannot be categorized according to any of the types defined in the *Visualization Toolkit*. This implies that source objects interfacing with multidimensional data are responsible for converting the data they interface with into one of the types defined in **vtk**. This can be a difficult process, requiring you to write interface code.

Other visualization systems treat this problem differently. In these systems a dataset type is defined that can represent multidimensional data. This dataset type is essentially an *n*-dimensional matrix. Additional filters are defined that allow the user to extract pieces of the dataset and assemble them into a more conventional dataset type, such as a volume or structured grid. After mapping the data from multidimensional form to conventional form, standard visualization techniques can be applied. (Future implementations of **vtk** may include this functionality. At the current time you must map multidimensional data into a known **vtk** form.)

To demonstrate these ideas we will refer to Figure **9–50**. This is an example of multidimensional financial data. The data reflects parameters associated with monetary loans. In the file `financial.txt` there are six different variables: TIME_LATE, MONTHLY_PAYMENT, UNPAID_PRINCIPLE, LOAN_AMOUNT, INTEREST_RATE, and MONTHLY_INCOME. (Note: this is simulated data, don't make financial decisions based upon this!)

We will use Gaussian splatting to visualize this data (see "Splatting Techniques" on page 395). Our first step is to choose dependent and independent variables. This choice is essentially a mapping from multidimensional data into an unstructured point dataset. In this example we will choose MONTHLY_PAYMENT, INTEREST_RATE, and LOAN_AMOUNT as our (*x*, *y*, *z)* point coordinates, and TIME_LATE as a scalar value. This maps four of six variables. For now we will ignore the other two variables.

We use vtkGaussianSplatter to perform the splatting operation (i.e., conversion from unstructured points to volume dataset). This is followed by an isosurface extraction. We splat the data two times. The first time we splat the entire population. This is to show context and appears as gray/wireframe in the figure. The second time we splat the data and scale it by the value of TIME_LATE. As a result, only payments that are late contribute to the second isosurface.

The results of this visualization are interesting. First, we see that there is a strong correlation between the two independent variables MONTHLY_PAYMENT and LOAN_AMOUNT. (This is more evident when viewing the data interactively.) We see that the data falls roughly on a plane at a 45 degree angle between these two axes. With a little reflection this is evident: the monthly payment is strongly a function of loan amount (as well as interest rate and payment period). Second, we see that there is a clustering of delinquent accounts within the total population. The cluster tends to grow with larger interest rates and shrink with smaller monthly payments and loan amounts. Although the relationship with interest rate is expected, the clustering towards smaller monthly payments is not. Thus

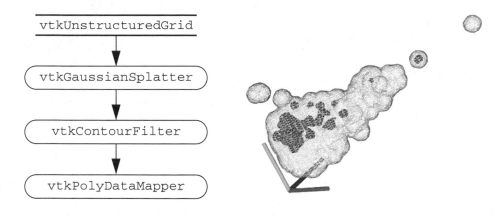

```
// construct pipeline for delinquent population
vtkGaussianSplatter *lateSplatter = vtkGaussianSplatter::New();
  lateSplatter->SetInput(dataSet);
  lateSplatter->SetSampleDimensions(50,50,50);
  lateSplatter->SetRadius(0.05);
  lateSplatter->SetScaleFactor(0.005);
  lateSplatter->DebugOn();

vtkContourFilter *lateSurface = vtkContourFilter::New();
  lateSurface->SetInput(lateSplatter->GetOutput());
  lateSurface->SetValue(0,0.01);
  lateSurface->DebugOn();

vtkPolyDataMapper *lateMapper = vtkPolyDataMapper::New();
  lateMapper->SetInput(lateSurface->GetOutput());
  lateMapper->ScalarVisibilityOff();

vtkActor *lateActor = vtkActor::New();
  lateActor->SetMapper(lateMapper);
  lateActor->GetProperty()->SetColor(1.0,0.0,0.0);
```

Figure 9–50 Visualization of multidimensional financial data. Visualization network, output image, and sample C++ code are shown (`finance.cxx`). The gray/wireframe surface represents the total data population. The dark surface represents data points delinquent on loan payment.

our visualization has provided a clue into the data. Further exploration into the data may reveal the reason(s), or we may perform additional data analysis and acquisition to understand the phenomena.

One important note about multidimensional visualization. Because we tend to combine variables in odd ways (e.g., the use of MONTHLY_PAYMENT, INTEREST_RATE, and LOAN_AMOUNT as *(x, y, z)* coordinates), normalization of the data is usually required. To normalize data we simply adjust data values to lie between (0,1). Otherwise our data can be badly skewed and result in poor visualizations.

Connectivity

Many useful visualization algorithms often borrow from other fields. Topological connectivity analysis is one such technique. This technique is best categorized as a method in computational geometry, but serves many useful purposes in computer graphics and visualization.

To illustrate the application of connectivity analysis, we will use an MRI dataset generated by Janet MacFall at the Center for In Vivo Microscopy at Duke University. The dataset is a volume of dimensions 256^3 and is included on the CD-ROM. The data is of the root system of a small pine tree. Using the class vtkSliceCubes, an implementation of marching cubes for large volumes, we generate an initial isosurface represented by 351,118 triangles. (We have placed the file pine_root.tri on CD-ROM. This is a faster way of manipulating this data. If you have a large enough computer you can process the volume directly with vtkVolume16Reader and vtkMarchingCubes.)

Figure **9–51**(a) shows the initial dataset. Notice that there are many small, disconnected isosurfaces due to noise and isolated moisture in the data. We use vtkConnectivityFilter to remove these small, disconnected surfaces. Figure **9–51**(b) shows the result of applying the filter. Over 50,000 triangles were removed, leaving 299,480 triangles.

The vtkConnectivityFilter is a general filter taking datasets as input, and generating an unstructured grid as output. It functions by extracting cells that are connected at points (i.e., share common points). In this example the single largest surface is extracted. It is also possible to specify cell ids and point ids and extract surfaces connected to these.

Decimation

Decimation is a 3D data compression technique for surfaces represented as triangle meshes. We use it most often to improve rendering interactive response for large models.

Figure **9–52** shows the application of decimation to the data from the pine root example. The original model of 351,118 triangles is reduced to 81,111 triangles using a combination of decimation and connectivity. The decimation parameters are fairly conservative. Here we see a reduction of approximately 55 percent.

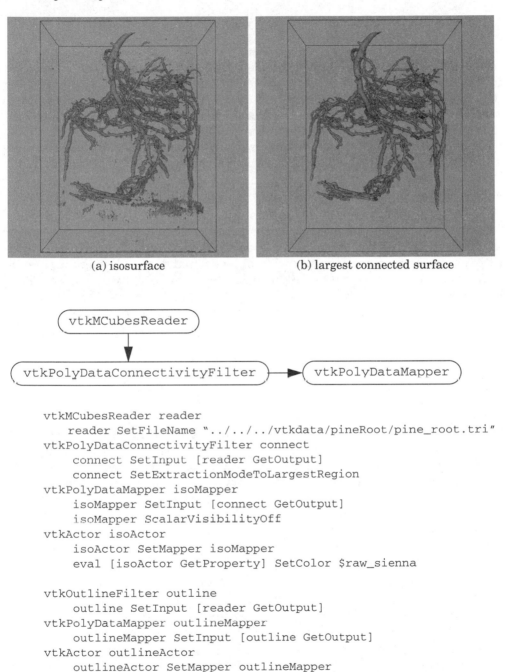

(a) isosurface   (b) largest connected surface

```
vtkMCubesReader reader
    reader SetFileName "../../../vtkdata/pineRoot/pine_root.tri"
vtkPolyDataConnectivityFilter connect
    connect SetInput [reader GetOutput]
    connect SetExtractionModeToLargestRegion
vtkPolyDataMapper isoMapper
    isoMapper SetInput [connect GetOutput]
    isoMapper ScalarVisibilityOff
vtkActor isoActor
    isoActor SetMapper isoMapper
    eval [isoActor GetProperty] SetColor $raw_sienna

vtkOutlineFilter outline
    outline SetInput [reader GetOutput]
vtkPolyDataMapper outlineMapper
    outlineMapper SetInput [outline GetOutput]
vtkActor outlineActor
    outlineActor SetMapper outlineMapper
```

Figure 9–51 Applying connectivity filter to remove noisy isosurfaces (`connPineRoot.tcl`). Data is from 256^3 volume data of the root system of a pine tree.

The most common parameters to adjust in the `vtkDecimate` filter are the `TargetReduction`, `InitialError`, `ErrorIncrement`, `MaximumIterations`, and `InitialFeatureAngle`. `TargetReduction` specifies the compression factor (numbers closer to one represent higher compression). Because of topological, decimation criterion, aspect ratio, and feature angle constraints this reduction may not be realized (i.e., `TargetReduction` is a desired goal, not a guaranteed output). The `InitialError` and `ErrorIncrement` control the decimation criterion. As the filter starts, the decimation criterion is set to `InitialError`. Then, for each iteration the decimation criterion is incremented by `ErrorIncrement`. The algorithm terminates when either the target reduction is achieved, or the number of iterations reaches `MaximumIterations`. The `InitialFeature-Angle` is used to compute feature edges. Smaller angles force the algorithm to retain more surface detail.

Other important parameters are the `AspectRatio` and `MaximumSubIter-ations`. `AspectRatio` controls the triangulation process. All triangles must satisfy this criterion or the vertex will not be deleted during decimation. A sub-iteration is an iteration where the decimation criterion is not incremented. This can be used to coalesce triangles during rapid rates of decimation. `MaximumSub-Iterations` controls the number of sub-iterations. This parameter is typically set to two.

Texture Clipping

Texture mapping is a powerful visualization technique. Besides adding detail to images with minimal effort, we can perform important viewing and modelling operations. One of these operations is clipping data to view internal structure.

Figure **9–53** is an example of texture clipping using a transparent texture map. The motor show consists of five complex parts, some of which are hidden by the outer casing. To see the inside of the motor, we define an implicit clipping function. This function is simply the intersection of two planes to form a clipping "corner." The object `vtkImplicitTextureCoords` is used in combination with this implicit function to generate texture coordinates. These objects are then rendered with the appropriate texture map and the internal parts of the motor can be seen.

The texture map consists of three regions (as described previously in the chapter). The concealed region is transparent. The transition region is opaque but with a black (zero intensity) color. The highlighted region is full intensity and opaque. As can be seen from Figure **9–53**, the boundaries appear as black borders giving a nice visual effect.

The importance of texture techniques is that we can change the appearance of objects and even perform modelling operations like clipping with little effort. We need only change the texture map. This process is much faster relative to the alternative approach of geometric modelling. Also, hardware support of texture is becoming common. Thus the rendering rate remains high despite the apparent increase in visual complexity.

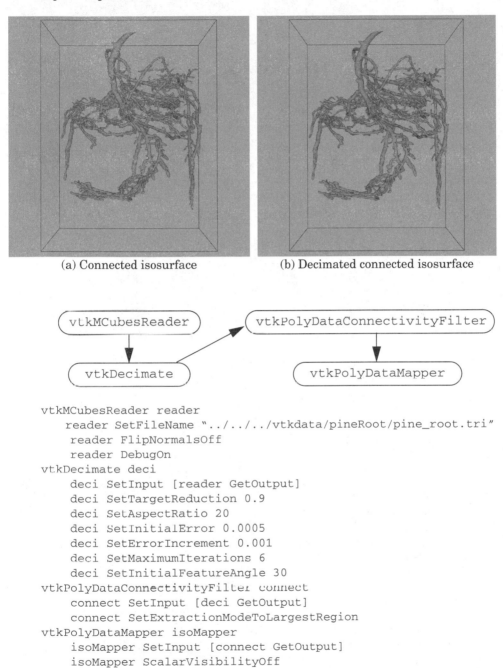

(a) Connected isosurface (b) Decimated connected isosurface

```
vtkMCubesReader reader
    reader SetFileName "../../../vtkdata/pineRoot/pine_root.tri"
    reader FlipNormalsOff
    reader DebugOn
vtkDecimate deci
    deci SetInput [reader GetOutput]
    deci SetTargetReduction 0.9
    deci SetAspectRatio 20
    deci SetInitialError 0.0005
    deci SetErrorIncrement 0.001
    deci SetMaximumIterations 6
    deci SetInitialFeatureAngle 30
vtkPolyDataConnectivityFilter connect
    connect SetInput [deci GetOutput]
    connect SetExtractionModeToLargestRegion
vtkPolyDataMapper isoMapper
    isoMapper SetInput [connect GetOutput]
    isoMapper ScalarVisibilityOff
```

Figure 9–52 Applying connectivity and decimation filters to remove noisy isosurfaces and reduce data size (deciPineRoot.tcl). Data is from 256^3 volume data of the root system of a pine tree.

```
# texture
vtkStructuredPointsReader texReader
    texReader SetFileName "../../../vtkdata/texThres.vtk"
vtkTexture texture
    texture SetInput [texReader GetOutput]
    texture InterpolateOff
    texture RepeatOff

# read motor parts...each part colored separately
#
vtkBYUReader byu
    byu SetGeometryFileName "../../../vtkdata/motor.g"
    byu SetPartNumber 1
vtkPolyDataNormals normals
    normals SetInput [byu GetOutput]
vtkImplicitTextureCoords tex1
    tex1 SetInput [normals GetOutput]
    tex1 SetRFunction planes
vtkDataSetMapper byuMapper
    byuMapper SetInput [tex1 GetOutput]
vtkActor byuActor
    byuActor SetMapper byuMapper
    byuActor SetTexture texture
    eval [byuActor GetProperty] SetColor $cold_grey

# other parts follow...
```

Figure 9–53 Texture cut used to reveal internal structure of a motor. Two cut planes are used in combination with transparent texture (motor.tcl).

Delaunay Triangulation

Delaunay triangulation is used to construct topology from unstructured point data. In two dimensions we generate triangles (i.e., an unstructured grid or polygonal dataset) while in three dimensions we generate tetrahedra (i.e., an unstructured grid). Typical examples of structured points include points measured in space, or a dimensional subset of multidimensional data.

In the example of Figure **9–54** we show how to create a 2D Delaunay triangulation from a field of points. The points are created by generating random x and y coordinate values in the interval $[0, 1]$, and setting the z-value to a constant value (i.e., the points lie in an x-y plane). The points are then triangulated, and tubes and sphere glyphs are used to highlight the resulting points and edges of the triangulation.

One important concern regarding Delaunay triangulations is that the process is numerically sensitive. Creating triangles with poor aspect ratio (e.g., slivers) can cause the algorithm to break down. If you have a large number of points to triangulate, you may want to consider randomizing the point order. This approach tends to generate triangles with better aspect ratio and give better results. You may also want to consider other implementations of Delaunay triangulation that are more numerically robust. See [Edelsbrunner94] for an example.

9.6 Chapter Summary

Dividing cubes is a scalar contouring operation that generates points rather than surface primitives such as lines or polygons. Dense point clouds appear solid because of the limited resolution of computer images.

Vector fields have a complex structure. This structure can be visualized using streamribbons, streamsurfaces, and streampolygons. The topology of a vector field can be characterized by connecting critical points with streamlines.

Tensor fields consist of three orthogonal vector fields. The vector fields are the major, medium, and minor eigenvectors of the tensor field. Hyperstreamlines can be used to visualize tensor fields.

Dataset topology operations generate triangle strips, extract connected surfaces, and compute surface normals. Decimation is a polygon reduction algorithm that reduces the number of triangles in a triangle mesh. Implicit modelling techniques can be used to construct swept surfaces and volumes. Unstructured points are easy to represent but difficult to visualize. Splatting, interpolation, and triangulation techniques are available to construct structure for unstructured points. Multivariate visualization is required for data of dimension four and higher. Data must be mapped to three dimensions before standard visualization techniques can be used. Parallel coordinates techniques are also available to visualize multivariate data.

Modelling algorithms extract geometric structure from data, reduce the complexity of the data or create geometry. Spatial extraction selects dataset

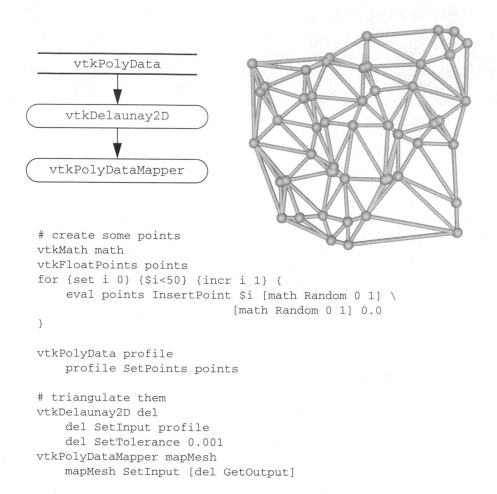

```
# create some points
vtkMath math
vtkFloatPoints points
for {set i 0} {$i<50} {incr i 1} {
    eval points InsertPoint $i [math Random 0 1] \
                              [math Random 0 1] 0.0
}

vtkPolyData profile
    profile SetPoints points

# triangulate them
vtkDelaunay2D del
    del SetInput profile
    del SetTolerance 0.001
vtkPolyDataMapper mapMesh
    mapMesh SetInput [del GetOutput]
```

Figure 9–54 Two-dimensional Delaunay triangulation of a random set of points. Points and edges are shown highlighted with sphere glyphs and tubes (`DelMesh.tcl`). Only the pipeline to generate triangulation is shown.

structure and associated data attributes lying within a specified region in space. Subsampling reduces data by selecting every nth data point. A related technique, data masking, selects every nth cell. Subsets of a dataset can also be selected using thresholding, which selects cells or points that lie within a range of scalar values. Probing resamples data at a set of points. The probe produces a dataset that has the topology of the probe with data values from the probed dataset. Generating triangle strips can reduce storage requirements and improve rendering speeds on some systems. If a dataset has multiple disjoint structures, a connectivity algorithm can uniquely identify the separate structures. For polygonal data that does not have vertex normals defined, normal generation algorithms can compute these values that are suitable for interpolation by Gouraud or Phong shading. Decimation, another data reduction technique, removes triangles in "flat" regions and fills the resulting gaps with new triangles. Unstructured points present a challenge because the data does not have topology. Splatting represents each point in the data with a structured point set and accumulates these splats using implicit modelling techniques. Triangulation techniques build topology directly from the unstructured points.

Multidimensional visualization techniques focus on data that has many scalar data values for each point. Parallel coordinates is an interesting approach that plots the scalar values for a data point along a parallel axis. The observer looks for trends and relationships between the lines that represent each point's data.

Texture algorithms use texture coordinates and texture maps to select or highlight portions of a dataset. Texture thresholding assigns texture coordinates based on a scalar value. The scalar value and texture map determine how a cell or portion of a cell is rendered. Boolean textures extend this concept to 2D and 3D. Careful design of a boolean texture map permits the "clipping" of geometry with combinations of implicit surfaces. Texture can also be used to animate vector fields.

9.7 Bibliographic Notes

Dividing cubes is an interesting algorithm because of the possibilities it suggests [Cline88]. Point primitives are extremely simple to render and manipulate. This simplicity can be used to advantage to build accelerated graphics boards, perform 3D editing, or build parallel visualization algorithms.

Many plotting and visualization systems use carpet plots extensively. Carpet plots are relatively easy to represent and render. Often 2D plotting techniques are used (i.e., lighting and perspective effects ignored). Check [Wang90] for additional information on rendering carpet plots.

In recent years a number of powerful vector visualization techniques have emerged. These techniques include streamsurfaces [Hultquist92], streampolygons [Schroeder91], vector field topology [Helman91] [Globus91], streamballs [Brill94], and vorticity visualization [Banks94]. The streamballs technique is a recent technique that combines techniques from implicit modeling. You may also wish to see references [Crawfis92] [vanWijk93] and [Max94]. These describe volume rendering and other advanced techniques for vector visualization, topics not well covered in this text.

Some abstract yet beautiful visualization images are due to Delmarcelle and Hesselink [Delmarcelle93]. Their rendering of hyperstreamlines reflect the underlying beauty and complexity of tensor fields.

Polygon reduction is a relatively new field of study. SIGGRAPH '92 marked a flurry of interest with the publication of two papers on this topic [Schroeder92a] [Turk92]. Since then a number of valuable techniques have been published. One of the best techniques, in terms of quality of results, is given by [Hoppe93], although it is limited in time and space because it is based on formal optimization techniques. Other interesting methods include [Hinker93] and [Rossignac93]. A promising area of research is multiresolution analysis, where wavelet decomposition is used to build multiple levels of detail in a model [Eck95]. The most recent work in this field stresses progressive transmission of 3D triangle meshes [Hoppe96], improved error measures [Garland97], and algorithms that modify mesh topology [Popovic97] [Schroeder97].

Triangle strip generation is an effective technique for achieving dramatic improvements in rendering speed and reductions in data handling. The reference by [Evans96] describes other triangle strip generation algorithms as well as presenting some of the most effective techniques to date.

The use of texture for visualization is relatively unexploited. This has been due in part to lack of texture support in most graphics software and hardware. This is now changing, as more vendors support texture and software systems (such as OpenGL) that provide an API for texture. Important references here include the boolean textures [Lorensen93] and surface convolution techniques [Cabral93] [Stalling95].

Unstructured or unorganized point visualization is likely to play a prominent role in visualization as the field matures and more complex data is encountered. Nielson et al. have presented important work in this field [Nielson91].

Multidimensional visualization is another important focus of visualization research [Bergeron89] [Mihalisin90]. Much real-world data is both unstructured and multidimensional. This includes financial databases, marketing statistics, and multidimensional optimization. Addressing this type of data is important to achieve future advances in understanding and application. Feiner [Feiner90] has presented a simple projection method combined with virtual reality techniques. [Inselberg87] has introduced parallel coordinates. These techniques have been shown to be powerful for many types of visual analysis.

9.8 References

[Banks94]
  D. C. Banks and B. A. Singer. "Vortex Tubes in Turbulent Flows: Identification, Representation, Reconstruction." In *Proceedings of Visualization '94*. pp. 132–139, IEEE Computer Society Press, Los Alamitos, CA, 1994.

[Bergeron89]
  R. D. Bergeron and G. Grinstein. "A Reference Model for the Visualization of Multidimensional Data." In *Proceedings Eurographics '89*. pp. 393–399, North Holland, Amsterdam, 1989.

[Bowyer81]
  A. Bowyer. "Computing Dirichlet Tessellations." *The Computer Journal*. 24(2):162–166, 1981.

[Brill94]
  M. Brill, H. Hagen, H-C. Rodrian, W. Djatschin, S. V. Klimenko. "Streamball Techniques for Flow Visualization." In *Proceedings of Visualization '94*. pp. 225–231, IEEE Computer Society Press, Los Alamitos, CA, 1994.

[Cabral93]

B. Cabral and L. Leedom. "Imaging Vector Fields Using Line Integral Convolution." In *Proceedings of SIGGRAPH '93*, pp. 263–270, Addison-Wesley, Reading, MA, 1993.

[Cline88]

H. E. Cline, W. E. Lorensen, S. Ludke, C. R. Crawford, and B. C. Teeter, "Two Algorithms for the Three-Dimensional Construction of Tomograms." *Medical Physics*. 15(3):320–327, June 1988.

[Crawfis92]

R, Crawfis and N. Max. "Direct Volume Visualization of Three Dimensional Vector Fields." In *Proceedings 1992 Workshop on Volume Visualization*. pp. 55–60, ACM Siggraph, New York, 1992.

[Delmarcelle93]

T. Delmarcelle and L. Hesselink. "Visualizing Second-Order Tensor Fields with Hyperstreamlines." *IEEE Computer Graphics and Applications*. 13(4):25–33, 1993.

[Eck95]

M. Eck, T. DeRose, T. Duchamp, H. Hoppe, M. Lounsbery, W. Stuetzle. "Multiresolution Analysis of Arbitrary Meshes." In *Proceedings SIGGRAPH '95*. pp. 173–182, Addison-Wesley, Reading, MA, August 1995.

[Edelsbrunner94]

H. Edelsbrunner and E. P. Mucke. "Three-dimensional alpha shapes." *ACM Transactions on Graphics*. 13:43–72, 1994.

[Evans96]

F. Evans, S. Skiena, A. Varshney. "Optimizing Triangle Strips for Fast Rendering." In *Proceedings of Visualization '96*. pp. 319–326, IEEE Computer Society Press, Los Alamitos, CA, 1996.

[Feiner90]

S. Feiner and C. Beshers. "Worlds within Worlds: Metaphors for Exploring *n*-Dimensional Virtual Worlds." In *Proceedings UIST '90* (ACM Symp. on User Interface Software). pp. 76–83, October, 1990.

[Garland97]

M. Garland and P. Heckbert. "Surface Simplification Using Quadric Error Metrics." In *Proceedings SIGGRAPH '97*. pp. 209–216, The Association for Computing Machinery, New York, August 1997.

[Globus91]

A. Globus, C. Levit, and T. Lasinski. "A Tool for Visualizing the Topology of Three-Dimensional Vector Fields." In *Proceedings of Visualization '91*. pp. 33–40, IEEE Computer Society Press, Los Alamitos, CA, 1991.

[He96]

T. He, L. Hong, A. Varshney, S. Wang. "Controlled Topology Simplification." *IEEE Transactions on Visualization and Computer Graphics*. 2(2):171–184, June 1996.

[Helman91]

J. L. Helman and L. Hesselink. "Visualization of Vector Field Topology in Fluid Flows." *IEEE Computer Graphics and Applications*. 11(3):36–46, 1991.

[Hinker93]

P. Hinker and C. Hansen. "Geometric Optimization." In *Proceedings of Visualization '93*. pp. 189–195, IEEE Computer Society Press, Los Alamitos, CA, October 1993.

[Hoppe93]

H. Hoppe, T. DeRose, T. Duchamp, J. McDonald, W. Stuetzle. "Mesh Optimization." In *Proceedings of SIGGRAPH '93*. pp. 19–26, August 1993.

[Hoppe96]

H. Hoppe. "Progressive Meshes." In *Proceedings SIGGRAPH '96*. pp. 96–108, The Association for Computing Machinery, New York, August 1996.

[Hultquist92]

J. P. M. Hultquist. "Constructing Stream Surfaces in Steady 3-D Vector Fields." In *Proceedings of Visualization '92*. pp. 171–178, IEEE Computer Society Press, Los Alamitos, CA, 1992.

[Inselberg87]

A. Inselberg and B. Dimsdale. "Parallel Coordinates for Visualizing Multi-Dimensional Geometry." In *Computer Graphics 1987 (Proceedings of CG International '87)*. pp. 25–44, Springer-Verlag, 1987.

[Lawson86]

C. L. Lawson. "Properties of n-Dimensional Triangulations." *Computer-Aided Geometric Design*. 3:231–246, 1986.

[Lorensen93]

W. Lorensen. "Geometric Clipping with Boolean Textures." in *Proceedings of Visualization '93*. pp. 268–274, IEEE Computer Society Press, Los Alamitos, CA, Press, October 1993.

[Max94]

N. Max, R. Crawfis, C. Grant. "Visualizing 3D Vector Fields Near Contour Surfaces." In *Proceedings of Visualization '94*. pp. 248–255, IEEE Computer Society Press, Los Alamitos, CA, 1994.

[Mihalisin90]

T. Mihalisin, E. Gawlinski, J. Timlin, and J. Schwegler. "Visualizing a Scalar Field on an n-Dimensional Lattice." In *Proceedings of Visualization '90*. pp. 255–262, IEEE Computer Society Press, Los Alamitos, CA, October 1990.

[Nielson91]

G. M. Nielson, T. A. Foley, B. Hamann, D. Lane. "Visualizing and Modeling Scattered Multivariate Data." *IEEE Computer Graphics and Applications*. 11(3):47–55, 1991.

[Popovic97]

J. Popovic and H. Hoppe. "Progressive Simplicial Complexes." In *Proceedings SIGGRAPH '97*. pp. 217–224, The Association. for Computing Machinery, New York, August 1997.

[Rossignac93]

J. Rossignac and P. Borrel. "Multi-Resolution 3D Approximations for Rendering Complex Scenes." In *Modeling in Computer Graphics: Methods and Applications*. B. Falcidieno and T. Kunii, eds., pp. 455–465, Springer-Verlag Berlin, 1993.

[Schroeder91]
W. Schroeder, C. Volpe, and W. Lorensen. "The Stream Polygon: A Technique for 3D Vector Field Visualization." In *Proceedings of Visualization '91*. pp. 126–132, IEEE Computer Society Press, Los Alamitos, CA, October 1991.

[Schroeder92a]
W. Schroeder, J. Zarge, and W. Lorensen. "Decimation of Triangle Meshes." *Computer Graphics (SIGGRAPH '92)*. 26(2):65–70, August 1992.

[Schroeder92b]
W. Schroeder, W. Lorensen, G. Montanaro, and C. Volpe. "Visage: An Object-Oriented Scientific Visualization System." In *Proceedings of Visualization '92*. pp. 219–226, IEEE Computer Society Press, Los Alamitos, CA, October 1992.

[Schroeder94]
W. Schroeder, W. Lorensen, and S. Linthicum, "Implicit Modeling of Swept Surfaces and Volumes." In *Proceedings of Visualization '94*. pp. 40–45, IEEE Computer Society Press, Los Alamitos, CA, October 1994.

[Schroeder97]
W. Schroeder. "A Topology Modifying Progressive Decimation Algorithm." In *Proceedings of Visualization '97*. IEEE Computer Society Press, Los Alamitos, CA, October 1997.

[Stalling95]
D. Stalling and H-C. Hege. "Fast and Independent Line Integral Convolution." In *Proceedings of SIGGRAPH '95*. pp. 249–256, Addison-Wesley, Reading, MA, 1995.

[Turk92]
G. Turk. "Re-Tiling of Polygonal Surfaces." *Computer Graphics (SIGGRAPH '92)*. 26(2):55–64, July 1992.

[vanWijk93]
J. J. van Wijk. "Flow Visualization with Surface Particles." *IEEE Computer Graphics and Applications*. 13(4):18–24, 1993.

[Wang90]
S-L C. Wang and J. Staudhammer. "Visibility Determination on Projected Grid Surfaces." *IEEE Computer Graphics and Applications*. 10(4):36–43, 1990.

[Watson81]
D. F. Watson. "Computing the n-Dimensional Delaunay Tessellation with Application to Voronoi Polytopes." *The Computer Journal*. 24(2):167–172, 1981.

[Wixom78]
J. Wixom and W. J. Gordon. "On Shepard's Method of Metric Interpolation to Scattered Bivariate and Multivariate Data." *Math. Comp.* 32:253–264, 1978.

[Yamrom95]
B. Yamrom and K. M. Martin. "Vector Field Animation with Texture Maps." *IEEE Computer Graphics and Applications*. 15(2):22–24, 1995.

9.9 Exercises

9.1 Describe an approach to adapt dividing cubes to other 3D cell types. Can your method be adapted to 1D and 2D cells?

9.2   Discuss the advantages and disadvantages of representing surfaces with points versus polygons.

9.3   Streamribbons can be constructed by either i) connecting two adjacent streamlines with a surface, or ii) placing a ribbon on the streamline and orienting the surface according to streamwise vorticity vector. Discuss the differences in the resulting visualization.

9.4   Write the following programs to visualize velocity flow in the combustor.
a) Use `vtkProbeFilter` and `vtkHedgeHog`.
b) Use `vtkProbeFilter` and `vtkStreamLine`.
c) Use `vtkProbeFilter` and `vtkWarpVector`.
d) Use `vtkProbeFilter` and `vtkVectorNorm`.
e) Use `vtkProbeFilter` and `vtkVectorDot`.

9.5   Describe a method to extract geometry using an arbitrary dataset. (That is, extract geometry that lies within the culling dataset.) (*Hint:* how would you evaluate in/out of points?)

9.6   The filter `vtkPolyDataNormals` is often used in combination with the filters `vtkSmoothPolyData` and `vtkContourFilter` to generate smooth isosurfaces.
a) Write a class to combine these three filters into one filter. Can you eliminate intermediate storage?
b) How much error does `vtkSmoothPolyData` introduce into the isosurface? Can you think of a way to limit the error?
c) What is the difference between the surface normals created by `vtkMarchingCubes` and `vtkPolyDataNormals`?

9.7   Assume that we have a database consisting of interest rate R, monthly payment P, monthly income I, and days payment is late L.
a) If R, P, I are all sampled regularly, how would you visualize this data?
b) If all data is irregularly sampled, list three methods to visualize it.

9.8   Why do you think triangle strips are often faster to render than general polygons?

9.9   The normal generation technique described in this chapter creates consistently oriented surface normals.
a) Do the normals point inside or outside of a closed surface?
b) Describe a technique to orient normals so that they point out of a closed surface.
c) Can surface normals be used to eliminate visible triangles prior to rendering? (*Hint:* what is the relationship between camera view and surface normal?)

9.10   Describe a technique to partially threshold a cell (i.e., to cut a cell as necessary to satisfy threshold criterion). Can an approach similar to marching cubes be used?

9.11 The class `vtkRendererSource` allows us to use the rendered image as a texture map (or structured points dataset). Write a program to construct iterated textures, that is textures that consist of repeated images. Can the same image be generated using texture coordinates?

9.12 Describe how you would modify the decimation algorithm to treat general polygons.

9.13 Several examples in the text (e.g., `deciFran.tcl` and `deciHawa.tcl`) use the class `vtkDecimate`. Modify these examples to use the topology modifying progressive decimation algorithm (implemented in `vtkDecimatePro`). How much greater reduction can you achieve?

## CHAPTER 10

Image Processing

*I*n this chapter we describe the image processing components of the *Visualization Toolkit*. The focus is on key representational ideas, pipeline issues such as data streaming and caching, and useful algorithms for improving the appearance and effectiveness of structured point visualizations.

10.1 Introduction

Image processing has been a mainstay of computing since the advent of the digital computer. Early efforts focused on improving image content for human interpretation. More recently image processing has been utilized by practitioners of computer vision, the goal being the processing of image data for autonomous machine perception [Gonzalez92]. From the perspective of data visualization, image processing is used to manipulate image content to improve the results of subsequent processing and interpretation. For example, a CT or MRI scan may generate spurious signal noise or require image segmentation. Using the techniques of image processing, noise can be removed and automatic and semi-automatic segmentation can be performed on a slice by slice (i.e., image by image basis). As a result, isosurface generation, volume rendering, and other 3D techniques can be improved in appearance, accuracy, and effectiveness by applying techniques from image processing.

Since the focus of this text is on 3D graphics and visualization, this chapter treats image processing in a limited way. However, we would like to emphasize the interrelationship of image processing, computer graphics, and visualization. Often texts and courses treat these as distinctly separate disciplines, when in fact they are closely related (see "Imaging, Computer Graphics, and Visualization" on page 5).

The material presented here was selected to demonstrate a number of important points. First, the data flow or pipeline approach presented earlier is directly applicable to image processing, with the added benefit that we can easily implement data streaming and caching due to the regular nature of image data. Second, image processing algorithms can improve the results of visualization. We will show this through a number of useful examples. And finally, from a practical point of view, we wanted to demonstrate a system architecture that includes imaging, graphics, and visualization.

10.2 Data Representation

In this section we will briefly describe the data representation behind the imaging pipeline. As we saw earlier (see "The Dataset" on page 118), a dataset consists of both a structure (topology and geometry) and data attributes. Although in principle an image can be represented as a structured points dataset, the special nature of image processing suggests a more complex representation, as we will soon see.

An image is typically used to refer to a 2D structured point dataset. More generally, in this chapter we will define an image as consisting of up to four dimensions: three spatial dimensions x, y, and z, and time t. The reason we add the time dimension is that images are frequently generated as a time series, and we often wish to access the data along the time axis. For example, we may plot the value at a point as a function of time.

As described in "Structured Points" on page 128, an image has both regular topology and geometry. The regularity of the data lends itself to many special operations. In particular, we can support *data caching* and *streaming*, and operating on *regions of interest* in the data.

Regions of Interest

When data has a regular spatial organization, it is possible to request the data in pieces or regions of interest. For example, a mapper may need only a region of the data for its display, so loading or processing the whole dataset would be inefficient. An example of this is a two-dimensional viewer that displays only one slice of a large structured volume. By loading slices only as they are needed, disk access can be reduced, and memory conserved.

Although regions of interest can have arbitrary shapes, the regular structure of the data samples determines optimal region configurations. An image stored in a Cartesian coordinate system easily divides into smaller rectangular

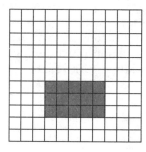
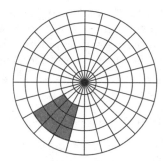

Axis aligned matrix   *Polar coordinate grid*
(rectangular region)   *(pie-shaped region)*

Figure 10–1 Axis aligned matrices naturally lend themselves to rectangular regions, and polar coordinate grids to pie-shaped regions.

regions, while data sampled on a polar coordinate grid is best divided into pie-shaped regions (Figure **10–1**). Therefore, operating on regions of data means that we process "windows" of data specified by *(min,max)* ranges of each dimension, or axis. For example, a region in a 2D image of dimensions 100 x 100 might be specified as *(25,49, 0,49)*, meaning that we would operate on a (25 x 50) window.

Streaming and Caching

The disadvantage of processing regions of interest is that the same data may be read and processed multiple times. If the viewer described above needs to cine (i.e., loop) through the slices, or interactively pan around a large image, it would be beneficial to have all the data loaded at once.

A compromise between the two extreme approaches of maintaining all data in memory or operating on small pieces is to update regions larger than requested, but not as large as the whole image. This is referred to as a data cache. Data caching anticipates future requests and works well in most cases. However, it breaks down when there is little or no coherence between subsequent requests.

With the region-processing model, the data objects can be thought of as caches that hold any number of regions. There are numerous caching strategies for saving and releasing regions that can be quite complex. The simplest strategy saves only a single region at any one time. If subsequent requests are completely contained in the cached region, no further processing is required. An alternative strategy might divide an image into tiled regions of all the same size. When a region larger than the tile is requested, multiple tiles are updated to cover the region. When designing a caching strategy, it is important to consider the overhead of copying data to change its format. Some of the advantages of complex strategies are lost when all the factors are considered.

Given the ability to operate on regions of data, it is a small step to *stream* operations on a whole dataset. Streaming is the process of pulling regions of data in a continual flow through the pipeline. For instance, a pixel histogram mapper could request single pixels as it accumulates values in its bins. Large datasets can be processed in this manner without ever having to load more than a few pixels at a time. If multiple processors are available, region processing can also be used to split a task into multiple pieces for load balancing and faster execution.

Attribute Data and Components

Unlike visualization algorithms that may generate normals, vectors, tensors, and texture coordinates, image processing algorithms generally process attribute data consisting of scalar data. Often the data is a single component (e.g., a gray-scale image), but frequently color images (three components of RGB, for example) may also be processed.

In the *Visualization Toolkit* imaging pipeline, attribute data is represented as *n*-dimensional component data. Refer to "Putting It All Together" on page 448 to see the implementation details for component data, regions of interest, streaming, and caching.

10.3 Algorithms

This section provides an overview and examples for important image processing algorithms. The importance of the algorithms is measured on their relevance to 3D data visualization. Topics include: removing noise, smoothing, reducing sampling artifacts, image enhancement, segmentation, and morphological operators such as erosion and dilation.

Image Restoration

Noise and other artifacts are inherent in all methods of data acquisition. Since artifacts can degrade the visual appearance and analysis of images, the first step of image processing is often restoration. Knowledge of the statistical properties of artifacts allows filters to selectively remove them with minimal impact on the underlying data. For example, most of the power of typical images lie in low frequencies, while white noise is evenly distributed across the frequency spectrum. In this situation, low-pass filters eliminate much of the noise, but leave most of the image intact.

A simple implementation of a low-pass smoothing filter is convolution with a kernel with all positive values. The typical kernels used for smoothing are either constant across a circular neighborhood, or have a Gaussian profile (see Figure **10–2**). Gaussian smoothing results in better-looking images than smoothing with constant kernels, but can be more computationally expensive because of the large kernel size necessary to capture the Gaussian profile. Smoothing becomes even more expensive when it is generalized to three-dimensional datasets, and three-dimensional kernels.

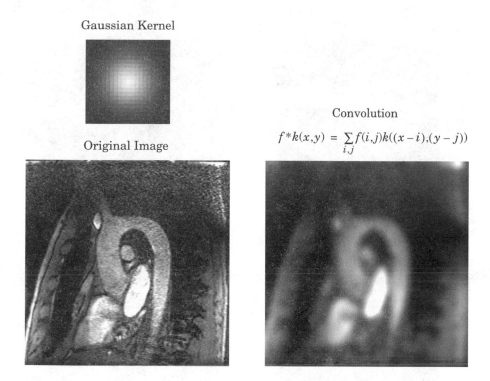

Gaussian Kernel

Original Image

Convolution

$$f*k(x,y) = \sum_{i,j} f(i,j)k((x-i),(y-j))$$

Figure 10–2 Low-pass filters can be implemented as convolution with a Gaussian kernel. The Gaussian kernel displayed on top has been magnified for this figure (`GaussianSmooth.tcl`).

One way to speed Gaussian smoothing is to decompose the filter into two 1D convolutions. Since the 2D Gaussian function is separable,

$$g(i,j) = \frac{1}{2\pi\sigma^2}\exp\left(\frac{i^2+j^2}{2\sigma^2}\right) = \frac{1}{\sqrt{2\pi}\sigma}\exp\left(-\frac{i^2}{2\sigma^2}\right)\frac{1}{\sqrt{2\pi}\sigma}\exp\left(-\frac{j^2}{2\sigma^2}\right) \quad \textbf{(10-1)}$$

smoothing along the x axis and then along the y axis with 1D Gaussian kernels is equivalent to convolving with a 2D Gaussian kernel. It is also possible to approximate Gaussian smoothing by convolving with a constant binary kernel multiple times.

Nonlinear Smoothing

One problem with simple smoothing to remove noise is that edges are blurred. Although high frequencies make up a small part of images, the human visual system is acutely sensitive to high frequencies in the spatial form of edges. In fact, most of the low frequencies in an image are discarded by the visual system

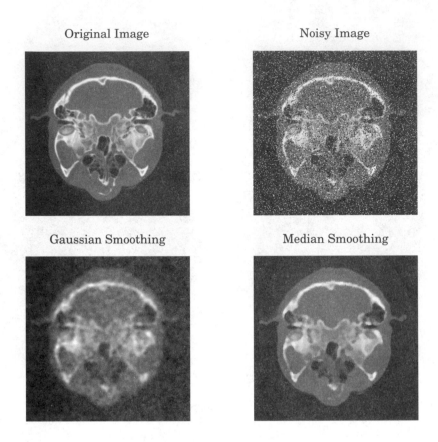

Figure 10–3 Comparison of Gaussian and Median smoothing for reducing low-probability high-amplitude noise (`MedianComparison.tcl`).

before it even leaves the retina. One approach to smoothing that preserves edges is anisotropic diffusion. This filter smooths relatively flat regions of an image, but does not diffuse across abrupt transitions. The diffusion is iterated until the desired level of noise reduction is reached. Two possible diffusion criteria are: Diffuse only when the gradient magnitude is below a specified value, or diffuse two pixels only when the difference between the pixels is lower than a specified constant.

A median filter also smooths while preserving edges. This filter replaces each pixel with the median value of the scalar values in a neighborhood centered on the pixel. Median filters are most effective on high amplitude noise that has a low probability of occurring (see Figure **10–3**). There are two ways to control the amount and scale of noise removed: The size of the neighborhood can be varied, or the filter can be applied multiple times. This median filter preserves edges; however, it does round corners and remove thin lines. The hybrid median filter was developed to address this behavior. It operates on a 5 x 5 neighborhood

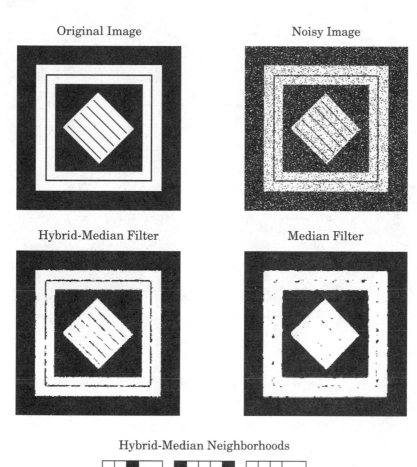

Figure 10–4 Comparison of median and hybrid-median filters. The hybrid filter preserves corners and thin lines, better than the median filter. The lower patterns represent the three neighborhoods used to compute the hybrid median (HybridMedianComparison.tcl).

around each pixel. The algorithm consists of two steps: first the median values of an "x"-shaped and "+"-shaped neighborhoods are computed, then the median of these two values and the center-pixel value is computed to give the final result. The hybrid median has a fixed size neighborhood, but can be applied multiple times to further reduce noise (Figure **10–4**).

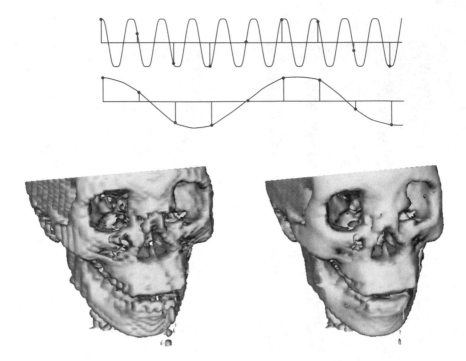

Figure 10–5 This figure demonstrates aliasing that occurs when a high-frequency signal is subsampled. High frequencies appear as low frequency artifacts. The lower left image is an isosurface of a skull after subsampling. The right image used a low-pass filter before subsampling to reduce aliasing (IsoSubsample.tcl).

Low Frequency Artifacts

An artifact called aliasing occurs when subsampling and is often associated with stair-stepping edges. Sampling theory proves that discrete sampled signals with spacing S, completely describe continuous functions composed of frequencies less than S/2. When a signal is subsampled, its capacity to hold high frequency information is reduced. However, the high frequency energy does not disappear. It wraps around the frequency spectrum appearing as a low frequency alias artifact (Figure **10–5**). The solution, which eliminates this artifact, is to low-pass filter before subsampling. Low-pass smoothing reduces the high frequency range of an image that would cause aliasing.

The same aliasing phenomena occurs when acquiring data. If a signal from an analog source contains high frequencies, saving the analog data in a discrete form requires subsampling that will introduce alias artifacts. For this reason, it is common practice to acquire data at high resolutions, then smooth and subsample to reduce the image to a manageable size.

Low-frequency artifacts, other than aliasing, can also occur when acquiring data. One example is base-line drift. As data is acquired over time, the average

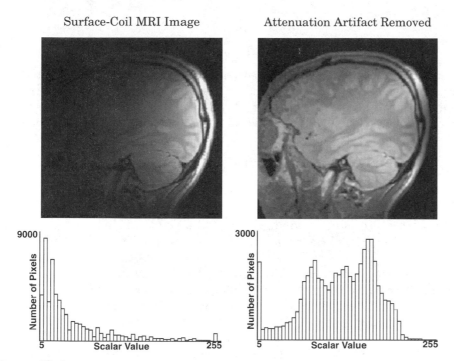

Figure 10–6 This MRI image illustrates attenuation that can occur due to sensor position. The artifact is removed by dividing by the attenuation profile determined manually. This histograms shows how the artifact hides information in the form of scalar value clusters (`Attenuation.tcl`).

value (base line) of the signal can slowly change. This drift can be removed with a high-pass filter after data acquisition. It is also possible to acquire a second dataset that isolates the baseline. Subtracting the baseline from the primary signal removes the drift artifact. In general, it is better to measure the artifact than risk making wrong assumptions that might adversely affect the actual data.

Another gradual change across an image is caused by sensor position. The amplitude of a measured signal usually attenuates as the source moves away from the sensor. An example of this attenuation artifact is seen in surface-coil-MRI images as shown in Figure **10–6**. If the attenuation profile is known, then the artifact can be removed by dividing the original data with the profile. Since this artifact can be characterized by a small set of parameters like sensor position and range, it is possible to automatically determine the attenuation profile from the data. Like most artifacts, nonuniform attenuation tends to hide the information in an image. Given a function that measures the amount of information in an image, gradient descent and other search strategies can find the optimal attenuation parameters.

Image Enhancement

Often datasets contain information or have dynamic range that cannot be completely displayed in a single image. X-Ray ComputedTomography (CT) datasets, for example, can have 10 times the scalar resolution of the typical computer monitor capable of displaying 256 shades of gray. One method used for conveying information buried in the large dynamic range of these medical datasets is to allow a user to interactively set the color map with a window-level transfer function. The user can then choose to display the range of data they find most important as shown in Figure **10–7**. The slope of the transfer function determines the amount of contrast in the final image. Slopes greater than one increase contrast, and slopes less than one decrease contrast. All contrast and information is lost in the scalar ranges where the transfer function is constant and has zero slope.

The short fall of simple window-level transfer functions are their limited shape. More general nonlinear transfer functions can be more appropriate for certain datasets. One example is the logarithmic transfer function, $f(x) = K \log(1 + x)$, which can be used to display image power spectrums (Figure **10–10**). Most of the pixels in the power spectrum represent high frequencies, and have small values. However the smaller population of low-frequency pixels often have large values. The logarithmic function has the largest slope near zero, and therefore leaves the most contrast for pixels with small values. However, when the constant K is chosen correctly, none of the large pixel values become completely saturated.

To take advantage of all the available display contrast, images should have a uniform distribution of intensities. For continuous images, this intensity distribution is called the *probability density function* (PDF). For discretely-sampled images with discrete scalar values, the image histogram has the same information as the PDF (Figure **10–7**). A histogram breaks the scalar range of an image into discrete nonoverlapping bins. Each bin has a pixel count that represents the number of pixels whose scalar value falls in that bin's range.

To achieve the goal of a uniform scalar histogram, transfer functions can be used to spread out clusters in the histogram and compress scalar ranges that are under-represented in the image. To maintain the general appearance of the image, the transfer function should be monotonically increasing so that the brightness relation is maintained. To spread out clusters in the histogram, the slope of the transfer function should be large where the scalar densities are the highest, and the slope should be small in empty regions of the histogram.

Histogram equalization is an algorithm that automatically generates a tailored transfer function to increase contrast in an image. For continuous images, the transfer function is simply the cumulative distribution function (CDF) which is defined as the integral of the PDF. By definition, the CDF function has a large slope where the PDF has the largest value, and therefore gives the greatest contrast to scalar ranges that occur most frequently in an image. The result of using the CDF as a transfer function is an image with an ideal constant scalar distribution. For discrete images and image histograms, a discrete version of the CDF function can be used. However, because of the discrete approximation, the resulting image is not guaranteed to have a constant histogram (Figure **10–8**).

High-pass filters can also be used to compress the range of an image. Since low frequencies account for much of the dynamic range of an image but carry little information, a high-pass filter can significantly decrease an image's scalar range and emphasize hidden details. The Laplacian filter, which is a second derivative operation, is one implementation of a high-pass filter. It eliminates constant and low frequencies leaving only high-frequency edges. The output of

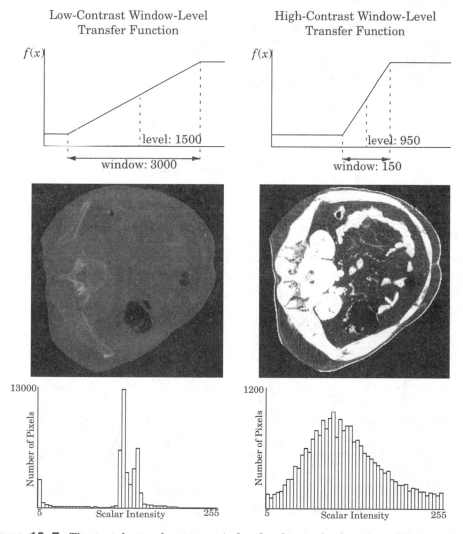

Figure 10–7 The top charts show two window-level transfer functions. The resulting images are displayed in the middle row. The bottom row shows image histograms of the images.

Original Image and Its Histogram

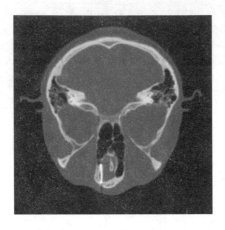 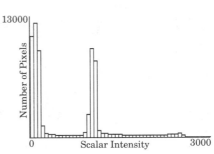

Computed Transfer Function

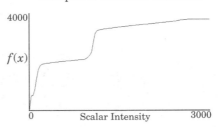

Resulting Image and Its Histogram

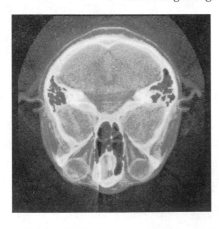 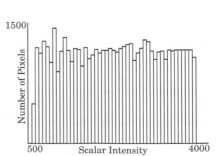

Figure 10–8 Histogram equalization automatically computes a transfer function that produces an image with a nearly constant scalar histogram (HistogramEqualization.tcl).

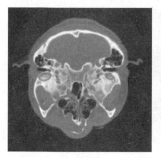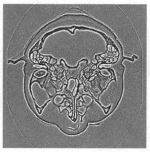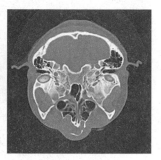

Figure 10–9 High-pass filters can extract and enhance edges in an image. Subtraction of the Laplacian (middle) from the original image (left) results in edge enhancement or a sharpening operation (right) (`EnhanceEdges.tcl`).

the Laplacian can be subtracted from the original image to produce edge enhancement or sharpening of an image (Figure **10–9**).

Frequency Domain

The Fourier transform belongs to a class of filters that fundamentally change the representation of an image without changing its information. The output of the Fourier transform is in the frequency domain. Each pixel is a complex number describing the contribution of a sinusoidal function to the original image. The magnitude of the pixel encodes the amplitude of the sinusoid, and the orientation of the complex pixel encodes the sinusoid's phase. Each pixel represents a sinusoid with different orientation and frequency. The reverse Fourier transform converts a frequency domain image back to the original spatial domain (Figure **10–10**).

Low-pass and high-pass filtering become trivial in the frequency domain. A portion of the pixels are simply masked or attenuated. Figure **10–11** shows a high pass Butterworth filter that attenuates the frequency domain image with the function H

$$H(u,v) = \frac{1}{1 + [C^{2n}/(u^2 + v^2)^n]} \tag{10-2}$$

The gradual attenuation of the filter is important. The ideal high-pass filter, shown in the same figure, simply masks a set of pixels in the frequency domain. The abrupt transition causes a ringing effect in the spatial domain (as the figure illustrates).

Although any filter that operates in the frequency domain can also be implemented in the spatial domain, some operations are less computationally expensive and easier to implement in the frequency domain. To perform similar filtering of Figure **10–11** in the spatial domain would require convolution with a large kernel and would be slow. In general, convolution with large kernels is

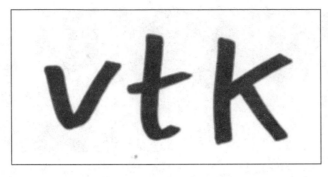

$$F(u,v) = \frac{1}{MN} \sum_{x=0}^{M-1} \sum_{y=0}^{N-1} f(x,y) \exp\left[-j2\pi\left(\frac{xv}{M} + \frac{vy}{N}\right)\right]$$

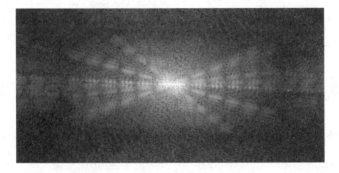

Figure 10–10   The discrete Fourier transform changes an image from the spatial domain into the frequency domain, where each pixel represents a sinusoidal function. This figure show an image and its power spectrum displayed using a logarithmic transfer function (VTKSpectrum.tcl).

more efficient when performed in the frequency domain. Multiplication, $\alpha\beta$, in the frequency domain, is equivalent to convolution, $a*b$, in the spatial domain (and vice versa). In these equations, α is the Fourier transform of a, and β is the Fourier transform of b.

In order to make frequency-domain processing feasible, it is first necessary to minimize the cost of transforming from the spatial to frequency domain and back. There exist fast algorithms that implement the Fourier transform and its inverse. First, the Fourier transform is decomposable, so a 2D transform can be implemented by first taking the 1D Fourier transform of all the rows, and then taking the Fourier transform of all the columns of an image. Second, the complexity of one-dimensional Fourier transforms can be reduced with an algorithm called the fast Fourier transform (FFT). It works by recursively factoring the number samples, N, into its prime components. If N is prime and not factorable, then the transform is completed in one step that is order $O(N^2)$ complexity. If N is divisible by two, the array of numbers is divided into two parts that are trans-

Ideal High-Pass Filter

Butterworth High-Pass Filter

$$H(u,v) = \begin{cases} 1 & if(u^2 + v^2 < C^2) \\ 0 & otherwise \end{cases}$$

$$H(u,v) = \frac{1}{1 + [C^{2n}/(u^2 + v^2)^n]}$$

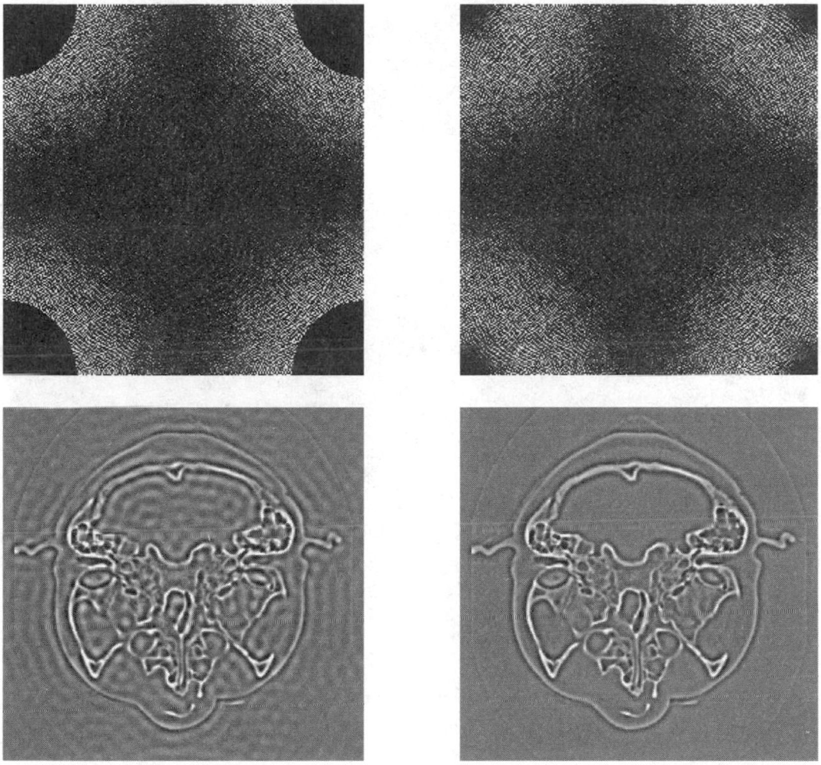

Figure 10–11 This figure shows two high-pass filters in the frequency domain. The Butterworth high-pass filter has a gradual attenuation that avoids ringing produced by the ideal high-pass filter with an abrupt transition (IdealHighPass.tcl).

formed separately and then combined. If N is a power of two, then the algorithm executes in order $O(N\log N)$ time. For this reason, it is more efficient to process images with sizes that are powers of two (e.g., 512 x 512) than other sized images. For non-power of two images it may be faster to pad the image to a size that is a power of two size before processing.

An important point about the discrete Fourier transform is that it treats the image as a periodic function. This means the pixels on the right border are adjacent to pixels on the left border. Since there is usually no physical relationship between these pixels, the artificial horizontal and vertical edges can distort the frequency spectrum and subsequent processing. To reduce these artifacts,

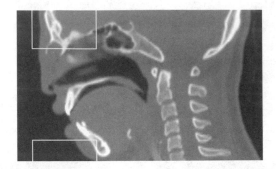

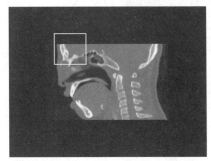
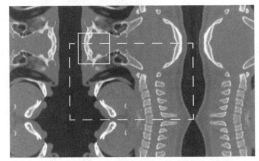

Figure 10–12 Convolution in frequency space treats the image as a periodic function. A large kernel can pick up features from both sides of the image. The lower-left image has been padded with zeros to eliminate wraparound during convolution. On the right, mirror padding has been used to remove artificial edges introduced by borders (Pad.tcl).

the original image can be multiplied by a window function that becomes zero at the borders. Another approach removes these artificial edges by smoothing only along the borders.

In both of these approaches, a portion of the original image is lost, so only the central portion of an image can be processed. If this is unacceptable, another solution is to double the dimensions of the original image with a mirror-padding filter. The intermediate image is periodic and continuous (Figure **10–12**).

Image Segmentation

Segmentation is the process of classifying pixels in an image or volume. It can be one of the most difficult tasks in the visualization process. One form of segmentation takes an image as input, and outputs a map that contains a classification for each pixel. The output of such a segmentation filter usually has binary or discrete values for each pixel; however, it is also possible to output a fuzzy classification where the pixel's scalar value represents a measure of confidence in the classification.

Correlation Kernel

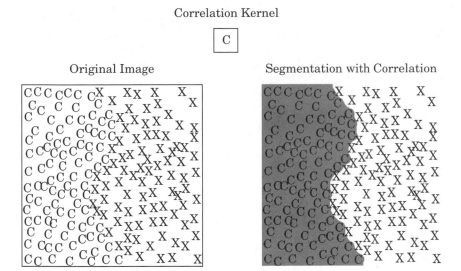

Original Image   Segmentation with Correlation

Figure 10–13 A pipeline containing correlation, thresholding, dilation, and erosion is used here to segment a region composed of "C"s. The left image shows the original image. The right image shows the segmented region superimposed on the original image.

A simple example of a one-parameter segmentation is a threshold filter used to mark bone in a CT dataset. Since bone has the largest scalar value, it is easy to select a threshold that separates bone from the rest of the image.

For other tissues and other imaging modalities, segmentation is usually more difficult. Noise in the image and overlapping scalar values of tissues can decrease the effectiveness of simple threshold segmentation. By using two parameters, the threshold can segment pixels with a range of scalar values. The extra parameter allows more control over the resulting segmentation, but also doubles the complexity of selecting the parameters.

Images can be preprocessed to segment images based on more complex features such as textures. Sometimes textures in tissues add information useful for segmentation. Texture sensitive filters like Laplacian and gradient magnitude can discriminate between different textures. Additional filters that can be used for texture segmentation are the range, variance, and correlation filters. The range filter simply reports the difference between the maximum and minimum values in a neighborhood around each pixel, and the variance filter computes the variance of the neighborhood pixels relative to the center pixel.

Figure **10–13** shows an example of how a correlation filter can be used for segmentation. A correlation filter is similar to convolution. The kernel is shifted across the image, and for each location the dot product between the image and the kernel gives a measure of correlation between the two. The output of the correlation filter is large everywhere the pattern occurs in the image, but small at other locations. Because the resulting map is sparse, additional postprocessing is required to find a uniform, segmented region. In this example, dilation followed by erosion was used to close the gaps between the patterns. (Dilations and erosion are discussed in the next section.)

Postprocessing

Although preprocessing can do a lot to improve segmentation results, postprocessing can also be useful. Morphological filters, which operate on binary or discrete images, can be useful for manipulating the shape of the segmented regions. In this brief discussion we will only consider operations that use circular footprints, even though these morphological filters can be defined much more generally. Erosion is implemented by removing pixels within a specified distance of a border. For each pixel not in the segmented region, all the neighbors in a circular region around the pixels are turned off. This erosion filter shrinks the segmented region and small isolated regions disappear.

The opposite of erosion is dilation. This filter grows the area of segmented regions. Small holes in the segmented region are completely closed. Any pixel not in the segmented region but near the region is turned on. Dilation and erosion are dual filters with nearly identical implementations. Dilating the "on" pixels is equivalent to eroding "off" pixels in a binary image (see Figure **10–14**).

Closing is the serial application of first dilation and then erosion. When an image is dilated small holes in the map disappear. However, dilation alone also grows the boundaries of the segmented regions. When dilation is followed by erosion in a closing operation, small holes are removed; however, the boundary of the segmented regions remain in the same general location. Opening is the dual of closing. Opening removes small islands of pixels. It is implemented with an initial erosion, followed by a dilation.

Connectivity filters can also remove small regions without affecting the remaining boundaries of segmented regions. This set of filters separate the segmented pixels into equivalence classes based on a neighbor relation. Two pixels belong to the same class if they are touching. There are two common neighbor relations in two-dimensional images: four connectivity considers pixels neighbors if they are edge neighbors, and eight connectivity considers pixels neighbors if pixels share any vertex.

After the pixels have been assigned an equivalence class, various methods are used to determine which groups of pixels will pass through the filter, and which classes will be eliminated. The island-removal filter is a connectivity filter that removes groups that have too few pixels. Seed connectivity allows the user to explicitly specify which groups will pass through the filter. The user or application specifies a set of seeds. Any group that includes a seed makes it through the filter. Groups that do not contain seeds are removed. This filter is similar to the seed-connectivity filter; however, the seeds are supplied in a second image. First the intersection between the segmented image and the seed image is taken. Each remaining pixel is then added to a set of seeds.

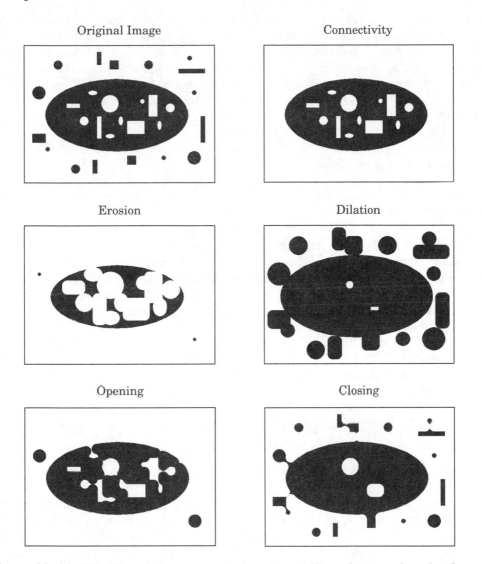

Figure 10–14 This figure demonstrates various binary filters that can alter the shape of segmented regions (MorphComparison.tcl).

Multispectral Segmentation

From everyday experience we know that it is easier to see structure and information in color images than in gray-scale images. This is because each pixel contains more information in the red, blue, and green components than a single component gray-scale pixel. One way to segment multispectral images is to separate the components and threshold them individually and then combine the resulting binary images with logic filters. This allows selection of rectangular patched areas in the color/component space of the pixels.

By using multiple thresholds combined with multiple levels of logic filters, it is possible to specify arbitrary areas in the component's space for segmentation. However, it can be easier and more efficient to transform the components into a different coordinate system before the threshold operation. The simplest example of this is to threshold a projection of the components. This is equivalent to a threshold after performing a dot product between the components of a pixel and a constant-direction vector. This divides the component space into two areas separated by a hyper-plane.

Another example of a coordinate transformation is conversion from red, green, blue (RGB) color component to hue, saturation, value (HSV) representation (see "Color" on page 39). Segmentation of images based on hue and color saturation is difficult in RGB space, but trivial in HSV space.

Color is not the only multispectral information that can be used for segmentation. It is possible to take advantage of multispectral segmentation even if the original dataset has only one component. Additional images can be created from spatial information of the images using spatial filters. These multiple images can then be combined into one multicomponent image, then multicomponent segmentation can proceed.

Typically, the number of free parameters in a filter is directly correlated to the dimensionality of the pixels; and although additional parameters make a filter more powerful, it also makes it more difficult to find an appropriate set of parameter values. There are supervised and unsupervised algorithms that can be used to automatically select the best set of segmentation parameters, but discussion of these is outside the scope of this book.

10.4 Putting It All Together

We suggest that you review the code accompanying the images in this chapter to see how to use the **vtk** imaging pipeline. In this section we will explain some of the implementation details of image data. We will also show how to mix the imaging and visualization pipelines, and how to use imaging filters to perform regression testing.

Data Representation

In the imaging pipeline, there are three major objects for representing and manipulating data. These are `vtkImageData`, `vtkImageRegion`, and `vtkImageCache`.

`vtkImageData` actually represents the image data. Internally, it refers to an instance of `vtkScalars`. Therefore, its native representation data type may be any one of `unsigned char`, `char`, `unsigned short`, `short`, `int`, `float`, or any concrete type of `vtkScalars`. `vtkImageData` is referred to by `vtkImageCache` and `vtkImageRegion`, and is generally not instantiated.

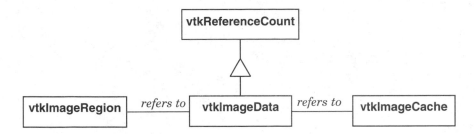

Figure 10–15 Representing image data.

vtkImageRegion is an object that refers to a region of data within a vtkImageData object. It hides the actual extent of the underlying data, and allows axes to be reordered so that data can be processed in a different order.

vtkImageCache supports the caching of data. In the imaging pipeline, vtkImageCache serves as input and output to the imaging filters. This is the object that is actually instantiated and manipulated by the user (we will demonstrate this in the next section).

In the **vtk** imaging pipeline, point attribute data is represented differently than in the visualization pipeline. In the imaging pipeline point attribute data is represented as n components per data point. Typically n is one for gray-scale data, or three for color data but, in general, can be any positive number.

Create an Image

This example demonstrates how to directly create an image using C++ code. Typically, you will use an image reader or procedurally create an image from a source object. The example shown here creates an vtkImageCache and then fills it with an image of interfering sinusoidal grids

$$F(x, y) = \left(\sin\left(\frac{x}{10}\right) + \sin\left(\frac{y}{10}\right) \right) \tag{10-3}$$

Although image caches contain similar data as structured points, the access interface is quite different. Since caches hold regions with arbitrary extents, direct manipulation of the scalar objects is less intuitive. Instead, scalar values are accessed through the cache individually given an (i, j, k, t) index into the image. To speed the data access, caches also support pointer arithmetic to access scalar values of neighboring samples. Scalar values are returned as void pointers that must be cast to the correct scalar type.

Gradient Magnitude

In this example we demonstrate a lengthy imaging pipeline. The basic purpose of the pipeline is to visualize information about the image gradient. The gradient

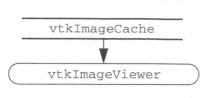

```
vtkImageCache *image = vtkImageCache::New();
vtkImageRegion *region;
float *ptr;
  image->SetWholeExtent(0,255,0,255,0,0,0,0);
  image->SetUpdateExtent(0,255,0,255,0,0,0,0);
  image->SetScalarTypeToFloat();
  region = image->GetScalarRegion();

for (j=0; j<256; j++)
  {
  y = j/10.0;
  for (i=0; i<256; i++)
    {
    x = i/10.0;
    ptr = (float *)(region->GetScalarPointer(i, j, 0, 0);
    *ptr = 128.0 * (sin(x) + sin(y));
    }
  }
region->Delete();
```

Figure 10–16 Creating an image of two interfering sinusoidal gratings in an image cache. The resulting image has dimensions 256x256.

direction and magnitude are mapped into the hue and saturation components of the color HSV space, respectively. The pipeline, resulting image (see the Color Plates as well), and a portion of the code are shown in Figure **10–17**.

The pipeline demonstrates some interesting tricks. The first three filters read CT data of the human head (vtkImageReader), magnify the image by a factor of four (vtkImageMagnify), and then smooth the data (since magnification uses linear interpolation, introducing some sharp edges). The next filter actually computes the 2D gradient (vtkImageGradient), placing the x-y gradient components into its output.

The next series of filters is where the fun begins. First, the data is converted to polar coordinates (vtkImageEuclideanToPolar). We use this filter because we want to operate in color HSV space (see "Color" on page 39). The image magnitude is to be mapped into saturation value, while the gradient direction is mapped into hue value (remember hue is represented as an angle on the HSV color wheel). The filter `vtkImageConstantPad` is used to add a third component to the data, since the gradient filter only generated two components, and we need three components to represent color. The `vtkImageExtractCompo-nents` is used to rearrange the components into HSV order. Finally, the data is converted back into RGB color space with `vtkImageHSVToRGB`. (This is necessary because the image viewer expects RGB values.)

Image Warping

In this example we combine the imaging and visualization pipelines. Imaging filters are used to read in an image (`vtkPNMReader`) and then smooth it (`vtkIm-ageGaussianSmooth`). The data, which is a structured points dataset, is then passed to the visualization pipeline as polygons (`vtkStructuredPointsGeom-etryFilter`). Next we warp the data in the direction perpendicular to the image plane using the visualization filter `vtkWarpScalar`. The pipeline, example output, and sample code are shown in Figure **10–18**.

One important note about this example. The input to `vtkStructured-PointsGeometryFilter` is of type `vtkImageCache`, not `vtkStructured-Points`. The reason this works is because the `SetInput()` method implemented in `vtkStructuredPointsFilter` is overloaded to take either structured points or images as input. When an image is provided as input, a hidden process creates an instance of `vtkImageToStructuredPoints`. This filter then performs the type conversion and returns a structured points dataset.

Regression Testing

In our work with **vtk**, we often need to perform software testing. The testing may be necessary because we've added new classes or features to the system, modified old code, or are simply testing a graphics library or new piece of hardware. We use a powerful testing procedure based on processing the output of the system, which is typically an image. We refer to the testing process as regression testing.

Regression testing is based on the following procedure. A test program (typically a Tcl/Tk script) is written that exercises a portion of the code. In our example, we will assume that we are testing a feature of implicit modelling. The output of the script is an image with a fixed view, as shown in Figure **10–19**(a). To perform the test, we compare the output of the test program with a previously stored image, or "valid" image (Figure **10–19**(b)). The valid image was generated when we initially created the object or objects to be tested, and is assumed to be the correct output. Then, we use a the filter `vtkImageDifference` to compare the test image with the valid image. This filter takes into account dithering and anti-aliasing effects, and creates an output image representing the difference between the test image and valid image (Figure **10–19**(c)). It also reports the dif-

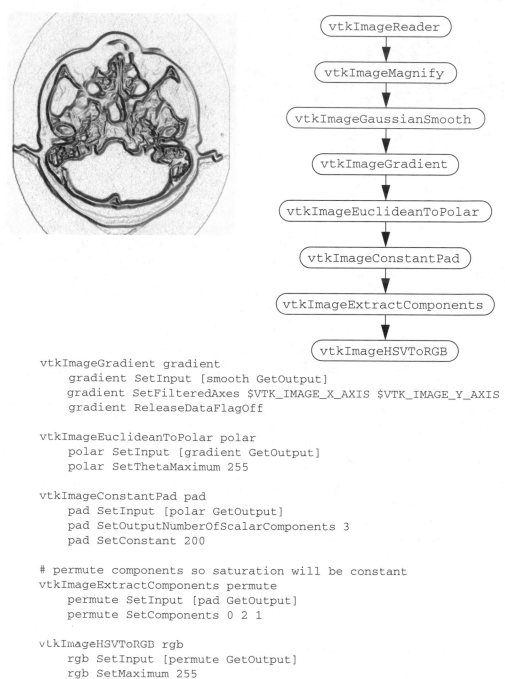

```
vtkImageGradient gradient
    gradient SetInput [smooth GetOutput]
    gradient SetFilteredAxes $VTK_IMAGE_X_AXIS $VTK_IMAGE_Y_AXIS
    gradient ReleaseDataFlagOff

vtkImageEuclideanToPolar polar
    polar SetInput [gradient GetOutput]
    polar SetThetaMaximum 255

vtkImageConstantPad pad
    pad SetInput [polar GetOutput]
    pad SetOutputNumberOfScalarComponents 3
    pad SetConstant 200

# permute components so saturation will be constant
vtkImageExtractComponents permute
    permute SetInput [pad GetOutput]
    permute SetComponents 0 2 1

vtkImageHSVToRGB rgb
    rgb SetInput [permute GetOutput]
    rgb SetMaximum 255
```

Figure 10–17 An imaging pipeline to visualize gradient information. The gradient direction is mapped into color hue value while the gradient magnitude is mapped into the color saturation (`ImageGradient.tcl`).

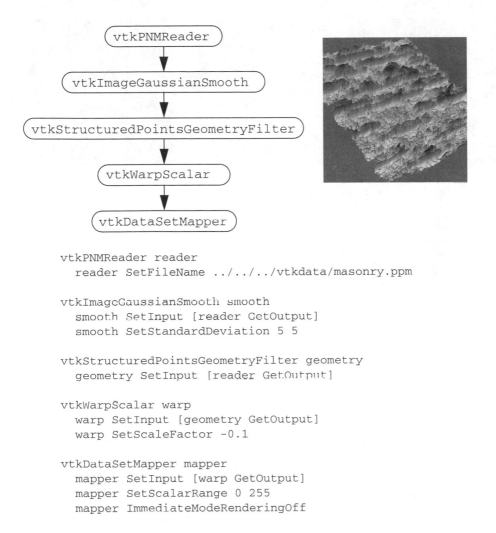

```
vtkPNMReader reader
    reader SetFileName ../../../vtkdata/masonry.ppm

vtkImageGaussianSmooth smooth
    smooth SetInput [reader GetOutput]
    smooth SetStandardDeviation 5 5

vtkStructuredPointsGeometryFilter geometry
    geometry SetInput [reader GetOutput]

vtkWarpScalar warp
    warp SetInput [geometry GetOutput]
    warp SetScaleFactor -0.1

vtkDataSetMapper mapper
    mapper SetInput [warp GetOutput]
    mapper SetScalarRange 0 255
    mapper ImmediateModeRenderingOff
```

Figure 10–18 Combining the imaging and visualization pipelines to deform an image in the z-direction (imageWarp.tcl).

ference in the images in terms of a pixel count. To determine whether the test is passed, we compare the pixel count with a threshold value (for example, 10 pixels).

Our regression testing procedure cannot test the original implementation of an object or objects. The developer must verify that the valid image is indeed correct. However, the process is invaluable for finding and correcting problems due to incremental code changes (e.g., bug fixes, enhancements, etc.) Furthermore, the test can be run as a batch process, with a simple pass/fail output, and an image to show the differences.

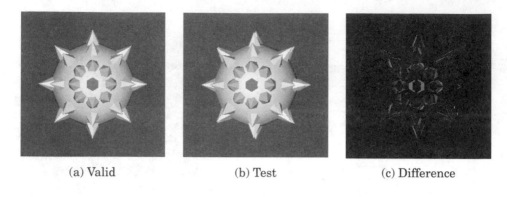

<table>
<tr><td>(a) Valid</td><td>(b) Test</td><td>(c) Difference</td></tr>
</table>

```
vtkRendererSource renSrc
    renSrc WholeWindowOn
    renSrc SetInput ren1

vtkPNMReader pnm
    pnm SetFileName "valid/$afile.ppm"

vtkImageDifference imgDiff
    imgDiff SetInput [renSrc GetOutput]
    imgDiff SetImage [pnm GetOutput]
    imgDiff Update

if {[imgDiff GetThresholdedError] < 10.0} {
    puts "Passed Test for $afile"
} else {
    puts "Failed Test for $afile with an error \
            of [imgDiff GetThresholdedError]"
    vtkPNMWriter pnmw
        pnmw SetInput [imgDiff GetOutput]
        pnmw SetFileName "$afile.error.ppm"
        pnmw Write
    vtkPNMWriter pnmw2
        pnmw2 SetInput [renSrc GetOutput]
        pnmw2 SetFileName "$afile.test.ppm"
        pnmw2 Write
}
```

Figure 10–19 Software regression testing using image processing. A test image is taken from the renderer and compared with a valid image stored on disk. (a) shows the valid image. (b) shows the test image (artificially modified by slight camera rotation). (c) shows the image difference. The code fragment above is extracted from the regression testing procedure.

10.5 Chapter Summary

Image processing can be used to improve 3D visualizations of structured point datasets (images and volumes). Important techniques include smoothing, filtering, morphological operators such as erosion and dilation, and segmentation.

Because of the regular topology and geometry of images, it is possible to design caching and streaming pipelines to reduce memory requirements. In the *Visualization Toolkit*, the imaging pipeline is integrated with the visualization pipeline. This capability enables the creation of applications that combine computer graphics, imaging, and visualization.

10.6 Bibliographic Notes

Many books are available describing imaging algorithms. Several are listed below including [Gonzalez92] and [Russ95]. The texts [Pavlidis82] and [Wolberg90] are imaging books with somewhat of a computer graphics and/or visualization slant. The text [Robb95] is an outstanding reference for medical imaging and visualization.

10.7 References

[Ballard82]
> D. H. Ballard, C. M. Brown. *Compute Vision*. Prentice Hall, Inc., Englewood Cliffs, NJ, 1982.

[Davies97]
> E. R. Davies. *Machine Vision Theory Algorithms Practicalities 2d ed*. Academic Press, San Diego, CA, 1997.

[Gonzalez92]
> R. C. Gonzalez, R. E. Woods. *Digital Imaging Processing*. Addison-Wesley Publishing Co., Reading, MA, 1992.

[Niblack86]
> W. Niblack. *An Introduction to Digital Image Processing*. Prentice Hall, Inc., London, 1986.

[Pavlidis82]
> T. Pavlidis. *Algorithms for Graphics and Image Processing*. Computer Science Press, Rockville, MD, 1982.

[Robb95]
> R. Robb. *Three-Dimensional Biomedical Imaging Principles and Practice*. VCH Publishers, New York, NY, 1995.

[Russ95]
> J. C. Russ. *The Image Processing Handbook 2d ed*. CRC Press, Inc, Boca Raton, FL, 1995.

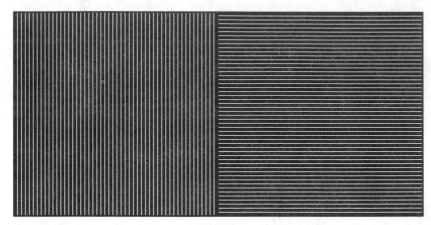

Figure 10–20 Sample image for segmentation exercise (`HVLines.tcl`)

[Wolberg90]
    G. Wolberg. *Digital Image Warping*. IEEE Computer Society Press, Los Alamitos, CA, 1990.

10.8 Exercises

10.1 Create an image pipeline that will segment the area with vertical lines in Figure **10–20** .

10.2 Decomposition can increase the speed of an operation.
    a) Prove that 3D Gaussian smoothing can be decomposed into three 1D operations.
    b) Determine the complexity of the decomposed filter and the same filter implemented as a 3D convolution.
    c) Under what conditions can constant smoothing be decomposed into 1D operations?

10.3 Create an image pipeline that shows the spectrum of a Gaussian image. What effect does increasing or decreasing the standard deviation have on the spectrum?

## CHAPTER 11

Interpreters and Tcl/Tk

*I*n this chapter we investigate interpreted languages for data visualization. We compare their strengths and weaknesses against traditional compiled languages. Then, we provide a quick introduction to the syntax of the interpreted language Tcl, how we integrated Tcl with the *Visualization Toolkit*, and some example programs.

11.1 Interpreted versus Compiled Languages

Programming languages can be categorized as either compiled or interpreted. These categories correspond to the way in which we interact with the language. In a compiled language, the source code is first compiled (i.e., translated into machine instructions), linked (modules gathered together and symbols resolved), and then executed. When an error is detected, the source code must be edited, recompiled and relinked before it can be tested. Programmers can spend significant amounts of time waiting on the compiler. An interpreted language requires no compilation or linking. Instead, instructions are typed directly to the computer, or a file is edited and reparsed, and the language instructions are carried out immediately. Using an interpreted language can drastically reduce development time, especially in situations where many small tweaks are required to achieve the desired result (e.g., developing user interfaces).

While development times may be reduced for interpreted languages, compilation results in the fastest execution times. Compilers produce executables that are more difficult to reverse-engineer, and they often have efficient methods to manipulate and represent complex data structures. While there are a few languages that support both interpretation and compilation, the most commonly used languages today are either of one type or the other.

For the software that accompanies this book, we decided to write our objects in the compiled language C++ because of its object-oriented capabilities, efficient execution speed, and large following. We also wanted to be able to rapidly develop applications (including graphical user interfaces) with the **vtk** toolkit, so we "wrapped" the Tcl interpreted language around the C++ objects. Tcl offers a simple interpreted language that can be imbedded into programs, plus the graphical user interface Tk. Tcl/Tk is widely used and is available free of charge.

The end result is a toolkit that offers you the choice of building interpreted or compiled applications. Moreover, because each object is implemented in a compiled language, even the interpreted applications execute relatively quickly. The interpreter is only used generally for high-level object manipulation, and is rarely involved in tight execution loops. Now let's take a look at some of the issues involved with our implementation of the Tcl interpreted language.

11.2 Introduction to Tcl

Tcl is an interpretive language developed by John Ousterhout during the late 1980's [Ousterhout94]. It was designed to provide a flexible command language that could be easily integrated with a variety of applications. Tcl itself is written in the C programming language, and has a well-defined API for integrating in new functions. Its syntax is very similar to C shell programming. The example script below illustrates some of its basic features. Any line that starts with a pound sign (#) is a comment and is ignored, command lines consist of a command name possibly followed by arguments. A semicolon or new line indicates the end of a command.

```
# Tcl script to compute the circumference of a circle
set pi 3.1416
set radius 2
set area [expr $pi*$radius*2.0]
puts $area
```

The set command takes two arguments: the name of a variable to create and its initial value. The second line in the example uses this command to create a variable named pi with a value of 3.1416. All variables in Tcl are stored as strings. Integer and floating-point values are converted to strings as necessary. The third line creates a variable named radius. In the fourth line a variable named area is created using the set command, but its initialization is more complex. Enclosing brackets allow you to use a Tcl statement as an argument to a command. The format of a nested statement is the same as any other, except that a pair of brackets enclose it. Inside the brackets we want to calculate the area of the circle so we use the expr command, which evaluates its arguments as a mathematical expression and returns the result. Notice that there are dollar signs in front of the two variables we created earlier. This causes Tcl to perform variable substitution and use the value of the variable, not just its name. The fifth line uses the puts command to print out the result that is stored in the variable area.

Now let's look at another example. The script below prints the numbers one through 10 and their squares. The first two lines are comments. The remaining lines are all part of a for command that takes four arguments. Each of these arguments is enclosed in braces (not brackets), which tells Tcl to take whatever is between them as the argument. Unlike brackets, no variable substitution or evaluation is done.

The first argument of a for loop is the initialization script. Before the loop starts iterating, it will evaluate its first argument, which in this case is a set command that creates and initializes a variable named num. The second argument is the test condition. This argument will be evaluated before each iteration through the loop. Looping continues until this expression becomes false. The third argument is evaluated at the end of each iteration. This argument is typically used to increment the loop variable. In the script below we use the incr command to increment the variable num. The fourth argument is the body of the loop that is evaluated with each iteration.

The braces are important because they prevent the arguments from being evaluated before they are passed to the for loop. Otherwise, the result of $num <= 10 would have been passed as the second argument, instead of the actual script $num <= 10. Double quotations perform a similar function, except that variable substitution does occur before the argument is passed to the command. In our example, the values for num and numsqr will be substituted before the enclosed string is passed to the puts command.

```
# Tcl script to print the numbers 1-10 and their squares
#
for {set num 1} {$num <= 10} {incr num} {
  set numsqr [expr $num*$num]
  puts "$num => $numsqr"
  }
```

That covers most of Tcl's basic syntax. The example scripts later in this chapter will help to clarify some of these points. There are hundreds of Tcl commands beyond what we introduced, and fortunately John Ousterhout's book, titled *Tcl and the Tk Toolkit*, covers them clearly and effectively.

11.3 How vtk is Integrated with Tcl

To use the Tcl interpreter with the *Visualization Toolkit* classes you need to understand a little about how the two are integrated. Between the C++ code of **vtk** and the Tcl interpreter, there is a layer of wrapper code. This code, written in the C programming language, controls the exchange of information between Tcl and **vtk**'s C++ methods.

For every class in **vtk** a command is added to Tcl with the same name as the class. These commands create instances of their respective classes. In the first line of the following example, the vtkActor command creates an instance of that class. The one argument to an instantiation command is the name to assign to the resulting instance.

Once an instance has been created, the instance name also becomes a command. This may seem a little odd at first, but it is well suited to the object-oriented nature of **vtk**. After creating an instance of vtkActor named actor, we can invoke methods on this instance by using its name as a command. In the second line of this example we use this technique to invoke the Print() method for the instance of vtkActor we just created. To invoke a method that takes arguments, you just add them onto the command as shown in the third line of this example.

```
vtkActor actor
   actor Print
   actor SetDebug 1
   puts [actor GetDebug]
set property [actor GetProperty]
   $property Print
   $property SetColor 1 0 0
   puts [$property GetColor]
```

Methods with return values can be used just like Tcl commands that return values. Since every return value in Tcl must be a string, the wrapper code will automatically convert integers and floating-point values into strings before returning them. For methods that return pointers, it's a bit more difficult. Since we cannot return the pointer, we must convert the pointer into a unique string name. To accomplish this we keep hash tables that convert between instance pointers and string names. Whenever you create a **vtk** object in a Tcl script, that object's name and instance pointer are stored in hash tables. If you use that name as an argument to a method, the string name will automatically be converted to an instance pointer using these hash tables. When a method needs to return a pointer to an instance that wasn't created in the Tcl script, we create a unique string name such as vtkTemp0, vtkTemp1, and so on. The pointer and generated name are also entered into the hash tables for future use. For example, in the fifth line of the above example, we use the set command to create a new variable called property. Its initial value is the result of invoking the Get-Property() method on our instance actor. Normally, this method returns a C++ pointer, but the wrapper code converts the pointer value into a generic string name and returns that. The sixth line shows how this result can then be used through the variable property.

Most of the arguments provided as the input and output to methods are simple types such as integers and floats. Where a method takes a fixed size array, such as float fargs[3], we break up the array into individual components. For example, in C++ and Tcl we use the following statements to invoke a method:

```
C++:         Instance->aMethod(int iarg, float fargs[3])

Tcl:         Instance  amethod iarg fargs1  fargs2  fargs3.
```

For methods that return a value or a pointer to an array we perform the opposite operation. That is, we return a single string consisting of the method return value or the components of the array. For methods that return arrays the components of the array are space delimited. We are limited to a single string because of the semantics of the Tcl language.

Pointers to objects are passed back and forth using either the name specified upon creation or their generated name as described above. The argument to user-defined functions (e.g. SetStartRender(void (*f)(void *), void *arg)) in C++ is a pointer to a function. In our Tcl implementation, you specify a string argument that will be interpreted when the user defined function is called. The following example prints out the message "Executing the mapper" at the start of polyMapper1's Render() method.

```
# excerpt from a Tcl script
polyMapper1 SetStartRender {puts "Executing the mapper"}
```

Because of the differences between C++ and Tcl, not all of the methods that are available from C++ are accessible in Tcl. We developed a program in Lex and Yacc to read in the C++ header files and automatically generate the wrapper code. After augmenting the information from the C++ header files with a hints file, it still does not provide enough flexibility for us to safely wrap some methods. The few methods that could not be wrapped are unavailable from the Tcl interpreter.

Special Tcl Commands

While there are some C++ methods not available to the Tcl interpreter, there are also special commands not available to C++. These commands are implemented in the wrapper code standing between the **vtk** C++ class library and the Tcl interpreter. They exist only in **vtk** and are not part of the standard Tcl language.

One of these special commands is ListMethods. The ListMethods command prints a list of all the methods available to an instance of a **vtk** object created in Tcl. It also lists the number of arguments that the method takes. For example (the % is the Tcl interpreter prompt):

```
% vtkLight light1
light1
% light1 ListMethods
Methods from vtkObject:
  Delete
  New
  GetClassName
  DebugOn
  DebugOff
  GetDebug
  SetDebug with 1 arg
  GetMTime
  Modified
  BreakOnError
  SetGlobalWarningDisplay with 1 arg
  GlobalWarningDisplayOn
  GlobalWarningDisplayOff
  GetGlobalWarningDisplay
Methods from vtkLight:
  New
  GetClassName
  Render with 2 args
  SetColor with 3 args
  GetColor
  SetPosition with 3 args
  GetPosition
  SetFocalPoint with 3 args
  GetFocalPoint
  SetIntensity with 1 arg
  GetIntensity
  ...
```

Note that the methods are listed according to the inheritance hierarchy. The `ListMethods` command is useful for learning about **vtk** objects or for reminding yourself of the exact form of a method.

Another special command is `ListInstances`. This command should be invoked in combination with a class. `ListInstances` lists all the instances of a particular class. For example:

```
% vtkActor actor
actor
% vtkActor actor2
actor2
% vtkActor ListInstances
actor actor2
```

This command is useful when you want to remember the name of a particular instance or wish to create a list of objects to operate on.

Finally, the `vtkCommand DeleteAllObjects` command can be used to delete all the **vtk** instances created in a Tcl session. You can use this command prior to reloading scripts to avoid creating instances of the same name and to free allocated memory.

Dynamic Libraries

You may have noticed in the example in the section "Interpreted Code" on page 73 an unusual command:

```
catch {load vtktcl}
```

The Tcl `load` command is used to dynamically load the **vtk** library. Only when this library is loaded do the **vtk** commands become available for use. The Tcl `catch` command is necessary because on some systems dynamic loading is not available or not needed. On these systems the `load` command will cause an error. The `catch` command prevents errors from causing the interpreter to abort. Thus we use the combination of `catch` and `load` to insure portability of Tcl scripts across different computer systems.

11.4 Examples

Figure **11–1** compares the C++ and Tcl code to render a cube. Notice how the pointers in C++ are dealt with from the Tcl script. Most of the code in this example can be used as a starting point for other scripts. The next example is a Tcl version modified from `Mace.cxx` presented previously in Figure **4–14**. In it we create the same visualization pipeline and then execute a `for` loop that modifies the actor's properties (see `mace.tcl`).

Near the end of the script, we set the `UserMethod()` of the `vtkRender-WindowInteractor` to `{wm deiconify .vtkInteract}`. This command lets us access an interpreter widget (the "interactor ui") into which we can type Tcl commands. This widget is created at the beginning of the example by sourcing the file `vtkInt.tcl`. We can then access this widget by typing "u" in the rendering window. The interpreter widget can be very useful for making small changes and immediately seeing the effects of them.

```
catch {load vtktcl}
# this is a tcl version of the Mace example
# get the interactor ui
source ../../examplesTcl/vtkInt.tcl

# Create the RenderWindow, Renderer and both Actors
#
vtkRenderer ren1
vtkRenderWindow renWin
    renWin AddRenderer ren1
```

```cpp
// C++ code to draw a cube
#include "vtk.h"

main ()
{
  vtkRenderer *ren1 =
      vtkRenderer::New();
  vtkRenderWindow *renWin =
      vtkRenderWindow::New();
    renWin->AddRenderer(ren1);
  vtkCubeSource *cubeSrc =
      vtkCubeSource::New();
  vtkPolyDataMapper cubeMpr =
      vtkPolyDataMapper::New();
  vtkActor *cube1 =
      vtkActor::New();

  cubeMpr->SetInput(
    cubeSrc->GetOutput());
  cube1->SetMapper(cubeMpr);
  ren1->AddActor(cube1);
  renWin->Render();
}
```

```tcl
# Tcl code to draw a cube
catch {load vtktcl}



vtkRenderer ren1

vtkRenderWindow renWin
  renWin AddRenderer ren1

vtkCubeSource cubeSrc

vtkPolyDataMapper cubeMpr

vtkActor cube1


cubeMpr SetInput \
  [cubeSrc GetOutput]
cube1 SetMapper cubeMpr
ren1 AddActor cube1
renWin Render
```

Figure 11–1 A comparison between the C++ and Tcl code to render a cube.

```tcl
vtkRenderWindowInteractor iren
    iren SetRenderWindow renWin

# create a sphere source and actor
#
vtkSphereSource sphere
vtkPolyDataMapper    sphereMapper
    sphereMapper SetInput [sphere GetOutput]
vtkLODActor sphereActor
    sphereActor SetMapper sphereMapper

# create the spikes using a cone source and the sphere source
#
vtkConeSource cone
vtkGlyph3D glyph
    glyph SetInput [sphere GetOutput]
    glyph SetSource [cone GetOutput]
    glyph SetVectorModeToUseNormal
    glyph SetScaleModeToScaleByVector
    glyph SetScaleFactor 0.25
vtkPolyDataMapper spikeMapper
    spikeMapper SetInput [glyph GetOutput]
```

```
vtkLODActor spikeActor
    spikeActor SetMapper spikeMapper

# Add the actors to the renderer, set the background and size
#
ren1 AddActor sphereActor
ren1 AddActor spikeActor
set cam1 [ren1 GetActiveCamera]
$cam1 Zoom 1.4
ren1 SetBackground 0.1 0.2 0.4
renWin SetSize 300 300
renWin Render

set sphereProp [sphereActor GetProperty]
set spikeProp [spikeActor GetProperty]

# Loop through some properties
#
for {set i 0} {$i < 360} {incr i 2} {
    ren1 SetBackground 0.6 0.0 [expr (360.0 - $i) / 400.0]
    $cam1 Azimuth 5
    $sphereProp SetColor 0.5 [expr $i / 440.0] \
            [expr (360.0 - $i) / 400.0]
    $spikeProp SetColor [expr (360.0 - $i) / 440.0] 0.5 \
            [expr $i / 440.0]
    renWin Render
}

# Enable user method to pop-up interactor
#
iren SetUserMethod {wm deiconify .vtkInteract}
iren Initialize

# prevent the tk window from showing up then start the event loop
wm withdraw .
```

11.5 User Interfaces with Tk

If you have been experimenting with the example Tcl scripts, you may have noticed an empty window appearing along with the rendering window. This window is intended to hold the user interface for your application. This user interface is written in Tk, an extension to Tcl. Tk provides support for common user-interface components such as push-buttons, text widgets and scroll bars. Developing applications using the Tk user interface is covered in John Ousterhout's book [Ousterhout94], as well as several other application-oriented books available at your local bookstore.

If you want to use Tcl and prevent the empty window from popping up, you can add the following lines to your scripts. They indicate that the top level window of the user interface should not be mapped (i.e., displayed) but otherwise nothing else changes.

```
# prevent the default tk window from showing up
wm withdraw .
```

A nice feature of Tk is that it is window system independent. You can create user interfaces that will work in both the X Window system and the Microsoft Windows windowing system. Thus, applications you build in Tcl/Tk are computer-platform independent. You also may be interested in one of the Tcl/Tk user-interface design tools. These tools allow you to lay out graphical user interfaces interactively by directly placing buttons, sliders, and other widgets in their correct position.

A Simple Example

Figure **11–2** shows an example of a simple user interface for a Tcl program. This example was created from the mace.tcl example by replacing the Tcl command "wm withdraw ." with the Tcl script shown in Figure **11–2**. The behavior of the application is as the color sliders (one for each color component red, green, blue) are moved, the actor spikeActor's color is modified, and the scene is rerendered. Note that the simple user interface does not prevent us from typing "u" in the rendering window to obtain the interpreter widget.

Using vtkTkRenderWidget

One of the features of the previous example is that the rendering window and the user interface are in separate windows. Although this may be desirable in some applications, often we wish to integrate the rendering window and user interface into a single window. Figure **11–3** is an example of such an integrated application.

Rendering window and Tcl/Tk integration is achieved using the special object vtkTkRenderWidget. This object acts like a Tk widget (a canvas, for example), but has a special method that allows it to interface with **vtk**. This method is illustrated in the following:

```
vtkRenderer Renderer
vtkTkRenderWidget .window -width 300 -height 300
set RenWin [.window GetRenderWindow]
$RenWin AddRenderer Renderer
```

Another nice feature of vtkTkRenderWidget is that it is possible to create event bindings in the widget. So you can create your own interactor style for manipulating actors, lights, or cameras, or for special features like image capture or animation sequences. A good example of this capability can be found in the Tcl

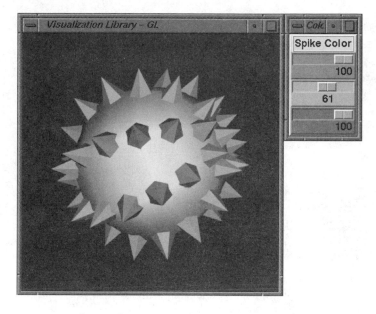

```
# Create user interface
#
frame .f
label .f.l -text "Spike Color"
scale .f.r -from 0 -to 100 -background #f00 \
-orient horizontal -command SetColor
scale .f.g -from 0 -to 100 -background #0f0 \
-orient horizontal -command SetColor
scale .f.b -from 0 -to 100 -background #00f \
-orient horizontal -command SetColor

set color [[spikeActor GetProperty] GetColor]
.f.r set [expr [lindex $color 0] * 100.0]
.f.g set [expr [lindex $color 1] * 100.0]
.f.b set [expr [lindex $color 2] * 100.0]

pack .f.l .f.r .f.g .f.b -side top
pack .f

proc SetColor {value} {
    [spikeActor GetProperty] SetColor [expr [.f.r get]/100.0] \
            [expr [.f.g get]/100.0] \ [expr [.f.b get]/100.0]
    renWin Render
}
```

Figure 11–2 Mace with a Tk user interface. Tcl script shown above is added to the mace example to create simple user interface shown (spikeColor.tcl).

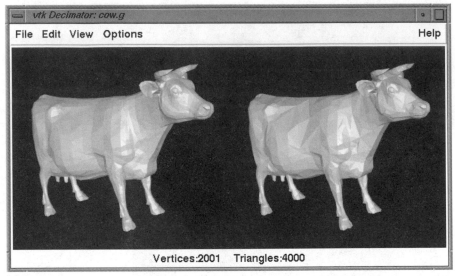

Figure 11–3 Example showing rendering window and graphical user interface integrated into a single application. We use the special Tcl/Tk widget `vtkTkRenderWidget` to allow us to place rendering windows into a Tcl/Tk application. (See the script `Decimate.tcl`.)

script `TkInteractor.tcl`, which creates an alternative user-interface interactor to the `vtkRenderWindowInteractor` used in previous sections of the book.

(Note: if you are compiling **vtk** on Unix systems you may have to take special steps to include `vtkTkRenderWidget`. This is because the compile process requires prior knowledge of the installation location for Tcl and Tk.)

11.6 Chapter Summary

In this chapter we discussed the differences between compiled and interpreted languages. We find ourselves most frequently working with interpreted languages, since our work tends to be rapid prototyping or small visualization programs. The *Visualization Toolkit* allows you to build applications with either compiled C++ or the Tcl/Tk interpretive language. This allows you to pick the environment that best suits you, or to mix them together, doing your prototyping in Tcl and then writing the final program in C++. We then described the basic syntax of Tcl and provided a few example scripts to explain how Tcl handles variables and recursive interpretation. We then looked at how **vtk** is wrapped with Tcl and what limitations that creates. The chapter concluded with a few example scripts and a brief discussion of combining Tk's user interfaces with **vtk**.

11.7 Bibliographic Notes

For more information on interpreted languages or interpreted graphics systems, you can turn to Ousterhout's book on Tcl and Tk [Ousterhout94]. You also might want to look into other popular languages such as Python, Perl or Scheme.If you are familiar with electronic news groups, then you might be interested in the following groups: `comp.lang.tcl`; `comp.lang.python`; or `comp.lang.scheme`. For information on Lex and Yacc [Levine92] provides a good starting point. For some background on the authors' experiences in the interpreted language LYMB you can look into [Schroeder92].

11.8 References

[Ousterhout94]
J. K.Ousterhout. *Tcl and the Tk Toolkit*. Addison-Wesley Publishing Company, Reading, MA, 1994.

[Levine92]
J. R. Levine, T. Mason, and D. Brown. *Lex & Yacc.* O'Reilly & Associates, Sebastopol, CA, 1992.

[Schroeder92]
W. J. Schroeder, W. E. Lorensen, G. D. Montanaro, and C. R. Volpe. "VISAGE: An Object-Oriented Scientific Visualization System." In *Proceedings IEEE Visualization `92*. IEEE Computer Society Press, Los Alamitos, CA, 1992.

11.9 Exercises

11.1 Create a Tcl script to perform the same visualization as presented in Figure **4–13**.

11.2 Extend Exercise 11.1 by adding a `for` loop that will azimuth the active camera through 360 degrees creating a short animation.

11.3 Describe the advantages and pitfalls of using the Tcl interface (as compared to C++) in **vtk**. Be sure to discuss the possible performance issues taking into account the compiled/interpreted hybrid nature of **vtk**. Also consider issues of scale associated with building large or complex applications in such an environment.

## CHAPTER 12

Visualization on the Web

*T*he early 1990s established the widespread use and accessibility of the World Wide Web. Once a network used primarily by researchers and universities, the Web has become something that is used by people throughout the world. The effects of this transformation have been significant, ranging from personal home pages with static images and text, to professional Web pages embedding animation and virtual reality. This chapter discusses some of those changes and describes how the World Wide Web can be used to make visualization more accessible, interactive, and powerful. Topics covered include the advantages and disadvantages of client-side versus server-side visualization, VRML, and Java3D, interwoven with demonstration examples.

12.1 Motivation

Before describing in detail how to perform visualization over the Web, it is important to understand what we expect to gain. Clearly people have been visualizing data prior to the invention of the Web, but what the Web adds is the ability for people throughout the world to share information quickly and efficiently. Like all successful communication systems, the Web enables people to interact and share information more efficiently compared to other methods. In many ways the Web shares the characteristic of computer visualization in its ability to communicate large amounts of data. For that reason, computer graphics and visualization are now vital parts of the Web, and are becoming widespread in their application.

To demonstrate these concepts we provide a simple example that illustrates the usefulness of the Web, and leads us into our first important topic: client-side versus server-side visualization.

One common problem for researchers has been how to share or publish results. Typically, this involved having one site perform the research, interact with the data, form conclusions, and then publish the results as a report. The report might include a few pictures and possibly even a short animation. Obtaining access to the report might be through a journal or conference. Subsequently, co-workers at other sites would read the report and respond via verbal communication or formal articles.

While certainly a viable means of sharing information, there are two important shortcomings in such a scenario. First, the report does not allow another researcher to interact with the visualizations. They are static pictures or pre-recorded animations. There is no opportunity to look from a different angle or change the parameters of the visualization. Second, access to the report may be limited or untimely. For example, some journals require as much as two years to accept, review, and publish an article. This time delay is too long for many technology-driven fields such as medicine, computers, or business. Such delays in receiving information can result in fruitless research or a failed business.

Using the Web this scenario changes significantly. It is now possible to create reports so that other researchers can interact directly with the data, including visualizing the results in an alternative form. The Web also provides the opportunity to publish results immediately so that anyone with Web access can view them. Additionally, results can be modified as your work progresses so that they are always up to date.

Another motivation for visualization over the Web is collaboration. If a researcher is performing a visualization of a dataset at one site, there are a number of hurdles preventing someone at another site from doing the same. For starters, the data, which could be sizable, must be copied, or sent from one site to the other. Then the software being used must be available at both sites which may not even be possible depending on the hardware available. The popularity of cross-platform systems such as AVS, IBM's Data Explorer, and **vtk** have helped this situation, but even then the software and data reside at both locations. This is frequently referred to as client-side visualization because all steps of the visualization are performed at the collaboration (or client) sites. In contrast, server-side visualization occurs when all of the visualization is done at one centralized location called the server. The results of the server-side visualization are then sent to collaboration sites.

The Web opens up the opportunity to perform mixed client/server visualization that has a number of benefits. First, let's consider the drawbacks to client-side only visualization. As mentioned in the preceding discussion, client-side visualization requires both the data and the software at the client. If the datasets are very large it may be impractical to transfer the data over the Web.

Since the server doesn't know what the client is going to do with the data, all of the data must be sent. Additionally, the client may not have sufficient memory or performance to perform the visualization. The advantages of client-side visualization are that the user has complete control over the visualization and can interact with or modify it at will.

With server-side visualization the most significant loss is in interaction. A server-side only visualization is much like publishing a report. The clients have very little control over the images and animations it produces. The advantage is that the results are easily viewed from any client without requiring special hardware or software. As we will see in the remaining sections, the advantage of using recently developed Web technology is that we can mix server-, and client-side visualization much more readily than before, providing the benefits of both.

12.2 Early Web Visualization

While the World Wide Web received most of its attention in the early 1990s, its foundations date back decades earlier to the Internet and ARPAnet. What made the 1990s so significant was the development of some standardized visual tools for exchanging information. The most common of these are the Web browsers such as Mosaic, Netscape Navigator, and Microsoft Explorer. These browsers provide a unified interface supporting many data (or content) types. The first content type to gain wide acceptance was HyperText Markup Language or HTML. HTML provides a way to format text and images in a document that can be shared across the Web. HTML also includes the ability to provide active links in one document that point to other documents on the Web. This helps to solve the problem of sharing results but it still limits the user to static images.

This problem was quickly solved as Web browsers started to support other content types including animation formats such as MPEG, AVI, and QuickTime. Now a link in a HTML document can load an animation sequence for the user to view and interact with. The next step was to allow the client to control the generation of the animation sequence on the server. To facilitate this process, a mechanism for the client to send general information to the server was introduced. The Common Gateway Interface (CGI) along with HTML forms serves this purpose. In this two-pronged approach, an HTML form collects information from the client, passes it to the server that executes a CGI-BIN script, and then finally produces a result for the client to view.

For example, consider a situation where you would like to perform an isosurface extraction from volume data and then generate a short animation rotating the camera around the isosurface. There are a number of ways to generate such an animation and create an MPEG file, which can then be linked into an HTML document. Figure **12–1** shows one example generated from the following HTML code:

```
<HEAD><TITLE>Sample MPEG Animation Page</TITLE></HEAD>
```

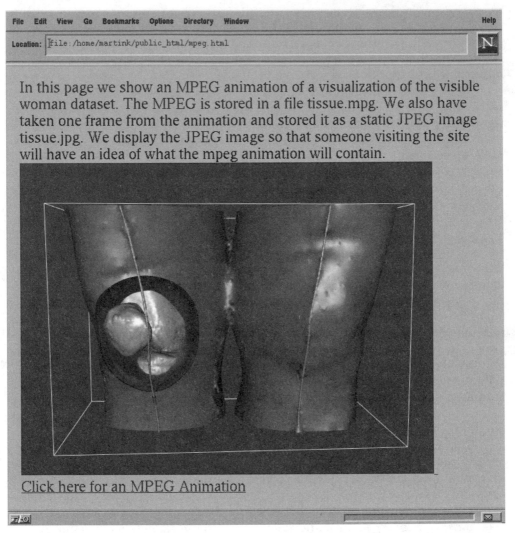

Figure 12–1 MPEG visualization example.

In this page we show an MPEG animation of a visualization
of the visible woman dataset. The MPEG is stored in a file
tissue.mpg. We also have taken one frame from the animation
and stored it as a static JPEG image tissue.jpg. We
display the JPEG image so that someone visiting the site will
have an idea of what the mpeg animation will contain.

```
<br>
<A HREF="tissue.mpg"><IMG SRC="tissue.jpg">
<br>Click here for an MPEG Animation</A>
```

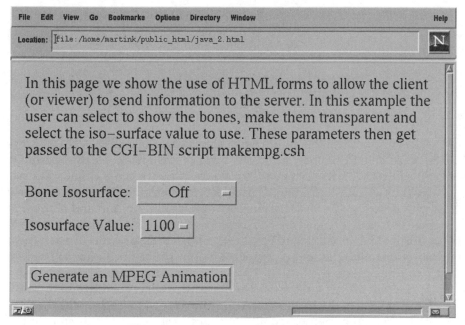

Figure 12-2 Example HTML form.

The title and text description are followed by <A HREF="tissue.mpg"> which associates the MPEG file, tissue.mpg, with whatever comes between the first <A> and the closing </A>. In this example there is a JPEG image and a line of text. Clicking on either of these will play the MPEG animation.

Now let's use CGI and an HTML form to enable the client to change the iso-surface value. The first step is to obtain the desired isosurface value from the client using an HTML form such as Figure **12-2**. The form was generated by the following HTML code:

```
<HEAD><TITLE>Sample MPEG Animation Page</TITLE></HEAD>

<FORM METHOD="POST" ACTION="/cgi-bin/makempg.csh">

In this page we show the use of HTML forms to allow the client
(or viewer) to send information to the server. In this example
the user can select to show the bones, make them transparent and
select the isosurface value to use. These parameters then get
passed to the CGI-BIN script makempg.csh</P>

<P>Bone Isosurface: <SELECT NAME=iso>
<OPTION SELECTED>Off
<OPTION>On
<OPTION>Transparent
</SELECT><BR>
```

```
Isosurface Value: <SELECT NAME=isoval>
<OPTION>1400 <OPTION>1200
<OPTION SELECTED>1100
<OPTION>1000 <OPTION>900
</SELECT><BR>

<P><INPUT TYPE="submit"
VALUE="Generate an MPEG Animation"></FORM></P>
```

The FORM keyword starts the definition of the HTML form. The ACTION keyword indicates what should happen when the form is submitted. In this example the server will run a CGI-BIN script called makempg.csh when a client submits this form. Next the two pull-down menus are declared with the SELECT keyword. The NAME keyword sets up an association between a string name and the value for this menu. This will be used by the script makempg.csh to access the values from the form. The OPTION and SELECTED keywords provide a mechanism to specify the values for the menu and what value the default should be. Finally, the last two lines create the button that will submit the form when pressed.

Once the client has submitted the form, the server will execute the CGI-BIN script and pass it the arguments from the form. The script will then generate a new MPEG animation based on the client's request and return it to the client.

While these examples demonstrate a closed loop of interaction between the client and server, there are two remaining problems. First, this approach places the entire computational load on the server. While this may be viable for some applications, some servers literally receive millions of client requests a day, severely straining server resources. Second, while the process is interactive, the lag time between making a change and seeing the result can be considerable, depending on the length of the animation and the communication bandwidth. Better solutions are now available to improve interactivity.

12.3 Virtual Reality Modeling Language (VRML)

HTML is a powerful tool for creating hypertext documents; however, it does not directly support 3D content. This limitation can be severe if we are interested in exploring 3D data, and do not know exactly what we wish to see, or what we wish to present to a user. As a result, an important development has been to create 3D worlds that the user can freely navigate. One application of this technology is Web content that allows customers to preview a hotel, resort, or vacation area by moving through a model representing the site. Such an application allows customers to preview a prospective business and directly experience what is available without relying on preconstructed views of the site.

As a result of this need for greater interactivity, a new content type appeared referred to as the Virtual Reality Modeling Language (VRML). The idea behind VRML was to create a standard definition for transmitting 3D content over the Web. Having its origins in an early system called Labyrinth, which

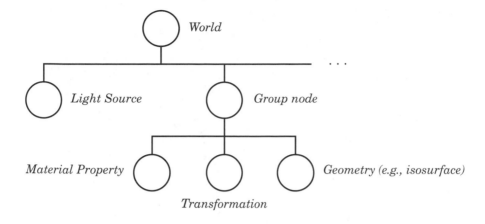

Figure 12–3 A simple scene graph.

is in turn based on Reality Lab from Rendermorphics, it quickly evolved to the VRML 1.0 specification based on Open Inventor from Silicon Graphics.

A VRML 1.0 file (typically with a `.wrl` extension, abbreviated from world) contains a scene graph representation of a 3D world (e.g., a scene). Consider Figure **12–3** which shows a simple scene. It is a directed graph that is traversed depth first from top to bottom with the content of the graph in its nodes (the circles). In this figure the top node is a group node that collects child nodes together. The light is a directional light node and the second group node represents an isosurface. The isosurface group node is represented by three children nodes: one to control the material properties, a general transformation, and finally the 3D geometry. VRML and Open Inventor support many different types of nodes including some support for animation. (See also "Alternative Visual Programming Models" on page 98.)

The basic idea behind VRML 1.0 is that the 3D content can be downloaded from the server and then interacted with the client. There are many Web browsers that support VRML and most take advantage of client-side graphics hardware if available. This helps address both the server-load problem and the interaction lag time associated with the earlier approach of server-generated MPEG animations. Like HTML, VRML supports active links so that navigating through a door in one VRML world can send you to new VRML (or HTML) sites.

To address many of the limitations in VRML 1.0, significant changes were made resulting in the VRML 2.0 standard. Where VRML 1.0 was primarily a static scene description with some very limited behaviors, VRML 2.0 adds audio, video, and integration with Web scripting languages and more. It is still essentially a data file, but with the capabilities of simulating much more realistic and immersive environments. Many visualization systems, including **vtk**, support exporting scenes as VRML files. Consider the following example:

```
vtkRenderer ren1
vtkRenderWindow renWin
    renWin AddRenderer ren1

# create pipeline
#
vtkPLOT3DReader p13d
    p13d SetXYZFileName "../../../vtkdata/combxyz.bin"
    p13d SetQFileName "../../../vtkdata/combq.bin"
    p13d SetScalarFunctionNumber 100
    p13d SetVectorFunctionNumber 202
vtkContourFilter iso
    iso SetInput [p13d GetOutput]
    iso SetValue 0 .38
vtkPolyDataNormals normals
    normals SetInput [iso GetOutput]
    normals SetFeatureAngle 45
vtkPolyDataMapper isoMapper
    isoMapper SetInput [normals GetOutput]
    isoMapper ScalarVisibilityOff
vtkActor isoActor
    isoActor SetMapper isoMapper
    eval [isoActor GetProperty] SetColor 0.3 0.4 0.5

vtkStructuredGridOutlineFilter outline
    outline SetInput [p13d GetOutput]
vtkPolyDataMapper outlineMapper
    outlineMapper SetInput [outline GetOutput]
vtkActor outlineActor
    outlineActor SetMapper outlineMapper

# Add the actors to the renderer, set the background and size
#
ren1 AddActor outlineActor
ren1 AddActor isoActor
renWin SetSize 500 500
ren1 SetBackground 0.1 0.2 0.4
```

This is a typical program within **vtk** that extracts an isosurface and bounding outline from a structured grid dataset. To export this result to a VRML data file we can use the vtkVRMLExporter as shown below:

```
vtkVRMLExporter exp
    exp SetRenderWindow renWin
    exp SetFileName Combustor.wrl
    exp Write
```

These four lines create an instance of vtkVRMLExporter, set its input to ren-Win (an instance of vtkRenderWindow), set a file name, and finally write out the result. This is different from previous examples where data was written out using vtkPolyDataWriter or other subclasses of vtkWriter. vtkVRMLExporter is a subclass of vtkExporter, not vtkWriter. The significant difference is that a writer takes a vtkDataSet as input and is responsible for writing out a single dataset. An exporter takes a vtkRenderWindow as input and is responsible for writing out an entire scene, possibly containing multiple actors, lights, textures, and material properties, in addition to any datasets.

If you consider a continuum from a static data file to a fully interactive visualization program, vtkWriter would be at one end, vtkExporter in the middle, and a **vtk** program at the other. VRML 1.0 would fall at the same place as vtkExporter and VRML 2.0 would fall between vtkExporter and an actual program due to its added support for behavior and script interaction. What VRML lacks from a visualization perspective is algorithms. VRML is a 3D multimedia content format and lacks direct support for applying visualization techniques or algorithms.

12.4 A VRML Visualization Server

We can improve on the earlier MPEG visualization server example by creating a VRML visualization server. The primary limitations of the MPEG approach were that the processing burden was on the server, and the client-side interaction was limited to requesting that a different MPEG animation be generated. In our improved example, the basic idea is the same as before. That is, we use a HTML form to define parameters for a visualization, which then spawns off a CGI-BIN script. The difference is that in this example the server will generate a VRML data file that is returned to the client. The client can then control the viewpoint and rendering of the VRML result. The data and visualization software still reside on the server, so the client is only required to have a VRML compatible Web browser.

The HTML form is essentially the same as the one used to generate Figure **12–2**. What changes is that the CGI-BIN script now needs to produce a VRML file instead of an MPEG. So instead of the form invoking makempg.csh, it will invoke a C++ executable named VRMLServer. This executable will parse the inputs from the form and then write out a VRML file to its standard output. The first part of the program parses the arguments from the form. The server passes these arguments as a single string to the program's standard input. At the same time an environment variable named CONTENT_LENGTH is set to the length of this input. In this example there are two values passed from the form: iso and isoval. According to convention they are separated by a "&" when passed to the CGI-BIN script. The following C++ code extracts these values from the input string and performs some quick error checking.

```
// first get the form data
env = getenv("CONTENT_LENGTH");
if (!env) return -1;
```

```
int inputLength = atoi(env);
// a quick sanity check on the input
if ((inputLength > 40)||(inputLength < 17)) return -1;
cin >> arg1;

if (strncmp(arg1,"isoval=",7) == 0)
  {
  isoval = atof(arg1 + 7);
  strcpy(isoType,arg1 + 11);
  }
else
  {
  isoval = atof(arg1 + inputLength - 4);
  strncpy(isoType,arg1 + 4,inputLength - 16);
  isoType[inputLength - 16] = '\0';
  }
```

This code is specific to the parameters in this example, but generic argument
extraction routines such as cgic (see http://www.boutell.com/cgic/) can
be used. Once the form data has been obtained, it can be used to set up the visualization pipeline as usual. In the following code, an isosurface is added to the
renderer based on the isoType input from the form. Likewise if isoType is set
to "Transparent" then that actor's opacity is set to 0.5.

```
// should we do the isosurface
if (strcmp(isoType,"Off"))
  {
  ren1->AddActor( isoActor );
  }
if (strcmp(isoType,"Transparent") == 0)
  {
  isoActor->GetProperty()->SetOpacity( 0.5 );
  }
```

Once the pipeline is set up, the last step is to generate the proper headers and
VRML output. The header is the keyword Content-type: followed by the keyword x-world/x-vrml that is the specification for VRML content. This is often
followed by a pragma indicating that the client browser should not cache the
data, typically because of the memory it would consume.

```
// Send out vrml header stuff
fprintf(stdout,"Content-type: x-world/x-vrml\n");
fprintf(stdout,"Pragma: no-cache\n\n");

// write out VRRML 2.0 file
vtkVRMLExporter *writer = vtkVRMLExporter::New();
writer->SetInput( renWin );
writer->SetFilePointer( stdout );
writer->Write();
```

Finally an instance of `vtkVRMLExporter` is created, assigned an instance of `vtkRenderWindow` as input, and set to write to standard output. When the `Write` method is applied, the exporter updates the visualization pipeline and produces the VRML output. The `vtkRenderWindow` is never rendered and no windows appear on the server. There is no need for an interactor because the interaction will be handled by the client's VRML browser. This program simply reads in a string of input (the parameters from the form) and then produces a string of output (the VRML data). It is also important to remember that CGI-BIN scripts are typically run from a different user id and environment than your own; file names and paths should be fully specified.

12.5 Visualization with Java

The examples discussed so far have addressed Web-based visualization in a number of ways. We have seen how to present preconstructed content such as images and animations using HTML, as well as creating interactive worlds with VRML. Each technique has its benefits but lacks the flexibility found in a custom-developed program. This is where Java stands out. Java's origins trace back to an embedded control language for small appliances and personal digital assistants. As such it was designed to work on a wide variety of hardware without recompilation and with high reliability. These same qualities are valuable to Web programming where a single program must run on many different machines without fail.

Since Java is a full programming language, any visualization application written in Java will run on any Java-compliant system. In addition, Java provides the flexibility to perform the visualization on the server, on the client, or even a mixture of both. A number of early Java programs (a.k.a., applets) have emerged that render simple geometry or play back image sequences. The current challenge is to perform "real" visualization within Java. As of this writing, Java has poor performance relative to C++ and lacks a direct connection to take advantage of 3D graphics hardware. In the future, with the introduction of Java3D, these problems may disappear leaving just one remaining problem: the lack of a visualization API. Fortunately, the *Visualization Toolkit* has been interfaced with Java so that it can be used from Java in a manner similar to its use in Tcl/Tk (see Chapter 11 for more information on Tcl/Tk).

While Java is a portable byte-compiled language, its designers realized it was important to have a way for developers to make calls to C or C++ routines. This mechanism is called the Java Native Interface, or JNI for short. The JNI provides a clean, well-defined way for native code such as C and C++ to work with Java. This allows a visualization system such as **vtk** to be used, which in turn provides a mechanism to access 3D graphics hardware (if available). Native code also allows performance critical functions to be handled in optimized C or C++ code instead of the currently lower-performing Java.

The downside to JNI and native code is that it sacrifices Java's portability somewhat. Where a pure Java program can be byte-compiled and run on any machine that supports Java, a program that relies on native code requires that the compiled native code be installed on the client. For each type of machine you want to support, you will need a compiled version of the native code. For a toolkit like **vtk** this means that the client would have to download the native **vtk** support (e.g., an object library) before being able to run **vtk**-Java applications. Once that is done, most applications described in this book can be made into a Web-based visualization. Depending on the needs of the application, the data can be left on the server and the results sent to the client, or the data could be sent to the client for both processing and viewing.

The following example shows how to use Java and **vtk** to display vibrational modes of a rectangular plate. In the preceding examples an HTML form was used to obtain input from the client. With Java we can construct a customized client-side user interface to obtain the required information.

The first step in this example creates the HTML code that in turn launches the Java applet.

```
<title>Vibrational Modes of a Rectangular Plate</title>
<h2>Vibrational Modes of a Rectangular Plate</h2>
This Java applet downloads a VTK data file into a Java String. It
then uses the InputString method of the VTK data reader to use this
string as its data. Then it creates a filter pipeline that takes
the original geometry and warps it according to the vector data.
There are four sets of vector data in this example. They correspond
to the first, second, fourth and eighth vibrational modes. The
geometry is color based on the amount of displacement.
<hr>
<applet code=App2.class width=400 height=500>
<param name=model value=plate.vtk>
</applet>
<hr>
```

The key lines are near the end where the `applet` keyword is used to start the App2 Java applet with a default window size of 400 by 500. Parameters are passed to the applet using the `param` keyword followed by key-value pairs. When the client encounters the `applet` keyword, it then requests that Java applet from the server and starts executing it. We will consider the Java code in App2 from a visualization perspective. A more complete introduction to Java programming can be found in numerous books (see "Bibliographic Notes" on page 494).

The first few lines of the applet import other classes that this application will use. VTKModel is a class that uses Java to read **vtk** data files across the Web. The `import vtk.*` line provides access to all of the native **vtk** objects.

```
import VTKModel;
import vtk.*;
import java.awt.*;
import java.applet.*;
import java.io.InputStream;
import java.net.URL;
```

Next comes the class definition for App2. As with most Java applets, this class extends the Applet class. It has a number of instance variables including many **vtk** objects that will be used to set up the visualization pipeline.

```
public class App2 extends Applet
    {
    VTKModel md;
    String mdname = null;
    String message = null;
    vtkPolyDataReader pr = null;
    vtkWarpVector warp = null;
    vtkGeometryFilter ds2poly = null;
    vtkCleanPolyData clean = null;
    vtkPolyDataNormals normals = null;
    vtkVectorDot color = null;
    vtkDataSetMapper plateMapper = null;
    vtkPanel panel = null;
    vtkActor a = null;
```

The init() method handles applet initialization. This is where parameters from the HTML page will be processed and the visualization pipeline and user interface will be set up. To place the rendering window within the user interface, we use the vtkPanel class that is a subclass of the Java Canvas class. This way the rendering window can be treated as if it were just another piece of the user interface.

```
public void init()
    {
    GridBagLayout grid = new GridBagLayout();

    this.setLayout(grid);
    panel = new vtkPanel();
    panel.resize(400,400);
    constrain(this,panel,0,0,8,8);
```

Next, this method checks to see if the model parameter is set, and opens a stream connection to the server that the VTKModel class uses to download the data file into a Java string. This is then passed to a vtkPolyDataReader at which point the data is now available to the native **vtk** code on the client.

```
InputStream is = null;
try
  {
    mdname = getParameter("model");
    if (mdname == null)
      mdname = "model.obj";
    is = new URL(getDocumentBase(), mdname).openStream();
    md = new VTKModel(is);
    // create the model
```

```
pr = new vtkPolyDataReader();
pr.ReadFromInputStringOn();
pr.SetInputString(md.GetData());
pr.SetVectorsName("mode1");
warp = new vtkWarpVector();
warp.SetInput(pr.GetOutput());
warp.SetScaleFactor(0.5);
```

The rest of the pipeline is set up as usual with the exception that a Java syntax is used instead of C++ or Tcl. (Due to **vtk**'s object-oriented design the variations from one language to another are minor.) At this point in the init() method the rest of the pipeline is set up along with some checkboxes and event handlers for the user interface. The visualization pipeline connects to the vtkPanel in a manner similar to the TkRenderWidget (see "Using vtkTkRenderWidget" on page 466). The vtkPanel has a method that returns the RenderWindow that can then be acted on as usual. Callbacks such as the StartRenderMethod() are available in Java as in C++ and Tcl. Within Java, the callback will invoke the public void method specified on the instance specified. For example:

```
panel.GetRenderer().AddActor(a);
panel.GetRenderer().SetStartRenderMethod(this,"aCallBack");
}

public void aCallBack()
  {
  System.out.println("Starting Render");
  }
```

The resulting applet is shown in Figure **12–4**.

This demonstrates one of the advantages of using Java for Web visualization. VRML would require that the geometry of each vibrational mode be sent to the client for viewing. With Java and **vtk** the geometry can be sent once along with a set of scalar displacements for each vibrational mode. Then as the client switches between modes, the geometry can be modified quickly by the client without any additional network traffic. In fact the client could mix vibrational modes or perform an animation showing the vibration of the plate all without having to go back to the server, and without requiring much more data than a single VRML model of the plate. If the client decided to examine another geometry, say the vibrational modes of a disc, then it would likely return to the server for the new data. This is the flexibility that Java provides.

12.6 Java3D

While native code (such as a **vtk** implementation) in Java provides one mechanism to perform hardware accelerated 3D graphics, there is an effort to provide such support as part of the standard Java API. This effort, called Java3D, is still

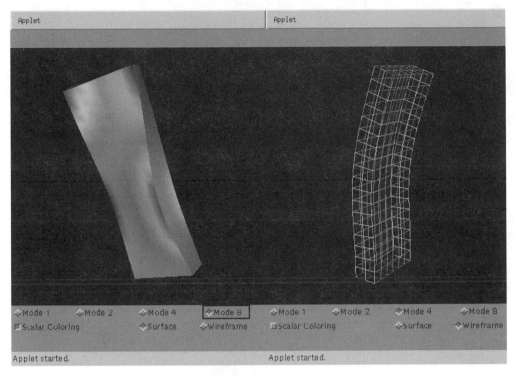

Figure 12–4 Two images from a Java (JNI) applet.

in development as of this writing but much of its basic structure has been finalized. Java3D provides both scene graph rendering similar to VRML, and high-level immediate mode rendering. The immediate mode rendering support is not as complete as libraries like OpenGL, but it does provide a good subset of its functionality. One significant advantage to using Java3D instead of the Java Native Interface is that visualization applets can be written in pure Java without any native code requirements (e.g., libraries on your system). While **vtk** does not currently support a pure Java implementation of its visualization algorithms, such a solution is viable if the promised performance improvements to Java occur.

To better understand the Java3D API, we'll walk through an example applet distributed with the original 1.0 specification. In this example, a colored cube is rendered as it rotates at a fixed rate.

First, let's consider the definition of the cube. Some of the details have been left out for brevity. The complete description of the cube is stored in a Java class we'll call `ColorCube`. It contains two class variables (`verts` and `colors`) that store the vertex positions and RGB colors. It has an instance of the `Shape3D` class that will be used by Java3D and a method, `getShape()`, to access it. Finally, `ColorCube` has a constructor that creates a `QuadArray`, inserts the `verts` and `colors` into it, and assigns it to the `Shape3D` instance variable.

```
public class ColorCube extends Object
    {
    private static final float[] verts =
        {
        // front face
        1.0f, -1.0f,  1.0f, 1.0f,  1.0f,  1.0f,
        -1.0f,  1.0f,  1.0f, -1.0f, -1.0f,  1.0f,
...
        // bottom face
        -1.0f, -1.0f,  1.0f, -1.0f, -1.0f, -1.0f,
        1.0f, -1.0f, -1.0f, 1.0f, -1.0f,  1.0f,
        };
    private static final float[] colors = {
        // front face (red)
        1.0f, 0.0f, 0.0f, 1.0f, 0.0f, 0.0f,
        1.0f, 0.0f, 0.0f, 1.0f, 0.0f, 0.0f,
...
        // bottom face (cyan)
        0.0f, 1.0f, 1.0f, 0.0f, 1.0f, 1.0f,
        0.0f, 1.0f, 1.0f, 0.0f, 1.0f, 1.0f,
        };
    private Shape3D shape;
    public ColorCube() {
        QuadArray cube = new QuadArray(24,
                        QuadArray.COORDINATES | QuadArray.COLOR_3);
        cube.setCoordinates(0, verts);
        cube.setColors(0, colors);
        shape = new Shape3D(cube, new Appearance());
        }
    public Shape3D getShape() {
        return shape;
        }
    }
```

Having defined the geometry, the entry point for a Java3D application is the applet. The HelloUniverse class extends the Applet class and provides the initialization code for this application. The constructor for this applet creates a Canvas3D object that is where the 3D information will be rendered. It then calls the createSceneGraph() method that performs the detailed setup of the scene graph including creating an instance of ColorCube. Then the constructor creates an instance of a UniverseBuilder given the Canvas3D and attaches the scene graph to the Universe. The UniverseBuilder is mostly boiler-plate code that handles setting up the view location (or platform) and attaching it to the Canvas3D.

```
public class HelloUniverse extends Applet
    {
    public HelloUniverse()
```

```
        {
        setLayout(new BorderLayout());
        Canvas3D c = new Canvas3D(graphicsConfig);
        add("Center", c);
        // Create a simple scene and attach it to the virtual universe
        BranchGroup scene = createSceneGraph();
        UniverseBuilder u = new UniverseBuilder(c);
        u.addBranchGraph(scene);
        }
    }
```

It is worth noting that in the createSceneGraph() method, the use of the previously defined ColorCube class and its insertion into the scene graph via the BranchGroup class. The setCapability() method is used to enable the cube's transform to be modified and underlies an important concept. To achieve the highest rendering rate, Java3D performs a number of optimizations on the scene graph. Many of these optimizations only work if certain properties of the nodes are guaranteed to not change. So by default most properties of a node are set to be "read only." To modify them after creation requires the specific call shown below.

```
    public BranchGroup createSceneGraph()
      {
      // Create the root of the branch graph
      BranchGroup objRoot = new BranchGroup();
      // Create the transform group node and initialize it to the
      // identity.  Enable the TRANSFORM_WRITE capability so that
      // our behavior code can modify it at runtime.  Add it to the
      // root of the subgraph.
      TransformGroup objTran = new TransformGroup();
      objTran.setCapability(TransformGroup.ALLOW_TRANSFORM_WRITE);
      objRoot.addChild(objTran);
      // Create a simple shape leaf node, add it to the scene graph.
      objTran.addChild(new ColorCube().getShape());
      // Create a new Behavior object that will perform the desired
      // operation on the specified transform object and add it into
      // the scene graph.
      Transform3D yAxis = new Transform3D();
      Alpha rotationAlpha = new Alpha(
         -1, Alpha.INCREASING_ENABLE, 0, 0, 4000, 0, 0, 0, 0, 0);
      RotationInterpolator rotator =
      new RotationInterpolator(rotationAlpha, objTran, yAxis,
          0.0f, (float) Math.PI*2.0f);
      BoundingSphere bounds =
        new BoundingSphere(new Point3d(0.0,0.0,0.0), 100.0);
      rotator.setSchedulingBounds(bounds);
      objTran.addChild(rotator);
      return objRoot;
      }
```

```
public void addBranchGraph(BranchGroup bg) {
  locale.addBranchGraph(bg);
  }
```

While Java3D has not been released as of this writing, it is fairly easy to see how a toolkit like **vtk** could be integrated with it. All the information for the geometry and point data is available and could be put into a `Shape3D` instance. The setup of the visualization pipeline would remain the same.

12.7 VRML, Java, and the EAI

The External Authoring Interface (EAI) provides VRML with the same combination of power and flexibility that Java3D has. The EAI provides a communication interface that allows Java and VRML to interact with each other. This is particularly powerful in that a Java applet can create a VRML world, add and delete nodes from the scene graph, and a VRML scene graph can invoke Java code or Java Script in response to an event. In many ways this is similar to the Java3D solution with the exception that VRML is being used for the rendering instead of the Java3D rendering engine. Both solutions have the benefit of Java as a general purpose language for handling programmatic and user-interface issues.

There are a number of ways to organize a visualization that uses the EAI. We will consider the most general method that starts with an HTML page that loads both a VRML world file and a Java applet in the traditional way. This example is loosely derived from work by David Brown. The Java applet starts by importing a number of classes including some VRML specific ones and then defining the instance variables that it will be using.

```
import java.awt.*;
import java.applet.*;
import java.lang.*;
import vrml.external.field.*;
import vrml.external.Node;
import vrml.external.Browser;
import vrml.external.exception.*;

public class visApplet extends Applet
  {
  // The Browser
  Browser browser = null;
  // Various UI widgets
  Button grow_button, shrink_button;

  // Various stuff in the VRML scene we hang on to
  Node root_node, sphere_node;
  EventInSFVec3f setScale = null;
  float currentScale = (float)1.0;
```

Next, the applet defines the init() method that will request a reference to the browser, invoke initScene() to build the VRML interface, and create the user interface. In this case the user interface is just two buttons on a white background.

```
/** Initialize the Applet */
public void init()
  {
  // Connect to the browser
  browser = Browser.getBrowser(this);
  if (browser == null) {
    die("init: NULL browser!");
  }
  System.out.println("Got the browser: "+browser);

  // Initialize some VRML stuff
  initScene();

  // Build a simple UI
  grow_button = new Button("Grow Sphere");
  add(grow_button);
  shrink_button = new Button("Shrink Sphere");
  add(shrink_button);
  // Misc other UI setup
  Color c = Color.white;
  System.out.println("Setting bg color to: " + c);
  setBackground(c);
  }
```

There is a simple error handling routine defined.

```
/** Handle a fatal error condition */
public void die(String s)
  {
  System.out.println("visApplet: FATAL ERROR!");
  System.out.println("--> " + s);
  System.out.println("visApplet: Aborting...\n");
  }
```

The initScene() method sets up the VRML scene and relies heavily on the EAI. For synchronization reasons, this method starts off by waiting a few seconds to assure that the VRML browser has time to initialize and read the VRML file specified by the HTML. Then it uses the browser.getNode("aName") method to obtain nodes from the scene graph. These nodes must be named using the DEF keyword in the VRML file. The first node it gets is the SPHERE node that happens to be a VRML transform. It uses the getEventIn() method to obtain a handle to the scale instance variable of this transform which will be used later.

```
/** Set up some stuff in the VRML scene */
public void initScene()
  {
  System.out.println("initScene()...");

  // wait a couple seconds
  try {
    Thread.currentThread().sleep(5000);
    }
  catch(InterruptedException e) {}

  // Get the "SPHERE" node
  try {
    sphere_node = browser.getNode("SPHERE");
    }
  catch(InvalidNodeException e){
    System.out.println("InvalidNodeException: " + e);
    die("initScene: SPHERE node not found!");
    return;
    }

  System.out.println("- Got the SPHERE node: " + sphere_node);
  try {
    setScale = (EventInSFVec3f)
    sphere_node.getEventIn("set_scale");
    }
  catch (InvalidEventInException e) {
    die("initScene: InvalidEventInException " + e);
    return;
    }
```

Then the same techniques are used to obtain the ROOT node of the scene graph. If you scan the VRML file that follows this example, you will see that the ROOT node is just an empty Group. After obtaining the node we request handles to its addChildren() and removeChildren() methods.

```
  // Get the "ROOT" node (a Group which we add to)
  try {
    root_node = browser.getNode("ROOT");
    }
  catch(InvalidNodeException e){
    System.out.println("InvalidNodeException: " + e);
    die("initScene: ROOT node not found!");
    return;
    }
  System.out.println("- Got the ROOT node: " + root_node);

  // Get the ROOT node's add/removeChildren EventIns
  EventInMFNode addChildren;
  EventInMFNode removeChildren;
```

```
    try {
      addChildren = (EventInMFNode)
      root_node.getEventIn("addChildren");
      removeChildren = (EventInMFNode)
      root_node.getEventIn("removeChildren");
      }
    catch (InvalidEventInException e) {
      die("initScene: InvalidEventInException " + e);
      return;
      }
```

Using the EAI, VRML can be created from a Java string as shown in the following code. This allows us to create geometry on the fly and add it to the scene graph using the addChildren() handle obtained above. The handles support matching setValue() and getValue() methods that modify and interrogate the scene graph respectively.

```
      // Create the VRML for a purple sphere
      Node[] shape;
      String purple_sphere =
        "#VRML V2.0 utf8\n" +
        "Transform {\n" +
        "   children Shape {\n" +
        "      appearance Appearance {\n" +
        "         material Material {\n" +
        "            diffuseColor 0.8 0.2 0.8\n" +
        "         }\n" +
        "      }\n" +
        "      geometry Sphere {}\n" +
        "   }\n" +
        "   translation 0 3 0" +
        "}\n";
      try {
        shape = browser.createVrmlFromString(purple_sphere);
        }
      catch (InvalidVrmlException e) {
        die("initScene: InvalidVrmlException: " + e);
        return;
        }
      // Add the sphere to the ROOT group
      addChildren.setValue(shape);
      System.out.println("initScene: done.");
      }
```

The events for the two buttons are processed in the action() method. One increases the scale of the sphere and the other decreases it. This is done using the handle to the SPHERE node's scale that was obtained in the initScene() method, and invoking the setValue() method with the appropriate arguments.

```
/** Handle actions from AWT widgets */
public boolean action(Event event, Object what)
  {
  if (event.target instanceof Button) {
  Button b = (Button) event.target;
  if (b == grow_button) {
    currentScale = currentScale * (float)1.2;
    float ascale[] = new float[3];
    ascale[0] = currentScale;
    ascale[1] = currentScale;
    ascale[2] = currentScale;
    setScale.setValue(ascale);
    }
  else if (b == shrink_button) {
    currentScale = currentScale / (float)1.2;
    float ascale[] = new float[3];
    ascale[0] = currentScale;
    ascale[1] = currentScale;
    ascale[2] = currentScale;
    setScale.setValue(ascale);
    }
  } // event.target instanceof Button
  return true;
  }
```

The last method in the applet draws a border around the two buttons when the applet needs to be repainted.

```
/** Override paint() to get more control over how we're drawn */
public void paint(Graphics g)
  {
  int w = size().width;
  int h = size().height;

  // Draw a simple border
  g.drawRect(0, 0, w-1, h-1);
  g.drawRect(1, 1, w-3, h-3);
  super.paint(g);
  }
}
```

An excerpt from the VRML file has been included below. Note the use of the DEF keyword to name nodes that can then be accessed from Java. The resulting Java/ VRML example can be seen in Figure **12–5**.

```
#VRML V2.0 utf8
#
Group {
  children [
```

```
    #
    # Some objects
    #
    DEF ROOT Group {}
    DEF SPHERE Transform {
      childrenShape {
        appearanceAppearance {
          materialMaterial {
            ambientIntensity0.283774
            diffuseColor0.0846193 0.56383 0.0595097
            specularColor0.13092 0.87234 0.0920716
            emissiveColor0 0 0
            shininess0.2
            transparency0
          }
        }
        geometrySphere {}
      }
      translation 4 0 0
    }
  ]
}
```

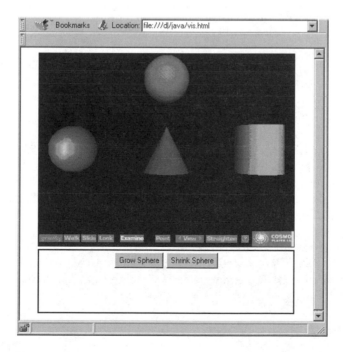

Figure 12–5 Java and VRML combined using the EAI.

12.8 The Future of Web Visualization

In the previous sections we provided an overview of some of the technologies important to applying visualization on the World Wide Web. Since Web-based technologies, computer graphics, and visualization are all rapidly growing fields, the likelihood of new development and change is high. However, we are confident that these technologies will remain important to the future. Eventually we expect 3D graphics and data visualization to become as pervasive as 2D graphical user interfaces and presentations are today. The main barriers to this development is the limited bandwidth of the Web, lack of familiarity (and difficulty of use) of 3D graphics and visualization, and limitations in computer hardware and software. We believe that technological advances will eventually minimize bandwidth and computer hardware limitations, while systems like **vtk** will make 3D graphics and visualizations easier to use.

One of the benefits of systems like **vtk** is that they are driven by their algorithmic content. The systems we have seen earlier such as OpenGL, HTML, VRML and Java, are implementations of a system or information protocol. Algorithmic systems, on the other hand, implement mathematical, logical, and design relationships that change much more slowly than system implementations. As a result, systems like **vtk** will remain vital for years to come, although the underlying implementation language and interface may change. To track future changes to **vtk** visit our Web pages at `http://www.kitware.com`.

12.9 Chapter Summary

Visualization over the Web opens up many forms of collaborative development, entertainment, and publishing that were previously restricted to a few individuals with access to custom software. There are many ways to perform visualization over the Web ranging from simple HTML pages with pictures, to complete Java-based applications. Deciding on the correct solution for Web visualization depends on three key factors: 1) the amount of interaction and control you want to provide to the user or client, 2) performance issues related to data size and client/server load balancing, 3) how much complexity you are willing to deal with. While the Java-based solutions can provide interaction, control, and load balancing, this involves added complexity. It may be that producing a static VRML file for your Web page is sufficient. Either way there are a host of tools available and more are on the way. The greatest challenge will likely be to create a future standard for the Web that includes not just 3D viewing but also visualization.

12.10 Bibliographic Notes

For a general introduction to HTML and CGI consider [Morris95] or [Graham95]. Both books provide a good introduction and include coverage for both UNIX and MS Windows-based systems. For more detailed coverage of CGI programming consider [Gundavaram96]. Mark Pesce [Pesce95] provides a n excellent introduction to VRML including its early genesis. [Ames96] is also a great VRML resource. *The Inventor Mentor* by Josie Wernecke [Wernecke94] is an excellent book for learning about Open Inventor and scene graphs. *Java in a Nutshell* [Flanagan96] is a good reference for Java and for someone who already knows how to program in another language For documentation on the Java Native Interface or Java3D, visit Sun's Web site at `http://java.sun.com`.

12.11 References

[Ames96]

> A. Ames, D. Nadeau, and J. Moreland. *The VRML Sourcebook.* John Wiley & Sons, Inc., New York, NY, 1996.

[Flanagan96]

> David Flanagan. *Java in a Nutshell.* O'Reilly & Associates, Inc., Sebastopol, CA, 1996.

[Graham95]

> I. S. Graham. *The HTML Sourcebook.* John Wiley & Sons, Inc., New York, NY, 1995.

[Gundavaram96]

> S. Gundavaram. *CGI Programming on the World Wide Web.* O'Reilly & Associates, Inc., Sebastopol, CA, 1996.

[Morris95]

> M. E. S. Morris. *HTML for Fun and Profit.* SunSoft Press, Prentice Hall PTR, Englewood Cliffs, NJ, 1995.

[Pesce95]

> M. Pesce. *VRML - Browsing and Building Cyberspace.* New Riders Publishing, Indianapolis, IN, 1995.

[Wernecke94]

> J. Wernecke. *The Inventor Mentor.* Addison-Wesley, Reading MA,1994.

Applications

We have described the design and implementation of an extensive toolkit of visualization techniques. In this chapter we examine several case studies to show how to use these tools to gain insight into important application areas. These areas are medical imaging, financial visualization, modelling, computational fluid dynamics, finite element analysis, and algorithm visualization. For each case, we briefly describe the problem domain and what information we expect to obtain through visualization. Then we craft an approach to show the results. Many times we will extend the functionality of the *Visualization Toolkit* with application-specific tools. Finally, we present a sample program and show resulting images.

The visualization design process we go through is similar in each case. First, we read or generate application-specific data and transform it into one of the data representation types in the *Visualization Toolkit*. Often this first step is the most difficult one because we have to write custom computer code, and decide what form of visualization data to use. In the next step, we choose visualizations for the relevant data within the application. Sometimes this means choosing or creating models corresponding to the physical structure. Examples include spheres for atoms, polygonal surfaces to model physical objects, or computational surfaces to model flow boundaries. Other times we generate more abstract models, such as isosurfaces or glyphs, corresponding to important application data. In the last step we combine the physical components with the abstract components to create a visualization that aids the user in understanding the data.

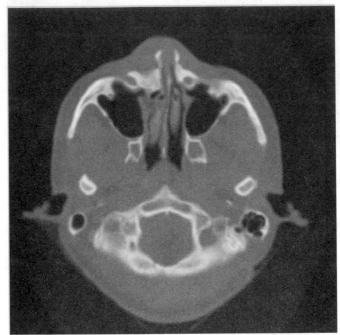

Figure 13–1 A CT slice through a human head.

13.1 3D Medical Imaging

Radiology is a medical discipline that deals with images of human anatomy. These images come from a variety of medical imaging devices, including X-ray, X-ray Computed Tomography (CT), Magnetic Resonance Imaging (MRI), and ultrasound. Each imaging technique, called an imaging modality, has particular diagnostic strengths. The choice of modality is the job of the radiologist and the referring physician. For the most part, radiologists deal with two-dimensional images, but there are situations when three-dimensional models can assist the radiologist's diagnosis. Radiologists have special training to interpret the two dimensional images and understand the complex anatomical relationships in these two-dimensional representations. However, in dealing with referring physicians and surgeons, the radiologist sometimes has difficulty communicating these relationships. After all, a surgeon works in three-dimensions during the planning and execution of an operation; moreover, they are much more comfortable looking at and working with three-dimensional models.

This case study deals with CT data. Computed tomography measures the attenuation of X-rays as they pass through the body. A CT image consists of levels of gray that vary from black (for air), to gray (for soft tissue), to white (for bone). Figure **13–1** shows a CT cross section through a head. This slice is taken perpendicular to the spine approximately through the middle of the ears. The gray boundary around the head clearly shows the ears and bridge of the nose.

The dark regions on the interior of the slice are the nasal passages and ear canals. The bright areas are bone. This study contains 93 such slices, spaced 1.5 mm apart. Each slice has 256^2 pixels spaced 0.8 mm apart with 12 bits of gray level.

Our challenge is to take this massive amount of gray scale data (over 12 megabytes) and convert it into information that will aid the surgeon. Fortunately, our visualization toolkit has just the right technique. We will use isocontouring techniques to extract the skin and bone surfaces. From experience we know that a density value of 600 will define the air/skin boundary, and a value of 1150 will define the soft tissue/bone boundary.

Medical imaging slice data is structured point data. Recall from Chapter 5 that for structured point data, the topology and geometry of the data is implicitly known, requiring only dimensions, an origin, and the data spacing.

The steps we follow in this case study are common to many three-dimensional medical studies.

1. Read the input.

2. For each anatomical feature of interest, create an isosurface.

3. Transform the models from patient space to world space.

4. Render the models.

This case study describes in detail how to read input data and extract anatomical features using isocontouring. Along the way we will also show you how to render the data. We finish with a brief discussion of medical data transformations.

Read the input

Medical images come in many flavors of file formats. This study is stored as flat files without header information. Each 16-bit pixel is stored with the bytes swapped. Also, as is often the case, each slice is stored in a separate file with the file suffix being the slice number.

Assume for the moment that **vtk** does not have a reader that can read the data in our format, and that we have to create an object to do that. This is an instructive example, because it demonstrates the process you may have to go through to read your own data.

Because of the object-oriented design of **vtk**, our task is not too difficult. In **vtk** terminology, our reader is a source and our data is structured points. So, we look for any existing objects that are of type `vtkStructuredPointsSource`. The object `vtkPNMReader` that reads Pozkanzer Portable Pixmap (PPM) files can serve as a guide.

As for any source object in **vtk**, we must provide at a minimum three methods: a constructor, `Execute()`, and `PrintSelf()`. We also need to decide what instance variables our object will require to perform its duties. From our experience with medical imaging data, we know that each slice is usually kept in a separate file with a suffix that is a number. The format of the number varies. Some files will be of the form prefix.1, prefix.2, ... while others will be of the form prefix.001, prefix.002, ... We could just choose the first style since that's the style our case study data uses, but we'll try to generalize the file naming so that others can use our object later. To make the file naming general, we introduce a FilePattern instance variable that holds a string that we can use to build a file name from a prefix and a number. Medical imaging files often have a header of a certain size before the image data starts. The size of the header varies from file format to file format. We handle this variance by introducing a HeaderSize instance variable. This will contain the number of bytes to skip over before getting to the image data. Since each pixel in our image data is two bytes long, the bytes may have to be swapped to be the proper format for our visualization application. We add a SwapBytes instance variable to indicate whether or not swapping is required. We also need a DataOrigin and DataSpacing to define where the first slice starts and what the x, y, z spacings are for the vtkStructured-Points. Finally, another complication is that sometimes one or more bits in each 16-bit pixel is used to mark connectivity between voxels, or for other purposes unrelated to the current case study. So we add a DataMask instance variable to allow us to mask out extraneous information.

To implement this object we could simply just write a single class to read the data. However, we realize that reading volume datasets may be a common activity, so we will create two separate classes: vtkVolumeReader and vtkVolume16Reader. The abstract class vtkVolumeReader will serve to define a common programming interface as well as data attributes and methods, while the concrete class vtkVolume16Reader will implement the actual functionality necessary to read our data.

We begin by defining the class vtkVolumeReader. (Here we show only the .h header file. See the .cxx file to see the actual implementation.) Subclasses of vtkVolumeReader will read one or more files and create a structured points dataset.

```
class VTK_EXPORT vtkVolumeReader : public
vtkStructuredPointsSource
{
public:
  vtkVolumeReader();
  const char *GetClassName() {return "vtkVolumeReader";};
  void PrintSelf(ostream& os, vtkIndent indent);

  // Description:
  // Specify file prefix for the image file(s).
  vtkSetStringMacro(FilePrefix);
  vtkGetStringMacro(FilePrefix);

  // Description:
  // The sprintf format used to build filename from FilePrefix
  // and number.
  vtkSetStringMacro(FilePattern);
```

```
    vtkGetStringMacro(FilePattern);

    // Description:
    // Set the range of files to read.
    vtkSetVector2Macro(ImageRange,int);
    vtkGetVectorMacro(ImageRange,int,2);

    // Description:
    // Specify the spacing for the data.
    vtkSetVector3Macro(DataSpacing,float);
    vtkGetVectorMacro(DataSpacing,float,3);

    // Description:
    // Specify the origin for the data.
    vtkSetVector3Macro(DataOrigin,float);
    vtkGetVectorMacro(DataOrigin,float,3);

    // Other objects make use of these methods
    virtual vtkStructuredPoints *GetImage(int ImageNumber) = 0;

protected:
  char *FilePrefix;
  char *FilePattern;
  int ImageRange[2];
  float DataSpacing[3];
  float DataOrigin[3];
};

#endif
```

This abstract class defines a number of instance variables and methods that any derived classes will need to use. The special method GetImage() is important because it defines a programming interface that all subclasses of vtkVolume-Reader must satisfy by implementing this method. We define this method because we expect that other objects in the system may need to access the data a slice (or image) at a time. (For example, the object vtkSliceCubes uses the method ReadImage().)

Next we create the subclass vtkVolume16Reader. This object implements vtkVolumeReader's abstract interface, and implements the methods we need to read our data. The header file, which reflects our design choices described above, is shown in the following:

```
#ifndef __vtkVolume16Reader_h
#define __vtkVolume16Reader_h

#include <stdio.h>
#include "vtkVolumeReader.h"
#include "vtkTransform.h"
```

```
#define VTK_FILE_BYTE_ORDER_BIG_ENDIAN 0
#define VTK_FILE_BYTE_ORDER_LITTLE_ENDIAN 1

class VTK_EXPORT vtkVolume16Reader : public vtkVolumeReader
{
public:
  vtkVolume16Reader();
  static vtkVolume16Reader *New() {return new vtkVolume16Reader;};
  const char *GetClassName() {return "vtkVolume16Reader";};
  void PrintSelf(ostream& os, vtkIndent indent);

  // Description:
  // Specify the dimensions for the data.
  vtkSetVector2Macro(DataDimensions,int);
  vtkGetVectorMacro(DataDimensions,int,2);

  // Description:
  // Specify a mask used to eliminate data in the data file (e.g.,
  // connectivity bits).
  vtkSetMacro(DataMask,short);
  vtkGetMacro(DataMask,short);

  // Description:
  // Specify the number of bytes to seek over at start of image.
  vtkSetClampMacro(HeaderSize,int,0,VTK_LARGE_INT);
  vtkGetMacro(HeaderSize,int);

  // Description:
  // These methods should be used instead of the SwapBytes methods.
  // They indicate the byte ordering of the file you are trying
  // to read in. These methods will then either swap or not swap
  // the bytes depending on the byte ordering of the machine it is
  // being run on. For example, reading in a BigEndian file on a
  // BigEndian machine will result in no swapping. Trying to read
  // the file on a LittleEndian machine will result in swapping.
  // As a quick note most UNIX machines are BigEndian while PCs
  // and VAX tend to be LittleEndian. So if the file you are reading
  // was generated on a VAX or PC, SetDataByteOrderToLittleEndian
  // otherwise SetDataByteOrderToBigEndian.
  void SetDataByteOrderToBigEndian();
  void SetDataByteOrderToLittleEndian();
  int GetDataByteOrder();
  void SetDataByteOrder(int);
  char *GetDataByteOrderAsString();

  // Description:
  // Turn on/off byte swapping.
  vtkSetMacro(SwapBytes,int);
  vtkGetMacro(SwapBytes,int);
  vtkBooleanMacro(SwapBytes,int);
```

```
    // Description:
    // Define a matrix to transform the data from slice space
    // into world space. This matrix must be a permutation matrix.
    // To qualify, the sums of the rows must be + or - 1.
    vtkSetObjectMacro(Transform,vtkTransform);
    vtkGetObjectMacro(Transform,vtkTransform);

    // Other objects make use of these methods
    vtkStructuredPoints *GetImage(int ImageNumber);

protected:
    void Execute();
    int    DataDimensions[2];
    short DataMask;
    int    SwapBytes;
    int    HeaderSize;
    vtkTransform *Transform;

    void TransformSlice (short *slice, short *pixels, int k,
                            int dimensions[3], int bounds[3]);
    void ComputeTransformedDimensions(int dimensions[3]);
    void ComputeTransformedBounds(int bounds[6]);
    void ComputeTransformedSpacing(float Spacing[3]);
    void ComputeTransformedOrigin(float origin[3]);
    void AdjustSpacingAndOrigin(int dimensions[3],
                            float Spacing[3], float origin[3]);
    vtkScalars *ReadImage(int ImageNumber);
    vtkScalars *ReadVolume(int FirstImage, int LastImage);
    int Read16BitImage(FILE *fp, short *pixels, int xsize,
                            int ysize, int skip, int swapBytes);
};

#endif
```

As you can see, the header file follows our idea of what this reader object should look like. We have introduced a few methods to perform various read operations. The key method, which is protected, is Read16BitImage(). This method has the task of actually reading the slice files. Two other methods, ReadImage() and ReadVolume(), utilize Read16BitImage() to read images and volumes, respectively. The method GetImage() satisfies the interface defined by the superclass vtkVolumeReader. There are several other methods created that deal with transforming the data as it is read. This is important since we often have to rearrange the data to be consistent with the physical structure from which it was derived.

Now let's walk briefly through the C++ code to see how we put things together. For the sake of brevity we will examine only the Execute() method. The Execute() method is required of any source or filter object. We initialize the filter, validate instance variables, read in the data as a scalar field, and store it as a structured points dataset.

```
void vtkVolume16Reader::Execute()
{
  vtkScalars *newScalars;
  int first, last;
  int numberSlices;
  int *dim;
  int dimensions[3];
  float Spacing[3];
  float origin[3];

  vtkStructuredPoints *output=
                          (vtkStructuredPoints *)this->Output;

  // Validate instance variables
  if (this->FilePrefix == NULL)
    {
    vtkErrorMacro(<< "FilePrefix is NULL");
    return;
    }

  dim = this->DataDimensions;

  if (dim[0] <= 0 || dim[1] <= 0)
    {
   vtkErrorMacro(<< "x, y dimensions " << dim[0] << ", " << dim[1]
                << "must be greater than 0.");
    return;
    }

  if ( (this->ImageRange[1]-this->ImageRange[0]) <= 0 )
    {
    numberSlices = 1;
    newScalars = this->ReadImage(this->ImageRange[0]);
    }
  else
    {
    first = this->ImageRange[0];
    last = this->ImageRange[1];
    numberSlices = last - first + 1;
    newScalars = this->ReadVolume(first, last);
    }

  // calculate dimensions of output transform
  ComputeTransformedDimensions (dimensions);
  output->SetDimensions(dimensions);

  // calculate spacing of output from data spacing and transform
  this->ComputeTransformedSpacing (Spacing);
```

```
    // calculate origin of output from data origin and transform
    this->ComputeTransformedOrigin (origin);

    // adjust spacing and origin if spacing is negative
    this->AdjustSpacingAndOrigin (dimensions, Spacing, origin);

    output->SetSpacing(Spacing);
    output->SetOrigin(origin);
    if ( newScalars )
      {
      output->GetPointData()->SetScalars(newScalars);
      newScalars->Delete();
      }
  }
```

The Execute() method is relatively straightforward. The structured point
dataset is defined by setting the origin, spacing, and dimensions. The scalar data
is obtained by reading the slice data, and then associating it with the dataset.
The only tricky part is the use of reference counting: We have to create the scalar
object (newScalars above), assign it to the dataset (with the SetScalars()
method), and then unregister our use of the object (with the Delete() method).
(If reference counting is a mystery to you, see Appendix A for more information.)

The method Read16BitImage() is the heart of this object. The methods
ReadImage() and ReadVolume() both make use of it. Here we will show the
C++ code for Read16BitImage(); you can view the code for ReadImage() and
ReadVolume() on the CD-ROM included with this book (note that the actual
source for this class contains more methods and additional features).

```
    int vtkVolume16Reader:: Read16BitImage (FILE *fp,
                                unsigned short *pixels, int xsize,
                                int ysize, int skip, int swapBytes)
  {
    int numShorts = xsize * ysize;
    int status;

    if (skip) fseek (fp, skip, 0);

    status = fread (pixels, sizeof (unsigned short), numShorts, fp);

    if (status && swapBytes)
      {
      unsigned char *bytes = (unsigned char *) pixels;
      unsigned char tmp;
      int i;
      for (i = 0; i < numShorts; i++, bytes += 2)
        {
        tmp = *bytes;
        *bytes = * (bytes + 1);
        * (bytes + 1) = tmp;
```

```
        }
      }

    if (status && this->DataMask != 0x0000 )
      {
      unsigned short *dataPtr = pixels;
      int i;
      for (i = 0; i < numShorts; i++, dataPtr++)
        {
        *dataPtr &= this->DataMask;
        }
      }

    return status;
  }
```

Observe that the instance variables HeaderSize (via the variable skip), Swap-Bytes (via the variable swapBytes), and DataMask all come into play in this method. Also, the data dimensions are used to compute the number of data items to read. We can easily check our new object with a simple test program:

```
#include "vtkVolume16Reader.h"
main () {
  vtkVolume16Reader *aVolume = vtkVolume16Reader::New();
  aVolume->SetDataDimensions(256, 256);
  aVolume->SetDataByteOrderToLittleEndian();
  aVolume->SetFilePrefix ("../../../vtkdata/fullHead/headsq");
  aVolume->SetImageRange(1, 93);
  aVolume->SetDataSpacing (.8, .8, 1.5);
  aVolume->Update();
  cout << "Our Volume: " << *aVolume;
}
```

The Update() method forces our object to Execute().

The first step, and for this case study the most complicated, is complete! We can read our input data and we tried to generalize our object so that others may use it later for data in a different format. Also, we created an abstract superclass so that future developers can take advantage of it to implement their own readers. Now we can begin to explore this interesting medical data.

Create an isosurface

We can choose from three techniques for isosurface visualization: volume rendering, marching cubes, and dividing cubes. We assume that we want to interact with our data at the highest possible speed, so we will not use volume rendering. We prefer marching cubes if we have polygonal rendering hardware available, or if we need to move up close to or inside the extracted surfaces. Even with hardware assisted rendering, we may have to reduce the polygon count to get reasonable rendering speeds. Dividing cubes is appropriate for software rendering. For this application we'll use marching cubes.

For medical volumes, marching cubes generates a large number of triangles. To be practical, we'll do this case study with a reduced resolution dataset. We took the original 256^2 data and reduced it to 64^2 slices by averaging neighboring pixels twice in the slice plane. We call the resulting dataset *quarter* since it has 1/4 the resolution of the original data. We adjust the DataSpacing for the reduced resolution dataset to 3.2 mm per pixel. Our first program will generate an isosurface for the skin.

The flow in the program is similar to most **vtk** applications.

1. Generate some data.

2. Process it with filters.

3. Create a mapper to generate rendering primitives.

4. Create actors for all mappers.

5. Render the results.

The filter we have chosen to use is vtkMarchingCubes. We could also use vtkContourFilter that will create an instance of vtkMarchingCubes through the use of C++ templates. To complete this example, we take the output from the isosurface generator vtkMarchingCubes and connect it to a mapper and actor via vtkPolyDataMapper and vtkActor. The C++ code follows.

```
// include class definitions
#include "vtkRenderer.h"
#include "vtkRenderWindow.h"
#include "vtkRenderWindowInteractor.h"
#include "vtkVolume16Reader.h"
#include "vtkPolyDataMapper.h"
#include "vtkActor.h"
#include "vtkOutlineFilter.h"
#include "vtkCamera.h"
#include "../patented/vtkMarchingCubes.h"
main ()
{
  // create the renderer stuff
  vtkRenderer *aRenderer = vtkRenderer::New();
  vtkRenderWindow *renWin = vtkRenderWindow::New();
    renWin->AddRenderer(aRenderer);
  vtkRenderWindowInteractor *iren =
                      vtkRenderWindowInteractor::New();
    iren->SetRenderWindow(renWin);
  // read the volume
  vtkVolume16Reader *v16 = vtkVolume16Reader::New();
    v16->SetDataDimensions(64,64);
    v16->SwapBytesOn();
    v16->SetFilePrefix ("../../../vtkdata/headsq/quarter");
```

```
    v16->SetImageRange(1, 93);
    v16->SetDataSpacing (3.2, 3.2, 1.5);

  // extract the skin
  vtkMarchingCubes *skinExtractor = vtkMarchingCubes::New();
    skinExtractor->SetInput(v16->GetOutput());
    skinExtractor->SetValue(0, 500);
  vtkPolyDataMapper *skinMapper = vtkPolyDataMapper::New();
    skinMapper->SetInput(skinExtractor->GetOutput());
    skinMapper->ScalarVisibilityOff();
  vtkActor *skin = vtkActor::New();
    skin->SetMapper(skinMapper);

  // get an outline
  vtkOutlineFilter *outlineData = vtkOutlineFilter::New();
    outlineData->SetInput(v16->GetOutput());
  vtkPolyDataMapper *mapOutline = vtkPolyDataMapper::New();
    mapOutline->SetInput(outlineData->GetOutput());
  vtkActor *outline = vtkActor::New();
    outline->SetMapper(mapOutline);
    outline->GetProperty()->SetColor(0,0,0);

  // create a camera with the correct view up
  vtkCamera *aCamera = vtkCamera::New();
    aCamera->SetViewUp (0, 0, -1);
    aCamera->SetPosition (0, 1, 0);
    aCamera->SetFocalPoint (0, 0, 0);
    aCamera->ComputeViewPlaneNormal();

  // tell the renderer our camera and actors
  aRenderer->AddActor(outline);
  aRenderer->AddActor(skin);
  aRenderer->SetActiveCamera(aCamera);
  aRenderer->ResetCamera ();
  aRenderer->SetBackground(1, 1, 1);

  // interact with data
  renWin->Render();
  iren->Start();
}
```

Figure **13–2** shows the resulting image of the patient's skin.

We can improve this visualization in a number of ways. First, we can choose a more appropriate color (and other surface properties) for the skin. We use the vtkProperty method SetDiffuseColor() to set the skin color to a fleshy tone. We also add a specular component to the skin surface. Next, we can add additional isosurfaces corresponding to various anatomical features. Here we choose to extract the bone surface by adding an additional pipeline segment. This consists of the filters vtkMarchingCubes, vtkPolyDataMapper, and

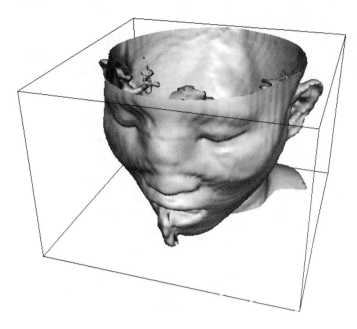

Figure 13–2 The skin extracted from a CT dataset of the head (medical1.cxx).

vtkActor, just as we did with the skin. Finally, to improve rendering performance on our system, we create triangle strips from the output of the contouring process. This requires adding vtkStripper. Figure **13–3** shows the resulting image, and the following is the C++ code for the pipeline.

```
// extract the bone
vtkMarchingCubes *boneExtractor = vtkMarchingCubes::New();
  boneExtractor->SetInput(v16->GetOutput());
  boneExtractor->SetValue(0, 1150);

vtkStripper *boneStripper = vtkStripper::New();
  boneStripper->SetInput(boneExtractor->GetOutput());

vtkPolyDataMapper *boneMapper = vtkPolyDataMapper::New();
  boneMapper->SetInput(boneStripper->GetOutput());
  boneMapper->ScalarVisibilityOff();

vtkActor *bone = vtkActor::New();
  bone->SetMapper(boneMapper);
  bone->GetProperty()->SetDiffuseColor(1, 1, .9412);
```

The *Visualization Toolkit* provides other useful techniques besides isocontouring for exploring volume data. The vtkStructuredPointsGeometry-Filter extracts geometry (e.g., lines, planes, or subvolumes) from objects of type

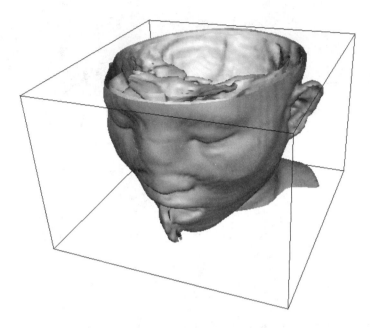

Figure 13–3 Skin and bone isosurfaces (medical2.cxx).

vtkStructuredPoints. Each point in the extracted geometry will have a scalar value from the original data. (Recall that in this case study the scalar value is the X-ray density.)

We can use this filter to extract three orthogonal planes corresponding to the axial, sagittal, and coronal cross sections that are familiar to radiologists. The axial plane is perpendicular to the patient's neck, sagittal passes from left to right, and coronal passes from front to back. For illustrative purposes, we render each of these planes with a different color lookup table. For the sagittal plane, we use a gray scale. The coronal and axial planes vary the saturation and hue table, respectively. We combine this with a translucent rendering of the skin (we turn off the bone with the C++ statement bone->VisibilityOff()). The following **vtk** code creates the three lookup tables.

```
// create a b/w lookup table
vtkLookupTable *bwLut = vtkLookupTable::New();
  bwLut->SetTableRange (0, 2000);
  bwLut->SetSaturationRange (0, 0);
  bwLut->SetHueRange (0, 0);
  bwLut->SetValueRange (0, 1);

// create a hue lookup table
vtkLookupTable *hueLut = vtkLookupTable::New();
  hueLut->SetTableRange (0, 2000);
```

```
  hueLut->SetHueRange (0, 1);
  hueLut->SetSaturationRange (1, 1);
  hueLut->SetValueRange (1, 1);

// create a saturation lookup table
vtkLookupTable *satLut = vtkLookupTable::New();
  satLut->SetTableRange (0, 2000);
  satLut->SetHueRange (.6, .6);
  satLut->SetSaturationRange (0, 1);
  satLut->SetValueRange (1, 1);
```

For each plane, we need a vtkStructuredPointsGeometryFilter, a vtk-
PolyDataMapper and a vtkActor. The C++ code is as follows:

```
// sagittal
vtkStructuredPointsGeometryFilter *saggitalSection =
    vtkStructuredPointsGeometryFilter::New();
  saggitalSection->SetExtent (32,32, 0,63, 0, 93);
  saggitalSection->SetInput (v16->GetOutput());
vtkPolyDataMapper *saggitalMapper = vtkPolyDataMapper::New();
  saggitalMapper->SetInput(saggitalSection->GetOutput());
  saggitalMapper->ScalarVisibilityOn();
  saggitalMapper->SetScalarRange (0, 2000);
  saggitalMapper->SetLookupTable (bwLut);
vtkActor *sagittal = vtkActor..New();
  sagittal->SetMapper(saggitalMapper);

// axial
vtkStructuredPointsGeometryFilter *axialSection =
    vtkStructuredPointsGeometryFilter::New();
  axialSection->SetExtent (0,63, 0,63, 46, 46);
  axialSection->SetInput (v16->GetOutput());
vtkPolyDataMapper *axialMapper = vtkPolyDataMapper:New();
  axialMapper->SetInput(axialSection->GetOutput());
  axialMapper->ScalarVisibilityOn();
  axialMapper->SetScalarRange (0, 2000);
  axialMapper->SetLookupTable (hueLut);
vtkActor *axial = vtkActor::New();
  axial->SetMapper(axialMapper);

// coronal
vtkStructuredPointsGeometryFilter *coronalSection =
    vtkStructuredPointsGeometryFilter::New();
  coronalSection->SetExtent (0,63, 32, 32, 0, 92);
  coronalSection->SetInput (v16->GetOutput());
vtkPolyDataMapper *coronalMapper = vtkPolyDataMapper::New();
  coronalMapper->SetInput(coronalSection->GetOutput());
  coronalMapper->ScalarVisibilityOn();
  coronalMapper->SetScalarRange (0, 2000);
  coronalMapper->SetLookupTable (satLut);
```

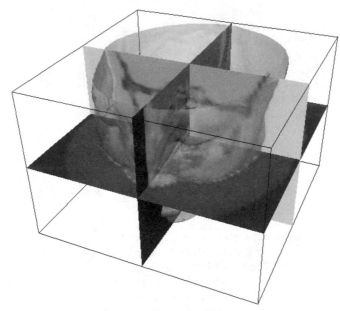

Figure 13–4 Composite image of three planes and translucent skin (medical3.cxx).

```
vtkActor *coronal = vtkActor::New();
   coronal->SetMapper(coronalMapper);
```

Figure **13–4** shows the resulting composite image.

In this example, the actor named skin is rendered last because we are using a translucent surface. Recall from "Transparency and Alpha Values" on page 212 that we must order the polygons composing transparent surfaces for proper results. We render the skin last by adding it to aRenderer's actor list last.

Representing the axial, coronal and sagittal planes with geometry is not efficient if your graphics system has texture mapping capabilities. (See "Exercises" on page 552.) Another approach, which you may want to try, is to create three polygons representing these planes. Then extract the data from the volume with the class vtkStructuredPointsGeometryFilter to create three images. These images can then be used as texture maps to color the planes.

We need to make one last point about processing medical imaging data. Medical images can be acquired in a variety of orders that refer to the relationship of consecutive slices to the patient. Radiologists view an image as though they were looking at the patient's feet. This means that on the display, the patient's left appears on the right. For CT there are two standard orders: top to bottom or bottom to top. In a top to bottom acquisition, slice i is farther from the patient's feet than slice i - 1. Why do we worry about this order? It is imperative in medical applications that we retain the left / right relationship. Ignoring the slice acquisition order can result in a flipping of left and right. To correct this, we need to transform either the original dataset or the geometry we have extracted. (See "Exercises" on page 552.) Also, you may wish to examine the implementation of the classes `vtkVolume16Reader` and `vtkImageReader`. These classes have special methods that deal with these issues of transforming data.

13.2 Creating Models from Segmented Volume Data

The previous example described how to create models from gray-scale medical imaging data. The techniques for extracting bone and skin models is straightforward compared to the task of generating models of other soft tissue. The reason is that magnetic resonance and, to some extent, computed tomography generates similar gray-scale values for different tissue types. For example, the liver and kidney in a medical computed tomography volume often have overlapping intensities. Likewise, many different tissues in the brain have overlapping intensities when viewed with magnetic resonance imaging. To deal with these problems researchers apply a process called segmentation to identify different tissues. These processes vary in sophistication from almost completely automatic methods to manual tracing of images. Segmentation continues to be a hot research area. Although the segmentation process itself is beyond the scope of this text, in this case study we show how to process segmented medical data.

For our purposes we assume that someone (or many graduate students) have laboriously labeled each pixel in each slice of a volume of data with a tissue identifier. This identifier is an integer number that describes which tissue class each pixel belongs to. For example, we may be given a series of MRI slices of the knee with tissue numbers defining the meniscus, femur, muscles, and so forth. Figure **13–5** shows two representations of a slice from a volume acquired from a patient's knee. The image on the left is the original MRI slice; the image on the right contains tissue labels for a number of important organs. The bottom image is a composite of the two images.

Notice the difference in the information presented by each representation. The original slice shows gradual changes at organ borders, while the segmented slice has abrupt changes. The images we processed in the previous CT example used marching cubes isocontouring algorithm and an intensity threshold to extract the isosurfaces. The segmented study we present has integer labels that have a somewhat arbitrary numeric value. Our goal in this example is to somehow take the tissue labels and create grayscale slices that we can process with the same techniques we used previously. Another goal is to show how image processing and visualization can work together in an application.

The Virtual Frog

To demonstrate the processing of segmented data we will use a dataset derived from a frog. This data was prepared at Lawrence Berkeley National Laboratories and is included with their permission on the CD-ROM accompanying this book.

The data was acquired by physically slicing the frog and photographing the slices. The original segmented data is in the form of tissue masks with one file per tissue. There are 136 slices per tissue and 15 different tissues. Each slice is 470 by 500 pixels. (To accommodate the volume readers we have in **vtk**, we processed the mask files and combined them all in one file for each slice.) We used integer numbers 1–15 to represent the 15 tissues. Figure **13–6** shows an original slice, a labeled slice, and a composite of the two representations.

Before we describe the process to go from binary labeled tissues to grayscale data suitable for isosurface extraction, compare the two images of the frog's brain shown in Figure **13–7**. On the left is a surface extracted using a binary labeling of the brain. The right image was created using the visualization pipeline that we will develop in this example.

Developing a Strategy

In the last example, we used C++ and created a program that was tailored to extract two surfaces: one of the skin and one of the bone. All the parameters for the surface extraction were hard-coded in the source. Since our frog has 15 different tissues; we seek a more general solution to this problem. We may have to experiment with a number of different parameters for a number of visualization and imaging filters. Our goal is to develop a general pipeline that will work not only our 15 tissues but on other medical datasets as well. We'll design the program to work with a set of user-specified parameters to control the elements of

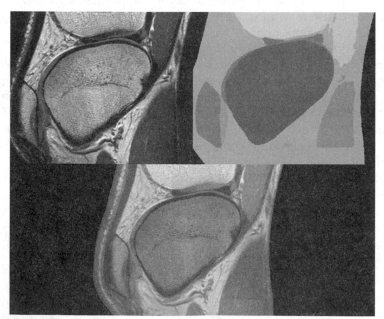

Figure 13–5 Magnetic Resonance Image of a knee (left); segmented tissue (right); composite (bottom). (Data and segmentation courtesy of Brigham and Women's Hospital Surgical Planning Lab.)

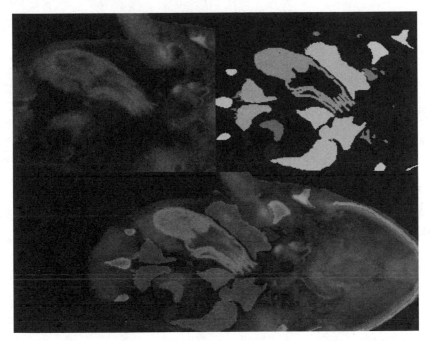

Figure 13–6 Photographic slice of frog (upper left), segmented frog (upper right) and composite of photo and segmentation (bottom). The purple color represents the stomach and the kidneys are yellow (frogSlice.tcl). (See Color Plates.)

the pipeline. A reasonable description might look like:

```
SLICE_ORDER hfsi
ROWS 470
COLUMNS 500
STUDY ../frogMasks/frogTissue
PIXEL_SIZE 1
SPACING 1.5
```

plus possibly many more parameters to control decimation, smoothing, and so forth. Working in C++, we would have to design the format of the file and write code to interpret the statements. We make the job easier here by using Tcl interpreter. Another decision is to separate the modelling from the rendering. Our script will generate models in a "batch" mode. We will run one **vtk** Tcl script for each tissue. That script will create a .vtk output file containing the polygonal representation of each tissue. Later, we can render the models with a separate script.

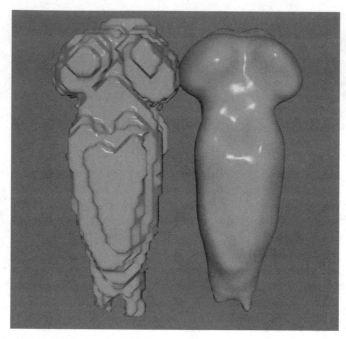

Figure 13–7 The frog's brain. Model extracted without smoothing (left) and with smoothing (right).

Overview of the Pipeline

Figure **13–8** shows the design of the pipeline. This generic pipeline has been developed over the years in our laboratory and in the Brigham and Women's Hospital Surgical Planning Lab. We find that it produces reasonable models from segmented datasets. Don't be intimidated by the number of filters (12 in all). Before we developed **vtk**, we did similar processing with a hodgepodge of programs all written with different interfaces. We used intermediate files to pass data from one filter to the next. The new pipeline, implemented in **vtk**, is more efficient in time and computing resources.

We start by developing Tcl scripts to process the volume data. In these scripts, we use the convention that user-specified variables are in capital letters. First we show the elements of the pipeline and subsequently show sample files that extract 3D models of the frog's tissues.

Read the Segmented Volume Data

We assume here that all the data to be processed was acquired with a constant center landmark. In **vtk**, the origin of the data applies to the lower left of an image volume. In this pipeline, we calculate the origin such that the x,y center of the volume will be (0,0). The DataSpacing describes the size of each pixel and the distance between slices. DataVOI selects a volume of interest (VOI). A VOI lets us select areas of interest, sometimes eliminating extraneous structures like the CT table bed. For the frog, we have written a small C program that reads the tissue label file and finds the volume of interest for each tissue.

The SetTransform method defines how to arrange the data in memory. Medical images can be acquired in a variety of orders. For example, in CT, the data can be gathered from top to bottom (superior to inferior), or bottom to top (inferior to superior). In addition, MRI data can be acquired from left to right, right to left, front to back (anterior to posterior) or back to front. This filter transforms triangle vertices such that the resulting models will all "face" the viewer with a view up of (0,-1,0), looking down the positive z axis. Also, proper left-right correspondence will be maintained. That means the patient's left will always be left on the generated models. Look in SliceOrder.tcl to see the permutations and rotations for each order.

All the other parameters are self-explanatory except for the last. In this script, we know that the pipeline will only be executed once. To conserve memory, we invoke the ReleaseDataFlagOn() method. This allows the **vtk** pipeline to release data once it has been processed by a filter. For large medical datasets, this can mean the difference between being able to process a dataset or not.

```
set originx [expr ( $COLUMNS / 2.0 ) * $PIXEL_SIZE * -1.0]
set originy [expr ( $ROWS / 2.0 ) * $PIXEL_SIZE * -1.0]
vtkPNMReader reader
  reader SetFilePrefix $STUDY
  reader SetDataSpacing $PIXEL_SIZE $PIXEL_SIZE $SPACING
  reader SetDataOrigin $originx $originy
    [expr $START_SLICE * $SPACING]
  reader SetDataVOI $VOI
  reader SetTransform $SLICE_ORDER
  [reader GetOutput] ReleaseDataFlagOn
```

Remove Islands

Some segmentation techniques, especially those that are automatic, may generate islands of misclassified voxels. This filter looks for connected pixels with the ISLAND_REPLACE label, and if the number of connected pixels is less than ISLAND_AREA, it replaces them with the label TISSUE. Note that this filter is only executed if ISLAND_REPLACE is positive.

```
set lastConnection reader
if {$ISLAND_REPLACE >= 0} {
  vtkImageIslandRemoval2D islandRemover
      islandRemover SetAreaThreshold $ISLAND_AREA
      islandRemover SetIslandValue $ISLAND_REPLACE
      islandRemover SetReplaceValue $TISSUE
      islandRemover SetInput [$lastConnection GetOutput]
  set lastConnection islandRemover
}
```

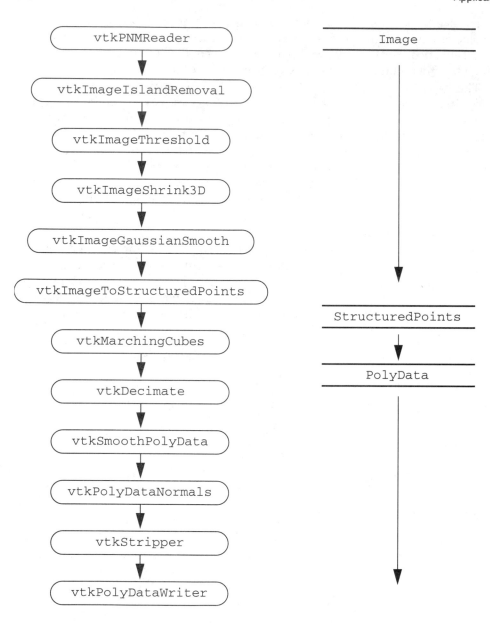

Figure 13–8   The segmented volume to triangle pipeline. Volume passes through image pipeline before isosurface extraction.

Select a Tissue

The rest of the pipeline requires gray-scale data. To convert the volume that now contains integer tissue labels to a gray-scale volume containing only one tissue, we use the threshold filter to set all pixels with the value TISSUE (the tissue of choice for this pipeline) to 255 and all other pixels to 0. The choice of 255 is somewhat arbitrary.

```
vtkImageThreshold selectTissue
    selectTissue ThresholdBetween $TISSUE $TISSUE
    selectTissue SetInValue 255
    selectTissue SetOutValue 0
    selectTissue SetInput [$lastConnection GetOutput]
```

Resample the Volume

Lower resolution volumes produce fewer polygons. For experimentation we often reduce the resolution of the data with this filter. However, details can be lost during this process. Averaging creates new pixels in the resampled volume by averaging neighboring pixels. If averaging is turned off, every SAMPLE_RATE pixel will be passed through to the output.

```
vtkImageShrink3D shrinker
    shrinker SetInput [selectTissue GetOutput]
    eval shrinker SetShrinkFactors $SAMPLE_RATE
    shrinker AveragingOn
```

Smooth the Volume Data

To this point, unless we have resampled the data, the volume is labeled with a value of 255 in pixels of the selected tissue and 0 elsewhere. This "binary" volume would produce stepped surfaces if we did not blur it. The Gaussian kernel specified in this filter accomplishes the smoothing we require to extract surfaces. The amount of smoothing is controlled by GAUSSIAN_STANDARD_DEVIATION that can be independently specified for each axis of the volume data. We only run this filter if some smoothing is requested,

```
set lastConnection shrinker
if {$GAUSSIAN_STANDARD_DEVIATION != "0 0 0"} {
  vtkImageGaussianSmooth gaussian
  gaussian SetDimensionality 3
  gaussian SetStandardDeviation $GAUSSIAN_STANDARD_DEVIATION
  gaussian SetRadiusFactor 1
  gaussian SetInput [shrinker GetOutput]
  set lastConnection gaussian
}
```

Generate Triangles

Now we can process the volume with marching cubes just as though we had obtained gray-scale data from a scanner. We added a few more bells and whistles to the pipeline. The filter runs faster if we turn off gradient and normal calculations. Marching cubes normally calculates vertex normals from the gradient of the volume data. In our pipeline, we have concocted a gray-scale representation and will subsequently decimate the triangle mesh and smooth the resulting vertices. This processing invalidates the normals that are calculated by marching cubes.

```
vtkMarchingCubes mcubes
    mcubes SetInput [toStructuredPoints GetOutput]
    mcubes ComputeScalarsOff
    mcubes ComputeGradientsOff
    mcubes ComputeNormalsOff
    eval mcubes SetValue 0 $VALUE
    [mcubes GetOutput] ReleaseDataFlagOn
```

Reduce the Number of Triangles

There are often many more triangles generated by the isosurfacing algorithm than we need for rendering. Here we reduce the triangle count by eliminating triangle vertices that lie within a user-specified distance to the plane formed by neighboring vertices. We preserve any edges of triangles that are considered "features".

```
vtkDecimate decimator
  decimator SetInput [mcubes GetOutput]
  eval decimator SetInitialFeatureAngle $DECIMATE_ANGLE
  eval decimator SetMaximumIterations $DECIMATE_ITERATIONS
  decimator SetMaximumSubIterations 0
  decimator PreserveEdgesOn
  decimator SetMaximumError 1
  decimator SetTargetReduction $DECIMATE_REDUCTION
  eval decimator SetInitialError $DECIMATE_ERROR
  eval decimator SetErrorIncrement $DECIMATE_ERROR_INCREMENT
  [decimator GetOutput] ReleaseDataFlagOn
```

Smooth the Triangle Vertices

This filter uses Laplacian smoothing described in "Mesh Smoothing" on page 388 to adjust triangle vertices as an "average" of neighboring vertices. Typically, the movement will be less than a voxel. Of course we have already smoothed the image data with a Gaussian kernel so this step may not give much improvement; however, models that are heavily decimated can sometimes be improved with additional polygonal smoothing.

```
vtkSmoothPolyDataFilter smoother
  smoother SetInput [decimator GetOutput]
  eval smoother SetNumberOfIterations $SMOOTH_ITERATIONS
  eval smoother SetRelaxationFactor $SMOOTH_FACTOR
  eval smoother SetFeatureAngle $SMOOTH_ANGLE
  smoother FeatureEdgeSmoothingOff
```

```
smoother BoundarySmoothingOff;
smoother SetConvergence 0
[smoother GetOutput] ReleaseDataFlagOn
```

Generate Normals

To generate smooth shaded models during rendering, we need normals at each vertex. As in decimation, sharp edges can be retained by setting the feature angle.

```
vtkPolyDataNormals normals
   normals SetInput [smoother GetOutput]
   eval normals SetFeatureAngle $FEATURE_ANGLE
   [normals GetOutput] ReleaseDataFlagOn
```

Generate Triangle Strips

Triangle strips are a compact representation of large numbers of triangles. This filter processes our independent triangles before we write them to a file.

```
vtkStripper stripper
   stripper SetInput [normals GetOutput]
   [stripper GetOutput] ReleaseDataFlagOn
```

Write the Triangles to a File

Finally, the last component of the pipeline writes the triangles strips to a file.

```
vtkPolyDataWriter writer
   writer SetInput [stripper GetOutput]
   eval writer SetFileName $NAME.vtk
```

Execute the Pipeline

If you have gotten this far in the book, you know that the *Visualization Toolkit* uses a demand-driven pipeline architecture and so far we have not demanded anything. We have just specified the pipeline topology and the parameters for each pipeline element.

```
writer Update
```

causes the pipeline to execute. In practice we do a bit more than just Update the last element of the pipeline. We explicitly Update each element so that we can time the individual steps. The script segmented8.tcl on the CD-ROM contains the more sophisticated approach.

Specifying Parameters for the Pipeline

All of the variables mentioned above must be defined for each tissue to be processed. The parameters fall into two general categories. Some are specific to the particular study while some are specific to each tissue. For the frog, we collected the study-specific parameters in a file frog.tcl that contains:

```
set SLICE_ORDER hfsi
set ROWS 470
set COLUMNS 500
set STUDY ../frogMasks/frogTissue
set PIXEL_SIZE 1
set SPACING 1.5
set VALUE 511.5
set SAMPLE_RATE "1 1 1"
set DECIMATE_REDUCTION .95
set DECIMATE_ITERATIONS 5
set DECIMATE_ERROR .0002
set DECIMATE_ERROR_INCREMENT .0002
set SMOOTH_ITERATIONS 0
set SMOOTH_FACTOR .01
set FEATURE_ANGLE 60
```

There is a specific file for each tissue type. This tissue-specific file reads in the frog-specific parameters, sets tissue-specific parameters, and then reads the pipeline script (we call it segmented8.tcl). For example, liver.tcl contains:

```
source frog.tcl
set NAME liver
set TISSUE 10
set START_SLICE 25
set END_SLICE 126
set VOI "167 297 154 304 $START_SLICE $END_SLICE"
source segmented8.tcl
```

Parameters in frog.tcl can also be overridden. For example, skeleton.tcl overrides the standard deviation for the Gaussian filter.

```
source frog.tcl
set NAME skeleton
set TISSUE 13
set VALUE 368.5
set START_SLICE 1
set END_SLICE 136
set ZMAX [expr $END_SLICE - $START_SLICE]
set VOI "23 479 8 473 0 $ZMAX"
set GAUSSIAN_STANDARD_DEVIATION "1.5 1.5 1"
source segmented8.tcl
```

Note that both of these examples specify a volume of interest. This improves performance of the imaging and visualization algorithms by eliminating empty space.

Another script, marching8.tcl, uses similar parameters but processes the original gray-scale volume rather than the segmented volume. This script is used in skin.tcl to extract the skin. The file marching8.tcl does not have the island removal or threshold pipeline elements since the data is already has gray-scale information.

Once the models are generated with the process just outlined, they can be rendered using the following tcl script called renactors.tcl.

```
#   Render Actors Created with segmented8.tcl/marching8.tcl
# Get the interactor ui
source ../vtkInt.tcl
source ../colors.tcl
```

First we create a Tcl procedure to automate the creation of actors from the model files. All the pipeline elements are named consistently with the name of the part followed by the name of the pipeline element. This makes it easy for the user to identify each object in more sophisticated user interfaces.

```
proc mkname {a b} {return $a$b}
# proc to make actors
# create pipeline
proc MakeActor { name r g b} {
   set filename  [eval mkname $name .vtk]
   set reader   [eval mkname $name PolyDataReader]
   vtkPolyDataReader $reader
     $reader SetFileName $filename
   set mapper [eval mkname $name PolyDataMapper]
   vtkPolyDataMapper $mapper
     $mapper SetInput [$reader GetOutput]
        $mapper ScalarVisibilityOff
   set actor [ eval mkname $name Actor]
   vtkLODActor $actor
   $actor SetMapper $mapper
   eval [$actor GetProperty] SetDiffuseColor $r $g $b
   eval [$actor GetProperty] SetSpecularPower 50
   eval [$actor GetProperty] SetSpecular .5
   eval [$actor GetProperty] SetDiffuse .8
   return $actor
}
```

After the familiar code to create required rendering objects, a single statement for each part creates an actor we can add to the renderer:

```
# Now create the RenderWindow, Renderer and Interactor
vtkRenderer ren1
vtkRenderWindow renWin
    renWin AddRenderer ren1
vtkRenderWindowInteractor iren
    iren SetRenderWindow renWin
# Add the actors to the renderer using the MakeActor proc#
ren1 AddActor [eval MakeActor lung $powder_blue]
ren1 AddActor [eval MakeActor heart $tomato]
ren1 AddActor [eval MakeActor liver $pink]
ren1 AddActor [eval MakeActor duodenum $orange]
ren1 AddActor [eval MakeActor blood $salmon]
ren1 AddActor [eval MakeActor brain $beige]
ren1 AddActor [eval MakeActor eye_retna $misty_rose]
ren1 AddActor [eval MakeActor eye_white $white]
ren1 AddActor [eval MakeActor ileum $raspberry]
```

```
ren1 AddActor [eval MakeActor kidney $banana]
ren1 AddActor [eval MakeActor l_intestine $peru]
ren1 AddActor [eval MakeActor nerve $carrot]
ren1 AddActor [eval MakeActor spleen $violet]
ren1 AddActor [eval MakeActor stomach $plum]
ren1 AddActor [eval MakeActor skeleton $wheat]
```

The rest of the script defines a standard view.

```
ren1 SetBackground 0.2 0.3 0.4
renWin SetSize 450 450
[ren1 GetActiveCamera] SetViewUp 0 -1 0
[ren1 GetActiveCamera] Azimuth 30
[ren1 GetActiveCamera] Elevation 30
[ren1 GetActiveCamera] Dolly 1.75
iren Initialize
iren SetUserMethod {wm deiconify .vtkInteract}
# prevent the tk window from showing up
wm withdraw .
```

Figure **13–9** shows four views of the frog generated with `renactors.tcl`.

This lengthy example shows the power of a comprehensive visualization system like the *Visualization Toolkit*.

- We mixed image processing and computer graphics algorithms to process data created by an external segmentation process.

- We developed a generic approach that allows users to control the elements of the pipeline with a familiar scripting language, tcl.

- We separated the task into a "batch" portion and an "interactive" portion.

Other Frog-Related Information

The folks at Lawrence Berkeley National Laboratory have an impressive Web site that features the frog used in this example. The site describes how the frog data was obtained and also permits users to create mpeg movies of the frog. There are also other datasets available. Further details on "The Whole Frog Project" can be found at `http://www-itg.lbl.gov/Frog`. Also, the Stanford University Medical Media and Information Technologies (SUMMIT) group has on-going work using the Berkeley frog. They are early **vtk** users. Enjoy their *Virtual Creatures* project at: `http://summit.stanford.edu/creatures`.

13.3 Financial Visualization

The application of 3D visualization techniques to financial data is relatively new. Historically, financial data has been represented using 2D plotting techniques such as line, scatter plots, bar charts, and pie charts. These techniques are especially well suited for the display of price and volume information for stocks, bonds, and mutual funds. Three-dimensional techniques are becoming more

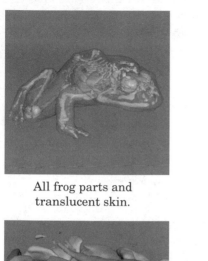

All frog parts and
translucent skin.

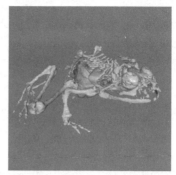

The complete frog without
skin.

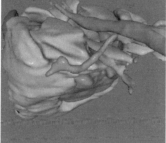

No skin or skeleton.

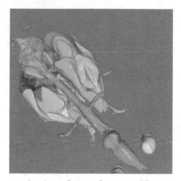

A view from the top. How
good is your biology?

Figure 13–9 Various frog images generated with `renactors.tcl`.

important due to the increased volume of information in recent years, and 3D graphics and visualization techniques are becoming interactive. Interactive rates mean that visualization can be applied to the day-to-day processing of data. Our belief is that this will allow deeper understanding of today's complex financial data and other more timely decisions.

In this example we go through the process of obtaining data, converting it to a form that we can use, and then using visualization techniques to view it. Some of the external software tools used in this example may be unfamiliar to you. This should not be a large concern. We have simply chosen the tools with which we are familiar. Where we have used an Awk script, you might choose to write a small C program to do the same thing. The value of the example lies in illustrating the high-level process of solving a visualization problem.

The first step is to obtain the data. We obtained our data from a public site on the World Wide Web (WWW) that archives stock prices and volumes for many publicly traded stocks. (This Web site has closed down since publication of the first edition. The data for this example are available on the CD-ROM.)

Once we have obtained the data, we convert it to a format that can be read into **vtk**. While **vtk** can read in a variety of data formats, frequently your data will not be in one of those. The data files we obtained are stored in the following format:

```
930830   49.375   48.812   49.250   1139.2   56.1056
930831   49.375   48.938   49.125   1360.4   66.8297
930902   49.188   48.688   48.750   1247.2   60.801
...
```

Each line stores the data for one day of trading. The first number is the date, stored as the last two digits of the year, followed by a two-digit month and finally the day of the month. The next three values represent the high, low, and closing price of the stock for that day. The next value is the volume of trading in thousands of shares. The final value is the volume of trading in millions of dollars.

We used an Awk script to convert the original data format into a **vtk** data file. (See "vtk File Formats" on page 595.) This conversion could be done using many other approaches, such as writing a C program or a Tcl script.

```
BEGIN {print "# vtk DataSet Version 2.0\n
Data values for stock\nASCII\n\nDATASET POLYDATA"}
{count += 1}
{ d = $1%100}
{ m = int(($1%10000)/100)}
{ if (m == 2) d += 31}
{ if (m == 3) d += 59}
{ if (m == 4) d += 90}
{ if (m == 5) d += 120}
{ if (m == 6) d += 151}
{ if (m == 7) d += 181}
{ if (m == 8) d += 212}
{ if (m == 9) d += 243}
{ if (m == 10) d += 273}
{ if (m == 11) d += 304}
{ if (m == 12) d += 334}
{ d = d + (int($1/10000) - 93)*365}
{dates[count] = d; prices[count] = $4; volumes[count] = $5}
END {
    print "POINTS " count " float";
    for (i = 1; i <= count; i++) print dates[i] " " prices[i] " 0 ";
    print "\nLINES 1 " (count + 1) " " count;
    for (i = 0; i < count; i++) print i;
    print "\nPOINT_DATA " count "\nSCALARS volume float";
    print "LOOKUP_TABLE default";
    for (i = 1; i <= count; i++) print volumes[i];
    }
```

The above Awk script performs the conversion. Its first line outputs the required header information indicating that the file is a **vtk** data file containing polygonal data. It also includes a comment indicating that the data represents stock values. There are a few different **vtk** data formats that we could have selected. It is up to you to decide which format best suits the data you are visualizing. We have judged the polygonal format (vtkPolyData) as best suited for this particular stock visualization.

The next line of the Awk script creates a variable named count that keeps track of how many days worth of information is in the file. This is equivalent to the number of lines in the original data file.

The next fourteen lines convert the six digit date into a more useful format, since the original format has a number of problems. If we were to blindly use the original format and plot the data using the date as the independent variable, there would be large gaps in our plot. For example, 931231 is the last day of 1993 and 940101 is the first day of 1994. Chronologically, these two dates are sequential, but mathematically there are (940101–931231=) 8870 values between them. A simple solution would be to use the line number as our independent variable. This would work as long as we knew that every trading day was recorded in the data file. It would not properly handle the situation where the market was open, but for some reason data was not recorded. A better solution is to convert the dates into numerically ordered days. The preceding Awk script sets January 1, 1993, as day number one, and then numbers all the following days from there. At the end of these 14 lines the variable, d, will contain the resulting value.

The next line in our Awk script stores the converted date, closing price, and dollar volume into arrays indexed by the line number stored in the variable count. Once all the lines have been read and stored into the arrays, we write out the rest of the **vtk** data file. We have selected the date as our independent variable and x coordinate. The closing price we store as the y coordinate, and the z coordinate we set to zero. After indicating the number and type of points to be stored, the Awk script loops through all the points and writes them out to the **vtk** data file. It then writes out the line connectivity list. In this case we just connect one point to the next to form a polyline for each stock. Finally, we write out the volume information as scalar data associated with the points. Portions of the resulting **vtk** data file are shown below.

```
# vtk DataFile Version 1.0
Data values for stock
ASCII

DATASET POLYDATA
POINTS 348 float
242 49.250 0
243 49.125 0
245 48.750 0
246 48.625 0
...
```

```
LINES 1 349 348
0
1
2
3
...

POINT_DATA 348
SCALARS volume float
LOOKUP_TABLE default
1139.2
1360.4
1247.2
1745.4
...
```

Now that we have generated the **vtk** data file, we can start the process of creating a visualization for the stock data. To do this, we wrote a Tcl script to be used with the Tcl-based **vtk** executable. At a high level the script reads in the stock data, sends it through a tube filter, creates a label for it, and then creates an outline around the resulting dataset. Ideally, we would like to display multiple stocks in the same window. To facilitate this, we designed the Tcl script to use a procedure to perform operations on a per stock basis. The resulting script is listed below.

```
catch {load vtktcl}
# this is a tcl script for the stock case study
# Create the RenderWindow, Renderer and both Actors
vtkRenderer ren1
vtkRenderWindow renWin
  renWin AddRenderer ren1
vtkRenderWindowInteractor iren
  iren SetRenderWindow renWin

#create the outline
vtkAppendPolyData apf
vtkOutlineFilter olf
  olf SetInput [apf GetOutput]
vtkPolyDataMapper outlineMapper
  outlineMapper SetInput [olf GetOutput]
vtkActor outlineActor
  outlineActor SetMapper outlineMapper
set zpos 0

# create the stocks
proc AddStock {prefix name x y z} {
  global zpos

  # create labels
```

```
    vtkTextSource $prefix.TextSrc
      $prefix.TextSrc SetText "$name"
      $prefix.TextSrc SetBacking 0
    vtkPolyDataMapper $prefix.LabelMapper
      $prefix.LabelMapper SetInput [$prefix.TextSrc GetOutput]
    vtkFollower $prefix.LabelActor
      $prefix.LabelActor SetMapper $prefix.LabelMapper
      $prefix.LabelActor SetPosition $x $y $z
      $prefix.LabelActor SetScale 0.25 0.25 0.25
      eval $prefix.LabelActor SetOrigin
                    [$prefix.LabelMapper GetCenter]
    # create a sphere source and actor
    vtkPolyDataReader $prefix.PolyDataRead
      $prefix.PolyDataRead SetFileName
                  "../../../vtkdata/$prefix.vtk"
    vtkTubeFilter $prefix.TubeFilter
      $prefix.TubeFilter SetInput [$prefix.PolyDataRead GetOutput]
      $prefix.TubeFilter SetNumberOfSides 8
      $prefix.TubeFilter SetRadius 0.5
      $prefix.TubeFilter SetRadiusFactor 10000
    vtkTransform $prefix.Transform
      $prefix.Transform Translate 0 0 $zpos
      $prefix.Transform Scale 0.15 1 1
    vtkTransformPolyDataFilter $prefix.TransformFilter
      $prefix.TransformFilter SetInput
                        [$prefix.TubeFilter GetOutput]
      $prefix.TransformFilter SetTransform $prefix.Transform
    # increment zpos
    set zpos [expr $zpos + 10]
    vtkPolyDataMapper $prefix.StockMapper
      $prefix.StockMapper SetInput
              [$prefix.TransformFilter GetOutput]
    vtkActor $prefix.StockActor
      $prefix.StockActor SetMapper $prefix.StockMapper
      $prefix.StockMapper SetScalarRange 0 8000
      [$prefix.StockActor GetProperty] SetAmbient 0.5
      [$prefix.StockActor GetProperty] SetDiffuse 0.5

    apf AddInput [$prefix.TransformFilter GetOutput]

    ren1 AddActor $prefix.StockActor
    ren1 AddActor $prefix.LabelActor
    $prefix.LabelActor SetCamera [ren1 GetActiveCamera]
}

# set up the stocks
ddStock GE "GE" 94 46 4
AddStock GM "GM" 107 39 14
AddStock IBM "IBM" 92 70 16
AddStock DEC "DEC" 70 19 26
```

```
# Add the actors to the renderer, set the background and size
#
ren1 AddActor outlineActor
ren1 SetBackground 0.1 0.2 0.4
renWin SetSize 1200 600

# render the image
[ren1 GetActiveCamera] SetViewAngle 10
ren1 ResetCamera
[ren1 GetActiveCamera] Zoom 2.8
[ren1 GetActiveCamera] Elevation 90
[ren1 GetActiveCamera] SetViewUp 0 0 -1
iren Initialize

# prevent the tk window from showing up then start the event loop
wm withdraw .
```

The first part of this script consists of the standard procedure for renderer and interactor creation that can be found in almost all of the **vtk** Tcl scripts. The next section creates the objects necessary for drawing an outline around all of the stock data. A vtkAppendPolyData filter is used to append all of the stock data together. This is then sent through a vtkOutlineFilter to create a bounding box around the data. A mapper and actor are created to display the result.

In the next part of this script, we define the procedure to add stock data to this visualization. The procedure takes five arguments: the name of the stock, the label we want displayed, and the x, y, z coordinates defining where to position the label. The first line of the procedure indicates that the variable ren1 should be visible to this procedure. By default the procedure can only access its own local variables. Next, we create the label using a vtkTextSource, vtkPoly-DataMapper, and vtkFollower. The names of these objects are all prepended with the variable "$prefix." so that the instance names will be unique. An instance of vtkFollower is used instead of the usual vtkActor, because we always want the text to be right-side up and facing the camera. The vtkFol-lower class provides this functionality. The remaining lines position and scale the label appropriately. We set the origin of the label to the center of its data. This insures that the follower will rotate about its center point.

The next group of lines creates the required objects to read in the data, pass it through a tube filter and a transform filter, and finally display the result. The tube filter uses the scalar data (stock volume in this example) to determine the radius of the tube. The mapper also uses the scalar data to determine the coloring of the tube. The transform filter uses a transform object to set the stock's position based on the value of the variable zpos. For each stock, we will increment zpos by 10, effectively shifting the next stock over 10 units from the current stock. This prevents the stocks from being stacked on top of each other. We also use the transform to compress the x-axis to make the data easier to view.

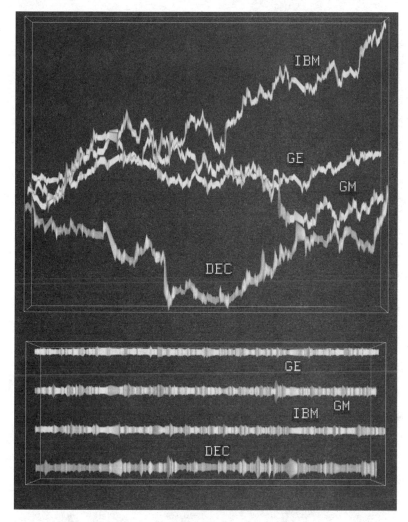

Figure 13–10 Two views from the stock visualization script. The top shows closing price over time; the bottom shows volume over time (`stocks.tcl`).

Next, we add this stock as an input to the append filter and add the actors and followers to the renderer. The last line of the procedure sets the follower's camera to be the active camera of the renderer.

Back in the main body of the Tcl script, we invoke the `AddStock` procedure four times with four different stocks. Finally, we add the outline actor and customize the renderer and camera to produce a nice initial view. Two different views of the result are displayed in Figure **13–10**. The top image shows a history of stock closing prices for our four stocks. The color and width of these lines correspond to the volume of the stock on that day. The lower image more clearly illustrates the changes in stock volume by looking at the data from above.

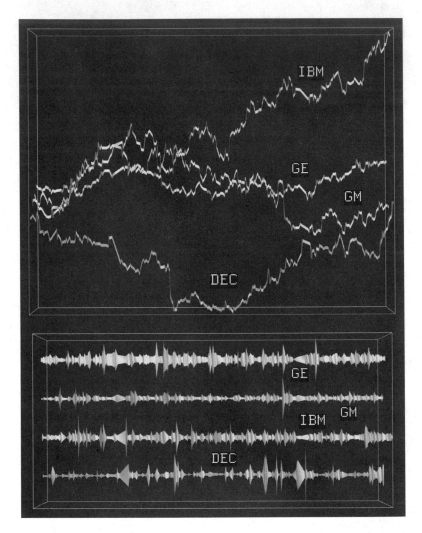

Figure 13–11 Two more views of the stock case study. Here the tube filter has been replaced by a ribbon filter followed with a linear extrusion filter.

A legitimate complaint with Figure **13–10** is that the changing width of the tube makes it more difficult to see the true shape of the price verses the time curve. We can solve this problem by using a ribbon filter followed by a linear extrusion filter, instead of the tube filter. The ribbon filter will create a ribbon whose width will vary in proportion to the scalar value of the data. We then use the linear extrusion filter to extrude this ribbon along the y-axis so that it has a constant thickness. The resulting views are shown in Figure **13–11**.

13.4 Implicit Modelling

The *Visualization Toolkit* has some useful geometric modelling capabilities. One of the most powerful features is implicit modelling. In this example we show how to use polygonal descriptions of objects and create "blobby" models of them using the implicit modelling objects in **vtk**. This example generates a logo for the *Visualization Toolkit* from polygonal representations of the letters v, t, and k.

We create three separate visualization pipelines, one for each letter. Figure **13–12** shows the visualization pipeline. As is common in **vtk** applications, we design a pipeline and fill in the details of the instance variables just before we render. We pass the letters through a vtkTransformPolyDataFilter to position them relative to each other. Then we combine all of the polygons from the transformed letters into one polygon dataset using the vtkAppendPolyData filter. The vtkImplicitModeller creates a volume dataset of dimension 64^3 with each voxel containing a scalar value that is the distance to the nearest polygon. Recall from "Implicit Modelling" on page 184, that the implicit modelling algorithm lets us specify the region of influence of each polygon. Here we specify this using the SetMaximumDistance() method of the vtkImplicitModeller. By restricting the region of influence, we can significantly improve performance of the implicit modelling algorithm. Then we use vtkContourFilter to extract an isosurface that approximates a distance of 1.0 from each polygon. We create two actors: one for the blobby logo and one for the original polygon letters. Notice that both actors share the polygon data created by vtkAppendPolyData. Because of the nature of the **vtk** visualization pipeline (see "Implicit Control of Execution" on page 102), the appended data will only be created once by the portion of the pipeline that is executed first. As a final touch, we move the polygonal logo in front of the blobby logo. Now we will go through the example in detail.

First, we read the geometry files that contain polygonal models of each letter in the logo. The data is in **vtk** polygonal format, so we use vtkPolyDataReader. t

```
vtkPolyDataReader *letterV = vtkPolyDataReader::New();
   letterV->SetFileName ("v.vtk");

vtkPolyDataReader *letterT = vtkPolyDataReader::New();
   letterT->SetFileName ("t.vtk");

vtkPolyDataReader *letterK = vtkPolyDataReader::New();
   letterK->SetFileName ("k.vtk");
```

We want to transform each letter into its appropriate location and orientation within the logo. We create the transform filters here, but defer specifying the location and orientation until later in the program.

```
vtkTransform *VTransform = vtkTransform::New();
vtkTransformPolyDataFilter *VTransformFilter =
     vtkTransformPolyDataFilter::New();
```

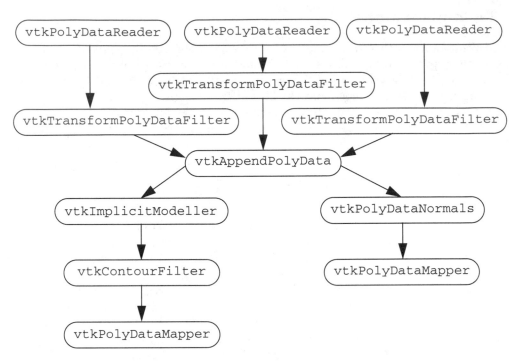

Figure 13–12 The visualization pipeline for the **vtk** blobby logo.

```
    VTransformFilter->SetInput (letterV->GetOutput());
    VTransformFilter->SetTransform (VTransform);

vtkTransform *TTransform = vtkTransform::New();
vtkTransformPolyDataFilter *TTransformFilter =
    vtkTransformPolyDataFilter::New();
    TTransformFilter->SetInput (letterT->GetOutput());
    TTransformFilter->SetTransform (TTransform);

vtkTransform *KTransform = vtkTransform::New();
vtkTransformPolyDataFilter *KTransformFilter =
    vtkTransformPolyDataFilter::New();
    KTransformFilter->SetInput (letterK->GetOutput());
    KTransformFilter->SetTransform (KTransform);
```

We collect all of the transformed letters into one set of polygons by using an instance of the class vtkAppendPolyData.

```
vtkAppendPolyData *appendAll = vtkAppendPolyData::New();
appendAll->AddInput (VTransformFilter->GetOutput());
appendAll->AddInput (TTransformFilter->GetOutput());
appendAll->AddInput (KTransformFilter->GetOutput());
```

Since the geometry for each letter did not have surface normals, we add them here. We use vtkPolyDataNormals. Then we complete this portion of the pipeline by creating a mapper and an actor.

```
// create normals
vtkPolyDataNormals *logoNormals = vtkPolyDataNormals::New();
    logoNormals->SetInput (appendAll->GetOutput());
    logoNormals->SetFeatureAngle (60);

// map to rendering primitives
vtkPolyDataMapper *logoMapper = vtkPolyDataMapper::New();
    logoMapper->SetInput (logoNormals->GetOutput());

// now an actor
vtkActor *logo = vtkActor::New();
    logo->SetMapper (logoMapper);
```

We create the blobby logo with the implicit modeller, and then extract the logo with vtkContourFilter. The pipeline is completed by creating a mapper and an actor.

```
// now create an implicit model of the letters
vtkImplicitModeller *blobbyLogoImp = vtkImplicitModeller::New();
    blobbyLogoImp->SetInput (appendAll->GetOutput());
    blobbyLogoImp->SetMaximumDistance (.075);
    blobbyLogoImp->SetSampleDimensions (64,64,64);
    blobbyLogoImp->SetAdjustDistance (0.05);

// extract an iso surface
vtkContourFilter *blobbyLogoIso = vtkContourFilter::New();
    blobbyLogoIso->SetInput (blobbyLogoImp->GetOutput());
    blobbyLogoIso->SetValue (1, 1.5);

// map to rendering primitives
vtkPolyDataMapper *blobbyLogoMapper = vtkPolyDataMapper::New();
    blobbyLogoMapper->SetInput (blobbyLogoIso->GetOutput());
    blobbyLogoMapper->ScalarVisibilityOff ();

// now an actor
vtkActor *blobbyLogo = vtkActor::New();
    blobbyLogo->SetMapper (blobbyLogoMapper);
    blobbyLogo->SetProperty (banana);
```

To improve the look of our resulting visualization, we define a couple of organic colors. Softer colors show up better on some electronic media (e.g., VHS video tape) and are pleasing to the eye.

```
vtkProperty *tomato = vtkProperty::New();
    tomato->SetDiffuseColor(1, .3882, .2784);
```

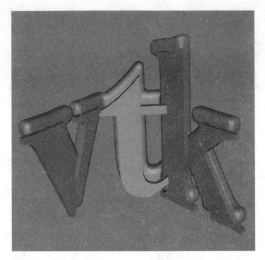

Figure 13–13 A logo created with vtkImplicitModeller(vtkLogo.cxx).

```
tomato->SetSpecular(.3);
tomato->SetSpecularPower(20);


vtkProperty *banana = vtkProperty::New();
    banana->SetDiffuseColor(.89, .81, .34);
    banana->SetDiffuse (.7);
    banana->SetSpecular(.4);
    banana->SetSpecularPower(20);
```

These colors are then assigned to the appropriate actors.

```
logo->SetProperty (tomato);

blobbyLogo->SetProperty (banana);
```

And finally, we position the letters in the logo and move the polygonal logo out in front of the blobby logo by modifying the actor's position. The resulting image is shown in Figure **13–13**.

```
VTransform->Translate (-16,0,12.5);
VTransform->RotateY (40);
KTransform->Translate (14, 0, 0);
KTransform->RotateY (-40);

// move the polygonal letters to the front
logo->SetPosition(0,0,6);
```

13.5 Computational Fluid Dynamics

Computational Fluid Dynamics (CFD) visualization poses a challenge to any visualization toolkit. CFD studies the flow of fluids in and around complex structures. Often, large amounts of supercomputer time is used to derive scalar and vector data in the flow field. Since CFD computations produce multiple scalar and vector data types, we will apply many of the tools described in this book. The challenge is to combine multiple representations into meaningful visualizations that extract information without overwhelming the user.

CFD analysts often employ finite difference grids. A finite difference grid represents the discretization of the problem domain into small computational cells. The grid allows the analyst to create a large system of equations that can then be solved on a computer. The grid is topologically uniform in *i-j-k* space, but the corresponding physical coordinates need not be uniformly distributed. This is what we call a structured grid dataset in **vtk**.

There are a number of techniques we can use when we first look at the complex data presented by CFD applications. Since we need to apply several algorithms to the data, and since there will be many parameter changes for these algorithms, we suggest using the Tcl interpreter rather than C++ code. Our strategy for visualizing this CFD data includes the following:

1. Display the computational grid. The analyst carefully constructed the finite difference grid to have a higher density in regions where rapid changes occur in the flow variables. We will display the grid in wireframe so we can see the computational cells.

2. Display the scalar fields on the computational grid. This will give us an overview of where the scalar data is changing. We will experiment with the extents of the grid extraction to focus on interesting areas.

3. Explore the vector field by seeding streamlines with a spherical cloud of points. Move the sphere through areas of rapidly changing velocity.

4. Try using the computational grid itself as seeds for the streamlines. Of course we will have to restrict the extent of the grid you use for this purpose. Using the grid, we will be able to place more seeds in regions where the analyst expected more action.

For this case study, we use a dataset from NASA called the LOx Post. It simulates the flow of liquid oxygen across a flat plate with a cylindrical post perpendicular to the flow [Rogers86]. This analysis models the flow in a rocket engine. The post promotes mixing of the liquid oxygen.

We start by exploring the scalar and vector fields in the data. By calculating the magnitude of the velocity vectors, we derive a scalar field. This study has a particularly interesting vector field around the post. We seed the field with multiple starting points (using points arranged along a curve, referred to as a *rake*) and experiment with parameters for the streamlines. Streampolygons are particularly appropriate here and do a nice job of showing the flow downstream from the post. We animate the streamline creation by moving the seeding line or rake back and forth behind the post.

Following our own advice, we first display the computational grid. The following Tcl code produced Figure **13–14**.

```
# read data
vtkPLOT3DReader pl3d
   pl3d SetXYZFileName "../../../vtkdata/postxyz.bin"
   pl3d SetQFileName "../../../vtkdata/postq.bin"
   pl3d SetScalarFunctionNumber 153
   pl3d SetVectorFunctionNumber 200
   pl3d DebugOn
   pl3d Update

# computational planes: the floor
vtkStructuredGridGeometryFilter floorComp
   floorComp SetExtent 0 37 0 75 0 0
   floorComp SetInput [pl3d GetOutput]
vtkPolyDataMapper floorMapper
   floorMapper SetInput [floorComp GetOutput]
   floorMapper ScalarVisibilityOff
vtkActor floorActor
   floorActor SetMapper floorMapper
   [floorActor GetProperty] SetColor 0 0 0
   [floorActor GetProperty] SetRepresentationToWireframe

# the post
vtkStructuredGridGeometryFilter postComp
   postComp SetExtent 10 10 0 75 0 37
   postComp SetInput [pl3d GetOutput]
vtkPolyDataMapper postMapper
   postMapper SetInput [postComp GetOutput]
   postMapper ScalarVisibilityOff
vtkActor postActor
   postActor SetMapper postMapper
   [postActor GetProperty] SetColor 0 0 0
   [postActor GetProperty] SetRepresentationToWireframe

# plane upstream of the flow
vtkStructuredGridGeometryFilter fanComp
   fanComp SetExtent 0 37 38 38 0 37
   fanComp SetInput [pl3d GetOutput]
vtkPolyDataMapper fanMapper
   fanMapper SetInput [fanComp GetOutput]
   fanMapper ScalarVisibilityOff
vtkActor fanActor
   fanActor SetMapper fanMapper
   [fanActor GetProperty] SetColor 0 0 0
   [fanActor GetProperty] SetRepresentationToWireframe
```

```
# outline
vtkStructuredGridOutlineFilter outline
    outline SetInput [pl3d GetOutput]
vtkPolyDataMapper outlineMapper
    outlineMapper SetInput [outline GetOutput]
vtkActor outlineActor
    outlineActor SetMapper outlineMapper
    [outlineActor GetProperty] SetColor 0 0 0

# Create graphics stuff
vtkRenderer ren1
vtkRenderWindow renWin
    renWin AddRenderer ren1
vtkRenderWindowInteractor iren
    iren SetRenderWindow renWin

# Add the actors to the renderer, set the background and size
#
ren1 AddActor outlineActor
ren1 AddActor floorActor
ren1 AddActor postActor
ren1 AddActor fanActor
```

To display the scalar field using color mapping, we must change the actor's representation from wireframe to surface, turn on scalar visibility for each vtk-PolyDataMapper, set each mapper's scalar range, and render again, producing Figure **13–15**.

```
postActor SetRepresentationToSurface
fanActor SetRepresentationToSurface
floorActor SetRepresentationToSurface

postMapper ScalarVisibilityOn
postMapper SetScalarRange [[pl3d GetOutput] GetScalarRange]
fanMapper ScalarVisibilityOn
fanMapper SetScalarRange [[pl3d GetOutput] GetScalarRange]
floorMapper ScalarVisibilityOn
floorMapper SetScalarRange [[pl3d GetOutput] GetScalarRange]
```

Now, we explore the vector field using vtkPointSource. Recall that this object generates a random cloud of points around a spherical center point. We will use this cloud of points to generate streamlines. We place the center of the cloud near the post since this is where the velocity seems to be changing most rapidly. During this exploration, we use streamlines rather than streamtubes for reasons of efficiency. The Tcl code is as follows.

```
# spherical seed points
vtkPointSource rake
    rake SetCenter -0.74 0 0.3
```

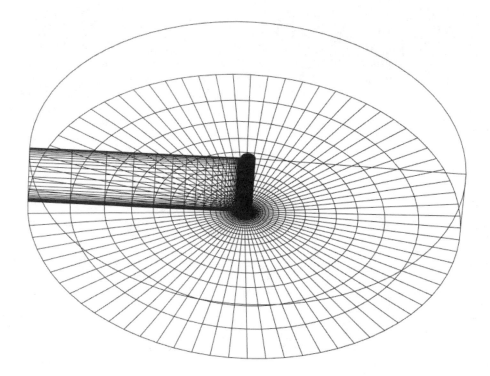

Figure 13–14 Portion of computational grid for the LOx post (LOxGrid.tcl).

```
    rake SetNumberOfPoints 10
vtkStreamLine streamers
    streamers SetInput [pl3d GetOutput]
    streamers SetSource [rake GetOutput]
    streamers SetMaximumPropagationTime 250
    streamers SpeedScalarsOn
    streamers SetIntegrationStepLength .2
    streamers SetStepLength .25
vtkPolyDataMapper mapTubes
    mapTubes SetInput [streamers GetOutput]
    eval mapTubes SetScalarRange [[pl3d GetOutput] GetScalarRange]
vtkActor tubesActor
    tubesActor SetMapper mapTubes
```

Figure **13–16** shows streamlines seeded from four locations along the post. Notice how the structure of the flow begins to emerge as the starting positions for the streamlines are moved up and down in front of the post. This is particularly true if we do this interactively; the mind assembles the behavior of the

Figure 13–15 Scalar field displayed on three computational grids.

streamlines into a global understanding of the flow field.

For a final example, we use the computational grid to seed streamlines and then generate streamtubes as is shown in Figure **13–17**. A nice feature of this approach is that we generate more streamlines in regions where the analyst constructed a denser grid. The only change we need to make is to replace the rake from the sphere source with a portion of the grid geometry.

```
vtkStructuredGridGeometryFilter seedsComp
   seedsComp SetExtent 10 10 37 39 1 35
   seedsComp SetInput [pl3d GetOutput]
streamers SetSource [seedsComp GetOutput]
# create tubes
vtkTubeFilter tubes
    tubes SetInput [streamers GetOutput]
    tubes SetNumberOfSides 8
```

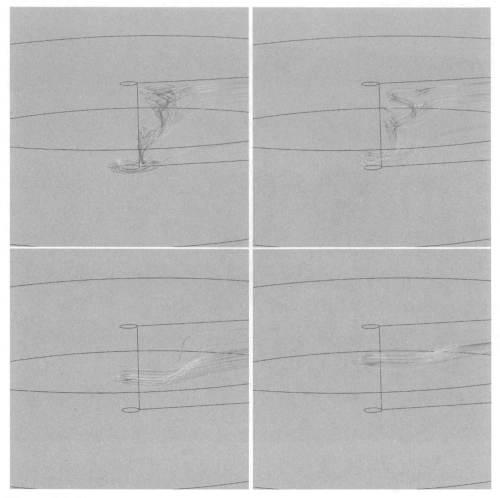

Figure 13–16 Streamlines seeded with spherical cloud of points. Four separate cloud positions are shown.

```
    tubes SetRadius .08
    tubes SetVaryRadiusOff
# change input to streamtubes
mapTubes SetInput [tubes GetOutput]
```

There are a number of other methods we could use to visualize this data. As we saw in "Vector Field Topology" on page 367, there are regions where the velocity vanishes. We can use the object vtkVectorTopology to identify these region(s) and generate streamlines. Another useful visualization would be to identify regions of vorticity. We could use Equation **9-12** in conjunction with an isocontouring algorithm (e.g., vtkContourFilter) to creates isosurfaces of large helical-density.

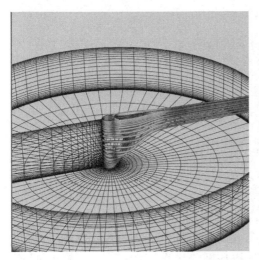 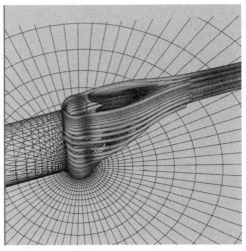

Figure 13–17 Streamtubes created by using the computational grid just in front of the post as a source for seeds (`LOx.tcl`).

13.6 Finite Element Analysis

Finite element analysis is a widely used numerical technique for finding solutions of partial differential equations. Applications of finite element analysis include linear and nonlinear structural, thermal, dynamic, electromagnetic, and flow analysis. In this application we will visualize the results of a blow molding process.

In the extrusion blow molding process, a material is extruded through an annular die to form a hollow cylinder. This cylinder is called a *parison*. Two mold halves are then closed on the parison, while at the same time the parison is inflated with air. Some of the parison material remains within the mold while some becomes waste material. The material is typically a polymer plastic softened with heat, but blow molding has been used to form metal parts. Plastic bottles are often manufactured using a blow molding process.

Designing the parison die and molds is not easy. Improper design results in large variations in the wall thickness. In some cases the part may fail in thin-walled regions. As a result, analysis tools based on finite element techniques have been developed to assist in the design of molds and dies.

The results of one such analysis are shown in Figure **13–18**. The polymer was molded using an isothermal, nonlinear-elastic, incompressible (rubber-like) material. Triangular membrane finite elements were used to model the parison, while a combination of triangular and quadrilateral finite elements were used to model the mold. The mold surface is assumed to be rigid, and the parison is assumed to attach to the mold upon contact. Thus the thinning of the parison is controlled by its stretching during inflation and the sequence in which it contacts the mold.

Figure **13–18** illustrates 10 steps of one analysis. The color of the parison indicates its thickness. Using a rainbow scale, red areas are thinnest while blue regions are thickest (see Color Plates). Our visualization shows clearly one problem with the analysis technique we are using. Note that while the nodes (i.e., points) of the finite element mesh are prevented from passing through the mold, the interior of the triangular elements are not. This is apparent from the occlusion of the mold wireframe by the parison mesh.

To generate these images, we used a Tcl script shown in Figure **13–19** and Figure **13–20**. The input data is in **vtk** format, so a vtkUnstructuredGrid-Reader was used as a source object. The mesh displacement is accomplished using an instance of vtkWarpVector. At this point the pipeline splits. We wish to treat the mold and parison differently (different properties such as wireframe versus surface), but the data for both mold and parison is combined. Fortunately, we can easily separate the data using two instances of class vtkConnectivity-Filter. One filter extracts the parison, while the other extracts both parts of the mold. Finally, to achieve a smooth surface appearance on the parison, we use a vtkPolyDataNormals filter. In order to use this filter, we have to convert the data type from vtkUnstructuredGrid (output of vtkConnectivityFilter) to type vtkPolyData. The filter vtkGeometryFilter does this nicely.

13.7 Algorithm Visualization

Visualization can be used to display algorithms and data structures. Representing this information often requires creative work on the part of the application programmer. For example, Robertson et al. [Robertson91] have shown 3D techniques for visualizing directory structures and navigating through them. Their approach involves building three dimensional models (the so-called "cone trees") to represent files, directories, and associations between files and directories. Similar approaches can be used to visualize stacks, queues, linked lists, trees, and other data structures.

In this example we will visualize the operation of the recursive Towers of Hanoi puzzle. In this puzzle there are three pegs (Figure **13–21**). In the initial position there are one or more disks (or pucks) of varying diameter on the pegs. The disks are sorted according to disk diameter, so that the largest disk is on the bottom, followed by the next largest, and so on. The goal of the puzzle is to move the disks from one peg to another, moving the disks one at a time, and never placing a larger disk on top of a smaller disk.

The classical solution to this puzzle is based on a divide-and-conquer approach [AhoHopUll83]. The problem of moving n disks from the initial peg to the second peg can be thought of as solving two subproblems of size $n–1$. First move $n–1$ disks from the initial peg to the third peg. Then move the nth disk to the second peg. Finally, move the $n–1$ disks on the third peg back to the second peg.

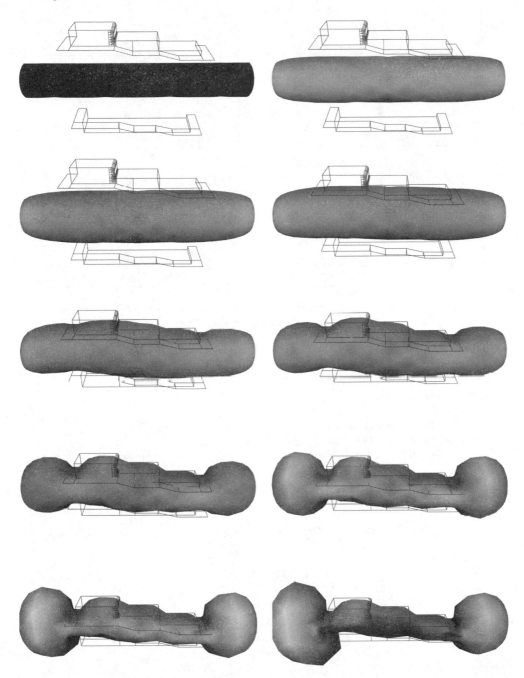

Figure 13–18 Ten frames from a blow molding finite element analysis. Mold halves (shown in wireframe) are closed around a parison as the parison is inflated. Coloring indicates thickness - red areas are thinner than blue (`blow.tcl`)

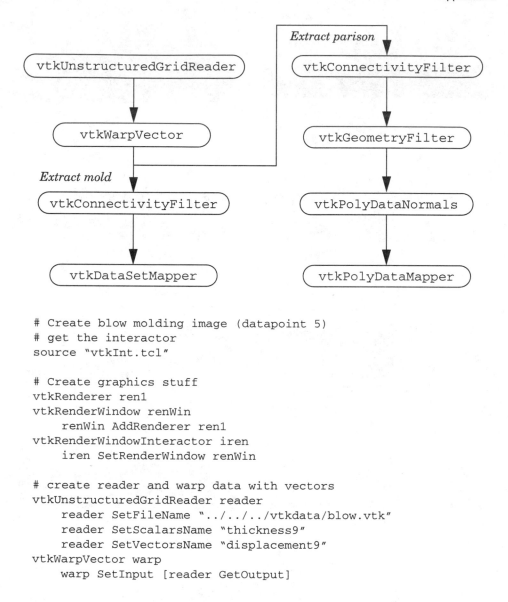

```
# Create blow molding image (datapoint 5)
# get the interactor
source "vtkInt.tcl"

# Create graphics stuff
vtkRenderer ren1
vtkRenderWindow renWin
    renWin AddRenderer ren1
vtkRenderWindowInteractor iren
    iren SetRenderWindow renWin

# create reader and warp data with vectors
vtkUnstructuredGridReader reader
    reader SetFileName "../../../vtkdata/blow.vtk"
    reader SetScalarsName "thickness9"
    reader SetVectorsName "displacement9"
vtkWarpVector warp
    warp SetInput [reader GetOutput]
```

Figure 13–19 Tcl script to generate blow molding image. Network topology and initial portion of script are shown (Part one of two).

The solution to this problem can be elegantly implemented using recursion. We have shown portions of the C++ code in Figure **13–22** and Figure **13–23**. In the first part of the solution (which is not shown in Figure **13–22**) the table top, pegs, and disks are created using the two classes vtkPlaneSource and

```
# extract mold from mesh using connectivity
vtkConnectivityFilter connect
    connect SetInput [warp GetOutput]
    connect SetExtractionModeToSpecifiedRegions
    connect AddSpecifiedRegion 0
    connect AddSpecifiedRegion 1
vtkDataSetMapper moldMapper
    moldMapper SetInput [connect GetOutput]
    moldMapper ScalarVisibilityOff
vtkActor moldActor
    moldActor SetMapper moldMapper
    [moldActor GetProperty] SetColor .2 .2 .2
    [moldActor GetProperty] SetRepresentationToWireframe

# extract parison from mesh using connectivity
vtkConnectivityFilter connect2
    connect2 SetInput [warp GetOutput]
    connect2 SetExtractionModeToSpecifiedRegions
    connect2 AddSpecifiedRegion 2
vtkGeometryFilter parison
    parison SetInput [connect2 GetOutput]
vtkPolyDataNormals normals2
    normals2 SetInput [parison GetOutput]
    normals2 SetFeatureAngle 60
vtkLookupTable lut
    lut SetHueRange 0.0 0.66667
vtkPolyDataMapper parisonMapper
    parisonMapper SetInput [normals2 GetOutput]
    parisonMapper SetLookupTable lut
    parisonMapper SetScalarRange 0.12 1.0
vtkActor parisonActor
    parisonActor SetMapper parisonMapper

# Add the actors to the renderer, set the background and size
ren1 AddActor moldActor
ren1 AddActor parisonActor
ren1 SetBackground 1 1 1
renWin SetSize 750 400

iren Initialize
iren SetUserMethod {wm deiconify .vtkInteract}

# prevent the tk window from showing up then start the event loop
wm withdraw .
```

Figure 13–20 Tcl script to generate blow molding image (Part two of two).

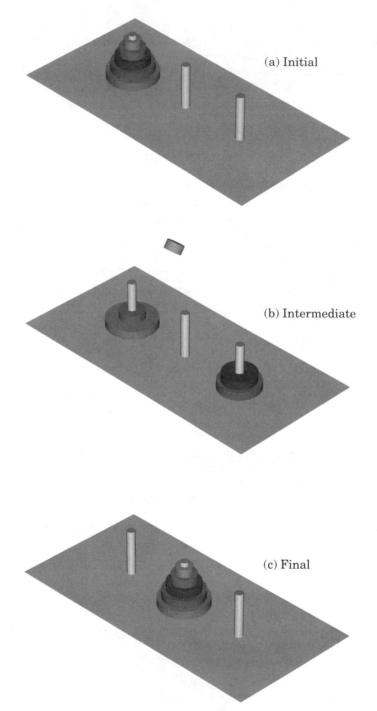

Figure 13–21 Towers of Hanoi. (a) Initial configuration. (b) Intermediate configuration. (c) Final configuration (Hanoi.cxx).

```
// Recursive solution of Towers of Hanoi. Parameters are number
// of disks,originating peg, final peg, and intermediate peg.
static void Hanoi (int n, int peg1, int peg2, int peg3)
{
  if ( n != 1 )
    {
    Hanoi (n-1, peg1, peg3, peg2);
    Hanoi (1, peg1, peg2, peg3);
    Hanoi (n-1, peg3, peg2, peg1);
    }
  else
    {
    MovePuck (peg1, peg2);
    }
}
```

Figure 13–22 C++ code for recursive solution of Towers of Hanoi (Hanoi.cxx).

vtkCylinderSource. The function Hanoi() is then called to begin the recursion. The routine MovePuck() is responsible for moving a disk from one peg to another. It has been jazzed up to move the disk in small, user-specified increments, and to flip the disc over as it moves from one peg to the next. This gives a pleasing visual effect and adds the element of fun to the visualization.

Because of the clear relationship between algorithm and physical reality, the Towers of Hanoi puzzle is relatively easy to visualize. A major challenge facing visualization researchers is to visualize more abstract information, such as information on the Internet, the structure of documents, or the effectiveness of advertising/entertainment in large market segments. This type of visualization, known as information visualization, is likely to emerge in the future as an important research challenge.

13.8 Chapter Summary

This chapter presented several case studies covering a variety of visualization techniques. The examples used different data representations including polygonal data, volumes, structured grids, and unstructured grids. Both C++ and Tcl code was used to implement the case studies.

Medical imaging is a demanding application area due to the size of the input data. Three-dimensional visualization of anatomy is generally regarded by radiologists as a communication tool for referring physicians and surgeons. Medical datasets are typically structured point data (or volumes) or 2D images that form volumes. Common visualization tools for medical imaging include isosurfaces, cut planes, and image display on volume slices.

```
// Routine is responsible for moving disks from one peg to the next
//.
void MovePuck (int peg1, int peg2)
{
  float distance, flipAngle;
  vtkActor *movingActor;
  int i;

  NumberOfMoves++;
  // get the actor to move
  movingActor = (vtkActor *)pegStack[peg1].Pop();
  // get the distance to move up
  distance = (H - (L * (pegStack[peg1].GetNumberOfItems() -1)) + rMax
            / NumberOfSteps;
  for (i=0; i<NumberOfSteps; i++)
    {
    movingActor->AddPosition(0,distance,0);
    Renwin->Render();
    }
  // get the distance to move across
  distance = (peg2 - peg1) * D / NumberOfSteps;
  flipAngle = 180.0 / NumberOfSteps;
  for (i=0; i<NumberOfSteps; i++)
    {
    movingActor->AddPosition(distance,0,0);
    movingActor->RotateX(flipAngle);
    Renwin->Render();
    }
  // get the distance to move down
  distance = ((L * (pegStack[peg2].GetNumberOfItems() - 1)) - H -
rMax) / NumberOfSteps;
  for (i=0; i<NumberOfSteps; i++)
    {
    movingActor->AddPosition(0,distance,0);
    Renwin->Render();
    }
  pegStack[peg2].Push(movingActor);
}
```

Figure 13–23 Function to move disks from one peg to another in the Towers of Hanoi example. The resulting motion is in small steps with an additional flip of the disk.

Next, we presented an example that applied 3D visualization techniques to financial data. In this case study, we began by showing how to import data from an external source. We applied tube filters to the data and varied the width of the tube to show the volume of stock trading. We saw how different views can be used to present different pieces of information. In this case, we saw that by viewing the visualization from the front, we saw a conventional price display. Then, by viewing the visualization from above, we saw trade volume.

In the modelling case study we showed how to use polygonal models and the implicit modelling facilities in **vtk** to create a stylistic logo. The final model was created by extracting an isosurface at a user-selected offset.

Computational fluid dynamics analysts frequently employ structured grid data. We examined some strategies for exploring the scalar and vector fields. The computational grid created by the analyst serves as a starting point for analyzing the data. We displayed geometry extracted from the finite difference grid, scalar color mapping, and streamlines and streamtubes to investigate the data.

In the finite element case study, we looked at unstructured grids used in a simulation of a blow molding process. We displayed the deformation of the geometry using displacement plots, and represented the material thickness using color mapping. We saw how we can create simple animations by generating a sequence of images.

We concluded the case studies by visualizing the Towers of Hanoi algorithm. Here we showed how to combine the procedural power of C++ with the visualization capabilities in **vtk**. We saw how visualization often requires our creative resources to cast data structures and information into visual form.

13.9 Bibliographic Notes

The case studies presented in the chapter rely on having interesting data to visualize. Sometimes the hardest part of practicing visualizing is finding relevant data. The Internet is a tremendous resource for this task. Paul Gilster [Gilster94] has written an excellent introduction to many of the tools for accessing information on the Internet. There are many more books available on this subject in the local bookstore.

In the stock case study we used a programming tool called AWK to convert our data into a form suitable for **vtk**. More information on AWK can be found in *The AWK Programming Language* [Aho88]. Another popular text processing languages is Perl [Perl95].

If you would like to know more about information visualization you can start with the references listed here [Becker95] [Ding90] [Eick93] [Feiner88] [Johnson91] [Robertson91]. This is a relatively new field but will certainly grow in the near future.

13.10 References

[Aho88]
    A. V. Aho, B. W. Kernighan, and P. J. Weinberger. *The AWK Programming Language*. Addison-Wesley, Reading, MA, 1988.

[AhoHopUll83]
    A. V. Aho, J. E. Hopcroft, and J. D. Ullman. *Data Structures and Algorithms*. Addison-Wesley, Reading, MA, 1983.

[Becker95]
    R. A. Becker, S. G. Eick, and A. R. Wilks. "Visualizing Network Data." *IEEE Transactions on Visualization and Graphics*. 1(1):16–28,1995.

[deLorenzi93]
    H. G. deLorenzi and C. A. Taylor. "The Role of Process Parameters in Blow Molding and Correlation of 3-D Finite Element Analysis with Experiment." *International Polymer Processing*. 3(4):365–374, 1993.

[Ding90]
    C. Ding and P. Mateti. "A Framework for the Automated Drawing of Data Structure Diagrams." *IEEE Transactions on Software Engineering*. 16(5):543–557, May 1990.

[Eick93]
    S. G. Eick and G. J. Wills. "Navigating Large Networks with Hierarchies." In *Proceedings of Visualization '93*. pp. 204–210, IEEE Computer Society Press, Los Alamitos, CA, October 1993.

[Feiner88]
    S. Feiner. "Seeing the Forest for the Trees: Hierarchical Displays of Hypertext Structures." In *Conference on Office Information Systems*. Palo Alto, CA, 1988.

[Gilster94]
    P. Gilster. *Finding It on the Internet: The Essential Guide to Archie, Veronica, Gopher, WAIS, WWW (including Mosaic), and Other Search and Browsing Tools*. John Wiley & Sons, Inc., 1994.

[Johnson91]
    B. Johnson and B. Shneiderman. "Tree-Maps: A Space-Filling Approach to the Visualization of Hierarchical Information Structures." In *Proceedings of Visualization '91*. pp. 284–291, IEEE Computer Society Press, Los Alamitos, CA, October 1991.

[Perl95]
    D. Till. *Teach Yourself Perl in 21 Days*. Sams Publishing, Indianapolis, Indiana, 1995.

[Robertson91]
    G. G. Robertson, J. D. Mackinlay, and S. K. Card. "Cone Trees: Animated 3D Visualizations of Hierarchical Information." In *Proceedings of ACM CHI '91 Conference on Human Factors in Computing Systems*. pp. 189–194, 1991.

[Rogers86]
    S. E. Rogers, D. Kwak, and U. K. Kaul, "A Numerical Study of Three-Dimensional Incompressible Flow Around Multiple Post." in *Proceedings of AIAA Aerospace Sciences Conference*. vol. AIAA Paper 86-0353. Reno, Nevada, 1986.

13.11 Exercises

13.1 The medical example did nothing to transform the original data into a standard coordinate system. Many medical systems use RAS coordinates. R is right/left, A is anterior/posterior and S is Superior/Inferior. This is the

patient coordinate system. Discuss and compare the following alternatives for transforming volume data into RAS coordinates.
a) `vtkActor` transformation methods.
b) `vtkTransformFilter`.
c) Reader transformations.

13.2 Modify the last medical example (`medical3.cxx`) to use `vtkTexture` instead of `vtkStructuredPointsToGeometryFilter`. Compare the performance of using geometry with using texture. How does the performance change as the resolution of the volume data changes?

13.3 Change the medical case study to use dividing cubes for the skin surface.

13.4 Combine the two scripts `segmented8.tcl` and `marching8.tcl` into one script that will handle either segmented or grayscale files. What other parameters and pipeline components might be useful in general for this application?

13.5 Create polygonal / line stroked models of your initials and build your own logo. Experiment with different transformations.

13.6 Enhance the appearance of Towers of Hanoi visualization.
a) Texture map disks, base plane, and pegs.
b) Create disks with central holes.

13.7 Use the blow molding example as a starting point for the following.
a) Create an animation of the blow molding sequence. Is it possible to interpolate between time steps? How would you do this?
b) Create the second half of the parison using symmetry. What transformation matrix do you need to use?

13.8 Start with the stock visualization example presented in this chapter.
a) Modify the example code to use a ribbon filter and linear extrusion filter as described in the text. Be careful of the width of the generated ribbons.
b) Can you think of a way to present high/low trade values for each day?

Software Guide

*O*ur focus in this text has been visualization architecture, algorithms, and applications. We have avoided discussing lower-level software design and implementation details for the most part. Instead, we have included a C++ software library that we feel demonstrates important concepts in a simple, easily understood manner. If you are interested in using this software, we recommend that you read the first section "Software Conventions" in this appendix. If you plan on extending the software or are especially interested in understanding its internal organization, read the "Development Guide" as well.

A.1 Software Conventions

We adopted a number of conventions during the design and implementation of the *Visualization Toolkit*. We did this to make the software easy to understand and use. Hopefully, you will spend more time learning about visualization than the idiosyncrasies of our software. Understanding the following conventions is a good starting point towards this goal.

Naming Conventions

There are a number of simple naming conventions in **vtk**. Becoming familiar with these conventions will help you better understand and use the software library. In general, we use long, descriptive names for classes, instance variables, and methods. Each name begins with a capital letter, and separations between words are indicated by case change (e.g., NumberOfPoints). Specific conventions are as follows.

Class Names. Each class name begins with the prefix vtk. (The prefix prevents name clashes when mixing C++ libraries).

File Names. File names are the same as the name of the class they contain. We use the suffix .h for include files and .cxx for source files.

Data Member Names. We use long, descriptive names beginning with a capital letter and case change to indicate word separation. When referring to data members we use an explicit this-> pointer. We find that the resulting code is easier to understand and less confusing.

Automatic Variables. Automatic variables generally begin with a lowercase letter. Our major convention is to make the variable names descriptive.

#define. We use all uppercase with the underscore character separating words. All constants should start with "VTK_" prefix. If a constant will only be used and defined within one .cxx file, then you can name it whatever you want, although we still encourage you to use the "VTK_" prefix.

On-Line Documentation

We have provided a minimal, but complete, set of documentation for **vtk**. The documentation exists in at least three forms. First, all documentation is embedded directly in the source code. The include files (.h) contain the object synopsis and description as well as virtual and inline method descriptions. The source files (.cxx) contain additional method descriptions. Second, we have extracted this embedded information and reformatted it into HTML pages. You can view the source code directly to obtain information, or you can use an HTML browser. The latter part of this text (see "Object Synopsis" on page 564) contains this information formatted for your convenience. To use this information effectively, you will need to follow a few guidelines.

Documentation is inherited. Often, methods (especially virtual methods) are documented in a base class and not in its derived classes. Or some functionality may be present and documented in a base class, so the derived class inherits this as well.

Methods are documented once. Typically, there are two or more forms for a method; for example, SetColor(float,float,float) and SetColor(float *). Documentation is provided for only one of the methods, since the action performed is identical for both, even though the arguments are in different forms.

Standard or obvious methods are not documented. Constructors, destructors, standard methods (see following section), or obvious methods are not documented. Obvious methods are methods that are obvious from context and need no additional description.

Standard Methods

Objects in **vtk** use the same names for common methods. Becoming familiar with these methods will help you understand the source code. Some of these methods are only applicable when coding in C++ (e.g., the New() method is never called from an interpreted language such as Tcl.)

<class>::New(). This static class method is used to instantiate objects. We refer to this method as an "object factory" since it is used to create instances of a class. In **vtk**, every New() method should be paired with the Delete() method. (See "Achieving Device Independence" on page 66, and "Creating, Deleting, and Reference Counting Objects" on page 562).

<class pointer> *MakeObject(). This method is effectively a virtual constructor. That is, invoking this method causes an object to make a copy of itself and then return a pointer to the new object.

void Delete(). Use this method to delete a **vtk** object created with the New() or MakeObject() method. Depending upon the nature of the object being deleted, this may or may not actually delete the object. For example, reference-counting objects will only be deleted if their reference count goes to zero (see "Creating, Deleting, and Reference Counting Objects" on page 562).

void DebugOn()/DebugOff(). Turn debugging information on or off.

void Print(). Print out the object including superclass information.

char *GetClassName(). Return the name of the class.

void Modified(). This updates the internal modification time stamp for the object. This method should be called whenever the object has been modified.

unsigned long GetMTime(). Return the last modification time of an object. The value is guaranteed to be unique and monotonically increasing.

Standard Array Methods

Additional standard methods exist for objects that manage memory. These methods are not common for all objects but are common to objects that allocate and delete memory. The majority of these objects can be thought of (and are often implemented as) arrays. Thus access is via an "id" or nonnegative integer number.

`int Allocate()`. Obtain memory via the `new` operator. If the object has allocated memory previously, the memory is extended only as necessary to obtain the allocation request. If memory allocation fails, a `0` is returned.

`void Initialize()`. Cause an object to release any memory acquired during previous allocation requests. The object is not deleted.

`void Reset()`. Memory acquired from previous allocation requests is retained and reused. The object's old data is overwritten.

`void Insert___(int id, data)`. This method is used to insert data into an object at location `id` (here the "___" is a place holder for a name like points, scalars, vectors, values, etc.). Memory allocation is performed as necessary, and the number of data items in the object is updated.

`int InsertNext___(data)`. This method also inserts data into an object, but at the end of the array. The location in the array is returned where the data is placed.

`void SetNumberOf___(int n)`. Use this method to simultaneously set the number of items in an array and allocate memory for the data. This method is usually followed by the `Set___()` method.

`void Set___(int id, data)`. Similar to the `Insert___()` and `InsertNext___()` methods, this method places data into the object at location `id`. The difference is that this method does not allocate memory or perform range checking. It's faster, but a more dangerous operation. One of the methods `SetNumberOf___()` or `WritePointer()` should always be called prior to using the `Set___()` method.

`<data type> Get___(int id)`. Return the data value (of appropriate type) at location `id`.

`<data *> WritePointer(int id, int n)`. This special method allows you to obtain a pointer inside the data object, and then directly manipulate the pointer for both memory read and write operations. It returns a pointer to data at location `id`, and allocates memory to write n data values. Use this method only when maximum performance is required, since it is a violation of object encapsulation.

`<data *> GetPointer(int id)`. Return a pointer at data location `id`.

Visualization Toolkit Macros

The *Visualization Toolkit* uses a number of `#define` macros (found in the file `vtkSetGet.h`). These macros greatly simplify programming tasks and enforce uniform object behavior. Their uses include setting and getting instance variables including proper treatment of modified time and reference counting, and provide simple output for debugging, warnings, and error conditions.

Many macros are used to create standard object methods. To properly understand the `.h` files you will need to know how these macros expand. A summary of these macros, with examples, follows.

vtkSetMacro(Name,Type) is used to set the value of instance variables. The macro expands into the method: void SetName(Type). For example, vtkSetMacro(Scale,float) expands to void SetScale(float).

vtkGetMacro(Name,Type) is used to get the value of an instance variable. The macro expands into the method: Type GetName(). For example, vtkGetMacro(Scale,float) expands to float GetScale().

vtkBooleanMacro(Name,Type) is used to create convenience methods for boolean (i.e., true/false or 1/0) instance variables. The macro expands into the two methods: void NameOn() and void NameOff(). For example, vtkBooleanMacro(Visibility, float) expands into void VisibilityOn() and void VisibilityOff().

vtkSetStringMacro(Name) is used to set the value of a character string instance variable. The macro expands into the method void SetName(char *). For example, vtkSetStringMacro(Filename) expands into void SetFilename(char *).

vtkGetStringMacro(Name) is used to get the value of a character string instance variable. The macro expands into the method char *GetName(). For example, vtkGetStringMacro(Filename) expands into char *GetFilename().

vtkSetObjectMacro(Name,Type) is used to set instance variables that are pointers to other objects (i.e., an association). The macro expands into the two methods void SetName(Type *) and void SetName(Type &). For example, vtkSetObjectMacro(Transform,vtkTransform) expands into void SetTransform(vtkTransform *) and void SetTransform(vtkTransform &).

vtkGetObjectMacro(Name,Type) is used to get instance variables that are pointers to other objects. The macro expands into the method Type *GetName(). For example, vtkGetObjectMacro(Transform,vtkTransform) expands into vtkTransform *GetTransform().

vtkSetReferenceCountedObject(Name,Type) is used to set instance variables that are pointers to reference counted objects. (The use of a reference counted object may need to be Registered() or UnRegistered(), as appropriate.) The macro expands into the two methods void SetName(Type *) and void SetName(Type &). For example,
vtkSetReferenceCountedObjectMacro(Points,vtkPoints) expands into void SetPoints(vtkPoints *) and void SetPoints(vtkPoints &).

`vtkSetVector2Macro(Name,Type)` is used to set instance variables that are arrays of length `[2]`. The macro expands into the two methods `void SetName(Type,Type)` and `void SetName(Type array[2])`. For example, `vtkSetVector2Macro(HueRange, float)` expands into `void SetHueRange(float,float)` and `void SetHueRange(float array[2])`.

`vtkSetVector3Macro(Name,Type)` is used to set instance variables that are arrays of length `[3]`. The macro expands into the two methods `void SetName(Type, Type, Type)` and `void SetName(Type array[3])`. For example, `vtkSetVector3Macro(Color,float)` expands into `void SetColor(float,float,float)` and `void SetColor(float array[3])`.

`vtkSetVector4Macro(Name,Type)` is used to set instance variables that are arrays of length `[4]`. The macro expands into the two methods `void SetName(Type, Type, Type, Type)` and `void SetName(Type array[4])`. For example, `vtkSetVector4Macro(WorldPoint,float)` expands into `void SetWorldPoint(float,float,float,float)` and `void SetWorldPoint(float array[4])`.

`vtkSetVectorMacro(Name,Type,Count)` is used to set instance variables that are arrays. The macro expands into the method `void SetName(Type data[Count])`. For example, `vtkSetVector(Bounds,float,6)` expands into `void SetBounds(float data[6])`.

`vtkGetVectorMacro(Name,Type,Count)` is used to get an array of data. The macro expands into the two methods `Type *GetName()` and `void GetName(Type data[Count])`. (The first macro returns a pointer to the data, the second copies the data into user-provided array.) For example, `vtkGetVector(Color,float,3)` expands into `float *GetColor()` and `void GetColor(float data[3])`.

`vtkDebugMacro(msg)` is used to print out debugging messages. (Debugging messages are printed when the `Debug` instance variable is true, otherwise no messages appear.) The `msg` parameter is a text string that includes the `iostream` operator `<<`. For example, `vtkDebugMacro(<<"S="<<s)` expands into (in a nutshell) `cerr << "Debug: (some info)" << "S=" << s << "\n"`.

`vtkWarningMacro(msg)` is used to print out warning messages. (Warning messages are informational in nature — the system behaves normally but an unusual situation has been encountered.) The `msg` parameter is a text string that includes the `iostream` operator `<<`. For example `vtkWarningMacro(<<"S="<<s)` expands into (in a nutshell) `cerr << Warning: (some info)" << "S=" << s << "\n"`.

`vtkErrorMacro(msg)` is used to print out error messages. (Error messages indicate that a significant problem has been encountered.) The `msg` parameter is a text string that includes the `iostream` operator `<<`. For example `vtkWarningMacro(<<"S="<<s)` expands into (in a nutshell) `cerr << ERROR: (some info)" << "S=" << s << "\n"`.

`vtkGenericWarningMacro(msg)` is used to print out warnings or error messages in code without a local `instance` pointer. For example, non-method or templated functions have no `instance` pointer. The `msg` parameter is a text string that may include the `iostream` operator `<<`. For example `vtkGenericWarningMacro (<<"S="<<s)` expands into (in a nutshell) `cerr << Generic Warning: (some info)" << "S=" << s << "\n"`

Modal Variables and Methods

Some instance variables are often *modal*. By this we mean that they represent one of a finite number of states. The simplest modal variable is a boolean variable (e.g., visibility and associated methods `VisibilityOn()` and `VisibilityOff()`). We saw in the previous section how to manage these variables using the boolean macros to create the "On" and "Off" style methods. This approach works well for boolean variables, but if the variable can take on more than two values (i.e., 0 and 1), then the approach breaks down.

For these modal variables we use a special form of the `Set` method. The usual form of the `Set` method takes an instance variable name and at least one other parameter defining the value of the instance variable. For example, in C++

```
aProperty->SetColor(r, g, b);
```

For modal variables, we use the form `Set_name_To_value` with no arguments. Some examples include

```
SetDataByteOrderToBigEndian()
SetRepresentationToWireframe()
SetInterpolationToGouraud()
SetIntegrationDirectionToForward()
```

Pointers, References, and Copying

The object-oriented paradigm encapsulates data and procedures into objects. One implication of this is that access into the internal data representation of an object is not allowed. Thus, the proper way to obtain information from an object is to copy information from the object into an accessible memory location.

From a software development point of view, this results in robust, safe systems. Unfortunately, copying data can be unacceptably inefficient. For example, if an object contains 1,000,000 `float` values, copying this data results in both computational and memory overhead.

In **vtk** we address this dilemma by offering a choice. Most every data access method comes in a pair. The first returns either a pointer or reference to an object or memory location; the second copies data into user provided memory, or offers a copy constructor or equivalent method to copy an object. Typical examples are shown in Figure **A–1**.

As a user you may choose to copy or reference data. Bear in mind this cautionary note: *Pointers and references often refer to dynamic data, that is, data that may be deleted or may change during program execution.* We guarantee that data referred to by a pointer or reference will not change as long as another **vtk** method is not executed. Use pointers and references quickly, and for reasons of efficiency. Otherwise, use the safer object-oriented approach and copy the data.

If you do decide to copy data, make sure that you free all memory. Automatic variables will be freed when scope is exited, but objects created with the `MakeObject()` or `new` methods must be deleted by you (using the `Delete()` method).

Creating, Deleting, and Reference Counting Objects

Objects in **vtk** are not created and deleted using the C++ methods `new` and `delete`. Instead, we use the static class method `New()` to instantiate an object, and the instance method `Delete()` to delete an object. For example, to create an instance of an actor (in C++) we would use:

```
vtkActor *actor = vtkActor::New();
```

Return Reference or Pointer

```
float *GetColor();
float *x= this->GetPoint(id);
vtkIdList *l= cell->GetPointIds();
vtkCell *c = this->GetCell(id);
```

Copy Data

```
float c[3]; void GetColor(c[3]);
float x[3]; this->GetPoint(id,x[3]);
vtkIdList l = *(cell->GetPointIds());
vtkCell *c = this->GetCell(id)->MakeObject();
```

Figure A–1 Example methods to access data by pointer or reference; or to copy data.

and then to delete the instance

```
actor->Delete()
```

(In Tcl we would use `vtkActor actor` to create the object, and `actor Delete` to delete it.)

We call the static class method `New()` an *object factory* because it is used to create instances of objects. Although the `New()` method appears to return a pointer to an object of declared type, in practice we can return an object of declared type or one of its *subclasses*. In the above example on an OpenGL system, the `New()` method actually returns a pointer to an object of type `vtk-OpenGLActor`. This is how we can create device independent applications using **vtk**. (Note: in this example, the system creates the appropriate object type by querying the environment variable `VTK_RENDERER`, or by choosing the default renderer if the environment variable is not set. Allowable values of `VTK_RENDERER` are OpenGL, GL (on SGI), Starbase (on HPs), and XGL (on Sun computers).)

The power of object factories goes beyond achieving graphics device independence. Using this same technique we could easily create subclasses of algorithms that would adapt to the type of hardware that they execute on. For example, the `vtkImageFFT` imaging filter could be used as a base class to derive a hardware accelerated Fast Fourier Transform object (call the derived class `vtkImageHardwareFFT`). Then, when the `vtkImageFFT::New()` method was invoked on systems supporting FFT in hardware, an instance of `vtkImage-HardwareFFT` would be created and returned. On other systems, the software implementation (i.e., `vtkImageFFT` object) would be returned.

Another related concept to object creating and deletion is *reference counting*. Reference counted objects are objects that keep track of the number of other objects that refer to them. These objects exist as long as they are referred to by other objects. Once their reference count goes to zero, they will self-destruct. This behavior has important implications if you are planning to do heavy-duty development programming using **vtk**.

Reference counting is implemented as follows. Every reference counted object (call it O for convenience) when constructed (using `New()`) has a reference count of 1. When O is used by another object (call it U), the using object registers its use of O by executing O's `Register()` method. This bumps O's reference count to 2. When U no longer uses (or references) O it executes O's `UnRegister()` method. Thus the reference count is decremented to a value of 1. At this point a call to O's `Delete()` method will reduce the reference count to 0 and O will destruct.

From the previous discussion we can create two simple rules for creating reference counted objects. First, for every `New()` method there must be a matching `Delete()` method. And second, for every `Register()` method there must be a matching `UnRegister()` method. If these rules are observed, you will avoid memory leaks and memory corruption problems. (The only exception to this rule is when objects are created using the `MakeObject()` method. In this case there should still be a matching `Delete()` method.)

In filter implementations these rules result in code that can appear misleading at first glance. A snippet of code is shown in the following.

```
points = vtkFloatPoints::New();
...//filter does its thing
output->SetPoints(points);
points->Delete();
```

In this example `points` (a reference counted object) is created with the `New()` method and then associated with the filter output using the `SetPoints()` method. Then the `points` are deleted with the `Delete()` method. Although it might appear that points has been deleted, in actuality the `SetOutput()` registers the use of `points` by the `output` object. Hence the `Delete()` method does not destroy `points`; instead, it simply decrements the reference count.

This scheme works well except for one situation: creating automatic variables that are reference counted objects. In this case the object is created with a reference count of one. Then, when scope is exited, the object is automatically deleted by the compiler. This results in warnings from **vtk**, since a reference counted object with a nonzero reference count is being deleted. To remedy this situation you can use the method `ReferenceCountingOff()` as follows.

```
{
  vtkFloatPoints pts;
  pts.ReferenceCountingOff();
  ...//other stuff
} //scope is exited and pts deleted automatically
```

We strongly discourage you from instantiating **vtk** objects as automatic variables. Memory leaks and dangling pointers are the likely outcome, and this capability may not be supported in future versions of **vtk**.

A.2 Object Synopsis

The following is an alphabetical list of the classes in the *Visualization Toolkit*. Each list item consists of the class name and a brief synopsis of its functionality. We have grouped objects in the synopsis according to functionality. These functional groups are as follows.

- *Foundation.* Foundation objects supply basic functionality for other objects throughout the *Visualization Toolkit*. These objects often serve as base classes (e.g., vtkObject), as computational classes (e.g., vtkMath), or provide fundamental data representation capability (e.g., vtkFloatArray).
- *Cells.* Cells are the fundamental abstraction of visualization data. Datasets are composed of collections of various types of cells. The object vtkCell

specifies an abstract interface for all cells.

- *Datasets.* Dataset objects are the fundamental visualization data types. These objects are input to and output from sources, filters, and mappers. The abstract object `vtkDataSet` specifies an interface that all derived classes must provide.

- *Pipeline.* Pipeline objects include reference counted objects and abstract classes for the visualization network architecture. Reference counted objects do the dirty work of representing cells and datasets. They are used in the visualization pipeline and are frequently passed from one object to the next during network execution. The abstract classes enforce network topology via type checking, and provide various methods to manipulate visualization classes.

- *Sources.* Source objects initialize visualization networks. Source objects have no other objects as input, and frequently read from external data files (i.e., readers) or create data from instance variables (i.e., procedural objects). Source objects create one or more datasets on output. (See *Readers/Writers/ Importers / Exporters.*)

- *Filters.* Filter objects have at least one input dataset and generate one or more datasets on output. The compiler enforces the way filters can be connected together. That is, the `SetInput()` method controls which types of objects can be input. The output of a filter is determined by the type returned from its `GetOutput()` (or equivalent) method.

- *Mappers.* Mappers terminate the visualization network. Mapper objects take one or more input objects. Writers are mapper objects that write data to a file. Device mappers are objects that map visualization data to a particular display device or graphics library. (See *Readers/Writers/ Importers / Exporters.*)

- *Readers/Writers/ Importers / Exporters.* Readers and writers are special types of sources and mappers that read or write data to and from files. Importers read from a file as well, but an entire scene (i.e., lights, cameras, renderers, actors, etc.) is defined rather than just visualization data. Similarly, exporters write files that define an entire scene.

- *Graphics.* Graphics objects provide the core rendering functionality. These allow manipulation of lights, cameras, and actors, as well as various actor properties and rendering attributes (e.g., renderer background color). Graphics also includes classes to support volume rendering.

- *Volume Rendering.* While volume rendering can be considered part of the graphics classes, we've broken it out here so you can see the basic architecture. The volume classes are similar to the graphics classes, the major difference being that the rendering is implemented in software, and does not depend on any graphics library.

- *Imaging.* Imaging objects are special filters that treat structured points datasets (i.e., images in 2D and volumes in 3D). The imaging classes also contain viewers and other tools for viewing and manipulating images.

- *OpenGL Renderer.* There are a variety of renderers supported by the *Visualization Toolkit.* A representative renderer is OpenGL. The description of objects in other rendering libraries is the same as for the objects in openGL.

- *Tcl/Tk.* Glue classes provided to enhance interfacing to Tcl/Tk graphical user interfaces.

- *Window-System Specific.* Certain objects are specific to a particular window system (i.e., X Window System or Windows). These objects capture user events such as key press and mouse motion.

Foundation

vtkActorCollection — a list of actors

vtkBitArray — dynamic, self-adjusting array of bits

vtkByteSwap — perform machine dependent byte swapping

vtkCellArray — object represents cell connectivity

vtkCellLinks — object represents upward pointers from points to list of cells using each point

vtkCellTypes — object provides direct access to cells in vtkCellArray and type information

vtkCharArray — dynamic, self-adjusting character array

vtkCollection — create and manipulate unsorted lists of objects

vtkContourValues — helper object to manage setting and generating contour values

vtkDataSetCollection — maintain an unordered list of dataset objects

vtkDoubleArray — dynamic, self-adjusting double-precision array

vtkEdgeTable — keep track of edges (edge is pair of integer ids)'

vtkFloatArray — dynamic, self-adjusting floating-point array

vtkIdList — list of point or cell ids

vtkImplicitFunctionCollection — maintains a list of implicit functions

vtkIndent — a simple class to control print indentation

vtkIntArray — dynamic, self-adjusting integer array

vtkLightCollection — a list of lights

vtkMath — performs common math operations

vtkMatrix4x4 — represents and manipulates 4x4 transformation matrices

vtkMultiThreader.h — A class for performing multithreaded execution

vtkObject — abstract base class for most of the vtk objects

vtkPiecewiseFunction — Defines a 1D piecewise function.

vtkPolyDataCollection — maintain a list of polygonal data objects

vtkPriorityQueue — an list of ids arranged in priority order

vtkReferenceCount — subclasses of this object are reference counted vtkRenderWindowCollection — a list of RenderWindows

vtkRendererCollection — a list of renderers

SetGet — standard macros for setting/getting instance variables

vtkShortArray — dynamic, self-adjusting short integer array

vtkStack — create and manipulate lists of objects

vtkStructuredPointsCollection — maintains a list of structured points data objects

vtkTimeStamp — record modification and/or execution time

vtkTimerLog — Timer support and logging

vtkTransformCollection — maintain a list of transforms

vtkUnsignedCharArray — dynamic, self-adjusting unsigned character array

vtkUnsignedShortArray — dynamic, self-adjusting unsigned short integer array

vtkVoidArray — dynamic, self-adjusting array of void* pointers

vtkVolumeCollection — a list of new volumes

Cells

vtkCell — abstract class to specify cell behavior

vtkCellType — define types of cells

vtkEmptyCell — an empty cell used as a place-holder during processing

vtkLine — cell represents a 1D line

vtkPixel — a cell that represents an orthogonal quadrilateral

vtkHexahedron — a cell that represents a 3D rectangular hexahedron

vtkPolyLine — cell represents a set of 1D lines

vtkPolyVertex — cell represents a set of 0D vertices

vtkPolygon — a cell that represents an n-sided polygon

vtkQuad — a cell that represents a 2D quadrilateral

vtkTetra — a 3D cell that represents a tetrahedron

vtkTriangle — a cell that represents a triangle

vtkTriangleStrip — a cell that represents a triangle strip

vtkVertex — a cell that represents a 3D point

vtkVoxel — a cell that represents a 3D orthogonal parallelepiped

Datasets

vtkDataSet — abstract class to specify dataset behavior

vtkPointData — represents and manipulates point attribute data

vtkPointSet — abstract class for specifying dataset behavior

vtkPolyData — concrete dataset represents vertices, lines, polygons, and triangle strips

vtkRectilinearGrid — a datset that is topologically regular with variable spacing in the three coordinate directions

vtkStructuredData — abstract class for topologically regular data

vtkStructuredGrid — topologically regular array of data

vtkStructuredPoints — topologically and geometrically regular array of data

vtkUnstructuredGrid — dataset represents arbitrary combinations of all possible cell types

General Pipeline

vtkAGraymap — scalar data in intensity + alpha (grayscale + opacity) form

vtkAPixmap — scalar data in rgba (color + opacity) form

vtkBitScalars — packed bit (0/1) representation of scalar data

vtkBitmap — scalar data in bitmap form

vtkCastToConcrete — works around type-checking limitations

vtkCellLocator — octree-based spatial search object to quickly locate cells

vtkCellPicker — select a cell by shooting a ray into graphics window

vtkColorScalars — abstract class represents scalar data in color specification

vtkCone — implicit function for a cone

vtkCylinder — implicit function for a cylinder

vtkDataSetFilter — filter that takes vtkDataSet as input

vtkDataSetToDataSetFilter — abstract filter class

vtkDataSetToPolyDataFilter — abstract filter class

vtkDataSetToStructuredGridFilter — abstract filter class

vtkDataSetToStructuredPointsFilter — abstract filter class

vtkDataSetToUnstructuredGridFilter — abstract filter class

vtkFilter — abstract class for specifying filter behavior

vtkFloatNormals — floating-point representation of 3D normals

vtkFloatPoints — floating-point representation of 3D points

vtkFloatScalars — floating-point representation of scalar data

vtkFloatTCoords — floating-point representation of texture coordinates

vtkFloatTensors — floating-point representation of tensor data

vtkFloatVectors — floating-point representation of 3D vectors

vtkGraymap — scalar data in grayscale form

vtkImplicitBoolean — implicit function consisting of boolean combinations of implicit functions

vtkImplicitDataSet — treat a dataset as if it were an implicit function

vtkImplicitFunction — abstract interface for implicit functions

vtkImplicitVolume — treat a volume as if it were an implicit function

vtkImplicitWindowFunction — implicit function maps another implicit function to lie within a specified range vtkIntPoints — integer representation of 3D points

vtkIntScalars — integer representation of scalar data

vtkLocator — abstract base class for objects that accelerate spatial searches

vtkLogLookupTable — map scalar values into colors using logarithmic (base 10) color table

vtkLookupTable — map scalar values into colors or colors to scalars; generate color table

vtkNormals — abstract interface to 3D normals

vtkPixmap — scalar data in RGB (color) form

vtkPlane — performs various plane computations

vtkPlanes — implicit function for convex set of planes

vtkPointLoad — computes stress tensors given point load on semiinfinite domain

vtkPointLocator — quickly locates points in 3-space

vtkPointSetFilter — filter that takes vtkPointSet as input

vtkPointSetToPointSetFilter — abstract filter class

vtkPolyDataConnectivityFilter — extract polygonal data based on geometric connectivity

vtkPolyDataFilter — filter that takes vtkPolyData as input

vtkPolyDataToPolyDataFilter — abstract filter class

vtkPoints — abstract interface to 3D points

vtkQuadric — evaluates implicit quadric function

vtkRectilinearGridFilter — filter that takes vtkRectilinearGrid as input

vtkRectilinearGridToPolyDataFilter — abstract filter class

vtkScalarTree — organizes data according to scalar values (used to accelerate contouring operations)

vtkScalars — abstract interface to array of scalar data

vtkShortScalars — short integer representation of scalar data

vtkSphere — implicit function for a sphere

vtkSphereTree — generates sphere tree to approximate a polygonal model.

vtkStructuredGridFilter — filter that takes vtkStructuredGrid as input

vtkStructuredGridToPolyDataFilter — abstract filter class

vtkStructuredPointsToStructuredPointsFilter — abstract filter class

vtkStructuredPointsFilter — filter that takes vtkStructuredPoints as input

vtkStructuredPointsToImage — Converts structured points to an image.

vtkStructuredPointsToPolyDataFilter — abstract filter class

vtkStructuredPointsToStructuredPointsFilter — abstract filter class

vtkTCoords — abstract interface to texture coordinates

vtkTensor — supporting class to enable assignment and referencing of tensors

vtkTensors — abstract interface to tensors

vtkTransform — a general matrix transformation class

vtkUnsignedCharScalars — unsigned char representation of scalar data

vtkUnsignedShortScalars — unsigned short representation of scalar data

vtkUserDefined — interface to user-defined data

vtkVectors — abstract interface to 3D vectors

vtkWindowLevelLookupTable — maps scalar values into colors or colors to scalars; generate color table

Sources

vtkEarthSource — creates the continents of the Earth as a sphere

vtkConeSource — generates polygonal cone

vtkCubeSource — creates a polygonal representation of a cube

vtkCylinderSource — generatse a cylinder centered at origin

vtkDiskSource — creates a disk with hole in center

vtkLineSource — creatse a line defined by two end points

vtkOutlineSource — creates wireframe outline around bounding box

vtkPlaneSource — creates an array of quadrilaterals located in a plane

vtkPointSource — creates a random cloud of points

vtkPolyDataSource — abstract class whose subclasses generate polygonal data

vtkRectilinearGridSource — Abstract class whose subclasses generates rectilinear grid data

vtkRendererSource — take a rendered image into the pipeline

vtkSphereSource — create a sphere centered at the origin

vtkStructuredGridSource — abstract class whose subclasses generates structured grid data

vtkTextSource — creates polygonal text

vtkTexturedSphereSource — create a sphere centered at the origin

vtkUnstructuredGridSource — abstract class whose subclasses generate unstructured grid data

vtkSource — abstract class specifies interface for visualization network source (or objects that generate output data)

vtkStructuredPointsSource — abstract class whose subclasses generate structured points data

vtkVectorText — creates polygonal text

Filters

vtkAppendFilter — appends one or more datasets together into a single unstructured grid

vtkAppendPolyData — appends one or more polygonal datasets together

vtkAxes — create an x-y-z axes

vtkBooleanStructuredPoints — combine two or more structured point sets

vtkBooleanTexture — generate 2D texture map based on combinations of inside, outside, and on region boundary

vtkBrownianPoints — assign random vector to points

vtkCleanPolyData — merges duplicate points and remove degenerate primitives

vtkClipPolyData — clips polygonal data with user-specified implicit function

vtkConnectivityFilter — extracts data based on geometric connectivity

vtkContourFilter — generates isosurfaces/isolines from scalar values

vtkCursor3D — generates a 3D cursor representation

vtkCutter — cuts a `vtkDataSet` with user-specified implicit function

vtkDashedStreamLine — generates a constant-time dashed streamline in an arbitrary dataset

vtkDecimate — reduces the number of triangles in a mesh

vtkDecimatePro — reduces the number of triangles in a mesh

vtkDelaunay2D — creates 2D Delaunay triangulation of input points

vtkDelaunay3D — creates 3D Delaunay triangulation of input points

vtkDicer — divide a dataset into spatially aggregated pieces

vtkDividingCubes — creates points lying on isosurface

vtkEdgePoints — generates points on isosurface

vtkElevationFilter — generates scalars along a specified direction

vtkExtractEdges — extracts cell edges from any type of data

vtkExtractGeometry — extracts cells that lie either entirely inside or outside of a specified implicit function

vtkExtractGrid — selects a piece (e.g., volume of interest) and/or subsample structured grid dataset

vtkExtractTensorComponents — extracts parts of tensor and create a scalar, vector, normal, or texture coordinates.

vtkExtractUnstructuredGrid — extracts a subset of unstructured grid geometry

vtkExtractVOI — select a piece (e.g., volume of interest) and/or subsample structured points dataset

vtkExtractVectorComponents — extracts components of vector as separate scalars

vtkFeatureEdges — extracts boundary, nonmanifold, and/or sharp edges from polygonal data

vtkFeatureVertices — extracts boundary, nonmanifold, and/or sharp vertices from polygonal data (operates on line primitives)

vtkGaussianSplatter — splats points with Gaussian distribution

vtkGeometryFilter — extracts geometry from data (or convert data to polygonal type)

vtkGlyph3D — copies oriented and scaled glyph geometry to every input point

vtkHedgeHog — creates oriented lines from vector data

vtkHyperStreamline — generates hyperstreamline in arbitrary dataset

vtkImplicitModeller — computes distance from input geometry on structured point dataset

vtkImplicitTextureCoords — generates 1D, 2D, or 3D texture coordinates based on implicit function(s)

vtkLinearExtrusionFilter — sweeps polygonal data creating a "skirt" from free edges and lines, and lines from vertices

vtkLinkEdgels — links edgels together to form digital curves.

vtkLinkSurfels — links edgels together to form digital curves.

vtkMarchingCubes — generates isosurface(s) from volume

vtkMarchingSquares — generates isoline(s) from structured points set

vtkMaskPoints — selectively filter points

vtkMaskPolyData — samples subset of input polygonal data

vtkMergeFilter — extracts separate components of data from different datasets

vtkMergePoints — merges exactly coincident points

vtkNormalEncoder — encode volume gradients and gradient magnitudes, build shading table

vtkOBBTree — generates oriented bounding box (OBB) tree

vtkOutlineFilter — creates wireframe outline for arbitrary dataset

vtkPolyDataNormals — computes normals for polygonal mesh

vtkProbeFilter — samples data values at specified point locations

vtkRectilinearGridGeometryFilter — extracts geometry for a rectilinear grid

vtkRecursiveDividingCubes — creates points lying on isosurface (using recursive approach)

vtkReverseSense — reverses the ordering of polygonal cells and/or vertex normals

vtkRibbonFilter — creates oriented ribbons from lines defined in polygonal dataset

vtkRotationalExtrusionFilter — sweeps polygonal data creating "skirt" from free edges and lines, and lines from vertices

vtkSampleFunction — samples an implicit function over a structured point set

vtkShepardMethod — samples unstructured points onto structured points using the method of Shepard

vtkShrinkFilter — shrinks cells composing an arbitrary dataset

vtkShrinkPolyData — shrinks cells composing of dataset type `vtkPolyData`

vtkSliceCubes — generates isosurface(s) from volume four slices at a time

vtkSmoothPolyDataFilter — adjusts point positions using Laplacian smoothing

vtkSpatialRepresentationFilter — generates polygonal model of spatial search object (i.e., a vtkLocator)

vtkStreamLine — generates streamline in arbitrary dataset

vtkStreamPoints — generates points along streamer separated by constant time increment

vtkStreamer — abstract object implements integration of massless particle through vector field

vtkStripper — creates triangle strips and/or polylines

vtkStructuredGridGeometryFilter — extracts geometry for structured grid

vtkStructuredGridOutlineFilter — creates wireframe outline for structured grid

vtkStructuredPointsGeometryFilter — extracts geometry for structured points

vtkSubPixelPositionEdgels — adjusts edgel locations based on gradients.

vtkSweptSurface — given a path and input geometry generate an (implicit) representation of a swept surface

vtkTensorGlyph — scales and orients glyph according to tensor eigenvalues and eigenvectors

vtkTextureMapToBox — generates 3D texture coordinates by mapping points into bounding box

vtkTextureMapToCylinder — generates texture coordinates by mapping points to cylinder

vtkTextureMapToPlane — generates texture coordinates by mapping points to plane

vtkTextureMapToSphere — generates texture coordinates by mapping points to sphere

vtkThreshold — extracts cells where scalar value of every point in cell satisfies threshold criterion

vtkThresholdPoints — extracts points whose scalar value satisfies threshold criterion

vtkThresholdTextureCoords — computes 1D, 2D, or 3D texture coordinates based on scalar threshold

vtkTransformFilter — transform points and associated normals and vectors

vtkTransformPolyDataFilter — transform points and associated normals and vectors for polygonal dataset

vtkTransformTexture — transforms (scale, rotate, translate) texture coordinates

vtkTriangleFilter — creates triangle polygons from input polygons and triangle strips

vtkTriangularTCoords — 2D texture coordinates based for triangles.

vtkTriangularTexture — generates 2D triangular texture map

vtkTubeFilter — filter that generates tubes around lines

vtkUnstructuredGridFilter — filter that takes an unstructured grid as input

vtkVectorDot — generates scalars from dot product of vectors and normals (e.g., show displacement plot)

vtkVectorNorm — generates scalars from Euclidean norm of vectors

vtkVectorTopology — marks points where the vector field vanishes (singularities exist).

vtkVoxelModeller — converts an arbitrary dataset to a voxel representation

vtkWarpScalar — deforms geometry with scalar data

vtkWarpTo — deforms geometry by warping towards a point

vtkWarpVector — deforms geometry with vector data

Mappers

vtkMapper — abstract class specifies interface to map data to graphics primitives

vtkDataSetMapper — map vtkDataSet and derived classes to graphics primitives

vtkPolyDataMapper — map vtkPolyData to graphics primitives

Readers, Writers, Importers, Exporters

vtkBYUReader — read MOVIE.BYU polygon files

vtkCyberReader — read Cyberware laser digitizer files

vtkDataReader — helper class for objects that read vtk data files

vtkDataSetReader — class to read any type of vtk dataset

vtkMCubesReader — read binary marching cubes file

vtkPLOT3DReader — read PLOT3D data files

vtkPNMReader — read pnm (i.e., portable anymap) files

vtkPolyDataReader — read vtk polygonal data file

vtkRectilinearGridReader — read vtk rectilinear grid data file

vtkSLCReader — read an SLC volume file.

vtkSTLReader — read ASCII or binary stereo lithography files

vtkStructuredGridReader — read vtk structured grid data file

vtkStructuredPointsReader — read vtk structured points data file

vtkUGFacetReader — read EDS Unigraphics facet files

vtkUnstructuredGridReader — read vtk unstructured grid data file

vtkVolume16Reader — read 16 bit image files

vtkVolumeReader — read image files

vtkIVWriter — export polydata into OpenInventor 2.0 format.

vtkBYUWriter — write MOVIE.BYU files

vtkDataSetWriter — write any type of vtk dataset to file

vtkDataWriter — helper class for objects that write vtk data files

vtkMCubesReader — write binary marching cubes file

vtkPNMWriter — write out structured points as a PNM file

vtkPolyDataWriter — write vtk polygonal data

vtkRectilinearGridWriter — write vtk rectilinear grid data file

vtkSTLWriter — write stereo lithography files

vtkStructuredGridWriter — write vtk structured grid data file vtkStructuredPointsWriter — write vtk structured points data file

vtkTIFFWriter — write out structured points as a TIFF file

vtkUnstructuredGridWriter — write vtk unstructured grid data file

vtkWriter — abstract class to write data to file(s)

vtk3DSImporter — imports 3D Studio files.

vtkImporter — importer abstract class

vtkExporter — abstract class to write a scene to a file

vtkIVExporter — export a scene into OpenInventor 2.0 format.

vtkOBJExporter — export a scene into Wavefront format.

vtkRIBExporter — export a scene into RenderMan RIB format.

vtkVRMLExporter — export a scene into VRML 2.0 format.

Graphics

vtkActor — represents an object (geometry & properties) in a rendered scene

vtkAssembly — create hierarchies of actors

vtkAssemblyPaths — a list of lists of actors representing an assembly hierarchy

vtkCamera — a virtual camera for 3D rendering

vtkCardinalSpline — computes an interpolating spline using a cardinal basis

vtkFollower — a subclass of actor that always faces the camera

vtkKochanekSpline — computes an interpolating spline using a Kochanek basis.

vtkLODActor — an actor that supports multiple levels of detail

vtkLight — a virtual light for 3D rendering

vtkMFCInteractor — provide an event driven interface

vtkPicker — select an actor by shooting a ray into a graphics window

vtkPointPicker — select a point by shooting a ray into a graphics window

vtkProjectedPolyDataRayBounder — Bound a ray according to polydata

vtkProp — represents an object for placement in a rendered scene

vtkProperty — represent surface properties of a geometric object

vtkRIBProperty — Renderman (RIB) Property

vtkRenderWindow — create a window for renderers to draw into

vtkRenderWindowInteractor — provide event driven interface to rendering window

vtkRenderer — abstract specification for renderers

vtkSpline — spline abstract class

vtkTexture — handles properties associated with a texture map

vtkWorldPointPicker — find world x,y,z corresponding to display x,y,z

Volume Rendering

vtkColorTransferFunction — Defines a transfer function for mapping a property to an RGB color value.

vtkRayBounder — abstract class defines API for objects that bound ray-casting operations

vtkRayCaster — a helper object for the renderer that controls ray casting

vtkViewRays — provides view ray information for efficiently casting rays

vtkVolume — represents a volume (data & properties) in a rendered scene

vtkVolumeMapper — Abstract class for a volume mapper

vtkVolumeProperty — represents the common properties for rendering a volume.

vtkVolumeRayCastCompositeFunction — ray cast function for composite operation

vtkVolumeRayCastFunction — abstract class defines API for volume ray casting functions

vtkVolumeRayCastMapper — Abstract class for mappers that use depth buffer (PARC) algorithms

Imaging

vtkImageAnisotropicDiffusion2D — edge preserving smoothing

vtkImageAnisotropicDiffusion3D — edge preserving smoothing

vtkImageAppendComponents — collects components from two inputs into

vtkImageButterworthHighPass — frequency domain high pass

vtkImageButterworthLowPass — simple frequency domain band pass

vtkImageCache — caches are used by `vtkImageSource` (this is the output data type of an imaging filter)

vtkImageCanvasSource2D — paints on a canvas

vtkImageCast — cast the input type to match the output type

vtkImageClip — reduces the image extent of the input

vtkImageCompressRange — reduces range of positive pixel values

vtkImageConnector — helper class for image connectivity filters

vtkImageConstantPad — makes image larger by padding with constant

vtkImageContinuousDilate3D — dilate implemented as a minimum

vtkImageContinuousErode3D — erode implemented as a maximum

vtkImageConvolution1D — performs a 1D convolution

vtkImageCopy — make a copy of the data

vtkImageData — similar to structured points

vtkImageDecomposedFilter — contains multiple 1D filters

vtkImageDifference — compute differences between images

vtkImageDilateErode3D — dilates one value and erodes another

vtkImageDilateValue1D — dilates a value on one axis

vtkImageDistance — 2D image distance map

vtkImageDistance1D — one step of creating a distance map

vtkImageDivergence3D — scalar field from vector field

vtkImageDotProduct — dot product of two vector images

vtkImageDuotone — for printing Duotone color images

vtkImageElipsoidSource — create a binary image of a ellipsoid

vtkImageEuclideanToPolar — converts 2D Euclidean coordinates to polar coordinates

vtkImageExport — gets data out of the pipeline as generic memory

vtkImageExtractComponents — outputs a single component

vtkImageFFT — generates Fast Fourier Transform

vtkImageFFT1D — 1D Fast Fourier Transform

vtkImageFeatureAnd — connectivity with seeds in second image

vtkImageFileReader — reads images from a single binary file

vtkImageFilter — generic filter that has one input

vtkImageFlip — flip image along specified axes

vtkImageFourierCenter — shifts constant frequency to center for

vtkImageFourierCenter1D — shifts constant frequency to center for

vtkImageFourierFilter — superclass that implements complex numbers

vtkImageGaussianSmooth — smooths on a 3D plane

vtkImageGaussianSmooth1D — smooths on one axis

vtkImageGaussianSource — create an image with Gaussian pixel values

vtkImageGradient — computes the gradient vector

vtkImageGradientMagnitude — computes magnitude of the gradient

vtkImageHSVToRGB — converts HSV components to RGB

vtkImageHistogram — generates a histogram for an image

vtkImageHistogramEqualization — apply histogram equalization

vtkImageHybridMedian2D — median filter that preseverse lines and corners

vtkImageIdealHighPass — simple frequency domain band pass

vtkImageIdealLowPass — simple frequency domain band pass

vtkImageImport — feed generic memory into image pipeline

vtkImageInPlaceFilter — filter that operates in place

vtkImageIslandRemoval2D — removes small clusters in masks

vtkimageLaplacian — computes divergence of gradient

vtkImageLogic — applies Boolean operations such as and, or, xor, nand, nor, not

vtkImageMIPFilter — compues maximum intensity projections of pixel values

vtkImageMagnify — magnifies an image by integer values

vtkImageMagnify1D — magnifies an image along a single axis

vtkImageMagnitude — collapses components with magnitude function

vtkImageMarchingCubes — generate isosurface(s) from volume/images

vtkImageMask — combines a mask and an image

vtkImageMathematics — perform arithmetic operations on an image including add, subtract, multiply, divide, invert,

vtkImageMatte — adds a border to an image

vtkImageMean — smooths on a 3D plane

vtkImageMean1D — mean of a neighborhood

vtkImageMedian3D — replace each pixel with median value of surrounding pixels

vtkImageMedianFilter — abstract superclass for median filters

vtkImageMirrorPad — extra pixels are filled by mirror images

vtkImageMultipleInputFilter — generic filter that has n inputs

vtkImageSphereSource — create a binary image of a sphere

vtkImageNonMaximumSuppression — suppresses non-maximal gradient values

vtkImageOpenClose — perform opening or closing on an image

vtkImageOpenClose3D — performs opening or closing on a 3D image

vtkImagePadFilter — super class for filters that fill in extra pixels

vtkImagePermute — permutes axes of input

vtkImageRDuotone — reverse operation of duotone — combines two images

vtkImageRFFT — reverse Fast Fourier Transform

vtkImageRFFT1D — performs a 1D reverse fast Fourier transform

vtkImageRGBToHSV — converts RGB components to HSV

vtkImageRange3D — dilate implemented as a minimum

vtkImageReader — superclass of binary file readers

vtkImageRegion — piece of an image

vtkImageResample — resamples an image using linear interpolation

vtkImageResample1D — resamples an image (along one axis) using linear interpolation

vtkImageSeedConnectivity — seed connectivity with user-defined seeds

vtkImageSeriesReader — reads a series of 2D images

vtkImageShiftScale — upper threshold on pixel values

vtkImageShrink3D — subsamples an image

vtkImageSimpleCache — caches the last region generated

vtkImageSinusoidSource — create an image with sinusoidal pixel values

vtkImageSkeleton2D — skeleton of 2D images

vtkImageSobel2D — computes a vector field using Sobel functions

vtkImageSobel3D — computes a vector field using Sobel functions

vtkImageSource — source of data for pipeline

vtkImageSpatialFilter — filters that operate on pixel neighborhoods

vtkImageSubsample3D — subsamples an image with an integer stride

vtkImageThreshold — flexible threshold

vtkImageToStructuredPoints — interfaces image pipeline to **vtk** visualization pipeline

vtkImageTwoInputFilter — generic superclass for filter that have two inputs

vtkImageTwoOutputFilter — superclass of filters that have two outputs

vtkImageVariance3D — variance in a neighborhood

vtkImageViewer — display a 2D image

vtkImageWrapPad — makes an image larger by wrapping existing data

Tcl-Tk Specific

vtkTkImageViewerWidget — a Tk Widget for viewing **vtk** images

vtkTkRenderWidget — a Tk Widget for vtk 3D graphics/volume renderering

OpenGL Renderer

vtkOpenGLActor — OpenGL actor

vtkOpenGLCamera — OpenGL camera

vtkOpenGLLight — OpenGL light

vtkOpenGLPolyDataMapper — a `vtkPolyData` mapper for the OpenGL library

vtkOpenGLProperty — OpenGL property

vtkOpenGLRenderWindow — OpenGL rendering window

vtkOpenGLRenderer — OpenGL renderer

vtkOpenGLTexture — OpenGL texture map

Window System Specific

vtkImageXViewer — display a 2D image in an XWindow

vtkImageWin32Viewer — display a 2D image in an Win32Window

vtkWin32MappedInteractor — provide an event driven interface

vtkWin32OpenGLRenderWindow — OpenGL rendering window

vtkWin32RenderWindowInteractor — provide an event driven interface

vtkXRenderWindow — a rendering window for the X Window system

vtkXRenderWindowInteractor — an X event-driven interface for a render window

For additional information, such as object inheritance, see the object diagrams. More extensive documentation (including descriptions of methods and instance variables) is available from on-line documentation included on the CD-ROM. Note that this synopsis is not complete: Some objects are omitted for compactness. Most of the omitted objects are from graphics libraries (SGI GL and HP Starbase, for example).

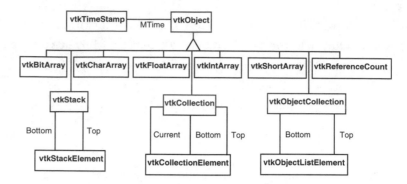

Figure A–2 Foundation object diagram.

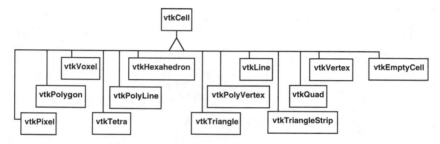

Figure A–3 Cell object diagram.

A.3 Object Diagrams

The following section contains abbreviated object diagrams using the OMT graphical language. The purpose of this section is to convey the essence of the software structure, particularly inheritance and object associations. Due to space limitation, not all objects are shown, particularly "leaf" (i.e., bottom of the inheritance tree) objects. Instead, we choose a single leaf object to represent other sibling objects. The organization of the objects follows that of the synopsis.

Foundation

The foundation object diagram is shown in Figure **A–2**. These represent the core data objects, as well as other object manipulation classes.

Cells

The cell object diagram is shown in Figure **A–3**. Currently, 12 types are supported in **vtk**.

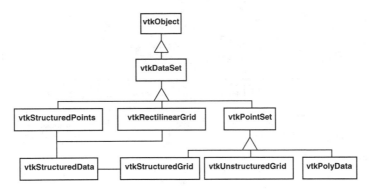

Figure A–4 Dataset object diagram.

Datasets

The dataset object diagram is shown in Figure **A–4**. Currently, four concrete dataset types are supported. Unstructured point data can be represented by any of the subclasses of vtkPointSet. Rectilinear grids are represented using vtk-StructuredGrid.

Pipeline

The pipeline object diagram is shown in Figure **A–5**. These are the core objects to represent data.

Sources

The source object diagram is shown in Figure **A–6**.

Filters

The filter object diagram is shown in Figure **A–7**.

Mappers

The mapper object diagram is shown in Figure **A–8**. There are basically two types: graphics mappers that map visualization data to the graphics system and writers that write data to output file (or other I/O device).

Graphics

The graphics object diagram is shown in Figure **A–9**. The diagram has been extended to include some associations with objects in the system. If you are unfa-

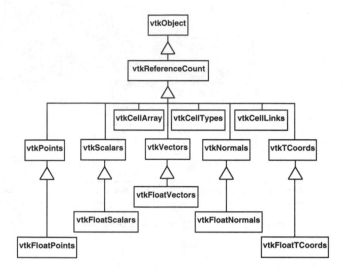

Figure A–5 Pipeline object diagram.

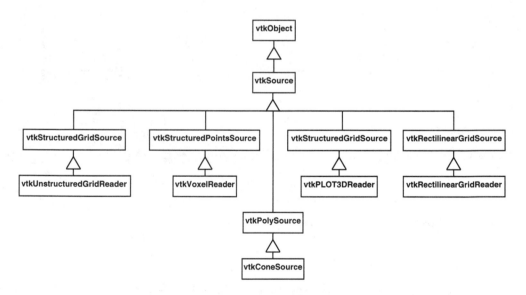

Figure A–6 Source object diagram.

miliar with the object-oriented graphics notation see Rumbaugh et al., *Object-Oriented Modeling and Design*. (Full reference in Chapter 2 reference section.)

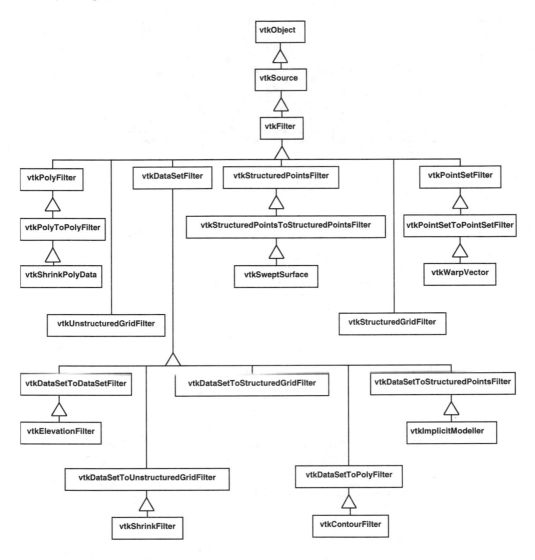

Figure A–7 Filter object diagram.

Volume Rendering

The volume rendering class hierarchy is shown in Figure **A–10**. Note that volume rendering and surface rendering are integrated together via the renderer. The renderer maintains a list of both actors and volumes and handles compositing the image.

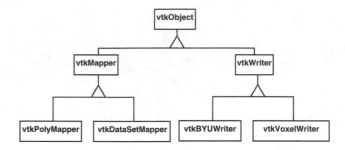

Figure A–8 Mapper object diagram.

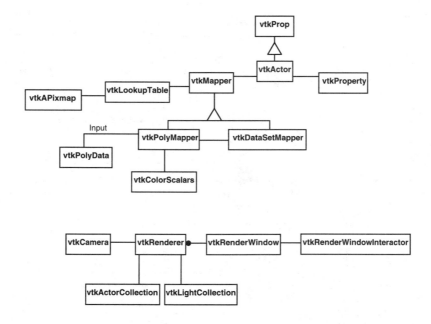

Figure A–9 Graphics object diagram.

Imaging

The imaging object diagram is shown in Figure **A–11**. Imaging integrates with the graphics pipeline via the structured points dataset. Also, it is possible to capture an image from the renderer via the vtkRendererSource object, and then feed the image into the imaging pipeline.

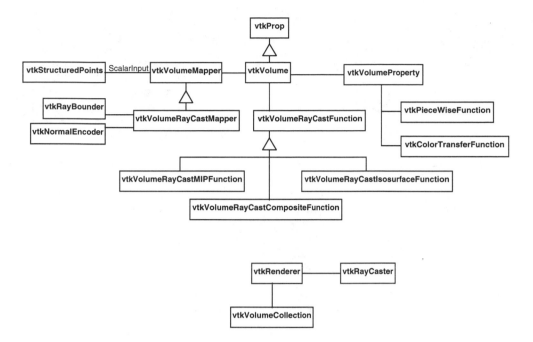

Figure A–10 Volume rendering object diagram.

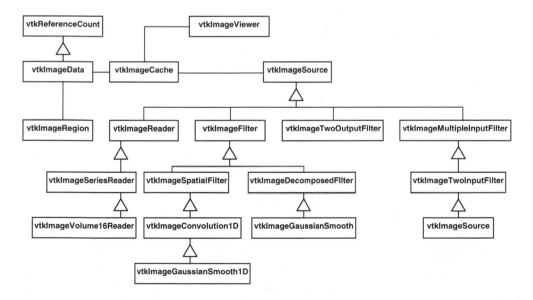

Figure A–11 Imaging object diagram.

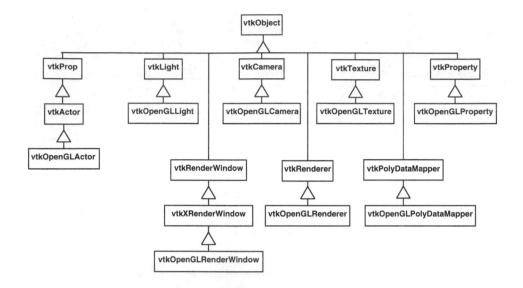

Figure A–12 OpenGL / graphics interface object diagram.

OpenGL Renderer

The OpenGL renderer object diagram is shown in Figure **A–12**. Note that there are other rendering libraries in **vtk**. The OpenGL object diagram is representative of these other libraries.

A.4 Development Guide

In this section we've included general tips for extending the *Visualization Toolkit* C++ class library.

Reference Counting

We saw in Chapter 4 how reference counting is used to conserve memory resources. To implement reference counting we derive a class from vtkReferenceCount. This object defines two methods: Register() and UnRegister(), and an instance variable ReferenceCount. The Register() method increments the reference count while the UnRegister() method decrements the count. When the reference count returns to zero, the object invokes its own destructor.

In order for the reference counting mechanism to work correctly, we have to create and assign a reference counted object properly. When a reference counted object is first created, *its count is initially one*. When the object is assigned to another object, its count is incremented by one. Of course, each additional object association bumps the reference count by one. The reference count is reduced as using objects are deleted or no longer use the reference counted object. Therefore, the correct procedure when dealing with reference counted objects is to create it with the `New()` method, assign it to another object or use it as necessary, and then free it with the `Delete()` method. Please refer to "Creating, Deleting, and Reference Counting Objects" on page 562 for more information on reference counting and example use of reference counted objects.

Modified Time

Correct execution of the visualization network requires tracking object modification times. In **vtk** an objects modification time is a unique, monotonically increasing unsigned integer. During network execution, modified times are compared between objects. If the input to a process object has been changed, or the object itself has been changed, then the process object must reexecute. In most cases tracking modified time is handled automatically via methods inherited from the objects superclass(es), or by using the standard **vtk** Set/Get macros. In some special cases you may have to understand the modified time mechanism to properly design and implement an object.

Every subclass of `vtkObject` inherits the standard `GetMTime()` method. This virtual method generally provides the proper default behavior. However, if an object A depends upon object B (i.e., B is either an instance variable or association), and B can be modified independently of A, then A must implement its own `GetMTime()` method. In this method both the modified times of A and B must be compared, and the larger value must be returned. Of course, if A depends upon more than one object, then a comparison is required between the modified time of each object.

A good example to look at is the filter `vtkTransformFilter`. This filter has a pointer to a `vtkTransform` object. Because the transform object can be modified independent of `vtkTransformFilter`, the filter must check both its own modified time as well as the transform object's modified time.

One special note. In the example above, B must not be a data flow input to A. The `GetMTime()` method must return the modified time of the local object, not of the network. Comparison between the local process object and its inputs is handled by the network update procedure (i.e., when invoking `Update()`).

Network Updates

The implicit execution technique implemented in **vtk** requires repeated network updates as process objects are modified or input datasets change. This process is implemented using two methods: `Execute()` and `Update()`. The `Update()` method compares object modification time with its input modified time, and if necessary, executes (via `Execute()`) the process object. In most cases this procedure is handled automatically by methods inherited from the object's superclasses. However, there are cases where you will have to understand the network update mechanism to properly implement a process object.

The Update() method must be overloaded if the object has more than one input, more than one output, or does not use the standard Input/Output instance variables. The basic procedure is to issue an Update() method to each input, and then compare modified times between the input objects and the filters execute time. If the modified time of any input object is greater than the local object's execute time, or the local object's modified time is greater than its execution time, then the local object must reexecute. In addition, the local process object may have released data to conserve memory. If this is so, then it must reexecute. See vtkFilter for an example of the network update procedure. You may also want to refer to "Multiple Input / Output" on page 103.

Deriving a New Source Object

Source objects initiate a visualization network. They read data from a file or communications device, or procedurally generate it. To create a new source object you must decide what kind of **vtk** specific data type to generate: vtkPolyData, vtkStructuredPoints, vtkUnstructuredGrid, or vtkStructuredGrid, or vtkRectilinearGrid. (Or, if none of these is suitable, you will have to define your own dataset type.)

Your new source object should be a subclass of vtkSource. For the data types currently in **vtk** there are convenience base classes available for subclassing: vtkPolyDataSource, vtkStructuredPointsSource, vtkStructuredGridSource, vtkUnstructuredGridSource, and vtkRectilinearGridSource. If you use these objects as base classes, you need only to create standard constructors, destructors, instance variable methods, and the single most important method: Execute(). Execute() is the method that is invoked during pipeline execution to generate output data. Good examples of source objects to study are vtkConeSource or vtkPlaneSource.

The body of the source object Execute() method generally consists of five major parts (refer to Figure **A–13**).

1. *Declaration.* Variables are declared, including the appropriate **vtk** types, pointers, and references. A pointer to the output of the source is declared and initialized using the GetOutput() method to perform any typecasting.

2. *Initialization.* In this step we insure the validity and consistency of the input. We may also include debugging information since it provides feedback to users about entry into the filter and other important statistics.

3. *Allocation.* Visualization data is allocated using the object factory New() method. (See "Creating, Deleting, and Reference Counting Objects" on page 562 for more information.)

4. *Body.* The body of the algorithm follows. Data values are created as appropriate.

5. *Output.* The visualization objects allocated in step 3 are set as output. This includes any geometry, topology, and point attributes objects. You may wish

to provide debugging output such as summarizing results to the user. Also any objects you've created with the `new` operator should be deleted with the `Delete()` operator as necessary.

The details of each step will vary depending upon the particular data type.

Deriving a New Filter Object

Filter objects transform input data into output data. The key to deriving a new filter object is to identify the type of input and output data. The data types you choose depend upon the desired level of generality and performance.

The more general a filter is, the larger the number of dataset types it can process. The advantage of general filters is that if a new type of data is created, a general filter can immediately accommodate it. For example, filters that input `vtkDataSet` can process any new or existing type of data, since every data type is a subclass of `vtkDataSet`. General filters are typically not as efficient as filters written with a particular data form in mind. We saw an example of this in Figure **6–38**. You will have to decide what the cost of generality means to your application.

You also may wish to create filters based on the inherent type of the data. The filter `vtkStructuredGridGeometryFilter` is used to extract geometry from topologically regular grids expressed via a local *i-j-k* coordinate system. Such a filter makes sense only in the context of structured data. Since it is impossible to extract unstructured geometry or polygonal geometry using a *i-j-k* indexing scheme, the filter is not applicable to those data types.

Care must also be used when selecting the output form of a filter. Usually the filtering algorithm dictates the output data type, but if you have a choice we encourage you to choose the most general form. A more general output form means that your filter can be connected to a greater number of other filters.

Once you have decided upon your input and output data types, you can implement your filter. A number of special classes exist for you to derive your filter from. These classes combine the instance variable `Input` and `Output` and the methods `GetOutput()` and `SetInput()` into a single class. Examples include the following.

> `vtkDataSetToDataSetFilter`. Given an input dataset, generate an output dataset. The most general of all filters.

> `vtkDataSetToPolyDataFilter`. Given an input dataset, generate polygonal data on output.

> `vtkDataSetToStructuredPointsFilter`. Given an input dataset, generate structured points on output.

> `vtkDataSetToStructuredGridFilter`. Given an input dataset, generate a structured grid on output.

> `vtkDataSetToUnstructuredGridFilter`. Given an input dataset, generate unstructured grid data on output.

```
void vtkLineSource::Execute()
{
  int numLines=this->Resolution;
  int numPts=this->Resolution+1;
  float x[3], tc[2], v[3];
  int i, j;   .
  int pts[2];
  vtkFloatPoints *newPoints;
  vtkFloatTCoords *newTCoords;
  vtkCellArray *newLines;
  vtkPolyData *output = this->GetOutput();
```

                    Declaration

```
  vtkDebugMacro(<<"Creating line");
  newPoints = vtkFloatPoints::New();
  newPoints->Allocate(numPts);
  newTCoords = vtkFloatTCoords::New();
  newTCoords->Allocate(numPts,2);
  newLines = vtkCellArray::New();
  newLines->Allocate(newLines->EstimateSize(numLines,2));
```

Initialization

Allocate

```
  // Generate points and texture coordinates
  for (i=0; i<3; i++) v[i]= this->Point2[i]-this->Point1[i];
  tc[1] = 0.0;
  for (i=0; i<numPts; i++)
    {
    tc[0] = ((float)i/this->Resolution);
    for (j=0; j<3; j++) x[j] = this->Point1[j] + tc[0]*v[j];
    newPoints->InsertPoint(i,x);
    newTCoords->InsertTCoord(i,tc);
    }

  //  Generate lines
  for (i=0; i < numLines; i++)
    {
    pts[0] = i;
    pts[1] = i+1;
    newLines->InsertNextCell(2,pts);
    }
```

Body

```
  // Update ourselves and release memory
  output->SetPoints(newPoints);
  newPoints->Delete();
  output->GetPointData()->SetTCoords(newTCoords);
  newTCoords->Delete();
  output->SetLines(newLines);
  newLines->Delete();
```

Output

Figure A–13 Example source object implementation. This is the Execute()
method from vtkLineSource.

vtkPolyDataToPolyDataFilter. Input and output polygonal data.

vtkPointSetToPointSetFilter. General filter to create a point set from an input point set. Point sets are data that explicitly represents points with a point array (i.e., subclasses of vtkPoints).

vtkRectilinearGridToPolyDataFilter. Filters of this type take rectilinear grid datasets as input and generate poly data on output.

vtkStructuredGridToPolyDataFilter. Create polygonal data from any type of structured data.

vtkStructuredPointsToPolyDataFilter. Given input structured points, create polygonal data on output.

vtkStructuredPointsToStructuredPointsFilter. Input and output structured points.

You should derive your objects from these abstract classes, if possible. To actually create your filter, implement the usual standard constructor, destructor, and instance variable methods. Finally, the algorithm itself is implemented in the Execute() method. Good examples of filter objects to study are vtkWarp-Vector or vtkContourFilter.

The body of the filter object Execute() method follows the same five steps that the source object does. There are a few important differences. A filter object has an Input instance variable of general type vtkDataSet. Input may have to be cast to the appropriate input type, as enforced by its superclass. The value of Input is guaranteed to be non-NULL upon entry into the Execute() method. Also, in the body of the method, use the convenience methods of vtkPointData to copy and interpolate data whenever possible. Example code illustrating this process is shown in Figure **A–14**.

Deriving a Reference Counted Object

Reference counted objects are objects that are used by datasets to represent data arrays. These objects are passed between filters as network execution proceeds. They are subclasses of vtkReferenceCount. Examples of reference counted objects include vtkPoints, vtkScalars, vtkVectors, vtkNormals, vtkT-Coords, and their subclasses.

The subclasses of these objects depend upon type-specific arrays for implementation. For example, vtkFloatPoints is used to represent arrays of floats and is a concrete class of vtkPoints. In turn, the class vtkFloatArray is used to represent the data within vtkFloatPoints. Hence, to derive a reference counted object, you must identify the appropriate abstract superclass (e.g., vtk-Points) as well as the particular type you are interested in representing (e.g., float, int, short, or your own type). Then you must create or identify a previously defined type-specific array to support the object you wish to derive. For examples of similar classes, see vtkFloatPoints or vtkIntScalars.

```
void vtkWarpVector::Execute()
{
  vtkPoints *inPts;                                    ⎤
  vtkFloatPoints *newPts;                              |
  vtkPointData *pd;                                    |
  vtkVectors *inVectors;                               |
  int i, ptId, numPts;                                 ⎬  Declaration
  float *x, *v, newX[3];                               |
  vtkPointSet *input=(vtkPointSet *)this->Input;       |
  vtkPointSet *output=(vtkPointSet *)this->Output;     ⎦

  vtkDebugMacro(<<"Warping data with vectors");        ⎤
                                                       |
  inPts = input->GetPoints();                          |
  numPts = inPts->GetNumberOfPoints();                 |
  pd = input->GetPointData();                          ⎬  Initialization
  inVectors = pd->GetVectors();                        |
                                                       |
  if ( !inVectors || !inPts )                          ⎦
    {
    vtkErrorMacro(<<"No input data");
    return;
    }

  newPts = vtkFloatPoints::New();                      ⎤  Allocation
  newPts->SetNumberOfPoints(numPts);                   ⎦
//
// Loop over all points, adjusting locations
//
  for (ptId=0; ptId < numPts; ptId++)                  ⎤
    {                                                  |
    x = inPts->GetPoint(ptId);                         |
    v = inVectors->GetVector(ptId);                    |
    for (i=0; i<3; i++)                                ⎬  Body
      {                                                |
      newX[i] = x[i] + this->ScaleFactor * v[i];       |
      }                                                |
    newPts->SetPoint(ptId, newX);                      |
    }                                                  ⎦
//
// Update ourselves and release memory
//
  output->GetPointData()->CopyNormalsOff();y           ⎤
  output->GetPointData()->PassData(input->GetPointData()); ⎬  Output
  output->SetPoints(newPts);                           |
  newPts->Delete();                                    ⎦
```

Figure A–14 Example filter object implementation. This is the `Execute()` method from `vtkWarpVector`.

Deriving a New Dataset

Deriving a new dataset means creating a subclass of vtkDataSet. You must design your new dataset to satisfy the abstract interface specified by vtk-DataSet. In addition, you may need to construct additional source, filter, and mapper objects, as appropriate. Try to take advantage of the abstract classes vtkPointSet and vtkStructuredData if you can, since they implement many of the virtual functions found in vtkDataSet.

Deriving a New Cell Type

Deriving a new cell type means creating a subclass of vtkCell. To derive a new cell you must design your new cell type to satisfy the abstract interface specified by vtkCell, you must modify CellType.h, and you must modify the dataset vtkUnstructuredGrid.

To modify CellType.h you must add a #define to associate a numeric tag with the cell name. This tag is used internally by the class vtkUnstructuredGrid and vtkCell::GetCellType() to map cells into appropriate data structures.

The class vtkUnstructuredGrid is modified since it must represent every cell type. Hence the method vtkUnstructuredGrid::GetCell() must be modified accordingly.

One special note: If you create a new cell type you must implement methods to return the "boundary" faces and edges of the cell. These boundary faces and edges are expressed as a type of cell, so they must be valid cell types. This may require implementing new cell types to represent the boundaries of the cell as well.

Interfacing to a Rendering Library

The *Visualization Toolkit* has been designed to accommodate different types of rendering libraries. This includes both *retained* as well as *immediate-mode* rendering libraries.

Retained libraries typically implement a two-step rendering process. In the first step, a library-specific data structure or display list is built. In the second step, the structure is traversed and displayed. The build process is often slow, while the traversal is relatively fast. An example of a retained library is PHIGS.

Immediate-mode libraries display immediately upon loading graphics data. Only a single step is required to render data.

In **vtk** you can interface to both retained and immediate-mode renderers. The key is to modify the Render() method appropriately. In an immediate-mode renderer you simply execute the instructions necessary to load the graphics data. In a retained-mode renderer you must first build a display list, and then traverse the list to actually render it. Some graphics libraries (such as OpenGL) actually support either immediate mode or display list (i.e., retained mode) rendering.

(Use the methods `vtkMapper::ImmediateModeRenderingOn/Off()` to select between immediate and retained-mode rendering.)

To construct a new renderer for **vtk**, you must construct two general types of objects: the renderer and graphics primitives. The renderer is responsible for coordinating lights, cameras, actors, and actor properties. This entails proper initialization and control of the graphics library. Graphics primitives are lower-level objects that define the lights, cameras, geometry, and properties to the graphics library. They are responsible for converting internal **vtk** data to the appropriate form, and loading the data into the library. (Start by studying the OpenGL object diagram in Figure **A–12**.)

We encourage you to use our object design to implement your rendering library interface. The advantages are device independence and system consistency. You may need to extend the graphics classes, particularly the lights or property classes, in order to provide access to special graphics functionality.

Deriving a New Mapper Object

Mappers interface the visualization pipeline to the graphics system or are used to write data to file. If you need to add a graphics mapper, you may also have to modify the graphics system, so please read that section as well.

Mappers are similar to graphics primitives in that they also implement the `Render()` method. Mappers must create the appropriate device primitives (e.g., points, polygons, lines, etc.) by interfacing to the renderer. Mappers may also need to map data through a lookup table. Follow the example set by `vtkPoly-DataMapper` as a starting point.

Writers are usually easy to implement. The single method `WriteData()` must be implemented (besides the usual constructor/destructor and instance variable methods).

Introducing User-Defined Data

The *Visualization Toolkit* supports user-defined data in the visualization network. This is an array of pointers to `void*` data. Thus user-defined data can be arbitrarily complex.

The nature of this support is that user-defined data will be passed through the network if it is present and if the filters are such that they copy data from input to output. No mechanism to read, write, or display user-defined data is available in **vtk**. To introduce user-defined data into the network you will have to add some or all of this functionality.

Improving Performance

The *Visualization Toolkit* has been written to demonstrate visualization algorithms and architecture. Often, we have not made a serious attempt to optimize performance. If you wish to improve performance, we suggest you begin by eliminating virtual function access to data, and replace them with `inline` functions.

The reference counted objects such as `vtkPoints`, `vtkScalars`, `vtkVec-`
`tors`, `vtkNormals`, and `vtkTCoords` are particularly important. These abstract
objects specify an interface to concrete classes such as `vtkFloatPoints` or
`vtkIntScalars`. This design provides the benefit that new concrete types can
be introduced without modifying any other objects. The downside is that data is
accessed via virtual function pointers.

If you wish to eliminate virtual access, you will have to select a single representation type such as `float` or `double`. (For example, if the representation
type `float` is chosen, all point coordinates would be represented with floating-
point numbers.) Once a type is chosen, modify the abstract classes so that they
become concrete. Make sure that you use `inline` data access functions.

A variation of this idea is to allow some data types to be abstract, while others are concrete. As an example, you might allow scalars to be of various types
(`char`, `short`, `int`, `float`), while all other data is represented with `floats`.
This idea can be taken further by implementing templated functions and retrieving data pointers. See the `vtkMarchingCubes` object for an example.

Another area to improve performance is to tune the interface to the graphics libraries. The *Visualization Toolkit* has been designed to be portable across a
variety of graphics libraries. Thus, we have sacrificed performance for flexibility
and portability. If your application is to run with a particular library or your data
is of a particular form, you can often take advantage of characteristics of the
graphics library. For example, some graphics libraries allow you to load large
amounts of data (i.e., a display list) with a single function call. By converting the
vtk data structures into a display list, rendering can be greatly accelerated.

A.5 vtk File Formats

The *Visualization Toolkit* provides a number of source and writer objects to read
and write various data file formats. The *Visualization Toolkit* also provides some
of its own file formats. The main reason for creating yet another data file format
is to offer a consistent data representation scheme for a variety of dataset types,
and to provide a simple method to communicate data between software. Whenever possible, we recommend that you use formats that are more widely used.
But if this is not possible, the *Visualization Toolkit* formats described here can be
used instead. Note, however, that these formats are not supported by many other
tools.

The visualization file formats consist of five basic parts.

1. The first part is the file version and identifier. This part contains the single
    line: # vtk DataFile Version x.x. This line must be exactly as shown
    with the exception of the version number x.x, which will vary with differ-
    ent releases of **vtk**. (Note: the current version number is 2.0. Version 1.0
    files are compatible with version 2.0 files.)

2. The second part is the header. The header consists of a character string ter-

```
# vtk DataFile Version 2.0 ](1)
Really cool data ](2)
ASCII | BINARY ](3)
DATASET type  ](4)
...
POINT_DATA n  ](5)
...
```

Part 1: Header

Part 2: Title (256 characters maximum, terminated with newline \n character)

Part 3: Data type, either ASCII or BINARY

Part 4: Geometry/topology. *Type* is one of: STRUCTURED_POINTS STRUCTURED_GRID UNSTRUCTURED_GRID POLYDATA RECTILINEAR_GRID

Part 5: Dataset attributes. The number of data items *n* of each type must match the number of points in the dataset.

Figure A–15 Overview of five parts of **vtk** data file format.

minated by end-of-line character \n. The header is 256 characters maximum. The header can be used to describe the data and include any other pertinent information.

3. The next part is the file format. The file format describes the type of file, either ASCII or binary. On this line the single word ASCII or BINARY must appear.
4. The fourth part is the dataset structure. The geometry part describes the geometry and topology of the dataset. This part begins with a line containing the keyword DATASET followed by a keyword describing the type of dataset. Then, depending upon the type of dataset, other keyword/data combinations define the actual data.
5. The final part describes the dataset attributes. This part begins with the keyword POINT_DATA, followed by an integer number specifying the number of points. Other keyword/data combinations then define the actual data values.

An overview of the file format is shown in Figure **A–15**. The first three parts are mandatory, but the other two are optional. Thus you have the flexibility of mixing and matching dataset attributes and geometry, either by operating system file manipulation or using **vtk** filters to merge data. Keywords are case insensitive, and may be separated by whitespace.

Before describing the data file formats please note the following.

- *dataType* is one of the types `bit`, `unsigned_char`, `short`, `int`, `float`, or `double`. These keywords are used to describe the form of the data, both for reading from file, as well as constructing the appropriate internal objects. Not all data types are supported for all classes.

- All keyword phrases are written in ASCII form whether the file is binary or ASCII. The binary section of the file (if in binary form) is the data proper; i.e., the numbers that define points coordinates, scalars, cell indices, and so forth.

- Indices are 0-offset. Thus the first point is point id 0.

- If both the data attribute and geometry/topology part are present in the file, then the number of data values defined in the data attribute part must exactly match the number of points defined in the geometry/topology part.

- Cell types and indices are of type `int`.

- Binary data must be placed into the file immediately after the "newline" (`\n`) character from the previous ASCII keyword and parameter sequence.

- The geometry/topology description must occur prior to the data attribute description.

Binary Files

Binary files in **vtk** are portable across different computer systems as long as you observe two conditions. First, make sure that the byte ordering of the data is correct, and second, make sure that the length of each data type is consistent.

Most of the time **vtk** manages the byte ordering of binary files for you. When you write a binary file on one computer and read it in from another computer, the bytes representing the data will be automatically swapped as necessary. For example, binary files written on a Sun are stored in big endian order, while those on a PC are stored in little endian order. As a result, files written on a Sun workstation require byte swapping when read on a PC. (See the class `vtk-ByteSwap` for implementation details.) The **vtk** data files described here are written in big endian form.

Some file formats, however, do not explicitly define a byte ordering form. You will find that data read or written by external programs, or the classes `vtkVolume16Reader`, `vtkMCubesReader`, and `vtkMCubesWriter` may have a different byte order depending on the system of origin. In such cases, **vtk** allows you to specify the byte order by using the methods

```
SetDataByteOrderToBigEndian()
SetDataByteOrderToLittleEndian()
```

Another problem with binary files is that systems may use a different number of bytes to represent an integer or other native type. For example, some 64-

bit systems will represent an integer with 8-bytes, while others represent an integer with 4-bytes. Currently, the *Visualization Toolkit* cannot handle transporting binary files across systems with incompatible data length. In this case, use ASCII file formats instead.

Dataset Format

The *Visualization Toolkit* supports five different dataset formats: structured points, structured grid, rectilinear grid, unstructured grid, and polygonal data. These formats are as follows.

- Structured Points
  The file format supports 1D, 2D, and 3D structured point datasets. The dimensions n_x, n_y, n_z must be greater than or equal to 1. The data spacing s_x, s_y, s_z must be greater than 0. (Note: in the version 1.0 data file, spacing was referred to as "aspect ratio". ASPECT_RATIO can still be used in version 2.0 data files, but is discouraged.)

  ```
  DATASET STRUCTURED_POINTS
  DIMENSIONS nx ny nz
  ORIGIN x y z
  SPACING sx sy sz
  ```

- Structured Grid
  The file format supports 1D, 2D, and 3D structured grid datasets. The dimensions n_x, n_y, n_z must be greater than or equal to 1. The point coordinates are defined by the data in the POINTS section. This consists of *x-y-z* data values for each point.

  ```
  DATASET STRUCTURED_GRID
  DIMENSIONS nx ny nz
  POINTS n dataType
  ```
  $p_{0x} \, p_{0y} \, p_{0z}$
  $p_{1x} \, p_{1y} \, p_{1z}$
  ...
  $p_{(n-1)x} \, p_{(n-1)y} \, p_{(n-1)z}$

- Rectilinear Grid
  A rectilinear grid defines a dataset with regular topology, and semiregular geometry aligned along the *x-y-z* coordinate axes. The geometry is defined by three lists of monotonically increasing coordinate values, one list for each of the *x-y-z* coordinate axes. The topology is defined by specifying the grid dimensions, which must be greater than or equal to 1.

```
DATASET RECTILINEAR_GRID
DIMENSIONS nx ny nz
X_COORDINATES  nx dataType
```
$x_0 \, x_1 \dots x_{(nx-1)}$
```
Y_COORDINATES  ny dataType
```
$y_0 \, y_1 \dots y_{(ny-1)}$
```
Z_COORDINATES  nz dataType
```
$z_0 \, z_1 \dots z_{(nz-1)}$

- Polygonal Data
  The polygonal dataset consists of arbitrary combinations of surface graphics primitives vertices (and polyvertices), lines (and polylines), polygons (of
  various types), and triangle strips. Polygonal data is defined by the POINTS
  VERTICES, LINES, POLYGONS, or TRIANGLE_STRIPS sections. The POINTS
  definition is the same as we saw for structured grid datasets. The VERTI-
  CES, LINES, POLYGONS, or TRIANGLE_STRIPS keywords define the polygonal dataset topology. Each of these keywords requires two parameters: the
  number of cells *n* and the size of the cell list *size*. The cell list size is the
  total number of integer values required to represent the list (i.e., sum of
  numPoints and connectivity indices over each cell). None of the keywords
  VERTICES, LINES, POLYGONS, or TRIANGLE STRIPS is required.

```
DATASET POLYDATA
POINTS n dataType
```
$p_{0x} \, p_{0y} \, p_{0z}$
$p_{1x} \, p_{1y} \, p_{1z}$
...
$p_{(n-1)x} \, p_{(n-1)y} \, p_{(n-1)z}$

```
VERTICES n size
```
$numPoints_0, \, i_0, \, j_0, \, k_0, \dots$
$numPoints_1, \, i_1, \, j_1, \, k_1, \dots$
...
$numPoints_{n-1}, \, i_{n-1}, \, j_{n-1}, \, k_{n-1}, \dots$

```
LINES n size
```
$numPoints_0, \, i_0, \, j_0, \, k_0, \dots$
$numPoints_1, \, i_1, \, j_1, \, k_1, \dots$
...
$numPoints_{n-1}, \, i_{n-1}, \, j_{n-1}, \, k_{n-1}, \dots$

```
POLYGONS n size
```
$numPoints_0, \, i_0, \, j_0, \, k_0, \dots$

$numPoints_1, i_1, j_1, k_1, ...$
...
$numPoints_{n-1}, i_{n-1}, j_{n-1}, k_{n-1}, ...$

TRIANGLE_STRIPS n $size$
$numPoints_0, i_0, j_0, k_0, ...$
$numPoints_1, i_1, j_1, k_1, ...$
...
$numPoints_{n-1}, i_{n-1}, j_{n-1}, k_{n-1}, ...$

- Unstructured Grid
  The unstructured grid dataset consists of arbitrary combinations of any possible cell type. Unstructured grids are defined by points, cells, and cell types. The CELLS keyword requires two parameters: the number of cells n and the size of the cell list $size$. The cell list size is the total number of integer values required to represent the list (i.e., sum of $numPoints$ and connectivity indices over each cell). The CELL_TYPES keyword requires a single parameter: the number of cells n. This value should match the value specified by the CELLS keyword. The cell types data is a single integer value per cell that specified cell type (see Cell.h or Figure **A–16**).

  DATASET UNSTRUCTURED_GRID
  POINTS n $dataType$
  $p_{0x} p_{0y} p_{0z}$
  $p_{1x} p_{1y} p_{1z}$
  ...
  $p_{(n-1)x} p_{(n-1)y} p_{(n-1)z}$

  CELLS n $size$
  $numPoints_0, i, j, k, l, ...$
  $numPoints_1, i, j, k, l, ...$
  $numPoints_2, i, j, k, l, ...$
  ...
  $numPoints_{n-1}, i, j, k, l, ...$

  CELL_TYPES n
  $type_0$
  $type_1$
  $type_2$
  ...
  $type_{n-1}$

Attribute Format

The *Visualization Toolkit* supports the following point attributes: scalars (single-valued as well as color scalars of 1, 2, 3, and 4 bytes), vectors, normals, texture coordinates (1D, 2D, and 3D), and 3×3 tensors. In addition, a lookup table using the RGBA color specification can be defined as well.

Each type of point attribute data has a *dataName* associated with it. This is a character string (without embedded whitespace) used to identify a particular data. The *dataName* is used by the **vtk** readers to extract data. As a result, more than one point attribute of the same type can be included in a file. For example, two different scalar fields, pressure and temperature, can be contained in the same file. (If the appropriate *dataName* is not specified in the **vtk** reader, then the first data of that type is extracted from the file.)

- Scalars
  Scalar definition includes specification of a lookup table. The definition of a lookup table is optional. If not specified, the default **vtk** table will be used (and *tableName* should be "default").

  SCALARS *dataName dataType*
  LOOKUP_TABLE *tableName*
  s_0
  s_1
  ...
  s_{n-1}

  The definition of color scalars varies depending upon the number of values (*nValues*) per scalar. If the file format is ASCII, the color scalars are defined using *nValues* float values between (0,1). If the file format is BINARY, the stream of data consists of *nValues* unsigned char values per scalar value.

  COLOR_SCALARS *dataName nValues*
  $c_{00} \, c_{01} \cdots c_{0(nValues-1)}$
  $c_{10} \, c_{11} \cdots c_{1(nValues-1)}$
  ...
  $c_{(n-1)0} \, c_{(n-1)1} \cdots c_{(n-1)(nValues-1)}$

- Lookup Table
  The *tableName* field is a character string (without imbedded white space) used to identify the lookup table. This label is used by the **vtk** reader to extract a specific table.

  Each entry in the lookup table is a rgba[4] (*red-green-blue-alpha*) array (*alpha* is opacity where *alpha=0* is transparent). If the file format is ASCII, the lookup table values must be float values between (0,1). If the file format is BINARY, the stream of data must be four unsigned char values per table entry.

LOOKUP_TABLE *tableName size*
$r_0\, g_0\, b_0\, a_0$
$r_1\, g_1\, b_1\, a_1$
...
$r_{size\text{-}1}\, g_{size\text{-}1}\, b_{size\text{-}1}\, a_{size\text{-}1}$

- Vectors

  VECTORS *dataName dataType*
  $v_{0x}\, v_{0y}\, v_{0z}$
  $v_{1x}\, v_{1y}\, v_{1z}$
  ...
  $v_{(n\text{-}1)x}\, v_{(n\text{-}1)y}\, v_{(n\text{-}1)z}$

- Normals
  Normals are assumed normalized $|n| = 1$.

  NORMALS *dataName dataType*
  $n_{0x}\, n_{0y}\, n_{0z}$
  $n_{1x}\, n_{1y}\, n_{1z}$
  ...
  $n_{(n\text{-}1)x}\, n_{(n\text{-}1)y}\, n_{(n\text{-}1)z}$

- Texture Coordinates
  Texture coordinates of 1, 2, and 3 dimensions are supported.

  TEXTURE_COORDINATES *dataName dim dataType*
  $t_{00}\, t_{01} \cdots t_{0(dim\text{-}1)}$
  $t_{10}\, t_{11} \cdots t_{1(dim\text{-}1)}$
  ...
  $t_{(n\text{-}1)0}\, t_{(n\text{-}1)1} \cdots t_{(n\text{-}1)(dim\text{-}1)}$

- Tensors
  Currently only 3×3 real-valued, symmetric tensors are supported.

  TENSORS *dataName dataType*
  $t^0_{00}\, t^0_{01}\, t^0_{02}$
  $t^0_{10}\, t^0_{11}\, t^0_{12}$

$$t^0_{20} \; t^0_{21} \; t^0_{22}$$

$$t^1_{00} \; t^1_{01} \; t^1_{02}$$
$$t^1_{10} \; t^1_{11} \; t^1_{12}$$
$$t^1_{20} \; t^1_{21} \; t^1_{22}$$

$$\dots$$
$$t^{n-1}_{00} \; t^{n-1}_{01} \; t^{n-1}_{02}$$
$$t^{n-1}_{10} \; t^{n-1}_{11} \; t^{n-1}_{12}$$
$$t^{n-1}_{20} \; t^{n-1}_{21} \; t^{n-1}_{22}$$

Examples

The first example is a cube represented by six polygonal faces. There are scalar data associated with the eight vertices. A lookup table of eight colors is also defined.

```
# vtk DataFile Version 2.0
Cube example
ASCII
DATASET POLYDATA
POINTS 8 float
0.0 0.0 0.0
1.0 0.0 0.0
1.0 1.0 0.0
0.0 1.0 0.0
0.0 0.0 1.0
1.0 0.0 1.0
1.0 1.0 1.0
0.0 1.0 1.0
POLYGONS 6 30
4 0 1 2 3
4 4 5 6 7
4 0 1 5 4
4 2 3 7 6
4 0 4 7 3
4 1 2 6 5
POINT_DATA 8
SCALARS sample_scalars float
LOOKUP_TABLE my_table
0.0
1.0
2.0
3.0
4.0
5.0
6.0
7.0
LOOKUP_TABLE my_table 8
0.0 0.0 0.0 1.0
1.0 0.0 0.0 1.0
```

```
0.0 1.0 0.0 1.0
1.0 1.0 0.0 1.0
0.0 0.0 1.0 1.0
1.0 0.0 1.0 1.0
0.0 1.0 1.0 1.0
1.0 1.0 1.0 1.0
```

The next example is a volume of dimension $3 \times 4 \times 5$. Since no lookup table is defined, either the user must create one in **vtk**, or the default lookup table will be used.

```
# vtk DataFile Version 2.0
Volume example
ASCII
DATASET STRUCTURED_POINTS
DIMENSIONS 3 4 6
ASPECT_RATIO 1 1 1
ORIGIN 0 0 0
POINT_DATA 72
SCALARS volume_scalars char
LOOKUP_TABLE default
0 0 0 0 0 0 0 0 0 0 0 0
0 5 10 15 20 25 25 20 15 10 5 0
0 10 20 30 40 50 50 40 30 20 10 0
0 10 20 30 40 50 50 40 30 20 10 0
0 5 10 15 20 25 25 20 15 10 5 0
0 0 0 0 0 0 0 0 0 0 0 0
```

The third example is an unstructured grid containing all 12 cell types. The file contains scalar and vector data.

```
# vtk DataFile Version 2.0
Unstructured Grid Example
ASCII

DATASET UNSTRUCTURED_GRID
POINTS 27 float
0 0 0    1 0 0    2 0 0    0 1 0    1 1 0    2 1 0
0 0 1    1 0 1    2 0 1    0 1 1    1 1 1    2 1 1
0 1 2    1 1 2    2 1 2    0 1 3    1 1 3    2 1 3
0 1 4    1 1 4    2 1 4    0 1 5    1 1 5    2 1 5
0 1 6    1 1 6    2 1 6

CELLS 11 60
8 0 1 4 3 6 7 10 9
8 1 2 5 4 7 8 11 10
4 6 10 9 12
4 5 11 10 14
6 15 16 17 14 13 12
6 18 15 19 16 20 17
4 22 23 20 19
3 21 22 18
```

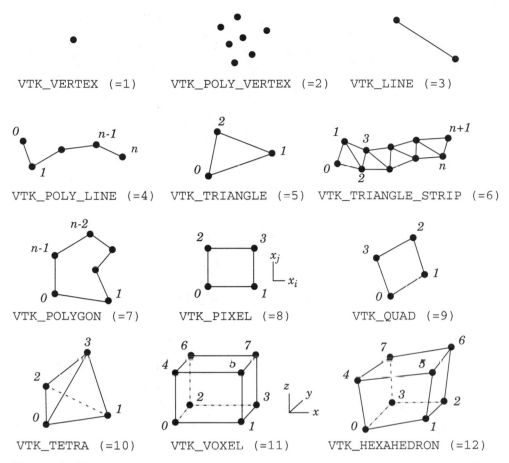

Figure A–16 Cell type specification. Use the include file CellType.h to manipulate cell types.

```
3 22 19 18
2 26 25
1 24

CELL_TYPES 11
12
12
10
10
7
6
9
5
5
3
1
```

```
POINT_DATA 27
SCALARS scalars float
LOOKUP_TABLE default
0.0    1.0    2.0    3.0    4.0    5.0
6.0    7.0    8.0    9.0    10.0   11.0
12.0   13.0   14.0   15.0   16.0   17.0
18.0   19.0   20.0   21.0   22.0   23.0
24.0   25.0   26.0
VECTORS vectors float
1 0 0   1 1 0   0 2 0   1 0 0   1 1 0   0 2 0
1 0 0   1 1 0   0 2 0   1 0 0   1 1 0   0 2 0
0 0 1   0 0 1   0 0 1   0 0 1   0 0 1   0 0 1
0 0 1   0 0 1   0 0 1   0 0 1   0 0 1   0 0 1
0 0 1   0 0 1   0 0 1
```

Additional examples are available in the data examples directory.

B

CD-ROM Organization

*N*ow that we have dealt with the complexities of data visualization, we face the greatest challenge of all: reading and extracting information from the CD-ROM. This appendix quickly discusses what is on the CD-ROM, how to access it, and potential problems you may encounter. Since the contents of the CD-ROM may not be up-to-date, you may wish to occasionally check the *Visualization Toolkit* Web site http://www.kitware.com.

B.1 Introduction

The CD-ROM that comes with this book has been designed to work with both Unix and Microsoft Windows systems. Since these two systems store their information differently, there will be some parts of the CD-ROM that only apply to Unix systems and vice versa. (The major difference is in the newline characters used on PC's and Unix systems. There are also some executables that only run on Windows '95/NT systems.)

The following sections give a synopsis of what material is on the CD and how to access it. We recommend that you start by viewing the README.html file. This file includes installation instructions and other system documentation.

The following is a list of the files and directories found on the CD-ROM.

- README.html - HTML (Hyper-Text Markup Language) files for **vtk**. This Web page (and referenced pages) contain installation instructions, object manual pages, example code and resulting images, color plates, and extensively documented applications.

- SETUP.exe - a PC executable that installs **vtk** binaries and libraries (dlls). If you execute this file, **vtk** will be installed on your PC along with some example code and data.

- vtk - **vtk** source code directory for PCs. If you are compiling **vtk** on a PC you will access this directory.

- vtkunix - **vtk** source code directory for Unix systems.

- vtkdata - this directory and subdirectories contain data used by the examples in the book including the C++, Tcl, and Java examples. You might take a minute to read the README.html and README files found here, since they give credit to some of the creators of the data.

- patented - PC libraries containing patented code. You can replace the dlls installed with SETUP.exe with those found in this directory. Do not use these dlls in commercial application without a license grant from the appropriate patent holder.

There are a several other directories and files not listed here. These are typically used as repositories for the HTML pages, or are used as part of the PC installation process.

B.2 Microsoft Windows Systems

This CD-ROM is designed to work with Microsoft Windows95 or Microsoft WindowsNT. It will not work properly under Microsoft Windows 3.0, 3.1, or 3.11.

Installing Precompiled Binaries

Installing the pre-compiled executables on Windows systems requires running the program SETUP.EXE on the CD-ROM. This will guide you through an installation process, create a program group, and set up a number of examples. You can run the examples by invoking them from the Start>Programs>Visualization Toolkit menu selection. This process should be quick and easy.

Compiling Source Code

Source code for **vtk** under Windows is kept in the directory vtk. There is a README.html file in that directory installation instructions. In a nutshell, the installation process is as follows:

- Run the executable `vtk\pcmaker\Debug\pcmaker.exe`. You'll have to supply information about where you want to compile the **vtk** code, where your compile is located and the type of compiler (MS Visual C++ or Borland), and whether you want a debug or optimized version.

- `pcmaker` will run for 5-10 minutes (depending on your system) building dependencies and makefiles.

- After `pcmaker` completes, change directories into where you requested **vtk** be built. Then change directories into `vtkdll` and type `nmake` to begin the compile process for that dll. (The compilation process may take an hour or more.) If you desire to build dlls for Tcl and Java, do the same for `vtktcl` and `vtkjava`.

After you've built the desired libraries, you may want to place into the appropriate system folders.

B.3 Unix Systems

Precompiled binaries and/or libraries are not included for Unix systems on the CD-ROM. If you are developing on a Unix system, you'll have to compile **vtk** first.

On a Unix system, use the source code in `vtkunix`. To build **vtk**, you'll have to use the `configure` process to build dependencies and makefiles. The `configure` process will take into account your system architecture, the location of include files, and the rendering resources available.

In a nutshell, this is the procedure you'll follow to compile **vtk**. You can choose to leave the source code on the CD, but if you're building different architectures or editing code you probably want to copy the `vtkunix` directory onto a local disk. In the directions that follow, we assume that you've created a directory `/usr/people/joe/vtk-sgi` into which you wish to place your object code and libraries, and that the source code exists in `/usr/people/joe/vtk`. Also, the instruction below assumes that you have Tcl/Tk installed on your system.

- `cd /usr/people/vtk-sgi`

- `/usr/people/joe/vtk/configure --with-tcl`

- edit the `user.make` file (set debug flags etc.)

- `make`

You may want to run `configure --help` to see other options. For example, using `--with-shared` lets you build shared libraries. Or, `--with-tkwidget` lets you instantiate a special Tcl/Tk widget that you can place into Tk user-interface applications.

B.4 Problems

If you run into problems, we recommend that you contact us on the **vtk** mailing list, or send us e-mail. Find us at `http://www.kitware.com`.

Glossary

API. An acronym for application programmer's interface.

Abstract Class. A class that provides methods and data members for the express purpose of deriving subclasses. Such objects are used to define a common interface and attributes for their subclasses.

Abstraction. A mental process that extracts the essential form or unifying properties of a concept.

Alpha. A specification of opacity (or transparency). An alpha value of one indicates that the object is opaque. An alpha value of zero indicates that the object is completely transparent.

Ambient Lighting. The background lighting of unlit surfaces.

Animation. A sequence of images displayed in rapid succession. The images may vary due to changes in geometry, color, lighting, camera position, or other graphics parameters. Animations are used to display the variation of one or more variables.

Antialiasing. The process of reducing aliasing artifacts. These artifacts typically result from undersampling the data. A common use of antialiasing is to draw straight lines that don't have the jagged edges found in many systems without antialiasing.

Azimuth. A rotation of a camera about the vertical (or view up) axis.

Attribute. A named member of a class that captures some characteristic of the class. Attributes have a name, a data type, and a data value. This is the same as a data member or instance variable.

Base Class. A superclass in C++.

Binocular Parallax. The effect of viewing the same object with two slightly different viewpoints to develop depth information.

Boolean Texture. A texture map consisting of distinct regions used to "cut" or accentuate features of data. For example, a texture map may consist of regions of zero opacity. When such a texture is mapped onto the surface of an object, portions of its interior becomes visible. Generally used in conjunction with a quadric (or other implicit function) to generate texture coordinates.

C++. A compiled programming language with roots in the C programming language. C++ is an extension of C that incorporates object-oriented principles.

CT (Computed Tomography). A data acquisition technique based on X-rays. Data is acquired in a 3D volume as a series of slice planes (i.e., a stack of n^2 points).

Cell. The atoms of visualization datasets. Cells define a topology (e.g., polygon, triangle) in terms of a list of point coordinates.

Cell Attributes. Dataset attributes associated with a cell.

Class. An object that defines the characteristics of a subset of objects. Typically, it defines methods and data members. All objects instantiated from a class share that class's methods and data members.

Clipping Plane. A plane that restricts the rendering or processing of data. Front and back clipping planes are commonly used to restrict the rendering of primitives to those lying between the two planes.

Color Mapping. A scalar visualization technique that maps scalar values into color. Generally used to display the variation of data on a surface or through a volume.

Compiled System. A compiled system requires that a program be compiled (or translated into a lower-level language) before it is executed. Contrast with *interpreted systems*.

Composite Cell. A cell consisting of one or more primary cells.

Concrete Class. A class that can be instantiated. Typically, abstract classes are not instantiated but concrete classes are.

Connectivity. A technique to extract connected cells. Cells are connected when they share common features such as points, edges, or faces.

Contouring. A scalar visualization technique that creates lines (in 2D) or surfaces (in 3D) representing a constant scalar value across a scalar field. Contour lines are called isovalue lines or isolines. Contour surfaces are called isovalue surfaces or isosurfaces.

Constructor. A class method that is invoked when an instance of that class is created. Typically the constructor sets any default values and allocates any memory that the instance needs. See also *destructor*.

Critical Points. Locations in a vector field where the local vector magnitude goes to zero and the direction becomes undefined.

Cutting. A visualization technique to slice through or cut data. The cutting surface is typically described with an implicit function, and data attributes are mapped onto the cut surface. See also *boolean texture*.

Dataset. The general term used to describe visualization data. Datasets consist of structure (geometry and topology) and dataset attributes (scalars, vectors, tensors, etc.).

Dataset Attributes. The information associated with the structure of a dataset. This can be scalars, vectors, tensors, normals, texture coordinates, or user-defined data.

Data Extraction. The process of selecting a portion of data based on characteristics of the data. These characteristics may be based on geometric or topological constraints or constraints on data attribute values.

Data Flow Diagram. A diagram that shows the information flow and operations on that information as it moves throughout a program or process.

Data Object. An object that is an abstraction of data. For example, a patient's file in a hospital could be a data object. Typical visualization objects include structured grids and volumes. See also *process object*.

Data Member. A named member of a class that captures some characteristic of the class. Data members have a name, a data type, and a data value. This is the same as an attribute or instance variable.

Data Visualization. The process of transforming data into sensory stimuli, usually visual images. Data visualization is a general term, encompassing data from engineering and science, as well as information from business, finance, sociology, geography, information management, and other fields. Data visualization also includes elements of data analysis, such as statistical analysis. Contrast with *scientific visualization* and *information visualization*.

Decimation. A type of polygon reduction technique that deletes points in a polygonal mesh that satisfies a co-planar or co-linear condition and replaces the resulting hole with a new triangulation.

Delaunay Triangulation. A triangulation that satisfies the Delaunay circumsphere criterion. This criterion states that a circumsphere of each simplex in the triangulation contains only the points defining the simplex.

Delegation. The process of assigning an object to handle the execution of another object's methods. Sometimes it is said that one object forwards certain methods to another object for execution.

Demand-driven. A method of visualization pipeline update where the update occurs only when data is requested and occurs only in the portion of the network required to generate the data.

Derived Class. A class that is more specific or complete than its superclass. The derived class, which is also known as the subclass, inherits all the members of its superclass. Usually a derived class adds new functionality or fills in what was defined by its superclass. See also *subclass*.

Destructor. A class method that is invoked when an instance of that class is deleted. Typically the destructor frees memory that the instance was using. See also *constructor*.

Device Mapper. A mapper that interfaces data to a graphics library or subsystem.

Diffuse Lighting. Reflected light from a matte surface. Diffuse lighting is a function of the relative angle between the incoming light and surface normal of the object.

Displacement Plots. A vector visualization technique that shows the displacement of the surface of an object. The method generates scalar values by computing the dot product between the surface normal and vector displacement of the surface. The scalars are visualized using color mapping.

Display Coordinate System. A coordinate system that is the result of mapping the view coordinate system onto the display hardware.

Divergence. In numerical computation: the tendency of computation to move away from the solution. In fluid flow: the rapid motion of fluid particles away from one another.

Dividing Cubes. A contour algorithm that represents isosurfaces as a dense cloud of points.

Dolly. A camera operation that moves the camera position towards (*dolly in*) or away (*dolly out*) from the camera focal point.

Double Buffering. A display technique that is used to display animations more smoothly. It consists of using two buffers in the rendering process. While one buffer is being displayed, the next frame in the animation is being drawn on the other buffer. Once the drawing is complete the two buffers are swapped and the new image is displayed.

Dynamic Memory Model. A data flow network that does not retain intermediate results as it executes. Each time the network executes, it must recompute any data required as input to another process object. A dynamic memory model reduces system memory requirements but places greater demands on computational requirements.

Dynamic Model. A description of a system concerned with synchronizing events and objects.

Effective Stress. A mathematical combination of the normal and shear stress components that provide a measure of the stress at a point. Effective stress is a scalar value, while stress is represented with a tensor value. See *stress*.

Eigenfields. Vector fields defined by the eigenvectors of a tensor.

Eigenvalue. A characteristic value of a matrix. Eigenvalues often correspond to physical phenomena, such as frequency of vibration or magnitude of principal components of stress.

Eigenvector. A vector associated with each eigenvalue. The eigenvector spans the space of the matrix. Eigenvectors are orthogonal to one another. Eigenvectors often correspond to physical phenomena such as mode shapes of vibration.

Elevation. A rotation of a camera about the horizontal axis.

Entity. Something within a system that has identity. Chairs, airplanes, and cameras are things that correspond to physical entities in the real world. A database and isosurface algorithm are examples of nonphysical entities.

Event-driven. A method of visualization pipeline update where updates occur when an event affects the pipeline, e.g., when an object instance variable is set or modified. See also *demand-driven*.

Execution. The process of updating a visualization network.

Explicit Execution. Controlling network updates by performing explicit dependency analysis.

Exporter. An object that saves a **vtk** scene definition to a file or other program. (A scene consists of lights, cameras, actors, geometry, properties, texture, and other pertinent data.) See also *importer*.

Fan-in. The flow of multiple pieces of data into a single filter.

Fan-out. The flow of data from a filter's output to other objects.

Feature Angle. The angle between surface normal vectors, e.g., the angle between the normal vectors on two adjacent polygons.

Filter. A process object that takes at least one input and generates at least one output.

Finite Element Method (FEM). A numerical technique for the solution of partial differential equations. FEM is based on discretizing a domain into elements (and nodes) and constructing basis (or interpolation) functions across the elements. From these functions a system of linear equations is generated and solved on the computer. Typical applications include stress, heat transfer, and vibration analysis.

Finite Difference Method. A numerical technique for the solution of partial differential equations (PDEs). Finite difference methods replace the PDEs with truncated Taylor series approximations. This results in a system of equations that is solved on a computer. Typical applications include fluid flow, combustion, and heat transfer.

Flat Shading. A shading technique where the lighting equation for a geometric primitive is calculated once, and then used to fill in the entire area of the primitive. This is also known as faceted shading. See also *gouraud shading* and *phong shading*.

Functional Model. The description of a system based on what it does.

Generalization. The abstraction of a subset of classes to a common superclass. Generalization extracts the common members or methods from a group of classes to create a common superclass. See also *specialization* and *inheritance*.

Geometry. Used generally to mean the characteristic position, shape, and topology of an object. Used specifically (in tandem with topology) to mean the position and shape of an object.

Glyph. A general visualization technique used to represent data using a meaningful shape or pictorial representation. Each glyph is generally a function of its input data and may change size, orientation, and shape; or modify graphics properties in response to changes in input.

Gouraud Shading. A shading technique that applies the lighting equations for a geometric primitive at each vertex. The resulting colors are then interpolated over the areas between the vertices. See also *flat shading* and *Phong shading*.

Hedgehog. A vector visualization technique that represents vector direction and magnitude with oriented lines.

Height Field. A set of altitude or height samples in a rectangular grid. Height fields are typically used to represent terrain.

Hexahedron. A type of primary 3D cell. The hexahedron looks like a "brick." It has six faces, 12 edges, and eight vertices. The faces of the hexahedron are not necessarily planar.

Homogeneous Coordinates. An alternate coordinate representation that provides more flexibility than traditional Cartesian coordinates. This includes perspective transformation and combined translation, scaling, and rotation.

Hyperstreamline. A tensor visualization technique. Hyperstreamlines are created by treating the eigenvectors as three separate vectors. The maximum eigenvalue/eigenvector is used as a vector field in which particle integration is performed (like streamlines). The other two vectors control the cross-sectional shape of an ellipse that is swept along the integration path. See also *streampolygon*.

Image-Order Techniques. Rendering techniques that determine for each pixel in the image plane which data samples contribute to it. Image-order techniques are implemented using ray casting. Contrast with *object-order techniques*.

Implicit Execution. Controlling network updates by distributing network dependency throughout the visualization process objects. Each process object requests that its input be updated before it executes. This results in a recursive update/execution process throughout the network.

Implicit Function. A mathematical function of the form $F(x, y, z) = c$, where c is a constant.

Implicit Modelling. A modelling technique that represents geometry as a scalar field. Usually the scalar is a distance function or implicit function distributed through a volume.

Importer. An object that interfaces to external data or programs to define a complete scene in **vtk**. (The scene consists of lights, cameras, actors, geometry, properties, texture, and other pertinent data.) See also *exporter*.

Information Visualization. The process of transforming information into sensory stimuli, usually visual images. Information visualization is used to describe the process of visualizing data without structure, such as information on the World Wide Web; or abstract data structures, like computer file systems or documents. Contrast with *scientific visualization* and *data visualization*.

Inheritance. A process where the attributes and methods of a superclass are bestowed upon all subclasses derived from that superclass. It is said that the subclasses inherit their superclasses' methods and attributes.

Instance. An object that is defined by a class and used by a program or application. There may be many instances of a specific class.

Instance Variable. A named member of a class that captures a characteristic of the class. Instance variables have a name, a data type, and a data value. The phrase, instance variable, is often abbreviated as ivar. This is the same as an attribute or data member.

Intensity. The light energy transferred per unit time across a unit plane perpendicular to the light rays.

Interpolate. Estimate a value of a function at a point p, given known function values and points that bracket p.

Interpolation Functions. Functions continuous in value and derivatives used to interpolate data from known points and function values. Cells use interpolation functions to compute data values interior to or on the boundary of the cell.

Interpreted System. An interpreted system can execute programs without going through a separate compilation stage. Interpreted systems often allow the user to interact and modify the program as it is running. Contrast with *compiled systems*.

Irregular Data. Data in which the relationship of one data item to the other data items in the dataset is arbitrary. Irregular data is also known as unstructured data.

Iso-parametric. A form of interpolation in which interpolation for data values is the same as for the local geometry. Compare with *sub-parametric* and *super-parametric*.

Isosurface. A surface representing a constant valued scalar function. See *contouring*.

Isovalue. The scalar value used to generate an isosurface.

Jacobian. A matrix that relates one coordinate system to another.

Line. A cell defined by two points.

MRI (Magnetic Resonance Imaging). A data acquisition technique based on measuring variation in magnetic field in response to radio-wave pulses. The data is acquired in a 3D region as a series of slice planes (i.e., a stack of n^2 points).

Mapper. A process object that terminates the visualization network. It maps input data into graphics libraries (or other devices) or writes data to disk (or a communication device).

Manifold Topology. A domain is manifold at a point p in a topological space of dimension n if the neighborhood around p is homeomorphic to an n-dimensional sphere. Homeomorphic means that the mapping is one to one without tearing (i.e., like mapping a rubber sheet from a square to a disk). We generally refer to an object's topology as manifold if every point in the object is manifold. Contrast with *nonmanifold topology*.

Marching Cubes. A contouring algorithm to create surfaces of constant scalar value in 3D. Marching cubes is described for volume datasets, but has been extended to datasets consisting of other cell types.

Member Function. A member function is a function or transformation that can be applied to an object. It is the functional equivalent to a data member. Member functions define the behavior of an object. Methods, operations, and member functions are essentially the same.

Method. A function or transformation that can be applied to an object. Methods define the behavior of an object. Methods, operations, and member functions are essentially the same.

Modal Lines. Lines on the surface of a vibrating object that separate regions of positive and negative displacement.

Mode Shape. The motion of an object vibrating at a natural frequency. See also *eigenvalues* and *eigenvectors*.

Model Coordinate System. The coordinate system that a model or geometric entity is defined in. There may be many different model coordinate systems defined for one scene.

Motion blur. An artifact of the shutter speed of a camera. Since the camera's shutter stays open for a finite amount of time, changes in the scene that occur during that time can result in blurring of the resulting image.

Morph. A progressive transformation of one object into another. Generally used to transform images (2D morphing) and in some cases geometry (3D morphing).

Multiple Input. Process objects that accept more than one input.

Multiple Output. Process objects that generate more than one output.

Multidimensional Visualization. Visualizing data of four or more variables. Generally requires a mapping of many dimensions into three or fewer dimensions so that standard visualization techniques can be applied.

Nonmanifold Topology. Topology that is not manifold. Examples include polygonal meshes, where an edge is used by more than two polygons, or polygons connected to each other at their vertices (i.e., do not share an edge). Contrast with *manifold topology*.

Normal. A unit vector that indicates perpendicular direction to a surface. Normals are a common type of data attribute.

Object. An abstraction that models the state and behavior of entities in a system. Instances and classes are both objects.

Object Model. The description of a system in terms of the components that make up the system, including the relationship of the components one to another.

Object-Order Techniques. Rendering techniques that project object data (e.g., polygons or voxels) onto the image plane. Example techniques include ordered compositing and splatting.

Object-Oriented. A software development technique that uses objects to represent the state and behavior of entities in a system.

Octree Decomposition. A technique to decompose a cubical region of three-dimensional space into smaller cubes. The cubes, or octants, are related in tree fashion. The root octant is the cubical region. Each octant may have eight children created by dividing the parent in half in the x, y, and z directions.

Object Factory. An object used to construct or instantiate other objects. In **vtk**, object factories are implemented using the class method New().

OMT. *Object Modelling Technique*. An object-oriented design technique that models software systems with object, dynamic, and functional diagrams.

Operation. A function or transformation that can be applied to an object. Operations define the behavior of an object. Methods and member functions implement operations.

Overloading. Having multiple methods with the same name. Some methods are overloaded because there are different versions of the same method. These differences are based on argument types, while the underlying algorithm remains the same. Contrast with *polymorphic*.

Painter's Algorithm. An object-order rendering technique that sorts rendering primitives from back to front and then draws them.

Parametric Coordinates. A coordinate system natural to the geometry of a geometric object. For example, a line may be described by the single coordinate s even though the line may lie in three or higher dimensions.

Parallel Projection. A mapping of world coordinates into view coordinates that preserves all parallel lines. In a parallel projection an object will appear the same size regardless of how far away it is from the viewer. This is equivalent to having a center of projection that is infinitely far away. Contrast with *perspective projection*.

Particle Trace. The trajectory that particles trace over time in fluid flow. Particle traces are everywhere tangent to the velocity field. Unlike streamlines, particle lines are time-dependent.

Pathline. The trajectory that a particle follows in fluid flow.

Perspective Projection. A mapping of world coordinates into view coordinates that roughly approximates a camera lens. Specifically, the center of projection must be a finite distance from the view plane. As a result closer, objects will appear larger than distant objects. Contrast with *parallel projection*.

Phong Shading. A shading technique that applies the lighting equations for a geometric primitive at each pixel. See also *flat shading* and *Gouraud shading*.

Pitch. A rotation of a camera's position about the horizontal axis, centered at its viewpoint. See also *yaw* and *roll*. Contrast with *elevation*.

Pixel. Short for picture element. Constant valued elements in an image. In **vtk**, a two-dimensional cell defined by an ordered list of four points.

Point. A geometric specification of position in 3D space.

Point Attributes. Data attributes associates with the points of a dataset.

Polygon. A cell consisting of three or more co-planar points defining a polygon. The polygon can be concave but without imbedded loops.

Polygonal Data. A dataset type consisting of arbitrary combinations of vertices, polyvertices, lines, polylines, polygons, and triangle strips. Polygonal data is an intermediate data form that can be easily rendered by graphics libraries, and yet can represent many types of visualization data.

Polygon Reduction. A family of techniques to reduce the size of large polygonal meshes. The goal is to reduce the number of polygons, while preserving a "good" approximation to the original geometry. In most techniques topology is preserved as well.

Polyline. A composite cell consisting of one or more lines.

Polymorphic. Having many forms. Some methods are polymorphic because the same method in different classes may implement a different algorithm. The semantics of the method are typically the same, even though the implementation may differ. Contrast with *overloading*.

Polyvertex. A composite cell consisting of one or more vertices.

Primary Cell. A cell that is not defined in terms of other cells.

Probing. Also known as sampling or resampling. A data selection technique that selects data at a set of points.

Process Object. A visualization object that is an abstraction of a process or algorithm. For example, the isosurfacing algorithm marching cubes is implemented as a process object. See also *data object*.

Progressive Mesh. A representation of a triangle mesh that enables incremental refinement and derefinement. The data representation is compact and is useful for transmission of 3D triangle meshes across a network. See also *polygon reduction*.

Properties. A general term used to describe the rendered properties of an actor. This includes lighting terms such as ambient, diffuse, and specular coefficients;

color and opacity; shading techniques such as flat and Gouraud; and the actor's geometric representation (wireframe, points, or surface).

Quadric. A function of the form
$$f(x, y, z) = a_0 x^2 + a_1 y^2 + a_2 z^2 + a_3 xy + a_4 yz + a_5 xz + a_6 x + a_7 y + a_8 z + a_9.$$ The quadric equation can represent many useful 3D objects such as spheres, ellipsoids, cylinders, and cones.

Quadrilateral (Quad). A type of primary 2D cell. The quadrilateral is four sided with four vertices. The quadrilateral must be convex.

Reader. A source object that reads a file or files and produces a data object.

Reference Counting. A memory management technique used to reduce memory requirements. Portions of memory (in this case objects) may be referenced by more than one other object. The referenced object keeps a count of references to it. If the count returns to zero, the object deletes itself, returning memory back to the system. This technique avoids making copies of memory.

Region of Interest. A portion of a dataset that the user is interested in visualizing. Sometimes abbreviated ROI.

Regular Data. Data in which one data item is related (either geometrically or topologically) to other data items. Also referred to as structured data.

Rendering. The process of converting object geometry (i.e., geometric primitives), object properties, and a specification of lights and camera into an image. The primitives may take many forms including surface primitives (points, lines, polygons, splines), implicit functions, or volumes.

Resonant Frequency. A frequency at which an object vibrates.

Roll. A rotation of a camera about its direction of projection. See also *azimuth*, *elevation, pitch,* and *yaw.*

Sampling. Selective acquisition or sampling of data, usually at a regular interval. See also *probing.*

Scalar. A single value or function value. May also be used to represent a field of such values.

Scalar Range. The minimum and maximum scalar values of a scalar field.

Scalar Generation. Creating scalar values from other data such as vectors or tensors. One example is computing vector norm.

Scene. A complete representation of the components required to generate an image or animation including lights, cameras, actors. properties, transformations, geometry, texture, and other pertinent information.

Scene Graph. A hierarchical, acyclic, directed tree representation of a scene. The graph order (depth first) controls when objects are processed by the graphics system.

Scientific Visualization. The process of transforming data into sensory stimuli, usually visual images. Generally used to denote the application of visualization to the sciences and engineering. Contrast with *data visualization* and *information visualization*.

Searching. The process of locating data. Usually the search is based on spatial criteria such as position or being inside a cell.

Segmentation. Identification and demarcation of tissue types. Segmentation is generally applied to CT and MRI data to associate soft tissue with a particular body organ or anatomical structure.

Simplex. The convex combination of n-independent vectors in n-space forms an n-dimensional simplex. Points, lines, triangles, and tetrahedra are examples of simplices in 0D, 1D, 2D, and 3D.grid

Source. A process object that produces at least one output. Contrast with *filter*.

Specialization. The creation of subclasses that are more refined or specialized than their superclass. See also *generalization* and *inheritance*.

Specular Lighting. Reflected lighting from a shiny surface. Specular lighting is a function of the relative angle between the incoming light, the surface normal of the object, and the view angle of the observer.

Splatting. A method to distribute data values across a region. The distribution functions are often based on Gaussian functions.

State Diagram. A diagram that relates states and events. Used to describe behavior in a software system.

Static Memory Model. A data flow network that retains intermediate results as it executes. A static memory model minimizes computational requirements, but places greater demands on memory requirements.

Strain. A nondimensional quantity expressed as the ratio of the displacement of an object to its length (normal strain), or angular displacement (shear strain). Strain is a tensor quantity. See also *stress*.

Stress. A measure of force per unit area. Normal stress is stress normal to a given surface, and is either compressive (a negative value) or tensile (a positive value). Shear stress acts tangentially to a given surface. Stress is related to strain through the linear proportionality constants E (the modulus of elasticity), v (Poisson's ratio), and G (modulus of elasticity in shear). Stress is a tensor quantity. See also *strain*.

Streakline. The set of particles that have previously passed through a particular point.

Streamline. Curves that are everywhere tangent to the velocity field. A streamline satisfies the integral curve $\frac{d}{ds}\vec{x} = \vec{v}(x, t')$ at some time t'.

Streampolygon. A vector and tensor visualization technique that represents flow with tubes that have polygonal cross sections. The method is based on integrating through the vector field and then sweeping a regular polygon along the streamline. The radius, number of sides, shape, and rotation of the polygon are allowed to change in response to data values. See also *hyperstreamline*.

Streamribbon. A vector visualization technique that represents vectors with ribbons that are everywhere tangent to the vector field

Streamsurface. A surface that is everywhere tangent to a vector field. Can be approximated by generating a series of streamlines along a curve and connecting the lines with a surface.

Streamwise Vorticity. A measure of the rotation of flow around a streamline.

Structured Data. Data in which one data item is related (either geometrically or topologically) to other data items. Also referred to as regular data.

Structured Grid. A dataset whose structure is topologically regular but whose geometry is irregular. Geometry is explicit and topology is implicit. Typically, structured grids consist of hexahedral cells.

Structured Points. A dataset whose structure is both geometrically and topologically regular. Both geometry and topology are implicit. A 3D structured point dataset is known as a volume. A 2D structured point dataset is known as a pixmap.

Subclass. A class that is more specific or complete than its superclass. The subclass, which is also known as the derived class, inherits all the members of its superclass. Usually a subclass will add some new functionality or fill in what was defined by its superclass. See also *derived class*.

Sub-parametric. A form of interpolation in which interpolation for data values is of higher order than that for the local geometry. Compare with *iso-parametric* and *super-parametric*.

Subsampling. Sampling data at a resolution at less than final display resolution.

Superclass. A class from which other classes are derived. See also *base class*.

Super-parametric. A form of interpolation in which interpolation for data values is of lower order than that for the local geometry. Compare with *iso-parametric* and *sub-parametric*.

Surface Rendering. Rendering techniques based on geometric surface primitives such as points, lines, polygons, and splines. Contrast with *volume rendering*.

Swept Surface. The surface that an object creates as it is swept through space.

Swept Volume. The volume enclosed by a swept surface.

Tcl. An interpreted language developed by John Ousterhout in the early 1980s.

Tk. A graphical user-interface toolkit based on Tcl.

Tensor. A mathematical generalization of vectors and matrices. A tensor of rank k can be considered a k-dimensional table. Tensor visualization algorithms treat 3×3 real symmetric matrix tensors (rank 2 tensors).

Tensor Ellipsoid. A type of glyph used to visualize tensors. The major, medium, and minor eigenvalues of a 3×3 tensor define an ellipsoid. The eigenvalues are used to scale along the axes.

Tetrahedron. A 3D primary cell that is a simplex with four triangular faces, six edges, and four vertices.

Texture Animation. Rapid application of texture maps to visualize data. A useful example maps a 1D texture map of varying intensity along a set of lines to simulate particle flow.

Texture Coordinate. Specification of position within texture map. Texture coordinates are used to map data from Cartesian system into 2D or 3D texture map.

Texture Map. A specification of object properties in a canonical region. These properties are most often intensity, color, and alpha, or combinations of these. The region is typically a structured array of data in a pixmap (2D) or in a volume (3D).

Texture Mapping. A rendering technique to add detail to objects without requiring extensive geometric modelling. One common example is to paste a picture on the surface of an object.

Texture Thresholding. Using texture mapping to display selected data. Often makes use of alpha opacity to conceal regions of minimal interest.

Thresholding. A data selection technique that selects data that lies within a range of data. Typically scalar thresholding selects data whose scalar values meet a scalar criterion.

Topology. A subset of the information about the structure of a dataset. Topology is a set of properties invariant under certain geometric transformation such as scaling, rotation, and translation.

Topological Dimension. The dimension or number of parametric coordinates required to address the domain of an object. For example, a line in 3D space is of topological dimension one because the line can be parametrized with a single parameter.

Transformation Matrix. A 4×4 matrix of values used to control the position, orientation, and scale of objects.

Triangle Strip. A composite 2D cell consisting of triangles. The triangle strip is an efficient representation scheme for triangles where $n + 2$ points can represent n triangles.

Triangle. A primary 2D cell. The triangle is a simplex with three edges and three vertices.

Triangular Irregular Network (TIN). An unstructured triangulation consisting of triangles. Often used to represent terrain data.

Triangulation. A set of nonintersecting simplices sharing common vertices, edges, and/or faces.

Type Converter. A type of filter used to convert from one dataset type to another.

Type Checking. The process of enforcing compatibility between objects.

Uniform Grid. A synonym for structured points.

Unstructured Data. Data in which one data item is unrelated (either geometrically or topologically) to other data items. Also referred to as irregular data.

Unstructured Grid. A general dataset form consisting of arbitrary combinations of cells and points. Both the geometry and topology are explicitly defined.

Unstructured Points. A dataset consisting of vertex cells that are positioned irregularly in space, with no implicit or explicit topology.

User-Defined Data. A data attribute beyond the typical data attributes scalars, vectors, tensor, normals, and texture coordinates. Typically, a function of visualization application.

Visualization. The process of converting data to images (or other sensory stimuli). Alternatively, the end result of the visualization process.

Vector. A specification of direction and magnitude. Vectors can be used to describe fluid velocity, structural displacement, or object motion.

Vector Field Topology. Vector fields are characterized by regions flow diverges, converges, and/or rotates. The relationship of these regions one to another is the topology of the flow.

Vertex. A primary 0D cell. Is sometimes used synonymously with point or node.

View Coordinate System. The projection of the world coordinate system into the camera's viewing frustrum.

View Frustrum. The viewing region of a camera defined by six planes: the front and back clipping planes, and the four sides of a pyramid defined by the camera position, focal point, and view angle (or image viewport if viewing in parallel projection).

Visual Programming. A programming model that enables the construction and manipulation of visualization applications. A typical implementation is the construction of a visualization pipeline by connecting execution modules into a network.

Visualization Network. A series of process objects and data objects joined together into a dataflow network.

Volume. A regular array of points in 3D space. Volumes are often defined as a series of 2D images arranged along the z-axis.

Volume Rendering. The process of directly viewing volume data without converting the data to intermediate surface primitives. Contrast with *surface rendering*.

Vorticity. A measure of the rotation of fluid flow.

Voxel. Short for volume element. In **vtk**, a primary three-dimensional cell with six faces. Each face is perpendicular to one of the coordinate axes.

Warping. A scalar and vector visualization technique that distorts an object to magnify the effects of data value. Warping may be used on vector data to display displacement or velocity, or on scalar data to show relative scalar values.

World Coordinate System. A three-dimensional Cartesian coordinate system in which the main elements of a rendering scene are positioned.

Writer. A type of mapper object that writes data to disk or other I/O device.

Yaw. A rotation of a camera's position about the vertical axis, centered at its viewpoint. See also *pitch* and *roll*. Contrast with *azimuth*.

Z-Buffer. Memory that contains the depth (along the view plane normal) of a corresponding element in a frame buffer.

Z-Buffering. A technique for performing hidden line (point, surface) removal by keeping track of the current depth, or z value for each pixel. These values are stored in the z-buffer.

Zoom. A camera operation that changes the field of view of the camera. Contrast with *dolly*.

Index

A

abstract class **24–28**, *611*
    and subclass 25
    example 27
    in vtk 565, 591
abstraction 21, *611*
    cell 335–337
    dataset 334–335
    during design 26
    point attribute 337–339
accumulation buffer 252
    antialiasing 252
actor 39
    geometry 54–55
    orientation 75
    origin 75
    position 75
    rotation 75
    surface properties 43–46
algorithm visualization
    application 544–549
algorithms
    image processing **432–448**
    modelling 154, **177–187**
    multidimensional **400–401**
    scalar 154, **155–167**
    tensor 154, **174–177**
    texture **402–407**
    vector 154, **167–174**
aliasing **250–252**
    image artifact 436
alpha **212–214**, 403, *611*
ambient light 43, *611*
animation *611*
    using texture 216, **405–407**, *624*
anisotropic diffusion 434
antialiasing *611*
    using accumulation buffer 252
aPE 111
API *611*
Application Visualization System, see AVS
applications **497–549**
    algorithm visualization 544–549
    computational fluid dynamics 537–542
    financial 524–532

    finite element method 543–544
    implicit modelling 533–536
    medical imaging 498–513
    segmented volume data 513–524
array methods 557
artificial intelligence (AI)
    versus intelligence amplification 7
aspect ratio 384
association
    in object model 26
attachment point 368
attenuation artifact 437
attribute 21, *611*
AVS 94, 111, **130**
    and vtk 131
awk 527
azimuth 47, *611*

B

base class 24, *611*
base curve 363
bilinear interpolation 313
binary files
    in vtk 597–598
binocular parallax *612*
boolean operators **180**
boolean texture **404–405**, 422, *612*
boundary point 383
bounding box 326
Bresenham 224

C

C++ 30, 32, 458, 555, *612*
    and Tcl 463
    application 533–536
caching 431–432
camera **46–49**
    azimuth 47
    dolly 49
    elevation 49
    focal point 46
    manipulation 47
    pitch 49
    position 46
    roll 49

W

X

Y

Z

LICENSE AGREEMENT AND LIMITED WARRANTY

READ THE FOLLOWING TERMS AND CONDITIONS CAREFULLY BEFORE OPENING THIS DISK PACKAGE. THIS LEGAL DOCUMENT IS AN AGREEMENT BETWEEN YOU AND PRENTICE-HALL, INC. (THE "COMPANY"). BY OPENING THIS SEALED DISK PACKAGE, YOU ARE AGREEING TO BE BOUND BY THESE TERMS AND CONDITIONS. IF YOU DO NOT AGREE WITH THESE TERMS AND CONDITIONS, DO NOT OPEN THE DISK PACKAGE. PROMPTLY RETURN THE UNOPENED DISK PACKAGE AND ALL ACCOMPANYING ITEMS TO THE PLACE YOU OBTAINED THEM FOR A FULL REFUND OF ANY SUMS YOU HAVE PAID. *THESE TERMS APPLY TO ALL LICENSED SOFTWARE ON THE CD EXCEPT THAT THE TERMS FOR USE OF ANY SHAREWARE OR FREEWARE ON THE CD ARE AS SET FORTH IN THE ELECTRONIC LICENSE LOCATED ON THE CD.*

1. **GRANT OF LICENSE:** In consideration of your agreement to abide by the terms and conditions of this Agreement, the Company and software developers grant to you a nonexclusive right to use the copy of the enclosed software program (hereinafter the "SOFTWARE"). The Company and software developers reserve all rights not expressly granted to you under this Agreement.

2. **OWNERSHIP OF SOFTWARE:** You own only the magnetic or physical media (the enclosed disks) on which the SOFTWARE is recorded or fixed, but the software developers retain all the rights, title, and ownership to the SOFTWARE recorded on the original disk copy(ies) and all subsequent copies of the SOFTWARE, regardless of the form or media on which the original or other copies may exist. This license is not a sale of the original SOFTWARE or any copy to you.

3. **COPY RESTRICTIONS:** This SOFTWARE and the accompanying printed materials and user manual (the "Documentation") are the subject of copyright. You may not copy the Documentation or the SOFTWARE, except that you may make a single copy of the SOFTWARE for backup or archival purposes only. You may be held legally responsible for any copying or copyright infringement which is caused or encouraged by your failure to abide by the terms of this restriction.

4. **USE RESTRICTIONS:** You may not reverse engineer, disassemble, decompile, modify, adapt, translate, or create derivative works based on the SOFTWARE or the Documentation without the prior written consent of the software developers.

5. **TRANSFER RESTRICTIONS:** The enclosed SOFTWARE is licensed only to you and may not be transferred to any one else without the prior written consent of the Company and software developers. Any unauthorized transfer of the SOFTWARE shall result in the immediate termination of this Agreement.

6. **TERMINATION:** This license is effective until terminated. This license will terminate automatically without notice from the Company and become null and void if you fail to comply with any provisions or limitations of this license. Upon termination, you shall destroy the Documentation and all copies of the SOFTWARE. All provisions of this Agreement as to warranties, limitation of liability, remedies or damages, and our ownership rights shall survive termination.

7. **MISCELLANEOUS:** This Agreement shall be construed in accordance with the laws of the United States of America and the State of New York and shall benefit the Company, its affiliates, and assignees.

8. **LIMITED WARRANTY AND DISCLAIMER OF WARRANTY:** The Company warrants that the SOFTWARE, when properly used in accordance with the Documentation, will operate in substantial conformity with the description of the SOFTWARE set forth in the Documentation. The Company does not warrant that the SOFTWARE will meet your requirements or that the operation of the SOFTWARE will be uninterrupted or error-free. The Company warrants that the media on which the SOFTWARE is delivered shall be free from defects in

materials and workmanship under normal use for a period of thirty (30) days from the date of your purchase. Your only remedy and the Company's only obligation under these limited warranties is, at the Company's option, return of the warranted item for a refund of any amounts paid by you or replacement of the item. Any replacement of SOFTWARE or media under the warranties shall not extend the original warranty period. The limited warranty set forth above shall not apply to any SOFTWARE which the Company determines in good faith has been subject to misuse, neglect, improper installation, repair, alteration, or damage by you. EXCEPT FOR THE EXPRESSED WARRANTIES SET FORTH ABOVE, THE COMPANY DISCLAIMS ALL WARRANTIES, EXPRESS OR IMPLIED, INCLUDING WITHOUT LIMITATION, THE IMPLIED WARRANTIES OF MERCHANTABILITY AND FITNESS FOR A PARTICULAR PURPOSE. EXCEPT FOR THE EXPRESS WARRANTY SET FORTH ABOVE, THE COMPANY DOES NOT WARRANT, GUARANTEE, OR MAKE ANY REPRESENTATION REGARDING THE USE OR THE RESULTS OF THE USE OF THE SOFTWARE IN TERMS OF ITS COR-RECTNESS, ACCURACY, RELIABILITY, CURRENTNESS, OR OTHERWISE.

IN NO EVENT, SHALL THE COMPANY OR ITS EMPLOYEES, AGENTS, SUPPLIERS, OR CONTRACTORS BE LIABLE FOR ANY INCIDENTAL, INDIRECT, SPECIAL, OR CONSEQUENTIAL DAM-AGES ARISING OUT OF OR IN CONNECTION WITH THE LICENSE GRANTED UNDER THIS AGREE-MENT, OR FOR LOSS OF USE, LOSS OF DATA, LOSS OF INCOME OR PROFIT, OR OTHER LOSSES, SUSTAINED AS A RESULT OF INJURY TO ANY PERSON, OR LOSS OF OR DAMAGE TO PROPERTY, OR CLAIMS OF THIRD PARTIES, EVEN IF THE COMPANY OR AN AUTHORIZED REPRESENTATIVE OF THE COMPANY HAS BEEN ADVISED OF THE POSSIBILITY OF SUCH DAMAGES. IN NO EVENT SHALL LIABILITY OF THE COMPANY FOR DAMAGES WITH RESPECT TO THE SOFTWARE EXCEED THE AMOUNTS ACTUALLY PAID BY YOU, IF ANY, FOR THE SOFTWARE.
SOME JURISDICTIONS DO NOT ALLOW THE LIMITATION OF IMPLIED WARRANTIES OR LIABILITY FOR INCIDENTAL, INDIRECT, SPECIAL, OR CONSEQUENTIAL DAMAGES, SO THE ABOVE LIMITATIONS MAY NOT ALWAYS APPLY. THE WARRANTIES IN THIS AGREEMENT GIVE YOU SPE-CIFIC LEGAL RIGHTS AND YOU MAY ALSO HAVE OTHER RIGHTS WHICH VARY IN ACCORDANCE WITH LOCAL LAW.

ACKNOWLEDGMENT

YOU ACKNOWLEDGE THAT YOU HAVE READ THIS AGREEMENT, UNDERSTAND IT, AND AGREE TO BE BOUND BY ITS TERMS AND CONDITIONS. YOU ALSO AGREE THAT THIS AGREEMENT IS THE COMPLETE AND EXCLUSIVE STATEMENT OF THE AGREEMENT BETWEEN YOU AND THE COMPANY AND SUPERSEDES ALL PROPOSALS OR PRIOR AGREEMENTS, ORAL, OR WRITTEN, AND ANY OTHER COMMUNICATIONS BETWEEN YOU AND THE COMPANY OR ANY REPRESENTATIVE OF THE COMPANY RELATING TO THE SUBJECT MATTER OF THIS AGREEMENT.

Should you have any questions concerning this Agreement or if you wish to contact the Company for any reason, please contact in writing at the address below.

Robin Short
Prentice Hall PTR
One Lake Street
Upper Saddle River, New Jersey 07458

About the Software

Overview

The Visualization Toolkit version 2.0 is a system for 3D computer graphics and visualization. With vtk you can visualize geometry from CAD systems, view medical data such as MRI or CT scans, examine the results of computer simulations, display multivariate or financial data, and create applications that transform your own data into 3D visualizations. With vtk2.0 you receive source code for a C++ class library with over 500 objects, both Tcl/Tk and Java interfaces to the class library, hundreds of megabytes of data files, and several hundred programming examples in C++, Tcl/Tk, and Java. The included HTML manual pages help you quickly learn how to use each class and extend existing examples to create your own applications.

System Description

The software has been designed and implemented based on object-oriented principles. With vtk2.0 you create applications by piecing together existing objects. Examples of objects include graphical components such as lights, cameras, actors, and transformation matrices; data objects such as images, volumes, or structured and unstructured grids; and algorithm objects such as contouring, decimation, Delaunay triangulation, and implicit modeling.

How To Use the Software

Typically you build an application by writing C++, Tcl/Tk, or Java code to manipulate the vtk classes. vtk has been designed to be operating system and graphics library independent—you can create applications on a PC and run them unchanged on a Unix system. And, if you use Tcl/Tk or Java, the user interface is transportable between windowing systems as well.

Operating Systems

vtk2.0 will run on Windows '95 and NT systems, and installs easily by executing "Setup.exe" on the CD-ROM. You may also modify and compile the source code under the Microsoft Visual C++ and Borland compilers. We have included a program that efficiently manages the compile process.

On Unix systems you must compile the source code using a configure process that automatically constructs makefiles, and then run "make" to compile the code. vtk2.0 compiles on most Unix systems including Linux, Sun, SGI, HP, and IBM. Some Unix executables are also available on the Web site listed below.

For More Information

Visit our Web site "www.kitware.com".

Technical Support

Prentice Hall does not offer technical support for this software. However, if there is a problem with the CD, you may obtain a replacement copy by emailing us with your problem at:

discexchange@phptr.com

You can obtain commercial support and consulting from Kitware at "www.kitware.com".